What They Said
in 1973

What They Said
In 1973

The Yearbook of Spoken Opinion

•

Compiled and Edited by

ALAN F. PATER

and

JASON R. PATER

MONITOR BOOK COMPANY, INC.

FIFTH ANNUAL EDITION

Printed in the United States of America

Library of Congress catalogue card number: 74-111080

ISBN number: 0-9600252-6-X

WHAT THEY SAID is published annually by
Monitor Book Company, Inc.
Beverly Hills, Calif.

To

The Newsmakers of the World . . .

May they never be at a loss for words

Preface to the First Edition (1969)

Words can be powerful or subtle, humorous or maddening. They can be vigorous or feeble, lucid or obscure, inspiring or despairing, wise or foolish, hopeful or pessimistic . . . they can be fearful or confident, timid or articulate, persuasive or perverse, honest or deceitful. As tools at a speaker's command, words can be used to reason, argue, discuss, cajole, plead, debate, declaim, threaten, infuriate, or appease; they can harangue, flourish, recite, preach, discourse, stab to the quick, or gently sermonize.

When casually spoken by a stage or film star, words can go beyond the press-agentry and make-up facade and reveal the inner man or woman. When purposefully uttered in the considered phrasing of a head of state, words can determine the destiny of millions of people, resolve peace or war, or chart the course of a nation on whose direction the fate of the entire world may depend.

Until now, the *copia verborum* of well-known and renowned public figures—the doctors and diplomats, the governors and generals, the potentates and presidents, the entertainers and educators, the bishops and baseball players, the jurists and journalists, the authors and attorneys, the congressmen and chairmen-of-the-board—whether enunciated in speeches, lectures, interviews, radio and television addresses, news conferences, forums, symposiums, town meetings, committee hearings, random remarks to the press, or delivered on the floors of the United States Senate and House of Representatives or in the parliaments and palaces of the world—have been dutifully reported in the media, then filed away and, for the most part, forgotten.

The editors of *WHAT THEY SAID* believe that consigning such a wealth of thoughts, ideas, doctrines, opinions and philosophies to interment in the morgues and archives of the Fourth Estate is lamentable and unnecessary. Yet the media, in all their forms, are constantly engulfing us in a profusion of endless and increasingly voluminous news reports. One is easily disposed to disregard or forget the stimulating discussion of critical issues embodied in so many of the utterances of those who make the news and, in their respective fields, shape the events throughout the world. The conclusion is therefore a natural and compelling one: the educator, the public official, the business executive, the statesman, the philosopher—everyone who has a stake in the complex, often confusing trends of our times—should have material of this kind readily available.

These, then, are the circumstances under which *WHAT THEY SAID* was conceived. It is the culmination of a year of listening to the people in the public eye; a year of scrutinizing, monitoring, reviewing, judging, deciding—a year during which the editors resurrected from almost certain oblivion those quintessential elements of the year's *spoken* opinion which, in their judgment, demanded preservation in book form.

WHAT THEY SAID is a pioneer in its field. Its *raison d'etre* is the firm conviction that presenting, each year, the highlights of vital and interesting views from the lips of prominent people on virtually every aspect of contemporary civilization fulfills the need to give the *spoken* word the permanence and lasting value of the *written* word. For, if it is true that a picture is worth 10,000 words, it is equally true that a verbal conclusion, an apt quote or a candid comment by a person of fame or influence can have more significance and can provide more understanding than an entire page of summary in a standard work of reference.

The editors of *WHAT THEY SAID* did not, however, design their book for researchers and scholars alone. One of the failings of the conventional reference work is that it is blandly written and referred to primarily for facts and figures, lacking inherent "interest value." *WHAT THEY SAID*, on the other hand, was planned for sheer enjoyment and pleasure, for searching glimpses into the lives and thoughts of the world's celebrities, as well as for serious study, intellectual reflection and the philosophical contemplation of our multifaceted life and mores. Furthermore, those pressed for time, yet anxious to know what the newsmakers have been saying, will welcome the short excerpts which will make for quick, intermittent reading—and rereading. And, of course, the topical classifications, the speakers' index, the subject index, the place and date information—documented and authenticated and easily located—will supply a rich fund of hitherto not readily obtainable reference and statistical material.

Finally, the reader will find that the editors have eschewed trite comments and cliches, tedious and boring. The selected quotations, each standing on its own, are pertinent, significant, stimulating—above all, relevant to today's world, expressed in the speakers' own words. And they will, the editors feel, be even more relevant tomorrow. They will be re-examined and reflected upon in the future by men and women eager to learn from the past. The prophecies, the promises, the "golden dreams," the boastings and rantings, the bluster, the bravado, the pleadings and representations of those whose voices echo in these pages (and in those to come) should provide a rare and unique history lesson. The positions held by these luminaries, in their respective callings, are such that what they say today may profoundly affect the future as well as the present, and so will be of lasting importance and meaning.

ALAN F. PATER
JASON R. PATER

Beverly Hills, California

viii

Table of Contents

Preface to the First Edition (1969)   *vii*

About the 1973 Edition   *xi*

Editorial Treatment   *xv*

Abbreviations   *xix*

The Quote of the Year   *xxi*

PART ONE: NATIONAL AFFAIRS

The Presidential Inaugural Address	25
The State of the Union Address	28
The American Scene	44
Civil Rights	55
Commerce / Industry / Finance	67
Crime / Law Enforcement	98
Education	112
The Environment	124
Foreign Affairs	148
Government	165
Labor / Economy	198
Law / The Judiciary	222
National Defense / The Military	230
Politics	242
The Watergate Affair	268
Social Welfare	309
Transportation	320
Urban Affairs	326
Women's Rights	331

PART TWO: INTERNATIONAL AFFAIRS

The Americas	339

Asia and the Pacific   348
    The War in Indochina   363
Europe   392
The Middle East / Africa
    The Middle East   417
    Africa   443
War and Peace   446

PART THREE: GENERAL

The Arts   455
Fashion   460
Journalism   464
Literature   484
Medicine and Health   491
The Performing Arts
    Motion Pictures   502
    Music   519
    The Stage   527
    Television and Radio   535

Personal Profiles   544
Philosophy   552
Religion   566
Space / Science / Technology   572
Sports   577

Index to Speakers   597
Index to Subjects   610

About the 1973 Edition . . .

This is the fifth annual edition in the *WHAT THEY SAID* series. Five years represent a not insignificant milestone and, since the first volume was published for 1969, we have endeavored to produce not only a singular and vital reference work each year but also to build a unique bookshelf-history of the passing parade of our times in a manner and spirit nowhere else attempted or obtainable. With this fifth volume, we can see the collection taking realistic form.

Each of the preceding four years, as recorded in *WHAT THEY SAID*, has produced its own individual history. Similarly, 1973, which this present volume covers, was a year for issues that will long be remembered and talked about as being synonymous with that year. Certainly, words like "energy crisis," "detente," "impeachment" and "Watergate" became familiar subjects in 1973 and are thoroughly discussed, dissected and analyzed in the opinions expressed by the speakers in *WHAT THEY SAID IN 1973*.

However, as in all years, the headline-grabbing events are but the topmost layer of a multi-faceted world going about its business in an infinite maze of pursuits that generate their own significance and make their own mark on the history of our world. Thus, words like "ecology," "women's liberation," "mass transit," "pornography," etc., make their imprint on our daily lives, sometimes in a more direct manner than the major headline stories.

And so, this latest volume in the *WHAT THEY SAID* series continues to present stimulating discussion on these and virtually all other consequential issues on the contemporary scene.

New features in the 1973 volume:

(A) All quotations are now individually numbered, and the subject index is keyed to this numbering system rather than to the page alone. The numbering system will continue as a regular feature in all future editions of the series.

(B) 1973 having been a Presidential inaugural year, the full text of President Nixon's inauguration address is included in this volume.

(C) A sub-category dealing exclusively with the Watergate affair appears immediately following the *Politics* section.

With no intention of being a complete news summary of 1973, following are some of the happenings reflected in many of this year's quotations . . .

Civil Rights:

As a protest against conditions faced by the American Indian, a group of Indians for a time occupied the town of Wounded Knee, S.D.

Commerce/Industry/Finance:

The Number One story in this area was the devaluation of the U.S. dollar in the face of strong fluctuations in foreign rates. Also generating much discussion were the U.S. sale of grain to the Soviet Union and U.S.-Soviet trade in general; the continued use of gold as a monetary standard; protectionism; and the social responsibilities of business and industry.

Crime/Law Enforcement:

Capital punishment remained a contested issue, as did prison reform; and a new FBI Director, Clarence M. Kelley, was appointed after Acting Director L. Patrick Gray III departed his post as a result of the Watergate investigation.

The Environment:

One of the top issues in the world this year was the energy crisis, spurred by gasoline and petroleum-product shortages, partly as a result of the Arab embargo of oil shipments to countries they considered friendly or sympathetic to Israel.

Foreign Affairs:

"Detente" became one of 1973's most frequently-used words, in this case meaning detente between the U.S. and the Soviet Union and between the U.S. and Communist China. The President's war-making powers were also frequently discussed and debated, some believing he has too much unilateral authority in this area and that it should be shared with Congress, and others feeling that the nature of foreign policy demands a Presidential leverage over war-and-peace. Terrorism on an international scale became more common, especially in connection with the Middle East conflict.

Government:

Concern over secrecy in government, Executive privilege, and public confidence in elected officials generally, was accentuated by the Watergate affair. Congress was worried about loss of legislative authority to the President and Presidential impoundment of Congressionally-allocated funds.

Labor/The Economy:

Inflation continued as a top-priority item, as did, also, wage-price controls and the various "phases" of Nixon Administration economic programs.

National Defense/The Military:

The volunteer Army got its first major test this year, and there was growing debate about further cuts in military spending and growing Soviet military strength.

Politics:

Garnering most of the headlines was the Watergate affair, dramatized by the televised Senate hearings. Watergate came to represent not merely the break-in at Democratic headquarters in

Washington, but also the break-in at Daniel Ellsberg's psychiatrist's office in California, and political campaign financing and tactics in general. Vice President Agnew resigned his office in face of charges of bribery, kickbacks and income-tax evasion.

The Americas:

Chilean President Salvador Allende was overthrown and died in the coup. Juan Peron returned to Argentina and was elected President. Pressure grew in the U.S. to improve relations with Cuba.

Asia:

President Ferdinand Marcos established martial law in the Philippines; exchanges continued between the U.S. and Communist China; relations improved between the Soviet Union and India.

Indochina:

A peace agreement ostensibly "ended" the war in Indochina, but throughout most of the year conflict continued in various hotspots in the area, such as Cambodia, where the U.S. bombing sparked heated debate in the U.S. Congress. A condition of the peace agreement was the release, by North Vietnam, of American prisoners of war; but many in the U.S. were not satisfied that all had been let go. Also as a result of the peace agreement, debate commenced in the U.S. over post-war reconstruction aid to North Vietnam.

Europe:

In Greece, a coup deposed President George Papadopoulos; a plan was developed for shared Catholic-Protestant rule in Northern Ireland; Britain and Iceland feuded over fishing rights; Soviet Party Chairman Leonid Brezhnev visited the United States; Soviet author Alexander Solzhenitsyn came under increasing pressure to stop writing against his government; U.S.-Soviet relations were ostensibly improving. Controversy continued in Britain over its already-accomplished entry into the European Common Market, and the perennial controversy over U.S. troops in Europe persisted.

The Middle East:

War broke out again between Israel and her Arab neighbors, then gradually diminished and ended through international negotiations, conducted chiefly by U.S. Secretary of State Henry Kissinger. Other events of the year in this area included Israel's shooting down of a Libyan commercial airliner; a major Israeli raid on Arab guerrillas in Beirut; Austria's capitulation to Arab terrorists by closing a transit facility for Israel-bound Soviet Jews; and the Arab cutback of oil shipments to countries friendly to Israel.

The Arts:

The U.S. Supreme Court ruled that local communities, cities or states could establish pornography and obscenity standards in their own areas.

Journalism:

The confidentiality of reporters' news sources remained a subject of discussion this year, as did the continuing debate of government vs. the news media.

Medicine and Health:

There was increasing call for a U.S. national health-insurance program.

Sports:

Baseball's designated-hitter rule was adopted by the American League, and Henry Aaron came ever closer to reaching, and possibly breaking, Babe Ruth's home-run record.

Editorial Treatment

ORGANIZATION OF MATERIAL

Special attention was given to the arrangement of the book—from the major divisions down to the individual categories and speakers—the objective being a logical progression of related material, as follows:

(A) The categories are arranged alphabetically within each of three major sections—

Part One:	"National Affairs"
Part Two:	"International Affairs"
Part Three:	"General"

In this manner, the reader can quickly locate quotations pertaining to particular fields of interest (see *Indexing*, next page). It should be noted that some quotations contain a number of thoughts or ideas—sometimes on different subjects—while some are vague as to exact subject matter and thus do not fit clearly into a specific topic classification. In such cases, the judgment of the Editors has determined the most appropriate category.

(B) Within each category, the speakers are in alphabetical order.

(C) Where there are two or more quotations by one speaker within the same category, they appear chronologically by date spoken or date of source.

SPEAKER IDENTIFICATION

The occupation, profession, rank, position or title of the speaker is given as it was *at the time the statement was made*. Thus, due to possible changes in status during the year, a speaker may be shown with different identifications in various portions of the book, or even within the same category. In the case of speakers who hold more than one position or occupation simultaneously, the judgment of the Editors has determined the most appropriate identification to use with a specific quotation.

THE QUOTATIONS

All quotations are printed verbatim, as reported by the source, except in cases where the Editors of *WHAT THEY SAID* have eliminated extraneous or overly-long portions. In such cases, *ellipses* are always inserted—and in no instance has the meaning or intention of any quotation been altered. (Material enclosed in brackets is by the Editors, or by the source, and is used to explain or clarify.) Special care has been exercised to make certain that each quotation stands on its own merits and is not taken "out of context." The Editors, however, cannot be responsible for errors made by the original newspaper, periodical or other source, i.e., incorrect reporting, mis-quotations or errors in interpretation.

DOCUMENTATION AND SOURCES

Documentation (circumstance, place, date) of each quotation is provided as fully as could be obtained, and the sources are furnished with all quotations. In some instances, no documentation details were available, and in those cases only the sources are given. Following are the sequence and style used for this information—

>Circumstance of quotation, place, date/Name of source, date: section (if applicable), page number.

>Example: *Before the Senate, Washington, Dec. 4/The Washington Post, 12-6:(A)13.*

The above example indicates that the quotation was delivered before the Senate in Washington on December 4. It was taken for *WHAT THEY SAID* from *The Washington Post*, issue of December 6, section A, page 13. (When a newspaper publishes more than one edition on the same date, it should be noted that page numbers may vary from edition to edition.)

When the source is a television or radio broadcast, the network or station is indicated along with the date of the broadcast (obviously, pages and section numbers do not apply).

Two asterisks (**) used in place of the source information indicate that the speaker supplied the quotation to *WHAT THEY SAID* directly.

INDEXING

(A) To find all quotations by a particular person, regardless of subject, use the *Index to Speakers.*

(B) To find all quotations on a particular subject, regardless of speaker, turn to the appropriate category (see *Table of Contents*) or use the detailed *Index to Subjects.*

(C) To find all quotations by a particular person on a particular subject, turn to the appropriate category and then to that person's quotations within that category.

The *Index to Speakers* is keyed to the page number. The *Index to Subjects* is keyed to both the page and the quotation number on that page (thus, 210:3 indicates quotation number 3 on page 210); the quotation number appears at the upper right corner of each quotation on every page.

The reader will find that the basic categorization format of *WHAT THEY SAID* is itself a useful subject index, inasmuch as all related quotations are grouped together by their respective categories. All aspects of journalism, for example, are relevant to each other; thus, the section *Journalism* embraces all aspects of the news media. Similarly, all quotations on Vietnam are together in the section *The War in Indochina*; so a particular speaker's views on any phase of the war can be found in that section under his name.

SELECTION OF CATEGORIES

The selected categories reflect, in the Editors' opinion, the most widely-discussed public-interest subjects, those which readily fall into the over-all sphere of "current events." They represent topics continuously covered by the mass media because of their inherent relevance to the changing world scene. Most of the categories are permanent; they appear in each annual edition of *WHAT THEY SAID*. However, because of the transient character of some subjects, there may be categories which appear one year and are not repeated.

SELECTION OF SPEAKERS

The following persons are *always* considered eligible for inclusion in *WHAT THEY SAID*: top-level officials of all branches of national, state and major local governments (both U.S. and foreign), including all United States Senators and Representatives; top-echelon military officers; college and university presidents, chancellors and professors; chairmen and presidents of major corporations; heads of national public-oriented organizations and associations; national and internationally known diplomats; recognized celebrities from the entertainment and literary spheres and the arts generally; sports figures of national stature; commentators on the world scene who are recognized as such and who command the attention of the mass media.

The determination of what and who are "major" and "recognized" must, necessarily, be made by the Editors of *WHAT THEY SAID* based on objective personal judgment.

Also, some persons, while not recognized as prominent in a particular professional area, have nevertheless attracted an unusual amount of attention in connection with a specific issue or event. These people, too, are considered for inclusion, depending upon the circumstances involved.

SELECTION OF QUOTATIONS

The quotations selected for inclusion in *WHAT THEY SAID* obviously represent a decided minority of the seemingly endless volume of quoted material appearing in the media each year. The process of selection is scrupulously objective insofar as the partisan views of the Editors are concerned (see *About Fairness*, below). However, it is clear that the Editors must decide which quotations *per se* are suitable for inclusion, and in doing so look for comments that are aptly stated, offer insight into the subject being discussed, or into the speaker, and provide—for today as well as for future reference—a thought which readers will find useful for understanding the issues and the personalities that make up a year on this planet.

ABOUT FAIRNESS

The Editors of *WHAT THEY SAID* understand the necessity of being impartial when compiling a book of this kind. As a result, there has been no bias in the selection of the quotations, the choice of speakers or the manner of editing. Relevance of the statements and the status of the speakers are the exclusive criteria for inclusion, without any regard whatsoever to the personal beliefs and views of the Editors. Furthermore, every effort has been made to include a multiplicity of opinions and ideas from a wide cross-section of speakers on each topic. Nevertheless, should there appear to be, on some controversial issues, a majority of material favoring one point of view over another, it is simply the result of there having been more of those views expressed during the year, reported by the media and objectively considered suitable by the Editors of *WHAT THEY SAID* (see *Selection of Quotations,* preceding page). Also, since persons in politics and government account for a large percentage of the speakers in *WHAT THEY SAID,* there may exist a heavier weight of opinion favoring the political philosophy of those in office at the time, whether in the United States Congress, the Administration, or in foreign capitals. This is natural and to be expected and should not be construed as a reflection of agreement or disagreement with that philosophy on the part of the Editors of *WHAT THEY SAID.*

Abbreviations

The following are abbreviations used by the speakers in this volume. Rather than defining them each time they appear in the quotations, this list will facilitate reading and avoid unnecessary repetition.

ADR:	asset depreciation range
AFL-CIO:	American Federation of Labor-Congress of Industrial Organizations
AIM:	American Indian Movement
ALP:	Australian Labor Party
AMA:	American Medical Association
ANZUS:	Australia-New Zealand-United States Treaty Council
CATV:	community antenna (cable) television
CBS:	Columbia Broadcasting System
CIA:	Central Intelligence Agency
DH:	designated hitter
EPA:	Environmental Protection Agency
FBI:	Federal Bureau of Investigation
FCC:	Federal Communications Commission
FDA:	Food and Drug Administration
FTC:	Federal Trade Commission
GATT:	General Agreement on Tariffs and Trade
GM:	General Motors
GNP:	gross national product
HEW:	Department of Health, Education and Welfare
HUD:	Department of Housing and Urban Development
IDA:	International Development Association
IRA:	Irish Republican Army
IRS:	Internal Revenue Service
ITT:	International Telephone & Telegraph Corporation
MGM:	Metro-Goldwyn-Mayer, Inc.
MIRV:	multiple individually-targetable re-entry vehicle (missile)
MNC:	multinational corporation
NAACP:	National Association for the Advancement of Colored People
NASA:	National Aeronautics and Space Administration
NATO:	North Atlantic Treaty Organization
NBC:	National Broadcasting Company
NFL:	National Football League
NOW:	National Organization for Women
NYSE:	New York Stock Exchange
OAS:	Organization of American States

ABBREVIATIONS

OEO: Office of Economic Opportunity
OMB: Office of Management and Budget
PBS: Public Broadcasting Service
POW: prisoner of war
SACB: Subversive Activities Control Board
SALT: strategic arms limitation talks
TV: television
UFO: unidentified flying object
U.K.:   United Kingdom
UN: United Nations
U.S.:   United States
USOC: United States Olympic Committee
U.S.S.R.: Union of Soviet Socialist Republics
VC: Viet Cong
VD: venereal disease
WBA: World Boxing Association
WBC: World Boxing Council
WPA: Works Progress Administration
YMCA: Young Men's Christian Association
YWCA: Young Women's Christian Association

Party affiliation of United States Senators and Congressmen—
C: Conservative-Republican
D: Democrat
I: Independent
R: Republican

The Quote of the Year

"No foreign policy—no matter how ingenious—has any chance of success if it is born in the minds of a few and carried in the hearts of none."

—HENRY A. KISSINGER

Assistant to the President of the United States for National Security Affairs (Secretary of State as of Sept. 22); before International Platform Association, Washington, August 2.

PART ONE

National Affairs

The Presidential Inaugural Address

Following is the full text of President Richard M. Nixon's Second Inaugural Address, as delivered in Washington, January 20, 1973:

Mr. Vice President, Mr. Speaker, Mr. Chief Justice, Senator Cook, Mrs. Eisenhower, and my fellow citizens of this great and good country we share together:

When we met here four years ago, America was bleak in spirit, depressed by the prospect of seemingly endless war abroad and of destructive conflict at home.

As we meet here today, we stand on the threshold of a new era of peace in the world. The central question before us is: How shall we use that peace?

Let us resolve that this era we are about to enter will not be what other postwar periods have so often been: a time of retreat and isolation that leads to stagnation at home and invites new danger abroad.

Let us resolve that this will be what it can become: a time of great responsibilities greatly borne, in which we renew the spirit and the promise of America as we enter our third century as a nation.

World Peace

This past year saw far-reaching results from our new policies for peace. By continuing to revitalize our traditional friendships, and by our missions to Peking and to Moscow, we were able to establish the base for a new and more durable pattern of relationships among the nations of the world. Because of America's bold initiatives, 1972 will be long remembered as the year of the greatest progress since the end of World War II toward a lasting peace in the world.

The peace we seek in the world is not the flimsy peace which is merely an interlude between wars, but a peace which can endure for generations to come.

It is important that we understand both the necessity and the limitations of America's role in maintaining that peace.

Unless we in America work to preserve the peace, there will be no peace.

Unless we in America work to preserve freedom, there will be no freedom.

Foreign Policy

But let us clearly understand the new nature of America's role, as a result of the new policies we have adopted over these past four years.

We shall respect our treaty commitments.

We shall support vigorously the principle that no country has the right to impose its will or rule on another by force.

We shall continue, in this era of negotiation, to work for the limitation of nuclear arms, and to reduce the danger of confrontation between the great powers.

We shall do our share in defending peace and freedom in the world. But we shall expect others to do their share.

The time has passed when America will make every other nation's conflict our own, or make every other nation's future our responsibility, or presume to tell the people of other nations how to manage their own affairs.

Just as we respect the right of each nation to determine its own future, we also recognize the responsibility of each nation to secure its own future.

Just as America's role is indispensable in preserving the world's peace, so is each nation's role indispensable in preserving its own peace.

Together with the rest of the world, let us resolve to move forward from the beginnings we have made. Let us continue to bring down the walls of hostility which have divided the world for too long, and to build in their place bridges of understanding—so that, despite profound differences between systems of government, the people of the world can be friends.

Let us build a structure of peace in the world in which the weak are as safe as the strong—in which each respects the right of the other to live by a different system—in which those who would influence others will do so by the strength of their ideas and not by the force of their arms.

Let us accept that high responsibility not as a burden, but gladly—gladly because the chance to build such a peace is the noblest endeavor in which a nation can engage, and gladly also because only if we act greatly in meeting our responsibilities abroad will we remain a great nation, and only if we remain a great nation will we act greatly in meeting our challenges at home.

Life in America

We have the chance today to do more than ever before in our history to make life better in America—to ensure better education, better health, better housing, better transportation, a cleaner environment—to restore respect for law, to make our communities more livable— and to ensure the God-given right of every American to full and equal opportunity.

Because the range of our needs is so great —because the reach of our opportunities is so great—let us be bold in our determination to meet those needs in new ways.

Just as building a structure of peace abroad has required turning away from old policies that have failed, so building a new era of progress at home requires turning away from old policies that have failed.

Abroad, the shift from old policies to new has not been a retreat from our responsibilities, but a better way to peace.

And at home, the shift from old policies to new will not be a retreat from our responsibilities, but a better way to progress.

Abroad and at home, the key to those new responsibilities lies in the placing and the division of responsibility. We have lived too long

with the consequences of attempting to gather all power and responsibility in Washington.

Abroad and at home, the time has come to turn away from the condescending policies of paternalism—of "Washington knows best."

A person can be expected to act responsibly only if he has responsibility. This is human nature. So let us encourage individuals at home and nations abroad to do more for themselves, to decide more for themselves. Let us locate responsibility in more places. And let us measure what we will do for others by what they will do for themselves.

Dependence on Government

That is why today I offer no promise of a purely governmental solution for every problem. We have lived too long with that false promise. In trusting too much in government, we have asked of it more than it can deliver. This leads only to inflated expectations, to reduced individual effort, and to a disappointment and frustration that erode confidence both in what government can do and in what people can do.

Government must learn to take less from people so that people can do more for themselves.

Let us remember that America was built not by government, but by people—not by welfare, but by work—not by shirking responsibility, but by seeking responsibility.

In our own lives, let each of us ask—not just what will government do for me, but what can I do for myself?

In the challenges we face together, let each of us ask—not just how can government help, but how can I help?

Your national government has a great and vital role to play. And I pledge to you that, where this government should act, we will act boldly and we will lead boldly. But just as important is the role that each and every one of us must play, as an individual and as a member of his own community.

From this day forward, let each of us make a solemn commitment in his own heart: to bear his responsibility, to do his part, to live his ideals—so that together, we can see the dawn of a new age of progress for America, and together, as we celebrate our 200th anniversary as a nation, we can do so proud in the fulfillment of our promise to ourselves and to the world.

As America's longest and most difficult war comes to an end, let us again learn to debate our differences with civility and decency.

And let each of us reach out for that one precious quality government cannot provide—a new level of respect for the rights and feelings of one another, a new level of respect for the individual human dignity which is the cherished birthright of every American.

Faith in America

Above all else, the time has come for us to renew our faith in ourselves and in America.

In recent years, that faith has been challenged.

Our children have been taught to be ashamed of their country, ashamed of their parents, ashamed of America's record at home and its role in the world.

At every turn we have been beset by those who find everything wrong with America and little that is right. But I am confident that this will not be the judgment of history on these remarkable times in which we are privileged to live.

America's record in this century has been unparalleled in the world's history for its responsibility, for its generosity, for its creativity and for its progress.

Let us be proud that our system has produced and provided more freedom and more abundance, more widely shared, than any system in the history of the world.

Let us be proud that in each of the four wars in which we have been engaged in this century, including the one we are now bringing to an end, we have fought not for our selfish advantage, but to help others resist aggression.

And let us be proud that by our bold, new initiatives, by our steadfastness for peace with honor, we have made a breakthrough toward creating in the world what the world has not known before—a structure of peace that can last, not merely for our time, but for generations to come.

We are embarking here today on an era that presents challenges as great as those any nation or any generation has ever faced. We shall answer to God, to history, and to our conscience for the way in which we use these years.

As I stand in this place, so hallowed by history, I think of others who have stood here before me. I think of the dreams they had for America, and I think of how each recognized that he needed help far beyond himself in order to make those dreams come true.

Today I ask your prayers that in the years ahead I may have God's help in making decisions that are right for America, and I pray for your help so that together we may be worthy of our challenge.

Let us pledge together to make these next four years the best four years in America's history, so that on its 200th birthday America will be as young and as vital as when it began, and as bright a beacon of hope for all the world.

Let us go forward from here confident in hope, strong in our faith in one another, sustained by our faith in God who created us, and striving always to serve His purpose.

The State of the Union Address

This year, rather than delivering the tradition-al State of the Union Address, President Rich-ard M. Nixon broadcast a series of State of the Union addresses on national radio. They are presented here in chronological order.

NATURAL RESOURCES AND
THE ENVIRONMENT

Every year since George Washington's time, the President of the United States has sent a message to the Congress about the state of our American Union and the measures which he felt the Legislative and Executive Branches of government should take in partnership to improve it.

This year, I am presenting my State of the Union report not just in one speech but in several messages on individual topics to permit more careful consideration of the challenges we face. And because both the President and the Congress are servants of the people, I am inviting the people to join with us in consider-ing these issues, by discussing them in a series of radio talks.

Today I want to talk with you about the first of these detailed messages, the one on the state of America's natural resources and environment, which I will send to the Con-gress later this week.

President Abraham Lincoln, whose memory we are honoring this week, observed in his State of the Union message in 1862 that "A nation may be said to consist of its territory, its people, and its laws. The territory," he said, "is the only part which is of certain durability."

In recent years, however, we have come to realize that what Lincoln called "territory"— that is, our land, air, water, minerals, and the like—is not of "certain durability" after all. Instead, we have learned that these natural resources are fragile and finite, and that many have been seriously damaged or despoiled.

To put it another way, we realized that self-destructive tendencies were endangering the American earth during the 1960s in much the same way as conflicting political forces had endangered the body politic during the 1860s.

Progress Since 1969

When we came to office in 1969, we tack-led this challenge with all the power at our command. Now, in 1973, I can report that America is well on the way to winning the war against environmental degradation—well on the way to making our peace with nature.

Day by day, our air is getting cleaner. In virtually every one of our major cities, the levels of air pollution are declining.

Month by month, our water pollution pro-blems are also being conquered, our noise and pesticide problems are yielding to new initia-tives, our parklands and protected wilderness areas are increasing.

Federal Expenditures

Year by year, our commitment of public funds for environmental programs continues to grow. Some people claim that we are not spending enough. But they ignore the fact that Federal spending for protection of our environment and natural resources has in-creased four-fold in the last four years. In the area of water quality alone, it has grown fif-teen-fold. In fact, we are now buying new facilities nearly as fast as the construction industry can build them. Spending still more money would not buy us more pollution-con-trol facilities but only more expensive ones.

In addition to what government is doing in the battle against pollution, our private indus-tries are assuming a steadily growing share of responsibility in this field. Last year industrial spending for pollution-control jumped by 50 per cent. This year it could reach as much as $5 billion.

Foreign Cooperation

As befits America's world leadership role, we are also moving vigorously with other nations to preserve the global environment. The United States-Soviet environmental cooperation agreement which I signed in Moscow last year makes two of the world's greatest industrial powers allies against pollution. Another agreement which we concluded last year with Canada will help to clean up the Great Lakes. The ocean-dumping curbs passed by the Congress at my urging have put this country in the forefront of the international effort to protect the seas.

Congressional Inaction

We can be proud of our record in this field over the past four years. But a record is not something to stand on; it is something to build on. Nineteen important natural resources and environmental bills which I submitted to the last Congress were not enacted. In the coming weeks, I shall once again send these urgently-needed proposals to the Congress so that the unfinished environmental business of the 92nd Congress can become the first environmental achievements of the 93rd Congress.

Let me highlight three of the other major subjects which we will be addressing in 1973: wise land use, energy, and a healthy, expanding farm economy.

Land Use

Land in America is no longer a resource we can take for granted. We no longer live with an open frontier. Just as we must conserve and protect our air and our water, so we must conserve and protect the land—and plan for its wise and balanced use. Some progress is being made—but antiquated land-use laws, overlapping jurisdictions, and outdated institutions are still permitting haphazard development which can spoil both the utility and the beauty of the land.

That is why I will urge passage again this year of legislation designed to encourage states to establish effective means of controlling land use. That is why I will reintroduce my proposals to bring coherence to Federal mining and mineral leasing laws, better management of the Federal lands, and enlightened regulation of surface and underground mining.

Energy Crisis

The energy crisis was dramatized by fuel shortages this winter. We must face up to a stark fact: We are now consuming more energy than we produce in America. A year and a half ago I sent to the Congress the first Presidential message ever devoted to the energy question. I shall soon submit a new and far more comprehensive energy message containing wide-ranging initiatives to insure necessary supplies of energy at acceptable economic and environmental costs. In the meantime, to help meet immediate needs, I have temporarily suspended import quotas on home heating oil east of the Rocky Mountains.

Energy policy will continue to be a matter of the highest priority, as shown by my budget proposal to increase funding for energy research and development even in a tight budget year.

Agriculture

One of the most precious natural resources since our earliest days has been American agriculture. Our farmers have kept us the best-fed, best-clothed nation in the history of mankind, while enabling us to export farm products at a level that will reach an all-time annual record of $10 billion this year. Net farm income last year also reached a record high—over $19 billion, an increase of 30 per cent over four years.

This Administration has responded to the farmer's desire for less Federal intervention by giving him expanded opportunity in planting his acreage. The day is gone when Washington can enlarge its role on the farm at the expense of the farmer's freedom to make his own decisions. The goal of all our farm policies and programs is just the reverse. We want freer markets and expanded individual responsibility. We want to keep the farmer on his land and the government off.

I shall recommend a number of additional initiatives to preserve and enhance our natural resources in the State of the Union report on this topic to the Congress later in the week.

These, then, are the basic principles which should continue to guide all our efforts in environment and natural resources policy in the future.

Balance Needed

First, we must strike a balance so that the protection of our irreplaceable heritage becomes as important as its use. The price of economic growth need not and will not be deterioration in the quality of our lives and our surroundings.

Government's Role

Second, because there are no local or state boundaries to the problems of our environment, the Federal government must play an active, positive role. We can and will set standards. We can and will exercise leadership. We are providing necessary funding support. And we will provide encouragement and incentive for others to help with the job. But Washington must not displace state and local initiative. We shall expect the state and local governments—along with the private section—to play the central role in this field.

Costs

Third, the costs of pollution should be more fully met in the free marketplace, not in the Federal budget. For example, the price of pollution-control devices for automobiles should be borne by the owner and the user, not by the general taxpayer. People should not have to pay for pollution they do not cause.

Individual's Role

Fourth, we must realize that each individual must take the responsibility for looking after his own home and workplace. These daily surroundings are the environment where most Americans spend most of their time. They reflect people's pride in themselves and their consideration for their communities. Your backyard is not the domain of the Federal government.

Challenges

Finally, we must remain confident that America's technological and economic ingenuity will be equal to our environmental challenges. We will not look upon these challenges as insurmountable obstacles. Instead, we shall convert the so-called crisis of the environment into an opportunity for unprecedented progress.

Now is the time to stop the hand-wringing and roll up our sleeves and get on with the job. Now is the time to reject the doomsday mentality which says we are destined to pollute ourselves out of existence.

Defeatism

The advocates of defeatism warn us of all that is wrong. I remind them and all Americans of our genius for responsive adaptability and our enormous reservoir of spirit. The destiny of our land, the air we breathe, the water we drink is not in the mystical hands of an uncontrollable agent; it is in our hands. A future which brings the balancing of our resources—preserving quality with quantity—is a future limited only by the boundaries of our will to get the job done.

Each one of us has a personal stake in the task ahead. The choice is always ours, for better or for worse. Above all, we need pride in this beautiful country of ours, belief in our own strength and resourcefulness.

One of the most memorable experiences I have had as President occurred last year during my visit to the People's Republic of China when the Chinese Army Band played *America* the Beautiful. This song of tribute to our nation was also played at my inauguration four years ago and again this year.

No one will sing America the Beautiful with greater feeling than our prisoners of war as they return home from years of Communist captivity in Indochina.

America is a beautiful country. By our commitment to conservation, restoration and renewal, let us resolve to make America even more beautiful for the generations to come.

Washington, Feb. 14, 1973.

THE AMERICAN ECONOMY

Tomorrow I will send to the Congress the economic section of my State of the Union report.

One fact stands out above all others in this report: For the first time in nearly 20 years, we can look forward to genuine prosperity in a time of peace.

For most people, talking about the economy brings to mind some vast, complicated machine. Today, I want to talk about the economy in personal terms—about its impact on you and your family.

Basically the economy affects you in three ways.

First, it affects your jobs, how plentiful they are, how secure they are, how good they are. Second, it affects what you take home from those jobs, and how much you can buy with your income, and, finally, it affects how much you can spend on your own and how much you have to pay back to the government in taxes.

Let's look briefly at each of these elements.

Jobs

To begin with, the job picture today is very encouraging. The number of people at work in this country rose by 2-3/10 million during 1972, the largest increase in 25 years. Unemployment fell from the six per cent level in 1971 to five per cent last month. This record is even more remarkable since so many more people have been seeking jobs than usual. Nearly three million Americans have been released from defense-related jobs since 1969, including over one million veterans. Women and teenagers have also been looking for work in record numbers. Yet, jobs for all these groups have increased even faster.

The reason for this success is that the economy grew by six and one-half per cent last year, one of the best performances in the past quarter-century. Our economic advisers expect a growth rate of nearly seven per cent in 1973. That would bring unemployment down to around the 4-1/2 per cent level.

Income

The second great question is how much you take home from your job, how much it will buy for you. Here the news is also good. Not only are more people working, but they are getting more for their work. Average per capita income rose by seven and seven-tenths per cent during 1972. That is well above the average gain during the previous 10 years. Most important, however, is that these gains were not wiped out by rising prices, as they often were in the 1960s.

Inflation

The Federal government spent too much, too fast, in that period, and the result was runaway inflation. Your wages may have climbed very rapidly during those years, but not your purchasing power. Now that has changed. The inflation rate last year was cut nearly in half from what it was four years ago. The purchasing power of the average worker's take-home pay rose more last year than in any year since 1955. It went up by four and three-tenths per cent, the equivalent of two extra weekly paychecks.

We expect to reduce inflation even further in 1973, for several reasons. The fundamental reason is the nation's growing opposition to big spending. We have a good chance now, the best in years, to curb the growth of the Federal budget. That will do more than anything else to protect your family budget.

31

Productivity

Other forces are working for us, too. Productivity increased sharply last year, which means the average worker is producing more and, therefore, can earn more without driving prices higher. In addition, the fact that real spendable earnings rose so substantially last year will encourage reasonable wage demands this year. Workers will not have to catch up from an earlier slump in earnings.

Wage/Price Controls

Finally, we now have a new system of wage and price controls, one that is the right kind of system for 1973. The idea that controls have virtually been ended is totally wrong. We still have firm controls. We are still enforcing them firmly. All that is changed is our method of enforcing them.

The old wage and price control system depended on a Washington bureaucracy to approve major wage and price increases in advance. Although it was effective while it lasted, this system was beginning to produce inequities and to get tangled in red tape. The new system will avoid these dangers. Like most of our laws, it relies largely on self-administration, on the voluntary cooperation of the American people. But if some people should fail to cooperate, we have the will and we have the means to crack down on them.

We would like Phase III to be as voluntary as possible, but we will make it as mandatory as necessary. Our new system of controls has broad support from business and labor, the keystone for any successful program. It will prepare us for the day when we no longer need controls. It will allow us to concentrate on those areas where inflation has been most troublesome—construction, health care, and especially food prices.

Food Prices

Let me focus for a moment on food prices. They have risen sharply at the wholesale level in recent months, so that figures for retail prices in January and February, when they are published, will inevitably show sharp increases. In fact, we will probably see increases in food prices for some months to come.

The underlying cause of this problem is that food supplies have not risen fast enough to keep up with the rapidly rising demand. But we must not accept rising food prices as a permanent feature of American life. We must halt this inflationary spiral by attacking the causes of rising food prices on all fronts.

Our first priority must be to increase supplies of food to meet the increased demand. Your government is already moving vigorously to expand our food supplies. We are encouraging farmers to put more acreage into production of both crops and livestock. We are allowing more meat and dried milk to come in from abroad. We have ended subsidies for agricultural exports, and we are reducing the government's agricultural stockpiles. We are encouraging farmers to sell the stock they own.

Now, measures such as these will stop the rise of wholesale food prices and will slow the rise of retail food prices. Unfortunately, they cannot do much about prices in the next few months, but they will have a powerful effect in the second half of the year. They will bring relief to the American housewife without damaging the prosperity of our farmers.

Farm income today is higher than ever, and it will go even higher as we increase farm production.

For all of these reasons, we have a good chance to reduce the overall inflation rate to 2-1/2 per cent, or less, by the end of 1973. That means your dollars will go further at your local shop or supermarket.

Taxes

The third important economic question concerns how much money you control for yourself and how much you pay out in taxes. Here the picture is also promising.

Since 1950, the share of the average family's income taken for taxes in the United States has nearly doubled, to more than 20 per cent. The average person worked less than one hour out of each 8-hour day to pay his taxes in 1950. Today he works nearly 2 hours each day for the tax collector. No wonder someone once described the taxpayer as a person who doesn't have to take a Civil Service examination to work for the Federal government.

Federal Programs

In fact, if tax cuts had not been adopted during our first term, the average worker's pay increase last year would have been wiped out entirely by increased taxes. The only way to stop tax increases is to stop spending more than our present tax rates produce in revenue. That is why we are cutting back on Federal programs that waste the taxpayers' money; for example: on housing programs that benefit the well-to-do but shortchange the poor, health programs that build more hospitals when hospital beds are now in surplus, educational bonuses that attract more people into teaching when tens of thousands of teachers already cannot find jobs.

These old programs may have appealing names, they may sound like good causes, but behind the fancy label often lies a dismal failure. Unless we cut back now on the programs that have failed, we will soon run out of money for the programs that can succeed.

It has been charged that our budget cuts show a lack of compassion for the disadvantaged. The best answer to this charge is to look at the facts.

We are budgeting 66 per cent more to help the poor next year than was the case four years ago; 67 per cent more to help the sick; 71 per cent more to help older Americans, and 242 per cent more to help the hungry and malnourished. Altogether, our human-resources budget is nearly double that of four years ago when I came into office.

We have already shifted our spending priorities from defense programs to human-resources programs. Now we must also switch our spending priorities from programs which give us a bad return on the dollar to programs that pay off. That is how to show we truly care about the needy.

The question is not whether we help, but how we help. By eliminating programs that are wasteful, we can concentrate on programs that work. Our recent round of budget cuts can save $11 billion in this fiscal year, $19 billion next fiscal year, $24 billion the year after. That means an average saving of $700 over the next three years for each of America's 75 million taxpayers.

Foreign Trade

Let me turn, finally, to one other major economic decision we made last week—our proposal to change the relative value of the dollar in trading abroad.

We took this step because of a serious trade imbalance which could threaten your prosperity. America has recently been buying more from other countries than they have been buying from us. Now, just as a company cannot go on indefinitely buying more than it sells, neither can a country.

Changing the exchange rate will help us change this picture. It means our exports will be priced more competitively in the international marketplace, and they should, therefore, sell better. Our imports, on the other hand, will not grow as fast. But this step must now be followed by reforms which are more basic.

First, we need a more flexible international monetary system, one that will lead to balance without crisis. The United States set forth fundamental proposals for such a system last September. It is time for other nations to join us in getting action on these proposals.

Second, American products must get a fairer shake in world trade so that we can extend American markets and expand American jobs. If other countries make it harder for our products to be sold abroad, then our trade imbalance can only grow worse. That is why I will soon propose to the Congress new trade laws which would make it easier for us not only to lower our trade barriers when other countries lower theirs, but also to raise our barriers when that is necessary to keep things fair.

Our overall goal is to reduce trade and investment barriers around the world, but they cannot decline for one country and remain high for others. My proposals will allow us to work more effectively for a new trading system which is equitable for all.

Even as we reduce the foreign barriers that keep us from competing abroad, we must also strengthen our ability to compete. This means working more efficiently as well as working hard, so that we can increase our productivity. It means taking greater pride in our work. It means fighting harder to slow inflation, and it means keeping Federal spending down.

Outlook for 1973

If we do these things, 1973 can usher in a new era of prolonged and growing prosperity for the United States. Unlike past booms, this new prosperity will not depend on the artificial stimulus of war. It will not be eaten away by the blight of inflation. It will be solid. It will be steady. It will be sustainable.

If we act responsibly, this new prosperity can be ours for many years to come; if we don't, then as Franklin Roosevelt once warned, we could be wrecked on the rocks of loose fiscal policy. The choices are ours. Let us choose responsible prosperity.

Washington, Feb. 21, 1973.

AMERICA'S HUMAN RESOURCES

At the beginning of each new year, as we reflect on the state of our American Union, we seek again a definition of what America means. Carl Sandburg came close to capturing its real meaning in three simple words that became the title for one of his greatest poems: "The People, Yes."

America has risen to greatness because again and again when the chips were down, the American people have said yes—yes to the challenge of freedom, yes to the dare of progress, and yes to the hope of peace—even when defending the peace has meant paying the price of war.

America's greatness will endure in the future only if our institutions continually rededicate themselves to saying yes to the people— yes to human needs and aspirations, yes to democracy and the consent of the governed, yes to equal opportunity and unlimited horizons of achievement for every American.

It is in this spirit of rededication that I will send to the Congress in the next few days the fourth section of my 1973 State of the Union report—a message on the progress we have made, the steps we now must take, in helping people to help themselves through our Federal programs for human resources.

1973 is a year full of opportunity for great advances on this front. After more than ten years of war, we have successfully completed one of the most unselfish missions ever undertaken by one nation in the defense of another, and now the coming of peace permits us to turn our attention more fully to the works of compassion, concern and social progress at home.

Government Funding

The seriousness of your government's commitment to make the most of this opportunity is evidenced by the record level of funding for human-resources programs proposed in our new budget—$125 billion—nearly twice the amount that was being spent on such programs when I took office in 1969.

Programs

Let us look behind this impersonal label, "human resources," let us see some examples of the way these programs are helping to provide a better life for the American people.

Social Security cash benefits for the elderly and the disabled in fiscal year 1974 will be twice what they were four years ago.

Next year, five million additional poor, aged and disabled persons will receive increased health benefits.

Hundreds of counties, which previously had no food programs to assure nutrition for the needy, have them now—hunger is being eliminated from American life.

Hundreds of school districts, which were giving black or brown children inferior educations in separate school systems at the time we took office, now give all their children an equal chance to learn together in the same schools.

A new student assistance system is being established to bring higher education within reach of every qualified student in America.

We have launched a national drive for the conquest of cancer, we have advanced a workable proposal to provide comprehensive health insurance for every American family.

Health and education benefits for our veterans have been substantially increased, high-priority job programs have decreased the unemployment rate among Vietnam-era veterans by almost one-third during the past year alone.

Sweeping reforms have been set in motion to assure our senior citizens of quality nursing-home care and of a better chance to live with dignity in homes of their own.

Legislative proposals to increase self-determination and economic opportunity for the American Indian have been laid before the Congress; they will be resubmitted to the Congress this year.

Outlays for civil-rights activities in 1974 will be more than $3 billion—that's three and one half times what they were at the beginning of this Administration. With this support, we are closer today than ever before to the realization of a truly just society, where all men—and all women—are equal in the eyes of the law.

These achievements, and others that I will outline in my message to the Congress, constitute a record to be proud of, a good beginning to build on.

But there are certain other aspects of the state of our Union's human resources which urgently need reform.

Program Failures

During the 1960s, the Federal government undertook ambitious, sometimes almost utopian, commitments in one area of social policy after another, elbowing aside the state and local governments and the private sector, and establishing literally hundreds of new programs based on the assumption that any human problem could be solved simply by throwing enough Federal dollars at it.

The intention of this effort was laudable, but the results in case after case amounted to dismal failure. The money which left Washington in a seemingly inexhaustible flood was reduced to a mere trickle by the time it had filtered through all the layers of bureaucrats, consultants and social workers, and finally reached those whom it was supposed to help. Too much money has been going to those who were supposed to help the needy and too little to the needy themselves. Those who make a profession out of poverty got fat; the taxpayer got stuck with the bill; and the disadvantaged themselves got little but broken promises.

We must do better than this. The American people deserve compassion that works—not simply compassion that means well. They deserve programs that say yes to human needs by saying no to paternalism, social exploitation and waste.

In order to bring our programs up to this standard, we have carefully reviewed each of them with three questions in mind:

How can we reform the decision-making process to bring it closer to the people whom these decisions will affect?

How can we get more value and productivity out of every tax dollar devoted to human resources?

How can we reform our approach to the delivery of services so as to give people the assistance they need without taking away their freedom or decreasing their self-reliance and their self-respect?

Reforms

Here are some of the reforms we propose:

To give the people served a better and greater voice in education and manpower training programs, we propose to convert them from narrow, fragmented, categorical programs—closely controlled from Washington—into new special revenue-sharing programs which will provide Federal funds to be used within broad areas as each state and community judges best to meet its own special needs.

To make the Federal health-care dollar go further, we propose to eliminate programs whose job is done—such as hospital-construction subsidies which, if continued, would only worsen the national oversupply of hospital beds and further inflate medical costs. The savings achieved would help to make possible increases in other areas—such as over $100 million more next year in cancer and heart-disease research.

To make the economic-opportunity dollar go further, we propose to transfer most of the anti-poverty programs now conducted by the Office of Economic Opportunity into the appropriate Cabinet departments, thereby making them more efficient by linking them with other related Federal activities.

To ensure that all of our people are provided with a decent income under circumstances that will increase human dignity rather than eroding such basic values as the family structure and the dignity of work, we will work with the Congress to improve the welfare system. A system which penalizes a person for going to work and rewards a person for going on welfare is totally alien to the American tradition of self-reliance and self-respect. That is why reforming the present welfare system has been, and will continue to be, one of our major goals.

The overall effect of these reforms will be the elimination of programs that are wasteful so that we can concentrate on programs that work. They will make possible the continued growth of Federal efforts to meet human needs—while at the same time helping to prevent a ballooning budget deficit that could lead to higher taxes, higher prices and higher interest rates for all Americans.

Despite what some people say, fiscal responsibility is not just a rich man's concern. If we were to spend our economy into a tailspin in the name of social welfare, we would only be punishing those we sought to help. Over the course of our history, the free American economy has done more to combat poverty and to raise our standard of living than any government program imaginable. The stable, healthy growth of our economy must remain the cornerstone of all of our human-resources policies in the 1970s.

Idealism

To our great credit, we Americans are a restless and impatient people—we are a nation of idealists. We dream of eradicating poverty, and hunger, discrimination, ignorance, disease and fear, and we would like to do it all today. But in order to reach these goals, we need to connect this warm-hearted impatience of ours with another equally American trait—and that is level-headed common sense.

We need to forge a new approach to human services in this country—an approach which will treat people as more than just statistics—an approach which recognizes that problems like poverty and unemployment, health care and the costs of education are more than cold abstractions in a government file drawer.

I know how tough these problems are because I grew up with them. But I also know that with the right kind of help and the right kind of spirit they can be overcome.

I believe that no American family should be denied good health care because of inability to pay. But I also believe that no family should be deprived of the freedom to make its own health-care arrangements without bureaucratic meddling.

I believe that no boy or girl should be denied a quality education. But I also believe that no child should have to ride a bus miles away from his neighborhood school in order to achieve an arbitrary racial balance.

I believe that no American family should have to suffer for lack of income, or to break up because the welfare regulations encourage it. But I also believe that we should never make it more comfortable or more profitable to live on a welfare check than on a paycheck.

I believe that government must be generous and humane. But I also believe that government must be economically responsible. We must reform or end programs that do not work. We must discontinue those programs that have served their purpose, so that our limited resources can be applied to programs that produce 100 cents worth of human benefits for every tax dollar spent.

Cooperation at all Levels

Working together to meet human needs and unlock human potential is the greatest adventure upon which any people can embark. I pledge continued, strong Federal leadership in this work. But we have learned the hard way that Washington cannot do the whole job by itself. State and local governments, private institutions and each individual American must do their part as well.

Let us give all our citizens the help they need. But let us also remember that each of us bears a basic obligation to help ourselves and to help our fellow man, and no one else can assume that obligation for us—least of all the Federal government.

If we shirk our individual responsibility, the American dream will never be more than a dream. But if the people say yes to this challenge, and if government says yes to the people, we can make that dream come true in the lives of all Americans.

Washington, Feb. 24, 1973.

COMMUNITY DEVELOPMENT

I want to report to you today on the quality of life in our cities and towns.

A few years ago we constantly heard that urban America was on the brink of collapse. It was one minute to midnight, we were told, and the bells of doom were beginning to toll. One history of America in the 1960s was even given the title, "Coming Apart."

Today, America is no longer coming apart.

Progress Since the 1960s

One of the most difficult problems of the 1960s was the alarming increase in crime—up 122 per cent from 1960 to 1968. Today, the rate of crime is dropping in more than half of our major cities.

Civil disorders have also declined.

The air is getting cleaner in most of our major cities.

The number of people living in substandard housing has been cut by more than 50 per cent since 1960.

The nation's first new transit system in more than 20 years has just been opened in San Francisco. Another is under construction in Washington, D.C.; others are planned in Atlanta and Baltimore.

City governments are no longer on the verge of financial catastrophe. Once again the business world is investing in our downtown areas.

What does all this mean for community life in America? Simply this: The hour of crisis has passed. The ship of state is back on an even keel, and we can put behind us the fear of capsizing.

We should be proud of our achievements; but we should never be complacent. Many challenges still remain. In approaching them, we must recognize that some of the methods which have been tried in the past are not appropriate to the 1970s.

Government Involvement

One serious error of the past was the belief that the Federal government should take the lead in developing local communities. America is still recovering from years of extravagant, hastily-passed measures, designed by centralized planners and costing billions of dollars—but producing few results.

I recently learned of a city where $30 million was paid for an urban-renewal project. But instead of getting better, the physical condition of the target neighborhood actually got worse.

In one of our huge, high-rise public housing projects, less than one-third of the units are now fit for human habitation and less than one-fifth are even occupied.

In another city, urban renewal was supposed to salvage and improve existing housing. $30 million was spent over 12 years—but the results were so meager that the planners finally gave up and called in the bulldozers. Now almost half of the project's 200 acres lies vacant, unsold.

Some of our programs to help people buy or improve housing are also backfiring. Too many of the owners fail to meet their payments, and the taxpayer gets stuck with the bill. He also gets stuck with the house—and the added expense of looking out for it. As a result, over 90,000 Federally-subsidized housing units are now owned by the Federal government—your government—over 14,000 in one metropolitan area alone.

Now, these examples are not unusual. This does not mean that the people in charge of these programs were dishonest or incompetent. What it does mean is that they are human—and that no human being, accountable only to an office in Washington, can successfully plan and manage the development of communities which are often hundreds or thousands of miles away.

There are too many leaks in the Federal pipeline. It is time to plug them up. That is why we are changing our entire approach to human and community development. We are putting an end to wasteful and obsolete programs and replacing them with ones that work.

Budget Cutbacks

Our 1974 budget would eliminate seven outmoded urban-development programs. It would suspend four ineffective housing programs.

We are not pulling the rug out from under anyone who has already been promised assistance. Under commitments already made, we will subsidize an estimated 300,000 housing starts this year and will provide housing assistance to more than 2 million low- and moderate-income families.

But we are stopping programs which have failed. We are determined to get a dollar's worth of service out of every dollar's worth of taxes. The high-cost, no-result boondoggling by the Federal government must end.

This means we will continue to press for greater efficiency and better management in Federal programs. But it also means giving the lead role back to grassroots governments again. The time has come to reject the patronizing notion that Federal planners, peering over the point of a pencil in Washington, can guide your lives better than you can.

Revenue Sharing

Last October, at Independence Hall in Philadelphia, I signed into law a general revenue-sharing bill. This bill allocates 30 billion Federal dollars over the next five years for state and local governments to use however they like.

Revenue-sharing represents a new Declaration of Independence for state and local governments. It gives grassroots governments a new chance to stand on their own feet.

Revenue-sharing money can be used to put more policemen on the beat, to build new schools, to lower property taxes—or for whatever other purpose you and your local leaders think best.

Let me emphasize one point which is often misunderstood. General revenue-sharing money is new money. It was never intended to replace programs we are now cutting back. To replace those programs, I am asking the Congress to create four new special revenue-sharing programs.

One of these new revenue-sharing bills, the Better Communities Act, would provide $2.3 billion in its first year of operation. This aid will have no strings attached as long as it is used for community development. Your local leaders can go on spending it the way Washington was spending it, if they like. But they would also be free to work out better plans without having to get Washington's approval.

We have several other proposals which deserve the support of every American taxpayer.

New Proposals

One is our recommendation for a new Department of Community Development. This department will pull together programs which are now scattered among different departments or agencies. It would put them under a single roof. I first made this proposal nearly two years ago. It is time for the Congress to act on it. As a first step toward getting better coordination in this field, I have already appointed a Counsellor to the President for Community Development.

Another key recommendation is our $110 million proposal to help state and local governments build up their administrative skills and planning expertise.

In the field of housing, we must stop programs that have been turning the Federal government into a nationwide slumlord. One of my highest domestic priorities this year will be the development of new policies that eliminate waste and target aid to genuinely needy families.

One of our highest priorities must be to improve transportation. In the past 20 years, Federal money has helped build the world's best system of modern highways. Our Administration has committed $19 billion to this goal. Now we must concentrate on moving people within our cities as effectively as we move them between our cities. We must help our communities develop urban mass-transit systems of which Americans can truly be proud.

I propose that our states and communities be given the right to use a designated portion of the Highway Trust Fund for capital improvements in urban public transportation, including improvements in bus and rapid rail systems.

Changing the way we use the Highway Trust Fund should be one of the top items on our national agenda. If we do not act now, our children will grow up in cities which are strangled by traffic, raked by noise, choked by pollution.

By opening up the Highway Trust Fund today, we can open up great new vistas for our cities tomorrow.

I have also asked that Federal funding authority for mass-transit capital grants be doubled—from $3 billion to $6 billion. And I have recommended that the Federal share of mass-transit projects be raised to 70 per cent.

All of these steps will help us meet the challenge of mass transit.

Perhaps no program means more to those it helps than does disaster aid. But it is not enough for government merely to respond to disasters. We should also take actions to prevent disasters or reduce their effect.

I will soon send recommendations to the Congress to revamp and improve disaster aid. I hope the Congress will also support an important proposal I have already made—moving disaster assistance out of the Executive Office of the President and into the Department of Housing and Urban Development, where it can be coordinated with other community aid.

Urban vs. Rural Areas

Too often, people think of community development solely in terms of the big city. In fact, less than 30 per cent of our people live in places with a population of more than 100,000. This is approximately the same number who live in rural America. The proportion of our people living in cities with a population of over 1 million is no greater today than it was 50 years ago.

In an age when people move a great deal, the growth of our great cities and that of our smaller communities are directly linked. A balanced approach to community development must keep small-town America clearly in sight.

Our Administration will use every effective means to help develop smaller communities, to bring new vitality to the American countryside.

Community Spirit

Perhaps the most important factor in the crisis mentality of the 1960s was the growing sense on the part of the average individual that the circumstances of his life were increasingly beyond his control. Nothing is more important in improving our communities than giving people a sense of control again, letting them know that they can make a difference in shaping the places where they live.

If the spirit of community means anything, it means a spirit of belonging, a spirit of responsibility, a spirit of participation. Restoring this "spirit of community" is the ultimate purpose of all the community-development efforts of our Administration.

"A great city," Walt Whitman wrote, "is that which has the greatest men and women." Only by appealing to the greatness that lies within our people can we build and sustain the kind of communities we want for America.

Washington, March 4, 1973.

LAW ENFORCEMENT AND DRUG ABUSE

Nothing is so precious to Americans as the freedoms provided in our Constitution. In order that these freedoms may be enjoyed to their fullest, there must be another freedom—freedom from the fear of crime.

The senseless shooting of Senator John Stennis in January gave tragic emphasis to the fact that there is still a high risk of crime on our nation's streets. These acts of violence are the natural residue of an atmosphere in America that for years encouraged potential lawbreakers.

Responsibility for Crime

Americans in the last decade were often told that the criminal was not responsible for his crimes against society; but that society was responsible.

I totally disagree with this permissive philosophy. Society is guilty of crime only when we fail to bring the criminal to justice. When we fail to make the criminal pay for his crime, we encourage him to think that crime will pay.

Such an attitude will never be reflected in the laws supported by this Administration, nor in the manner in which we enforce those laws. The jurisdiction of the Federal government over crime is limited, but where we can act, we will act to make sure that we have the laws, the enforcement agencies, the courts, the judges, the penalties, the correctional institutions and the rehabilitation programs we need to do the job.

Next week I will propose a revision of the entire Federal Criminal Code, modernizing it and strengthening it, to close the loopholes and tailor our laws to present-day needs. When I say "modernize," incidentally, I do not mean to be soft on crime; I mean exactly the opposite.

Our new code will give us tougher penalties and stronger weapons in the war against dangerous drugs and organized crime. It will rationalize the present patchwork quilt of punishments for crime. It will substantially raise current limits on monetary fines and it will restrict the present absurd use of the insanity defense.

Capital Punishment

I am further proposing that the death penalty be restored for certain Federal crimes. At my direction, the Attorney General has drafted a statute consistent with the Supreme Court's recent decision on the death penalty. This statute will provide capital punishment for cases of murder over which the Federal government has jurisdiction, and for treason and other war-related crimes.

Contrary to the views of some social theorists, I am convinced that the death penalty can be an effective deterrent against specific crimes. The death penalty is not a deterrent so long as there is doubt whether it can be applied. The law I will propose would remove this doubt.

The potential criminal will know that if his intended victims die, he may also die. The hijacker, the kidnapper, the man who throws a fire bomb, the convict who attacks a prison guard, the person who assaults an officer of the law—all will know that they may pay with their own lives for any lives that they take.

This statute will be a part of my proposed reform of the Federal Criminal Code. However, because there is an immediate need for this sanction, I have directed the Attorney General to submit a death-penalty statute as a separate proposal so that the Congress can act rapidly on this single provision.

Drug Abuse

Drug abuse is still Public Enemy No. 1 in America. Let me tell you about some of the tragic letters I have received at the White House from victims of drugs.

One tells about a five-year-old boy hospitalized in Missouri. Someone gave him LSD.

One is from a boy, 18 years old, who had

spent 11 months in a mental hospital trying to get rid of his drug addiction. He started with marijuana. He is asking me for help because his 14-year-old brother has begun to use drugs.

Another is from a mother in California. Her son committed suicide. He could not end his drug habit, so he ended his life.

One of the things that comes through so forcefully in these letters is the sense of despair of people who feel they have no place to turn for help, and so they write to the White House. I intend to help them.

We have already made encouraging progress in the war against drug abuse. Now we must consolidate that progress and strike even harder.

One area in which I am convinced of the need for more immediate action is that of putting heroin pushers in prison and keeping them there. A recent study by the Bureau of Narcotics and Dangerous Drugs revealed that more than 70 per cent of those accused of being narcotics violators are freed on bail for a period of three months to one year between the time of arrest and the time of trial. They are thus given the opportunity to go out and create more misery, generate more violence, commit more crimes while they are waiting to be tried for these same activities.

The same study showed that over 25 per cent of the federally-convicted narcotics violators were not even sentenced to jail. When permissive judges are more considerate of the pusher than they are of his victims, there is little incentive for heroin pushers to obey the law, and great incentive for them to violate it. This is an outrage. It is a danger to every law-abiding citizen, and I am confident that the vast majority of Americans will support immediate passage of the heroin-trafficking legislation I will propose to the Congress next week.

This legislation will require Federal judges to consider the danger to the community before freeing on bail a suspect for heroin trafficking. That is something they cannot legally do now. It will require a minimum sentence of five years in prison for anyone convicted of selling heroin. It will require a minimum sen-

tence of 10 years to life imprisonment for major traffickers in drugs. And for offenders with a prior conviction for a drug felony, those who persist in living off the suffering of others, it will require life imprisonment without parole.

This is tough legislation, but we must settle for nothing less. The time has come for soft-headed judges and probation officers to show as much concern for the rights of innocent victims of crime as they do for the rights of convicted criminals.

Marijuana

In recent days, there have been proposals to legalize the possession and use of marijuana. I oppose the legalization of the sale, possession or use of marijuana. The line against the use of dangerous drugs is now drawn on the side of marijuana. If we move the line to the other side and accept the use of this drug, how can we draw the line against other illegal drugs? Or will we slide into an acceptance of their use, as well?

My Administration has carefully weighed this matter. We have examined the statutes. We have taken the lead in making sanctions against the use of marijuana more uniform, more reasonable. Previously, these sanctions were often unrealistically harsh. Today, 35 states have adopted our model statute on drugs, including marijuana. I hope others will.

But there must continue to be criminal sanctions against the possession, sale or use of marijuana.

Law enforcement alone will not eliminate drug abuse. We must also have a strong program to treat and assist the addict. Two-thirds of my proposed anti-narcotics budget goes for treatment, rehabilitation, prevention and research. We are approaching the point where no addict will be able to say that he commits crimes because there is no treatment available for him.

By providing drug offenders with every possible opportunity to get out of the drug culture, we need feel no compunction about applying the most stringent sanctions against those who commit crimes in order to feed their habits.

State and Local Enforcement

The crimes which affect most people most often are not those under Federal jurisdiction, but those in which state and local governments have jurisdiction. But while the Federal government does not have full jurisdiction in the field of criminal law enforcement, it does have a broad, constitutional responsibility to insure domestic tranquility. That is why I am doing everything I can to help strengthen the capacity of state and local governments to fight crime.

Since I took office, Federal assistance for state and local law-enforcement authorities has grown from over $100 million to over $1 billion. We are training over 40,000 law-enforcement officers in the control and prevention of drug abuse.

This year more than 1,200 state and local police officers will graduate from the new FBI Academy, and I plan to increase assistance next year to local law enforcement to over $1,200,000,000.

Costs of Crime

Crime costs Americans twice. It costs first in lives lost, in injuries, in property loss, in increased insurance rates, in being fearful for your own safety as you go about your work.

And second, crime costs in the taxes that go to maintain police forces, courts, jails, other means of enforcement.

It is a breach of faith with those who are paying the cost of crime, human as well as financial, to be lenient with the criminal. There are those who say that law and order are just code words for repression and bigotry. That is dangerous nonsense. Law and order are code words for goodness and decency in America.

Crime is color-blind. Let those who doubt this talk to the poor, the minorities, the inner-city dwellers, who are the most frequent victims of crime. There is nothing disgraceful, nothing to be ashamed of, about Americans wanting to live in a law-abiding country.

I intend to do everything in my power to see that the American people get all the law

and order they are paying for. Our progress in this effort has been encouraging. The latest FBI figures show that for the first nine months of 1972, the growth rate of serious crime in America was reduced to one per cent. That is the lowest rate of increase since 1960.

In 83 of our major cities, serious crime has actually been reduced, and in the District of Columbia it has been cut in half since 1969. Convictions for organized crime have more than doubled in the last four years. The rate of new heroin addiction has dramatically decreased.

These are the positive results of refusing to compromise with the forces of crime, refusing to accept the notion that lawlessness is inevitable in America. We have the freedom to choose the kind of nation we want, and we do not choose to live with crime.

Citizen Involvement

The Federal government can help provide resources. It can help provide leadership. It can act with its own jurisdiction. But in the end, one of the best resources we have, one of the greatest safeguards to public peace, is the active concern of the law-abiding American citizen. The war against crime is not just the job of the FBI and the state and local police; it is your job, everybody's job. It is the very essence of good citizenship to act when and where we see crime being committed.

Citizens in some high crime areas have gathered together to work with the police to protect lives and property, to prevent crime. They have recognized the simple fact that we are going to have a crime problem as long as we are willing to put up with it, and most Americans are not willing to put up with it any longer.

When I saw and heard the remarks of our returning prisoners of war, so strong and confident and proud, I realized that we were seeing men of tough moral fiber, men who reflected, despite their long absence from America, what America is all about.

Just as they are returning home to America, I believe that today we see America returning to the basic truths that have made us and kept us a strong and a free people. I am encouraged by that vision. It points the way toward a better, safer future for all Americans. It points the way toward an America in which men and women and children can truly live free from fear in the full enjoyment of their most basic rights.

To accept anything less than a nation free from crime is to be satisfied with something less than America can be and ought to be for all our people.

Washington, March 10, 1973.

The American Scene

Carl Albert
United States Representative, D-Oklahoma

1

Americans are talking about new "rights" which, if we do our job, will become, as other "rights," permanent parts of the American tradition. What are some of these "rights"? The right to breathe air that is clean, to drink water that is pure. The right to a job for everyone who wants to work. The right of every consumer to be protected in the marketplace. The right of every woman to be treated as equally as every man. The right to adequate health care regardless of age or ability to pay. The right of every citizen to be treated as an individual no matter how large or complex our society becomes. This expanding Bill of Rights will demand our attention in the months ahead; for a right, no matter how widely-recognized it is, does not automatically become a reality.

Quote, 5-27:496.

Mildred C. Bailey
Brigadier General, United States Army;
Director, Women's Army Corps

2

I am sure that there are some among you who see little beauty or adventure in today, with the enormous problems that confront us . . . Through the marvel of mass media, you, in your brief lifetimes, have been eyewitnesses to political assassinations; floods and famines; pollution; military combat and death; crime in the streets; riots, disorders, demonstrations; cop-outs and bombings; the drug scene; racial unrest; and so much more. Viewed only from the perspective of all that is wrong with this world, the picture becomes one of discouragement and disillusionment. Bad news, served in large portions at breakfast, lunch and dinner for a sufficiently long period of time, has had a less than salutary effect on our dispositions as well as our outlooks for the future. But the picture is out of focus. There are times when I am almost convinced that anyone with good news to report is a voice crying in the wilderness. Somehow, the sounds of progress do not seem to be heard quite so clearly as the sound of turbulence in its many forms. Dissension seems to attract far more attention than accord; a sensational murder case far more attention than murder prevented. If only we could devote some part of each day to listening to what *good* is happening throughout the land, perhaps we would be better prepared to cope with all the bad that is constantly paraded before our eyes.

At University of Wisconsin commencement,
Stevens Point, May 13/
Vital Speeches, 7-1:566.

Lloyd M. Bentsen
United States Senator, D-Texas

3

It has become unfashionable for an American to wear his patriotism on his sleeve. But I had rather see it worn there, right out in the open, than carried around in a billfold. When patriotism is expressed in dollars and cents, democracy has lost all meaning.

Quote, 8-12:149.

Heinrich Boll
West German author

4

You have all sceneries here [in the U.S.]. You have [the] Watergate [political-espionage affair], and you have press freedom. You have desert and you have New York; terrible provincialism and terrible up-to-dateness. Being American means the chance to be what you want.

New York/
The New York Times, 5-15:30.

Kingman Brewster, Jr.
President, Yale University

1

If the moral quality of our country is to be restored, it will not be by vindictiveness or even by puritanical rectitude. It will come from a rediscovery that power without humanity is unworthy.

Before Yale University graduating class,
New Haven, Conn., June 3/
The New York Times, 6-4:26.

Alistair Buchan
Professor, Oxford University, England;
Former director, International Institute
for Strategic Studies, London

2

The U.S. is still the world's great experimental society, and it does not behoove Europeans to look down their noses at it because we, for the time being, have more successfully solved some problems of crime and environment. This is simply because American problems are on a much, much larger scale.

Time, 3-12:46.

Warren E. Burger
Chief Justice of the United States

3

The mindless violence of the 1960s seems to have stemmed in part from a confused, immature idea that human beings will be happier and life will be better if they "act out what they feel"—and as soon as they feel it; in short, to elevate emotion over reason and experience as the guiding force of conduct, and ignore all rules. Instant gratification at all cost seemed, at times, to be the order of the day. Yet, a most encouraging sign has emerged with some of these protest leaders running for public office and some being elected, making clear that the system is indeed open to all. This has the added benefit of subjecting those who challenge the social and political order to the chastening experience of bearing responsibility and being accountable at the ballot box. The protests of the 1960s, like others over our 200-year history, were not totally devoid of reason, however, except in their resort to

violence. The hard truth is that there was and is much that needs change in our social, political and economic institutions; but there never has been a time in history when this was not true . . . However painful we find it, we should ask whether at least some of those who challenged the system in the 1960s did not correctly perceive that the world is in a period of great change and that what was good enough 50 or 40 or even 30 years ago is not necessarily good enough for today or for the future. The underpinnings, the fundamentals of our institutions, are sound and valid; but we must be willing to re-examine the methods of implementation and make orderly adjustments from time to time.

At College of William and Mary/
The National Observer, 7-21:11.

John Chancellor
News commentator,
National Broadcasting Company

4

There's a crisis of confidence in the United States. We have learned to live with and to accept things we don't believe. Do we believe the car company when it says it can't meet a pollution deadline? Do we believe a manufacturer who says he can't clean up a dirty river? Do we believe the label on the box which reads "super-giant size"? Do we believe that salesman who says the product will last? A lot of us don't believe; but we have become accustomed to not believing, and that's the heart of the crisis. The medicine we need is plain words honestly spoken. We need to start meaning what we say.

At Sidwell Friends School/
The Washington Post, 6-13:(A)18.

Kenneth B. Clark
Professor of Psychology,
City College of New York

5

Social progress is never charted in a straight line. It has its ups and downs, like on a graph. But those of us who are working in this area continue to work because we believe that, in spite of the ups and downs, the over-all trend is up, and that keeps us going. I've thought

(KENNETH B. CLARK)

about that many times in the last 10 years, and particularly during the last four years. And I keep telling myself that, in spite of regressions which seem to be coming with greater and greater frequency, American society has to be moving toward greater humanity.

Interview, New York/
The New York Times Magazine, 3-18:15.

William Sloane Coffin
Chaplain, Yale University

1

When I was a kid, I was told America was a melting pot. Now I know it is a pressure cooker.

At Southern Methodist University
Women's Symposium, April 5/
The Dallas Times Herald, 4-6:(C)2.

John B. Connally, Jr.
Former Secretary of the Treasury
of the United States;
Former Governor of Texas

2

We have inflation, high food prices; but other nations have more inflation and higher food prices. Americans pay $2.50 a pound for good steak, but in Japan it costs $14 a pound. Every once in a while, a preacher runs off with the collection plate and the choir director, but not all preachers are that bad. There are some politicians who are bad apples, but not all politicians. When we get frustrated, let's step back a bit and reflect on where we are, in perspective. Despite all her faults and frailties, no nation has done more: We have fed better and more, housed better and more, offered more freedoms, more progress, more advantages than any other system on the face of the earth.

Los Angeles Times, 9-20:(1)28.

Silvio O. Conte
United States Representative,
R-Massachusetts

3

Through 186 years we have learned that it

is not an easy thing to follow the precepts of self-government which our Constitution lays out. It is not a simple thing to follow the will of the majority while, at the same time, protecting the rights of the minority. We have failed this and other tests presented by our Constitution many times. Yet, in spite of our failures, our nation's journey is marked by success unrivaled in the history of civilization.

Quote, 11-18:496.

Alistair Cooke
Chief United States correspondent,
"The Manchester (England) Guardian"

4

[On the U.S. today]: I myself think that I recognize several of the symptoms Edward Gibbon saw so acutely in the fall of Rome, which arise not from external enemies but from inside the country itself: a love of the show and luxury; a widening gap between the very rich and the very poor; the exercise of military might in places remote from the centers of power; an obsession with sex; freakishness in the arts masquerading as originality and enthusiasm pretending to be creativeness; and a general desire to live off the state, whether it's a junkie on welfare or a government-subsidized airline.

On his "America" TV program, May 15/
Los Angeles Times, 5-17:(4)19.

Thomas J. Coyne
Associate Professor of Finance,
University of Akron (Ohio)

5

Most still believe that a democratic system is run by the majority, when in fact it often is not. The truth is that democracy, as practiced in the United States, tends to be run by the best-organized minority.

Plainview (Tex.) Daily Herald,
1-14:(A)6.

Marlene Dietrich
Actress, Singer

6

The need for caring has gone out of America. Everything is governed by money and power, which are the biggest evils of our times. People talk to each other with money. It's not considered rude to ask each other how much money you earn. In Europe, it's unheard of . . . When I came to America 40 years ago, it wasn't like that. But now they've got two cars in every garage and two chickens in every pot. There's nothing left to achieve, so they walk around the moon and put their feet up and watch TV.

Interview, New York/
The Washington Post, 1-7:(G)2.

William O. Douglas
Associate Justice,
Supreme Court of the United States

1

I think the heart of America is sound, the conscience of America is bright and the future of America is great. The thing that holds all of us together is not the wording of the Constitution or the separation of powers—it's the mucilage of goodwill.

News conference/
The Wall Street Journal, 11-1:18.

Sam J. Ervin, Jr.
United State Senator,
D-North Carolina

2

Freedoms are exercisable by fools as well as by wise men, by agnostics or atheists as well as by the devout, by those who defy our Constitution and laws as well as by those who conform to them, and by those who hate our country as well as by those who love it. We cannot over-magnify the value of these freedoms. To be sure, the exercise of our freedoms may require us to put up with a lot of intellectual rubbish. But our country has nothing to fear from them, however much they may be abused, as long as it leaves truth free to combat error. Liberty is hard to win, but easy to lose. She stands in constant peril at the hands of those who doubt the wisdom of America's commitment to liberty and who fear the exercise of liberty by others.

Quote, 12-30:634.

John H. Fischer
President, Teachers College,
Columbia University

3

It is unlikely that any large number of Americans would ever approve a social, economic or educational system that undertook to assure equal position, equal income or equal influence for all. To choose that course would be to abandon a central tenet of the concept of individual freedom: the right of every person to make the most and the best of his or her own capacities. Competition still appeals mightily to us, and to compete is necessarily to assume different capabilities and to anticipate different outcomes. But our commitment to competition goes hand-in-hand with our insistence that the competition be fair. Whatever the individual's capability, we do not want it unjustly restricted. And when we act at our most humane, we insist that, if an individual has been unfairly impeded, he is entitled to whatever help is necessary to correct the error or right the wrong. Fair is fair, we say; and that belief is as firm and clear among us as our readiness to let the best man or woman win and to applaud the winner.

At Teachers College dinner, San Francisco,
March 18/Vital Speeches, 5-15:470.

Henry Ford II
Chairman, Ford Motor Company

4

The U.S. came out of World War II as the proud and powerful leader of the free world. We thought for a long time that we could prevent aggression, stimulate economic growth and build democracy throughout the world. We had high hopes for the UN, the Alliance for Progress, the War Against Poverty. We were going to eliminate racial prejudice, rebuild the cities, provide decent housing for every American and send men to the moon. We have, of course, sent men to the moon. But none of the other goals has been achieved . . . We thought we could achieve everything we wanted and admired all at once. We were so taken by the glitter of our goals and our faith in ourselves that we failed to notice all the obstacles in the way and our limited

47

(HENRY FORD II)

means of overcoming them. And, as a result, we wasted much of our efforts and resources on fruitless tasks. And even when we made progress, we called it failure because we did not get all the way to unreachable goals. Measured by the targets we set for ourselves, we have failed. Measured by more humble standards, we have accomplished a great deal. We should not feel ashamed or defeated because we have failed to accomplish the impossible. But I hope we have learned that we can accomplish more at less cost and with less damage to our national spirit if we set our goals with a little humility. I am not saying that we should settle back into complacent stagnation; we need to have new worlds to conquer. But we also need to recognize that conquest is almost always gradual and incomplete; that for everything we do, there is something else we cannot do.

At Glassboro (N.J.) State College
50th Anniversary program/
The Wall Street Journal, 11-1:18.

Erich Fromm
Psychoanalyst

1

An excess of material things way beyond the necessaries of life has numbed most Americans to the point where they are indifferent to violence. There has been material expansion; we have grown soft from it at a sacrifice of, what shall I call it, well, the soul. And Americans on the whole have accepted the logic of machinery, which is to demonstrate how machinery works. The ultimate purpose of making a gun is to fire it . . . The United States bombed Vietnam, if not back to the Stone Age, at least to the Bronze, slaughtering hundreds of thousands of hapless peasants in the Indochina war. Our society is also internally destructive. In the last decade or so, a million people have been killed in highway accidents. We produce cars with built-in obsolescence. Knowing the possible dangers, we continue to pollute the environment. And we subsidize violence on the screen—movies, in which human life is depicted as brutish and

cheap . . . There is still a moral residue in America composed of our religious and humane tradition in which the proper goal of society is to serve its members. It is a good society, a democratic society, which offers a religious or ethical vision of itself and sees itself also as a power for good in the world.

Interview, New York/
The New York Times, 12-15:33.

Lillian Gish
Actress

2

Our country is great. We aren't falling to pieces. As I travel around the country, I am struck by the fact that never in my lifetime have so many people had so much. We should be proud. Instead, we have become almost apologetic. Now that we are approaching our 200th birthday as a nation, I want every state to put its story on screen. There is power in what has happened in our land. Why not tell it? Every state has something special to offer. It wouldn't take a lot of effort or a lot of money. It should start with the Governors of our states, and the colleges can film all the stories. It would bring back a pride in our country, in our states and in ourselves.

Interview, Dallas/
The Dallas Times Herald, 11-7:(F)1.

Eric F. Goldman
Professor of History, Princeton University;
Former Special Consultant to the
President of the United States

3

We look at the '60s, and our vision is blurred. There was so much that was violent and snarling that we say, "This is the most horrible decade we've ever had." We agree with [author] John Updike who called it "a slum of a decade." The problem is to put it into perspective and to remember that, just as the Vietnam war tore apart public opinion, the 1920s saw a disillusionment with World War I that cut very deeply and very broadly in the United States. Or we speak of "the urban crisis." If you look at the late 1880s and 1890s, there was trouble among the farmers—distress and a militant demand for change

—which was probably as serious as the present urban crisis. We speak of the ravages of inflation. But certainly inflation is no worse a problem than 1873 or 1893 and, of course, 1929—all of which brought major depressions. Yet something else has to be said—namely, that while we've had all of these miseries at one time or another in the past, we have never had so many of them simultaneously. And in our time they are climaxed by a political mess [the Watergate political-espionage affair] which is, without question, unparalleled.

Interview/
U.S. News & World Report, 11-26:57.

Barry M. Goldwater
United States Senator, R-Arizona

1

We are living in a nation that is performing admirably in time of great distress—taking shock and bad news in its stride, with gravity and calm. It is a nation, while only 200 years old, that is displaying a poise and confidence in time of trouble that bespeaks a maturity that has surprised the entire world and served notice on the world that the United States of America intends to remain strong and play its allotted role in the leadership of the free world.

San Francisco Examiner & Chronicle,
9-16:(This World)2.

Billy Graham
Evangelist

2

I believe America stands at the threshold of Divine judgment today. Morally, socially, economically, politically and spiritually, we are in deep spiritual trouble. We must reorder our priorities. We all admit that we need some sweeping social reforms—and in true repentance we must determine to do something about it. But our greatest need is a change in heart. Almost everyone I talk to seems to sense that a hurricane is about to break on the world of cataclysmic proportions.

At White House pre-Christmas worship service,
Washington, Dec. 16/Los Angeles Times,
12-17:(1)4.

John D. Harper
Chairman,
Aluminum Company of America

3

The belief is too widely shared in the country today that the American dream has already been dreamed. One public-opinion poll after another has found a steep decline in confidence in government, business, schools, the courts, churches, unions and every other institution of society. Many people believe we are mired down in insurmountable problems —crime in the streets, dishonesty in government, pollution of the environment, inflation, drugs, a shortage of food, spiraling prices, corporations grown huge and heartless. One result has been that people are dropping out of society, in some cases quite literally . . . I don't believe that our people have renounced the American dream or that the Republic is about to collapse. It's simply that we've come so far so fast that we've overtaken many of our goals and now we're searching for new endeavors worthy of the name . . . My own remedy for our national malaise is straightforward. It has been prescribed during other days of doubt and frustration. It is effective in each new time of crisis, because it taps the wellspring of energy that exists in every one of us. I am speaking about a revival of patriotism, a revival that well could be the spark that our society so badly needs today. I believe it is essential that we regain some of the patriotic vision and energy the early patriots had. We need both to keep our national perspective in these troubled times. There is much in our past that can renew our faith, rebuild our confidence and restore to us our sense of inspiration and national purpose.

Before Society of Mining Engineers,
Pittsburgh, September/
The New York Times, 10-7:(3)14.

Mark O. Hatfield
United States Senator, R-Oregon

4

We witness a country torn apart with division and lacking the spiritual foundation which would restore its vision and purpose. We, as a people, through our own acqui-

(MARK O. HATFIELD)

escence to corruption and waste, have helped to create a moral abyss that produces a disdain for honesty and humility in high levels of national leadership.

Before the Senate, Washington, Dec. 20/
Los Angeles Times, 12-21:(1)4.

Bob Hope
Actor, Comedian

1

Maybe the best thing about our system is the opportunity it gives people to make something of their lives. I think most people want the good life; they want to live in nice houses and eat well and have some of the material things. And if you don't want them, nobody's forcing you to have them, right? All our system offers anybody is a chance to make good and live well. It's not perfect, but it's the best there is. Let's face it, Bing [Crosby] was from a very poor Catholic family. And Frank Sinatra was from a very poor Italian family. In what other country in the world could a meatball and a piece of spaghetti command so much bread?

Interview, North Hollywood, Calif./
Playboy, December: 110.

Edward M. Kennedy
United States Senator, D-Massachusetts

2

The mood [of the country] is one of malaise. Whether it will stay that way is a difficult question to answer. You see it when you give speeches; you saw it in the [1972 Presidential] campaign. I was active when the country was challenged by President Kennedy and Robert Kennedy—my brothers—and the response from the American people impressed me as positive and constructive in attempting to solve problems. Americans have been at their best when they have been challenged to do something for community and country. Now there is an appeal to other practices.

Interview, Charlottesville, Va./
The Washington Post, 4-22:(A)2.

Harold B. Lee
President, Church of Jesus Christ
of Latter-day Saints (Mormon)

3

We're living in a time of great crisis. The country is torn with scandal and with criticism, with fault-finding and condemnation, and there are those who have downgraded the image of this nation probably as never before in history . . . Men may fail in this country; earthquakes may come; seas may heave themselves beyond their bounds; there may be drought and disaster and hardship. But this nation, founded upon principle laid down by men whom God raised up, will never fail.

At Ricks College, Rexburg, Idaho/
Los Angeles Times, 11-10:(1)29.

Walter Lippmann
Author; Former political columnist

4

[President Nixon's] role in American history has been that of a man who had to liquidate, defuse, deflate the exaggeration of the romantic period of American imperialism and American inflation. Inflation of promises, inflation of hopes, the Great Society, American supremacy—all that had to be deflated because it was all beyond our power and beyond the nature of things. His role has been to do that. I think on the whole he's done pretty well at it.

Interview/
The Washington Post, 3-25:(C)1.

Richard W. Lyman
President, Stanford University

5

Neither venality nor cynicism are exactly new phenomena, though our present circumstances do suggest a high tide of both that surpasses all previous high-water marks in the history of this republic.

San Francisco Examiner & Chronicle,
6-24:(This World)2.

Norman Mailer
Author

6

I have an absolute huge distrust of the

American government. When you have a country as morally dastardly as this, you begin to question the whole shape of the country.

New York, Feb. 6/
The New York Times, 2-7:45.

William F. May
Chairman, American Can Company

1

Where are we as a society? In my view, we are beset by instabilities—instabilities that have led us into a mood of national cynicism that is weakening our ability to think clearly and corroding our will to act decisively. I ought to make plain that, when I say cynicism, I mean just that, and not skepticism. Skepticism is healthy and an essential pre-condition of intelligent debate and considered action. Cynicism is a different mood—destructive, apathetic, sullen, ugly. It leads to quarreling for the sake of quarreling. It prevents you from recognizing the truth when you see it. Unlike skepticism, it is the enemy, not the friend, of sensible analysis, proper accommodation and rapid progress. Cynicism has brought on a decline in public confidence in our institutions in the last six or seven years—vital, fundamental institutions such as church, government, business, the military and even the Supreme Court.

Before American Society
of Corporate Secretaries,
White Sulphur Springs, W.Va., June 29/
Vital Speeches, 8-15:653.

Wilbur D. Mills
United States Representative, D-Arkansas

2

[Saying the Watergate political-espionage affair and other problems are not bringing the U.S. to a state of paralysis, unable to function]: On many occasions during my long tenure here, I have seen—as other members have seen—national leaders trying to convey across the oceans the simple fact that the American system is unlike other systems. It is not organized as other systems are organized; it does not function as others function. As the history of this century has demonstrated time and again, the American system has corrective

powers and curative powers uniquely its own. What we see—or should see—in operation today is a system functioning at its best, curing and correcting itself, purging itself, holding true to its course. The courts are functioning. The grand juries are functioning. The Congress is functioning. The conscience of the American people is functioning powerfully. Far from being a system in or at the edge of crisis, this system today is more accurately past the crisis and moving out of the valley. We have been confronted by the challenge, and everything now occurring confirms the great truth that both the American people and their American system are more than equal to that challenge. In this perspective, then, it is unrealistic and wholly out of proportion to dwell on the prospect that we may be heading for paralysis . . . These times demand—and these great people we all serve demand—far more of their elected leadership than pontification about the "sickness" of this society, or about the loss of that society's standards, values or directions. I believe the American people are sick to the gills of all this self-debasement. They want, and we must give them, positive, wholesome and confident leadership in both what we do and what we say.

Before the House, Washington, May 30/
U.S. News & World Report, 6-18:26.

Richard M. Nixon
President of the United States

3

. . . the time has come for us to renew our faith in ourselves and in America. In recent years, that faith has been challenged. Our children have been taught to be ashamed of their country, ashamed of their parents, ashamed of America's record at home and its role in the world. At every turn, we have been beset by those who find everything wrong with America and little that is right. But I am confident that this will not be the judgment of history on these remarkable times in which we are privileged to live. America's record in this century has been unparalleled in the world's history for its responsibility, for its generosity, for its creativity and for its progress. Let us be proud that our system has produced and

(RICHARD M. NIXON)

provided more freedom and more abundance, more widely shared, than any system in the history of the world.

Inauguration address, Washington, Jan. 20/
U.S. News & World Report, 2-5:87.

Burt F. Raynes
Chairman,
National Association of Manufacturers

1

. . . there is a whole body of alien philosophies abroad in the land that, while they may not profess socialism, are pushing us more and more in that direction . . . It is tough to counter such philosophies because they don't really stand *for* anything: They are against the system, against the establishment, against business, sometimes against labor. About all they seem to be *for* is the right to enjoy the necessities, comforts and amenities of life in this country without working for them.

Before Detroit Economic Club, Feb. 5/
Vital Speeches, 3-15:339.

Donald T. Regan
Chairman, Merrill Lynch, Pierce,
Fenner & Smith, Inc.

2

I know we [in the U.S.] are going through quite a period now. What with the revelations of [the] Watergate [political-espionage affair], inflation, the weakness of the dollar and the like, this is not the happiest time, particularly on Wall Street. Nevertheless, more Americans than ever are employed. More people have more money than they ever had in their lives. We are feeding, or helping to feed, the people of the three largest nations in the world— [Communist] China, Russia and India; and we were able to do this with fewer farmers than ever. Our technological progress is continuing. We maintain our supremacy in the fields of aviation, electronics, computers, chemicals, drugs. And in spite of its apparent woes over the last six months, we do have the finest

capital-raising mechanism the world has ever seen.

Interview, New York/
Los Angeles Times, 8-1:(2)7.

Hyman G. Rickover
Admiral, United States Navy

3

I have seen this nation pass through perilous times. We have survived these dangers and emerged from them stronger. Once again the times are perilous. Statesmen, the press and the citizenry who advocate their own beliefs on specified issues cannot free themselves from all responsibility for the over-all outcome of national affairs.

At ceremony making him a full Admiral,
Washington, Dec. 3/
The New York Times, 12-4:55.

Wilson Riles
California State Superintendent
of Public Instruction

4

In America, Henry Ford pioneered the age. Colonel Sanders perfected it. And we all seem to be on the verge of accepting a technological life which produces identical automobiles and tasty chicken, but also bores us to tears.

San Francisco Examiner & Chronicle,
8-12:(This World)2.

John D. Rockefeller III
Philanthropist

5

Have we lost our way? Is this great nation really on the decline, or can we come together in renewed dedication to live out the promise that was articulated so well 200 years ago? We will find out the answer to that question during the Bicentennial Era. For the Bicentennial offers us an opportunity to rediscover our roots and sense of identity. It offers us common ground, a chance to unite in common purpose if we will but take it and make the most of it. The inspirational quality of the Bicentennial depends to a considerable extent on our sense of history—on our ability to understand and truly appreciate the importance of the American experiment to ourselves and indeed to the entire world. If the Bicentennial counts for nothing else, Americans generally should come away with at least a better understanding of their country's heritage. The plain fact is that, except at a certain abstract level, most Americans are remarkably ignorant about their own history. I can say this because I am one of them. Not until I became concerned about the Bicentennial did I sense more fully the rich drama of our past, of its relevance to our situation today and our prospects for tomorrow. Only by knowing our heritage better can we fully understand our unfinished agenda. For the past is never really past; it lives within us and around us, and we ignore it at our peril.

Winthrop Rockefeller Lecture,
University of Arkansas, Fayetteville,
May 2/Vital Speeches, 7-15:599.

Nelson A. Rockefeller
Governor of New York

1

The hard reality is that there has been a blurring of sharp focus on what is right and wrong in America. There has been a growing tendency to cut corners, to think it's smart to beat the system—whether it's fixing a ticket or dealing with organized crime, cheating on exams, lying to the public, padding expense accounts or chiseling on welfare. The shock of [the] Watergate [political-espionage affair] must make all Americans realize that we must return to our basic belief in individual honesty and integrity.

Opening the Gubernatorial election campaign
of Charles Sandman, Jr., Cherry Hill, N.J.,
Sept. 17/The New York Times, 9-18:47.

George W. Romney
Former Secretary of Housing and
Urban Development of the United States;
Former Governor of Michigan

2

. . . with public confidence at a fearsomely low ebb, with wide-spread cynicism about the ability of the individual citizen's views or actions to make a difference, we need to demonstrate anew that the most powerful force in America is the concerned action of concerned, informed citizens.

At National Municipal League's
National Conference on Government, Dallas/
The Dallas Times Herald,
11-18:(B)5.

Hugh Scott
United States Senator, R-Pennsylvania

3

I think we should continue to have faith in the American people—in their judgment, in their wisdom, in their acuity, and in the fact that they really do listen and they really do care. There, of course, lies, in my opinion, the ultimate security of the Republic.

Quote, 12-2:529.

John P. Spiegel
President,
American Psychiatric Association

4

If you compare us with the Scandinavian countries or with England, Iceland and so forth, we have a lot more turbulence. But those are homogeneous societies. Our lack of homogeneity has something to do with our turbulence. We have a big image of a melting pot; but when you look beneath it, we are full of immigrants and people of different racial origins who have a hard time seeing eye to eye.

San Francisco Examiner & Chronicle,
10-21:(This World)2.

Kakuei Tanaka
Prime Minister of Japan

5

The U.S. has many domestic problems, and some Americans may be deeply concerned about the way their country is being run. But of all the 3.7 billion people on this earth, Americans have the most stable economy, they have an abundance of resources available within their own country, and they have more investments abroad than any other country. So in terms of broad economic activity, the influence of the United States, as such, has not changed at all. When you think in terms of capability in exercising economic, political

(KAKUEI TANAKA)

and military power, the weight of the U.S. in world affairs has not declined at all. I expect it to continue to be as important as it has been in the past. We Japanese hope that Americans will continue to have confidence in their power—and at the same time be willing to exercise the responsibility that is incumbent upon a great country.

Interview, Tokyo/
U.S. News & World Report, 11-26:83.

Rod Taylor
Actor

1

. . . it's high time we got back to taking pride in this great, big, wonderful country of ours. I'm so sick of these loud-mouthed detractors. You bet I'm a flag-waver—right in there with that great big, wonderful John Wayne. God, I love that man. He believes in his country and his government and stands right out there to be counted. I was born in Australia, but I couldn't love the U.S.A. more if I'd been born in the Alamo. And you may quote me.

Interview, Los Angeles/
Los Angeles Herald-Examiner, 5-13:(D)2.

Carl Vinson
Former United States Representative,
D-Georgia

2

My confidence in the nation is unshaken. Not one particle. It's the people that make the nation, and the people are the same as 50 years ago.

San Francisco Examiner, 11-29:40.

Lowell P. Weicker, Jr.
United States Senator, R-Connecticut

3

. . . let's hope the United States is never a totally orderly, neat, safe place. The excitement of this country is in its hurly-burly, in the way we trade punches. There's nothing to be scared of there; really there isn't. What are we supposed to go back to? I don't recall the United States ever has been a peaceful and quiet concept. Not ever. Never.

Interview, Washington/
The National Observer, 4-7:5.

Ralph D. Abernathy
President,
Southern Christian Leadership Conference

1

If black people are to be free, they have got to go into their own pockets and pay for their freedom. And I guess it's understandable. I don't guess any people would pay for another people's freedom. Martin Luther King said that when he said the power structure never gives its privileged and lofty positions without a struggle. Frederick Douglass said it another way: that too many of us want to reap the harvest without plowing the ground. We want the rain, void of the thunder and the lightning. It is true that we may not get everything that we fight for; but whatever we get, we must fight for it. Black people must be willing to pay the price for their freedom. If they do not have money, then they must form the troops that are necessary for demonstrations and everything else; and I don't think that the days of demonstrations are over, either.

Interview, Atlanta/
The Washington Post, 8-19:(C)5.

Tom Bradley
Mayor of Los Angeles

2

The contemporary black movement is an integral part of our national society. The demand by black people for equal education, for example, is a help to all people. The drug problem which affected the black communities was unnoticed or ignored, but after many years other Americans also felt the impact of this dread disease because the problem was not answered in the early stages. We have reached a point where the basic humanism of the movement is getting its due recognition and where the movement is transcending the restrictions which have been placed on it by

narrow definition of race.

Los Angeles Times, 7-29:(6)4.

William E. Brock III
United States Senator, R-Tennessee

3

I believe no public policy should be made on the basis of race, creed or color. I believe that busing [school] children to achieve racial balance cannot be morally distinguished from busing them to achieve racial segregation, because in either instance the effect is to impose upon a free people the coercion of a tyrannical government.

Before Senate Judiciary Committee,
Washington, April 10/
The Dallas Times Herald, 4-11:(A)22.

Yvonne B. Burke
United States Representative,
D-California

4

The black movement is alive and well. So long as poverty, unemployment and discrimination plague our society, the movement will flourish. The gap between black and white America is greater today than in 1960. The rate of unemployment among blacks is double that of white workers; joblessness for black teen-agers is nearly 40 per cent. A quarter of all black families received some sort of public assistance in 1971. No, the millenium is not yet at hand for America's black citizens. The need for the black movement continues. We shall go on pressing for the birthright guaranteed to every American by our laws and history.

Los Angeles Times, 7-29:(6)5.

Stokely Carmichael
Black activist

5

In 1966, 1967 and 1968, Stokely was yell-

(STOKELY CARMICHAEL)

ing, "Go out and kill them." In 1973, such a speech would be a waste of time and we [blacks] would have missed the boat. We must seek and create a new system through a scientific and systematic program. We must be preoccupied with building, not destroying.

San Francisco Examiner & Chronicle,
2-4:(This World)2.

Kenneth B. Clark
Professor of Psychology,
City College of New York

1

Integration in and of itself is an end, because segregation was an end. The end of segregation was to show some human beings were less worthy of respect. Segregation in schools had no other purpose except to remind blacks and whites that blacks had an inferior status in society. It performed that purpose very well.

Interview, New York/
The Christian Science Monitor, 6-5:16.

2

As I see it, the center of gravity for the civil-rights movement shifted almost abruptly from Southern to Northern urban. In the South, the purposes of the civil-rights movement were pretty clear and specific and direct: There were segregated schools, segregated transportation, segregated waiting-rooms, terror—things for which there were apparently rather direct, specific remedies. Now, when that was changed, we all looked at it and said, "My God, progress has been made." And we celebrated the progress. But the black in the Northern cities saw his kids were just as retarded in reading as they ever were; his home was just as deteriorated as it ever was. He was in the same fix he had been in before this great progress had ever occurred, you see. So he started getting mad. And his white allies in the North—who could deal with their guilt and racial ambivalence by contributing to the NAACP and the Urban League—found the restless natives next door. And they weren't prepared for this; and so they reacted by saying: "These ungrateful so-and-so's. I con-

tributed to the NAACP and I contributed to the Urban League. I'm a white liberal. I'm without prejudice. What do they want from me?" Their response was backlash. You got this damned cycle of white backlash, white ambivalence, reacting to Northern urban black frustration. And this, then, generated what I call the era of realism.

Panel discussion, New York/
The New York Times, 8-30:31.

Charles W. Colson
Former Special Counsel to the
President of the United States

3

Busing [of school children for racial balance] was the straw that broke the camel's back. There are limits to the powers of government to tell individuals how to live their lives. When it strikes close to home—busing or the union hall—then there are practical limits to what people will accept from government. It is like every other historic pattern in our society: if the pendulum swings too hard one way, it bounces back.

The Washington Post, 4-11:(A)10.

Leon F. Cook
President,
National Congress of American Indians

4

This is what we [Indians] are asking: remove the shackles put on us by a government that tried to destroy us. We want to move into the mainstream—but preserve our heritage at the same time.

U.S. News & World Report, 4-2:30.

Walter Cronkite
News commentator,
Columbia Broadcasting System

5

[On busing of school children for racial balance]: . . . I've got to be honest about it: That never seemed to me to be the right solution. I think breaking down housing patterns—mixing up the neighborhoods, to use the phrase of some people—is the answer, rather than putting kids in buses for three, four and five hours a day. I don't care whether you're black or white, the neighborhood school is a fundamental concept. Admittedly, I've always believed that you must break down the patterns of segregation and prejudice through schooling; you've got to start with the child. But I think that busing, as hard as it's been to sell to people, is too easy a solution. I think that other solutions—like housing integration and equal employment opportunity—may be tougher, may take longer, may be more expensive, but I think they've got to be better.

Interview, New York/
Playboy, June:86.

John H. Fischer
President, Teachers College,
Columbia University

1

Despite the lingering yearnings of a declining fraction of Americans, it has become abundantly clear that any hope of sustaining legal support of racial segregation is finished. A few will no doubt continue to make such political capital as they can of jealousy and bigotry, but the day is gone when the black man could be expected to submit to inferior treatment and to do it quietly. Not only are black and other minority Americans expecting now to enjoy the full rights of first-class citizenship, they are expecting—and expected by growing numbers of their countrymen—to participate without restriction and on equal terms with majority groups and to take part in every aspect of American life. In short, we are living together, and the togetherness is going to increase.

At Teachers College dinner,
San Francisco, March 18/
Vital Speeches, 5-15:469,470.

Gerald R. Ford
Vice President of the United States

2

I strongly feel that there's a better way than busing [of school children for racial balance] to improve educational opportunity for the disadvantaged. I think compensatory education—where you put more money in to provide more and better teachers and facilities—

that's the way to improve education for all, particularly the disadvantaged. And that's really the worthwhile goal. But as for arbitrary court action seeking to get a numerical racial balance as a means of improving education—I think that's the wrong approach.

Interview, Washington/
U.S. News & World Report, 12-17:29.

Milton Friedman
Professor of Economics,
University of Chicago

3

The fact is that blacks are far better off in the U.S. than they are under other systems. Let's get some facts straight. The average income of blacks here is far higher than the average income of *all* the people in the Soviet Union. The official [U.S.] government definition of the poverty line in the U.S. is higher than the average income in the Soviet Union; it's higher than the income received by 90 per cent of the people on the world's surface. Now, that doesn't mean blacks aren't subject to injustice; of course they are. Of course there's discrimination. I'm opposed to it; I'd like to see it eliminated. But the point is that—even with discrimination—blacks are far better off under our present system than they would be under alternative kinds of systems; and changing the system isn't going to eliminate people's prejudices.

Interview, Ely, Vt./
Playboy, February:68.

Kent Frizzell
Assistant Attorney General
of the United States

4

[On an accord reached between the government and Indians who have taken over Wounded Knee, S.D., in protest over treatment of the American Indian]: I don't think any great victory has been won by anyone at Wounded Knee. I think we have all learned something here and now hope we will go on and improve conditions between whites and Indians. I think what we have learned is that all of us have failed in the past to live up to our agreements. We're going to do a better job

(KENT FRIZZELL)

in the future to see that these agreements are kept.

Wounded Knee, S.D., April 5/
The Washington Post, 4-6:(A)12.

Leonard Garment
Special Consultant to the President
of the United States

1

Our midrange objective is to persuade the Congress, and specifically the Senate and House Interior Committees, to get busy and hold hearings on the President's [Nixon] landmark Indian-policy legislation, which has been waiting for Congressional action now for almost three years. On July 8, 1970, the President sent a special message to the Congress which proposed an entirely new and progressive set of policies for Indian people. It is ironic, bordering on tragic, to realize that if Congress had enacted this legislation, the principal grievances among Indian people—which have given rise to such tensions as broke out [currently] at Wounded Knee [S.D.]—would be well on their way to being effectively handled. This is compounded when we realize how fully, in fact how emotionally, the American people are now in a mood to redress the old wrongs and give Indians a better deal. To many Americans today, I believe, almost no Indian "demand" seems unreasonable; almost no Indian militant appears too way-out.

Interview, Washington/
The Christian Science Monitor, 3-29:1.

Billy Graham
Evangelist

2

America today has the finest civil-rights laws the world has known. But the problem is deeper than law. The problem is the human heart.

At rally, Durban, South Africa,
March 17/The New York Times,
3-18:(1)7.

Richard G. Hatcher
Mayor of Gary, Indiana

3

This new wave of black Mayors like [Los Angeles' Thomas Bradley] won't have the same problems [Cleveland's recent Mayor Carl] Stokes, Kenneth Gibson of Newark and I had when we came in. Our election brought out all the racists. And we really had to take the brunt of heavy opposition from every corner—the local news media, city council, county officials at every level, the state legislature and Governor's office. I don't think Bradley will have to contend with this . . . Our election was kind of like Jackie Robinson breaking the ice in big-league baseball in '47. He had to take stuff that other blacks following him didn't. Many of the battles we had to fight have now been won. As a result, there's now an accommodation with powerful interests like the business community, politicians or [labor] unions. Our right to exist as Mayors has been established. Tom won't have to establish his legitimacy to govern.

Interview, Gary, Ind./
Los Angeles Times, 7-2:(1)22.

Carl Holman
President,
National Urban Coalition

4

Integration has clearly come to have a different meaning and a different weight. It has become—and no one ever dreamed this earlier—it has become almost an obscenity to many young blacks, and a good many older blacks see it that way now. It is at least enough of a loaded word so that almost nobody uses it without putting in an apologetic or I suppose belligerent word: "Yes, I don't mind telling people I believe in integration."

The Washington Post, 4-8:(A)20.

5

The problem is that white people simply don't take black people seriously. Racial equality is one thing when it's being promised, but it obviously means something else to whites when blacks actually try to get jobs under a Philadelphia Plan, actually attend an integrated school, or seek to share some economic or political power. Then there is resistance, and you get the feeling they never were serious in the first place.

The Washington Post, 4-11:(A)10.

Linwood Holton
Governor of Virginia

1

We have been closely associated, we whites in the South, with black people from the very beginning of the time they came here in 1619. We know how to get along together. We know how; and government and business and individuals in the South are recognizing that the black citizen is a full citizen, that he has complete opportunities and that we must see —we, as the establishment, whether we are black or white—must see that everybody has that opportunity to go forward, in housing, in schooling, in jobs and job opportunities. That feeling is developing very completely throughout the South; and it is my judgment that you are seeing today the best example of black and white people living together in the South of anywhere, not only in the nation, but in the world. There is no place else where the black people and white people live together as they do today in the South. The rest of the nation is going to see this New South; the rest of the nation is going to realize that direct conciliation can take place. The leadership will have come from Virginia and other states in the South, and I am very proud of that.

TV-radio interview, San Francisco/
"Meet the Press,"
National Broadcasting Company, 6-3.

Benjamin L. Hooks
Commissioner,
Federal Communications Commission

2

Blacks in America will never really wield power unless they are given positions in government—appointed or elective—which will certainly make their voices actually count from coast to coast.

Television interview/
Daily Variety, 2-6:1.

Stephen Horn
Acting Chairman,
United States Commission
on Civil Rights

3

If the evidence shows that Federal policies have deprived the Navajos [Indians] of their civil rights, then a policy which provides for a large measure of self-determination for the Navajo people would seem to be the first step toward restoring those rights. Too often the discussion has focused on the simple extremes of paternalism versus termination, rather than on self-determination for tribes and individuals and how that self-determination might most effectively be achieved.

At U.S. Commission on Civil Rights hearing,
Window Rock, Ariz., Oct. 22/
Los Angeles Times, 10-23:(1)19.

Jesse L. Jackson
Civil-rights leader

4

The opposite of segregation is not integration. Martin [Luther King] didn't dream about a completely integrated world. He knew this is a pluralistic society and that ethnics tend to keep an identity. It's not a contradiction.

The New York Times,
8-26:(1)44.

Maynard H. Jackson, Jr.
Vice Mayor of Atlanta

5

Anyone looking for the civil-rights movement in the streets is fooling himself. Politics is the civil-rights movement of the '70s. Politics is the last non-violent hurrah.

The New York Times,
8-26:(1)44.

Barbara Jordan
United States Representative, D-Texas

6

The sense of urgency about civil rights seemed to melt away when the ghettos stopped burning . . . However, the problems remaining are immense . . . The effort to extend the concept of equality to include all

(BARBARA JORDAN)

men of all colors cannot yet be abandoned.

*Before the House,
Washington, Jan. 31/
U.S. News & World Report, 2-12:40.*

Vernon E. Jordan, Jr.
*Executive director,
National Urban League*

1

Good faith is what's killed us [in the civil-rights movement]. I mean, relying on people's good faith. We relied on good faith under the Plessy vs. Ferguson concept of separate but equal. And so the white kids got the good buses and the black kids got the raggedy buses. In Atlanta in 1951, when I was in the 11th grade, I used a geometry textbook that had been used in 1935 by a white student at Tech High School . . . the whole business of not being trustworthy is based on history.

The Washington Post, 4-8:(A)20.

2

The civil-rights issues of the '60s have changed. In the '60s, the issue was the right to sit on the bus; today the issue is where that bus is going and what does it cost to get there. In the '60s, the issue was the right to eat at the lunch counter; today the issue is the hunger and malnutrition that stalk the land. In the '60s, the issue was fair employment opportunity; today that can no longer be separated from full employment of black people and equal access to every kind and level of employment up to and including top policy-making jobs. This demands a more sophisticated, tougher strategy than the marches and demonstrations of the past. We are no longer engaged in a moral struggle for the conscience of the nation; nor is the civil-rights thrust still focused on the Old Confederacy. If we've learned anything about the new issues, it is that racism is not just a Southern phenomenon, but that it is endemic to all America. And we have learned, too, that other sections of the country can react with as much violence, repression and irrationality

today as the South has historically.

*Before National Newspaper Publishers
Association, Houston, June 21/
Vital Speeches, 7-15:587.*

Herman Kahn
Director, Hudson Institute

3

My own attitude is that the phrase "benign neglect," which is credited to Daniel P. Moynihan, the President's former adviser on social issues, is now, with a few relatively minor exceptions, exactly the right policy for handling a good many of the racial issues in the next few years. Both of the words in "benign neglect" are important: "benign"—we want to be helpful, we are not interested in perpetuating racist inequalities and strife; "neglect" —it obviously will take a while to make serious changes in the racial area, even after we get things going in the right direction, as I think we've done. Now we have to wait a generation, and it is important to emphasize the need for self-help and individual enterprise and initiative. I might make a point about this. For the last 200 or 300 years in Western culture, we have emphasized, increasingly, the treatment of causes, not symptoms. Generally speaking, that's a good idea; but it has two difficulties. One is that often we don't know how to treat the causes; we're really too dumb, or we haven't accumulated enough knowledge yet. Secondly, it takes time to treat causes; it may take 10 or 20 or 30 years. What we should do in many cases, therefore, is to treat the causes and point the system in the right direction; then go to work on symptoms, because we usually know how to deal with those and can get results more quickly.

*Interview/
U.S. News & World Report, 3-12:47.*

Edward M. Kennedy
United States Senator, D-Massachusetts

4

Let no one think I come to lecture you [Southerners] on that racial injustice which has proven to be as deeply-imbedded and resistant in the cities of the North as in the counties of the South. Indeed, Southerners may know even better than others of the need for leadership to free all men, white and black, from hatred and the consequences of hatred. We are no more entitled to oppress a man for his color than to shoot a man [Alabama Governor George Wallace] for his beliefs.

At Independence Day celebration,
Decatur, Alabama, July 4/
The Washington Post, 7-5:(A)6.

Richard G. Kleindienst
Attorney General of the United States

1

[On President Nixon's civil-rights policies]: This is an area where the political rhetoric of the times has been most unfair to the President. It's extremely important to Democratic politicians to claim that President Nixon doesn't care about blacks and minorities and that he has no commitment to civil rights. This is necessary to the Democrats because, if they gave the Administration credit, some blacks would vote for Republican candidates, and if a significant number of blacks voted independently, the ability of Democrats to get elected in Northern cities and states would be seriously affected . . . Our record in civil-rights enforcement has been a great one.

Interview, Washington/
Los Angeles Times, 2-11:(8)8.

Thomas H. Kuchel
Former United States Senator,
R-California

2

Look at civil rights, or to use what I think is a better phrase, equality of opportunity. When I came to Washington [in the mid-1950s], there wasn't even a black on the *Redskins* [football team]. It was difficult for a black to go into a hotel and order a bottle of beer. Now look at the hotels and the restaurants! Take a look in the banks, in the stores and offices, in the professions. There has been a tremendous step forward. We even have a black Mayor of Washington—a good man, no question about that. I know many people don't give [the late President Dwight]

Eisenhower much credit on civil rights; but I think he did a great deal to get things moving on voting rights and equal opportunity in jobs and in breaking down barriers in restaurants, theatres and hotels. And let's not forget Little Rock!

Interview, Washington/
Los Angeles Times, 7-17:(2)7.

Peter MacDonald
Chairman,
Navajo (Indian) Tribal Council

3

Most Indian tribes know what they want, where they want programs and in what time-frame they want to accomplish these things; but the problem comes at the top. Every action of the Navajo Council is subject to the approval of the [Federal] Bureau of Indian Affairs, and we have 30 or 40 major pieces of tribal legislation outstanding all the time for as long as two years. This is ridiculous. They tell us to go ahead and do our own thing, but they act as if they didn't want us to accomplish these things at all. Instead of rallying behind us on programs, it's often true that they come back and say, "Rewrite this sentence; we don't understand." Then a few months later, they want us to rewrite another sentence. And pretty soon, another fiscal year has passed, and they come back and say, "Why don't you do it all over again?" For a big nation like the Navajos, these delays are very detrimental. We must move fast.

Before U.S. Commission on Civil Rights,
Window Rock, Ariz., Oct. 22/
The New York Times, 10-23:8.

Benjamin E. Mays
President, Atlanta Board of Education

4

. . . 20 years or so ago, when school desegregation was just starting in the South, Atlanta schools were 70 per cent white and 30 per cent black. Now they're 80 per cent black and 20 per cent white. It's a matter of white flight and private schools, the old story. Massive busing [of school children for racial balance] would be counter-productive at this point. We'd end up with no whites to bus.

(BENJAMIN E. MAYS)

Then what would happen to Atlanta and all this progress and growth we're always bragging about?

Atlanta/
The New York Times, 4-25:20.

George S. McGovern
United States Senator, D-South Dakota

1

I'm against AIM [the American Indian Movement]. I don't like their tactics and regard them as a group of rip-off artists exploiting Indian problems for their own selfish ends. They're law-breakers and they're violent.

San Francisco Examiner & Chronicle,
9-9:(This World)2.

Russell Means
An official of the
American Indian Movement (AIM)

2

I can't speak for AIM outside South Dakota, but the leadership of AIM in the state has decided to give the United States and the white man another chance to change the way Indian affairs are handled . . . On July 4, 1976, white America is planning to celebrate its 200th birthday. If nothing has changed for Indian people by that time, we will make sure it is an unhappy birthday. We feel the government can put into Indian affairs the same effort it put into Vietnam, the United Nations and other areas—the kind of positive government aspects that have been denied Indians.

Before Senate Subcommittee on Indian affairs,
Washington, June 17/
The Dallas Times Herald, 6-18:(A)9.

Lloyd Meeds
United States Representative,
D-Washington

3

Unemployment on the Oglala Sioux [Indian] reservation is 50 per cent. It's 40 per cent on the Navajo reservation. You don't find unemployment on an Indian reservation in the country of less than 35 per cent. And I remember a great depression in this country when there was 25 per cent unemployment nationally. Well, these Indian tribes are minor nations. And they are in a depression all the time.

The Christian Science Monitor, 7-16:2.

Parren J. Mitchell
United States Representative,
D-Maryland

4

If the Supreme Court decision on integration can be violated [through lax government enforcement], what's to prevent the next attack coming against fair-employment laws, and the next against access to public accomodations? In my most pessimistic moods, I can see us duplicating the events that took place 100 years ago in the post-Reconstruction era. We [blacks] had achieved some rights and some political power, and we lost it all. That, it seems to me, is the greatest danger.

The Washington Post, 4-11:(A)10.

5

I am not at all assured in my own mind that even the most liberal of liberal whites is prepared to take that quantitative jump into total equality [for blacks]. I don't mean equal opportunity. I mean total equality. That means power in decision-making all through society. I'm talking about the power to influence decisions that affect our lives. And that's where even the most liberal whites draw the line.

The Washington Post, 4-11:(A)10.

6

Racism isn't dead. What we have now is the Administration of Richard M. Nixon and its benevolent, smooth, velvet racism.

Before Houston chapter, National Association
for the Advancement of Colored People/
The Dallas Times Herald, 11-18:(A)30.

Walter F. Mondale
United States Senator,
D-Minnesota

7

I have said many times that I do not support busing [of school children] for the purpose of racial balance . . . [But] I do not think the court should be denied the authority to eliminate discrimination when they find it. Sometimes when they do find it, it is necessary for them in their judgment to order some busing. When they do, I have stood up and protected the right in its court to do so. And may I say this: The issue is not a matter of social policy. The Congress, to my knowledge, has never voted to require busing. The sole issue is this: Where the court finds that a school district is discriminating and violating the Constitution of the United States, will it continue to have the power to eliminate that discrimination? That is the issue. It is not a social-policy question. It is a question of whether we believe in the Constitution of the United States.

TV-radio interview, Washington/
"Meet the Press,"
National Broadcasting Company, 9-30.

Rogers C. B. Morton
Secretary of the Interior of the United States

1

It is difficult to generalize when describing the characteristics of the [American] Indian community. There is great variance in point of view and attitude among individuals and wide differences in the styles and approach to life from tribe to tribe. On the fringe of all of this there has grown up in the wake of the black-militant movement in this country a revolutionary Indian movement. Dramatic violence is their pattern. The occupation of Alcatraz, *Nike* [missile] sites, the Federal office building in Washington, the village of Wounded Knee [S.D.] and others all fall into it. Their effort is symbolic rather than substantive. They believe that the pursuit of their cause transcends their criminal methods. Their demands are vague and change from day to day. They do not represent a constituted group with whom the government can contract or can serve. Some of their leaders are star-struck with self-righteousness; some are renegades; some are youthful adventurers; some have criminal records. They come forth with great gusto when there is hell to raise; otherwise, they are loosely-organized, slipping from one expensive-to-the-taxpayers event to the next under a cloak of false idealism. The bloody

past is the color of their banner; publicity is the course of their future. There is no way to relive the past. History is full of atrocities. You don't break the poverty cycle by reliving the Sioux massacre at Wounded Knee. And you gain little revenge by glorifying the fall of Custer.

The National Observer, 3-31:13.

Lucien N. Nedzi
United States Representative,
D-Michigan

2

It is unfortunate that some Federal judges have become like moths fatally attracted to a flame. They have ordered [school] busing in the face of overwhelming public opinion to the contrary, in the face of the fact that busing for racial balance across district lines is a radical departure from case law and tested educational practice, and in the absence of any persuasive evidence that education or racial harmony will be therefore improved.

Human Events, 3-3:6.

Richard M. Nixon
President of the United States

3

We pass laws, laws providing and guaranteeing rights to equal opportunity. But there is no law that can legislate compassion; there is no law that can legislate understanding; there is no law that can legislate an end to prejudice. That only comes by changing the man and changing the woman.

At National Prayer Breakfast,
Washington, Feb. 1/Time, 2-12:9.

Charles Rangel
United States Representative,
D-New York

4

While the members of the [Congressional Black] Caucus might be Democrats in name or on a local basis, there is no permanent marriage; for our only absolute loyalty and responsibility is to our constituency, our people. If the Democrats wish to embrace the [Alabama Governor] George Wallaces and malevolent posion that they represent, if the Demo-

(CHARLES RANGEL)

crats wish to cooperate with the most venal and corrupt Administration in America's history [the Nixon Administration], and if the Democrats wish to deny the humanity of black people by ignoring their needs, then the Caucus would sooner cut bait and fish no more.

Before Black Caucus, Washington,
Sept. 29/San Francisco Examiner, 10-1:13.

Elliot L. Richardson
Secretary of Defense
of the United States

1

We are working against a legacy of deep-rooted and wide-spread discrimination against minorities and women. The challenges we face are intensified by societal changes which have made rising expectations and growing frustrations a double-edged manager's nightmare. But succeed we must; the symptoms will not go away, and more explanation of the complexities of the roots of present injustices will not redress the grievances of those who deserve a fair share of the American dream.

San Francisco Examiner & Chronicle,
3-18:(This World)2.

Elliot L. Richardson
Attorney General of the United States

2

My view on busing [of school children for racial balance] is that it should not be allowed to get in the way of education. The purpose of desegregation is to advance equality of educational opportunity. We should keep our eyes clearly on that objective. When prolonged busing gets in the way of education, then the means are being put ahead of the ends.

Interview, Washington/
U.S. News & World Report, 9-3:27.

Bayard Rustin
Executive director,
A. Philip Randolph Institute

3

The term "black capitalism" doesn't mean

a damn thing to the black masses. It only means that middle-class blacks got richer. If white capitalists who control trillions of dollars in this country permit wretched whites to exist in places like Appalachia, why does anyone think that black capitalists will free their brothers in the ghetto?

The New York Times, 8-26:(1)44.

4

I wouldn't lead another [civil rights] march on Washington [such as in 1963] if they paid me $10 million. The time for marches is past. It's time for the tedious, dry-as-dust work of knocking on doors to get people registered, setting up baby sitters, getting people to the polls. This is not dramatic, like following Martin Luther King up and down the South. Southerners will not be bombing churches to stir us to action. We [blacks] have to stir ourselves.

The Washington Post, 8-26:(A)14.

Stanley S. Scott
Special Adviser to the
President of the United States

5

He [President Nixon] would rather get things done than put on a show. Black people had better get away from this emotional thing and become pragmatic. It's better to have a President who is a doer than a President who is a showman . . . Let's face it, the [1972] election is over. If blacks plan to make any substantive gains in the next four years, they are going to have to work with Richard Nixon. Unfortunately, there is an unwarranted apprehension among blacks to the White House. But I'm confident that by 1976 this President will have made broad initiatives in the domestic scene that this country will be proud of.

Interview, Fayette, Miss./
The New York Times, 2-11:(1)27.

Louis Stokes
United States Representative, D-Ohio

6

. . . the civil-rights thrust of the 1960s has now turned the corner. In the 1970s the civil-rights movement has moved over into the political arena and the economic-development arena. The '60s set the groundwork for the movement of the '70s. We were able in the '60s to get the laws we needed—to get the equal-employment legislation on the books, for example. There is no need for us in the '70s to continue the demonstrations and that kind of thing. To a large degree, we don't really need any more laws. What we do need is more progress on the laws we already have to help create additional progress, to make them more effective as they relate to black people. The movement of the '70s has to concern itself with implementing laws put on the books in the '60s. What we need . . . is to give a black perspective not only to those laws but to new legislation that comes along.

Interview, Washington/
Los Angeles Times, 10-26:(2)7.

Caspar W. Weinberger
Secretary of Health, Education
and Welfare of the United States

1

[On busing of school children for racial balance]: This [Nixon] Administration . . . believes that integration is very necessary and desirable, and that we should remove all vestiges of any discrimination in schools or in housing or in jobs. But the wrong way to achieve that is by forced busing to try to produce some kind of artificial statistical quota to make school enrollments match civilian populations. As far as cutting off Federal funds [to schools that refuse to integrate] is concerned, when it is concluded what the law actually requires, then if there are violations of that law, Federal funding certainly would be cut off as a means of enforcing that law. This is the policy of the Nixon Administration.

Interview, Washington/
U.S. News & World Report, 3-19:49.

John C. Whitaker
Under Secretary of the Interior
of the United States

2

[On the current Indian rights protest at Wounded Knee, South Dakota]: Two-and-a-half years ago, the President [Nixon] submitted seven bills to Congress that would have placed Indians on the threshold of a new era in which the Indian's future could be determined by Indians. If these had been passed, maybe the obvious lawlessness, like at Wounded Knee and the take-over of the Bureau of Indian Affairs and the genuine frustrations of Indian people, might have been avoided.

News conference, Washington, March 16/
The New York Times, 3-17:14.

Roy Wilkins
Executive director, National Association
for the Advancement of Colored People

3

I am worried for the [civil-rights] gains of the 1960s. We are marking time and trying to hold onto as many gains as we can. I am afraid for the thinking of the country—the thinking which does not include the Negro, which regards him as an outsider for whom "we are doing the best we can." Blacks who did more than their share of fighting and dying in Vietnam are coming home with less . . . to twice the unemployment rates of white veterans, and they see all the programs that help poor people being cut off. This is a dismal picture. No Negroes are going to endure it.

The Washington Post, 4-11:(A)10.

4

We [black people] have an investment in America, an investment in blood and tears, in lives dead and revered, and in lives which are triumphant over insults and barriers and persecution. We aren't going anywhere. We are staying right here. This is our land. For good or bad, it owns us. And we own it! We have bought it and our futures here with sacrifices and heroism, with humility and love. It belongs to us and we shall never give up our claim and run away. We are proud of our race, of our color, of our history as Americans. We are so proud of it that we demand that it be accepted on an equality with every other minority or majority in this nation. We want to stand on an equal footing with our fellow Americans and help make our country what it was supposed to be. "Our Constitu-

(ROY WILKINS)

tion is color-blind," wrote Mr. Justice Harlan, a lone voice in 1896. Today, that voice and that tough ideal has become—because of you and those from every race like you—the sound and fervor of a multitude. Your victory is certain if you finish the task you have so magnificently advanced.

At NAACP convention, Indianapolis, July 3/Vital Speeches, 9-1:686.

1

I don't pay any attention to those people who say the Negro hasn't made any progress since the march on Washington [in 1963] . . . I can stand at the entrance to almost any office building in Manhattan today and watch the office workers come out at 5 o'clock, and it's all salt and pepper. Ten years ago they'd all be white.

The New York Times, 8-26:(1)44.

Hosea Williams
Director, Atlanta chapter,
Southern Christian Leadership Conference

2

. . . blacks were duped into seeking economic power and blacks were duped into seeking political power, and all powers are useless unless preceded by the most gracious and powerful power of all—and that's the power of self-respect. Integration has failed; it didn't work. One of the main reasons integration has failed is that the black man does not respect himself. No man can respect you if you don't respect yourself. We've got to back up and get our thing together. The second reason that integration failed is that white men cannot shed 400 years of racism just like that. With the racism in the white man's mind, he cannot accept the black man as his equal; so the white man's goal was never to integrate but to assimilate: He wanted the black man to be like him, with a white mind.

At Southern Christian Leadership Conference convention, Indianapolis/ The Dallas Times Herald, 8-19:(A)24.

Andrew Young
United States Representative,
D-Georgia

3

The black masses have not seen any results [in improvement of their lives]. The progress that middle-class blacks have made has not really served the needs of the black masses. So the average black guy on the street is pretty cynical right now. The most cynical would be the young veteran coming back from Vietnam who's apt to end up as a Black Panther or Black Muslim.

The Washington Post, 4-11:(A)10.

Spiro T. Agnew
Vice President of the
United States

1

This [Nixon] Administration is not seeking a trade bill that will make it possible to bind up the status quo. We believe that the status quo has never been a very safe place to remain . . . This Administration wants foreign trade to continue to be a creative force for progress. We want each country to do what it is best suited for, so that all of us, here at home and around the world, can derive the greatest benefit from man's productive capabilities. And we want to continue to aid the growth of the developing countries for the same reason. We realize that the transition to a completely open world economy will take time. But we are committed to the creation of an international economy characterized by a maximum practical movement of trade and freedom of investment, because we believe this freedom will create the greatest good for the greatest number of all of our peoples.
Before Michigan Manufacturers Association,
Lansing, June 11/The Washington Post,
6-13:(A)7.

Robert O. Anderson
Chairman,
Atlantic Richfield Company

2

The oil depletion allowance once had validity and good purpose, but unfortunately it has become an absolute battlefield for the industry. It's hard to advocate giving up a financial resource, but the domestic oil producers have recently had a low rate of return on invested capital, and I have a strong feeling that we have to reintroduce the dynamics of the marketplace back into the industry.
Los Angeles Times, 12-25:(3)9.

Roy L. Ash
Director, Federal Office of
Management and Budget

3

[On recent large U.S. grain exports which resulted in higher food prices in the U.S.]: The cent-a-pound higher you pay for bread will, in the long run, allow you to buy gasoline at a lesser price . . . exporting wheat generates the foreign exchange and maintains the strength of the dollar that allows us to buy oil abroad at a lower price than we would have to pay if we didn't have the strong dollar that comes from exports . . . We gain by selling to other countries that at which we are so much more efficient than they and buying from other countries that at which they are more efficient than we. And we all gain, because we get the lower prices of their product.
San Clemente, Calif./
Los Angeles Herald-Examiner, 8-30:(A)5.

James R. Barker
Chairman,
Moore & McCormack Company, Inc.

4

Businesses aren't run by geniuses. It is a matter of putting one foot after another in a logical fashion. The trick is in knowing what direction you want to go.
Interview/The New York Times, 9-2:(3)5.

Raymond Barre
Former vice president,
European Economic Community
(Common Market)

5

In spite of, or because of, official statements, people are convinced that the international value of currencies will tend to change frequently, if not continuously. The gold fever, the rise in the prices of basic commodities, of real estate, of paintings, the system-

67

(RAYMOND BARRE)

atic search for capital gains, are the main symptoms of a generalized monetary incredulity . . .

The Washington Post, 6-14:(A)31.

Birch Bayh
United States Senator, D-Indiana

1

While the average American worker labors an average of only 37 hours a week, the average farmer works 50 hours a week and earns less for his time. Farmers receive an average of only 5.4 per cent return on their investment, whereas there is a 10 to 12 per cent return on investment in industry.

Quote, 4-29:385.

Jacob D. Beam
Former United States Ambassador
to the Soviet Union

2

[On U.S.-Soviet trade]: The big problem in all forms of trade is payment. Even if we are willing to get involved in these big deals with the Soviets, where are they going to get the money to pay us? That is going to be a continuing problem, perhaps a problem of increasing intensity, a major source of possible disappointment.

Interview/
U.S. News & World Report, 7-9:25.

Lloyd M. Bentsen
United States Senator, D-Texas

3

[Saying last year's U.S. grain sale to the Soviet Union benefited the Soviets at the expense of U.S. consumers]: The Russians handled the [Nixon] Administration like the fairway barkers handled the city slicker at the county fair. Not only was the Soviet Union able to obtain sorely-needed wheat from the United States in copious quantities, but she was able to get it at bargain-basement rates that would have made the old Yankee traders blush.

The Dallas Times Herald, 7-12:(A)5.

Victor G. Bloede
Chairman,
Benton & Bowles, advertising

4

[Criticizing harrassment of advertising]: Take away advertising and you are left with a choice between the unworkable—total public financial support of the press—and the unthinkable—government regulation . . . I suggest that the time has come for American newspapers—which have fought so gloriously for freedom of speech and expression over the decades—to expand the scope of their struggle to include all segments of the communications spectrum—including advertising.

At meeting of American Publishers
Association Bureau of Advertising,
New York, April 24/
The New York Times, 4-25:55.

John S. F. Botha
South African Ambassador
to the United States

5

[Along with the dollar,] gold is the other main pillar of the present [international monetary] system. Gold also must continue to play its part, as a reserve asset, and as an underpinning for the dollar. Gold commands confidence because it is the only international asset held by monetary authorities that is not a liability of another monetary institution. It is also the only instrument of reserves that is subject to complete national control. To phase gold out of the system would mean a reduction in that element of monetary reserves which enjoys most confidence.

Before International Club of California,
San Francisco/
San Francisco Examiner & Chronicle,
3-18:(C)10.

Thornton F. Bradshaw
President,
Atlantic Richfield Company

6

Atlantic Richfield's profits last year are a matter of public record—$191 million. Tell that to the average person and he thinks that's a whale of a lot of money, and it is. But it represents a return of slightly more than 6 per cent on invested capital. That is less than the cost of borrowed money. Over a period of time, you can go out of business that way. And certainly you cannot attract capital on that basis. The industry should be making 10 or 11 per cent. It doesn't come anywhere near that . . . The oil companies are large, because they have to be. In this day and age we are dealing with vast projects—a $4 million dry hole in Alaska before we discovered the field at Prudhoe Bay, and a cost of $220 million for a single refinery completed several years ago. Looking ahead, it will require $250 million for just one shale-oil plant in Colorado, and about $700 million for a single tar-sands plant in Canada.

Interview/
U.S. News & World Report, 7-30:28.

Leonid I. Brezhnev
General Secretary,
Communist Party of the Soviet Union

1

[On U.S.-Soviet economic cooperation]: It is alleged at times that the development of such cooperation is one-sided and only benefits the Soviet Union. But those who say so are either completely ignorant of the real state of affairs or deliberately turn a blind eye to the truth. And the truth is that broader and deeper economic cooperation in general, and the long-term and large-scale deals which are now either being negotiated or have already been successfully concluded by Soviet organizations and American firms, are bound to yield real and tangible benefits to both sides. This is something that has been confirmed quite definitely by American businessmen whom I have had an opportunity to talk with both in this country and, earlier, in Moscow. It was in that context that we discussed the matter with [U.S.] President Nixon, too. To this I would like to add that both the Soviet leadership and, as I see it, the United States government attach particular importance to the fact that the development of long-term economic cooperation will also have beneficial political consequences. It will consolidate the present trend toward better Soviet-American relations generally.

Television address to the American people,
San Clemente, Calif., June 24/
The New York Times, 6-25:18.

Yale Brozen
Professor of Business Economics,
University of Chicago

2

. . . does advertising create [product] loyalties impossible for new entrants to erode, and thereby erect a barrier to entry? The simple answer is that advertising does exactly the opposite: Advertising is used to create *disloyalty*. Firms do not advertise to get the customers they already have; that is a waste of money. They advertise to get the customers they do not yet have. They try to let people know they have a product—a product which may satisfy their desires better than those for which they are now spending their money. Firms use advertising to make customers of other firms and buyers of other products *disloyal*. A business advertises when it has what it believes is a better product. It shouts to the world, "Don't be loyal to those other brands and other products. Here is a product about which you may not know. Come try it." Any firm offers a product which it hopes will be so satisfactory to some consumers for the price that they will come back and buy again and again. It is the *product* which creates loyalty. No advertising is going to hypnotize anyone into repeatedly purchasing an unsatisfactory product. All advertising can do is get the customers a firm does not yet have to come try the product. All it can do is create disloyalty. Then the product better deliver or the advertiser will find that the customers he has attracted will spread the word about how unsatisfactory the product is, and he will be dead-killed by his own advertising. That is why superior products are extensively advertised and inferior [ones] are not.

At American Marketing Association
Public Interest in Advertising seminar,
Washington, May 24/**

Carroll G. Brunthaver
Assistant Secretary of Agriculture
of the United States

1

One fact that has come home most sharply to all of us this year is that our agricultural future cannot be appraised within a strictly domestic context. We must attack the question: what is happening in other countries, and what does this mean to the future of our own agriculture? U.S. wheat exports in this marketing year are equivalent to three-fourths of the 1972 crop. Soybean exports exceed one-half of last year's crop. Feed-grain exports will total over a billion bushels. With overseas customers making up those proportions of our commodity markets, it is obvious that we have to take careful account of developments in other countries. The way other people live, and want to live, become basic to our production and marketing strategy—almost as essential to planning as are trends in our own country. It is apparent that the growth in world demand is more than just a demand for food. It's a change in the nature and quality of that demand. You might call it the protein principle—the idea that, as incomes rise, people will demand more and better-quality proteins.
The National Observer, 3-17:10.

Jeffrey M. Bucher
Governor,
Federal Reserve Board

2

[On President Nixon's recently-announced devaluation of the dollar]: Devaluation is just like an aspirin: it takes care of the temperature, for a while.
Los Angeles Times, 2-14:(1)1.

Frank J. Burgert
President, Interlake, Inc.

3

Prosperity for every American worker comes essentially from production. Production comes from tools. Tools come from invested money . . . which usually comes from profit. Thus, the real heroes of our private-enterprise system are 31 million investor-stockholders and many more million indirect owners of business and insurance policies. In their search for profits, they've helped create companies, provided tools, provided jobs, built towns, built our nation. Thus, capital spending is a key to economic growth, and this is why capital investment is so important. When the AFL-CIO asks our government to eliminate capital-investment incentives for business, they're cutting off the life blood of business, which produces 77 per cent of the gross national product and generates 87 per cent of personal and corporate income taxes.
At Steel Mark Appreciation Dinner,
Steubenville, Ohio, May 16/
Vital Speeches, 7-15:595.

Arthur F. Burns
Chairman,
Federal Reserve Board

4

. . . the underlying reason for the high level of interest rates is the persistence of inflation since 1965. Inflationary expectations have by now become fairly well entrenched in the calculations of both lenders and borrowers. Lenders commonly reckon that loans may be repaid in dollars whose real value will deteriorate because of inflation, and they therefore tend to hold out for nominal rates of interest high enough to insure them a reasonable real rate of return. Borrowers, on their part, anticipating repayment in cheaper currency, are less apt to resist rising costs of credit. The marking up of nominal rates of interest during periods of inflation is a process that is much too familiar to economic historians. Businessmen and laymen have also seen its recent manifestation in other countries . . . I want to emphasize the simple truth that inflation and high interest rates go together and that both the one and the other pose perils for economic and social stability in our country.
Before Joint Congressional
Economic Committee, Washington, Aug. 3/
U.S. News & World Report, 8-20:71.

Earl L. Butz
Secretary of Agriculture
of the United States

5

Since World War II, there has been no

major famine any place in the world, in part because of the deployment of U.S. foodstuffs. But in the long run, and for much of the world, Malthus, the man who wrote that population would outrun food supply, was close to the truth. With population continuing to grow in a world beset by drought or by excessive moisture, by plant diseases, by other forces that offset the "green revolution," the Number One problem in many parts of the world is: how do we feed all the people? . . . We are richly blessed in this country. I think we are going to recognize increasingly that the United States has the world's largest bread-basket in its contiguous land mass of fertile soil, adequate rainfall, good growing climate and well-capitalized farms. As world population continues to grow, American farmers are going to be called upon to bring the rest of these idle acres back into production, and they will be free to plant and realize more of their income out of the marketplace, and less out of the Federal Treasury.

Interview, Washington/
U.S. News & World Report, 2-5:35.

1

[Arguing against export controls on farm products]: I want to maintain America's credibility as a dependable supplier of farm products. Our farm exports last year were nearly $13 billion. This was a substantial factor in improving our farm income. It was a substantial factor in bolstering the domestic economy. It was a substantial factor in balancing our international payments. We had a net trade deficit last year of around $4 billion. If it had not been for agricultural trade, that deficit would have been 9 or 10 billion dollars. As Americans, we are heavy importers of energy, of petroleum, of electronics, of coffee, of shoes, of a wide variety of things like that; and we must pay for them some way. The best way is the export of farm products. This is the one area in the American economy where we are by far and away more efficient than anybody else in the world.

Interview/U.S. News & World Report,
9-24:24.

Alexander Calder, Jr.
Chairman, Union Camp Corporation

2

. . . a lot of security houses that have sent men here to write up the company have said ours is one of the best management groups in our industry. I think this has been the most important part of my job—helping build this management group. It goes back to having "bench strength." If I were run over by a truck tomorrow, this company could sail right along without losing a beat. I think the day of the one-man head of a company is long gone. Oh, you have to have the buck stop somewhere; but you have a management group that's capable of doing my job.

Interview, Wayne, N.J./
Nation's Business, April:64.

John Chamberlain
Political columnist

3

. . . the consumer movement, as twisted by [consumerist] Ralph Nader into a growingly totalitarian pattern that relies on Federal ukases, is, in reality, anti-consumer. Naderism, if followed to its logical end, would kill many products before the manufacturers, responding to voluntary consumer direction, could get rid of imperfections. A government exercising a rigid police function might indeed keep a dangerous drug from reaching the market. On the other hand, it might kill a penicillin if a few bad side effects were to turn up before the drug had really proved that it could wipe out venereal disease.

Before Florida Soft Drink Association,
Disney World, Fla./Human Events, 11-17:17.

William P. Clements, Jr.
Deputy Secretary of Defense
of the United States

4

The basic truth is that, from the days of the Barbary pirates to our own reliance upon the petroleum supertanker, the absolute freedom of the seas has been a goal which no United States government could ever allow to

71

be compromised.

At keel laying of "U.S.S. Texas,"
Newport News, Va., Aug. 18/
The Dallas Times Herald, 8-19:(A)26.

Eugene P. Conese
President, Irvin Industries, Inc.

1

A lot of attention is paid to the rabble-rousers in Congress telling the press and the public that the 50, 100 or 500 largest corporations pay no, or next to no, Federal income taxes. When you pin them down, when you want to get a name of a specific company that does not pay taxes . . . they begin to mumble. When you press them very hard and when you finally get a company name from them and then you look its tax status up, you find that either the company suffered a loss last year, or had a substantial loss carry-forward, or had a substantial foreign tax credit. But the man on the street thinks that he is being ripped off because he has to pay his taxes while the corporate fat-cats are getting a tax-free ride. The loophole mentality has affected even the House Ways and Means Committee which shapes our corporate tax policy. The Committee recently held hearings on whether the 7 per cent investment tax credit and ADR are tax loopholes that should be removed from the tax books. Does it make sense to restrain and reduce investment when the economy is approaching full capacity operation? Does it make sense to discriminate against investment, the prime source of productivity gains—especially when the U.S. is falling seriously behind the productivity gains of Japan, West Germany and France, and when we are being flooded by imports from countries which subsidize investment?

At St. John's University Business Conference,
May 1/Vital Speeches, 6-1:505.

John B. Connally, Jr.
Former Secretary of the Treasury of the
United States; Former Governor of Texas

2

The President needs freedom to swap cuts in United States tariffs for matching concessions from other nations, and he needs freedom when necessary to raise tariffs and impose quotas. There are people in some ivory towers around this country whose feelings are hurt because the old days [of liberal trade policy] are over. But a negotiating process which always negotiated the United States down and other coutries up should be buried deep and permanently.

Before Wharton Graduate Business School
Club of New York, March 27/
The New York Times, 3-28:63.

Reginald Connor
Minister of Minerals
and Energy of Australia

3

There are only three certainties in life today: death, taxes and successive, progressive and ever-more-frequent devaluations of the U.S. dollar.

Before Parliament, Canberra/
Time, 3-26:46.

G. Bradford Cook
Chairman, Securities and Exchange
Commission of the United States

4

[On "inside" corporate information]: . . . future earnings, pending negotiations for important contracts or possible mergers, recent corporate product discoveries which are not yet publicly known should not be confided to . . . financial analysts unless the company is willing to make a public announcement at the same time regarding these otherwise non-public matters . . . Where a widely-circulated rumor has pushed a stock up or down by a significant amount, and insiders are aware of its falsity, the Commission would have real concern if insiders traded during the period prior to the release of corrective information, whether it be through filings with the Commission or by a corporate release.

Before American Society of
Corporate Secretaries, Washington, April 19/
The New York Times, 4-20:42.

Kurt Debus
Director, John F. Kennedy Space Center,
National Aeronautics and Space
Administration of the United States

1

I think more and more businesses, even small businesses, will have to think in more international terms. The marketplace has become international. Look at the [European] Common Market. The questions of where and what to invest are becoming international. What space is . . . doing is opening satellites up fully for commercial use. Commercial satellites will be launched by anyone who wants one up there: a company, a large farmer, a university, anyone who wants to see more or reach more people. The business world will go into orbit, you might say.

Interview, Kennedy Space Center, Fla./
Nation's Business, April:48.

John D. de Butts
Chairman,
American Telephone & Telegraph Company

2

Possibly you have heard the story of the businessman who, having laid out a thousand dollars for a parrot he was assured could speak five different languages, gave instructions to the pet shop to deliver this bird to his home that very afternoon. Arriving home that evening full of anticipation, he asked his wife whether the bird had been delivered. Yes, it had. "Where is he?" said the businessman. "In the oven," his wife replied. "My God, in the oven!" said the businessman. "Why, that bird speaks five languages." "Well," said his wife, "why didn't he speak up?" Not many of us speak five languages; but what I hope to suggest this evening is that if we businessmen wish to avoid a roasting, we had better be a little more outspoken with the one we have.

The Wall Street Journal, 4-12:16.

Herbert S. Denenberg
Insurance Commissioner of Pennsylvania

3

The life-insurance industry—however pure its motives and morals—is inflicting confusion on the public, with policies the public cannot

understand, with a pricing system that prevents intelligent shopping, with agents that are often incompetent and with many companies that are unsound financially. We know that the average buyer doesn't have the foggiest idea of whether he's getting a good buy or a fleecing when he buys life insurance . . . The tens of thousands of policies that clutter the market are designed to confuse the buyer—not to protect him. They are designed to provide competition by confusion.

Before Senate Antitrust and
Monopoly Subcommittee, Washington,
Feb. 23/The New York Times, 2-24:43.

John H. Dent
United States Representative,
D-Pennsylvania

4

For some unknown reason, men and women, intelligent toward every other kind of a problem that we face, seem to have a blank mind when it comes to considering the real dangers and the grave impact of excessive imports on the American economy. The great danger to the production facilities themselves is that they are being closed down and phased out. The loss of jobs deprives Americans of an opportunity to earn a living in the kind of work that they would like to do and have been doing for years. George Ball conjectured that this nation should dispense with the so-called "unsophisticated" industry. Well, we phased out those "unsophisticated" industries, throwing the baby out with the bath, and destroyed hundreds of thousands of American jobs for that great number of Americans who need that type of work the most and in whose numbers are high percentages of unemployment. In my humble opinion, this nation cannot survive on distribution and consumption. We must have, first and primary, production of goods and services.

Before House Ways and Means Committee,
Washington, June 14/Vital Speeches, 8-15:660.

Valery Giscard d'Estaing
Minister of Economy and Finance of France

5

The Americans believe that at the present

(VALERY GISCARD d'ESTAING)

time it is in their interest to have a very flexible monetary system, because such a system will lead other countries to revalue their currencies. But what will happen most probably is that other countries will end up devaluing their currencies. Once the U.S. balance of payments is close to equilibrium, then other countries will find themselves in a deficit situation, and in order to correct the deficit, they will devalue their currencies. And so this flexibility in the monetary system which the Americans are striving for now, in the belief that it will be advantageous for them, will turn against them the day the U.S. has a balance-of-payments surplus. This is why one should not base reasoning in monetary matters on what has happened in the past. What we must seek is a monetary system which will function in the foreseeable situation of the 1980s.

Interview, Paris/
U.S. News & World Report, 7-23:52.

John Diebold
Management consultant

1

We hear a lot about the "social responsibility" of business—that companies ought to devote more of their profits to good works. That's great; but it misses the whole point. The way to harness business to work with government in meeting social problems is to use the same system business uses in serving its customers: you make it terribly expensive to do things which hurt society, and you make it very attractive—very profitable—to accomplish what society wants done . . . The thing that makes business so effective in responding to the changing requirements and demands of the consumer is not any special morality or capability on the part of its management, but the feedback control of the profit system. So I think the job of government is to set up incentives and constraints in such a way that business makes money doing what society most needs done.

Interview, Washington/
U.S. News & World Report, 1-29:43.

Nicolaas Diederichs
Minister of Finance of South Africa

2

Gold is the only element in the monetary system which commands respect, whether we like it or not.

San Francisco Examiner & Chronicle,
7-29:(This World)2.

Coy G. Eklund
President, Equitable Life Assurance Society of the United States

3

My belief is that corporate enterprise in America, at this point in time, has received the social-responsibility message, understands its meaning and is increasingly acting upon it with earnestness and purpose. Top management and board members have come to realize that their business conduct must have both financial acceptability and social responsibility; that social irresponsibility is something closely akin to financial irresponsibility. What I am saying is that business leaders increasingly accept and act upon the belief that business can prosper and survive best through behavior compatible with the workings of the total life-support system, and that either social or ecological degradation of the environment in which business operates would not only impair but eventually bring down the profit-making corporation.

Before National Urban League, Washington,
July 24/Vital Speeches, 8-15:659.

Lewis A. Engman
Chairman, Federal Trade Commission

4

I cannot accept the suggestion from some quarters that we [at the FTC] are picking on big advertisers [in exposing advertising fraud] while ignoring the little ones. This is analogous to the man who gets a parking ticket and complains that the cop isn't out catching robbers—except that the reverse is implied here. The FTC is catching some of the robbers, and now they want us to concentrate on the working violations. I assure, we will do both.

Before Los Angeles County Bar Association,
May 31/Los Angeles Times, 6-1:(3)17.

1

What is the consumer's recourse when he finds himself stuck with a $10 toaster which burns his bread to a crisp, and the store manager tells him his warranty is invalid? What is the consumer's recourse when he orders and pays for the yellow lawn furniture, and two weeks later they deliver the purple? For that matter, what is his recourse if they do not deliver any lawn furniture until the day of the first big snow storm in November? What is the consumer's recourse when he continues to be billed for goods he never bought, and all the computer will do is add on monthly charges and spew out letters threatening a law suit? . . . The simple fact is that, for vast and increasing numbers of consumers with valid complaints, there is nothing to be done after two hours of haranguing the salesman, the supervisor, the department chief, the customer-service girl and the store manager other than to drive 15 miles back home, kick the dog, yell at his children and curse his wife.

Before International Association of Insurance Counsel, Toronto, July 6/ The Washington Post, 7-7:(C)7.

Peter M. Flanigan
Assistant to the President of the United States for International Economic Affairs

2

If you had money you wanted to invest anywhere in the world, one of the considerations that would be important to you would be, "What are the chances of nationalization of my investment?" I can't imagine any country less likely to nationalize than the United States; it's entirely contrary to our principles. And we would be jeopardizing our own enormous investments abroad if we supported nationalization. We have consistently said to people that we welcome foreign investment here. We're delighted to have people come and put their money here. There are no inhibitions, no barriers, and we think it's a good opportunity.

Interview, Washington/ U.S. News & World Report, 5-28:62.

Henry Ford II
Chairman, Ford Motor Company

3

We're going to have to spend billions of dollars to import petroleum into this country. The Arabs are going to have tens of billions, maybe hundreds of billions, and there's nothing to prevent them from coming to the U.S. and investing in the stock market. The Arabs may end up in control of most of the big companies in this country. It's a very serious possibility.

Interview/Fortune, May:191.

4

[On the U.S. trade deficit]: I don't think anybody pays enough attention to it. Washington really isn't doing anything about it. We're going to end up just like Britain. We're going to be a service country. We won't be able to produce against other countries at a reasonable price to the consumer; so the consumer is going to buy from overseas, and we'll be just a nation of fixers and spare-parts makers.

Interview/Fortune, May:284.

5

[On Federal controls on business]: We now have a silent partner who has no equity in our business but has a strong voice in management. They control everything we do, practically speaking. They control the design of our product—both from an operating standpoint and a looks standpoint. They control our prices, control our salaries, control our wages, control our profits.

Interview/Fortune, May:284.

6

Running a big country well is a very hard, complicated job—even harder than running a big company well. When government regulates business, neither can do its job well unless they discuss their differences rationally, understanding each other's problems, and help each other get the job done. Too often, instead of working together, they are pitted against each other, with the public cheering and booing from the sidelines. When this happens, everyone loses—especially the public.

Quote, 11-18:488.

John Kenneth Galbraith
Professor of Economics,
Harvard University

1

I do not think the "money doctors" will find a real solution [to the international monetary crisis]. As long as President Nixon's financial advisers think that God is a good conservative man with Republican sympathies, nothing will happen.

Quote, 4-1:289.

Carl A. Gerstacker
Chairman, Dow Chemical Company

2

We appear to be moving in the direction of what will not really be multinational or international companies as we know them today, but what we might call "anational" companies—companies without any nationality, belonging to all nationalities.

At White House Conference on the
Industrial World Ahead, Washington/
The New York Times Magazine, 3-18:24.

Richard C. Gerstenberg
Chairman, General Motors Corporation

3

Every nation, all around the world, wants to expand its trade with other nations. But every nation, unfortunately, is not working to achieve the ideal of free world trade. Almost everywhere, lip service is paid to international cooperation and to the need to reduce tariffs, import quotas, special taxes and other barriers to the free flow of commerce. But all too often, even in the United States, there is a feeling that free trade is something the "other guy" should practice. As a result, a stagnant cloud of protectionism still hangs over many of the world's trade centers. It is surprising that, even today, when we talk about the Earth as a spaceship in which all of the world's people are traveling together, that high tariffs and other barriers to trade are not recognized for what they are: short-sighted, penny-in-the-hand, futile graspings for security—and all at the expense of the proven bene-

fits of free trade.

Before Financial Executives Institute,
New York, Oct. 22/
Vital Speeches, 12-15:144.

4

We would all be wise to bear in mind what our late President John F. Kennedy once said: "Every time we lift a problem to the government, to that extent we limit the liberties of the people." The problems of American business are not best resolved in Washington. It is idle and foolish for us to believe that we can pack up our problems of competition, of costs, of productivity and [of] customer satisfaction and send them to Washington for solution. The problems of business are too complex, too subtle, too closely involved with the public mood and temperament to be handled by some bureaucracy, remote both in place and in feeling. Instead, the problems we face are ours to resolve as we have always done. And this, I submit, is best accomplished in a climate of freedom.

Before Financial Executives Institute,
New York, Oct. 22/
Vital Speeches, 12-15:146.

J. Paul Getty
Industrialist

5

The non-conformist, the leader and originator, has an excellent chance to make $1 million in the business world. He can wear a green toga instead of a gray flannel suit, drink yak's milk rather than martinis, drive a kibitka instead of a Cadillac, and vote a straight Vegetarian ticket; it will not make the slightest difference. Ability and achievement are what counts, no matter how unconventional the man.

Los Angeles Herald-Examiner, 7-4:(A)8.

Weldon B. Gibson
President,
Stanford Research Institute-International

6

I believe the trend of events is leading toward the growth of world corporations that during the next two or three decades can be increasingly described with these words: de-nationalized ownership, management and financing with no more than a fourth to a third of sales, assets and labor force within any one country.

Before Public Relations Society of America,
Honolulu, Nov. 13/
San Francisco Examiner, 11-13:58.

Barry M. Goldwater
United States Senator, R-Arizona

1

The real tragedy of [the] Watergate [political-espionage affair] has been that it has again distracted our attention at a very, very crucial time . . . The result of this diversion has been startling in terms of what has happened to the dollar overseas and the stock market here at home. Here we are, after two devaluations of the dollar in a 14-month period, and those in control of Congress still want to continue deficit spending on a vast scale, union leaders continue to demand wage boosts far, far in excess of increases in the rate of productivity, and welfare recipients throughout the country continue to step up on their demands for even higher payments. Now, this is what ails the dollar.

Before Rotary Club, San Francisco, July 10/
Los Angeles Herald-Examiner, 7-11:(A)5.

Edwin H. Gott
Chairman, United States Steel Corporation

2

I don't know what this country would do without big business. When I look at how far this country we all love has come—in food, in communications, in transportation—it's all due entirely to big business.

Interview/The Wall Street Journal,
2-28:12.

Armand Hammer
Chairman, Occidental Petroleum Corporation

3

[On his business dealings]: I am first and foremost a catalyst. I bring people and situations together. That's the big thing—bringing

the deal together.

Interview/
The New York Times, 5-20:(3)15.

John D. Harper
Chairman, Aluminum Company of America

4

Business seems to have lost its voice just when it needs it most . . . On the other hand, the more radical opponents of business are at no loss for words. They hammer away at the system . . . and increasing numbers of Americans are listening to them and believing them because they hear few other voices.

U.S. News & World Report, 10-8:49.

Leslie Harris
Vice president,
Interpublic Group of Companies

5

Belief in advertising is at an all-time low. A recent Opinion Research study put us [in advertising] at the bottom of the list in terms of public confidence. But at least we were in distinguished company: The U.S. Supreme Court got the same rating.

Before Los Angeles Advertising Club/
Daily Variety, 4-27:15.

Philip A. Hart
United States Senator, D-Michigan

6

Free enterprise is dead in some segments of our economy and seemingly on its death bed in others. It, however, is not beyond cure. The medicine I propose is a large dose of antitrust.

At National Computer Conference,
New York, June 4/
The New York Times, 6-5:53.

Mark O. Hatfield
United States Senator, R-Oregon

7

The price of gold should be established in a free market, and this price should have neither a ceiling nor floor guaranteed by the United States government.

Washington, Jan. 16/
San Francisco Examiner, 1-17:8.

Edward Heath
Prime Minister of the United Kingdom

1

[On U.S.-European trade negotiations]: We will get nowhere unless both sides of the Atlantic put clearly on the table what is their position and stop trying to pretend that they are the ones who are knights in shining armor and that it's the other chap who is the rogue . . . The U.S. has higher tariffs than the European Community across the board. That is the first thing. Secondly, it has high protectionism for its agriculture. So if it wants to discuss [Europe's] Common Agricultural Policy, then it has also to discuss the high protectionism for American agriculture . . . Let's have all the facts. Let's review them coolly and rationally and then see how we can remove the obstacles on each side of the Atlantic to an expansion of trade.

Interview/Newsweek, 5-28:48.

Margaret M. Heckler
United States Representative,
R-Massachusetts

2

Women now constitute 44 per cent of the labor force and in these changing economic times deserve as much right to access to credit as do men. It is documented that creditors are often unwilling to extend credit to a married woman in her own name—despite the fact that in some instances she may be the major breadwinner in the family. Today, women are in the professions, the factories, the stores and offices—in fact, are earning steady incomes in all walks of life. If women are to be such active participants in the economic scheme of things, then women are entitled to equal involvement in the way America does business.

Quote, 12-23:605.

Walter W. Heller
Professor of Economics, University
of Minnesota; Former Chairman,
Council of Economic Advisers
to the President of the United States

3

I think that we are in a position, vis-a-vis the rest of the world, that was improved by the Smithsonian Agreement, when we depreciated the dollar by 11, 12, 10 per cent, something like that; but it may be we are still over-valued. It may be that there ought to be a further adjustment in the value of the dollar, and I don't think we should consider that the end of the world, if we have to devalue. Obviously, we would rather have the rest of the world do the job for us by up-valuing their currencies. But if, as part of the deal, we had to depreciate our dollar a little bit further in terms of gold, I think we have demonstrated that that isn't going to be the worst thing that could happen.

TV-radio interview,
Washington/"Meet the Press,"
National Broadcasting Company, 2-11.

Jesse A. Helms
United States Senator,
R-North Carolina

4

My people know . . . that they are paying more for food because of the grain deal last year with the Soviet Union. They know that we sold too much, too cheap, too secretly. They know now that our graneries are nearly empty. They know that the scarcity of wheat and the scarcity of feed grains has driven up the prices in the whole food chain. They know that this triggered the [Nixon] Administration's disastrous attempt at price controls, which, in turn, drove chickens, beef and pork off the market . . . We are talking about a deal that has had major impact upon U.S. life, and it is only one of [Secretary of State Henry] Kissinger's agreements. I greatly fear that his much-lauded agreements will also end up with the Soviets taking us for a ride. The issue is one of competence, and I have concluded that Dr. Kissinger has failed the test.

Before the Senate,
Washington, Sept. 21/
Human Events, 10-6:6.

William A. Hewitt
Chairman, Deere & Company

5

The mechanism of the United States economy, together with the benefits it derives from a nationally-regulated international flow of technology, capital and goods, is difficult enough to digest and even harder to describe. Yet, the protectionist forces seem to be attempting to reduce the issue to a simple matter of "imports plus overseas investment equals fewer jobs for American workers." That is a gross and an inaccurate over-simplification. Such reasoning assumes that only other nations benefit from U.S. purchases and investments in those nations. Trade and investment, however, are mutually-rewarding to both parties. Imports provide the foreign exchange that other countries need to purchase U.S. products. In other words, imports finance exports. Exports, in turn, are effective employment catalysts. About 25,000 jobs are created by every $1 billion of goods that we export from this country . . . Imports also aid consumers, including the farmer. They give him a wider choice of products and prices, whereas tariffs and quotas tend to limit his choice, raise prices and nurture inflation. Over the long pull, trade restrictions also stifle exports.

At University of Illinois/
The Christian Science Monitor, 5-5:18.

1

I subscribe to the idea that "Communication is the beginning of understanding." The more we trade with our ideological adversaries, the more chance there is of fostering greater understanding among nations, including those nations who have been squared off against one another in the cold war that started at the end of World War II. The more we trade with our ideological adversaries, the more we will spread the benefits of more and better food and fiber throughout the world, and thus soften the temptation of nations to raid their neighbor's storehouse. The more we trade with our ideological adversaries on a mutually-beneficial basis, the more we will gain from one another and the more we will progress in the common quest for a more comfortable and more cultured civilization. Conversely, if nations with different ideologies insist on remaining in their mutually-isolated compartments in the world, antagonism is bound to grow, hostility will flourish and the

potential for outright conflict will be increased.

The National Observer, 5-19:15.

Edwin M. Hood
President,
Shipbuilders Council of America

2

U.S. trade and commerce, increasingly over the past decade, has been handled by the ships of other nations. More than 95 per cent of the critical materials without which the American economy could not function are imported by foreign-flag shipping. Only 5 per cent of all oil imports are brought to our shores in American bottoms. Our sealift capacity suffers from the infirmities of obsolescence and inadequacy. Even with last year's record level of new contracts, considerable shipyard capacity remains idle. The availability of the world's sea lanes can now be effectively frustrated by the expanding prowess of Russian naval and maritime strength. Our imbalance of trade, and to a large degree the persistent imbalance of international payments, can be attributed to the quality of our over-all marketing effectiveness throughout the world.

Before Casco Bay Council of the
Navy League, Brunswick, Me.,
April 24/Vital Speeches, 6-1:489.

Roman L. Hruska
United States Senator, R-Nebraska

3

[Warning against antitrust and monopoly legislation that may break up large U.S. industries]: Big industries abroad have expanded 120 per cent in the past five years. The rate of growth in this country has been only 60 per cent. If that growth rate continues, we will be outstripped in another four or five years. We can break up these industries here, but we can't break them up over there.

Nation's Business, November:35.

Hubert H. Humphrey
United States Senator, D-Minnesota

4

As we look ahead to vigorous competition in world trade—and it will be just that—let me

(HUBERT H. HUMPHREY)

share a few thoughts with my fellow Americans who are here. It is time for business, government, labor and agriculture to arrive at a common trade policy. In the real world of today, government and business must be working partners in the field of foreign trade; surely we should have learned this by now from our experience with other countries. These national partnerships must, however, abide by international standards such as GATT. Let's be candid—American industry has traditionally been geared to its domestic markets and to assured foreign markets. As a result, our trade, financial and economic policies are not designed to meet the competitive realities of the present. In the years ahead, we must refashion policies. We must be more competitive, more innovative. We must be export- and investment-minded. We must use the tools of market research to maximize our export potential. We must start doing all these things, and start doing them now . . . Those in control of economic and trade policy in our respective nations must come to a new recognition of the interdependence of politics and trade—both in their own countries and abroad. They must realize that international trade and economics is too important to leave either to the economists or the politicians alone. It is time for you and I—the American public, the Japanese public and the European public, as well as their respective leaders—to begin to understand each other and work together. In this way, we can help provide the leadership which will prevent us from continuing on a collision course which only spells disaster. We can and must develop trade, investment and monetary policies which allow us to grow together rather than grow apart.

At Conference on International Trade,
San Juan, Puerto Rico, January/
Vital Speeches, 2-1:238.

Lee A. Iacocca
President, Ford Motor Company

1

[On his industry's relations with government]: I think we could do a better job by saying, "That's your cup of tea; this is mine. Now, let's get to work. We'll have a council or a forum where there are areas you feel you want to encroach upon, and me on yours." We've got to talk first, rather than [the government] saying, "Hold it; I got the Federal seal and I'm going to *order* you to do it." We can legislate all of the auto problems in the world on a piece of paper. But if our industry caused the problems, unless the government changes our system completely, only I and the others [in the industry] can unravel them. If you think some bureaucrat can do that, you're wrong.

Interview, Detroit/Parade, 5-20:9.

2

I've made 15 trips to Europe since I've been on this job. The last one, in March, it pained me as an American that nobody wanted American dollars. They'd ask, "Don't you have some other currency? Don't you have some German marks?" I stopped in shame. Right after the war, you could buy marks by the bushel basket. Now, what the hell happened in 25 years? Here's the damned dollar, George Washington still on it, and nobody wants it. They won't even take it as a tip. *That's* what the hell happened.

Interview, Detroit/Parade, 5-20:9.

3

I'm a bigger consumerist than [lawyer-consumer advocate] Ralph Nader. I do everything Nader does, with one exception: I gotta worry about paying for it because I'm a big tycoon.

Interview/The New York Times, 5-23:71.

Frank N. Ikard
President, American Petroleum Institute

4

[Arguing against a proposed government oil corporation]: Twenty years ago, a penny would move a gallon of oil from Texas to New York by tanker. At the same time, a penny would also move a postcard from Texas to New York through the government postal service. Today, private enterprise still requires only a penny to move a gallon of oil from Texas to New York. But a postcard costs six cents . . . Americans enjoy the greatest supply of energy at the cheapest price in the world, including all the countries with nationalized agencies. Most of the oil that has been discovered in the world has been discovered by American companies.

Dec. 18/
The Dallas Times Herald, 12-19:(A)4.

Henry M. Jackson
United States Senator, D-Washington

1

I co-sponsored the East-West Trade Relations Act in 1971. But East-West trade must be *mutually* beneficial. Look what happened in last year's grain deal. The Russians bought [U.S.] wheat at subsidized prices of $1.60 a bushel when they should have been paying the full price. The American taxpayer ended up subsidizing the Russian housewife to the tune of more than $300 million, and the American housewife ended up paying higher prices for beef and other grain-based foodstuffs. Our shipping and grain-transportation systems have been severely disrupted. On that deal at least, the Soviets got the wheat and we got the chaff. Why should we underwrite credits to the Soviet Union? Are they doing that sort of thing for us? We're so anxious to do business —any kind of business—that we'll agree to anything. I recall that Lenin, in discussing the grave economic difficulties in the Soviet Union in the 1920s, said: "But, comrades, don't let us panic. If we give the bourgeoisie enough rope, they'll hang themselves." Karl Radek, a member of the C.P. Central Committee and co-worker of Lenin, asked: "Where are you going to get the rope to give the bourgeoisie?" Replied Lenin: "From the bourgeoisie."

Interview/
U.S. News & World Report, 6-18:35.

2

We [the U.S.] are sliding into the foreign-aid business with respect to the failing Soviet economy. The Soviet Union, for example, has recently borrowed substantial sums at the rate of interest lower than the [U.S.] prime rate. No American corporation—no American home-owner—can do that. Agricultural commodities in vast amounts have been purchased by the Soviet Union at prices lower than those paid by American consumers; and both the grain

itself, and its financing and transportation, have been subsidized by the American taxpayer.

Before the Senate, Washington/
The National Observer, 7-7:3.

3

The oil companies are the most important utility in the United States. They make possible other utilities—telephone, electric and so on. Serious consideration should be given to public-utility-type regulation [of oil firms].

Before California Correspondents
Association, Washington, Nov. 30/
Los Angeles Times, 12-1:(1)26.

Neil H. Jacoby
Professor of Economics,
Graduate School of Management,
University of California, Los Angeles

4

The idea that giant corporations "dominate" our society is pure myth. The United States is not now, and is not becoming, a "corporate economy" in the sense that big business corporations dominate American society. Our country has a heterogeneous economy with respect to the sizes and types of its enterprises, and is a pluralistic society with respect to the number and power of its institutions. Corporate economic power is effectively constrained by market competition. Corporate political power is effectively countervailed by the power of labor unions, farm organizations, professional societies and a host of consumerist and environmentalist blocs.

Lecture, Los Angeles, Oct. 4/
Los Angeles Herald-Examiner, 10-5:(A)14.

Nicholas Johnson
Commissioner,
Federal Communications Commission

5

[Criticizing advertisers]: [They sell] a lifestyle or religion known as materialism: the idea that what's important in your life is what's outside yourself—your auto or some appliance.

Television interview/
Los Angeles Times, 5-18:(4)23.

James H. Jones
President,
First National Bank of Commerce,
New Orleans

1

It is time to deny that old philosophy that the further away we [in business and banking] are from the political structure, the more pure we might be . . . The further away we are, the more isolated, the more self-centered, self-serving, the more incapable we are of fulfilling our community responsibilities.

At Southern Methodist University
Southwestern Graduate School of Banking/
The Dallas Times Herald, 8-15:(D)11.

Mary Gardiner Jones
Commissioner, Federal Trade Commission

2

The consumer's welfare and interests have always been the announced and avowed objective of all economic activity. Yet, it has also been a universally-accepted notion that profit is the direct and accepted measure of corporate performance . . . Consumer satisfaction . . . is assumed to exist if the company's operations are profitable. Herein lies a critical fallacy in corporate thinking about the extent to which their conduct in fact serves the day-to-day interests and concerns of the consumer . . . Corporations may have very little incentive [for instance] to be certain that the materials which they produce or the buildings which they construct are as fire-safe as possible. Indeed, it is unlikely that they will be concerned at all with fire safety beyond essential compliance with existing regulations . . .

Before National Fire Protection Association,
St. Louis/The Christian Science Monitor,
7-2:10.

Edgar F. Kaiser
Chairman,
Kaiser Industries Corporation

3

Business must communicate to the public —not just our younger generation—a number of proofs; namely, that wages for workers, taxes for government, dividends for shareholders, contributions for education, investment for product improvement, expansion and with it more jobs, and last but not least, environmental improvement—all these benefits of business to society depend absolutely and entirely on profitability.

San Francisco Examiner, 1-18:34.

Thomas E. Kauper
Assistant Attorney General,
Antitrust Division, Department of
Justice of the United States

4

My own sense of priorities puts a heavy emphasis on price fixing and merger activity aimed at reducing competition. Price fixing is a crime, and corporate officials who engage in it ought to go to jail.

Time, 9-24:110.

Donald M. Kendall
Chairman, PepsiCo, Inc.

5

. . . we [the U.S.] have to be tough in our trade negotiations. The day of the Marshall Plan approach is over. We could afford the Marshall Plan. We were in a position like the Japanese are now, with big surpluses. But we can't afford that kind of program today. We need negotiators who know what they're talking about, and who are tough. I don't mean unfair . . . I believe the United States can still compete in this world. I don't think we need protection from our neighbors and trading partners—just fair conditions.

Interview, Washington/
U.S. News & World Report, 1-22:67.

6

I predict the Soviet Union and the United States will be each other's major trading partner. We will benefit in having improvement in trade and payment balances; there will be a multiplier effect on domestic output and employment and greater economics of scale for U.S. industry . . . I look forward to a bright outcome toward normal Soviet-American trade and benefits in the lives of both our people that will far transcend commercial gain.

COMMERCE / INDUSTRY / FINANCE

There's a greater emphasis on the part of the Soviet people today for consumer goods which are essential to enhance the quality of their daily lives. This will assist us in mutual initiatives toward peace and away from the nightmare prospect of mutual annihilation.

Before Downtown Rotary Club,
Dallas, Oct. 10/
The Dallas Times Herald, 10-10:(F)9.

Richard G. Kleindienst
Attorney General of the United States

1

There was a time when, so far as Washington was concerned, American business was in the doghouse. This [Nixon] Administration's approach is entirely different. We believe that, through mutual education as to the meaning and intent of the law, mistakes by business can be avoided and many head-on confrontations on both sides can be obviated. We are not lying in ambush, hoping that you [in business] will make a misstep and fall into one of our legal snares. If you do, after our sincere efforts to keep you acquainted with the law, then the processes of justice will most certainly have to take over. But we assume you are innocent until proven guilty.

At Federal Bar Association Ninth Circuit
conference, Phoenix, March 28/
The New York Times, 3-29:75.

Jacques Kosciusko-Morizet
French Ambassador to the United States

2

[Saying European countries will be unwilling to go along with further U.S. dollar devaluation and that the U.S. must stabilize the dollar]: No reasonable country can accept the fact that the level of its economy is decided by the irrational movements of the money markets, that the revaluation of its currency and the subsequent loss of competitiveness result automatically from the fluctuations imposed by the irresponsible monetary policy of another country.

At meeting sponsored by French Chamber
of Commerce in the United States/
Los Angeles Times, 1-22:(3)9.

Irving Kristol
Professor of Urban Values,
New York University

3

One hears much about the "work ethic" these days, and I certainly appreciate the nostalgic appeal of that phrase. But next time you hear a banker extolling the "work ethic," just ask him if he favors making installment buying illegal. When I was very young, it was understood that the only people who would buy things on the installment plan were the irresponsibles, the wastrels, those whose characters were too weak to control their appetites. "Save now, buy later" is what the work ethic used to describe. To buy now and pay later was the sign of moral corruption—though it is now the accepted practice of our affluent society. A people who have mortgaged themselves to the hilt are a dependent people—and ultimately they will look to the state to save them from bankruptcy. The British have a wonderful colloquial phrase for installment purchasing—they call it buying on "the never-never." The implication is that through this marvelous scheme you enter a fantasy world where nothing is denied you, and where the settling of all accounts is indefinitely postponed. This is a consumer's utopia—and more and more it is as such a consumer's utopia that our bourgeois society presents itself to its people.

At Hillsdale (Mich.) College,
April/Vital Speeches, 6-1:503.

William J. Kuhfuss
President,
American Farm Bureau Federation

4

Restriction on [U.S.] agricultural exports is putting a strain on our trade relations with our best overseas customers for farm products and is not in the best interests of American agriculture or the American economy. Export limitations destroy the confidence of other countries in the United States as a reliable source of supply and may intensify our serious balance-of-payments problem.

News conference, New York, July 18/
The New York Times, 7-19:47.

R. Heath Larry
Vice chairman,
United States Steel Corporation

1

[On business-government relations]: If we wish to achieve an optimum growth pattern, we cannot continue to point at the role of government on the one hand—or the role of business in the market system on the other—as if each were inevitably in opposition to the other. We need, rather, to bring forth and retain the best capabilities of both.

Before National Association of Manufacturers,
March 7/The New York Times, 3-8:57.

Mary Wells Lawrence
Chairman, Wells, Rich, Greene, advertising

2

There is very little glory in advertising. If you sell the product, you get the rewards. It was childish a few years ago; now it is very adult, very complex; it requires a good deal of work . . . I don't think it's fun.

Interview/
The Dallas Times Herald, 6-13:(E)10.

Pierre Liotard-Vogt
Managing director,
Nestle Company, S.A.

3

Multinationals have gotten a bad image because of things like the International Telephone and Telegraph business in Chile. But this really was the exception, and it has been shown that what IT&T did also did not work. The multinational company cannot go along concentrating on growth, new products and markets in the self-knowledge that it is doing nothing wrong. It has to take time to tell what it is doing. If it does not, there is a tendency now for people to wonder what it is doing, to be suspicious. I know of no multinational company that is a superpower; because, as we have seen in the case of the oil companies, even the smallest countries can take them over if they want to.

Interview, New York/
The New York Times, 5-21:53.

Lee Loevinger
Lawyer; Former Assistant Attorney General,
Antitrust Division, Department of
Justice of the United States

4

It has been said so often that it has become a banality that the price of liberty is eternal vigilance. Yet it is still true, and it is peculiarly appropriate to remind business that the cost of freedom, like the cost of success, is continuous effort. Business must continually earn its freedom, and indeed its very right to exist and operate, by meeting the demands of its contemporary environment for both material productivity and social responsibility. But freedom cannot exist for business alone. Freedom for business means a free society with freedom for all. This requires that business, as one of the major institutions in society, must bear its full share of responsibility for serving those public interests that make freedom possible. Thus, in the final analysis, the social responsibility of business in a democratic society is nothing less than the duty to do its best to help provide freedom and dignity to every member of society. Good citizenship is good business; and in the long run, the best economic course is to be guided by contemporary ethics.

Lecture, New York University/
The National Observer, 5-19:15.

Robert W. Long
Assistant Secretary of Agriculture
of the United States

5

The new Americans born in the next three decades will expect much more of their food. They will insist that it be available when they want it, in or out of season; that it taste as it did when picked; be in a "grade AA" state of wholesomeness; provide a full measure of nutritional value; and be ready to fix with little or no fuss. And they will probably get it—to an even greater extent than today. During the past 30 years, food technologists began the task with creations that included frozen foods, fortified foods, year-round produce, and "instant" beverages and mixes. In the coming 30 years, new advances on the horizon in the way food is grown, processed, transported and prepared will make even recent innovations look old-fashioned.

Lecture at Franklin Institute, Philadelphia/The National Observer, 6-30:11.

Carl H. Madden
Chief economist,
Chamber of Commerce of the United States

1

[On multinational corporations]: . . . across one country after another there are overtones of suspicion against MNCs. For one thing, the very speed of their growth causes their accomplishments to be taken for granted while their shortcomings are emphasized. U.S.-based MNCs are understandably linked with criticisms of U.S. policies and actions that are reflected in the recent weakness of the dollar. Some foreign governments and critics have viewed MNCs as seeking excessive power, basing an indictment of all on evidence of a few alleged instances. Some [labor] unions fear the threat to their leadership of MNCs who appear able to move employment across national boundaries. The rising shortage of raw materials has dramatically strengthened the bargaining power of developing countries having such resources under development by MNCs. In Europe especially, MNCs are under suspicion because they have easily overstepped national cultural, political and economic institutional differences that even nationals working toward international or bloc integration have been unable to surmount. Indeed, the MNC is a convenient scapegoat for domestic critics, particularly when it has generated strong competition in local markets previously isolated from all but domestic influences.

At Georgetown University Bankers Forum, Warrenton, Va., Sept. 15/ Vital Speeches, 11-15:86.

William McChesney Martin, Jr.
Former Chairman,
Federal Reserve Board

2

The American dollar in the post-war world has been the principal bulwark of the international payments system as well as the best currency in the world in which to save. This is no longer true, and now no one has complete confidence in saving in any currency. This accounts for the speculation in gold, and this at a time when the world needs capital formation desperately.

Before Senate Finance Subcommittee, Washington, June 1/ The New York Times, 6-2:39.

Paul W. McCracken
Former Chairman,
Council of Economic Advisers
to the President of the United States

3

[On President Nixon's recently-announced devaluation of the dollar]: You go back two years and the mere talk of devaluation was sinful. [But] we have found, after all, that the exchange rate is just a price—there's nothing mystical about it. We have found we can adjust exchange rates without the world coming to an end.

Interview/ Los Angeles Times, 2-14:(1)1.

George Meany
President, American Federation
of Labor-Congress
of Industrial Organizations

4

What I have said to the President [Nixon] before, and what I have said to the Secretary of State, is that I would start with a very simple proposal that any nation that closes a [trade] door on us—on our [American] products—that we should turn around and close the door on them. Just as simple as that. What he [Nixon] is proposing is that sort of approach, so that he can negotiate with certain options. For instance, everybody knows that the best consumer market in the whole world is the United States. These countries—a good number of them—lock out American products from their own countries, but they want to sell here in the United States. I think there are other areas—for instance, we are competing with industries in various parts of the world that are subsidized by government.

(GEORGE MEANY)

I think the President wants to be in a position to say to a particular country, "Well, I am going to put an import tax on the products from your country." And he could put that import tax on in order to meet this subsidy.

Miami Beach, Feb. 19/
U.S. News & World Report, 3-5:79.

1

I never met a corporation yet that had a conscience.

Before House Ways and Means Committee,
Washington, March 7/
Los Angeles Times, 3-8:(1)6.

2

[On U.S. commercial dealings with Communist nations]: Our corporations would serve their country and even their own vital interests if they applied the following rule: The decisive consideration in commercial transactions with dictatorships is that such deals must serve the national interest of our country and its free society, and not simply be concerned with making a fast buck by helping the Communist regimes bail out of their economic difficulties and thus strengthening them for further subversion and aggression.

The New York Times, 6-17:(3)4.

Akio Morita
President, Sony Corporation (Japan)

3

We see the appearance [in the U.S.] of legislation that would restrict trade by compulsion or apply import surcharges . . . This type of effort to reduce the competitive strength of a trading partner . . . is the suppression of competitive strength by artificial means . . . Countries that would wish to sustain the system of free economy must have the courage to exert their own efforts to compete adequately. If a country works hard to increase its competitive strength, then other countries have to work harder to compete.

Before Foreign Correspondents Club,
Tokyo, June 15/
Los Angeles Times, 6-18:(3)9.

Samuel Neaman
Chairman, McCrory Corporation

4

Business [today] is much bigger. At the top sits a man who now has to make more decisions for more people. Everybody looks to him and says: "Make the decision." They want him to do it so they can escape the responsibility. "You make the decision so I can criticize," they say. We have gone from small business to large business, and we will have to learn that large business will have to delegate, to break itself into smaller components. We shouldn't put too much power into a central position; not because it's bad, but because it's impossible to control so many decisions and make them with enough knowledge.

Interview, New York/
Nation's Business, November:47.

James J. Needham
Chairman, New York Stock Exchange

5

[Large institutional investors that now dominate NYSE trading are] concentrating their activity in an ever-narrowing circle of investment choices . . . to the unjustified neglect of literally hundreds of other high-quality stocks . . . Now, no one is suggesting that the answer to these problems is for institutional investors to go out on a speculative binge. But it is certainly pertinent to inquire why the large institutions persist in tightening their concentration in a favorite 18 or favorite 50 or favorite 100 stocks while ignoring hundreds of other choice investment opportunities. One wonders whether the analysts are really at work.

Before Financial Analysts Federation,
Washington, May 9/
The Washington Post, 5-10:(D)17.

6

If the small investor is to have confidence in the workings of the securities industry, the Exchange and member firms must work to show him that his business is welcome and, indeed, essential to the securities marketplace and the national economy.

The Christian Science Monitor, 6-29:4.

E. L. Nicholson
Chairman and president,
CNA Financial Corporation

1

Many of the best potential business leaders in our country will never surface because they have [been] turned off on business in their youth. We are losing to our competitors in this league—education, government, research, social services, professions, travel, doing nothing. They are siphoning off too much of the talent needed for future generations of able business leadership.

Before Pennsylvania Chamber of Commerce,
Philadelphia/Quote, 10-28:413.

Richard M. Nixon
President of the United States

2

[Although the Administration favors free trade,] that's only half the story. We are talking about the other side as well. We must go up as well as down [with trade barriers]. That's the only way to get a fair deal and a fair shake for American products abroad. We have gone into too many [trade] negotiations abroad in which all we have done is negotiate down, whereas the others have negotiated up. We are going to ask Congress for the right for our negotiators to go up or down. Only if we go up can we get them to go down on some of the restrictions they have.

Washington, Feb. 13/
Los Angeles Times, 2-14:(1)16.

3

. . . we believe that the dollar is a sound currency and that this international attack upon it by people who make great sums of money by speculating—one time they make a run on the mark and the next time it is on the yen, and now it is on the dollar—we will survive it. Let me say there will not be another devaluation. I would say, second, we are going to continue our program of fiscal responsibility so that the dollar will be sound at home and, we trust as well, abroad. And we are also going to continue our efforts to get the other major countries to participate more with us in the goal that we believe we should all achieve, which we set out at the time of

the Smithsonian and the other agreements, and that is of getting an international monetary system which is flexible enough to take care of these, what I believe are, temporary attacks on one currency or another.

News conference, Washington, March 2/
The New York Times, 3-3:12.

Mohammad Reza Pahlavi
Shah of Iran

4

[On the price of oil]: Of course it's going to rise. Certainly! And how! You can spread the bad news and add that it comes from someone who knows what he's talking about. I know everything there is to know about oil, everything. I'm a real specialist, and it's as a specialist that I tell you the price of oil must rise. There's no other solution. However, it's a solution you of the West have wished on yourselves; or, if you prefer, a solution wished on you by your ultra-civilized industrial society. You've increased the price of the wheat you sell us by 800 per cent, and the same for sugar and cement. You've sent petrochemical prices rocketing. You buy our crude oil and sell it back to us, refined as petrochemicals, at a hundred times the price you've paid us. You make us pay more, scandalously more, for everything; and it's only fair that, from now on, you should pay more for oil. Let's say . . . 10 times more.

Interview/Los Angeles Times, 12-30:(6)4.

Wright Patman
United States Representative, D-Texas

5

[On recent devaluations of the dollar]: A few more of these international monetary agreements and the U.S. dollar will be approaching the status of banana-republic currency.

At Joint Congressional Economic
Committee hearing, Washington, Feb. 20/
The Dallas Times Herald, 2-21:(D)10.

6

. . . the average American—the plain people—have been left to compete with the corporate giants, the speculators, the gamblers and the fast-buck artists for available credit at

(WRIGHT PATMAN)

9, 10, 11 per cent—and even up to 36 per cent and more on many small loans. In my opinion, we can no longer accept these 18th-century monetary policies—all the soft, soothing words of the Federal Reserve Chairman notwithstanding. We must develop policies which will assure allocation of credit resources to areas of greatest need, such as housing, small business and farming sectors—to sectors that cannot compete with the corporate giants and the speculators at exhorbitant interest charges.

At House Banking Committee hearings,
Washington, Sept. 10/
Los Angeles Herald-Examiner, 9-11:(A)8.

Nikolai S. Patolichev
Minister of Foreign Trade
of the Soviet Union

1

[Advocating more U.S.-Soviet trade]: I am a devout supporter of more contacts, contacts, contacts which would bring more contracts, contracts, contracts.

Before National Association of Manufacturers,
Washington, June 22/
The New York Times, 6-23:9.

H. Ross Perot
Industrialist

2

[Advocating that everybody be allowed up to $100,000 in capital-gains earnings free of capital-gains taxes]: Let's look at the big issue. The big issue is the fact that we're [the U.S.] being out-performed by international competitors, the Japanese and the Germans. Too many dollars are going there. Jobs are being threatened in this country as a result of that . . . As I look at what we have to do in the next 10 years in our country to regain our competitive position, to have "Made in U.S.A." stamped on everything, it finally boils down to we've got to raise more money than we ever raised before in the history of our country. We've got to modernize our plants so that the American worker, with the highest standard of living in the world, keeps his job, has a better job and we create new jobs. That takes money . . . The only place in the world that there's that much money is in the pockets and the savings accounts of the working Americans. You can't get it from the wealthy people; there's not that much there. The working Americans have that much money to invest . . . We've got to give them an incentive . . . We've got to make it extremely attractive for him to invest his money. So all I did was study what the people who are out-performing us are doing. The Japanese have no capital-gains tax. The Germans have no capital-gains tax. I say let's give the man who is trying to get a stake in life, who's trying to get started, trying to build something for his family, the first $100,000 tax-free . . .

Television interview/
The Washington Post, 4-15:(H)1.

Donald T. Regan
Chairman, Merrill Lynch, Pierce,
Fenner & Smith, Inc.

3

Business is in the practical situation where it must perform more than its traditional functions. Traditionally, business must produce material goods and services required by all Americans. It must provide jobs for a growing population that insists on a decent standard of living. It must make enough profit to pay taxes to support the services and good works of government at all levels. But business must also, for pragmatic reasons, carry on good works of its own. Today, business is asked, indeed it is expected, to do more than it ever has before. It is asked to meet not just its broad objectives to producing goods and services at minimum cost, to employ people and to pay its taxes. Business must also make a contribution to protecting the environment and in some ways directly to help the poor. And some of the actions in business that are aimed at social improvement can be justified even to the most hard-eyed shareholder: In the long-run, social benefits benefit business. But only a strong business community can do all this. When weak, it cannot serve society in any way.

> *At Young Men's Christian Association*
> *annual meeting, Philadelphia, May 3/*
> *Vital Speeches, 7-1:576.*

1

[Urging capital-gains laws more favorable to the investor]: The willingness of individuals to put capital at risk, even at modest risk, is essential to the health of our system. Our tax structure should be built to encourage, not discourage, such risk-taking . . . Perhaps the starting point for capital-gains treatment should be with an asset held up to three months. Perhaps funds that are re-invested should get special treatment.

> *Before Senate Finance Subcommittee,*
> *Washington, July 24/*
> *Los Angeles Times, 7-25:(3)10.*

James M. Roche
Former chairman,
General Motors Corporation

2

I have observed, with concern, the many proposals for substantial changes in the rules governing our securities markets. Most of these proposals originated in the abnormal bull market of the late '60s. Because they are so important to the corporate structure of our country as well as the securities industries, it is crucial, I believe, that they be re-examined in light of the sober realities of today. Change is often essential, particularly in a dynamic society. But change must be constructive; it must be realistic. Today, for example, changes based on the assumption that brokerage rates are too high, that the industry's profits are excessive, are not realistic. Changes based on the assumption that the securities exchanges are a "club" which can be partitioned, disbanded or disrupted without full knowledge of the potential consequences of such action can do untold damage to our nation and would serve no constructive purpose. Quite properly, there are many different ideas as to what should be done to protect the advantages we have and to accomplish needed improvements. No one can—or should want to —resist useful change. Our task is to identify

what can and should be changed and how.

> *Before Securities Industry Association,*
> *White Sulphur Springs, W. Va., May 9/*
> *Vital Speeches, 6-15:526.*

David Rockefeller
Chairman,
Chase Manhattan Bank, New York

3

[Advocating the granting of most-favored-nation status to the Soviet Union to promote U.S.-Soviet trade]: The lack of that status does threaten the potential growth of Soviet exports to the U.S. and hence the ability of the Soviet Union to purchase American products. And it represents a real psychological barrier to improved relations, because the Soviets are opposed to doing business with countries that discriminate against their goods. I know there are aspects of Soviet life that we as Americans don't like. And there are aspects of our society that they don't like. I favor the free flow of people and ideas across national borders and the full development of every person's talents. The question is how to promote such personal contacts and exchanges of ideas which are essential to the breaking down of barriers between East and West. Increased commercial relations are one important way of getting each side to better know the other. If the most-favored-nation issue proves a stumbling block to a broader range of economic exchanges, we may lose a good opportunity to refashion the world along more rational and more cooperative lines.

> *Interview, Washington/*
> *U.S. News & World Report, 8-13:40.*

Robert V. Roosa
Partner, Brown Brothers,
Harriman & Company; Former Undersecretary
for Monetary Affairs, Department
of the Treasury of the United States

4

The mushrooming expansion in the number of transactions among nations, as the scale of their economies has grown, and the enormous growth in capital flows—which now account for a larger volume of payments than do trade

(ROBERT V. ROOSA)

transactions in the world as a whole—have created new potentials, and more compelling motives, for massive shifts from one currency to another. These are the conditions of progress. They are also the conditions for monetary crisis—regardless of whether the world's currencies have established parities subject to disruptively large flows of reserves, or loosely flexible exchange rates subject to disruptively large fluctuations that throttle trade. It will not be enough to exalt "flexibility," for that can mean many things, including the creation of a shooting gallery for mere speculators. Constructive flexibility will have to be developed within newly-agreed "rules of the road," to avoid converting exchange rates into tools of degenerative economic warfare. That will not be easy. It is in the context of such comprehensive reform that the dollar can, if we wish it to, regain a crucial place within a truly multilateral, international monetary system. But that will require us to recognize an inherent duality between the maintenance of a reasonably stable value of the dollar at home and maintenance of the conditions for confidence in the dollar abroad.

Before Economic Club of New York/
The New York Times, 4-5:45.

Edward B. Rust
President,
Chamber of Commerce of the United States;
President, State Farm Insurance Companies
1

As businessmen, our focus must always be on the quality of the service or product we offer, simply because this is the first expectation people have of us. The manufacturer who landscapes the factory site but hedges the obligations in his product warranty has a misplaced sense of priorities. It's at this basic level that we must begin to rebuild faith in the institution of business. We need to regenerate a dedication to quality, to value and to service . . . This, I believe, is what Ralph Nader and other consumerists are saying; and I find it hard to disagree with them on that point. You will notice that you rarely find consumerists criticizing a business for its failure to involve itself in social programs on the periphery of that business. Nader's focus is usually on the first business of business: its products and services. His primary insistence is on products that perform as they are supposed to, on warranties that protect the buyer at least as much as the seller, on services that genuinely serve. He has been described in some quarters as "an enemy of the system"; but if we are willing to look objectively at his activities, I think we are forced to the conclusion that his commitment is to make the system work.

Before National Association of Life
Underwriters, Chicago, Sept. 18/
Los Angeles Times, 9-26:(2)7.
2

We in business sometimes complain that the public—and our young in particular—don't understand or appreciate the free-enterprise system. But I must observe that, when business sees consumerism and its spokesmen as enemies of that system, then business is demonstrating its own failure to understand the healthy tensions and competing pressures that must always be present in that system, if it is to survive.

Quote, 11-18:484.

Paul A. Samuelson
Professor of Economics,
Massachusetts Institute of Technology
3

There has been a resurgence of protectionism in the land of the over-valued dollar —America. The disease is bad. If you don't believe me, go to any trade union, or go to any business group. In commercial circles, I hear the Japanese have become "Japs" again.

At Newsweek magazine news conference on
Japanese-American economic affairs, Tokyo/
San Francisco Examiner, 3-14:66.

Irving S. Shapiro
Vice chairman,
E. I. du Pont de Nemours & Company
4

. . . I am a devoted and optimistic advocate of what I call one-world economics. There are no geographical boundaries to the material needs of people and no justification in morals or ethics for some nations to be haves and others to be have-nots. Our economic system, like our politics, sprang from national origins; and when its capability was limited, its incentives were linked to national well-being. But there has been a change. Now, thanks mainly to technology and industrialization and to developments in communication and transportation, production capacity with its supporting structure has matured to the point that it can look beyond national boundaries to the task of meeting needs on a world-wide scale . . . The demands of the world-wide market, as we see it, are by no means uniform; not everybody wants television sets, and some people prefer cotton to nylon. The mechanism for supplying the demands is not uniform, either; it includes multinationals, of course, but is based on thousands of national companies and state enterprises of varying size and function. In one-world economics, the objective is to fill whatever material needs exist wherever they are, and, as in any good business deal, there are benefits for both sides. Business can make a fair profit to satisfy its objectives while helping nations and people improve their well-being to satisfy theirs. Unlike one-world politics, one-world economics is within reach. The productive system is proven out, and much of it is in place. What remains is to harness it effectively to the world-wide task.

Before United Nations Group
of Eminent Persons, New York,
Sept. 11/Vital Speeches, 10-15:20.

George P. Shultz
Secretary of the
Treasury of the United States

1

Our trade position must be improved. If we cannot accomplish that objective in a framework of freer and fairer trade, the pressures to retreat inward will be intense. We must avoid the risk, for it is the road to international recrimination, isolation and autarky.

Washington, Feb. 12/
Los Angeles Times, 2-14:(2)6.

[Criticizing last year's sale of U.S. wheat to the Soviet Union]: I think it is a fair statement that they [the Soviets] were very sharp in their buying practices, and I think that we should follow the adage [that], if we are burned the first time, why, maybe they did it; but if we get burned twice, that is our fault, and we shouldn't have that happen.

News conference, Washington,
Sept. 7/The New York Times, 9-8:1.

Howard K. Smith
News commentator,
American Broadcasting Company

3

One of the best things to come out of World War II was a resolve by the nations of the world to liberate trade among them, cut away traffic and other barriers that had paralyzed the world in depression, let the most productive national industries prevail on the world market. That freedom enabled American industry to grow apace, and the existence of a wide-open world market enabled the war-torn nations to recover. Well, with recovery bad old habits are being indulged. The European Common Market has come into existence, girding itself around with protections against our trade. Japan has done the same to protect its growth. We have resorted to a trick called voluntary quotas which are, in fact, walls against them selling to us. Now before Congress is the Burke-Hartke bill which would carry paralysis to its logical conclusion—erect barriers against almost all foreign products, keep our lazy industries lazy, raise all our prices by lack of foreign competition and eventually provoke other nations to shut out our goods entirely. The President [Nixon] in his trade message has offered an alternative. He asked Congress for some clout to negotiate an all-around reduction of the rising thickets of protection before it is too late. Congress now faces the most important choice it will have to make this year: Burke-Hartke and a stagnant, lazy, protected U.S. economy, or the President's way—freer trade, a competitive economy, rising world prosperity. To me, the choice seems easy.

> *News commentary,*
> *American Broadcasting Company, April 10/*
> *The Christian Science Monitor, 4-26:16.*

Christopher Soames
Vice President for External Affairs,
European Common Market Commission

1

[On increasing U.S.-European trade by lowering tariffs and other trade restrictions]: . . . the European [Economic] Community cannot go much further along this road unless the United States also decides, as we earnestly hope it will, to offer comparable market access. We, too, have our electorates to convince and our lobbies to answer. It is a real necessity, political as well as economic, for us to be able to say that the Community is not alone in making this essential contribution.

> *Before business leaders,*
> *New York, Oct. 30/*
> *The Dallas Times Herald, 10-31:(F)7.*

William I. Spencer
President,
First National City Bank, New York

2

[Arguing against protectionism]: This failure of the average citizen to perceive the relationship that exists between the state of the global economy and the quality of his personal life has served to fuel the fires of protectionism in America and elsewhere. It makes no sense for the United States to curb the imports of any nation which gives us a fair deal in the marketplace. We want to import enough coffee to keep us awake and enough wine to make us mellow. And most important of all, we want to import enough gas and oil to appease our seemingly insatiable appetite for energy.

> *Before businessmen, Hong Kong,*
> *June 21/The New York Times, 6-22:47.*

Stuart Symington
United States Senator, D-Missouri

3

Substantial questions continue to be raised about the fairness of various aspects of our Federal tax laws. Is it fair to permit gains on capital investments held for less than a year to be taxed, in effect, at half the rates imposed on income which a taxpayer earns in wages? Are depletion allowances for oil and gas wells and other natural deposits too generous when compared to depreciation authorized for other business enterprises? Is it reasonable to allow individuals to become non-taxpayers altogether by virtue of the fact that they possess capital and choose to invest all resources in local and state government bonds? Questions of fairness are balanced by other and often correlating questions concerning the consequences of tax breaks and the success of these laws in achieving asserted objectives of social and economic benefits for all citizens. For example: Does the foreign tax credit applied to multinational corporations encourage plant location, say, in France, rather than in Missouri? Can the deferral of tax until repatriation of corporate profits earned abroad be justified in balance-of-payments terms? Our tax laws need sifting from the standpoint of equity and in regard also to their consequences and asserted social and economic benefits. When programs to assist low-income Americans are being repeatedly attacked as ineffective by the Nixon Administration, which plans budget savings through their elimination, this Congress can and should make certain that low- and middle-income Americans are not discriminated against in the operation of our tax laws.

> *The Washington Post, 4-15:(C)6.*

Herman E. Talmadge
United States Senator, D-Georgia

4

[On abolishing farm price-support programs]: If we could abolish all programs of every kind in this country and live in an absolute free market, I would favor doing that. Under those conditions, I think farmers would get along as well as anyone else. But I haven't heard anyone advocating repealing the minimum wage. They are not going to; on the contrary, they are advocating increasing it, and they have already urged that it be increased from $1.60 an hour to $2.50 an hour. I haven't heard anyone advocating repealing collective bargaining. They are not going to. And your farm price support is merely a minimum living for farmers, similar to the minimum wage. As long as we continue to have that, we have got to have some price supports for farm commodities, or else make peons out of all of them.

TV-radio interview,
Washington/"Meet the Press,"
National Broadcasting Company, 3-25.

Kakuei Tanaka
Prime Minister of Japan

1

You Americans have had your burdens and suffering in Asia and have paid your price. We would like to help you. Take the latest dollar crisis. The U.S. alone could not solve it; therefore, Japan participated in the solution. And the same has been true in tariff negotiations. We want to expand world trade, not to contract it. The world's moral leadership must be American, and the American position must be defended. We only hope the dollar will become stronger. It must maintain its role as the key currency.

Interview, Tokyo/
Los Angeles Herald-Examiner, 3-31:(A)10.

Stanley Tannenbaum
Chairman,
Kenyon and Eckhardt, advertising

2

At a time when there is almost universal belief that most advertising is basically dishonest, we [in advertising] have the facts to persuade the skeptics and the cynics that our house is clean . . . and we are too mousey or busy or indifferent or dumb to communicate the facts to the people [the public] who can make us or break us.

At American Association of Advertising
Agencies Western Region Convention,
Santa Barbara, Calif., Oct. 15/
Los Angeles Times, 10-16:(3)13.

Arthur R. Taylor
President,
Columbia Broadcasting System

3

Businessmen are far too defensive about accusations that they "meddle" in politics. There's no need for such attitudes. There are any number of reasons why corporations must and should involve themselves in the political process—not less than in the past but more. Everyone has a right to speak out and take positions to protect and foster their own interests and the interests they serve. The Founding Fathers premeditated that condition. The policies and decisions of governmental bodies at all levels, from the regulatory agencies to Congress itself, vitally affect the operations of business firms. The attitude that when business talks to government there must be some dirty, underhanded hanky-panky going on is narrow and rigid. One problem is that people apparently perceive the business-government relationship to be far more corrupt than experience indicates is accurate. Business, in fact, is probably one of the least-organized and least-aggressive sectors of society in terms of explaining its needs and positions to the government. Quite apart from protecting self-interest, it seems that corporate participation in politics is a matter of broad social responsibility. Corporations have resources of talent and knowledge that can be, and are, highly useful to legislators and government officials at all levels. Businessmen have an obligation to offer government the benefit of their special knowledge. There's no reason why business should be silent and aloof while everyone else speaks out. Indeed, it has been my experience that legislators want and appreciate factual testimony and expert opinion from business executives who have done their homework on complex legislative proposals.

At Amherst (Mass.) College,
Jan. 18/Vital Speeches, 6-1:493.

Nobuhiko Ushiba
Japanese Ambassador to the United States

4

Both Japan and the United States want a freer and fairer environment for the expansion

(NOBUHIKO USHIBA)

of world trade. We also want a more flexible and more stable world monetary system to finance this trade and to facilitate the flow of international investment. In the final analysis, however, the decision which will restore equilibrium to both our bilateral and our multilateral economic relations will not be governmental decisions but business decisions. Governments must reach agreement on the rules which influence business decision-making, but only the entrepreneur can decide with what, when and how to compete in world markets. It is the cumulative decisions of international businessmen which ultimately determine the vitality and prosperity of world trade.

Before Chicago Association of Commerce and Industry, Feb. 7/ The Washington Post, 2-22:(A)18.

Jay Van Andel
Chairman, Amway Corporation

1

If you are going to develop a business, you had better not get too involved in details of an operation. You had better stay on the promotion side. I think that's why many small businessmen stay small. You know, it's like the garage mechanic who likes to stay under the car and the restaurant owner who never gets out of the kitchen.

Interview/ Nation's Business, October:68.

C. William Verity
Chairman, Armco Steel Corporation

2

I spend an awful lot of time talking to students who know very little about the challenges and excitement of the steel business. Some of their professors, who have never been in industry, who have never seen a steel plant, fill them full of a bunch of junk. They tell them that the people in steel are nothing but big polluters who care only about profits; that steel workers are nothing but clock-punchers who have no challenges. So the students decide that, if they want to do something for humanity, they should go into the Peace Corps or into government. I try to tell them there is excitement in the steel business, where things are really done to provide what people want . . . I've probably spent too much time in this youth area, but one result is that a lot of bright students want to work for Armco. What you put in at the bottom today is what is going to be running your company 25 years from now. If you have really creative, bright young people coming into your company today, you don't have to worry about the future.

Interview/ Nation's Business, August:58.

Paul A. Volcker
Under Secretary for Monetary Affairs, Department of the Treasury of the United States

3

I am not at all happy about what seems to me an unnecessary depreciation of the dollar in recent weeks or about the size of some of the fluctuations in exchange rates from day to day. But I am satisfied that, during a period of great uncertainty in financial markets, exchange market pressures have been absorbed and diffused in a manner consistent with our basic goals and requirements and those of other nations. Specifically, economic policies at home and abroad have not been distorted by the need to deal with massive flows of speculative capital in an atmosphere of crisis. International business has not been impaired.

Before Joint Congressional Economic Subcommittee, Washington, June 26/ The Washington Post, 6-27:97.

Rawleigh Warner, Jr.
Chairman, Mobil Oil Corporation

4

The horrendous Watergate [political-espionage affair] developments [are a reminder that] the need for integrity has never been greater. Even in as large an organization as my company, people tend to take their cue from the top—for good or for ill. [Leaders in large organizations] need not only personal probity, but must work, quite consciously, to generate openness and honesty in the organization.

Accepting New York University Graduate
School of Business Administration's
C. Walter Nichols Award, New York,
May 25/The New York Times, 5-26:44.

1

There is nothing mysterious about business. In a large business, you have to break down the units to manageable size, set goals to be achieved, select the best people, give them authority and responsibilities, and reward those who do the job. The secret is personnel selection and delegation of duties . . . I would put integrity at the top among ingredients a businessman must have. Without it, a person doesn't have anything to build on. Basic integrity must be at the top of any organization, and the philosophy must spread down through the ranks. The vast majority of businessmen I know have integrity.

Interview, New York/
Nation's Business, September:54.

W. L. Wearly
Chairman, Ingersoll-Rand Company

2

Multinational enterprise is nothing basically new. And yet there are those who see the multinational corporation as a "new Devil" —just as they once saw automation as a "new Devil." And as they were wrong in claiming that automation destroyed jobs, they are also wrong in claiming that multinational corporations export jobs.

The Wall Street Journal, 1-30:16.

Donald E. Weeden
Chairman, Weeden & Company, investments

3

[Saying the securities industry needs change in its dealings with customers]: I sometimes wonder whether there is a relationship, or at least an analogy, between the flight from Wall Street and the rush to legalized gambling. Perhaps the real difference between the [race] track and the [stock] market is not in the odds but in the convenience.

Before National Investor Relations Institute/
The New York Times, 10-25:77.

4

I believe that we are about to see a dramatic change in how stocks are marketed, to whom and at what cost. Five years from now you may well see a Wall Street that has little resemblance to the financial world we presently know. For more than a century, we rested on the conviction that securities trading had to be funneled into one physical place in order to make the best markets. The place was the New York Stock Exchange. And we all made very good money off of the rest of the country. Now comes the explosion of communications technology plus the computer able to handle enormous volumes of data, and investors and their brokers all over the country are asking each other "why send everything to New York?" That is a tough question. Why should an investor in California send his order to New York? So long as he can buy or sell at the same prices as in New York, why go to all the trouble? Certainly not because of any reverence for tradition. And certainly not in order to maintain jobs and revenues in old beloved New York . . . Wall Street could easily go the way of the luxury ocean liners, clinging to outmoded, expensive ways of doing business, while the public finds other ways to invest or otherwise spend discretionary income. You have to work on Wall Street to understand the extent of the *Titanic* mentality in some quarters. Happily, there is a new generation of leaders who want no part of "the public be damned" approach. They see the potential diversification of the securities industry. They are afraid neither of the computer nor of new marketing techniques. Above all, they see the challenge for an affluent society to find new ways to broaden ownership of capital assets.

Before City Club of New York/
The New York Times, 12-16:(3)12.

Frederic W. West, Jr.
Executive vice president,
Bethlehem Steel Corporation

5

[Arguing against nationalization]: Ever since nationalization, British Steel Corporation has been deep in the red all but two years.

(FREDERIC W. WEST, JR.)

And last year, one of those two profitable years, its return on sales of nearly $4 billion was just $7 million. Keep that profit of $7 million in mind when I tell you that British Steel recently announced a tremendous modernization and expansion program, with the government contributing $3½ billion. To put things into perspective, if the company went on making $7 million a year, it'd take 500 years for their profits to add up to $3½ billion.

At business award dinner, Canisius College, Buffalo, N. Y./The Wall Street Journal, 11-23:4.

Marina v. N. Whitman
Member, Council of Economic
Advisers to the President
of the United States

1

Under present conditions, with major food items in short supply the world over, foreign consumers are competing briskly with our own consumers for the output by American farmers. This means that, if domestic prices are artificially held below world prices, producers will sell more of their output abroad as long as they are free to do so. Or, in the case of agricultural commodities such as grains and soybeans, whose prices are not themselves controlled, there is the danger that foreign demand may drive those prices up to the point where domestic producers who must buy those items for feed, and who face ceilings on the prices of the meat and poultry and eggs that they produce, are forced to operate at a loss. It is in order to prevent this sort of situation that the President [Nixon] has asked the Congress for authority to impose controls on exports of grains and soybeans, should available supplies of these commodities turn out to be insufficient to satisfy both domestic needs and unrestricted exports without continuing increases in their prices. In the short run, it may turn out that restricting exports of the key commodities I have just mentioned is essential to make the freeze

workable or to stabilize food prices during Phase 4 [of the President's economic program]. But this course of action would be simply the lesser of two evils, and certainly not one we would want to have to rely on as an anti-inflationary weapon over the long run. It goes against much that we have been working hard to achieve: improving our balance of trade and balance of payments, stabilizing the value of the dollar in foreign exchange markets, and enabling Americans to reap the classical gains from trade by selling what we produce most efficiently at the best prices we can get. We have worked hard to establish a reputation as a reliable source of supply and to help cement our political relationships with other nations by mutually-beneficial commercial relationships. All these goals are far more likely to be achieved if we are able to stabilize food prices to the American consumer by expanding the production of the American farmer rather than by restricting exports of our agricultural products.

Before American Home Economics Association, Atlantic City, N.J., June 25/Vital Speeches, 8-15:657.

Leonard Woodcock
President,
United Automobile Workers of America

2

[Criticizing proposals that would give the President of the United States great control over the raising and lowering of U.S. tariffs]: The breathtaking range of powers that would be placed in the President's hands would represent another major step in the dangerously anti-democratic process, already carried much too far, of transferring Congressional authority to the Executive. These powers could be used either to liberalize trade or to increase protectionism. Given the unpredictability of the present occupant of the White House [Nixon] and the even greater difficulty of predicting what future Presidents might do with the powers that they would inherit under the proposed legislation, Congress and the American people are being asked to buy a pig in a poke with respect to the nation's future trade policies.

Before House Ways and Means Committee,
Washington, May 15/
The Washington Post, 5-18:(A)9.

1

The business of the people has fallen on hard times, while the business of the great corporations prospers as never before.

TV-radio interview/"Meet the Press,"
National Broadcasting Company, 9-2.

Walter B. Wriston
Chairman,
First National City Bank, New York

2

To put it all in perspective, you have to remember that the current problem of the dollar is a monument to the success of United States policies. We emerged from the Second World War with a productive capacity disproportionate to the rest of the world, with a pretty good system of government and with a generous bent of mind. There was no economic power that was close to what the United States was then. But as we pumped out funds through the Marshall Plan, as American capital was exported abroad, as our know-how moved out and other countries got organized, the success of all those moves helped to build the economies of the rest of the world. And their currencies began to take on strength. So the relative position of the United States has changed very markedly in the last 20 years. Our deliberate policy was to raise up others. What is happening today is something you could have foreseen some years ago.

Interview, Washington/
U.S. News & World Report, 3-26:20.

Crime • Law Enforcement

Spiro T. Agnew
Vice President of the United States

1

[On domestic government surveillance and wiretapping]: I believe in any method of collecting information if it's related to the national security, so long as it's not abused; and certainly we expect the President, being the only person that all the people of the United States have entrusted with this responsibility, should be able to make a proper judgment on that . . . I have an ordinary individual's repugnance to the idea that somebody is snooping on someone else. So the kind of wiretapping that's done illegally I find reprehensible and totally abhorrent. One of the things I would never do is tap another person's conversation, regardless of how advantageous it might be to me individually.

Interview/
The New York Times Magazine, 6-24:42.

Lloyd M. Bentsen
United States Senator, D-Texas

2

The Attorney General has gotten so political in recent years that if we're going to have a non-partisan FBI, we have to have an independent FBI . . . For years the Justice Department stayed clear of politics. But in 1960, President [John] Kennedy appointed his campaign manager Attorney General; and in 1968, President Nixon appointed his campaign manager Attorney General . . . You had a strong character in [the late FBI Director J. Edgar] Hoover, and he was able to turn aside political pressures. But not every man is as strong-willed as J. Edgar Hoover.

Washington/
The Dallas Times Herald, 4-14:(A)7.

Alan Bible
United States Senator, D-Nevada

3

White-collar crime is the type of crime that can have a serious influence on the social fabric of the nation and is costing the American consumer millions of dollars in higher prices and lost tax revenues . . . We have heard it said that a little man can steal a bottle of milk from a doorstep, and he goes to jail in a hurry. But a business tycoon can steal thousands or millions of dollars and probably won't ever see the inside of a prison.

U.S. News & World Report, 3-12:53.

Richard Blum
Criminologist, Stanford University

4

It's widely believed, especially on the part of the public, that heroin addiction causes crime. All the research I've read suggests that people cause crime, and sometimes those people use heroin.

San Francisco Examiner & Chronicle,
4-15:(This World)2.

Dolph Briscoe
Governor of Texas

5

Where fair laws are administered fairly and firmly, criminal behavior is discouraged. It's when respect for law declines that your [the police's] job gets tougher. Public confidence and public support of fair and just and even-handed law enforcement must be raised to an all-time high if we are to see a genuine improvement in the fight against unlawful activity. That means that we cannot turn our heads at one unlawful situation just because it is popularly accepted by some . . . It means that those who hold public office must be willing to talk straight about law enforcement, and mean it when we say that all the laws of the state must be enforced equally across the board.

Before Central Texas Peace Officers
Association, Temple, Tex., Aug. 23/
The Dallas Times Herald, 8-24:(A)5.

Warren E. Burger
Chief Justice of the United States

1

If anyone is tempted to regard humane prison reform as "coddling criminals," let him visit a prison and talk with inmates and staff. I have visited some of the worst prisons and have never seen any signs of "coddling," but I have seen the terrible results of the boredom and frustration of empty hours and a pointless existence.

Quote, 3-11:218.

Don Byrd
Chief of Police of Dallas

2

[Saying the fight against crime is everybody's responsibility]: We [the police] go out and tell businessmen, "Here's the way to protect your stuff." You go back, and a certain percentage hasn't paid any attention at all; none at all. What control do we have over that as a police agency? None. In the community, what turns a youngster into a criminal? What makes him steal cars and graduate from one crime to another? I tell you we have no control over that. The churches, the schools, the families, the communities have that control. We do not. We can pull the crime down some. [But] we can't pull it down where it needs to be, and keep it there.

Interview, Dallas/
The Dallas Times Herald, 12-19:(A)16.

Robert C. Byrd
United States Senator, D-West Virginia

3

Considering the vast intelligence network that is under the control of the FBI, with thousands of computerized dossiers gathered by the FBI, it is obvious that the FBI can reach so far into the lives of all Americans that no Administration—Democratic or Republican—should have direct political control

of the agency through a compliant and politicized Director.

Before the Senate,
Washington, Feb. 19/
U.S. News & World Report, 3-5:21.

Charles F. Campbell
Warden, Fort Worth (Tex.)
Federal Correctional Institute

4

[On his prison's low-pressure, co-ed policy]: We aren't ready to stand up and beat our chests and say, "Hey, look at us; we're a success." That remains to be seen. But we do feel we are making headway. I would like to think that this program will one day be looked back on as the pilot experiment that led to similar institutions throughout the country. The basic theory on which we operate is a simple one. We believe that people are people first and prisoners second. There is more about them with which we can identify than condemn.

Interview/Parade, 2-11:15.

Norman A. Carlson
Director, Federal Bureau of Prisons

5

The only thing we can say with any degree of certainty is that we still know very little about how to deal effectively with offenders. It is ludicrous to pretend otherwise.

Quote, 11-4:444.

Donald F. Cawley
Police Commissioner of New York City

6

This Department can point to no decision of the [U.S. Supreme] Court which has been especially helpful or hindering. The Court enunciates the Constitutional law of the land, and we are mandated to follow. Within that framework we do our job. We cannot pass our responsibility to do the job off on any court decision or decisions. The alleged fact that the decisions of the Supreme Court play a role in the day-to-day operation of a major police department is close to a myth.

The New York Times, 7-29:(1)31.

Ramsey Clark
Former Attorney General
of the United States

1

[FBI] intelligence not for prosecutional purposes—and a lot of it is inadmissible in court anyway—should be segregated and ultimately abolished. To engage in the accumulation of information about individuals and groups as an end in itself is socially unjustifiable.

The New York Times, 3-26:30.

John B. Connally, Jr.
Former Secretary of the Treasury
of the United States;
Former Governor of Texas

2

If I were President, I can foresee a time when I might ask for a wiretap on someone . . . When it's a question of the security of the nation and the right of the individual, the legal rights of the individual must give way.

News conference, Washington, Sept. 10/
The Washington Post, 9-11:(A)12.

Edward M. Davis
Chief of Police of Los Angeles

3

. . . the catching of a felon never justifies the catcher becoming a felon himself; the end does not justify the means when we are talking about the law. I hope that no American police executive is ever caught committing a felony to catch a felon. We were lectured about this, weren't we? In *People v. Cahan* and *Mapp v. Ohio*, and case after case—it's an ancient lesson. The sacred thing that we have to remember is reverence for the law and how it should be the political religion of the land. Really, I think perhaps we ought to change the oath we [law officers] take. We take an oath to uphold the Constitution. I think we ought to add to that oath something about reverence for the law, not just upholding and enforcing the law.

Before Los Angeles County (Calif.)
Peace Officers Association/
Los Angeles Times, 6-6:(2)7.

Sam J. Ervin, Jr.
United States Senator,
D-North Carolina

4

I came up here during Joe McCarthy days, when [the late Senator] Joe McCarthy saw a Communist hiding under every rose bush; and I have been here fighting the no-knock laws and preventive-detention laws and indiscriminate bugging by people who've found subversives hiding under every bed. In this nation, we have had a very unfortunate fear. And this fear went to the extent of deploring the exercise of personal rights for those who wanted to assemble and petition the government for redress of grievances.

At Senate Watergate hearings, Washington,
June 14/The New York Times, 6-15:19.

5

Governmental surveillance can take many forms. Just recently, I learned that in cities from San Francisco, California, to Mount Vernon, New York, high-powered cameras have been set up to keep track of individuals and their activities. These cameras are so sensitive they can read an automobile license plate five blocks away. They can focus on an individual as he talks with friends and associates and can follow him as he walks down the street. They can peek through the windows of the homes of innocent Americans and record what is going on inside. It seems to me that this is the very sort of secret prying into the private lives and activities of individuals which bodes much evil for our democracy. These cameras represent the tools of tyranny and totalitarianism which seeks total control over the lives of individuals. They are, in my opinion, utterly inappropriate in a society which values the privacy and civil liberties of the individual.

At Miami University, Hamilton, Ohio,
June 28/Vital Speeches, 9-1:679.

Michael Fooner
Law-enforcement consultant

6

To explain crime as being caused by poverty, bad housing, unemployment and similar social ills is to bypass the realities of "where it's at." On the contrary, crime—in this country and abroad—will be found on analysis to be closely related to wealth and prosperity, and to the greed for power. The crime trend correlates with the gross national product.

Before International Police Association,
Anaheim, Calif., Oct. 25/
Los Angeles Times, 10-26:(2)3.

L. Patrick Gray III
Acting Director,
Federal Bureau of Investigation

1

Rehabilitation is fine for those convicted felons who show signs of being able to profit from such measures . . . it is a useless gesture for those who resist every such effort, or take advantage of such effort to gain early release and do it all over again. The real purpose of incarceration is to protect society . . . and if rehabilitation is going to contribute to the protection of society in a given case, let's rehabilitate; if not, let's incarcerate and protect society. The objective of the criminal-justice system is the protection of society, not just the protection of the rights of the accused.

At National Conference on Criminal Justice,
Washington, Jan. 25/
The National Observer, 2-24:17.

H. R. Haldeman
Former Assistant
to the President of the United States

2

With regard to leaks of information, especially in the national-security area, it became evident in 1969 that leaks of secret information were taking place that seriously jeopardized a number of highly-sensitive foreign-policy initiatives that had been undertaken by the [Nixon] Administration, including the ending of the war in Vietnam, the Middle East crisis, nuclear arms limitation and the establishment of new relationships among the great powers. These initiatives were closely interrelated; leaks about any one of them could seriously endanger all of them; and such leaks were taking place. In order to deal with these leaks, a program of wiretaps was instituted in 1969

and continued into early 1971. The President has stated that each of these taps was undertaken in accordance with procedures that were legal at the time and in accord with longstanding practice in this area. This program was authorized by the President of the United States, and the wiretaps were determined by coordination between the Director of the FBI, the President's Assistant for National Security Affairs and the Attorney General of the United States.

At Senate Watergate hearings, Washington,
July 30/The New York Times, 7-31:24.

Eric Hoffer
Philosopher

3

City streets will be safe when courage is celebrated and honored as a chief virtue . . . We need shopkeepers and bank tellers who will defy holdup men. We need citizens who will fly at a mugger's throat. We need women who will scratch and bite and gouge out the eyes of anyone who molests them . . . [The average American today is] infinitely less pugnacious, less quarrelsome and less ready to take offense than he was in the past. The great majority of Americans are afraid to open their mouths. They will not get into a fight no matter what you call them, and will not get involved even when they see people murdered before their own eyes. They are afraid to get angry.

At U.S. Conference of Mayors,
San Francisco, June 19/
Los Angeles Times, 6-20:(1)22.

Harold E. Hughes
United States Senator, D-Iowa

4

[Arguing against capital punishment]: If the death penalty is mandated for some crimes, juries will be less likely to convict than where some discretion is granted; and kidnapers and [airliner] hijackers who have already been involved in killing, when closed in upon, will see nothing to lose by further killing.

Radio address, March 17/
San Francisco Examiner, 3-17:2.

(HAROLD E. HUGHES)

1

It is not just the nameless law-breaker who robs or kills or pushes narcotics who should be brought to justice. White-collar crime is just as serious. Fraud, bribery, rent-gouging and price-fixing ought to be included, not to mention political espionage, burglary and sabotage, such as were involved in the notorious Watergate case.

Radio address, March 17/
San Francisco Examiner, 3-17:2.

2

[On President Nixon's recent crime message in which he called for stricter enforcement and punishment]: The recommendations are a regression to punishments and sentencing methods that have long since been professionally discredited, so far as deterring criminal acts or correcting criminal tendencies are concerned. They are a long voyage into the night of the past.

Quote, 4-8:313.

Joseph H. Jackson
President, National Baptist Convention, U.S.A.

3

I believe the climate in which we live is not conducive to eliminating capital punishment. I don't say capital punishment is a forward moral step; but it reflects the fact that the elimination of it was not the thing to do at that time. I believe in life. I believe in freedom for the individual. But if a person develops more of the raging lion and tiger than of the man, it's better for society to destroy the tiger than allow the tiger freedom to destroy human beings.

Interview/
Los Angeles Times, 10-13:(1)31.

John Kaplan
Professor of Law, Stanford University

4

In large areas of the U.S., there is no substantial cause for criminals to fear the criminal law. The reason is that government is not willing to pay the money it would take to really get tough.

Time, 3-26:69.

Nicholas deB. Katzenbach
Former Attorney General
of the United States

5

[The FBI] ought to have a political independence in terms of its Director and personnel. The tradition of the place ought to be the tradition [the late Director J. Edgar] Hoover put on it: free of partisan politics if not of ideals and ideas and maybe ideology, but a professional organization with a professional ethic.

Interview/The New York Times, 3-26:30.

Clarence M. Kelley
Chief of Police of Kansas City, Mo.;
Director-designate, Federal Bureau
of Investigation

6

I think that one of the things that has made it difficult for the news media and the police to get together is that, on occasion, the police are too apprehensive—and without good reason—about the press. And the press many times is too demanding on the police in going into matters which clearly are not that type of thing that should be revealed, such as the progress of a pending investigation or the revelation of a criminal record, or something of that type. On the other hand, the police should recognize that the press and other news media form a strong forum or a platform for exposure of tactics by the police which can be oppressive—even illegal. And while some may term it a threat, I would say, rather, that it's a barrier to inroads into rights and the privileges of people.

Interview/
The Dallas Times Herald, 6-17:(A)34.

7

I subscribe to the theory that society has to place some restrictions on the police. The police, after all, constantly are depriving people of liberty. But the pendulum can swing too far the other way. There is no question that police activity can be hampered by a too-severe interpretation of Constitutional rights.

Interview/The New York Times, 6-18:18.

Clarence M. Kelley
Director, Federal Bureau of Investigation

1

I promise to serve only justice and to avoid any other force or influence which hurts the cause of justice. I pledge to enforce the laws of the United States without taking [a] self-interpreting stance and with the vigor necessary to rid us of the predators who deny us full measure of our rights and freedoms. I further pledge that these same laws will apply to me personally as well as officially.

At his swearing-in ceremony,
Kansas City, July 9/
Los Angeles Herald-Examiner, 7-10:(A)6.

2

I have been astonished by the impression some people have that the FBI is engaged in elaborate clandestine operations infringing on Constitutional rights [of] the citizenry. I am dismayed by allegations that cloak-and-dagger tactics of the FBI threaten to make it a Gestapo—a menace to American freedom. I feel we must convey to the American people the truth about what the FBI does, and by what authority the FBI does it.

Before National Newspaper Association,
Hot Springs, Ark., Oct. 11/
The Washington Post, 10-12:(A)32.

3

I know it almost borders on heresy to say that maybe police are not always adequately attuned to the times. I think that we as a profession have a most commendable over-all record of keeping abreast of the times. However, just keeping up to date is not enough. We must look farther ahead. We must endeavor to anticipate change—and plan accordingly. All too frequently, I believe, people in law enforcement—on all levels and jurisdictions—have not really recognized the unprecedented rate of change in our society and how we are being affected . . . The whole concept of change—its rapidity, its complexity, its ambiguity—is often bewildering to us who are in command positions. The first reaction is to say, "I don't see any change," or "This type of change won't affect me or my department," or "I'll just wait and the change will

go away." The natural tendency is to stay with the traditional, the proven, what we have now—and, I can assure you, such a reliance can only lead us into great trouble.

Before International Association of Chiefs
of Police, San Antonio, Tex./
The National Observer, 10-13:17.

4

[On subversion]: I don't know whether it's increasing. But it still exists. And I'm afraid we as a people have relaxed our vigilance quite a bit. There have been many countries which have fallen because of their negligence in protecting what they had. When you talk about such things, sometimes people accuse you of waving the flag and that type of thing. But I am seriously concerned about the security of our nation—and I don't want to take any chances with it. This is not just a matter of patriotism or sentiment. It's a matter of preserving what we've got.

Interview, Washington/
U.S. News & World Report, 10-15:52.

5

In the field of narcotics, there is quite a large field of thought that marijuana should be legalized. I, frankly, do not accept that idea, because marijuana brings about psychological dependency. And it's been my personal observation that it is easy to go from a minor offense to a major. For example, the youngster who starts off by stealing a car, unless stopped, is likely to go to robbery. After the first step, the second one is not so difficult. So it is with marijuana. It's easy to go from that into the hard narcotics.

Interview, Washington/
U.S. News & World Report, 10-15:53.

6

We of the FBI recognize and wholeheartedly uphold the right and need of the people to be fully and accurately informed of our performance and policies . . . And we pledge ourselves to truth . . . truth regarding our operations . . . truth in reporting our investigations. We are prepared to accept the people's verdict.

Before National Newspaper Association/
Quote, 12-2:537.

Edward J. Kiernan
President, International Conference
of Police Associations

1

[Advocating restoration of capital punishment]: How long are you going to gamble with the families of police officers as the chips in this no-limit game? . . . It is a fact of life that our present laws only protect the killers while the police officer is forced to try to do his job knowing that society is playing Russian roulette with his life. In the past, attempts to mandate the death penalty were opposed by the so-called bleeding hearts because of their reluctance to take a human life. Their obvious lack of concern for the police officer who gave his life was excused by the theory that this is part of the job of being a policeman. They worry about the families of the killer, but they shed no tears for the families of the dead officer . . . We have tried the easy way out and it obviously has not worked. Please, before it is too late, try our way.

Before Senate Judiciary Subcommittee,
Washington, June 13/
Los Angeles Times, 6-14:(1)20.

Richard G. Kleindienst
Attorney General of the United States

2

Generally speaking, I don't believe that the death penalty accomplishes an overriding social purpose. I don't believe, generally speaking, the death penalty acts as a deterrent to crime. And unless you can demonstrate to me that it acts as a deterrent, then I don't think it's justified in an enlightened society. However, I do think there are some areas of possible criminal activity where the death penalty can be a deterrent, and that is usually the kind of criminal activity that is of such cold-blooded, premeditated, thought-out type—a kidnaping, an assassination, a bombing of a public building, a skyjacking, the killing of a prison guard. There are three or four or five specific areas where there is justification for a death penalty.

News conference, Washington,
Jan. 4/The New York Times, 1-5:22.

3

This [Nixon] Administration has been successful in doing what the two previous Administrations fell short on, and that is making a marshaled, coordinated, effective, efficient use of total Federal resources in this fight [against organized crime]. I think, if the motive power maintains itself in this vital area, by '74, '75, '76, '77, some years within the reasonable future, I believe we are going to say to ourselves this whole sad phenomenon called organized crime is going to be effectively a past chapter of American history. I firmly believe that, within a reasonable period of time, organized crime is going to be reduced to an ordinary irritant in our society.

News conference, Washington, Jan. 6/
The Dallas Times Herald, 1-7:(A)8.

Philip M. Klutznick
Chairman, research and policy committee,
Committee for Economic Development

4

The stake of this nation's business community in preventing crime and assuring justice stems not only from the economic reality that crime costs business an estimated $16 billion a year and boosts prices paid by its customers. Far more important, crime undermines the very spirit of a free American society.

Before Philadelphia Crime Commission,
Jan. 25/The New York Times, 1-26:53.

John V. Lindsay
Mayor of New York

5

We're becoming a nation of hustlers. Mugging is simply part of hustling. The can't-make-it rate in the ghetto is at least 30 per cent. That is the crime problem. Only the availability of meaningful work will end the hustling. We're kidding ourselves if we think there is another solution.

San Francisco Examiner & Chronicle,
5-13:(This World)2.

Robert List
Attorney General of Nevada

6

[Arguing against a National Advisory Commission on Crime suggestion that handguns be banned]: If honest citizens are stripped of their protection, the criminal element would run rampant. Criminals don't ordinarily obtain guns in a lawful manner and hence don't register them. Gun registration serves only to let authorities know which honest citizens own guns. I do agree with one Commission recommendation. That is the suggestion that the legislatures pass laws to provide long prison terms for criminals who commit a felony with a handgun. That is putting the penalty where it belongs—in the lap of the criminal. Honest citizens must be able to protect themselves.

Carson City, Nev./
The Dallas Times Herald, 8-20:(C)9.

John L. McClellan
United States Senator, D-Arkansas

1

I think there's some justification for limited gun-control. The problem is—and it gives me deep concern—that if we can't enforce our laws against carrying guns that many states have now, how can we expect to enforce a law prohibiting the ownership or possession of a gun? What disturbs me is that the good citizen will be disarmed and the criminal will not be. He'll have the gun. The "bad guys" will still be armed while the "good guys" will be disarmed. As an illustration, let's go back to prohibition. Those who wanted liquor got it. Those who want guns today will get them, unless we can have better law enforcement than we have now.

Interview, Washington/
U.S. News & World Report, 3-26:72.

2

. . . it isn't the enactment of a given law that deters the criminal. The only thing that will deter the commission of crime is the reasonable certainty of detection, prosecution, conviction and punishment of the criminal. I do believe punishment is a deterrent to crime. The duty to rehabilitate the criminal, when possible, is a responsibility of society. But the coddling of a criminal—as if society owed him a special kind of consideration or treated him as if he had no corresponding obligation to

society—is wrong; it is absurd.

Interview, Washington/
U.S. News & World Report, 3-26:72.

3

[On his favoring restoration of capital punishment]: I certainly do. I remember when we were debating the explosions-and-bombings bill which was later included in the Organized Crime Control Act, and Senator Philip Hart offered an amendment to eliminate capital punishment. He said a number of people on death row in prisons had been interviewed, and they all stated the death penalty didn't deter them from committing the crime. Well, obviously it didn't, because they committed the crime. But I thought a better test would be—and so stated in debate—to ask them this: "If you had known at the time you committed the crime or just before you committed it that you would be electrocuted if you did it, would you have committed the crime?" I think that's a better test, and had it been used, their answers would have been different. Laws on the books don't deter. It's the enforcement of those laws that is the deterrent.

Interview, Washington/
U.S. News & World Report, 3-26:72.

Robert B. McKay
Dean, New York University Law School;
Chairman, New York City
Board of Correction

4

Prisons don't rehabilitate, [and the proper approach is to] keep as many [people] as possible out of the system; and those that are in, get them out . . . The main thing is to de-populate the jails. They don't serve any function but detention, and they don't always even do that. We have to figure out ways to divert men and women from them.

News conference, New York, April 15/
The New York Times, 4-16:39.

Patrick V. Murphy
Police Commissioner of New York City

5

We as police are frustrated because we can't have good crime-control until the state

(PATRICK V. MURPHY)

assumes more responsibility . . . The failure to control crime is the failure of the states —not only our own state but all the states. The Mayor can't do anything about that. The state must do it. It will take funds. Dedicated court officers and correction officials are powerless to make the system work.

New York, Jan. 5/
The New York Times, 1-6:33.
1

We should not underestimate the value of good [police] leadership. Policemen want to be thanked for a good job. We haven't treated the policeman with dignity . . . Every policeman is making such powerful decisions on the street. That's power. Our management is still in the 19th century.

Interview, New York/
Los Angeles Times, 1-25:(1)29.

Richard M. Nixon
President of the United States
2

[On gun-control]: Let me say personally, I have never hunted in my life. I have no interest in guns and so forth. I am not interested in the National Rifle Association or anything from a personal standpoint. But I do know that, in terms of the United States Congress, what we need is a precise definition which will keep the guns out of the hands of the criminals and not one that will impinge on the rights of others to have them for their own purposes in a legitimate way.

News conference, Washington, Jan. 31/
The New York Times, 2-1:20.
3

Americans in the last decade were often told that the criminal was not responsible for his crimes against society, but that society was responsible. I totally disagree with this permissive philosophy. Society is guilty of crime only when we fail to bring the criminal to justice. When we fail to make the criminal pay for his crime, we encourage him to think that crime will pay.

Radio address to the nation, March 10/
The Washington Post, 3-11:(A)4.

In recent days, there have been proposals to legalize the possession and use of marijuana. I oppose the legalization of the sale, possession or use of marijuana. The line against the use of dangerous drugs is now drawn on this side of marijuana. If we move the line to the other side and accept the use of this drug, how can we draw the line against other illegal drugs? Or will we slide into an acceptance of *their* use as well? My Administration has carefully weighed this matter. We have examined the statutes. We have taken the lead in making sanctions against the use of marijuana more uniform, more reasonable . . . But there must continue to be criminal sanctions against the possession, sale or use of marijuana.

Radio address to the nation, March 10/
The Washington Post, 3-11:(A)4.
5

Contrary to the views of some social theorists, I am convinced that the death penalty can be an effective deterrent against specific crimes. The death penalty is not a deterrent so long as there is doubt whether it can be applied . . . [By reinstating the death penalty,] the potential criminal will know that, if his intended victims die, he may also die. The hijacker, the kidnaper, the man who throws a fire bomb, the convict who attacks a prison guard, the person who assaults an officer of the law, all will know that they may pay with their own lives for any lives that they take.

Radio address to the nation, March 10/
The Washington Post, 3-11:(A)4.

Glenn A. Olds
President,
Kent (Ohio) State University
6

I think a person that engages in hard-drug traffic, particularly to hook the young, ought to be shot. I personally view the consequence, both of the habit and the impact of hard drugs, to be murder. It's a more dangerous kind of murder, in my view, than that which results from a gun.

News conference, Kent, Ohio/
The Dallas Times Herald, 3-2:(C)8.

Claude Pepper
United States Representative, D-Florida

1

It is the American public who must realize that the overwhelming majority of people who go to prison will one day return. We are going to have to either put offenders away and keep them there indefinitely, or we are going to have to support more effective rehabilitation efforts. For without them, we will all be forced to cope with the end results of our current prison system: recidivism, growing crime, future Atticas.

Quote, 6-17:567.

Charles H. Percy
United States Senator, R-Illinois

2

One of the very serious impediments to a prisoner's being able to re-integrate himself successfully into the community is the lack of a vocational skill, and the resultant lack of a job. With no job, branded as an ex-con, and with little money to fall back on, two out of every three prisoners return to crime. The present training of prisoners is hopelessly inadequate. Chances are very slim that an offender will return to a life of crime if he is able to get a job immediately upon release. However, if he cannot get that job, the chances are very great that he will return to crime. Thus, a direct correlation exists between the ability of an ex-offender to get a job and the likelihood of his not returning to a life of crime.

Quote, 11-11:470.

Rocky Pomerance
Chief of Police
of Miami Beach, Fla.

3

The police identify with the victim of crime. We see the victims at the worst time. We see them when they are hysterical with grief because a loved one has been killed. We see them when they are down because they've been burglarized or assaulted. So it's not unusual that police should take a "harder line" when they think of the victims' problems. We see the victims first. When we catch the person we think did the crime, we're upset just like the victim is upset. It never surprises me that the police feel strongly about the innovative programs of work-release [of prisoners] and so forth. While ultimately such things may be the answer, you'll never be able to convince the man whose wife has been killed or raped by someone participating in one of these programs. Our cumulative daily experience comes to focus in participation in the victim's frustration.

Interview/The National Observer, 3-31:13.

Ronald Reagan
Governor of California

4

I don't believe those who voted [in California] to re-establish capital punishment did so out of any feelings of vengeance or because they were bloodthirsty zealots. They simply believe that criminals who murder innocent women and children, who gun down police and engage in political assassination will not be deterred by anything less than the ultimate penalty—and the people are right . . . For a number of years, we have had a moratorium on capital punishment. Unfortunately, it has not been a total moratorium. Last year alone, there were 1,789 executions in California. The executions took place on our streets, in the victims' homes and in places of business. One thousand, seven hundred and eighty-nine innocent people in our state were executed with no recognition of their Constitutional rights or of the moratorium that only gave shelter to their executioners.

At California Chamber of Commerce
breakfast, Sacramento, Sept. 7/
Los Angeles Times, 9-8:(1)23.

5

[On gun control]: I am opposed to taking guns away from law-abiding citizens, because the criminal is always going to have his. We [he and his crime-control task force] think that the proper gun control is to say to the criminal: "If you are going to use a gun, the penalty is going to be a lot higher than if you try robbing somebody's house without a gun."

(RONALD REAGAN)

And we think this could be the effective deterrent.

Interview/Human Events, 10-13:20.

Abraham A. Ribicoff
United States Senator, D-Connecticut

1

[Current drug-law enforcement efforts] have allowed many major traffickers to prove themselves better organized than the Federal agencies pursuing them. Despite a seven-fold increase in funding of Federal drug-law enforcement over the past five years, the situation today remains one of major heroin traffickers being identified by the hundreds but being apprehended only by the dozens; of heroin being smuggled into the nation each year by the tons but being seized only by the pounds.

Washington, March 28/
The New York Times, 3-29:26.

Elliot L. Richardson
Attorney General of the United States

2

The first concern of the administration of justice is the individual; the second is truth. The first of these demands fairness; the second demands fearlessness. I will endeavor to be faithful to both.

On being sworn in as Attorney General,
Washington/Quote, 7-8:26.

3

We ought to level with people as to just how little we know about how to treat drug addicts, criminal offenders, alcoholics. The truth of the matter is we're not very good at any of these things. One of the reasons why we have not been willing to level with people in the past is that most people have simply not wanted to know that our correctional institutions didn't correct. It was more comfortable for them to believe that, if we had enough machine tools in there and we had enough probation officers, that people would get straightened out. The fact of the matter is

that our record nationally in this is extremely poor.

Interview, Washington/
U.S. News & World Report, 9-3:26.

Frank L. Rizzo
Mayor of Philadelphia

4

. . . ask me about criminals—those thugs who lie in wait to beat, rob, murder. I've been a policeman all my life. I know what they [criminals] are capable of. I'm sometimes astounded by the misplaced compassion we give those creeps. This is where I become a conservative. You read stories on why people become criminals, read where a guy steals to provide for his family. I've arrested a lot of criminals in my career, and I've yet to apprehend the first one who bought milk for his kids with the loot or paid his rent. You know what they do with the money? Broads, drink and gamble. They just don't want to work.

Interview, Philadelphia/
Los Angeles Times, 1-21:(1)16.

Nelson A. Rockefeller
Governor of New York

5

[On drug abuse]: Lots of wonderful young people have died—and hundreds of thousands more have been and are being crippled for life. Addiction has kept on growing. A rising percentage of our high-school and college students, from every background and economic level, have become involved, whether as victims or pushers or both. The crime, the muggings, the robberies, the murders associated with addiction continue to spread a reign of terror. Whole neighborhoods have been as effectively destroyed by addicts as by an invading army. We face the risk of undermining our will as a people—and the ultimate destruction of our society as a whole.

State of the State address, Albany,
Jan. 3/The New York Times, 1-4:28.

William D. Ruckelshaus
Acting Director, Federal Bureau of Investigation

6

Despite the unease which some may feel, I

have not found the FBI to be an organization of free-lance busybodies snooping at random and amassing dossiers on individual private excesses or the sins of our most celebrated citizens. Such comic-opera characterization is not only misleading but dangerous in its presumption of sinister motivation on the part of some of the most able, best-trained and dedicated men and women who have ever served this republic.
At Ohio State University commencement, June 8/Los Angeles Times, 6-9:(1)23.

1

The Director [of the FBI] must be able to conceptualize how the FBI fits into our societal fabric at any given historical moment. He must recognize the permissible limits of investigative techniques—what is permissible in wartime or times of extreme emergency is impermissible when the threat to our country's security is minimal—and he must communicate forcefully those limits to FBI agents. Needless to say, this takes an individual of considerable capacity. Further, the necessity to America of our major Federal law enforcement agency's not exceeding a wise exercise of its power is too important to leave to the judgment of one man. There must be effective oversight . . . In my opinion, neither the Legislative nor the Executive oversight or check is sufficient today and needs to be strengthened.
At Ohio State University commencement, June 8/The Washington Post, 6-14:(A)30.

2

[On whether the FBI is becoming a "secret police"]: . . . it is a Federal investigative agency, and in that sense a police force. It does have information which it keeps secret. The question is whether the information is legitimately gathered in a free society and whether it is legitimately kept secret. And as long as we keep asking ourselves questions of legitimacy, the chances are—while we may disagree on a given point as to whether it is legitimate or not—we're at least going to avoid the real excesses that occur with secret police when you end up with the kind of secret police they had in Nazi Germany or some truly totalitarian state. That's why I always get back to the fact that checks are so

important, that Congressional oversight is so crucial, that they keep asking these questions: "Why are you doing it?" "Why are you asking about this kind of thing?" Maybe it's legitimate. But they ought to keep asking those questions so that the person who is running the FBI is asking himself these questions, too, rather than saying, "We'll do whatever we want, because nobody is ever going to ask us about it or know about it."
Interview, July 13/ The New York Times Magazine, 8-19:35.

Donald E. Santarelli
Administrator, Law Enforcement Assistance Administration of the United States

3

Our present correctional system too often calls upon society to pay a double price. In the first place, society pays to incarcerate an offender; then it pays when the man victimizes society once again after his release.
Oct. 14/Los Angeles Times, 10-15:(1)15.

Hugh Scott
United States Senator, R-Pennsylvania

4

In recent weeks, the intelligence community and the White House have borne the onus of criticism from certain quarters for the use of wiretaps on National Security Council employees and newsmen. Further, an [Nixon] Administration proposal for the use of special measures to protect the domestic security in the turbulent days of 1970 has served as the focus for domestic political opponents. The impression has been left with the American people that somehow wiretaps, the clandestine operations, were tactics dreamed up by internal-security agencies and individuals—solely within the Nixon Administration. This is an utterly false impression . . . At my request, the President has agreed to make public certain preliminary statistics and to have completed over the next few weeks a more detailed survey of national-security wiretaps and other clandestine and covert activities undertaken in the United States in recent years . . . While the use of wiretaps for national-security reasons was most widespread in the post-war, cold-war years, it diminished under Dwight Eisenhower, was stepped up again under Attorney General Robert F. Kennedy, and was reduced under Attorney General Ramsey Clark, and remains today, in the first years of the '70s, at about one-half the level of the early to mid '60s.

The Christian Science Monitor, 6-27:16.

Whitney N. Seymour, Jr.
Former United States Attorney
for the Southern District of New York

1

Over the course of years, the [Federal] Bureau [of Investigation] has become a monolithic institution, much too dependent on the personality of the individual who serves as its Director, and much too tied up in administrative regulations and internal checks and balances to do a truly effective job. The FBI has escaped criticism for these tendencies because no one has dared to raise a voice against it. But every one of us in law enforcement can cite some of its weaknesses.

At John Jay College of Criminal Justice
commencement, New York, June 3/
The New York Times, 6-4:31.

William A. Stanmeyer
Associate Professor, Georgetown University;
Director, Center for Law and Education

2

A major reason that crime has gone up 11 times faster than population, that shoplifting is destroying retail business, that bus drivers no longer carry change, that drug-abuse is leeching away the lives of 10 per cent of our high-school children, that airline passengers face daily risk of hijack, that a rape occurs every 15 minutes . . . is that, just when we need more-effective law enforcement, the courts have set out, generally, to render it impotent. Just when we most need to strengthen the certainty of sanction, we weaken it! We have seen to it that crime does pay. And the criminal knows it. Because of strained legal interpretations, American criminal jurisprudence has lost the common-sense

flexibility that characterizes the British system, our legal forebear, and which, though somewhat diminished even in England, is likely to increase in their practice long before the law-abiding citizens here at last insist that we leave the mountaintop of Constitutional theory and return to the marketplace of plain reason.

At Hillsdale (Mich.) College/
The Wall Street Journal, 4-23:12.

John V. Tunney
United States Senator, D-California

3

I'm not at all convinced the death penalty is a deterrent. But if the justification is deterrence, then do it in a public place where people can see it and maybe it will be a deterrent.

San Francisco Examiner,
3-25:(This World)2.

Roy Wilkins
Executive director,
National Association for the Advancement
of Colored People

4

[On the Nixon Administration]: We shall not comment on the irony of a "law and order" Administration punishing penny-ante Negro crime, while plotting in the highest echelons of government the theft of liberties and freedom of a whole people. Not that stealing, under any circumstances, is right. Not that Negro crime in instances is not heinous and horrible. Not that murder is petty, whether the accused be black or white. But nothing can match the oily preachments on law of one whose dark code is a belief that the end justifies the means.

At NAACP convention, Indianapolis,
July 3/The Washington Post, 7-4:(A)9.

James Q. Wilson
Chairman, department of government,
Harvard University

5

We . . . must seriously re-examine our correctional system. On the basis of almost every piece of reliable evidence that has been gathered so far, the present system is not rehabilitating criminals in large numbers. This should not surprise us. It was an act of hubris to suppose that we could devise an institution, staffed by mediocre men and women, in which persons who have been engaged in repeated criminal acts and who are now well past the age of consent can, under unpleasant circumstances, somehow be talked out of it; or that by exposing convicted criminals to handicrafts, to making license plates, or to weaving mattresses we can rehabilitate them . . . We should decide, I believe, that the correctional system has only two legitimate functions: that of protecting society by segregating certain people for certain periods of time, and, secondly, that of creating a penalty so that at least some persons will think that the costs of criminal activity outweigh the gains. Such a result can be achieved without requiring longer criminal sentences. But I think it will require more certain sentences, if not necessarily more severe ones.

Before Coalition for a Democratic Majority, May 24/ Vital Speeches, 9-1:691.

Marvin E. Wolfgang
Professor of Law, University of Pennsylvania

1

There is no keen and precise estimate of the extent to which fear of crime changes people's behavior. But it's enormous: They take taxis instead of walking; they barricade their houses; they construct medieval fortresses; they close up their cities tight after dark.

The Washington Post, 5-27:(A)12.

Stephen M. Young
Former United States Senator, D-Ohio

2

I disagree with the [Nixon] Administration over why the crime rate is coming down in Washington, D.C. People are locking themselves up at night. There are not as many mugees to be mugged.

Quote, 5-13:434.

Evelle J. Younger
Attorney General of California

3

The time has come for the state to help [medically and financially] the victim of a crime as much as it helps the criminal who committed it.

Sacramento, Jan. 3/ San Francisco Examiner, 1-4:9.

4

[Saying gun laws will not end the handgun problem]: [You can't] get handguns out of the hands of bad guys [through legislation]. My own personal feeling is, if I had some magic power—[if] I could say some magic words—and all the cheap handguns in the world disappeared, that would be wonderful. But . . . I just don't see how we could do it legislatively.

Before California Peace Officers Association, Sacramento/ Los Angeles Times, 2-9:(1)2.

5

[Prisons] are condemned as failures because they do not rehabilitate convicts; but prisons are not intended to rehabilitate . . . Though we can and should try our very best to rehabilitate the convict, let's not condemn the entire criminal-justice system . . . for failing to perform a function it was never intended to perform. It should be made clear that prisons cannot rehabilitate inmates—only inmates can rehabilitate inmates. Prisons can and do offer opportunities and encourage those men who want to help themselves . . . The principle function of prisons is to keep the bad guys away from the good guys—not to serve as rehabilitation centers.

Before International Police Association, Anaheim, Calif., Oct. 26/ Los Angeles Times, 10-27:(2)1,10.

Education

Russell Adams
Director, Department of African Studies,
Howard University

1

I think that, if black studies are to survive, they must be academically rigorous, vocationally relevant and socially useful. The stronger institutions, black and white, will support black studies, for these studies have pointed up fundamental academic and social oversights in the American system.

U.S. News & World Report, 1-29:32.

Reubin Askew
Governor of Florida

2

. . . we have placed on the shoulders of our public schools—almost alone—tremendous social, political and economic burdens—burdens that should be borne by the total community, not just the schools, not just the courts, not any one element of our society, regardless of what that element might be. We've asked public schools, in far too many cases, to act as parents as well as instructors, and we've been angered by their inability to do so. But worst of all, we've allowed our public schools to be effectively isolated from the people, often limiting citizen involvement to the raising of funds for painting the teachers' lounge or to the setting of dates for a cookie sale. It's no wonder, then, that education has come upon difficult times.

Quote, 12-9:558.

William S. Banowsky
President, Pepperdine University

3

Never has there been a better time to restore the relationship between the business and education communities—a relationship which has suffered during the past 10 to 15 years. Students still have long hair, but it is

just a fashion. They now have a sense of gratitude for the past accomplishments, a sense of humor which shows intelligence, and a greater appreciation of history . . . their attitudes are more constructive and positive.

Before Southern California Business Men's
Association, Los Angeles, May 1/
Los Angeles Herald-Examiner, 5-2:(A)6.

Don Barnhart
South Dakota State Superintendent
of Public Instruction

4

[On Nixon Administration cuts in "impact aid" to school districts]: The Federal government has abandoned its responsibility to protect local government. I'm waiting for the day in this country where we can have cost overruns for children, the same as we have for weapons to kill.

The Washington Post, 4-18:(A)2.

Lerone Bennett, Jr.
Senior editor, "Ebony" magazine

5

The predominantly black [educational] institution is challenged in this country. There are those who do not believe blacks can contribute knowledge to this world or to administer institutions. But we need the black school to produce the black intellectuals who can deal with the fundamental problems that black people have in this country.

At luncheon sponsored by Howard University's
Project Awareness, Washington, Jan. 23/
The Washington Post, 1-24:(B)3.

Alexander M. Bickel
Professor of Law, Yale University

6

The disruptive tactics of students have at times amounted to the assumption of control in faculty decision-making; and they are not to be tolerated for this fundamental reason. Whatever the tactics of students—even if they are entirely civil, and however embarrassingly unfashionable it may be to insist on power and privilege—administrators and faculties should realize that inroads on the autonomy of the latter are inroads on academic freedom; the abandonment of faculty control, or any part of it, over appointments, curriculum and academic standards is the abandonment of the ends of the university.

At conference of the International Council on the University Emergency, Venice, Italy, Oct. 14/The New York Times, 10-14:(1)13.

William G. Bowen
President, Princeton University

1

[On finances and budget-cutting at the university]: For a place like Princeton . . . survival is not the issue. What is at issue is our ability to preserve quality and do some important new things. That's less dramatic but not less important. What I worry about is a kind of slow deterioration of academic quality and initiative . . . the danger is in losing one's momentum.

Los Angeles Times, 5-14:(2)5.

B. Frank Brown
Chairman, National Commission on the Reform of Secondary Education

2

. . . high schools are in a state of extreme intellectual despair. At least half of the teaching in secondary schools today is devoted in one way or another to social relationships, and this is watering down the curriculum. The farther we get from the more rigorous academic courses in English, math and science, the more these scores are going to decline.

U.S. News & World Report, 12-31:39.

Earl L. Butz
Secretary of Agriculture of the United States

3

. . . in our ongoing affluent society, we can't have all chiefs. Somebody has to milk the cows, tend the looms and generate the

power. That goes for college people as well. Society's demand for increased productivity will place special stress on our technically-oriented educational institutions—on the hard sciences, on engineering and on the practical instruction which transforms knowledge and brain power into ability.

At University of North Carolina commencement, Charlotte/ The National Observer, 5-26:13.

Kenneth B. Clark
Professor of Psychology, City College of New York

4

Black studies are as revolting as the form of segregation we fought against—even more so because they are insidious. They are allegedly buying peace [on campus], but at the expense of the education of black students.

U.S. News & World Report, 1-29:30.

James Coleman
Professor of Social Relations, Johns Hopkins University

5

It's impossible to conceive of equal educational opportunity in a society, simply because of the fact that the main educational opportunity comes from family, and families give unequal attention and unequal genetic resources and unequal financial resources to their children.

The Washington Post, 4-8:(A)20.

Charles C. Edwards
Assistant Secretary for Health, Department of Health, Education and Welfare of the United States

6

[On Federal aid for medical-student education]: Frankly, we are now questioning very seriously whether it is appropriate for the Federal government to bear so substantial a share of the cost of preparing individuals for careers that offer about the highest earning power in our society. We simply have to question whether taxpayers should continue to be expected to subsidize tuition costs for medical students, but not for students in

(CHARLES C. EDWARDS)

other fields whose income expectations fall far below that of physicians.

Before Association of American Medical Colleges, Washington, Nov. 5/
Los Angeles Herald-Examiner, 11-5:(A)2.

John H. Fischer
President,
Teachers College, Columbia University

1

In face of growing massism, the school must serve as a strong countervailing force on behalf of individuality . . . The essence of our effort to see that every child has a chance must be to assure each an equal opportunity, not to become equal, but to become different —to realize whatever unique potential of body, mind and spirit he or she possesses.

Before American Association of School Administrators, San Francisco, March 18/
San Francisco Examiner, 3-19:9.

2

Several days ago, a friend suggested to me that we at Teachers College ought to be thinking about why the education of the principals in the Watergate [political-espionage] affair did not develop in them more dependable character qualities. It's a fair question and an old one. In one form or another, the relation between education and character has occupied philosophers and pedagogs for several millenia. But a matter more fundamental than character weakness in a few dozen individuals is why our system of universal education has not engendered in our population as a whole a keener appreciation of moral values, a higher level of expectation toward our political system and higher standards for judging our elected officials. Why do we so regularly expect mediocrity and accept mendacity in public office? To be sure, our Constitution embodies a scheme of checks and balances because our forefathers were familiar with the hazards of unrestrained power and other predictable human weaknesses. But our polity rests mainly on the assumption that, when ordinary men and women are suitably informed, they may be expected most of the time to make political choices with intelligence, with reason and in good faith. To support that assumption and to give it continuing validity is one of the principal functions of popular education in a democracy. If our education is falling short in performing that function, we had better know about it and we had better be doing something about it.

Before Teachers College 1973 graduates/
The National Observer, 7-7:15.

Edmund J. Gleazer, Jr.
President, American Association
of Community and Junior Colleges

3

The community colleges have a tremendously complicated educational task. This is because of the great variety of students attracted and the commitment of the institutions to meet them where they are . . . Community colleges are increasingly attractive to students who might otherwise have gone to the university. This attests to the higher levels of academic achievement there . . . Students coming out of high school are often undecided about a career. They are not pressed to make a decision in the community colleges. The colleges serve the need for "passage," movement out of the educational system to adulthood.

Interview/
The Christian Science Monitor, 4-14:(B)1.

S. I. Hayakawa
President, San Francisco State University

4

How anybody dresses is indicative of his self-concept. If students are dirty and ragged, it indicates they are not interested in tidying up their intellects either.

Interview, San Francisco/
Los Angeles Herald-Examiner, 4-8:(B)3.

5

. . . essentially a university is a place for study, reflection and vigorous argument—not for gangsterism, street fighting and crap like that.

Interview, San Francisco/
Los Angeles Herald-Examiner, 4-8:(B)3.

S. I. Hayakawa
Former president,
San Francisco State University

1

Schooling takes too much of a person's time between the ages of 12 and 20. Seventy-five per cent of crimes are committed by people under 21. I think it is because, for many who are not scholastically inclined, school is a prison. They rebel against the whole thing.

Interview, San Francisco/
Los Angeles Times, 11-25:(1)12.

James M. Hester
President, New York University

2

Regrettably, some members of universities have not always lived up to the ideals of academic life. In particular, the intolerance exhibited by some on college campuses during the era of protest betrayed the basic conditions of the academic world. This provided powerful ammunition to the critics of universities. For a considerable part of the public, the academic mystique was shattered. The academic mystique is the quality of specialness that has long been attached to academic life. That specialness implies dedication to goals that are higher than material rewards and to the highest standards of objectivity, honesty and justice. The academic mystique signifies reverence for a calling that is of profound consequence to the qualitative advancement of the entire society. This calling, therefore, deserves special respect, special support and special protection. But the mystique becomes a sham when members of the academic world forsake the community's ideals. Then universities have no greater standing in society than any other enterprise.

At New York University commencement,
June 5/Vital Speeches, 9-1:692.

Roger W. Heyns
President, American Council on Education

3

If we [in education] are going to be effective in our relations with government, we must be willing participants in the process of re-examination. We can claim no exemption from it. Government spends enormous amounts for education; and I suggest that the realities call for us to examine whether we can increase the usefulness of these existing resources to the health of the institution and the consequent health of society.

Before American Association of Colleges,
San Francisco/
San Francisco Examiner, 1-16:18.

Walter J. Hickel
Former Secretary of the Interior
of the United States

4

[Education is] a process of reality . . . of preparation to make decisions based on options the intellects provide.

Before American Association of School
Administrators, San Francisco, March 19/
San Francisco Examiner, 3-20:5.

Marjorie S. Holt
United States Representative,
R-Maryland

5

If we are to rescue our children from mediocrity, we must abolish the [educational] programs that use them as guinea pigs for social experimentation, while neglecting to nourish their minds. We must clear the schools of constant assault on culture, intellect and tradition, lest we drown in the mire of "relevance" and psychological education. We should be teaching our children a body of knowledge comprised of what T.S. Eliot called "the permanent things," and not the faddish social theories that are doomed to be replaced by equally short-lived ideas. If we do not want to bring up vague-minded robots that march to the tune of the drummer of the day instead of to the heartbeat of the universe, we must save the schools before they move further in the direction they are taking. We must return to quality education before it is too late.

Quote, 11-18:485.

Sidney Hook
Former Professor of Philosophy,
New York University

1

Is it expecting too much of effective general education that it develop within students a permanent defense against gullibility? It is astonishing to discover how superstitious students are, how vulnerable to demagogic appeal, to empty show and eloquence.

At "The Philosophy of the Curriculum"
conference, New York/
The New York Times, 9-23:(1)36.

Chet Huntley
Former news commentator,
National Broadcasting Company

2

I am saddened and dismayed when I examine the list of activities for which academic credit is now given in some school systems. Is your school system giving academic credit for football and basketball and tennis? How about pottery-making or flower-arranging? Drama? Glee club and band? And what about monitoring? In many school systems, academic credit is given for monitoring . . . that's a messenger service in which a student interrupts classroom such-and-such to tell teacher Smith that she is wanted on the telephone, or student Jones that he'll have to take the bus to get home today. Academic credit is frequently given for participation in student government; and student government is usually nothing more than a thinly-disguised popularity contest. Academic credit is given for contribution to the school paper, for cheerleading and pom-pom waving, for making announcements over the closed-circuit radio or television system. A credit for monitoring is given the same value as a credit for trigonometry or for the ability to write a sonnet. Academic credit is given for these activities which we used to pursue after school hours for the sake of pride, for publicity and recognition, for the pursuit of excellence, or for the sheer joy of it.

Before National School Board Association,
Anaheim, Calif. April 7/
Vital Speeches, 7-15:602.

Robert M. Hutchins
Chairman, Center for the Study
of Democratic Institutions

3

. . . an educational system operates within severe limitations. It is limited by the background and ability of its pupils and the environment in which they live. It is limited by the prejudices of taxpayers. It cannot proclaim a revolution and survive.

The Fresno (Calif.) Bee, 2-7:(A)18.

Herman Kahn
Director, Hudson Institute

4

Education by definition is a narrowing of the eyes. It says, "This is important. This is the way to look at things." It trains you to look at the relevant data on the relevant issues. But at the same time, it may tell you to ignore lots of things which are not relevant to what you're interested in. When you spend a lot of time in learning things in school, you sometimes lose track of, sort of, common sense.

Interview/
The Washington Post, 7-1:(C)1.

Russell Kirk
Author

5

We have succeeded in schooling a great many people—too many at college and university levels because neither their own interests nor the employment market justify today so grand a production of people with academic degrees. We have not yet succeeded in *educating* a great many people—for which sorry fact the declining sales of serious books are some evidence. We have not developed so successful a system of popular instruction as Switzerland has, nor yet so admirable a system of higher education as Britain used to have. The typical product of our schools and colleges is mediocre intellectually—no triumph, no disaster. But the times demand more than mediocrity. Our failure to quicken imagination accounts, in large part, for our national difficulties, now formidable. Our public men tend to lack moral imagination and strength of will; our communities grow ugly and violent because vision and courage are wanting. Mediocrity in a pattern of education may not be disastrous in itself, and yet it may contribute gradually to private and public decadence. Mediocre appeals for "excellence" will not suffice in the absence of real educational reform. Who at P.S. 137 really aspires to impart wisdom and virtue? Who at Behemoth University has any time for such abstract ends? And yet, if those with power in the educational establishment remain unconcerned with wisdom and virtue, the ethos of sociability and material success will evaporate gradually, or perhaps swiftly—leaving a vacuum possibly to be filled by force and a master.

At Hillsdale (Mich.) College/
The National Observer, 7-21:11.

Hernan LaFontaine
Director of bi-lingual education,
New York City Public School System

1

[Criticizing standardized school tests]: To test or not to test—that is the question. Whether 'tis nobler in the mind to suffer the slings and arrows of outrageous measurement, or to take arms against a sea of standardized tests and, by opposition, end them.

The New York Times, 3-25:(4)9.

Robert L. Lamborn
Executive director,
Council for American Private Education

2

[On private education]: People want to have alternatives to public education . . . It's part of our national tradition to encourage a vigorous diversity in education to match the high value our country has placed on individuality and freedom of choice.

Interview, Washington/
The New York Times, 11-4:(1)18.

Richard W. Lyman
President, Stanford University

3

To be effective, liberal education must enable people to learn the difference between wish and achievement—and how to blend the two. It must assist everyone, regardless of vocational expectations, in learning how to think critically. And that does not mean merely how to become skeptical of the Establishment—that's too easy and requires no disciplined thought whatsoever. It means how to amass, consider and weigh evidence; how to distinguish among kinds of knowledge, not for the purpose of denigrating some and elevating others but so as to know what one knows, and what the limits and qualifications on that knowledge are. This doesn't mean that we should lessen the attention we pay to the preparation of young men and women to be good doctors, lawyers, merchants, or chiefs of government or industry. What it does mean is that training is not enough. Training without education means the development of a person's capacities in a one-sided and dangerous way. It produces expertise without wisdom, widely recognized as an explosive and unstable compound . . . The unique strength of American higher education, for all its sins of omission and commission, has been its ecumenical quality, its effort to bridge the gap between *Academia* and the world of practical affairs. This is a heritage we would be very foolish to lose in the heat of some sham battle over what higher education is all about. It is about the mind, the spirit, *and* about coping with the real world.

Addressing an alumni assembly/
The National Observer, 6-16:10.

William C. MacInnes
President, University of San Francisco

4

The euphoria [for education] of the 1960s was wonderful. There were government grants. Growth was the measure of success. A college president who did not increase his enrollment believed himself to be in trouble. But the government has turned economy-minded. It's a new style today. I even saw an advertisement for a college campus for sale. We are undergoing realignment. What we must do now is offer something for somebody who chooses to go to college. A college cannot be a baby-sitting institution for late adolescents. It is not a refuge and no longer is it a

(WILLIAM C. MacINNES)

protection from the draft. I think it is a healthy shake-out. Now we must seek students who want to become educated. I don't think the gate should be open to everyone who walks past a university.

Interview, San Francisco/
San Francisco Examiner, 3-8:3.

Marya Mannes
Author, Journalist

1

I believe that an education which fails to make the reading of the great literature of the past as relevant as the important works of the present is no education at all. And the universities which abandon this bridging of time as the base of all wisdom are not worth their charter.

At Portland (Ore.) State University/
Quote, 4-1:294.

Sidney P. Marland, Jr.
Assistant Secretary for Education,
Department of Health, Education and
Welfare of the United States

2

We must begin . . . to plan and carry out a reasoned, rational and practical reform of the teaching profession. We must begin to change the way teachers teach, the efficiency with which their professional skills and intellectual talents are used or misused in the schools, the number of children they work with and the circumstances under which they perform that work. We must take, in sum, a new view of the teacher's place in our system of education—giving the teacher the opportunity not only to be more responsive to student needs, but also to find a far greater degree of professional fulfillment and satisfaction, and a larger degree of engagement in the decisions affecting the schools. In the face of greatly-increasing expectations, at a time in history when technology and contemporary organizational techniques are reforming virtually every human enterprise, teaching remains a highly labor-intensive system, and education

as an institution remains a cottage industry.

At Rhode Island College commencement,
June 8/Vital Speeches, 8-1:625.

3

There is manifest in this country—to my knowledge for the first time in our history—an active loss of enchantment with our schools . . . from kindergarten through graduate school . . . For the first time, Americans in significant numbers are questioning the purpose of education, the competence of educators and the usefulness of the system in preparing young minds for life in these turbulent times.

U.S. News & World Report, 9-3:28.

William J. McGill
President, Columbia University

4

[On the public attitude toward politically-active universities]: Public support for higher education for the first time in a generation is beginning obviously to diminish . . . The public watches these struggles [between education and politics] and then wonders whether our central commitment is to education or to politically-toned social activism. In the wake of such skepticism, the enthusiasm which undergirded earlier and major public commitments of Federal resources to higher education . . . has disappeared.

At ceremony honoring 1972 Nobel Prize
winners, Columbia University, March 20/
The New York Times, 3-21:45.

John D. Millett
Vice president,
Academy for Educational Development;
Former chancellor, Ohio Board of Regents

5

The primary product this Academy has been selling since 1962 is master planning [for higher education]. The trouble is, there are empire-builders among state-university presidents. And there are heads of private institutions who don't want to give up any of their power and prestige. I tell the people in private institutions: "You've got to make a choice —you can be autonomous or you can be

affluent, but you can't be both."
U.S. News & World Report, 5-21:46.

Malcolm C. Moos
President, University of Minnesota

1

This class [of '73] represents a generation that was born too old too soon. It has gone through an incredible corridor of mindless violence, and it has seen a lot and learned a lot in the process. It has learned that confrontation doesn't seem to work and that "compromise" isn't necessarily a dirty word.
Interview/
The New York Times, 6-18:22.

Leland B. Newcomer
President, La Verne (Calif.) College

2

One of the reasons that young people aren't going to college is that they've found college isn't the only way to get an education and that getting a degree isn't a guarantee of a job. This hurts college enrollments; but I think it's a very healthy thing.
U.S. News & World Report, 4-23:44.

Barbara Newell
President, Wellesley College

3

The current trend toward coeducation has increased rather than lessened male domination of American higher education. In spite of affirmative action guidelines, most educational institutions have but token women faculty members along with their token black faculty. It is naive to believe that any movement for educational equity for women can come out of such colleges and universities. This leadership will have to be sustained by [women's] colleges like Wellesley . . . Women's colleges take their students seriously, as individuals. Women at Wellesley have to run their own lives. We take it as our obligation to develop the talents of each individual fully, unhampered by stereotypes. And if we're really successful, God willing, we'll work ourselves out of a job.
The Christian Science Monitor, 12-28:(B)2.

Ewald B. Nyquist
New York State Commissioner of Education;
President, State University of New York

4

Unfortunately, many teachers have a fear of being replaced by machines, of losing their jobs. Too often this fear is the result of inadequate training. The average teacher or administrator has not always been afforded the desirable pre-service or in-service training which would provide him or her with knowledge about, and technical skill in, the effective use of the many technological systems available. More important, little attention has been given to show them how to integrate technology in the teaching process. All too often, emphasis has been on how to use technology as an "add-on" rather than as an integrated teaching tool or technique. The users also have not been involved adequately in the decision to install technological support systems. Most decisions have been made by a few technical managers. In all candor, I think it should be said that if productivity is to increase in education—a labor-intensive occupation—technology will have to be employed, some teachers and personnel will be replaced; but I should think this can be accomplished largely by attrition.
At annual conference of District
Superintendents of Schools, Albany, N.Y.,
Jan. 4/Vital Speeches, 2-15:277.

5

. . . there are thousands of people—men and women of all ages—who contribute in important ways to the life of the communities in which they live even though they do not have a college degree. Through native intelligence, hard work, and sacrifice, many have gained in knowledge and understanding, have developed and expanded their cultural and aesthetic horizons and, thus, have become significant contributors to society. And yet, the social and economic advancement of these people has been thwarted in part by the emphasis that is put on the possession of credentials presumptively attesting to intellectual competence and the acquisition of skills. As long as we remain a strongly "credentialed" society, and until courts decide other-

(EWALD B. NYQUIST)

wise, employers will not be disposed to hire people on the basis of what they know, rather than on what degrees and diplomas they hold. If attendance at a college is the only road to these credentials, those who cannot or have not availed themselves of this route, but have acquired knowledge and skills through other sources, will be denied the recognition and advancement to which they are entitled. Such inequity should not be tolerated. The costs of traditionalism are too high.

At conference sponsored by Cleveland Commission on Higher Education, Cleveland, July 18/ Vital Speeches, 9-1:698.

1

Present-day education is still predicated on a number of myths: that the school or college is the exclusive place of education; that youth is the exclusive age of learning; that knowledge flows exclusively from the teacher; that education is properly measured by the accumulation of credits; that there is a rhythm or pattern of intellectual curiosity or social maturity common to all; that it is dangerous or counter-productive to mix young and old people in the same classrooms; that education must be experienced in unbroken sequences of 12 to 16 years; that prolonged adolescence is a good thing and that the more education one gets before working the better; that degrees and diplomas are the only indicators of talent and competence and the only instruments by which upward social and economic mobility may be acquired; and that admission to college can best be determined by such quantitative criteria as high-school grades and College Board scores.

At Conference on Non-Traditional Studies, Glens Falls, N.Y., Oct. 31/ Vital Speeches, 12-15:156.

Thomas B. Ragle
President, Marlboro (Vt.) College

2

Students come to us less educated now. Literacy is falling among youth. They read less and less, and write less and less. Eighty per cent of our incoming freshmen don't meet our reading standards.

Interview, Marlboro, Vt./ The Christian Science Monitor, 7-21:10.

James S. Rausch
General secretary,
United States Catholic Conference

3

[Criticizing a U.S. Supreme Court ruling against state aid for parochial schools]: The U.S. Catholic Conference is in fundamental disagreement with the majority decision of the Supreme Court today. To conclude, as the Court has done, that religious sponsorship of elementary or secondary schools cuts off their patrons from benefits which other citizens enjoy, is to penalize many Americans on religious grounds—something itself contrary to the traditions of this nation. This is a denial of the civil rights of millions of citizens.

The Christian Science Monitor, 6-26:8.

Burt F. Raynes
Chairman,
National Association of Manufacturers

4

I do not find it surprising that so many youngsters coming out of our schools are "turned off" on business and industry. They are being molded by a system that has become a sort of "shadow government" in itself —one that subsists in a government-financed hothouse, shielded from the necessity of competing in the real world. I submit that in our schools today you will find little understanding of or appreciation for the realities of our country's economic life. Is it surprising, then, that a large number of the graduates of these schools of ours reject the free-enterprise system that has built this country—and its schools?

Before Detroit Economic Club, Feb. 5/ Vital Speeches, 3-15:339.

Donald T. Regan
Chairman, Merrill Lynch, Pierce,
Fenner & Smith, Inc.

5

There has never been what I know of as an

easy time for the average person to send kids to college. But due to the great rise in the state universities and the like, there are more people than ever that can get to college and take less share of the family's income dollar. I admit if you want to go to a few of the best-known private schools that have remained small and aren't tax-supported, the cost has risen, yes. But it still doesn't cost too much for the average student to go to the state university. . . .

Interview, New York/
Los Angeles Times, 8-1:(2)7.

Paul C. Reinert
President, St. Louis University

1

The day of the strong, totally autonomous independent [educational] institution is past. Given the limitations of our academic resources and the inexhaustible list of education needs, it is imperative that the programs of all types of institutions, public and private, large and small, be somehow interrelated and integrated into a total plan serving the public need. This means that we are all going to have to accept some restraints on our ambitions.

Before Association of American Colleges,
San Francisco/The New York Times, 1-22:14.

2

Master planning is the most important single governance issue that U.S. higher education will face during the next 10 years. As I see it, this is the path out of the woods. You have a situation now where the public sector finds itself over-expanded in some parts of each state and the private sector is at the same time under-enrolled. You have hard-to-come-by dollars being spent in states where unused accommodations exist, with students getting turned away from public colleges while private ones stand empty. You have new institutions springing up in the backyards of existing ones, and schools getting money to initiate programs already being offered by neighboring institutions. This sort of condition has cost us dearly, and we're finally in agreement—I hope—that an end must come to it.

U.S. News & World Report, 5-21:44.

Edwin O. Reischauer
Professor, Harvard University;
Former United States Ambassador to Japan

3

There is no better way of making you conscious of things outside your own culture than to learn a foreign language, particularly one of a very different sort, like Japanese, Chinese or Hindi. We ought to teach such languages earlier in education, when children enjoy it and learn easily. It might change their attitude about the world. Yet language is being taught increasingly less than before and at the wrong time. Language in the primary school is one thing children can do and like doing. Language requirements at high school or college are almost inevitably a bore; people hate them.

Interview, Cambridge, Mass./
Los Angeles Times, 10-19:(2)7.

Paul Reiss
Vice president for academic affairs,
Fordham University

4

Many universities are heading into real trouble, and the [faculty labor-] union issue is going to make it worse. Our situation is typical. We had to hire many younger teachers during the time of growth, and many acquired tenure. The result is that our tenured posts are filled, to a great extent, and many by younger professors; and openings in the future are going to be far fewer than they normally would have been. I can see this situation leading to discontent among young teachers, who may turn to the union as offering some security.

U.S. News & World Report, 9-10:37.

John T. Rettaliata
President, Illinois Institute of Technology

5

. . . the long tradition of universities in providing an atmosphere of thought and choice and reason made possible the implementation of new knowledge and skills. That, then, is the true role of higher education—to endow the men and women who pass through

(JOHN T. RETTALIATA)

our colleges and universities with the intellectual capacity to discover and understand factual knowledge, coupled with the capacity to evaluate and discriminate and make choices based on reason. The role of higher education is to develop intellectual leadership, to foster unusual human talent, to equip the individual with the rational tools for humane innovation and growth. Some may argue that our colleges and universities have played their role poorly; that higher education has become an exercise in reciting facts, rather than learning; that higher education aims at employment, rather than understanding. There is, of course, some truth in that argument. But simply because higher education has been an effective path to well-paying jobs in no way diminishes its broader goal . . . Universities have great staying power. They have existed in totalitarian societies and in democratic societies. They have flourished in rural communities and in urban centers. They have served a world slow to change, and they are serving a world in the midst of change. Through it all, they have preserved a basic identity. They remain unique instruments for the development of man.

At ITT Parents Day, April 29/
Vital Speeches, 8-1:636,637.

Wilson Riles
California State Superintendent
of Public Instruction

1

High-school diplomas today don't measure performance. They don't even represent a minimum level of performance. There are many who advocate two kinds of diplomas —one saying the student attained a certain performance level and another saying the student attended 12 years. I think that would be detrimental. We should strive, instead, to raise all students to a certain level so we can say that the diploma at least represents a certain level of accomplishment. And I don't think that level should be eighth grade.

Interview, Sacramento/
San Francisco Examiner & Chronicle,
4-29:(A)15.

Charles B. Saunders, Jr.
Deputy Assistant Secretary for Education,
Department of Health, Education and
Welfare of the United States

2

Federal programs in education have grown to the point where they impose heavy administrative burdens on officials at state and local levels. In no other field is Federal aid more complex: There are more than 100 programs in the Office of Education—and dozens more in some 26 other agencies . . . I find no evidence that the Federal bureaucracy, or even Congress in its wisdom, knows how to solve the educational problems which characteristically differ from region to region, state to state, school district to school district and child to child.

At National Municipal League's National
Conference in Government, Dallas,
Nov. 15/The Dallas Times Herald,
11-16:(A)12.

Barbara Sizemore
Superintendent of Schools
of the District of Columbia

3

Something has gone wrong at the classroom level, more specifically in the teaching-learning process, and I think this is true all over the country, not only in big cities . . . My concern, of course, is for the poor, because that's obviously where we're failing. We're failing the affluent, too; but we can't even teach the poor to read . . . That's our most glaring and obvious failure. To sweep it under the rug I think would be a terrible injustice.

Interview/The Washington Post, 9-2:(B)1.

John Wayne
Actor

4

[On college professors]: It takes 15 years of kissing somebody's backside for a professor to get a chair somewhere, and then he's a big-shot in a little world, passing his point of view on to a lot of impressionable kids. He's never really had to tough it out in this world of ours, so he has a completely theoretical view of how it should be run and what we should do for our fellow man.

Interview, Newport Beach, Calif./
Good Housekeeping, February:132.

The Environment

Spiro T. Agnew
Vice President of the United States

1

[Because of pollution,] we are told we should . . . dismantle our technology. There is another, more rational approach: The technology that causes pollution can also cure it.

At Drexel University commencement/
The New York Times, 6-18:22.

Carl Albert
United States Representative,
D-Oklahoma

2

Our environmental achievements over the past 10 years are dwarfed by what remains to be done. I wish I could agree with [President] Nixon's recent statement that "We are well on the way to winning the war against environmental degradation." However, the problem has been and still is very critical. The war is not close to being won . . . I do not intend to paint a dismal picture of the environment just to take issue with the President. This crisis goes beyond partisan politics to the very heart of our existence.

Radio address, Washington, Feb. 23/
Fresno (Calif.) Bee, 2-24:(A)3.

Roy L. Ash
Director,
Federal Office of Management and Budget

3

There have been a lot of alarming statements about the energy crisis. But I feel it won't be as bad as some fear. Unemployment may go up a bit, but not as drastically as predicted. I don't want to suggest it isn't a problem or a crisis, but it doesn't have to be a catastrophe.

Washington, Nov. 26/
The Washington Post, 11-28:(B)2.

Les Aspin
United States Representative,
D-Wisconsin

4

[Saying there are stockpiled crude-oil inventories in the Midwest that could be used to produce petroleum]: This is just one more piece of evidence that this summer's gasoline shortage is probably being created by the big oil companies. There is simply not a plausible explanation for Midwest refineries to operate at only 85 per cent capacity with new and growing inventories of crude available, except a conscious decision to hold back production.

Washington, June 2/
The Dallas Times Herald, 6-3:(A)32.

James Biddle
President,
National Trust for Historic Preservation

5

We Americans must decide if we want to preserve what we have or if we just want to pave it over, high-rise it and factory it. We've got to decide at what point your land ceases to be your land, at what point you must yield to over-all planning. It is the economic pressures that are the most destructive for preservation. Our philosophy at present seems to be that for land the best use is its highest development, the most profitable use, that there are no other values of equal importance. We find in the preservation business that our biggest problem is the belief that, if it's good, it's got to make money.

Washington/
San Francisco Examiner & Chronicle,
4-1:(B)6.

Alain Bombard
French marine biologist

6

Until there is an international agreement on

environmental problems, there's not much that can be done [about pollution]. You in the U.S. spend a considerable amount to purify your water. But given the cost, it's obvious you cannot do much more without handicapping yourself in your trade competition with other nations such as Japan. All countries and all peoples are so linked by the seas that international cooperation is the only answer to our mutual problems. Do you realize that 150 miles beyond the little beach at Saint-Tropez, which is so famous in France and around the world, there is pollution from the city of Genoa, 250 miles away? What can you do about something like this? Well, that's up to the economists and the ecologists. As for myself, I don't believe in vast projects such as trying to reach zero economic growth; I don't think that's realistic. But we could create products which are recyclable. We could try to agree on measures to stop tankers from flushing out their fuel compartments at sea. We could get industries to agree to put anti-pollution measures into their factories. That's where the start has to be made.

Interview, Amiens, France/
U.S. News & World Report, 6-11:52.

Norman E. Borlaug
Director, International Maize and Wheat
Improvement Center, Mexico City

1

It is my belief that food is the moral right for all who are born into this world. The question of how many should be born into this world is another issue. Without food, all other components of social justice are meaningless. I am also convinced that world order and peace cannot be built nor maintained on empty bellies and abject poverty. This should be readily apparent to even political ideologists and to advocates of utopian environments. The continued success of the Green Revolution will hinge, however, upon whether agriculture will be permitted to continue to use the inputs of agricultural chemicals, including chemical fertilizers and pesticides which are absolutely necessary to cope with hunger. If world agriculture is denied the use of these chemicals because of the adoption of unwise legislation in the affluent nations, where such legislation has been and continues to be by powerful lobby groups who subsequently indirectly attempt to impose their wills on the developing nations by political pressures, then crop production will again stagnate and social and political upheavals will be sure to follow. Prime Minister Indira Gandhi succinctly stated the position of India—and other countries of the developing world—at the 1972 Stockholm United Nations Conference on the Environment when she said: "Is it morally right for the affluent nations to deny the developing nations the use of science and technology, which is absolutely essential to improving the standard of living of [their] people, even if it produces some minor adverse effects on the environment?" I concur completely with this point of view.

At New Mexico State University
commencement, May 12/
Vital Speeches, 7-1:556.

H. A. Boucher
Lieutenant Governor of Alaska

2

[On the energy crisis]: If people only knew the tremendous reversal of attitudes and behavior that they and this nation will be forced to undergo starting right now, they never would have permitted the folly of our Alaskan [oil] pipeline delay. Today's energy crisis, with its power blackouts and all the rest, is only a foretaste of what is coming and has been coming ever since the late 1960s. That's when America suddenly ceased being self-sufficient in energy. It seems almost impossible for our people to grasp what this means. They think of their country as a land of boundless riches—which it never was—and think they can go right on living the good life of creature comforts made possible by their cars, air conditioners, adjustable heat and all those gizmos from waffle irons to automatic toothbrushes. What made us a powerful superstate, with the highest living standard in the world, was the cheap domestic energy supply we have been squandering. Energy, and the oil which gives most of it, is the very lifeblood of our civilization. Now we are no longer self-

(H. A. BOUCHER)

sufficient, and the price will be going up and up from now on. It is not exaggerating to say that the energy problem already has become the most difficult one now confronting our nation, and not only domestically but internationally as well. For the first time in our history, the wolf is at our own door, and he won't go away.

New York/
San Francisco Examiner & Chronicle,
5-13:(B)2.

Tom Bradley
Mayor of Los Angeles

1

The Federal government did not take the necessary actions to plan for, and even possibly avert, the current [energy] crisis. And there is no question that, when the time comes to apportion blame, our oil [company] giants also are going to bear very heavy responsibility . . . I call upon Congress and the President [Nixon] to set aside ill-conceived proposals for surcharge taxes on gasoline or a ban on Sunday driving or weekend closing of gas stations. These would punish the people who could least afford it. Instead, and only if absolutely necessary—and I now think this is to be the case—a carefully-structured system of gasoline rationing should be adopted.

Television broadcast, Los Angeles, Nov. 25/
Los Angeles Times, 11-26:(1)27.

James L. Buckley
United States Senator, C-New York

2

There are certain environmentalists who can never be satisfied even by going back to the kerosene lamp, which the public is not going to do. Many other environmentalists understand there has to be a middle ground. One thing I fear is the possibility of a backlash. There was a breakthrough in the whole environmental mood of the country in the late 1960s, which made all our legislative gains possible. You have to have public support. But if certain environmentalists press things so hard that the public believes their goals are

unreasonable or threaten severe dislocations, such as prolonged blackouts or rationing of fuel, we could have a backlash that could set us far behind where we are today.

Nation's Business, April:33.

Arthur F. Burns
Chairman, Federal Reserve Board

3

I think it's a good thing that the Arab states have cracked down on giving us oil supplies at this time. It will force us to become self-sufficient now instead of years from now when we might be much less well-prepared. We can do it, and I don't see that the crisis will lead to a recession.

Washington, Nov. 26/
The Washington Post, 11-28:(B)2.

Earl L. Butz
Secretary of Agriculture of the United States

4

Farmers are criticized for using herbicides, pesticides and nutrients essential for bountiful crop production. If this trend continues, it will only lead to lower efficiency on farms and higher food costs. The inevitable result will be a net decrease in efficiency, and added costs will have to be built into the retail food price to maintain the volume of food production required by a growing nation . . . The only reason we can sustain 210 million people in this country with a high-protein diet is that we have modified the environment. Without harming it or endangering animal species, including our own, we must modify the environment to our use, with full awareness of the level of risks involved.

Before National Canners' Association,
San Francisco, Jan. 26/
Los Angeles Times, 1-27:(1)11.

Robert C. Byrd
United States Senator, D-West Virginia

5

[Advocating the softening of current environmental regulations]: The inescapable fact is that, if we are going to avoid a paralyzing stoppage in almost every phase of our national life, we are just going to have to make accommodations . . . All of us would like to see Minnehaha living once again in the wigwam of Nokomis, by the shining big-sea-water. But that wigwam is now a power plant, and Minnehaha—who used to live in the wigwam—is making $200 a week working in the office of the president of the power plant, while Hiawatha is working his tail off in the plant to keep up the payments on a split-level, a station wagon and a boat. Like it or not, ours is an industrial society; and unless we are prepared to sacrifice our entire lifestyle, we will remain an industrial society.

Before Peabody Coal Co. stockholders,
St. Louis, Aug. 10/
The Washington Post, 8-11:(A)2.

John Chamberlain
Political columnist

1

The trouble with the environmentalist movement in the U.S. was that it fell into the hands of the elitists who despise anything that smacks of trade. The movement was dominated by well-to-do folk of the Park Avenue pink variety who, unlike the common people, live by clipping coupons. To these people, Disneylands are for the rabble. When the Walt Disney enterprises proposed building an Alpine ski resort in the Sierra Nevada Mountains that would be attractive to the average purse, I thought what a fine thing it would be for Los Angeles. People could get in a car Friday night, spend two exhilarating days in snow and scenery, and be back at work Monday morning. But the elitists of the Sierra Club would not have it that way. They wanted to preserve the high Sierras, all of them, for the pack-tripper. But who can afford taking a month off for an expensive pack trip? The Sierra Club may mean well, but must we preserve all of our wilderness domain—and we still have a lot of it in a nation that is geographically only 2 per cent urbanized—for the lucky rich who can seek solitude at their own whim?

Before Florida Soft Drink Association,
Disney World, Fla./Human Events,
11-17:16.

Edward N. Cole
President, General Motors Corporation

2

[On the fuel shortage]: We're not for [gasoline] rationing, to begin with. We think that in peacetime it just cannot be managed. I don't think there is any good way that you can fairly ration any commodity in a peacetime economy. What we favor is this: Gasoline—or energy—should be allowed to seek its normal price level in the marketplace, eliminating the restrictions on price at the wellhead for natural gas and allowing liquid and solid fuels to seek their levels and encouraging the entrepreneur to go in and spend the money for research and development. That will bring fuels into the market at the lowest possible price to the consumer. Next best to this would be added taxes, if the tax receipts were devoted to encouragement of exploration, refining, or research and development. The third and the most undesirable thing would be rationing, which we don't think can work.

Interview, Washington/
U.S. News & World Report, 12-31:34.

John B. Connally, Jr.
Former Secretary of the Treasury
of the United States;
Former Governor of Texas

3

We're a wasteful people. We're an extravagant people. We're a profligate race and nation. We've used too much of the world's goods and too much of our resources in too extravagant of a fashion.

Before Southern Medical Association,
San Antonio, Tex., Nov. 13/
The Dallas Times Herald, 11-14:(A)24.

Alistair Cooke
Chief United States correspondent,
"The Manchester (England) Guardian"

4

As for the woes we share with the world that you can see from your window—overpopulation, pollution of the atmosphere, the cities and the rivers, the destruction of nature —I find it impossible to believe that a nation [the U.S.] which produced such ingenious

(ALISTAIR COOKE)

human beings as Jefferson and Eli Whitney, John Deere, McCormack, Kettering, Oppenheimer, Edison, Benjamin Franklin, is going to sit back and let the worst happen . . .

On his "America" TV program, May 15/
Los Angeles Times, 5-17:(4)19.

John Z. DeLorean
Former vice president and general manager,
Chevrolet Division,
General Motors Corporation

1

I feel very strongly that the energy crisis is a very good thing, coming at this particular time. The Arab supply of crude oil was 6 per cent; their refined, which came to us mostly through Italy, was another 5 per cent or 6 per cent. For them to cut off or reduce our supplies made a very small impact. But if we had gone along, and this had happened around 1980 when it was estimated that our dependence on Arab oil would be 45 per cent or 50 per cent, we would have been faced by absolute catastrophe: no industry running, no airplanes flying; no autos running, only basic transportation to enable us to grow and distribute food; barely enough heating of homes or hospitals to keep people from freezing to death; schools closed. It is a good thing it happened now. This energy crisis is going to precipitate a tremendous amount of American ingenuity.

Interview, Washington/
Los Angeles Times, 12-11:(2)7.

Charles J. DiBona
Special Energy Consultant
to the President of the United States

2

We [the U.S.] have enough coal for centuries, we have potential resources of billions of barrels of oil and we have trillions of cubic feet of natural gas. In fact, we have enough of these fuels to last for as long as our economy depends on conventional fuels.

News conference, Los Angeles, May 14/
Los Angeles Times, 5-15:(2)8.

William O. Doub
Commissioner, Atomic Energy
Commission of the United States

3

In my view, the relatively small risk from nuclear power plants combined with the considerable environmental benefits from reduced air pollution make nuclear power perhaps the most attractive source of energy for this country's growing electrical needs. This view is doubly enforced when the national-security aspects and balance-of-payment concerns arising from continuing reliance on foreign fuels are factored into the cost-benefit equation.

San Francisco Examiner, 10-2:34.

Rene Dubos
Former Professor of Microbiology,
Rockefeller University

4

If we were to make the effort to save energy in the design of our buildings, in the expenditure of energy in the automobile, in the whole planning of our cities, it would not only save energy and solve our immediate energy problems fairly rapidly, but I think we would improve the quality of life. I think it is most immoral, in any case unethical, to scare the American public into the fear of shortage of energy by telling them, "See, if we cut down on the amount of gasoline that you use or electricity that you use, you will spoil your life. You won't be able to have a dishwasher. You won't be able to heat your house or to have an air conditioner." This is absolute dishonest nonsense.

Quote, 9-2:222.

Bob Eckhardt
United States Representative, D-Texas

5

If the Environmental Protection Agency is to be the enforcement agency of such laws as the Clean Air Act and the Federal Water Pollution Control Act, it must be out from under the dominion of the Executive Branch . . . As long as the administration of EPA serves at the pleasure of the President, he [the EPA Director] is then subject to the *dis-*

pleasure of the President, which may at times include the displeasure of the President's political supporters.

Washington, March 8/
The Dallas Times Herald, 3-9:(A)6.

William A. Egan
Governor of Alaska

1

[Saying the proposed Alaska oil pipeline would present minimal danger to the environment]: Never before in the history of this country has engineering been used so much to protect the environment. The most rigid engineering and scientific stipulations have been undertaken. I feel that those who have followed what we have been doing sincerely feel that much has been done to protect the environment. I should certainly feel this is a model for the nation that we can develop our resources in a safe, environmental way.

News conference, Los Angeles, Oct. 5/
Los Angeles Times, 10-6:(1)28.

Paul R. Ehrlich
Professor of Biology, Stanford University

2

[Man] is systematically diminishing the capacity of the natural environment to perform its waste disposal, nutrient cycling and other vital roles at the same time that the growing population and rising affluence are creating larger demands for these natural services. Whole species of plants and animals are being decimated or exterminated by intentional or inadvertent poisoning, by too intensive harvesting and, especially, by destruction of habitat. These are not trivial losses to be mourned only by nature-lovers and bird-watchers; they represent dangerous and irreversible tinkering with the natural systems on which the planet's carrying capacity for human beings is dependent. Ecology is not a fad but a scientific discipline whose practitioners attempt to decipher the complex relationships among organisms and their physical environment. Slowly, painstakingly, but steadily, ecologists are providing scientific substance to notions once held by conservationists largely on esthetic grounds: that one does not exter-

minate any population or species lightly; that man's fate is inextricably tied to nature; that all human beings, including those millions who may never set foot in the wilderness, have a stake in unexploited land.

At International Planned Parenthood
Federation workshop, Tokyo/
The National Observer, 7-14:17.

John D. Ehrlichman
Assistant to the President
of the United States for Domestic Affairs

3

[On why the Nixon Administration is allocating to localities only $5 billion of the $11 billion Congressionally-appropriated for water-pollution control]: There are only so many contractors who can build sewer plants. There is only a certain amount of sewer equipment that can be purchased. It becomes obvious that there is no point in going out and tacking dollar bills to the trees. That isn't going to get the water clean.

Interview, Washington, Feb. 4/
The Washington Post, 2-5:(A)4.

Maurice Ewing
Director of earth and planetary sciences,
University of Texas, Galveston

4

My views on oil spills just don't coincide with those stated in some of the scare head-lines. There are occasional oil spills at sea, but claims of the damage done are very much over-stated. Natural oil leaks or seeps from the earth contribute much more to the pollution of the ocean than man's spills do. By drilling oil wells in the coastal waters, you are actually cleaning up oil seepages in the long run . . . Some 35 years ago, when I was at sea, I saw something on the horizon that looked like a sunken ship. As I approached it, I could see it was a vast collection of floating material, trash and Sargassum weeds. I guess it must have covered 20 or 30 acres. The sea had brought the material together by what you might liken to an underwater tornado. You see, even before anyone ever heard about pollution and off-shore oil, there was debris in

(MAURICE EWING)

the ocean. But nature knows how to handle such things.

Dallas, March 30/
The Dallas Times Herald, 4-1:(A)36.

John F. Finklea
Director, United States Environmental
Research Center

1

The Federal government has spent less on the research and development effort responding to the Clean Air Act than it has on a single north-south interstate highway across the state of North Carolina. Needless to say, if dirty air were considered even a remote threat to national security, the needed research-and-development effort would be under way.

At National Academy of Science
conference on air pollution, Oct. 5/
The Washington Post, 10-6:(A)2.

Richard G. Folsom
President,
American Society of Mechanical Engineers

2

There is no present crisis in the fossil-fuel resources, but there is an imbalance between use and availability of different kinds of low-cost fossil fuels. The situation is headed for crisis conditions if we continue to do what we are now doing. What we need [to awaken public awareness of the need for cutting use of certain fuels] is a Pearl Harbor in energy. If I had some way to freeze all the gasoline pumps across this nation tomorrow morning, that would do it.

Before National Energy Forum, March 19/
The Washington Post, 3-20:(A)11.

Henry Ford II
Chairman, Ford Motor Company

3

I'm more worried by [the energy crisis] than any other problem. I'm not worried about gasoline for automobiles, but the whole infrastructure of the U.S. We've got to heat our homes, run our plants to employ people.

People want air conditioning and a lot of other things that they're used to, and I don't see the power system of this country meeting the needs. What with the environmentalists crapping all over any suggestion before it's even tried—a fellow can't build a power plant that's not going to do something to somebody somewhere. If it goes on, we're going to have plant closedowns. There are lots of plants that are in trouble right now. In Ohio, there isn't any more natural gas and you can't increase the size of a plant. I hope to hell New York goes dark for a week. Then maybe something will happen; people will have more babies, I guess. But I'll tell you, something will get done if New York shuts down for a week. I'm not sure anything else will move it quick enough.

Interview/Fortune, May:191.

Lewis W. Foy
President, Bethlehem Steel Corporation

4

. . . I've got bad news—I mean bad news for anyone who thinks this country's in terrible shape and that only radical changes can set things right. I'm thinking, for example, of the far-out environmentalists, the kind of people who have been preaching that doomsday is just around the corner, that the air is too dangerous to breathe, that our rivers and lakes are getting dirtier every day. And they've almost convinced us that "Lake Erie is dead." Well, I've got baↄ news for those people. Last fall, the Pennsylvania Fish Commission announced the all-time record-size game fish caught in Pennsylvania during the 1972 season. Four prize fish were caught, and guess what: Three of them were hooked in Lake Erie—the "dead" lake. But the news early in June was even "worse." The Fish Commission reported that the record for rainbow trout has already been broken twice in 1973, and the report goes on to say this: "At the rate rainbow records are falling in Lake Erie and its tributaries, nothing seems to be permanent." I'd call that very bad news for the prophets of doom; because if you can't convince the fish that Lake Erie is dead, how can you convince the people?

Before International Platform
Association, Washington, Aug. 1/
Vital Speeches, 8-15:649.

S. David Freeman
Director,
Energy Policy Project (Ford Foundation)   1

What we are finding out so painfully this winter [during the current energy shortage] is that energy is the lifeblood of modern society and that it flows into every vein of our governmental body and affects every aspect of people's lives. The coordinated development of energy policy must take place at the highest level of national government and must involve state and local governments as well. And, most important, it must involve the American citizen. Energy policy for too long has been left to a few major oil companies and large utilities, and [to] Federal agencies dominated in their thinking by the energy "establishment."

The Christian Science Monitor, 12-18:(B)1.

Robert W. Fri
Acting Administrator, Environmental
Protection Agency of the United States

    2

[On EPA proposals that would discourage the use of automobiles in urban areas to control air pollution]: . . . we are basically attacking the problem by asking people to change their habits—their long-standing and intimate relation to private automobiles. This is a fundamental change, but the only one that fundamentally will work.

June 15/The Washington Post, 6-16:(A)1.

Milton Friedman
Professor of Economics,
University of Chicago

    3

Even the most ardent environmentalist doesn't really want to stop pollution. If he thinks about it and doesn't just talk about it, he wants to have the *right amount* of pollution. We can't really *afford* to eliminate it— not without abandoning all the benefits of technology that we not only enjoy but on which we depend. So the answer is to allow only pollution that's worth what it costs, and not any pollution that isn't worth what it costs. The problem is to make sure that people bear the costs for which they are responsible. A market system rests fundamentally on such an arrangement. If you hit me with your car and you damage me, you are obliged to pay me—at least until we have no-fault insurance. The problem of pollution is that, if you emit noxious smoke that damages me, it's difficult for me to know who's done the damage and to require you to be responsible for it. The reason the market doesn't do it is that it's hard to do. The resolution does have to be through governmental arrangements, but in the form of effluent taxes rather than emission standards. I prefer such taxes to emission standards because taxes are more flexible. If it's more expensive for a company to pay the tax than emit the pollutant, it will very quickly raise its own emission standards.

Interview, Ely, Vermont/
Playboy, February:58.

Armond Fruchart
Oceanographer

    4

Man, in the year 2000, probably will not die of hunger but of suffocation, for lack of clean air, or of thirst, for lack of pure water. If he survives these, he may die of boredom, unable to enjoy leisure and recreation on a polluted coast.

San Francisco Examiner & Chronicle, 6-10:
(This World)2.

Carl A. Gerstacker
Chairman, Dow Chemical Company

    5

Pollution-control will continue on forever if we see it simply as a drag on earnings, as a necessary nuisance classified as overhead. If we see the opportunity in pollution and exploit that opportunity to the hilt, then we will help our earnings, and we will solve our pollution problems and . . . the nation's pollution problems.

Nation's Business, February:51.

Richard C. Gerstenberg
Chairman,
General Motors Corporation

1

[On the current "energy crisis"]: Please, I disagree with that term. "Energy Crisis" suggests that our own survival is at stake or that we have reached a great turning point. If everyone keeps talking about a crisis, they will create one; some folks seem to have their mind on creating one. I don't mean you will get gas every time you want it and every place you want it. I suspect we are going to have to pay more for gas. There will be temporary shortages until supplies catch up with demand. I don't look at this as anything we won't resolve.

Interview, Washington/
Los Angeles Times, 6-22:(2)7.

2

I am an environmentalist; I like to hunt and fish for trout. But I don't think we can retain the out-of-doors just to satisfy the trout fishermen in this country. We have got to think of the general public. I am the kind of guy who thinks we ought to grow; and if we are going to grow, we have to find new sources for all the things we need, and fuel is one of the things high on the list. We have got to grow and look forward, and we can't have this zero-growth business. No growth, no hope—that is not for America.

Interview, Washington/
Los Angeles Times, 6-22:(2)7.

Fred T. Hartley
President,
Union Oil Company of California

3

I do not regard it [the energy crisis] as a diminishing threat. On the contrary, I do not see how we can go through the next few years—or more likely few months—without some kind of energy curtailments . . . Consumers of all kinds are demanding more and more. You might even say Americans are on an energy-consumption binge.

Before shareholders, Los Angeles, April 30/
Los Angeles Times, 5-1:(3)7.

Ken Hechler
United States Representative,
D-West Virginia

4

[On strip mining]: The hills of Appalachia are bleeding. With all the emphasis at my command, I report to this Committee that a revolution is brewing in America. The people are not going to stand by any longer while strip miners rip up their homeland. If Congress just passes an innocuous [anti-strip-mining] bill designed to quiet the public outcry while meeting the demands of the lobbying organizations, then there'll be a Boston tea party which won't be a tea party.

Before Senate Interior and Insular
Affairs Committee, Washington,
March 13/The New York Times, 5-14:24.

Hubert H. Humphrey
United States Senator, D-Minnesota

5

[Criticizing the Nixon Administration's energy policy]: Right now we don't have enough gasoline to plow the fields in Minnesota. The next crisis is not going to be fuel but food, a genuine food crisis in the United States because all of these things are related . . . We must have some jerk planning this . . . There is no known way, at least for the next five years, to alleviate the energy crisis.

At Senate Foreign Relations Committee
hearing, Washington, May 30/
The Washington Post, 5-31:(A)16.

Sherman Hunt
President,
Texas Mid-Continent Oil & Gas Association

6

[On the current oil shortage]: To a disastrous degree, Congress and the courts have allowed the environmental pressure groups of our society to dictate the energy policies of the country . . . To satisfy these extremists, we have deprived ourselves of billions of barrels of oil and trillions of cubic feet of gas.

Before Texas Governor's Energy Advisory
Council, Dallas/The Dallas Times Herald,
11-23:(A)10.

Frank N. Ikard
President, American Petroleum Institute

1

Charges that the nation's oil companies have conspired to contrive a gasoline shortage are false. These charges—made without a shred of supporting evidence—are being repeated often and insistently. As a result, they have become an example, almost without parallel in American history, of unsupported statements gaining an air of credibility through repetition. Factors outside the industry—not conspiracy within the industry—have combined to create the present energy supply problem.

June 23/
San Francisco Examiner, 6-24:(A)11.

Henry M. Jackson
United States Senator, D-Washington

2

[Advocating construction of the proposed Alaska oil pipeline]: The pipeline has been stalled far beyond any reasonable time. We need those 10 billion barrels of oil going to waste up there in Alaska, and we need them pronto. Our fuel needs, the need to reduce our imbalance of payments, the need to be as independent as possible of growing Arab political pressures—all these are far more important than unfounded or exaggerated claims of potential ecological damage. I am not going to wait much longer to see the pipeline being built. If this whole matter is still bogged down in litigation by next winter, I am going to move in the Senate to have the United States government build the pipeline—just as the government built the Little Big Inch line in World War II.

San Francisco Examiner & Chronicle,
7-22:(B)2.

3

Among the oil-consuming nations, the United States is in a particularly difficult position. We have only a five-day oil reserve—the amount in our pipelines. Great Britain has 105 days reserve, Sweden has more than 120 days and Western Europe is planning for a 90-day reserve. The United States is in the precarious position that any major disruption

of supply could bring this country to a standstill.

San Francisco Examiner, 10-15:34.

Reginald H. Jones
Chairman, General Electric Company

4

The energy picture is not a picture of a doomsday crisis. We have a temporary shortage of certain clean fuels, and nuclear plants have been delayed in coming on line. We must act now to encourage the development of the abundant United States energy reserves and resources by such steps as allowing natural gas gradually to seek its competitive price level, which would reduce demand and spur the development of large-scale coal gasification. While we should take full advantage of low-cost imported oil and liquefied natural gas, we should provide incentive for rapid development of our indigenous energy resources. We need a more orderly and expeditious procedure for siting and licensing today's nuclear power plants while pushing ahead with breeder-reactor development. Through such steps, our nation can return to energy abundance through a combination of nuclear and fossil-fueled resources.

Interview, New York, Jan. 25/
The New York Times, 1-26:49.

Robert W. Kastenmeier
United States Representative,
D-Wisconsin

5

One might think from the TV commercials of the American Petroleum Institute that the nation is in danger of running out of oil and other energy resources. That certainly is not the case. Much of the so-called energy crisis is being concocted in the board rooms and public-relations offices of the nation's major oil companies.

March 26/
The Washington Post, 3-27:(C)3.

Kerryn King
Senior vice president, Texaco, Inc.

6

We simply have to face the fact that we are

(KERRYN KING)

living hand-to-mouth when it comes to oil and gas. If oil imports were cut off tomorrow, we would be closing factories within three weeks.

Quote, 11-4:434.

Dudley Kirk
Professor of Population Studies,
Stanford University

1

In the United States, too much attention has been given to the population "crisis," described in terms of population growth. Much of this discussion has been superficial and cast in the language of doomsday rhetoric . . . Our present population size and density are not in themselves the chief cause of our pollution, crime, racial strife and the multitude of other social ills that we are facing at the present time. Countries like Great Britain, with ten times our density of population, have far less crime, less social disorganization, and indeed less pollution. The problems are not so much those of sheer numbers as they are where and how we choose to live. The United States has roughly the world average in population density, but our population is very unevenly distributed over our land area . . . Much of the environmental and social disorganization we experience as growth problems —urban sprawl, trash disposal, over-use of recreation areas—are really caused by affluence. And increasing segregation by class, race, age and exposure to conflicts in values are a result of mobility.

Before American Institute of Architects,
San Francisco/
San Francisco Examiner & Chronicle,
5-13:(Sunday Homes)A.

Henry A. Kissinger
Secretary of State of the United States

2

. . . we must bear in mind the deeper causes of the energy crisis: It is not simply a product of the [recent] Arab-Israeli war [and the resultant cutback of Arab oil supplies to pro-Israeli countries]; it is the inevitable consequence of the explosive growth of world-wide demand outrunning the incentives for supply. The Middle East war made a chronic crisis acute, but a crisis was coming in any event. Even when pre-war production levels are resumed, the problem of matching the level of oil that the world produces to the level which it consumes will remain. The only long-term solution is a massive effort to provide producers an incentive to increase their supply, to encourage consumers to use existing supplies more rationally and to develop alternate energy sources.

Before the Pilgrims organization,
London, Dec. 12/
The New York Times, 12-13:28.

Charles A. Lindbergh
Aviator

3

I believe our civilization's latest advance is symbolized by the park rather than by satellites and space travel. In establishing parks and nature reserves, man reaches beyond the material values of science and technology. He recognizes the essential value of life itself, of life's natural inheritance irreplaceably evolved through earthy epochs, of the miraculous spiritual awareness that only nature in balance can maintain. As our civilization advances—if our follies permit it to advance—I feel sure we will realize that progress can be measured only by the quality of life—all life, not human life alone. The accumulation of knowledge, the discoveries of science, the products of technology, our ideals, our art, our social structures, all the achievements of mankind have value only to the extent that they preserve and improve the quality of life. This is why I say that parks symbolize the greatest advance our civilization has yet made.

At dedication of Lindbergh Interpretive
Center, Lindbergh State Park,
Little Falls, Minn./
The National Observer, 10-6:14.

John A. Love
Director, Federal Office of Energy Policy

4

I am afraid we are faced with two imperatives—the environment and energy—and we cannot take an extreme view on either end. [It is no solution] to have all the energy you need if you can't breathe [or to have] the cleanest air in the world and have no energy.

Before House Banking Subcommittee,
Washington, July 30/
The Dallas Times Herald, 7-31:(A)4.

1

I do want to point out that the U.S. is in much better condition than most other industrial nations of the world in regard to energy. Obviously, the most extreme comparison is Japan, which imports about 95 per cent of its energy and almost 100 per cent of its oil. We do have major domestic production of over 9 million barrels [of oil] a day if you count natural-gas liquids, etc. We do have more oil to be found off each of our coasts. We do have Alaska coming in. We do have this tremendous quantity of coal and shale. We've got technical know-how to develop new sources of energy. If we can bring a great-enough sense of urgency to the problem, I think that it can be solved—perhaps not on the basis that we double our supply of energy every 10 or 15 years, but we can certainly have an adequate supply.

Interview, Washington/
U.S. News & World Report, 11-12:100.

Charles F. Luce
Chairman,
Consolidated Edison Company, New York

2

About 70 per cent of the electricity that New York will use this winter will be provided by heavy residual oil. More than half of that oil comes from Arabic exporting countries that have announced they're going to place an embargo on oil shipments to the U.S. The only hope we see at the moment of keeping the lights on up and down the East Coast is to temporarily suspend the air-pollution requirements to permit utilities to burn higher-sulphur fuels, and at the same time to impose strict conservation measures, not only on the use of electricity, but on the use of all kinds of energy.

U.S. News & World Report, 11-12:18.

Tom McCall
Governor of Oregon

3

Advocates of growth at almost any price are, of course, tough adversaries of social planners and environmentalists. An example is the former president of a backlash organization in my state who gave a speech in California in February. He contended that some people in the environmental movement are "revolutionaries" bent on destroying the American economic system. I hope he wasn't referring to a group of 60 junior high school students from Warrenton, Oregon—the proposed site of a $175 million aluminum plant that would provide 800 jobs. Those 60 students visited me in my office just a few days ago. I asked how many of them wanted the aluminum plant constructed. Not a single hand went up. They said, "We want things just like they are." But, I said, Warrenton's economy is sagging, and this will help pick up the slack. No, they said. "We want things just like they are." I wouldn't label these children "revolutionaries," or crackpots. They just don't want anybody messing around with their part of the world. The world is being messed with plenty. As planners, our job is to assure that the mess is brought into some semblance of order.

Before American Society of Planning
Officials, Los Angeles/
Los Angeles Times, 5-2:(2)9.

4

A place without people is always more beautiful than a place with people, no matter how beautiful the people are.

San Francisco Examiner, 10-8:32.

Michael McCloskey
Executive director, Sierra Club

5

The environmental movement can succeed only if it can find ways to advance its cause that are consistent with the other legitimate goals of our people. And job security is paramount among these. Environmental protection cannot come at the cost of social justice; and conversely, progress toward social justice will become short-lived if it is earned

(MICHAEL McCLOSKEY)

at the price of a healthy environment. Our two movements [ecology and labor] cannot be mutually exclusive, and both of us have learned that a mercenary society that is callous about the fate of workers and the unemployed is just as apt to be callous about the fate of public self and the rights of other living things in future generations. We have both suffered from the callousness of industries that don't care, whose only goal is profit, who fight every reform, who oppose our every program, who never stop discouraging us and who never tire of misleading the public. We have suffered the same things and from the same people. With the forces arrayed against us, we need to work together if we are to have any chance of succeeding.

Before Oil, Chemical and Atomic Workers' Union, Toronto/Los Angeles Times, 9-23:(6)8.

Edward C. McDonagh
Chairman, department of sociology,
Ohio State University

1

[On the gasoline shortage]: With the loss of mobility, a certain amount of boredom will set in. We will become more indoor oriented. Television will probably expand programming, and we will have a slower existence than we have become accustomed to. The dreams of the future will dim; but what dreams do come true will mean so much more. While we will not be going to the restaurant or having that long vacation, when we do eat out or travel it will be enjoyed that much more. The next several years will indeed be a slowing and a sobering period, but with the possibility that, in changing our mode of living, we are, perhaps, avoiding a real ecological catastrophe that might have laid in wait for future generations.

Columbus, Ohio/
The Dallas Times Herald, 11-28:(A)26.

George F. McDonnell
President,
Zurich-American Insurance Companies

2

If there is a silver lining in the energy crisis, it's shining on the insurance industry. Less miles being driven, at slower speeds, old accident-causing factory equipment being taken off steam, workers on less overtime—it should all add up to less accidents and less claims. If nation-wide daylight saving time is adopted, it should also mean less accidents and some improvement in the crime problem, as people do more of their traveling in daylight hours.

Chicago, Nov. 8/
The New York Times, 11-9:67.

John J. McKetta, Jr.
Professor of Chemical Engineering,
University of Texas, Austin

3

[On the fuel shortage]: There is no way the United States can become independent or self-sufficient in fuel production by 1980 or even by 1990, even by a drastic decrease in fuel use and a great increase in fuel production . . . Even if we brought in a new oil field immediately that produced 100 million barrels a day, it wouldn't even wet the bottom of the bucket. If President Nixon put $10 million today into drilling new wells, we still couldn't catch up with the nation's demand in our lifetime.

Before North Texas chapter of Society of Petroleum Engineers, Arlington, Nov. 20/The Dallas Times Herald, 11-21:(A)2.

Margaret Mead
Anthropologist

4

The brightest person we have ever produced used only one tenth of his brain. By using our brain and technology together, we can recycle material and stop treating our air and seas as garbage pails.

San Diego, Calif., 6-21:(A)2.

Arnold R. Miller
President,
United Mine Workers of America

5

[On the current energy "crisis" proclaimed by the energy industry]: The United Mine

Workers agrees that the energy problems facing the nation are serious; but the current campaign to stampede public opinion hardly serves the national interest. In the present "crisis atmosphere," the interests of the American worker and the consumer public will likely be ignored, and the narrow interests of corporate profit will likely dominate the debate. We face an emergency crisis today because government has failed to develop a national approach to our energy needs, but has instead allowed corporate interests to develop and supply the nation's energy in accordance with their instincts for profit alone.

News conference, Washington, April 16/
The New York Times, 4-17:26.

Wilbur D. Mills
United States Representative, D-Arkansas

1

[On oil and gas depletion allowances]: Some will say that it's not fair for the individual who goes out wildcatting for oil and gas to have his gross income from a well reduced by 22 per cent before you begin to apply tax. They say that's a loophole, and therefore the tax law is not fair in this respect. But if you want oil and gas in the United States, you have to offer a tax inducement to get investment there. Without this inducement, people won't put their money into it. Then what are you faced with? We're already in a crisis in our supply of energy. By the year 1985, unless we change, the importation of fuels into the United States will be running at the rate of $20 billion a year. Now, what will that do to our balance of payments at that time? We must face up to the fact that energy is a growing and continuing crisis. I don't think we want to de-stimulate through tax changes in this area of energy supply. We've got to further stimulate our domestic supplies.

Interview/
U.S. News & World Report, 4-16:58.

Rogers C. B. Morton
Secretary of the Interior of the United States

2

Regrettably, too many of our people fail to recognize the dimensions of the energy crisis. They say, "Give me energy, but don't run power-transmission lines or gas lines across my lands." They say, "Give me secure domestic supplies of gas and oil, but don't provide equitable economic incentives for exploration, development and production" . . . They say, "Give me an energy policy that leads to secure energy supplies, but don't ask me to pay a fair price for it." They say, "Give me a workable national energy policy, but don't dam, dig, mine or drill in my state." They say, "Give me an energy policy that maximizes national security, but don't infringe on our trade and defense relationships within the world community." Too many Americans are still unaware of the consequences we face, and the growing threat a dependence on unstable, expensive and interruptible foreign energy sources holds for our future.

At "Interpipe '73" conference, Houston,
Oct. 30/U.S. News & World Report,
11-12:20.

3

With almost 40 per cent of the world's known coal reserves, the U.S. literally has coal to burn for centuries. We have relegated coal to an orphan status in the energy family. In fact, one of the major reasons we have lost self-sufficiency [in energy] is that we depend most on those fuels—oil and natural gas—that we have in shortest supply.

Before National Association of Manufacturers,
New York/The Dallas Times Herald,
12-9:(A)11.

Larry Moss
President, Sierra Club

4

I am heartened by the fact that most of those fighting the environmental battle five or six years ago are still fighting it today. I think there have been fewer leadership defections from our cause than from others, like the civil-rights or anti-war movements. Fewer among us have moved on to other things. It leads me to believe that we recognize the environmental battle for what it is—a lifetime commitment.

Interview, Washington/
The Christian Science Monitor, 9-19:16.

Edmund S. Muskie
United States Senator, D-Maine

1

An orderly and equitable ocean regime has become both more vital to nations and more difficult for them to agree upon. They are more dependent than ever before on access to critical areas of the ocean, on its ecological health, and on its mineral and food resources. As ocean users multiply—and as competition among them intensifies—the classical political question of "who gets what" is thrust to the center of the debate over the future of the oceans. With wise answers to this question, international cooperation and justice can prevail in the ocean. With short-sighted answers, 70 per cent of the earth's surface could become an arena for serious international tension and conflict. We must nurture a new sense of international community toward the ocean. With it must come an over-arching conception of the common good, a capacity for handling our inevitable disputes peacefully, and a set of new political habits and reciprocity, good faith and mutual accountability for our activities in the ocean. These goals are no longer utopian hopes. They now are the imperatives of prudent diplomacy.

Before Law of the Sea Institute,
Kingston, R.I., June 21/ Quote, 9-16:273.

Ralph Nader
Lawyer; Consumer advocate

2

[Arguing against nuclear power plants because of safety hazards]: Can we as a society rely on a technology that has to be perfect forever, or the alternative is massive social disaster? I think the answer to that has got to be no. We have no right as human beings to inflict that kind of risk on future generations in terms of the kind of environment we are going to bequeath to them . . . To put all of our energy eggs into one fragile nuclear basket may well go down in history as the most prominent act of technological suicide this country has ever advocated.

At Western Governors Conference,
Gleneden Beach, Ore., Sept. 25/
Los Angeles Times, 9-26:(1)3.

Richard M. Nixon
President of the United States

3

. . . we must remain confident that America's technological and economic ingenuity will be equal to our environmental challenges. We will not look upon these challenges as insurmountable obstacles. Instead, we shall convert the so-called crisis of the environment into an opportunity for unprecedented progress. Now is the time to stop the hand-wringing and roll up our sleeves and get on with the job. Now is the time to reject the doomsday mentality which says we are destined to pollute ourselves out of existence. The advocates of defeatism warn us of all that is wrong. I remind them and all Americans of our genius for responsive adaptability and our enormous reservoir of spirit. The destiny of our land, the air we breathe, the water we drink, is not in the mystical hands of an uncontrollable agent. It is in *our* hands. A future which brings the balancing of our resources, preserving quality with quantity, is a future limited only by the boundaries of our will to get the job done.

Radio address to the nation,
Washington, Feb. 14/
The New York Times, 2-15:28.

4

The immediate [energy] shortage will affect the lives of each and every one of us. In our factories, our cars, our homes, our offices, we will have to use less fuel than we are accustomed to using. Some school and factory schedules may be realigned. And some jet airplane flights will be canceled. This does not mean that we're going to run out of gasoline, or that air travel will stop, or that we will freeze in our homes or offices any place in America. The fuel crisis need not mean genuine suffering for any American. But it will require some sacrifice by all Americans. We must be sure that our most vital needs are met first, and that our least-important activities are the first to be cut back; and we must be sure that, while the fat from our economy is being trimmed, the muscle is not seriously damaged . . . Now, some of you may wonder whether we're turning back the clock to another age. Gas rationing, oil shortages, reduced speed limits—they all sound like a way of life we left behind with Glenn Miller in the war of the '40s. Well, in fact, part of our current problem also stems from war—the war in the Middle East. But our deeper energy problems come not from war but from peace and from abundance. We are running out of energy today because our economy has grown enormously and because, in prosperity, what were once considered luxuries are now considered necessities . . . Now our growing demands have bumped up against the limits of available supply. And until we provide new sources of energy for tomorrow, we must be prepared to tighten our belts today.

Broadcast address to the nation, Washington, Nov. 7/The New York Times, 11-8:32.

1

[On his objective in trying to meet the current energy crisis]: It can be summed up in one word that best characterizes this nation and its essential nature, and that word is independence. From its beginning 200 years ago and throughout its history, America has made great sacrifices of blood and treasure to achieve and maintain its independence. In the last third of this century, our independence will depend on achieving and maintaining self-sufficiency in energy. What I have called Project Independence-1980 is a series of plans and goals set to ensure that, by the end of this decade, Americans will not have to rely on any source of energy beyond our own. As we look to the future, we can do so confident that the energy crisis will be resolved, not only for our time, but for all time. We will once again have those plentiful supplies of inexpensive energy which helped to build the greatest industrial nation and one of the highest standards of living in the world. The capacity for self-sufficiency in energy is a great goal, and an essential goal. We are going to achieve it.

Broadcast address to the nation, Washington, Nov. 25/Los Angeles Times, 11-26:(1)12.

2

There are only 7 per cent of the people of the world living in the United States, and we use 30 per cent of all the energy. That isn't bad; that is good. That means we are the richest, strongest people in the world, and that we have the highest standard of living in the world. That is why we need so much energy, and may it always be that way.

Before Seafarers International Union, Washington, Nov. 26/ The Washington Post, 11-27:(A)4.

Mohammad Reza Pahlavi
Shah of Iran

3

[On the coming scarcity of oil and the resultant increases in price instituted by oil-producing countries]: Oil should only be used for derivatives like petrochemicals. It seems a sin to use it for heating houses and lighting electrical bulbs. Why not develop coal, atomic energy, solar energy? In the past, the [oil companies] did not attach too much importance to the problem. They took oil and profited. They closed all the coal pits. They didn't bother to find other sources of energy. They fixed low prices. Now they will have to pay the price.

Interview, Teheran, Dec. 20/ Los Angeles Herald-Examiner, 12-21:(A)16.

Charles H. Percy
United States Senator, R-Illinois

4

[On the energy crisis]: We [the U.S.] are going to be in an increasingly proportionately strong position as against Europe and Japan. We don't need Mid-Eastern oil that much. We have huge resources—500 years' resources of coal alone. We can work on shale oil. We can do more exploration of oil in this country. I think we have many resources that we can draw upon. We don't have our backs up against the wall in this issue at all, and the Arab states [who have cut back on oil shipments to pro-Israeli countries] should know that.

TV-radio interview, Washington/ "Meet the Press," National Broadcasting Company, 11-11.

Peter G. Peterson
Former Secretary of Commerce
of the United States

1

Energy is the new international issue for as far ahead as we can see. It is tied to trade, money, politics and everything else.

Interview/
The Washington Post, 7-9:(A)18.

James Pitts
Director,
California Air Pollution Research Center

2

I'm concerned about the energy crisis . . . I don't question its existence. What I question is why the heck, with all of the resources of industry, government and the universities, the public has had this situation essentially "sprung" on it. Where were the contingency plans? We seem to have contingency plans for every other eventuality.

Riverside, Calif./
Los Angeles Herald-Examiner, 11-23:(B)1.

George Porter
Scientist; Director, Royal Institution
of Great Britain

3

If sunbeams were weapons of war, we would have had solar energy centuries ago . . . I have no doubt that we will be successful in harnessing the sun's energy and that the lights will not go out in the 21st century.

Before British Association for the
Advancement of Science,
Canterbury, England/
The Dallas Times Herald, 8-26:(A)39.

William Proxmire
United States Senator, D-Wisconsin

4

[On the fuel shortage]: Every day that we postpone putting a program into effect that will meet this shortage is costing us hundreds of thousands of barrels of oil, and that means a cruel shortage this winter. Whatever we do to meet this shortage is going to be painful and costly. When the President [Nixon] said that if all of us sacrifice a little no one would suffer, he was wrong. Some will suffer. No matter what we do, some will lose their jobs. Indeed, some thousands already have lost their jobs—in airlines, in some manufacturing plants and elsewhere. And no matter what we do, it's going to get worse. The problem is how to keep the present painful crisis from becoming an economic catastrophe . . . Not for months, not for a year or two, but for several long years we face the painful experience of slowing down, traveling less, becoming far more thrifty and less extravagant with our precious energy resources. It's going to be a long, cold, expensive road.

Broadcast address, Dec. 2/
Los Angeles Times, 12-3:(1)22.

Dixy Lee Ray
Chairman, Atomic Energy Commission
of the United States

5

The public has been unconsciously nurtured to fear atomic energy. Part of this has been the scientist's fault. If you're a scientist, you probably wouldn't want the rest of the world to think what you did was easy . . . We have to overcome this built-in fear. It takes time, but we have to pay attention to it. If you know what something is, the fright will disappear.

Interview, Germantown, Md./
Los Angeles Times, 2-16:(4)4.

Ronald Reagan
Governor of California

6

[Criticizing environmentalists]: There seems to be an organized, well-financed lobby determined to preserve the natural habitat and comfort of every species except man. Well, it is time to remember that people are ecology, too.

Before American Association of State
Highway Officials, Los Angeles, Nov. 12/
Los Angeles Times, 11-13:(1)30.

Edwin O. Reischauer
Professor, Harvard University; Former
United States Ambassador to Japan

7

I am thinking of the inevitable imbalance

between limited resources and unlimited demand, with the world population doubling every 35 years and increasing even more rapidly in terms of per capita consumption in the more advanced parts of the world. And there will be a long-term increase in consumption in the poorer parts, too. The pinch of resources and consumption will get worse and worse, and will have to be handled internationally. Oil already is; food, too, to a great extent. Great surplus areas feed huge deficit areas. There will have to be a global kind of approach. The national approach will no longer suffice in dealing, for example, with pollution of the seas and the world's atmosphere, which may be disasters for us all.

Interview, Cambridge, Mass./
Los Angeles Times, 10-19:(2)7.

John P. Roche
President, American Iron and Steel Institute

1

The over-all effort by this nation's steel makers to control pollution and improve the environment is producing a remarkable record of progress . . . Our control efforts currently result in the removal of 91 per cent of all particulate emissions into the air and 94 per cent of water pollutants. That 94 per cent is a far better record than is achieved by the nation's major municipalities through their waste water treatment systems. Even with this strong record, the industry is the first to state that more needs to be accomplished. The steel industry is moving as rapidly as possible to meet its environmental-quality goals despite the enormous financial burden that the task imposes.

May 21/The New York Times, 5-22:24.

David Rockefeller
Chairman,
Chase Manhattan Bank, New York

2

The problem of economic betterment continues to be one of the major problems that all of us should be concerned with, even though in the last 25 years we have really come to understand that there are other elements in life which have an equally important,

or at least very important, impact. It may well be, for example, that there are people in Europe whose standard of living in purely economic terms is less than that of many Americans, but who, overall, may find greater satisfaction in life than their counterparts in this country. Their ability to live pleasantly may be greater because their surroundings are more gracious, it is easier for them to commute to work, they have less pollution and crime, they have more ready opportunities for cultural advantages at lower rates. My point here is that I don't think that the standard of living in the statistical sense is necessarily a measure of happiness or satisfaction or whatever you want to call it. Therefore, I don't think you can have a single goal in the sense of only trying to improve the per capita gross national product. On the other hand, this remains an important measure of satisfaction; for without it, clearly, it is pretty difficult to be able to enjoy very much of the good things of life. The over-all objectives of society today are more complex than they were. But those who are so fascinated by the quality of life may overlook the importance of the economic side of the standard of living . . . People in this country tend to be faddists and become obsessed with a particular concern or goal and fail to recognize the problems on the other side. Maybe we had to have to some extent a hysterical approach originally to get people aware of the [environmental] problem; but now that they are, we had better settle back to a more realistic recognition that we are not going to have perfection in either direction. What we can have, if we go about it right, is a balance between growth and environmental problems.

Interview, New York/
Los Angeles Times. 4-10:(2)7.

Nelson A. Rockefeller
Governor of New York

3

In recent years, the people of our state and the country have gradually come to adopt new values in relation to our environment and evidenced a willingness to forego certain economic advantages to achieve these values . . .

(NELSON A. ROCKEFELLER)

In this period of change that we as a state and as a society are experiencing, people are beginning to question whether all growth is automatically good—beginning to look at the quality of life as well as the quantity of our gross national product.

Explaining his veto of a bridge over
Long Island Sound, June 20/
The Washington Post, 6-21:(A)3.

William D. Ruckelshaus
Administrator, Environmental Protection
Agency of the United States

1

[On his decision to give automobile manufacturers one more year, until 1976, instead of 1975, to install new pollution-control catalytic converters on all new cars, except in California where 1975 will remain the deadline]: This is a terribly complex and important decision that involves the whole mix of our nation's struggle for a cleaner environment. Involved in this decision are billions of dollars, hundreds of thousands of jobs, probably the single most important segment of our economy, the largest aggregate man-made contributor to air pollution and the ambivalence of the American public's intense drive for healthy air and apparently insatiable appetite for fast, efficient and convenient automobiles. The ultimate effect of the decision will touch more than 200 million people . . . [The decision was made] to phase in the catalysts [in California] because of the potential societal disruption in attempting to apply this new technology across all car lines in one year. In weighing this potential against the minimal impact on air quality of this decision versus an outright denial of the suspension request, I believe it is the better part of wisdom to phase in the catalyst.

News conference, Washington, April 11/
The New York Times, 4-12:22.

Leo J. Ryan
United States Representative,
D-California

2

[On the energy shortage]: The President

[Nixon] has deliberately confused the issue by equating driving at 50 miles an hour and not lighting your Christmas trees with patriotism. He hasn't ordered Detroit to stop making big cars. Instead, he closes down gas stations during a day [Sunday] that for many people is the only time they can go shopping. He ignores his own life—jetting from Key Biscayne to San Clemente to Camp David to the White House—which makes a total mockery of what he has asked of the American people. If he wants to set an example, let him stay in the White House and light his Christmas tree with the fuel from one of his jets.

Los Angeles Times, 11-30:(4)23.

Glenn T. Seaborg
Professor of Chemistry, University of California, Berkeley; Former Chairman, Atomic Energy Commission of the United States

3

The wise use of energy—and considerably more than we are using now—can restore nature and rejuvenate man. It can help us to turn desert areas green again, help us rebuild the environment, build the foundations for peace, open frontiers for many beyond this planet and insure the continued progress of mankind. If tomorrow we were to suffer an instant cutback of, say, 20 to 30 per cent of our total energy consumption, we would probably witness the collapse of Western civilization as we know it.

Before American Institute of Architects,
San Francisco/
San Francisco Examiner & Chronicle,
5-13:(Sunday Homes)A.

George P. Shultz
Secretary of the Treasury of the United States

4

People from the oil-producing countries are swaggering quite a bit these days and telling us not only about our energy policy but also about our foreign policy and other things. The one thing that seems to impress them is the effort to develop our own resources . . . through a strong and imaginative research-and-development program. A country that has produced atomic energy from a standing start in four years and that has put a man on the moon from a standing start in eight years is certainly going to be able to learn how to use these energy resources and do so promptly. I find when I say that [to leaders of oil-producing nations], that is the one thing that tends to cool off the swagger just a bit . . . There is no threat. There is no "if." We are engaging in a research-and-development program designed to see how we can use the resources we have, economically and in a compatible manner with our aspirations about the kinds of environment we want to live in. That's not an "if." That's not a threat. That's a statement of our policy we intend to stay with.

At Foreign Correspondents Club,
Tokyo, Sept. 13/
Los Angeles Times, 9-14:(3)16.

Forrest N. Shumway
President, The Signal Companies

1

The United States has been an energy waster since time immemorial. The philosophy of the people has been built on cheap energy. The utilities have spent their entire lives trying to sell more and more. I can remember, when we built a building in downtown Los Angeles, we were told by the utility, "Leave all the lights in the building on. It's spectacular. It'll be good advertising for you, and it costs just about as little to leave them on as it does to hire a guy to go around and shut them off."

Interview/
The Dallas Times Herald, 4-9:(D)7.

William E. Simon
Deputy Secretary of the Treasury
of the United States

2

[On the rising demand for gasoline]: Part of this rise in demand can be explained by growth in the population, growth in the economy and the increasing number of cars on the road. But demand has also risen significantly because of the many power-using devices added to cars. These include automatic transmissions, air conditioners, various safety features, and the changes made in automobiles since

1970 in compliance with EPA regulations issued under the mandate of the Clean Air Act . . . While gasoline demand has been growing at about 6 per cent per year, the volume of crude oil processed by refiners has risen only 3 per cent per year. We are now extremely short of refinery capacity and, at the time of the President's [Nixon] energy message which announced the new oil import program, no new refineries were under construction. Furthermore, expansion of existing refineries had ceased. Growth in the capacity of the industry had come to an end because the industry found that it was more profitable to invest abroad than in the United States.

Before Senate Committee, Washington/
The Washington Post, 7-18:(A)26.

3

We [the U.S.] import one-third of our oil, and oil accounts for 46 per cent of out total energy. That means that oil from abroad accounts for around 15 per cent of the total, or that the U.S. is 85 per cent self-sufficient. But we mustn't be beholden to foreign sources for even that much.

The Washington Post, 11-14:(A)24.

William E. Simon
Administrator, Federal Energy Office

4

[On the energy crisis]: We have been a nation of great energy wastrels. We have been accustomed to an over-abundance of cheap energy. That day has ended. This country now faces the choice between comfort and convenience, or jobs. [Though industries will be forced to conserve energy,] our main thrust will be to get the consumer to save, so that there will be the least possible effect in industrial production and employment.

News conference, Washington/
The National Observer, 12-15:3.

5

One of my biggest jobs is going to be keeping the American people and the government awake after this [Arab oil] embargo ends so that they realize that [the energy] problem is going to be with us for a long, long time. And it's going to be tough to do that. After I became Chairman of the [govern-

(WILLIAM E. SIMON)

ment-wide] Oil Policy Committee last December, I testified 40 to 50 times between January and July; made speeches all over the country. Everything everybody else is saying now was said then. People don't listen. Crisis acts as a catalyst to get people to understand.

Interview, Washington/
The National Observer, 12-29:1.

Maurice F. Strong
Executive Director,
United Nations Environment Program

1

I am not among the prophets of a planetary doomsday. I do not foresee as inevitable a global cataclysm in which the natural system breaks down from unsupportable physical burdens imposed by the multifarious and sometimes frenetic activities of the human race. However, I am persuaded that prospects of serious breakdowns in specific areas with tragic consequences for large numbers of people are very real—even imminent—and that we can no longer risk the ad hoc responses that have characterized our reaction to these emergencies in the past. As much as schools need fire drills and ships need life-boat drills, does not Space Ship Earth need emergency survival systems?

Fairfield Osborn Memorial Lecture,
Rockefeller University, New York,
Oct. 18/The New York Times, 10-21:(1)19.

2

Two hundred million Americans use more energy for air-conditioning alone than China's population of 700 million for all purposes. I believe it is highly questionable whether any country has a permanent right to a disproportionate share of the world's resources.

News conference, New York,
Nov. 21/The New York Times, 11-22:11.

Edward Teller
Physicist

3

Because the environmentalists protested that reactors would raise water temperatures slightly, the whole nuclear-reactor program has

been delayed at least two years. This will change as soon as America has its first big [power] blackout, maybe even sooner. I differ from the environmentalists. I like people more and fish less.

San Francisco Examiner & Chronicle,
1-28:(This World)2.

Russell E. Train
Administrator, Environmental Protection
Agency of the United States

4

We're at a point in the environmental effort corresponding to midcourse correction in a space flight. We set out several years back on a very ambitious unprecedented program of environmental reform, necessarily without all the pertinent data on execution of the program. We're now in the inevitable stage of adjusting to realities. The whole environmental effort is under pressure at the moment. Costs to industries, citizens and communities are beginning to become evident. At the same time, the benefits of our efforts, which are going to be very real, have not become equally evident. But shortly we'll see cleaner air and water and improved conditions all around, so that the average citizen can recognize it . . . Energy problems are providing an opportunity for people to attack the environmental movement. Advertisements constantly imply that environmentalists have blocked new [oil] refining capacity, for instance. That's complete hot air. The charge that environmental programs will impede economic activity is totally wrong. It's just the opposite. It's environmental burdens like the toll on human health that are the real constraints on growth.

Interview, Washington, Sept. 12/
The New York Times, 9-13:40.

5

There are some who tell us that all we have to do to warm things up [during the current energy crisis] is to tear up the Clean Air Act, throw it into the nearest furnace and let it go up in smoke that will lift air pollution over the nation's cities to even more dangerous levels. There are some who tell us that the environmental effort is responsible for the energy crisis and that to solve our energy problems we need only rid ourselves of all these irksome environmental restrictions and roadblocks . . . Let me be blunt about it: What these people say is simply not true, and they know it. [The environmental movement] is not responsible for the energy crisis. It did not start the Arab-Israeli war. It did not make us deeply and dangerously dependent upon Arab oil. It had absolutely nothing to do with our failure until this year to abolish the oil import quotas or to adequately expand our refinery capacity.

Before Town Hall of California,
Los Angeles, Dec. 18/
Los Angeles Times, 12-19:(1)3.

Darrell M. Trent
Acting Director,
Federal Office of Emergency Preparedness

1

Clearly, we cannot retreat from our commitments to protect the environment. But we also have a heavy responsibility to see to it that our homes, offices, schools, hospitals and factories have adequate energy supplies. Environmental protection and sufficient energy are two vital national goals, and one cannot be pursued to the neglect of the other.

At Seatrade Conference on Energy,
New York, March 26/
The New York Times, 3-27:63.

John V. Tunney
United States Senator, D-California

2

[On the catalytic converter pollution-control device to be required on all new cars by 1976]: . . . the catalytic converter is the wrong device at the wrong time. What we need, very simply, is an entirely new alternative to the conventional internal-combustion engine—an alternative that is efficient, reasonably priced and smog-free.

April 11/The New York Times, 4-12:21.

Edmund J. Turk
Chairman,
Ohio Public Utilities Commission

3

[On the energy shortage]: In the next few

years, you are going to see a radical change in the lifestyle of Americans. For instance, we may have to close the schools this December, January and February. You mark what I'm saying here tonight. Maybe you'll remember it when you're eating breakfast in your kitchen wearing an overcoat and earmuffs. A lot of factories are going to close; and when they do, you're going to see people begging the government to take the fuel away from their houses so the factories can stay open.

Cleveland/
The New York Times, 11-14:65.

Morris K. Udall
United States Representative, D-Arizona

4

The harsh truth is that eventually, if civilization is to remain on this planet, we need permanent, renewable, clean, large-scale energy sources that consume nothing and pollute nothing . . . Some non-damaging trade-offs may be necessary, but when the tough decisions come, the environment cannot be sold out. If we are sensible, we can both balance the energy budget and make our peace with nature's eternal laws.

U.S. News & World Report, 7-30:34.

C. William Verity
Chairman, Armco Steel Corporation

5

Our feeling is that there will be a more reasonable approach to solving environmental problems when the public realizes [that] first, they have to pay the bill, and secondly, they have to make a judgment on whether the benefits are worth the cost . . . Few people recognize what a tremendous amount of recycling the steel industry does. At Armco, we buy about two million tons of scrap a year, much of it automobile scrap. In fact, our company alone recycles the equivalent of a million automobiles a year, so there are that many fewer junked cars cluttering up the landscape. And you can imagine how many of these eyesores are recycled by the entire steel industry.

Interview/Nation's Business, August:58.

Stephen A. Wakefield
Assistant Secretary for Energy and Minerals,
Department of the Interior of the
United States

1

The one thing about the job of energy conservation that impresses me more than anything else is the universal nature of the claim it is going to present against us and our activities. There is no big single bonanza of energy savings that we can discover and utilize that is going to let the rest of us home free. It is idle to think that the whole burden can be borne by the industrial sector, leaving the consumer untouched and unbothered. Everybody, and everything, is going to have to give. For it is here, in the arena of conservation, that the energy crisis ceases to be a distant abstraction and becomes an immediate, gripping, painful particularity. It is here that the anonymous "we" becomes that very personal "me," and people make this translation only with great difficulty and reluctance . . . Just as our patterns of energy consumption are all interrelated, so are the patterns of the efforts needed to deal with our energy problems. We will have to solve them together. There just isn't any other way.

At Maryland State Chamber of Commerce
Legislative Conference, Bedford, Pa.,
Sept. 25/Vital Speeches, 11-15:84.

Carl Walske
President, Atomic Industrial Forum

2

[On the current energy shortage]: In Washington today there is an awareness of our need to rely on nuclear power—such as did not exist one year ago. On the public side, while the critics are raising their voices ever louder, there is at the same time a rapid escalation in the awareness of the man in the street over his energy problems. Believing as I do in the rightness of the nuclear solution, I consider this to be a moment of opportunity —and deep responsibility—for the nuclear industry . . . I am an unmitigated optimist: If we do our work, things will work out well.

San Francisco/
Los Angeles Times, 11-23:(1)28.

Barbara Ward
Economist

3

[On the energy crisis]: I think some of the things that are happening now are potentially salutary. The energy crisis is making people rethink some of their attitudes regarding growth-at-all-costs. And if the first thing you have to do before man changes his mind is to know what his mind has to change about, I think maybe we are there.

New York/
The Christian Science Monitor, 11-30:19.

Rawleigh Warner, Jr.
Chairman, Mobil Oil Corporation

4

I have one fundamental disagreement with them [environmentalists]: They never put a cost to what they want. They simply decide what they want and, regardless of cost to everybody else, that's their only goal. In our society there is always a relative cost of things. Now, what they should do is try to determine the impact on others. If they did, they would set lower goals . . . Still, I think we can get along. I hope so. But if the environmentalists are going to be successful in putting capricious demands on businesses, then they are going to end up with one result: The United States is going to be substantially non-competitive in world trade. If anyone thinks we are in trouble today on our balance of trade, then let them wait a while. We really are heading for trouble. I don't mean to say we shouldn't have clean air and water, and an attractive countryside; I'm for those things. But there has to be a moderate approach to the standards that are set.

Interview, New York/
Nation's Business, September:54.

Caspar W. Weinberger
Secretary of Health, Education and Welfare
of the United States

5

[On the gasoline shortage]: I don't know that at this point it is necessary to increase [gasoline] taxes or to ration. The principal thing, I think, that is required at this moment is conservation of existing supplies at the same time we are making every effort to increase the supply . . . I'm not at all convinced that a high tax on various forms of energy is going to increase the supply. I certainly hope we can avoid rationing, because that involves a whole new extension and addition to governmental power and authority, besides being a terribly annoying and intrusive sort of activity.

Interview, Washington, Nov. 17/
The New York Times, 11-18:(1)34.

Blaine J. Yarrington
President, Standard Oil Company (Indiana)

1

[On the current gasoline shortage]: We already are allocating to distributors, service stations, farmers and industry on the basis of their 1972 purchases; that began on May 1. Along with this, we have switched to a strong conservation message in our advertising—TV, radio, newspapers and magazines. This is quite a change for us after years of training our people to get out there and sell. Suddenly, we are saying: "Please don't come in and ask for so much." We have also started educating our distributors and service-station operators to the fact that this crisis is real. Next, we will be mailing conservation messages to our credit-card customers. For some strange reason, a lot of people seem to think all this talk of shortages is just conversation . . . The problem is going to be with us at least through 1975. It is going to take that long to build more refining capacity in this country and the superports needed for more oil imports from abroad. The pinch will be worse in 1974 and 1975 than this year—unless Americans start practicing conservation in a big way.

Interview, Washington/
U.S. News & World Report, 6-4:26.

Samuel W. Yorty
Mayor of Los Angeles

2

Fish have become much more important to these people ["environmental extremists"] than the ability of our people to have jobs and to create the standard of living or improve it. I believe in building. I think that great civilizations are known more for what they build than for what they postpone . . . We've got a lot of people in this country who are very sincere but who have been taken over by people who call themselves environmentalists, who are really just out to be obstructionists. Almost everything that we try to do is blocked in court or blocked in some other channel by those who think that the way to preserve the United States of America and our living standard is not to produce anything any more, not to build anything, certainly not to build any tunnels or any dams, because if you build a dam, you block up a stream, and who knows, you may interfere with some of the movement of the fish . . .

Before Beavers organization,
Los Angeles, Jan. 18/
Los Angeles Times, 1-20:(2)10.

Evelle J. Younger
Attorney General of California

3

We will never again see land used with the freedom from all restrictions as it was in the 19th century, and we will not see the unchecked growth and urban development which has characterized most of this country.

San Francisco Examiner & Chronicle,
10-21:(This World)2.

Foreign Affairs

James Abourezk
United States Senator, D-South Dakota

1

[On Henry Kissinger's nomination for Secretary of State]: I will oppose Kissinger not only for his disregard of Congress, but of the American people in general. What has been wrong with our foreign policy since 1945 is that it has been conducted in secret by a few people.

Washington, Sept. 13/
The Washington Post, 9-14:(A)19.

Creighton W. Abrams
General and Chief of Staff,
United States Army

2

Detente is expressed by some as a fact; it is applauded by still others as a policy; saluted by still others as a new era; and it provides the basis—at least the semantic basis—for some who would reduce military capabilities to what I believe would be a dangerous level . . .

The Washington Post, 10-25:(A)41.

Leonid I. Brezhnev
General Secretary,
Communist Party of the Soviet Union

3

Some . . . claim that detente is impossible unless some changes are affected in the internal order of the socialist countries. Others give the impression of not actually opposing the detente, but declare with amazing frankness their intention to use the process of detente to weaken the socialist system and, ultimately, to secure its destruction. For the public at large, this tactic is presented as a concern for human rights or for a so-called "liberalization" of our system. Let us call a spade a spade.

With all the talk of freedom and democracy and human rights, this whole strident campaign serves only one purpose: to cover up the attempts to interfere in the internal affairs of the socialist countries, to cover up the imperialist aims of this policy. They talk of "liberalization," but what they mean is the elimination of socialism's real gains and the erosion of the socio-political rights of the peoples of the socialist countries . . . We are being told: "Either change your way of life or face a cold war." But what if we should reciprocate? What if we should demand modification of bourgeois laws and customs that go against our ideas of justice and democracy as a condition for normal relations between states? Such a demand, I expect, would not improve the outlook for the healthy development of relations between states. It is impossible to fight for peace while impinging on the sovereign rights of other peoples. It is impossible to champion human rights while torpedoing the principles of peaceful coexistence.

At World Peace Congress, Moscow,
Oct. 26/Vital Speeches, 11-15:73.

Zbigniew Brzezinski
Director, Institute on Communist Affairs,
Columbia University

4

I think [President] Nixon and [Secretary of State Henry] Kissinger are running into great difficulty, precisely because, in their desire to be realistic and conservative, they have given the public the impression that no fundamental values—moral, human or religious—are at stake in foreign affairs. In a democracy like America, foreign policy must be supported through moral concerns of the people.

The Washington Post, 10-7:(A)8.

Alastair Buchan
Professor, Oxford University, England;
Former director, International Institute
for Strategic Studies, London

1

Unless [U.S. Secretary of State Henry] Kissinger can change now that he is the head of a great department, he may prove to have outlived his usefulness and to have become an anachronism more trusted by adversaries than friends. Henry Kissinger may perceive that the best use to which he can put his reputation and his remaining time in office will not be to reorganize the world—for which he has no mandate—but to lay the foundations of reforms that would give greater confidence in the consistency of an American foreign policy at the mercy of the vagaries of personality and political change.
BBC radio lecture, London/
Los Angeles Times, 12-3:(1)8.

Earl L. Butz
Secretary of Agriculture of the United States

2

When President Nixon went to Peking and Moscow last year, one of the powerful tools he had in his diplomatic kit was this bountiful food supply we have in America . . . [Food] is a truly international language. It knows no barrier. It pierces every Curtain—Iron and Bamboo. That's the language the United States is prepared to speak—forcefully, powerfully and on a sustained basis.
Nation's Business, June:30.

Frank Church
United States Senator, D-Idaho

3

[On funds spent for the Agency for International Development]: The American people have reason to question whether their money is being spent wisely when their dollars wind up in the Swiss bank accounts of Cambodian Generals and their tanks are used to kill Greek and Thai students.
Los Angeles Times, 12-6:(1)4.

Ramsey Clark
Former Attorney General of the United States

4

The fundamental human rights—that's what we're talking about. Don't we know that, when a Jewish family in Kharkov or Riga [U.S.S.R.] cannot exercise the fundamental human right to travel, the dignity of humanity everywhere is demeaned? What do we stand for? Look at what we do when it's chrome or humanity in Rhodesia. We side with chrome. When it's gold or diamonds in South Africa, with all the dignity and beauty of those noble [black] people there who suffer so much segregation and violence, do we side with humanity or with gold and diamonds? And what will it be in the Middle East finally? Do you have to be Jewish to love Israel? Not on your life. You have to care about humanity, about the vitality and freedom of the human spirit, about democratic institutions. And if it comes to a choice between humanity and oil, there is no choice.
At dedication of Andrew Goodman Building
of Walden School, New York/
The National Observer, 11-17:19.

A. W. Clausen
President, Bank of America

5

Detente is not an accomplished fact; it is never a static condition. It is a living relationship. Detente does not involve a change of heart. It involves a new perception of self-interest. It is all too easy to succumb to cynicism or to let memories of past wrongs so color our thoughts that we fall behind in the quest for a lasting detente. To achieve a world at peace, a world where the quality of life has meaning, both East and West must temper hard realism with a lot of perseverance and a bit of faith.
San Jose, Calif./
Los Angeles Herald-Examiner, 11-8:(A)14.

John B. Connally, Jr.
Former Secretary of the Treasury
of the United States;
Former Governor of Texas

6

[During the past 25 years,] we [the U.S.] gave of our strength, we shared our abundance, we shielded the weak with our armament—in the hope that other people in their

(JOHN B. CONNALLY, JR.)

own way might choose for themselves a life of peace and prosperity. We were not the world's policeman, but we were the world's best friend—the one free country able and willing to become a leader without the desire for the territory or treasure of any other nation. We possessed the power to become a tyrant, but we did not.

At Vietnam Veterans Homecoming Celebration, Dallas/ The Dallas Times Herald, 6-5:(A)12.

1

America's foreign-policy decisions are not immune from criticism. But I submit to you that the free world has less cause to worry when the United States fulfills its commitments and surely would have far greater cause to worry if the United States began ignoring its commitments.

Before Institute of Directors, London/ The New York Times, 11-18:(4)17.

William L. Dickinson
United States Representative, R-Alabama

2

[Saying he favors a bill curbing the President's war-making powers]: Some people have said this would inhibit the President. Well, if the question is on committing U.S. forces on foreign soil, I want it to inhibit him.

Nov. 7/ Los Angeles Herald-Examiner, 11-8:(A)2.

Lev E. Dobriansky
Professor of Economics, Georgetown University

3

Whether in the economic, political, cultural and other spheres of our expansive activity, let us always bear in mind that the first asset is peoples, our contacts with them, our knowledge and appreciative understanding of them, and our harmonious relations with them. This is prerequisite to all else if the bonds and cement of prolific interdependence are to be durable. In the process of our own cosmopolitan development, for much of the non-Communist world the old "ugly American" is a thing of the past. But one is somewhat uncertain, though the opportunity is great, about the possible resurgence of American ugliness in contacts with the peoples which have been called the captive nations in the Communist world, from the Danube to the Pacific. Here, too, despite the uncertainties, the opportunity for thriving knowledge, restructured conceptions and an understanding quintessential to world peace and eventual freedom is the most challenging and engaging.

At University of Alabama commencement, Huntsville, May 27/ Vital Speeches, 8-15:648.

William O. Douglas
Associate Justice, Supreme Court of the United States

4

The most alarming trend in government is the unimpeded growth of the President's war powers. Some people have the rather naive view that the [Supreme] Court should never enjoin a war. But that's not the issue. The question is whether an individual, having passed the physical and shown ability to shoulder a gun, should be sent overseas to fight in a war that Congress hasn't declared. I believe that any time an individual is coerced by his government, then he has an action. If my position were sustained, the undeclared war would not be enjoined; the only people sent to fight in it would be those who want to fight.

Interview/Time, 11-12:93.

Alec Douglas-Home
Foreign Secretary of the United Kingdom

5

We all start from the premise that detente, representing the opposite of tension, is desirable. We have all had more than enough of stress and strain. Detente is, or ought to be, the essence of good-neighborliness, a quality of which we certainly need more today. The danger is that detente is a word that may mean different things to different people. It can be what in modern jargon is called a "hurrah" word, sounding all right but bearing little relation to reality.

The New York Times, 12-2:(4)17.

Sam J. Ervin, Jr.
United States Senator, D-North Carolina

1

[Saying that Presidents and Congresses have been too loose with the public's money, as in the foreign-aid program]: If an individual were to borrow money to give it away, his friends and family would institute an inquisition in lunacy against him and have a guardian appointed on the grounds that he's not capable of managing his own affairs. But in the last 40 years, if a politician advocated the country borrowing money to give it away, he would likely be elected President or Senator or Congressman, or wind up as Secretary of State.

Interview/
The New York Times Magazine, 5-13:86.

2

Unfortunately, there are those persons who have so little regard for the principle of separation of powers as to embrace the notion that the so-called realities of modern international relations require almost exclusive Executive control over foreign policy . . . There is not one syllable in the Constitution and not one word of verified historical evidence to support the view that the President has broad discretion to act without the collaboration and consent of the Congress in foreign affairs.

At "Pacem in Terris" conference,
Washington, Oct. 11/
The New York Times, 10-12:6.

Gerald R. Ford
Vice President of the United States

3

In foreign policy I have said—and I really say it emphatically—I consider myself an internationalist. I'm a reformed isolationist who, before World War II, was mistaken like a lot of people. Through a series of events—military service and otherwise—I have become, I think, a very ardent internationalist.

Interview, Washington/
U.S. News & World Report, 12-17:29.

J. William Fulbright
United States Senator, D-Arkansas

4

[Presenting a bill that would phase out U.S. foreign military grants and military assistance missions over a two-year period]: The cold war is over. Yet the policies of the era linger on in the military aid program. It is time to wipe out this relic of the past. The bill I am introducing today will give it a fitting burial.

Before the Senate, Washington,
April 3/The New York Times, 4-4:4.

5

[Criticizing Senator Henry Jackson's proposal of linking U.S. trade with the Soviet Union to the relaxation of Soviet emigration policies]: Learning to live together in peace is the most important issue for the Soviet Union and the United States; too important to be compromised by meddling—even idealistic meddling—in each other's affairs. It is simply not within the legitimate range of our foreign policy to instruct the Russians in how to treat their own people, any more than it is [Soviet Communist Party Secretary] Leonid I. Brezhnev's business to lecture us on our race relations or on such matters as the Indian protest at Wounded Knee [S.D.]. We would, quite properly, resent it, and so do they. Consider how the American people would have responded if Brezhnev had canceled his recent visit because of the Watergate [political-espionage affair], or taken the occasion to lecture us on political corruption. We would, of course, tell Brezhnev to get stuffed, regardless of our own dismay over the Watergate . . . This does not mean that we cannot sometimes pressure another country—even a big country like the Soviet Union—into changing its domestic policies. If the Russians want our trade badly enough, they will bend to the Jackson amendment; they largely have already. But let us not pretend that this is a victory for human rights; at most it is a victory for the rights of a small fraction of the millions of persecuted people upon the earth, and they are by no means the worst persecuted. It is a victory, moreover, purchased at the cost of intruding in the internal affairs of a proud and powerful nation; a nation which can no more be expected to endure our intrusions than we would endure theirs; a nation—and this is the central point—whose cooperation is absolutely

(J. WILLIAM FULBRIGHT)

essential if we are to protect the most fundamental of all human rights: the right of innocent people to stay alive in the age of nuclear weapons.

Before American Bankers Association,
Washington, July 11/
Los Angeles Times, 7-19:(2)7.

1

Why indeed should we cooperate with the Soviet Union, a country whose social system is inimical to our own? The answer is simplicity itself: We have to get along with the Russians because, in matters of world peace, we cannot get along without them. The threat of nuclear destruction has become a commonplace, so much so that we tend to dismiss it. But the fact remains that the leaders of the two nations have the means at their disposal at any time to destroy each other's cities and much or most of each other's populations. American pioneer families helped each other to build cabins and clear the land because the job was too big to do alone; cooperation was a matter of survival. Similarly, the Bedouin Arabs have an ancient etiquette of hospitality —a traveler across the desert cannot be refused food and water, because the host knows that he, too, may someday journey across the desert; here, too, it is a matter of survival, not of affection or friendship or religion or ideology. That is the sum and substance of it: In matters of war and peace, Russians and Americans are wanderers in the same desert, and in that desert it is not ideology that counts but food and water—the "food and water" of trade, arms control, political cooperation and cultural exchange.

Before American Bankers Association,
Washington, July 11/
Vital Speeches, 9-15:706.

2

There is very little in international affairs about which I feel certain, but there is one thing of which I am quite certain: the necessity of fundamental change in the way nations conduct their relations with each other. There is nothing in the human environment to prevent us from bringing about such fundamental change. The obstacles are within us, in the workings of the human mind. But just as it is the source of many of our troubles, the inventive mind of man is sometimes capable of breaking through barriers of prejudice and ancient attitude.

Quote, 11-25:514.

Barry M. Goldwater
United States Senator, R-Arizona

3

If we give any indication to the rest of the world that we're going to become an isolated country again, and to disarm unilaterally, I think every ally we have will start looking for somebody else to be allied with. I have a hunch that many of them would tend toward the Soviets, because they see Red China as a bigger threat to peace than they do the Soviets.

Interview/
U.S. News & World Report, 10-15:77.

4

[Criticizing the Congressional override of President Nixon's veto of a bill limiting Presidential war-making authority, and giving more war powers to Congress after an initial period]: Since the Revolutionary War, the dangers of Congress meddling in military affairs have been recognized. We came very close to losing that war for that same reason, and the Founding Fathers recognized Congress should have nothing to do with it . . . If I were an enemy of the United States and knew I could provoke the United States to war and have 60 days to prepare internal pressure, I'd be the happiest man in the world.

At Idaho State University, Nov. 7/
The Dallas Times Herald, 11-8:(A)12.

John T. Gurash
Chairman, INA Corporation

5

. . . [I was] leafing through a 1946 issue of *Time* magazine and reading the headlines in that post-war year: Europe and Japan were on their knees. America had an unchallenged nuclear monopoly. Russia and China were a monolithic Communist bloc. And just about the only signs of American business abroad were Hershey bars and nylon stockings. The advertisements?—every one of them for American products. And what do we read in *Time* magazine today? Europe and Japan are at the height of prosperity, with a combined economic clout greater than the United States'. Dozens of countries are making news—countries that didn't *exist* in 1946. And mutual suspicions have divided Russia and China. The advertisements?—Sony and Volkswagen, BOAC and Fiat, Nikon and Volvo; the American products are nearly outnumbered. Change is what has happened. For years we have been playing by the rules of the post-war period. Now, a quarter-century later, the rules no longer apply. The early 1970s will probably go down as the time all the changes came to a head: the entry of Britain to the Common Market; the double devaluation of the dollar; the SALT talks; and President Nixon's visits to China and Russia. The cold war has finally ended. The test now is to make sure an economic war doesn't break out in its place.

Before British-American Chamber of Commerce, London, May 21/ Vital Speeches, 7-15:588.

W. Averell Harriman
Former United States Ambassador-at-Large

1

Most people think of detente as a love affair. It isn't that. It just means that a few things have been settled. The trouble with [President] Nixon is that he blows up his successes too high, and then he has to create a crisis to get back to basics again.

Time, 11-12:71.

Mark O. Hatfield
United States Senator, R-Oregon

2

I think no President of either political party would now venture out again on this [Vietnam] type of undeclared Executive-initiated and Executive-declared war—because of the repercussions that would obviously follow. But as far as the office of the President is concerned, the very circumstance under which this Vietnam war occurred still persists. And unless the Congress is willing to take specific

action to circumscribe the power of the President to engage in such unilateral warfare, the stage is still set for any time in the future . . . I think the so-called war-powers-of-the-President bill, which has been introduced to define some of the "emergency situations" under which any President would be expected to act, is such an action that would help prevent future Vietnams.

Interview, Washington/ The Christian Science Monitor, 1-29:3.

Jesse A. Helms
United States Senator, R-North Carolina

3

During recent times, when more and more overtures have been made to the West about trade, when detente is on everybody's lips, the Soviet Union has become even more repressive, cracking down on freedom of expression, political dissent, and punishing outside contacts by ordinary citizens. We are told that the cold war is over, but they are still shooting people at the Berlin Wall. The more desperate the Soviets become for economic benefits from the free world, the more rigidly they crack down on their people in an attempt to offset the effect of contacts with free people. Thus, the existing nature of our trade with Communists, instead of providing for more freedom, can unintentionally have the effect of contributing to oppression, instead of relieving it—unless we conduct our negotiations so as to bring liberty into the bargain. The Soviets need trade and investment more than we need the opportunities they offer. For the sake of freedom, we must not lose our advantage.

Before World Anti-Communist League, London, Sept. 1/ Vital Speeches, 10-1:766.

Will Herberg
Professor of Philosophy and Culture, Drew University, Madison, N.J.

4

Americans can't conceive of anything good without seeing themselves as missionaries. Now that they've burned their fingers in Vietnam, they don't want to get involved in

(WILL HERBERG)

remote wars; but they're all in favor of spreading the American way all over the world. The American way is not seen as limited to Americans; it's the right way of life for everybody. So we speak of our "mission" in the world and launch "crusades" on the behalf of the American way.

Interview/
U.S. News & World Report, 6-4:58.

Thomas L. Hughes
President, Carnegie Endowment for International Peace; Former Assistant Secretary and Director of Intelligence and Research, Department of State of the United States

1

There is nothing further that [President] Nixon can add to the formulation and conduct of American foreign policy for the next three years which can't be done better without him. He is at once superfluous and destabilizing. For his remaining time in the White House, he has to be regarded as a foreign-policy problem, not a foreign [-policy] asset. Those who are concerned about neo-isolationism and the flight from foreign policy should see Mr. Nixon's continuation in office as an insuperable obstacle to the rebuilding of an American consensus on world affairs. Those who worry about the disintegration of respect for leadership and authority in foreign policy cannot hope for recovery while he remains. Some think that those abroad who discern weakness in Washington could be tempted to take advantage. Some think that those in Washington who anticipate that perception could be tempted to take risks and perceive threats that are not there. Mr. Nixon is hardly a dispassionate element either way. Increasingly, he will become a growing destabilizer of both causes and effects . . . The foreign policy of this country should no longer be required to carry the burden of a discredited Chief Executive [as a result of the Watergate political-espionage affair]. The responsible and dedicated foreign-policy personalities of the government should no longer be asked to run interference for a malefactor in high office.

Far from being the most persuasive reason for him to stay, foreign policy has become another persuasive reason for him to leave.

Before Women's National Democratic Club/
The Washington Post, 12-23:(B)5.

Hubert H. Humphrey
United States Senator, D-Minnesota

2

I believe in what some call the theory of "linkage" in international relations. Events in different parts of the world are linked together when great powers with concerns in many areas of the world are involved.

At Bnai Zion award dinner, New York,
Feb. 18/The New York Times, 2-19:7.

Henry M. Jackson
United States Senator, D-Washington

3

[On detente between the U.S. and Communist nations]: Without bringing about an increasing measure of individual liberty in the Communist world, there can be no genuine detente. When reading the Western press and listening to Western broadcasts is no longer an act of treason, when families can be reunited across national borders, when emigration is free—then we shall have a genuine detente between peoples and not a formula between governments for capitulation on the issue of human rights.

At Yeshiva University commencement,
New York, June 4/
The Washington Post, 6-5:(A)7.

Herman Kahn
Director, Hudson Institute

4

[President Nixon] basically accepts the idea that we will remain the world's policeman—but not intervene as easily and rapidly as before. He is developing a "Nixon Doctrine" . . . that people and nations should rely basically on self-help . . . [This would not] have worked internationally against Adolf Hitler, who could be stopped only by a grand, closely-coordinated alliance. But in current conditions, where neither Communism nor Fascism is really on the march [and] no other ideological movement is sweeping the world . . . an emphasis on self-help makes sense internationally.

Interview/
U.S. News & World Report, 3-12:43.

Edward M. Kennedy
United States Senator, D-Massachusetts

1

The failure of the [Nixon] Administration to respond diplomatically before [the current Arab-Israeli] war broke out can be seen only in the context of our over-all weakness in foreign policy. The obvious push by the Soviet Union to advance its own interests in the Middle East, its obvious disregard for human rights within its own borders, while the [Nixon] Administration offers unduly generous trade concessions [to the Soviets]—these are the obvious signs of our nation's excessive reliance on the promise of detente and our failure to meet, let alone anticipate, the dangers that surround it.

At AFL-CIO convention,
Bal Harbour, Fla., Oct. 19/
The Washington Post, 10-20:(A)2.

Henry A. Kissinger
Assistant to the President of the United States
for National Security Affairs

2

For years, one of the shibboleths of our [the U.S.'s] political debate has been that, with the end of the war in Vietnam, we could restore our priorities and recover our unity. It is true that, during the war, debate dissolved increasingly into a sterile chant of competing liturgies. But the end of the war has produced a strange lassitude and uncertainty . . . We have been shaken by the realization of our fallibility. It has been painful to grasp that we are no longer pristine—if ever we were. Later than any nation, we have come to the recognition of our limits. In coming to a recognition of our limits, we have achieved one of the definitions of maturity. But the danger is that we will learn that lesson too well; that, instead of a mature recognition that we cannot do everything, we will fall into the dangerous and destructive illusion that we cannot do

anything . . . In the 1920s, we were isolationists, because we thought we were too good for this world. We are now in danger of withdrawing from the world because we believe we are not good enough for it. The result is the same, and the disastrous consequences would be similar.

Before Federal City Club, Washington/
Los Angeles Times, 4-17:(2)7.

3

We have entered a truly remarkable period of East-West diplomacy. The last two years have produced an agreement on Berlin, a treaty between West Germany and the U.S.S.R., a SALT agreement, the beginning of negotiations on a European Security Conference and on mutual balanced force reductions, and a series of significant, practical bilateral agreements between Western and Eastern countries, including a dramatic change in bilateral relations between the U.S. and U.S.S.R. Yet, this very success has created its own problems. There is an increasing uneasiness—all the more insidious for rarely being made explicit—that superpower diplomacy might sacrifice the interests of traditional allies and other friends. Where our allies' interests have been affected by our bilateral negotiations, as in the talks on the limitations of strategic arms, we have been scrupulous in consulting them; where our allies are directly involved, as in the negotiations on mutual balanced force reductions, our approach is to proceed jointly on the basis of agreed positions. Yet, some of our friends in Europe have seemed unwilling to accord America the same trust in our motives as they received from us or to grant us the same tactical flexibility that they employed in pursuit of their own policies. The United States is now often taken to task for flexibility where we used to be criticized for rigidity. All of this underlines the necessity to articulate a clear set of common objectives together with our allies. We do not agree on all policies. In many areas of the world our approaches will differ, especially outside of Europe. But we do require an understanding of what should be done jointly and of the limits we should impose on the scope of our

(HENRY A. KISSINGER)

autonomy.

At Associated Press luncheon,
New York, April 23/
Los Angeles Times, 4-25:(2)7.

1

No foreign policy—no matter how ingenious—has any chance of success if it is born in the minds of a few and carried in the hearts of none.

Before International Platform Association,
Washington, Aug. 2/
The Washington Post, 8-4:(D)2.

2

Is it possible to insulate foreign policy from the general difficulties we are facing as a nation? I don't know the answer, but that is the question that torments me.

Interview/The Washington Post, 8-5:(C)6.

Henry A. Kissinger
Secretary of State-designate
of the United States

3

If we are going to achieve the lasting peace which we seek and if we are going to leave behind a foreign-policy tradition that will be carried on on a non-partisan basis in succeeding Administrations, we have an obligation to explain our philosophies purposes and policies to the public. After my confirmation, I intend to invite leaders of various opinion-forming elements in this country to the State Department to advise us on how [we] can most-effectively discharge this responsibility. We will do our best to conduct foreign policy in as open a manner as is consistent with the goals which we all share, which is to bring about a lasting peace.

News conference, San Clemente, Calif.,
Aug. 23/The New York Times, 8-24:12.

4

. . . the consensus on which foreign policy was conducted in the late 1940s and through the 1950s and 1960s is eroding in part because the conditions in the world have changed so enormously. In the late 1940s and in the 1950s, foreign policy was essentially designed to prevent what was considered a monolithic Communism from militarily overrunning the world. Today, we are conducting a foreign policy in which, at one and the same time, we are engaged in detente with the Soviet Union and the People's Republic of [Communist] China and, on the other hand, we are trying to strengthen the traditional friendships with Europe and Japan. On the one hand, we are stressing the need for adequate defense budgets, and, on the other, we are conducting negotiations for the limitation of strategic arms. This requires a complexity of thought and sophistication on the part of the American public that was not called for in the 1940s and the 1950s.

News conference, San Clemente, Calif.,
Aug. 23/The Washington Post, 8-26:(A)19.

5

We face problems now that no past generation has faced; they are common problems of humanity. They are food, energy, environment, communication. Up until Western imperialism, there was no world history. There was only regional history. When we talk about the Roman Empire, we talk about people who hardly knew the Chinese existed. Most great cultures developed independently. Now we are in close contact each day, yet it is a fact of our existence that we have never really assimilated. Yes, we must re-think where we are.

Interview, San Clemente, Calif./Time, 9-3:15.

6

. . . we have as a country to ask ourselves the question whether it should be the principal goal of American foreign policy to transform the domestic structure of societies with which we deal or whether the principal exercise of our foreign policy should be directed toward affecting the foreign policy of those societies. Now, I recognize there is a certain connection between domestic policy and foreign policy. But if we adopt as a national proposition the view that we must transform the domestic structure of all countries with which we deal, even if the foreign policy of those countries is otherwise moving in a more acceptable direction, then we will find ourselves massively involved in every country in the world.

At Senate Foreign Relations Committee hearing on his confirmation, Washington, Sept. 7/The New York Times, 9-10:20.

Henry A. Kissinger
Secretary of State of the United States

1

Foreign policy is explained domestically in terms of justice. But what is defined as justice at home becomes the subject of negotiations abroad. It is thus no accident that many nations, including our own, view the international arena as a forum in which virtue is thwarted by the clever practice of foreigners.

At "Pacem in Terris" conference, Washington, Oct. 8/ The Washington Post, 10-12:(A)30.

2

The United States and the Soviet Union are, of course, ideological and to some extent political adversaries. But the United States and the Soviet Union also have a very special responsibility. We possess, each of us, nuclear arsenals capable of annihilating humanity. We, both of us, have a special duty to see to it that confrontations are kept within bounds that do not threaten civilized life. Both of us, sooner or later, will have to come to realize that the issues that divide the world today, and foreseeable issues, do not justify the unparalleled catastrophe that a nuclear war would represent. And therefore, in all our dealings with the Soviet Union, we have attempted to keep in mind and we have attempted to move them to a position in which this overriding interest that humanity shares with us is never lost sight of. In a speech at "Pacem in Terris," I pointed out that there are limits beyond which we cannot go. I stated that we will oppose the attempt by any country to achieve a position of predominance, either globally or regionally, that we would resist any attempt to exploit a policy of detente to weaken our alliances, and that we would react if a relaxation of tensions were used as a cover to exacerbate conflicts in international trouble spots . . . It is easy to start confrontations; but in this age we have

to know where we will be at the end, and not only what pose to strike at the beginning.

News conference, Washington, Oct. 25/Los Angeles Times, 10-26:(1)23.

3

Let me explain what we understand by "detente." We do not say that detente is based on the compatibility of domestic systems. We recognize that the values and ideology of both the Soviet Union and the People's Republic of [Communist] China are opposed and sometimes hostile to ours. We do not say that there are no conflicting national interests. We do say that there is a fundamental change in the international environment compared to any other previous period, a change which was expressed by President Eisenhower more than 20 years ago when he said, "There is no longer any alternative to peace" . . . So we do not say that we approve of the domestic evolution of the Soviet Union or of other Communist countries with which we are attempting to coexist. Nor do we accept that detente can be used for military expansion, or for threatening weaker countries, or for undermining our traditional friendships. But we do make a conscious effort to set up rules of conduct and to establish a certain interconnection of interests—and, above all, to establish communications between the top leaders and between officials at every level—that makes it possible in times of crisis to reduce the danger of accident or miscalculation. This has been our policy with the Soviet Union, and it is the policy we have pursued as well with the People's Republic of China.

News conference, Washington, Dec. 27/ U.S. News & World Report, 1-7('74):64.

Melvin R. Laird
Secretary of Defense of the United States

4

[Although there may well be fighting] in various sections of the world during the next five to 10 years, I can say that, as far as American involvement in that fighting [is concerned], we have applied the Nixon Doctrine, and as we look to the next five to 10 years, we are no longer in the position where the United States is the cop on every beat. Our

(MELVIN R. LAIRD)

allies are in a position where they can take on that responsibility in their own neighborhoods.

News conference, Washington, Jan. 19/
Los Angeles Times, 1-20:(1)23.

Melvin R. Laird
Counsellor to the President
of the United States for Domestic Affairs;
Former Secretary of Defense

1

There is great talk of [U.S.-Soviet] detente. But the only manner in which detente can be proven is by deeds, not words. The Soviet Union, as far as I'm concerned, has not been performing as if detente were here.

At breakfast session with reporters,
Washington, Oct. 16/
The Washington Post, 10-28:(A)2.

Clare Boothe Luce
Former American diplomat and playwright

2

. . . for a long time in the United States, "balance of power" was a dirty word. Then it became increasingly clear to thoughtful people, as the power of Soviet Russia grew, that we were locked into a bipolar position with them, and that this stalemate could be broken only by the growth of new powers that would keep the seesaw balanced. That was the great advance we made when we opened the door to [Communist] China. It restored a balance of power, which would indicate that we might have 50 years without a big war.

Interview, New York/
The New York Times Magazine, 4-22:54.

Mike Mansfield
United States Senator, D-Montana

3

I'm just against foreign aid. [Twenty-seven years after World War II,] the old guard is hanging on, trying to preserve something that long ago outlived its usefulness. I don't know why we have approximately 100 bases in Japan; I don't know why we have bases in

Africa and elsewhere.

News conference, Washington, Feb. 3/
The Washington Post, 2-4:(A)18.

4

The presence of so many U.S. forces on foreign soil presumes a policy that heavily favors the military option . . . The commitment and level of U.S. forces abroad has determined our policy, rather than our policy determining the level of U.S. forces abroad.

Before Senate Foreign Relations
Subcommittee on Arms Control,
Washington, July 25/
The Washington Post, 7-26:(A)7.

Francis J. McNamara
Executive Secretary, Subversive Activities
Control Board of the United States

5

[On the imminent elimination of the SACB]: I'm not bitter. I'm not disappointed. [It bugs me when] people come in here with smug looks on their faces and suggest that anyone who still thinks the Soviet Union is trying to take over the world is a stupid ass. I'm amazed that people actually believe the Soviet Union no longer wants to bury us.

Interview, Washington, June 30/
The Washington Post, 7-1:(A)22.

George Meany
President, American Federation of Labor-
Congress of Industrial Organizations

6

. . . I can't buy the idea that, through rapprochement, we've reached a basis of accommodation with the Soviet Union or with the Chinese Communists. Now the Soviet Union, they're looking for all sorts of favors, and they're getting them. But what are they doing? What are they doing at the UN? Are they with us or are they with the terrorists, supported by the Arab governments, that murdered our diplomats? That's who they're with. They're not with us. They're with the Arab zealots; they're with Black September; they're with the Palestinian guerrillas; they're with people who murdered the Israeli athletes in Munich [during last year's Olympics]; and they're with the people who murdered our

diplomats just a few weeks ago [in Sudan].
So, this is not a basis of accommodation
where there's give and take on both sides. It
seems we're giving.

Interview, Washington/
The National Observer, 5-5:24.

Thomas H. Moorer
Admiral, United States Navy;
Chairman, Joint Chiefs of Staff

1

It is unrealistic to think that this nation
can withdraw from the world, live in isolation,
and live at the same time—untroubled by
those who want what we have—in peace. We
are involved world-wide because we have interests world-wide—interests which involve all elements of our national power: political, economic and military.

Before Commonwealth Club,
San Francisco, Feb. 9/
San Francisco Examiner, 2-10:4.

Fred Warner Neal
Professor of Political Science,
Reed College, Portland, Ore.

2

. . . whereas [President] Nixon is perforce
committed to detente, it is questionable
whether the detente policy could survive were
he to be replaced. Vice President [Gerald]
Ford, for example, doesn't have Mr. Nixon's
background, his finesse, his national constituency or his personal investment in the detente
policy; he is much more open to being swayed
by the powerful cold-war forces still at work
in the country. The words of Senator [Henry]
Jackson and his fellow opponents of detente
are what our people have been hearing for 25
years, whereas the words of [Secretary of
State Henry] Kissinger, [Senator J. William]
Fulbright and others in support of detente are
not. There is a ready-made public against
detente . . . there is almost no conscious,
organized public for it. It is ironic, indeed,
that one has to turn to President Nixon, the
former cold-warrior par excellence, as a guarantee against a return to cold-war policies, but

that seems to be the situation.

Lecture, Reed College/
The Washington Post, 12-23:(B)4.

Richard M. Nixon
President of the United States

3

It is important that we understand both
the necessity and the limitations of America's
role in maintaining [the] peace. Unless we in
America work to preserve the peace, there will
be no peace. Unless we in America work to
preserve freedom, there will be no freedom.
But let us clearly understand the new nature
of America's role, as a result of the new
policies we have adopted over the past four
years. We shall respect our treaty commitments. We shall support vigorously the principle that no country has the right to impose its
will or rule on another by force. We shall
continue, in this era of negotiation, to work
for the limitation of nuclear arms, and to
reduce the danger of confrontation between
the great powers. We shall do our share in
defending peace and freedom in the world.
But we shall expect others to do their share.
The time has passed when America will make
every other nation's conflict our own, or
make every other nation's future our responsibility, or presume to tell the people of other
nations how to manage their own affairs. Just
as we respect the right of each nation to
determine its own future, we also recognize
the responsibility of each nation to secure its
own future. Just as America's role is indispensable in preserving the world's peace, so is
each nation's role indispensable in preserving
its own peace.

Inauguration address, Washington, Jan. 20/
U.S. News & World Report, 2-5:86.

4

[On the recent execution of two American
diplomats by Palestinian guerrillas in Sudan]:
I was noting a well-intentioned comment by
one individual who raised a question as to
whether the United States, in this instance,
might have been better advised to bring pressure on another government to release 60 who
were held in prison in order to save the lives

(RICHARD M. NIXON)

of the two. I disagree with that. All of us would have liked to have saved the lives of these two very brave men, but they knew and we knew that, in the event we had paid international blackmail in this way, it would have saved their lives, but it would have endangered the lives of hundreds of others all over the world; because once the individual, the terrorist or the others has a demand that is made that is satisfied, he then is encouraged to try again. And that is why the position of your government has to be one in the interest of preserving life, of not submitting to international blackmail or extortion any place in the world . . . The nation that compromises with the terrorists today could well be destroyed by the terrorists tomorrow.

Washington/The National Observer, 3-17:10.

1

Our policy in the world for the next four years can be summarized quite simply: Where peace is newly planted, we shall work to make it thrive. Where bridges have been built, we shall work to make them stronger. Where friendships have endured, we shall work to make them grow.

State of the World Address, May 3/
Los Angeles Times, 5-4:(1)12.

Thomas P. O'Neill, Jr.
United States Representative,
D-Massachusetts

2

[Saying he favors a bill curbing the President's war-making powers]: If the President [Nixon] can deal with the Arabs and he can deal with the Israelis and he can deal with the Soviets, he ought to be able to deal with the Congress of the United States [when it comes to authorizing a war situation].

Washington, Nov. 7/
Los Angeles Herald-Examiner, 11-8:(A)2.

John O. Pastore
United States Senator,
D-Rhode Island

3

[On U.S. foreign policy]: We still identify

ourselves, to our long-range detriment, with unpopular governments because they are anti-Communist or on our side, whatever that means. We need a foreign-aid program, but we need [one] considerably different, considerably smaller than the one we've got, which can reasonably be described as a jerry-rigged boondoggle.

Before Catholic Association of
College Alumni, Cranston, R.I., Dec. 9/
The Dallas Times Herald, 12-10:(A)2.

William Proxmire
United States Senator,
D-Wisconsin

4

[Advocating a reduction of U.S. foreign intelligence operations]: Our foreign covert operations have brought little but embarrassment abroad and confusion at home. They should be cut to the bone. In the day of sophisticated electronic devices, no longer is there a sound justification for covert operations to defend the U.S. from surprise attack.

April 8/The Washington Post, 4-9:(A)4.

Itzhak Rabin
Former Israeli Ambassador
to the United States

5

. . . Israel is lucky. Israel has the will and wits to defend Israel. Besides China and one or two more, there are not many nations friendly to America that you can say so much about today. But neither Israel, nor China, nor any of the other nations now in the circle of America's friends can possibly achieve successful self-defense in a new kind of world in which America has ceased to be a great power.

Washington/Los Angeles Times, 4-12:(2)7.

John R. Rarick
United States Representative,
D-Louisiana

6

The Communist struggle for world conquest will not be won in some distant jungle, but through the indecision of the free nations

. . . and Washington is the weakest point.

At anti-Communist rally, Washington,
April 14/The Washington Post, 4-15:(A)18.

Edwin O. Reischauer
Professor, Harvard University;
Former United States Ambassador to Japan

1

I would certainly give credit to the President [Nixon] and [National Security Affairs adviser] Henry Kissinger for their handling of American relations with former adversaries, but I don't think this was as difficult as many people make out. The American public was more than ready for it. The [Communist] Chinese wanted it. The Soviets wanted it. It would have taken quite a bit of leadership to have kept us from having it. But I don't fault them on our relationships with foreign adversaries. I think they have been disastrous on the more important thing: the relationships with our friends.

Tokyo/Los Angeles Times, 7-29:(4)4.

William P. Rogers
Secretary of State
of the United States

2

[Saying war-making powers should be shared by the President and Congress]: There are few significant matters which can be accomplished by Presidential order alone . . . the fact that even a minor skirmish could lead to a confrontation of the major powers and raise the specter of nuclear war serves to emphasize the desirability of appropriate Congressional participation in decisions which risk involving the United States in hostilities . . . We must be sure that such decisions [involving war or the risk of war] reflect the effective exercise by the Congress and the President of their respective Constitutional responsibilities.

Before Senate Foreign Relations Committee,
Washington/The Washington Post, 4-10:(A)18.

3

When we have discussions with other governments, we talk over the international situation and each of us generally refers to domestic matters as well. But experience has taught us that public condemnation or criticism of other governments is non-productive. We strongly support the idea that the internal affairs of a country or government have to be decided by the people and government concerned. So we are not going around the world expressing public comments about the acts of other governments, because we find it counter-productive. And we also have encouraged other governments not to do that about us.

News conference, Seoul, South Korea,
July 20/The Dallas Times Herald, 7-20:(A)3.

Benjamin S. Rosenthal
United States Representative,
D-New York

4

. . . "grandmotherly" diplomacy is over. Americans tend to engage in exaggerated myths about their foreign policy. Grandmotherly diplomacy is the idea that we have a delightful, charming, dependable and unique relationship with Europe because all of our grandmothers and great grandmothers came from Europe . . . we can't rely on our grandmothers any more. We must rely on ourselves. As President Nixon has said, 1973 is the year of Europe. We must act as a mature nation. Our relationship must continue to be dependent on events and performances and not on grandmotherly relationships.

At dinner for European parliamentarians,
Washington, Oct. 30/
The Washington Post, 11-1:(B)3.

Dean Rusk
Former Secretary of State
of the United States

5

I think one can detect around the country a rather general mood of withdrawal from world affairs. This is reflected not only in the national decision that has been made by the American people and the Congress and the President to get out of Southeast Asia. One sees it in the growing demands to withdraw our troops from NATO, to eliminate or make deep cuts in foreign aid, to impose severe restrictions on imports, and in a rather general feeling that we should forget the rest of the

(DEAN RUSK)

world and take care of our problems here at home. Now, this may be an understandable temporary reaction to the prolonged agony of Vietnam. It could be the beginnings of a cycle of isolationism comparable to, say, the '20s and the '30s. I hope, myself, that this is temporary, because we have on our plate in the coming years some major issues that are vital to this country; such things as the law of the sea, the nuclear arms race and nuclear war, and how you build a durable peace, problems of the environment on an international scale, the population problem right round the globe, better answers in the field of race-relations—not only in this country, but as our example might have an impact on similar problems elsewhere—and the coming problem of reduction in the supply of non-renewable resources such as critical minerals and fossil fuels. These are extraordinarily important national issues for us, but they can only be resolved on an international basis—that is, by a responsible and active participation by the United States in world affairs . . . So I hope very much that, if there is this mood of withdrawal, that it is a temporary phenomenon and that we'll decide what our role ought to be in world affairs. Maybe it will be different in important respects than in the past, but that we not try to find a foxhole to hide in; because with these problems that I'm talking about, there's no place to hide; there's no way to escape them.

Interview/The Washington Post, 8-5:(C)4.

1

. . . foreign policy is that part of our public business which we ourselves cannot control. The Congress, the President, the courts, state and local governments, within Constitutional limits, can pretty well decide what we do about our domestic affairs. But when we move beyond that national frontier, we're dealing with about 140 other governments, no one of which simply salutes when

we speak. So we often want to accomplish things which we can't accomplish because others simply won't act the way we want them to act.

Interview/The Washington Post, 8-5:(C)4.

John A. Scali
United States Ambassador/Permanent Representative to the United Nations

2

No nation has American aid forced upon it. They ask for it. And we give it without any demand that they become a faithful ally of the United States. If a nation does not want our aid, well, then, they need not apply.

*At United Nations
Security Council meeting, Panama City/
The Christian Science Monitor, 3-22:8.*

Arthur M. Schlesinger, Jr.
*Historian; Professor of Humanities,
City University of New York*

3

With checks, both written and unwritten, inoperative, with Congress impotent, the Executive establishment feeble and subservient, press and television intimidated, national opinion disdained, foreign opinion rejected, the fear of dismissal eliminated, our President [Nixon] is free to indulge his most private resentments and rages in the conduct of foreign affairs, and to do so without a word of accounting to Congress and the American people.

*San Francisco Examiner & Chronicle,
1-14:(This World)2.*

James R. Schlesinger
*Director, Central Intelligence Agency
of the United States*

4

Intelligence has got to be absolutely first class. It has got to be based on complete intellectual integrity. It is very important that we call them as we see them . . . And that is my intention. And it shall remain my intention.

Before Senate Armed Services Committee,
Washington, April/
Los Angeles Times, 5-2:(1)25.

James R. Schlesinger
Secretary of Defense of the
United States

1

Detente is a velvet glove—a mailed fist in a velvet glove. Should we be discussing the beauty and texture of the glove, or the import of the mailed fist?

Interview, Washington/
The Christian Science Monitor, 9-1:1.

Hugh Scott
United States Senator,
R-Pennsylvania

2

[Referring to U.S. involvement in Vietnam]: Never, never, never again will I want to see our country militarily involved in another country's problem.

Washington, Jan. 26/
San Francisco Examiner, 1-27:2.

Norodom Sihanouk
Exiled former Chief of State
of Cambodia

3

If the United States intervenes in every country where there are domestic quarrels, it will have a fair amount of work to do.

San Francisco Examiner & Chronicle,
4-15:(This World)2.

Stuart Symington
United States Senator, D-Missouri

4

[Because of Vietnam,] we [the U.S.] have lost the respect of the world, and the only reason some nations have anything to do with us is because they think we have some money left.

Before Senate Democratic caucus,
Washington, Jan. 4/
Los Angeles Times, 1-5:(1)8.

5

No economy, not even the economy of the United States, can continue to police the world and baby-sit the world indefinitely.

Washington, March 15/
The New York Times, 3-16:15.

Barbara Tuchman
Author, Historian

6

The most baneful myth of our time has been the myth of the Communist monolith. We now discover, happily if belatedly, that the supposed Sino-Soviet unity is in fact a bitter antagonism of two rivals wrapped in hate, fear and mutual suspicion. The error has been the costliest since the myth that appeasement could contain Hitler. It never had much to do with facts, but was rather a reflection of fears and prejudices. Knee-jerk reactions to fear and prejudice are not the best guide to a useful foreign policy, which I would define as the conduct of relations and exercise of influence in the service of an enlightened self-interest. The question remains, what can be done to narrow the gap between information from the field and policy-making at home. First, it remains essential to maintain the integrity of Foreign Service reporting, not only for the sake of what may get through, but to provide the basis for a change of policy when the demand becomes imperative. Second, some means must be found to require that preconceived notions and emotional fixations be periodically tested against the evidence. Perhaps legislation could be enacted to enforce a regular pause for rethinking, for questioning the wisdom of an accepted course of action, for cutting one's losses if necessary. Failing that, I pass to a final suggestion which is not proposed as a joke: It is to abolish the Presidency, because it seems to me that too much power and therefore too much risk is now subject to the idiosyncrasies of a single individual at the top, whoever he may be. I would substitute a committee of five to be elected as a slate put forward by each party, and to have a single five-year term with a rotating chairman, each to serve for one year. The idea needs a little working out, which I leave for the moment to anyone here who

(BARBARA TUCHMAN)

may want to consider it.

Before Foreign Service officers
of the 1940s/
The National Observer, 3-10:10.

Kurt Waldheim
Secretary General of the
United Nations

1

Real detente means true understanding of the values and interests of others. It must involve all nations. It must embrace economic, cultural and humanitarian cooperation. It does not require that any nation should surrender its sovereignty, its independence, its system of government or its ideology. It does require that all nations should try to understand and certainly to tolerate the systems and attitudes of others. It is not an easy process.

At European Conference on
Security and Cooperation, Helsinki/
Los Angeles Times, 7-4:(1)19.

Ardeshir Zahedi
Iranian Ambassador to the
United States

2

I never thought I would be a good diplomat, because I hate to lie and I hate people who lie to me.

Interview, Washington/
The Washington Post, 4-22:(L)3.

Government

Spiro T. Agnew
Vice President of the United States

1

[On his being Vice President]: It's an intellectual frustration for a man who's spent his time in Executive government making decisions to suddenly find that he cannot make decisions any more, that he can only recommend that they be made. It's not a debilitating frustration or a frustration that makes me want to abandon the Vice-Presidency . . . It's simply an adjustment from a line responsibility to an advisory responsibility; and it's hard to make, it really is. In the first year that I was Vice President, I would find myself saying, "Well, now we are going to do this"; and then I would come back and say, "We're not going to do anything; we're going to ask the President if it's not a good idea to do this." So the Vice-Presidency has its frustrations, and it's a tremendous adjustment for someone who has been [as Governor of Maryland] a single Executive.

Interview, Washington, May 15/
The Washington Post, 5-16:(A)7.

2

I still cannot see myself actively going out and opposing a Presidential policy as long as I sit in this office. I don't think that's what the Vice President is intended to do. He would not be Vice President but for the selection of the President, and having accepted the job on those terms, he should not let his personal ambitions propel him . . .

Interview, Washington, May 15/
The Washington Post, 5-16:(A)7.

3

Any man who goes into the political arena expects to receive some wounds [from his political critics]. But the public men who govern best are the ones who have the courage to govern as they think best. For if a President allows himself to be forbidden the per-

formance of his elective purpose because of the condemnation of critics, however well-intentioned, then he ceases to govern at all. I can assure you, ladies and gentlemen, that this [Nixon] Administration is not going to allow that to happen. The President, like other Presidents before him, is not concerned with popularity or glory, but rather with his responsibilities to the country.

Before International Boilermakers' Union,
Denver, Aug. 15/
Los Angeles Times, 8-16:(1)18.

Carl Albert
United States Representative,
D-Oklahoma

4

[On President Nixon's impoundment of Congressionally-allocated funds]: He's trying to make a legislator out of himself, and it's not the business of the President of the United States to assume Congress' responsibility for the fiscal affairs of the nation, as I see it, whether it's good or bad. I'm more interested in preserving the Constitution, the separation of powers, than I am in the President being right on every budget estimate he makes. You know, he makes mistakes, too.

Television interview, Jan. 28/
San Francisco Examiner, 1-29:3A.

John B. Anderson
United States Representative,
R-Illinois

5

[Criticizing Attorney General Richard Kleindienst for saying that the President, if he chose, could prohibit all of the 2.5 million Executive Branch employees from testifying before Congress]: Until the present, I have not been inclined to take an overly-restrictive view of Executive privilege. It seemed to me quite reasonable to allow the President to

165

(JOHN B. ANDERSON)

enjoy confidential relations with his direct advisers regarding matters of national security. But I feel compelled to stress before the Committee today in the strongest terms possible my utter shock and dismay at the testimony presented yesterday by Attorney General Kleindienst. [His statement] was not only unnecessarily provocative and contemptuous of Congress, but, more importantly, it contained such an alarming and dangerous expansion of the notion of Executive privilege that I can see only one course of action: Congress must immediately pass legislation strictly limiting Executive privilege, lest the delicate balance of shared power between the two Branches be ruptured permanently.

At joint Senate Subcommittee hearing,
Washington, April 11/
The Washington Post, 4-12:39.

Roy L. Ash
Director, Federal Office of
Management and Budget

1

[On Nixon Administration's restraints imposed on government spending and programs]: I was asked in a Congressional hearing the other day, "Isn't it terrible that as you, the Executive Branch, now begin to restrain this great momentum that we have built into all of our Federal programs, you're creating all kinds of shocks in the system?" It was likened to a train that was moving along the track at high speed. If you put on the brakes too fast, you create many shocks throughout the string of cars, sometimes damaging the cargo in that train. And my answer to that was: "Maybe that's right. Maybe there are some shocks, and maybe it damaged the cargo a bit. But if that train had been allowed to proceed full speed down the track, it was about to run head-on into another one coming full speed in the other direction; and then I think we would have had a considerably greater shock." That's what we've been trying to avoid: the head-on collision with economic catastrophe. We'll acknowledge that there are some shocks in the process of slowing this momentum—but consider the alternative.

Interview, Washington/
U.S. News & World Report, 4-30:95.

2

As the Congress is presently organized, it is very difficult for them [to set national priorities and establish goals of fiscal responsibility]. Maybe we're facing the question of what is the role required of the Congress today. Members must represent their individual constituencies at home as well as the nation as a whole. Can they effectively organize to represent the whole? I'm optimistic. I think it is possible that the Congress can find within itself the means to represent both of these sometimes conflicting interests at the same time.

Interview, Washington/
U.S. News & World Report, 4-30:95.

Thomas L. Ashley
United States Representative, D-Ohio

3

If general revenue-sharing came up today, it would be defeated soundly in Congress . . . "New Federalism" will never fly or even get off the ground if, as at the present time, it is based on the negation or impairment of the responsibility of Congress.

At conference sponsored by Woodrow Wilson
International Center, Washington, May/
The Washington Post, 6-19:(A)10.

George W. Ball
Former Under Secretary of State
of the United States

4

Today, our government is no longer open, but conducted in an atmosphere of secrecy and furtiveness in which a great part of its effort is directed not toward gaining the confidence and consent of the people, but concealing its own activities from public scrutiny. Powers were concentrated in the White House [by the Nixon Administration] to the point where the traditional departments of government became mere appendices.

At New School for Social Research
commencement, New York/
The New York Times, 6-6:38.

James D. Barber
Chairman, department of political science,
Duke University

1

It's difficult, in many ways, to talk about the Presidency as an institution, in the same way as we talk about Congress or the courts as institutions. The Presidency is so highly personalized. It centers on one individual, to whom all the other actors in the Presidential establishment look for their cues. And one way or the other, they'll find those cues. They'll discern from the President's apparent purposes what they ought to do . . . Institutions, including the Presidency, are largely in the participants' minds. They are not physical structures. They are a set of expectations that the actors have about what they should do and what is wanted from them.

Panel discussion, New Orleans/
The Washington Post, 9-16:(C)1.

Birch Bayh
United States Senator, D-Indiana

2

[Advocating lowering of the House and Senate minimum age requirements to 22 and 27 years respectively]: Young people today are mature and well-educated enough to serve in the Congress. They've earned that right by participating in all aspects of society, from paying taxes to serving in the armed forces, to taking part in responsible political and community activity. Most important, they have something constructive to offer by serving in the Congress: courage and energy, creativeness and idealism—attributes always in short supply anywhere in our society.

Parade, 3-25:7.

3

Anyone who wants milk and honey and rose petals and violet water had better not run for the Senate, because this body has to deal with controversial issues.

Quote, 12-9:554.

Lloyd M. Bentsen
United States Senator, D-Texas

4

[Saying Congress must hold the line on spending or it will lose control of the Federal purse-strings to the Presidency]: The issue is whether or not inflation and taxes will be curbed. The principle is the survival of representative government. The average American understands the President's [Nixon] pledge to oppose an increase in taxes. And he is impressed when he hears the President say that it's time to get big government off your back. Unless we in Congress can make our case in terms just that direct and just that relevant, we're going to lose the power of the purse . . . [Letting the President usurp that power] will be a transfer of power from elected officials closest to the people to one man in the White House and an army of Executive bureaucrats.

Before the Senate, Washington, Feb. 20/
The Dallas Times Herald, 2-21:(A)10.

5

[Criticizing the volume of paperwork in government]: Too often, we in Congress write one page of law—in clear and simple terms—only to see the bureaucrats transform that one page into 50 pages of guidelines and regulations that confound the public without really reflecting what Congress was trying to do. The Lord's Prayer has only 56 words; Lincoln's Gettysburg Address only 266; the Ten Commandments have 297 words; and the Declaration of Independence only 300. But a recent order from the Federal government dealing with the price of cabbage contained 26,911 words.

Washington/
The Dallas Times Herald, 4-1:(A)40.

Alexander M. Bickel
Professor of Law, Yale University

6

In order to remain independent, the Presidency must have a substantial measure of privacy of decision-making . . . If Congress could freely penetrate, investigate and expose the decision-making process of the Presidency, it could go a very long way toward controlling it and destroying its independent separateness.

Los Angeles Times, 7-24:(1)10.

Harry A. Blackmun
Associate Justice,
Supreme Court of the United States

1

I once heard a president of a great university describe government in nautical terms. He said that an enlightened autocracy is like a great sailing ship: It is beautiful to observe as it rides before fair winds. Usually it runs its course and reaches the harbor that was its goal. But sometimes it encounters adversity, and often, when it does, it sinks. A well-tuned democracy, on the other hand, is like a raft: It may not sink, but one's feet are *always* wet.

At American Bar Association
Prayer Breakfast, Washington, Aug. 5/
The National Observer, 8-18:13.

Daniel J. Boorstin
Director, National Museum
of History and Technology

2

. . . there are hundreds of people who write on White House stationery. This is a new phenomenon. In fact, it's a phenomenon which has astonished, and properly astonished, some Senators who asked [a] Counsellor of the President if he ever saw the President and he said he didn't. And I think there are something like 40 persons who bear some title such as Counsellor to the President or something of that sort. Now, this is a relatively new phenomenon: the opportunity for the President to get out of touch with the people who speak in his name . . . The Executive Office of the President has expanded beyond all bounds and has tended to supersede the Executive Branch of the government. Some drastic reconsideration of that is in order. American citizens in general do not realize the extent of the Executive Office. The dangers of that growth have been dramatized in [the] Watergate [political-espionage affair], and in several ways: first, by making it possible for people to use or seem to use the authority of the President without his knowledge; and then, by making it possible for a President to say—with some credibility—that he didn't know what was going on; that is an equally

disastrous fact and one which should give us pause. The Executive Office of the President ought to be scrutinized. I cannot believe that the responsibility of the Office is served by its proliferation. How many of these people and how many of these White House "positions" were simply superfluous? As I watched some of the Watergate hearings, I kept asking myself what all those people—[former Presidential Counsel John] Dean and others—were doing there in the first place. Was there really an honest job there that needed doing?

Interview/
The Dallas Times Herald, 7-15:(B)3.

3

We have to recognize that one of the distinctions between democracy and other forms of government is that, while democracy is messy on the surface, other forms of government are messy underneath. In fact, in most countries in the world . . . the sorts of things that are reported with such horror in the Watergate [political-espionage] episode wouldn't even make the newspapers.

San Francisco Examiner & Chronicle,
7-15:(This World)2.

4

I think the passage of the 22nd Amendment in the Constitution [limiting Presidents to two terms] was a mistake. I think that the proposal for a six-year term for the President is also misguided. I think one of the points in having a representative government is to have the elected person in power always subject to the possibility of being re-elected or not being re-elected . . . That was a very short-sighted and, I think, malicious Constitutional amendment. It doesn't belong in the Constitution. And I think that the notion that it is desirable to have a President who can give his full attention to the "Presidency" and not worry about re-election is quite a mistake. What we want is a President who will be thinking about the prospects of re-election and will wonder what reaction the public will have to what he's doing as President. That's what we mean by representative government.

Interview/
The Washington Post, 7-21:(A)14.

Tom Bradley
Mayor-elect of Los Angeles

1

Unless we [in the various levels of government] work together to solve our common problems, all of us will fail . . . They [the public] are not really concerned about titles. They're concerned about whether or not we give good services to them, whether or not we improve the quality of life for them . . . They don't really make that distinction as to whether or not we come from the state or the Federal government or the city. If the air is polluted, they blame us in government . . . if our streets are clogged with automobiles to the point where we can hardly travel on the freeways and highways, they don't blame city hall, they blame all of us.

Before California State Assembly,
Sacramento, June 14/
Los Angeles Times, 6-15:(1)3.

William E. Brock III
United States Senator, R-Tennessee

2

I think the differences between the White House and Congress are extremely serious. But perhaps I would look at it in a somewhat different light than some other members of Congress. I think it's presumptuous of Congress to criticize the Executive for taking over some of the powers we lawmakers have abdicated. If the Congress wants to have more say in the establishment of national needs and national policy, then it must restructure itself so as to be able to establish those priorities. Congress is not so structured today.

Interview/
U.S. News & World Report, 2-12:38.

James L. Buckley
United States Senator, C-New York

3

Anyone who thinks that Congress is going to return to co-equality [with the Presidency] is fooling himself. The responsibility is focused in Washington, and the power is focused in the White House. But I think we're going to see some reassertion of Congressional scrutiny and Congressional power.

At Capitol Hill Club reception,
Washington, May 23/
The New York Times, 5-24:26.

McGeorge Bundy
President, Ford Foundation; Former Special Assistant to the President of the United States for National Security Affairs

4

Precisely because national security can be an important reason for secrecy, it's important to keep the amount of material that has to be kept secret to an absolute minimum. The notion that everything stamped "classified" relates to national security is preposterous.

San Francisco Examiner & Chronicle,
7-1:(This World)2.

Arthur F. Burns
Chairman, Federal Reserve Board

5

The fact that the Federal budget has in recent years gotten out of control should be a matter of concern to all of us. Indeed, I believe that budgetary reform has become essential to the resurgence of our democracy.

At George Washington University School of Government and Business Administration commencement/The New York Times, 6-18:22.

James MacGregor Burns
Professor of Political Science,
Williams College, Williamstown, Mass.

6

[Criticizing some members of Congress for trying to restrain the Executive power of President Nixon]: Those who praised and promoted Presidential power in behalf of social progress during the Roosevelt, Truman and Kennedy years, and who now wish to diminish the President's capacity for economic and social leadership, are exhibiting short memories. And they may be helping to produce in the future another impasse in which an innovative, progressive and socially-conscious President will be trying vainly to enact and implement programs thwarted by an essentially un-reformed and mal-representative Congress.

San Francisco Examiner, 3-15:23.

(JAMES MacGREGOR BURNS)

1

. . . one of the most blighting aspects of the Nixon Presidency—and I would say this is true to some extent of his predecessors—is the over-glamorization of the Presidency; not only the kind of thing that happens in the White House with these fancy-dressed people around there and all the excessive ceremony, which I think takes us too far away from the old Jeffersonian image of the plebian Presidency, but the response of the press—and I would actually lay some of the responsibility at the hands of you gentlemen of the press, your tendency to respond to the efforts of the White House to glamorize itself. I would like to see an attempt to cut this down, not to swallow the President's pronouncements as so terribly important . . . I would say that to de-mystify the Presidency you should pay less attention to some of these ceremonial efforts and should look even more critically at some of the President's pronouncements.

TV-radio interview, Washington/
"Meet the Press,"
National Broadcasting Company, 7-8.

Earl L. Butz
Secretary of Agriculture
of the United States

2

In the last 30 years, we have grown accustomed to the flow of power to Washington. We have gotten used to sending our money to Washington to be spent for us through nationally-stereotyped programs. One of the reasons that we [in the Nixon Administration] so strongly endorse the New Federalism is that we know it is easier to get responsible expenditures and responsive programs at the local level. The New Federalism indeed fits into the Nixon Administration's goal of getting a dollar's worth of government for every dollar spent.

Before Economic Society of
Southern Florida, Miami, Aug. 8/
Vital Speeches, 9-1:688.

Harry F. Byrd, Jr.
United States Senator, I-Virginia

3

The way I look at the question of Congres-

sional power of the purse is this: The real power Congress has is the power *not* to appropriate. That power goes back nearly a thousand years, when the representatives of the people of Britain became exercised about the extravagances of their King and took upon themselves the power of the purse which, in essence, is the power not to give the King unlimited funds. So that the power the U.S. Congress has is the power not to appropriate. Once Congress appropriates, then, to a considerable degree, the power of the purse passes out of the hands of Congress and into the hands of the Chief Executive, because it is the Chief Executive who can determine—and he is about the only person who really can determine it—the timing of the expenditures and the degree of the expenditures. So I cannot agree with the argument of those of my colleagues who contend that the President must spend all the money the Congress appropriates. I do not believe that is logical.

Before the Senate, Washington/
Human Events, 5-19:5.

Robert C. Byrd
United States Senator, D-West Virginia

4

[Advocating that remaining Cabinet members be subject to reconfirmation by the Senate when a President is re-elected for a second term]: It is ironic that the President must face the people after four years and respond to criticism over his policies and performance, while the men who perform most of the work of the Executive Branch of government do not.

Los Angeles Times, 5-3:(1)21.

Erskine Childers
President of the Republic of Ireland

5

People have come too much to rely on governments to create their societies, and that should be the function of their citizens—to decide the way they shall live, their social and moral patterns.

Interview, Dublin/
San Francisco Examiner & Chronicle,
7-22:(This World)25.

Lawton M. Chiles, Jr.
United States Senator, D-Florida

1

[Saying there should be more Senate Committee meetings open to the public]: When we read the polls and find that Congress ranks behind used-car dealers with regard to the respect that the public holds for them, then I do not think we can believe that the public believes that what we are doing is correct. They do not trust us, and one reason why they do not trust us is the number of closed doors we have here . . . I was in the Florida Legislature. I heard the argument against open meetings there. It was argued that Senators can sit together and work things out better if meetings are not open. But the legislation to open up the system was adopted . . . The Florida Legislature went from perhaps 48th in the nation to where it was rated fourth in the study conducted by the Citizens Committee or Conference on State Legislatures . . . I believe one of the finest things the Florida Legislature did was to open up its doors in order to restore some public confidence to the work that it was doing.

Before the Senate, Washington/
The Washington Post,
3-9:(A)26.

Shirley Chisholm
United States Representative, D-New York

2

[Criticizing the way Congress operates]: They have no organized system of getting legislative work done. The Congress usually meets all year round; there's no time for families. There's a constant state of anxiety because of the way in which business is done . . . All day long you're running back and forth for quorum calls; we're constantly hearing those bells in our office, and we're jumping up and down like jumping jacks. You can't think clearly that way. There's no continuity of thought.

Washington, July 5/
The New York Times,
7-6:28.

William E. Colby
Director, Central Intelligence Agency
of the United States

3

I take it as a major charge [as CIA Director] to fulfill both meanings of the word "intelligence." The one is the official meaning of an intelligence organization . . . but the second meaning is the application of the human quality of intelligence to be able to analyze facts and come out with assessments and judgments about them.

At his swearing-in ceremony, Washington,
Sept. 4/The Washington Post, 9-5:(A)2.

John B. Connally, Jr.
Former Secretary of the Treasury
of the United States;
Former Governor of Texas

4

If we don't quit blaming the President for everything that goes wrong, we're going to destroy the Presidency and, in time, our democracy. We live in very troubled times, and Congress, with all due respect, can't run this nation. The only way the nation can be run is through the Executive Branch of government. If we destroy the Presidency, we destroy the United States as you and I know it.

Los Angeles Times, 9-20:(1)28.

Alistair Cooke
Chief United States correspondent,
"The Manchester (England) Guardian"

5

[Presidential advisers have] really the force of a Politburo. The defect of the Constitution is that it does not allow Congress to pass on the men who will be the most powerful men in the country. The nub is that they are not accountable to Congress. They are all experts in artful deceit—which is what advertising is all about. Politics becomes an extension of wartime tactics.

Before Women's National Democratic
Club, Washington, May 29/
The Washington Post, 5-30:(B)2.

John Sherman Cooper
United States Senator,
R-Kentucky

1

Congress has got to reorganize its procedures. I agree with the President [Nixon] that Congress, as an institution, and its committees and means of dealing with the problems of government, are archaic. Congress is limited in its personnel, its staff; Congress can't cope with the thousands of employees in the Executive Branch. There is a great need for modern ways of working, of getting the best equipment, such as computers.

Interview,
Washington/
The Washington Post, 1-2:(A)4.

Norris Cotton
United States Senator,
R-New Hampshire

2

[On President Nixon's impounding of Congressionally-allocated funds]: In at least two recent instances, Congress has increased appropriation bills in defiance of the budget recommendations of the President and of its own appropriation committees to such an extent that the whole body knew it had reached a fantastic figure impossible to justify. To remedy this, Congress actually inserted a provision authorizing the President to reduce any or all items up to a certain per cent. There never has been a more blatant example of spinelessness on the part of a legislative body. After this weak-kneed behavior, it's truly amazing to hear the outcries that the President is usurping the powers of Congress by refusing to spend part of the funds it has appropriated. How can he do otherwise? He has no power to impose new taxes to produce the money to satisfy these demands, nor can he keep on borrowing without exceeding the debt limit that Congress has determined. If he has cut in the wrong places, that, too, is the fault of the Congress for not facing up to its Constitutional duty by doing its own pruning.

Human Events, 2-17:1.

Alan Cranston
United States Senator,
D-California

3

The Presidency must be a constant target of vigilance—by the Congress, the courts, the people, and by the occupant of the White House himself—lest it exceed Constitutional restraints. There is far less danger of arbitrary use of power by the Congress which, in a very real sense, is the spiritual embodiment of representative democracy. The very pluralism and factionalism that are decried as weaknesses of Congress are also the sources of its strengths.

Quote, 8-26:204.

4

Freedom is safe only where governmental power is diffused. No society will long remain free where governmental power remains overly concentrated in the hands of one man. Concentrated power tends to become the absolute power.

Quote, 9-9:241.

Walter Cronkite
News commentator,
Columbia Broadcasting System

5

[On the leaking of classified government documents to the press, etc.]: . . . I don't think an individual is entitled to know what is inside secret files while they're still secret. Please understand, however, that I'm for complete declassification of secret papers. Over-classification is one of the areas in which the Federal government is terribly culpable. But I think we have to get at it through legal means. I don't believe we have any right to violate the law. I'm a real old-fashioned guy in that sense: I believe in law and order.

Interview, New York/
Playboy, June:78.

John C. Culver
United States Representative, D-Iowa

6

Since I've come to Congress, almost every one of the major public-policy questions before the country is different and new . . .

and yet, if you look at the scaffolding of committee jurisdiction, you can't help but be struck with the fact that so much of it mirrors a 19th-century America. We have a Committee on Agriculture, but we have no committee on urban America, where 77 per cent of our people live.

Interview, Washington/
The Washington Post, 4-12:(H)2.

William O. Douglas
Associate Justice,
Supreme Court of the United States

1

I've been in Washington, D.C., long enough to realize that people here get the idea that they sort of run the country, own the country, control the country. But we're all pretty minor characters . . . The people of this country are the sovereigns. They can make it exactly the kind of country they want.

News conference, Washington, Oct. 29/
Los Angeles Times, 10-30:(1)5.

John D. Ehrlichman
Assistant to the President
of the United States for Domestic Affairs

2

[On President Nixon's impounding of Congressionally-allocated funds]: The Congress appropriates, but the President is charged by law with expending; and the laws impose on him the duty to make savings and to spend only at a rate which is not wasteful.

Interview, Washington, Feb. 4/
The Washington Post, 2-5:(A)4.

John D. Ehrlichman
Former Assistant to the President
of the United States for Domestic Affairs

3

Our political system and our real governmental institutions are not just the buildings and the laws and the traditions that one sees here in the city of Washington. Our government and our politics are only as idealistic as the people in those buildings who administer the laws and run the campaigns and fulfill the traditions . . . We are either going to have highly-motivated able people running the po-

litical campaigns and filling the offices in government or we will surely have seat-warmers and hacks who will fill these places, and the country will be the worse for it. People must be attracted who will come here to fight for what they believe in and to work long hours to get things done. I hope that young people don't stay away; I hope they come here and apply their idealism and their enthusiasm and their high moral principles. I hope they come and test their ideas and their convictions in this marketplace. I hope they do come and do better . . . If you [young people] go to work for the President and the Executive Branch, there are very few in the Congress or the media that are going to throw rosebuds at you. If you favor change in what our government is and what it does in our society, you will have to fight for it. No such thing has been won here by default, at least not recently. And be prepared to defend your sense of values when you come here, too. You will encounter a local culture which scoffs at patriotism and family life and morality just as it adulates the opposite; and you will find some people who have fallen for that line. But you will also find in politics and government many great people who know that a pearl of great price is not had for the asking, and who feel that this country and its heritage are worth the work, the abuse, the struggle and the sacrifices. Don't stay away. Come and join them and do it better.

At Senate Watergate hearings,
Washington, July 30/
The New York Times, 7-31:23.

Julie Nixon Eisenhower
Daughter of President Richard Nixon

4

[Saying President Nixon relaxes best away from the White House]: This is just a pressure-box atmosphere. If we could live anywhere else, it would be just great. I guess it's because the phones are always ringing. People are always around. It's a museum. It's not really a home. Beyond that, my father is the kind of man who needs time away, where he can think. It's the beautiful view, to be able to look out and see the trees and see the

(JULIE NIXON EISENHOWER)

flowers, to look up from the blue chair at Camp David and think. It's such a different feeling.

Interview, Washington/
The New York Times, 11-4:(1)81.

Sam J. Ervin, Jr.
United States Senator,
D-North Carolina

1

[Saying the Presidential appointment of the Director of the Office of Management and Budget should be subject to Senate confirmation]: The Director of the OMB in many respects is the deputy President of the United States. This agency has become the arm by which the President exercises power over every facet of the Executive Branch. Certainly, the Congress and the American people should have an opportunity to scrutinize any official who will exercise powers as extensive as those possessed by the OMB and to pass upon his qualifications.

Washington, Jan. 23/
The Washington Post, 1-25:(A)16.

2

I consider the question of Executive impoundment of [Congressionally-] appropriated funds very crucial. Now, if Congress does recapture the power of the purse, it has a solemn obligation to make sure that funds appropriated are compromised to the money on hand.

Interview/
U.S. News & World Report, 2-12:38.

3

The history of mankind shows that governments have an insatiable thirst for power. This desire for power will carry them to tyranny unless it is prevented.

Time, 2-19:22.

4

[On the refusal of some White House aides to testify before Congressional Committees]: I'd recommend to the Senate [that] they send the Sergeant-at-Arms of the Senate to arrest a White House aide or any other witness who refuses to appear . . . The President [Nixon] has some peculiar notions about Executive privilege. And I'd suggest to the White House aides that, if anybody has to go to jail on account of the invocation of Executive privilege, that it will not be the President—it will be the White House aides.

TV-radio interview/"Face the Nation,"
Columbia Broadcasting System, 3-18.

5

[Addressing a Justice Department witness who testified that Presidential impoundment of Congressionally-authorized funds is Constitutional but who could not come up with exact citations to that effect from the Constitution]: You remind me, sir, of the preacher in North Carolina who was fired by his congregation, and they gave no reason for firing him. So he went to the chairman of the board of deacons and he asked why he had been expelled from his job as parson. He asked the chairman, "Don't I argufy?" The chairman said, "You sure do argufy." He asked, "Don't I sputeify?" He said, "You sure do sputeify." So the preacher said, "Well, what's the trouble?" The chairman said, "You don't show wherein" . . . [I] am compelled to say that, like the preacher, you did not show wherein.

At Senate committee hearing, Washington/
The Christian Science Monitor, 4-13:3.

6

In recent years, the First Amendment's guaranty of freedom of expression has come under considerable attack. All branches of government, at almost every level, have been tempted to interfere with the gathering, editing, publication or distribution of information to the American people. Increased government subpoenaing of newsmen, the Justice Department's effort to enjoin publication of [the] so-called "Pentagon Papers" and expanding government control and regulation of broadcasting are just a few of the reminders that government cannot be trusted to honor the commandments of the First Amendment.

Quote, 6-10:530.

7

Some people believe in a doctrine of inherent powers [of the Presidency]. I do not believe the President has any power at all except such as the Constitution expressly gives him or such as are necessarily inferred from the expression of those powers. I think the Constitution was written that way to keep the President, and of course the Congress, from exercising tyrannical power.

At Senate Watergate hearings, Washington, July 25/The Washington Post, 7-26:(A)27.

1

I think we've had the unfortunate thing of glorifying high officials lately and attributing to them all wisdom; and those of us who stay on the Washington scene find out that they are just like the rest of us, that they too have feet of clay. And I wouldn't disillusion young people; I think they ought to recognize all human beings have feet of clay.

The Washington Post, 8-12:(F)3.

Daniel J. Evans
Governor of Washington

2

I am for [President] Nixon's special revenue-sharing program. The concept is vital. The program of categorical grants has bogged down. Special revenue-sharing means that a greater part of the dollar goes to the ultimate beneficiary.

U.S. News & World Report, 3-12:77.

3

In my view, there is nothing more essential than that the President of the United States be given the opportunity to see and be seen—personally and informally—by the people . . . The modern-day tragedy of the Presidency is that he is quite literally the prisoner of Pennsylvania Avenue.

At National Press Club, Washington/ Los Angeles Times, 9-3:(2)7.

Houston I. Flournoy
California State Controller

4

The Federal government, which has a current deficit estimated at $30 billion, is sending revenue-sharing checks to the states which have a reported surplus this year that approximates $18 billion. At least 30 states, in addition to California, are considering tax reduction or rebates. A number of states are reportedly using their revenue-sharing funds to invest, at least temporarily, in Federal securities. In other words, the Federal government is borrowing these funds back from state and local governments in order to pay their bills which include these payments to the state.

San Francisco Examiner, 3-22:30.

Gerald R. Ford
United States Representative, R-Michigan; Vice President-designate of the United States

5

We are going to have to trim back on legislation, now on the way to Congressional passage, which would break the President's budget by a highly inflationary $7 billion. If necessary, the President [Nixon] stands ready to veto some of these budget-busting bills, however well-intentioned they may be. If necessary, he will also continue to use the fiscal tool of reserving expenditure of certain appropriated funds. But I would hope that we can begin now to move away from this kind of Executive-Legislative confrontation . . . toward a new spirit of constructive cooperation . . . I want to make a contribution to this process.

Before Southern Manufactured Housing Institute, Knoxville, Tenn., Oct. 19/ Los Angeles Herald-Examiner, 10-19:(A)2.

6

I don't think the President has unlimited authority in the area of Executive privilege . . . However, I don't think Congress and the public have an unlimited right to personal communications between the President and his advisers or any documents that go between a President and his advisers.

At Senate Rules Committee hearing on his nomination for Vice President, Washington, Nov. 1/ The Washington Post, 11-2:(A)8.

Gerald R. Ford
Vice President-designate of the United States

7

. . . truth is the glue that holds government

(GERALD R. FORD)

together; compromise is the oil that makes government go.

At House Judiciary Committee hearing on his nomination for Vice President, Washington/The Christian Science Monitor, 11-16:14.

Gerald R. Ford
Vice President of the United States

1

Unquestionably, there has been a transition of power from the Congress to the Executive. I think most of it took place during World War II and subsequent periods of military conflict. There has also been some authority given up by Congress, even in peacetime. In many instances, I would say the Congress has done this willingly. But, to some extent, Congress may have been bludgeoned into it. I hear these cries that Congress is not going to give up any more power to the President and is going to retrieve some that it has already given up. Yet, in this legislation to deal with the energy emergency, Congress is giving up potentially more authority than it has given up in almost any other area . . . I wish Congress would stop protesting about loss of power one day and then giving up more power the next day, figuratively speaking.

Interview, Washington/ U.S. News & World Report, 12-17:30.

J. William Fulbright
United States Senator, D-Arkansas

2

[On government classification, such as of the "Pentagon Papers" on Vietnam leaked to the press in 1971]: Most of the material should not have been secret in the first place. You are almost bound to get this kind of leak. I still don't see the harm that came from it, other than the fact that there is involved a violation of the law [by those who leaked them]. That is bad. I don't believe in trusting the judgment of anyone and everybody to make that decision. In other words, I can disapprove of the leaking of documents, but at the same time I disapprove just as heartily of the abuse of the classification power.

Interview, Washington/ The Christian Science Monitor, 7-18:8.

Barry M. Goldwater
United States Senator, R-Arizona

3

[On the dismissal of the "Pentagon Papers" case because of government misconduct]: As we all know, nothing was settled at the time Judge W. Matthew Byrne, Jr., dismissed the charges against Daniel Ellsberg and Anthony Russo, Jr., for the theft and distribution of classified government material known in the press as the "Pentagon Papers." After all these months of litigation, we still do not know whether people who steal classified information and make it public are to be held accountable under the laws. Nor do we know whether the defense contention that laws protecting classified information run counter to the First Amendment [has] any legal validity. Thanks to a group of ill-advised government officials who felt that it was proper and necessary to take the law into their own hands to speed the conviction of civilians who had taken the law into their own hands, there are now no rules governing the theft and dissemination of classified government documents. Thanks to a group of self-appointed government officials . . . it is now possible for anybody with a purpose to leak any kind of information he can get his hands on. Thanks to stupidity on the part of the government, nothing was settled [at the trial] in Los Angeles. Ellsberg and Russo were not convicted of their crimes; nor were they vindicated on the charges. In fact, nobody won in the "Pentagon Papers" case except muckrakers in the press who trade upon revealing secret government information and zealots within the government who believe, like Ellsberg, that their judgment is superior to that of men elected to operate the government, and who feel that any means—even stealing classified materials—is justified to make their point with the public.

Before the Senate, Washington, May 14/ The Washington Post, 5-16:(A)18.

Fred I. Greenstein
Professor of Law, Politics and Society,
Princeton University

1

. . . we all know that the invisible Presidency and the institutionalized Presidency in an expanded White House have been a particular phenomenon of the period since the New Deal. It's not just the way in which the Presidency has taken over the Executive Office Building and the catacombs underneath, but the way in which it has successfully mined the entire Federal government and the military establishment for its physical wherewithal.

Panel discussion, New Orleans/
The Washington Post, 9-16:(C)1.

Mark O. Hatfield
United States Senator, R-Oregon

2

"Community control"; "home rule"; "participatory democracy"—whatever the nomenclature used, it refers to restoring the sovereignty of the people through powerful, community-based self-government. It is what I prefer to call "neighborhood government" . . . this requires that far more of the money which is paid to government remain at the local level. This must not be confused with revenue-sharing, which I regard, quite candidly, as a hoax which will probably increase rather than diminish the power of the Federal government. Let me give you a challenge. Take some unit of local government—a small country, a town, a neighborhood—and analyze its taxes. Discover how much its citizens and corporations are paying to the Federal and even the state government. Then calculate how much they are getting in return from that government in services. Then do an inventory of the needs of the community—the number of hospital beds, of schools, of better houses, of tutorial programs, etc. And finally, decide whether that community would better meet its needs if it could retain a high portion of those tax revenues, utilizing them directly and locally as they see fit. The United States is becoming a badly-planned, centralized society. We must act to take the only other realistic option—a de-centralized society with planning and self-government empowered at the local level.

Before Ripon Society/
The Washington Post, 1-4:(A)14.

3

Most people believe the Federal government has grown too big, that it spends far too much money, that what it does spend is frequently wasted, that it has lost touch with the citizens, that it employs too many presumptuous bureaucrats and that it blunders on, not in control of itself nor controlled by others. And they are right.

San Francisco Examiner & Chronicle,
4-22:(This World)2.

4

We have demanded of our President a combination of a tribal chief, a bishop, an instigator of political reform, an economic manipulator and a soothsayer for all of our fears for the future. No man can hold that kind of responsibility without the collective prayers of all Americans and without having to share that responsibility with all Americans.

San Francisco Examiner, 11-12:32.

Lawrence J. Hogan
United States Representative, R-Maryland

5

[Saying Congressional salaries are too low]: . . . all of us [in Congress] who come from the private sector see our personal finances eroding year after year while our contemporaries continue to have increases and are making substantially more money than we are . . . I have seen my colleagues in very serious financial situations, trying to educate their children in college and trying to borrow money to mortgage their future just to be able to afford their children what their contemporaries in the outside world just take for granted.

Human Events, 7-28:3.

William H. Hudnut III
United States Representative, R-Indiana

5

[Abraham Lincoln] kept reminding the American people that government was the public's business, that political pragmatism

177

(WILLIAM H. HUDNUT III)

must yield to political morality and that doing the right as God gave him to see the right should never be abandoned for the sake of political expediency. An awareness of the transcendent sovereignty of God, before whose throne the nations rise and pass away, is necessary if we are going to avoid moral decay, both personal and national.

Sermon at White House worship service, Washington, Oct. 14/ San Francisco Examiner, 10-15:18.

Harold E. Hughes
United States Senator, D-Iowa

1

I have long believed that government will change for the better only when people change for the better in their hearts.

News conference, Des Moines, Iowa, Sept. 6/The New York Times, 9-7:23.

2

This nation is on the edge of a precipice. The government will not make the decisions that are necessary unless the people set higher standards and demand these decisions. We raked across the world with our misuse of power; we are raping our natural resources for private profit—and the government will not solve these problems unless the people require it.

Quote, 10-21:386.

Hubert H. Humphrey
United States Senator, D-Minnesota

3

The budgetary process of the United States makes a mockery of democracy. There is no room for citizens or Congressional participation until the budget comes here to us [from the Executive Branch] as a total package conceived in the most complete secrecy.

San Francisco Examiner, 2-23:38.

William H. Hunt
Chairman, Louisiana-Pacific Corporation

4

. . . there is a growing sense of despair in the ability of the government to solve the nation's ills. I am not referring here to philos-

ophies of the political left or right, but rather to a mood which one senses among the people themselves. They see that the government has poured vast sums into social programs, they see that the government has passed endless laws, they see that agencies have adopted endless regulations, and they ask themselves: "What good has it done?" Maybe the real debate in our society takes place beyond the pale of government. Maybe the real debate in our society takes place among the people themselves. It's the people who have shaped our institutions, and it's the people who will change our institutions. And maybe the primary function of government is to make sure the people have the ability to throw their weight around . . . If we preserve our freedom to act and react, we will create the sort of society which best serves us all.

At California State University, San Diego, May 10/Vital Speeches, 8-15:647.

Lee A. Iacocca
President, Ford Motor Company

5

One of the things the government can't do is run anything. The only things our government runs are the Post Office and the railroads, and both of them are bankrupt.

Quote, 6-17:553.

Jenkin Lloyd Jones
Editor and publisher, "The Tulsa Tribune"

6

[On the 18-year-old vote]: In the state of New York, on the eve of one's twenty-first birthday, one is still supposed to be such a child that one isn't supposed to know enough not to shoot a cop. But we have decided that three years before reaching age twenty-one, one knows enough to pick a President of the United States.

Before Ohio Chamber of Commerce, Columbus, March 14/ Vital Speeches, 5-15:474.

Barbara Jordan
United States Representative, D-Texas

7

Congress must regain the will to govern. We

cannot forget that last October the House passed a spending ceiling which surrendered all discretion over budget cuts to the President, reflecting Congress' appalling willingness to shrug off the responsibility for difficult decisions and leave them to the President. We must be willing to take the political heat involved in making hard choices between competing public needs.

Before the House, Washington, April 18/The New York Times, 4-24:22.

Vernon E. Jordan, Jr.
Executive director, National Urban League

1

The proposed [Nixon] special revenue-sharing approach breaks faith not only with poor people, but with local governments as well. What Washington gives with one hand it takes with the other. Mayors who once hungered for no-strings-attached bloc grants are now panicked by the realization that the funds they receive will be inadequate to meet the needs of their communities and will be less than their cities get in the current categorical-aid programs. In addition, there is the probability that future special revenue-sharing funds will continue to shrink. Rather than shifting power to the people, the new American counter-revolution creates a vacuum in responsible power. We must not forget, as so many have, that Federal programs today embody local initiatives and local decision-making. The myth of the Washington bureaucrat making decisions for people 3,000 miles away is false. The money often comes from the Federal Treasury; the broad program goals and definitions of national need come, as they should, from Congress. But the specific program proposals, their implementation and their support come from local governments, citizens and agencies. Those Federal dollars that are now deemed tainted actually enable local citizens to meet local problems under the umbrella of national financial and moral leadership. To shift the center of gravity away from national leadership [through revenue-sharing] is to compound the drift and inertia that appear to

categorize our society today.

At National Press Club, Washington/ The Christian Science Monitor, 4-10:(B)16.

Jack Kemp
United States Representative, R-New York

2

[Approving of President Nixon's Federal budget which cuts back on expenditures in some areas]: The budget squeeze has promptly separated the "bad guys" from the "good guys." The bad guys are marked as plainly as in any Western: They like the new budget because they don't care about the poor or the environment; they ignore our great social needs; they don't want to pay taxes and want only to cater to their crude materialistic values. The good guys do care, and they are outraged at the program cuts; they are willing to see taxes go up; and they can point to any number of ways of bringing in revenues by taxing types of income they may wish they had but do not. This tendency of the good guys to fund their social concern with other people's money explains why right now they sound so unconvincing.

Before the House, Washington, Feb. 8/Vital Speeches, 3-15:350.

Edward M. Kennedy
United States Senator, D-Massachusetts

3

Almost never in its arguments does the Postal Service raise its sights above the dollar sign. I would have liked to see some substantial indications that the Service is sensitive to more than just the economic argument, some recognition that other basic issues are also at stake in the present controversy [over increasing postage rates]—issues like freedom of the press, the First Amendment, the flow of ideas in our free society, and a deep-rooted hallowed historical practice going back to the days of Benjamin Franklin. If only we could be convinced that the Postmaster General is paying as much attention to the Constitution and American history as he is to his office balance sheet.

Feb. 8/Quote, 3-25:276.

179

(EDWARD M. KENNEDY)

No government can grant us . . . freedom.[1] We must find [freedom] for ourselves. We cannot find it when the conditions of our daily life are determined by remote officials in distant places. States and communities and individuals must reclaim that power which has been absorbed by bureaucracies ignorant of their needs and interests.

At Independence Day celebration,
Decatur, Alabama, July 4/
The Christian Science Monitor, 7-7:6.

George Kinnear
President,
National Association of Tax Administrators

Qualified authorities say that we have a more than adequate tax base in this country to support government at all levels. But our present intergovernmental fiscal structure cannot allocate support to the lower governmental levels in an efficient manner. The Federal government has the most growth-responsive revenues, while state and local governments have the most rapidly growing expenditure requirements. Washington also has a great advantage because the larger a government's territorial dimensions, the less concern it has that taxpayers will move to escape taxes. Also, its opportunities to benefit from the economies of large-scale operations are greater. The relation between state and local revenues and the development of an efficient, coordinated tax structure is a subject that has been too long ignored. It calls for emergency consideration. Our system of Federalism requires vitality and efficiency at all levels of government, and this requires well-planned coordination.

Interview/Nation's Business, April: 74.

Henry A. Kissinger
Assistant to the President
of the United States for
National Security Affairs

I first saw government at a high level in the early 1960s—at a time which is now occasionally debunked as overly brash, excessively optimistic, even somewhat arrogant. Some of these criticisms are justified. But a spirit prevailed then which was quintessentially American: that problems are a challenge, not an alibi; that men are measured not only by their success but also by their striving; that it is better to aim grandly than to wallow in mediocre comfort. Above all, government and opponents thought of themselves in a common enterprise—not in a permanent, irreconcilable contest.

Before Federal City Club, Washington/
Los Angeles Times, 4-17:(2)7.

Henry A. Kissinger
Secretary of State-designate
of the United States

[On the Nixon Administration's relations with Congress]: . . . what do we mean by bipartisanship? We do not ask for rubber-stamping, and we cannot expect unanimity. Serious people obviously will continue to have differences. Where profound disagreements exist, it would be self-defeating to paper them over with empty formulae. We, in turn, cannot give up basic principles, nor can we promise to act only when there is bipartisan agreement, though this will be our preference. But we shall work to shape a broad consensus on our national goals and to confine differences to tactical issues. When our views differ, we shall strive not to press the debate to a point that tears the over-all fabric of the national consensus . . .

At Senate Foreign Relations Committee
hearing on his confirmation, Washington/
The National Observer, 9-15:3.

Melvin R. Laird
Counsellor to the President of the
United States for Domestic Affairs

For foreign policy and national security, the President gave us the Nixon Doctrine and its principles of partnership, strength and a willingness to negotiate. The Nixon Doctrine and the concept of burden-sharing in foreign policy is not much different than the concept of revenue-sharing, which is the cornerstone of our domestic policy. In both concepts, you put some faith and trust in the ability of the people who are living with the problem at the local level—whether in Marshfield, Wisconsin, or Saigon [South Vietnam]—to have the competence, the will and the desire to solve the problems that threaten them if only they can get the resources. Vietnamization has proved itself so far, just as revenue-sharing is proving itself. What we need more than ever is the continued understanding and support of Congress and the American people to keep implementing these programs that are so much more in keeping with the demands and the requirements of the final third of the twentieth century.

Interview, Washington/
U.S. News & World Report, 9-17:35.

Alfred M. Landon
Former Governor of Kansas

1

Even those "liberals" who advocated centralization of power are now seeing the end result. In 1936, I pointed out exactly what was going to occur when I talked about the centralization of power in Washington—the short-circuiting of the state governments by encouraging municipalities to deal directly with the Federal government in Washington. Now this long march of what was called "liberal" legislation is reaching a point which appalls some of those who advocated that kind of legislation; and they're beginning to call for a reversal. They see how far the Congress has gone in yielding power [to the Executive], not only in permitting a planned economy by the Federal government, but things such as the Gulf of Tonkin Resolution which President [Lyndon] Johnson interpreted as giving him a free hand to assume the guardianship of all Asia. What we have today as a result of that trend of the last 40 years are big government, big business and big labor —and individuals don't count for much.

Interview, Topeka, Kan./
U.S. News & World Report, 5-21:23.

Christopher Lasch
Historian

2

The people, because they have been lied to so often, have grown suspicious of men in power. They are convinced that only untrustworthy people are likely to rise to power in political institutions . . . Indeed, they are losing confidence in all of our institutions and are sinking into earthly cynicism.

At Center for the Study of Democratic
Institutions, Santa Barbara, Calif./
The Dallas Times Herald, 12-16:(A)28.

Robert L. Leggett
United States Representative,
D-California

3

[Urging Congress to reassert its governmental powers]: Let's face it: We're naive idiots. We've abdicated our powers to the President and his Cabinet, the Governors and the cities. It's going to take a powerful lot of organizing to get out of this mess.

The Sacramento (Calif.) Bee, 1-10:(A)19.

John V. Lindsay
Mayor of New York

4

[On the time he spent as a Congressman in the House of Representatives]: I liked the House; I found it a remarkable institution. But I think if you stay there too long everybody tends to become mediators. You become a skilled craftsman at the business of legislating, but you tend to become isolated in a curious way. There's too much marble all around.

Interview, New York/
The New York Times, 12-23:(1)20.

Arthur S. Link
Professor of American History,
Princeton University

5

. . . the imperial dimensions of the Presidency do not mean that the incumbent of that office has to yield to the seductive temptations the office holds out. The Presidency requires a man of very great moral

(ARTHUR S. LINK)

strength—more so than any other office in the world, because it does have such power, such opportunities for the exercise of power. The Presidency does not have the restraints on it, for example, that the British cabinet system does or that other major governments impose.

Interview, Princeton, N.J./
Los Angeles Times, 5-16:(2)7.

Walter Lippmann
Author; Former political columnist

1

[On President Nixon's use of Executive privilege to prevent his aides from testifying before Congress]: While there obviously has to be some kind of Executive privilege, it must be used with the utmost discretion and restraint. Our system of government will simply not work if any principle is pushed to an extreme. There must be respect for the rules on the part of everybody—the President, the Congress, the courts. The men who wrote the Constitution were rational gentlemen. They knew the system they were devising could not work unless the rules were respected. Their primary assumption was that the kind of people who were running the government would play by the rules. If the President refuses to do this, nothing works and you don't have our Constitutional system.

Interview/
The Washington Post, 3-25:(C)4.

George H. Mahon
United States Representative, D-Texas

2

The differences between the White House and Congress are very serious, because I do not feel the President [Nixon] has the broad authority which he has exercised to impound [Congressionally-appropriated] funds. I don't think he has the authority under the law just to, willy-nilly, eliminate programs or drastically to reduce them on the ground that he doesn't think they're effective. After all, a law is a law. I think that's going to be a major issue.

Interview/
U.S. News & World Report, 2-12:37.

Frederic V. Malek
Deputy Director,
Federal Office of Management and Budget

3

[Defending the Federal revenue-sharing program against charges that some funds are being squandered by local governments for low-priority projects such as bridle paths and tennis courts]: One community's necessity is another community's trivia. And it is not up to Washington or anyone else to tell local communities how to spend their funds. The officials in the communities should make the decision. If wrong, they will be locally accountable.

At U.S. Conference of Mayors,
San Francisco, June 18/
Los Angeles Times, 6-19:(1)20.

Marvin Mandel
Governor of Maryland

4

I think that what is happening as a result of [the] Watergate [political-espionage affair] is that we are seeing a revival of the institutions, the very institutions of government, the Judiciary, the Congress, taking over and re-establishing itself as an important part of our Constitutional government. Where the Executive has pre-empted the field for quite a few years, now the other institutions of government are reasserting themselves, and I think the confidence of the people will be restored because of that.

TV-radio interview,
San Francisco/"Meet the Press,"
National Broadcasting Company, 6-3.

Mike Mansfield
United States Senator, D-Montana

5

. . . the President [Nixon], fundamentally, is a loner . . . But unfortunately, when you get away from Washington, if you do it too much, you lose touch with events as they are really happening, and you don't have the contacts you should have. The end result is that the government suffers to a degree because of the lack of this cooperation, this accommodation, this partnership which is so vital to the functioning of this republic. If you don't have this relationship of President and Congress, it throws the whole ship of state out of kilter . . . Our government operates on a very delicate balance; and when that balance is disturbed, we get into serious difficulties.

Interview, Washington/
The Christian Science Monitor, 6-25:2.

Charles McC. Mathias, Jr.
United States Senator, R-Maryland

1

. . . breaches of public trust [in government] have occurred in large measure because men of great ability and talent have been loyal to their superiors or their department . . . rather than living up to their solemn oath to defend the Constitution and the law . . . If there is a conflict of loyalties which a high official cannot resolve, he should be expected to resign from his office. The only way to restore confidence and trust throughout our society is for everyone who shares the privilege of leadership to obey the law, and to meet the small questions and the great issues with equal courage.

Before the Senate, Washington, March 29/
The Washington Post, 3-30:(A)7.

David R. Mayhew
Associate Professor of Political Science,
Yale University

2

The only important thing a Vice President does is take over if a President dies. It makes little difference what a Vice President does while he waits. It makes a great deal of difference what kind of man is doing the waiting.

The National Observer, 11-17:7.

Eugene J. McCarthy
Former United States Senator,
D-Minnesota

3

I would eliminate the office of the Vice President and simply set up one process by which the President can be replaced if he dies

or is disabled, and another to be used if he is in disgrace, is either impeached or resigns under pressure.

Rome, Nov. 11/
Los Angeles Times, 11-12:(1)16.

Paul N. McCloskey, Jr.
United States Representative, R-California

4

For too long, I think, we have sought to deify our national leaders. A President is a man, not a God. His task is to see that the laws are faithfully executed, not to rule as some sort of emperor with divine guidance. A little humility in the White House could be a refreshing thing.

At Senate confirmation hearing for
Vice President-designate Gerald Ford,
Washington/
San Francisco Examiner & Chronicle,
11-11:(A)12.

Paul W. McCracken
Former Chairman,
Council of Economic Advisers to the
President of the United States

5

We must avoid the assumption that red ink [in the Federal budget] is akin to fiscal sin. [However] we must avoid the opposite mistake of trying to dismiss it as if only the hair shirts, those who haven't cottoned to modern wisdom, should worry about it.

The Dallas Times Herald, 1-30:(D)5.

Frank McGee
Television commentator, "Today" show,
National Broadcasting Company

6

Will Rogers once said, "As our government deteriorates, our humor increases." If that is true, this should be the most hilarious time in our history.

Quote, 11-11:457.

George S. McGovern
United States Senator, D-South Dakota

7

[Criticizing the increasing power and influence of the Presidency]: Fundamentally, we

(GEORGE S. McGOVERN)

have experienced an exhaustion of important institutions in America. Today, only the Presidency is activist and strong, while other traditional centers of power are timid and depleted . . . This is not the way of a government of laws or even of men, but of one man. Today, the United States seems to be moving dangerously in that direction. The Congress seems incapable of stopping what it opposes or of securing what it seeks . . . And it may fairly be asked whether the Congress of the United States in the seventh decade of this century is in peril of going the way of the [British] House of Lords in the first decade. The difference is that the diminution of the Lords made English government more democratic, while the diminution of the Congress makes American government more dictatorial.

Lecture at Oxford University, England, Jan. 21/The Washington Post, 1-22:(A)1,5.

1

[On the increasing power of the Executive Branch in government-spending decisions]: . . . today in Washington, at the center of our system, Congress and the Executive are more at odds than at any time in recent years. The real issue is not the size of the budget, but what is the most sensible way to allocate that budget; not whether we should reduce wasteful programs, but who should decide what is wasteful and determine national priorities . . . It does no good to talk about bringing power closer to the people and reducing the power of the bureaucracy when, in fact, a more powerful bureaucracy is making decisions the people's representatives may not approve and cannot change.

Before South Dakota Legislature, Pierre, Feb. 12/ The Washington Post, 2-13:(A)6.

2

I concede that public and partisan debate makes a democracy's decision-making process messier and more confusing than a dictatorship's. [But] I believe that strength resides in the more disorderly democratic process that can never be made up for by the tidiness of absolutism.

At "Pacem in Terris" conference, Washington, Oct. 11/The Washington Post, 10-12:(A)2.

George Meany
President, American Federation of Labor-Congress of Industrial Organizations

3

The tools of those [in government] who would invade an individual's right of privacy are the tools of repression, thought-control and tyranny. Wiretaps, hidden microphones, closed-circuit television monitoring people innocently pursuing their daily lives, lie detectors, tape recorders, personnel questionnaires, computer data banks, peepholes, cameras, spyglasses, private detectives—all have been and are being used to intrude upon the privacy of individuals under the guise that this is "necessary" . . . Certainly, an Administration is inconvenienced at times by a free press or by demonstrators exercising their rights of assembly and petition. But it is far better for any Administration to be inconvenienced than that freedom be banished. The issue today is the rights of the people. Are they to be protected? Is government to be permitted to decide which laws are going to be obeyed by whom and when? Are Americans going to be governed by laws or by whim?

Labor Day message, Washington, Aug. 31/ The New York Times, 9-1:36.

Wilbur D. Mills
United States Representative, D-Arkansas

4

Far from being a system in or at the edge of crisis, this system today is more accurately past the crisis and moving out of the valley . . . There may be a state of shock within some quarters of the Executive Branch; but let no one in this or other lands forget that the Executive Branch is not the sum of the government of the United States. It is here on this [Capitol] Hill that the people are represented . . . it is here [in the Congress] that the voices of the American people are being heard saying, "Get America moving again."

Before the House, Washington, May 30/ The Washington Post, 5-31:(A)4.

Newton N. Minow
Former Chairman,
Federal Communications Commission

1

We think the Congress has been asleep to the importance of television [coverage of Congressional sessions]. We think Congress has been negligent in carrying its views and its issues to the people. We think it wrong that the number of people who can attend a Congressional session now is limited to the number of people who can get passes to sit in the small visitors' gallery . . . Congress should be on television, live on all the networks, to carry their views live to the American people.

News conference, New York, Oct. 24/
The Washington Post, 10-25:(A)5.

Walter F. Mondale
United States Senator, D-Minnesota

2

[New laws are needed to maintain] an open and legal Presidency, with strong safeguards to protect against the abuses of Presidential power . . . We have begun to create a monarchy out of an office intended to be the bulwark of a democracy.

Before the Senate, Washington, Sept. 17/
San Francisco Examiner, 9-17:15.

3

I want a strong President, who is strong enough to do what needs to be done to meet our adversaries overseas, to solve our problems here at home. But what bothers me is that, in my opinion, over the last 40 years—I think we see the ultimate under this President [Nixon], but it has been true under previous Presidents —through a series of developments and precedents our Presidents have really gotten to such a point that they seem larger than the law . . . Increasingly, Presidents seem to feel they have the power to break the law, and those around them apparently feel they have the power to break the law. We have got a new system of what you might call official lawlessness; and the American people have gotten a whiff of this now and they want it stopped.

TV-radio interview, Washington/
"Meet the Press,"
National Broadcasting Company, 9-30.

4

We have permitted the institution of the Presidency to become larger than life and larger than the law. And one way in which we've done that is to permit an almost unlimited expenditure of funds to permit the President to live in the way he deems that he should . . . Now, I think the President should live in luxury. I think he should live at a level that permits him to receive and entertain foreign dignitaries and do what needs to be done. But I think there ought to be a limit on his expenses, just as on every other American's, as to how much of this he needs. And I think it's gone too far.

Los Angeles Times, 10-16:(1)22.

Malcolm C. Moos
President, University of Minnesota

5

The conflict between the need to know and the right not to tell in the highest councils of government has become the spectre that haunts every headline. Hanging over all of us like the deadliest of all mists is not disillusionment, not despair, not disenchantment, not even distrust—but disbelief. Stated with the bark off of it, it has become difficult to believe in the existence of objective truth.

At University of Notre Dame commencement,
May 20/Quote, 8-26:208.

John E. Moss
United States Representative, D-California

6

[Criticizing President Nixon's appointment of General Alexander Haig as his Assistant and White House Chief of Staff]: The Haig matter is only the latest, most vivid illustration of this cumulative erosion of the barrier separating political roles and military professionals . . . Increasing reliance by American Presidents on the [White House] National Security Council and its staff, instead of the State Department, means that an organization with strong military orientation has replaced an overwhelmingly civilian institution as the central advisory organ for American foreign policy . . . General Haig hails from a hierarchical rather than egalitarian organization. He is oriented to a group rather than to rights of

185

(JOHN E. MOSS)

individuals. He stresses obedience and discipline rather than freedom of expression. While I am sure he is a decent, honorable man, the President, by placing him in the most de facto political position in Washington, has elevated those very virtues that are the blatant negation of what this nation and our society stand for.

June 11/The Washington Post, 6-13:(A)14.

Edmund S. Muskie
United States Senator, D-Maine

1

[Criticizing President Nixon's new budget that shifts more responsibility to state and local governments through revenue-sharing, etc.]: Does the new budget really deliver on that promise to help local initiative, or does it, as I suspect, simply shift to local taxpayers new burdens that will only deepen popular resentment of government? . . . Self-reliance means that state government or local government or those least able to pay the costs will have to pay the bills . . . [Most cities use revenue-sharing funds] for capital improvements, official salaries, public safety and tax relief. In one instance, the money is being spent to remodel a public golf course . . . a priority that, as a golfer, I commend, but as a legislator, I question.

At National Legislative Conference,
Washington, Feb. 2/
The Washington Post, 2-3:(A)2.

2

Most of the instruments that are available to us as a Congress in trying to check Executive authority are very crude—such things as impeachment or the outright refusal to appropriate any money for a particular department. I think what we have to demonstrate to this President [Nixon] is that this is a determined Congress—determined to re-assert its Constitutional authority and responsibility, and that it doesn't dismiss some of these crude means. But it is not going to advertise what it may use. It's going to be as selective

as the President has tried to be in gradually expanding his authority at the expense of the Congress and the people.

TV-radio interview/"Issues and Answers,"
American Broadcasting Company, 2-4.

3

[On a Nixon Administration proposal that would make it a crime to make public almost any kind of government-classified information on defense or foreign policy, whether or not the classification was proper]: Classified information, you should know, is any document or record or other material which any one of over 20,000 government officials might have decided—for reasons they need never explain —should be kept secret. It is any piece of paper marked top secret, secret or confidential, because someone, sometime, supposedly decided that its disclosure could prejudice the defense interests of the nation. In practice, however, classified information is material which some individual in the government decides he does not want made public. He could make that decision to hide incompetence. Many have. He could be trying to conceal waste. Many have. He could even be attempting to camouflage corrupt behavior and improper influence. Many have. He could simply be covering up facts which might embarrass him or his bosses. Many have. Classified information is the 20 million documents the Pentagon's own most-experienced security officer has estimated to be in Defense Department files. Classified information is the 26-year backlog of foreign-policy records in the State Department archives. And most of that information is improperly classified—not out of evil motives, but out of a mistaken interpretation by conscientious employees of what security actually requires . . . We already have the criminal sanctions we need against disclosure of true defense secrets. To expand the coverage of those penalties can only stifle the flow of important but not injurious information to the press and, therefore, to the public. With the criminal penalties already in the law and with the proven record of responsible behavior by the great majority of government employees and newsmen, the only purpose behind further expansion of the secrecy laws would be the effort to silence dissent within the government and hide incompetence and misbehavior. New penalties will not further deter espionage and spying. They will only harm those who want the public to know what the government is doing. Nothing could be better designed to restrict the news you get to the pasteurized jargon of official press releases than a law which would punish a newsman for receiving sensitive information unless he returned the material promptly to an authorized official. Nothing could damage the press more than a provision which would make a newsman an accomplice in crime unless he revealed the source of information disclosed to him. The Administration proposal carries an even greater danger in the power it would give to the officials who now determine what shall be secret and what be disclosed. Not only would they be able to continue to make those decisions without regard to any real injury disclosure might cause, they would be empowered to prosecute anyone who defied their judgment. Their imposition of secrecy could not be reviewed in the courts. And a violation of their decision would be a crime involving not only government employees but journalists as well.

At Frostburg (Md.) State College,
April 1/The New York Times,
4-9:37.

1

We in Congress fear, as all Americans fear, the threat of one-man rule. We in Congress distrust, as all Americans distrust, any President who would suggest that only he knows what is best for America. This notion of one-man rule—over the budget, over inflation and over the Watergate [political-espionage] hearing—constitutes an abuse of the President's power . . . That is why many members of Congress disagree not only with the policies the President [Nixon] has proposed, but also with his rejection of Congress' role in developing these policies.

Broadcast address,
Washington, April 2/
U.S. News & World Report, 4-16:26.

Ralph Nader
Lawyer;
Consumer advocate

2

The major problem with Executive privilege is that the Congress has not in any meaningful way challenged [its use by President Nixon and other Presidents]. All of the Executive privilege crises of the past have been resolved by settlement that, almost without exception, has confirmed the very dubious power of the Executive to claim it.

At joint Senate Subcommittee hearing,
Washington/
The Dallas Times Herald,
4-13:(A)6.

Richard E. Neustadt
Professor of Government,
Harvard University

3

Somehow I don't see a trend to increased power for the institution [of the Presidency] in the political fate of Truman, Johnson and Nixon. It is true that Truman carried off the Korean war, Johnson shoved us into Vietnam and Nixon allowed his staff to go all over the place doing all kinds of shenanigans without the respect shown to the other parts of the government that other Presidents have shown. But if you look at what happened to the Presidents who asserted their authority more sharply, with less circumspection about Congress, it turns out that Truman and his party were thrown out of office for the Korean war; Johnson was, in effect, forced to quit over Vietnam; and look at Nixon! I find it hard to be downhearted or see a worrisome trend-line in an institution in which public retribution comes so fast . . . It is too bad that the king can get us into things that people decide they don't like, but look how the system clobbers the king! Where's the trend-line to increasing [Presidential] power in that? These three Presidents pushed their claim to independent judgment and authority hard and were terribly penalized politically for doing so. Presidential power, as I see it, is as contingent as ever, as uncertain as can be. The press and an atten-

(RICHARD E. NEUSTADT)

tive public can do just enormous harm to a President's ambition.

Interview, Cambridge, Mass./
Los Angeles Times, 12-27:(2)7.

Richard M. Nixon
President of the United States

1

The Presidency is a very demanding position, physically, mentally and emotionally. [Unless a man has] a remarkable physique in all these respects, he should not seek the Presidency at an age up in the late 60s . . . The Presidency has many problems, but boredom is the least of them.

Interview on his 60th birthday, Washington,
Jan. 9/San Francisco Examiner, 1-9:2.

2

. . . I offer no promise of a purely governmental solution for every problem. We have lived too long with that false promise. In trusting too much in government, we have asked of it more than it can deliver. This leads only to inflated expectations, to reduced individual effort and to a disappointment and frustration that erode confidence both in what government can do and in what people can do. Government must learn to take less from people so that people can do more for themselves. Let us remember that America was built not by government, but by people; not by welfare, but by work; not by shirking responsibility, but by seeking responsibility. In our own lives, let each of us ask—not just what will government do for me, but what can I do for myself? In the challenges we face together, let each of us ask—not just how can government help, but how can I help? Your national government has a great and vital role to play; and I pledge to you that, where this government should act, we will act boldly and we will lead boldly. But just as important is the role that each and every one of us must play, as an individual and as a member of his own community.

Inauguration address, Washington,
Jan. 20/U.S. News & World Report, 2-5:87.

3

I believe in the battle—whether it's the battle of a campaign or the battle of this office, which is a continuing battle. It's always there wherever you go. I, perhaps, carry it more than others because that's my way . . . You can't be relaxed. The *Redskins* [football team] were relaxed in their last game of the regular season, and they were flat, and they got clobbered. You must be up for the great events—up, but not uptight. Having done it so often, I perhaps have a finer-honed sense of this. But you can overdo it, over-train and leave your fight in the dressing room.

Interview/
Time, 1-22:11.

4

. . . we are cutting back on Federal programs that waste the taxpayers' money —for example, on housing programs that benefit the well-to-do but short-change the poor, health programs that build more hospitals when hospital beds are now in surplus, educational bonuses that attract more people into teaching when tens of thousands of teachers already cannot find jobs. These old programs may have appealing names, they may sound like good causes; but behind the fancy label often lies a dismal failure. Unless we cut back now on the programs that have failed, we will soon run out of money for the programs that can succeed.

Radio address to the nation,
Feb. 21/
Vital Speeches, 3-15:323.

5

Under the doctrine of separation of powers, the manner in which the President personally exercises his assigned Executive powers is not subject to questioning by another branch of government. If the President is not subject to such questioning, it is equally appropriate that members of his staff not be so questioned, for their roles are, in effect, an extension of the Presidency.

March 12/
The New York Times, 5-23:29.

1

[On a suggestion that members of the House of Representatives be elected for four years instead of the current two years]: Personally, I have long favored the four-year term for members of the House, with half of the members elected every two years. Members serving for two-year terms have to spend one of every two years running for re-election, with the result that they serve one year and run one year. This not only places an enormous burden on the member himself; it also can work to the disadvantage of his constituents and of the country. By reducing the extraordinary campaign burden on its members, I believe the House of Representatives could be made a more effective instrument of government.

Radio address, May 16/
U.S. News & World Report, 5-28:105.

2

[On secrecy in government]: I want to be quite blunt. Had we not had secrecy, had we not had secret negotiations with the North Vietnamese, had we not had secret negotiations over a period of time with the [Communist] Chinese leaders, let me say quite bluntly, there would have been no limitation of arms for the Soviet Union and no summit; and had we not had that kind of security and that kind of secrecy that allowed for the kind of exchange that is essential, you men [former Vietnam prisoners of war] would still be in Hanoi rather than Washington today. And let me say, I think it is time in this country to quit making national heroes out of those who steal secrets and publish them in the newspapers. Because, gentlemen, you see, in order to continue these great initiatives for peace, we must have confidentiality, we must have secret communications. It isn't that we are trying to keep anything from the American people that the American people should know. It isn't that we are trying to keep something from the press that the press should print. But it is that what we are trying to do is to accomplish our goal, make a deal. And when we are dealing with potential adversaries, those

negotiations must have the highest degree of confidentiality . . . And by our secrets, what I am saying here is not that we are concerned about every little driblet here and there; but what I am concerned about is the highest classified documents in our National Security Council files, in the State Department, in the Defense Department, which if they get out, for example, in our arms-control negotiations with the Soviets, would let them know our position before we ever got to the table. They don't tell us theirs; they have no problem keeping the secrets. I don't want, and you don't want, their system and that kind of control; but I say it is time for a new sense of responsibility in this country and a new sense of dedication of everybody in the bureaucracy that if a document is classified, keep it classified.

Before former U.S. Vietnam prisoners
of war, Washington, May 24/
The Washington Post, 5-27:(C)6.

3

Now more than ever we need to foster between the Executive and the Congress a spirit of responsible partnership [that] must rest on the foundation of mutual respect between the Executive and the Legislature. We have fought hard for our positions; we will continue to fight hard for them. In fact, we have a duty to fight vigorously for those things we believe in. But as we battle for our views, let us remember that we can accommodate our positions without abandoning our principles.

At unveiling of cornerstone of Everett
McKinley Dirksen Congressional Research
Center, Pekin, Ill., June 15/
The New York Times, 6-16:28.

Sam Nunn
United States Senator, D-Georgia

4

The U.S. Postal Service is slower than the sands of an hour-glass, and not nearly as dependable.

Quote, 3-25:265.

Thomas P. O'Neill, Jr.
United States Representative,
D-Massachusetts

1

According to his [President Nixon's] definition, a program is fiscally irresponsible if he has not recommended it in his budget. Congress has no intention of accepting the President's budget recommendations, part and parcel, without question . . . the President can shake his finger all he wants. The Congress is not about to be bullied away from its Constitutional responsibilities as guardian of the purse.

The New York Times, 6-24:(4)2.

Wayne Owens
United States Representative, D-Utah

2

[On President Nixon's impoundment of Congressionally-allocated funds]: Insulated with "four more years," the President of the United States, in pursuit of his own legislative and political ends, terminates by arbitrary Executive fiat programs which he could not defeat in the orderly, lawful process of our government. And Congress, in its docile, dependent mood, at times seems determined to give the President what he wants, up to and including the Congressional birthright.

Before the House, Washington, April 18/
The New York Times, 4-24:22.

Robert Packwood
United States Senator, R-Oregon

3

[Congressional] reforms are not going to make any difference unless there is the will in Congress to want to govern. We can set policy, we can take back the powers [lost to the Executive Branch] if we want. But we have said "can't, can't, can't" so long, it has become an excuse for "won't."

Time, 1-15:17.

Wright Patman
United States Representative, D-Texas

4

[On state lotteries, state-run off-track betting and other forms of state-controlled gambling]: Today, the craze of gambling as an easy road to enrich the public coffers is gaining favor throughout the nation. This is a tragic development. These schemes . . . are being packaged in typical Madison Avenue style. We are told that a little gambling—backed by the state—will help educate children and provide other benefits . . . This is the purest form of hogwash.

Before the House, Washington, April/
U.S. News & World Report, 7-23:25.

Peter G. Peterson
Former Secretary of Commerce
of the United States

5

[On his experience as Secretary before being ousted]: The experience may have been costly, but it was also priceless.

Quote, 1-28:73.

Howard Phillips
Acting Director,
Federal Office of Economic Opportunity

6

[On the Nixon Administration's government reforms and program cutbacks]: . . . our goal is not to enhance Federal power, but to disperse it; not to reduce the resources available to help people, but to give the people themselves greater control over their allocation. We do not justify our social reforms on the basis of economy; although, under the President's budget, tax increases will be avoided by keeping the growth of program expenditures in line with economic growth. No, the argument for the changes which are being made . . . across the Federal bureaucracy is that, in the final analysis, this is a people's government, whose authority and resources derive entirely from the people.

Before Middlesex County Bar Association,
Boston, March 21/
The Christian Science Monitor, 4-12:18.

J. J. Pickle
United States Representative, D-Texas

7

L.B.J. [the late President Lyndon B.

Johnson] gave me one guiding principle. He said: "When you vote, vote for the people."

San Francisco Examiner, 2-12:32.

William Proxmire
United States Senator, D-Wisconsin

1

[Criticizing government officials being chauffeured around in limousines]: In view of the stringent fiscal straits in which we find ourselves, the cut-backs for low-income housing and programs to aid low-income farmers, and the controls placed on the wage of American workers, [the limousines should stop rolling]. It is absurd for the Secretary of HUD and four of his assistants and Under Secretaries to be chauffeured around Washington at the same time the agency has frozen funds for public housing.

Washington, Jan. 16/
San Francisco Examiner, 1-17:2.

2

I am perhaps one of the very few Northern Democrats who agree with [President Nixon's] impoundment [of Congressionally-allocated funds]. I think it is correct. The President has no alternative if he is to be fiscally responsible. President [John] Kennedy did it in 1962 for a wing of B-52s. Congress passed a defense-appropriations bill with this $10 billion for B-52s in it, and Kennedy just refused to spend the money. Not a word was said about it. Nobody criticized him.

Interview/Human Events, 2-17:3.

Thomas F. Railsback
United States Representative, R-Illinois

3

[On the impeachment of a President]: You have to apply a different standard to a President's impeachment than to a judge's, because a judge serves "during good behavior" and has that job for life; but a President doesn't hold office for the same duration. We probably should treat a Presidential impeachment with even more care and apply a more limited definition of "high

crimes and misdemeanors" than to any other Federal office-holders.

The National Observer, 11-17:6.

Ronald Reagan
Governor of California

4

Before 1930, Federal, state and local governments were taking 15 cents out of every dollar you earned. By 1950, it was 30 cents. Today, government's share of every dollar you earn is more than 43 cents. Obviously, freedom itself is in danger if we continue this rate of increase.

TV-radio address, Sacramento, Feb. 8/
Los Angeles Times, 2-9:(1)1.

Elliot L. Richardson
Secretary of Defense of the United States

5

At issue is our national response to the often necessary and seemingly inescapable growth of centralized government and the concomitant submergence of the individual, the community and the states to Washington-based authority. At stake, I believe, is nothing less than the future of the individual—and of individual liberty—in the United States. The last 40 years have seen us turning increasingly to central authority. And the trend continues to this day . . . It is an issue that is receiving a good deal of careful thought by this Administration in its comprehensive concept of "The New Federalism"—a blueprint for revitalizing government that outlines ways to make our institutions more responsive to individual needs. Beyond that, "The New Federalism" is a way of reversing the flow of power to Washington, to start it flowing back, in President Nixon's words, "to the states, to the communities, and most important, to the people" . . . For the increasingly-evident fact is that neither the President, nor the Congress, nor a centralized bureaucracy, can keep neighborhood streets safe, clean up local pollution, meet local public health emergencies, un-snarl local traffic problems, or pick up local garbage. Such problems require local concern, local decisions and local action. The answer to the drift of power toward the center must be

(ELLIOT L. RICHARDSON)

a determination by citizens to wage an un-ending campaign to achieve local, personalized autonomy.

New York/
The New York Times, 1-31:37.

Elliot L. Richardson
Attorney General of the United States

1

These are times when the institutions of our government are under stress. It is not because the structure is not sound. It is sound. If there are flaws, they are in our-selves. The task is not one of redesign but one of renewal and reaffirmation.

At his swearing in as Attorney General,
Washington, May 25/Los Angeles Times,
5-27:(1)1.

2

Confidence is not a structure built of stone that can withstand the buffeting winds of ac-cusation and mistrust. It is the expression, rather, of trust itself. It is as fragile as it is precious, as hard to restore as it is easy to destroy. And yet it is obvious that trust is necessary to the very possibility of free self-government. The good health of the body politic needs the tonic of skepticism, but it cannot long survive massive doses of cynical acid . . .

Before American Bar Association,
Washington, Aug. 8/
The Washington Post, 8-11:(A)16.

3

We are at a point where society's expecta-tions from government are so numerous and so clamorous that we can no longer afford to indulge a response to problems which pretends to be able to solve them when we don't really know how to solve them at all. This is the "don't just stand there—do something" syndrome, and in past years there has been some excuse for it. But I think the time has come to blow the whistle on it, because I think its consequence has contributed to the erosion of confidence in government.

Interview, Washington/
U.S. News & World Report, 9-3:25.

William P. Rogers
Secretary of State of the United States

4

. . . I believe that it is very important for the United States not to become so obsessed with security matters that laws are freely vio-lated [by the government]. I think one of the things that provides security for Americans is the fact that we are a law-abiding nation, and that is protection for all individuals and a protection for individual rights. So I think great care should be shown before any extra-legal action is undertaken. On the other hand, I think, as Secretary of State—and I know how the President [Nixon] feels about this—it is very discouraging when you are in the mid-dle of very sensitive negotiations to have things leaked from the government, papers stolen and made public, in a way which we believe, the government believes, can adversely affect our security interests. Now, where to draw the line is a very difficult question to answer . . . But generally speaking, I lean toward strict observance of legal requirements and only support a variance from that in very unusual circumstances.

News conference, Washington, Aug. 20/
The Washington Post, 8-21:(A)4.

William B. Saxbe
United States Senator, R-Ohio

5

[Saying he will not seek re-election next year]: It's been a wonderful experience [serv-ing in the Senate]. There are many things to impress you, and also many things to depress you. The future of the country lies with Con-gress—and in many ways it could do a lot better job . . . It should be the one that makes the decisions. [But] if they can set things up where they can take action by doing nothing, they will.

Washington, Oct. 9/
The Washington Post, 10-10:(A)2.

Hugh Scott
United States Senator, R-Pennsylvania

6

Government is too fat because Congress-men vote too much lard.

The Dallas Times Herald, 1-21:(B)2.

1

This talk of Congress being powerless, let's examine it. The Congress manages to pass on all of the President's Constitutional appointees. Congress gives all the money to the President. The Congress handles all of the taxing power of the country. Thus, a good deal of this talk about how impotent Congress is is really talk designed by an opposition Congress in a confrontation.

Interview, Washington/
The Christian Science Monitor, 1-25:3.

2

The 500 members of Congress always think they know better than that single fellow downtown [the President]. Yet, they keep noticing that he is, by Orwellian measure, more equal than they are. Here the Founders are to blame: They created a strong Executive, which primarily distinguishes our system from the more usual parliamentary system. If the Presidency has become too powerful and Congress too weak—as I concede that they have in recent times—it is, I believe, because we have dealt with a great Depression and three wars since the 1920s. Congress was happy to turn the Depression over to a strong President. And wars cannot be fought and peace achieved by committee—certainly not by a committee of 535.

Time, 2-12:13.

3

[Saying President Nixon had been isolated by his recent White House staff]: I know that everyone from the Vice President down had trouble with the men around the President. I had such trouble with them that I had no conversation with [former Presidential Assistant John] Ehrlichman after last January that I can recall, other than some purely social occasion when I may have run into him. The attitude was: "We know best and we are conveying the President's wishes." I have discovered to my own satisfaction in conversations with various Cabinet members that they had serious doubts that the messages they gave to Ehrlichman or [former Presidential Assistant H. R.] Haldeman were in some cases actually transmitted to the President. The decisions were made by them and referred to the Cabinet members. This was a horrible, inexcusable

way to run a government.

Interview, Washington/
The Christian Science Monitor, 7-3:12.

Austin Smith
Chairman, Parke, Davis & Company

4

There are supposed to be three branches of government: Legislative, Executive and Judicial. But regulatory agencies have become the fourth, and some believe in some ways the most powerful. The stage seems to be set for some agencies to become investigator, prosecutor, judge and jury, with authority to act on the spot.

Quote, 2-4:107.

Howard K. Smith
News commentator,
American Broadcasting Company

5

I have said this before, but it is more topical now. What we need in our political system is the British-type vote of confidence. That is, when serious issues arise, the Legislature is virtually required to debate, then vote whether it has confidence in the Executive. If the Executive wins, he can govern with new vigor. If he loses, he is replaced by someone in which there is confidence. By that system, the long angry divisions over Vietnam, with Congress carping but never voting, would not have happened. [The late President Lyndon] Johnson would have won and been able to negotiate from strength, or lost and been replaced by someone who would pull us out. In the case of [the] Watergate [political-espionage affair], Nixon might have been retired months ago, but without legal prejudice. While government went on under trusted management, he could prove his innocence on his own time, and possibly make a comeback. In Britain, Gladstone made three comebacks as Prime Minister; Churchill, as Cabinet Minister, made three, ending up as his nation's greatest Prime Minister. The praise you hear for our system of built-in indecision is sentimental, not rational. It is like being proud of your Model T because it has always been in the family—overlooking the fact that the motor jams every time you want to go somewhere.

News commentary,
American Broadcasting Company/
The National Observer, 12-1:13.

Elmer B. Staats
Comptroller General of the United States

1

The Federal government is an institution, and I am aware that institutions are not popular with the young. One doesn't have to be young to dislike some institutions or some things about institutions. But it must be faced that nothing runs in today's complex world without an institution of some kind to manage it. If one institution is thrown out, it will be replaced by another. Institutions are something we have to live with, cope with and, for those of us who are unlucky enough, manage. Moreover, institutions are not unassailable. They can be influenced, altered, redirected and corrected. The White House is an institution in the United States, like the Congress, the Supreme Court and so on. We have just seen [in the Watergate political-espionage affair] how one of these [the White House], insulated as it may unfortunately have been from the force and direction of popular will, suddenly changed its organization and direction in an hour of crisis. Whatever cynical thoughts may have suggested in the weeks when this crisis was building up, there came a time when the more constructive forces, always strong in our democracy, prevailed. The institution of democracy, that old and inefficient form of government, was at work—something for which, obviously, we should always be grateful.

At University of South Dakota
commencement, May 12/
Vital Speeches, 7-1:547.

Adlai E. Stevenson III
United States Senator, D-Illinois

2

What this institution [the Congress] needs is power [in its relations with the Presidency]. Our wounds are self-inflicted. The weaknesses

will come back to haunt us. I want a strong Executive, but I also want to restore the system of checks and balances. We can't do that through a series of confrontations between Congress and the Executive, where one kicks the other because it is crippled. The President did that to us, and now we are doing that to the President.

The New York Times Magazine, 9-23:83.

Meldrim Thomson, Jr.
Governor of New Hampshire

3

Federal bureaucrats do not like states. They love regional government. It is a concept foreign to our Federal Constitution, where not once does the word "region" appear. Yet, bureaucrats fight for it because salaries are plush, the pastures of wasteful frivolity lush, and the power of the people nonexistent. Today it is difficult for a state to stand straight and clean above its dependence on [the] Federal government. About 30 per cent of our state budget comes from Federal funding of one kind or another. Not only do most of these funds have strings attached to them, but the regulatory twine manipulates the Federal puppets in an incessant whirling-dervish ecstasy of Do's and Dont's . . . If President Nixon's New Federalism, so essential to the continued life of our republic, is to be effective, the states must reassert their sovereignty. This will be difficult but not impossible. Today's office-holders must embrace the ideals of yesterday's Founding Fathers and be willing to make the same sacrifice of property and lives which they mutually pledged to each other. The struggle is for raw power. Upon the outcome rests the freedom of Americans and the ultimate hope of all mankind.

At testimonial for former OEO Director
Howard Phillips, Alexandria, Va./
Vital Speeches, 11-15:93.

Charles Thone
United States Representative, R-Nebraska

4

Postal Service advertising, its $3.2 million information program and its headquarters move from a building that was paid for to the swankiest new office complex in Washington are some of the reasons why second- and third-class postage rates just went up and letter postage will soon go from 8 to 10 cents. I think the Postal Service should devote its attention to moving the mail . . .

Los Angeles Times, 9-10:(1)2.

John G. Tower
United States Senator, R-Texas

1

[The Federal government] at long last will be operating in the black [by fiscal year 1975]. The President [Nixon] had the courage, the guts, to impound programs which were widely accepted, in the interest of furthering fiscal responsibility. The President feels the time has come to order our priorities and live within our means . . . The Constitutional question has been raised if the President has the authority to withhold [Congressionally-] appropriated funds. The record reveals that past Presidents withheld appropriated funds to a greater degree than President Nixon.

Before Texas State Republican Executive Committee, Feb. 10/ The Dallas Times Herald, 2-11:(A)4.

Al Ullman
United States Representative, D-Oregon

2

Getting better control of the budget by Congress is a question of basic use of power. The only way we can get it back is to bite the bullet, take the responsibility and limit ourselves. It's a big bite.

San Francisco Examiner, 1-16:24.

W. Allen Wallis
Chancellor, University of Rochester (N.Y.)

3

. . . "the object of power," as Orwell has said, "is power. Power is not a means, it is an end." It becomes an overriding end when government dwarfs and overwhelms all other sources of power combined, being the only power not subject to a greater power.

At Roberts Wesleyan College commencement, Rochester, N.Y./ The National Observer, 6-30:6.

Earl Warren
Former Chief Justice of the United States

4

Some of the major maladies of American government arise not from an excess bureaucratic posture and resistance to innovation, but rather from non-professional behavior, from action without authorization, or from action without adequate respect for the law. Nothing is more destructive of good government than the confusion of personal loyalty with institutional loyalty. The loyalty of a career public servant belongs not to any holder of public office, but to the standards of his profession and the institutions of our nation.

At Rockefeller Public Service Awards ceremony, Washington/ The Dallas Times Herald, 12-6:(A)14.

Lowell P. Weicker, Jr.
United States Senator, R-Connecticut

5

It was Lord Brice, I think, who, after he reviewed the colonies following the [U.S.] Revolutionary War, was asked what was the difference between a monarchy and a democracy. He said a monarchy's like a ship under full sail: every line and sheet in place, the decks scrubbed, and every man at his place. It's just magnificent, and the reason for it is that there's one man in charge—the captain. The only problem is that, if he's the wrong man, the ship can go on an iceberg. Democracy's like a raft: Everybody's feet are getting wet all the time, but you know the damn thing isn't going to sink. That's true, I think.

Interview, Washington/ The National Observer, 4-7:5.

Caspar W. Weinberger
Secretary of Health, Education and Welfare of the United States

6

The share of the gross national product that's devoted to government is now over 34 per cent; and it just seems to me that, when you get a third of the whole national effort devoted to supporting government, it becomes increasingly difficult to maintain a viable, effective private sector. It isn't the increase in

(CASPAR W. WEINBERGER)

the number of dollars that worries me. It's the increase in the amount of authority and power in government that those dollars represent. My worry is that, as government gets bigger, individual human freedom gets smaller; and I think that's not really consistent with the premises that went into the founding of the country.

Interview/Los Angeles Times, 2-25:(6)7.

1

[Supporting the Nixon Administration's cut-back of certain government programs to save money]: [As the April 15 income-tax deadline approaches,] each taxpayer will be playing an unwilling part in a tragedy of waste. Many of these precious dollars will be burned up in unnecessary administrative costs and in programs that are inefficient. The choice before the public is clear: President Nixon's budget with present taxes or the special-interests spenders' plans with higher taxes.

News conference, Washington, March 27/
Los Angeles Times, 3-28:(1)21.

Aaron Wildavsky
Dean, Graduate School of Public Policy,
University of California, Berkeley

2

We now have a President [Nixon] who has attempted to run foreign policy without the Senate, domestic and budgetary policy without the House and a political campaign without his party. He has adopted an essentially Gaullist view of the Presidency. He says, "I'm the only one who counts to the people; and if anybody, including Congress, disagrees with me, so much the worse for them." But I think that it is not really inherent in Nixon. I think that, if he were able to get benefits and praise from the ordinary conduct of his job, he would have been less likely to do this. It's very difficult for any President now to achieve satisfaction, because the demands we make on him are essentially contradictory or so difficult that no one knows how to achieve them.

Panel discussion, New Orleans/
The Washington Post, 9-16:(C)1.

John J. Williams
Former United States Senator, R-Delaware

3

One [political] party is just as honest as the other, and one party has just as many instances of corruption as the other. It is not the question of which Administration is in power at the time that corruption develops, but how that Administration handles it . . . It is important that people of this country, particularly young people, be able to look up to their public officials and have confidence in their integrity. When these young people read about what's going on today, I can understand how they get cynical about the Administration and the Establishment. Yet, even with all the experience I have had with corruption at various times in the last 24 years, and in the light of all I have heard before or since, I still think that the overwhelming percentage of American people, regardless of their political affiliation, are basically honest. And that applies to government officials and employees. But the facts of life being what they are, you have to be eternally on guard under any Administration. The answer to corruption is prompt, firm action when anything develops. You just can't compromise on it when it happens.

Interview, Millsboro, Del./
Los Angeles Times, 4-2:(2)7.

Malcolm Wilson
Governor of New York

4

. . . I believe the greatest service government can perform is to help people find the best within themselves, and the worst that government can do is to suffocate self-expression and self-reliance with government-imposed solutions to every human problem.

Inaugural address, Albany, N.Y.,
Dec. 18/The New York Times, 12-19:78.

Ralph W. Yarborough
Former United States Senator, D-Texas

5

The reason Japan is growing is because they have men with wisdom, experience and knowledge. The thing that is overlooked in this country [the U.S.] is experience. They don't elect inexperienced kids or movie stars to run the government in Japan.

Interview, Austin, Tex./
The Dallas Times Herald, 8-12:(G)1.

Ronald L. Ziegler
Press Secretary to the President
of the United States

1

The President [Nixon] doesn't have any "yes men" around him. It's absurd to suggest I never argue with the President. Some think it's a virtue for an adviser to march into the Oval Office and shout, "No, I disagree." That doesn't come close to understanding an aide's role. When he asks my opinion, I give it to him as straight as I know how. When I disagree with the course of action, I say so. I guarantee you that, if I were a "yes man," I wouldn't still be around here.

Los Angeles Times, 12-29:(1)8.

Labor · The Economy

Roy L. Ash
Director,
Federal Office of Management and Budget

1

An eminent economist to whom I've just been talking and I both agreed that a major contributing factor to inflation is the expectation by some that the Congress may not see eye-to-eye with the President on spending, and that maybe he's not going to be able to hold spending within his ceilings. There are those who say, "Aha, if the President is not going to be able to come in at 250 billions this year and at 269 next year, the Federal government is going to be out borrowing lots more money"—and there go interest rates. One view is that by its present actions the Congress is signaling to the American people and to the world that you can expect more inflation. Look at this flurry of programs Congress is considering. It's hardly saying to the public that it intends to hold expenditures down; it's saying something quite the opposite. I think it would be very helpful if the Congress came out today and said, "We're going to spend no more than 250 billions this fiscal year, and we're going to have a 269-billion ceiling in 1974, and we're going to operate our machinery so that it will come in at that." That would be a signal to this country and to the world that would be taken as a very good one, because it would say we are going to hold inflation.

Interview, Washington/
U.S. News & World Report, 4-30:94.

2

Let me tell you why tax increases may not at all be the way to go: In the first place, the Federal government, local governments and the states are now spending 36 per cent of our gross national product. At some point, enough government is enough. What happens when it gets to 40 or 50 per cent? Remember that this 36 per cent share compares with 25 per cent 20 or so years ago. So the first reason not to raise taxes is that there's already enough government. A second reason is that it takes months to get a bill through Congress, and at the end of that time it might not be good economic policy to raise taxes. Finally, there is a third reason not to raise taxes: In the minds of some people, a tax increase is not just a way to achieve a better budget balance, it is merely an invitation to spend more Federal money.

Interview/
U.S. News & World Report, 9-17:94.

John Balles
President,
Federal Reserve Bank of San Francisco

3

A [price] freeze is like holding a thermometer under water: The temperature doesn't really reflect the true condition of the patient.

Interview, June 13/
Los Angeles Times, 6-14:(3)19.

Benjamin F. Biaggini
President,
Southern Pacific (Railway) Company;
Former member, Federal Pay Board

4

As a company and an industry [railroads] long under heavy regulation, we are very concerned about any more of it. We feel Phase 4 [of the Nixon Administration economic plan] should move positively toward less regulation for the United States economy generally and toward more freedom in pricing and other legitimate decision areas of our American business system.

The New York Times, 7-8:(3)13.

Arch N. Booth
President,
Chamber of Commerce of the United States

1

[The Nixon Administration's economic] Phase 4 is another in a series of charades that prolongs the dangerous illusion that economic problems can be solved by government edict, rather than government responsibility. It is an improvement on the [price] freeze, which has been a disaster. The folly of controls is that they delude the American public. They are used to cover up the failure of the government's fiscal and monetary policies, and they delay the day when we can return to a free and balanced economy.

July 18/The New York Times, 7-19:1.

Peter J. Brennan
Secretary of Labor-designate
of the United States

2

[On compulsory arbitration]: I am against compulsion in working out differences between people. Once you accept compulsion in one field, you start on the inevitable road to compulsion in every segment of life. I do not think that compulsion is what our country was founded on.

At his confirmation hearing before
Senate Labor and Public Welfare Committee,
Washington/U.S. News & World Report,
2-5:76.

Peter J. Brennan
Secretary of Labor of the United States

3

I just feel the concern of the working people in the country is that they want to make a decent living, they want to be able to pay fair prices for the merchandise, things they need; and food, of course, is one of the main things that every family needs. But the working man and woman, which we all are part of, we all have to realize that we have to make certain sacrifices; we have to cooperate, and I think this is the time, right now, that we must look this whole [economic] situation over and say what we will do as Americans to

cooperate. Forget all the experts and all those telling us what is good and what is bad, what do we think; and I have great confidence in the American people, that they have an idea what is good for them and for the country. And if we can just get some program moving they can all get behind, I think it will get around to solving themselves.

Los Angeles Times, 7-27:(2)7.

4

. . . I think both labor and management are getting more sophisticated in their negotiations. If a dispute can be settled across the table by free collective bargaining—give and take on both sides—it's a much better way to handle the business than a strike or a lockout by the employer. The rank-and-file members in many unions would rather have this because they find that, if they strike for another 5 cents in the weekly paycheck, it may cost them thousands of dollars in lost wages, and they never make that up. Now, sometimes there's a larger principle involved, and then you may have a strike. That's where the big strikes will come in the future, rather than just for another nickel or dime.

Interview, Washington/
U.S. News & World Report, 7-30:40.

5

I want to do the best I can for the country and the working man and woman; and that includes management, because the first thing I ever learned bargaining for workers—the best contract I could get—didn't mean a damn thing if somebody wasn't there at the end of the week to pay the checks and pay for fringe benefits. So for me or any labor man to try to kill off the person that he had just signed the agreement with would be ridiculous. So you can't put them out of business. You have to make sure that they make their profit and they can take care of their obligations as far as the agreement goes. And I think this is all management wants to hear. And I'm happy to say that many labor leaders are moving in that direction now; they want to survive, and they want management to survive.

Interview, Washington/
U.S. News & World Report, 7-30:44.

Dolph Briscoe
Governor of Texas

1

This nation is on the verge of economic chaos—and has been for four years—but all we get are vague reassurances that things will be better next month, or the month after that. The Republicans keep trying to re-launch the economy with words and slogans, as if the economy were a hot-air balloon. Like Herbert Hoover, they keep trying to convince us that prosperity is just around the corner . . . I believe the people are tired of high-flown promises followed by shoddy performance. They're not going to accept this brand of economic chaos much longer. That is why the Democratic Party is on the move again.

At Democratic rally, El Paso, Tex.,
Aug. 18/The Dallas Times Herald, 8-19:(A)4.

James L. Buckley
United States Senator, C-New York

2

No matter how much we may try to disguise the fact, the climate for a vigorous free economy is being eroded by inflation, protectionism and government intervention and controls. We have been losing ground, and the principal blame must be placed at the door of government, at the door of Congress for its habit of creating programs without adequately assessing their practical consequences, and at the door of our bureaucracies for the seeming glee with which they so often abandon the rule of common sense as they generate their forms and regulations.

Nation's Business, April:31.

3

I'm not quite sure that there are glaring inequities in our tax system, although it needs to be constantly reviewed. There are some problems, but not the major ones you hear when people talk about tax reform. Most of the so-called loopholes—tax-free income from municipal bonds, interest on mortgage payments, the depletion allowance, you name it—were deliberately adopted for reasons of policy or equity which at the moment seemed good. Maybe they have outlived their usefulness. But I think it should be recognized that,

once there is a set of rules, the business community has no choice but to operate within those rules; they become an economic fact of life. To discontinue suddenly something that has become ingrained in the economic process is inequitable. We need to strive for simplicity. The more complicated the structure—rules, regulations, etc.—the larger the opportunity there is to manipulate within the rules. The kind of reform that appeals to me would be a trade-off—eliminating all of these goodies in exchange for a 20 per cent tax rate, something of that sort.

Nation's Business, April:32.

4

I would like to see all [wage-price] controls removed at this point, with a strongest-possible statement by the President of the United States to the people of the United States explaining the A-B-Cs of economics that the people really understand; and that is that we are going to have inflationary forces so long as we insist on over-spending. So long as we insist on racking up huge deficits, they get crammed into the monetary system and force up prices. I think that this last round, this Stage 3½ [economic program] or whatever they call it, is a classic demonstration of why controls don't work and of the perversity. You create shortages; you are going to develop black markets; you drive products off the marketplace. It is time we got down to fundamentals and stop trying to paper over inflation rather than going into its root causes.

TV-radio interview,
Washington/"Meet the Press,"
National Broadcasting Company, 7-15.

Arthur F. Burns
Chairman, Federal Reserve Board

5

I have found it necessary to revise my ideas about the proper role of government in specific economic matters. Experience is a demanding teacher, and my respect for it has led me at times to favor governmental actions that I abhorred in my youth.

At symposium celebrating the 250th anniversary of Adam Smith, Kirkaldy, Scotland/
The New York Times, 6-7:77.

Earl L. Butz
Secretary of Agriculture of the United States

1

Part of the reason food prices are up is that farmers are getting more for things they produce. It is plain wrong for consumers to expect farm-food producers to work for 20 per cent less than the rest of the population. The good old days of 50-cent steaks, 17-cent gasoline and cars for less than $1,000 are gone. You can't have both—high wages and low prices.

Before National Canners Association,
San Francisco, Jan. 26/
San Francisco Examiner, 1-26:4.

2

. . . the cost of farm products is only part of the cost of food in the supermarket, and it is the smallest part. The biggest part of the price Mrs. Housewife pays at the check-out counter is due to the cost of processing and distributing food after it leaves the farm. The farmer gets 40 cents of the consumer's food dollar. When people talk about the high price of food, that 40 cents is the wrong rabbit to chase. They ought to be chasing the 60-cent rabbit. Let's take the price of bread as a case in point. Twenty-five cents is the price for a one-pound loaf of white bread in many cities. The wheat in that loaf at farm value today is worth about 2.8 cents, and other farm-produced ingredients add another cent. You could take all the wheat and other farm products out of that loaf of bread, and still pay 21 cents for the wrapper. I have over-simplified that. But the question is: why don't we attack the 21 cents, not the 3.8? And yet, if you listen to the flak going around the country today, you would think that the price of bread has gone sky-high because of the grain we sold to Russia. The truth is that, if bread is high-priced, it is because of all the other costs involved in putting it inside that wrapper.

Interview, Washington/
U.S. News & World Report, 2-5:33.

3

During the last two months, we had seasonal wintertime rises in farm prices, largely due to weather and transportation shortages. Newspapers and press stories have blown these seasonal monthly rises into preposterous annual increases . . . That use of statistics is like saying, if you have a cold this week, it is at the annual rate of 52 colds a year. This kind of arithmetic is preposterous, and the urban newspapers ought to know better.

At National Agricultural Outlook
Conference, Feb. 20/
The Dallas Times Herald, 2-21:(A)19.

4

[On why some Nixon Administration sources talk about the possibility of farm price controls while he and the President are outspokenly against them]: That's because there are still some damn fools in the Administration who don't agree with me. The Democrats don't have a monopoly on damn fools.

News conference, Washington,
March 20/The New York Times, 3-21:22.

5

To the housewives of America, I say: Take another look: Inflation has raised the cost of your food. Bigger spending by Congress has broken the Federal budget; the resulting budget deficits have fanned the fires of inflation; inflation, in turn, has raised your prices; and this is what has broken your family budget. Housewives who are boycotting food: Take your placards and your signs, take your pickets and your lines, take your microphones and march to the doors of Congress. There you will find those budget-breakers, those spenders, those fiscally irresponsible people who have raised the price of your grocery cart, raised the price of your family car, raised the price of your medical care, raised the level of your rent, raised the level of your interest rates and raised your taxes. Unless these spenders are sobered by your uprising, they will raise both your costs and your taxes once again. Just as you housewives practice selective shopping at the grocery store to get your family's nutrition at a price that you can afford, it is time for you, the housewives of America, to march to the doors of Congress, point a finger at those budget-breaking Congressmen who are responsible for fanning inflation, and start being more selective about

(EARL L. BUTZ)

shopping for fiscally-responsible Congressmen who will get you the government you can afford.

*Before National Press Club,
Washington, April 3/
Human Events, 4-14:10.*

1

[Arguing against strong government controls on food prices]: You end up with empty counters; you end up with black markets; you end up with special deals; you end up with a situation that people simply don't like. It is what we had in World War II when we had food rationing, and our people wanted it ended as soon as they could get it ended.

*TV-radio interview/"Meet the Press,"
National Broadcasting Company, 4-8.*

2

[The] work ethic needs now, as never before, to be reinforced by incentive. America attained greatness because, for nearly two centuries, the American people produced under a competitive incentive system—the chance to earn, to innovate, to own, to be different, to keep something for themselves, to maximize their individual worth in some close relationship to their own dedication and hard work . . . America would be in less of a predicament today—with inflation at home and burdensome trade deficits—if we had not fallen behind Japan and Western Europe in our rate of productivity increase. Our society must break free from the insidious trend toward the reliance of people on government for their security, income and well-being.

*At University of North Carolina
commencement, Charlotte/
The National Observer, 5-26:13.*

3

You'll get back to 79-cent roasts about the time you get back to the 60-cent minimum wage, about the time you get back to $1000 for a new Chevrolet car, about the time you get back to getting your bathroom repaired for $19.50 instead of the $80 it now costs. [The country is] permanently on a higher

price level, and it's across the board.

*Before Economic Society of Southern
Florida, Miami, Aug. 8/
San Francisco Chronicle, 8-9:9.*

4

The private sector of the economy remains the wellspring of initiative, of innovation, of production and of well-being. This is not an old-fashioned, obsolete concept. It is as modern as today. It has worked in this country for 197 years. In spite of our efforts to hobble it, in spite of our efforts to cripple it, in spite of the growth of big government, in spite of Federal domination, our free-enterprise economy still works. This is the wisdom behind Phase 4 [of the Nixon Administration's economic program]—and why Phase 5 will be Phase-Out.

*Before Economic Society of Southern
Florida, Miami, Aug. 8/
Vital Speeches, 9-1:688.*

Mortimer Caplin
*Former Commissioner, Internal Revenue
Service of the United States*

5

The American tax system . . . is one of the wonders of the world. No other nation has the level of compliance we have; and I'm talking about nations close to our traditions —England and Canada and many others. Sure, we have a very tough statute with criminal penalties and broad investigative powers in the hands of revenue agents. But there is a tradition of tax compliance in this country going back to the Revolution. We were born with the cry of taxation on our lips, and we've been a very tax-conscious nation. We had a whiskey rebellion one time when we didn't like excise taxes on corn liquor. We do have a high level of education, and we do have a religious streak in the country. But mainly, the people, I believe, are essentially honest. I say this after traveling all over the country, studying statistics on millions of returns. I think Americans are an unusually honest people, despite the ills of the day. But they do cry for leadership, and they do want to make sure they're not being taken advantage of.

They like the fact that their neighbor is paying his fair share, too. And if the fellow down the street is somehow beating the game, it has a corrosive effect.

Interview/
The Washington Post, 12-16:(B)5.

Ewan Clague
Former Commissioner,
Bureau of Labor Statistics,
Department of Labor of the United States

1

In about 10 years, you are going to have fewer people entering the labor force and, on the other end, more and more people retiring earlier and living longer. It will be a real shrinkage in the work force, and that is going to be trouble. To encourage retirement at age 55, this nation has got to be crazy.

The Washington Post, 3-25:(A)20.

A. W. Clausen
President, Bank of America

2

If Europe has only lukewarm faith in this country's ability to control homefront inflation, we can attribute some little part of it to the historic delays, lags and procrastinations that have typified our use of fiscal weapons in fighting inflation . . . It is absolutely critical —as soon as possible—to show the world that we not only will keep the rate of inflation in check but that we are determined to reduce the level of inflation further than it has been to date. There is a solution to this problem which I believe merits serious consideration by both the Congress and the White House. I suggest that the President propose—and the Congress take the necessary legislative steps to enact—a contingency stabilization tax purposely constructed to puncture the balloon of inflationary expectations. Specifically, this contingency tax would consist of an individual and corporate income tax surcharge which would not take effect unless triggered automatically by an abnormal increase in the rate of inflation. It could go on or off—as circumstances warranted and without political flimflam.

Before Los Angeles World Affairs Council,
March 30/Vital Speeches, 5-1:441.

3

Gentlemen and scholars may disagree on whether inflation is an insidious infiltrator or a violent adversary. But it doesn't matter whether inflation appears in the guise of a cat burglar wearing tennis shoes or as a storm trooper with hobnailed boots. Inflation is our economy's Public Enemy Number One.

Before New York University
Money Marketeers, April 25/
Quote, 6-10:539.

4

In the present economic environment, existing wage and price controls do little to contain the over-all forces of inflation. Moreover, they distort the flows of production and trade and discourage needed capital investment. In my opinion, their band-aid effect is out-worn, and they now should be removed as impediments to the corrective process. Controls ultimately contribute to inflation. They wind up inflationary expectations like a trap spring.

New York, Dec. 17/
San Francisco Examiner, 12-17:60.

James M. Collins
United States Representative, R-Texas

5

Taxpayers will pay more than $2 million in food stamps to [labor] strikers in fiscal 1973. A major loophole has been found and is being exploited . . . When there is little or no economic pressure on the rank-and-file union member to settle a strike, he does not push for a settlement, and the union is able to hold out longer for bigger pay increases. As a result of the abuse of food stamps, the most effective pressure on unions today is removed.

Before the House, Washington, May 15/
The Dallas Times Herald, 5-16:(A)7.

John B. Connally, Jr.
Former Secretary of the Treasury
of the United States; Former Governor
of Texas

6

I have never heard so much unjustified prognosis of gloom and doom [about the economy]. Here we are in the middle of a

(JOHN B. CONNALLY, JR.)

broad economic expansion of enormous proportions, yet there are people constantly talking about, "Well, it's terrible, but we're facing a recession." Now, I don't know how you answer these things.

June 20/Los Angeles Times, 6-21 (3)15.

1

The future of this country in the decade of the '70s and into the '80s is going to be determined not by political intrigue or military diplomacy or political diplomacy, but by economic diplomacy.

*Before California Republican State
Committee, San Diego, Sept. 8/
Los Angeles Herald-Examiner, 9-10:(A)3.*

Frederick B. Dent
Secretary of Commerce of the United States

2

The more we can avoid [wage-price] controls, the healthier the economy will be in the long run, because controls build in economic pressures which sooner or later must be satisfied. Undoubtedly, part of the inflationary pressures we felt in February and March were the result of the working out of inequities and pressures built up under Phase 2, and which everyone recognized would have to be satisfied . . . Many feel the record of Phase 3 is suspect. But the combination of prosperity in the country, pressures from almost twice the rate of inflation in foodstuffs and perverse effects of the devaluation of the dollar are economic forces that were difficult for any control system to restrain.

*Interview, Los Angeles, May 2/
Los Angeles Times, 5-3:(3)13.*

3

Where in this land are voices being heard . . . calling for patience for us to work out of our difficulties without destroying the character of this magnificent [free-enterprise] system which has given us so much? Can we find in the business community staunch defenders of this system? Where are the businessmen who are counseling their friends and neighbors to have confidence that the resilience of this system can best restore economic order with-

out the distortions which are inevitably brought upon us by government regulations? We have so very much to lose, and yet there are so few who are concerned with defending and broadening the appreciation of what we have. The genius of America has been our ability to accomplish through incentives all the things to which we ascribe proper priority. Yet, during the recent debate here in Washington as to how far back we would roll prices, who was speaking up to point out the danger of shortages, disincentives, rationing, black markets and all the rest of the economic evils that would have befallen our society?

Nation's Business/September:34.

William L. Dickinson
United States Representative, R-Alabama

4

America's [labor] unions have lulled their workers to sleep and have them believing welfare and food stamps are a "right." Most large unions have a liaison man between the welfare people and the labor union. The union contacts this man prior to a strike, and he sets the machinery in motion so that strikers will be immediately eligible for food stamps when the strike starts.

Human Events, 4-14:3.

John Diebold
Management consultant

5

We are producing new machines that are more technically complex and more powerful than ever before. But our methods of management, and our human relations in offices and factories, have not kept pace. In many ways, the huge strides we have made in technology are at the heart of today's social tumult and upheaval. Most people spend more than a third of their working lives on the job. It seems to me that, in our increasingly educated society, every person ought to be free to decide what level of pressure and challenge he wants put upon him. And he should be equally free to opt out without any adversary relationship with his boss.

*Interview, Washington/
U.S. News & World Report, 1-29:42.*

Michael DiSalle
Director,
Federal Office of Price Stabilization

1

The only way to get food prices down is to "keep them down on the farm after they've seen parity."

San Francisco Examiner & Chronicle,
4-22:(This World)2.

Otto Eckstein
Professor of Economics, Harvard University;
Former member, Council of Economic Advisers to the President of the United States

2

[The basic reason for the current fast-moving inflation is that] the whole world's economy is in a period of strong expansion right now. This is bound to run up prices in the short run, as supplies are relatively inelastic over a short period. That has happened everywhere—in Europe and Japan, for example, as well as in this country. In the United States, the [Nixon] Administration did right in applying its Phase 1 freeze on prices and wages, but it should have been kept on for six months rather than three. Then came the controls of Phase 2, which were simply too weak all around. Phase 3, in turn, was widely interpreted by the business community as signaling the end of controls. Consequently, with Phase 3 there has been an explosion of prices—one that was not at all necessary at this time.

U.S. News & World Report, 4-23:26.

Edgar R. Fiedler
Assistant Secretary for Economic Policy,
Department of the Treasury of the
United States

3

The public's attention has been diverted from the basic inflation problem—supply and demand. The American people have not been educated. Price and wage controls can make a contribution to the anti-inflation effort—as they did in part in 1972. But what happens to inflation during 1973 and 1974 does not depend in the main on the [government]

controls program. What it does depend on, fundamentally, is the economic pressure of demand upon supply.

News conference, Los Angeles, April 10/
Los Angeles Times, 4-11:(3)11.

Milton Friedman
Professor of Economics,
University of Chicago

4

Technically, inflation isn't terribly difficult to stop. The real problem is that the favorable effects of inflation come early, the bad effects late. In a way, it's like drink. The first few months or years of inflation, like the first few drinks, seem just fine. Everyone has more money to spend and prices aren't rising quite as fast as the money that's available. The hangover comes when prices start to catch up. And, of course, some people are hurt worse than others by inflation—usually people without much political voice: the poor and retired people on fixed incomes. Some people aren't hurt at all. And others profit enormously. When you start to take some action *against* inflation, on the other hand, the bad effects are felt right away. People are out of work. Interest rates go up. Money gets tight. It's unpleasant. Only later do the good effects of an end to rising prices show up. The problem is getting through the painful cure without wanting another drink. The greatest difficulty in curtailing inflation is that, after a while, people begin to think they'd rather have the sickness than the cure. What they don't realize is that, once the cure has taken effect, it's possible to have both economic growth and price stability. But as we saw with [President] Nixon, there is terrible public pressure to junk the cure and go back to being sick—or drunk, to continue the metaphor.

Interview, Ely, Vermont/
Playboy, February:52.

John Kenneth Galbraith
Professor of Economics, Harvard University

5

A [wage-price] controls program won't be effective until it is administered by people

(JOHN KENNETH GALBRAITH)

who believe in it. Right now [under the Nixon Administration], it's like the hierarchy of the Catholic Church being put in charge of birth control.

Newsweek, 6-25:71.

1

. . . the teaching of economics is a disguise for the exercise of power—part of the power system itself. Every year economists intellectually condition thousands of students and much of the public through writing and pronouncements. Contrary to what these economists say, economic forces do not work out for the best, except for the powerful.

Interview, Newfane, Vt./Parade, 9-9:11.

2

[President Nixon's advisers] stand about in the same relation to economic affairs as [evangelist] Billy Graham does in relation to sin. It's something that they preside over but they don't do anything about.

News conference, Boston, Dec. 2/
San Francisco Examiner, 12-3:6.

Richard C. Gerstenberg
Chairman, General Motors Corporation

3

I now suggest that the day has passed when the dialogue between [labor] union and management must be couched in the tired rhetoric of divisiveness. I now suggest that we have come to a time when we can acknowledge that we have far more in common than in conflict, when we can jointly pay our respects to the buried animosities of the past while we pay tribute to what we have jointly achieved despite them. These differences have no place in our country today; they have gone the way of the sweatshop.

U.S. News & World Report, 4-2:88.

4

Any way you look at it, our business is awfully good at the minute. People are spending money, yet they are concerned. I guess inflation is the main worry. We will always have a certain inflation; but the recent inflation in particular things, notably food, is far beyond what we can live with. No part of the money a guy spends, day to day, does he become more conscious of than what his wife has to pay for food. This food thing touches the housewife every day, and she complains to her husband, and this brings a hell of a lot of pressure on the [labor] unions to ask more than they might have otherwise. It's awfully important that we get the price of food under control.

Interview, Washington/
Los Angeles Times, 6-22:(2)7.

5

. . . there is no question that wage and price controls were a good prescription for an ailing economy when they were instituted back in August of 1971. For some time thereafter, our economy continued to benefit from close and careful surveillance and supervision. But now we feel the patient is sufficiently on the way to recovery to be taken off medication which, in any case, cannot be administered indefinitely. The competitive market that has served this nation for so long is robust, it is healthy, and it is resourceful. Given the opportunity to operate again in freedom, it will be again.

Before Financial Executives Institute,
New York, Oct. 22/
Vital Speeches, 12-15:145.

C. Jackson Grayson, Jr.
Former Chairman, Price Commission,
Federal Cost of Living Council

6

I prefer to see the whole wage-price burden put back on business and labor. It should be made clear that the responsibility is theirs, not the government's. The more decisions that are shoved on to Washington, the more the public tends to feel that private parties can't be trusted to handle them. That, in turn, can lead to greater public control of our private-enterprise system—which, in my view, would mean less efficiency and a loss of our personal freedoms.

Interview, Washington/
U.S. News & World Report, 3-5:37.

C. Jackson Grayson, Jr.
*Dean, Southern Methodist University
School of Business;
Former Chairman, Price Commission,
Federal Cost of Living Council*

1

[On the time he spent on the Price Commission]: It was a tremendous learning experience. I saw the tremendous complexities and interrelationships of the economy. It gave me a new understanding of how, when you affect one part of the economy, it ripples through other parts. You can't view any one single action by itself. For example, the supply of anchovies off the coast of Peru influences the price of soybean meal, which in turn shows up in the price of cattle feed.

*Interview, New York/
The Christian Science Monitor, 5-26:6.*

Matthew Guinan
*President,
Transport Workers Union of America*

2

No matter how sophisticated the leaders of industry and labor may become, labor must retain the only truly effective weapon it has —the strike.

*At labor conference, San Francisco/
U.S. News & World Report, 6-25:71.*

Paul Hall
*President, Seafarers International
Union of North America*

3

Labor and management in the maritime industry must cooperate or die. Hell, we've had men in recent months shut down a ship just because there was no chocolate ice cream on board; not because there was no ice cream on the damned ship, you understand, but because they didn't have the right kind of ice cream. We in the maritime unions know we have the guts and muscle to fight if we have to. But maritime [labor] strikes have outlived their purpose. If the maritime industry is to be rejuvenated, there must be no strikes, no work stoppages, no interferences with the flow of ships and their cargo.

Interview/Los Angeles Times, 7-4:(1)10.

Michael J. Harrington
*United States Representative,
D-Massachusetts*

4

The passage by the House yesterday of the amendment to prohibit food stamps for workers on strike was an action lacking both wisdom and fairness . . . The integrity of the collective-bargaining process would have been strengthened, not diminished, by allowing working people and their families to receive food stamps if they qualified in other respects. Many union families would not have so qualified, but the stamps would have insured that members at the lower tip of the income spectrum could participate in strike activity. As for the responsibility of government, it continues to lie in making certain that collective bargaining is truly an adversary process between two capable parties. It is my opinion that cutting off food stamps will greatly interfere with this process.

*Before the House, Washington, July 20/
The Washington Post, 7-24:(A)20.*

John S. Harrison
*Executive vice president,
Aluminum Company of America*

5

. . . I am confident that our economic system will survive, if for no other reason [than] that it is the most successful and adaptable one ever devised by man. It allows man to do what he does best—express himself, be daring and creative; to succeed if he is clever and aggressive; to fail—entirely on his own—if he can't cut it. It seems to me that such a system—based on individual ability —must ultimately outlive all attempts to confine or restrict it. The fact that its essential ingredient—individual reward for taking risk and succeeding in competition—the fact that this has to be re-invented from time to time and added to other systems—is compelling evidence of its unique vitality.

*At Junior Achievement conference,
University of Indiana, Aug. 15/
Vital Speeches, 9-15:716.*

Jesse A. Helms
United States Senator,
R-North Carolina

1

Public assistance to *either* side in a labor dispute violates the rights of the opposing party. Public assistance in the form of the distribution of food stamps to strikers' households has the undeniable effect of giving a distinct economic advantage to the union in the collective-bargaining contest. The duration of strikes has increased significantly since the advent of welfare payments to strikers. To continue these payments will only fuel this trend, thus bringing more pressures on our already troubled economy and further undermining the principles of free collective bargaining which is so vital to the American free-enterprise system.

Before the Senate, Washington/
Human Events, 8-11:4.

Walter E. Hoadley
Executive vice president,
Bank of America

2

Everyone is so occupied with the next 30 minutes or the next 60 days, they don't see the long-range consequences [of economic policy such as wage-price controls]. There's very little prospect of getting things back to normal in this decade . . . Whether you number them or not, we're going to be going through phases indefinitely from here on out. We're going to be trying everything. What works, we'll use until it stops working. But there won't be any enduring solutions.

Newsweek, 6-25:71.

James D. Hodgson
Former Secretary of Labor
of the United States

3

[For four years as Labor Secretary, I sat] and watched just about everyone grow increasingly fed up with the big [labor] strike. Along would come some strike—in railroads, longshore, autos, or whatever—and the protest would mount. The inconvenienced public wailed, union members saw their modest savings wiped out, corporate profits plummeted, communities suffered from bad business and bad feeling, the government saw its economic goals threatened. Only the foreign competitors cheered.

Interview/Los Angeles Times, 7-4:(1)10.

Sidney Homer
Investment banker

4

We have tried a dozen painless, ineffective cures for our inflation. We have compromised with it. We have in this way lived through our "economic Munich" and are now suffering the consequences. Democracies, when faced with burdensome problems, have a way of trying all sorts of temporary palliatives before they get their courage up to really fight the evil. We have arrived at that point where a vigorous democracy finally wakes up to its problem and often acts courageously and effectively. Perhaps we will.

At Southern Conference on Teacher
Retirement, Dallas/
The Dallas Times Herald, 6-6:(D)14.

Hubert H. Humphrey
United States Senator, D-Minnesota

5

Across the board—from the price of gold, to balance of payments, to stock-market decline, to consumer confidence, to increasing interest rates—the economic policies of this [Nixon] Administration spell disaster.

At Congressional Joint Economic
Committee hearing, Washington,
May 23/The Washington Post, 5-24:(D)17.

6

I know that excess [government] spending is inflationary. But the question is what do you spend it for. It is not inflationary to take care of your health. It is not inflationary to educate your children. It is not inflationary to train people who have little or no skill, to make them somebody's skilled workers. It is not inflationary to make your streets safe. It is not inflationary for you to have a decent home. I'll tell you what's inflationary: to waste money on military weapons that may or may not be needed; to waste money on excessive interest charges. I'll tell you what's inflationary: to leave people unemployed; to let them go down the drain.

Quote, 5-27:488.

Henry M. Jackson
United States Senator, D-Washington

1

I believe that an American President, to be effective, must have the confidence of business and labor. I think the President must be personally involved in trying to bring about price-wage stability in which you have long-range price-wage guidelines. I see the need for some tough controls for a long time to come. I don't like controls, but this [Nixon] Administration has been "on-again, off-again" and as soon as a control system starts to work—like Phase 2—they dump it. The result has been a disaster. Most thoughtful businessmen agree with me.

Interview, Washington/
"W": a Fairchild publication, 10-19:9.

2

This [Nixon] Administration has done more to unbalance our economy, to indulge the greed of the rich while denying the need of the poor, than any in memory. It makes the Harding Administration look like Boy Scouts and the Hoover Administration look like economic geniuses . . . Back in October of 1968, then-candidate Nixon said: "I do not believe Americans should be forced to choose between unemployment and un-American [wage-price] controls." Well, there is a promise he has kept, because he hasn't forced us to choose—he has given us both.

At AFL-CIO convention,
Bal Harbour, Fla., Oct. 19/
San Francisco Examiner, 10-19:10.

Thomas E. Kauper
Assistant Attorney General,
Antitrust Division, Department of
Justice of the United States

3

[On the free-enterprise system]: This is probably not the kind of thing I'm supposed to say, but I have always had a little doubt about how committed the general public really is to the notion of competition.

The Dallas Times Herald, 8-6:(C)6.

E. Douglas Kenna
President,
National Association of Manufacturers

4

[On President Nixon's Phase 4 economic program]: With chaotic conditions in the production and distribution of goods already painfully apparent, Phase 4 seems likely to further aggravate the mounting adverse effects of controls. Furthermore, the failure to provide for equal treatment of wages in a rigid restraint program ignores by far the largest element of production costs.

San Francisco Examiner & Chronicle,
7-29:(This World)10.

Edward M. Kennedy
United States Senator, D-Massachusetts

5

They [the Nixon Administration] have imposed a heavy burden of taxation upon every working man, permitting a wealthy few to withhold their fair contribution to the cost of the nation. Our ancestors took up arms against unjust taxation. Now our government denies us that which they battled to secure. They have forced upon this nation policies which mask the hopes and fair expectations of all who labor. High interest rates, for example, do not damage the banks which collect them, nor disturb the wealthy who deduct them. But they damage every consumer who must make higher payments for his house, his car and television. And they can cripple the small businessman who must borrow to finance his operation or equipment. Not content with the depredations of unjust taxes and high interest, they are responsible for inflation which penny-by-penny, day-by-day, lowers the earnings and savings, pensions and insurance of the great majority, even while profits soar.

At Independence Day celebration,
Decatur, Ala., July 4/
The Washington Post, 7-5:(A)6.

Theodore W. Kheel
Director,
Institute of Collective Bargaining
and Group Relations

1

In my judgment, the prospect of a [labor] strike in the vast majority of bargaining situations can never be outmoded, unaccepted, outlawed or rendered obsolete without doing more damage than the relief the public will supposedly get. The strike and collective bargaining are Siamese twins. They cannot be severed. But that does not mean that strikes cannot be avoided. [Strikes] are still with us and will likely be as long as the Constitution remains in force.

At labor conference, San Francisco/
U.S. News & World Report, 6-25:70.

Virginia H. Knauer
Director,
Federal Office of Consumer Affairs

2

[On consumer boycotts of high-priced food products]: I do not favor boycotts, but I do favor selective purchasing. From my own experience, I have found a shopper can generally trim as much as 10 per cent off her food budget through such tactics as using unit pricing, avoiding impulse buying, cutting back on convenience shopping, using shopping lists and so on. In place of higher-cost meats, I urge the substitution of lower-price protein such as eggs, cheese, poultry, fish, beans and organ meat. Even the cheapest cuts of meat can be turned into a gourmet meal with imagination and a few spices.

Interview/
The Dallas Times Herald, 3-11:(A)46.

William J. Kuhfuss
President,
American Farm Bureau Federation

3

[Criticizing the Nixon Administration's freezes on agricultural prices]: We were about to crest on food costs this year when they bowed to political pressure. Too many people are trying to discredit profitability, the greatest motivator ever devised for an enterprise

system. The freeze took the profit out of poultry and milk because grain costs kept rising; and what happened?—chicks are killed and milk cows sold for slaughter. It will take time to recover, and prices will be driven up. No other country has the production capacity we have, if the market is allowed to operate. But legislation and management decisions look to the past and so make mistakes; but the market tends to look at the present and ahead to the future, and so it makes more-intelligent decisions.

The Christian Science Monitor, 7-13:5.

R. Heath Larry
Vice chairman,
United States Steel Corporation

4

I share the President's [Nixon] concern about the present rate of inflation . . . But the real contributors to rising price indexes are matters such as food, energy and raw materials, which are more subject to world-market influences than to domestic controls.

Interview/
U.S. News & World Report, 7-2:18.

Hans Mast
Chief economist, Swiss Credit Bank,
Zurich

5

Most likely, we are headed for a cumulative recession—in Europe and world-wide. While production is slowing down, cost inflation keeps speeding up. The results will be a worsening profit squeeze, cutbacks in investment programs, weakening consumer demand, higher unemployment. Monetary uncertainty makes things worse. It's a depressing picture.

U.S. News & World Report, 12-17:57.

Paul W. McCracken
Former Chairman, Council of Economic
Advisers to the President of the
United States

6

We have a very peculiar profile of consumer sentiment at the moment. In general, consumer sentiment is quite bearish. On the other hand, people think it's a good time to buy because of their fear of price rises later. Traditionally, inflation is associated with reduced plans to buy. This time, increased fear of inflation and higher prices is causing people to buy. This creates a very interesting and very difficult problem for us. The problem is, there's evidence of over-buying, anticipatory buying. Once that fades out of the picture, and if this generally bearish consumer sentiment takes over—especially if this happens at the same time as other checks on inflation —we could have an air pocket around the turn of the year.

San Francisco Examiner & Chronicle,
6-10:(This World)20.

George W. McKinney, Jr.
Senior vice president,
Irving Trust Company, New York

1

[On stopping inflation]: Step number one in this process is to get rid of direct controls over wages and prices and interest rates. These controls have accelerated the inflation. They have stimulated faster growth of the nation's money supply and have caused interest rates to rise more rapidly to higher levels than would otherwise have been the case. They have led to overly-relaxed fiscal and monetary policies and have further weakened the international position of the dollar. Finally, they are building up further distortions that make it increasingly difficult to stop the basic inflationary problem itself. We can only solve our inflationary problems by avoiding excessively stimulative fiscal and monetary measures, particularly during periods of economic slack, for a number of years. It's a difficult prescription; but, until we follow it, our domestic monetary muddle—and therefore our international monetary muddle—will be a fact of life.

At Contrary Opinion Forum,
Vergennes, Vt., Oct. 6/
Vital Speeches, 12-1:103.

George Meany
President, American Federation of Labor-
Congress of Industrial Organizations

2

. . . American workers face 1973 in the unshaken belief that trade-unionism will serve them as well in the future as it has in the past. They pay no heed to the editorialists, wrong so often in the past, who claim unions are weaker, divided, unprepared for the battles that lie ahead. These purveyors of gloom couldn't be more wrong . . .

New Year statement/
The Fresno (Calif.) Bee, 1-25:(A)26.

3

[Advocating price controls on farm products, restoration of rent controls and enactment of an excess-profits tax]: If the Congress fails to make the Economic Stabilization Act fair and equitable, then workers and consumers will be stampeded by food prices, gouged by landlords, fleeced by money-lenders and squeezed by profit-hungry corporations.

Before House Banking Committee,
Washington, March 28/
Los Angeles Times, 3-29:(1)5.

4

Since August 15, 1971 [when President Nixon announced Phase 1 economic controls], America has seen the folly of giving the President blank-check authority in this [wage and price] field . . . but an important lesson can—and must—be learned from this experience: that the Congress must be explicit in the authority it grants the President on economic measures. Be explicit. Spell out what you mean. Don't use general terms or leave room for "interpretations" which may bear no resemblance to Congressional intent. In other words, tell the Administration what the Congress deems fair and equitable. Write it into law.

Before House Banking Committee,
Washington/The Christian Science Monitor,
4-6:6.

5

[Criticizing the performance of new Labor Secretary Peter Brennan and President Nixon's assertion that Brennan fights for what he believes and is a "team player"]: If Pete is on the team and that is a team, then I submit he will have to admit that he cannot be on two competing teams at the same time. The team idea is propaganda, mere propaganda. If that's a baseball team, the pitcher and the catcher

(GEORGE MEANY)

are named Richard. The first, second and third basemen and the shortstop are named Nixon. Right field, center field, left field —those guys are named Milhous. In fact, I don't even think Pete's on the taxi squad.

At conference of construction trade unions, Washington, April 16/ The Washington Post, 4-17:(A)1.

1

[On why labor strikes are not as readily used by unions today as in the past]: Things are different today. Simply because collective bargaining has raised living standards and improved and stabilized the financial circumstances of a great many workers, these workers now have a great deal more to lose. They have mortgage payments, car payments, college tuition payments—things that did not burden them 20 or 30 years ago. So with every year that passes, strikes become a more serious matter to workers, and, I would guess, to managements as well.

The New York Times, 4-22:(1)46.

2

The right [of labor] to negotiate with management is an empty promise if it does not include the right to strike. That is the basic economic weapon—ultimately the only weapon—workers have to insure that their employers come to the bargaining table in good faith.

The New York Times, 4-24:33.

3

. . . the record shows that [organized] labor has been successful—and it's on the record; it can be documented—in passing beneficial legislation which affects all workers. They all get the benefit. In other words, every worker in this country, un-organized or organized—has workmen's compensation. Every worker in this country has unemployment insurance, un-organized or organized. Workers who get old have Medicare and so forth, un-organized or organized. All of these things were put on the statute books through the efforts of the minority who are organized. They weren't put on there by the employers; they weren't put on there by the politicians.

Employers and politicians didn't get together and say this is a good thing to do. All of these things—and this can be documented—all came from the efforts of the organized worker. Because he's organized, he can exert some influence. Now, the beneficiary of all these things is the un-organized worker. And the un-organized worker benefits—and this can be documented, too—he benefits from our wage increases. Every time organized workers get an increase, un-organized workers also, within a reasonable length of time, get an increase. Now, they don't get the same, but they do go up. And this is the history of every industry, every profession, every calling in the country; every mechanic, every building-trades mechanic, every machinist—his wages go up. The little machine shops that are un-organized, their wages go up.

Interview, Washington/ The National Observer, 5-5:18.

4

The fellow that started out to control this economy is a fellow by the name of [President Richard] Nixon, and he started out to control it in 1969 and he has just messed it up. It is up to him and to the Congress to come up with something equitable. I don't think a rigid control or freeze now on prices and wages in their present relationship would be fair. Certainly, low-income workers should be exempted from controls. I certainly think there would have to be room for a substantial catch-up on the part of wages before any sort of lid is applied to them—and no lid at all unless prices, rents, profits and interest rates are controlled just as effectively. I personally think that the only answer is controls right across the board, just the same as we had in wartime. Now, of course, the argument here is that, well, we can do this but we have to create a great big bureaucracy. Well, if the alternative is creating a great big bureaucracy or to see this economy go into a complete tailspin, then I think we've got to create the bureaucracy. If this is not going to be done, there should be no controls, and certainly none on working people alone.

Interview, Washington/ The National Observer, 5-5:24.

1

[Accusing the Nixon Administration of "doctoring" economic statistics for its own political purposes]: They can't seem to break the habit of deceit. This is a cold-hearted Administration; but it wants to be loved, and so it lies. It wants to act like Scrooge, but at the same time to look like Santa Claus; and boy, that takes quite a makeup job.

Before A. Philip Randolph Institute,
Washington, May 18/
The Dallas Times Herald, 5-20:(A)23.

2

Once upon a time, long ago, [labor] unions were looked upon as unpatriotic, as un-American conspiracies. Patriotism was the exclusive possession of the followers of Alexander Hamilton, the so-called upper classes . . . the union organizer was denounced as an outside agitator, while his employer was often exalted as the pillar of the community; and, for some reason I could never understand, he was almost always a Republican. How times have changed; or perhaps i should say how the stereotypes have changed. Today, the worker is portrayed as the pillar of the status quo, and his patriotism is "out of style," "excessive," if not downright "ridiculous." On the other hand, the employer is, in many cases, gloating over the prospect of trade deals with the Soviets, while his secretary is booking tickets for the [Communist] Chinese ballet, his wife is at the country club contemplating acupuncture for her next face lift, and his kids are most likely organizing Jane Fonda fan clubs and picketing the White House against American policy.

Accepting Congressional Medal of Honor
Society's Patriots Award/
The Wall Street Journal, 7-2:10.

3

My answer [to inflation] is to take all [wage-price] controls off. Take whatever chaos comes from the removal of all controls. I think more and more people are coming to the idea that this might be the answer. There is one thing about it: It would be equitable . . . if everything was left to the free market. As it is now, wages are controlled, [but] what else is controlled?

Interview/U.S. News & World Report, 9-10:78.

Arnold R. Miller
President,
United Mine Workers of America

4

Whether safety reduces production or whether it does not, we don't intend to bargain away our lives for a few more tons a day. The United Mine Workers of America is going to enforce safety to the letter, with no ands, ifs or buts. And if that is not acceptable to some coal operators, they had better find a new way of making a living. Coal miners in West Virginia and Kentucky and Pennsylvania and in other coalfields are tired of dying so that men in board rooms of New York and Boston and Pittsburgh can get rich.

At UMW convention, Pittsburgh,
Dec. 3/The New York Times, 12-4:51.

Wilbur D. Mills
United States Representative, D-Arkansas

5

[Arguing against investment-income tax increases such as on capital gains]: I've always been told that you can sheer a sheep each year, but you can only skin him once.

At House Ways and Means Committee
hearing, Washington, Feb. 5/
Los Angeles Times, 2-6:(1)1.

6

True [tax] equity is impossible to obtain under the present structure of the [Internal Revenue] Code. If we can't do something about that, we'll never have a law that will not be susceptible to criticism on the grounds that it is not totally and completely equitable. Take the case of capital gains. Capital has to be invested for us to grow, to produce additional employment, additional goods to be consumed, and so on. If you carry tax equity on capital gains to the point that you upset the balance and cause a decline in economic activity, you can bring on a depression right quick. In carrying out a desire for equity, you can only go so far without destroying some objective that has been written into the tax law.

Interview, Washington/
U.S. News & World Report, 4-16:54.

Walter F. Mondale
United States Senator, D-Minnesota

1

[On high-income persons who paid little tax in 1971 because of the minimum-tax loophole]: These favored taxpayers paid an average tax of only 4 per cent on their loophole income. That's a smaller rate than a wage-earner making $6,000 a year pays . . . These new Treasury figures show clearly how inadequate the minimum tax is. Thousands of wealthy Americans are piling up huge amounts of income every year from capital gains, oil depletion allowances, stock options, real estate tax shelters and other tax loopholes, and paying a smaller percentage of it in taxes than working people making $6,000 a year.

Washington, April 15/
Los Angeles Times, 4-16:(1)7.

2

The minimum wage has not been increased since 1966, and prices during that period have risen by more than 3.5 per cent. But the President [Nixon] says a $2-an-hour minimum wage, that doesn't even make up for inflation, is inflationary.

At Wisconsin COPE conference, Milwaukee,
Sept. 8/The Washington Post, 9-9:(A)11.

Edmund S. Muskie
United States Senator, D-Maine

3

Our taxes . . . fall hard and heavy on the vast bulk of low- and middle-income Americans, on the men and women whose main source of income is their salaries and wages or the earnings of their small stores, workshops and farms. Too often, the wealthy have umbrellas. We started with the idea of collecting taxes in direct proportion to ability to pay them. We have strayed from that path, and it is now time to go back to that sound beginning.

Before the Senate, Washington, Jan. 23/
Los Angeles Herald-Examiner, 1-23:(A)8.

Yasuhiro Nakasone
Minister of International Trade and
Industry of Japan

4

What shocks us most is that the United States has become so weak that it has to shock us. We find not only that the dollar is flabby, but, more basically, there is inflation, reduction in your labor productivity, a marked decline in work hours and in the quality of the goods we buy from you. All this disturbs us greatly.

Interview, Tokyo/
The New York Times, 3-23:35.

Richard M. Nixon
President of the United States

5

Since 1950, the share of the average family's income taken for taxes in the United States has nearly doubled, to more than 20 per cent. The average person worked less than 1 hour out of each 8-hour day to pay his taxes in 1950. Today he works nearly 2 hours each day for the tax collector. No wonder someone once described the taxpayer as a person who doesn't have to take a civil-service examination to work for the Federal government. In fact, if tax cuts had not been adopted during our first term, the average worker's pay increases last year would have been wiped out entirely by increased taxes. The only way to stop tax increases is [for government] to stop spending more than our present tax rates produce in revenue.

Radio address to the nation, Feb. 21/
Vital Speeches, 3-15:323.

6

. . . since we have been hearing so much in the past few months about what is wrong with the American economy, let us look at some of the things that are *right* about our economy. We can be proud that the American economy is by far the freest, the strongest and the most productive economy in the whole world. It gives us the highest standard of living in the world. We are in the middle of one of the biggest, strongest booms in our history. More Americans have jobs today than ever before. The average worker is earning more today than ever before. Your income buys more today than ever before. In August, 1971, I announced the new economic policy. Since then, the nation's output has increased by a phenomenal 11½ per cent, a more rapid growth than in any comparable period in the last 21 years. Four-and-a-half million new civilian jobs have been created—more than in any comparable period ever. At the same time, real per capita disposable income —meaning what you have left to spend after taxes and after inflation—has risen by 7½ per cent. This means that, in terms of what your money will actually buy, in the past year and a half your annual income has increased by the equivalent of four extra weeks' pay. When we consider these facts, therefore, we can see that, in terms of jobs, of income, of growth, we are enjoying one of the best periods in our history.

Broadcast address to the nation, Washington, June 13/Los Angeles Times, 6-14:(1)22.

1

The Phase 4 that follows the [just-announced 60-day price] freeze will not be designed to get us permanently into a controlled economy. On the contrary, it will be designed as a better way to get us out of a controlled economy, and to return us as quickly as possible to the free-market system. We are not going to put the American economy in a straitjacket. We are not going to control the boom in a way that would lead to a bust. We are not going to follow the advice of those who have proposed actions that would lead inevitably to a permanent system of price and wage controls. Such actions would bring good headlines tomorrow and bad headaches six months from now for every American family, in terms of rationing, black markets and eventually a recession leading to more unemployment . . . Let there be no mistake: If our economy is to remain dynamic, we must never slip into the temptation of imagining that in the long run controls can substitute for a free economy or permit us to escape the need for discipline in fiscal and monetary policy. We must not let controls become a narcotic—and we must not become addicted. There are all sorts of seemingly simple gimmicks that would give the appearance or offer the promise of controlling inflation—but that would carry a dangerous risk of bringing on a recession, and that would not be effective in holding down prices. Rigid, permanent controls always look better on paper than they do in practice.

Broadcast address to the nation, Washington, June 13/Los Angeles Times, 6-14:(1)22.

Wright Patman
United States Representative, D-Texas

2

We are headed toward a period in which we will see the highest interest rates in the history of this nation . . . We are headed for another real economic mess—another recession fueled by misguided monetary policies and hesitant economic stabilization efforts. Without question, the crunch is going to put home-building into another recession; and once again we are faced with the uncontrollable situation where about half the population is literally priced out of the housing market.

At Commercial Bank Presidents Conference, New York, July 24/The New York Times, 7-25:59.

Joseph A. Pechman
Director of economic studies, Brookings Institution

3

[Saying income-tax loopholes should be plugged]: It makes no sense for a nation with a median family income close to $11,000 to pretend that it cannot take care of its poor in a dignified way, improve its education system, remove some of the blight from its cities and support other public services adequately because it has reached the limits of its taxable capacity. Tax rates are high in this country because certain kinds of income largely escape taxation.

The Christian Science Monitor, 3-12:6.

Charles H. Percy
United States Senator, R-Illinois

4

I know it is very unpopular to say that you support any kind of tax increase. But I'd be quite willing to consider whatever means are necessary to control inflation.

News conference, Chicago, Sept. 17/ Los Angeles Herald-Examiner, 9-18:(B)8.

W. R. Poage
United States Representative,
D-Texas

1

The only way to hold down food prices is to encourage an adequate supply of food production. The only way to encourage the farmer to produce more is to give him adequate incentive. As the farmer's returns increase, his production will increase. And when production meets demand, farm prices will fall.

The Dallas Times Herald, 3-11:(A)38.

Bertram L. Podell
United States Representative, D-New York

2

The most recent casualty of Phase 4 [of the Nixon Administration's economic program] is a consumer item that is very popular in my district—the bagel. For the past few years, the price of bagels had stabilized at eight to ten cents. Then Mr. Nixon arranged for the sale of one-quarter of America's wheat harvest to the Soviet Union, giving inside information to a few speculators who were thus able to make a fortune on the deal. Finally, and incredibly, the President removed all price controls on wheat. The result was a substantial increase in the cost of flour. As a result, my constituents are now paying 12 to 15 cents for a bagel—an increase of between 20 to 50 per cent . . . The blame lies squarely with President Nixon and Secretary of Agriculture Earl Butz. The noted economist, John Kenneth Galbraith, recently remarked that having these men administer price controls is analogous to putting the Paulist Fathers in charge of a birth-control clinic . . . Much more is at stake than merely the price of bagels. The President's electoral mandate gave him the responsibility to represent the interests of all the people, not just the wealthy few. It is time for Mr. Nixon to wake up to the realities of the consumers' nightmare, and by his actions to justify the faith placed in him by so many Americans.

Before the House, Washington/
The Dallas Times Herald, 9-19:(E)2.

William Proxmire
United States Senator, D-Wisconsin

3

The recent devaluation [of the U.S. dollar] may have been necessary. But it is a confession of the failure of our government policies to keep America as strong and competitive as it was, and it will cost your family $50 to $100 a year in higher prices . . . the devaluation will reduce the competition for steel and auto companies and others. You'll pay more for the refrigerator you buy, and also more the next time you trade in your car.

Radio address to the nation,
Washington, Feb. 28/
Los Angeles Herald-Examiner, 2-28:(A)10.

Ronald Reagan
Governor of California

4

Government itself has been the biggest single cause of inflation, through deficit spending, and because government year in and year out has been consuming a bigger and bigger share of the national income through higher and higher taxes. The typical citizen must work longer to pay his family's taxes than he does to pay for their food, shelter and clothing combined. We work from January until some time in May just to pay our taxes.

San Francisco Examiner, 2-5:26.

5

[Arguing against consumer boycotts of high-priced meat]: Anyone is upset when prices—and particularly food prices—go up as much as they do. [But] no one knows exactly who to blame, [so boycotting is pointless]. If I am right, and I think I am right, acts of God [such as weather conditions in farm areas] had something to do with the present food prices. I'm not in favor of boycotting Him . . . The people should be reminded that in this country, as in no other country in the world, food is the lowest part, literally, of the family expense . . . We put food on the tables of America for about 15 per cent of the people's earnings.

News conference, Sacramento, March 27/
Los Angeles Times, 3-28:(1)3.

1

To suggest a tax increase to cure inflation is like telling a drunk that another drink will cure him.

News conference, Sacramento, April 24/
Los Angeles Times, 4-25:(1)8.

2

We will not whip inflation by shrugging our shoulders and saying it is somebody else's problem. It is everybody's problem. If we are to have lower prices, there must be greater efficiency—in our factories, on our farms, in our offices. And if we are to assure our prosperity, our people can no longer afford to pay a higher and higher percentage of their income in taxes. We must bring government spending under control if the wage gains our people make are to be real instead of an endless cycle of pay increases followed by higher tax deductions, followed by legitimate demands for even higher wages so that the people can pay even higher taxes. This is the classic cycle that leads to inflation. And that, along with our other economic problems, is why our people have difficulty making ends meet.

Before American Legion, Anaheim, Calif.,
June 22/Human Events, 7-14:14.

Abraham A. Ribicoff
United States Senator, D-Connecticut

3

What every housewife ought to know if national predictions about a looming egg shortage are right, is exactly where the problem and the blame really lie. The problem is simply that the nation's agri-business, the giant corporate farm industry, is not affected by the price freeze. A Midwestern corn-grower can charge what he wants. But the feed manufacturer and the poultry farmer to whom he sells can no longer pass on the increases to the shopper. To blame are the [Nixon] Administration and the overwhelming majority of Congress who have buckled under pressure from powerful agri-business lobbies to give growers the only profit in the long chain from the farm to the table. So when people scream about fewer eggs or thinner chickens, remember that the freeze stops at the silo door of agri-business. The question, then, is not

"which comes first, the chicken or the egg?" but who comes first, the agri-business executive or the consumer?

The Washington Post, 7-15:(C)6.

Edward B. Rust
President, State Farm Insurance Companies;
President-elect, Chamber of Commerce
of the United States

4

Somehow, management and labor must recognize that they have a common threat to their existence—our ability to compete in international markets. To the extent that we continue to have constant troubles between management and labor, we are impairing our success. A fellow told me a long time ago [that] it's hard to figure out how you sink one half of a ship without taking everybody else down with it. So we really need an educational process, and that sounds idealistic, I'm afraid. It's hard to bring about an economy where everybody understands that, if he pushes too hard in one place, he's going to push something out of place somewhere else.

Interview/Nation's Business, May:58.

Ronald A. Sarasin
United States Representative,
R-Connecticut

5

When we remove the [price] freeze, there's no question we'll see higher prices; but over the longer haul, the only way to bring prices down is to increase the supply . . . Price freezes don't solve problems. We have tinkered with the economy; and every time we have, we've loused it up a little bit more.

Television interview/
The Washington Post, 8-12:(A)14.

A. Schaefer
Chairman, Union Bank of Switzerland

6

Not only wage levels and indirect profits, as well as capital expenditures and corporate sales, but also inflation and the real growth of the economy are being determined more and more by the attitudes, perception and the

(A. SCHAEFER)

degree of economic responsibility shown by labor and labor organizations. If labor makes use of its greater political power to push through exaggerated claims for higher wages and benefits, longer vacations, shorter working hours and so forth, that do not take into proper consideration the actual capabilities of the economy, a situation results in which economic growth, full employment and price stability are jeopardized. The increased pressures on companies can be only partially offset by rationalizing their operations. When the wage level advances four times faster than labor's aggregate productivity—which, for example, has been the case in Switzerland for some time now—business and industry will, whenever possible, raise prices to make up that percentage of wage increases which cannot be offset by gains in productivity. This is done, of course, because, to forego profits, capital-spending projects and the allocation of funds for research would not only spell the end of individual companies, but the collapse of the entire economy as well.

Before Economic Club of Detroit,
Jan. 8/Vital Speeches, 2-1:243.

George P. Shultz
Secretary of the Treasury of the United States

1

[Under Phase 2 of the Nixon Administration's economic stabilization program, corporations and union bargainers] were driving their cars according to a specified speed; and before you could change the speed of your car, you had to go to Washington to get permission. In Phase 3, we say the rules are the same, the traffic laws are the same, and you sort of adjust to the conditions as you see them on a self-adjusting basis. But if you speed, you're going to get picked up. And if you're a drunken driver, you're going to lose your license. We can do that, and we will do that.

Before New York City Savings Bonds
Committee, Jan. 31/
The New York Times, 2-1:49.

2

The housewife, who wields the most powerful anti-inflation weapon through her buying decisions, can bring about stabilization by refusing to pay high meat prices. It is a clear fact that the housewives of America are damn smart people.

News briefing/Newsweek, 4-9:20.

3

The genius of our income-tax system is voluntary compliance . . . No amount of policing will achieve compliance if that willingness should disappear.

Washington/
The Christian Science Monitor, 5-1:9.

4

We don't have a free economy today. We've got a heavily-regulated economy; and, at least as I view it, we must untangle ourselves from that web and get back to a greater degree of freedom. I am labeled as an ideologue and I have lots of critics . . . Well, the people who write that think that they are delivering an insult to me; and I want to say, finally, that I consider it a compliment. I do have a set of ideals, a set of convictions and observations about what a good economy and a good society is; and freedom of enterprise —free markets, free collective bargaining—is a central element in it as far as I'm concerned.

Before Grocery Manufacturers of America,
White Sulphur Springs, W. Va./
The Wall Street Journal, 6-25:10.

William E. Simkin
Former Director,
Federal Mediation and Conciliation Service

5

I suspect that responsible labor leaders —almost across the board—are looking at the [labor] strike in a way that differs materially from commonly-held notions. The right to threaten a strike—and to fulfill that threat when necessary—is still cherished by most. But the actual exercise of the strike is becoming more and more distasteful. All too often, the gains are substantially less than the costs.

At labor conference, San Francisco/
U.S. News & World Report, 6-25:71.

Richard P. Simmons
President,
Allegheny Ludlum Steel Corporation

1

I take violent exception to the behavioral scientists who feel that everything from earthquakes down is caused by our failure to give our workers job adjustments. They point to the assembly line and the boredom of the job and say industry has to develop another way to build things to interest workers in their jobs. Of 80 million people, how many work on assembly lines? Our people will work overtime within reason. Are they willing to eliminate their jobs? Of course not. Would you? We could spend eight hours over a keg of beer and discuss this.

Interview, Pittsburgh/
The New York Times, 3-25:(3)7.

Howard K. Smith
News commentator,
American Broadcasting Company

2

There is no villain [in high meat prices]. Supermarkets operate on low profits and count on volume to make money. Meat packers' profits are about 1 per cent, very low. Feed-lot operators are actually losing money as their feed prices rise, and some are stopping production. True, breeders and farmers are making money; but they live in debt and uncertainty so much it is hard to begrudge them some good years. The problem, when you get to basics, is demand has simply exploded against limited supply. Each American demands twice as much beef as two decades ago, and there are many more Americans. The war-ravaged countries have grown rich suddenly and have strongly increased their demand for our meat and foods. The price leap is therefore inevitable. Supply will increase; but it may never increase enough to match the rising demand. So prices are likely to continue rising—though the rate of rise may slow as [price] controls fall away and breeders are reassured against their eternal fear of over-production. Meanwhile, we will have to take comfort in the fact that, even in inflation, food takes less of the budget of an American family than of an average family anywhere else in the world.

News commentary,
American Broadcasting Company, Aug. 6/
The Christian Science Monitor, 8-29:14.

Edgar B. Speer
Chairman,
United States Steel Corporation

3

. . . I fail to see any great economic wisdom in containing the forces of inflation by restricting the profits that are the basis for expanding production. It may be politically expedient over a short period of time—but in the long run it is economic folly. In fact, with the need for capital already great and growing in almost every sector of the national economy, the "long run" may be shorter than we think . . . Economic controls aren't some new device created by modern economists. In ancient China, Egypt, Greece, Rome—in fact, for more than 4,000 years—the idea has persisted that governments can hold down prices simply by making it illegal to raise them. Yet in all this time, under all manner of circumstances, the results have usually been shortages and economic chaos, generating greater problems for the same people that the controls were supposed to protect. The results are much the same here in the 20th century. Almost daily, shortages and dislocations caused by the current economic controls are becoming more evident. And while the government says it is trying to find a way out of controls, there are hints that it may recommend some type of permanent agency which could, as *Business Week* phrased it, "keep the Federal government in the controls business forever." Frankly, I believe it's time to put more freedom back into our free economy. It's not that I distrust the planners here in Washington. It's just that I have a lot more faith in the private judgments of the American public, whether they're acting as consumers or producers, whether they consider themselves part of labor or management, whether they are packaging, selling, or buying real estate. In other words, I'd rather see the cost of living controlled by the millions of private decisions

(EDGAR B. SPEER)

that are made every day in the supermarkets of this nation than by some super-authority located in our nation's Capitol. The only true test of whether a product is worth its price, or a company worth its profit, is that ultimate decision that's made at the point of sale.

Before Society of Industrial Realtors,
Washington, Nov. 10/
Vital Speeches, 1-1('74):182.

Herbert Stein
Chairman, Council of Economic Advisers
to the President of the United States

1

In 1969, the rate of inflation, as measured by the Consumer Price Index, was 6.1 per cent. In 1972, after we got past the bulge which followed the end of the [wage-price] freeze, the rate of inflation was 3.0 per cent. It has been my experience that people are almost always skeptical, and often infuriated, when you tell them that the rate of inflation has declined. They are likely to counter by asking indignantly, "What about hamburger? Or beefsteak?" I have been accused of suggesting that the way to beat the high cost of living is to stop eating. That is not my position, although there is a Jewish proverb which says that, if we didn't have to eat, we would all be rich. However, I do recognize that people have to eat. But it is also true that man does not live by hamburger alone. And the fact that the prices of non-food items have been rising less-rapidly makes the rapid rise of food prices more tolerable.

Before Virginia Council on Economic
Education, Richmond/
The National Observer, 3-3:13.

2

. . . one of the legacies of the 1971 price-control venture is the belief that a freeze is the cure for what ails you. This is simply a longing for the naivete and irresponsibility of childhood. No one would want to freeze prices and wages, even for a short period, if he were capable of a more flexible and sophisticated system . . . But even if it were desirable to do so, it is not possible to recapture

more than once in a generation the combination of national innocence and morale which makes a freeze endurable. I understand, of course, why the idea of a freeze is so popular with Congressmen: It is the only kind of price-control that can be applied by an Act of Congress. Other, more sophisticated and adaptable systems have to be run almost entirely by Administrative discretion . . . We [in the Administration] have not been lured into exclusive reliance on controls, but have fought for the necessary measures on both the demand and supply sides . . . And while we were and are reluctant price-fixers, we have tried hard to make the controls work, have even enjoyed doing so at times, but have remained determined that at the end of the tunnel there should be freedom, not more tunnel.

Before American Statistical Association,
New York, April 20/
The Washington Post, 4-21:(C)7.

Stanley S. Surrey
Professor of Law, Harvard University;
Former Assistant Secretary of the
Treasury of the United States

3

. . . tax reform is really a moral issue. It is not just a technical exercise to be engaged in by skilled experts. It is an effort to restore fundamental morality to a tax system by ending both its unfairness and the cynical, immoral way the tax game is played today by those with money and knowledgeable advisers.

Before House Ways and Means Committee,
Washington, Feb. 5/
Los Angeles Times, 2-6:(1)18.

Thomas J. Watson, Jr.
Chairman of the executive committee,
and former chairman of the board,
International Business Machines Corporation

4

My . . . guess is that all American industry is going to have to move slowly toward a non-layoff policy. I know it would be very hard for the auto industry to cope with it. But I do know that in Europe the concept of broad layoffs to suit the needs of management is pretty obsolete. I think it will be here, too, in the years ahead.

Interview, Armonk, N.Y./
Nation's Business, February:45.

William W. Winpisinger
General vice president,
International Association of Machinists

1

I submit that it is not statesmanship but suicide for [labor] unions to surrender their right to strike as long as 200 corporations control two-thirds of the nation's total productive capacity, as long as the richest 1.6 per cent of the population holds 30 per cent of all the assets in the private sector, and as long as workers' incomes are thousands of dollars below what even the government says is needed for a moderate standard of living.

Interview/Los Angeles Times, 7-4:(1)10.

Leonard Woodcock
President,
United Automobile Workers of America

2

We'd have been better off if there had been no [wage-price] controls at all. We were on our way to economic stabilization in 1971 when the deep freeze was put on. It is doubtful at best that the price controls in effect since August 1971 significantly altered the course that prices would have taken in their absence. Wage controls, on the other hand, have been all too effective and have inflicted grave inequities upon workers.

News conference, Detroit, Jan. 16/
San Francisco Examiner, 1-17:2.

3

We [labor unions] are challenging, in effect, whether human beings exist for the sake of production and profit, or whether we are engaged in production for the sake of human beings.

August/The New York Times, 9-23:(4)3.

Edwin H. Yeo
Vice chairman, Pittsburgh National Bank

4

You know what Phase 4 [of the Nixon Administration's economic program] reminds me of? It's like sticking your foot out the door of a car to slow it down when the braking system is shot.

The New York Times, 8-19:(3)1.

Law · The Judiciary

Howard H. Baker, Jr.
United States Senator, R-Tennessee

1

[On his experience as a lawyer]: I'll tell you what my daddy told me after my first trial. I thought I was just great. I asked him, "How did I do?" He paused and said, "You've got to guard against speaking more clearly than you think."

Interview/The Washington Post, 6-24:(K)2.

David L. Bazelon
Chief Judge, United States Court of Appeals for the District of Columbia Circuit

2

Challenging an expert and questioning his expertise is the lifeblood of our legal system—whether it is a psychiatrist discussing mental disturbances, a physicist testifying on the environmental impact of a nuclear power plant, or a General Motors executive insisting on the impossibility of meeting Federal auto-pollution standards by 1975. It is the only way a judge or a jury can decide whom to trust.

The Dallas Times Herald, 5-13:(E)12.

Lloyd M. Bentsen
United States Senator, D-Texas

3

[On his bill that would give courts greater discretion in deciding whether evidence in a criminal case is admissable]: [The bill would] prevent the criminal from escaping unpunished simply because a policeman violates a minor technicality in obtaining clear physical evidence of his guilt. The exclusionary rule, through which the courts protect our Constitutional right against unreasonable search and seizure, has become an inflexible loophole through which a criminal can walk to freedom.

The Dallas Times Herald, 2-18:(E)9.

Harry A. Blackmun
Associate Justice,
Supreme Court of the United States

4

We [on the Supreme Court] never have the moments and the hours to put our feet on the window sills and reflect a bit.

San Francisco Examiner, 2-13:30.

Irwin Brownstein
Justice, New York State Supreme Court

5

There is a growing tendency in this country to consolidate power in the Executive Branch of the government. I consider this a dangerous trend, particularly for our judiciary. A judiciary controlled by the Executive Branch quickly loses its independence.

News conference, New York,
April 7/The New York Times, 4-8:(1)32.

Warren E. Burger
Chief Justice of the United States

6

The Federal court system is for a limited purpose, and lawyers, the Congress and the public must carefully examine each demand they make on that system. People speak glibly of putting all the problems of pollution, of crowded cities, of consumer class-actions and others in the Federal courts. We should look more to state courts familiar with local conditions and local problems.

San Francisco Examiner, 1-15:24.

7

One of the great strengths of the [U.S.] Supreme Court, with few parallels anywhere, is that historically it has never in any significant degree retreated before public opinion, the pressure of Congress or exhortations of the Executive Branch. The Justices' duty is to stand firm in defense of basic Constitutional values as they see them, even against momentary tides of public opinion. As the years pass, the critics may prove to have been more correct on some matters than the Justices. The Constitution's authors allowed for that, too. Their design, and the laws of nature, provide for change in the Judiciary through the selection of new members by an elected President and Senate, so that, over the long range of history, the Judiciary is not too far from public opinion.

Interview/
The Reader's Digest, February:95.

1

No matter what coercive powers of enforcement governments may assert, the peoples in country after country in all ages have demonstrated that man was meant to be free, but that this ideal can be realized only under the rule of law. And this must be a rule that places restraints on individuals and on governments alike. This is a delicate, a fragile, balance to maintain. It is fragile because it is sustained only by an ideal that requires each person in society, by an exercise of free will, to accept and abide the restraints of a structure of laws. If it seems a contradiction to say that to preserve freedom we must surrender some freedom, it is no more so than to say, as Christians have been saying for 2,000 years, that "he that loseth his life . . . shall find it."

At Law Day Service, St. John's Cathedral,
Jacksonville, Fla., April 29/
Vital Speeches, 6-15:516.

2

[Complaining of the increased workload of the Supreme Court]: No person who looks at the facts can rationally assume that nine justices today can process four or five times as many cases as did the past Courts that included Taft, Holmes, Brandeis, Cardozo or Hughes . . . and do this task as it ought to be done. To suggest, as has been done, that additional law clerks can take up the increased load may flatter the ego of law clerks, but I suggest that the public and the profession want the decisional functions of the Supreme

Court of the United States to be exercised by judges.

State of the Judiciary address before
American Bar Association, Washington,
Aug. 6/Los Angeles Times, 8-7:(1)13.

3

A truly qualified advocate—like every genuine professional—resembles a seamless garment, in the sense that legal knowledge, forensic skills, professional ethics, courtroom etiquette and manners are blended in the total person. There are some few lawyers who scoff at the idea that manners and etiquette form any part of the necessary equipment of the courtroom advocate. Yet, if one were to undertake a list of the truly great advocates of the past 100 years, I suggest he would find a common denominator: They were all intensely individualistic, but each was a lawyer for whom courtroom manners were a key weapon in his arsenal. Whether engaged in the destruction of adverse witnesses or undermining damaging evidence or in final argument, the performance was characterized by coolness, poise and graphic clarity, without shouting or ranting, without baiting witnesses, opponents or the judge.

Lecture, Fordham University Law School,
Nov. 26/Los Angeles Times, 12-28:(2)7.

4

. . . in spite of all the bar examinations and better law schools, we are more casual about qualifying the people we allow to act as advocates in the courtroom than we are about licensing electricians. The painful fact is that the courtrooms of America all too often have Piper-Cub advocates trying to handle the controls of Boeing-747 litigation.

Lecture, Fordham University Law School,
Nov. 26/San Francisco Examiner, 11-27:9.

Joseph P. Busch
District Attorney,
Los Angeles County, California

5

[On why juries are necessary in criminal trials]: While we always presume that judges are impartial and are going to listen to the

(JOSEPH P. BUSCH)

evidence and seek the truth . . . and apply the law fairly and equally to reach the desired result, the search for the truth is the real crux of the trial. That is why we have people under oath, confrontations and cross-examinations. But in searching for the truth, a judge does not have any more ability than you or I to find what the truth is. Truth cannot be taught to people; it is inherent, something that you feel, observe. That's one of the reasons that, when you have instructions to the jury, they're told about credibility and how to determine it, to look at the person accused and the witnesses, their demeanor, everything about them, not just their words. And when you have a jury, there are 12 persons searching for the truth. And when we talk about a criminal case, these 12 persons, after they have arrived at what they believe the facts and the truth to be, are sworn to follow the law. They can't substitute their ideas of what the law should be. They have to follow what the judge tells them is the law . . . I think the system that commits 12 persons from the community to join in and determine what justice should be rendered in a particular case is a very valid one in that it gives a great sense of security to the populace to know that justice can be rendered this way. That's why I think that jury trials should exist for the serious crimes and that the people have the right to a jury trial. Because of this cross-section of the community searching for the truth and applying the law, it's a solace to the collective minds of the community.

Interview, Los Angeles/
Los Angeles Herald-Examiner, 3-25:(A)12.

John B. Connally, Jr.
Former Secretary of the Treasury
of the United States;
Former Governor of Texas

1

We're leading ourselves into believing the [U.S.] Supreme Court is the ultimate arbiter of all disputes, and I don't believe it. I think there are times when the President of the United States would be right in not obeying a decision of the Supreme Court.

News conference, Washington, Sept. 10/
The Washington Post, 9-11:(A)1.

William O. Douglas
Associate Justice,
Supreme Court of the United States

2

[On being a Supreme Court Justice]: It's about a four-day-a-week job. But that's a matter of working habits, a matter of energy . . . Those three days with nothing to do much except take a walk, go out West on a trek, go to Europe, fly down to Knoxville for three days in the Smokies—these times of being away from the desk are a time when you are digesting a lot of things that have come in during those four days. It's one of the best decision-making processes. At the end of a 25-mile hike, your work is pretty well done.

Interview, Washington, Oct. 28/
The New York Times, 10-29:29.

3

The first opinion the Court ever filed had a dissenting opinion. Dissent is a tradition of this Court . . . A person writing a dissent is free-wheeling. When someone is writing for the Court, he is hoping to get eight others to agree with him, so many of the majority opinions are rather stultified.

Interview, Washington, Oct. 28/
The New York Times, 10-29:29.

4

The great contribution of the (Earl) Warren Court was making principles of equality and harmony a reality rather than a theory. But the court has never been comprised of stereotyped people. Now there are different men on the Court, all of them honest and dedicated, but dedicated to different parts of the Constitution. That sort of shifting attention has been true from the beginning of the Court, and it will always be true. The shift has been over-emphasized, anyway. Those who really study the cases will realize that lately there is no solid bloc, no phalanx, no automatic line-up of certain people against others. It shifts on every type of case. We're all independent, we all go here under our own steam, and we're not subject to political or Presidential pressure. And that's the way it works.

Interview/Time, 11-12:93.

1

I do wish the news media were more interested in doing in-depth stories on the [Supreme] Court and [on] justice. They're interested in one Justice throwing an inkwell at another one, but they don't always help the Court educate as it should. The Court's great power is its ability to educate, to provide moral leadership.

Interview/Time, 11-12:94.

Sam J. Ervin, Jr.
United States Senator, D-North Carolina

2

Judges ought to have wisdom as well as knowledge. I can recall defending a man who was running a big moonshine still right in his house. And I pleaded him guilty. Then the prosecutor, who got his pay from fees for each conviction, asked him where he got his still, figuring he might get some more cases. The man said, "I ain't gwine tell ya." The prosecutor asked the judge to make him answer. But the judge said, "This man is indicating to me he has a code of ethics. It may not be as good as some others, but it would do injury to his conscience to make him answer. Motion denied." That judge had wisdom.

The Washington Post, 2-5:(A)4.

3

An old lawyer in St. Louis made a speech some time ago in which he said, "Do not waste your time looking up the law in advance, because you can find some Federal district court that will sustain any proposition you make."

At Senate Watergate hearings, Washington/
The Dallas Times Herald, 6-20:(A)8.

Arthur J. Goldberg
Former Associate Justice,
Supreme Court of the United States

4

Law will not endure nor justice be attained

if the government itself has both flouted the law and sought to hide its crime.

At Law Day ceremony, Washington,
May 1/Los Angeles Times, 5-2:(1)24.

L. Patrick Gray III
Acting Director,
Federal Bureau of Investigation

5

The accused on trial is not the only person whose inalienable rights are on the line in a criminal case. The people in whose name the prosecution is brought have a rather substantial set of rights on the line, too.

At National Conference on Criminal Justice,
Washington, Jan. 25/
The New York Times, 1-26:7.

Fred E. Inbau
Professor of Criminal Law,
Northwestern University

6

[On the U.S. Supreme Court]: In contrast to the Warren Court, the Burger Court is coming back to a state of realism and is striking a better balance between individual civil liberties and the rights of law-abiding citizens to live in reasonable safety of life and limb. The Warren Court was excessively concerned with the rights of individuals accused or suspected of crimes, and the rights of the public at large were given only secondary consideration. A combination of factors has brought about this change: a general public rejection of soci·l permissiveness and also the appointment to the Court of four members who are in sympathy with this rejection concept. The majority of the present Court will continue its efforts to strike a proper balance and reach an accommodation of these two competing interests and values.

Interview/
U.S. News & World Report, 7-16:30.

Albert E. Jenner, Jr.
Lawyer; President,
National Conference on Uniform State Laws

7

Evidentiary rules vary so widely that a New York lawyer can walk into a courtroom in

(ALBERT E. JENNER, JR.)

Chicago or Los Angeles and literally not know whether some piece of evidence he wants to introduce will be admissible. That's an intolerable situation.

Los Angeles Times, 3-19:(1)12.

Richard G. Kleindienst
Attorney General of the United States

1

There are many reasons for trial delay, not the least of which are brought about by the defense. The experienced defendant who knows he is guilty has everything to gain from delay. He will start by choosing an overworked defense attorney whose appearance is required in many courts and whose enforced absence will be a repeated cause for continuances. And many a veteran defense counsel has a whole bagful of pretrial motions, many of them simply designed to delay. For as we know, delay erodes the prosecution's case. Where the delay moves from months to years, evidence is lost and witnesses disappear or suffer loss of memory. Meanwhile, if the defendant is out on bail, he may be preying on the community. On the other hand, there can be many other causes of delay not due to the defense. And if the defendant stays in jail, either because he cannot raise bail or is charged with a non-bailable offense, then there is a clear injustice to him in any protracted delay before he is proven guilty or innocent. I am not advocating pure speed for its own sake, at the expense of justice. Some judges have dismissed charges arbitrarily after a certain lapse of time or a certain number of continuances, thus, in my opinion, aggravating the problem rather than solving it, by giving criminals a new hunting license against society. If anything, the threat to society in this instance is even worse than in cases where the defendant is released pending trial, since the defendant whose case is arbitrarily dismissed is not only freed physically but is freed of any respect for the law whatever. The criminal-justice system in the United States is falling far short of its job. It must make drastic reforms to restore itself as the foundation-stone of American democracy.

Before National District Attorneys Association, Beverly Hills, Calif., March 7/The New York Times, 4-19:43.

Philip B. Kurland
Professor of Law, University of Chicago

2

. . . it is necessary to remember that the [U.S.] Supreme Court is not the government of the United States, but only a part of it. Its primary function remains—in part because its capacities will allow it no more—to restrain the misbehavior of other governmental bodies. It is over-burdened with problems that should better be left outside its ken: some too large, others too small to call on the limited resources that the Court can bring to bear. This is not to demean the Court's role, but to preserve it. It remains the one governmental institution above all others capable of affording some protection, however temporary, to individuals and minorities against the incursion of majorities.

The National Observer, 4-14:16.

Joseph McLaughlin
Dean, Fordham University Law School

3

I'm not so sure that most Americans have had a lot of respect for the law. For the past 10 or 15 years . . . we had people openly flouting the law as the way of changing the law. I think we have begun a whole process of disrespect.

"W": a Fairchild publication, 11-30:4.

David Melinkoff
*Professor of Law,
University of California, Los Angeles*

4

Lawyers as a group are no more dedicated to justice or public service than a private public utility is dedicated to giving light. The profession is a public profession because it exists to satisfy a public need. But individual lawyers are members of that public profession to satisfy private personal needs.

San Francisco Examiner & Chronicle, 7-22:(This World)2.

Robert W. Meserve
President, American Bar Association

1

Today, lawyers are educated and licensed as if they could eventually do everything which constitutes the practice of law. The myth of omni-competence we know is precisely that—a myth. Our economic and social life is far too complex to support such a reality. We have provided specific ethical prohibitions against undertaking to do things which we know, or should reasonably know, that we can't do. I personally believe that the lawyer's own sense of his or her capabilities is and ought to be the primary basis of professional restraint . . . If each lawyer does in fact only a *few* among an almost unlimited range of tasks, why must each lawyer be exposed to the same educational experience? Why should all lawyers go to law school for three years? Surely, effective training for some tasks can be accomplished in substantially less time, even if some specialized skills may take even longer to acquire. Why should all lawyers take only traditional law courses in law school? Studies in scientific or technical areas may be far more useful in preparing *some* kinds of lawyers than much of the traditional curriculum. Why should only law students go to law school? Much of what even the traditional law school offers can be of value to students from other disciplines. The basic question is: Why should all lawyers be educated as if they were going to do the same kind of job when demonstrably they are not going to do so?

Before New York State Bar Association/
The National Observer, 2-17:10.

Louis Nizer
Lawyer

2

The difference between an office lawyer and a trial lawyer is as great as between an internist and a surgeon. Both require high talents, but the specialized skills and tools are so different that they may as well be in different professions.

Newsweek, 12-10:75.

Lewis F. Powell, Jr.
Associate Justice,
Supreme Court of the United States

3

[On the judicial caseload problem]: We have created here in America the most litigous society in the history of mankind. Our courts tend to play a more active role under our form of government than under any other system with which I am familiar.

At Judicial Conference of the Fifth Circuit,
El Paso, Tex., April 11/
The Washington Post, 4-12:(A)9.

William H. Rehnquist
Associate Justice,
Supreme Court of the United States

4

[Saying periodic changes and alterations in Court procedures are desirable]: We should certainly not lightly tinker with a system which is working well, but we should not hesitate to recognize and deal with a problem to the system when it does manifest itself. The end to be accomplished, after all, is the retention of the Supreme Court in its place at the apex of the nation's judicial pyramid, in substance as well as in form, fully capable of transacting the business that Congress intends to come before it. The Supreme Court has continued to occupy this high place . . . not in spite of periodic changes in its method of doing business, but because of such changes.

Before American Bar Foundation Fellows,
Cleveland, Feb. 10/
The New York Times, 2-12:13.

Charles S. Rhyne
Lawyer; Former president,
American Bar Association

5

If the American public loses its respect for our courts, one-third of our governmental system of checks and balances will be stripped of its power. This is axiomatic, for no organ has power absent either respect or fear; and fear has never been an arm of democracy. If one of our three branches of government may be destroyed, none are safe. Unless our court system can maintain its position of dignity

227

(CHARLES S. RHYNE)

and respect in the eyes of our public, the foundation of our way of life is in danger. The truth inherent in this reasoning is sufficiently grave to merit our thoughtful, objective consideration. We [lawyers] have a duty and a responsibility to perform in maintaining the confidence of the public in our courts. Such confidence is the foundation of our whole system of government, and we must never allow it to be impaired or destroyed.

Before Long Beach (Calif.) Bar Association,
May 1/Vital Speeches, 6-1:485.

Nelson A. Rockefeller
Governor of New York

1

The courts and related institutions have been created to serve the people's need. When size, staffing or procedures are inadequate, then they must be made adequate to the task for which society created them.

Albany, N.Y., Jan. 25/
The New York Times, 1-26:1.

William B. Saxbe
United States Senator, R-Ohio

2

[Saying he expects to be nominated by President Nixon to be the new Attorney General]: I feel very strongly that the Justice Department is the very heart and soul of our country, because government without law is tyranny, and I would like to re-establish a real sound belief in our system of justice and in our country.

Washington, Oct. 31/
The Washington Post, 11-1:(A)21.

Gordon Schaber
Dean, University of the Pacific Law School

3

The practice of law in most courtrooms today is about as modern as performing surgery in a barbershop.

San Francisco Examiner, 3-9:38.

Bernard Schwartz
Professor of Law,
New York University Law School

4

[On the U.S. Supreme Court]: You see in the Burger Court a pause in the expansion of Constitutional rights. During the 1950s and 1960s, you had a veritable explosion in this area, and now we have a period of consolidation. In certain areas—namely, racial and sexual discrimination—the Court is still breaking new ground. In other areas—such as the rights of criminal defendants, for example—I think the development was so rapid that some of the Justices did not want to break new ground. We are in a period of ebb tide because of the need to consolidate. You can't live in a constant state of Constitutional revolution. The time comes to consolidate, and that is what the Burger Court is doing. The Court, isolated though it is, feels the touch of public opinion. As far as the future is concerned, I see more of the same for a while. The turbulence of the 1960s gives way to a period of taking stock. We are looking to see how far we have gone and where we go from here. This is as true for the law as for society at large.

Interview/
U.S. News & World Report, 7-16:30.

John J. Sirica
Chief Judge,
United States District Court
for the District of Columbia

5

. . . a great intellectual doesn't make a great trial judge. A man who's been a trial lawyer is a better judge of human nature than Professor X at Harvard, who's probably never been in the well of a courtroom . . . So Sirica's not an intellectual. Who cares! The important question is whether a judge is honest and does he have the courage of his convictions to do what is right at the moment.

Interview/
The New York Times Magazine, 11-4:34.

Herbert Jay Stern
United States Attorney for New Jersey

1

How are we going to effectively advocate respect for the law to some young man or woman who has seen only poverty, despair, filth and decay, when he or she learns that the Mayor and the president of the city council of his very own city, Jersey City—the very men who trumpeted law and order—have a secret, numbered, joint bank account in Florida, with $1,310,000 in cash in it? What happens when they know that a former gubernatorial candidate kept a special Swiss bank account for payoffs; when they see the former speaker of the New Jersey Assembly leave the halls of that august body to the raucous cheers and applause of the members to begin serving a jail term in Federal prison? I suggest to you, my fellow members of the bar, that if we will have law, if we will have order, then we are going to have to start by imposing them on the "top" of society, not on its "bottom." . . .

Before lawyers, New York/
The Washington Post, 12-10:(A)2.

Lyman M. Tondel, Jr.
Chairman, standing committee on
ethics and professional responsibility,
American Bar Association

2

I think that, for whatever reason, too few law schools and colleges have paid too little attention to the importance of inculcating ethical standards [in the legal profession]. There is always the fear that the teaching will be subjective and that people will teach their own standards . . . but I think that problem is minimized when you get to the law-school level . . . I think that ethics is a very subtle thing to teach—it's not two-plus-two equals four—but I firmly believe that schools could do a much better job than they're doing . . .

The Christian Science Monitor, 7-27:4.

A. L. Wirin
Former chief counsel,
American Civil Liberties Union

3

The American criminal [justice] system is accusatory in nature, not inquisitional. Under the inquisition, authorities rely on interrogating the defendant and forcing him to succumb to coercion, abuse, the third-degree and even torture to prove his innocence. In our accusatory system, the burden of proof is on the authorities—the government—and it is up to them to prove their case without relying on the testimony of the accused. [The vice of the inquisition system,] apart from its obvious inhumanity, [is that it] encourages the defendant to confess his guilt, even when he is innocent, to avoid abuse.

Los Angeles Times, 9-22:(1)14.

National Defense • The Military

Creighton W. Abrams
General and Chief of Staff,
United States Army

1

. . . first it was a "war to end all wars." Then we weren't going to make the mistakes of the First World War. Then we got the UN People said we weren't going to fight another war because nuclear weapons were too dangerous. Who was going to start a war when we and the Soviets and others have nuclear weapons? Well, we've had two very costly wars since then. Each time people start saying those things, the Army is reduced in size; our money is reduced. The thing that worries me is that we Americans will let the Army go down to 500,000 men, then to 300,000, and so on. I wish maybe more than anyone in this room that there will never be another war. But the way things have happened in this century, no one in the Army can base his thinking on the assumption that war won't occur. Actually, our decision to go to war has always been sort of an irrational thing in terms of the military force we had available. It wasn't because we had good military forces or that we had anything but faith that we might win. At the beginning of each war there was no way you could put the situation through systems-analysis and predict victory. The analysis would have predicted a defeat every damn time in this century.

Interview, Washington/
U.S. News & World Report, 8-6:40.

2

In this period of possible detente—not real peace, but possible detente—we are opposed by formidable strength. We face, at various places around the world, strong and capable adversaries, becoming stronger all the time. These are facts. As our relations throughout the world improve, we should consider that we have more and more to gain by preventing another war; and the only way I know how to do that, the only way that has worked in the past, is by maintaining our own strength, our own capability and our own resolve to defend our security, our freedom, and those of our allies . . . And so for the Army today, this means we must be ready, prepared to stand for the country. We must have effective, potent and credible strength to defend the nation's security and its freedom. Insuring that the Army is prepared is my most fundamental duty and is the Army's primary mission at all times.

Before Association of the U.S. Army,
Oct. 16/Human Events, 11-10:5.

3

[On the all-volunteer Army]: The Army should be representative, and if it's not, then it's not an Army of the United States. It has got to be that way; and if we can't do it, then we should say so and find another solution . . . I don't know any other way [than a return to the draft].

July/Los Angeles Herald-Examiner, 11-4:(B)7.

Roy L. Ash
Director,
Federal Office of Management and Budget

4

. . . we don't believe Congress should—and don't believe the people would—support a policy of balancing the budget through the device of allotting to the defense program whatever is left over after all other programs have been provided for. That is, we don't believe that Congress would be wise to pass all the domestic appropriations, subtract them from the total available and say the remainder is all that there is for defense. That would be very unwise in terms of meeting our highest priority—national defense.

Interview/
U.S. News & World Report, 9-17:93.

Les Aspin
United States Representative, D-Wisconsin

1

[Criticizing the fancy dress of military officers' servants]: Military officers shouldn't have personal servants in the first place. But as long as they do, they should at least let them dress like soldiers, instead of like characters in a musical comedy . . . Our Generals and Admirals seem to have lost their heads. They're putting on ludicrous, aristocratic airs.

Washington/
The Dallas Times Herald, 8-24:(A)17.

Ben B. Blackburn
United States Representative, R-Georgia

2

The American strategic advantage due to existence of our MIRVs has been erased by a successful test of a Soviet MIRV SS-18. [The MIRV was] the only area of sophisticated military technology in which the United States had enjoyed a definite lead. We have received disturbing reports regarding a continuing and increasing flow of sophisticated American technology to the Soviet Union and to some of the Warsaw Pact countries. Most of the technology being transferred has a direct military application . . . Transfer of American capital, goods and technological know-how having an immediate military utility to the Soviet Union and Warsaw Pact governments is, to me, a direct contribution to the Soviets' ability to ultimately destroy our country and our allies.

News conference, Washington/
The Dallas Times Herald, 12-12:(D)10.

Leonid I. Brezhnev
General Secretary,
Communist Party of the Soviet Union

3

The military budgets of the NATO countries are being increased by 2 to 3 billion dollars a year, and these are figures indicative of ever-newer types of weapons of destruction: new and ever-more destructive nuclear bombs and warheads, new and ever-more powerful missiles, tanks and planes, warships and submarines. The qualitative improvement of

weapons has assumed unprecedented proportions. Attempts are being made to justify this by claiming that it could allegedly help secure success at the Arms Limitation Talks by creating "bargaining points." Quite obviously, these "bargaining points" will, in fact, yield nothing except an intensification of the arms race. As for the Arms Limitation Talks, their success does not require any new military programs, but a sincere desire, backed by mutual restraint, to check the arms race.

At World Peace Congress, Moscow,
Oct. 26/Vital Speeches, 11-15:71.

George S. Brown
General, United States Air Force;
Commander, Air Force Systems Command

4

Over the past decade, there has grown up an erroneous public image of the Department [of Defense] as a vast organization with a life and purpose all its own: too large to be effectively managed; expending a disproportionate bulk of our national wealth; and dedicated to periodically raising the specter of threats to the national security. The fact is, however, that the Department of Defense has no separate life of its own. It is not an end in itself, but simply a *means* to the end of protecting and preserving the national security. In the final analysis, it is the people of the United States who determine our national goals and objectives, including the defense and security of the nation. The military services are the instruments of the people. They are constituted and supported by the representatives of the people, and serve to achieve national goals.

Before Economic Club, Detroit,
May 21/Vital Speeches, 7-1:567.

George S. Brown
General and Chief of Staff,
United States Air Force

5

However little we may like the term—or the way it has been used over the past few years—we *are* part of a military-industrial complex. In the free-enterprise economy of our democratic society, and with the technological

(GEORGE S. BROWN)

sophistication of modern weaponry, I know of no other reasonable way to develop and produce the weapon systems that the security of the nation demands. The system works. It has been notably effective. Major war has been deterred, and smaller conflicts have been kept from going global. In no small part, these achievements have been possible because, up to now, the United States has had superior weapons in sufficient numbers to prevent and to limit war. Up to now. We are at a point in our history where that kind of effectiveness will no longer be possible, unless it is matched by an equal measure of tough, economy-minded *efficiency*. All of us must recognize certain basic truths. First, defense costs, like costs everywhere, have been climbing steadily. Second, even if defense spending could be maintained at a fixed level in current dollar terms, there is an erosion of real purchasing power. Third, this has necessitated reduction in force size. Fourth, the reduced force structure makes it more than ever imperative to offset the numerical inferiority with qualitatively superior weapons systems. But, fifth, the cost of these systems has also been climbing so rapidly that we face such alternatives as reduced quality, lesser numbers, or just not going forward at all with some programs that are needed. These factors can only degrade the effectiveness of our defense forces, unless we move in the direction of greatly increased *efficiency* in the way we do business. Cost-consciousness, cost avoidance, cost reduction, will have to be our way of life.

Before National Security Industrial
Association, Washington, Sept. 13/
Vital Speeches, 10-1:761.

Howard H. Callaway
Secretary of the Army of the United States

1

[On racial quotas for the all-volunteer Army]: We don't plan to put in quotas now. If it came to a quota, we'd let everyone know why we're doing it, and I think we'd have the support of the blacks and whites of America, because we'd have a good, sound program. We

don't want the Army to be all-anything. We want it to be a broad cross-section of America.

Interview, Washington, Aug. 26/
The Washington Post. 8-27:(A)2.

2

It is an exciting time for me to be Secretary of the Army as we enter a historic time, a time of basic change as we try to do what has never been done before. The Army has set out to provide security for this great country, to keep our global commitments, to stand ready to face an aggressor on a moment's notice —and to do all this with an Army of volunteers. No nation in history has tried to meet such massive and complex commitments without compelling people to serve, through one form of conscription or another. It is a challenge . . . and one which I assure you we will do our utmost to meet. There are influential voices throughout the land today who do not fully understand the need for this Army. They recognize, as we all do, that this is an era of detente, and not of defiance; it is an era of negotiation and cooperation, rather than conflict and confrontation. But it is not yet a time when we have achieved an era of peace. For while we have ample testimony about detente and cooperation, we can still see that the military forces of the Warsaw Pact nations are steadily growing, becoming larger, more modern and better able to impose their will upon us or upon our allies if we do not remain strong.

At United Way Kickoff Luncheon,
Atlanta, Sept. 25/
Vital Speeches, 11-1:34.

3

[On whether there should be a military draft]: There is a great debate among a great many of the people who are the strongest supporters of the Army—people who serve on the Armed Forces Committees of Congress and who have traditionally been thought of as supporters of the Army, people in the American Legion and the Veterans of Foreign Wars, the other veterans' organizations. They continually look at the issue as a choice between a draft or a volunteer Army, and most want the draft. Most think that it's a duty to serve your country and that everybody should do it. But the question today is not over the draft, but whether the Army can succeed or fail in the environment it is in. The alternative to succeeding with a volunteer Army is not a draft, but failure.

Interview/
U.S. News & World Report, 10-15:65.

Mark W. Clark
General, United States Army (Ret.)

1

. . . as a commander in modern-day warfare, with so many sophisticated weapons —atomic weapons—you've got to learn to live with the political considerations of your government when fighting your battle, whether you like it or not.

Interview, Charleston, S.C./
Human Events, 3-31:16.

William P. Clements, Jr.
Deputy Secretary of Defense
of the United States

2

From the results achieved to date and the outlook for the next several years, I am convinced that the volunteer [armed] force is working and will continue to do so . . . Doomsayers and pessimists will have to turn to other pursuits to find more fertile ground. We shall make the volunteer force a great success, and all of us can take pride in our accomplishment.

Before Air Force Sergeants Association,
Washington, Aug. 29/
The Dallas Times Herald, 8-30:(A)5.

Clark M. Clifford
Former Secretary of Defense
of the United States

3

Is it not clear that today we simply do not need all the military forces which we now maintain? [The United States is maintaining,] in the face of substantially reduced international tensions and substantially consolidated U.S. international objectives, practically

as large a force as we did in 1964, when global confrontation seemed to be much sharper and America's goals more ambitious.

At "Pacem in Terris" convocation of Center
for the Study of Democratic Institutions,
Washington, Oct. 9/
The New York Times, 10-10:4.

Alan Cranston
United States Senator, D-California

4

[On President Nixon's decision to close some military bases in the U.S. as an economy measure]: We're sacrificing jobs here at home so that the President can keep his bases overseas. We should be putting that money to work here at home in areas that create jobs for Americans rather than jobs for Icelanders, Germans, Spaniards and countless other foreigners.

U.S. News & World Report, 4-30:42.

Barry M. Goldwater
United States Senator, R-Arizona

5

The sobering realities are that we have not designed and fielded new air-superiority fighters in the last 15 years, and we have not added any advanced strategic bombers in the last 22 years . . . to borrow from General [Dwight] Eisenhower, "No real security resides in a second-best Air Force." Our air arm is aging badly. We need new blood . . . It is essential that we get the B-1 into the inventory as soon as possible to replace the B-52, which was designed in the late 1940s and built in the 1950s and 1960s. The B-1 will be a superb aircraft, capable of matching the Soviet Backfire. Compared to the B-52, the B-1 will use half as much runway, fly much faster, carry two-and-one-half times more payload, have greater range and require less fuel. But the problem is that the Backfire is either operational now or sure to be by 1974, while even if we can get the needed funds to continue development of the B-1, the new bomber won't be operational until about 1980.

At Wings Club, New York/
Los Angeles Herald-Examiner, 9-28:(A)14.

(BARRY M. GOLDWATER)

1

My pet gripe is that we have four tactical air forces: Army, Navy and Marines, as well as the Air Force itself. This is one of the glaring examples of repetition that we don't need. My guess is it costs us between 12 and 14 billion dollars to have four tactical air forces. We're the only country that does. It's political. You have the Army fighting the idea that the Air Force should do it. The Air Force fights the idea that anybody else but the Air Force should do it. I personally think it's an Air Force role and mission, and it should have it.

Interview/
U.S. News & World Report, 10-15:77.

Andrew J. Goodpaster
General, United States Army;
Supreme Allied Commander/Europe

2

Our people like to think that peace is the natural condition of man, that armies are temporary nuisances, and that conflicts of interest can be solved by a simple policy of good-will; [that] since this is a period of detente, an "era of negotiation," forces can be reduced. But we must learn, and our people must learn, that in order to achieve a meaningful and enduring relaxation of tensions, we must maintain our capability for defense. Detente without defense is a delusion—and an especially dangerous delusion at that.

At Washington (D.C.) Institute of
Foreign Affairs, Sept. 26/
Vital Speeches, 10-15:26.

Mark O. Hatfield
United States Senator, R-Oregon

3

[Advocating dismantling of the Selective Service System]: If there is not any need [now] for the President to have the authority to induct men into the military, then I believe there is no reason why the draft structure should remain . . . The time needed to set up a system, give physical examinations and transport the men to their training stations would be virtually the same with or without a draft system continuing on a stand-by basis.

Washington, Feb. 7/
Los Angeles Times, 2-8:(1)23.

F. Edward Hebert
United States Representative, D-Louisiana

4

[Arguing against unilateral reductions in U.S. military strength]: We are in a time when negotiations are going on [between the U.S. and the Soviet Union] which we all hope will lead to greater arms control, a reduction of arms development and lessening of tension in the world. Neither now, nor at any time in history, has anybody won at a conference table what they were not in a position to defend on the battlefield . . . Detente and negotiations to improve world stability are products of our strength; they are not a reason for dismantling that strength.

Before the House, Washington, July 30/
U.S. News & World Report, 8-13:32.

Hubert H. Humphrey
United States Senator, D-Minnesota

5

Since it doesn't appear that tomorrow morning the Russians are going to attack, we ought to be using our time building our defense and weapons systematically, in a manner that saves us money, that eliminates as much waste as possible. I was in Moscow on the day that [U.S. astronaut] Neil Armstrong landed on the moon. I saw what happened in the Soviet Union. They went around muttering to themselves in so many words: "My God, they did it! These crazy Americans—five years behind us in space—they mobilized, they set up an objective, they committed their resources, they did it within a time frame, they brought together the technical ability, the finance, the management, and they did it." That amazing space-flight success told them something that no weapons system in the world could tell them—namely, that if we have to do it, we can do it. That's why I think we could stretch out *Trident* and other expensive weapons systems. The Russians know we can build them. If they start dragging their feet in those SALT talks, they know we can and will go ahead . . . We've got so many nuclear weapons, so many things with which to defend ourselves, that they're trying to catch up with us instead of our catching up with them. There is not one responsible person in this government today that says we're weaker than the Soviet Union. So, given this leadership, we can afford to make some cuts in our defense budget.

Interview/
U.S. News & World Report, 10-15:78.

Henry A. Kissinger
Secretary of State-designate
of the United States

1

If we don't stop the arms race now, we are going to get into a whole new realm of technology in which it will be very difficult to put the genie back in the bottle.

Before Senate Foreign Relations Committee,
Washington, Sept. 11/
Los Angeles Herald-Examiner, 9-12:(A)5.

Melvin R. Laird
Counsellor to the President of the
United States for Domestic Affairs;
Former Secretary of Defense

2

There is talk of detente, but the security of the U.S. is not assured by such talk—it takes deeds and ironclad guarantees as well . . . The Soviet Union is pressing forward with the fastest-growing military establishment and research-and-development program of any nation in the world today. That's why it's so important, as we move into the mutual and balanced force reduction area, as we move into the talks on SALT II, that we assure our continued technological superiority and get some verifiable agreements that have teeth in them and mean something—something that really guarantees a two-sided agreement to slow down an arms build-up.

Interview, Washington/
U.S. News & World Report, 9-17:39.

3

The top legislative priority of the President of the United States always must be adequate protection of the national security of this country, and an adequate defense structure so that we have a realistic deterrent and can maintain our commitments—our basic treaty commitments which have been approved under our Constitutional process by the United States Senate. That's the highest priority; and it must always be the highest priority in our Federal system.

Interview, Washington/
U.S. News & World Report, 9-17:100.

Joseph Luns
Secretary General,
North Atlantic Treaty Organization

4

It is . . . not easy to pursue both detente and defense. Detente—even if only a small beginning is made—tends to create a false euphoria which induces people to forget that they have to continue to make sacrifices for their security. I should like to go even a step further by stressing that only by maintaining a military balance will it be possible to create real detente. I don't see how you can fruitfully negotiate equitable agreements leading to further detente from weakness.

Interview, Brussels/Human Events, 4-14:9.

Forbes Mann
Senior vice-president, LTV Corporation

5

It is tragic indeed that the world should spend 6.4 per cent of its total output on its military forces. But it is even more tragic to recall the price paid by those who in the past have too sorely tempted the appetites of would-be aggressors. We should perhaps remind ourselves that the price paid by each American to maintain our nation's military strength comes to about one dollar per day.

Quote, 2-18:154.

Mike Mansfield
United States Senator, D-Montana

6

. . . I think that the defense bill can be cut drastically—I would hope somewhere in the vicinity of 5 or 6 billion dollars. Too much has been spent on too many exotic weapons. Too many of these weapons have not proven out. I think the loss, on that basis, is in excess

(MIKE MANSFIELD)

of $40 billion today. Something should be done about the 600,000 military personnel, plus 400,000 dependents, we have at bases overseas—not including the U.S. civilian employees and foreign nationals who are working and being paid by the U.S. There ought to be a further reduction in the size of the military —although I must note in all candor that President Nixon, since he has been in office, has reduced the military forces from 3.5 million to about 2.2 million. But I think that total could be cut to about 1.8 million. When troops are withdrawn overseas, they shouldn't be stationed here in the United States; they ought to be discharged.

Interview/
U.S. News & World Report, 10-1:27.

George S. McGovern
United States Senator, D-South Dakota

1

It may be that our national security is in peril. But if that is true, it is not because we have given the Pentagon too little. In part, it is because we have offered up too much for arms and too little for the other sources of national strength.

Before Senate Appropriations Committee,
Washington, Sept. 13/
The New York Times, 9-14:4.

Walter F. Mondale
United States Senator, D-Minnesota

2

The ratio of high-ranking officers to enlisted men [in the military] is far out of proportion . . . The grade structure has become so top-heavy with high-ranking officers that it's shaped not like a pyramid but like a balloon.

Washington, Aug. 15/
Los Angeles Times, 8-16:(1)11.

Thomas H. Moorer
Admiral, United States Navy;
Chairman, Joint Chiefs of Staff

3

People who wear the uniform of the country give up many freedoms in order that those

who do not may have freedom. The military is not a democracy and never will be.

Before Commonwealth Club,
San Francisco, Feb. 9/
San Francisco Examiner, 2-10:4.

4

The desire for "no more Vietnams," "no more confrontations," can easily become a persuasion for those who will advocate that the best way to avoid confrontation is to reduce the ways and means to confront—reduce military presence, reduce weapons which feed the so-called military-industrial complex, reduce defenses which are purportedly too costly anyway. Such warnings, no matter how well intentioned, are misleading.

San Francisco Examiner & Chronicle,
2-18:(This World)2.

5

Of course we are number one. And we must remain number one. The American people will never support a second-rate defense capability . . . If we don't build the defenses we need, then all other questions become moot.

Interview, Dallas/
The Dallas Times Herald, 6-3:(A)25.

6

[Four years ago,] the military profession was being derided and demeaned to an extent unprecedented during my lifetime. [Now] the world has moved appreciably closer to a lasting peace. If we expect to continue and advance negotiations leading to improved conditions of enduring peace, continued military strength is an essential stabilizing element in a world of change and turmoil.

At U.S. Military Academy graduation
ceremony, West Point, N.Y.,
June 6/The New York Times, 6-7:50.

7

[On the effect on the military of the current fuel shortage]: We can live with the shortage as a short-term thing. But if we continue at a lowered tempo, there will be progressive deterioration of combat readiness. We're just like a football team, and if you don't practice during the week, you may not be able to play the game on Saturday.

Time, 12-10:47.

Richard M. Nixon
President of the United States

1

Our defense budget today takes the lowest percentage of our gross national product in 20 years. There is nothing I would like better than to be able to reduce it further. But we must never forget that we would not have made the progress toward lasting peace that we have made in this past year if we had not had the military strength that commanded respect. This year we have begun new negotiations with the Soviet Union for further limitations on nuclear arms. We shall be participating later in the year in negotiations for mutual reduction of forces in Europe. If, prior to these negotiations, we unilaterally reduce our defense budget or reduce our forces in Europe, any chance for successful negotiations for mutual reduction of forces or limitation of arms will be destroyed. There is one unbreakable rule of international diplomacy: you can't get something in a negotiation unless you have something to give. If we cut our defenses before negotiations begin, any incentive for other nations to cut theirs will be completely removed. If the United States reduces its defenses and others do not, it increases the danger of war. Only a mutual reduction of forces will reduce the danger of war. We must maintain our strength until we get agreements under which other nations will join us in reducing the burden of armaments. What is at stake is whether the United States shall become the second-strongest nation in the world. If that day should ever come, the chances of building a new structure of peace in the world would be irreparably damaged, and free nations everywhere would live in mortal danger. A strong United States is not a threat to peace; it is the free world's indispensable guardian of peace and freedom.

TV-radio address to the nation, Washington, March 29/Los Angeles Times, 3-30:(1)14.

2

I am for limitations of armaments . . . I am for, certainly in the nuclear field, doing everything that we can to reduce that danger that is hanging over the world today. But I also know that it is vitally important that in this field of limitation of armaments, that we remember that the United States of America is not a threat to the peace of the world. I have traveled in most of the countries of the world. I have been to the Communist countries and to the free countries. I have yet to talk to a world leader who believes that the United States of America threatens his peace or his freedom. A strong United States is a force for peace; a weak United States means that the peace will be threatened. And so that is why I say at this point, not that we want to be strong in order to dominate anybody else—that period is long gone, if it ever did exist in our own minds—but what we need to recognize is that we now have a balance in the world. We must maintain that balance, and that is why let us keep our defenses up. Oh, take the fat off wherever we possibly can; but keep them [the defenses] up and be sure in negotiations we go down only if the other side goes down. And if we do that, then we contribute to the peace of the world, in which we are all so very much interested.

At reception for former U.S. Vietnam prisoners of war, Washington, May 24/ The New York Times, 5-25:16.

3

This Memorial Day, 1973, is the occasion for all of us to express special gratitude for the sacrifices of those brave men who have given their lives to protect America's freedom over the past two centuries. Today, as we honor the memory of our wartime dead, we are able for the first time in 12 years to do so as a peacetime nation, with all of our fighting forces home from Vietnam and all our prisoners set free, their heads held high. The men and women who fell in America's wars, from Bunker Hill to Khe Sanh and Hue, have brought the promise of lasting peace on earth closer for us all. Let us prove that their heroism was not in vain. Let us work together to erect a new structure of peace upon the firm foundations they fought so nobly to build.

Memorial Day radio address to the nation, Key Biscayne, Fla., May 28/ Los Angeles Times, 5-29:(1)6.

Otis G. Pike
United States Representative, D-New York

1

[Describing the difficulties of "flying a desk" in order to illustrate his advocacy of eliminating flight pay for desk-bound military officers]: If the IN basket is continually loaded on the starboard, or right-hand, side of the desk, and the OUT basket is continually empty on the port, or left-hand, side of the desk, wood fatigue sets in, the landing gear tends to buckle and the whole fuselage crashes down on your feet. Happily, most of these Colonels and Generals and Admirals have been flying these desks for a long, long time, and have learned to keep their feet on top of the desk, out of danger's way . . . [Describing a Rear Admiral who spun too fast in his swivel chair when he heard he might lose his flight pay]: Unfortunately, his shoulder boards were at that particular angle of attack which, combined with his rapid rotation, caused him to become airborne. Unfortunately, also, the window had been left open because the air conditioning was too cold that day, and Rear Admiral J. Heavy Bottomley went soaring out of the window and into space, where he achieved an orbit with an apogee of 190 miles and a perigee of 125 miles. He is visible to the naked eye out there as he circles the earth once every 91 minutes. He is particularly beautiful just before sunrise and just after sunset with the light flashing on the stars on his shoulder boards; but some of the effect is lost in the daytime. I am told that he will be passing over the Washington Monument just after sunset on the Fourth of July.

Before the House, Washington,
June 28/The Washington Post, 6-29:(A)2.

William Proxmire
United States Senator, D-Wisconsin

2

[Advocating the abolishment of the Selective Service System]: The continuation of this huge bureaucracy at a time when no one is being drafted is probably the biggest single boondoggle now going on in the government. It is a ridiculous and wasteful expenditure of funds. We stopped the draft, but the bureaucracy goes on forever.

Washington, March 12/
San Francisco Examiner, 3-12:2.

3

There are now more Generals, Admirals, Lieutenant Generals, Vice Admirals, Colonels, Captains, Lieutenant Colonels and Commanders [in the U.S. military] than at the height of World War II; but there are 10 million fewer men in the military. There are too many chiefs, too many command echelons, too many headquarters, too much self-indulgence, too much money and too little performance . . . At a cost of over $5 million yearly, the Pentagon keeps 62 helicopters near Washington to ferry high-ranking officers from place to place. Some 45 limousines are on stand-by for Pentagon brass, complete with chauffeurs if requested. Precisely 178 planes are assigned to senior military officers at an annual cost of $39.2 million, many of which are used as personal aircraft; one recently was remodeled at the direction of the General who uses it at a cost of $430,000 to include a luxury interior, bar, stereo system, plush furniture and special exterior paint. Many senior officers in command positions receive rent-free quarters estimated to be worth far beyond the total of their housing allotment. In addition to the normal basic pay, quarters and subsistence of $40,030, a full General or Admiral receives the equivalent of $3,106 in Federal tax advantages. Exactly 29,457 non-flying officers are paid flight pay costing $75.6 million a year.

Before the Senate, Washington, July 18/
Los Angeles Times, 7-19:(1)5.

Elliot L. Richardson
Secretary of Defense of the United States

4

I know the pressures of social need, and I know the pinch of too few resources and too many problems. But I also know that the success of our undertaking to secure a generation of peace demands that we maintain a clear sufficiency of military strength.

U.S. News & World Report, 4-9:80.

Hyman G. Rickover
Admiral, United States Navy

1

If we ever want to make any progress in the Pentagon, somebody is going to have to reduce the number of officers, the number of Generals and Admirals and senior civilians, because every time one of those jobs is set up, each one of them gets a large staff. Each staff has to make work, so pretty soon the energy of the entire enterprise is taken up in doing, undoing, redoing and satisfying everybody higher up; and soon all productive work stops.

Congressional testimony/
Quote, 12-30:639.

Dean Rusk
Former Secretary of State
of the United States

2

[On amnesty for U.S. Vietnam-war draft-dodgers]: If I were in the Congress, I would want to give some thought as to how what we do now affects the ability of the Congress to call up men in some future contingency. Because if they are called and everyone says, "thank you very much, but I'll have some of your amnesty instead," then this nullifies the power of Congress in this field.

Nashville, Tenn., March 21/
The Washington Post, 3-23:(A)12.

Phyllis Schlafly
Commentator, "Spectrum,"
Columbia Broadcasting System

3

The weapons that the Soviets are building have no usefulness except to destroy or blackmail the United States. According to [Deputy] Secretary [of Defense William] Clements, they are spending more money on weapons than we are, out of an economy which is only half as rich. They are even outspending us in research and development. For years we were told that the Soviets only wanted to achieve parity, or equality. But they achieved parity in 1967, and they kept on building even faster. Meanwhile, the United States has been in a strategic-weapons freeze for the last six years. We have not built one single additional interconti-

nental ballistic missile, one single additional *Polaris*-type submarine, one single new strategic bomber, or one single space weapon. We gave up building these weapons in order to show our good faith. Did the Soviets reciprocate? No; they kept right on building, faster than ever. You don't have to take my word for it. It is all formalized in the SALT agreements which our government signed in Moscow in 1972. They guarantee the Soviets a nuclear superiority over us of at least 3 to 2.

Before Commonwealth Club,
San Francisco, July 13/
Human Events, 9-8:20.

James R. Schlesinger
Secretary of Defense of the United States

4

It is an enchanting illusion that you can simply take large amounts of money out of the defense budget and get only fat and not muscle. It was an illusion in 1949, and it is an illusion that we can ill afford today.

Interview, Washington, Aug. 30/
The Washington Post, 8-31:(A)1.

Howard K. Smith
News commentator,
American Broadcasting Company

5

[President] Nixon's Moscow visit left the Russians racing to build the world's strongest navy, while ours is static. His agreement on missiles, which weapons Russia is now "MIRV-ing" or multiplying, will make Russia the world's strongest strategic power in 10 years. She is already the strongest conventional power. Meanwhile, our allies in Europe continue their happy holiday from history and cut their forces. In the United States, Vietnam has damaged support for any military effort, and [the] Watergate [political-espionage affair] has wounded our confidence in our ability to lead. It is not the public mood to believe it now; but in 10 years it may be highly topical. A Cuban missile-like crisis then, with Russia indubitably superior, won't come out the same way the last one did. Don't take

(HOWARD K. SMITH)

my word for it; listen to the Russians.

News commentary,
American Broadcasting Company,
Aug. 29/Human Events, 9-22:3.

1

. . . We are mistaken to let our defense establishment decline, as it is doing. Our Mediterranean fleet is antiquated, outrun and outgunned by Russia's ships. We have no match for their SAM-6 [missiles] . . . They have 13 airborne divisions to get to any scene of confrontation quickly—we have two. With our skeleton Army of volunteers, we shall have less in the future. Many commentators and cartoonists depict the Pentagon as bloated with money, while our social problems get leavings. The opposite is true. We are spending less of our GNP on defense now than any time since the immediate aftermath of World War II. Defense gets 18 per cent of our budget—social and economic problems get 72 per cent. Unless we do something about it, the day will surely come when there will be a confrontation, and the Russians won't back down, and we won't be able to do a thing about it.

News commentary,
American Broadcasting Company, Oct. 26/
The Christian Science Monitor, 11-8:(B)12.

John C. Stennis
United States Senator, D-Mississippi

2

. . . our military posture cannot be neglected. We are not going to retreat now from world affairs. I'll be happy if we can reduce the cost of defense programs and weapons —and we ought to be able to reduce them some. But there is an ever-increasing cost for them and for manpower. I do think we have to be careful not to swing too far, now that we have a Vietnam settlement, and forget our military obligations and preparedness.

Interview/
U.S. News & World Report, 2-12:39.

3

I think young girls who are willing to go into the [military] service should be encour-

aged. It seems to me that they should be given more and more places and used more and more by the services—especially the Air Force and the Army—but not for combat. They are an abundant source of talent, and more extensive experiments of their use should be made.

Before the Senate, Washington,
Sept. 24/The New York Times, 9-24:13.

Adlai E. Stevenson III
United States Senator, D-Illinois

4

The notion persists that world power and influence—national security—are directly related to the size of the defense budget. The idea that domestic problems might be solved simply by throwing dollars at them finds no advocates; yet we allow the same notion to drive us to compulsive, nearly indiscriminate, expenditures for weapons, military personnel and power.

Quote, 12-16:598.

Maxwell D. Taylor
General, United States Army (Ret.);
Former Chairman, Joint Chiefs of Staff

5

The national mood that followed Vietnam has inevitably been one marked by an anti-military bias and a distrust of military solutions to foreign-policy problems. It's a phenomenon we have seen after former wars, when the man in uniform symbolizes an unpleasant national experience. He becomes a scapegoat for the past. We see this now in the critical attitude toward the armed forces, in complaints over bloated defense budgets, in the charges—some justified, some exaggerated —of inefficiency of the Pentagon, of overruns in defense contracts, in suspicion of collusion in the military-industrial complex.

Interview/Los Angeles Times, 12-19:(2)7.

Strom Thurmond
United States Senator, R-South Carolina

6

We must not allow vital areas of weapon procurement and research and development to suffer in this period of [defense] budget restraints. What good will it do us to have the best-paid Army in the world if it has only broomsticks with which, to fight?

Before Adjutants General Association,
Arlington, Tex., April 16/
The Dallas Times Herald, 4-17:(A)6.

1

I know of no organization that exists between the military and industry that would adversely affect the country. The term "military-industrial complex" is used by those opposed to the military establishment to prejudice the American people against the military.

The Christian Science Monitor, 6-14:3.

Walter Walker
General, United States Army; Former
Commander-in-Chief for Northern Europe,
North Atlantic Treaty Organization

2

There is no parallel in history with the money and effort that Russia is continuing to put into a massive armaments buildup, which has no usefulness except to destroy or blackmail us.

Before Conservatives, London, Sept. 26/
San Francisco Examiner, 9-27:16.

M. F. Weisner
Admiral and Commander-in-Chief of the
Pacific Fleet, United States Navy

3

[The] U.S. Navy is again becoming smaller . . . with a 40 per cent decrease since 1969, from 926 active fleet ships to approximately 555 ships. This staggering reduction in the fleet, compelled by budgetary limitations . . . will continue until 1975 when new ships now under construction will be delivered to the fleet at a faster rate than old ones are retired . . . In terms of present capability, the most serious potential challenge to our use of the sea lanes is the Soviet Navy. [The U.S.S.R. has a] submarine fleet of over 300 submarines, of which almost one-third are nuclear powered, as well as a modern and growing surface fleet. Many of their submarines, surface ships and aircraft are equipped with anti-ship cruise missiles, a capability we are just beginning to develop. A possible confrontation affecting the free use of the sea by us or our allies anywhere in the world is a serious matter.

At Navy Day luncheon at the
Commercial Club, San Francisco, Oct. 25/
San Francisco Examiner, 10-26:5.

Elmo R. Zumwalt, Jr.
Admiral, United States Navy;
Chief of Naval Operations

4

[Aircraft] carriers are the backbone of our sea control and force-projection capabilities, as well as our over-sea presence. They are the most impressive maritime representatives of American interests overseas.

The Christian Science Monitor, 8-28:4.

Politics

Bella S. Abzug
United States Representative, D-New York

1

Behind the carefully-cultivated facade of middle-American values that the Nixon Administration presents to the public—John Wayne's movies, country music, football and Billy Graham—exists a philosophy and a power structure that is single-hearted in its devotion to the needs of big business and the military establishment, and that with all the shortsightedness of a Calvin Coolidge or Herbert Hoover neglects the needs of ordinary Americans.

Before Commonwealth Club, San Francisco, March 23/San Francisco Examiner, 3-24:6.

Spiro T. Agnew
Vice President of the United States

2

My relationship with the President [Nixon] has had no bumpy spots in the road at all. We've never had any trouble communicating. I'm not a person who runs to the President for reassurance every time someone is speaking about a coolness between us. And he's often said to me that one of the oldest games in national politics is to drive a wedge between the President and the Vice President.

Interview, Washington/ The Christian Science Monitor, 3-27:12.

3

. . . I'm weak [politically] among what you might call the liberal intellectuals. I'm weak in the opinion media, and I'm weak among their clients—the doctrinaire young and doctrinaire black, and the poor who consider their poverty as a permanent status rather than a temporary disability to be overcome. And the reason I'm weak among the doctrinaire young, black and poor is because those categories are the clients of the intellectuals that I mentioned. I think some of this is

changing. I've been very careful about trying to consult with intellectuals on a regular basis —some who are not conservatives. Some I consult with are more traditionally liberal—not "New Left," but people like Irving Kristol and Herman Kahn and some who probably are considered a little more liberal. I never lose a chance when I can get with these people to talk with them, because I want to see what makes them reach their conclusions.

Interview/U.S. News & World Report, 5-7:34.

4

I can assure you of this: that if I go after the [1976 Republican Presidential] nomination, it will be because I think I can get it, and once having achieved it, that I think I can be elected. I'm not going to go through any long effort and exercise for the honor of seeking the nomination. If I go after it, it will be because I think I can be elected.

Interview, Washington, May 15/ The Washington Post, 5-16:(A)7.

5

I think that I'd like to see us get to public financing [of political campaigns]. I'm coming to the conclusion it's the only answer . . . if you're going to raise any substantial amounts of money, you have to go to people of means. People of means are usually people who have extensive business connections. And with the complexities of government relations with business in all the regulated fields, it's virtually impossible to avoid the drawing of some links, however tenuous they might be, between an individual contributor and some suit that he may have . . . with a government regulatory agency . . . So I think the only answer, in order to dispel this public lack of confidence . . . is public financing. I think we have to come to it. That won't cure all the abuses, but I think that will help.

Interview, Washington/ Los Angeles Herald-Examiner, 8-7:(A)8.

1

[On his being investigated for accepting bribes and kickbacks when he was Governor of Maryland]: . . . I have no intention to be skewered in this fashion. And since I have no intention to be so skewered, I have called this press conference to label as false and scurrilous and malicious these rumors, these assertions and accusations that are being circulated . . . I'm denying that outright and I'm labeling them—and I think a person in my position at a time like this might be permitted this departure from normal language—as damned lies.

News conference, Washington, Aug. 8/
The New York Times, 8-9:20.

2

[On charges that he received bribes and kickbacks while Governor of Maryland]: I have been completely destroyed, in my judgment. My political future is zero . . . I am fighting for my integrity and my reputation. That is more important now than any political office.

The New York Times, 10-7:(4)1.

Spiro T. Agnew
Former Vice President of the United States

3

My decision to resign [as Vice President] and enter a plea of *nolo contendere* [no contest, to tax evasion] rests on my firm belief that the public interest requires swift disposition of the problems which are facing me. I am advised that a full legal defense of the probable charges against me [bribery and kickbacks] could consume several years. I am concerned that intense media interest in the case would distract public attention from important national problems—to the country's detriment. I am aware that witnesses are prepared to testify that I and my agents received payments from consulting engineers doing business with the State of Maryland during the period I was Governor. With the exception of the admission that follows, I deny the assertions of illegal acts on my part made by the government witnesses. I admit that I did receive payments during the year 1967 which were not expended for political purposes and that, therefore, these payments were income

taxable to me in that year, and that I so knew. I further acknowledge that contracts were awarded by state agencies in 1967 and other years to those who made such payments, and that I was aware of such awards. I am aware that government witnesses are prepared to testify that preferential treatment was accorded to the paying companies pursuant to an understanding with me when I was the Governor. I stress, however, that no contracts were awarded to contractors who were not competent to perform the work, and in most instances state contracts were awarded without any arrangement for the payment of money by the contractor. I deny that the payments in any way influenced my official actions. I am confident, moreover, that testimony presented in my behalf would make it clear that I at no time conducted my official duties as County Executive or Governor of Maryland in a manner harmful to the interests of the county or state, or my duties as Vice President of the United States in a manner harmful to the nation, and further assert that my acceptance of contributions was part of a long-established pattern of political fundraising in the state. At no time have I enriched myself at the expense of the public trust. In all the circumstances, I have concluded that protracted proceedings before the grand jury, the Congress and the courts, with the speculation and controversy surrounding them, would seriously prejudice the national interest. These, briefly stated, are the reasons I am entering a plea of *nolo contendere* to the charge that I did receive payments in 1967 which I failed to report for the purposes of income taxation.

At U.S. District Court, Baltimore, Oct. 10/
U.S. News & World Report, 10-22:23.

4

[On charges against him of bribery and kickbacks which resulted in his resignation as Vice President]: . . . public officials who do not possess large personal fortunes face the unpleasant but unavoidable necessities of raising substantial sums of money to pay their campaign and election expenses. In the fore-front of those eager to contribute always have been the contractors seeking non-bid state awards.

(SPIRO T. AGNEW)

Beyond the insinuation that I pocketed [while in Maryland public office] large sums of money—which has never been proven and which I emphatically deny—the intricate tangle of criminal charges leveled at me, which you've been reading and hearing about during these past months, boils down to the accusation that I permitted my fund-raising activities and my contract-dispensing activities to overlap in an unethical and unlawful manner. Perhaps, judged by the new post-Watergate political morality, I did. But the prosecution's assertion that I was the initiator and a Grey Eminence in an unprecedented and complex scheme of extortion is just not realistic. Portraying the prosecution's witnesses, who have long been experienced and aggressive in Maryland politics, as innocent victims of illegal enticements from me is enough to provoke incredulous laughter from any experienced political observer. All knowledgeable politicians and contractors know better than that. They know where the questionable propositions originate. They know how many shoddy schemes a political man must reject in carrying out his office . . . Let me reiterate here that I have never —as county executive of Baltimore County, as Governor of Maryland or as Vice President of the United States—enriched myself in betrayal of my public trust.

Broadcast address to the nation, Washington,
Oct. 15/Los Angeles Times, 10-16:(1)7.

Herbert E. Alexander
Executive director,
Citizens' Research Foundation,
Princeton, N.J.

1

In recent years there has been much comment about the high cost of politics. The rise has been dramatic. I estimate that $400 million was spent in 1972 for all elective and party politics in this country at all political levels, in campaigns for nomination and for election. This represents a 33 per cent increase from 1968. It represents an increase of almost 300 per cent since 1952, when the first national total was estimated. But political

costs need to be considered in perspective. Considered in the aggregate, politics is not over-priced. It is under-financed. $400 million is just a fraction of 1 per cent of the amounts spent by governments at all levels; and that is what politics is all about—gaining control of governments to decide policies on, among other things, how tax money will be spent. $400 million is less than the amount spent in 1972 by the two largest commercial advertisers in the United States.

Before Senate Commerce Subcommittee
on Communications, Washington/
The New York Times, 3-30:39.

Howard H. Baker, Jr.
United States Senator, R-Tennessee

2

[On whether he will be running for the Presidency in 1976]: I have had my private conference with myself about running . . . and I reached a few fundamental conclusions: One, I don't have to think seriously about it for the moment. Two, to do it would be a disservice to the duties I'm trying to perform. Three, I don't think I'd like to be President; my personal self says it's a bum trip . . . but four, I would not be afraid to be President.

Interview/
"W": a Fairchild publication, 7-13:17.

Joseph R. Biden, Jr.
United States Senator, D-Delaware

3

When we say that the American political system is the best money can buy, it is not a compliment, it is an epitaph.

Before the Senate, Washington/
The New York Times, 8-4:13.

4

I've heard it mentioned here that we better go softly on public financing of elections, because we need to preserve the two-party system. Well, I think unless we go very heavily on public financing of elections, we are going to lose the two-party system. One of the reasons I think the two parties are in such jeopardy is not because the small contributor is worried about being pushed out of the picture, but because the small contributor, in my opinion, feels "what in the hell difference does it make whether I make the small contribution, because those Democrats are the product of big labor, and those Republicans are the product of big business? And what difference does it make if I contribute $5, $10, $50 or $100?" And I think, if anything, a significant step toward public financing would increase the two-party system effort.

Before Senate Rules and Administration Subcommittee on Privileges and Elections, Washington/The Washington Post, 10-1:(A)22.

Julian Bond
Georgia State Legislator

1

It's plain that, for too many young people, [electing a new President] means little more than a change of photographs at the Post Office or a new picture for darts on dormitory walls.

At Princeton University/ The New York Times, 3-28:47.

Peter J. Brennan
Secretary of Labor of the United States

2

When I come down here, somebody asks me, "How do you feel being down here in Washington with all the bureaucrats and all the politicians?" I fortunately was born and raised in a city where all that nonsense started. And I don't say this in any insulting way—but I find this to be the minor leagues compared to New York City.

Before American Society of Association Executives, Washington, March 20/ The Wall Street Journal, 4-4:16.

Kingman Brewster, Jr.
President, Yale University

3

[Saying there must be reductions in the cost of politics]: I mean reducing the cost of running for office; and that requires, first of all, forcing the television stations and networks to give prime time without cost to

legitimate political candidates for state-wide and national office . . . The practical question would be, how do you distinguish between the serious and the frivolous candidates? I would use the British system of requiring candidates to post a bond which would be forfeited if they don't get a certain minimum vote—say 10 per cent of the total. This is a way of keeping frivolous candidates off the ballot. I would keep frivolous candidates away from television by a similar self-policing device.

Interview, New Haven, Conn./ Los Angeles Times, 6-19:(2)7.

Dolph Briscoe
Governor of Texas

4

Instead of going into hibernation, the Democratic Party is going into high gear . . . The situation in our country today is serious, and the people of America are doing some serious thinking about the directions our country has taken under Republican rule. The national economy is in flames as a result of the current [Nixon] Administration's game plan. The national conscience is in ashes as a result of [the] Watergate [political-espionage affair]. The answer to both problems can be found right here today—here in the mind and heart of the Democratic Party.

Before Texas State Democratic Executive Committee, Beaumont, July 21/ The Dallas Times Herald, 7-22:(A)17.

5

I want to tell you today that this [dirty tactics in political campaigns such as the Watergate political-espionage affair] is not politics as usual, from Democrats or Republicans . . . Don't let those who are caught jimmying open the doors of their opponents' offices, or tapping the lines of their opponents' phones, or attempting to sabotage activities of other candidates convince you that they are acting no differently than every other politician. Politics . . . is not a dirty business. It is not a free ticket to an easy fortune.

At University of Houston commencement, Aug. 18/ The Dallas Times Herald, 8-19:(A)29.

Patrick J. Buchanan
Special Consultant to the President
of the United States

1

I suppose it isn't unfair to recognize a sort of middle-class, fifties-generation lack of style among us [Nixon Administration aides]. But we're not ashamed, because we're making it work for the good of the nation.
The New York Times, 3-21:41.

2

[Criticizing allegations that unfair Republican campaign tactics won the 1972 Presidential election for Richard Nixon]: If one looks back over the political history of this country, there is only one other man, other than Richard Nixon, who has been his party's nominee for President or Vice President five times. That is Franklin Roosevelt. No other individual in our political history has served in both of the same high offices for so long a period of time as has the incumbent President. He is not the leader of a majority party. He has been—since 1946—a member of the minority party in American politics. And thus, this political career, I believe, is all the more impressive. That political record . . . is no accident. It is no fluke. And that election of 1972 was not stolen. And the mandate that the American people gave to this President and his Administration cannot and will not be frustrated or repealed or overthrown as a consequence of the incumbent tragedy [of Watergate].
At Senate Watergate hearings,
Washington, Sept. 26/
The Washington Post, 9-27:(A)13.

James L. Buckley
United States Senator, C-New York

3

[On his political-campaign philosophy in view of "dirty tricks" used by some politicians in their campaigns]: Run the best campaign for yourself on the issues, and don't worry too much about the curves that are thrown, because the electorate is generally too smart to be taken in by the curves . . . I just don't see how you can legislate people into the highest standards of behavior. Obviously,

we want the highest possible ethics, but I don't think we can legislate sleight-of-hand out of existence.
The New York Times, 6-24:(1)43.

McGeorge Bundy
President, Ford Foundation;
Former Special Assistant to Presidents
John Kennedy and Lyndon Johnson
for National Security Affairs

4

At its center, the present [Nixon] Administration has behaved in a lonely and mistrustful fashion, not only with its real opponents, but with all sorts of people and institutions that would gladly have been its friends, if not its political allies. In that sense, it has been a model of the mind of narrow thinking which is the main enemy of mutually-respecting independence.
San Francisco Examiner & Chronicle,
11-11:(This World)2.

George Bush
Chairman, Republican National Committee

5

There's a certain one-upmanship involved when there's wrongdoing, or the appearance of wrongdoing, on the part of people in public life. For a fleeting moment, one or the other candidate will gain briefly, one or the other party will gain briefly; but as time goes by, the loser is the political process itself.
Before National Press Club, Washington,
April 18/Los Angeles Times, 4-19:(1)6.

6

Frankly, I get worried when somebody says, " . . . let's let the Federal government finance all campaigns for the Presidency." The idea would soon spread to campaigns for the House and Senate and other offices. There is a key role—an honest, open role—for contributory participation. You cut that off when you mechanically apply price tags. The strength of our system comes from people participating —be it through money or energy—and any reform must maintain that principle . . . My own experience in Congress, as a member of the House, is that the overwhelming majority of members of both sides are honorable men.

When they accept a campaign donation, they're not for sale. Most people who give contributions don't expect special favors. They might expect a philosophy from a Congressman that they can support, but they aren't trying to buy something.

Interview/
U.S. News & World Report, 6-4:81.

1

As somewhat of an idealist, it bothers me that people think that the whole [American political] system is corrupt or that nobody can get fair play and there's no point in participating. This whole disenchantment, particularly among young people, is disturbing. In the long run, however, I'm confident that, when this whole Watergate [political-espionage] thing is over, people are going to say we have a pretty damn special system. It works, and it doesn't stop in high places. Justice is really an interaction of several entities—the courts, press, Committees of Congress—which have a way of cleansing our system. People don't see that now because we're wringing our hands over problems of the moment.

Interview/Nation's Business, December:32.

Earl L. Butz
Secretary of Agriculture of the United States

2

[Saying the Nixon Administration's accomplishments outweigh its faults]: Many things these days and in this Administration will become a chapter, a permanent chapter, in this history of good. We must accentuate these accomplishments; we must not let those chapters get lost among the footnotes of history that will ultimately carry the record of the bad and the sordid.

At National 4-H Congress, Chicago/
The New York Times, 11-29:53.

Robert C. Byrd
United States Senator, D-West Virginia

3

I think that what we [Democrats] have got to do is get rid of the pro-welfare giveaway image, the pro-permissiveness image, the pro-busing image, the meat-axe cuts of defense funds, and get back into the middle of the stream.

San Francisco Examiner & Chronicle,
1-7:(This World)2.

Jimmy Carter
Governor of Georgia

4

The mood of the people, in my opinion, is one of basic conservatism. But . . . conservatism does not mean racism. It does not mean stubborn resistance to change. It does not mean callousness or unconcern about our fellow human beings. I think it means a higher valuation of the human being, of individuality, self-reliance, dignity, personal freedom. But I also think it means increased personal responsibility through governmental action for alleviating affliction, discrimination and injustice . . . As more of our citizens choose to exercise their exciting new freedom and as the conglomerate and more unselfish will of the people is felt on government, I predict that we shall see an emergence of what might be called benevolent conservatism. There are many conservative people who care.

Before National Press Club, Washington,
Feb. 9/The Washington Post, 2-11:(D)6.

Jimmy Carter
Governor of Georgia;
Chairman, National Democratic Campaign
Committee

5

[On the Democratic Party's loss in last year's Presidential election]: . . . we lost because the public image of our Party alienated much of the traditionally Democratic vote in this country—because we had allowed ourselves to be perceived as a party that had little or no respect for the basic principles held by most Americans . . . What we do need is to realize that you cannot be perceived as making light of a man's religious and moral convictions, calling him a racist if he is concerned about busing [of school children for racial balance], a Neanderthal if he worries about crime and a square if he is scared to death

247

(JIMMY CARTER)

about drug abuse—and then expect him to vote your way just because his father and his grandfather have always voted Democratic.

Interview, Atlanta, May 12/
The New York Times, 5-13:(1)48.

Emanuel Celler
Former United States Representative,
D-New York

1

[Richard] Nixon is probably the most political President who ever sat in the White House, but he is congenitally devious. When you talk to Nixon, you have no idea if his words actually reflect what's in his mind. It's something like kissing a girl through a handkerchief.

Plainview (Tex.) Daily Herald, 3-13:4.

John B. Connally, Jr.
Former Secretary of the Treasury of the
United States; Former Governor of Texas;
1972 chairman, Democrats for Nixon

2

I think the problem the Democrats have is to try to change the course of the Party, not to go out and start castigating people because they didn't vote for [George] McGovern [in last year's Presidential election]. I have no apologies to make because I did not vote for McGovern. I didn't think he was the man to be elected; I thought it would have been almost tragic for the country if he had been. If I have to choose between a political future in the Democratic Party and supporting a man who I think is not qualified to be President, the choice is very easy for me. I'll sacrifice whatever my future is in any party.

Interview/
The Dallas Times Herald, 3-6:(A)13.

3

In recent history, it is the Republican Party which has invited broader participation from people in all walks of life; which has worked more effectively for economic growth and fiscal responsibility; which has sought opportunity for all without the burden of bigger government and higher taxes; and which stands for expanded international trade, more realistic monetary policies and responsible American leadership in the free world. I believe that in our time the Republican Party best represents the broad views of most Americans whatever their [formal] political affiliation. I believe that it can best provide the strength and stability to unite our people to deal effectively with our problems. I know that it now best represents my own personal convictions. Accordingly, I am today announcing my decision to affiliate with the Republican Party and make any contribution I can to help it meet the needs and aspirations of all Americans.

Announcing his switch from the
Democratic Party, at news conference,
Houston, May 2/
The New York Times, 5-3:34.

Alan Cranston
United States Senator, D-California

4

Political big money imperceptibly but inevitably erodes the impartiality of our best men and our best institutions. It gives the contributor an advantage over the non-contributor in the functioning of our democracy. It is a growing cancer which can destroy our body politic. It must be cut out.

Quote, 9-2:221.

5

[Vice President-designate Gerald Ford] may seem bland and uninspiring to those whose tunnel-vision politics is limited to a compulsion for the charismatic leader. But I think he will prove to be a man of solidity in a time of turbulence.

Before the Senate, Washington, Nov. 26/
Los Angeles Times, 11-27:(1)13.

Robert J. Dole
United States Senator, R-Kansas

6

There's a lack of understanding [by some Nixon Administration White House aides] of the legislative process and the people in it, even though I concede we're [members of

Congress] prima donnas, too. It's the attitude —lack of understanding. It always appears we're being pushed around, directed and asked to respond; but there's very little sympathy when we have a problem, whether it's closing a base in Kansas or whatever. They say, "We can bring you two Nixon pens, but otherwise we can't help you." The boys with power don't have much time for Senators and Congressmen.

The Washington Post, 4-29:(A)14.

John D. Ehrlichman
Former Assistant to the President
of the United States for Domestic Affairs

1

[Responding to charges by former Presidential Counsel John Dean that the Nixon Administration was excessively concerned about public demonstrations, etc.]: Today, the Presidency is the only place in the nation where all the conflicting considerations of domestic and international politics, economics and society merge; it is there that street violence and civil rights and relations with Russia and their effect on China and the Cambodian military situation, and a thousand other factors and events, are brought together on the surface of one desk and must be resolved. Some of these events in 1969 and 1970 included hundreds of bombings of public buildings in this country, a highly-organized attempt to shut down the Federal government, which you will all remember, intensive harassment of political candidates and violent street demonstrations which endangered life and property. Taken as isolated incidents, these events were serious. Taken as part of an apparent campaign to force upon the President a foreign policy favorable to the North Vietnamese and their allies, these demonstrations were more than just a garden variety exercise of the First Amendment. Just as, and because, they affected the President's ability to conduct foreign policy, they required the President's attention and concern. Had he and his staff been ignorant of the significance of such a campaign, or merely indifferent, they, that is the President and his staff, would have been subject to the proper criticism of all citizens

interested in securing a stable peace in Southeast Asia and the return of our POWs. But the President did understand these events to be important in the over-all foreign-policy picture, and they received balanced attention along with other events and factors.

At Senate Watergate hearings,
Washington, July 24/
The New York Times, 7-25:27.

2

[Supporting the use of political intelligence by a candidate to investigate an incumbent's personal habits which might adversely affect his performance in office]: . . . I think that each candidate who contests the candidacy of an incumbent has the obligation to come forward and contest the fitness of that incumbent for office, both in terms of his voting record and in terms of his probity, and in terms of his morals, if you please, and any other facts that [are] important or germane to the voters of his district or state or the country, for that matter. I think a candidate for office assumes that burden of proof. He assumes the burden of proof of showing the unfitness of the incumbent; and I don't think in our political system that is limited to his voting record or his absenteeism. If it were, we would countenance the perpetration of scoundrels in office who were thieves or who were fraudulent or who were profligate or who were otherwise unfit for office. So I think it's perfectly competent for a challenger to meet head-on the issue of the fitness of an incumbent . . . I know of my knowledge of incumbents in office who are not discharging their obligation to their constituents because of their drinking habits, and it distresses me very much; and there is a kind of unwritten law in the media that that is not discussed, and so the constituents at home have no way of knowing that you can go over here in the [Senate or House] Gallery and watch a member totter onto the floor in a condition of at least partial inebriation, which would preclude him from making any sort of a sober judgment on the issues that confront this country. Now, I think this is important for the American people to know. And if the only way that

(JOHN D. EHRLICHMAN)

it can be brought out is through his opponents in a political campaign, then I think
that opponent has an affirmative obligation to
bring that forward.

At Senate Watergate hearings,
Washington, July 27/
The Washington Post, 7-28:(A)13.

Sam J. Ervin, Jr.
United States Senator, D-North Carolina

1

[Criticizing the Nixon Administration]: I
would suggest two books that should be in
the White House. One is the Constitution of
the United States, and the other is Dale
Carnegie's book, *How to Win Friends and Influence People.*

Time, 2-19:22.

2

I think the Nixon Administration has been
the most repressive Administration as far as
basic rights are concerned ever since John
Adams had the Congress pass the Alien and
Sedition Act.

News conference, Washington,
March 26/Los Angeles Times, 3-27:(1)9.

3

[On President Nixon's victory over Senator
George McGovern in last year's election]: I
think after the election [in which] Nixon got
such a tremendous vote—why, he thought he
had a great mandate from the people. In my
judgment, he overlooked the fact it was not
because they loved Caesar more, but Brutus
less.

Interview/
The New York Times Magazine, 5-13:80.

4

[Arguing against a bill which would permit
election registration by postcard]: If this bill
is passed without some stringent amendments,
there is going to be a general resurrection of
the dead on every election day.

Human Events, 5-19:3.

5

One clear thing about elections is that
some men who are not willing to steal a
penny of another man's money are willing to

steal elections.

Quote, 6-17:560.

6

[Saying he will not seek re-election next
year]: Since time takes a constantly-acceler-
ating toll of those of us who live for many
years, it is simply not responsible for me to
assume that my eye will remain undimmed
and my natural force stay unabated for so
long a time . . . Here [in Morganton, N.C.]
we [he and his wife] hope to dwell for a time
among the people who have known us best
and loved us most, and to watch the sun set
in indescribable glory.

Before the Senate, Washington,
Dec. 19/Los Angeles Times, 12-20:(1)4.

Harry S. Flemming
Former Special Assistant to the
President of the United States

7

Giving up politics is like giving up smoking.
It's easier said than done.

The Washington Post, 7-8:(K)3.

Hiram L. Fong
United States Senator, R-Hawaii

8

[Arguing against a bill which would permit
election registration by postcard]: If this bill
passed, we will be registering cemetery lists,
we will be registering tombstones, we will be
registering vacant places, and we will be registering fictitious people.

Human Events, 5-19:3.

Gerald R. Ford
United States Representative, R-Michigan;
Vice President-designate of the United States

9

[On his being nominated for Vice Presi-
dent]: My thoughts have been mixed: pride in
the confidence which President Nixon has
shown for me and deep satisfaction that apparently it is shared by hundreds of other old
friends and colleagues, in the Congress and
throughout the country. I have felt a touch of
sadness at the thought of leaving the House of
Representatives, which has been my home for
nearly half my life. I have also felt something
like awe and astonishment at the magnitude

of the new responsibilities I have been asked to assume. At the same time, I have a new and invigorating sense of determination and purpose to do my best to meet them. Perhaps the worst misgivings I have about the Vice-Presidency are that such contacts with all kinds of people would be more difficult—and that my friends might stop calling me Jerry.

At Senate Rules Committee hearing
on his nomination for Vice President,
Washington, Nov. 1/
The New York Times, 11-2:23.

1

. . . I would say I am a moderate on domestic issues, a conservative in fiscal affairs and a dyed-in-the-wool internationalist in foreign affairs.

At hearing on his nomination for
Vice President, Washington/
The New York Times, 11-11:(1)52.

Gerald R. Ford
Vice President of the United States

2

I am a Ford, not a Lincoln. My addresses will never be as eloquent as Lincoln's. But I will do my best to equal his brevity and plain speaking.

At his swearing-in ceremony as
Vice President, Washington,
Dec. 6/The National Observer, 12-15:2.

Bill Frenzel
United States Representative,
R-Minnesota

3

If there's any way to turn off the voter it's to line up a bunch of candidates in front of him on TV. The public would be so sick of us that we'd have to drag them to the polls in a paddy wagon. It seems to me, if you really want to ruin a guy's candidacy, you give him a half hour on TV. Five minutes could probe the depths and valleys of most candidates.

Before House Subcommittee, Washington,
Oct. 2/The Washington Post, 10-3:(A)2.

Eric F. Goldman
Professor of History, Princeton University;
Former Special Consultant to the
President of the United States

4

[On President Nixon's White House aides]: This staff takes on a function of its own, removed from the President. Under [Lyndon] Johnson we used to say that the staff was like a wheel with spokes: They all led to the hub, which was Lyndon Johnson. He knew everything that happened, every leaf that fell on the White House lawn.

The National Observer, 5-5:1.

Barry M. Goldwater
United States Senator, R-Arizona

5

[On political espionage against him during the 1964 Presidential campaign]: I was bugged by the other [Democratic] side and paid no attention to it. They had even put television monitors across the elevator in my apartment building. A bachelor across the hall caught on and said, "Hey, I bring chicks up here and I don't want to get caught." So I didn't say anything; I just took my clippers and dismantled the thing.

Before Phoenix Heard Museum supporters,
Phoenix, April 25/
The New York Times, 4-27:10.

6

The thing that bothers me is, here I have spent over a third of my life trying to build the Republican Party, adding my little bit to it, having been successful in the South and in the Southwest, and then all of a sudden, as I near the end of my time in politics, I wonder —what the hell's it all been for? Here we are just drifting around; more Independents than Democrats or Republicans. And we need a two-party system. I feel terribly let-down, frankly. That is the feeling that prevails over every other feeling. I just—I get up in the morning and I think, oh, well, what the hell, what can you do?

Television interview/
"The Watergate Year,"
Columbia Broadcasting System, 6-17.

(BARRY M. GOLDWATER)

1

[On Senator Edward Kennedy's criticism of the Watergate political-espionage affair]: The South had another visitor from the North recently when Senator Edward Kennedy celebrated the Fourth of July in Decatur, Alabama, in an unlikely meeting with Governor George C. Wallace. In a speech which was obviously the opening gun of Kennedy's drive for the Presidency in 1976, the Senator constituted himself as both judge and jury in the Watergate affair. I say that one does not have to excuse or condone any of the stupid illegalities of the Watergate affair to suggest that Senator Kennedy is the last person in the country to lecture us on such matters. Until all the facts involving the Chappaquiddick tragedy [in which a woman riding in Kennedy's car was drowned] are made known, the American people can do without moralizing from the Massachusetts Senator. Oh, I know he is running for President, but that's no excuse.

At Young Republican National Convention,
Atlanta, July 12/
Los Angeles Herald-Examiner, 7-13:(A)4.

2

No sincere conservative that I know would ever adopt the idea that the end justifies the means . . . Actually, that premise belongs to the other side. It was used on me in 1964. And that was the premise which led the liberals in the academic world and in the media to defend or pooh-pooh Mr. [Daniel] Ellsberg's theft of confidential and classified government material [the "Pentagon Papers"]. That premise also was the one that led to the virtual enshrining by the liberals of Angela Davis, the Berrigan brothers, the peace rioters and the war dissenters, even though serious violations of the law were involved. It was the liberals, not the conservatives, who promoted the idea that dissenters should choose what laws they would obey and which they would ignore. It was the liberals, not the conservatives, who urged the burning of draft cards and cheered the desertion of military men because they felt the war in Vietnam was special and illegal and because they disagreed with its objectives.

Before Young Americans for Freedom,
Washington, Aug. 16/
The Christian Science Monitor, 8-23:16.

3

I believe unquestionably that the Republican victory in the Presidential election in 1972 was a victory for conservatism over the forces of leftist radicalism. Whether you agree with everything President Nixon accomplished in his first term of office or whether you believe that some Administration moves ran counter to our basic conservative tenets, the fact remains that, when the voters went to the polls in 1972, the choice was between all-out capitulation to the New Left or support for the nearest thing this country has seen in 40 years to a conservative Administration . . .

Human Events, 8-25:5.

4

I've always said that you'll find about the same amount of honesty within a political body that you will find in any group. I don't know what the figure is; maybe it's 3 or 4 per cent that are crooked. I don't care whether they are members of the YMCA board, the Red Cross or the Episcopal Church. The average man in politics is very honest and sincere and with all the ethics in the world. The trouble is that only a handful can muddle up the whole thing.

Interview, Phoenix/
"W": a Fairchild publication, 9-21:2.

5

[On Vice President Agnew's resignation because of charges of bribery and kickbacks against him]: In effect, [Agnew] was tried and judged in a manner completely foreign to the proper pursuit of justice in the United States, a manner which convicted him by headlines and newscasts based on leaks of official information, but before a single legal charge had been filed. I hope that never again in my lifetime will I witness this kind of abuse of an American citizen by people in responsible positions.

Washington, Oct. 10/
The Washington Post, 10-11:(A)19.

This particular President [Nixon] is the most complete loner I have ever known. How you can change that I don't know. I have been trying my damnest to get him to be a little more human and to come down and speak with the boys and girls and find out what the Legislative Branch is thinking. When you talk about the arrogance, the rudeness, that is an individual matter which we are hopeful we can correct. But I wouldn't bet a lot of money.

San Francisco Examiner & Chronicle,
11-18:(This World)2.

[On President Nixon]: I've never known a man to be such a loner in any field . . . business, profession, politics, or what . . . I can't sit here and tell you who his [political] advisers are. I know that Mel Laird has quit mainly because the President won't listen to him. Bryce Harlow is reportedly quitting for the same reason. Now, I can't believe, with all due respect to General [Alexander] Haig—he's one of the most brilliant men I've run into —that Nixon would listen to General Haig on political matters when General Haig doesn't know anything about political matters . . . I just can't believe he would listen to [Ronald] Ziegler. That, in my opinion, would be something disastrous. Again, there is nothing personal, but Ziegler doesn't understand politics. The President, I think, thinks of himself as the supreme politician in this country. And being a loner, I think he sits by himself and tells himself what he's going to do. Now, we went through this "gesture" period of having Congressmen and Senators down to see him —but it seems to have ended. And this is what I was afraid of—that it would be a one-pitch goal and that would end it. And as a result, he's not getting advice. That's his problem; he's not getting it. And when he gets it, he doesn't listen to it.

Interview/
The Christian Science Monitor, 12-18:2.

H. R. Haldeman
Former Assistant to the President
of the United States

[On the Nixon Administration]: I had the rare privilege for four years of serving on the White House staff under one of America's greatest Presidents and with the most outstanding, dedicated and able group of people with whom I have ever worked. Those who served with me at the White House had complete dedication to the service of this country. They had great pride in the President they served and great pride in the accomplishments of the Nixon Administration in its first four years. I cannot imagine anything more satisfying than [to] have had the opportunity to play a part in the first Nixon Administration —which brought about the end of America's longest and most difficult war [Vietnam]; the end of the cold war which had been a fact of life for as long as many of us can remember; the opening of communications and dialogue with the leaders of the Soviet Union and the leaders of the People's Republic of [Communist] China; the building of a structure that can well lead not to just one but many generations of peace; the start of the return of power of government to the people by revenue-sharing and Federal reorganizations; the whole new approach to domestic programs designed to bring those programs into line with the real people. We all felt and still feel that the first four years was a time of laying the groundwork for even greater accomplishments in the second term; and we have complete faith that the promise will be met.

At Senate Watergate hearings, Washington,
July 30/The New York Times, 7-31:24.

William D. Hathaway
United States Senator, D-Maine

The mandate of last November's election belongs to Richard Nixon and Spiro Agnew, not their political party. While winning the White House, Republicans actually lost strength in the Senate and among the nation's Governors. Given this fact, who is to say with any assurance what the mandate of 1972 was? . . . If the President leaves office [because of the Watergate political-espionage affair], the mandate of last year is negated; it seems

(WILLIAM D. HATHAWAY)

logical to me to allow the people themselves to decide who shall then receive what only they can rightfully give.

The Washington Post, 11-14:(A)27.

Linwood Holton
Governor of Virginia

1

In general, we Republicans believe that each person should have the opportunity to strive and make his or her own place in our society, while our Democratic friends are more inclined to subordinate the individual to the group, thereby placing less emphasis on individual initiative and more on collective action . . . A majority of the American people [would support basic Republican principles and candidates] if they were better aware of where we stand. Here, I think, is the tragic flaw: We simply have not communicated. We have got to let people know what it means to be a Republican, what Republicanism stands for.

Before Ripon Society,
Arlington County, Va., Nov. 30/
The Washington Post, 12-1:(A)2.

Harold E. Hughes
United States Senator, D-Iowa

2

The politician in this country is probably in greater danger of being struck down than in almost any other Western country. Americans don't like to hear that; but our history proves it. Just in the past 10 years: Jack Kennedy, Robert Kennedy, Martin Luther King, George Wallace. Surely there must be some way in which we can dampen the anger which politics generates in the hearts of our people.

Parade, 10-28:5.

Hubert H. Humphrey
United States Senator, D-Minnesota

3

. . . if there is one thing that raises suspicion, it is big money. American politics has become so expensive. I have been in it, and I must say that the most unhappy feeling I have is about contributors and contributions and having to demean oneself in order to raise the money necessary to conduct a campaign, particularly on a national basis. This is just wrong, and yet—pray tell me—are we to turn politics over to the sons of the rich? Is it going to be a rich man's playground? Or how is a man of modest means going to run for office?

Interview, Washington/
The Christian Science Monitor, 3-19:8.

4

[On the necessity for compromise in the Democratic Party]: . . . some people think it's immoral to win—that you have to make a compromise or two and that's somehow unworthy of us. Franklin Roosevelt once said you have to make adjustments and compromises to be in a position to make the great decisions. We are a coalition party and always have been. We don't rank with the purity of ivory soap. Sometimes we've tried to be that pure and have floated right out of existence.

The Dallas Times Herald, 4-13:(B)2.

5

. . . I do not intend to be a candidate [for President] in 1976. I have had my run at it. I tried to do well. I hope that I have been a constructive force in American politics. I will settle for that.

TV-radio interview, Washington/
"Meet the Press,"
National Broadcasting Company, 7-1.

Robert M. Hutchins
Chairman, Center for the Study of
Democratic Institutions

6

If I were asked to name the single change in my lifetime that seems to me to have had the worst effect on American politics, I would say that it is the tremendous expenditures now required to get elected to anything.

Quote, 10-7:338.

Daniel K. Inouye
United States Senator, D-Hawaii

1

Having been in politics since 1954, I wasn't particularly naive about big money. But I never dreamed that so much—$60 million of Republican funds and about $37 million of Democratic funds—was involved in the '72 [election] campaign. I was also not aware of the dirty tricks, the espionage, the arm-twisting, the shady, scurvy, slimy tactics, the corruption of young men by older men who preached law and order. And this bugging of telephones! It's been shocking! And what a horrible commentary on our democracy! . . . At a time when the Vice President of the United States [Agnew] has resigned and the President [Nixon] himself is under fire and the whole political system is under a dark cloud of suspicion, I believe that legislators, politicians have to reassure the people that honesty and openness and decency are still the character ingredients of the men they elected.

Interview/Parade, 11-11:5.

Herman Kahn
Director, Hudson Institute

2

Intellectuals are constantly searching for things that will show us [the U.S.] to be a totalitarian state. In 1970, I had at least two dozen phone calls from college-faculty people asking if it was true that the Hudson Institute had done a study for the Nixon Administration on how to call off the 1972 elections. It was a crazy rumor, of course, and nobody paid any attention to it *except* for a few of the biggest minds on the campuses. When you suffer from nightmares like that, you're at least paranoiac if not manic.

Interview, Hudson Institute/
The Reader's Digest, April:76.

Edward M. Kennedy
United States Senator, D-Massachusetts

3

Today, in spite of the enormous progress we have made in so many other areas of public life, we are still using voter registration methods which were, perhaps, sophisticated at the turn of the century, but which are generations out of date today, as obsolete as the Pony Express or the Model T Ford.

The Sacramento (Calif.) Bee, 2-17:(A)15.

4

[Advocating government financing of all Federal election campaigns and limits on individual campaign contributions]: Of all the lessons of [the] Watergate [political-espionage affair], perhaps the one that is most obvious today is the lesson that money is a vastly corrosive power in American politics. There could be no more powerful formula for compounding the cynicism of our citizens over Watergate than for Congress to ignore this opportunity to shut off the vast rivers of cash and contributions that flood our political system in every election campaign.

Before Senate Rules and Administration
Committee, Washington, June 6/
The New York Times, 6-7:32.

5

[Alabama Governor George Wallace and I have] differing opinions on some important issues. But we have one thing in common: We don't [referring to the Watergate political-espionage affair] corrupt, we don't malign, we don't compile lists of enemies whose careers and lives are to be shattered because of their disagreement. We don't use the tactics of a criminal or the power of the law in order to silence those whose ideas of politics are different from our own. For if there is one thing George Wallace stands for, it is the right of every American to speak his mind and be heard fearlessly and in any part of the country. It is in that spirit that I come here today. For that is the spirit of America. And I don't believe that either Governor Wallace or I, the people of Massachusetts or the people of Alabama, are going to give up that right to anyone, however great his power and however high his office.

At Independence Day celebration,
Decatur, Ala., July 4/
Los Angeles Herald-Examiner, 7-5:(A)2.

6

The [Nixon] Administration, masquerading as conservative, has taken the most radical

255

(EDWARD M. KENNEDY)

steps toward dismembering the spirit of our [American] Revolution and the protections of the Constitution. They administer the nation's business through men hidden in the White House—men responsible neither to Congress nor the public, and who cannot be compelled to account for their actions or even to disclose them. They have transformed the public institutions into instruments of intimidation and control—turning to their own benefits not only agencies of intelligence and law enforcement, but an immense mechanism of economic sanction and rewards.

At Independence Day celebration, Decatur, Ala., July 4/ Los Angeles Times, 7-5:(1)25.

1

This [Nixon] Administration has had its foot in its mouth, its hand in your pocket, its tongue in its cheek, its finger in the air, its eye on Dow Jones.

At AFL-CIO convention, Bal Harbour, Fla., Oct. 19/ The New York Times, 10-20:16.

John V. Lindsay
Mayor of New York

2

The art of politics is the key in any area of government, particularly in the elective arena. You have to have a mixture of good politicians and good specialists. Politicians have to learn to become good professionals in management. You can get into a lot of trouble if you don't have politicians on your team.

At urban affairs conference, New York, March 20/The New York Times, 3-21:45.

Russell B. Long
United States Senator, D-Louisiana

3

I do not see anything wrong with a man making a large [political-campaign] contribution as long as we have the private system of financing campaigns; nor can I see, when we have a limitation on what a candidate can spend, that there is anything wrong about letting a man run representing the fat cats,

just as a man can run to represent the rank and file. Let us put it in its worst possible light. It may be that those with great wealth —it may very well be the most reactionary and self-serving people in the country—are very voracious in what they would expect a man elected to public office to do; but in fairness, in a democracy, one would think they would be entitled to support a man in office, and that man would be entitled to explain his side of the argument, and if all had an equal opportunity to try to get votes and get the greater support, in the last analysis it would be a question not of which side a man came from, but rather whose argument made better sense to the public. So in the last analysis, when we try to move toward a system where both sides will have the same amount of money to spend and the same opportunity to be heard—and hopefully we can work it out in such a fashion that both would have an equal opportunity to present their case to the public—why should it make a real difference whether one man was supported by people who made large contributions and the other was supported by people who made small contributions, or indeed whether he put up his own money? In the last analysis, it should be a question of what the public thinks about the matter.

Before the Senate, Washington/ The Washington Post, 8-22:(A)20.

Clare Boothe Luce
Former American diplomat and playwright

4

The New Left thing has expended itself. If anything, we are moving back to a political center. We don't want any revolutions around here. We want to do it the way we've done it for 200 years: two steps forward, one step back. That is the way we want to go.

Interview, New York/ The New York Times Magazine, 4-22:50.

Frank Mankiewicz
1972 Presidential campaign manager for Senator George McGovern

5

The entry fee for politics has become too

high. It is becoming limited to the rich, the famous and those willing to mortgage themselves.

Quote, 5-27:481.

Mike Mansfield
United States Senator, D-Montana

1

Once again, in the last [1972] election the flaws in the electoral system were paraded before the nation. In my judgment, both Congressional and Presidential campaigns are too repetitive, too dull and too hard on candidates and electorate. Most serious, the factor of finance begins to overshadow all other considerations in determining who runs for public office and who does not, in determining who gets adequate exposure and who does not. It is not healthy for free government when vast wealth becomes the principal arbiter of questions of this kind. It is not healthy for the nation for politics to become a sporting game of the rich. This Congress must look and look deeply at where the nation's politics are headed. In my judgment, ways must be found to hold campaign expenditures within reasonable limits. Moreover, to insure open access to politics, I can think of no better application of public funds than, as necessary, to use them for the financing of elections, so that public office will remain open to all, on an unfettered and impartial basis, for the better service of the nation.

Before Senate Democratic Caucus,
Jan. 4/
The Washington Post, 1-11:(A)18.

2

Last year, the American people re-elected [President] Nixon by a very large majority, but at the same time added to the Democratic majority in the Senate while reducing the Democratic majority in the House only slightly. Americans really plumped for a divided government, a government based on checks and balances. In that way, it's possible for us to counterbalance each other and, hopefully, work in the best interests of the people as a whole . . . For President Nixon to get the

vote that he did indicates Americans had a certain degree of compatability with the programs which he was advocating and the policies which he was endeavoring to pursue. But at the same time, I think it indicated a certain amount of confidence in the Congress—a recognition of the fact that, if there is going to be a stabilizing factor, it could well be in the body of men and women who represent the people most closely and who are nearest to them at all times.

Interview/
U.S. News & World Report, 10-1:28.

George S. McGovern
United States Senator, D-South Dakota

3

[On his defeat in last year's Presidential election]: My confidence in the ability to get to people with appeals based on simple, old-fashioned virtues like trust and decency has been shattered.

Interview, Washington/
San Francisco Examiner, 1-9:2.

4

[Saying he campaigned too much when he ran for President last year]: Campaigning in three or four cities a day is a thing of the past. I don't think anyone will ever run for President that way again . . . Looking back on my travel schedule, I don't know how I did it. And I did it for two years—and [President] Nixon never left the White House.

Interview, Washington/
Los Angeles Times, 1-10:(1)4.

5

To those who charge that liberalism has been tried and found wanting, I answer that the failure is not in the idea, but in the course of recent history. The New Deal was ended by World War II. The New Frontier was closed by Berlin and Cuba almost before it was opened. And the Great Society lost its greatness in the jungles of Indochina.

Lecture at Oxford University, England,
Jan. 21/The New York Times, 1-22:38.

6

[The Democratic Party today] consists largely of fragments and factions . . . with no principles, no programs, living only from day

(GEORGE S. McGOVERN)

to day, caring only for the prerequisites of office, doing nothing and, worse, not caring that nothing is done.

Lecture at Oxford University, England, Jan. 21/The Dallas Times Herald, 1-22:(A)6.

1

[On his running for the Presidency last year]: The whole campaign was a tragic case of mistaken identity—starting right with the [Democratic] Convention. What I saw as the most moving political experience that had taken place in this country in many years, I found out later, looked on television as if it were the take-over of the good old Democratic Party by a bunch of freaks and long-haired kids and aggressive women. People watching on television got a distorted picture of me. They came away feeling I was some kind of a radical avante-garde type, an elitist, someone outside the mainstream. While I saw myself as being right in the heart of the American tradition—from a farm state, a clergyman's son. I'd worked my way through school, gone off to war, come back to the ministry and teaching, and then achieved elective office against overwhelming odds. What could be more squarely in the apple-pie tradition? The trouble was, all people saw on television were a few of my outspoken supporters out front; and they came away thinking that was me.

Interview, Pierre, S.D./ The New York Times Magazine, 5-6:88.

2

[On his losing last year's Presidential election]: It almost makes you weep. To think of the kind of people I could have brought into government, compared to what we have in there now. We would have transformed the spirit of America. We would have lifted the hopes of the country, revived optimism. Our government could have given the people a sense of being part of a country that was living up to the dreams and the hopes of its people. You know, people are very unhappy today—even Republicans. Last November could have been a turning point comparable

to the Roosevelt period, the Jefferson period. The country was ripe for it. If only we could have gotten by the hurdle of that election.

Interview, Pierre, S.D./ The New York Times Magazine, 5-6:88.

3

I want to say that there were 20 million Americans who supported my candidacy [for President] in 1972. Doubtless, many of them were shattered emotionally by the results —overwhelmingly defeated. But I think we served a purpose that will very well stand the test of time. I think that, while we made some honest mistakes in 1972, it is increasingly clear to the American people that we did not lie to them; we did not burglarize anybody's files; we did not wiretap; we did not bribe anyone; and we did not mishandle campaign funds. We did not get much credit for setting those standards in 1972. We are getting the credit now, in my opinion [as a result of the Watergate political-espionage affair]. The campaign is beginning to come into focus. And I think that history is going to be kind to the 1972 McGovern campaign.

Interview, Washington/ The Christian Science Monitor, 7-5:10.

George Meany
President, American Federation of Labor-Congress of Industrial Organizations

4

The President [Nixon] is a master politician; he's the best I've seen in the White House politically. He knows all the angles and he works very hard to get blue-collar support, white-collar support, no-collar support, fur-coat support, mink-coat support. He wants all the votes; and that's the measure of a politician, of his efficiency—he wants all the votes. So if you mean he's working to try to get the traditional middle-class Democratic vote, well, that's normal; that's what he should do; that's part of the political game . . . Now, of course, he got a good share of the so-called middle-class vote last election [1972]. But he didn't get it, I don't think, from a positive angle at all; I don't think he got it for anything he did. I think he got it because he had an opponent by the name of [George] McGovern that nobody could trust.

Interview, Washington/
The National Observer, 5-5:24.

1

[Criticizing the tactics of President Nixon's 1972 re-election campaign aides]: What was going on was not campaign [contribution] collection—what these people were doing was extortion. They were going up to big corporations and saying: "Get it up, get it up. You want to do business with the government, you have to get so much up." They were putting a tax on them. Hell, it was just like the old gangster regime where they came down the street to tell the storekeeper: "You're going to stay in business? Fifty dollars a month." The next one $100 a month. As far as I am concerned, the morals of this Committee to Re-elect were not any better than the morals of the gangsters.

News conference, Washington, Aug. 30/
The New York Times, 9-2:(1)34.

2

After five years of [President] Richard Nixon, this great and once-proud nation stands before the world with its head bowed —disgraced not by its enemies abroad but by its leaders at home . . . Today, knowing what we know, we can say that this torn and tattered Administration has lost the moral authority to lead either at home or abroad. [The Nixon Administration has] sounded a trumpet of retreat and withdrawal—retreat from decency at home and withdrawal from principle everywhere else. Never in history has a great nation been governed so corruptly.

At AFL-CIO convention,
Bal Harbour, Fla., Oct. 18/
The New York Times, 10-19:21.

Richard B. Morris
Professor of History, Columbia University

3

We no longer have men in public life of the stature of our Founding Fathers. The impact of immediacy created by TV has placed a premium, not on reflection and reason, but on the glib answer and the bland statement. The politician is concerned with public relations, not with public principles. In the founding of the nation, we needed charismatic figures, but today we could do with honest ones.

New York/
The New York Times, 5-6:(1)56.

Richard M. Nixon
President of the United States

4

I would say that my view, my approach, is probably that of a Disraeli conservative: a strong foreign policy, strong adherence to basic values that the nation believes in and the people believe in, and to conserving those values and not being destructive of them, but combined with reform—reform that will work, not reform that destroys.

Interview/
The New York Times Magazine, 2-11:12.

5

We live in a time when many people are cynical about politics and politicians. In this profession—as in any—there is much that could be improved. But there is also much to admire. It would be a tragedy if we allowed the mistakes of a few to obscure the virtues of most—or if we let our disappointment with some aspects of the system turn into despair with the system as a whole. The system is working. The way to make it work better is to bring more good people into it.

At dedication of research center named for
the late U.S. Senator Everett M. Dirksen,
Pekin, Ill., June 15/
Los Angeles Herald-Examiner, 6-15:(A)2.

6

There are a great number of people in this country that didn't accept the [Presidential election] mandate of 1972. After all, I know that most of the members of the press corps were not enthusiastic . . . about either my election in '68 or '72. That is not unusual. Frankly, if I had always followed what the press predicted or the polls predicted, I would never have been elected President. But what I am saying is this: People who did not accept the mandate of '72, who do not want the

(RICHARD M. NIXON)

strong leadership that I want to give, who do not want to cut down the size of our government bureaucracy that burdens us so greatly and to give more of our government back to the people, people who do not want these things, naturally, would exploit any issue—if it weren't [the] Watergate [political-espionage affair], anything else—in order to keep the President from doing his job. And so I say I impute no improper motives to them. I think they would prefer that I fail. On the other hand, I am not going to fail. I am here to do a job, and I am going to do the best I can. And I am sure the fair-minded members of this press corps—and that is most of you—will report when I do well, and I am sure you will report when I do badly.

News conference, San Clemente, Calif.,
Aug. 22/The National Observer, 9-1:6.

1

I've made my mistakes, but in all of my years of public life I have never profited from public service. I have earned every cent. And in all my years of public life, I have never obstructed justice. People have got to know whether or not their President is a crook. Well, I'm not a crook. I earned everything I've got.

Before Associated Press
Managing Editors Association,
Disney World, Fla., Nov. 17/
San Francisco Examiner, 11-18:(A)1.

Robert Packwood
United States Senator, R-Oregon

2

[Addressing President Nixon]: All of us, Mr. President, whether we're in politics or not, have weaknesses. For some, it's drinking. For others, it's gambling. For still others, it's women. None of these weaknesses applies to you. Your weakness is credibility. This has always been your short-suit with the news media and the general public.

At White House discussion, Washington,
Nov. 15/The New York Times, 11-17:18.

Henry E. Petersen
Assistant Attorney General,
Criminal Division, Department of
Justice of the United States

3

[Saying members of Congress criticize the Justice Department for not enforcing political campaign contribution laws, and yet they don't pass enforceable laws or appropriate sufficient funds for enforcement]: They know where the money has to come from. And they sit up there and moan that there's no enforcement. They're all so goddamned hypocritical up there about these things. If they weren't so goddamned hypocritical, they would have passed statutes a long time ago that could be enforced. They make me sick! This hypocrisy just makes me ill! That pious attitude by the politicians with respect to campaign contributions just makes me apoplectic!

Interview/
The Washington Post, 12-2:(H)6.

Raymond K. Price, Jr.
Special Assistant to the President
of the United States

4

We [Nixon Administration aides] recognize we're perceived as "dull" [by the public and the press], and to some extent we are. But then, we're not here to make this another Camelot.

The New York Times, 3-21:41.

William Proxmire
United States Senator, D-Wisconsin

5

[On President Nixon's shuffling and re-shuffling of posts and aides in his Administration in the wake of the Watergate political-espionage affair]: A house-cleaning was called for. But this stuttering, stop-go, in-out administration of national affairs is becoming a sorry joke. The nation is ill-served when the top men in our government are being shuffled around like a deck of cards in a drunken poker game.

San Francisco Examiner & Chronicle,
5-20:(This World)8.

Harry Reasoner
News commentator,
American Broadcasting Company

1

The great problem with setting up a system for public financing of [political] campaign costs is to establish it fairly—fair, that is, to incumbents and the people who want to oust them, to major parties and to new groups who want to gain strength. Quite naturally, the incumbents are less interested in being fair to challengers than the challengers are, and since it is the incumbents who have to pass any legislation, and the present system favors them, we may still be discussing high-sounding proposals—and living with the present wretched system—two or three Presidents and a dozen Congresses from now. The best proposal, it has seemed to me, was the one first outlined in 1965 by a non-partisan commission originally appointed by President Kennedy. It provided that only individuals could contribute to campaign costs, that there would be a limit on the amount an individual could give—$50, or something like that—that he could give it to any qualified candidate or party—and that he could then deduct it, all of it, from his income tax. This system would not shut out new candidates or new parties, and it would preserve the necessity for incumbents to court their employers.

News commentary,
American Broadcasting Company/
The Christian Science Monitor, 12-31:(B)8.

George E. Reedy
Former Press Secretary to
President Lyndon B. Johnson

2

. . . I don't think that President Nixon ever had much if any political power, at any time. He was elected [in 1972] on a lot of negatives: McGovern scared the hell out of a lot of people and they went over and voted for Nixon. His major amount of power has been that the majority of the American people are loyal to their President and they are willing to obey the laws and follow his leadership. But that power is rapidly vanishing because of the impact of [the] Watergate [political-espionage affair]. And I think that he won't have too much for the next couple of years, and by and large it will be negative power. He will be able to keep up the house-keeping function of the White House, and he will be able to do the sorts of things a President can do if he doesn't have to go to Congress . . . but if he has to go to Congress for something, I think he will be in an awful lot of trouble.

New York/
The Dallas Times Herald, 8-17:(A)20.

Ed Reinecke
Lieutenant Governor of California

3

So often the conservative is pictured as rock solid, unmoving. But a true political conservative is an intellectual liberal, because he believes in individual freedoms. He believes in trying it.

Interview, Sacramento/
Los Angeles Times, 11-10:(2)10.

James Reston
Vice president and columnist,
"The New York Times"

4

[On a news conference recently held by Vice President Agnew in which he denied that he was involved in bribes and kickbacks while he was Governor of Maryland]: My main feeling about the Agnew development is that the Vice President conducted the most honest press conference in Washington in years. He didn't duck the charges that he was being investigated as a crook. Instead, he faced the music and in the end made a cogent comparison between the way he deals with such controversy and the way [President] Nixon does. Agnew has always maintained that, no matter what he says about the press, newsmen are always welcome to drop into his office for a good argument. I've always been able to. These days, it's almost thrilling to find a public official who can be congratulated for his accessibility.

Interview, Martha's Vineyard, Mass./
"W": a Fairchild publication, 8-24:4.

Elliot L. Richardson
*Former Attorney General
of the United States*

1

[On his experience with the Nixon Administration White House staff]: To me they were amateurs, because they thought it was smart to be "smart." One thing I've learned is that you can't work the angles, because you cut yourself on them. You can't play politics like a three-cushion billiard shot. You can spin the process of calculation too far. The simple way is so much simpler.

*News conference, Nov. 27/
San Francisco Examiner, 11-28:10.*

Donald W. Riegle, Jr.
United States Representative, D-Michigan

2

[On the Republican Party]: I think it's a party that has been subjected to one-man rule from the Nixon White House. The Republican Party has more and more become sort of a country-club-type party that is dominated by a handful of people at the top of the Executive Branch of government, where dissenters have been purged from the Party, had their patriotism questioned and so on.

The Dallas Times Herald, 3-12:(A)11.

Frank L. Rizzo
Mayor of Philadelphia

3

I'm no politician. I have no respect for politicians. They deal in human souls and talk with forked tongues.

*Interview/
Los Angeles Times, 2-15:(2)1.*

Nelson A. Rockefeller
Governor of New York

4

Maybe history will look at [President] Nixon and say it could have been done differently, but that he did something fundamental . . . People have had it with government, with business, with the church . . . They're disillusioned . . . Our established institutions' credibility is at a low ebb. I'm clear, I'm not confused on my feelings about the need to change . . . on our responsibility in the world . . . We've got to shape it . . . In a way, that's what Nixon is doing . . . A lot of good stuff will go down in the process, and in a way the people recognize it . . . But I think they respect him. I think this is a time for gut feeling rather than intellectual feeling, and maybe this is why the intellectuals have got such trouble . . .

*Interview, New York, February/
The New York Times Magazine, 4-29:67.*

William P. Rogers
Secretary of State of the United States

5

[Financing of political campaigns is so] rotten [that] otherwise honorable men can be corrupted by it. When so much money is floating through the political system with so little effective accounting for it, that fact invites evil.

*Before college students, Aug. 7/
U.S. News & World Report, 8-20:28.*

William D. Ruckelshaus
*Former Acting Director,
Federal Bureau of Investigation*

6

No one can deny the wrenching effect of political scandal, and no one can excuse it. But the worst political scandal in this country is not the Watergate [political-espionage affair] but the inattention we pay to the political process. It is not only a matter of voter apathy, but of citizen apathy. Politics with a small "p" is not supposed to be left to professionals; in the end, that only invites manipulation and cynical huckstering. Politics is supposed to be the process of collective decision-making, and as such we are all supposed to be part of that process. If we dismiss it as dirty, as unworthy of our concern and active participation, we insure cynical abuse of the process.

*At Ohio State University commencement/
The National Observer, 7-14:17.*

Dean Rusk
*Former Secretary of State
of the United States*

1

It seems to me that it is important for our government to have highly sophisticated means of intelligence in the kind of world in which we live; but I'm deeply concerned about any indication that these powerful methods be used by any Administration—Democrat or Republican—for partisan political purposes. A good deal of information comes in from a variety of sources which could be politically damaging to one's opponents, and I do not believe that those who are in government are entitled to use that information or those means in the free-swinging hurly-burly of the political processes by which the American people determine who are to represent them in Washington.

Interview/The Washington Post, 8-5:(C)4.

Pierre Salinger
*Former Press Secretary to
President John F. Kennedy*

2

[On the incident in 1969 when the car Senator Edward Kennedy was driving plunged into a pond near Chappaquiddick Island, Mass., killing a woman companion]: Chappaquiddick was a personal tragedy. It happened to involve a United States Senator; but it did not [as in the Watergate political-espionage affair] involve a President of the United States in the process of carrying out his Constitutional responsibilities. Yes, I know there was a covering letter from the judge on the Kennedy testimony, saying he didn't believe Kennedy's story; but at least the testimony was made public. And Kennedy did not have to be subpoenaed; he voluntarily turned himself in. They may be talking Chappaquiddick in Washington, but just go outside of the nation's capital. They'd take Kennedy for President any day. He's the last living [Kennedy] heir. He's got the name. He's been a good Senator.

*Interview, Washington/
"W": a Fairchild publication, 9-7:15.*

William B. Saxbe
United States Senator, R-Ohio

3

[On the Nixon Administration]: I don't know whether it's one of the most corrupt [Administrations], but it's one of the most inept. They just couldn't plan a scenario as ridiculous as what's been going on; and if it keeps on, they're going to have to get them clown suits.

*Columbus, Ohio, Oct. 11/
The New York Times, 11-2:22.*

4

[On his decision not to run for the Senate again]: My dad was a cattle buyer. That's what I always intended to be. I don't know where I went wrong.

*Interview, Washington/
The Dallas Times Herald, 10-28:(D)14.*

William B. Saxbe
*United States Senator, R-Ohio;
Attorney General-designate of
the United States*

5

[On why, after he had been critical of the Nixon Administration, he accepted the nomination for Attorney General from President Nixon]: You sit around the Senate for years and think of what you can do. You shoot your mouth off. [Then] they hand you the ball. You can't go home and sit on the porch.

Nov. 1/The New York Times, 11-2:22.

Richard M. Scammon
Political analyst

6

[Saying Senator Edward Kennedy may not have a good chance of capturing the Presidency in 1976]: Sure Kennedy's the front-runner. [But] so was [Senator Edmund] Muskie [in the 1972 nominating campaign]. There's a feeling Kennedy's accident-prone. There's the playboy image, the lack of maturity. Americans have a reverence about the Presidency, the White House, U.S. One, all that.

Human Events, 4-14:2.

Eric Sevareid
News commentator,
Columbia Broadcasting System

1

[On former Vice President Agnew's recent resignation because of bribery and kickback charges against him]: Agnew preached the old-fashioned virtues and practiced the old-fashioned vices.

Quote, 11-4:433.

Maurice H. Stans
1972 chairman, Finance Committee
to Re-elect the President (Nixon)

2

. . . the idea is being purveyed in some circles that no one gives a substantial amount of money to a [political] campaign without buying something in return, without the expectation of a favor. That is a lie, and it is belittling to our self-respect as a people. I would like to give a couple of examples. Clement Stone of Chicago, pretty well-known now, gave $2 million to elect the President. He gave a lot in 1968. He is a very wealthy man and he can afford it. He believes in the President [Nixon]; he knows him as a friend. Clement Stone has never asked for anything from his government or the Administration in return. He has done it because he believes it is a public service from a man of wealth. I would like to give you another case. Ray Kroc is a man in Chicago who is responsible for the development of the McDonald hamburger chain . . . Now, what happened after his contribution became known? First, the press accused him of making the contribution so that he can influence the Price Commission on matters affecting his company. Secondly, he was accused of making the contribution so that he could get a lower minimum wage for the young people who work for his company. He was insulted by these insinuations and falsehoods; they were vicious and unfair, completely conjecture without any fact whatever.

At Senate Watergate hearings,
Washington, June 13/
The New York Times, 6-14:41.

Robert S. Strauss
Chairman,
Democratic National Committee

3

[On polls that show the people believe that "dirty tactics" are used by both Democratic and Republican candidates in political campaigns]: I think one of the great disservices that's being done to the American public today is being done when they say, "Everybody does it; it is done all the time." Everybody doesn't do it. Sound, responsible professionals don't do it in the political process. Republicans don't do it and Democrats don't do it. It just isn't done all the time. Senator [Hugh] Scott and Congressman [Gerald] Ford don't do it, and Carl Albert doesn't do it and the Majority Leader [Mike] Mansfield doesn't do it, and neither do their colleagues up there. I think this is a great disservice to this whole process of trying to sell the American people on the fact that it is done all the time. It just isn't.

TV-radio interview, Washington/
"Meet the Press,"
National Broadcasting Company, 5-27.

4

Since the first of the year, we've seen the Republicans denied the three big things they've been able to elect a President on. First, they said they were the businessman's party—they knew how to run the business of this country better than those Democrats. Obviously, that's wrong; look at the runaway inflation and tinker-toy approach to domestic affairs, the unbelievably stupid, if not sinister, sale of grain to Russia. The Republicans said they were an economy party. We've got the wildest inflation we've ever had, the highest interest rates we've ever had, and they haven't cut down on spending. And they said, "We're the law-and-order party." They didn't bring law and order. They couldn't even keep law and order in the White House. They burgled, they stole, they took illegal campaign contributions from corporations.

Interview, Dallas, Aug. 25/
The Dallas Times Herald, 8-26:(A)36.

1

[On the resignation of Vice President Agnew because of charges of bribery and kickbacks against him]: I refuse to buy this posture they are trying to put him in as the brave, heroic, self-sacrificing man who resigned in the nation's interests. He didn't serve this nation. He held the welfare of this nation in one hand and [by pleading guilty to a lesser charge] bargained for his freedom. I find nothing heroic, nothing brave and nothing to serve the nation in that.

At Western States Democratic Conference, Los Angeles, Oct. 14/ San Francisco Examiner, 10-15:20.

2

The result of last week's elections show that Americans are coming back to the Democratic Party because we are again responding to what the people want. [The] Watergate [political-espionage affair] wasn't the reason. It was much deeper than that. It was a total failure of the Republican Administration to govern or come to grips with the human and moral problems of this time.

At Democratic fund-raising dinner, Greenville, Tex., Nov. 12/ The Dallas Times Herald, 11-13:(A)7.

James R. Thompson
United States Attorney
for the Northern District of Illinois

3

[Commenting, as Special Assistant Attorney General in the case, on the resignation, and plea of guilty to a lesser charge, of former Vice President Agnew because of bribery and kickback charges against him]: If the case had gone to trial and if those witnesses had testified . . . conviction would have resulted. He would have been sentenced to a very large number of years in the Federal penitentiary, and should have been . . . It is the strongest case of bribery and extortion I have ever seen. He was a crook; there's no question about it.

San Francisco Examiner, 10-11:3.

Barbara Tuchman
Author, Historian

4

Our government is fundamentally an agreement capable of binding a ruler. [President] Nixon has turned the government into a monarchy. In a sense, [Presidents] Kennedy and Johnson were monarchists, but Nixon has violated the Bill of Rights. The so-called domestic intelligence program in 1970, the lies about Cambodia, the milk lobby . . . he shows a total disregard for the Constitution.

Interview/ "W": a Fairchild publication, 9-21:16.

John V. Tunney
United States Senator, D-California

5

[On a White House "enemies" list referred to by former Presidential Counsel John Dean during the Senate Watergate hearings]: I just can't help but wonder how much government business was left undone while they [in the Nixon Administration] were preparing that list, and contracting it and expanding it. It's so petty and trivial and absurd—except for the fact that they were going to get the IRS to go after [people on the list]. It makes you wonder about the President's ability to choose his staff. Around the Democratic cloakroom here in Washington, it's a badge of honor to be on that list.

Los Angeles Times, 7-8:(Calendar)11.

Robert F. Wagner
Former Mayor of New York

6

In political life, you get used to being attacked by peanut politicians.

Television interview, New York, March 25/The New York Times, 3-26:46.

George C. Wallace
Governor of Alabama

7

[On his being paralyzed from the waist down as a result of an assassination attempt last year]: When I was campaigning for the Presidency in 1972, and during my campaigns for Governor of Alabama, I used to say, "Stand up for America." Well, I can't do

(GEORGE C. WALLACE)

much standing up any more, but I can sure do a lot of sitting down for America.

The New York Times, 3-27:47.

1

... at one time the media tried to make it out as if we [in Alabama] were all way off somewhere out of the mainstream and that what we talked about in Alabama wasn't good and it was evil; and yet when I had the opportunity to go [campaigning for the 1972 Democratic Presidential nomination], as of May, 1972, I had a million votes more than any other national Democratic candidate. And I'm proud that the average man in places like Michigan, Maryland, Wisconsin and Pennsylvania had the feeling that we in Alabama are right about some of these things. So now they visit us: the President [Nixon] coming to Alabama and Mississippi, and the Vice President [Agnew], and Senator [Hubert] Humphrey and Senator [Edmund] Muskie, and Senator [Edward] Kennedy. Why, he [Kennedy] was in Alabama on July 4, and the speech he made sounded like it was written in Saraland, Alabama; it sounded like the things that have been said in Prichard and Mobile and Chickasaw—and I'm very proud of that fact ... I'm very proud that there may be some political converts in this country. They may be walking down the political sawdust trail, asking repentance of the people for saying, "We didn't trust you; but now maybe what you've been talking about, and the things you think, are better than what some of our Ivy League planners have been thinking for you."

Mobile, Ala./
The National Observer, 10-6:5.

Earl Warren
Former Chief Justice of the United States

2

Politics is not guerrilla warfare where booby traps are laid for the opposition. [The late President] Truman was always "Give 'em hell Harry," but always on the issues and not on personalities.

Quote, 6-3:505.

Lowell P. Weicker, Jr.
United States Senator, R-Connecticut

3

This [Senate] seat is everything I dreamed about when I was a kid. I looked upon politicians as I looked upon baseball and hockey players: They were my idols. That isn't the case today. Even my own two young boys —their dad's in politics and they take some pride in that; but believe me, believe me, does the politician stand alongside the rock star now? No; no way. The politician has become almost a laughable type of figure.

Interview, Washington/
The National Observer, 4-7:5.

Aaron Wildavsky
Dean, Graduate School of Public Policy,
University of California, Berkeley

4

The institution I think is performing worst now is not the Presidency and not Congress but the [political] parties. If there is any group of people that ought to hold the President to account, that should be telling him off when he oversteps his boundaries, it is the party leaders. Our problem is that we don't have a significant corps of party leaders who have a stake in more than this President [Nixon] and this Presidency, and who can, therefore, help set boundaries for acceptable political behavior. Without suggesting panaceas, I think what we want is to have a variety of healthy and, to some degree, contentious, political institutions.

Panel discussion, New Orleans/
The Washington Post, 9-16:(C)4.

Caroline Wilkins
Co-Chairman,
Democratic National Committee

5

When I talk to women, I find there are three groups. The older ones, who have worked in the Party for years—some of whom felt excluded at the last national convention —don't want to demand a place, but feel they should be recognized for the work they have done in the past. They don't want to be shuttled about like a piece of furniture. Then, there are the younger women—the issue-oriented—who are going to talk about abortion and lesbianism come hell or high water. There's no quieting them. Finally, there is the other group of younger women who are the envelope-stuffers and coffee-makers, the women who keep the Party going between elections. There is room for all of them. And that is what we are trying to do now. People in the Party want to get it back together again and are trying very, very hard to understand each other and get along.

Interview, Washington/
Los Angeles Times, 4-26:(4)14.

Charles Wilson
United States Representative, D-Texas

1

In Texas, being a "liberal" was being against the lobby, for the utilities regulation bill and against a food tax. Up here [in Wash-

ington], I see a disturbing inclination on the part of the liberals just to blatantly vote for spending bills . . . [If being a "big lib" in Washington] means you've got to vote for spending you don't believe in, I guess I'll be a conservative.

Interview, Washington/
The Dallas Times Herald, 5-4:(E)29.

Evelle J. Younger
Attorney General of California

2

All my career I've striven to be respected rather than loved. For all the wild cheers at a political convention, I'd rather have the quiet votes on election day. I've been to too many celebrations in June that have turned into wakes in November.

Interview, San Francisco/
Los Angeles Times, 11-13:(2)4.

THE WATERGATE AFFAIR

Spiro T. Agnew
Vice President of the United States

1

Somehow, out of all of the confusion about Watergate has come the public concept that the Senate has a right to be a grand jury in this matter. I think it's wrong for the Senate to be involved in the same investigation that the grand jury is at this point. I think that if the grand jury had folded up and not done its job, and the Senators thought there were other things that had to be dredged out that were concealed in the normal legal process of the criminal proceeding, they would have a right at that point to continue an investigation. But the proper forum for investigations of allegations of criminality is a grand jury, where the safeguards of secrecy, sworn testimony and the usual due process of law are available—and not in a televised political forum.

Interview/U.S. News & World Report, 5-7:32.

2

I do not attempt to assert that certain individuals are without fault, or that the Watergate matter is a defensible lark. But I do state that the Republican Party is not involved, not indicted and not responsible.

San Francisco Examiner & Chronicle,
6-10:(This World)2.

3

Justice Felix Frankfurter once wrote, ". . . The history of liberty has largely been the history of the observance of procedural safeguards." How very pertinent his observation is to us as the Watergate story unfolds. What is critically lacking, as the Senate Committee does its best to ferret out the truth, is a rigorous set of procedural safeguards. Lacking such safeguards, the Committee, I am sad to say, can hardly hope to find the truth and can hardly fail to muddy the waters of justice beyond redemption. Some people have argued

that rules of evidence and guarantees of due process don't matter so much in the Ervin hearings because nobody is really on trial up there. The mission of the hearings, this argument runs, is purely one of information-gathering. But Chairman Ervin himself has suggested otherwise. "My colleagues and I are determined," he said on the day the hearings began, "to uncover all the relevant facts . . . and to spare no one, whatever his station in life may be." To me, ladies and gentlemen, that phrase, "spare no one," sounds very much like an adversary process, a trial situation. There is no escaping the fact that the hearings have a Perry Masonish impact. The indefatigable (TV) camera will paint both heroes and villains in lurid and indelible colors before the public's very eyes in the course of these proceedings . . . There is no question whatever that some men, despite their innocence, will be ruined by all this—even though I am sure that the Senate intended nothing of the kind when it commissioned this investigation.

Before National Association of
State Attorneys General, St. Louis,
June 11/The National Observer, 6-23:5.

4

Watergate does show one thing: In a job as big as the Presidency, you can't watch everything. You're at the mercy of people carrying out your instructions. I don't think there's any foolproof way in which a person who heads a large enterprise can protect himself against people who work for him. You want people with initiative. You don't want people who check with you before doing anything, because that's of no value to you. When you stimulate initiative, you bring about the situation where sometimes people make a misjudgment based on their analysis and not on yours. There isn't any other way. We're all locked into the people we work for.

Interview/Time, 7-2:17.

1

The preoccupation with anything and everything related to Watergate is the most obvious, but not necessarily the most insidious, by-product of the affair. Far more dangerous, in my opinion, is the persecutorial atmosphere hanging over the American political system . . . Our opponents will argue that the strength of our free system lies in our willingness to wash our dirty linen in public; and to some extent they are right. But even a strong garment cannot be put through the washing machine over and over without wearing out; and I happen to think that the Watergate jeans are losing their blue and beginning to fall apart. We all know that Presidents must take some heat. Well, President Nixon has been standing there and taking it ever since [Senate Watergate Committee Chairman Senator Sam] Ervin has been doing his rain dance in that Washington committee room . . . We have reached the watershed of Watergate. In spite of that, it is obvious that some in this country are going to continue to attempt to milk this issue dry. Those embittered critics of this Administration and this party who could not discredit us at the polls in November [last year] will make every effort—no matter how reckless—to discredit us now . . . I realize that some of you may be somewhat discouraged because of the unrelenting attacks. These are difficult times for all of us. But if our adversaries really think that we Republicans are going to simply lie down and let them roll over us, they can't know very much about Republicans.

At rally honoring
Representative Leslie Arends, St. Charles, Ill.,
Sept. 8/The Washington Post, 9-9:(A)2.

2

Unfortunately, there will always be some individuals who do not abide by the rules and ethics of fair play. A lack of faith either in their cause or in the system itself drives them to the use of improper or illegal methods. This, of course, was the tragedy of Watergate. Certain individuals, exercising poor judgment and acting unethically, tried to circumvent laws and accepted standards of conduct in order to serve their cause. The irony, of course, is that, in doing so, they damaged their cause all out of proportion to the small advantage they sought. By betraying principle, they did far graver damage than the opposition could ever have done. But it would be a mistake to assume that what they did is typical of political campaigns. They were only a small minority compared to the millions . . . who worked within the framework of law and proper conduct.

Before National Federation of
Republican Women, Los Angeles, Sept. 29/
The New York Times, 9-30:(1)60.

George D. Aiken
United States Senator, R-Vermont

3

I am speaking out now because the developing hue and cry for the President's [Nixon] resignation suggests to me a veritable epidemic of emotionalism. It suggests that many prominent Americans, who ought to know better, find the task of holding the President accountable as just too difficult. Those who call for the President's resignation on the ground that he has lost their confidence risk poisoning the well of politics for years to come. Within less than 10 years, we have seen one Presidency destroyed by an assassin's bullet; another by a bitter and divisive war. To destroy the third in a row through the politics of righteous indignation cannot possibly restore confidence either at home or abroad. The men who wrote our Constitution were fully aware how waves of emotionalism, if given an easy electoral outlet, could reduce any political system to anarchy. That's why, in a nation governed by its laws, they provided that Presidents should rule for four years. They laid down that that period of rule could be interrupted only after Congress had framed a charge of high crimes and misdemeanors and had conducted a trial itself based on those charges. To ask the President now to resign and thus relieve the Congress of its clear Congressional duty amounts to a declaration of incompetence on the part of the Congress . . . The President's public explanations

(GEORGE D. AIKEN)

of the Watergate mess have been astonishingly inept. But this is not of itself an impeachable offense, nor does it suggest that the President be scolded, publicly, in the presence of a Congressional Committee. It is the clear duty of the House, through whatever procedure it chooses, to frame a charge of impeachment and to set itself a deadline for the task. If a charge is framed and voted, the Senate's clear duty is to proceed in a trial with all deliberate speed . . . May I now pass on to this Congress advice which I received from a fellow Vermonter: "Either impeach him or get off his back."

Before the Senate, Washington, Nov. 7/
The New York Times, 11-8:35.

John B. Anderson
United States Representative, R-Illinois

1

Until it has been amply demonstrated to the American people that the last shadowy element in this [Watergate] tragedy has been brought to light, our institutions of government will remain under a cloud.

April 30/Los Angeles Times, 5-1:(1)9.

2

[A possible explanation of why Watergate happened]: They [top aides of President Nixon] were knowledgeable and intelligent people, but they had no political experience. The reins of power were concentrated almost exclusively in people who had never been elected to office, didn't deal with politicians, simply didn't know. [Former domestic adviser] John Ehrlichman was a very intelligent, capable man, but he had no knowledge of politics. [Former Presidential Assistant H. R.] Haldeman might as well have been on another planet.

The Washington Post, 7-29:(C)1.

Howard H. Baker, Jr.
United States Senator, R-Tennessee;
Vice Chairman,
Senate Watergate Committee

3

Although juries will eventually determine

the guilt or the innocence of persons who have been and may be indicted for specific violations of the law, it is the American people who must be the final judge of Watergate.

At Senate Watergate hearings, Washington,
May 17/The New York Times, 5-20:(4)1.

4

The [Senate Watergate] Committee has been criticized from time to time for its absence of rules of evidence, the right of confrontation, of cross-examination by counsel, and a number of other legal concepts that we do not have. But we do not have defendants, either; and we are not trying to create defendants. We are trying to find fact, to establish circumstances, to divine the causes, to ascertain the relationships that make up in toto the so-called Watergate affair.

At Senate Watergate hearings, Washington,
July 23/Los Angeles Times, 7-24:(1)8.

James D. Barber
Chairman, department of political science,
Duke University

5

In considering the effect of the Watergate case, you must remember . . . that [President] Nixon has a real appetite for crises. In his book, *Six Crises*, he says that, while these crises were no fun, life consists of more than just a search for enjoyment; those who stay on the sidelines are "vegetables;" meeting crises, on the other hand, is challenging and creative. These have been recurring themes in Nixon's thinking. He only feels alive when he is in the midst of tense deliberateness, all keyed up, wound up and under strain. That is familiar to him, and he gives the impression that moments of crisis have been gratifying to him. In the midst of this [Watergate] crisis, he goes to Church on Easter. The sermon is about sin, but he comes out smiling and greeting the parishioners and reportedly calls up [implicated Presidential aides] Dean and Haldeman and wishes them Happy Easter. The familiar smiling photo shows him far from feeling uncomfortable. He knows what it feels like. That's been the story of his life . . . Most people would think, "If I were in Nixon's shoes these days, I would be damn uncomfortable, worried and upset." I don't think he is. I think he is probably in a very real sense happier than in most times of his Presidency. All this business about life being a battle, a struggle, a contest appeals to him.

Interview, Durham, N.C./
Los Angeles Times, 4-30:(2)7.

Stephen Barber
Washington bureau chief,
"London Daily Telegraph"

1

Actually, the British aren't too worried about Watergate, because we deal with your government, not persons. The United States is a going concern, and it's not going to collapse over this rash of scandals.

At Dallas Women's Club, Nov. 7/
The Dallas Times Herald, 11-8:(C)5.

Robin Beard
United States Representative,
R-Tennessee

2

Sure, I'm concerned [about Watergate]. The worst of it is that it damages what little credibility people felt toward their officials. Most of the elected officials in both parties are honest. But I think we have here a situation in which some people, through total naivete or stupidity or whatever, made some just unbelievable decisions. There were some bad mistakes made. But I'll tell you right now, I believe in standing behind the President [Nixon]. I believe in giving him the same rights we give to the [Daniel] Ellsbergs and Angela Davises of this world. And I think when this case is all through, the system will be stronger. This little cancerous growth will be removed. We'll survive.

Before Rotary Club, Franklin, Tenn./
The Washington Post, 8-12:(A)1.

Samuel Beer
Professor of Government,
Harvard University

3

It's important to remain rational and not

get carried away [by Watergate]. There's such a hate-Nixon campaign going on right now that we shouldn't indulge in the same thing that [the late Senator] Joe McCarthy did. In a few years, the Democrats will have their guy in the White House, and the Republicans will be looking for the same thing.

The National Observer, 5-5:10.

Lucy Wilson Benson
National president,
League of Women Voters

4

Recently, a campaign official predicted that Watergate wouldn't have the dire effect on the 1974 elections that some are predicting. Why? Because, he stated, it "is not a gut issue. It doesn't affect your pocketbook, your health, your wife's safety or your son's life." I believe that it just may be the gutsiest issue this country has ever faced. And this isn't just another idle superlative. For what Watergate boils down to is the proper use of power—and power is what politics is all about. It boils down to the style and form of government; the restoration of some form of functional equilibrium between the Executive and Legislative Branches; and the public's right to know. It reduces to some key questions: Is our democratic system of self-government, as set forth in the Constitution, still viable? Or has our society grown so complex that only rigid management and programmed manipulation can hold its seams together? The answers to these questions are answers which, indeed, will affect the lives, health, pocketbooks and the rights of every one of us. The answers are our future. Justice Louis Brandeis once described government as "the potent, omnipresent teacher. For good or ill, it teaches the whole people by its example."

At Carleton College, Northfield, Minn./
The Washington Post, 7-22:(C)6.

Harry A. Blackmun
Associate Justice,
Supreme Court of the United States

5

. . . the pall of the Watergate, with all its revelations of misplaced loyalties, of strange

271

(HARRY A. BLACKMUN)

measures of the ethical, of unusual doings in high places, and by lawyer after lawyer after lawyer, is upon us. It is something that necessarily touches us all, irrespective of political inclination.

At American Bar Association
Prayer Breakfast, Washington,
Aug. 5/The National Observer, 8-18:13.

Derek C. Bok
President, Harvard University

1

The critical question is whether Watergate will arouse the interest of the country and its officials to a sufficient extent to cause us to take a hard look at the underlying problems that led to these unpleasant incidents . . . It is superficial to believe that Watergate is simply an accident involving a few unscrupulous men who happened to occupy positions of power . . . It is impossible to rely so heavily on large political contributions from persons affected by government action without running a constant risk of illicit donations and undue influence over government officials. It is very difficult to permit clandestine, unsupervised activities in certain spheres of government, such as foreign affairs, without having some public officials succumb to the temptation of using similar tactics under circumstances that are clearly offensive and inappropriate. Now that Watergate has revealed the dangers of excessive Executive power, there is a possibility for serious deliberation, for a conscientious search for new arrangements and adjustments that will recognize the efficiency and expertise of the Executive Branch while guarding against the dangers of unresponsive or uncontrolled use of power.

Interview/
The Christian Science Monitor, 7-25:16

Kingman Brewster, Jr.
President, Yale University

2

When my contemporaries ask me, "What is the impact of the Watergate scandal on the young?" I have to reply, "Very slight! They are not surprised. Their basic response is, 'What would you expect?' " That is too bad; but it's so.

At Yale University baccalaureate service/
The New York Times, 6-18:22.

3

I have been one of those who have felt that there is more good than bad coming out of the Watergate. I say this in the sense that there is a kind of vindication of the system in terms of its major Constitutional components —an independent press, an independent judiciary and Congress—all playing their part. In spite of the trauma, I don't think this will leave us weaker, but rather stronger, because people do have reason to believe that the system, with its checks and balances, can work. Out of this experience will come greater respect for the checks and balances. Therefore, the uptight law-and-order extremists or the free-slugging activists will stand less chance of prevailing after this catharsis than before. The young were cynical before. I believe this is going to improve rather than destroy their confidence. It shows the system is capable of curing its own illnesses.

Interview, New Haven, Conn./
Los Angeles Times, 6-19:(2)7.

Leonid I. Brezhnev
General Secretary,
Communist Party of the Soviet Union

4

[Saying his visit to the U.S. next month to confer with President Nixon will not be cancelled because of Watergate]: America stays where it is. The time remains as it was. What do you expect, an earthquake?

News conference, Bonn, West Germany,
May 20/The New York Times, 5-21:3.

Edward W. Brooke
United States Senator, R-Massachusetts

5

There's no doubt some legislation has passed and some hasn't been passed, at least in part, because of Watergate. The bombing ban on Cambodia would not have passed the House nor in the degree it did in the Senate.

Votes on the part of Congress to correct the imbalance between the Executive and Legislative Branches have accelerated—measures such as impoundment, Congressionally-imposed ceilings on spending. Perhaps one of the healthy by-products of Watergate is that Congress is seizing the opportunity to restore some balance of power. Watergate might give moderate Republicanism an opportunity to be heard in the councils of the Republican Party; for too long it has not been given a proper hearing. Watergate is still going to be around in 1976 Presidential politics. Morality in government will be an issue.

Interview/
U.S. News & World Report, 7-30:21.

1

[Calling on President Nixon to resign]: It has been like a nightmare, and I know that he doesn't want to hurt the country and I certainly don't want to prejudice the case. He might not be guilty of any impeachable offense. On the other hand, there is no question that President Nixon has lost his effectiveness as the leader of this country, primarily because he has lost the confidence of the people of the country; and I think, therefore, that in the interests of this nation that he loves, that he should step down, should tender his resignation.

TV-radio interview/
"Issues and Answers,"
American Broadcasting Company, 11-4.

James L. Buckley
United States Senator, C-New York

2

[On President Nixon's refusal to furnish certain White House tapes bearing on the Watergate affair to the Senate Committee]: I think he has painted himself into a very tight corner, unnecessarily and foolishly. I think clearly in the instant case the consensus of the American people will be that the President, while he has the right to exercise the [Executive] privilege, ought not to be exercising it.
The New York Times, 7-25:32.

James MacGregor Burns
Professor of Political Science,
Williams College, Williamstown, Mass.

3

[On what brought about the Watergate affair]: I think it was a coming into the White House of a group of men who had many abilities, but who had no guiding vision. There was no great purpose that informed these people. There have been all sorts of crises and all sorts of compromises and concessions and weaknesses in the Presidency in the past; for example, under Franklin Roosevelt. But with Presidents like Roosevelt and [John] Kennedy and others, there was always a kind of guiding objective they kept in mind. And I think the people in the [Nixon] White House found themselves without such a vision. The only vision was service to the President and helping him realize his ambitions. And I think when you don't have this kind of guiding vision, all sorts of other practical and impractical things come into operation, and people lose their way.

TV-radio interview, "Meet the Press"/
The Wall Street Journal, 7-20:8.

George Bush
Chairman, Republican National Committee

4

The [Republican] Party is not involved in the alleged infidelity of the few . . . The Party has been untainted by anything to do with Watergate. I'll be darned if we are going to let the ugliness of Watergate obscure the positive record of the President [Nixon].
San Francisco Examiner & Chronicle,
5-20:(This World)2.

Robert C. Byrd
United States Senator, D-West Virginia

5

[On the Watergate affair]: Members of Congress react to opinion back home. If the grass-roots support of the President [Nixon] diminishes, it will be reflected in a weakening of his support in Congress. The President has friends on both sides of the aisle in Congress.

(ROBERT C. BYRD)

We all want to see the office of the President untainted. But he can't emerge unscathed. This blemish will remain with the Administration until the crack of doom.

U.S. News & World Report, 5-7:20.

Ramsey Clark
Former Attorney General
of the United States

[1]

If I have learned anything from Watergate, it is that there is a higher probability that people who engage in demagoguery about law and order tend to feel less constrained by the rules of law.

Interview, New York/
Los Angeles Times, 11-4:(6)7.

Charles W. Colson
Former Special Counsel to President Nixon

[2]

[Criticizing former Presidential Counsel John Dean's testimony at the Senate Watergate hearings which implicated President Nixon in the Watergate cover-up]: It really bothers me to see the Dean testimony given as much weight as it is given. If it is one-on-one, the President vs. Dean, I can't put them even in the same league; I think it is a tragedy if the American people do. I hope that all of this is put in perspective. See, up until now you really haven't heard from people who have been personally involved with the President. The first person that made any direct-testimony allegations involving the President was Dean; and he really has based it upon only three meetings, one of which his own testimony discredits. So I think it will be a great tragedy if one week of John Dean, with people patting him on the head for being such a good boy to come forward and put all this stuff on the record—99 per cent of which is his own sins and errors—I just hope that, when others come forward with a different point of view, that they will be given at least comparable creditability to Mr. Dean. At which point, I might add, I don't think there

will be a whole lot for the President to answer.

Interview, Washington/
The Christian Science Monitor, 7-9:6.

Henry Steele Commager
Professor of History, Amherst College

[3]

I think Watergate will promote greater honesty among public officials, at least in the immediate future. They'll watch their step, mainly because they don't want to get caught. I think the same will hold true of businesses and corporations in this country. I don't think the American people are going to become more cynical because of Watergate. On the contrary, I think they'll feel their government has been strengthened as a result of this air-cleaning.

Interview/
"W": a Fairchild publication, 9-21:16.

John B. Connally, Jr.
Former Secretary of the Treasury of the
United States; Former Governor of Texas;
1972 chairman, Democrats for Nixon

[4]

[On the Watergate affair]: The Republican Party didn't do it. One of the things we need to put into perspective was that the act of individuals ought not to be attributed to the mass of members who belong to a political party. I don't think that any future activity within this nation should be judged in terms of its chronology of BW [before Watergate] or AW [after Watergate]. I feel very strongly about Watergate. I think too much of it goes on in this country and in and out of government. And I think it ought to be stopped. I'm convinced of that. I think this illegal act, and those who participated in it, ought to be punished. But I don't think it ought to blind us to the realization that we have great problems in this country. And I don't think that incident, however reprehensible, ought to be used as a shield against what the President [Nixon] has done that has been so much in the interest of this country. I think the President has done an incredibly effective job in dealing with the foreign relations of this country and has shown great courage in dealing with our domestic problems.

At news conference announcing his switch to the Republican Party, Houston, May 2/ Los Angeles Times, 5-3:(1)25.

1

There is not a Republican in this room who has to hang his head in shame because of Watergate or any other political scandal. The political system is not simon pure in our nation. It never has been; never will be. Occasionally we get a bad apple. If we're honest enough to purge him from our midst and say we made a mistake and go on about our business, we'd be a whole lot better off. Watergate is not our Waterloo unless we let it be.

Before California Republican State Committee, San Diego, Calif., Sept. 8/ Los Angeles Herald-Examiner, 9-10:(A)3.

2

If those who have charged forth so bravely with their demands for impeachment of the President [Nixon] really think they have a case, then it's time for them to put up or shut up . . . There is an element of hatred in this [Watergate] controversy–the smell of a vendetta–and if wise and cooler heads in both political parties don't take control, we are in for a much greater national trauma than we have heretofore experienced . . . Denials notwithstanding, it is abundantly clear that some members of Congress have schemed to use the confirmation of the new Vice President [Gerald Ford] as a means to undermine and discredit the President. They deemed Gerald Ford to be a hostage to be held in the dungeons of the Congressional Committee while they deliberated how to get the President to quit or how to impeach him. Wise heads may have prevailed, but it's still a sorry spectacle –a calculated move to win a political victory regardless of how much it demoralized and divided the American people. Isn't that in the same category of dirty tricks that the other side was accused of?

Before American Dental Association, Houston, Oct. 28/ Los Angeles Times, 10-29:(1)10.

John T. Connor
Chairman, Allied Chemical Corporation; Former Secretary Of Commerce of the United States

3

[On the Watergate affair]: Impeachment of the President [Nixon] is not the answer. His impressive record–in handling the Vietnam troop withdrawal, the return of our prisoners, the establishment of new hopeful relationships with Russia and [Communist] China, and the needed realignments of our foreign and domestic responsibilities–leads inevitably to the conclusion that his continuity in office is well deserved. An alternative is available in this national emergency: a "coalition" government that would include some Democratic leaders of integrity and experience who have been elected by the people to public positions of importance. Although unusual, that solution would not be without precedent. President Franklin D. Roosevelt called upon outstanding Republicans such as Harry L. Stimson, Frank Knox and Robert P. Patterson in World War II to achieve national unity. They served in his Cabinet and Administration with great distinction . . . A coalition government would have a reasonable chance of achieving sufficient national unity and public support to get us through this serious Constitutional crisis.

Interview/Newsweek, 5-14:39.

Alistair Cooke
Chief United States correspondent, "The Manchester (England) Guardian"

4

It is hard to know what the people think. If you read *Time* and *Newsweek* this week, you see the President [Nixon] all but impeached. Yet the polls indicate opinion is against impeachment . . . I believe the people who are indignant are very indignant, and the people who are indifferent are sunk in apathy. There is a lot of raging apathy. The rest of the people are bewildered, and quite a few are frightened.

Interview, San Francisco/ San Francisco Examiner, 11-5:23.

Owen Cooper
President, Southern Baptist Convention

1

There is a lesson for us in Watergate. It shows us that wrongdoing is no respecter of persons, that exalted position offers no immunity from crime, that misuse of money is the root of all kinds of evil. If from Watergate we learn that there are moral standards, that there are Christian ethics, that there is right and wrong, then Watergate may have been worth the price.

Quote, 8-5:122.

Norris Cotton
United States Senator, R-New Hampshire

2

It [Watergate] is a reflection that he [President Nixon] had such a bunch of jackasses around him in the first place. The problem was too much campaign money around and too many nuts thinking up silly ways to spend it.

Los Angeles Times, 7-15:(1)11.

Archibald Cox
Professor of Law, Harvard University;
Special government prosecutor for
Watergate

3

[Saying the Senate's televised Watergate hearings could prejudice the case against those involved in Watergate and thus result in their escaping legal punishment]: There is much more to this question than whether one or two people go to jail. Confidence in our institutions is at stake. We must find a way both to expose the truth and to punish the wrongdoers. Failure to convict persons in high office shown guilty of crime—even as a consequence of the Senate hearings—could well shatter public confidence in our governmental institutions, particularly confidence in our system of justice. At a time when the nation's concern about crime has focused attention on our system of justice, it would be discriminatory and therefore demoralizing for the powerful to go scot-free while ordinary citizens are sen-

tenced to prison.

Before Senate Watergate Committee,
Washington/
U.S. News & World Report, 6-18:17.

4

[On President Nixon's refusal to turn over White House tapes relating to Watergate]: Careful study before requesting the tapes convinced me that any blanket claim [by the President] of [Executive] privilege to withhold this evidence from a grand jury is without legal foundation. It therefore becomes my duty promptly to seek subpoenas and other available legal procedures for obtaining the evidence for the grand jury . . . The effort to obtain these tapes and other documentary evidence is the impartial pursuit of justice according to law. None of us should make assumption about what the tapes will show. They may tend to show that there was criminal activity—or that there was none. They may tend to show the guilt of particular individuals, or their innocence. The one clear point is that the tapes are evidence bearing directly upon whether there were criminal conspiracies, including a conspiracy to obstruct justice, among high government officials.

July 23/The Washington Post, 7-24:(A)17.

5

. . . there has been and is evidence—not proof, perhaps, but clearly prima-facie evidence—[in the Watergate affair] of serious wrongdoing on the part of high government officials; wrongdoing involving an effort to cover up other wrongdoing. It appeared that the papers, documents and recordings of conversations in the White House, including the tapes, would be relevant to getting the truth about these incidents. I'm referring not only to the Watergate incident itself, but to other things involving electronic surveillance, break-ins at a doctor's office and the like. Last night we were told that the court order [requiring Mr. Nixon to turn over this material] would not be obeyed, that the papers, memoranda and documents of that kind would not be provided at all; and that, instead of the tapes, a summary of what they showed would be provided. I think it is my duty as the special prosecutor, as an officer of the court and as the representative of the grand jury, to bring to the court's attention what seems to me to be non-compliance with the court's order.

News conference, Washington, Oct. 20/
The New York Times, 10-21:(1)60.

Walter Cronkite
News commentator,
Columbia Broadcasting System

1

I have a feeling that when this [Nixon] Administration is squared away—whether by resignation, impeachment or accommodation —we are in for a period of considerable moral soul-searching which may straighten us out for a good number of years to come. People have become so fed up with subterfuge, dishonesty and lack of candor that we are going to find them demanding of their politicians a straight-forwardness such as we haven't had for many generations . . . Watergate just happened to come along at the same time as the demand for honesty in relations between the sexes, in advertising, in ecology, in almost everything. It just stumbled into that great big elephant trap that had already been built for it. That's what is forcing the President's hand right now. He simply has to do something to satisfy that nation-wide demand for a thorough cleansing of our way of life.

Interview, New York/
The Christian Science Monitor, 12-26:(B)8.

Carl T. Curtis
United States Senator, R-Nebraska

2

[Criticizing the motives of some persons who are pushing the Watergate investigation]: [Watergate has] brought into being a deter-mined and militant coalition whose objective is not justice but rather to "get Nixon" . . . [They are] the Nixon-haters, a group of polit-ico-sadists of the type who enjoyed their ef-forts to destroy [the late President] Lyndon Johnson over the [Vietnam] war issue—a small segment of newsmen who prefer politi-cal propaganda over objective reporting, a few extreme partisans whose sense of justice is numbed by their desire for political gain, and those politicians who are willing to exploit any issue for personal publicity.

Before the Senate, Washington, June 14/
The Washington Post, 6-15:(A)18.

Samuel Dash
Chief Counsel,
Senate Watergate Committee

3

In Phase One [of the Senate Watergate hearings], everything was concentrated in Washington, because it involved an incident that occurred here. But the espionage oc-curred all over the country, and the campaign finance matters are all over the country. It's now a nationwide investigation . . . These will be perhaps the most important phases of the investigation. It will require the Commit-tee to be more creative in the legislative area. After all, we don't really need new laws against wiretapping, burglary and eavesdrop-ping. But this whole area of what's fair or foul in Presidential elections is very murky, and we'll be getting into it for the first time.

Interview/
San Francisco Examiner & Chronicle,
8-12:(A)10.

John W. Dean III
Former Counsel to President Nixon

4

It's my honest belief that, while the Presi-dent [Nixon] was involved [in Watergate], he did not realize or appreciate at any time the implications of his involvement. And I think that, when the facts come out, I hope the President is forgiven.

At Senate Watergate hearings,
Washington, June 25/
The Christian Science Monitor, 6-27:2.

5

The Watergate matter was an inevitable outgrowth of a climate [in the White House] of excessive concern over the political impact of demonstrators, excessive concern over leaks, an insatiable appetite for political intelligence, all coupled with a do-it-yourself White House staff, regardless of the law. The White House was continually seeking intelligence informa-

(JOHN W. DEAN III)

tion about demonstration leaders and their supporters that would either discredit them personally or indicate that the demonstration was in fact sponsored by some foreign enemy. There were also White House requests for information regarding ties between major political figures—specifically, members of the U.S. Senate—who opposed the President's war policies.

At Senate Watergate hearings, Washington, June 25/The Washington Post, 8-12:(A)11.

1

[Accusing President Nixon of okaying a pay-off to already-convicted Watergate conspirators to prevent them from implicating White House aides]: I told the President about the fact that there were money demands being made by the seven convicted defendants, and that the sentencing of these individuals was not far off . . . I told the President about the fact that there was no money to pay these individuals to meet their demands. He asked me how much it would cost. I told him that I could only make an estimate that it might be as high as a million dollars or more. He told me that that was no problem; and he also looked over at [former Presidential Assistant H. R.] Haldeman and repeated the same statement.

At Senate Watergate hearings, Washington/ The National Observer, 7-7:4.

Robert J. Dole
United States Senator, R-Kansas

2

[On Republican Party aides who have been implicated in the Watergate affair]: I've been fussing for months at some of the people whose names are now emerging. If there was trouble within the Party, it was with some of these people who we are now hearing about . . . They were people who felt they were a cut above the rest of the Party, and now we may find out they were a cut below. [Hopefully, the Republican Party] is bigger than one person or group of people. We simply cannot let a handful of men and women drag the Party down. Some of the people who have

been named, innocent or not, came in at the top of the political structure. They didn't have any political experience. They never knocked on a door or ran for political office. They were given a lot of power, and perhaps they didn't know what to do with it.

Washington, April 19/ Los Angeles Times, 4-20:(1)7.

3

With all the problems we have, particularly with inflation, we ought to be devoting our time to these issues and these problems and letting the grand jury and the courts get along with the Watergate [investigation]. I think the people have had enough of watching the seven Senators [on the Watergate Committee] try Richard Nixon on television.

Washington, Aug. 30/ Los Angeles Herald-Examiner, 8-30:(A)2.

Peter H. Dominick
United States Senator, R-Colorado

4

There can be no more deals and no more technical arguments about evidence. Nothing short of complete disclosure [of what President Nixon knows about Watergate] will be adequate to restore the confidence of the American people. The President should divulge everything he has personal knowledge of and should permit complete access to all tapes, papers, files, documents and memoranda which have been requested by the Senate Watergate Committee and the special prosecutor. I am reluctant to talk about impeachment, but the genie is already out of the bottle, and it cannot be put back in.

Time, 11-19:20.

Winfield Dunn
Governor of Tennessee

5

[On the possibility of President Nixon resigning because of Watergate]: I don't think the President will ever occupy the prominent position in the future he did in the past, but we [Republican Governors] have more to gain through the re-establishment of his credibility than by anything else. Unless additional information is revealed that proves his culpability, we'd all be shocked by his resignation.

The New York Times, 11-18:(1)49.

Pierre S. du Pont IV
United States Representative, R-Delaware

1

From my own point of view, it [Watergate] is very serious. It goes to the heart of things, because our system damned well won't work if people don't have respect for their leadership. There just is no excuse for high-ranking public officials condoning or encouraging violations of the law.

The New York Times, 4-26:34.

John D. Ehrlichman
Former Assistant to the President of the United States for Domestic Affairs

2

[On his experience while working at the White House]: It was a climate of vigorous dedication to getting things accomplished. And an awful lot of good people worked very long, hard hours and got a lot of good stuff done. I think this business about climate and fear and oppression and all this kind of thing is terribly unfair to those people. And one of the abiding concerns I have in this whole [Watergate affair] episode is that all these good guys who were there—and a lot of them are still there—are somehow or another going to be tarred for having been there. And it's not right. You take . . . that whole crowd of young, able, dedicated guys who dealt with these problems on farm bills and rural electrification and Indians and welfare and schools and busing and all these things that we were dealing with. They come at 7 o'clock in the morning and they go home at 9 o'clock at night, and they were there Saturdays and they were there Sundays. And I just hate to think they're going to, somehow or another, have less than the full appreciation that the country ought to give them for what they've done.

Interview, Washington/
The Washington Post, 7-15:(A)1.

3

[On the break-in at the office of the psychiatrist of Daniel Ellsberg, who leaked the secret "Pentagon Papers" to the press]: You get into these conflicting duty situations . . . at times, and you have to take the main chance. You have to do the thing that is more important to the country and not do the other thing. It occurred to me the other day that it's very much analogous to the dilemma of this Committee, where you are confronted with the conflicting rights of individuals who may be prejudiced by this whole process on the one hand, and what you consider to be the larger national interest. And you have resolved that conflict in favor of the larger national interest, even though some individuals may be harmed in the long pull by the process. And I can understand that. The larger national interest [in the Ellsberg break-in] was in finding out all we could about who and in what circumstances these vital national secrets, these top secret documents, were compromised . . . My disapproval [after being informed of the break-in] was because these people, as far as I knew, had been sent out there to do an investigation. I was under the assumption that it would be conducted as a normal investigation, not as some kind of a second-story job; and when I heard this, my initial reaction to it was somebody has not exercised good judgment.

At Senate Watergate hearings,
Washington, July 25/
The Washington Post, 7-26:(A)27.

Sam J. Ervin, Jr.
United States Senator, D-North Carolina;
Chairman, Senate Watergate Committee

4

[Criticizing the Nixon Administration's insistence that no White House aides will testify at public Senate hearings on the Watergate affair, but would appear at non-public grand jury hearings and non-public Senate hearings]: Divine right went out with the American Revolution and doesn't belong to White House aides. What meat do they eat that makes them grow so great? I am not willing to elevate them to a position above the great mass of the American people. I don't think we have any such thing as royalty or nobility that

(SAM J. ERVIN, JR.)

exempts them. I'm not going to let anybody come down at night like Nicodemus and whisper something in my ear that no one else can hear. That is not Executive privilege; it is Executive poppycock.

News conference, Washington,
April 2/Time, 4-16:10.
1

[Opening the Senate hearings on the Watergate affair]: Today, the Select Committee on Presidential Campaign Activities begins hearings into the extent to which illegal, improper or unethical activities were involved in the 1972 Presidential election campaign . . . We are beginning these hearings today in an atmosphere of the utmost gravity. The questions that have been raised in the wake of the June 17 [1972] break-in strike at the very undergirding of our democracy. If the many allegations made to this date are true, then the burglars who broke into the headquarters of the Democratic National Committee at the Watergate were, in effect, breaking into the home of every citizen of the United States. And if these allegations prove to be true, what they were seeking to steal was not the jewels, money or other property of American citizens, but something much more valuable—their most precious heritage: the right to vote in a free election.

At Senate Watergate hearings,
Washington, May 17/
U.S. News & World Report, 5-28:106.
2

[Challenging President Nixon's refusal to supply the Senate Committee with White House papers on Watergate by claiming Executive privilege/separation of powers in the Constitution]: Since there is nothing in the Constitution requiring the President to run for re-election, I don't think that Executive privilege covers any political activities whatsoever . . . I also take the position that Executive privilege does not entitle a President to have kept secret information concerning criminal activities of his aides or anybody else, because there is nothing in the Constitution that authorizes or makes it the official duty of a President to have anything to do with criminal activities.

At Senate Watergate hearings,
Washington, July 11/
The Washington Post, 7-12:(A)8.
3

The [Watergate] evidence thus far introduced . . . tends to show that men upon whom fortune had smiled benevolently and who possessed great financial power, great political power and great governmental power undertook to nullify the laws of man and the laws of God for the purpose of gaining what history will call a very temporary political advantage.

At Senate Watergate hearings,
Washington, July 19/
The Washington Post, 7-20:(A)24.
4

[On President Nixon's refusal to turn over to the Committee White House tapes bearing on Watergate]: . . . I think that high moral leadership demands that the President make available to this Committee any information in the form of tapes or records which will shed some light on that crucial question: How did it happen that burglars were caught in the headquarters of the opposition [Democratic] party with the President's campaign funds in their pockets and in their hotel bedrooms at the time? And I don't think the people of the United States are interested so much in abstruse arguments about the separation of powers or Executive privilege as they are in finding the answer to that question.

At Senate Watergate hearings,
Washington, July 23/
The Washington Post, 7-24:(A)18.
5

. . . I think that the Watergate tragedy is the greatest tragedy this country has ever suffered. I used to think that the Civil War was our country's greatest tragedy, but I do remember that there were some redeeming features in the Civil War in that there was some spirit of sacrifice and heroism displayed on both sides. I see no redeeming features in Watergate.

At Senate Watergate hearings,
Washington, July 23/
The Washington Post, 7-24:(A)18.

1

[On imminent litigation to force President Nixon to supply the Committee with White House tapes related to Watergate which the President has refused to do under subpoena]: The chair recognizes that there is no precedent for litigation of this nature, but there originally was no precedent for any litigation. And I think this litigation is essential if we are to determine whether the President is above the law and whether the President is immune from all of the duties and responsibilities in matters of this kind which devolve upon all the other mortals who dwell in this land.

At Senate Watergate hearings,
Washington, July 26/
The Washington Post, 7-27:(A)22.

2

[On President Nixon's statement that the Committee is out to implicate him in the Watergate scandal]: The Committee doesn't want to get anything but the truth. The country is in a tragic state when the President expresses the belief that the Committee, a nonpartisan committee, is trying to implicate him. It's unfortunate that he has that attitude . . . Like President Nixon, I would be quite happy if the Committee could complete its investigation and report on this tragedy. And I pray we can write a report saying the President was without blame legally and morally for the Watergate affair.

Before Gaston County Chamber of
Commerce, Gastonia, N.C., Aug. 16/
San Francisco Examiner, 8-17:22.

Gerald R. Ford
United States Representative, R-Michigan;
Vice President-designate of the United States

3

[Denying that President Nixon is a "crippled" President because of Watergate]: If Richard Nixon can achieve all that he has done for this country in the last few weeks [reduced unemployment, brought new Middle East peace hopes, etc.] as a "cripple," then he is the very best argument this nation ever had for hiring the handicapped.

Before National Association of Realtors,
Washington, Nov. 13/
Los Angeles Times, 11-14:(1)23.

Wendell H. Ford
Governor of Kentucky

4

I believe that Watergate is sinking in with the people. If the President [Nixon] is in trouble, then we're [politicians] all in trouble. The fallout from Watergate is going to make mountains out of molehills in politics.

Stateline, Nev./
U.S. News & World Report, 6-18:22.

John W. Gardner
Chairman, Common Cause

5

The Watergate is not primarily a story of political espionage nor even of White House intrigue. It is a particularly malodorous chapter in the annals of campaign financing. The money paid to the Watergate conspirators before the break-in [at Democratic headquarters]—and the money passed to them later —was money from campaign gifts. It was not found in a pea patch. It was money presumably given to ensure [President] Nixon's re-election.

April 23/The Washington Post, 4-24:(A)9.

6

When [President] Nixon says we must put this [Watergate] behind us in order to deal with more important things, he fails to see that this is the most important thing. The responsiveness of our government, the extent [to] which the functioning of our government was broken down, is the most important question facing the American people today . . . The President, at the time of his election, spoke of the American people as children. He didn't seem to recognize that those children set the terms of his power under our system. They own the place. The name on the mailbox is "the people." And if we don't have that kind of system, if it isn't a government of laws, then anyone in this audience can be the next victim—their phone can be tapped, their mail opened, their doctor's files rifled. Anything can happen once you break that structure of law.

Television interview, Aug. 19/
San Francisco Examiner, 8-20:11.

Eric F. Goldman
Professor of History, Princeton University;
Former Special Consultant to the President
of the United States

1

[On whether Watergate is a worse scandal than Teapot Dome in the 1920s]: Much worse. A number of people say, "Corruption is a natural part of American political life." They can point to the Administrations of Grant and Harding and to the fact that the average Congressman today is a far more ethical man than at most times in the past. Yet there's a fundamental difference. The corruption of American political life in the past has largely had to do with the stealing of money. As we all know, the charges now do not have too much to do with the stealing of money. What you have are charges that some men who are quite ethical about money and a number of other things—in the name of a cause, the re-election of President Nixon—have been trying to steal power. That kind of corruption is far more dangerous to a democracy. And modern technology—electronic eavesdropping, for instance—raises its capacity for damage.

Interview/
U.S. News & World Report, 11-26:57.

Barry M. Goldwater
United States Senator, R-Arizona

2

I've been getting letters and calls from Republican friends of mine all around the country. And they are saying, "No more money to the Republican National Committee until this is cleared up." When you find staunch, hardworking Republicans refusing to help the Party, well, I can tell you we're having a hell of a time selling tickets to the Republican gala dinner in May here in Washington. And it is because of Watergate . . . I see the issue out of this as "can you trust Dick Nixon?" It gets right down to that. All of us who support Nixon are to be on the line in the 1974 election. When they say, "Are you still supporting the President?" I'd say, "I'm still supporting the President." And I'd say that even if—no, I won't say that. I might not support him if it

turns out he knew all about this and kept his mouth shut. But I don't think he knows about it . . . [But] what worries me is that, unless the President comes out with something—"We did it," or, "We didn't"; "This is the reason," or, "This is not the reason"; "We're involved," or, "We are not involved" —unless he does this in the relatively near future, it's just another dirty piece of meat like the ITT [political-favoritism affair] and the other little things that have been happening that the Democrats can make real hay out of whether they are true or not.

Interview, Washington/
The Christian Science Monitor, 4-12:1,8.

3

[On the effect of Watergate on the next Presidential election]: It's going to have its effect; there's no question of it. I don't think it's going to have a major effect, although there will be a large bloc of voters who will never forgive the Republican Party. Even though the Party had absolutely nothing to do with it, they'll never forget the word Republican as it relates to Watergate any more than the old-timers would forget the Depression as related to [Herbert] Hoover, even though Hoover had nothing at all to do with the Depression.

Television interview/
"The Watergate Year,"
Columbia Broadcasting System, 6-17.

4

[On Senator Edward Kennedy, who was involved in the death of a driving companion at Chappaquiddick Island, Mass., in 1969, and his criticism of the Watergate political-espionage affair]: Until all the facts involving the Chappaquiddick tragedy are made known, the American people can do without moralizing from the Massachusetts Democrat . . . In a speech [on July 4] which was obviously the opening gun of Kennedy's drive for the Presidency in 1976, the Senator for Massachusetts constituted himself as both judge and jury in the Watergate affair. He spoke with unctuous righteousness about such things as "mischief" and "honor" and "exemption from restraints," and all of his remarks were obviously directed to the Watergate charges, although he didn't mention them as such. I say that one does not have to excuse or condone any of the stupid illegalities of the Watergate affair to suggest that Senator Kennedy is the last person in the country to lecture us on such matters.

At National Young Republicans
Convention, Atlanta, July 12/
Los Angeles Times, 7-13:(1)25.

1

[On President Nixon's refusal to supply the Senate Watergate Committee with White House tapes which relate to Watergate]: I think the President has made a mistake by refusing to release these tapes. It's not a question of separation of powers or a Constitutional confrontation–that's a smokescreen. The important question here is the honor and the veracity of the President of the United States. I think the President must release these tapes and he must come before the Senate Watergate Committee and the television cameras and tell the truth.

Interview/
San Francisco Examiner & Chronicle,
7-29:(A)10.

2

Because the Nixon Administration is more conservative than liberal, of course, attempts already are being made to try and equate the irregularities of the Watergate affair with conservative principles generally. This is the thing we must guard against and fight against. This is the "big lie" being used by liberal politicians to take maximum unjustified advantage of the Watergate crimes . . . In fact, it is my firm conviction that the Nixon Administration would not find itself in the situation it does today if it had been manned at the top by staff people strongly committed to the principles of conservatism. It was not the existence of conservative ideology in the White House or in the Committee for the Re-election of the President which brought on the stupidities and the irregularities of the Watergate. Rather –and let me emphasize and underline this assertion–it was the lack of ideology and the lack of experience and the lack of a deeply-rooted philosophy of life which brought on the unfortunate and unforgivable activity that

has been uncovered in the Watergate investigation.

Before Young Americans for Freedom,
Washington, Aug. 16/
The Christian Science Monitor, 8-23:16.

3

[On the national tumult caused by Watergate]: I'm asking in the name of reason, in the name of sanity, of justice and enlightenment, in the name of the great God above, for a moment of quiet thought and reflection. If we can have such a moment to quiet the hysteria that grips us, we may be able to proceed to the task ahead; to put in order our house of government; to eliminate the incompetent, punish the guilty, and to make sure that what has happened will not happen again–but all this in an orderly, deliberate fashion. To the Congress, to the White House, to the [Nixon] Administration, to the press and the news media, to the pulpits and the universities, to each and every one of us, I plead for restraint in this crisis. For us to stay on this road of unreason means stark tragedy. Finally, in the words of the street, "Cool it!" Give us time to think, and look at the road ahead.

Nov. 4/U.S. News & World Report, 11-19:26.

Katharine Graham
Publisher, "The Washington Post"

4

[On her newspaper's reporting of the Watergate affair]: By pursuing that tangled matter as far as we did, and by refusing to be put off by vague, misleading White House statements, *The Post* incurred the bitter, lasting hostility of many figures in the [Nixon] Administration and the President's re-election campaign team . . . It might have been more comfortable for us if we had been content to treat the Watergate arrests as a routine case of breaking and entering. But again, if we had failed to pursue the facts as far as they led, we would have denied the public any knowledge of an unprecedented scheme of political surveillance and sabotage.

At Gallaudet College colloquium,
Washington, March 2/
The Washington Post, 3-3:(C)2.

L. Patrick Gray III
Former Acting Director,
Federal Bureau of Investigation

1

[On his possession and burning, while Acting Director, of supposed Watergate-related files on the instructions of then-Presidential aides John Dean and John Ehrlichman]: At the time I accepted the two files from Dean and Ehrlichman, at the time I destroyed them . . . I believed that I was acting faithfully, loyally, properly and legally pursuant to instructions given me by top assistants to the President of the United States. I have come to believe, however, what I should have realized then, that my acceptance of the documents in the first place, and my keeping them out of the normal FBI files, was a grievous misjudgment. My destroying them and resistance of disclosure only compounded the error. That the documents were not in fact Watergate evidence, while legally significant, does not lessen my present belief that I permitted myself to be used to perform a mere political chore. I shall carry the burden of that act with me always.

At Senate Watergate hearings,
Washington, Aug. 3/
The Washington Post, 8-4:(A)11.

2

[On his involvement in the Watergate affair]: In the service of my country, I withstood hours and hours of depth-charging, shelling, bombing; but I never expected to run into a Watergate in the service of a President of the United States, and I ran into a buzz-saw, obviously.

At Senate Watergate hearings,
Washington, Aug. 6/
The New York Times, 8-7:20.

Robert P. Griffin
United States Senator, R-Michigan

3

. . . I think the American voter is a very sophisticated, very knowledgeable group of people. They have followed this Watergate mess on television. They are familiar with those responsible in general and realize that most of the people that we generally refer to

as politicians had nothing to do with it. In fact, one of the ironic things is that most of the people who really were involved in Watergate and those kind of adventures were not politicians.

TV-radio interview, Washington/
"Meet the Press,"
National Broadcasting Company, 10-7.

Edward J. Gurney
United States Senator, R-Florida;
Member, Senate Watergate Committee

4

I feel that Watergate has been overblown and over-played in these hearings and by the media. I think the Committee spent more time than it needed to spend. I think we could have accomplished as much as we did in perhaps even one-half the time we did, and not expose the nation and people to this dirty-linen hearing every day.

Radio interview, Washington,
Aug. 8/San Francisco Examiner, 8-9:11.

5

The only concrete contributions we [the Watergate Committee] have made have been to force down the stock market, up the price of gold, devalue the American dollar, hurt the economy and destroy the confidence of people in the American political system.

San Francisco Examiner & Chronicle,
11-11:(This World)2.

Alexander M. Haig, Jr.
Assistant to the President
of the United States

6

Watergate is important, and we all have differing sensitivities about it. But there has been an over-fixation on Watergate. We have just so much time at the helm, and we don't have any time to waste. Not that Watergate attention is wasted time. It isn't that. It's that we *really* do have a number of items before us that are of vital importance to the people of America—and frankly to the world, because we are a world power and can't shrink from that. These moments we have to deal with these problems are precious to me and my staff.

Interview, Washington/
The Washington Post, 9-30:(A)12.

1

Under no circumstances would we ever be true to the preservation of the powers of the office of the President to permit any [Watergate] investigator a . . . free-rein fishing expedition into the vital discussions that occur in the President's office.

TV-radio interview/
"Meet the Press,"
National Broadcasting Company, 10-28.

H. R. Haldeman
*Former Assistant to the President
of the United States*

2

I am fully confident that when all the truth is known in the proper forum and in its totality, that there will be no question as to my position in this matter [Watergate] and my non-involvement in any way, shape or form in any improper or illegal acts, whether they be acts of commitment, acts of cover-up or anything else that might be considered. I was not involved in the planning or the execution of the Watergate, as I have consistently said. I was not involved in any cover-up of the Watergate in any way, as I have consistently said. And that will become clearly known and understood as the truth comes out.

Interview, Washington, June 15/
The Washington Post, 6-16:(A)8.

3

One of the great tragedies of our time is that, for the moment at least, a cloud hangs over the accomplishments of the past four years and the promise of the next four years because of Watergate, its aftermath and related matters. This has spawned an unceasing barrage of charges and counter-charges, allegations, innuendo, hearsay, rumor, speculation, hypothesis, which I devoutly hope these hearings and the concurrent work of the Justice Department and the special prosecutor will bring to an early and definite conclusion so that the nation and its leadership can again

turn their thoughts and their efforts to more productive enterprises.

At Senate Watergate hearings,
Washington, July 30/
The New York Times, 7-31:24.

Philip A. Hart
United States Senator, D-Michigan

4

The level of decency among politicians is at least as high as it is among lawyers. Most of the bandits and bad actors in Watergate are not politicians. Whatever they are, they're not politicians.

Time, 5-21:33.

Wayne L. Hays
United States Representative, D-Ohio

5

[On televised Watergate testimony by Nixon Administration aides]: Anyone who can watch the crew of neo-Nazi bastards on television and believe that this Administration has the best interests of the American people at heart thinks with greater perspicacity than I can possibly muster.

Canton, Ohio, Sept. 6/
San Francisco Examiner, 9-7:9.

Jesse A. Helms
United States Senator, R-North Carolina

6

People are sick and tired of hearing about it [Watergate]. Rightly or wrongly, the people think it's much ado about nothing, that it's a political vendetta. They feel the economy, inflation, the fuel shortage, things like that, over-shadow the importance of Watergate.

Interview/The Washington Post, 7-29:(E)2.

Ernest F. Hollings
*United States Senator,
D-South Carolina*

7

The Watergate affair is sending shock waves through our entire political system, further weakening our important institutions of government, and further shaking the people's faith and confidence in all those who represent and govern them. The men who burglar-

(ERNEST F. HOLLINGS)

ized the Watergate and bugged their friends and enemies alike, who hired campaign spies and saboteurs by the platoon, were frightened men—afraid of the people, afraid of operating in the open, afraid of the democratic system. And their fear of open participatory politics led them right into the tragic folly of subversion symbolized by the Watergate.

At Democratic fund-raising dinner,
Washington, May 23/
The Washington Post, 5-24:(A)24.

Hubert H. Humphrey
United States Senator, D-Minnesota

1

I think the affair [Watergate] is despicable. It's the most tawdry side of politics . . . politics at its worst. The whole idea of wiretapping and snooping just is cheap and needs to be condemned as something unworthy of the American political process. But the public essentially feels that this is a matter between sets of politicians. It isn't as if something had been stolen from the trust funds. It isn't as if there had been misappropriation of money. Therefore, I don't believe that the Watergate will be a political turning-point issue, causing millions of Americans to pull away from the President [Nixon] and move back to the Democratic [Party] side. I regret this indifference; but the letters I'm getting indicate this is true.

Interview, Washington/
The Christian Science Monitor, 3-19:8.

2

. . . this whole Watergate mess casts a shadow over all public people, over the entire political process of this nation; and we are going through what I consider a period of cleansing, and I only hope that the cleansing process will be a lasting one. I think lessons are being learned here in this Watergate situation that will live with this republic for years to come—and some very good lessons. Every public official will be more cautious, more careful about his personal and public conduct. We have become too easy—easy living, too

permissive in many ways in this country. It is about time that we began to live by the doctrines of truth and the Constitution . . . and start to embrace integrity rather than gimmickry, get away from this image-making and get back to substance. We have had too much cosmetics in everything—cheap advertising, cheap politics; and now we are beginning to pay the price in corrupted government.

TV-radio interview,
Washington/"Meet the Press,"
National Broadcasting Company, 7-1.

E. Howard Hunt
Convicted Watergate conspirator and
former Central Intelligence Agency official

3

[On why he participated in Watergate]: There is a built-in bias by the intellectual community, including the news media, against people who want to preserve the best of our country's heritage. As for me, I don't want to exchange the good of this country for the uncertainties of change . . . I was not aware that my activity constituted a Federal offense. I never personally went into Democratic offices, and I thought the most they could get me on was second-degree burglary . . . I cased the situation thoroughly, and I'm good at it. I appraised the risk as very high and the potential return as very low. I recommended against it, but it wasn't my decision. I can tell you this: If it had been a CIA operation and I'd been in charge, it never would have happened.

Interview/Time, 1-29:20.

4

I guess it's obvious now that the Watergate thing was planned by a small group of people —[former Attorney General John] Mitchell, [1972 Nixon campaign finance vice chairman Jeb] Magruder, maybe a few others. We [the convicted men who carried out the Watergate plan] were just legmen in that operation following decisions made by others, and yet we're the only ones who have suffered from it so far . . . I saw a picture of Magruder making a river raft trip, visiting London, preparing to hit the lecture circuit and make some money. I can't for the life of me understand. Here are the prime conspirators walking around on the streets, free on bond. But there's no end in sight for me [in prison]. I think it's ironic and inequitable.

Interview/Time, 8-27:18.

Edward Hutchinson
United States Representative, R-Michigan

1

The President [Nixon] hasn't committed an impeachable offense, in my opinion. And any attempt to move along the line of impeachment at this time would be highly partisan . . . There isn't any evidence of criminality involving him—that I know anything about. The impeachment power should be very narrowly construed when you talk about using it, because the trauma of impeachment is something this country ought not go through if it can at all be avoided . . . If a President, in the trough of unpopularity, can be forced from office—if it can happen once—then it can happen more regularly, and that would lend great instability to the office of the President.

The National Observer, 11-17:6.

Daniel K. Inouye
United States Senator, D-Hawaii;
Member, Senate Watergate Committee

2

It is not our business [at the Senate Watergate hearings] to shackle the President [Nixon] and drag him to the committee room and force him to testify. But if he wishes to present his case to us, we would afford him all the courtesies and accommodate him on his terms as to time and place. Deep within us, we're hoping that our proceedings will somehow clear the White House . . . But I must say that, as of this moment, if the testimony of [former Presidential Counsel] John Dean is permitted to remain unrebutted, then the President looks very bad.

At University of Hawaii, July 3/
Los Angeles Times, 7-5:(1)28.

3

[On President Nixon's refusal to turn over to the Committee White House tapes relevant to Watergate]: If this were a criminal matter, I would say the tapes were absolutely neces-

sary, essential. In our case, I think we can proceed and file an adequate report without the tapes. It is not our job to determine the guilt or innocence of anybody.

Television interview, Sept. 9/
San Francisco Examiner, 9-10:13.

Henry M. Jackson
United States Senator, D-Washington

4

I believe that we have reached the point where the President [Nixon] must appear before an appropriate forum and lay his [Watergate] cards on the table. The American people are no longer willing to have a continuity of crises which we have had now all this year. The real issue is whether or not there is enough confidence left for the President to govern this nation. I believe that an appropriate forum would be the [Senate] Watergate Committee. This view, I think, is being shared now by more and more members of the Senate. For example, Senator [Barry] Goldwater feels that this would be an effective course of conduct. We just can't litigate for the next three years of his [Nixon's] office all of the issues that have been raised and are being raised daily. We have reached the point where a lot of my friends don't want to turn on TV. They don't want to pick up the morning newspaper because of the bad news. We can't afford, I think, the continuity of these crises.

TV-radio interview,
Washington/"Meet the Press,"
National Broadcasting Company, 11-4.

Herbert W. Kalmbach
Former personal attorney to President Nixon

5

[On his raising money to "pay off" Watergate defendants on orders of top White House aides]: The fact that I had been directed to undertake these actions by the number two and number three men on the White House staff made it absolutely incomprehensible to me that my actions in this regard could have been regarded in any way as improper or unethical.

At Senate Watergate hearings, Washington/
The Christian Science Monitor, 7-17:10.

Edward M. Kennedy
United States Senator, D-Massachusetts

1

The Watergate mentality is at the core of the fight between Congress and President Nixon. The same arrogance, the same imperialism, the same blind judgment that led to Watergate is also the attitude that led to other controversies in foreign and domestic policy. The bombing of Cambodia, the doctrines of impoundment and unlimited Executive privilege, the harassment of the press, the imprisonment of news reporters [for their refusal to reveal news sources]—you know the abuses as well as I. They are legion, and their name is Watergate.

Before American Society of Newspaper
Editors, Washington, May 4/
Los Angeles Times, 5-5:(1)25.

2

The body politic of America is on the operating table today. Watergate is the wound, an independent prosecutor must be the surgeon and Congress must supervise the operation on behalf of all the people of the country. If we do not heal the wound, if we do not investigate the case completely, if we allow a prosecutor to be appointed who is independent in name but not in fact, then we shall be sewing up the wound with the infection still inside.

At Syracuse (N.Y.) University
commencement, May 12/
The Dallas Times Herald, 5-13:(A)36.

3

There is no partisan or political advantage to be gained from Watergate. We can all take pride that the strongest voices urging a full and fair investigation of the case are voices in the President's own party.

At Syracuse (N.Y.) University
commencement/The New York Times,
6-18:22.

Henry A. Kissinger
Assistant to the President of the
United States for National Security
Affairs

4

I have no question that the President [Nix-
on] will insist on the full disclosure of the [Watergate] facts, and that, when this is accomplished and the human tragedies are completed, the country will go on. Then we have to ask ourselves whether we can afford an orgy of recriminations or whether we should not keep in mind that the United States will be there longer than any particular crisis —whether all of us do not have an obligation to remember that faith in the country must be maintained and its promise should be eternal.

At Associated Press luncheon,
New York, April 23/
The Washington Post, 4-24:(A)1.

Egil Krogh, Jr.
Former Assistant Director,
White House Domestic Council

5

[On his involvement in the 1971 break-in at the office of Daniel Ellsberg's psychiatrist]: I feel that the decision made in 1971 to go forward with the covert operation was a mistake, and I felt that it was a mistake immediately thereafter when the details of its execution were presented to me . . . I have some real regrets over what has taken place, in terms of injuring innocent persons; but at the time in 1971, when this job was presented to me as something of extraordinary national importance, what I undertook was fully authorized and lawful.

Before newsmen after pleading innocent
to indictment charges, Los Angeles,
Sept. 6/Los Angeles Times, 9-7:(1)26.

Melvin R. Laird
Counsellor to the President of the
United States for Domestic Affairs

6

All of the news from the Congress has been tied in with the [Watergate] hearings, pretty much. Everything coming out of Washington as far as the country['s] ills [are] concerned has been in connection with these hearings. Those legislators who have been working on other areas such as highways, education, agriculture, energy and some of the big economic issues are not hearing too much from their constituents about these major problems. The Congress reacts according to the needs and demands of their constituents.

Interview, San Clemente, Calif.,
Aug. 21/The New York Times, 8-22:24.

Alfred M. Landon
Former Governor of Kansas

1

The ultimate verdict on how the Presidency is affected [by Watergate] will rest on how thoroughly this sordid affair has been explored and the guilty ones prosecuted. So far, there has been no proof that the President [Nixon] was personally involved. There are no issues involving national unity or national purpose in the Watergate case or its ramifications. The issues there involve law and order and moral standards; Americans are not divided on maintaining those. They are divided on whom to trust and who let them down. That is temporarily elusive. But the facts are in the process of being clearly established by our customary judicial processes and a Senatorial investigating committee.

Interview, Topeka, Kan./
U.S. News & World Report, 5-21:23.

Arthur S. Link
Professor of American History,
Princeton University

2

This [Watergate] is the greatest moral crisis of the Presidency. It is unprecedented. There is nothing analogous to it in the past, nothing. There is a crisis, and one of enormous magnitude, because it involves the integrity not only of the office but of the President, too; and that is the tragedy of it. The peculations of the Harding and Grant Administrations—and no one can condone such corruption—were sores on the body politic but not cancers in the body itself. They didn't subvert democratic processes. They didn't corrupt entire Administrations. The difference now is that Watergate—and Watergate is just the tip of the iceberg, I am afraid—makes it clear that at least the White House staff and part of the Nixon Administration set out deliberately,

knowingly, in a systematic way to subvert and destroy the very processes through which the American democracy must operate . . . The only way we can preserve the two-party system is by observing certain definite rules of the political game. These rules are pretty wide and allow a great deal of latitude for things that ought not happen. Heretofore, however, the rules have been observed. The parties have been like two great organisms fighting each other: They will engage in all kinds of antics, like the war dance of whooping cranes, and all kinds of rhetoric. Yet, instinctively they seem to know that some things you can't do and still preserve the two-party system. You can't attempt to destroy the other party. You can't attempt to subvert the other party's decision-making and choice of candidates. That never happened before. This is a rather fundamental right if you are going to have a two-party system. And most fundamentally, the leaders of the two parties have to remain within the laws and not engage in wiretapping, burglary and so on.

Interview, Princeton, N.J./
Los Angeles Times, 5-16:(2)7.

Clare Boothe Luce
Former American diplomat and playwright

3

I'm sorry I can't go into any great flights over the immorality of government—perhaps because I've lived too long and seen too many scandals in government, under both parties. You know, nobody is very far from the Boss Tweed era in American politics. So I am not as shocked as the newspaper people are or pretend to be [over Watergate]. I think it was regrettable; above all, I think it was a damned stupid thing to do. And it's been badly handled, probably because the President [Nixon] wasn't involved. If he had been, he'd have been on top of it like a shot.

Interview, New York/
The New York Times Magazine, 4-22:53.

4

. . . thank God for Watergate, because Watergate has caused a great questioning among the people of this country. It has made

(CLARE BOOTHE LUCE)

them ask, "How come the President has all that power?"

Interview, Honolulu/ Newsweek, 11-26:38.

Jeb Stuart Magruder
1972 deputy director, Committee for the Re-election of the President (Nixon)

1

[On the Watergate political-espionage affair]: I did help organize the Committee for the Re-election of the President beginning in May of 1971, and I remained there throughout the entire campaign. Unfortunately, we made some mistakes in the campaign which have led to a major national concern. For those errors in judgment that I made, I take full responsibility. I am, after all, a mature man, and I am willing to face the consequences of my own acts. These mistakes were made by only a few participants in the campaign. Thousands of persons assisted in the campaign to re-elect the President, and they did nothing illegal or unethical. As far as I know, at no point during this entire period, from the time of planning of the Watergate to the time of trying to keep it from the public view, did the President have any knowledge of our errors in this matter. He had confidence in his aides, and I must confess that some of us failed him.

At Senate Watergate hearings, Washington, June 14/The New York Times, 6-15:18.

Marvin Mandel
Governor of Maryland

2

What we are witnessing, [in Watergate] piece by piece, is a massive scheme by a cynical and callous power-elite to remake a nation in its own image. The arrogant private army of corrupters had its origin in the hyphenated law firms of Wall Street, the advertising agencies of Madison Avenue and Disneyland, and the board rooms of the most powerful industrial giants in America . . . We have witnessed in the past several weeks an erosion of confidence in the very institutions of government, those venerable and sacred offices of public trust: the Justice Department, the Federal Bureau of Investigation, the Central Intelligence Agency, the Treasury Department, the Department of Transportation, the Securities [and] Exchange Commission, and the Presidency itself. So far, 15 ranking Presidential and governmental officials have resigned, and two former Cabinet officers have been indicted. And the end apparently is not in sight . . . The ethic of government for a few terrible months had become the ethic of the boardroom—of industrial espionage—of snooping and spying, of bribery and stealing, of pilfering the competition's secrets, of packaging the Presidency, of picking its morals off a drive-in movie marquee. I do not assign guilt, or convict in public. I simply point out that the names of Mitchell, Stans, Mardian, Colson, Dean, Magruder, Kleindienst, Haldeman, Ehrlichman, Krogh—and all the other closet conspirators—have never appeared on a ballot anywhere in this nation. Not a single one is or was responsible, or responsive, to any electorate or constituency in America.

At Mount St. Mary's College commencement, Emmitsburg, Md., May 27/The Washington Post, 5-28:(A)1,12.

Mike Mansfield
United States Senator, D-Montana

3

Frankly, I don't see what can be gained by the President [Nixon] resigning [because of Watergate], and I don't advocate it. People would just be left to come to their own conclusions about the allegations concerning the President . . . All we have heard so far are allegations . . . allegations have been raised, innuendo has been raised, but no proof has been forthcoming. Whether a person is a President or a plumber, every citizen is innocent until proven guilty.

Washington, Nov. 8/ The Dallas Times Herald, 11-9:(A)25.

Charles McC. Mathias, Jr.
United States Senator, R-Maryland

4

[The total disclosure of all White House

evidence related to Watergate is] the only way you are going to get rid of the confusion which has grown instead of diminished as a result of the piecemeal disclosures. Unless there is this kind of a disclosure, I think the alternatives to impeachment [of President Nixon] become less and less and less. Each one of these disclosures, each one of these failures to produce evidence that's been promised, nibbles away at credibility. It's the greatest argument that I can think of for a massive, complete, total disclosure of all the evidence that is available at one time. That's the only way we're ever going to get Watergate behind us. The physical evidence is there . . . not only tapes, but memoranda, documents, papers . . . things [special Watergate prosecutor] Archibald Cox requested, for example, before his dismissal. They haven't been produced. Why not?

TV-radio interview/"Face the Nation,"
Columbia Broadcasting System, 11-25.

Eugene J. McCarthy
Former United States Senator,
D-Minnesota
1

I don't think any good would be served by impeaching him [President Nixon] or even by his resignation at this point. The foreign policy of the country is being conducted just as well now as before the president got in trouble. And if the Congress and the Democrats assert themselves on the domestic issues, I think they can do more about domestic problems now that he's on the defensive than if he were stronger and more popular.

Rome, Nov. 11/
Los Angeles Times, 11-12:(1)16.

James W. McCord
Convicted Watergate conspirator
2

[On why he became involved in Watergate]: There were a number of reasons . . . One of the reasons—and a very important reason to me—was the fact that the Attorney General himself, Mr. John Mitchell, at his offices, had considered and approved the operation, according to [convicted Watergate plan-

ner G. Gordon] Liddy; secondly, that the Counsel for the President, Mr. John Dean, had participated in those decisions with him; that one was the top legal officer for the United States in the Department of Justice and the second gentleman was a top legal officer in the White House.

At Senate Watergate hearings, Washington/
U.S. News & World Report, 5-28:27.

George S. McGovern
United States Senator, D-South Dakota
3

The Watergate scandal is not, as the President [Nixon] implied, typical of the political process. Our politics is better than that. And Watergate is worse than the tactics of any national campaign in my memory or modern times. What was wrong with Watergate was not just that the President's associates got caught, but what they did. The standard of conduct set by the Committee to Re-elect the President was simply unprecedented. I have no doubt that the ethical standards of American politics can be improved. But we must wonder about Mr. Nixon's reference to "campaign excesses that have occurred on all sides." I emphatically reject the notion that I or my colleagues or my Party in the Presidential election [of 1972, when he was the Democratic nominee] condoned or would have countenanced activities of a criminal nature.

Before American Society of Newspaper
Editors, Washington, May 2/
The New York Times, 5-3:33.
4

Watergate may also cause us to look more closely at political labels and catchphrases. The men around the Committee to Re-elect the President [Nixon, in 1972] said that they were conservatives and that their opponents were radicals. But it is not conservatism to turn the political process into an all-out war in which not only the other party but also police and prosecutors are considered "the enemy"—in which one side abuses the electoral system by using spies, wiretaps and paramilitary tactics. Many of the men who wrote our Constitution were proud conservatives. They ordained for us a politics of decency

(GEORGE S. McGOVERN)

and civility; they knew this was the only way to secure liberty and stability. And those who have taken their name but betrayed their principles and broken the law are not conservatives in any true sense, but criminals.

At Bethesda Chevy Chase High School,
Gathersburg, Md./
The Christian Science Monitor, 7-24:16.

1

The President [Nixon] has made it very hard for us to accept the argument that he advances that he had nothing to do either with the cover-up of the Watergate incident or its original planning. I think it's premature for any of us in the Congress to be advocating impeachment at this point. But . . . if the President remains steadfast in his refusal to turn over the [Watergate-related White House] tapes, even if the courts hold that he has an obligation to do so, then the Congress will have no other recourse except to give serious consideration to impeachment . . . I would like to believe that the President is innocent either of any knowledge of the Watergate incident or of the cover-up, but he's making it increasingly hard for any of us to hold to that view . . . I can't buy the notion that there's some kind of peculiar right that the President has to place himself above the rights of inquiry of the Congress of the United States.

TV-radio interview/"Face the Nation,"
Columbia Broadcasting System, 8-19.

2

[Calling for President Nixon's impeachment]: We demand justice be done. The agency is Congress and the remedy is impeachment. It is time to tell those who have violated the trust of the people, "Enough!" . . . [With each passing day, it] becomes harder to believe what the White House says. It is plain to see this Administration is simply incredible. When people ask if the United States can afford to place on trial the President, if the system can stand impeachment, my answer is, "Can we stand anything else?"

At University of North Carolina,
Chapel Hill, Nov. 28/
San Francisco Examiner, 11-29:15.

George Meany
President, American Federation of Labor-
Congress of Industrial Organizations

3

[On revelations that President Nixon has been taping his White House conversations]: I never had the slightest idea that my conversations with the President were being recorded. It is so fantastic as to be almost unbelievable. God bless the blunderers at Watergate, because if they hadn't been so clumsy, Americans would never have known about this.

U.S. News & World Report, 7-30:19.

4

[On President Nixon's firing of special Watergate prosecutor Archibald Cox and related incidents]: Events of the last several days prove the dangerous emotional instability of the President of the United States . . . We firmly believe there must be a completely independent investigation of the scandals in this Administration. The President has so destroyed the people's confidence in government that . . . he should resign or be impeached. But meanwhile the Congress should move immediately to establish an independent office of special prosecutor, completely removed from the President's authority.

At AFL-CIO convention,
Bal Harbour, Fla., Oct. 24/
Los Angeles Times, 10-25:(1)20.

John N. Mitchell
Former Attorney General of the
United States; 1972 director, Committee for
the Re-election of the President (Nixon)

5

[On the Watergate political-espionage affair]: I deeply resent the slanderous and false statements about me concerning the Watergate matter reported as being based on hearsay and leaked out. I have previously denied any prior knowledge of or involvement in the Watergate affair and again reaffirm such denials.

March 29/Time, 4-30:15.

6

[On the Watergate political-espionage affair]: I never approved any bugging plans during any period of the [1972 Presidential] campaign . . . I have heard discussions of such plans. They have always been cut off at all times; and I would like to know who it was that kept bringing it back and back and back.

Washington/Newsweek, 4-30:21.

1

[On why he did not advise President Nixon last year of the Watergate affair after he had learned of it]: Because I did not believe that it was appropriate for him to have that type of knowledge; because I knew the actions he would take, and it would be most detrimental to his political [re-election] campaign . . . He was not involved [in Watergate]; it wasn't a question of deceiving the public as far as Richard Nixon was concerned; and it was the other people that were involved in connection with these activities . . . I believe at that particular time—and maybe in retrospect I was wrong—but it occurred to me that the best thing to do was just to keep the lid on through the election . . . I'm sure that, knowing Richard Nixon, the President, as I do, that he would just lower the boom [on those responsible for Watergate] . . . and it would come back to hurt him in connection with his re-election . . . In my mind, the re-election of Richard Nixon, compared with what was available on the other side, was so much more important that I put it in just that context.

At Senate Watergate hearings,
Washington, July 10/
Los Angeles Times, 7-11:(1)16.

Martha (Mrs. John N.) Mitchell
Wife of the former
Attorney General of the United States

2

[Saying the White House, not her husband, should bear the blame for the Watergate affair]: They tried to make my husband the fall-guy. But he's the good guy . . . John Mitchell was the honest one in the whole lousy bunch of SOBs. And who do you think he has been protecting?—Mr. President [Nixon]. Mr. Mitchell and I went to Washington to help this country. We didn't make one iota of profit from anything. Where do you think

all this originated? Do you think my husband is that stupid?

News conference, New York, May 18/
Los Angeles Herald-Examiner, 5-19:(A)1.

3

[On Watergate's effect on her husband]: I love him very much. He loves me because I've stood up for him. But he is defending the President [Nixon] who planned the whole goddamned thing . . . He [her husband] never moves; he won't see our friends; he's broken up. That's what the doctors say. He's remote. He's been taken. He took a tremendous loss. Nixon cut him off, and his law firm has been miserable to him. He stays in the apartment 24 hours a day . . . [Nixon] bleeds people. He draws every drop of blood and then drops them from a cliff. He'll blame any person he can put his foot on. I've never seen anything like it in history. We need a new government.

New York, Aug. 27/
Los Angeles Times, 8-28:(1)17.

Walter F. Mondale
United States Senator, D-Minnesota

4

I believe that he's [President Nixon] responsible for the political culture that he created. All of these key people around him, whether he knew it or not, had the same theme, the same idea [with Watergate]. They were conspiratorial. They had contempt for the law. They felt they could do anything they wanted to . . . They would rifle a doctor's files; they would sponsor perjury; they would hire spies; they would wiretap; they would disrupt meetings; they would try to twist the FBI and the Internal Revenue Service and the CIA to affect political campaigns. And it may be that Mr. Nixon didn't know about it. But everybody he put in charge of it knew about it. And I think he's responsible for creating that kind of climate.

Los Angeles Times, 10-16:(1)22.

Malcolm C. Moos
President, University of Minnesota

5

It must be faced that the sum of all the

(MALCOLM C. MOOS)

allegations [connected with the Watergate affair] is that we were the victims of a coup d'etat or an attempted coup. I weigh my words carefully. I am aware that the strict definition of a coup d'etat is "a sudden decisive exercise of force whereby the existing government is subverted." But surely, an attempt to capture or retain control of a government by illegal means is action of the same degree.

San Francisco Examiner & Chronicle,
6-17:(This World)2.

Edmund S. Muskie
United States Senator, D-Maine

1

Without the Senate investigation into the Watergate scandal, we might not know how close we came to tyranny.

The Dallas Times Herald, 9-13:(B)2.

2

The Senate [Watergate] Committee is not a perfect instrument for determining all the truth. Issues of criminal guilt or innocence can only be resolved in court. But the truth about official conduct that is grossly improper—if not technically illegal—can only be made known through a Congressional investigation that has captured America's attention.

Quote, 11-18:484.

Richard M. Nixon
President of the United States

3

I will simply say, with regard to the Watergate case, what I have said previously: that the investigation conducted by Mr. [John] Dean, the White House Counsel . . . indicates that no one on the White House staff at the time he conducted the investigation—that was last July and August—was involved or had knowledge of the Watergate matter. And as far as the balance of the case is concerned, it is now under investigation by a Congressional Committee, and that Committee should go forward, conduct its investigation in an even-handed way, going into charges made against

both candidates, both political parties.

News conference, Washington,
March 2/The New York Times, 3-3:12.

4

Whatever may appear to have been the case before, whatever improper activities may yet be discovered in connection with this whole sordid [Watergate] affair, I want the American people, I want you, to know beyond the shadow of a doubt that, during my term as President, justice will be pursued fairly, fully and impartially, no matter who is involved. This office is a sacred trust, and I am determined to be worthy of that trust . . . Who, then, is to blame for what happened in this case? For specific criminal actions by specific individuals, those who committed those actions must, of course, bear the liability and pay the penalty. For the fact that alleged improper actions took place within the White House or within my campaign organization, the easiest course would be for me to blame those to whom I delegated the responsibility to run the campaign. But that would be a cowardly thing to do. I will not place the blame on subordinates, on people whose zeal exceeded their judgment and who may have done wrong in a cause they deeply believed to be right. In any organization, the man at the top must bear the responsibility. That responsibility, therefore, belongs here in this office. I accept it. And I pledge to you tonight from this office that I will do everything in my power to insure that the guilty are brought to justice and that such abuses are purged from our political processes in the years to come, long after I have left this office.

TV-radio address to the nation, Washington,
April 30/The New York Times, 5-2:32.

5

Some people, quite properly appalled at the abuses that occurred, will say that Watergate demonstrates the bankruptcy of the American political system. I believe precisely the opposite is true. Watergate represented a series of illegal acts and bad judgments by a number of individuals. It was the system that has brought the facts to light and that will bring those guilty to justice—a system that in this case has included a determined grand jury, honest prosecutors, a courageous judge, John Sirica, and a vigorous free press. It is essential now that we place our faith in that system, and especially in the judicial system. It is essential that we let the judicial process go forward, respecting those safeguards that are established to protect the innocent as well as to convict the guilty.

TV-radio address to the nation, Washington, April 30/The New York Times, 5-2:32.

1

In any American political process, one of the most difficult tasks of all comes when charges are made against high officials in an Administration . . . Many times in the history of our country, Administrations fail to meet the test of investigating those charges that may be embarrassing to the Administration . . . We have had such a situation [with Watergate]. We have been confronted with it . . . [But] all Americans can have confidence in the fact that the new Attorney General nominee, Elliot Richardson, and a special prosecutor he will appoint will get to the bottom of this thing. They will see to it that all guilty are prosecuted and brought to justice. That is the pledge I make tonight.

At Republican fund-raising dinner, Washington, May 9/ Los Angeles Times, 5-10:(1)18.

2

Any suggestion that this President [because of Watergate] is ever going to slow down while he is President or is ever going to leave this office until he continues to do the job and finishes the job he was elected to do, anyone who suggests that, that is just plain poppycock. We are going to stay on this job until we get the job done. Because after all, you see, when we put all of the events that we read about, the things we see on television, in perspective, and then we think of the ages, we think of the world and not just our own little world, we think of the nation and not only our little part of that nation, we realize that here in this office is where the great decisions are going to be made . . . And what we were elected to do, we are going to do.

And let others wallow in Watergate; we are going to do our job.

Before White House staff, Washington, July 20/ The Washington Post, 7-21:(A)10.

3

[Saying that people are too concerned with Watergate, while the important issues of the day are being ignored]: . . . the petty, little, indecent things that seem to obsess us at a time when the world is going by . . . Let others spend their time dealing with the small, murky, unimportant, vicious things. We will spend our time building a better world.

At dinner for Japanese Prime Minister Kakuei Tanaka, Washington, July 31/ Los Angeles Times, 8-1:(1)1.

4

On May 22, I stated in very specific terms —and I state again to every one of you listening tonight—I had no prior knowledge of the Watergate operation; I neither took part in nor knew about any of the subsequent cover-up activities; I neither authorized nor encouraged subordinates to engage in illegal or improper campaign tactics. That was and is the simple truth. In all of the millions of words of testimony [at the Senate Watergate hearings], there is not the slightest suggestion that I had any knowledge of the planning for the Watergate break-in. As for the coverup, my statement has been challenged by only one of the 35 witnesses who appeared [former Presidential Counsel John Dean]—a witness who offered no evidence beyond his own impressions, and whose testimony has been contradicted by every other witness in a position to know the facts.

Broadcast address to the nation, Washington, Aug. 15/Los Angeles Times, 8-16:(1)20.

5

After 12 weeks and 2 million words of televised testimony [at the Senate Watergate hearings], we have reached a point at which a continued, backward-looking obsession with Watergate is causing this nation to neglect matters of far greater importance to all of the American people. We must not stay so mired in Watergate that we fail to respond to chal-

(RICHARD M. NIXON)

lenges of surpassing importance to America and the world. We cannot let an obsession with the past destroy our hopes for the future . . . Either we, your elected representatives here in Washington, ought to get on with the jobs that need to be done—for you—or every one of you ought to be demanding to know why. The time has come to turn Watergate over to the courts, where the questions of guilt or innocence belong. The time has come for the rest of us to get on with the urgent business of our nation.

Broadcast address to the nation, Washington, Aug. 15/Los Angeles Times, 8-16:(1)20.

1

As we look at Watergate in a longer perspective, we can see that its abuses resulted from the assumption by those involved that their cause placed them beyond the reach of those rules that hold a free society together. That attitude can never be tolerated in this country. However, it did not suddenly develop in 1972. It became fashionable in the 1960s, as individuals and groups increasingly asserted the right to take the law into their own hands, insisting that their purposes represented a higher morality. Then, their attitude was praised in the press and from some of our pulpits as evidence of a new idealism. Those who insisted on the old restraints, and who warned of the overriding importance of operating within the law and by the rules, were accused of being reactionaries. That same attitude brought a rising spiral of violence and fear, of riots and arson and bombings, all in the name of peace and justice. Political discussion turned into savage debate. Free speech was brutally suppressed as hecklers shouted down or even physically assaulted those with whom they disagreed. Serious people raised questions about whether we could survive as a free democracy. The notion that the end justifies the means proved contagious. Thus it is not surprising, even though it is deplorable, that some persons in 1972 adopted the morality that they themselves had rightly condemned, and committed acts that have no place in our political system . . . We must recognize that one excess begets another, and that the extremes of violence and discord in the 1960s contributed to the extremes of Watergate. Both are wrong. Both should be condemned. No individual, no group and no political party has a corner on the market on morality in America.

Broadcast address to the nation, Washington, Aug. 15/Los Angeles Times, 8-16:(1)20.

2

[On his refusal to turn over to investigators White House tapes related to Watergate]: . . . a much more important principle is involved in this question than what the tapes might prove about Watergate. Every day a President of the United States is required to make difficult decisions on grave issues. It is absolutely necessary, if the President is to be able to do his job as the country expects, that he be able to talk openly and candidly with his advisers about issues and individuals. This kind of frank discussion is only possible when those who take part in it know that what they say is in strictest confidence . . . If I were to make public these tapes, containing blunt and candid remarks on many different subjects, the confidentiality of the office of the President would always be suspect. It would make no difference whether it was to serve the interests of a court, of a Senate Committee or the President himself—the same damage would be done to the principle, and it would be irreparable. Persons talking with a President would never again be sure that recordings or notes of what they said would not suddenly be made public. No one would want to advance tentative ideas that might later seem unsound. No diplomat would want to speak candidly in those sensitive negotiations which could bring peace or avoid war. No Senator would want to talk frankly about the Congressional horse-trading that might get a vital bill passed. No one would want to speak bluntly about public figures here and abroad. That is why I shall continue to oppose efforts which would set a precedent that would cripple all future Presidents by inhibiting conversations between them and those they look to for advice. This principle of confidentiality of Presidential conversations is at stake in the question of the tapes. I must and shall oppose any efforts to destroy this principle, which is so vital to the conduct of the Presidency.

Broadcast address to the nation, Washington, Aug. 15/Los Angeles Times, 8-16:(1)20.

1

Watergate is an episode that I deeply deplore; and had I been running the [1972 Presidential] campaign rather than trying to run the country, and particularly the foreign policy of this country at this time, it would never have happened. But that is water under the bridge; it is gone now. The point that I make now is that we are proceeding as best we know how to get all those guilty brought to justice in Watergate; but now we must move on from Watergate to the business of the people . . . I shall not resign. I have 3½ years to go, or almost 3½ years. And I am going to use every day of those 3½ years trying to get the people of the United States to recognize that, whatever mistakes we have made, that in the long run this Administration, by making this world safer for their children, and this Administration, by making their lives better at home for themselves and their children, deserves high marks rather than low marks.

News conference, San Clemente, Calif., Aug. 22/The National Observer, 9-1:6.

2

[On his firing of special Watergate prosecutor Archibald Cox]: The matter of the [Watergate-related White House] tapes has been one that has concerned me because of my feeling that I have a Constitutional responsibility to defend the office of the Presidency from any encroachments on confidentiality which might affect future Presidents in their abilities to conduct the kind of conversations and discussions they need to conduct to carry on the responsibilities of this office. And of course, the special prosecutor felt that he needed the tapes for the purpose of his prosecution. That was why, working with the Attorney General [Richardson], we worked out what we thought was an acceptable compromise—one in which . . . Senator [John] Stennis would hear the tapes and would provide a complete and full disclosure not

only to judge Sirica but also to the Senate [Watergate] Committee. Attorney General Richardson approved this proposition, Senator [Howard] Baker, Senator [Sam] Ervin approved of the proposition. Mr. Cox was the only one that rejected it. Under the circumstances, when he rejected it and indicated that, despite the approval of the Attorney General, of course of the President, and of the two major Senators on the Ervin Committee, when he rejected the proposal, I had no choice but to dismiss him.

News conference, Washington, Oct. 26/The New York Times, 10-27:14.

3

Next week the Acting Attorney General, Mr. Bork, will appoint a new special prosecutor [succeeding Archibald Cox, who was fired by the President] for what is called the Watergate matter. The special prosecutor will have independence, he will have total cooperation from the Executive Branch, and he will have as his primary responsibility to bring this matter which has so long concerned the American people—bring it to an expeditious conclusion. Because we have to remember that under our Constitution it has always been held that justice delayed is justice denied, it's time for those who are guilty to be prosecuted and for those who are innocent to be cleared. And I can assure you, ladies and gentlemen and all our listeners tonight, that I have no greater interest than to see that the new special prosecutor has the cooperation from the Executive Branch and the independence that he needs to bring about that conclusion.

News conference, Washington, Oct. 26/The New York Times, 10-27:14.

4

As a result of the deplorable Watergate matter, great numbers of Americans have had doubts raised as to the integrity of the President of the United States. I've even noted that some publications have called on me to resign the office of President of the United States. Tonight I would like to give my answer to those who have suggested that I resign. I have no intention whatever of walk-

(RICHARD M. NIXON)

ing away from the job I was elected to do. As long as I am physically able, I am going to continue to work 16 to 18 hours a day for the cause of a real peace abroad, and for the cause of prosperity, without inflation and without war, at home. And in the months ahead, I shall do everything that I can to see that any doubts as to the integrity of the man who occupies the highest office in this land —to remove those doubts where they exist. And [I] am confident that, in those months ahead, the American people will come to realize that I have not violated the trust that they placed in me when they elected me as President of the United States in the past. And I pledge to you tonight that I shall always do everything that I can to be worthy of that trust in the future.

Broadcast address to the nation, Washington, Nov. 7/The New York Times, 11-8:32.

Basil A. Paterson
Vice chairman,
Democratic National Committee

1

Watergate will not elect a [Democratic] President. Watergate will not elect a Governor. Watergate won't even elect a city councilman. Issues and candidates win elections. We [Democrats] must mobilize the electorate by talking about inflation, by talking of the daily scandal faced by men and women trying to feed and clothe their families.

At Young Democrats convention,
Louisville, Ky./
The Washington Post, 8-11:(A)12.

Charles H. Percy
United States Senator, R-Illinois

2

[Advocating a special independent prosecutor to investigate the Watergate affair]: A simple and very basic question is at issue: Should the Executive Branch investigate itself? I do not think so, and neither, I am convinced, do a majority of my colleagues. In introducing this resolution [calling on President Nixon to name a special prosecutor], I

am not attempting in any way to question the integrity or ability of Attorney General-designate Elliot Richardson, a distinguished public servant for whom I have the highest regard. But Mr. Richardson cannot be regarded as independent of the Executive Branch of the government . . . Let us get on with the important task of governing; but let us remember that we cannot govern unless we have the support of the people. The best way of ensuring the faith and the trust of the people is to appoint a special prosecutor whose motives, actions and conclusions cannot possibly be questioned.

Washington, May 1/
The Washington Post, 5-2:(A)26.

3

Responsible Republicans believe that Watergate was reprehensible and that it is wrong to try to whitewash it by pointing to the instances of excesses or misdeeds on the part of the Democrats . . . We must exercise absolute restraint in what we infer from the actions taken by others until we have absolute proof. But this should never deter us. However the chips may fall, this ship of state is strong enough to survive any kind of storm. And we will come out the better for it if we go about the process deliberately, dispassionately and with thoroughness and care.

Washington/
The Christian Science Monitor, 5-11:1.

4

The stark facts about the President's [Nixon] position with respect to Watergate would seem to be these: either he was completely unaware of activities being carried out in his name and ostensibly directed by some of his closest subordinates, or else he knew about them and at least did not express his disapproval. Neither of these choices can be contemplated without dismay. But if there is a logical alternative, it is the President's responsibility to make it known to us.

At Knox College commencement,
Galesburg, Ill., June 2/
The New York Times, 6-3:(1)45.

5

The Congress cannot dictate to the President [Nixon] the way to handle Watergate.

We can only offer advice and apply pressure, both public and private, to reach the desired result. That is our prerogative and duty. But to suggest that, because of the exigencies of the times, we can force the President to take the witness stand in the Senate Caucus Room is once again to say that the end justifies the means. We should have had our fill of that type of thinking by now.

Before the Senate, Washington,
June 25/The Washington Post, 6-25:(A)15.

1

We know that, as a result of Watergate and the surrounding events, the Republican Party has been wounded and stands ready to be hurt even mor seriously in the elections of 1974. That is t a pretty prospect; and I for one feel it is not a fair one. Those men responsible for Watergate will have their own crosses to bear in the months and years to come. But those of us in the regular Republican organization are going to have to answer for their mistakes, because the American public is going to hold us, to some degree, guilty by association.

Before Kansas Republicans, Wichita/
T. e Dallas Times Herald, 9-10:(C)3.

Howard Phillips
Former Acting Director,
Federal Office of Economic Opportunity

2

Now that the liberal establishment has badly crippled [by exploiting the Watergate political-es: nage affair] President Nixon's capacity for leadership, their greatest fear is that Mr. Nixon might leave office soon enough for Vice President Agnew to pick up history's mandate, with the moral authority to carry forward the work which Richard Nixon began. For me, at least, this is the meaning of the charges now being directed at the Vice President [bribery and kickbacks while he was Governor of Maryland] . . . Many of the President's lifelong liberal enemies now speak openly of a scenario in which they connive to retain in office an emasculated Richard Nixon, divested of real power, yet permitted to enjoy the trappings and ceremony of Presidential

office, while they are free to grasp the substance of power, awaiting and plotting the arrival of a new liberal reign in 1976. Richard Nixon is too much a patriot and a man of integrity to let that scenario unfold. He cares too much for our system of checks and balances to let the institution of the Presidency become an empty ceremonial shell. If he determines that he is unable to resume effective leadership in both domestic and foreign policy—with his appointees accountable to his authority—I am convinced that he would resign rather than permit himself to become the helpless pawn of his enemies or the cause of grave systemic damage.

Before Young Americans for Freedom,
Washington/The New York Times, 9-4:33.

William Proxmire
United States Senator, D-Wisconsin

3

[On the Watergate political-espionage affair]: When former White House Counsel John Dean is reported throughout this country to have privately told the grand-jury investigators that the President [Nixon] was directly involved in a Watergate cover-up, President Nixon is being tried, sentenced and executed by rumor and allegation. As the Senator who succeeded Joe McCarthy in the United States Senate, I find this kind of persecution and condemnation without trial McCarthyism at its worst . . . Doesn't the President have the same right [that] every other American has to be innocent until proven guilty? Doesn't a man who has spent more than 20 years in the pitiless glare at the summit of national political life deserve to be believed when he directly tells the nation that he had no knowledge of these matters, until there is proof that he lied? Doesn't he deserve at least this measure of faith until proven a liar?

Before the Senate, Washington, May 8/
Los Angeles Herald-Examiner, 5-8:(A)2.

Ronald Reagan
Governor of California

4

[On a poll showing much of the public thinks President Nixon had advance knowl-

(RONALD REAGAN)

edge of Watergate]: That is a tribute and a testimonial to the ability of those who have been doing their best to blow this and carry it as far along as to the next election as they can . . . This will involve elements of the communications media. This will involve representatives of the Senate Investigating Committee. They have got hold of a good thing from their standpoint.

News conference, Sacramento, April 24/
Los Angeles Times, 4-25:(1)8.

1

They [those responsible for Watergate] did something that was stupid and foolish and was criminal—it was illegal. Illegal is a better word than criminal, because I think criminal has a different connotation. I think the tragedy of this is that men who are not criminals at heart, and certainly not engaged in criminal activities, committed a criminal or illegal act and now must bear the consequences. These are men whose lives are being very much changed by this. I doubt if any of them would even intentionally double-park.

News conference, Sacramento, May 1/
Los Angeles Times, 5-2:(1)25.

Harry Reasoner
News commentator,
American Broadcasting Company

2

[Comparing Watergate with previous political scandals]: I suggest that this is the first documented time when the felonies and the lies were perpetrated for reasons of ideology rather than greed. So far as we know so far, no individual was stealing money; these men, up to a high level, were breaking and entering and perjuring to achieve what they believed to be something good for the country—the destruction of the Democratic Party, maybe, or the establishment of some general kind of thought control. You can sort of understand President Harding's Interior Secretary, Albert Fall—he [in the Teapot Dome scandal] wanted money; and human greed, if not acceptable in high office, is, at least, not a novelty. But

what apparently has motivated the men in this [Nixon] Administration was a deep desire to eliminate the untidiness of the American system—the slovenly tolerance of a loud opposition and a free press, the permission that the Founding Fathers carelessly gave the people to hold wrong opinions. That is what is dangerous. [Convicted Watergate conspirator] E. Howard Hunt, pleading guilty to a felony, said, "Anything I have done I believe was in the best interest of my country." This is scary.

News commentary,
American Broadcasting Company, May 2/
The Christian Science Monitor, 5-12:16.

Henry S. Reuss
United States Representative, D-Wisconsin

3

The plain fact is that [President] Nixon, whatever his involvement in the Watergate, has presided over a corrupt government. The plain fact is that he has waited an unconscionably long time to do anything about it. A third plain fact is that he has forfeited public confidence. Since he has accepted full responsibility for his Administration, Mr. Nixon should consider resigning for the good of the country. As a member of that Administration, so should [Vice President] Agnew, though there is no suggestion of his implication in the Watergate.

May 11/
Los Angeles Herald-Examiner, 5-12:(A)2.

John J. Rhodes
United States Representative, R-Arizona

4

I can't imagine the Republican members of the House or Senate really panicking because of what they might deem to be an adverse atmosphere caused by Watergate. Watergate, I still think, in the long run will prove to have been a possibly passing thing and not a permanent thing insofar as the body politic of this country is concerned.

TV-radio interview/"Face the Nation,"
Columbia Broadcasting System, 12-23.

Elliot L. Richardson
*Former Attorney General
of the United States*

1

[On his quitting as Attorney General in response to President Nixon's firing of Watergate special prosecutor Archibald Cox over the Watergate tapes affair]: At stake in the final analysis is the very integrity of the governmental process I came to the Department of Justice to help restore. My own single most important commitment to this objective was my commitment to the independence of the special prosecutor. I could not be faithful to this commitment and also acquiesce in the curtailment of his authority. To say this, however, is not to charge the President with a failure to respect the claims of the investigative process; given the importance he attached to the principle of Presidential confidentiality, he believed that his willingness to allow Senator [John] Stennis to verify the subpoenaed tapes fully met these claims. The rest is for the American people to judge. On the fairness with which you do so may well rest the future well-being and security of our beloved country.

*News conference, Washington, Oct. 23/
Los Angeles Times, 10-24:(1)12.*

2

Behind the layers of secrecy successively peeled back by persistent investigation [of Watergate], we caught an ugly glimpse of the abuse of power. It has been a frightening glimpse, not so much for what it reveals as for what it portends. The significant point, it seems to me, is this: Even if the evils of Watergate were assumed to be no worse than the kindred but unremarked acts of past Administrations, the fact that Americans now recoil from such things is a reassuring sign that our instinct of value-preservation is still alert and sensitive. Just as in a simpler age our forebears came to realize that they could no longer tolerate robber barons, we have come to realize that we can no longer tolerate the embezzlement of political trust.

*At Appeal of Conscience Foundation
dinner, New York, Dec. 11/
The New York Times, 12-12:30.*

Samuel I. Rosenman
*Former Special Counsel to Presidents
Franklin Roosevelt and Harry Truman*

3

[On the Watergate political-espionage affair]: If the Watergate had happened in England or Canada, this government would have had to resign, and there would have to have been another election. There should be some remedy here where elections can be shown by legal evidence to have been so permeated by illegalities that you can't tell how the voters may have voted without the fraud. The thing that made me throw up more violently than anything else was listening to [President] Nixon suggest that this kind of corruption has always gone on in American politics. He never cited a single instance. The current scandal is stuff that goes to the very essence of the American electoral system. There have been many cases where "floaters" were used to go in and vote illegally; I grew up in a system in New York where it was almost commonplace for "floaters" to go into a voting place and cast five, ten, fifteen illegal votes. But Watergate is something which shocks the imagination. Here the whole idea was to sabotage the complete electoral process by methods which were clearly as illegal as putting in "floaters" to vote, but doing it on a gigantic scale. And these revelations are spreading! That is why I am so pessimistic about the state of the union.

*Interview, New York/
Los Angeles Times, 5-17:(2)7.*

William D. Ruckelshaus
*Acting Director,
Federal Bureau of Investigation*

4

One of the problems which Watergate elucidates is the paucity of time and thought we give to the question of public morality in this country . . . The tawdriness of current revelations should be no excuse to shun an active role in the political process. In fact, I believe it should provide further incentive and determination to alter the circumstances which led

(WILLIAM D. RUCKELSHAUS)

to the abuses.
At Ohio State University commencement/
The New York Times, 6-18:22.

Dean Rusk
Former Secretary of State
of the United States

1

[On Watergate]: I think it is very important that we Americans remind ourselves that 99-point-X per cent of the men and women in government are honorable, decent people trying to do the right job, and that we not let the malefactions of, after all, a relatively few people, even in high places, create a sense of cynicism and disillusionment about the political system itself. I think all the facts are going to come out, and I think appropriate action will be taken. What those facts will show, and what that action will be, I'm not prepared to say yet. But we must not lose confidence in this extraordinarily resilient constitutional system of ours, because it's rooted in the notion of individual freedom. And to me that's very important . . . What is important from the international point of view is that capacity of the President and the Secretary of State to speak effectively and with authority on behalf of the American people in the conduct of our foreign relations. Anything which weakens the ability of the President to do that necessarily limits what he can accomplish in his negotiations with foreign nations. So I would hope that we would get all the facts out, take the necessary action and get this business [Watergate] behind us as soon as possible so that we can get on with the public business.
Interview/The Washington Post, 8-5:(C)4.

Pierre Salinger
Former Press Secretary to the late
President John F. Kennedy

2

What disturbs me most [about Watergate] is how it portrays the mentality of these men and of Nixon himself. I've been saying for 20 years that Nixon is a haunted, paranoid man

who thinks everyone is out to get him. He was traumatized in '47 during the Hiss case; he said the liberals were out to get him. In '52 he was traumatized when his slush fund was discovered. In '60 he was traumatized because he thought the election was stolen . . . Then he got to the point where he was traumatized by one demonstrator outside the White House fence. I think all the Watergate activities—the domestic intelligence plans, the burglaries, the bugging—are just a reflection of those fears. And I think the whole scandal would have passed over if he had had the good judgment to separate himself from his political friends like [former Presidential Assistants John] Ehrlichman and [H. R.] Haldeman right away.
Interview, Washington/
"W": a Fairchild publication, 9-7:15.

Ronald A. Sarasin
United States Representative, R-Connecticut

3

No one can be very proud of what the [Senate] Watergate hearing shows. But we are learning a lesson from it—that our system of law works, and that no one is above the law, not those involved in Watergate and not those on the other side of the political spectrum who break into draft boards or steal papers from the Pentagon . . . I'm not willing to condemn the President [Nixon] at this point. I think he's entitled to the presumption of innocence that everyone's entitled to. And nobody seems to give him that. We keep waiting for him to prove his innocence. Well, that burden isn't on anyone in this country. And it isn't on him.
Before Rotary Club, Danbury, Conn./
The Washington Post, 8-12:(A)14.

William B. Saxbe
United States Senator, R-Ohio;
Attorney General-designate of the
United States

4

The big question is: Was he [President Nixon] privy to any of the machinations before Watergate or any of the cover-up after? He told me [last week], as directly as he could, that he was not. I must go into this new job [as Attorney General] with that belief. Any prejudices I had before that must be put aside. I must be objective or I can't perform the duties I [will] take an oath to perform . . . I've got to judge guilt or innocence on the basis of hard proof and not upon the basis of, "it would be normal to believe this or it would be reasonable to believe this." You can do all these things as a private citizen or even as a Senator, but you can't do this as a judge or as a prosecutor or as an Attorney General. [From a lawyer's standpoint,] there is no hard evidence of collusion, conspiracy, cover-up on the part of the President. That's what the question is.

Interview, Nov. 6/
Los Angeles Times, 11-7:(1)8.

William J. Scherle
United States Representative, R-Iowa

1

I don't think Watergate has damaged the President's standing with Republicans in Congress; nor do I think it has damaged President Nixon as a man or a President. Certainly, though, it has created a reluctance of people to feel as close to him as they did before. I don't think Congressional Republicans will necessarily want to back away from the White House. We look for more harmony, less confrontation, more compromise and certainly more accessibility to the White House. In the past, the Republican leadership would go down to the White House and were told what to do. It was all a one-way street. Now when the leadership goes down there, *they* establish the agenda. There's more harmony now; there's more agreement.

Interview/
U.S. News & World Report, 7-30:20.

Hugh Scott
United States Senator, R-Pennsylvania

2

[On the resignations of several key White House aides because of Watergate]: This is a

bad day at Credibility Gap. The lack of grace has led to a fall from grace.

Before the Senate, Washington,
April 30/Los Angeles Times, 5-1:(1)9.

3

[On former Presidential Counsel John Dean's testimony implicating President Nixon and White House aides in Watergate]: The only evidence that these people [on the Senate Watergate Committee] are deducing is the statement of non-corroborated self-confessed felon "honest" John Dean, a statement which will not be corroborated by anyone else, in my judgment, in the court . . . It is an attempt to get the President on the basis of this little rat [Dean] seeking to find some way to reduce the [Watergate] penalty upon himself.

At dinner for Representative Robert McClory,
Waukegan, Ill., July 13/
The Washington Post, 7-15:(A)11.

Eric Sevareid
News commentator,
Columbia Broadcasting System

4

200 years of this republic show just four outbreaks of major scandal in the Federal Executive: patronage scandals in Jackson's time; the corruption of Grant's time; of Harding's time; and now Watergate and associated crimes and misdemeanors. Oddly, these infections occurred almost exactly 50 years apart. If that's significant, then virtue should be blossoming around here the rest of this century. But we may never go back to the old-fashioned concepts of governmental virtue. Big-power status has changed much. In 1929, Secretary of State Stimson indignantly rebuffed the idea of espionage or counter-espionage. Gentlemen, he said, do not read other people's mail.

Commentary,
Columbia Broadcasting System, May 10/
The Christian Science Monitor, 5-24:14.

5

It is hardly debatable any longer that this law-and-order Administration has turned out to be as lawless as any on record, and perhaps it already holds the record. The Nixon Presi-

(ERIC SEVAREID)

dency will be discussed for decades, not only because of its policy judgments good and bad, but also because of this President's judgments of other human beings. Maybe the psychologists can help the historians figure out why Mr. Nixon was attracted to these kinds of men [his aides involved in Watergate], and why these kinds of men were attracted to Mr. Nixon. The body count is already far too high to be explained by happenstance or ill luck.

Commentary,
Columbia Broadcasting System, Oct. 11/
The Christian Science Monitor, 10-17:20.

R. Sargent Shriver
1972 Democratic Vice-Presidential nominee

1

[Saying President Nixon should resign because of Watergate]: [His] resignation might be the greatest single contribution he could make to this country's well-being. The higher patriotism asks more of us than that we rally to the support of a discredited President. It asks instead that we restore the credibility of our leadership even if that means a change of leaders.

The Christian Science Monitor, 5-21:1.

John J. Sirica
Chief Judge, United States District Court
for the District of Columbia

2

[On President Nixon's refusal to turn over to the court Watergate-related tapes and documents]: In all candor, the court fails to perceive any reason for suspending the power of courts to get evidence and rule on questions of privilege in criminal matters simply because it is the President of the United States who holds the evidence.

Aug. 29/
The Christian Science Monitor, 9-15:14.

Chesterfield Smith
President, American Bar Association

3

[Saying a Congressional impeachment investigation should be instituted against Presi-

dent Nixon rather than calls for Nixon to resign]: A forced resignation of the President could only leave within the breasts of many of our people a feeling that perhaps evidence sufficient to justify impeachment was not really here and that the whole affair was nothing more than a political assassination . . . It is my personal position that there can be no matter more important to us on the domestic scene, nor more detrimental to our foreign relations, than a continuation of this political never-never land where a majority of our citizens do not believe the President and suspect his motives and every move he makes.

Before American Life Insurance Association,
Washington, Nov. 27/
The New York Times, 11-28:34.

Howard K. Smith
News commentator,
American Broadcasting Company

4

Watergate was immoral and illegal. But what has mystified most is, it was unnecessary. [President] Nixon was likely to win [the 1972 election] easily. So, why swat a fly with a cannon? Trying to answer this for myself, I have settled on three explanations: One, we forget the atmosphere when the plans were laid. Cities had been afire, campuses out of control, American flags burned by demonstrators. Some conservatives felt the nation was far on the way to subversion. They felt justified, indeed duty-bound, to fight fire with fire, to spy on and sabotage those they considered dupes of subversives. Two, in the 1960 Presidential election, Nixon took defeat with grace. But many ardent supporters felt it had been stolen by what they called the ruthless Kennedy organization, allegedly faking the few thousand votes that carried Texas and Illinois. When the Watergate plans were laid, they firmly expected another Kennedy—Ted —would be their opponent in 1976. This time, they were resolved to excel in ruthlessness. Three, money. Most campaigns are hand-to-mouth. This one overflowed with money—a temptation that seemed almost a command to do the dirty work big. Once the resulting, elaborate machinery began moving, like the German Army mobilizing in 1914, it couldn't be stopped. It developed a life of its own, though the target had now become a beatable [George] McGovern. These thoughts justify nothing. But they explain an otherwise inexplicable, useless, self-defeating scandal.

News commentary,
American Broadcasting Company, May 4/
The Christian Science Monitor, 5-22:(B)12.

Maurice H. Stans
1972 chairman, Finance Committee
to Re-elect the President (Nixon)

1

In the course of all the things that have happened since June 17 [of 1972, the date of the Watergate break-in], a lot of innocent people have been drawn through the mire of unrelenting publicity, insinuations, accusations. There have been very damaging effects on their business and on their personal lives. It is very unfair; somebody has got to speak up for those people. So when the Committee concludes its work and writes its report, I hope it will make it clear that such people, and by name, are innocent victims of this tragedy. I put myself in that category. I volunteered or was drafted, whatever the case may be, because I believed in my President. You know by now from what you have heard, but I know you cannot feel, the abuse to which I have been subjected because of the association I fell into. All I ask, Mr. Chairman and members of the Committee, is that, when you write your report, you give me back my good name.

At Senate Watergate hearings,
Washington, June 13/
The New York Times, 6-14:41.

Fortney H. Stark
United States Representative, D-California

2

[Saying President Nixon might stage a military coup in order to remain in power if it was proved he was involved in Watergate wrongdoing]: Considering the President's irrational behavior and the existence of an aristocratic military elite in this country, it is not inconceivable that a military takeover could be attempted. The President could easily manufacture an "extreme national emergency," tell his Generals to take command, and send Congress and the Supreme Court packing.

Before Supervisors Association of Naval
Air Rework Facility at Alameda (Calif.)
Naval Air Station, Nov. 2/
Los Angeles Herald-Examiner, 11-4:(A)2.

Adlai E. Stevenson III
United States Senator, R-Illinois

3

[Expressing concern about the independence of President Nixon's new choice for special Watergate prosecutor, Leon Jaworski, after the President's firing of Archibald Cox]: I don't know what terms were offered Mr. Jaworski, but it would be unwise to depend on them as we did before. I keep thinking of the immortal words of Zsa Zsa Gabor at the beginning of one of her innumerable marriages: "This time, darling, it's for real." That's what the President is saying: "This time, darling, it's for real."

Nov. 1/Los Angeles Times, 11-2:(1)6.

Robert S. Strauss
Chairman,
Democratic National Committee

4

Everyone is tired of Watergate, and we're ashamed more than we're tired. The things that shame us we don't want to hear about. But on the other hand, the people want to know that the system works and the truth will come out. Unfortunately, the President [Nixon] and some of his people have done this thing sort of like a strip show: They take off one tiny thing at a time and keep the public's eyes glued on the stage. If they had just come forward and told the story, the American public would forgive the sins of omission and commission. The American public is very forgiving of the Presidency; they want to forgive him and get on to solving some of their problems . . . The country needs some kind of restoration of confidence in this President, and it can't have it until the

(ROBERT S. STRAUSS)

President goes to the people. Even though I have the most partisan job in the world as chairman of the party out of power, my first concern is my country.

Interview, Dallas, Aug. 25/
The Dallas Times Herald, 8-26:(A)36.

Barbara Tuchman
Author, Historian

1

If the people involved in Watergate go uncorrected, then clearly such people will have the go-ahead in the next Administration. There will be more operators, detectives and big-shot lawyers on future Presidential staffs. If, for the sake of avoiding a hornet's nest, we let the Nixon Administration finish its term, then all the revelations on Watergate will be meaningless. What are we prepared to let our government get away with?

Interview/
"W": a Fairchild publication, 9-21:16.

John V. Tunney
United States Senator, D-California

2

I do not look at it [Watergate] as a partisan issue. The men who were involved happened to be Republicans. Actually, they are just power-mad, arrogant individuals—outlaws. The Democrats have a lot of outlaws, too.

Washington, May 1/
Los Angeles Times, 5-2:(1)24.

3

He [President Nixon] must leave office for the common good. The people do not believe him, and he has shamed them. Our country simply cannot sustain three more years of such distrust, despair and disillusionment. The mystical bond that unites the governed with the governor has been severed. In the name of common decency, Mr. Nixon should put his nation ahead of himself and step aside so that the process of national renewal and revitalization can begin.

Before the Senate, Washington, Oct. 30/
The New York Times, 10-31:30.

Jerome R. Waldie
United States Representative, D-California

4

There's no way [President] Nixon's credibility and integrity can ever be restored [as a result of Watergate]. He will be enormously crippled for the rest of his term, and that's a tragedy for him and the country.

April 30/Los Angeles Times, 5-1:(1)9.

Ben J. Wattenberg
Political analyst

5

What does Watergate really mean? Take the paralysis-of-government argument: He [President Nixon] can't function; he's already through. And yet, meanwhile, the bombs are falling in Cambodia, the Census Bureau is functioning, they're collecting our taxes, they're still delivering the mail late—you know, everything goes on. Also, the comparison has been made with Harding. Now, this is very, very unfair: Harding was a do-nothing, nothing President. Nixon, as much as I might want to begrudge it, has done some monumental things in the last few years. And the idea that Richard Nixon is going to be remembered for [Presidential aides H. R.] Haldeman and [John] Ehrlichman and a bunch of creeps who bugged the Watergate—when he also ended the [Vietnam] war and established relations with [Communist] China and Russia and set up the SALT treaty—is unlikely. This guy has been a historic President, like it or not.

At discussion on Watergate, Washington/
The Washington Post, 5-20:(C)4.

Lowell P. Weicker, Jr.
United States Senator, R-Connecticut;
Member, Senate Watergate Committee

6

[Specific violation of the law] is not the only issue involved [in Watergate], although some people in the [Nixon] Administration would like to have it drawn that way as narrowly as possible. It's just as bad in my book for certain persons at the Presidential level to condone illegal practices . . . I don't give a damn if there's a law on the books against it or not . . . Do I have a broader picture that I am trying to substantiate? The answer is yes. Do I think it goes beyond Watergate? The answer is yes. Somebody had to start it. Somebody had to abet it. [Watergate defendants E. Howard] Hunt and [G. Gordon] Liddy and [James W.] McCord, et al, didn't just get together in a barroom one night and decide they were going to do something gratuitous for the Republican Party.

News conference, Washington,
March 26/
The Washington Post,
3-27:(A)10.

1

The polls show that the American people think something like Watergate goes on all the time in politics. Well, the hell it does. It doesn't go on all the time. Politics is my profession, and I'm proud of it. This has been my life, for God's sake, since 1960, and in every conceivable race—state legislature, Mayor, Congressman, Senator. And this Watergate thing is totally new to me. It's absolutely necessary that we restore faith in the political system.

Washington/
Los Angeles Times, 4-22:(1)13.

2

[Saying Watergate should not reflect negatively on Republicans in general]: . . . I'm here as a Republican, and I think I express the feelings of the 42 other Republican Senators and the Republicans of Connecticut and the feelings of the Republican Party far better than those who committed illegal, un-Constitutional and gross acts. Republicans do not cover up. Republicans do not go ahead and threaten. Republicans do not go ahead and commit illegal acts. And God knows, Republicans don't view their fellow Americans as enemies to be harassed. But rather, I can assure you that this Republican, and those that I serve with, look upon every American as a human being to be loved and won.

At Senate Watergate hearings,
Washington, June 28/
The New York Times, 6-29:26.

Gough Whitlam
Prime Minister of Australia

3

I realize that the American President [Nixon] and the American Presidency would not be in their present parlous position [because of Watergate] if the present President were to have regular press conferences as the present Australian Prime Minister does, and if the American Administration were answerable to the American Congress as the Australian government is answerable to the Australian Parliament.

Before Parliament, Canberra/
Los Angeles Times, 6-1:(1)17.

Aaron Wildavsky
Dean, Graduate School of Public Policy,
University of California, Berkeley

4

Among people in public administration, it has been usually fashionable to denigrate bureaucratic loyalties as absolutely the worst kind of thing. You know: "They're parochial. They love their bureau. They don't care about anything else." But in Watergate, the people who stood up best were those in the Justice Department, the FBI, the CIA who felt strongly about their agencies, who could think of themselves as surrounded by colleagues who had a code of professional behavior. Those who did worst were the faceless, bright young men of the Nixon Administration, who revered a Presidential figure at some distance, but seemingly had no church, no family, no sense of values. So they had to be taught, and the [Watergate Committee] Senators gave them little sermons: "Young man, don't you understand that what you did was terrible?" And obviously they did not so understand, or they would not have done it.

Panel discussion, New Orleans/
The Washington Post, 9-16:(C)4.

John J. Williams
Former United States Senator,
R-Delaware

5

Corruption can over-shadow. [President]

(JOHN J. WILLIAMS)

Nixon has done a good job in many areas—terrific in getting out of Vietnam. I think people feel that. But something like Watergate can detract from the good he has done. Sometimes people remember something like this long after they forget the good. That is unfortunate, but that is life. The Truman Administration went down in history as a corrupt Administration, yet I never found anything wrong that he or members of his family were involved in or that he or members of his family ever profited from any wrong-doing. Yet, it was Truman's failure to take forceful action or cooperate more freely with Congress that caused him to get tagged with a corrupt Administration. History has shown that always this has happened. I hope this [Nixon] Administration will heed the lessons of history. If they don't, they can go down with a comparable rating with those others who have ignored the lesson.

Interview,
Millsboro, Del./
Los Angeles Times, 4-2:(2)7.

Ralph D. Abernathy
President,
Southern Christian Leadership Conference

1

Lockheed [Aircraft Corp.] is on welfare; the banks, the oil companies, the non-tax-payers, IT&T all are on welfare. But when the poor get money, it is "welfare"; when the rich get government money, it is "Federal subsidies."

Lecture, University of San Francisco,
March 6/San Francisco Examiner, 3-7:16.

Spiro T. Agnew
Vice President of the United States

2

[Urging more supervision of legal-assistance attorneys]: A poverty lawyer, after all, is a person in that community who has no public accountability—such as an elected official has —and who receives his money from Washington. At the same time, he receives no direction from Washington, because the very nature of his legal function makes it necessary that he be independent. So what you have is publicly-funded social activism without public responsibility.

Television interview/
U.S. News & World Report, 1-29:47.

3

Humanitarianism and social concern are not measured by the sheer number of public programs and dollars that are committed, but by results—by improvements in the lot of the poor and disadvantaged—not by improvements in the lot of the self-appointed political activists who claim to be their saviors.

Before Suffolk County Republicans,
Hauppauge, N.Y., March 29/
The New York Times, 3-30:18.

Carl Albert
United States Representative, D-Oklahoma

4

[On President Nixon's cut-backs in Federal spending for the poor and elderly]: Congress will not tolerate the callous attitude of an Administration that seems to have no compassion for the down-and-out citizens of this country . . . It is apparent that big business will not suffer from the Nixon budget cuts. The rich won't suffer, either. [Instead,] you, the average American taxpayer . . . will continue to pay a disproportionately large share of your income in Federal taxes while getting fewer Federal services in return. The American people deserve far more; this nation, if it is to survive, requires far more . . . [The recently-announced Nixon budget] certainly does not point us toward a brighter tomorrow. It is a budget without a sense of the affirmative. It is a budget with its hands in its pockets and its eyes on the ground.

Radio address, Feb. 11/
The Washington Post, 2-12:(A)18;
Los Angeles Times, 2-12:(1)4.

Robert M. Ball
Commissioner, Social Security
Administration of the United States

5

What I hope and expect is that, whatever changes are made [in the Social Security System] will be made within the framework of the proven principles of a work-related contributory insurance system. Social Security is not just another government program raising money through taxes and then separately determining what benefits should be paid out. We need to look at the system of contributions and benefits together as a single system. It just is not right to attack the program because it is not financed through progressive

(ROBERT M. BALL)

taxes. If you are going to continue the values of a contributory system, people have to contribute to it.

Before Commonwealth Club,
San Francisco, Jan. 5/
San Francisco Examiner, 1-6:5.

1

Social Security is not an annuity. It is insurance against the loss of earned income. It is one of those simple social inventions that has changed the world.

Before Senate Committee on Aging,
Washington, Jan. 15/
San Francisco Examiner, 1-16:2.

E. Clinton Bamberger
Dean of Law,
Catholic University of America

2

[Arguing against increased government supervision of poverty-program attorneys as suggested by Vice President Agnew]: Mr. Agnew's suggestion would lead to socialization of the legal profession. It is up to the local board to decide what types of cases to handle. From then on, it is strictly a matter between the lawyer and his client; and no government official, or anybody else, has the right to interfere with that relationship. That's the way it works for the rich, and that's the way it should work for the poor.

U.S. News & World Report, 1-29:47.

Clark W. Blackburn
General director,
Family Service Association of America

3

The day of taking the family for granted should be drawn to a close. We must consider what we can do as a united effort to help all families in a program of family development. We have more than three centuries of marriage and divorce history behind us now. Surely the time has come when all social legislation, including, for example, income-tax structures, Social Security benefits, medical-care programs, housing supplements, retirement bene-

fits, be re-evaluated in the light of supporting the family as an essential social institution and one of our greatest national assets.

Interview, New York/
San Francisco Examiner & Chronicle,
3-18:(Sunday Scene)15.

Robert B. Carleson
Commissioner of Welfare
of the United States

4

. . . the original concept of welfare in this country was to assist the aged, the blind, the disabled, and primarily the children and the people who were helpless, who were either orphans, or part orphans, and their mothers who would have to care for them. In other words, it would help those people who were really incapable of helping themselves. And what has happened is that, over the years, through a combination of statutes that have been changed both at the Federal and state level and regulations that have been adopted, we've gotten to the point now where the welfare system is trying to take care of a lot of people who really were not meant to be cared for in the first place, many of whom are capable of helping themselves whether entirely or partially. So I think what really has to be done to reform the welfare system is to tighten up the eligibility requirements to insure that only those who are really in need are eligible for welfare and to require those people who have obligations to meet those obligations.

Interview/Human Events, 4-28:12.

Richard J. Daley
Mayor of Chicago

5

I hope Congress will set day-care as a priority. It is much more productive than aid to dependent children. I don't think President Nixon understood the problem or he wouldn't have vetoed child-care. I think sometimes the President is poorly advised. The war on poverty, even if not a whopping success, did a lot. The programs I like are day-care, pre-school, bi-lingual programs for Spanish-speaking, helping assistants to work in education, and taking care of senior citizens, helping them to enjoy life. If there is no help for that, what is government for?

San Francisco/
U.S. News & World Report, 7-2:66.

Frederick B. Dent
Secretary of Commerce of the United States

1

[On criticism of Nixon Administration cut-backs in some social programs]: Special interest groups, which have a vested interest in the Federal largesse involved, are bombarding the public with sob stories proclaiming that each and every program labeled "anti-poverty" is responsible for keeping the United States from burning down for the last four summers. Aside from the ugly, threatening implications of such charges, they [the anti-poverty "middlemen" in the government bureaucracy] are attempting to mislead the American people on the ability of programs to perform effectively to help the poor. This Administration rejects the new "trickle-down" theory that, if we provide funds for the anti-poverty middlemen, benefits will "trickle down" to those truly in need.

Before American Society of Association
Executives, Washington, March 20/
The New York Times, 3-21:21.

Gerald R. Ford
United States Representative, R-Michigan

2

If you take a good look at welfare legislation, you will see that it is a guaranteed annual income for idleness.

Before Potato Chip Institute
International, San Francisco, Jan. 29/
San Francisco Examiner, 1-30:9.

John W. Gardner
Chairman, Common Cause

3

[On government social programs]: We have a tendency now to leap into something with tremendous enthusiasm—no planning, no experimentation—and spend a tremendous amount of money, and then go into a kind of

tailspin when it doesn't work immediately. And we're like moody children: we're enthusiastic and then we're terribly pessimistic.

The Washington Post, 4-8:(A)20.

Kermit Gordon
President, Brookings Institution

4

If you're focusing on efforts to improve economic conditions of those at the bottom of the pile, the most effective, but not exhaustive, device is sustained prosperity and high demand for labor. Now, this has nothing to do with aid to education or the poverty program or anything else . . . Just look at what happened in the 1960s to the proportion of the population below the poverty line—an enormous drop from over 40 million, I think, to about 24 million. Well, the poverty program and improvements in the welfare system and Social Security were all minor factors; but the major and overwhelmingly important factor was a strong demand for labor . . . This is kind of a social solvent whose power is unmatched by any categorical type of government program.

The Washington Post, 4-8:(A)20.

Richard G. Hatcher
Mayor of Gary, Ind.

5

. . . as a moral and practical matter, our society cannot raise the expectations of the down-trodden in this nation and then dash those expectations. In so doing, this society would be daring an understandably desperate people. It would be inviting them to abandon what little hope they have in our system of laws. It would be taking a reckless gamble with the stability of this nation.

Before Senate Intergovernmental Relations
Subcommittee, Washington, Feb. 21/
The New York Times, 2-22:20.

Harold E. Hughes
United States Senator, D-Iowa

6

[Criticizing Nixon Administration budget cuts in poverty and health programs]: The little old lady eating a boiled egg in a room

(HAROLD E. HUGHES)

. . . the children, the poor, the disabled, the handicapped, the alcoholic, the drug addict —they are the people the Administration thinks are contributing to inflation in this country.

Before the Senate, Washington, Feb. 8/
The Washington Post, 2-9:(A)1.

Hubert H. Humphrey
United States Senator, D-Minnesota

1

[On the Senate's sustaining President Nixon's veto of a $2.6 billion bill for rehabilitating the handicapped]: [It's] just a goddamned outrage, a national shame. I'm ashamed to be in the Congress. Mr. Nixon with his mandate has declared war on the maimed. It's a day of infamy for the White House.

Washington, April 3/
The Dallas Times Herald, 4-4:(A)4.

Vernon E. Jordan, Jr.
Executive director, National Urban League

2

Our nation's leaders must know that they represent not only corporations, but welfare mothers; not only labor unions, but the unorganized unemployed; not only big farm owners, but migrant workers. Black people in this hard and crucial time need to be heard, need to be dealt with as equals, need to fully participate in the decisions that determine our survival. The black ghetto is as fitting a place for negotiation as the Kremlin. The Chicago slum is as fitting a place for a Presidential visit as the Great Wall of China. The Indian reservation is as fitting a place for a politician's concern as Hanoi.

Quote, 1-7:15.

3

[Criticizing Federal budget cutbacks for social programs]: I would hate to have to explain to a poor black family in Bedford-Stuyvesant that's chained to an over-crowded slum apartment because of the housing-subsidy freeze that this is really the best of all possible worlds. I would hate to have to explain to a poor black farm worker in Mississippi that the record gross national product means he's living in a golden era. And I would hate to have to explain to an unemployed Vietnam veteran who can no longer enter a Federal manpower-training program that he is being adequately repaid for his sacrifices. Life in 1973 may be better for some people, but it is not better for black Americans. We are afflicted with unemployment rates more than double those for white workers. Black teenage unemployment is near 40 per cent. Unemployment and under-employment in the ghettos of America is from one-third to one-half of the work force. The total number of poor people in this country has risen sharply in the past several years. No, this is no Eden in which we live, and we cannot complacently agree that there is no longer a need for Federal social-service programs.

At National Press Club, Washington,
March 16/Vital Speeches, 5-1:419.

4

The gut issues of today—better schools, jobs and housing for all, personal safety and decent health care—are issues that transcend race. So long as they are falsely perceived as "black issues," nothing constructive will be done to deal with them. White Americans must come to see that its cities, its needs and its economic and physical health are at stake. The needs of blacks and whites are too strongly intwined to separate.

At National Press Club, Washington,
March 16/
The Dallas Times Herald, 3-17:(A)5.

Edward M. Kennedy
United States Senator, D-Massachusetts

5

[On President Nixon's policy of impounding Congressionally-allocated social welfare funds]: Just as the Presidential doctrine of Executive privilege under the Constitution was never intended to be a license to cover up corruption, so the Presidential doctrine of impoundment was never intended to be a license to annihilate whole domestic programs

. . . Just as capital punishment is not the answer to the problems of crime and law enforcement in modern American life, so capital punishment is not the answer to the problems in our social programs. So long as the Administration persists in trying to turn its budget-cutting knife into a guillotine for social programs, the current confrontation between Congress and the President will continue; and the nation will be the loser.

Before National Association of Counties,
Washington, April 4/
The Washington Post, 4-5:(A)7.

Melvin R. Laird
Counsellor to the President of the
United States for Domestic Affairs

1

I'm against cash assistance for housing. I'm against cash assistance in the food-stamp program. I'm against cash assistance as far as health is concerned. But eventually you've got to get all these separate cash programs brought together and have an income-strategy program and not piecemeal separate cash programs all over the government.

The Washington Post, 10-28:(A)2.

George C. Martin
President,
National Association of Home Builders

2

The Federal government has been involved in housing since 1932. It deserves to be there and needs to be there at a time when more and more people are being priced out of their opportunity for shelter. When we can spend $16 billion in Europe in 30 years after the war, when we can spend $2.5 million on a space satellite that is malfunctioning and when we can spend $80 billion in defense and then say we only have one per cent of our [Federal] budget for housing, there is something drastically wrong with our country's priorities . . . Today there is an inventory of available housing of less than one per cent. In 1960 there were 80,000 more available units, while we have 25 million more people today. Because our industry has had two or three good years, those in government think we ought to

cool our heels for a while, like in 1966 and 1969. We are not going to listen to the myths that say we have over-built and that there is no need for government assistance in housing.

At Pacific Coast Builders Conference,
San Francisco, June 13/
Los Angeles Herald-Examiner, 6-14:(C)6.

George S. McGovern
United States Senator, D-South Dakota

3

[The American people have been] oversold on social programs . . . they are wary of buying even sensible and essential social progress from any political leader.

Lecture at Oxford University, England,
Jan. 21/The Washington Post, 1-22:(A)1.

4

I think the President [Nixon] is setting a time-bomb in this country with the way he has dealt with the problems of the disadvantaged. No matter how unpleasant it is to contemplate, the fact remains that there are millions of people in this country on the poverty level. There are dependent children; there are mothers who are incapable of supporting their families; there are old people who are eking out their lives on inadequate incomes.

Interview/The Washington Post, 4-15:(C)7.

Margaret Mead
Anthropologist

5

The country is in terrible disarray. Richest and strongest of nations we may be, but we seem to have lost any concern for those who are young or weak, old or poor . . . [America has slid into] a pit of deterioration, corruption, apathy, indifference and outright brutality toward the weak, the sick, the young and the poor . . . We can now take into account both the dreadful consequences of valuing a budget more than caring for people and cutting services to human beings to save funds for oil subsidies, strip mining, and more and more deadly weapons.

Before Senate Labor and Public Welfare
Subcommittee, Washington, Sept. 25/
The New York Times, 9-26:17.

Walter F. Mondale
United States Senator, D-Minnesota

1

[Criticizing President Nixon's new budget proposals]: Aside from Social Security, this budget is nothing less than a disaster. This budget would, among other things, eliminate 180,000 desperately-needed jobs; end the Federal aid for low- and moderate-income housing; slash health research, aid to education, Medicare benefits for the aged; and abolish practically every effort to strengthen rural America. While nearly 100 programs to help people would be destroyed, the defense and foreign-aid budgets would rise dramatically, and not a single tax loophole for the rich would be closed . . . Without consulting Congress, he [Nixon] is destroying the poverty program . . . By Executive order he has ended virtually all of our housing and rural-development programs. We are not witnessing a policy of restraint. We are witnessing a retreat from our commitment to social and economic justice.

Radio address, March 2/
The Washington Post, 3-3:(A)5.

Gaylord Nelson
United States Senator, D-Wisconsin

2

It is bitterly ironic that after waging war for years in Southeast Asia—a war which Congress never declared—this [Nixon] Administration now proposes a cease-fire in the war on poverty here at home [by cut-backs in Federal programs] . . . And while abandoning the poor in rural areas and poverty-stricken inner cities here at home, the Administration is proposing a $7 billion program to rehabilitate the countries of Southeast Asia.

U.S. News & World Report, 3-5:12.

Richard M. Nixon
President of the United States

3

It has been charged that our budget cuts show a lack of compassion for the disadvantaged. The best answer to this charge is to look at the facts. We are budgeting 66 per cent more to help the poor next year than

was the case four years ago; 67 per cent more to help the sick; 71 per cent more to help older Americans; and 242 per cent more to help the hungry and malnourished. Altogether, our human-resources budget is nearly double that of four years ago when I came into office. We have already shifted our spending priorities from defense programs to human-resources programs. Now we must also switch our spending priorities from programs which give us a bad return on the dollar to programs that pay off. That is how to show we truly care about the needy. The question is not whether we help, but how we help. By eliminating programs that are wasteful, we can concentrate on programs that work. Our recent round of budget cuts can save $11 billion in this fiscal year, $19 billion next fiscal year, $24 billion the year after. That means an average saving of $700 over the next three years for each of America's 75 million taxpayers.

Radio address to the nation, Washington,
Feb. 21/Vital Speeches, 3-15:323.

4

To our great credit, we Americans are a restless and impatient people; we are a nation of idealists. We dream of eradicating poverty and hunger, discrimination, ignorance, disease and fear, and we would like to do it all today. But in order to reach these goals, we need to connect this warmhearted impatience of ours with another equally American trait—and that is level-headed common sense. We need to forge a new approach to human services in this country—an approach which recognizes that problems like poverty and unemployment, health-care and the costs of education are more than cold abstractions in a government file drawer. I know how tough these problems are, because I grew up with them. But I also know that, with the right kind of help and the right kind of spirit, they can be overcome.

Radio address to the nation, Washington,
Feb. 24/Vital Speeches, 3-15:326.

5

Too much money has been going to those who were supposed to help the needy and too little to the needy themselves. Those who make a profession out of poverty got fat, the taxpayer got stuck with the bill, and the disadvantaged themselves got little but broken promises. We must do better than this. The American people deserve compassion that works—not simply compassion that means well. They deserve programs that say yes to human needs by saying no to paternalism, social exploitation and waste.

> Radio address to the nation,
> Washington, Feb. 24/
> Vital Speeches, 3-15:326.

1

There are too many leaks in the Federal pipeline. It is time to plug them up. That is why we are changing our entire approach to human and community development. We are putting an end to wasteful and obsolete programs and replacing them with ones that work. Our 1974 budget would eliminate seven outmoded urban-development programs. It would suspend four ineffective housing programs. We are not pulling the rug out from under anyone who has already been promised assistance. Under commitments already made, we will subsidize an estimated 300,000 housing starts this year and will provide housing assistance to more than 2 million low- and moderate-income families. But we are stopping programs which have failed. We are determined to get a dollar's worth of service out of every dollar's worth of taxes. The high-cost, no-result boondoggling by the Federal government must end. This means we will continue to press for greater efficiency and better management in Federal programs. But it also means giving the lead role back to grassroots governments again. The time has come to reject the patronizing notion that Federal planners, peering over the point of a pencil in Washington, can guide your lives better than you can.

> Radio address to the nation,
> Washington, March 4/
> Vital Speeches, 4-1:356.

2

I have submitted to Congress for the next fiscal year the largest budget in our history —$268 billion. The amount I have requested in this budget for domestic programs in such fields as health, housing, education and aid to the elderly, the handicapped and the poor is twice as big as the amount in my first budget four years ago. However, some members of Congress believe the budget in these areas should be even higher. If I were to approve the increases in my budget that have been proposed in the Congress, it would mean a 15 per cent increase in your taxes, or an increase in prices for every American. That is why I shall veto the bills which would break the Federal budget which I have submitted. If I do not veto these bills, increased prices or taxes would break the family budget of millions of Americans. This is not a battle between Congress and the President. It is *our* battle. It is *your* money and *your* prices and *your* taxes I am trying to save. Twenty-five years ago, as a freshman Congressman, I met President [Harry] Truman in this office. I remember he had a sign on the desk. It read, "The buck stops here." That meant, of course, that a President can't pass the buck to anyone else when a tough decision has to be made. It also means that *your* buck stops here. If I do not act to stop the spending increases which Congress sends to my desk, *you* will have to pay the bill.

> TV-radio address to the nation,
> Washington, March 29/
> Los Angeles Times, 3-30:(1)14.

Charles H. Percy
United States Senator, R-Illinois

3

In the 1960s, we built new colleges and classrooms for the young people from the "baby boom" of World War II. We poured Federal monies into massive social programs to improve their lives. Indeed, the whole structure of American life was changed to accommodate them. We are left now, as they grow into adulthood, with more than enough facilities for the young and not enough for the old.

> Quote, 12-30:652.

Howard Phillips
Acting Director,
Federal Office of Economic Opportunity

1

There's been a tremendous amount of money given to people through the poverty program to organize welfare demonstrations, to organize rent strikes . . . [and] to give support to organizations . . . involved in the peace movement. We've even had some grantees that have gotten involved in gay liberation. Frankly, I think that sort of thing has very little to do with poverty. [It is] a violation of my civil liberties for the Federal government to subsidize . . . political activity.

Newsweek, 3-5:20.

2

. . . we reject that notion of [poverty-program] legal services which defines poverty as a political, rather than an economic, problem; which argues that, after a certain point, it is inefficient to represent individual clients whose causes are not of concern to "poor people as a class" and which justifies the use of poverty funds to represent affluent clients because the issues are perceived as "class" issues. We will shortly be submitting to the Congress legislation for a legal-services corporation which will truly place the needs of the poor first, before the political objectives of program attorneys or elected officials. We believe it is a proposal which will stand the test of time, providing high-quality legal assistance, no matter which national Administration may be in power.

Before Middlesex County Bar Association,
Boston, March 21/
The Christian Science Monitor, 4-12:18.

3

[On the closing of the OEO and elimination or shifting of anti-poverty programs]: What we're doing is making the Federal government's anti-poverty activities more effective. They haven't really been effective in eliminating poverty in the past. What the President [Nixon] wants is to reorganize the Federal anti-poverty effort in such a manner as to enhance its real benefit to the poor. We propose to eliminate the middleman—the anti-poverty bureaucrat—and see that the money intended for the poor really goes to their direct benefit. The old approach of trickling down dollars for the poor through a vast array of poverty contractors and professionals has only alleviated poverty for the middlemen. We are also reorganizing Federal anti-poverty activities so that more decisions are placed in the hands of elected officials who can be held accountable for success or failure, rather than leaving those decisions to the discretion of people employed by the Federal bureaucracy. We are, in effect, providing local option . . . People frequently ask me, "How can you decide that a program in my community is good or bad?" My answer to them is that I can't decide. That's precisely why it's so important that we return decision-making authority to people at the local level who are in a better position to make such assessments.

Interview/
U.S. News & World Report, 5-21:71.

W. R. Poage
United States Representative, D-Texas

4

The [Nixon] Administration wiped out the emergency-loan program in disaster areas. Along with this, the water-bank program was eliminated. And then the rural electric and the rural telephone rate was increased by 250 per cent. All of this is bound to adversely affect the quality of rural living . . . and all of this was done in spite of the fact that the Congress had provided specific authority and specific funds for these programs.

San Francisco Examiner & Chronicle,
1-7:(This World)7.

Elliot L. Richardson
Secretary of Health, Education and
Welfare of the United States

5

In spite of our progress, our institutions are failing to live up to our rising expectations. Budgets have spiraled upward, priorities have been reordered; yet to extend the present range of HEW services equitably to those in need would require seemingly impossible allocations of resources—an additional 20 million trained personnel and an additional $250 billion—a sum equal to the entire Federal budget. There is an increasingly pervasive sense not only of failure but of futility. In many fundamental respects, the human-service system is developing beyond the scope of control by government and the people. The legislative process has become a cruel shell game, and the service system has become a bureaucratic maze—inefficient, incomprehensible and inaccessible.

Washington, Jan. 18/
The New York Times, 1-19:16.

Nelson A. Rockefeller
Governor of New York

1

[Saying the current welfare system allows people to be on welfare who shouldn't be]: Christian principles have been behind most of our social programs; but it has reached the point where it has gotten out of hand . . . We've got a system that is building in the people a desire to cheat.

At Tennessee Prayer Breakfast, Nashville/
The New York Times, 3-23:31.

Beulah Sanders
Chairman,
National Welfare Rights Organization

2

Children are being denied the basic necessities of food, clothing and health care because Federal officials sit on their duffs.

Los Angeles Times, 2-15:(1)2.

Bradley R. Schiller
Economist, University of Maryland

3

Public anti-poverty activity has, for the most part, been a bread-and-circus kind of affair. We have allotted, grudgingly to be sure, huge sums of money to [feed], clothe and house the poor in the hope, perhaps, of achieving social tranquility. At the same time, we subjected the poor to a kaleidoscope of training and education activities, holding out false promises of job opportunity. Yet, we have done close to nothing to create the job opportunities . . .

The Washington Post, 4-10:(A)10.

Hugh Scott
United States Senator, R-Pennsylvania

4

[On President Nixon's impoundment of Congressionally-allocated social welfare funds]: All this furor you hear about people saying the President is depriving the underprivileged, or the poor, or people who want to be educated or want health services or somebody else, is just a lot of hogwash. What the President is saying is the Congress appropriated $261 billion for a $250 billion budget [last year]. You can't spend more than you make, and the government can't do it without taxing. The President is acting because Congress didn't have enough plain guts to act in this situation.

Jan. 27/The Washington Post, 1-28:(A)3.

R. Sargent Shriver
Former Director,
Federal Office of Economic Opportunity

5

[Criticizing OEO Acting Director Howard Phillips]: The wrecking crew is in there. As they say in the murder trials, the victim [the OEO] was killed with a blunt instrument. That's what Mr. Phillips is. He's not a sophisticated individual; he's a blunt instrument . . . He's an absolutist—one of those people who sees everything in black and white . . . [The Nixon Administration doesn't] like poor people. Poor people are not the most attractive people. They are not Frank Sinatra. If you like to play golf, poverty isn't the subject you like to talk about on the 19th green.

News conference, Washington, March 15/
The Washington Post, 3-16:(A)12.

6

President Nixon wants to stop the war on poverty . . . His action in dismantling the Office of Economic Opportunity, which was the headquarters of the war on poverty, is tantamount to closing up the Labor Department with respect to workingmen, or closing up the Agriculture Department with respect to the farmers. Now, it's true, of course, that you could close up the Agriculture Department and still continue farm programs someplace else. You could also close up the Labor

317

(R. SARGENT SHRIVER)

Department and still continue work with organized labor and with working people and manpower programs. But I think the farmers would react very strongly against closing up the Agriculture Department. I think [AFL-CIO president] George Meany would react very strongly if you tried to close up the Labor Department. They would look upon the Labor Department or the Agriculture Department as a symbol of the government's interest in their problems. Poor people have looked upon OEO in a similar way.

Interview/
U.S. News & World Report, 5-21:72.

Louis Stokes
United States Representative, D-Ohio

1

Over the past four years, we have learned that self-reliance is a virtue demanded only from minorities, the poor and the disadvantaged. No one has told Lockheed and Penn Central to pull themselves up by their bootstraps. People are helpless when they are un-educated, poor, at the mercy of drug addicts or pushers, out of work, living in unsanitary and indecent housing or when living costs continue to spiral. The Nixon Administration intends to keep those necessary tools locked away—and will award the key only to the privileged and the powerful.

Before the House, Washington, Jan. 31/
The New York Times, 2-1:23.

John G. Tower
United States Senator, R-Texas

2

The so-called war on poverty was politically conceived, politically administered and politically motivated. It came out of a Marxist concept of trying to organize the poor into a group and creating a political force of some kind. I don't think increased political consciousness has resulted. I think all that community action does is probably give a little money to an organized group which may not even represent a majority within the minority. I think it's been counter-productive to the

extent that there is probably less popular support for social and economic programs than there was seven or eight years ago.

The Washington Post, 4-13:(A)18.

Caspar W. Weinberger
Secretary of Health, Education and
Welfare of the United States

3

I think we have made significant strides with reduction of poverty in some areas; but I think most of those are probably attributable to the improvement of the economy, which has provided jobs in the private sector. I think that's the only permanent way to do it, and the only realistic way to do it. I don't think we are ever going to do it by simply paying community organizers. There are a lot of services that people in lower-income brackets have to have. The government's role can well be toward encouraging the provision of those services by someone other than governments. If no one can be found, I am not so doctrinaire that I would oppose government doing it; but I do oppose turning to government first.

Interview/Los Angeles Times, 2-25:(6)7.

4

I think in many ways Republicans are infinitely more liberal in the sense of willingness to try new approaches. I find the most intense conservatism seems to be in the social-welfare, human-rights field, in the sense that anyone associated with any of these programs in the past doesn't want to change anything . . . It's the source of our greatest difficulty . . . Congress will let you start something new, but not if you're going to abolish something old.

The Christian Science Monitor, 8-17:1.

5

I am skeptical about a guaranteed-income policy. I think that, by itself, it would not provide the necessary incentive for people on welfare to leave, but on the contrary would add a very large number to the rolls who are now working. I would like to see the income of those people increased by providing them with the qualifications to hold better jobs, and the creation of an economic climate that will encourage private industry to provide more jobs. These are some of the areas we are working in. We're going right back to the beginning to devise a new reform program, and we are not content simply to resubmit what Congress has three times refused to enact. We don't want an issue; we want a program.

Interview, Washington/
Nation's Business,
October:26.

Transportation

Spiro T. Agnew
Vice President of the United States

1

The automobile is not a monster, but it will become one if we allow ourselves to become totally dependent upon it for our urban transportation . . . The reason people now drive their automobiles into town is not necessarily because they want to do so, but because there are all too often no alternatives.

At rapid-transit seminar,
Los Angeles, March 20/
Los Angeles Herald-Examiner, 3-20:(A)2.

Alan S. Boyd
President,
Illinois Central Gulf Railroad

2

Railroads move more than three times as much freight per gallon of fuel than does highway carriage. They occupy less land, and do so less obtrusively, than do alternate modes, per unit of transport created. By pursuing present trends toward bigger rail cars, more modern facilities and more efficient operations, railroads can increase their capacity *seven times*—without using even one more acre for rights-of-way.

Before American Soybean Association,
Des Moines, Iowa, Aug. 21/
Vital Speeches, 9-15:724.

Claude S. Brinegar
Secretary of Transportation of the
United States

3

Quite clearly, there is a healthy rail system trying to crawl out of the Northeastern (railroad) wreck. All of us working together can help it escape.

Washington, March 26/
The Washington Post, 3-27:(A)1.

4

[Advocating a law requiring mandatory use of seat belts in automobiles]: I would like to be able to tell my children: "Fasten your belt. You'll break the law if you don't." You do a lot of things because of the law. You stop at a stop sign—at least I do—in the middle of the night even when nobody's coming, because of the law. And I think a lot more people would wear their seat belts if there were a law requiring them to. The Australians report good results from voluntary compliance with their new law. If we got the total up from the 25 per cent who wear them now to even 50 per cent, we'd obviously save a lot of lives.

Interview, Washington/
U.S. News & World Report, 7-23:39.

5

Eventually, congested areas may find it necessary to price freeway space very much the way we price movie theatres. The seats are cheaper in the early afternoon than they are at night. If you want to use the freeway or expressway at 7 a.m., you may have to have a sticker on your car that says: "I paid for the privilege," while later in the day you will travel without a sticker.

San Francisco Examiner, 8-21:30.

6

While our Department's program to expand mass transit and to increase the strength of the national rail system are worthwhile steps in the right direction, nothing can really make the necessary fuel-saving unless we significantly improve the energy efficiency of the family automobile—the user of over 50 per cent of our transportation fuels. Let's face it, our cars are too heavy, too inefficient and driven too much. In the national interest, we must recognize that we cannot long continue in this direction.

San Francisco Examiner, 10-11:36.

Secor D. Browne
Chairman, Civil Aeronautics Board
of the United States

1

As far as new technical possibilities in transportation are concerned, we have all kinds—and so far, no way to use most of them. I think the U.S. is essentially stuck with two widely-used modes of transportation: the car and the airplane. Feet, and most other kinds, are hardly used at all.

Quote, 2-18:160.

John Z. DeLorean
Former vice president and general manager,
Chevrolet Division, General Motors
Corporation

2

I think auto executives are some of the most insulated men in the country. They work together, party together. They're out of touch with what the real world is like or what people are concerned about. And when you consider the effect on the world the product has . . .

Interview, Bloomfield Hills, Mich./
Los Angeles Times, 5-28:(1)5.

Jean Drapeau
Mayor of Montreal

3

[Saying public mass transportation should be attractive]: Airlines pay a great deal of attention to what their planes look like. The average person only rides in an airplane once or twice a year. Why shouldn't what he rides *every day* be attractive, too?

Interview, Montreal/
Los Angeles Times, 6-7:(1-B)1.

Richard C. Gerstenberg
Chairman, General Motors Corporation

4

I don't see any revolutionary change coming [in the use of automobiles]. The average guy has become accustomed to the freedom the auto gives him. A car gives a guy more personal liberty than he can get in any [other] way, shape or form. On the other hand, I think we are going to have to find a

better way to move people in and around our big cities other than by the private auto. GM is working on improved transit buses and locomotives for commuter lines. We have got to find better commuter stuff than we have now.

Interview, Washington/
Los Angeles Times, 6-22:(2)7.

William P. Gwinn
Former chairman,
United Aircraft Corporation

5

Before the end of the century, swift vertical take-off transports capable of operating from small landing areas are likely to be in use. These would take care of the medium flights not included in our high-speed long-distance service. I believe supersonic commercial service will come eventually, despite the great production costs and technical problems. I think space travel will be commonplace one day . . . It is likely by the turn of the century that rockets will be sufficiently developed for commercial air transportation. Just think of blasting off from New York and landing in Manila about 45 minutes later! By then, perhaps all points on the globe will be within daily commuting time of each other. There are predictions that, by the 21st century, there will be people living in a satellite city circling the earth at an altitude of hundreds of miles. Perhaps your favorite airline will be carrying tourists to such a scientific community.

Before Wings Club, New York/
San Francisco Examiner & Chronicle,
5-20:(B)3.

Lee A. Iacocca
President, Ford Motor Company

6

We believe the auto complements [mass] transit systems. You can't take a plane or a train without getting there first in a car. However, we have gotten to the point where, in some areas like downtown New York, there's no room for any more cars . . . I don't know how you lick the over-all problem of a sprawling city like Los Angeles or De-

(LEE A. IACOCCA)

troit. A monorail system, for example, is a fast-moving system . . . from point A to point B. But big cities don't go from A to B. They go from A to B to C and to D. You might need 50 rails, costing billions of dollars . . . I think we have to innovate, try something in the big cities to complement the car. Perhaps we could pass a law and say commuters can't drive to work unless there are four guys in a car. But I don't think anybody is going to try that, although the Environmental Protection Agency has suggested such a solution. Unfortunately, that could destroy people's mobility.

Interview/
San Francisco Examiner, 11-5:37.

Arthur F. Kelly
President, Western Airlines

1

[On the gasoline shortage]: . . . we must regard public conveyances, such as airlines —which use only 5 per cent of the nation's annual petroleum consumption—not as the problem, but as a solution to the problem . . . while we understand the necessity for conservation and want to do our part, we believe that the public transportation system —both air and ground—must not be permitted to deteriorate. It is too important to the over-all economy.

At Town Hall forum, Los Angeles, Nov. 6/
Los Angeles Times, 11-7:(3)18.

E. Spencer Miller
President, Maine Central Railroad

2

Of two things I am certain. First, Congress will not shape a comprehensive railroad policy, but will temporize. Second, any plan it develops will shun a direct, above-the-table, straightforward approach in the direction of preserving free enterprise; and, instead, will kowtow to every pressure group with votes, entailing so many concessions that government ownership will be inevitable.

Human Events, 2-24:12.

Edmund S. Muskie
United States Senator, D-Maine

3

In the American auto industry today, the spirit of competition appears to be lacking and the zest for change lost. There appears to be little enthusiasm to develop technology which comes to grips with social and economic problems.

At Senate Air and Water Pollution
Subcommittee hearing, Washington,
May 23/Los Angeles Times, 5-24:(3)19.

John Portman
Architect; Urban developer

4

You are not going to take away the automobile from people, because people are going to want maximum freedom of movement. However, the principle is not to take away the automobile but to conserve the use of the automobile by, among other things, keeping the wife away from the steering wheel for every move she makes. Now her every errand is related to wheels. If we could produce the kind of environment where she would need wheels only 25 per cent of the time, then we would have made one hell of a contribution [to alleviating the energy crisis] . . . Let me make it clear that I am not against the wheel. No one is going to take my car. All I am saying is that the automobile is being badly misused, and we should put it in its proper place, which is to use it only out of necessity.

Interview, Atlanta/
Los Angeles Times, 5-4:(2)11.

Jennings Randolph
United States Senator, D-West Virginia

5

When I first came to the [Capitol] Hill in 1933, I became a member of the House Committee on Roads. Even before that, I had envisioned a need for a super-highway system. I was so bold as to draw lines on a map outlining where it would go. Then I introduced legislation. I didn't see it as a process of machines laying concrete and asphalt. I saw it as a process of one part of America getting to know another part of America.

The Washington Post, 4-16:(A)3.

Louis C. Ripa
Chairman, Porter and Ripa Associates,
engineering

1

[Saying the answer to mass transit is cooperation between competing modes of transportation]: This cooperation can be achieved through establishing hubs linking key rail, bus, air and automobile transportation routes into an over-all inter-connecting system. From these transportation hubs, travelers or commuters could make speedy connections to major airports, to city centers and to other key congested areas . . . Many of you can remember when women had to shop [a] half-dozen or more stores for food—the grocer, vegetable store, butcher shop, fish market, dairy outlet, and so on. Then came the supermarket, and all food shopping could be accomplished in one place, under one roof. In transportation, we need a similar concept.

At International Road Federation
World Meeting, Munich/
The New York Times, 11-23:24.

W. F. Rockwell, Jr.
Chairman, Rockwell International

2

Transportation is synonymous with livability, the freedom to move about anywhere we wish and as quickly as we wish in common safety with our neighbors. To achieve that freedom, we need new and improved ways of getting people and freight into, out of and around our cities. Mobility has been a prominent characteristic of the American people for more than 200 years . . . The river of mobility flows today just as strongly as it did 200 or 100 or 25 years ago. The people will not accept an immobile America. They will not accept as a vision of the future the current waist-high weeds on train tracks in some major passenger terminals throughout the country. Economic history has shown us, time and time again, that the demands for mobility are always met . . . The demand is still here; but sometimes, in the clamor of protest, dissent

and obstruction, I wonder if we can hear the voices of the people.

Before National Defense Transportation
Association, Washington, Sept. 24/
Vital Speeches, 10-15:21,22.

William J. Ronan
Chairman, New York State
Metropolitan Transportation Authority

3

[Urging Federal subsidies for mass-transit systems]: The day is clearly past for expecting local transit systems to be able to operate out of the fare box.

Before House Banking Subcommittee on
Urban Mass Transportation, Washington,
March 21/The New York Times, 3-22:78.

Norton Simon
Industrialist

4

[Advocating a single publicly-owned railway system rather than government nationalization]: The railroads are in the middle of a massive financial crunch. A number of marginal lines are near bankruptcy, and the taxpayers are being asked to provide the bail. Pending legislation is at best a Band-aid. If not amended, current proposals will lead to more problems, more money and eventually excessive subsidies not well conceived, or complete nationalization. The railroads are being permitted to run down, in many cases deliberately. Service and maintenance are becoming worse. This has resulted in accidents, delays in shipments and higher costs to users. What led to the collapse and temporary bail-out of the Penn Central is being repeated. The general public will have to foot the bill again, again and again.

New York, Nov. 8/
Los Angeles Times, 11-9:(3)17.

Clark E. Stair
Vice president, research and development,
Firestone Tire and Rubber Company

5

We have come a long way since the days only 30 years ago when tires with rubber inner tubes had to be inflated every week.

(CLARK E. STAIR)

The development of impermeable compounds —mostly using butyl polymers—has resulted in tremendous improvement in tire air retention, but unfortunately has also led to consumer neglect. In fact, tires have become probably the most neglected components of a car—even though they are among the most important from the standpoint of control and safety —because they have become so dependable. In the early days of the auto industry, the motorist who ventured out without extra tubes and tires and a tire pump was foolhardy indeed. Today's motorist barely ever looks at his tires, much less checks the air pressure. He feels so confident about tires that he forgets about them. All of us must do something about this lulled reaction, because until we can aim government and public attention at neglected and worn-out tires—coupled with inadequate roads and the need for improved driving habits—the total picture of tire-related highway safety will remain hazy. The beam will continue to be aimed at the new tires and not at where the problem actually lies.

Before Akron (Ohio) Rubber Group,
Jan. 26/Vital Speeches, 4-1:363.

James R. Sullivan
Senior vice president for reorganization
planning, Penn Central Railroad

1

Over the past several decades, the government has poured $300 billion into subsidizing our competitors—trucks, waterways and airlines—while we [the railroads] have gotten hardly a penny.

Interview, Philadelphia/
Los Angeles Times, 3-27:(1)12.

Stewart L. Udall
Former Secretary of the Interior
of the United States

2

[On the gasoline shortage]: Take a good look at these big new automobiles, because there is never going to be anything like them in the world again. Look at the big array of machines; look at the big new models every

year. We are seeing the final act. We are going to have to cut the weights, the sizes. We are going to have to slowly reduce the number. We are going to have to go to the simple, durable, low-horsepower automobiles. If we are wise, we will put more of the money we are spending on building highways into all kinds of public transportation—everything from bikeways through cities to better buses and trains.

Interview, Bethesda, Md./
Los Angeles Times, 5-28:(2)7.

Wesley C. Uhlman
Mayor of Seattle

3

[On the success of his city's experiment with free downtown bus service]: It far exceeded what had been expected. I had been told it couldn't work—I guess because it never had been tried anywhere else . . . Americans are in love with their cars. They are sold as sex symbols on television and purchased as sex symbols . . . The only way to break up a love affair is to offer an attractive alternative. And I think that our alternative has successfully broken up the love affair.

Interview, Seattle/
Los Angeles Times, 10-29:(1)3.

John A. Volpe
Secretary of Transportation
of the United States

4

Skyjackings are like bank robberies: There will always be some, no matter what.

Plainview (Tex.) Daily Herald, 1-11:6.

Lowell P. Weicker, Jr.
United States Senator, R-Connecticut

5

American railroads are being killed by highways, waterways and airports built and maintained by the government. Rails are the most efficient, cleanest and least land-hungry of all forms of surface transportation.

Quote, 6-24:591.

6

[Advocating the nationalization of U.S.

passenger railroads]: This will not simply be a proposal to expand Amtrak. It means that the Federal government will be running the trains, passenger trains, and no more of these quasi-government corporations that put our essential service[s] into the twilight zone . . . The people of the United States are fully aware that private corporations and bankrupt trusteeships have failed to provide either what is possible or what our minimum transportation requirements call for. We are at the end of the line.

Washington, Sept. 10/
San Francisco Examiner, 9-11:9.

Frederic W. West, Jr.
Executive vice president,
Bethlehem Steel Corporation

1

In 1971, the deficits for some [nationalized railway] systems ran like this: British Railways, $198 million; French National Railways, $128 million; German Federal Railway, $725 million; Japanese National Railways, $884 million. You might think that the taxpayers in those countries benefit through lower shipping charges, but you'd be wrong. Average ton-mile freight rates overseas are much higher than they are in this country—often twice as high. As for operating efficiency, listen to this: For every mile of track, the ratio of employees overseas as compared with the U.S. average ranges from 3-to-1 in France to 12-to-1 in Japan. And that's how it is. Nationalization inevitably throws a crushing burden on the taxpayers, and it's not only true of railroads.

At business award dinner,
Canisius College, Buffalo, N.Y./
The Wall Street Journal, 11-23:4.

William R. Wilson
Vice president,
Lockheed Aircraft Corporation

2

[On Europe's attempt to develop a commercial aircraft-manufacturing industry to compete with the U.S.]: People tend to overreact to this so-called European threat. We [the U.S.] control nearly 90 per cent of the world aerospace market. They aren't going to run us out of business. While we sit over here viewing European competition with alarm, they sit over there viewing us with utter terror.

U.S. News & World Report, 8-20:44.

Henri Ziegler
Director-general, Sud-Aviation (France)

3

[On the cancellation by several international airlines of their orders for the British-French supersonic *Concorde*]: We are pursuing the program. We are neither discouraged nor will we change our opinion on the quality of the plane as confirmed by the tests. Regular supersonic transport is an irreversible trend.

San Francisco Examiner, 2-7:35.

Urban Affairs

Joseph L. Alioto
Mayor of San Francisco

1

When he [President Nixon] suggests . . . that the crisis is over in American cities, first of all we [Mayors] are pleased to have that intelligence, because most of us couldn't figure it out on our own; we are pleased to have that. The other side is, maybe he isn't getting the information, maybe it is being kept from him, as to the real problem of the American cities . . .

TV-radio interview, San Francisco/
"Meet the Press,"
National Broadcasting Company, 6-17.

Ben Boo
Mayor of Duluth, Minn.

2

. . . the [President] Nixon philosophy toward the cities has, in my judgment, been exactly what the cities have been needing so long. He proposes a strong local government, that decisions be made at the local level. He has proposed revenue-sharing, both general and special, which gives the right of decisions at the local level. And that is why I believe that his plan is good for the cities.

TV-radio interview, San Francisco/
"Meet the Press,"
National Broadcasting Company, 6-17.

Frank Fasi
Mayor of Honolulu

3

Your mother takes care of the family, keeps the house clean, keeps you out of trouble, tells you what you can do and cannot do and punishes you when you do something wrong. That's the same thing a Mayor does, except he must do it for an entire city.

Before Cub Scouts/Quote, 2-4:97.

Peter C. Goldmark
Inventor; Former president and director
of research, Columbia Broadcasting
System Laboratories

4

When people started moving to the suburbs, they thought they would be going far enough. They were afraid to go farther away because they wanted to have the advantages of the nearby big cities and the rural charm of the suburbs. Today, they have neither. The city doesn't have the amenities and there is little of the rural charm left in the suburbs.

Interview, Stamford, Conn./
The Dallas Times Herald, 3-16:(A)20.

Richard G. Hatcher
Mayor of Gary, Ind.

5

The cities are increasingly viewed as repositories for the poor, the black, the Latin, the elderly—those who are relatively powerless against the interests of stronger and more affluent elements of our society.

Before Senate Intergovernmental Relations
Subcommittee, Washington, Feb. 21/
The New York Times, 2-22:20.

John V. Lindsay
Mayor of New York

6

I've learned that most of the Mayors everywhere perhaps aren't powerless people, but they show it and they behave that way. They're all at the mercy of state systems and state legislatures; they're all creatures of other bodies; they have no fundamental role. The development of the country was such that the major cities were thought to be cesspools of pestilence, crime and corruption. Some of the Mayors are very brave on the subject; but some of them are absolutely scared to death to speak out on any subject, because they feel that they're weak to begin with and they mustn't get further weakened. So there is a lot to the notion of powerlessness among Mayors.

Interview, New York/
The New York Times, 12-23:(1)20.

Sol M. Linowitz
Former chairman, National Urban Coalition

1

. . . too many of us have tried to isolate ourselves against the problems of our urban society. Too many people have sought to flee to the suburbs and tried to leave the city's problems behind. So today we are near the end of a long countdown for our cities—cities that are over-crowded, dirty, crime-ridden, poor and discouraged, cities that have become prisons which trap millions of people in hopeless and abject poverty. We stand at the edge of a crisis, but we seem incapable of summoning the will and the resources to rebuild the cities and reclaim the lives of the people living in them . . . We hear leaders in the government—and much of the press—telling us that our cities have "cooled off." We hear the President [Nixon] saying that the crisis of the cities is over. But the inescapable fact is that the crisis is not over. The hard fact is that the only "cooling off" that has taken place has been in the commitment of the government and of the American people to correct the festering problems of urban America . . . What we need is a determination on the part of all of us—in government, in industry, in labor, in education, in every segment—to make our society whole again and to recognize that these urgent problems of our cities deserve the highest priority. Quite clearly, this challenge is everybody's business.

Los Angeles Times, 11-13:(2)7.

James T. Lynn
Secretary of Housing and
Urban Development of the United States

2

[On criticism by some Mayors that Federal revenue-sharing would eventually provide less money for them than categorical grants provide]: Some big cities will receive less down the line, and it is possible that some cities

would receive less in the first year [of revenue-sharing] than they receive in the current year. But it is also possible that they would get nothing next year under the categorical-grant program.

Washington, April 19/
The New York Times, 4-20:1.

3

I think it is time to dispel the myth that there is somebody in Washington, D.C., who knows better than the people themselves what is needed for community development in their cities. There is plenty of room for diversity in what the communities may do. After all, the problems and opportunities of communities in this country aren't the same. Our communities do have common aims and desires. They want happiness for their people, employment, a sound economic base, a decent environment. But every community is different, and the best means of accomplishing these objectives are different. So I think we are going to see a wide diversity of what people consider their top priorities from city to city. That's the strength of what we're trying to do. When mistakes are made with a Federal program, you make a mistake for all 50 states of the union. But if we have a few communities that make mistakes—all right, they're still mistakes, but they affect only the people in those communities, and the officials who make these mistakes have to answer to the local voters.

Interview, Washington/
U.S. News & World Report, 6-18:54.

Henry W. Maier
Mayor of Milwaukee

4

The crisis in our cities cannot be solved by Presidential proclamation that the urban crisis is over. Nor can it be solved by the "Vietnamization" of our urban problems—the pulling out of vitally-necessary Federal programs and paying the cities to try to cope with an already over-burdened property tax, the most unpopular and unfair tax in the land.

Before ad hoc Senate committee,
Washington, June 14/
The New York Times, 6-15:62.

(HENRY W. MAIER)

1

President Nixon has announced that "The crisis of our cities is past." No one knows better than the Mayors of America that the crisis of our cities is not past. But President Nixon's callous disregard of the needs of the people who populate our cities makes it crystal clear that this nation will not be able to come to grips with the pressing problems which beset our cities unless we elect a veto-proof Congress in 1974 and a Democratic national Administration in 1976.

News conference, San Juan, P.R.,
Dec. 5/The New York Times, 12-6:23.

George Meany
President, American Federation of Labor-
Congress of Industrial Organizations

2

[President Nixon said] a few weeks ago we've solved the problems of our cities—of our inner cities. Well, by God, he had better go to some of our inner cities. The problems of crime, drugs—there are very few inner cities of America where people can walk the streets in safety. And still he says, well, gee, isn't it great; we've solved the problem; crime is on the wane. Well, I just don't buy that.

Interview, Washington/
The National Observer, 5-5:24.

Richard M. Nixon
President of the United States

3

Too often, people think of community development solely in terms of the big city. In fact, less than 30 per cent of our people live in places with a population of more than 100,000. This is approximately the same number who live in rural America. The proportion of our people living in cities with a population of over 1 million is no greater today than it was 50 years ago. In an age when people move a great deal, the growth of our great cities and that of our smaller communities are directly linked. A balanced approach to community development must keep small-town

America clearly in sight.

Radio address to the nation, Washington,
March 4/Vital Speeches, 4-1:357.

Abraham A. Ribicoff
United States Senator, D-Connecticut

4

[On President Nixon's assertion that the city crisis is over]: The crisis in the cities isn't over. Anyone who lives or works in or visits the cities knows the crisis is still with us. If the crisis in our cities is over, why has serious crime gone up 30 per cent in the past four years? If the crisis in our cities is over, why are schools on the verge of bankruptcy and collapse in Chicago, Detroit, Philadelphia, Portland, Oregon, and elsewhere? If the crisis in our cities is over, why has there been no bus service available in many Connecticut cities for more than 100 days? If the crisis in our cities is over, why do almost five million homes lack proper plumbing? [The nation's Mayors] agree with me that no Federal program should be continued if it doesn't work. They support the President's theory that local leaders should be given the responsibility for running their cities. But they vigorously object to the President's meat-ax approach for ending urban problems. The Mayors say they can't save their cities without Federal financial help.

Radio address, March 10/
The Washington Post, 3-11:(A)4.

Daniel Rose
Partner, Rose Associates, real estate

5

A great many thoughtful observers have come to the conclusion that the high-density, mixed-use central cities as we have known them are impractical and inefficient and that they no longer answer our needs of today. These men challenge the belief that most people would prefer to live in cities, and maintain that they would choose suburban life even if the cities were safe, attractive and agreeable and no more expensive than alternatives. These observers feel that the automobile has liberated us from dependence on the old high-density city . . . [but] even if these men are correct, the relentless logic of an ecologically-minded society bent on conserving resources won't permit all of us the luxury of living in Dullsville even if we wish to. For the endlessly sprawling American suburb is the most economically wasteful human settlement known to man . . . Besides, if safe, big cities are just more fun to be in.

At New School Center for New York
City Affairs, October/
The New York Times, 11-25:(3)12.

Gay Talese
Writer

1

I spent most of this year in southern California and pondered moving there, but it was never a serious thought. California has more space. I've got a suntan; I played tennis every day; I had a swimming pool—all the trappings of the good life. I returned to a [New York] brownstone on a dusty, dirty street with grim, angry people fighting for parking spaces—and I love it. New York is ugly; it's over-programmed, over-crowded, over-neurotic and over-skilled, but it's where I think I can do my best work. It's where the most stimulating and interesting minds are. You feel the pressure of having to be at your best—and you have to be at your best in order to stay here. It's not a place for the slow-footed or slow-witted. The word that most characterizes New York is "energy," and that's what you miss in other places. Even the failings of New York are the same elements that produce energy. This is a vertical city. Buildings are jammed shoulder-to-shoulder; it's all very tight. There are maybe 10,000 people in one block in some sections of the city, all living vertically, all bumping into each other, fighting for that small piece of space. This kind of contact produces an electrical effect. California is horizontal. There's all that spread-out space, but you're not able to be in touch with people. They're all in their cars out there, the air conditioning is always on and the windows are jammed closed. You can never really touch each other.

Interview, New York/
"W": a Fairchild publication, 3-23:20.

Wesley C. Uhlman
Mayor of Seattle

2

Most of us [Mayors] have applauded the President's [Nixon] idea of New Federalism and revenue-sharing, but it has not turned out to be the savior of the cities we thought it would be. Instead, it's a Trojan Horse, full of impoundments and cutbacks and broken promises.

Before Senate Intergovernmental Relations
Subcommittee, Washington, Feb. 21/
The Washington Post, 2-22:(A)1.

Louie Welch
Mayor of Houston

3

I think it is impossible to exaggerate the problems of the cities, because they are the problems of the people.

TV-radio interview, San Francisco/
"Meet the Press,"
National Broadcasting Company, 6-17.

Walter B. Wriston
Chairman,
First National City Bank, New York

4

As a provider of vital services, city government is highly vulnerable to those who threaten to disrupt it. An impending strike by transportation workers, sanitation men, teachers, firemen or police has always caused the city to capitulate in "the public interest." When this happens, as we all know, the big [labor] unions tend to engage in games of one-upmanship, leapfrogging over one another to escalate their demands. There is, of course, no simple or obvious solution; but the city must begin to eliminate some of the bureaucratic rigidity and waste that make the majority of citizens so susceptible to the often unreasonable demands of any raucous minority. Throughout the nation, city and state taxpayers are becoming evermore disenchanted with the idea of paying more and more for less and less. So, increasingly in many urban areas, city governments are turning to private enterprise for police protection, garbage col-

(WALTER B. WRISTON)

lection, fire-fighting, education, the distribution of welfare checks and food stamps and the processing of income-tax returns. Discipline imposed by the profit motive often enables private companies to perform these functions more cheaply and efficiently. If they do not measure up, they cannot impose themselves on the body politic in perpetuity; they cannot even hold the city captive by going on strike; they are simply replaced.

Before Regional Plan Association,
New York, April 5/
Vital Speeches, 6-1:483.

Anne Armstrong
Counsellor to the President
of the United States

1

If you talk about the militant fringe of the Women's Lib movement—the protestors—I think they've hurt the cause of progress for women. They've turned off a lot of people who were ready to listen to rational arguments and accept women on their merits . . . Personally, I'm not one who is bitter at all on this subject. There has been definite progress in the role of women. Perhaps the progress is not as fast as we would like, but it is steady and it is sure. There is still discrimination against women in this country, but what discrimination still exists is diminishing, so that within a few years we will be able to say truthfully that we have full opportunity for women.

Interview, Washington/
U.S. News & World Report, 5-14:67.

Brigitte Bardot
Actress

2

Women get more unhappy the more they try to liberate themselves. A woman is a tender and sweet person. She will lose that if she tries to be like a man.

Television interview/
Los Angeles Times, 4-10:(1)2.

Liz Carpenter
Former Press Secretary to
Lady Bird (Mrs. Lyndon) Johnson

3

Women have been stepped upon, crept upon and slept upon [too long]. We still find something in men to love, but we're going to love them much more when they right the old wrongs and get with the 20th century. Make no mistake about it. There is a little bit of the liberationist in every woman. Most of us are somewhere between the gentle perception of an Anne Morrow Lindbergh and the biting brilliance of a Germaine Greer—between the poet and the zealot. Yet every intelligent person, man and woman, realizes that there are still millions of women being exploited —overtly and subtly. We literally have a nation crawling with over-qualified women who are under-confident.

At Matrix Awards dinner of Dallas
Professional Chapter of Women in
Communications, Dallas, Feb. 23/
The Dallas Times Herald, 2-24:(A)5.

Midge Decter
Author

4

[On her criticism of the women's-liberation movement]: I have become the figure at the center of resistance to the movement. Women who two years ago would have been very fierce in the face of resistance to the movement say to me, "You've picked the lunatic fringe of this movement [as representative of the whole movement], and that's not fair." But as they go on and on with that kind of conversation, you find out that they adhere to the very ideas they describe as lunatic . . . You know, it's become almost impossible to talk accurately about relations between men and women, because the whole thing has become so ideological. Everything fits into the ideological slots, and I don't think men and women are telling the truth any more.

Interview, New York/
The New York Times, 3-21:41.

Carl N. Degler
Professor of American History,
Stanford University

5

The women's movement is the most radical

331

(CARL N. DEGLER)

social phenomenon in all history; it makes the impact of Marxism seem old hat.

The Christian Science Monitor, 4-4:11.

Catherine S. East
Executive Secretary, President's Citizen's Advisory Council on the Status of Women

1

The term "women's liberation" can be appropriately applied only to a small segment of the women's rights movement . . . the branch of the movement that had its origin in the student activities of the early '60s. These women, primarily radical feminists, have thus far been mainly concerned with analyzing the origins, nature and extent of women's subservient role in society, with an emphasis on the psychology of oppression . . . The women's rights movement is largely composed of the kind of women that are in the National Association of Women Lawyers, the General Federation of Women's Clubs, the National Federation of Business and Professional Women's Clubs, the Women's Equity Action League, the YWCA and the League of Women Voters; and they are, by and large, pretty conservative as a group. It's these organizations that have secured passage of the Equal Rights Amendment by Congress and are lobbying for state ratification. It is these groups that are working for reforms in education and in other areas of society. They are not trying to overthrow the government, abolish the family or force all women into employment. They are seeking . . . to make the family a real partnership and to make freedom of choice for women a reality.

The Christian Science Monitor, 4-17:(B)12.

Edward D. Eddy
President, Chatham College

2

What is the traditional role of American women? Marriage. A son. Two daughters. Breakfast. Ironing. Lunch. Bowling; maybe a garden club; or, for the very daring, non-credit courses in ceramics. Perhaps an occasional

cocktail party. Dinner. Football or baseball on TV. Each day the same. Never any growth in expectations—unless it is growth because the husband has succeeded. The inevitable question: "Is that all there is to life?" . . . In what Gloria Steinem might call a chauvinist statement, Andre Malraux has proclaimed: "A man is what he does." Now, as if for the first time, the question is posed to all women: "What are *you* going to do? What are *you* going to be?" The modern woman begins to answer, but it is not the answer to which we are accustomed. She says, "I have chosen to be a wife and mother." Or, "I have chosen to pursue a career in business—to be a doctor; to run a lab; to go into politics." A woman should have—must have—the same options as a man. She must choose the life she wants for herself, competing on an equal basis with men.

Before Rotary Club, Pittsburgh,
Jan. 3/Vital Speeches, 2-15:274.

Betty Friedan
Founder, National Organization for Women

3

In 1966, when we were organizing NOW to take women into the mainstream of society, into full equality with men, I suggested we call it National Organization FOR Women, because men must be a part of our movement. More and more men are supporting the movement in this country because they are tired of being polarized by "the masculine mystique." I see no reason to make enemies of friends.

News conference, University of Texas,
Arlington, March 29/
The Dallas Times Herald, 3-30:(C)4.

Mary W. Gray
Professor of Mathematics and Statistics,
American University

4

There are women who will tell you that they have never been discriminated against. This may well be true. But frequently from there they go on to infer that no women are discriminated against. They feel that, if any woman is good enough and willing to work hard enough, she can succeed. Actually, I frequently tend to agree. But then I ask: Why should a woman have to work twice as hard —for half as much money—as a man?

Before American Association for the
Advancement of Science/
The National Observer, 1-20:18.

Germaine Greer
Author; Women's rights advocate

1

The result [of the women's movement] must be a better life for us all. I don't mean more comfortable, because God knows for the first few generations it won't be, because we have an enormous intellectual weight upon our shoulders; we have to invent a way of life which was never before possible. But at least we can argue in the true sense of "better" that we have a more moral existence when women act out of free choice, when they contract themselves to people out of free choice, when they produce work which is their best, when they are able to face criticism, when they have enough intellectual and spiritual muscle not to break down and be hidden by uxorious husbands from the pressure of cultural examination.

Before Cambridge (University) Union,
England/The Christian Science Monitor, 4-4:11.

2

Despite a lifetime of service to the cause of sexual liberation, I have never caught a venereal disease, which makes me feel rather like an arctic explorer who has never had frostbite.

Quote, 5-13:434.

Martha W. Griffiths
United States Representative,
D-Michigan

3

What we need in this country is a President whose own wife or daughter has just once been subjected to the ordinary kind of discrimination that women face every day. And we need a woman on the Supreme Court. Those Justices are living in the middle ages where women are concerned. So far, only four of the nine have held that sex is a "suspect classification" in discrimination cases.

San Francisco Examiner & Chronicle,
8-26:(A)13.

Wilma Scott Heide
President,
National Organization for Women

4

When did Congress begin to take us seriously on the Equal Rights Amendment? When about 20 of us from Pennsylvania NOW interrupted a Senate Subcommittee on Constitutional amendments, February 17, 1970! When did the Office of Federal Contract Compliance of the U.S. Labor Department begin to implement Executive Order 11375 and issue Order # 4 with goals and timetables to be applied to women? When we repeatedly visited, sat in the Labor Secretary's office and got on or took over their closed circuit television program in 14 cities in July, 1970! When did *The New York Times* and others desegregate want ads? When NOW picketed! . . . We could share thousands of other examples that, when polite letters, proffered meetings, documented evidence, detailed offensiveness to our personhood do not penetrate and/or produce significant behavioral change, then it is irresponsible of us not to change our behavior and tactics . . . In urging the courage of our convictions, I truly regret the necessity. It seems part of my personal preference to quietly persuade, softly negotiate change, cite the justice of our case. Yet, we haven't always the "luxury" of relative passivity or even limited activity. Our militancy and programs to get out into what has been "man's world" must be seen as a rejection of nearly total passivity through self-denial and vicarious half-lives. That so-called "man's world" is our world and it's in trouble. We're hell-bent or heaven-bent— depending on one's view—to join it, determine the action and redirect it, share it, lead it— differently we hope, but participate we will.

Before National Organization for Women,
Washington, February/
Vital Speeches, 5-1:427.

Theodore M. Hesburgh
President, University of Notre Dame;
Former Chairman, United States Commission
on Civil Rights

1

It is an illusion to equate the problems of blacks and Chicanos with those of women. If and when women put their minds and efforts seriously to the solution of the inequalities that exist between themselves and men—not a one-way street—they will make rapid progress in righting the wrongs, as is now beginning to happen. Not so for the deep-rooted inequities that blacks—men, and more especially women —suffer. The color problem is far more difficult . . . far more influenced by deep-seated prejudices than the problem of gender.

Before American Council on Education,
Washington, Oct. 6/
The New York Times, 10-8:12.

Leo Kanowitz
Professor of Law, Hastings College
of the Law, San Francisco

2

Man, in his accepted dominant role, pays a heavy price today by social custom and legal regulation, through his compulsory military service, being excluded from state protective labor laws, loss of preference in child custody cases and his basic support obligations in marriage and after divorce. These are all direct products of our basic system according the male a superior role. But the many indirect detriments to all of us are the greater social problems. Much crime, juvenile delinquency, marital discord, racism stem from the tensions set off internally by the disparity of sex-role expectations and the individual's abilities or desires. There is a real possibility the international problems of war and peace are traceable to the psychological by-products of the sex roles assigned by the major societies of the world.

Interview,
Hastings College of the Law,
Jan. 3/San Francisco Examiner,
1-4:23.

Juanita M. Kreps
Professor of Economics,
Duke University

3

In [the] future world, the kinds of jobs held by women will be far more varied than heretofore; equal pay for equal work will be assured not only by law but by commonly-accepted practice; the work-life of a woman, even when she has children, will be longer . . . there will be greater numbers of single women and more women as heads of households . . . women's aspirations will be high, for they are going to expect good jobs and good pay even as they expect to offer superior performance . . . It seems unlikely that American women, particularly the college-educated, will again give home work and child care the central role they occupied in, say, the 40s and 50s. The greater the societal need to restrict family size, moreover, the greater will be women's participation in market jobs.

Before Ellen Browning Scripps Association,
Los Angeles/Los Angeles Times, 3-4:(4)5.

Anita Loos
Author

4

The people I'm furious with are the women's liberationists. They keep getting up on soapboxes and proclaiming that women are brighter than men. That's true, but it should be kept very quiet or it ruins the whole racket.

Interview, New York/
The New York Times, 4-26:39.

Clare Boothe Luce
Former American diplomat and playwright

5

I think it's ridiculous to think that women will continue to consent to spending their whole lives in a three-room flat cooking their husband's dinner out of the deep freeze . . . Women had better begin thinking of jobs and careers for themselves because they'll either end up stir-crazy or on relief. So it isn't a question of great and noble ideas about equal-

ity—but simply of being sensible.
Interview, New York/
The Christian Science Monitor, 5-4:10.

Golda Meir
Prime Minister of Israel

1

I was never a feminist. But I never accepted that a woman, as a woman, is inferior. But I don't think the opposite is true either.
Before Labor Party, Jerusalem/
The Washington Post, 2-9:(A)21.

Ira M. Millstein
Lawyer; Former Chairman, National
Commission on Consumer Finance of
the United States

2

[On the difficulty of women obtaining retail and bank credit]: A lot of women are still not aware they should be entitled to credit. Until they are conscious that a woman with income is a person entitled to credit—period— that marital status shouldn't interfere, that she should be judged as any wage-earner for better or worse, what good would it do to put another law on the books? As soon as women start stamping their feet and raising hell and getting to the right person in the credit-granting office, it will get done.
The New York Times, 3-25:(1)35.

Mohammad Reza Pahlavi
Shah of Iran

3

Nobody can influence me, nobody at all— and a woman still less. In a man's life, women count only if they're beautiful and graceful and know how to stay feminine . . . This Women's Lib business, for instance. What do these feminists want? Equality, you say? Indeed! I don't want to seem rude, but . . . You [women] may be equal in the eyes of the law, but not, I beg your pardon for saying so, in ability.
Interview/
Los Angeles Times, 12-30:(6)1.

Dixy Lee Ray
Chairman-designate, Atomic Energy
Commission of the United States

4

I don't have any illusions that I was appointed because of my scientific experience or expertise. If it hadn't been for the women's-liberation movement, I doubt that the President [Nixon] would have appointed me. I was appointed because I was a woman, and that's perfectly all right with me.
Interview/
The Christian Science Monitor, 2-23:12.

Jill Ruckelshaus
Assistant to the chairman, Republican
National Committee; Member, national policy
council, National Women's Political Caucus

5

For me, the women's movement is not class warfare. Men, as a class, are not the enemy. Our obstacles are tradition, inertia and education.
Before New York Couture Business Council/
Los Angeles Times, 1-8:(1)2.

Patricia Schroeder
United States Representative, D-Colorado

6

Of course I'm for women's rights. The only way we will get a higher quality of life is if everyone participates. Women have been told so often they can spectate and not participate, that they have thought they are not capable of participating. But yes; we are.
Interview, Washington/
The Christian Science Monitor, 3-21:14.

Gloria Steinem
Author; Editor, "Ms." magazine

7

The opposition [to the women's rights movement] is stiffening in the economic areas—from the powerful rich employer groups fighting the Equal Rights Amendment because they have figured out what equal pay will cost them, to the so-called liberal academicians because they see jobs being awarded on the basis of talent. The resistance is recognizing what

335

(GLORIA STEINEM)

the movement is about: power—the challenge to existing power. The struggle will get more difficult as we make gains. But the support for the movement has grown enormously. For the first time, it represents a plurality of the American women.

Interview, San Francisco/
San Francisco Examiner, 1-18:28.

1

There is a very deep understanding among all of us [in the women's rights movement] that we unite as a caste because we have been discriminated against as a caste . . . We must neither turn away the blue-haired woman speaking on equal pay or the blue-jeaned woman yelling for abortion.

At National Women's Political Caucus,
Houston, Feb. 9/
The Dallas Times Herald, 2-12:(D)1.

2

[Criticizing news coverage of the women's movement]: You [journalists] are using divide-and-conquer tactics to make Women's Lib appear not worthwhile. The problem of seriousness afflicts us most . . . When women libbers disagree, it's the fight that is emphasized, not the issues. When I join demonstrations for causes that are worth reporting, I am only quoted about Jackie Onassis and braburning. *Ms.* magazine was founded as a remedial publication, and until the press becomes a human press, there will be need for remedial publications.

Before American Newspaper Publishers
Association, New York, April 25/
Los Angeles Times, 4-27:(4)2.

3

I would like to remind us that the revolution which women are trying to make is one so long and so deep and so serious that it makes all the Watergates of the world seem like very small patriarchal episodes . . . Most important, I think, is to realize that we are

indeed talking about a revolution and not just a reform.

At Simmons College commencement,
Boston/The New York Times, 6-18:22.

N. Eldon Tanner
First-counsellor to the president,
Church of Jesus Christ of Latter-day
Saints (Mormon)

4

Satan and his cohorts are using scientific arguments and nefarious propaganda to lure women away from their primary responsibilities as wives, mothers and homemakers. We hear so much about emancipation, independence, sexual liberation, birth control, abortion and other insidious propaganda belittling the role of motherhood—all of which is Satan's way of destroying women, the home and family, the basic unit of society.

At Mormon conference,
Salt Lake City, Oct. 7/
Los Angeles Herald-Examiner, 10-8:(A)12.

Esther Vilar
Author

5

Women are no longer subject to the will of men. Quite the contrary. They have been given every opportunity to win their independence; and if, after all this time, they have not liberated themselves and thrown off their shackles, we can only arrive at one conclusion: There are no shackles to throw off.

San Francisco Examiner & Chronicle,
1-28:(This World)2.

Laurel Walum
Professor of Sociology,
Ohio State University

6

The more [women] try to have their cake and eat it too, the crummier the cake gets.

San Francisco Examiner & Chronicle,
9-9:(This World)2.

PART TWO

International Affairs

Raul Alarcon (Quesada)
*Cuban Ambassador/Permanent Representative
to the United Nations*

1

[On the recent coup overthrowing Chilean President Salvador Allende]: It is not difficult to know where the main responsibility lies. The trail of blood spilled in Chile leads directly to the dark dens of the [U.S.] Central Intelligence Agency and the Pentagon. If the Fascist military junta [in Chile] has bloody hands, [U.S. President] Nixon and his collaborators are guilty of instigating and masterminding the events in Chile.

*Before United Nations Security Council,
New York, Sept. 17/
The New York Times, 9-18:5.*

Salvador Allende (Gossens)
President of Chile

2

Anyone who seeks to subvert the workers' government will be smashed by the government and the people . . . Nothing is going to halt Chile on its march to socialism.

*Santiago, Feb. 5/
The New York Times, 2-7:9.*

3

I want to insist that Chile is not a socialist country. This is a capitalist country, and my government is not a socialist government. Neither, as the press likes to say, is it a Marxist government. I am a Marxist. That's something else. But the government is made up of Marxists, laymen and Christians. This is a popular, democratic, national revolutionary government—anti-imperialist. There is genuine democracy here. There is incredible freedom here, particularly freedom of the press and freedom of speech. I don't think there is any other country in the world where the President of the republic submits himself to the kind of verbal and written assaults that take place here.

*Interview, Santiago, June/
The Washington Post, 9-16:(C)2.*

4

There are people who want to drag us toward civil war. I will do everything possible, and impossible, to avoid this. Only the future will tell whether I will succeed. I'm sure we would probably win. But that isn't the problem. The problem is the country: The country would be destroyed; its economy would be ruined for many, many years. It would destroy the entire social fabric: Passions in every family would be set on fire; there would be fathers on one side and sons against us, or sons with us and their fathers against us. Even worse—and this is something I honestly say we have to avoid—if a revolt or civil war were successful in Chile, we would end up with a despotic government—a Fascist dictatorship!

*Interview, Santiago, June/
The Washington Post, 9-16:(C)2.*

David Barrett
Premier of British Columbia, Canada

5

[On his socialist provincial government's take-over of various private companies]: We have not expropriated anything. We purchased. We have no intention of expropriating. We clearly spelled out the areas that we will confine to ourselves—namely, the utility monopolies. Number one is the B.C. Telephone Company. But even in that case, we want to act through negotiations. Our aim is not to take over business, but to be partners with it. But we insist on accepting social and economic responsibility where private industry fails.

U.S. News & World Report, 7-16:55.

Lloyd M. Bentsen
United States Senator, D-Texas

1

In view of our [more friendly] attitude toward the Soviet Union and the People's Republic of [Communist] China, consistency demands a similar posture toward our close neighbor [Cuba]. If we learned anything from our experience with Communist China, we learned that 20 years of non-communication and isolation handicapped us as well as the Chinese. We learned that we cannot afford to live in ignorance of any other nation in this shrinking world . . . Improving relations with Cuba would be symbolic of new political maturity in the United States; of a new willingness to respect differences among peoples; and of a new realization that Latin America is seeking to fulfill its own destiny in its own way.

Before World Affairs Council,
Philadelphia/
Los Angeles Times, 12-20:(2)7.

Robert Bourassa
Premier of Quebec, Canada

2

We [in Quebec] want cultural sovereignty, because we are a French-speaking society; and we need economic Federalism, because we are North Americans.

San Francisco Examiner & Chronicle,
11-11:(This World)24.

Harry F. Byrd, Jr.
United States Senator, I-Virginia

3

The Nixon Administration should ignore the threats of Panamanian politicians. It should ignore the hypocritical howls from the United Nations. I say flatly and emphatically that U.S. security over the [Panama] Canal is not negotiable . . . Panama has been notoriously susceptible to political upheavals, with 44 Presidents having come and gone in 70 years. It was only a few years ago that the President was assassinated; the first Vice President then assumed office but was shortly deposed as having been involved in the assassination. Another Vice President then became President and he was thrown out the next year. A treaty compromising our rights in the Panama Canal would weaken this country's defense posture in the Western Hemisphere. It is ridiculous to think that the uninterrupted movement of commercial or military ships could be guaranteed under any Panamanian regime of the moment. There is no assurance that some Castro-type Communist government wouldn't seize control of Panama.

Human Events, 12-8:19.

Robert C. Byrd
United States Senator, D-West Virginia

4

The anti-hijacking agreement with Cuba fits very well into [the] ambience of detente between the United States and its former protagonists; and there are many who feel that the time is ripe for U.S. recognition of Cuba for this reason. The advocates of a new U.S. policy toward Cuba feel that the Nixon Administration is excluding Cuba from the politics of detente. They feel that, if talks can begin with [Communist] China, a nation which we fought on the battlefields of Korea not too long ago, and Russia, our traditional rival and foe, then we can begin to talk to the Cubans, close neighbors with whom mutual enmity developed over a relatively short span of years . . . At what point is a harsh, hard-line policy toward Cuba no longer a viable one, or perhaps even a counter-productive one? Are the obstacles as seen by the Administration and as posed by the Castro government too great to be overcome? Is the export-of-revolution policy that much a threat in Latin America today? Is the Soviet military and economic presence in Cuba permanent or might it not be subject to change, say, for example, through three-way negotiations between the United States, Cuba and the Soviet Union? Is it not within our self-interest to see the Soviet influence in Cuba neutralized, or at least diminished? Is not the compensation issue one for negotiation if the nations would just agree to sit down and talk? Are we not in danger of being isolated in the Western Hemisphere as more and more Latin American countries unilaterally resume relations with

Cuba in violation of what they consider an antiquated OAS policy? Is it not within our self-interest to consider our relationship with the rest of Latin America as one of unity and community which has evolved over a period of over 150 years?

Before the Senate, Washington/
The National Observer, 5-26:13.

Helder Camara
Roman Catholic Archbishop of Olinda
and Recife, Brazil

1

We would not be worthy of Christ if we remained silent before the institutionalized injustices that maintain two-thirds of the population of our nation in conditions unworthy of human beings, and on the other hand if we would not use our voice on behalf of those who are barbarously tortured and not infrequently killed by a number of paralegal methods that sadly bring back to memory the hideous days of Stalin and Hitler.

Before Pernambuco State Legislature,
Recife, May 31/The New York Times,
11-11:(1)8.

Fidel Castro
Premier of Cuba

2

On several occasions we have been in real danger of a direct aggression by the armed forces of the United States. This danger has existed and it will continue to exist while there is a Cuban revolution and while there is imperialism. There will always be a Cuban revolution, but Yankee imperialism will not live forever.

Addressing Cuban troops, Dec. 30/
The New York Times, 1-1('74):7.

Miguel Angel de la Flor
Foreign Minister of Peru

3

Imperialism has been and still is present in America in both its old and new manifestations, from which we [in Latin America]

must defend ourselves and make a common front.

Before Organization of American States,
Washington, April 5/
The Washington Post, 4-6:(A)4.

4

We don't oppose foreign investment; we want it and we need it. But we don't want it to occur the way it did prior to 1968 when it resulted in political and economic dependency. We're not prepared to accept it if it has strings attached of an economic or political nature. We want a society that is free, just and nationalistic. If to reach that stage we cannot find a friendly, sincere hand of one or another country, then I'm sorry, we have to keep our revolutionary process as top priority. It may take longer. Perhaps we will move more slowly economically, but we will certainly move faster in making the necessary social changes.

Interview, Lima/
Los Angeles Herald-Examiner, 8-5:(A)18.

Jose Juan de Olloqui
Mexican Ambassador to the United States

5

The Mexican way of doing things has transcended our frontiers. Few countries have presented principles so just and clear as those of Mexico. None of those principles is based on the imposition of rules of conduct to other nations, regions or hemispheres. On the contrary, they recognize the independence and self-determination of states. In brief, all those principles are based on peaceful solutions, in solidarity and cooperation with other nations and the observance of the statutes of the United Nations. Not only has Mexico reiterated those principles in all forums, but in all cases we have adjusted our conduct to them. In that way, Mexico raised its voice protesting in the League of Nations when Ethiopia was attacked. In the same manner, we defended the Spanish Republic, and we have protested every time there has been a violation of the Charter of the United Nations.

Before Inter-American Bar Association,
Washington, Jan. 16/
Vital Speeches, 3-1:301.

Daniel J. Flood
United States Representative,
D-Pennsylvania

1

. . . the Caribbean is our fourth front, in which the Panama Canal is the prime target for the control of the Western Hemisphere. The importance of this area was instinctively recognized by such leaders as Admiral Mahan, William Howard Taft, Theodore Roosevelt and Charles Evans Hughes and cannot be ignored, for the isthmus has become a focal point in the struggle for world power. The real issue there is not U.S. sovereignty over the Canal Zone versus Panamanian, but undiluted U.S. control of the Zone versus U.S.S.R. domination of the Panama Canal and the Caribbean region, with the Canal Zone serving as a Soviet base. Certainly . . . the Panama Canal is not a toy for diplomatic playboys but the strategic center of the Americas on which the eyes of the world are now focused. The time for diplomatic dalliance and weakness in regard to its juridical structure is over.

Before the House, Washington,
Feb. 8/Vital Speeches, 3-1:295.

Alastair Gillespie
Minister of Trade of Canada

2

[Saying Canada will continue to supply oil to the U.S. despite the Arab cutback of oil shipments]: Let there be no doubt about Canada's determination to continue to supply her traditional trading partners and friends. Canada does not, and will not, hold her friendships up for ransom.

At National Foreign Trade Convention,
New York/The Christian Science Monitor,
11-21:16.

Huang Hua
Communist Chinese Ambassador
to the United Nations

3

[Supporting Panama in its drive to oust the U.S. from control of the Panama Canal Zone]: The Panamanian government's position is just and its demand reasonable. We firmly support it. [The U.S.] imposed an unequal treaty on the Panamanian people, whereby it has forcibly occupied the Panama Canal, stationed large numbers of troops in the Canal Zone and enforced a colonial rule there.

Before United Nations Security Council,
Panama City/Los Angeles Herald-Examiner,
3-19:(A)2.

Robert A. Hurwitch
Deputy Assistant Secretary for Inter-
American Affairs, Department of State
of the United States

4

Cuba has not abandoned its goals of subverting other governments in the hemisphere. We are convinced that, regrettably, the time has not yet arrived when the Western Hemisphere can safely regard Cuba as no longer a threat to its peace and security or when we can take Cuba's leaders at less than their word.

Before Senate Latin America Subcommittee,
Washington, March 26/
Los Angeles Herald-Examiner, 3-27:(A)15.

5

[On U.S.-Cuban relations]: One could say there's a principle of consistency which dictates that, if you set out to improve relations with Peking and Moscow, and—at the end of the Indochina war—with Hanoi, you should have the same attitude toward Cuba. But, basically, the world is not the same everywhere; and to conduct foreign policy on such principles of consistency can lead you into a lot of trouble. Both the Soviet Union and the People's Republic of [Communist] China are large and populous areas that offer opportunities for trade and investment. Both of them are also military powers—one a superpower and the other potentially so. Now look at Cuba. It is small in area and population, and it is not as politically important as Russia and China. In fact, Cuba has been pretty much going downhill as a political force in the Hemisphere. I don't know of any countries in Latin America today, for example, that are seeking to emulate the Cuban model. Furthermore, Cuba is not militarily very powerful.

Cuba doesn't have much to offer the U.S. in terms of trade. Most of its future exports are mortgaged to the Soviet Union as payment for Russian aid. We no longer need Cuban sugar. We get along without smoking Cuban tobacco, although there are some connoisseurs, I suppose, who still have nostalgic twinges for a good Cuban cigar. And of course, Cuba still has some nickel that it used to sell us. None of these economic interests is very important to us. There is another important difference. The Soviet Union and the People's Republic of China have sought or indicated that they want to have an improved relationship with the United States. Cuba has not done that.

Interview, Washington/
U.S. News & World Report, 4-2:31.

C. L. R. James
Caribbean writer and historian

1

What is required [in the Caribbean] first is a federation—not a federation of the British-speaking islands alone, but a federation that includes Haiti, the Dominican Republic, Cuba, Jamaica, coming right down the list of islands including Guadalupe and Martinique, south to Aruba, including Guyana and what used to be Dutch Guiana and what is still French Guiana. There are enough people there to form a state, a modern state. The language differences today are not decisive. There are enough people to make some attempt to form a modern state. Those little islands by themselves cannot make it . . . Ten years ago, no one would have given to these ideas more than a sympathetic but somewhat indifferent interest. But today, the young people in the Caribbean and abroad are aware that they have to form a substantial modern Caribbean state or forever remain a number of small islands . . . too small to accommodate the demands of economic independence. The question of language is not a problem. The question of race is not a problem. Once the economic question is put in some kind of order . . . it would be comparatively easy for them to organize themselves into a unified state.

Interview, Washington/
The Washington Post, 8-25:(B)3.

Henry A. Kissinger
Secretary of State-designate
of the United States

2

What is in the interest of Mexico—in a wider sense—is in the interest of the United States. And what is in the interest of the United States is in the interest of Mexico. We shall apply this principle to all of Latin America.

Mexico City, Aug. 25/
San Francisco Examiner & Chronicle,
8-26:(A)21.

Raul Lastiri
President of Argentina

3

There should be a real understanding that governments should help people and not serve the interests of huge, multinational companies. Investments here frequently have made huge profits but left poverty and pain in their wake. If the genuine desire of the American [U.S.] people to help the people of Latin America is not strangled by the profit motive, Latin America once again will believe in the United States—not as a superpower but as an equal.

Los Angeles Herald-Examiner, 9-20:(A)10.

Eugene B. LeBailly
Lieutenant General, United States
Air Force; Chairman, Inter-American
Defense Board

4

Attempts to have the Latin-American governments concentrate on national-development projects to the exclusion of military needs have not been very successful. Our restrictions have not resulted in a direct switch of funds from "guns to butter," but only in a switch from the U.S. to Europe as principal arms supplier.

U.S. News & World Report, 1-22:54.

Gustavo Leigh (Guzman)
Member of the governing junta of Chile

5

[On the recent coup overthrowing President Salvador Allende]: This is not a time for

(GUSTAVO LEIGH [GUZMAN])

discussions, dialogues, meetings, forums or Congressional debates. We must pull this country out of its present chaos and clean it of undesirable, negative and dangerous elements. Only after achieving this aim shall we study the suitability of authorizing political parties.

Interview/
Los Angeles Herald-Examiner, 10-9:(A)4.

Carlos Andres Perez
President-elect of Venezuela

1

I believe that petroleum policy is going to be a great instrument toward toppling trade barriers that the developed countries are placing in front of the under-developed world. Petroleum is indispensable for the developed countries, but the conditions for supplying it will be set by us [the under-developed oil-producing countries] instead of by them, as happened in the past . . . I do not share any attitude which would contribute to generating strategic hatred toward the government or the people of the United States. But we will assume an extremely serious policy to demand from that great country more adequate treatment.

News conference, Caracas, Dec. 11/
San Francisco Examiner, 12-12:13.

Juan D. Peron
Former President of Argentina

2

[Criticizing terrorism and factional fighting in Argentina]: We have a revolution to accomplish; but for it to be valid, it must be one of peaceful reconstruction and without costing the life of a single Argentine . . . Every Argentine—however he thinks and whatever he feels—has the right to live in security and peace, and the government has the obligation to assure that. Whoever from any sector wants to alter that situation is a common enemy whom we must fight without quarter . . . The situation of the country is so grave that we all have to participate, or no one will ever

be able to do the job.

TV-radio address to the nation,
Buenos Aires, June 21/
Los Angeles Times, 6-22:(1)6.

3

[On his probable reassumption of power]: At my advanced age, I cannot have any other aspiration except to be useful to the country in the manner in which the country may demand . . . I am just a soldier in my country's service.

Broadcast address to the nation,
Buenos Aires/Newsweek, 7-23:29.

Juan D. Peron
Former President, and current candidate
for President, of Argentina

4

[On the recent coup overthrowing Chilean President Salvador Allende]: We are surrounded by threats; and when we see the defeat of one of our neighbors who, like us, wants to achieve freedom, we have to be on the alert. The example of Chile has to be valuable to us, because in the world of today we have to worry more about events beyond our borders than those inside our nations.

Buenos Aires, Sept. 21/
San Francisco Examiner, 9-22:4.

Augusto Pinochet (Ugarte)
President of the governing junta of Chile

5

We are a junta of old Generals without ambitions. We are men without a future who can bring a future. Democratic normality will eventually return to Chile.

Broadcast address, Santiago, Sept. 15/
The Washington Post, 9-17:(A)1.

6

[On the recent coup overthrowing President Salvador Allende]: I shall put my country back on its feet. In coordination with the other members of the junta, I shall draw up a plan to restore Chile's former standard of living, which it lost in the three years of this Marxist [Allende] government. The junta will not abolish social achievements. On the contrary, we plan to develop them legally, not illegally, as was being done.

Interview, Santiago, Sept. 16/
Los Angeles Times, 9-17:(1)6.

1

[On the recent coup overthrowing President Salvador Allende]: We [the junta] didn't want the job of running the country, but we have been forced to assume it, and we are putting all our efforts to the task. As soon as the country recovers and forgets about the chaos of the past, the nation will be turned back to those whom the Chilean people elect to run it.

News conference, Santiago, Sept. 21/
Los Angeles Times, 9-22:(1)3.

2

[On the recent coup overthrowing President Salvador Allende]: We received help [in the coup] from nobody. Put that all in capital letters. We did this ourselves, the true Chileans and the armed forces, with no help from the inside or the outside . . . We did this because the President [Allende] had exceeded the Constitutional limits of his office. He had made fools out of the Judiciary and the Legislative Branch. On the one hand, he told us [the military] that he did not want a civil war. Yet, day after day our intelligence service reported the presence of arms even in his own house. While he said to us that he was the victim of civil war, we had documentation that he was preparing for one.

Interview, Santiago/
Time, 10-1:28.

Galo Plaza
Secretary General,
Organization of American States

3

[On Latin-American countries' arms purchases]: Actually, we have a kind of balance. One country buys some *Mirages* [fighter planes], so another country feels it must do the same. But the second buys only about the same number as the first. So there is no real race. It's simply a matter of prestige, of the military establishment in each country keeping up with the times.

U.S. News & World Report, 1-22:54.

Harry Reasoner
News commentator,
American Broadcasting Company

4

[On the recent coup which overthrew Chilean President Salvador Allende]: Chile, in its respect for legal processes and its own Constitution, was an unique and wonderful signpost to the rest of Latin America. This was the only country below the Caribbean that always allowed its Presidents to serve out their terms, that seemed to have the political maturity the whole continent must achieve before this hemisphere is really calm and secure. So it is unreservedly bad news that Chile could find no way to make its majority effective at the ballot box. It is the kind of thing that happens when a country's extremes become larger than its middle.

News commentary,
American Broadcasting Company, Sept. 11/
The Christian Science Monitor, 9-22:14.

Raul Roa
Foreign Minister of Cuba

5

[Criticizing U.S. sovereignty over the Panama Canal Zone]: The highest aspiration of the Panamanian people was always that of a canal for humanity and not for an acquatic monopoly; a canal flanked by shipyards and factories, not by military bases and Green Beret factories.

Before United Nations Security Council,
Panama/San Francisco Examiner, 3-16:6.

William P. Rogers
Secretary of State of the United States

6

We made a decision four years ago to seek a less intrusive role in hemispheric affairs and to work in partnership with our neighbors rather than in [a] paternalistic manner. This decision did not imply any lessening of our interest in Latin America, but a shift in the manner in which we hoped to conduct our relations in the hemisphere . . . The President's [Nixon] policy toward Latin America was spelled out in October, 1969. It set us on the course we have been following, and will

(WILLIAM P. ROGERS)

follow. We're maintaining our commitments and our responsibilities, but we're relinquishing a directive role; that is, we are moving away from dependence toward interdependence. We're an active partner in the new relationship being built. We've reduced our visibility and lessened our dominance. At the same time, Latin American countries have developed their own solutions to problems and are assuming responsibilities that are rightfully theirs and not ours. That is what the Nixon Doctrine is all about. In situations in which we find ourselves in disagreement with our Latin-American neighbors, our policy and our desire is to work out solutions through negotiations, solutions based in reciprocity. This movement away from confrontation to negotiation is, of course, another one of the basic tenets of the Nixon Doctrine.

Interview, Mexico City/
San Francisco Examiner & Chronicle,
5-13:(A)2.

1

[Saying foreign investors should be compensated when they are ousted by their host country]: Each Latin American country must decide for itself whether it wants to, and how to, attract private investment. And it has the sovereign right to determine the rules under which such investment operates. Foreign investors must, however, be able to depend on the reliability of that determination, just as they must have confidence in the rules under which they are welcomed.

Bogota, Colombia, May 18/
The Washington Post, 5-20:(A)4.

John A. Scali
United States Ambassador/Permanent
Representative to the United Nations

2

[On Panama's insistence that the U.S. surrender its control over the Panama Canal]: The Panama Canal is not a work of nature or, as some have tried to put it, a "natural resource." The Canal is a very complex enterprise, and the working out of a new regime for it cannot be accomplished by the wave of

a hand or the quick stroke of a pen. It requires thoughtful and meticulous negotiation to achieve a fair reconciliation of interests. We have been and are prepared for such a negotiation.

Panama City, March 21/
Los Angeles Times, 3-22:(1)24.

Rufus Z. Smith
Deputy Assistant Secretary-designate for
Canadian Affairs, Department of State
of the United States

3

[On his appointment]: It's a unique job because there is no other official in the State Department of such senior rank dealing exclusively with the relations of another country. I believe my appointment reflects growing concern within the U.S. government and Congress of the importance and complexity of our relationship with Canada. And I hope it answers, to some degree, the charge by Canadians that the United States has been taking Canada for granted for too long.

Interview, Ottawa/
The Washington Post, 1-7:(A)27.

Osvaldo Sunkel
Chilean economist

4

[On the recent Chilean coup which overthrew the government of Salvador Allende]: The government of President Allende made an attempt at changing this structure of underdevelopment and dependence. It may have had many failings and committed many errors, but nobody can deny that it attempted to redress this economic and social structure by fundamentally democratic means . . . The Chilean experiment has ended with a catastrophic collapse of its economic and political systems—and the dramatic personal sacrifice of its leader and many of his followers. The conclusion for us here seems to be that it is not possible to try to restructure relations of dependence between under-developed countries and the transnational capitalist systems in a peaceful way. May I express a modest wish that you keep the Chilean drama in mind. It represents what under-developed and dependent countries have in mind, and fear, when they express concern over the asymmetric relationships between their countries and the international system, so heavily weighted in favor of developed countries and their multinational corporations.

Before United Nations panel on multinational corporations, New York, Sept. 13/The New York Times, 9-14:8.

Omar Torrijos (Herrera)
Head of Government of Panama

1

[Criticizing U.S. control of the Panama Canal Zone]: I want the moral backing of the world; and especially I want the people of the United States to know how we feel about the Canal. The Americans are very decent people, and when they realize what is happening here, they will feel a sense of shame, just as they did during the Vietnam war. That war wasn't stopped because of a lack of bombs, but because the American people did not want it. I think they can stop the neo-colonialism in the Panama Canal Zone in the same way.

March 11/The New York Times, 3-15:16.

2

[Saying the U.S. should surrender its "colonial" control of the Panama Canal to Panama]: We ask the world represented here to give us your moral support in this struggle, since our people is reaching the limit of its patience. We will never be an associated state, a colony or a protectorate. Nor will we add another star to the flag of the United States.

Before United Nations Security Council, Panama City, March 15/ The Washington Post, 3-16:(A)21.

3

Every minute of isolation [by the OAS] suffered by the brother people of Cuba constitutes 60 minutes of Hemispheric shame.

Before United Nations Security Council, Panama City, March 15/ The Washington Post, 3-16:(A)21.

Pierre Elliott Trudeau
Prime Minister of Canada

4

[On statements by some U.S. Congressmen that Canada is restricting oil supplies to the U.S. during the current Arab cut-back]: [I was] deeply distressed . . . to hear charges that Canada has been kicking the U.S. while it's down. Let's look at the facts. Far from reducing oil exports to the United States, Canada has been shipping to the U.S. more oil than ever before. Our projections for this year indicate we will ship to the U.S. 63 million barrels more oil than they purchased from us in 1972, an increase of 18 per cent. By increasing Canadian production, we have been able to respond to our neighbor's needs, while at the same time meeting our first responsibility, which is to ensure basic fuel requirements for Canadians. Consistent with that responsibility, the government's policy is—and will continue to be—to supply the U.S. from domestic production with all the help we possibly can.

Broadcast address, Ottawa, Nov. 22/ San Francisco Examiner, 11-23:16.

Asia and the Pacific

An Chi-yuan
Communist Chinese Chief Delegate to the
United Nations Economic Commission
for Asia and the Far East

1

What calls for special attention is the fact that a superpower [the Soviet Union] is stepping up its expansion in this region in an attempt to seize hegemony. It not only has instigated a war of aggression to dismember another country [Pakistan in 1971] but also has been making a show of force everywhere [in Asia], infringing on other countries' sovereignty and gravely menacing the peace and security of this region. Its doings have served to expose the essence of the so-called "Asian collective security system" it has been peddling everywhere. Its immediate aim in energetically advocating "Asian collective security" is to control and divide Asian countries and incorporate them gradually into its sphere of influence. Such a system can only bring new disasters to the people of Asia.

At United Nations ECAFE meeting,
Tokyo, April 12/
The Christian Science Monitor, 4-14:1.

Lawrence W. Beer
Professor of East Asian Politics,
University of Colorado

2

It may appear to many that at long last the United States and [Communist] China and Japan are going to get along together, and for some time to come . . . History, however, suggests that we and they are quite capable of sudden and dizzying shifts of attitude. We do not know, and neither do the Chinese know, what the domestic and international political situation of China will be after the passing of Mao Tse-tung and Chou En-lai. We do not know, and neither do the Japanese know, how

the United States and Japan will iron out the economic differences that arise in decades ahead. Nobody really knows what is ahead for Korea, Taiwan and Vietnam. We and they may be hopeful, but we have no reason for unrestrained euphoria as we look ahead. To complicate America's problem, the people of the United States have some very heavy psychological baggage to get rid of if our future relations with East Asia are to be less painful than our past relations.

Boulder, Colo., March/
Vital Speeches, 5-15:459.

Zulfikar Ali Bhutto
President of Pakistan

3

[Saying the U.S. should resume arms sales to his country which were stopped during the India-Pakistan war . . . in 1971]: Pakistan was once called the most allied ally of the United States. We are now the most non-allied ally of the United States.

Before American correspondents,
Rawalpindi, July 5/
The New York Times, 7-6:3.

4

The biggest folly India ever committed was to put its finger into the Bengal furnace [its war with Pakistan over the independence of Bangladesh in 1971]. They should not have been bowled over by their hate for Pakistan. The fall of Dacca was the beginning of the fall of India.

Interview, Rawalpindi, July 7/
The Washington Post, 7-8:(A)15.

5

In the past it used to be said by certain apologists of our neighbor, India, that India was arming herself feverishly because of a Chinese threat. In 1962 there was that boundary conflict; but now we are in 1973 and we all know that there is no possibility of a

Sino-Indian conflict. On the other hand, India is making anxious efforts to improve her relations with China. We therefore have a legitimate question to ask: Why then is India arming herself at the cost of fundamental economic responsibilities to her people? This question becomes all the more valid because, in the last 25 years, we [Pakistan] have been victims of Indian aggression on no less than four occasions.

TV-radio interview, New York/
"Meet the Press,"
National Broadcasting Company, 9-23.

Johannes Bjelke-Petersen
Premier of Queensland, Australia

1

[Criticizing his country's haste to accomodate Communist-bloc countries]: I want the free world to know that the dangerous, crash course the present Labor government is heading on is entirely unacceptable to the vast majority of Australians . . . In the space of four short months, we've had the top Russian man out here, the Viet Cong here, the North Vietnamese here. The welcome given these delegations by Cabinet Ministers, union leaders and Federal Senators causes me and many people deep concern . . . And to achieve this, we have ignored, even alienated old friends and cut old ties in America and Britain. We owe a great deal to America—in trade and in times of both war and peace—and most Australians want to maintain those close links. It has become quite clear that it is not [Prime Minister Gough] Whitlam who is running the government. The government is being run by the Communist-dominated unions, and the ALP is quite happy to go along just as long as it can remain in office . . . It's all very well to talk about being independent, about standing on your own feet. It sounds good and it reads good, and people say, "Oh, my word, yes, we'll do it." But this is a country of only 13 million people. And if you've got no army and you're cutting back on defense and you're antagonizing America and Britain, it's empty talk that doesn't mean much if it ever comes to a real showdown. We can't pretend we're a big power and isolate ourselves and say we'll

declare the Indian Ocean—as Whitlam did the other day—a neutralized zone and we'll live free and happy forever. It is a very naive attitude.

Interview, Brisbane, Australia/
Los Angeles Times, 5-16:(1A)1,10.

Leonid I. Brezhnev
General Secretary,
Communist Party of the Soviet Union

2

What strikes the eye is the total lack of principles in the foreign policy of the [Communist] Chinese leaders. They say that they are working for socialism and peaceful coexistence; but in fact, they go out of their way to undermine the international positions of the socialist countries and encourage the vitalization of the aggressive military blocs and closed economic groups of capitalist states. They style themselves proponents of disarmament, but in fact try to block all the practical steps designed to restrict and slow down the arms race and, defying world opinion, continue to pollute the earth's atmosphere by testing nuclear weapons. They keep assuring the world that they support the just struggle of the Arabs for the return of the territories seized by the aggressor [Israel] and for the establishment of a just peace in the Middle East, but at the same time are doing their utmost to discredit the real assistance rendered to the victims of aggression by their true friends, the Soviet Union and the other countries of the socialist community. They call themselves revolutionaries, but cordially shake the hand of a representative of the Fascist junta of Chilean reactionaries, a hand stained with the blood of thousands of heroes of the revolution, the sons and daughters of the working class, of the working people of Chile. Of course, a policy of this kind does not help strengthen peace and security. It injects an element of dangerous instability in international affairs.

At World Peace Congress, Moscow,
Oct. 26/Vital Speeches, 11-15:71.

3

We [the Soviet Union and India] will be together on our onward march. Only those who do not wish well for India, who do not

(LEONID I. BREZHNEV)

want India to be self-reliant and independent, are not happy with our friendship. Indian-Soviet friendship is one of the basic principles of our policy. The Soviet Union stood by you on several occasions in the past. In the future, too, in happiness and in sorrow, the Soviet Union will stand by India.

New Delhi, Nov. 27/
The New York Times, 11-28:3.

Chiang Ching-kuo
Premier of Nationalist China

1

In the past 20 years, the Chinese Communists have sent out numerous trial balloons and started many rumors about peace talks with us. But let me give you my word of honor that we will never enter into any negotiations with the Chinese Communists. Our decision in this respect is not based on political dispute or personal grudges. It is a matter of life or death.

Interview, Taipei, Jan. 22/
The New York Times, 1-23:4.

2

We plan to recover the [Communist] China mainland by 30 per cent military efforts and 70 per cent political efforts. We will emphasize the political rather than the military. It's not that we are going to invade a foreign country. We are just returning to our own territory and, therefore, political measures are more important than military ones.

Interview, Taipei, Jan. 22/
The New York Times, 1-23:4.

3

The Republic of [Nationalist] China is determined fearlessly to build Taiwan, Penghu, Kinmen and Matsu into a moral bastion in the world's fight against Communism and to transform itself into a dam of solid rock that will block the raging rapids of appeasement. We shall become a mighty force in the fight against slavery and aggression—a force with the vigor of life, creativity and potential. Our determination is based on a long-time understanding of Communism and cognizance of

how world affairs are developing . . . freedom and slavery or democracy and totalitarianism are in substance two totally antagonistic and irreconcilable systems. All Communist regimes follow the line of brute force, impose their will on the people and maintain their rule through terror, duress and extortion. To expect them to change their nature is as foolish as to hope for a pie in the sky. Peaceful coexistence with the Communists would make permanent the world order of half slave and half free.

Before Legislative Yuan, Taipei,
Sept. 25/Vital Speeches, 11-1:55.

4

Taiwan is Chinese territory. It belongs to the Chinese people. A Chinese government functions here. The Republic of [Nationalist] China exists, and the Communists [on the mainland] know it. Our agents move in and out and among the people on the mainland. Many people who have visited the mainland have also been here. They know how much better life is on Taiwan than on the mainland. They've told their friends living under the Communists about life here. We've received letters from the mainland recently saying our government was not very satisfactory when it was on the mainland, but even so it was still better than the Chinese Communist regime they have now. Also, many people on the mainland remember the firm anti-Communist stand of our President [Chiang Kai-shek] in the past, and they know he is and will continue to be anti-Communist. So he is still considered the leader of the Chinese people. Those are the reasons why the Communists worry about the Republic of China and the people on Taiwan.

Interview, Taipei/
U.S. News & World Report, 12-10:116.

5

When [Communist Chinese Premier] Chou En-lai practices "ping pong diplomacy," Americans should not forget the Americans who lost their lives in Korea and Vietnam. For the U.S. to recognize the Communist regime on the [Chinese] mainland would be a tremendous historical and moral decision. Before reaching that decision, the U.S. must take into consideration what I call the American spirit—the dedication to democracy and a free society. What we are doing here [in Nationalist China] is creating a free and open society, in contrast with the mainland which is totalitarian and a closed society. It is something to think about.

Interview, Taipei/
U.S. News & World Report, 12-10:116.

Chou En-lai
Premier of the People's Republic of
(Communist) China

1

Taiwan Province [Nationalist China] is our motherland's sacred territory, and the people in Taiwan are our kith and kin. We have infinite concern for our compatriots in Taiwan, who love and long for the motherland. Our compatriots in Taiwan can have a bright future only by returning to the embrace of the motherland. Taiwan must be liberated. Our great motherland must be unified. This is the common aspiration and sacred duty of the people of all nationalities of the country, including our compatriots in Taiwan. Let us strive together to attain this goal.

At Chinese Communist Party Congress,
Peking, Aug. 24/The New York Times, 9-1:6.

2

China is an attractive piece of meat coveted by all. But this piece of meat is very tough, and for years no one has been able to bite into it.

At Chinese Communist Party Congress,
Peking, Aug. 24/
The New York Times, 9-1:6.

Dalai Lama
Exiled former Chief of State of Tibet

3

The spirit of detente between Peking and Washington, [Communist] China's growing respect for the old traditions and culture—both their own and those of Tibet [which China rules]—are encouraging signs [for Tibetans]. Since 1959, the Chinese have treated Tibetans on a man-to-subhuman basis. It remains to be seen whether these first signs of leniency will

develop into a man-to-man relationship and whether this relationship will endure.

Interview, Dharamsala, India/
The Washington Post, 7-15:(C)2.

Sardar Mohammed Daud
President of Afghanistan

4

[On why he just led a coup which toppled the Afghan government of King Mohammed Zahir Shah]: Traitorous elements, in an attempt to carry out their sinister political designs, resorted to a strategem of divide and rule. But the patriots put up with it in hopes that this corrupt and effete government would eventually realize how appalling was the state of the country and try to reform it. But their hopes were not achieved; and the government became corrupt to such an extent that there was no longer any hope of reforming it. Hence, the patriotic people decided to liquidate this corrupt system and thus save the country from ruination.

Broadcast address to the nation, Kabul,
July 17/The Washington Post, 7-18:(A)20.

Luis Echeverria (Alvarez)
President of Mexico

5

[The Communist revolution in China was] one of the great revolutions of mankind. Although our political systems and our beliefs differ, we share the same fundamental aspirations.

At banquet in his honor,
Peking, April 19/
Los Angeles Herald-Examiner, 4-20:(A)4.

Takeo Fukuda
Director General, Japanese Administrative
Management Agency; Former Foreign
Minister of Japan

6

[On Japan's high inflation rate]: If this rate of inflation continues, it will become impossible to make either personal or business plans for the future. We won't be able to plan for our old age or for the education of our children. And the dream of salaried workers to own their own homes, at least by the age

(TAKEO FUKUDA)

of 40 or 50, will be destroyed. Without cracking inflation, trying to build a stable society and molding Japan into a "great peace nation" will be like trying to build a castle in a foundation of sand.

Los Angeles Times, 10-19:(1-A)1.

Indira Gandhi
Prime Minister of India

1

We welcome any effort toward peace [in Asia]. But we are aware of the dangers which still hover over us. Detente should not become an occasion to build new balances of power and to re-draw spheres of influence, or to reinforce the opinion of certain big powers that they alone can be responsible for shaping the destinies of small nations.

Before One-Asia Assembly, New Delhi/
The Christian Science Monitor, 2-9:3.

2

[India is] always under-valued, under-estimated, not believed. When we were fighting for independence without violence, you [the world] said: "How can you do it?" But we did it and we won. When we wanted to have a democracy, you said: "How can a country of illiterate people have a democracy that works?" But it worked and we had our democracy. When we wanted to have planning, you said: "This is a Communist thing; democracy and planning cannot get together." But they did go together, and today in India we are not starving any more. Finally, we announced that we would solve the over-population problem. You laughed at us, but even in that we are succeeding.

Interview/McCall's, June:99.

3

[On the 26th anniversary of India's independence]: We [in India] have together faced many a hurdle. Sometimes we come out with flying colors, sometimes success eluded us. Now we face our acid test as a nation, and if we are able to tackle it resolutely and courageously, we will have a future ahead of us burnished and bright like gold tried by fire . . . The question is whether we want to be a nation of those who cry, complain or quit in the face of difficulty, or a country of the courageous who squarely and boldly face their trials and privations. This question has to be answered today in our country by the young and the aged alike.

New Delhi, Aug. 15/
The New York Times, 8-16:10.

4

During the Bangladesh crisis, it was only the Soviet Union that understood the reality and came to our help. Once again, the Soviet Union has come to our aid by giving us two million tons of food grain. We are grateful for that. India and the Soviet Union will always remain friends. Very often, the Western press reports the Soviet Union is pressuring India. I want to make it clear here and now that the Soviet Union has never put any kind of pressure on India in the name of friendship and has never told us what we should do.

New Delhi, Nov. 27/
The New York Times, 11-28:3.

William E. Griffith
Professor of Political Science,
Massachusetts Institute of Technology

5

President Nixon's withdrawal of 500,000 troops from Vietnam has convinced the [Communist] Chinese that they need not fear a hostile American presence on their southern border. This, combined with mutual Chinese and American concern over the Soviet buildup in the Middle East, in the Mediterranean and in missile strength generally, has induced them to move toward partial detente with the United States. The single most important advantage to China in this detente is that the Russians can no longer feel so sure that if they were to attack China the United States would do nothing. The United States would probably not do much, but that's not the point. The point is: what do the Russians think? By ending the total antagonism between China and the United States, the Nixon visit to Peking [last year] has deterred the Russians from military adventures against China. And make no mistake: the Chinese fear the Soviet Union, which has a million troops on their border, far more than they fear the United States.

Interview/
The Reader's Digest, January:51.

Andrei A. Gromyko
Foreign Minister of the Soviet Union

1

In Asian affairs as in international affairs as a whole, the line pursued by the Soviet Union is that of peace, security and cooperation. The Soviet Union extends its hand to any state which supports these goals. One shining example of this is the continuous upward development of relations between the U.S.S.R. and India, a great peace-loving Asian power. This is also attested to by the experience of friendly relations between the Soviet Union and many other countries in Asia. We proceed from the premise that there are no problems in relations between the Soviet Union and the states of the Asian continent which could not be solved at the negotiating table. The Soviet Union has taken the initiative in the matter of establishing collective security in Asia. This idea is gradually gaining in strength, skepticism is dissipating and unfounded suspicions are disappearing.

Before United Nations General Assembly,
New York, Sept. 25/
The New York Times, 9-26:2.

Huang Hua
Communist Chinese Ambassador to the
United Nations

2

Some people argue that, since the two Germanys [East and West] could be admitted to the United Nations, why can't North and South Korea join simultaneously. The two Germanys were the outcome of World War II; but the present division of Korea was simply imposed on the Korean people as a result of U.S. aggression and intervention after World War II.

At United Nations, N.Y.,
Nov. 14/Los Angeles Times, 11-15:(1)5.

Yoshihiro Inayama
Chairman, Nippon Iron & Steel
Corporation (Japan)

3

The manners of Japanese who go abroad are bad. Many of the Japanese going abroad are farmers who only recently came into money by selling land. They don't have any idea of how to act; they are utterly without manners. Japanese in groups are quite different from Americans in groups. You don't see large groups of Americans at the Imperial Hotel making impositions upon and bothering other people. When we businessmen go abroad and see how Japanese tourists act, it turns our stomach.

Interview, Tokyo/
Los Angeles Times, 6-3:(6)1.

Herman Kahn
Director,
Hudson Institute (United States)

4

This year the Japanese economy will probably have a gross national product of $400 billion. That's a big GNP—and normally you would believe that a country that big, that much involved in foreign affairs and foreign trade, would have to take sides. But in fact, the Japanese get along with both Koreas, both Vietnams, both Germanys, both Chinas, both India and Pakistan, both the Soviet Union and United States, both the Israelis and the Arabs. For a people who have been known for a long time as a . . . people [who put stock in] "face" and have a short temper, that's very impressive.

Tokyo/Los Angeles Times, 8-12:(9)9.

Donald M. Kendall
Chairman, PepsiCo, Inc.

5

Out of our [U.S.'s] $6 billion [trade] deficit in 1972, about 4 billion was with Japan. It has reached the point where the problem can't be solved just by Japan changing the barriers they have against us. And there are many barriers. They have restrictions on the sale of U.S. computers and peripheral

(DONALD M. KENDALL)

equipment, for example, and on agricultural products, and on distribution—they won't permit us to have, for instance, more than a handful of Sears, Roebuck-type stores in Japan. The oil companies can't go into the Japanese market with their service stations, and so on, the way we allow the Japanese to work over here. Even if you changed all that, you would not crack the problem today. There is going to have to be currency realignment in Japan.

Interview, Washington/
U.S. News & World Report, 1-22:66.

Kim Jong Pil
Premier of South Korea

1

Just because Vietnam is over doesn't mean the United States should move its troops out of South Korea, too. History doesn't work that fast. A hasty decision to withdraw could cause real trouble in the area. The troops reflect the U.S. presence and affirm American interest in Asia. A few thousand soldiers are not important, but U.S. presence is. The United States can be the deciding factor in Asian stability during this period of Russian-Chinese tension.

Interview, Seoul, Feb. 24/
The Dallas Times Herald, 2-24:(A)5.

Norman Kirk
Prime Minister of New Zealand

2

We are a small country—in size, too small to be a military power; geographically too remote to be an industrial power; too restricted to be a financial power. But the strength, integrity and independence of our thought and social legislation can show the way for the bigger, stronger and more powerful nations. We can establish an order of priorities that all the world will respect, most countries will envy, many will imitate.

Los Angeles Times, 12-8:(1)24.

Henry A. Kissinger
Assistant to the President of the
United States for National Security
Affairs

3

Our contacts with the People's Republic of [Communist] China have moved from hostility toward normalization. We both believe that it is essential for the peace of the world that the United States and the People's Republic of China act with a sense of responsibility in world affairs; that we are part of an international community in which all nations have a stake in preserving the peace; and that, therefore . . . the normalization of relations between the United States and the People's Republic of China is not directed against other nations, but is part of a pattern that the President [Nixon] has pursued of building a structure of peace in which all nations can participate and in which all nations have a stake.

News conference, Washington,
Feb. 22/The National Observer, 3-3:7.

4

We, of course, continue to maintain diplomatic relations with Taiwan [Nationalist China]. The level of our troops on Taiwan is not the subject of negotiation [with Communist China], but will be governed by the general considerations of the Nixon Doctrine with respect to danger in the area. There exists no immediate plan for any withdrawal, but there will be a periodic review . . .

News conference, Washington,
Feb. 22/The National Observer, 3-3:7.

Henry A. Kissinger
Secretary of State of the United States

5

No matter what happens in the United States in the future, the friendship with the People's Republic of [Communist] China is one of the constant factors of American foreign policy.

At banquet, Peking, Nov. 13/
The Washington Post, 11-14:(A)13.

Alexei N. Kosygin
Premier of the Soviet Union

1

Tension does exist in our relations with [Communist] China, but it is because of no fault of ours. For some reason, the Chinese leaders have been shouting about a Soviet threat to China. It is a lie from beginning to end.

News conference, Stockholm, April 5/
Los Angeles Times, 4-6:(1)5.

Lee Kuan Yew
Prime Minister of Singapore

2

[On his small country's relations with superpowers]: When an elephant is on a rampage, if you are a mouse and don't know the habits of elephants, it can be a very painful business.

At White House dinner in his honor,
Washington, April 10/
The Washington Post, 4-12:(C)3.

Clare Boothe Luce
Former American diplomat and playwright

3

Ten years ago, in a speech at the Los Angeles Council on Foreign Affairs, I discussed the inescapable collision of interests between Soviet Russia and [Communist] China. My theme was that nationalism is still a stronger "ism" than any other "ism," including Communism. The speech laid a horrible egg. Not one person applauded. What I was saying seemed to them to be Communist, believe it or not. I was saying that the United States needed a strong friend in Asia, and that was China, and that the time was bound to come when the Chinese would need a strong friend in the West, and that, inescapably, would be the United States.

Interview, New York/
The New York Times Magazine, 4-22:54.

Raul Manglapus
Former Foreign Secretary
of the Philippines

4

[Asking the U.S. to denounce the current martial law in the Philippines instituted by President Ferdinand Marcos]: When is the American conscience going to speak up for the Philippine democracy you once loved so well and which you once even claimed to be your child? . . . We ask you only to speak up—not to intervene. We do not ask that American Marines be landed on our shores. We ask that aid be conditioned on the restoration of civil liberties. And we ask that, when our armed forces move to return us to democracy, your awesome military and economic presence does not move to object.

Before Commonwealth Club,
San Francisco, Aug. 10/
San Francisco Examiner, 8-10:4.

Ferdinand E. Marcos
President of the Philippines

5

[On the martial law in his country]: . . . I have no intention of setting up a dictatorship in the Philippines. What was done was in accordance with the old Constitution, which embodied the same basic principles that guided not only the commonwealth but also the Philippines under American law. It authorized the President to proclaim martial law in the event of invasion, insurrection or rebellion. Do not forget that President Lincoln in the 1860s utilized the power of martial law and considered it a part of the unwritten Constitution of the United States. It is a surprise for me to find American writers and contemporary observers ignorant of the problem, equating martial law with Hitler, Mussolini, and perhaps with Franco in Spain. They forget that a democracy must recognize the existence of a power to protect itself against certain crises.

Interview, the Philippines, January/
World, 4-24:16.

6

In our view, the rise of Japanese economic power in the Pacific is not necessarily a cause for apprehension; it could, in fact, contribute a lot to the development of the nations in the region. The common fear is, of course, that the economic strength of Japan may re-create the specter of a militarist Japan. This is, how-

(FERDINAND E. MARCOS)

ever, conjecture that can only be unfair to the Japanese people. Insofar as economic power is directly related to politics, I perceive the economic ascendancy of Japan today as pointing to an increased role for Japan in international relations. The way is open for this great nation to use its influence to mend the continuing tensions between nations.

Interview,
the Philippines, January/
World, 4-24:54.

Daniel P. Moynihan
United States Ambassador to India

1

Our [the U.S.'s] aims here [in India] are based on a major and minor premise. The major premise, and this is genuinely true, is that we would hope to see the Indian democracy succeed as we would hope to see our own democracy succeed. The minor premise is that, if we are to pursue this larger policy, we have to do so in a different way. For a long while, the U.S. saw India in a kind of dependent relationship. There was an aspect of "We know best; we know who India's allies should be; what their agricultural policies should be, what their family-planning programs should be." Well, that's over. What we've got to have is a new relationship, a relationship of equals.

Interview, New Delhi/
The New York Times, 9-11:2.

Mujibur Rahman
Prime Minister of Bangladesh

2

Pakistan has not recognized us, but 100 other countries have done so. I don't care about recognition from them [Pakistan]. If they do not accept reality, if they still think of Bangladesh as part of Pakistan, let them do so; let them live in a fool's paradise. All I want is for this to be an area of peace. That is our foreign policy.

Interview, Dacca, June 7/
The New York Times, 6-9:9.

Richard M. Nixon
President of the United States

3

[On U.S. aid and arms to India and Pakistan]: . . . the Indians are getting their $83 million in economic assistance; the Pakistanis are being allowed to go through with their purchases of the arms, non-lethal arms, and spare parts . . . This in no way, in no way, jeopardizes the peace in the area. After the war that broke Pakistan in half, India's superiority is so enormous that the possibility of Pakistan being a threat to India is absurd. All we are trying to do is seek good relations with both, and we trust in the future that our aid to both can be ones that will turn them toward peace rather than war. I should also say in India's case—while our aid there, our $83 million, was economic—India, as you know, purchases quite significant amounts of arms from the Soviet Union, and also has an arms capability itself. So there is no problem in terms of creating conditions which could lead to another outbreak of war by providing for simply keeping a commitment that the United States had made for the sale of spare parts and non-lethal arms to Pakistan.

News conference,
Washington, March 15/
The New York Times, 3-16:22.

4

[On his trip to Communist China last year]: Many of you [newsmen] in this room were on the trip to China, and sometimes I suppose the feeling must have developed, "Well, this is a one-shot deal." I never considered it that, and all of you who reported on it did not consider it that. It was the beginning, we trust, of a longer journey; a journey in which we will have our differences, but one in which the most populous nation in the world, and the United States of America, can work together where their interests coincide for the cause of peace and better relations in the Pacific and in the world.

News conference,
Washington, March 15/
The New York Times, 3-16:22.

Masayoshi Ohira
Foreign Minister of Japan

1

I think there will continue to be elements of instability, of poverty, of trouble and conflicts for a long time to come in Asia, including Southeast Asia. Therefore, to achieve real stability in this region is a task that surpasses the capabilities of one country, that surpasses the capability of Japan. We know our limitations in this respect. I think this is something that requires the participation of the United States, the European countries, the Soviet Union and [Communist] China. This is something we have to approach on a global scale, with a global mobilization of all the world's resources and power and technology and all the wisdom that exists in the world.

Interview, Tokyo, Jan. 25/
The New York Times, 1-26:10.

2

I think what is fundamentally necessary, or what is fundamentally to be desired, is for us both [the U.S. and Japan] to have an unshakable trust in each other, to have a very deep mutual understanding. I think this need for deep mutual understanding and mutual trust lies at the heart of any talk of policy objectives. When we view our actual relationship in this light, I am sorry to say that this mutual understanding and mutual trust are not yet sufficient or satisfactory either in Japan or in the United States. The relationship between Japan and the United States has not really matured . . . [One reason is that Americans emphasize contractual obligations] while in our country, this feeling of contractual relationship is weak.

Interview, Tokyo, Jan. 25/
The New York Times, 1-26:10.

3

The development of relations between Japan and the United States is something like relations between a man and his wife. Face to face with each other day and night, we are apt to grumble among ourselves. And at times, we are strongly tempted to have a love affair on the side. But the husband who lost his way and had an affair, however, will come to realize that his wife is his most important partner after all. And a love affair undertaken by the wife is the same. So, to deepen ties between Japan and the United States, let us make the most from the lessons we have learned from our "married" life together.

At dinner for Japanese and American
government officials, Tokyo/
The National Observer, 8-4:4.

Mohammad Reza Pahlavi
Shah of Iran

4

On Pakistan I can say this: that the integrity of Pakistan, what remains of Pakistan, is vital for us. If it was threatened and some separatist movement started, this would create an absolutely intolerable situation for us on our eastern frontier. But we are not encouraging Pakistan to adopt an aggressive, hostile attitude toward India. On the contrary, we would like these two countries to be friends, to cooperate. There is enough difficulty and evil to cope with than to think of making war. So our policy is not at all an aggressive or encouraging policy of warfare, but just warning that disintegration of Pakistan could not be tolerated by Iran . . .

TV-radio interview, Washington/
"Meet the Press,"
National Broadcasting Company, 7-29.

Jerry L. Pettis
United States Representative, R-California

5

[On his just-concluded trip to Communist China]: It was a little mind-boggling to visit a country where one-fourth of the human race resides and to find that, despite two revolutions since 1949, things appear to be very stable. It's a completely classless, pure Communist society. I certainly don't advocate it for us, but for them it has accomplished a great deal.

Washington, July 19/
The Dallas Times Herald, 7-20:(A)3.

Edwin O. Reischauer
Professor, Harvard University;
Former United States Ambassador to Japan

1

[On U.S. bases in Japan]: The Japanese got security at a bargain price. They spend less than 1 per cent of their gross national product on defense, while we [the U.S.] spend 7 per cent. But the psychological cost [to the Japanese] is very heavy—bases in the hands of people of a different culture and a different race.

San Francisco Examiner & Chronicle,
5-13:(This World)2.

David Rockefeller
Chairman, Chase Manhattan Bank, New York

2

[On his recent trip to Communist China]: The experience of going to a country as big as China, with as long a history as they've had, but which effectively for the last 24 years has been cut off from us, is a very exciting one— like visiting a new world. And I have to say that the Communists have accomplished a great many exciting and important things. They've deliberately cut themselves off from the rest of the world because they wanted to develop and consolidate an entire new structure of their society; and to a considerable extent they've succeeded in doing that. Now they are suddenly feeling that they're in a position where they can re-establish contacts with the rest of the world; and they recognize that we [the U.S.] and other industrial powers have many things that they don't have that they'd like to have in the way of technology and capital and goods. I think they're very serious about wanting to expand not only political but economic and cultural relationships. They are eager to learn about what's going on in our country.

Interview, Washington/
U.S. News & World Report, 8-13:37.

William P. Rogers
Secretary of State
of the United States

3

We have a security treaty [with Japan] which we believe is the keystone to peace in the Pacific. If we ever lose sight of that, if we fail to appreciate the fact [that] that relationship has . . . made it possible for the United States to move to create better conditions in relations with . . . the People's Republic of [Communist] China and the Soviet Union, then we've made a serious mistake.

Before America-Japan Society, Tokyo,
July 17/Los Angeles Times, 7-18:(1)4.

Carlos P. Romulo
Foreign Secretary of the Philippines

4

[On the current martial law in the Philippines]: It is not easy for Americans to understand martial law. To an American, martial law is like waving a red flag before a bull . . . [Democracy in the Philippines] never worked. We tried to be a carbon copy of American democracy in the Philippines without success. Democracy, American style, must have a bastion to fall on, a great and strong middle class. You have it in America. Here, we have only the very rich and the very poor . . . In developing societies, democracy as Americans know it and we have experienced and lived it, cannot successfully operate among us. We had too much politics, uninhibited politics. Our people had to have something that will help us develop and develop fast. If you had our Legislature and our licentious press, you couldn't develop as fast. To do that, you have to impose certain stern measures; and when you do, you don't expect to get everybody's approval. A person may not want to take castor oil, but he must take it if he needs it. You have to have surgery if you need it. Sometimes a scalpel is more merciful than to allow cancer to continue festering a man's body.

Interview, Manila/
Los Angeles Herald-Examiner, 2-5:(A)4.

5

[On the current martial law in the Philippines]: Democracy is far from dead in the Philippines. We must view the "new society" as a transitory stage, a period of preparation during which we try to fashion new social and political institutions which will give more concrete meaning to the abstract concept of democracy.

The Christian Science Monitor, 8-28:9.

Kenneth Rush
Deputy Secretary of State
of the United States

1

[On U.S.-Indian relations]: I see no great issues between us. There has been misunderstanding perhaps, on the part of both nations, as to the reasons why the other was carrying out actions that it did. I feel the leaders of the two countries are pushing forward toward understanding the action of the other in a much more satisfactory manner than in the past. I can say your Prime Minister and your government and our President and our government are trying very hard to understand each other better, which is the real basis for good relations among nations.

News conference, New Delhi, April 21/
The Dallas Times Herald, 4-22:(B)6.

Hugh Scott
United States Senator, R-Pennsylvania

2

I have been there [India] quite a few times, and all I get are lectures on how superior the Soviet Union is. I think we [the U.S.] have done more than enough for them. I would rather see India go to the Soviet Union or someone else for help. Frankly, in my opinion, their conduct has been no damned good.

Plainview (Tex.) Daily Herald, 1-2:6.

Norodom Sihanouk
Exiled former Chief of State of Cambodia

3

[Communist] China is still revolutionary despite the fact that she chooses to be your [the U.S.'s] friend. She must help the small peoples' revolutions in the Third World. Otherwise, how can she present herself to you as a big power? The greatness of China is based not only on the Chinese people but also on her prestige among the revolutionary peoples.

Interview, Peking/Time, 5-21:52.

Robert L. F. Sikes
United States Representative, D-Florida

4

It seems to be [Nixon] Administration policy to snuggle closer to the Communists at the expense of our long-term allies and friends. Unfortunately, this has caused a chain reaction whereby other countries now are declaring their friendship for Communist China, even at the cost of breaking relations with Free [Nationalist] China. This policy has caused the government on Taiwan and other governments world-wide to seriously evaluate whether Taiwan can preserve freedom if world nations continue to trade them off for the sake of expediency. It is small wonder the Communists on the mainland resent the continued existence of a Free China. It is a sore spot for them to have a capitalist democracy flourishing within the shadow of their Communist government and outstripping their Communist regime in all save regimentation. This is what the struggle over Taiwan is all about . . . Just as it is embarrassing for the Communists in Berlin to look over the wall and see the progress being made by the people of West Germany, so it is embarrassing for the Communists at Peking to peer across the Straits and see a flourishing and economically-strong Free China. Let us not play into Red China's hand by jeopardizing steadfast alliances for uncertain gains.

Human Events, 6-2:23.

Swaran Singh
Foreign Minister of India

5

I would like to see a decrease in American interest in this area. Perhaps the best thing for all concerned would be an American policy of . . . benign neglect.

Interview/Newsweek, 4-9:63.

Kakuei Tanaka
Prime Minister of Japan

6

To secure the peace [in Asia] that is being materialized at long last, the [Japanese] government wants to study the possibility of holding an international conference in which

(KAKUEI TANAKA)

Asian countries and Pacific nations would be represented . . . Japan, which has great economic power, should not merely be a recipient of peace, but should also participate willingly in the task of creating peace and thereby fulfill its responsibilities . . . International politics in Asia are, of course, far more complicated than those of Europe, and it will not be easy to construct the basis for a new stability in this part of the world. But if a place for serious discussions is established and if better measures can be found to carry out the post-[Vietnam] war reconstruction and to maintain peace on the Indochina Peninsula, that peace will eventually lead to the stability of all of Asia.

Before Parliament, Tokyo, Jan. 27/
The New York Times, 1-28:(1)17.

1

We have no intention of developing our own nuclear capacity. Nor are we about to tell the Americans to abandon all their bases [in Japan] and go home. Perhaps there will have to be some reduction, yes; but the more important American bases we want to stay here. We *never* will ask them to go—*never.*

Interview, Tokyo/Parade, 3-4:5.

2

There is absolutely no truth in the claim that militarism is reviving in Japan. The only military capacity we have is for our own defense—not for intervention in the affairs of others. We, after all, lost the war and were the first country to suffer a nuclear holocaust. We have not forgotten this so quickly—no matter what some outsiders may think.

Interview/Parade, 3-4:7.

3

[Saying Communist China has no aspiration to be a superpower]: . . . one-third of China's long frontier with Russia and India is restless and undefined. The Chinese population is rising at perhaps 2 per cent annually. Yet the gross national product is only half of Japan's. Therefore, they must concentrate on internal development. If China had truly wanted to be a global superpower, it would not

have encouraged the North Vietnamese to end their war [against South Vietnam and the U.S.].

Interview, Tokyo/
The New York Times, 3-30:39.

4

[On Japan's image in Asia]: I am not too apprehensive about this. We will give a lot more untied aid, through the World Bank, the IDA, the Asian Development Bank and the Vietnam Reconstruction Conference. We will act in such a way that nobody could see any economic invasion. But like the U.S., Japan will be called names.

Interview, Tokyo/Time, 5-7:35.

5

[Japanese] relations with [Communist] China will become important, but relations with the U.S. come first. The Japanese attitude toward China has been split around 50-50 pro and con closer relations. When it comes to the Soviet Union, the pros are only 10 per cent of our people. In the case of the U.S., I would say that about 70 per cent are supporters of the U.S. If Japan is to contribute to world peace, she must perfect her own security, and to do this she must cooperate closely with the U.S. In the economic and technological area, Japan must cooperate with the U.S. in helping under-developed nations.

Interview, Tokyo/Time, 5-7:35.

6

When you talk about nuclear deterrents, we are resolved not to own nuclear power or nuclear weapons. We have declared this intent domestically and internationally. It is under this assumption that we continue to maintain the treaty of security with the United States. We shall not have nuclear weapons, and we have remained and do remain and will remain under the nuclear umbrella of the United States.

Washington, Aug. 5/
Los Angeles Herald-Examiner, 8-6:(A)4.

7

Japan has no ambitions of territorial aggrandizement—in fact, has not had any since World War II. Japanese businessmen have no intention of trying to establish economic control over Asia. When aid and development projects are discussed, Japan's policy is to listen to the requests of the receiving countries so that we can meet their special and specific requirements. As for [Communist] China, it has 800 million people and its population is increasing by about 1.5 per cent each year. It is expected the total will reach about 1 billion by 1985, and perhaps 1.2 to 1.3 billion toward the end of this century. It is natural, therefore, that the Chinese are placing great emphasis upon self-help and independence in terms of their economic development. They have shown no signs of trying for predominance over Asia. Therefore, it seems to me Japan and China will not compete for leadership. That was exactly what the two nations declared in the joint communique issued last year when I visited China. We established that as one of the major principles governing our relationship.

Interview, Tokyo/
U.S. News & World Report, 11-26:83.

Nobuhiko Ushiba
Former Japanese Ambassador
to the United States

1

Japan is still suffering from a junior-partner complex, always suspicious of the big brother [the U.S.], believing that behind every move of [the big brother] lies a sinister intention to bully Japan. On the other hand, it was not so long ago when some Americans who are supposed to know Japan well stated publicly that the only way to get concessions from the Japanese was to clobber them over the head. They refused to take at face value Japanese endeavors to rectify the trade imbalance . . . Prejudices die hard in international politics, but it will be most important to get rid of these antiquated psychologies as soon as possible to promote an equal partnership.

Before Japan-America Society, Tokyo/
Los Angeles Times, 9-13:(1-A)6.

Gough Whitlam
Prime Minister of Australia

2

I don't believe there is any reason why any Australian Prime Minister can't get along with any United States President. I see no reason why the present Prime Minister can't get on with the present President. The Australian government was elected with a mandate to oppose continuation of the war in Vietnam, and to oppose Australian participation in it. This is the only point of difference between the United States Administration and the Australian government. In all other fields there are many opportunities, great opportunities, for cooperation between the United States and Australia. Our part of the world particularly will benefit from such fruitful, constructive, peaceful cooperation.

Sydney, Jan. 16/
The New York Times, 1-17:6.

3

Where the U.S. went wrong in its revulsion against the change of government [to Communist] in China—and where Australia went wrong in America's wake—was in believing that China was internationally an aggressive country. It never has been. It isn't now. I don't foresee that it will be. It is an amazingly docile country. More than any country in the world, the Chinese are satisfied to live in all senses within their own borders.

Interview/Time, 3-26:44.

4

Our relations with the United States are very important, but [are] only one aspect of our interests and obligations in our region and around the world. But . . . as we seek to widen and strengthen those other relations, we do not do so at the expense of existing ones. Naturally, there will be differences in approach to several international questions between Australia and the United States. I believe, however, we should explore constructively the wide areas of agreement which unite us, rather than seek to emphasize those few matters on which we are divided or take a different approach toward the same basic end. I believe that this alliance is old enough and strong enough to stand a little frankness on both sides. I believe that the friendship which we offer America now—namely, that of a robust middle power making its own assessments

(GOUGH WHITLAM)

and its own decisions in consultation with other interested countries—provides a better basis for a durable relationship of friendship between Australia and the United States than existed in the past. We do not wish to grandstand or thumb our noses at the United States. When our interests do not coincide and when we disagree with the United States, we shall, as a good friend should, say so firmly and frankly—usually, and preferably, in private.

At National Press Club, Washington, July 30/Vital Speeches, 9-1:682.

1

Nothing could be further from the truth than the suggestion that, under the new government, Australia is going isolationist. That is just as absurd as the idea that we are moving into a different ideological orbit. Precisely what we are trying to do is to break out of a kind of ideological isolationism which has limited the conduct of our affairs in the past. In our own region, in our dealings with all the countries of that region, we think it's time for an ideological holiday. That is why we have established diplomatic relations with a range

of governments as diverse as North Vietnam and the Vatican. It is, if you like, a policy of diplomatic even-handedness. It does not mean that Australia is not aligned. We are by definition aligned, through ANZUS. It does mean, however, that we propose that our dealings with all nations should be less ideologically oriented than hitherto.

At National Press Club, Washington, July 30/Vital Speeches, 9-1:682.

Takeshi Yasukawa
Japanese Ambassador to the United States

2

Our relations with the United States have changed considerably since the days of the American occupation [after World War II], but we haven't completely gotten rid of our complex toward the United States. When the United States says something, it is always interpreted as [applying] pressure, and too often it has been Japanese thinking to equate repulsing whatever the United States says with protecting Japan. In other words, to whatever the United States says, responding "no" has been considered the way to maintain our national interest.

News conference, Tokyo, June 15/ Los Angeles Times, 6-16:(1)14.

THE WAR IN INDOCHINA

Joseph P. Addabbo
United States Representative, D-New York

1

[Advocating a House vote to deny further funds to President Nixon for bombing in Cambodia]: We perhaps cannot stop the bombing by adopting this amendment . . . but we can express the intent of Congress to stop the bombing [and] avoid providing the Pentagon with the blank-check approval it wants to expand the bombing or to carry the Cambodian campaign into a further escalation. We can avoid being the rubber stamp of legitimacy that the President has asked us to be . . . The integrity of Congress is at stake.

Before the House, Washington/
The New York Times, 5-13:(4)2.

Spiro T. Agnew
Vice President of the United States

2

[On South Vietnamese President Nguyen Van Thieu]: [He is] a distinguished man; he is a decent man; he is a man of tremendous patriotism for his country; he is a scholar . . . I hope you'll have a chance to find out how absolutely outrageous the stories that have been passed about him as a callous dictator really are.

Before Lincoln Club, Los Angeles,
Feb. 12/Los Angeles Times, 2-14:(2)1.

3

[Arguing against amnesty for U.S. Vietnam-war draft-dodgers and deserters]: If we simply accepted all of these people back and said, "You're forgiven; you were right; it was an immoral war," what would happen if trouble broke out 10 or 20 years from now? We would have established a precedent that would encourage those who chose to evade their responsibilities to do so . . . These draft-dodgers and deserters have not admitted that they are wrong. On the contrary, they say that the

country is wrong and they are right. Until they recognize that it is they who have erred and not the country, we must be unyielding in how we treat them.

Before Veterans of Foreign Wars,
Washington, March 6/
Los Angeles Times, 3-7:(1)15.

4

The long and bitter debate in America over the Vietnam war has come to focus on one basic issue: whether the United States would honor its commitment to defend a brave ally against calculated aggression or whether, in the face of great difficulty and harsh criticism, it would simply cut its losses and abandon its commitments. The President [Nixon] chose the former course, knowing that the cold searching eye of history and the conscience of the American people would never condone his taking the easy way.

Before Veterans of Foreign Wars,
Washington, March 6/
The Washington Post, 3-7:(A)12.

5

[On the 1971 newspaper publication of the "Pentagon Papers," secret government documents on Vietnam]: [Never] has matter so flagrantly out-of-context been given such prominent attention [by the news media]. Never has the distillate of the tiny Pentagon dovecote, further refined and edited by the Vietnam phobic elements of the media, been so outrageously flaunted before the American public.

At dinner for U.S. Representative
Paul W. Cronin/Variety, 3-7:36.

6

The President [Nixon] believes that he must have the authority to continue [U.S.] bombing in Cambodia in order to achieve a negotiated settlement there and send the North Vietnamese troops packing, just as

363

they're required to do under the Paris [Vietnam peace] agreement. We're very close to peace now, and it would be an immense tragedy if we let the Paris accords become unraveled over the Cambodian issue.

Before Lions International, Miami Beach, June 28/The Washington Post, 6-29:(A)11.

Carl Albert
United States Representative, D-Oklahoma

1

[On the recently-concluded Vietnam peace agreement]: The treaty signed in Paris ends U.S. participation in that war. We're out of it, and I think we should stay out of it, and we will stay out of it.

*TV-radio interview/
"Face the Nation,"
Columbia Broadcasting System, 1-28.*

John B. Anderson
United States Representative, R-Illinois

2

[On intensified U.S. bombing of North Vietnam, including the Hanoi and Haiphong areas]: Congress has reached the turning point on Vietnam. People on my side of the aisle who have been semi-hawkish have really been converted by the bombing. They have no stomach for such tactics any more. I hope the [Nixon] Administration gets the message. Henry [Kissinger, National Security Affairs Adviser] has to come back from Paris with an agreement, and in a relatively short time.

*Interview, Washington/
The National Observer, 1-13:3.*

Bao Dai
*Exiled Former Chief of State
of South Vietnam*

3

I know that many Vietnamese, a silent majority in fact, regard me as the symbol of Vietnamese unity, and traditions remain strong in South Vietnam. For this reason, it is my duty to do all I can to try and contribute to this unity in South Vietnam and, in the long run, to that of the country as a whole. Whatever may happen, I am determined to return to Vietnam, where I belong, as a simple Vietnamese citizen. But this return, when it occurs, must not be regarded as it would be right now, as a personal or partisan political act which would detract from my role as a national arbiter in the higher interests of peace and unity.

*Tokyo, Feb. 12/
The New York Times, 2-13:20.*

Lloyd M. Bentsen
United States Senator, D-Texas

4

[On the just-concluded Vietnam peace agreement]: We are grateful that peace has come, that the war is over and our men will be coming home. But we must understand that a cease-fire doesn't mean that North and South Vietnam have resolved their political and military differences . . . North Vietnam can be expected to violate the agreement whenever it suits their purpose.

*Washington, Jan. 23/
The Dallas Times Herald, 1-24:(A)1.*

Philip Berrigan
Activist American Catholic priest

5

[On former U.S. Vietnam prisoners of war]: We are over-publicizing the war criminals that are coming home. But what else could we expect from the government but to distort the true nature of the men? The returning prisoners are just what [President] Nixon would want them to be, but they're going to have to come to terms with themselves . . . It's not that I am against them coming home, because these men have suffered grievously over the years for their actions in this war. However, they are just what the President wants them to be, and nothing could be more demeaning.

*At fund-raising dinner for "Camden 17,"
Wynnewood, Pa., Feb. 17/
Los Angeles Times, 2-19:(1)7.*

Mrs. Nguyen Thi Binh
Foreign minister, Provisional
Revolutionary Government of
South Vietnam (Viet Cong)

1

[On the recently-concluded Vietnam peace agreement]: We should like to believe that the American government has learned the lesson of this longest and most difficult war in its history; and that President Nixon now understands that no force, however brutal, and no maneuver, however perfidious, can oblige the Vietnamese people to renounce its fundamental rights.

News conference, Paris, Jan. 25/
The Washington Post, 1-26:(A)20.

Willy Brandt
Chancellor of West Germany

2

[Saying he has not publicly condemned U.S. Vietnam policy]: The pressing impatience with which people in Germany, too, await peace for Vietnam can well be understood. As the Federal Chancellor, I have believed that it was not right to join in vociferous protests, some of which had a false ring about them . . . We have chosen other ways and other forms of exerting our influence for peace and humanity.

Before Parliament at his second-term
inauguration, Bonn, Jan. 18/
Los Angeles Times, 1-19:(1)22.

Leonid I. Brezhnev
General Secretary,
Communist Party of the Soviet Union

3

[On the recently-concluded Vietnam peace agreement]: The struggle to end the war in Vietnam is one of the most important aspects of our foreign policy, of the peace program advanced by the 24th Congress of the Communist Party of the Soviet Union. And now the end is put to the war. One of the most dangerous—to be more precise, the most dangerous—seat of war in the world is being liquidated. Over many years, this war was used by the forces of aggression and reaction to intensify international tensions, to step up the arms race. This war created obstacles for establishing wide international cooperation. New possibilities for easing tensions, for consolidating security and world peace, open now. It can be expected that the political settlement in Vietnam will have a positive effect on the relations among the states that were involved in one way or another in the events in Indochina. Moreover, this shows that it is possible to find a peaceful and just solution of other conflicts.

At dinner honoring North Vietnamese,
Moscow, Jan. 30/
The New York Times, 1-31:17.

Edward W. Brooke
United States Senator, R-Massachusetts

4

[Advocating U.S. post-war reconstruction aid for Indochina]: Everyone wants reconstruction assistance, and I think it may be the big chip in bringing about adherence to the cease-fire. People are hurting, and they need assistance to build a life for themselves.

Saigon/
The Dallas Times Herald, 4-18:(E)2.

Joel T. Broyhill
United States Senator, R-Virginia

5

[On U.S. post-war reconstruction aid for North Vietnam]: If the roll were called [in the Senate] tomorrow afternoon, I'd respond with the loudest "No!" that you ever heard, and I'd push the [electronic voting] card in so hard that it'd probably break the computer circuit.

The Washington Post, 3-22:(B)15.

McGeorge Bundy
Former Special Assistant to the President
of the United States for National
Security Affairs

6

[Saying the "Pentagon Papers," made public by Daniel Ellsberg, were useless to North Vietnam]: It was because they [Hanoi] had a very extensive intelligence operation going on

(McGEORGE BUNDY)

that this material would be of marginal interest. My opinion is that they had this kind of information coming out of their ears.

At Ellsberg trial, Los Angeles, March 9/
The Dallas Times Herald, 3-10:(A)6.

Ellsworth Bunker
United States Ambassador
to South Vietnam

1

[On U.S. involvement in the Vietnam war]: I believe that history will determine that it has not been in vain. One small country has gained a chance at self-determination. Other nations nearby have gained the time to create a more stable Asia. And the great powers of the world have, through this war, evolved a way to replace confrontation with diplomacy . . . Now that I am leaving this country and this task, I simply want to say to you all—Americans and Vietnamese—that I am proud of you and proud to have been one of you in this work we shared. We have come to the end of a chapter, and we have fulfilled our commitment.

Farewell address upon departing his post
as Ambassador, Saigon/
Los Angeles Times, 5-11:(1)6.

2

I think our real success in Vietnam is that we have substantially achieved the principal objective that involved us in that divided country in the first place: to protect South Vietnam's right of self-determination, and to prove that America's commitments to its allies were, and remain, valid commitments. To do this it was necessary to send our troops into battle and give large amounts of economic aid, in order to create the security in which a viable political environment could be established. I think we succeeded in doing this. Vietnam is now on the threshold of a new era which we hope will become an era of durable peace. The cease-fire agreement is basically a good agreement that will work, if the parties who signed it abide by it. In the long run, I think they will. It is my hope that the many

violations of the agreement by North Vietnam will cease when the Communist leadership realizes they have more to gain than to lose by adhering to the terms of the agreement. In my opinion, North Vietnam needs peace now as badly as South Vietnam. For the past 20 years or more, North Vietnam has neglected construction of almost everything that was not directly related to the war against the South. It is time for both sides to mend the wounds of war and build economies and social structures that will result in a lasting peace.

Interview, Saigon/
U.S. News & World Report, 5-21:78.

Robert C. Byrd
United States Senator, D-West Virginia

3

[On U.S. post-war reconstruction aid to North Vietnam]: I'm against it, period. I'm against it now; I'll be against it six months from now; I'll be against it a year from now.

Washington, Feb. 15/
Los Angeles Times, 2-16:(1)6.

William M. Byrne, Jr.
Judge, United States District Court for
the Central District of California

4

[Dismissing the "Pentagon Papers" trial of Daniel Ellsberg and Anthony Russo because of government misconduct, bugging and burglary against the defendants]: [There has been] an extraordinary series of disclosures regarding the conduct of several governmental agencies . . . an unprecedented series of actions with respect to these defendants . . . The bizarre events have incurably infected the prosecution of this case . . . The only remedy available that would assure due process and a fair administration of justice is that this trial be terminated and the defendants' motion for dismissal be granted and the jury discharged.

Los Angeles, May 11/
The New York Times, 5-13:(4)1.

Chiang Ching-kuo
Premier of Nationalist China

5

It is our sincere hope that [U.S.] President

Nixon would firmly support South Vietnam, as it is the key factor in the Asian situation. If Vietnam is allowed to fall to the Communists, then other countries in the area, such as Thailand, Laos, Cambodia, Singapore and Malaysia, will also fall. South Vietnam, South Korea and Taiwan are the three crucial points in Asia. If they fall to the Communists, the entirety of Asia will go.

Interview, Taipei, Jan. 22/
The New York Times, 1-23:4.

Chou En-lai
Premier of the People's Republic
of (Communist) China

1

[On the U.S. signing of the Vietnam peace agreement]: The fact that the agreement was eventually signed is another convincing proof [that] no force on earth can check the great historical trend: namely, countries want independence, nations want liberation and the people want revolution.

At banquet honoring North Vietnamese,
Feb. 1/Los Angeles Herald-Examiner,
2-1:(A)2.

Mark W. Clark
General, United States Army (Ret.)

2

The adoption of a "no-win policy" [by the U.S.] in the Vietnam war was the beginning of the demoralization among the troops . . . Troops are perfectly willing to fight, but they want to win and they want their government to do everything it can to win . . . As for future military situations like Vietnam, we shouldn't rush into any of them unless we must and are going to shoot the works and win it.

Interview, Charleston, S.C./
Human Events, 3-31:16.

Ramsey Clark
Former Attorney General
of the United States

3

[Advocating amnesty for U.S. Vietnam-war draft-dodgers and deserters]: George Washington granted amnesty to those who rebelled

against the early Republic. Sixteen Presidents have granted amnesty. It's the greatest tradition that we have. It's the spirit of America.

Television debate/
U.S. News & World Report, 3-12:35.

John B. Connally, Jr.
Former Secretary of the Treasury of
the United States; Former Governor of Texas

4

[On the fact that former U.S. President Lyndon Johnson died at the time a Vietnam peace treaty was being signed]: It seems ironic, on this day, that his predecessors began the war in Southeast Asia and his successor [President Nixon] ended it. It was his fate to be the bridge over the intervening chasm of conflict that swept this country and the world. But he accepted that role without flinching; and no one would be happier today, no one would be more appreciative of the beginnings of peace and the President who achieved it, than the President who worked so long and so unselfishly for the tranquility that eluded him.

At President Johnson's burial,
L.B.J. Ranch, Texas, Jan. 25/
The Washington Post, 1-26:(A)16.

5

They [U.S. Vietnam veterans] kept the faith at a time of great crisis in our national history. They served when others of less faith turned their backs and copped out . . . Because of them [the veterans], the President of the United States was able to negotiate peace with honor. Because of them, Communist aggression in Southeast Asia was stopped for a decade—and in this troubled world, a stalemate is sometimes equivalent to success.

At Veterans Homecoming Celebration, Dallas/
The Dallas Times Herald, 6-5:(A)12.

Norris Cotton
United States Senator, R-New Hampshire

6

I voted consistently as what you might call a hawk for four years under Lyndon Johnson and for four years under Richard Nixon. But now that we've brought our men home, our prisoners home, I consider this a new ballgame. As far as I'm concerned, I want to get

(NORRIS COTTON)

the hell out of there [Indochina] as quickly as possible, and not risk being there to catch ourselves in more trouble.

News conference/
The National Observer, 5-26:2.

Pham Van Dong
Premier of North Vietnam

1

[On the just-concluded Vietnam peace agreement]: We are full of enthusiasm and very happy . . . Now we must lean on the agreement and on the texts to pursue our struggle to complete the revolutionary work carried out by the Vietnamese people. Let us brandish high the flag of peace, national independence and liberty.

Hanoi, Jan. 24/
Los Angeles Times, 1-25:(1)17.

2

Some people say we want to impose a Communist government on South Vietnam. It is a calumny.

Interview, Hanoi/The New York Times, 2-7:4.

James Doolittle
Lieutenant General,
United States Air Force (Ret.)

3

If we [the U.S.] can maintain a relationship with North Vietnam by assisting their reconstruction, and postpone or avoid war with them, I would be very inclined to do something which to me is anathema, which is to try to bribe someone or pay a ransom.

San Francisco Examiner & Chronicle,
4-22:(This World)2.

Nguyen Phu Duc
Foreign Minister of South Vietnam

4

The public and, if I may say so, the press in the free countries have been in a number of instances rather unfair to us. We are not perfect. Our shortcomings are blown out of proportion and dramatized, over-dramatized . . . We are portrayed as a country lacking com-

pletely in freedom [where] people are jailed for holding different opinions from the government . . . I think that many of these criticisms are not balanced. As you know, we are a country at war—not only a hot war, but a war of subversion . . . There have to be some restrictions to democratic liberties. We make no secret of it and no apology for it . . . If you look at the newspapers in South Vietnam, you'll see that many of them criticize the government . . . We say that in South Vietnam there are no political prisoners. We mean that people are not put in jail simply because they hold different views from the government . . . We are not a perfect society, but we have no monopoly on corruption and we don't condone corruption.

Interview, Sept. 23/
The New York Times, 9-24:11.

Daniel Ellsberg
Former government consultant,
Rand Corporation

5

I have not met a lawyer in this country who could say clearly that the acts that I admitted doing [in 1971]—copying the "Pentagon Papers," of which I had authorized possession, and giving those copies to the Senate Foreign Relations Committee, ultimately to the press—violated any law, including the three with which I was charged. It is an unexplored area. No one had ever been tried as a source to the papers or to Congress before; and my trial, as it was interrupted, didn't really settle the legal question, an extremely shadowy area. As I say, no one had ever supposed, before, [that] such acts did constitute a violation of the law, and that is why there had been no prosecutions.

TV-radio interview, Washington/
"Meet the Press,"
National Broadcasting Company, 5-20.

Sam J. Ervin, Jr.
United States Senator, D-North Carolina

6

. . . I have supported the President's [Nixon] position. I'd like to put an end to the war in Vietnam. It was a mistake ever to get involved in the war on the mainland of Asia. But I'm a great believer in going by the Constitutional processes; and the power to negotiate a settlement is certainly an Executive power; it's not a Congressional power . . . I think we would have been out of this war long ago if there hadn't been so much Congressional efforts to set deadlines . . . They're [the North Vietnamese] not going to negotiate if you tell them, in effect, that you're going to leave the field to them . . . I think all the effort to set a deadline . . . has impeded the making of peace.

Television interview, Jan. 4/
The Washington Post, 1-12:(A)22.

Daniel J. Flood
United States Representative,
D-Pennsylvania

1

[On U.S. involvement in the war]: If ever I saw a military merry-go-round, this is it; military in the sense of the general spectre of the great United States of America just exhausting itself.

At House Appropriations Committee hearing,
Washington, January/
The Washington Post, 2-11:(D)7.

Jane Fonda
American actress

2

[On reports by freed U.S. POWs that they were tortured while prisoners in North Vietnam]: There was most probably torture of POWs. Guys who misbehaved and treated their guards in a racist fashion or tried to escape were tortured. Some [U.S.] pilots were beaten to death by the people they had bombed when they parachuted from their planes. But to say that torture was systematic and a policy of the North Vietnamese government is a lie. And the guys [former POWs] are hypocrites. They're trying to make themselves look self-righteous, but they are war criminals according to law.

Interview/Newsweek, 4-16:51.

Hiram L. Fong
United States Senator, R-Hawaii

3

The bombing [by the U.S. in Cambodia] is more or less useless. Bombing can't hold a territory. If you continue, you're going to have more prisoners of war. And if there are more prisoners of war, you're going to have to go in and get them out . . . you get back into the same situation.

Washington, May 15/
The Washington Post, 5-16:(A)12.

J. William Fulbright
United States Senator, D-Arkansas

4

[On the recently-concluded Vietnam peace agreement]: I feel no one was victorious in the Vietnam peace. It was as good as we could have gotten, and I am happy about it. But it is a vague and ambiguous peace and the same one we could have gotten last October, or even in 1965, for that matter.

Before White River Production Credit
Association, Newport, Ark./
The Dallas Times Herald, 1-29:(A)17.

Indira Gandhi
Prime Minister of India

5

I cannot help feeling that the very manner of ending the Vietnam war may create new tensions. The cease-fire should not lull us into comfort that there will be peace all the way. To many nations, peace itself has often been war by other means.

San Francisco Examiner, 2-18:(This World)2.

6

[Accusing the U.S. of racist policies in Vietnam]: I would like to ask a question: Would this sort of war or savage bombing which has taken place in Vietnam have been tolerated for so long had the people [in Vietnam] been European?

Newsweek, 2-19:50.

Barry M. Goldwater
United States Senator, R-Arizona

7

[Praising President Nixon after the an-

(BARRY M. GOLDWATER)

nouncement of the just-concluded Indochina peace agreement]: Never before in American history has a President acted so courageously —not only in the face of opposition from an enemy abroad, but also in the face of un-precedented criticism at home. The American people owe him a debt of gratitude. His critics owe him an apology.

Washington, Jan. 23/
Los Angeles Times, 1-24:(1)16.

1

[On U.S. post-war reconstruction aid to North Vietnam]: The North Vietnamese were the culprits in this [war]. They could have ended the war before it caused any damage to their country. Their failure to do so caused many American deaths, and I don't think we should pay them for it. My mail is running heavily against it, and my feeling is that the American people will oppose it to a rather great extent.

Interview/
U.S. News & World Report, 2-19:23.

Billy Graham
Evangelist

2

[On U.S. involvement in the war]: I doubt-ed from the beginning over sending American troops anywhere without the will to win. We entered the war almost deliberately to lose it. You see, when the Russians went into Czecho-slovakia, they went with such overwhelming power that there was no battle. Nobody was killed. I don't think we should ever fight these long, drawn-out, half-hearted wars. It's like cutting a cat's tail off a half-inch at a time.

Interview, Washington/
The New York Times, 1-21:(1)42.

Marshall Green
Assistant Secretary for East Asia and
Pacific Affairs, Department of State
of the United States

3

[On current U.S. bombing in Cambodia even though a Vietnam peace agreement has

been signed]: It is related to our desire to see a cease-fire brought about in Cambodia. Our experience in these very difficult negotiations [with North Vietnam] shows that it takes a combination of a clenched fist with one hand and an open hand with the other to bring about negotiations with these characters in Hanoi.

Before House Foreign Affairs Subcommittee,
Washington, March 28/
The New York Times, 3-29:15.

Marshall Green
United States Ambassador to Australia

4

I don't think there is danger of another Vietnam [for the U.S.]. We are not going to be drawn into another affair like this without very careful consideration of all the possible consequences. In other words, the concept that somehow we are going to blunder into a situation, or that we will proceed in a way without giving careful thought to the conse-quences, I think is wrong.

Interview, Canberra, July 24/
The Washington Post, 7-25:(A)21.

Andrei A. Gromyko
Foreign Minister of the Soviet Union

5

[On the recently-concluded Vietnam peace agreement]: The agreement reached in Paris has been a result of the hard and courageous struggle of the Vietnamese people against ag-gression, a victory for a just cause, realism and common sense. It has been made possible, first of all, thanks to the heroic efforts of the Vietnamese people themselves, with whom all who hold dear the ideals of freedom and in-dependence could not but take sides. The combination of the staunchness of the Viet-namese and internationalist aid for Vietnam —moral, political and material—has been a major factor making for an end to the war. The Soviet Union has done its utmost to ren-der effective and efficient support to Vietnam, has always sided with the embattled Viet-namese people. And at this new stage, as be-fore in the years of stern trial, the Soviet

Union will invariably side with the just cause of Vietnam.

At International Conference on Vietnam, Paris, Feb. 27/Vital Speeches, 4-1:369.

H. R. Gross
United States Representative, R-Iowa

1

[Addressing Budget Director Roy Ash and arguing against U.S. post-war reconstruction aid for North Vietnam]: You tell us the President [Nixon] is determined to hold Federal spending to $250 billion in the next fiscal year. I'm all for that. I have been battling for economy in government spending for a long time. You also say the President is bent on holding down spending to $250 billion even if he has to withhold funds voted by Congress. Such a policy is very painful to millions of people throughout the country who consider these [impounded] programs vital and essential. Now, if that is going to be done, how can you justify spending money for North Vietnam? The only reason those Communists have experienced the ravages of war is because of their ruthless aggression. Yet, as I read the truce agreement, there is apparently provision in it, in Article 21, committing us to "help re-build and heal the wounds of North Vietnam and all of Indochina." There is absolutely no justification for anything like that. There is no justification for foreign aid in general, and even less so for assistance to North Vietnam.

At Republican legislators conference on the budget/Human Events, 3-10:8.

Mark O. Hatfield
United States Senator, R-Oregon

2

[Referring to President Nixon's use of the word "Communists" in defending his veto of a Congressional ban on bombing in Cambodia]: Just who are these Communists? Can they be the Communists so frequently toasted last week [during Soviet leader Leonid Brezhnev's U.S. trip] and whose flags were officially flown throughout Washington? Our bombs are not destroying an ideology—they are killing Cambodians opposing a feeble and corrupt

regime kept afloat by U.S. tax dollars.

June 28/The Washington Post, 6-29:(A)6.

Wayne L. Hays
United States Representative, D-Ohio

3

[On U.S. post-war reconstruction aid for North Vietnam]: Hell will be a skating rink before I vote for any foreign aid for that bunch of murderers.

The Washington Post, 1-25:(A)2.

F. Edward Hebert
United States Representative, D-Louisiana

4

[On U.S. bombing of North Vietnam]: We brought them to the conference table by bombing, and we brought them back by bombing. If bombing is necessary, bomb.

Washington/ San Francisco Examiner, 1-10:4.

Huang Hua
Communist Chinese Ambassador to the United Nations

5

[Saying Cambodian President Lon Nol should be deposed]: No justice-upholding countries should sit idly by and tolerate the willful intervention and aggression against a sovereign state or allow a traitorous puppet freak imposed on the Cambodian people by foreign forces to continue illegally to usurp the seat of the kingdom of Cambodia in the United Nations.

Before United Nations General Assembly, Dec. 4/Los Angeles Times, 12-5:(1)22.

Harold E. Hughes
United States Senator, D-Iowa

6

[On recently-disclosed secret U.S. bombing in Cambodia in 1969 and 1970]: I deeply believe that the peril to our free institutions created by these official practices of official deceit and secret warfare are more ominous than any problem confronting our country. No group within our society, however well-intentioned, can be permitted to make the momentous decision to wage secret warfare

(HAROLD E. HUGHES)

while officially deceiving the Congress and the public.

Before the Senate, Washington,
July 23/The New York Times, 7-24:5.

1

[On the Nixon Administration's agreement to stop U.S. bombing in Cambodia after August 15]: No thoughtful person can escape being apprehensive about whether or not our government really means business about stopping the Cambodian bombing, considering the history of deepening involvement, of secret large-scale military operations covered by falsified reports, and of deliberate violations of already-existing laws. Sacred and secret diplomatic commitments will be pled; the mythical light at the end of the tunnel will be cited again; once again we will be reminded of the impending bloodbath [should the U.S. withdraw its pressure], somehow strangely different and more deserving of our compassion than the blood-spilling of innocent people that is going on now under our own auspices.

Before the Senate, Washington,
July 27/The New York Times, 7-28:2.

Hubert H. Humphrey
United States Senator, D-Minnesota

2

[On possible U.S. post-war reconstruction aid for North Vietnam]: We have cities in America that are more devastated, or as much devastated today, as they are in Vietnam. When I look at the programs that are cut back [domestically] and I think about what requests are being made, I am going to take a good, long, hard look before I vote for proposals that will consume vast sums of our resources for overseas when we are in desperate need here at home in area after area.

The Christian Science Monitor, 2-24:5.

Daniel James, Jr.
Major General, United States Air Force;
Deputy Assistant Secretary for Public Affairs,
Department of Defense of the United States

3

[Criticizing members of the news media

who question the patriotic statements of U.S. Vietnam war prisoners returning to the U.S.]: [It is] always difficult for me to understand how reporters could write glibly about demonstrators who shout "God damn America" and "I hate the President," but who believe returning POWs have been coached to say "God bless America" and offer praise for their Commander-in-Chief.

Before Republican Congressional
Wives Club, Washington, March 14/
The Washington Post, 3-15:(A)23.

Jack Kemp
United States Representative, R-New York

4

[On current U.S. bombing in Cambodia]: The United States is not committed to any person or any form of government in Cambodia. Our government seeks only to bring about the cease-fire and withdrawal of all foreign troops as agreed to in Article 20 of the Paris [peace] agreements. Since the Communist forces have not observed the unilateral cease-fire proclaimed by the Cambodian government on January 28, but on the contrary are engaged in serious offensive military operations, U.S. air strikes—undertaken at the request of the Cambodian government—continue to be necessary to help defend their outnumbered forces against Communist offensive operations, until the terms of the Paris agreements endorsed by the 12-nation International Conference are finally implemented.

Human Events, 5-19:5.

Edward M. Kennedy
United States Senator, D-Massachusetts

5

While we hear a great deal from [Nixon] Administration spokesmen about the urgent need for airlifting military hardware and supplies to continue the war [in Cambodia], we hear nothing about the impact of our bombing on the people and land of Cambodia; we hear nothing about responding in any meaningful way to the urgent cries for help from the Cambodian people. The Administration chooses to throw a cloak of silence over the impact of the bombing and war on civilians . . . some three million men, women and children have become refugees since the American-sponsored invasion of that country three years ago. Civilian casualties number in the tens of thousands—and housing, food and medical conditions are rapidly deteriorating. The time is long overdue for America to stop sending its bombers over Cambodia and to start sending its diplomats to help arrange a cease-fire.

Washington, April 14/
The New York Times, 4-15:(1)22.

1

The human suffering and pain in Indochina stagger the imagination. It is difficult to comprehend the aggregate available statistics of war victims . . . We must join with others in answering their cries for help . . . Surely there can never be a peace with honor if America now walks away from the human debris of the war and neglects the urgent humanitarian needs of all the people in Indochina.

Quote, 4-29:396.

Henry A. Kissinger
Assistant to the President of the United States for National Security Affairs

2

[On the just-concluded Vietnam peace agreement]: We have had many armistices in Indochina. We want a peace that will last. And, therefore, it is our firm intention in our relationship to the Democratic Republic of [North Vietnam] to move from hostility to normalization and from normalization to conciliation and cooperation. And we believe that, under conditions of peace, we can contribute throughout Indochina to a realization of the humane aspirations of all the people of Indochina; and we will, in that spirit, perform our traditional role of helping people realize these aspirations in peace.

News conference, Washington, Jan. 24/
The New York Times, 1-25:20.

3

[On the just-concluded Vietnam peace agreement]: . . . it is obvious that a war that

has lasted for 10 years will have many elements that cannot be completely satisfactory to all the parties concerned. And in the two periods where the North Vietnamese were working with dedication and seriousness on a conclusion—the period in October and the period after we resumed talks on January 8—it was always clear that a lasting peace could come about only if neither side sought to achieve everything that it had wanted; indeed, that stability depended on the relative satisfaction and therefore on the relative dis-satisfaction of all of the parties concerned. And, therefore, it is also clear that whether this agreement brings a lasting peace or not depends not only on its provisions, but also on the spirit in which it is implemented. It will be our challenge in the future to move the controversies that could not be stilled by any one document from the level of military conflict to the level of positive human aspirations, and to absorb the enormous talents and dedication of the people of Indochina in tasks of construction rather than in tasks of destruction.

News conference, Washington, Jan. 24/
The Washington Post, 12-5:(A)10.

4

The real problem in relation to North Vietnam is that here is a country that has been almost constantly at war throughout its existence. It is a country with which we have made armistices in 1954, in 1962, and we've never made a genuine peace with it. Now we would like to explore the possibility of whether, after the experiences of the last decade, having established a pattern of coexistence with Moscow and Peking, it seems to us not inconceivable that, if we can coexist with Peking, we can coexist with Hanoi.

Television interview, Feb. 1/
The New York Times, 2-2:9.

5

The North Vietnamese are the most difficult people to negotiate with that I have ever encountered, when they do not want to settle. They are also the most effective that I have dealt with when they finally decide to settle. That is why we have gone through peaks and

(HENRY A. KISSINGER)

valleys in these negotiations of extraordinary intensity.

U.S. News & World Report, 2-5:67.

1

The basic purpose of my [recent] visit to Hanoi was not to work out an economic-aid program. The basic purpose of my visit to Hanoi was to establish contact with the leadership of the Democratic Republic of [North] Vietnam in order to see whether it would be possible to establish with it in Indochina something like the relationship that we have managed to establish with the People's Republic of [Communist] China in Asia in general. You have to consider that the leaders of the Democratic Republic of Vietnam have spent almost all of their lives either in prison or conducting guerrilla wars or conducting international wars. At no time in their lives have they had an opportunity to participate in a normal diplomatic relationship with other countries or to concentrate on the peaceful evolution of their countries and of their region. Now, for whatever reason, they have indicated some interest in at least exploring the possibility of a more constructive relationship and of a more peaceful evolution.

News conference, Washington, Feb. 22/
The New York Times, 2-23:14.

2

[Saying the U.S. would not be opposed to a peaceful, democratic Communist takeover of all of Vietnam]: If the performance of one part or the other [North or South Vietnam] is so clearly superior to that of the other that it tends to achieve moral superiority over the other, that is not an American concern. If the North Vietnamese are willing to compete peacefully, if they are willing to develop their country, if they are willing to rely on a political process, then we don't object to their objective.

Television interview, Washington, Feb. 25/
Los Angeles Herald-Examiner, 2-26:(A)2.

3

[Advocating U.S. post-war reconstruction aid for North Vietnam]: We are asking for support for the idea of such a program not on economic grounds, and not even on humanitarian grounds primarily, but on the grounds of attempting to build peace in Indochina and therefore to contribute to peace in the world.

News conference/Time, 3-5:16.

4

[Saying North Vietnam has violated the Vietnam peace agreement]: I think it is fair to say we have been very disappointed in the compliance by the North Vietnamese with the agreement . . . No one can seriously believe that we [the U.S.] are looking for pretexts to remain in Southeast Asia. No one can think that, after the agony that has been suffered, we would not welcome a peaceful evolution in this country [South Vietnam] as in all of Southeast Asia. Yet, it is a brutal fact that on the important clauses of the agreement . . . that all of these have been systematically, and I must say cynically, violated by the other side.

Before Associated Press,
New York, April 23/
Los Angeles Times, 4-24:(1)1,8.

5

[On his recent meeting with North Vietnam's Le Duc Tho and the resultant joint communique]: I have the impression that the realization that military victory cannot be achieved within Vietnam by either of the contending sides is becoming clearer. So as a result, while words themselves are never an ultimate guarantee, we hope that the peace can now be consolidated and the cease-fire more strictly observed; and also that this communique marks one further step on the road to the military disengagement of the United States from the conflict in Indochina.

News conference, Washington, June 14/
The New York Times, 6-15:10.

Nguyen Cao Ky
Former Vice President of South Vietnam

6

In South Vietnam the vast majority of the people are without a voice and are displeased with [President Nguyen Van] Thieu's leadership. But now they can only whisper among themselves. The press is controlled, and no politician has the opportunity or courage to say what this majority is thinking. Everyone is coming to me, asking me to stand up and speak for this majority. I am not yet functioning in the role of a leader, but as a spokesman for this silent majority. My national policy would include the "four yeses": yes to freedom of speech and political activity; I would say yes to collective leadership and to the participation and collaboration of all non-Communist groups in the South; yes to being honest with the people, and yes to carrying out a true social revolution that would end corruption as a first priority. The leader of a nationalist South Vietnam must be a leader whom the people understand, respect and support. If Thieu remains in power and his policies remain unchanged, I don't see any hope we will definitely defeat the Communists in the political struggle.

Interview, Saigon/Newsweek, 4-9:52.

Melvin R. Laird
Secretary of Defense of the United States

1

[On a hoped-for Vietnam cease-fire and peace agreement]: I hope and pray there will not be any killing in Vietnam or Laos or Cambodia or in Southeast Asia, but as a practical man I cannot assure you of that. I can assure you of . . . the success of our program to terminate American involvement in the killing and fighting . . . I don't want to get in a position where a year from now you can come back and say, "Well, you promised us all here there would be no more killing or fighting in Southeast Asia." I am not promising anybody that, under any kind of agreement, because I know the history of Southeast Asia . . . I am talking about every possible kind of agreement.

News conference, Washington, Jan. 19/
The Dallas Times Herald, 1-22:(A)5.

Pham Dang Lam
South Vietnamese Ambassador to Paris
peace talks

2

Unless they [North Vietnam] admit that

their design is to achieve the reunification of Vietnam their way and to place the whole of Vietnam under their domination, the Hanoi authorities cannot fail to acknowledge that there are two distinct states of Vietnam. [Both are] internationally recognized, each having its own political regime and exercising its sovereignty on its own territory, as in the cases of the two Germanys and the two Koreas.

At Paris peace talks, Jan. 4/
San Francisco Examiner, 1-4:1.

Lon Nol
President of Cambodia

3

The North Vietnamese have always liked war in the past and have hidden motives for returning to the conference table [in Paris]. In the near future, they hope to spread their aggression to Thailand and elsewhere. Even if they should accept a settlement, they are not in earnest.

News conference, Phnom Penh, Jan. 8/
The Washington Post, 1-9:(A)13.

Mike Mansfield
United States Senator, D-Montana

4

The Executive Branch [President Nixon] has failed to make peace by negotiation. It has failed to make peace by elaborating the war first into Cambodia, then into Laos and, this year, with blockade and renewed bombing, into North Vietnam. The effort to salvage a shred of face from a senseless war has succeeded only in spreading further devastation and clouding this nation's reputation.

Before Senate Democratic caucus, Washington/
The Christian Science Monitor, 1-5:2.

5

[On proposed U.S. post-war reconstruction aid to North Vietnam]: We have a moral obligation to give aid to the countries of Indochina, and I intend to support the President [Nixon] on this as another peace initiative. We have a moral obligation to do this because of the defoliation, napalming, the refugees and the partial destruction of the societies and

(MIKE MANSFIELD)

culture of Indochina.

Interview/
U.S. News & World Report, 2-19:23.

1

[Criticizing current U.S. bombing in Laos]: We're getting ourselves in deeper. We're getting involved in another civil war, and we have no Constitutional grounds to do so . . . I wonder if the time will ever come when we get out of Indochina lock, stock and barrel.

News conference, Washington, April 17/
The Washington Post, 4-18:(A)15.

2

[Criticizing current U.S. bombing in Cambodia]: Haven't we had enough war in Indochina? Aren't 50,000 American dead enough? Aren't 330,000 American wounded enough? I wonder when we're going to wake up to our responsibility. No interest of ours was involved [in Indochina] in the first place. No interest of ours is involved now.

Before the Senate, Washington,
May 3/Los Angeles Times, 5-4:(1)4.

3

In all of Indochina up to a few weeks ago, we [the U.S.] have dropped a total of 6.6 million tons of bombs. Do we recollect that, as of the end of World War II, in both the Pacific and European theatres, we dropped a total of 3.2 million tons of bombs? In this insignificant part of the world, an area in which we have never had any vital interest, an area which would have been better left alone, we have dropped 3.3 million more tons of bombs than we dropped on all our enemies during all of World War II.

Quote, 8-12:147.

Mao Tse-tung
Chairman, Communist Party of the
People's Republic of China

4

[Addressing North Vietnamese officials]: Our help to North Vietnam in the Vietnam war has been very little. We should thank *you.* It is you who have helped *us.* You have been fighting against U.S. imperialism for more than 10 years. We have helped each other all along.

Chungnanhai, Communist China, Feb. 1/
The Dallas Times Herald, 2-4:(A)2.

John Y. McCollister
United States Representative, R-Nebraska

5

[On possible U.S. post-war reconstruction aid for North Vietnam]: To hell with them. I would not vote a bus token to North Vietnam. If the North Vietnamese want money, they can get their good friends [former U.S. Attorney General] Ramsey Clark and [American actress] Jane Fonda to take up a collection for them.

Los Angeles Herald-Examiner, 4-5:(A)12.

George S. McGovern
United States Senator, D-South Dakota

6

[On last year's U.S. bombing of North Vietnam]: In the 12 days from December 18 to December 30, [President] Nixon undertook the cruelest and most insane act of a long and foolish war. He carried it out without a trace of Constitutional authority, and without so much as a glance toward Capitol Hill.

Before the Senate, Washington/
The Washington Post, 1-7:(A)18.

7

[Criticizing President Nixon's handling of U.S. policy in Indochina]: I don't know if Congress can do anything with the President. He doesn't consult with us; he doesn't talk to us; he doesn't tell us anything. He just does.

Interview, Washington/
San Francisco Examiner, 1-9:2.

8

I never advocated at any time during the [1972 Presidential] campaign, or since then, that we finance the rebuilding of North Vietnam by taking the money off the backs of old people in this country or taking it out of the school budget or taking it out of programs to save our cities. Yet, that is the predicament the President [Nixon] puts us in when he talks about using public tax funds to rebuild North Vietnam and at the same time impounds funds that the Congress designated to help our older people, our veterans, our school children and others who are in need in this country. I am not opposed to private American contributions, even in this context to help in the reconstruction of North Vietnam . . . but I am not going to support a program of public taxation to rebuild North Vietnam that comes out of the backs of the poor and the disadvantaged in this country.

TV-radio interview, Washington/
"Meet the Press,"
National Broadcasting Company, 3-11.

1

The [current U.S.] bombing of Cambodia and now the renewed bombing of Laos only mean more waste of dollars, new danger of captured [U.S.] prisoners and, some day, more proposals that we repay the damage. For God's sake, let's quit bombing Southeast Asia and begin rebuilding America.

Washington/
Los Angeles Herald-Examiner, 4-17:(A)1.

2

[On the recently-released U.S. Vietnam prisoners of war]: I believe that the nearly 29 million Americans who went out and worked their hearts out and voted for me [in the Presidential election] last fall had more to do with forcing the kinds of change that opened the way for the release of these prisoners than anything [President] Richard Nixon has done for 20 years.

At Jefferson-Jackson Day dinner, Pierre, S.D./
The New York Times Magazine, 5-6:84.

3

How could [President] Nixon get to be considered a peacemaker? When I heard that he had been nominated for the Nobel Peace Prize, I quite literally almost became sick to my stomach. After that totally insane, murderous bombing [of North Vietnam] at Christmas. And the bombing in Cambodia even now. I don't know what it is about him. It's almost as though he likes to show his muscles, and the only way he knows how is by hurting people.

Interview, Pierre, S.D./
The New York Times Magazine, 5-6:88.

K. Gunn McKay
United States Representative, D-Utah

4

Hundreds of thousands of American young men accepted military service as an obligation of their citizenship; and over 55,000 gave their lives in the course of the conflict. I believe it would be unfair to these young men if we were to extend amnesty unconditionally to those who have illegally avoided their obligations . . . I get the feeling that many who left the country now want to return with a clean slate, with no obligation of any sort to the United States. I cannot support this concept, nor can I rationalize granting repatriation for service in the Peace Corps or other volunteer service. I am unable to equate fighting in Southeast Asia with service in any of the civilian organizations.

Washington, Feb. 26/
The Salt Lake Tribune, 2-27:5.

George Meany
*President, American Federation of Labor-
Congress of Industrial Organizations*

5

[On his union's support over the years of U.S. Indochina policy]: We have supported the President [Nixon] the same as we supported President [Lyndon] Johnson before him on the theory that, in a war situation —and there was a war situation out there—that he's the Commander-in-Chief; that's our Constitutional set-up. I felt, and a great many of our people felt, that he was engaged in a fight to try to give these people in South Vietnam the right to choose a government for themselves, to try to save their freedom from oppression and the likely prospect of blood purges and slaughter at the hands of Communist aggressors. Well, we supported that. Now, of course, he's brought about a cease-fire, and we're supposed to be becoming quite friendly with the Communists and we supposedly have peace with honor; but I don't see it. Our people are still flying missions over there. I read the papers and I listen to the news and, well, there is not peace in that area. I am not going to fault him for his efforts; but when he

(GEORGE MEANY)

says that we've got it all behind us, I just can't buy that.

Interview, Washington/
The National Observer, 5-5:24.

Dale Milford
United States Representative, D-Texas

1

The Vietnam conflict has split this country more than any other factor since the Civil War. It would be foolish to go back and beat each other over the head by arguing who was right and who was wrong, and what mistakes we did or did not make in the past. It's obvious that both the President [Nixon] and those of us who supported him and the throngs of anti-war activists all wanted the same thing . . . peace. And now [with the just-concluded Vietnam peace agreement], we've got it.

Washington, Jan. 23/
The Dallas Times Herald, 1-24:(A)1.

Wilbur D. Mills
United States Representative, D-Arkansas

2

[On proposed U.S. post-war reconstruction aid for North Vietnam]: This will be an awful bitter pill for Congress to digest . . . I just don't like to give a bunch of fellows I can't describe as anything other than murderers and hoodlums money out of the Federal treasury.

Little Rock, Ark., Feb. 9/
Los Angeles Herald-Examiner, 2-10:(A)4.

Duong Van Minh
General, South Vietnamese Army (Ret.);
Former Chief of State of South Vietnam

3

[On the recently-concluded Vietnam cease-fire]: The peace negotiations were not conducted by the Vietnamese among each other. For the South Vietnamese, peace was concluded, once again, over their heads. To sum it all up, the Vietnamese problem can be settled only by the Vietnamese themselves. Allied power can neither make war nor peace in their stead.

Interview, Saigon, March 24/
The New York Times, 3-25:(1)3.

Thomas H. Moorer
Admiral, United States Navy;
Chairman, Joint Chiefs of Staff

4

I have always thought an invasion of North Vietnam would be a desirable move from a strictly military viewpoint. But as you know, there were many, many political complications that the United States struggled with in connection with this war, which was affected by the Geneva accords, the Laos agreements, things of this kind. The war was not fought in accordance with basic military principals alone.

San Francisco Examiner & Chronicle,
3-4:(This World)2.

5

I think the performance of our men in Vietnam was outstanding. They did more than anyone could have expected. You'll have to remember, too, that they were fighting in a war where it was difficult to distinguish friend from foe . . . Many of our citizens who should have known better kept telling our men that what they were doing was immoral and wrong and that we were the aggressors. But in spite of this, our men went on and did their duty. [American actress and anti-war activist Jane Fonda] has lived in a dream world all her life. I don't know what motivates her. The aid and assistance she gave the enemy was one of the saddest episodes of this unhappy war.

Interview, Dallas/
The Dallas Times Herald, 6-3:(A)1.

6

This gradual application of air power [which the late President Lyndon Johnson employed in Vietnam], with frequent bombing halts over the course of time, was intended to give the enemy cause and motivate him into seeking a political solution of the war. Instead, gradualism actually granted the enemy time to shore up his air defenses, disperse his military targets and mobilize his labor force for logistical repair and movement. Gradualism forced air power into an expanded and inconclusive war of attrition.

At Tail Hook Reunion,
Las Vegas, Nev., Sept. 8/
San Francisco Examiner & Chronicle,
9-9:(A)14.

Robert V. Moss, Jr.
President, United Church of Christ

1

[Advocating amnesty for U.S. Vietnam war draft-dodgers and deserters]: Amnesty does not mean forgiveness. Its root word is related to amnesia, and it means "to forget." Amnesty concerns the law's ability to undo what it has done in the past. To forgive a violation is to pardon. But amnesty is a legal action: to forget, to erase, to blot out in recognition of a greater interest—in this case, the reconciliation of a nation.

Chicago/
The Christian Science Monitor, 2-8:4.

Edmund S. Muskie
United States Senator, D-Maine

2

[On current U.S. bombing in Cambodia, even though a Vietnam peace agreement has been signed]: The bombing does not have the approval of the Congress nor has that approval been sought by the President [Nixon]. We believe that Americans want a complete and final end to our military involvement in South Asia, and that it is the responsibility of Congress to insist upon it.

Broadcast address, Washington,
April 2/Los Angeles Times, 4-3:(1)6.

Richard M. Nixon
President of the United States

3

Now that we have achieved an honorable [peace] agreement, let us be proud that America did not settle for a peace that would have betrayed our allies, that would have abandoned our prisoners of war, or that would have ended the war for us but would have continued the war for the 50 million

people of Indochina. Let us be proud of the two and a half million young Americans who served in Vietnam—who served with honor and distinction in one of the most selfless enterprises in the history of nations. Let us be proud of those who sacrificed—who gave their lives—so that the people of South Vietnam might live in freedom and so that the world might live in peace. In particular, I would like to say a word to some of the bravest people I have ever met: the wives, the children, the families of our prisoners of war and the missing in action. When others called on us to settle on any terms, you had the courage to stand for the right kind of peace, so that those who died and those who suffered would not have died and suffered in vain, and so where this generation knew war the next generation could know peace. Nothing means more to me now than the fact that your long vigil is coming to an end.

TV-radio address to the nation,
Washington, Jan. 23/
Los Angeles Herald-Examiner,
1-24:(A)9.

4

As this long and difficult war ends, I would like to address a few special words to each of those who have been parties to the conflict. To the people and the government of South Vietnam: By your courage, by your sacrifice, you have won the precious right to determine your own future. You have developed the strength to defend that right. We look forward to working with you in the future—friends in peace as we have been allies in war. To the leaders of North Vietnam: As we have ended the war through negotiations, let us build a peace of reconciliation. For our part, we are prepared to make a major effort to help achieve that goal. But just as reciprocity was needed to end the war, so too will it be needed to build and strengthen the peace. To the other major powers that have been involved, even indirectly: Now is the time for mutual restraint, so that the peace we have achieved can be kept. And finally, to the American people: Your steadfastness in supporting our insistence on peace with honor

(RICHARD M. NIXON)

has made peace with honor possible.

TV-radio address to the nation,
Washington, Jan. 23/
Los Angeles Herald-Examiner, 1-24:(A)9.

1

[On the just-concluded Vietnam peace agreement]: All parties must now see to it that this is a peace that lasts, and also a peace that heals . . . This will mean that the terms of the agreement must be scrupulously adhered to. We shall do everything the agreement requires of us, and we shall expect the other parties to do everything it requires of them.

TV-radio address to the nation,
Washington, Jan. 23/
U.S. News & World Report, 2-5:17.

2

. . . as far as amnesty [for U.S. Vietnam war draft-dodgers and deserters] is concerned, I have stated my views, and those views remain exactly the same. The war is over. Many Americans paid a very high price to serve their country—some with their lives; some as prisoners of war for as long as six to seven years; and of course, 2½ million—two to three years out of their lives—serving in a country far away in a war that they realize had very little support among the so-called better people—in the media and the intellectual circles and the rest; which had very little support, certainly, among some elements of the Congress, particularly the United States Senate; but which fortunately did have support among a majority of the American people . . . despite the fact that they were hammered night after night and day after day with the fact that this was an immoral war, that America should not be there, that they should not serve their country, that morally what they should do was desert their country. Certainly, as we look at all of that, there might be a tendency to say now—to those few hundreds who went to Canada or Sweden or someplace else and chose to desert their country because they had a higher morality —we should now give them amnesty. Now,

amnesty means forgiveness. We cannot provide forgiveness for them. Those who served paid their price. Those who deserted must pay their price; and the price is not a junket in the Peace Corps or something like that, as some have suggested. The price is a criminal penalty for disobeying the laws of the United States. If they want to return to the United States, they must pay the penalty. If they don't want to return, they are certainly welcome to stay in any country that welcomes them . . .

News conference, Washington, Jan. 31/
The New York Times, 2-1:20.

3

One cannot discuss peace in Vietnam itself without discussing Laos and Cambodia, because Laos and Cambodia opened the way to Vietnam . . . What happens in Indochina affects Thailand, Indonesia, Malaysia and Singapore.

San Clemente, Calif., Feb. 10/
The Washington Post, 2-11:(A)3.

4

One of the reasons I considered it vitally important that the war in Vietnam be ended in what I think was the right way, peace with honor, was that it was essential to demonstrate both to our allies in Europe, the Japanese and other allies, the Thai and so forth, and to potential adversaries, that the United States is a dependable ally. All the power in the world lodged in the United States means nothing unless those who depend upon U.S. power to protect them from the possibilities of aggression from other powers, which they themselves would not be able to do, all the power in the world here means nothing unless there is some assurance, some confidence, some trust that the United States will be credible, will be dependable . . . I would only suggest it is my conviction, very strongly, that in the perspective of history, that many of our allies, particularly, will look back and realize that, had we taken the easy way out—which we could have done years ago, certainly when I came into office in 1969—our failure there would have eroded and possibly destroyed their confidence in the

United States and, of course, enormously encouraged those who might have aggressive intentions toward us.

Informally to newsmen, Washington, Feb. 15/
U.S. News & World Report, 2-26:23.

1

Because the war has been so long, and because it has been so difficult, there is a tendency for us to forget how the United States became involved, and why. It would be very easy now, looking back, to point out the mistakes that were made in the conduct of the war, to even question whether or not the United States should have become involved in the first place. But let us get one thing very clear: when, during the course of President [John] Kennedy's Administration, the first men were sent to Vietnam for combat, when, during the course of President [Lyndon] Johnson's Administration, others were sent there to continue the activities in the military area, they were sent there for the most selfless purpose that any nation has ever fought a war. We did not go to South Vietnam, and our men did not go there, for the purpose of conquering North Vietnam. Our men did not go to South Vietnam for the purpose of getting bases in South Vietnam or acquiring territory or domination over that part of the world. They went for a very high purpose, and that purpose can never be taken away from them or this country. It was, very simply, to prevent the imposition by force of a Communist government on the 17 million people of South Vietnam. That was our goal and we achieved that goal; and we can be proud that we stuck it out until we did reach that goal.

Before South Carolina Legislature, Columbia,
Feb. 20/The New York Times, 2-21:22.

2

Because of what we did in Vietnam, the United States can now exercise more firm leadership in working for world peace. We would not have had the fruitful and productive negotiations and discussions with the Soviet Union, not have had the opening dialog with the People's Republic of [Communist] China, unless the United States had been strong, not only in arms but also in its will,

its determination . . . So as we look back on the war, American sacrifices are important because they were made not just for Vietnam, but for America's position of leadership in the whole world . . . The chances for us to build a peaceful world are better than at any time since World War II [because of America's stand in Vietnam].

Before South Carolina Legislature, Columbia,
Feb. 20/Los Angeles Times, 2-21:(1)14.

3

[Supporting U.S. post-war reconstruction aid for North Vietnam]: If the North Vietnamese, after 25 years of war, continue to think that their future will only be meaningful if they engage in continuing war, then we are going to continue to have war in that part of the world; and it would not only threaten South Vietnam . . . but Cambodia, Laos, the Philippines, the whole area. If, on the other hand, the people in North Vietnam have a stake in peace, then it will be altogether different, and so . . . we believe that once the Congress . . . considers this matter . . . that they will decide . . . that the interest of peace will be served by providing the aid. The costs of peace are great; but the costs of war are much greater.

News conference, Washington, March 2/
Los Angeles Times, 3-4:(1)6.

4

Tonight [when all U.S. POWs are on their way home and no U.S. military forces are stationed in Vietnam], I want to express the appreciation of the nation to others who helped make this day possible. I refer to you, the great majority of Americans listening to me tonight, who, despite an unprecedented barrage of criticism from a small but vocal minority, stood firm for peace with honor. I know it was not easy for you to do so. We have been through some difficult times together. I recall the time in November, 1969, when hundreds of thousands of protesters marched on the White House; the time in April, 1970, when I found it necessary to order attacks on Communist bases in Cambodia; the time in May, 1972, when I ordered the mining of Haiphong and air strikes on military targets in

(RICHARD M. NIXON)

North Vietnam in order to stop a massive Communist invasion in South Vietnam. And then perhaps the hardest decision I have made as President, on December 18, 1972—when our hopes for peace were so high and when the North Vietnamese stone-walled us at the conference table—I found it necessary to order more air strikes on military targets in North Vietnam to break the deadlock. On each of these occasions, the voices of opposition we heard in Washington were so loud they at times seemed to be the majority. But across America, the overwhelming majority stood firm against those who advocated peace at any price—even if the price would have been defeat and humiliation for the United States. Because you stood firm for doing what was right, [just-released U.S. prisoner-of-war] Colonel McKnight was able to say for his fellow POWs when he returned home, "Thank you for bringing us home on our feet instead of on our knees."

TV-radio address to the nation, Washington, March 29/Los Angeles Times, 3-30:(1)14.

1

North Vietnam . . . has persisted in violations of the Paris [peace] agreements. They have, for example, refused to withdraw the thousands of troops which they still maintain in Laos and Cambodia. They have poured huge amounts of military equipment into these areas and into South Vietnam. It would be a crime against the memory of those Americans who made the ultimate sacrifice for peace in Indochina, and a serious blow to this country's ability to lead constructively elsewhere in the world, for us to stand by and permit the settlement reached in Paris to be systematically destroyed by violations such as these. That is why we are continuing to take the necessary measures to insist that all parties to the agreements keep their word and live up to their obligations. It should be clearly understood by everyone concerned, in this country and abroad, that our policy is not aimed at continuing the war in Vietnam or renewing the war. Rather, it is aimed solely at preserving and strengthening the peace—a peace which we achieved at great cost in the past, and which holds such promise for the future.

At Armed Forces Day ceremony, Norfolk, Va., May 19/The Dallas Times Herald, 5-20:(A)1; The Washington Post, 5-20:(A)16.

2

[Defending unpublicized U.S. bombing in Cambodia in 1969-70]: These strikes weren't directed at the Cambodian Army or the Cambodian people. They were directed at the North Vietnamese invaders who at that time had occupied this area within Cambodia and were killing Americans from this area. And this is the significant thing: The Cambodian government did not object to the strikes. In fact, while they were in progress in the spring of that year, Prince [Norodom] Sihanouk, then the leader of the Cambodian government, personally invited me very warmly to make a state visit to the Cambodian capital. This is after the strikes had been going on for a long time. That's a pretty good indication of what he thought about what we were doing. Now, as for secrecy: As I've already indicated, the fact of the bombing was disclosed to appropriate government leaders [in the U.S.] . . . What is most important—and here is the bottom line—soon after this bombing started early in this Administration, there began a steady decline finally in American casualties along the Cambodian border [with South Vietnam], and the enemy was provided with one more incentive to move to the conference table, which they began to do. The secrecy was necessary to accomplish these goals—secrecy from the standpoint of making a big public announcement about it—although there was no secrecy as far as the [U.S.] government leaders who were concerned, who had any right to know or need to know. Had we announced the air strikes, the Cambodian government would have been compelled to protest, the bombing would have had to stop, and American soldiers would have paid the price for this disclosure and this announcement with their lives.

Before Veterans of Foreign Wars, New Orleans, Aug. 20/ The Wall Street Journal, 8-22:14.

Olof Palme
Prime Minister of Sweden

1

The period I went to school in the [United] States was the most important period of my life. For me and for most of my generation, American democracy—with its shortcomings, but also its great vitality—has been a great inspiration. Partly, at least, this explains our disappointment and distress over the Vietnam war, which for me stands as a contradiction to the basic tenets of American democracy.

Interview/The New York Times, 3-22:7.

William Proxmire
United States Senator, D-Wisconsin

2

Large-scale [U.S. post-war reconstruction] aid to North Vietnam is out of the question. One or two billion dollars for Hanoi has as much chance as a billion or two for the U.S. poverty program—and that is zero. No aid at any level will come until our prisoners of war are accounted for and all military activity is ended. That could be a very long time.

Interview/
U.S. News & World Report, 2-19:23.

Ronald Reagan
Governor of California

3

I challenge and question the right of any government to ask men to fight for their country and die for their country if that country isn't willing and doesn't believe in the cause enough to go forward and end the war by winning it . . . I think the war was badly fought for many years. My greatest criticism down through the years of the war was that, under two [U.S.] Administrations, they apparently were unwilling to win it and unable to end it.

News conference, Sacramento, Jan. 30/
San Francisco Examiner, 1-31:12.

Elliot L. Richardson
Secretary of Defense of the United States

4

[On current U.S. bombing in Cambodia]: I

realize there are some who sincerely believe that we should cease our involvement in Southeast Asia regardless of the consequences. Now that our POWs have returned and the last U.S. troops have withdrawn from Vietnam, it is tempting to withdraw from our commitments and to look inward to our own needs. The growth of such a new isolationism can lead as surely to war as could a policy of adventurism and over-involvement in world affairs. If by cutting off funds [for the bombing] the Congress announces that we are quitting regardless of how flagrantly the enemy violates the peace agreement, we could be removing the enemy's strongest incentive to live up to the hard-won Vietnam peace agreement. If the Congress does not support the President [Nixon] at this crucial point in time, it must also be willing to accept the responsibility for the undermining of the central achievement of the January [peace] agreement and for the prolonging of hostilities in Southeast Asia.

Human Events, 5-19:6.

Howard W. Robison
United States Representative, R-New York

5

I'm not sure I understand the President [Nixon] when he says he's against amnesty [for U.S. Vietnam-war draft-dodgers and deserters]. If he means blanket amnesty, then I'm against it, too. It's impractical, it's unfair, it's inequitable to those who served in the war and, particularly, to those who died in the war or who were wounded in the war. But I do believe the time is going to come when, if not Mr. Nixon, then another President or the Congress will have to say: These young men are in Canada or elsewhere and they are looking for some sort of resolution of their lives. We can leave them there and forget about them or let them come home at their own risk and face criminal proceedings, each and every one. That would clog up the criminal-court dockets a little more and it could be two years or so before some would have a trial. We can do that or we can be practical and begin to think about how you set up a review board of some sort, and try to encour-

(HOWARD W. ROBISON)

age resolution of the problem rather than just resist trying to find an answer to it.

Interview, Washington/
The Wall Street Journal, 6-18:12.

William P. Rogers
Secretary of State of the United States

1

[On the Vietnam peace agreement]: The widespread killing has been stopped; the level of military activity has declined substantially from the first days of the cease-fire; the International Control and Supervisory Commission has placed teams at seven key locations; after understandable initial difficulties, the Four-Party Joint Military Commission is now functioning and is meeting with the International Commission; and direct talks between the South Vietnamese parties are now under way in Paris. Of course, there are many remaining problems to be worked out. But so far, developments certainly support our expectations that the agreement will work, that the South Vietnamese people have a reasonable chance to sort out their own political destiny, and that peace with honor is being achieved.

Before House Foreign Affairs Committee,
Washington, Feb. 8/
The New York Times, 2-9:5.

2

[Advocating U.S. post-war reconstruction aid for North Vietnam]: It is certainly an understandable political argument to make that why should we help other nations—particularly one with which we have been at war —when we are not able to do all of the things that we would like to do at home . . . We will have a problem with Congress. And we will have to make it clear to Congress that this makes sense. We will have to consult with them and cooperate with them and try to involve their interest in this subject. It is not going to be easy; we recognize that. But we don't think it is going to fail. We think that, as in the past, Congress, when it finally finds out all the facts and gives full consideration to the problems and the implications of failing to

help—I think Congress will react responsibly. They did after World War II. They have done it in many instances. And I think they will again.

News conference, Washington, Feb. 15/
The New York Times, 2-16:14.

3

[Arguing against amnesty for U.S. Vietnam-war draft-dodgers and deserters]: Why shouldn't they suffer the consequences? Others had to be killed or maimed because these men shirked their duties . . . Every time a man deserted, someone else had to take his place. Some of our returning POWs may have been captured because they took the place of someone who shirked his responsibility. Someone else may have been killed because of them . . . We have laws in this country. The laws have to be obeyed. Those laws require that people serve their country.

Before Senate Foreign Relations Committee,
Washington, Feb. 21/
Los Angeles Herald-Examiner, 2-22:(A)4.

4

Peace must come to all of the nations of Indochina or it will not come permanently to any of them. The fall of Cambodia into North Vietnamese hands would endanger the framework of both the Vietnam cease-fire and the entire Indochina situation . . . The reason we are bombing in Cambodia is to bring about the implementation of the [peace] agreement. We are just as eager to stop the bombing as it is possible to be. And of course, we will do so just as soon as there is a cease-fire. This is in accord with our mutual agreement with North Vietnam. This is our only condition.

The Washington Post, 5-13:(A)9.

Kenneth Rush
Deputy Secretary of State
of the United States

5

In North Vietnam we have men who have been in power for over 30 years. They have known almost nothing but war. They are turning, we hope, toward peace. We want to help North Vietnam turn toward peace. How is the best way to do it? [U.S. post-World War II aid helped rehabilitate West Germany and Japan and they are now] two of our closest allies . . . two of the greatest contributors to peace in the world. I think the lessons we learned after World War II are the ones that should be applied to North Vietnam.

Washington, March/
U.S. News & World Report, 4-16:44.

William B. Saxbe
United States Senator, R-Ohio

1

[On intensified U.S. bombing of North Vietnam, including the Hanoi and Haiphong areas]: I have followed President Nixon through all his convolutions and specious arguments, but he appears to have left his senses on this . . . I have walked through the pea patch with him for the last time.

The National Observer, 1-13:3.

Helmut Schmidt
Minister of Finance, and former Minister of Defense, of West Germany

2

This war has never been a matter of the North Atlantic Alliance, but it did originate in relation to another alliance of the United States. Neither have the NATO partners ever been seriously consulted nor have they volunteered to give thoughtful advice. But nevertheless, this war has become a political and moral issue also to the European partners of the U.S. It is deeply disturbing not only to your nation but also to my people and the Europeans as a whole. I do not wish to give any impression of attempting interference and therefore do confine my personal judgment to one single sentence: This war must be ended, otherwise the danger of alienation might turn into reality and thereby deeply influence the development of European-American relations.

At Newberry (S.C.) College, Jan. 12/
The Washington Post, 1-17:(A)16.

Hugh Scott
United States Senator, R-Pennsylvania

3

[The idea of U.S. post-war reconstruction aid for North Vietnam] does go against the grain, [but] while I hate the whole idea of spending money in a country where we've been at war, there may be a rational reason for it. If we are engaged in the rehabilitation of a whole country and have a great input in the way the peace is kept, the investment is far cheaper than making war.

Washington, Feb. 15/
The New York Times, 2-16:14.

William L. Scott
United States Senator, R-Virginia

4

[Saying he will no longer support continued U.S. military operations in Indochina, such as the bombing of Cambodia]: We've been in this thing [the war] for so many years that there comes a point when we can't continue. It's unfortunate that North Vietnam hasn't lived up to the [peace] agreement, but I just don't see us, by unilateral agreement, continuing to try to enforce it . . . I like to be a team player, and I like to work with the [Nixon] Administration; but reasonable people sometimes disagree on things . . . We now have our prisoners of war back home, and the continued bombing may result in more American prisoners of war being taken . . . I believe that the people of our country are now tired of these continued war activities.

Washington, May 31/
The Washington Post, 6-1:(C)1,7.

Norodom Sihanouk
Exiled former Chief of State of Cambodia

5

You [the U.S.] say that you cannot allow Communism to take over Indochina, but you decide to be friends with China and the Soviet Union, the two most powerful Communist countries in history. Why do you accept friendship with Chinese and Soviet Communism and consider Indochinese Communism as dangerous? Indochina does not threaten the U.S. in any way. You are very far away. Why don't you let us live our lives? If we want to be Communists, why do you refuse us such a right?

Interview, Peking/Time, 5-21:52.

(NORODOM SIHANOUK)

1

[On his support for the Khmer Rouge, Cambodian Communists]: The Chinese, in their infinite wisdom, have taught me that one must choose between the main enemy and the secondary enemy. Now for [Communist] China, the main enemy is the Soviet Union and the secondary enemy is America . . . For me, the main enemy is American imperialism and the [Cambodian leader] Lon Nol's Fascism; the Communists are the secondary enemy. Conclusion: I have decided to back the secondary enemy in order to defeat the main enemy . . . Cambodia will become Communist, and it is only right that it become Communist, because the revolution that the Khmer Rouge have made in the liberated areas has succeeded. I was convinced of this by seeing it with my own eyes. The Khmer Rouge are serious people. They know how to build up a country, and they have done things that I never succeeded in doing . . . It is quite right that I should congratulate the Cambodian Communists and tell them: "You are fine people. You deserve to stay in power forever and nobody should push you out—not even Sihanouk. Sihanouk should no longer rule instead of you because he has not succeeded in doing what you have done. He wanted to; he dreamed of doing it; but he was not able to accomplish it. Besides, Sihanouk does not count. What counts is Cambodia. So even if one day you may throw him out, he will think as he does now. Yes, because he is bizarre. But he is not dishonest; and he is not a fool."

Interview, Brioni, Yugoslavia, June/
San Francisco Examiner & Chronicle,
8-12:(Sunday Punch)2.

2

I shall never forget the first contact I had with them [Americans] in 1953. I was trying to persuade the French to leave, and the Khmer Rouge [Cambodian Communists] were harassing me, saying that I was a traitor who had sold out to the French. I didn't know where to turn, and someone told me that the Americans weren't like the French; they believed in freedom and democracy and rejected colonialism. So I flew to Washington and requested a meeting with [Secretary of State John] Foster Dulles. I asked him for help in the name of freedom, democracy, etc., and he replied arrogantly: "Go home, Your Majesty, and thank God that you have the French. Without them, Ho Chi Minh [of North Vietnam] would swallow you in two weeks. Goodbye." And from that day on I have detested them [the U.S.]—them and their fake democracy, their fake freedom, their imperialism put through in the name of Christian civilization, their coups d'etat like the coup they made against me . . .

Interview, Brioni, Yugoslavia, June/
San Francisco Examiner & Chronicle,
8-12:(Sunday Punch)2.

3

It is now up to the Americans and the Cambodian Communists—the future masters of Cambodia—to determine whether or not they want to hold [peace] talks . . . The world must not let itself be fooled by [U.S. President] Nixon. You do not have to go to Peking or Moscow or Hanoi to look for peace. The key to peace lies in the hands of Mr. Richard Nixon. We formally accuse him of being the sole person responsible for this war. He is an arch-criminal with the deaths of tens of thousands of innocent Cambodians on his conscience.

Interview, Peking, July 10/
The New York Times, 7-12:3.

4

I am Chief of State. If the Cambodians want me in this position after the liberation, I will be happy to continue to be the concrete that unifies the people. If they won't have me, I will write, play music, paint, because in my deep soul I am an artist. It is not important what happens to Sihanouk. The only important thing is what happens to Cambodia.

Interview, Bucharest, Romania/
Newsweek, 7-16:35.

Sisouk Na Champassak
Minister of Defense and Finance of Laos

5

We are the first victims of the Vietnam

confrontation. We have been victims for 10 years. But now we have nothing. We are not even included in the big conference to be held 30 days after the signing of the peace agreement [between the U.S. and North Vietnam]. There is no guarantee of our security. The North Vietnamese are the aggressors, but we have no voice. But Hungary, Indonesia, India and Canada will be represented. There is no joy here.

Vientiane, Jan. 25/
The Dallas Times Herald, 1-25:(A)21.

Sosthene Fernandez
Major General and Chief of Staff,
Cambodian armed forces

1

[On the current fighting in Cambodia]: The Viet Cong barbarians didn't want to respect the [Indochina peace] accords they signed in Paris [earlier this year]. We declared unilaterally that we would stop all offensive action if the VC and North Vietnamese withdrew from Cambodia. But, instead, they attacked. We were obliged to counter-attack, to take the most violent measures, to kill as many VCs as we could. We have destroyed at least a third of them in every battle. We are courageous—that's why we have casualties. We are brave. We don't fear death.

Interview, Phnom Pehn/
Los Angeles Times, 5-14:(1)13.

2

Our only hope for survival is American bombing. I will pound on the American Embassy's doors until I receive assurance that the bombing will not stop.

Interview, Phnom Penh/
The Washington Post, 6-17:(A)3.

3

We will continue the fight until the North Vietnamese Communists leave our territory . . . If the North Vietnamese and the Viet Cong are still here [after the U.S. bombing stops Aug. 15], I will ask the U.S. to continue the air support . . . If things slowly and slowly get worse, the U.S. Congress will not close its eyes. The Americans will help us. If

Cambodia falls, the Americans will lose face, not the Cambodians.

Time, 7-23:47.

Souvanna Phouma
Premier of Laos

4

[On the just-concluded Vietnam peace agreement]: I think the Paris agreement will be respected by all sides. Today, we are not in the same situation as in 1962-63. The world is now living in an atmosphere of detente. Great powers are looking toward coexistence. I hope peace will be more durable this time.

Vientiane, Jan. 26/
San Francisco Examiner, 1-26:6.

5

[On the just-concluded cease fire agreement between the government and the Pathet Lao]: Thus will end—we hope—after more than two decades, the most useless, the saddest and the most absurd of the wars of our national history, in which Laotians have quarreled and killed each other with neither rhyme nor reason.

Radio address to the nation/
The New York Times, 2-25:(4)2.

Robert H. Steele
United States Representative, R-Connecticut

6

[On American actress Jane Fonda's criticism of U.S. Vietnam policy]: Mr. Speaker, I would like to nominate Academy Award-winning actress Jane Fonda for a new award: the rottenest, most miserable performance by any one individual American in the history of our country.

Before the House, Washington/
Newsweek, 4-16:51.

William H. Sullivan
Deputy Assistant Secretary for East Asia
and Pacific Affairs, Department of State
of the United States

7

. . . I think if there were an invasion by, let's say, East Germany into West Germany, we would still consider it an invasion, although it would probably be also considered a

(WILLIAM H. SULLIVAN)

civil war between the two elements of Germany. Vietnam, as is recognized by the 1954 agreements and as is endorsed by this [1973 peace] agreement, is essentially a single country, but it has been divided since 1954 by this provisional demarcation line; and if, in pursuit of their civil scraps with each other, these countries [North and South Vietnam], separate and apart during this period, attack one another, it is certainly an invasion. If the West Germans were to attack the East Germans, I think there would be no doubt what the reaction would be from the Soviets and the others associated with them.

TV-radio interview, Paris/
"Meet the Press,"
National Broadcasting Company, 1-28.

Nguyen Co Thach
Vice Foreign Minister of North Vietnam

1

When we [North Vietnamese] start a negotiation, we have two hypotheses. We have the long hypothesis and the short hypothesis. We are always ready for either. And that is why we always do so well.

Interview, Paris/
Newsweek, 6-18:45.

Thanom Kittikachorn
Prime Minister of Thailand

2

So long as violations of the [Vietnam] cease-fire and peace agreement continue to hamper a settlement in Indochina, Thailand regards its necessity still, in spite of all serious disadvantages we have to suffer, to make available our military facilities to the United States in order that there will be strict observance of the peace agreement with respect to . . . Cambodia and the Kingdom of Laos. We consider the present precarious situation in the two countries to directly affect the security and stability in Thailand and of the entire region.

At reception in his honor, Bangkok,
May 14/The Washington Post, 5-16:(A)23.

Nguyen Van Thieu
President of South Vietnam

3

[On the just-concluded Vietnam peace agreement]: This is only the beginning of the end of the Communist aggression by force. Another phase will now come, and it is going to be a political phase. This political struggle is inevitable. The political-struggle phase, although not as bloody, will be as tough and dangerous as the military-struggle phase. If South Vietnam still exists after 17 long years of hard struggle, then South Vietnam will not be lost to the Communists. As long as the 17 million people of South Vietnam, as long as the government, as long as the Constitution, and as long as the people and cadres remain, then the Republic of [South] Vietnam will survive. We are determined to step into the new phase of the struggle with strength. Only in this way will we win.

Radio address to the nation, Saigon,
Jan. 24/The New York Times, 1-25:23.

4

[Criticizing the recently-concluded Vietnam peace agreement]: What kind of peace is a peace that gives the North Vietnamese the right to have their troops here? What kind of a treaty is a treaty that de facto legalizes their presence? [U.S. President Nixon and his foreign-affairs adviser Henry Kissinger] were too impatient to make peace, too impatient to negotiate and sign. When you deal with Communists, you must never fix time limits. You must not tell them you want to repatriate your prisoners as soon as possible and reach peace as soon as possible. They only take advantage of you.

Interview/
Los Angeles Herald-Examiner, 1-31:(A)4.

5

[Addressing American journalists]: I simply want you to know that, as Vietnamese, we fully realize that many among you were skeptical about or even questioned the wisdom of the American involvement in Vietnam and quite often were critical of our shortcomings. We respect your opinion, but for us the truth remains that you [the U.S.] came to help us in time of danger; you kept your word to a small nation, even when the going was rough; and you kept it till the day an acceptable arrangement could be found to terminate the war. For this, we Vietnamese cannot but express our sincere and deeply-felt gratitude, which I hope you will help convey to the American people. As for your shortcomings, we simply say that we accept our part of the blame, all wars having their share of ugliness, let alone the fact that we had to confront a war that defies all simplifications or easy rationalizations.

At National Press Club, Washington,
April 5/The New York Times, 4-6:4.

1

I am very confident that our Army and our people are able to defend themselves against renewed aggression . . . I can assure you of one thing: never, never will I ask American troops to come back to Vietnam.

At National Press Club, Washington,
April 5/The Washington Post, 4-6:(A)1.

2

This is how I see things in coming years: The Communists will lie low for a time while trying to subvert us from within and sabotage our economic potential. If they should achieve a situation of great political and economic difficulties for us, there is bound to be a coup d'etat, probably to be staged by a group of military commanders bought off by them. From this coup will emerge a pro-Communist administration. [That is why the Communists] will not accept a general election, which necessarily will be conducive to a political rout [of] them and the annihilation of everything they have achieved through many years of hard labor in the South.

Interview/
The Washington Post, 7-29:(A)15.

Le Duc Tho
Member, North Vietnamese Politburo;
Negotiator at Paris peace talks

3

The fact that I arrive in Paris today for one more effort to peacefully settle the Vietnam problem shows once again the unswerving seri-

ous attitude and good will of the government of the Democratic Republic of [North] Vietnam. Had the U.S. side really had a good will and adopted a serious attitude, as the North Vietnamese side did, the Vietnam question would have been settled peacefully and rapidly . . . The Vietnamese people, who have been tempered during tens of years of fighting, are resolved not to cede to any pressure or threat, perseveringly stepping up their struggle against U.S. aggression for national salvation till the achievement of their basic national rights and the winning back of real peace and independence.

Paris, Jan. 6/
San Francisco Examiner, 1-6:1.

4

[On the just-concluded Vietnam peace agreement]: With the return of peace, the struggle of the Vietnamese people enters a new period. Our people, lifting high the banner of peace and of national accord, is decided to strictly apply the clauses of the agreement maintaining peace, independence and democracy and heading toward the peaceful reunification of its country. It will also have to rebuild its war-devastated country and consolidate and develop its friendly relations with all the peoples of the world, including the American people. Heavy tasks still await us in this new period. But the Vietnamese in the North, as in the South, at home as abroad, rich in their traditions of unity and perseverance in struggle, following a just policy, strengthened by the close solidarity of the peoples of Laos and Cambodia and benefiting from strong aid from the socialist countries and all the peace-loving countries of the world, will be able to smooth out all difficulties and victoriously accomplish their tasks.

News conference, Paris, Jan. 24/
The New York Times, 1-25:22.

5

It is our ardent wish that there be real, free and democratic general elections in South Vietnam so that the existing regime, of which the least one can say is that it is not democratic, is done away with. The question that arises is how, in the present situation of South

(LE DUC THO)

Vietnam, where not all arms have been laid down, where there are no democratic liberties —how, in these circumstances, one can hold elections conceived as truly democratic and free. This is why to talk of democratic and free elections before talking of cease-fire and democratic liberties amounts to putting the plow before the buffalo, or, if you will, before the bull. This is why, at the present moment, it is before everything else necessary in South Vietnam to achieve a veritable cease-fire, to respect democratic liberties and to effect national concord. It is on these bases that free and democratic general elections will be possible. That is our unvarying position.

News conference, Paris, June 14/
The New York Times, 6-15:11.

Robert Thompson
British authority on Southeast Asia

1

I am less impressed with the formalities of the cease-fire arrangements—or the good faith of the other [North Vietnamese] side—than with the fact that Russia and [Communist] China do not want any new flare-up of the semi-conventional war that has been going on here. It is very important to consider these new superpower relationships. It is not just Hanoi that is convinced of [U.S.] President Nixon's unpredictability and determination. He also has convinced Russia and China that, when it is necessary, he will use the power he has available. That includes American air power in the region. Every present factor is working against renewed fighting on a major scale.

Interview, Saigon/
U.S. News & World Report, 2-19:27.

Hoang Tung
Senior editor, "Nhan Dan," Hanoi

2

We have ended armed conflict but continue the struggle; however, not with military means. We are not in a hurry with reunification. It is now [our] policy not to use force to achieve this goal. The urgent quest now in

South Vietnam [is] to end conflict to make it possible to solve problems by political means . . . Being patient, we are ready to wait some time.

Interview, Hanoi/
Los Angeles Times, 3-17:(1)9.

Frederick C. Weyand
General, United States Army;
Commander, U.S. forces in South Vietnam

3

[On the final withdrawal of all U.S. ground combat forces from South Vietnam]: I depart with a strong feeling of pride in what we have achieved and what our accomplishment represents. All the American men and women who have served in this struggle join me today in wishing you [South Vietnamese] well. It is our sincere hope that the peace with honor that has been our goal will last forever.

At ceremony marking the withdrawal, Saigon,
March 29/Los Angeles Times, 3-30:(1)1.

Gough Whitlam
Prime Minister of Australia

4

For 20 years I have been appalled at the damage we of the West have done to ourselves and to other peoples by our Western ideological occupations, particularly in Southeast Asia. We are not going to be readily forgiven for throwing away the chance we had for a settlement in Indochina in 1954, after Korea, after Geneva. And if I had to sum up my own determination and that of my government in a single sentence, I would state that I am determined that nothing Australia does by action or inaction will contribute to a second, final loss of opportunity.

At National Press Club, Washington, July 30/
The Christian Science Monitor, 8-1:7.

Krister Wickman
Foreign Minister of Sweden

5

[On the just-concluded Vietnam peace agreement]: [South Vietnamese President Thieu's recent] aggressive speech and [U.S.] President Nixon's expression of support for the

Saigon regime augur no good for the future. We face an important step toward full independence in Vietnam, but there is still a tough road to go. We know that there will be a very hard political struggle between the parties in South Vietnam, and it is also clear that this struggle will be fought with military means.

Jan. 24/Los Angeles Times, 1-25:(1)19.

1

[Criticizing current U.S. bombing in Cambodia]: On one side stands a liberation movement with popular support, on the other an isolated terror regime led by [Cambodian President] Lon Nol. It is in support for this regime that bombs are falling over defenseless people in Cambodia.

May 1/The Washington Post, 5-2:(A)2.

Elmo R. Zumwalt, Jr.
Admiral, United States Navy;
Chief of Naval Operations

2

[On current U.S. bombing in Cambodia]: Without the bombing, it is almost certain Cambodia would fall . . . I believe if Cambodia falls, South Vietnam falls.

Before House Appropriations Subcommittee, Washington/The National Observer, 5-26:2.

Europe

Einar Agustsson
Foreign Minister of Iceland

1

What we have in mind is to get rid of the U.S. defense force [in Iceland]. We would like to return to the original agreement, which provided only for base facilities but no armed forces stationed in Iceland in peacetime.

News conference, Reykjavik, May 29/
Los Angeles Herald-Examiner, 5-30:(A)5.

Adamantios Androutsopoulos
Premier of Greece

2

[On the recent military coup installing him as Premier and toppling the government of George Papadopoulos]: Democracy and virtue cannot be imposed by law. Its achievement needs a reformation from within to cover all aspects of national life. When the country is ready, it will be led to elections . . . Without the reformation, parliamentary rule is a mask, a trap, a refuge and an empty reform . . . The hesitant, the panic-stricken, the defeatists, the apologists of anarchy can withdraw to the margins of national life under the cover of empty slogans, useless formulas and appeals to passion. Whatever obstacles lie in the path of the nation will be swept aside without hesitation.

Broadcast address to the nation,
Athens, Nov. 28/
Los Angeles Times, 11-29:(1)11.

Georgi A. Arbatov
Director, U.S.A. Institute,
Soviet Academy of Sciences

3

During my recent tours of the U.S., I was surprised that the ideas generated by the long cold war and by intensive anti-Soviet propaganda have faded away in the minds of most

Americans . . . The prevailing attitude toward the U.S.S.R. was not one of distrust and prejudice but of sincere interest and good-will. I can say that the attitude of people in my country toward Americans is the same. This, naturally, does not mean that the Soviet people favor America's social and economic institutions, [but] the mutual desire to live in peace and to work together—this, I believe, is the common sentiment of both sides. Naturally, mass sentiments in favor of peace do not always prevent dangerous turns in world development. Nevertheless, the sentiments and attitudes of whole nations make up a major force that cannot be ignored. This force has already played a significant role in bringing about favorable changes in Soviet-American relations.

Interview/Newsweek, 6-25:35.

Vladimir Ashkenazy
Pianist

4

[On life in the Soviet Union, which he fled 10 years ago]: Russia is a cocoon. All decisions are made for you. Whatever is in your brain they put there. Once I was free, I saw that what the Russians teach about the West is all lies. Even the most intelligent minds can't escape the effects of daily propaganda.

Newsweek, 3-26:99.

Worth Bagley
Admiral, United States Navy;
Commander, U.S. Naval Forces/Europe

5

If it is true that sea power is decisive—that no nation can control its destiny without it, no matter what other strengths it may have —then one is struck today with the divergent national attitudes toward this aspect of national security. If the respective national reliances on overseas trade, sources of energy and geographical links within defense alliances are kept in mind, the trends for the future are not encouraging. The nation building toward the greatest level of sea power—the Soviet Union—is least vulnerable and least dependent now in regard to each of these particulars. The continental and Mediterranean states, who lack either the flexibility of large heartland territory or the luxury of multiple coasts, have turned away from the maritime traditions that served and protected them in the past. The industrially-strong island nations, whose very existence allows no compromise with the sea, are in the act of rationalizing concessions on the character of sea power they require. It is comfortable, if not wholly satisfactory, to relate these developments to NATO defense concepts that followed logically from the dramatic invasion and land battles of Europe. Regardless of the logic applied, however, the growing Western inability to use and control the seas is becoming the Achilles heel of any NATO strategy. It narrows the range of response flexibility and raises questions as to the credibility of choices other than nuclear. But beyond that, the patterns of strategic thought that heretofore have been natural to the traditional maritime nations are losing the imagination and breadth that contributed so much to our history.

Before Pilgrim Club, London,
Oct. 15/Vital Speeches, 11-15:91.

George W. Ball
Former Under Secretary of State
of the United States

1

[The Soviet Union] is now deliberately concentrating on two objectives essential to its strategy of domination. First, it is striving to encourage the removal of the American presence and influence from Europe. Second, it is doing what it can to discourage Western European efforts to build effective institutions for common economic and political action . . . [If Moscow succeeded in these twin goals,] the Soviet Union would clearly loom as the major power on the European land mass, and the scurry of many nations to achieve accom-

modation could become a stampede.

Before House Foreign Affairs Subcommittee
on Europe, Washington, June 18/
The Washington Post, 6-19:(A)4.

2

[Arguing against U.S. troop cutbacks in Europe]: . . . one may still suspect that the Soviet leadership continues to cherish political ambitions in the West, although they may have changed their tactics . . . For us at this point to give away our bargaining counters before negotiations even start on the mutual troop withdrawal would not only raise questions about our steadfastness but our sanity.

Before House Foreign Affairs Subcommittee
on Europe, Washington, June 18/
The New York Times, 6-19:14.

Rainer Barzel
Member, West German Parliament

3

Growing neutralism and anti-Americanism are proceeding hand-in-hand in the [West German] government camp with the damnation of anti-Communism.

Los Angeles Times, 4-3:(1)17.

Jacob D. Beam
Former United States Ambassador
to the Soviet Union

4

They [Soviet leadership] would be satisfied with something they could claim as a dominating or, at least, equal role in world affairs. But they are not revolutionaries any more. They are hard-headed, practical people and know that total Communist victory is not going to happen—ever. There is a greater sense of purpose in developing Russia, in gradually boosting the living standards of the people, but not at the expense of Russia's military and industrial position. A Communist world —they recognize that as impractical as an immediate and realistic goal. As a political instrument, yes, it's important; but as a way of life, of world conquest—no.

Interview, Washington/
U.S. News & World Report, 5-28:43.

Lloyd M. Bentsen
United States Senator, D-Texas

1

We want our allies in Europe to realize it is impossible for us to provide the muscle [for Europe's defense] forever, and undesirable for us to provide it much longer . . . Clearly, the time has come to reduce our commitment. But we must do it reasonably and gradually, giving our NATO allies the time and opportunity to build the muscle that is needed to preserve the peace in Europe.

Before DeSoto Chamber of Commerce,
Dallas, Sept. 21/
The Dallas Times Herald, 9-23:(B)8.

Gianluigi Berti
Foreign Minister of San Marino

2

The world might learn a few lessons about peace from us. We haven't had a war for 500 years—since 1463. We don't have soldiers. We don't have an army, really, only a couple of hundred working citizens who put on fancy uniforms for ceremonial occasions. Like the Swiss, we have maintained our neutrality through the two world wars of this century. We are a small country. But we established our independence more than 1,000 years ago; and we have maintained our freedom, and this is our moral strength. We rarely have crime in San Marino. Even our police force is imported: carabinieri on loan from Italy.

San Marino/Los Angeles Times, 4-28:(1)1.

Pierre Billecoq
Minister of Transport of France

3

[On the proposed tunnel beneath the English Channel linking Britain and France]: It will be easier for you [British] to come and pick our roses of Picardy, and, for us, it will no longer be a long way to Tipperary.

At signing of tunnel agreement, London,
Nov. 17/The New York Times, 11-18:(1)3.

Willy Brandt
Chancellor of West Germany

4

The Atlantic Alliance remains the basis of our security. It also provides the backing for our policy of detente toward the East. The political and military presence of the United States is indispensable for keeping a balance of power in Europe. At the same time, the Federal government will endeavor to make the European pillar of the Alliance stronger . . . The freedom to contribute to detente and political equity is not something we get for nothing. We do not regard compulsory military service, defense budget and civil defense as mere necessities; we see them as a meaningful service for the free community of our citizenry; this service assists us in our work for peace.

Before the Bundestag, Bonn, Jan. 18/
Vital Speeches, 2-15:259.

5

The policy of detente can only be carried out in the world we live in, not in an experimental laboratory. This makes it a pressing necessity that we do not seek a position between the power blocs, but hold fast to our anchor in the Western system with its defensive ties; for only with the help of these ties can we achieve detente without illusions.

Before Social Democratic Party, Bonn/
Los Angeles Times, 3-19:(1)16.

6

The European contribution to common defense is now a much more substantial one than it was 10 years ago. Some of our friends in the United States sometimes overlook this fact. Much of the change is due to the efforts of my country. The European contribution, especially as far as army and air forces are concerned, is more important now than it was then. One could even say that the U.S. role within the [Atlantic] Alliance is no longer quite what it was. Nowadays, the European element plays a greater role, strategically as well . . . If it is true that an effective Alliance is not only in the interest of the United States, then it's not just a matter of the Americans helping the Europeans; it is a matter of how the two components of the Alliance agree to take care of their common interests . . . upholding a reasonable balance vis-a-vis the East is not only a question of nuclear arms, even though they play an important role. Accordingly, I think a considerable American presence [in Europe,] in addition to the nuclear deterrent, is vitally important for the Alliance.

Interview/
U.S. News & World Report, 4-30:38.

1

Political unity [between East and West Germany] is out of the question for the foreseeable future. But we must create conditions in which the German people, despite political division, can remain a cultural, historical and human community.

Before the Bundesrat, Bonn, May 25/
Los Angeles Herald-Examiner, 5-26:(A)4.

2

Speaking specifically about West Germany, I think we have gone a very long way to dispel the fears some of our neighbors had of us as a result of the war [World War II]. Even so, I feel we here in Germany must keep in mind that we cannot run away from our past; we cannot afford to forget it. I am constantly telling this to our young people. You see, for them, Nazism is something very remote, very difficult to understand. When they hear records of Hitler's speeches, for example, some of them even laugh, because Hitler sounds so incredible and ridiculous to them. But the fact remains, this frenzied rhetoric was given support by millions of our citizens. As a nation, we cannot forget this. And as for the new generation of Germans, even though they were not responsible for those things, they *do* have a responsibility to work for conditions that will make its recurrence impossible; that is, they *do* have a responsibility to work for a better Germany—and a better world.

Interview, Bonn/Parade, 9-23:5.

3

Let me say in all frankness, the presence of American forces in Europe is the decisive factor and one that will remain indispensable for a future that is at present unforeseeable. The presence of American troops must not be reduced in status to a symbolic contribution . . . I wish to emphasize that the American presence serves American interests just as ba-

sically as it serves ours.

Before Chicago Council on Foreign
Relations, Sept. 27/
Los Angeles Times, 9-28:(1)5.

4

[On the Arab cutback in oil supplies to various pro-Israel European countries]: Not all member states of the [European Economic] Community are currently affected in the same manner, but let us not delude ourselves. In fact, we are all equally affected, and none of us has the right to leave another alone with its troubles. If we accepted the weakening of one country, we would really be weakening the Community itself, and eventually each of its members. If we cannot hold together on this issue, we will accomplish nothing lasting in other fields.

At dinner in .his honor, Paris,
Nov. 26/The New York Times, 11-27:33.

Leonid I. Brezhnev
General Secretary,
Communist Party of the Soviet Union

5

The bonds between the Soviet Union and Czechoslovakia, between the Communists of the U.S.S.R. and Czechoslovakia, are now so deep and multiform, so natural for the whole way of our life, that our ideas and joys as well as our worries are identical in many respects.

Upon receiving the Order of the White Lion,
Prague, Feb. 23/
The New York Times, 2-24:3.

6

Taking place is a turn from the cold war and dangerous tension toward reasonable joint efforts to strengthen peace and develop mutually-advantageous cooperation. [The Soviet Union wants to overcome] Europe's bloody past not in order to forget it, but so that it would never be repeated. The policy of the Soviet Union in Europe, just as in other parts of the world, is first of all a policy of peace . . . From the same position we approach also our relations with such a state as the United States of America. We shall in the future, too, facilitate a favorable development

(LEONID I. BREZHNEV)

of Soviet-American relations on the principles of mutual respect and mutual advantage.

May Day address, Moscow, May 1/
Los Angeles Times, 5-2:(1)7.

1

The political barometer in Europe today shows ever more clearly that fair weather is ahead.

At ceremony honoring East German
Communist Party leader Erich Honecker,
East Berlin, May 13/
Los Angeles Herald-Examiner, 5-14:(A)4.

2

In the north and in the south of our vast country, in Siberia and in Central Asia, we are building giant power stations, hundreds of plants and factories, creating irrigation systems on territories that in size could vie with many a European state. Our goal is for the Soviet people to live better tomorrow than it lives today. Soviet people are tangibly aware of the fruits of these collective ·efforts. This, of course, does not mean that we in the Soviet Union have resolved all problems and face no difficulties. Problems that will take a lot of solving do exist, and apparently will always exist, in all times. But a specific feature of the problems facing us is that they are associated with the confident growth of the country, of its economic and cultural potential; and we are seeking their solution exclusively on the roads of further peaceful construction, of raising the cultural and living standards of the people, of developing our socialist society.

Television address to West German people
Bonn, May 21/The New York Times, 5-22:8.

3

[On improved Soviet-West German relations]: To be frank, it was not easy for the Soviet people, and hence its leaders, to open this new page in our relations. Memories of the past war, the tremendous sacrifices and destruction which the Hitler aggression brought us, are still raw in the minds of Soviet people. [But] the development of peaceful and mutually-beneficial relations [between Moscow and Bonn is] quite a real thing,

which exists and keeps growing in scope.

Television address to West German people,
Bonn, May 21/The National Observer, 6-2:4.

4

We do not have in the Soviet Union any law forbidding a Soviet citizen from leaving and going to another country if that departure is justified. But I'm sure any nation has a law where it is forbidden to certain categories of people connected with what is called national security from leaving their country. I am told there is such a law in Israel, too, and I'm sure the United States has similar rules.

News conference, Moscow, June 14/
Los Angeles Times, 6-15:(1)7.

5

By and large, we can say that quite a lot has already been done to develop Soviet-American relations. Yet, we are still only at the beginning of a long road. Constant care is needed to preserve and develop the new shoots of good relationships. Tireless efforts are needed in various fields. Patience is needed to understand the various specific features of the other side and to learn to do business with each other. I believe those who support a radical improvement in relations between the Soviet Union and the United States can look to the future with optimism, for this objective meets the vital interests of both our nations and the interests of peace-loving people all over the world. The general atmosphere in the world depends to no small extent on the climate prevailing in relations between our two countries. Neither economic or military might nor international prestige gives our countries any special privileges; but they do invest them with special responsibility for the destinies of universal peace and for preventing war. In its approach to ties and contacts with the United States, the Soviet Union is fully aware of that responsibility.

Television address to the American people,
San Clemente, Calif., June 24/
The New York Times, 6-25:18.

6

Sometimes in the West one can hear voices saying: "Since the Soviet Union and the other socialist countries are evincing great interest in solving questions of European security . . . could we not exercise pressure on them and extort some concessions from them?" . . . The reduction of tension in Europe is the common possession of all people on the continent, and its preservation and consolidation should be the common concern of all participants in the [European Security] Conference. We think that it should be a question not of some diplomatic exchange of merchandise, but of joint multilateral efforts and ultimately of working out an effective system to guarantee the security of all European countries and peoples and mutually advantageous cooperation among them.

At Communist rally, Sofia, Bulgaria,
Sept. 19/Los Angeles Times, 9-20:(1)11.

1

What do we expect from that [European Security] Conference and what are we hoping for? To put it in the most general terms, we want to see well-defined principles of relations between European states formulated unanimously, sincerely, with heart and soul, as they say, without diplomatic equivocations and misconstructions, approved by all the participants in the Conference and endorsed by all the peoples of the continent. I have in mind, for instance, such principles as the territorial integrity of all the European states, the inviolability of their frontiers, the renunciation of the use, or threat, of force in the relations between countries, non-interference in each other's internal affairs and the promotion, on that basis, of mutually-beneficial cooperation in diverse fields. We should like these principles to become sacred and indisputable in the day-to-day fabric of European affairs and of the psychology of the European peoples in order to become reality.

At World Peace Congress, Moscow,
Oct. 26/The New York Times, 10-27:10.

Marcelo Caetano
Prime Minister of Portugal

2

[Saying he put a brake on liberalization in Portugal because anarchist and socialist ideas were threatening the country's future]: I'm a

liberal; but there has to be a difference between generosity of thought and limitations of action. I myself was once an extremist . . . but the time comes when passion is replaced by reason.

Interview/
Los Angeles Herald-Examiner, 7-18:(A)13.

Robert Carr
Home Secretary of the United Kingdom

3

[Saying high governmental aides in Britain are career civil servants, not political appointees]: When governments change, only ministers change.

The Christian Science Monitor, 5-15:4.

Fidel Castro
Premier of Cuba

4

How can anyone call the Soviet Union imperialist? Let others lament the fact the Soviet Union has become an economic and military power. Cuba rejoices.

At conference of non-aligned nations, Algiers/
San Francisco Examiner & Chronicle,
9-16:(This World)14.

Nicolae Ceausescu
President of Romania

5

[On the growth of the European Common Market]: The West European countries are moving toward an integration that could create a powerful economic—and, of course, eventually also political—grouping. This poses a series of problems with respect to the development of cooperation among the European states. Cooperation must be based on full equality, with no restrictions. But the Common Market envisages the creation of restrictions [for example, trade barriers]. However, we hope ways will be found to eliminate them.

Interview/Time, 4-2:32.

Chiao Kuan-hua
Vice Foreign Minister of, and chief United Nations General Assmebly delegate from, the People's Republic of (Communist) China

6

The actions of the Soviet Union have amp-

(CHIAO KUAN-HUA)

ly shown that it is socialist in words, imperialist in deeds.

Before United Nations General Assembly,
New York, Oct. 2/
Los Angeles Herald-Examiner, 10-3:(A)18.

Erskine Childers
President of the Republic of Ireland

1

[On his being a Protestant in a predominantly Catholic country]: I have been a member of the Dail [Parliament] 35 years and a Minister for 22 years. I never found my religion had the slightest effect on my political career. The heads of the Protestant Church have made it quite clear that Protestants have a full and rewarding life in this country. But if election of a Protestant as President can demonstrate to the world at large, and especially to the Unionists [Protestant party] of Northern Ireland, that we live in an ecumenical state, then I am very glad. Maybe my election can help dispel the vestigial impressions of some people that we live in a sectarian state. I hope they will now see the light.

Interview, Dublin/
The New York Times, 7-4:15.

Chou En-lai
Premier of the People's Republic
of (Communist) China

2

Over the last two decades, the Soviet revisionist ruling clique, from Khrushchev to Brezhnev, has made a socialist country degenerate into a social-imperialist country. Internally, it has restored capitalism, enforced a Fascist dictatorship and enslaved the people of all nationalities, thus deepening the political and economic contradictions as well as contradictions among nationalities. Externally, it has invaded and occupied Czechoslovakia, massed its troops along the Chinese border, sent troops into the People's Republic of Mongolia, supported the traitorous [Cambodian President] Lon Nol clique, suppressed the Polish workers' rebellion, intervened in Egypt causing the expulsion of the Soviet experts, dismem-

bered Pakistan and carried out subversive activities in many Asian and African countries. This series of facts has profoundly exposed its ugly features as the new Czar and its reactionary nature, namely, socialism in words, imperialism in deeds. The more evil and foul things it does, the sooner the time when Soviet revisionism will be relegated to the historical museum by the people of the Soviet Union and the rest of the world.

At Chinese Communist Party Congress,
Peking, Aug. 24/
The New York Times, 9-1:6.

Lydia Chukovskaya
Soviet author

3

In our country we have an unwritten law which is stronger than any in our written code of laws . . . The one crime for which the authorities never forgive anyone: Every person must be severely punished for the slightest attempt to think independently.

San Francisco Examiner & Chronicle,
9-23:(This World)2.

William P. Clements, Jr.
Deputy Secretary of Defense
of the United States

4

The Soviet submarine fleet is not only capable, it is growing in size. In my opinion, these forces exceed Russia's requirements for defense of the homeland . . . [The Soviet Navy] shows every intention of establishing its presence throughout the world, whether the U.S. likes it or not.

Before Dallas Council on World Affairs,
April 13/Los Angeles Herald-Examiner,
4-14:(A)4.

John B. Connally, Jr.
Former Secretary of the Treasury
of the United States;
Former Governor of Texas

5

Britain's entry into the [European] Common Market is certainly not without repercussions in the Commonwealth and on the shores of my own land. But the United States applauds the British decision—a decision based upon Britain's national self-interest—because we are convinced that European unity is vital to the long-range economic and political stability of the entire world; and Britain is an essential cog in the machinery of a free, healthy and peaceful Europe.

Before Institute of Directors, London/ The New York Times, 11-18:(4)17.

Constantine II
Exiled King of Greece

1

[On the Greek government's decision to abolish the monarchy and declare a Presidential republic]: [It is] an illegal act by an illegal government. [If the people are denied a choice of government,] I shall be compelled to regard myself as the sole possessor of legality. I shall fight with all my strength as a soldier. I will have on my side the people of Greece and the armed forces . . . At this moment of great trial and crisis, I wish to assure the Greek people that I, King of the Hellenes, have not only the hope but the unshakable conviction that I shall return to my beloved country as guarantor of the dignity and of the Constitutional liberty of the Greek people, which alone give true meaning to the very concept of democracy . . . The real problem lies not in whether Greece should have a democracy with or without a King, but whether she should have a democracy at all, and whether the people of Greece has the right to be master of its fate and to enjoy its freedom.

News conference, Rome, June 2/ San Francisco Examiner & Chronicle, 6-3:(A)1;The New York Times, 6-3:(1)1,7.

2

[On the imminent referendum in Greece that asks for support of the current government of George Papadopoulos]: What else can it mean, except an exercise in brutal totalitarianism, when you [the Greek people] are offered no alternative solution? When you are given no choice? When opposition is forbidden? When there is no other candidate? When discussion is punished? When Greek men and Greek women are being dragged to the polls

to vote for a dictatorship?

San Francisco Examiner & Chronicle, 7-29:(This World)2.

Patrick Cooney
Minister of Justice of the Republic of Ireland

3

[On IRA violence in Northern Ireland]: The sickening spiral of violence which we have seen in the North has appalled every right-thinking person . . . The people who are allegedly fighting for the cause of unity [of the two Irelands] must learn that unity cannot be achieved by killing and bombing . . . I exhort all people to reject these men and to deny them support of any kind. I ask every member of the public, particularly those living in border areas, to cooperate and help the gardai [police] and the Army in carrying out their onerous duties.

The Christian Science Monitor, 4-18:6.

Alec Douglas-Home
Foreign Secretary of the United Kingdom

4

I can think of nothing more important in the world today than the maintenance of a close and friendly relationship between Europe and the United States. In an increasingly interdependent world, failure to find generally acceptable solutions [to U.S.-Europe trade problems] would place a great strain on the present structure of international relations. We cannot afford to enter negotiations on financial, economic or trading matters, let alone on defense matters, as adversaries.

Before Diplomatic and Commonwealth Writers Association, London, May 1/ The New York Times, 5-2:65.

5

What we would like to see in respect of the Soviet Union and countries of Eastern Europe is the kind of relationship between ordinary people which exists between Britain and France, Britain and Germany, Britain and Italy. In other words, freedom to move, freedom to speak, within the laws of the countries concerned.

News conference,
New York, Sept. 27/
Los Angeles Times, 9-28:(1)8.

1

The forces of NATO are not defensive in their purpose merely because we say so. By virtue of their numbers, equipment and dispositions, they are manifestly not intended for, nor capable of, aggression against Eastern Europe or anyone else. I hope that the purpose of the much larger forces maintained by the Warsaw Pact is equally defensive. But the fact remains—and it is a very uncomfortable fact—that the present size and composition of these forces give them an offensive capability which inevitably worries us Western Europeans. To create confidence, the Warsaw Pact countries must be ready to limit their numbers within a ceiling, and the graph of men and weapons must be shown to be turning down . . . Of course, arms are but the symptoms of the fear; they are not the cause. The cause of our anxiety is that the words in *Pravda*—those words about the complete and final victory of Communism—may really mean what they say.

The New York Times, 12-2:(4)17.

Elizabeth II
Queen of England

2

The [British] Commonwealth provides us with practical opportunities to cooperate, to serve each other and to break down defenses between peoples. If we fail, our successors will reflect sadly on a wonderful opportunity lost. If we succeed, we shall not only build a stronger and happier Commonwealth, but we shall also show that mankind is capable of living in peace and amity on a scale never achieved before.

On Commonwealth Day, May/
The New York Times, 8-2:2.

J. William Fulbright
United States Senator, D-Arkansas

3

Under the altered circumstances of Europe, the United States can safely reduce its own involvement by withdrawing some of our present force of about 300,000 men from the European continent. When American troops were first assigned to NATO in 1951, Western Europe was still enfeebled by the ravages of World War II; Stalin was alive and the Soviet threat, though probably exaggerated, was plausible. In the early 1970s, Western Europe is, for the most part, politically stable and economically powerful, with national economies healthier than that of the United States, and collective resources at least as great as those of the Soviet Union. At the same time . . . the Soviet Union has shown itself to be far more interested in formalizing the European status quo than in trying to alter it and shows no inclination to try to occupy Western Europe with ground forces. Indeed, the nuclear stalemate has made such an attack all but inconceivable. Under these circumstances, and for the sake of further advancing the East-West detente, we could safely and sensibly reduce the American ground forces in Europe to half its present numbers, or even fewer. A symbolic ground force is desirable as a demonstration of American loyalty to the North Atlantic Alliance, more specifically as token of the availability of American nuclear power for the defense of Europe; but there is no need of an American army of 300,000 men to protect Europeans against an all but inconceivable Soviet ground attack.

Before American Bankers Association,
July 11/Vital Speeches, 9-15:710.

4

If the cold war is running out, the essential reason is the running down of the Russian Revolution, which has come into its "Thermidor," that stage at which a revolution has run out of steam, its fire-breathing radicals exhausted or displaced, and normalcy and routine are restored.

The Washington Post, 7-22:(C)6.

1

[Arguing against the U.S. trying to gain more freedom for Soviet citizens in return for better U.S.-Soviet relations]: The Russian people have lived under dictatorship throughout their history. It is not for us, at this late date, to try to change that by external pressure, especially at a time when there is a better chance than ever to build a cooperative relationship between the Soviet Union and the United States.

At convocation sponsored by the Center for the Study of Democratic Institutions, Washington, Oct. 8/ The New York Times, 10-9:5.

Valery Giscard d'Estaing
Minister of Economy and Finance of France

2

Following our entry into the Common Market 15 years ago, we faced the need to reconstruct French industry. This was the first time since the 1914 war [World War I] that the French economy had opened up to the outside world. It was an economy grown old because of two world wars and because, between wars, nothing had been done to revitalize it. There were firms weakened by inflation and quite weak industrially. In this state of weakness, what we wanted to avoid was to let these weakened firms be brought up from abroad. We wanted them to reorganize themselves, and that's what they have done to a great degree. At present, we're not finished with this reorganization; but the large and medium-sized French firms can now hold their own with those in other industrialized countries. So the situation is different. We are now investing more abroad than foreigners are investing in France . . . So we are entering into a phase in which, on the one hand, the government is more easily accepting foreign investments in France and, on the other, French firms are investing more abroad, notably in North America.

Interview, Paris/ U.S. News & World Report, 7-23:51.

Phaidon Gizikis
President of Greece

3

[On the just-concluded military coup installing him as President and ousting the government of George Papadopoulos]: My only ambition is to contribute to the normal operation of the government, as well as to the consolidation of tranquility and unity among the Greek people. I shall carry out my duties with moderation, modesty and impartiality. Let us put aside the trifles that divide us and proceed united toward the great projects and major reforms the nation requires.

Broadcast address to the nation, Athens, Nov. 25/The New York Times, 11-26:14.

4

The Constitution of Greece shall be the work of all the Greeks. Its text shall represent all social trends and views. This charter, the work and achievement of the Greek people, acceptable to it in advance, shall become the fundamental law expressing its will on the country's future course and evolution.

Broadcast address to the nation, Athens, Dec. 31/The New York Times, 1-1('74):6.

Andrew J. Goodpaster
General, United States Army; Supreme Allied Commander/Europe

5

NATO is essential to the peace of one member as it is to all, and what makes it meaningful is that it is a collective force. In the past, treaties between nations did not keep the peace. NATO has. In the present situation, I would oppose any unilateral [U.S. force] reduction. We cannot cut our forces substantially; we can't cut them at all. We have exhausted the margin for reduction.

Human Events, 4-28:14.

6

[On proposals to withdraw U.S. troops from Europe]: I consider that the right question is not how long it has been since World War II. It is how long it is before World War III. The U.S. troops in Europe are there to keep World War III from taking place, and they have been succeeding . . . for nearly

401

(ANDREW J. GOODPASTER)

three decades . . . So don't just throw away what has maintained peace for our people. Evaluate the alternative carefully.

At Georgetown University Center for Strategic and International Studies, Washington/ U.S. News & World Report, 7-23:53.

Andrei A. Grechko
Minister of Defense of the Soviet Union

1

The Soviet Union is not preparing wars and does not intend to wage any to set up its political dominion or to change the social systems of other states. The Soviet Union has no need to extend its frontiers, but it is determined to defend resolutely what the Soviet people have created. The Soviet Union will follow firmly a policy aimed at strengthening peace, setting up a system of international security and preventing another world war. At the same time, however, the Soviet Union will keep in mind the fact that imperialism recognizes only force in international affairs.

At meeting of Soviet military commissars, Moscow, March 28/ U.S. News & World Report, 5-7:46.

William E. Griffith
Professor of Political Science, Massachusetts Institute of Technology

2

I don't believe . . . that the Soviet Union will very soon catch up with the West—even with increased East-West trade. The only way the Soviets could do that would be by reforming their inefficient economic system. In fact, they have decided *not* to reform their economic system, for fear of loss of political control, and to make up for the lack of reform by buying Western technology. This is bound not to work completely: You can import any amount of Western technology; but as long as you have inefficient management, you cannot use it effectively.

Interview/ The Reader's Digest, January:54.

Andrei A. Gromyko
Foreign Minister of the Soviet Union

3

Peace and socialism have been inscribed on our banner since the inception of the Soviet state. We remain loyal to this banner. The Soviet Union has no other foreign policy. It derives from the very nature of our social system.

At Conference on Security and Cooperation in Europe, Helsinki, Finland, July 4/ Vital Speeches, 8-1:614.

4

[On U.S.-Soviet relations]: The Soviet Union is convinced that if both sides strictly fulfill all the obligations assumed, including the rigorous observance of the cardinal principle of international relations, non-interference in each other's internal affairs—and that is what we proceed from—Soviet-American relations will be a permanent positive factor of international peace; and that is of historic importance.

Before United Nations General Assembly, New York, Sept. 25/ The New York Times, 9-26:3.

Horst Grunert
East German Ambassador/Permanent Observer to the United Nations

5

[On incidents of East German border guards shooting people trying to escape from his country]: I didn't speak with anyone who tried to leave our republic by violating the laws, so I don't know the intentions of these people. Maybe they were influenced by some of the mass media to believe that life in the so-called Western countries is more easy. I hope the mass media will try their best not to influence our young and inexperienced people to violate our laws, and then there will be no more incidents.

Before United Nations Correspondents' Association, New York, June 27/ Los Angeles Times, 6-28:(1)6.

Armand Hammer
Chairman,
Occidental Petroleum Corporation

1

[On his dealings with the Soviet Union]: I never believed their system would be as good as ours [the U.S.'s]. But we should let them find their own destiny. We are becoming more socialistic, and they are becoming more capitalistic; and somewhere in between there is a meeting ground.

Interview/
The New York Times, 5-20:(3)15.

Edward Heath
Prime Minister of the United Kingdom

2

My position is that I am perfectly happy to have mutually-balanced [West Europe-Soviet] force reductions, provided that it doesn't impair the security of Europe; and I think this is also the United States' position . . . I am not suggesting for a moment the Soviet Union is going to start walking across frontiers tomorrow, but what we have built up over the years is a balance of power in which Europe feels that it has got the basis of a sound security, and what is the point of throwing all that away? That I don't understand. And Europe is making a very, very substantial contribution to European defense and is going on building it up. What are the figures? Ninety per cent of the ground forces in Europe are European. Seventy-five per cent of the air forces are European. Eighty per cent of the naval forces are European. This is an Atlantic [U.S.-Europe] partnership in which we both play our part.

TV-radio interview, Washington/
"Meet the Press,"
National Broadcasting Company, 2-4.

3

The proposals we have put through give an opportunity for the [warring Catholic and Protestant] communities in Northern Ireland to work together, and to do so within a framework of their own organization of a political assembly . . . It may well be that extremists on either side will try to prevent this

. . . [but] the people in Northern Ireland have shown quite clearly by the recent plebiscite that they want to stay as part of the United Kingdom . . . When the time comes, if they want voluntarily to have a united Ireland, no government in Westminster will ever stand in the way.

Interview/Newsweek, 5-28:48.

4

I don't accept [the] myth [of an "English malaise"]. At the moment, we have an economy which is expanding again at the rate of 5 per cent; unemployment is falling; our reserves are very high; we have a floating pound which protects the reserves . . . We have reformed the whole of [our] industrial-relations legislation . . . and we now have an anti-inflationary policy which is giving us stability . . . These are all considerable achievements—and we have negotiated Britain into the European Economic Community. These aren't the proceeds of a nation in decline. These are the results of a new dynamism here in Britain.

Interview/Newsweek, 5-28:48.

5

There are those who favor the total integration of Northern Ireland in the United Kingdom, with no special local institutions for Northern Ireland. If all other possibilities had failed, Northern Ireland could no doubt be run fairly and efficiently under such a system. But what we are seeking is not merely fairness and efficiency. We are looking for a means to get to grips with the fundamental problem of Northern Ireland. That is to enable its people to live and work together and be responsible for the peaceful management of their own affairs.

London, Sept. 18/
The New York Times, 9-19:10.

6

I think it is accepted by the people of Britain already that we are a member of the [European Economic] Community and we're going to stay. There may be some who will try to make it an election issue; I don't think myself it will be. People, you know, have only got to ask themselves what would be our position—the United Kingdom, Scotland and

(EDWARD HEATH)

so on—if we were to announce we are now going to leave the Community. The rest of the world would be absolutely astonished, and they'd say, "You're going to pull out of an organization like this? You've got your problems, of course—you've only just joined—but look at all the opportunities for the future; and now you're going to cast them on one side?" I mean, the rest of the world would think we'd gone out of our minds. You only have to look at the other side of the question to see very clearly that the people of Britain now recognize that we're part of the Community and we're going to get benefits from it.

Interview, London/
The (Edinburgh) Scotsman, 9-26:11.

Hubert H. Humphrey
United States Senator, D-Minnesota

1

I look upon our [military] participation in Europe not only to protect Europeans, but also to protect Americans. I think it is important to have allies. I'd rather have the first line of defense away from New York City or Minneapolis. That first line is in Western Europe. As long as I can get my friends in Europe to commit their resources to their own defense and ours, I think we're in better shape.

Interview/
U.S. News & World Report, 10-15:78.

Richard H. Ichord
United States Representative, D-Missouri

2

[On the Soviet Union]: Can we afford to lose sight of the type of society with which we are dealing? I'm sure I do not have to remind you that even today, on the heels of the visit by the Soviet leader [Leonid Brezhnev], with all the gestures of friendship, the Soviet Union is still a nation which allows no freedom of press, no freedom of assembly, no freedom of religion, no freedom to emigrate to another country. We have no real evidence, nor can we safely conclude on the basis of

their own statements, that they have abandoned their long-range goal of world conquest.

Human Events, 7-21:4.

Henry M. Jackson
United States Senator, D-Washington

3

[Saying improved U.S.-Soviet trade relations should depend on Soviet willingness to permit more freedom in Eastern Europe]: Once we watched helplessly as barbed-wire fences and walls with watchtowers were built —not to keep people out, but to keep them in. We've seen people machine-gunned at the Berlin Wall or shipped off to prison camps. Their crime was the desire to be free. The thousands of Soviet citizens who wish to [emigrate] aren't criminals—they're just plain human beings who want to make a better life for themselves in another country [Israel] where they are welcome. While we're bargaining with the Russians over dollars and rubles, let's do some bargaining on behalf of helpless human beings. When we talk about free trade, let's talk about free people, too.

At National Press Club, Washington,
March 22/Quote, 7-29:110.

4

I look upon the Soviet Union as a nation that continues to be committed to totalitarianism. If anyone has any doubt about their aggressive attitude, ask the Czechs or the Chinese or ask [Yugoslavian President] Tito. They [the Soviets] do constitute a clear and present danger to freedom. Millions are still in slavery—Czechs, Romanians, Bulgarians. The idea that everything's changed, that detente is here—: the issue is freedom versus tyranny.

Interview/
The Washington Post, 4-2:(A)2.

5

[Criticizing U.S. trade with the Soviet Union as being too advantageous to the Soviets]: Are we being invited to stimulate the lagging Soviet economy, an economy made stagnant precisely because the lion's share of its technological resources have been siphoned off into military programs? Are we going to liberate the Soviet leaders from problems they cannot solve themselves, so that they can concentrate on further repression of their own people and the accumulation of military power for international coercion?

Los Angeles Times, 11-2:(2)7.

Abdul Salam Jalloud
Prime Minister of Libya

1

The Arab dollar or dinar must replace the American dollar in Europe. For Europe to get rid of its economic problems, it must depend on the Arab dollar, because it is based on the solid economic basis of black gold, which is oil.

*Interview, Tripoli/
San Francisco Examiner, 9-4:10.*

Michel Jobert
Foreign Minister of France

2

[On criticism of France's current nuclear tests in the South Pacific]: There has been a nuclear test explosion in these last few days, and others will follow . . . Why all this fuss, then? The fuss is running out of breath anyway, and will die out in the face of France's determination to insure her own defenses.

*San Francisco Examiner & Chronicle,
7-29:(This World)2.*

3

I am surprised to see that here and there people pretend to think there is a contradiction between the [European] desire to keep American troops in Europe and the rejection of imperious arbitration. How can anyone not see—or not wish to see—that the United States is in Europe first of all because of its own interest and that it is not in our own interest to reject them? These troops are in fact helping to maintain the indispensable balance, and by the same token we will have to take into account the possibility of their eventually leaving.

*At Western European Union assembly/
San Francisco Examiner & Chronicle,
12-9:(B)2.*

Olafur Johanneson
Prime Minister of Iceland

4

[Criticizing Britain's sending warships to protect British fishing boats in what Iceland claims are her territorial waters and what Britain claims are international waters]: The British Foreign Secretary is allowing himself to use strong, threatening words against a small and weaponless country. Iceland is one of 32 countries which have extended their fishing limits recently, but the British have not threatened any of them, and the British Foreign Secretary, Sir Alec Douglas-Home, has not even coughed.

*Radio broadcast, Reykjavik, May 28/
Los Angeles Times, 5-29:(1)7.*

Donald M. Kendall
Chairman, PepsiCo, Inc.

5

I think trade is going to be one of the main means of solving the problems between the United States and the Soviet Union. If I have ever seen a country where personal relationships are important, it's the Soviet Union. People react there as they would if you went out to some place in Ohio or Iowa and met somebody and became his friend. That has an impact in that community. It's the same way in the Soviet Union. The more American businessmen go over there and tell them about our country the better, because if there was ever a place where there is a lack of understanding about the United States, it's the Soviet Union. And I think this is also true on our side. When American businessmen go to the Soviet Union, they're going to develop personal relationships, and it's going to make, I believe, a tremendous impact. Because the biggest thing that's lacking is confidence and trust between both sides.

*Interview, Washington/
U.S. News & World Report, 1-22:70.*

Edward M. Kennedy
United States Senator, D-Massachusetts

6

There has been—and continues to be—a danger of isolating our NATO allies during

(EDWARD M. KENNEDY)

bilateral [U.S.] negotiations with the Soviet Union. There is a danger of giving the impression that we are prepared to reach agreements with Moscow at Europe's expense. And there is a danger of allowing serious conflict to develop in economic relations among Atlantic states—relations that have been neglected by this [Nixon] Administration for far too long . . . [The Administration] is even now issuing vague hints that the United States will reconsider its policies concerning the maintenance of U.S. troops on the continent—not after careful evaluation and consultation with the allies on the appropriate force structure, not through [mutual reductions with the Soviet Union], but in retaliation for an alleged lack of European enthusiasm and support for U.S. policies [in the Middle East].

Before the Senate, Washington, Nov. 2/
Los Angeles Herald-Examiner, 11-2:(A)2.

1

The iron regime of [Josef] Stalin is gone from the Soviet Union, and tensions between East and West have eased. But still we see Soviet men and women brutalized by the apparatus of state repression. Still we find writers and scientists and poets in prisons and the mental institutions of that vast country. Still we find Soviet Jews denied the right to free emigration. I believe the American people want their government to protest these crimes against the cause of human rights.

Quote, 11-25:521.

Henry A. Kissinger
Assistant to the President of the
United States for National Security Affairs

2

This year has been called the Year of Europe, but not because Europe was less important in 1972 or in 1969. The alliance between the United States and Europe has been the cornerstone of all post-war foreign policy. It provided the political framework for American engagements in Europe and marked the definitive end of U.S. isolationism. It insured the sense of security that allowed Europe to re-

cover from the devastation of the war. Nineteen seventy-three is the Year of Europe because the era that was shaped by decisions of a generation ago is ending. Our challenge is whether a unity forged by a common perception of danger can draw new purpose from shared positive aspirations. If we permit the Atlantic partnership to atrophy or to erode through neglect, carelessness or mistrust, we risk what has been achieved, and we shall miss our historic opportunity for even greater achievement. In the '40s and '50s, the task was economic reconstruction and security against the danger of attack. The West responded with courage and imagination. Today, the need is to make the Atlantic relationship as dynamic a force in building a new structure of peace, less geared to crisis and more conscious of opportunities, drawing its inspirations from its goals rather than its fears. The Atlantic nations must join in a fresh act of creation, equal to that undertaken by the post-war generation of leaders of Europe and America.

At Associated Press luncheon, New York,
April 23/Los Angeles Times, 4-25:(2)7.

3

The West no longer holds the nuclear predominance that permitted it in the '50s and '60s to rely almost solely on a strategy of massive nuclear retaliation. Because under conditions of nuclear parity such a strategy invites mutual suicide, the [Western] Alliance must have other choices. The collective ability to resist attack in Western Europe by means of flexible responses has become central to a rational strategy and crucial to the maintenance of peace. For this reason, the United States has maintained substantial conventional forces in Europe, and our NATO allies have embarked on a significant effort to modernize and improve their own military establishments. To maintain the military balance that has insured stability in Europe for 25 years, the Alliance has no choice but to address these needs and to reach an agreement on our defense requirements. This task is all the more difficult because the lessening of tensions has given new impetus to arguments that it is safe to begin reducing forces unilaterally. And unbridled economic competition can sap the impulse for common defense. All governments of the Western Alliance face a major challenge in educating their peoples to the realities of security in the 1970s.

At Associated Press luncheon, New York, April 23/Los Angeles Times, 4-25:(2)7.

Henry A. Kissinger
Secretary of State of the United States

1

[Criticizing a Senate vote to reduce U.S. forces in Europe]: It will be impossible to negotiate an agreement for the [mutual] reduction of forces [with the Soviet Union] when the United States unilaterally accomplishes what the negotiations are supposed to bring about. It will be very difficult, if not impossible, to convince our allies of the steadiness of American policy when the United States again unilaterally, before our discussions have well advanced, reduces its forces in Europe.

News conference, New York, Sept. 26/ The New York Times, 9-27:16.

2

[Arguing against the U.S. trying to gain more freedom for Soviet citizens in return for better U.S.-Soviet relations]: How hard can we press without provoking the Soviet leadership into returning to practices in its foreign policy that increase international tension? Are we ready to face the crises and increased defense budget that a return to cold-war conditions would spawn? Is it detente that has prompted repression—or is it detente that has generated the ferment and the demand for openness which we are now witnessing? . . . As long as we remain powerful we will use our influence to promote freedom as we always have. But in the nuclear age we are obliged to recognize that the issue of war and peace also involves human lives and that the attainment of peace is a profound moral concern.

At "Pacem in Terris" conference, Washington, Oct. 8/The New York Times, 10-9:5.

3

The relationship between the Soviet Union and the United States is an inherently ambiguous one. We have never said that detente indicates that we have parallel objectives, or that it indicates that we have compatible domestic structures. Our view has been that the detente is made necessary because, as the two great nuclear superpowers, we have a special responsibility to spare mankind the dangers of a nuclear holocaust . . . in this relationship one will always have an element both of confidence and of competition coexisting in a somewhat ambivalent manner. The relationship that has developed between the Soviet Union and the United States since 1971 has been one of considerable restraint, and there have been very frequent and very confidential exchanges between [Soviet] General Secretary [Leonid] Brezhnev and the President [of the U.S., Nixon]. At the same time, it is perfectly conceivable—and indeed, it has happened during the Middle East crisis—that long-standing commitments—ideological pressures—produce actions that bring these two sides into confrontation. At that point, it is important that enough confidence exists so that the confrontation is mitigated.

News conference, Washington, Nov. 21/ The New York Times, 11-22:18.

4

I would be less than frank were I to conceal our [the U.S.'s] uneasiness about some of the recent practices of the European community in the political field. To present the decisions of a unifying Europe to us as *faits accomplis* not subject to effective discussion is alien to the tradition of U.S.-European relations. This may seem a strange complaint from a country repeatedly accused of acting itself without adequately consulting with its allies. There is no doubt that the United States has sometimes not consulted enough or adequately—especially in rapidly moving situations—but this is not a preference; it is a deviation from official policy and established practice—usually under pressure of necessity. The attitude of the unifying Europe, by contrast, seems to attempt to elevate refusal to consult into a principle defining European identity. To judge from recent experience, consultation with us before a decision is pre-

(HENRY A. KISSINGER)

cluded, and consultation after the fact, has been drained of content. For then Europe appoints a spokesman who is empowered to inform us of the decisions taken but who has no authority to negotiate. We do not object to a single spokesman, but we do believe that, as an old ally, the United States should be given an opportunity to express its concerns before final decisions affecting its interests are taken, and bilateral channels of discussion and negotiation should not be permitted to atrophy—at least until European political unity is fully realized. To replace the natural dialogue with extremely formalistic procedures would be to shatter abruptly close and intangible ties of trust and communication that took decades to develop and that have served our common purposes well.

Before the Pilgrims organization, London, Dec. 12/The New York Times, 12-13:28.

1

There is one principal problem in our [the U.S.'s] relations with . . . Europe at this moment that only the Europeans can answer. All the other criticisms can be relatively easily taken care of. And that question is: What is to be the shape of the emerging unified Europe? Is this Europe to be organized on a basis which seeks its identity in exclusivity to our position—or at least in distance from the United States? Or is it prepared, while affirming its identity, to recognize that the opportunities of the future require Atlantic cooperation? As far as the United States is concerned, we have given our answer. All of our proposals, however they were advanced—from the proposal of the Atlantic Charter to the proposal of the common approach to energy—had one fundamental goal: to create a dialogue between ourselves and the Europeans in terms of the challenges that lay ahead of us and in terms of the common problems that needed to be solved. That offer is still open. We believe that some progress was made in our recent talks in Europe, and we will continue both the work on the declarations with the European community and with our Nato

partners, as well as the work on the Energy Action Group. But the United States is not concerned with developing some legal formula or with a document that responds to a single initiative. The problem before us is whether the nations of the Atlantic area, as well as Japan—faced with self-evident problems that affect them all—can develop a common approach, or whether they will consume themselves in the sort of rivalry that has destroyed other civilizations.

News conference, Washington, Dec. 27/ U.S. News & World Report, 1-7('74):64

Alexei N. Kosygin
Premier of the Soviet Union

2

[Criticizing suggestions that nations at the European Security Conference in Geneva demand concessions from Moscow over freedom of movement and information in the Soviet Union in return for detente and improved relations]: I want to emphasize that the Soviet Union does not intend to impose anything on anyone. But we reject all attempts to impose something on the Soviet Union, because that is contrary to our domestic and foreign policy. Success can be achieved only when all Conference participants are guided strictly by the principles of mutual respect and equality, not permitting one-sided advantages to be gained in the solution of international problems.

Belgrade, Yugoslavia, Sept. 24/ The Washington Post, 9-25:(A)21.

Georg Leber
Minister of Defense of West Germany

3

The development of a military balance of power sufficient for the political goals of the West—deterrence, crisis-management and defense—the evolution of a strong economic potential in Western Europe and the continuation of the close alliance between the U.S. and Western Europe—the framework of which has served time and again to define common interests and the ways and means of compromise—has produced the effect that the use of force in East-West relations no longer appears a suitable means of attaining political goals in Europe. Outside of the Warsaw Pact, ultimata, threats and pressure have not yielded the Soviet Union lasting successes in Europe. But this does not end the rivalry between the world powers and the controversy between Communist ideology and the free and democratic way of life. This rivalry has been limited only in the choice of means but not in objectives. If the military balance of power is neglected, the range of means for this competition might widen again. The same could be expected if the North Atlantic Alliance were to break apart. The maintenance of the balance of power and the normalization of relations between East and West limit the means in the continued struggle for the shape of Europe and the relations between the world powers. However, the normalization of relations with the Soviet Union and the East European countries cannot exceed the limits permitted by our ability to preserve the undisputed cohesion of the Western Alliance.

Before X. Internationale Wehrkunde Begegnung, Munich, Feb. 24/ Vital Speeches, 4-15:410.

Joseph Luns
Secretary General,
North Atlantic Treaty Organization

1

We want to maintain the military balance, but at a lower level; and this can only be done by the collective effort of the [Atlantic] Alliance. If NATO is disbanded, the effect would be far more serious than if the Warsaw Pact were dissolved, as the military cooperation in the Pact is based on a web of bilateral agreements, with the Soviet Union in the spider position. Disbanding the Warsaw Pact is not the same as disbanding Soviet forces. NATO exists in order to compensate for its numerically smaller forces through a system of collective security.

Interview, Brussels/Human Events, 4-14:9.

George Mavros
Acting leader, Center Union Party of Greece

2

[On the current Greek government which recently overthrew the regime of George Papadopoulos]: Greece is like a pilotless vessel in a storm. It is not governed. There is anarchy. Nobody can tell who is in power, not whether those now in control shall be in power tomorrow. Complete confusion reigns. According to rumors, rival groups and trends within the regime vie for power daily . . . The present regime, just as any other like it that may succeed it, shall collapse under the onus of the immense problems confronting it. Nothing can save it. Each day that goes by without restoration of democratic order merely aggravates the situation, exposing the nation to fatal dangers.

Dec. 31/The New York Times, 1-1('74):6.

Wilbur D. Mills
United States Representative, D-Arkansas

3

I cannot see the United States expanding commercial markets with the Soviet Union if the price is to be paid in the martyrdom of men of genius like [author Alexander] Solzhenitsyn and [physicist] Andrei Sakharov. Our insistence upon the liberalization of travel and immigration is by no means limited to only one category of Soviet citizens—members of the Jewish minority. The same principle must apply to all and, particularly, to these men whose creativity and courage have brought down upon them the wrath of the police-state mentality.

U.S. News & World Report, 9-24:79.

Dom Mintoff
Prime Minister of Malta

4

Never since the end of World War II has Southern Europe been more insecure than it is today. Symptoms are there for those who care to see them: dispute over Gibraltar, unrest in Cyprus and in Greece, the Arab-Israeli confrontation, etc. It is difficult to determine which of these is the most worrying—the black hatred devouring the hearts of Arabs and Israelis or the nonchalance and coolness with which the superpowers shake hands across Central Europe and bare their ugly teeth in the blue Mediterranean Sea.

At European Conference on Security and Cooperation, Helsinki, July 6/ Los Angeles Times, 7-7:(1)3.

Francois Mitterrand
French politician

1

[On how French voters approach an election]: On Monday, you throw artichokes at the prefecture. On Tuesday, it's potatoes. Wednesday, you put up roadblocks, and on Thursday you break windows. You tie up downtown Paris on Friday and boo the Minister of Finance. I don't know what you do on Saturday, but on Sunday you vote for the government.

Time, 3-26:49.

Mobutu Sese Seko
President of Zaire

2

Portugal is an economically, socially, culturally under-developed nation. It has no democracy. It has no military force. Its sole record is that of having the highest illiteracy level in Europe. Its force and its arrogance are supplied to it through its membership [in] NATO, because Portugal, with its colonies, is strategically necessary for that military organization.

San Francisco Examiner & Chronicle, 12-16:(This World)36.

Thomas H. Moorer
Admiral, United States Navy;
Chairman, Joint Chiefs of Staff

3

. . . some members of the U.S. Congress are now seeking a reduction of American armed-force strength in Europe. The objectives offered by the proponents of reduction are to reduce defense spending, help to alleviate the balance-of-payments strain and to contribute to detente and peace in the world. The underlying philosophy with respect to the American commitment to the defense of Europe is that

our intent will remain equally credible at the lower force levels. I respect the sincerity of those who hold such views, but I do not agree with them. I believe that unilateral reductions by the United States at this critical juncture would jeopardize the negotiations which will soon commence. We have persevered for more than 25 years awaiting the opportunity that now presents itself to achieve mutual accords on reducing the tensions in Europe. It would be a rash act indeed to initiate unilateral action which could undercut the goals and aspirations of our allies as well as ourselves. Consider this comparison: Since 1961 the United States has reduced its troop level in Europe by 35 per cent. The Soviets, on the other hand, have increased their troop levels by about 20 per cent in the last five years. Is it now prudent to believe that U.S. unilateral withdrawals would be greeted by reciprocal action on the part of the Soviets? I think not. We must be firm in our insistence that change be mutual, not unilateral.

At D.C. chapter of Navy League, Washington, Sept. 6/Vital Speeches, 10-1:739.

Edmund S. Muskie
United States Senator, D-Maine

4

[On possible U.S. troop cuts in Europe]: Few doubt the need for a strong, credible NATO. Few doubt that the military strength of the Alliance has played an important role in bringing about the much-improved East-West situation. But in view of our improved relations with the Soviets, in view of our own economic problems, and in view of the failure of the now-prosperous Europeans to assume a significantly larger share of the NATO burden, a number of questions have been raised about our present policies . . .

U.S. News & World Report, 8-13:31.

David O'Connell
Chief of Staff, Provisional wing,
Irish Republican Army

5

[Saying Britain should give up its authority over Northern Ireland]: There are those who say it is too much to ask Britain that she acknowledge the right of the Irish people to self-determination. We do not think so. We ask of England that which America gave to Vietnam, France to Algeria and Britain herself to her former colonies of Palestine, Cyprus and Aden. Britain . . . will gain universal respect by withdrawing from her first and last colony.

Observing the anniversary of the 1916 uprising that later resulted in Irish Republic independence, Belfast, April 22/ Los Angeles Times, 4-23:(1)4.

Olof Palme
Prime Minister of Sweden

1

Neutrality has never condemned us to be silent on world issues. Never. When we protested against Hungary, Czechoslovakia or the Berlin Wall in fairly strong language, we didn't hear anything from the [U.S.] White House [which is now complaining about Sweden's criticism of U.S. Vietnam policy] about our neutrality. There is a long-term political objective . . . It's all right for the superpowers to have detente . . . But one of the dangers is that, if the superpowers have a detente among themselves, they might feel free to push small countries around. The danger is this: that the enormous power of the superpowers will be a threat to the independence and right to exist of small countries. We have to speak up for the right of small countries to create their own future.

Interview/Time, 1-29:35.

2

[On the cooling of U.S.-Swedish relations because of Sweden's opposition to U.S. policy in Vietnam]: The war in Indochina is not a permanent phenomenon. We [his Social Democratic government in Sweden] might not be a permanent phenomenon. The Administration in Washington may not be a permanent phenomenon. But friendship between the American and Swedish people is a permanent phenomenon. That is important. Relations with the United States have always been good on a people-to-people basis. We spoke out very clearly on the war in Indochina, and I feel in

the long run this will strengthen rather than weaken our ties.

News conference/ The Christian Science Monitor, 9-18:9.

George Papadopoulos
President of Greece

3

[On the imminent referendum asking for voter approval of his policies]: It must be stressed that the revolution exists, will not resign and will not be overthrown by a vote of rejection . . . In the unlikely event voters reject the government proposals, it will simply mean rejection of the Constitutional changes. It will necessitate formulation of new proposals. But there is no force within or outside Greece capable of overthrowing the revolution.

Television address to the nation, July 27/ San Francisco Examiner & Chronicle, 8-5:(This World)12.

4

I declare before the Greek nation that I will keep strictly to the announced schedule regarding the stage-by-stage establishment of the democratic order . . . The new democracy is for all of us. Differences can exist and are even necessary under the democratic order. But passions and individualism undermine democracy, and self-discipline and superiority must be imposed.

Broadcast address to the nation, Athens, Aug. 19/ San Francisco Examiner, 8-20:13.

Claiborne Pell
United States Senator, D-Rhode Island

5

[Criticizing U.S. ties and military aid to the current Greek government]: To date, the [U.S. Nixon] Administration has given little or no evidence that it recognizes the validity of the concern which is widely expressed by those familiar with Greek affairs, regarding the possible long-term consequences of the junta's role and its American connection. We have, for far too long, allowed the junta to derive the benefits of United States military assis-

(CLAIBORNE PELL)

tance which flow from Greek military participation in the [NATO] Alliance while disregarding its responsibility to assure its own citizens their individual rights and liberties, the protection of which is the underlying reason for the Alliance itself.

The New York Times, 6-28:18.

Muammar el-Qaddafi
Chief of State of Libya

1

. . . you can't say that it was my stay in England [during his youth] which provoked my hatred against the English. There is a history of English dealings with the Arabs which goes back for decades, even before my birth. So the reason for our support of the Irish guerrillas [in Northern Ireland] is justified. It's a little country which has taken up arms to defend its rights and its freedom. We have given it our support.

Interview, Tripoli/
Los Angeles Herald-Examiner, 4-21:(A)1.

Abraham A. Ribicoff
United States Senator, D-Connecticut

2

Lavish toasts to peace are not very reliable guidelines. We must seek evidence that shows, for example, whether the Soviet Union is reconciled to the prospect of exchanging ideas and people with the West. But what do we actually find? A Valery Panov is not permitted to dance; Soviet newspapers are mockeries of the truth; and sane men are locked in insane asylums for speaking out against injustice.

Quote, 11-25:509.

Benjamin S. Rosenthal
United States Representative, D-New York

3

[Saying Europe should contribute more to its own defense and not be dependent on the U.S.]: So long as West Europe is booming and so long as the United States is having economic and psychological difficulties, we must have some change in the formula. We can't keep

going, hat-in-hand, saying, "Please do a little more." As long as the United States taxpayer is paying twice, three or four times as much, it's not right.

At House Foreign Affairs Committee hearing,
Washington, July 10/
The New York Times, 7-11:3.

Kenneth Rush
Deputy Secretary of State
of the United States

4

[If the U.S. nuclear umbrella were withdrawn,] European nations would have to choose between either vastly increasing their own nuclear capabilities or seeking accommodation with the Soviet Union . . . The same unacceptable choice between enlarged nuclear capabilities and accommodation would be forced on European nations were they to lose confidence in our commitment to the principle that European security and U.S. security are indivisible. Our unilateral withdrawal from our commitments in Western Europe would almost certainly produce such a loss in confidence.

Before Industrial College of the
Armed Forces, Washington, June 5/
The Washington Post, 6-6:(A)4.

5

If we reduce [U.S.] forces [in Europe] so that we don't have a credible conventional deterrence, three things will happen: The Russians will push harder for what they want, seeing no opposition; Europe will become fragmented . . . and each country will be unable to . . . resist political, economic and other pressures from Russia; and the United States would become . . . more isolationist, feeling Europe is not the front line of defense . . . Frankly, I do not think this country could survive as an isolationist nation.

Interview/
The Washington Post, 7-9:(A)8.

Andrei D. Sakharov
Soviet physicist

6

The Soviet Union has the same sort of

problems as the capitalist world: criminality and estrangement. The difference is that our society is an extreme case, with maximum un-freedom, maximum ideological rigidness and—and this is most typical—a society with maximum pretensions about being best, although it certainly isn't that . . . Realistically speaking, the Russian state represents an unprecedented concentration of economic and political power. But it is state capitalism, in which the state completely dominates economic life. The visa system secures divisions within our society. Territorial differences and injustices exist between different parts of the country. Moscow and other large cities are privileged when it comes to consumer goods, comforts, everyday life, cultural activity and so on.

Swedish television interview/
The New York Times, 7-5:10.

1

[On Soviet detente with the West]: Detente without democratization [in the Soviet Union], detente in which the West in effect accepts the Soviet rules of the game, would be dangerous. It would not really solve any of the world's problems and would simply mean capitulating in the face of real or exaggerated Soviet power. It would mean trading with the Soviet Union, buying its gas and oil, while ignoring all other aspects. I think such a development would be dangerous, because it would contaminate the whole world with the antidemocratic peculiarities of Soviet society; it would enable the Soviet Union to bypass problems it cannot resolve on its own and to concentrate on accumulating still further strength. As a result, the world would become helpless before this uncontrollable bureaucratic machine. I think that if detente were to proceed totally without qualifications, on Soviet terms, it would pose a serious threat to the world as a whole. It would mean cultivating a closed country, where anything that happens may be shielded from outside eyes, a country wearing a mask that hides its true face.

To Western reporters/
The New York Times Magazine, 11-4:47.

Walter Scheel
Foreign Minister of West Germany

2

[Saying a true test of East-West detente is if the Communist nations agree to allow freer movement of people, press, information and ideas in their countries]: The elementary requirements for contacts and exchanges of people all over Europe are part of the reality which politicians have to take into account. If the gap between our views on this reality is still too wide, then I think it would be a dictate of honesty to say so unambiguously. It would not be a catastrophe for Europe. Nor would it be the end of the process of detente. It would simply mean that the conditions are not yet mature enough to allow us to attain at this conference the ambitious goal we have set ourselves. At some time in the future, we could perhaps meet again for another multilateral effort.

At European Conference on Security and
Cooperation,
Helsinki, July 4/
Los Angeles Times, 7-5:(1)14.

Helmut Schmidt
Minister of Finance, and former Minister
of Defense, of West Germany

3

With the help of the United States, we in Europe have achieved a situation vis-a-vis the Soviet Union in which there is no single strand of imminent fear. Many people at present would not feel as urgent a need for close American military cooperation as they felt necessary at the time of the Soviet intervention in Czechoslovakia five years ago. [However, the governments of Europe know well that their security] depends to a great amount on the unchanged defense cooperation of the United States. [But] in a normal world, in which you have cooperation between countries as well as competition . . . you will not expect to have a new declaration of love every Monday morning at 9 o'clock . . . and it is unnecessary.

Interview/
The Christian Science Monitor, 4-17:(B)3.

Jean-Jacques Servan-Schreiber
Member, French National Assembly

1

France can mushroom into Europe only when political power is regionalized. But that's not enough. There has to be power at the European level, as well as at the local. We need different levels of power . . . Political nations, in the old sense, are not valid any more.

Interview, Nancy, France/
The Christian Science Monitor, 2-14:2.

Arnold Smith
Secretary General of the British
Commonwealth

2

[The Commonwealth] bridges the divides of race, color and religions, brings together developed and developing, and reaches into all the continents. Its composition is an antidote to regional exclusiveness or continental chauvinism. Commonwealth cooperation promotes cohesion, dulling the edge of racial passion and softening economic embitterment.

Ottawa, Canada, Aug. 1/
The New York Times, 8-2:2.

Christopher Soames
Vice President for External Affairs,
European Common Market Commission

3

We [in Europe] must acknowledge that, for matters which come under the generic heading of foreign policy, we can as yet boast but little European cohesion. We cannot expect to be considered a single political force unless and until we are ready to act as one.

May 8/The Washington Post, 6-3:(G)1.

Alexander I. Solzhenitsyn
Soviet author

4

[On reaction in the Soviet Union to his criticisms of Soviet life]: I received letters with threats, rather than demands; threats to make short work of me and my family. This summer such letters have come to me through the mail. Not to mention psychological mistakes, the many technical mistakes by the authors have convinced me these letters have been sent by KGB agents. For example, the incredible speed of delivery of these bandits' letters—less than 24 hours; only letters from the most important government organs go that fast. Another example of technical mistakes they make is that the KGB officials were in such a hurry that the envelopes were sealed only after the post office had stamped them . . . During the winter of 1971-72, I was warned through several channels—within the KGB's apparatus there are also people who are tormented by their fate—that they were preparing to kill me in a "car accident." But here we have a peculiarity, I would almost say an advantage of our social structure: Not a single hair falls or will fall from my head or from the heads of members of my family without the knowledge and approval of the KGB. That is the extent to which we are observed, shadowed, spied upon and listened to . . . If, for example, a letter that reaches me by post blows up, it will be impossible to explain why it didn't explode before in the hands of the censors. And since for a long time I have not suffered from serious diseases and since I don't drive a car and since because of my convictions under no circumstances of life will I commit suicide, then if I am declared killed or suddenly mysteriously dead, you can infallibly conclude, with 100 per cent certainty, that I have been killed with the approval of the KGB or by it.

Interview, Moscow/
The Christian Science Monitor, 8-30:5.

5

Citizenship in our country is not an inalienable natural right for every human being born on its soil. But it is a kind of coupon that is kept by an exclusive clique of people who in no way have proved that they have a greater right to Russian soil. And this clique can, if it does not approve of some citizen's convictions, declare him deprived of his homeland. I leave it to you to find a word yourselves for such a social structure.

Interview/Time, 9-10:30.

Axel Springer
West German publisher

1

I hate every kind of totalitarianism. What Germany did under Hitler was terrible, and we were destined to suffer for it. The division of Germany was our own fault—the result of our own criminal action. Still, no one can deny that the results of that division have produced a situation in which all Germans are not treated equally. In one part of Germany, there is a country where people are free to vote for whom they please, to read the newspapers and the books, to go to the films and plays of their own choosing. They have had the chance to begin anew, to rehabilitate themselves and to again become part of the decent, civilized world. But the people in the other [Communist] part of Germany were no more guilty than those of us over here [in the West]. They should not have to go on bearing the full burden of the past when it has been spared to those of us in West Germany. What Axel Springer wants is that those poor people on the other side of the wall [in East Germany] should have something like the same kind of chance that we have had. I do not have the right to sit here on an elegant sofa in a comfortable house and turn my back on those who are in East Germany sitting amidst misfortune. I cannot agree to any policy that says some Germans will be free while others are written off and forgotten.
Interview, West Berlin/
The Washington Post, 4-22:(B)2.

George Steiner
Scholar; Fellow, Churchill College,
Cambridge University, England

2

England has the enormous psychological problem of having 1,000 years of history behind it. The question is: what is there left to do? The past here has become so present that the great mood is looking back. Sometimes it seems as if there is nothing on television every night but war films, all looking back, at any war—the Boer War, Crimea, you name it. What are the books that sell 100,000 copies? *Mary,*

Queen of Scots, Wellington. What are the hit television films? *The Six Wives of Henry VIII,* Lord Clark's *Civilisation.* It's like a museum.
Interview/Time, 3-12:52.

Geoffery Stewart-Smith
Member of British Parliament

3

They [the Soviet Union] are advancing slowly everywhere—nothing dramatic, but a slow, remorseless extension . . . I'll give you one reason why. There are 630 members of this Parliament. About 80 are interested in foreign affairs, and of that number only about 50 care about defense. How do you measure that against a closed, monolithic society, motivated by total political warfare and a desire for global domination? We have no strategic aim but to make peace—which is fine unless you're dealing with a force to whom peace means control.
Interview/Human Events, 4-28:15.

Josip Broz Tito
President of Yugoslavia

4

[Saying the Communist Party should have strong authority]: We Communists have the right to interfere in everything. I am chairman of the League of Communists and I have the right to interfere. We have the right to interfere to insure the correct implementation of the general policy of the Party, the proper development of socialism, the proper development of social relations and brotherhood and unity, for which we shed a sea of blood.
Svetozarevo, Yugoslavia, April 4/
The New York Times, 4-8:(1)14.

Omar Torrijos (Herrera)
Head of Government of Panama

5

Like the Panama Canal Zone, Gibraltar is an outpost of international colonialism. When Panamà and Spain are freed of the Anglo-Yankee colonialism, I will come again to visit the Rock and to salute the Spanish flag on it.
The New York Times, 11-23:14.

William Whitelaw
British Secretary of State
for Northern Ireland

1

[On the just-announced British plan for insuring a share of political power for the Catholic minority in Northern Ireland]: We need
the good-will of everyone to make it work.
We knew we couldn't please everyone. But it
is a reasonable deal for reasonable people. The
unreasonable will always find reasons why it
will fail. They will say that the power-sharing
won't work. I say that it *must* work.

London, March 20/
The New York Times, 3-21:16.

Krister Wickman
Foreign Minister of Sweden

2

[On the cooling of U.S.-Swedish relations
because of Sweden's criticism of U.S. policy
in Vietnam]: Relations will probably never be
100 per cent perfect with [U.S.] President
Nixon, because he has taken such a personal,
emotional stand toward the present Swedish
government. Relations are not good with the
President, that's an obvious fact. Nixon will
never change his opinion on Sweden's stand
toward the Vietnam war, nor will the Swedish
government change its stand toward Vietnam.
These are facts, but they belong to history,
and we on the Swedish side don't regard them
as a reason for not having normal diplomatic
relations.

Interview, New York, Oct. 11/
The Dallas Times Herald, 10-12:(A)3.

Harold Wilson
Member of British Parliament;
Former Prime Minister of the United Kingdom

3

[On the 1968 Soviet invasion of Czechoslovakia and his current visit there]: [The visit
is] part of a general world-wide movement to
see that whatever happened in 1968 is now
past and over . . . Time has moved on now,
and I told them here that it was time to turn
one's back on 1968.

Prague/
The Christian Science Monitor, 4-30:14.

Leonid M. Zamyatin
Director general of Tass
(Soviet news agency)

4

[On U.S.-Soviet trade]: . . . when the development of trade is being discussed in a
long-term aspect, say for a period of 10 to 15
years, this creates a tremendous potential of
trust, and we regard this as one of the advantages of developing trade and economic
relations on a long-term basis . . . Our country is ready to conclude with the United
States large-scale deals based on mutual advantage. We can reach agreement on extensive
economic cooperation spanning a period of
decades. We have no intention of getting anything in the United States free of charge; and
neither do we intend the United States to get
anything from us free of charge.

News conference/
The Dallas Times Herald, 6-21:(A)27.

THE MIDDLE EAST

Saad al-Abdallah
Premier of Kuwait

1

We believe the Arab [oil] producer countries should define their stance and the manner in which they will use the oil weapons. You can be sure that, if we use this weapon [withholding oil from other nations] well, the somber period our region has known will come to an end and the balance will be on our side.

San Francisco Examiner & Chronicle,
9-30:(This World)2.

Belaid Abdesselam
Minister of Industry and Energy of Algeria

2

[On the Arab cutback of oil shipments to the U.S.]: We are not, and we have not been, contrary to what has been often reported, asking the United States to change its [Mideast] policy. We simply have asked the U.S. to fit its action to its stated policy. One of the tenets of U.S. policy has always been the refusal to recognize or accept the acquisition of territory by force. This is something that has not only been stated and repeated frequently by the United States, but also was voted by the United States as a member of the Security Council of the United Nations, which ordered the evacuation of Arab lands seized by Israel in the 1967 war. All we are asking is that these UN resolutions be carried out.

Interview/
U.S. News & World Report, 12-31:21.

James E. Akins
United States Ambassador to Saudi Arabia

3

Saudi Arabia cherishes its friendship with the U.S. King Faisal repeatedly says that our

[the U.S.'] true interests in the Middle East are in the Arab countries and that we must recognize this sometime. He is obsessed with Communism, and he's obsessed with the penetration of Communists into the Arab world, which he blames on our policy of one-sided backing of Israel.

Interview, Washington/
U.S. News & World Report, 9-10:94.

Yasir Arafat
Chairman,
Palestine Liberation Organization

4

For 25 years, [the United States'] only concern has been support for Israel—militarily, politically, financially and through the media —as if the U.S. sees nothing in the area but Israel. Certainly, this policy treads on the interests of the American people. As a result of Israeli blackmail, U.S. policy does not help the interests of the Middle East. It helps get the Jewish vote in the U.S. and Jewish election contributions. Obviously, this blackmail is eventually paid for by the ordinary American taxpayer. It is true that this U.S. support has changed the balance of power in the area in Israel's interest. But I ask: For how long will you [the U.S.] be able to guarantee such a balance? Did American military supremacy in Vietnam and Korea prove enough to guarantee complete and final separation?

Interview, Beirut/Time, 7-16:29.

Hafez al-Assad
President of Syria

5

[On the current Arab-Israeli war]: Right and justice are on our side. We are not dealers in death and destruction. We do not seek to kill but only to prevent our people being killed. We seek peace; we are working for peace for our people; we are defending our-selves today so as to enjoy peace in the fu-ture.

Address to Syrian people/
The Dallas Times Herald, 10-9:(B)2.

David Ben-Gurion
Former Prime Minister of Israel

1

I did not want war [with the Arabs in 1967]. But when it was thrust on us, we emerged stronger than would otherwise have been the case. Even so, I would have settled for peace and friendship with the Arabs at any time—and still would . . . Peace is the greatest adventure before us. But the end is not yet in sight; the war can go on for anoth-er 10 or 15 years. The only danger now is Egypt. We will be ready to give up all the conquered territory, except Jerusalem and the Golan Heights. But everything depends on the Russians and the Americans, and especially on the Russians; without them, the Egyptians can't wage war. For us, the need is for peace, to enable us to complete the task of building the Jewish state.

Interview, Sde Boker, Israel/
Los Angeles Times, 5-13:(6)7.

Houari Boumedienne
President of Algeria

2

The Palestinian problem, as we see it, will not be solved as long as Israel remains aggres-sive, hostile and oppressive, lodged as a for-eign body in the Middle East. Weak as the Arabs may be, they will continue to reject this foreign body until it decides to integrate in its human environment. What will bring such a change of heart about among Israelis? Only one thing: a hard struggle, carried into Israel by the Palestinians themselves.

Interview, Algiers/
The Christian Science Monitor, 9-28:11.

3

[On the Arab-Israeli conflict]: We [Arabs] must intensify our preparations for the deci-sive round of fighting from which we shall emerge victorious. We must make judicious use of our economic potential [the cutback of oil shipments to pro-Israeli countries] in this perhaps most dangerous juncture of the Arab nations' march through history.

At Arab summit meeting, Algiers/
San Francisco Examiner, 11-28:14.

Habib Bourguiba
President of Tunisia

4

Israel is in the position to fulfill the old Jewish dream, the dream of a state that stretches from the Nile to the Euphrates. The Israelis can do that. They have the might to do it, and the Arabs and all the under-devel-oped countries can do nothing to stop it, even if they were united.

Interview/
The Dallas Times Herald, 9-23:(A)3.

Leonid I. Brezhnev
General Secretary,
Communist Party of the Soviet Union

5

[On the renewed Arab-Israel warfare in the Middle East]: What is taking place there is a battle between Israel, the aggressor, and Egypt and Syria, the victims of aggression, who want to liberate their lands. [The Soviet Union re-mains a] convinced supporter of a fair and lasting peace . . . and of guaranteed security for all countries and peoples of the area which is so close to our frontiers. We are prepared as before to make our contribution toward en-suring such peace.

At luncheon honoring Japanese Prime Minister
Kakuei Tanaka, Moscow, Oct. 8/
Los Angeles Herald-Examiner, 10-8:(A)2.

6

[On the current Arab-Israeli war]: What are the vital reasons for military conflicts which periodically appear in this [Mideast] area, including the present one? From our point of view, the answer is clear: It is the occupation of Arab lands by Israel, as a result of its aggression and persistent unwillingness to consider the legitimate rights of the Arab people, and the support for this aggressive policy by those forces of the capitalist world which strive to obstruct free, independent development of progressive Arab states.

At World Peace Congress, Moscow, Oct. 26/
The New York Times, 10-27:10.

1

The hostile [Arab and Israeli] armies are confronting each other with their arms at the ready. It is clear that urgent measures must be taken to prevent new bloodshed and to establish a stable peace . . . This requires that the lands seized by Israel be returned to their legitimate owners, that justice with regard to the Arab people of Palestine be ensured and that the foundation be laid on this basis for durable, peaceful coexistence and good neighborly relations between the Arab states and the state of Israel. Otherwise, there will be neither peace nor tranquility in the area.

Before Indian Parliament, New Delhi,
Nov. 29/Los Angeles Times, 11-30:(1)14.

Chou En-lai
Premier of the People's Republic
of (Communist) China

2

The recent developments in the Middle East situation [the current Arab-Israeli war] have aroused general concern among the people throughout the world. The just struggle of the Arab people, including the Palestinian people, against aggression has won, and will continue to enjoy, the sympathy and support of all countries and people of the world who uphold justice. The essence of the Middle East issue is the contention of the superpowers for hegemony over this region. The superpowers are now trying hard to impose the solution they have concocted on the Arab people, including the Palestinian people. Even if they may appear to succeed for a time, they are doomed to failure. Tensions and turbulence will continually recur in the Middle East. The actions of the superpowers will only serve to further expose their true features as expansionists pursuing power politics. The efforts to deceive, betray and divide the Arab people, including the Palestinian people, will surely

arouse them to awaken further, strengthen their unity and carry forward their struggle against aggression and expansionism.

At banquet honoring Australian
Prime Minister Gough Whitlam, Peking,
Oct. 31/San Francisco Examiner, 11-1:18.

John B. Connally, Jr.
Unofficial adviser to President Nixon;
Former Secretary of the Treasury
of the United States

3

This nation [the U.S.] does not desert its allies or friends. We shall not begin by deserting Israel. At the same time, we do not believe our relationship with Israel must be exclusive of other relationships in the Middle East; and it must not be taken as a sign of estrangement from Israel if we seek to re-establish other old and valued friendships in the Middle East.

Before Union of Orthodox Jewish
Congregations of America, New York,
May 27/The Dallas Times Herald, 5-28:(A)1.

Stewart S. Cort
Chairman, Bethlehem Steel Corporation

4

[On the current oil cutback by Arab countries]: I think you see evidence here now of the dependence of Japan, Western Europe and the United States on Middle East oil; and whoever controls this oil and has access to it really has a knee on the Adam's apple of the industrialized West.

TV-radio interview/"Issues and Answers,"
American Broadcasting Company, 11-25.

Alan Cranston
United States Senator, D-California

5

[On U.S. involvement in the Middle East]: We are there for long-term strategic military and foreign policy reasons that pre-date the discovery of oil in Saudi Arabia. We are there because the free world is there, because Israel is there. And we are there because Hitler and Mussolini were there 30 years ago.

Before B'nai B'rith, Oakland, Calif., Nov. 17/
San Francisco Examiner & Chronicle,
11-18:(A)16.

Moshe Dayan
Minister of Defense of Israel

1

I think too much of America to think it will take dictation on foreign policy because some Arab king has oil.

Jerusalem/Newsweek, 2-19:49.

2

[On the recent Israeli raid on Arab guerrillas in Beirut]: In the future, Israel will act against the terrorists or organizations, insofar as possible, rather than in response to terrorist attacks . . . There could well be future cases in which Israel would have to act against a country, as a country, because of its responsibility for acts of terrorism. We cannot free Lebanon of its responsibility as a state for the acts of the terrorists who conduct their operations from its territory, and we do not intend solely to act against the terrorists personally . . .

Television interview, Jerusalem, April 13/
Los Angeles Herald-Examiner, 4-13:(A)1.

3

I do not support the great powers or the United Nations as guarantors of a peace agreement, or of an interim agreement, or any kind of agreement between us and the Arabs. I don't think that the great powers or any United Nations forces should play a role as a permanent element between us and our neighbors. I do not object to the big powers or Germany being mediators; but once the agreement is reached, I think we should face one another, we and the Arabs, with no third party in between either in the form of UN forces or guarantees. To that I object.

Interview, Jerusalem/
The Christian Science Monitor, 6-16:6.

4

I think that the problem of the Palestinians is as follows: There were about 700,000 Palestinians living where Israel is now—in Acre and in Jaffa and Ramle and so on. And during the war in 1948, they ran away. They fled. About the same number of Jews came from muslim countries—from Iraq and Syria, Morocco and Yemen—more than 700,000 to Israel . . . Now I think that there is no room for the

Arab refugees of 1948 to go back to old Israel. You can't undo what has been done. You can't turn the clock back. But I think that the Palestinians who live in the West Bank, the Palestinians who are in Jordan, the Palestinian refugees who are in Lebanon, Syria and Gaza Strip, should be settled. They should be rehabilitated, and then they will not long to go back to their old places, but will find their country within Jordan, Lebanon, Syria and so on.

Interview, Jerusalem/
The Christian Science Monitor, 6-18:3.

5

[Saying the U.S. forced Israel, during the current Arab-Israeli war, to allow relief convoys to reach trapped Egyptian troops in Sinai]: The food supply was not a humanitarian gesture. We had no choice. Or to be more precise, the alternatives to allowing food convoys were much worse . . . Anyone advocating we run the war in a state of rupture with the United States is advocating we can't possibly win.

Before the Knesset (Parliament), Jerusalem,
Oct. 30/The New York Times, 10-31:16.

Louis de Guiringaud
French Ambassador/Permanent Representative to the United Nations

6

[Rejecting Israel's view that it can maintain the status quo vis-a-vis the Arab states indefinitely through military superiority]: No matter how effectively it is used, force can never resolve the problems of the Middle East. Never in the course of history has force been successful in putting down resistance movements which have reflected authentic national aspirations.

At United Nations, N.Y., April 18/
Los Angeles Times, 4-19:(1)18.

Simcha Dinitz
Israeli Ambassador to the United States

7

The only place where there is no talking [negotiating] is the Middle East. But talk is the only way to get out of our [Arab-Israeli]

deadlock . . . The solution lies not on the Volga or Potomac Rivers, but along the Suez Canal. We and they must learn to live as neighbors.

News conference, Los Angeles, May 2/
Los Angeles Times, 5-3:(1)6.

Alec Douglas-Home
Foreign Secretary of the United Kingdom

1

We have stated again and again that we are totally committed to the existence [and security] of the state of Israel. Any suggestion to the contrary is totally without foundation.

The Christian Science Monitor, 11-8:3.

2

As long ago as 1970, I made a speech the implication of which was clear. It was that there could be no peace in the Middle East on a continuing basis of the occupation of Arab territories by Israeli forces. Such buffers would no longer provide Israel with physical security, I pointed out, because the Arabs would not rest until they had recovered their own territory. No one could impose a peace settlement on Israel. Nevertheless, the assessment was correct, and Israel would be wise to accept that there must be an alternative . . . By now, almost every country in the world, including the United States, is accepting that withdrawal and peace are synonymous. If that is so, the question then is: "What can be substituted for occupied buffer zones? How can Israel and her neighbors be protected against attack?"

News conference, London/
The Christian Science Monitor, 11-30:4.

Abba Eban
Foreign Minister of Israel

3

The first objective of Israel was to take Jewish history out of the control of external caprice and give it autonomy of its own. The biggest external impact of Israel has been on the Jewish people itself and the new belief it has inculcated in this people in their undiminished vigor and vitality. We have also proved something about the adaptability of democratic institutions through a whole range of challenges. Our experience refutes the common theme in developing countries that in danger and crisis you have to sacrifice democracy and establish more totalitarian forms of government. We have shown that there is almost no danger, condition or peril to which a democratic structure cannot be responsive.

Interview/Time, 4-30:40.

4

I would imagine that after six years they [the Arabs] must be less confident about what they call an imposed settlement than they were six years ago. They don't have many options. They can't really believe that terrorist violence—which, incidentally, is getting pushed further away out of the Middle East—can really have a radical effect. Therefore, the options are not very many. They are either to put up with the present situation, which they cannot want and which we don't think is ideal, or to change the present situation fundamentally by negotiations. There are really not many more options than that; and I think that there is a rational element in Arab policy and opinion that will in the last resort, be it soon or not, assert itself.

TV-radio interview, Herzlia, Israel/
"Meet the Press,"
National Broadcasting Company, 5-6.

5

Could anything be more absurd and squalid than to take a city, this particular city [Jerusalem], and cut it apart [into Arab and Israeli sectors]? What ought to be condemned about Jerusalem is not the unity and the peace of the past seven years, but the division and the bitterness of the past, of the years that went before. So there are some things about which we will be obdurate; other things which we will have to submit to the fortune of negotiation [with the Arabs]. That is what negotiation is . . . It is a process from which nobody should hope to emerge with one hundred per cent of what he hoped to achieve.

TV-radio interview, Herzlia, Israel/
"Meet the Press,"
National Broadcasting Company, 5-6.

(ABBA EBAN)

1

We have not been selfish enough to solve all our problems with such completeness as to leave the next generation without challenge. We bequeath to it the accumulated assets of these years—but also the unfinished quest.

Newsweek, 5-7:54.

2

Israel is the only successful exercise in parliamentary democracy among the developing states which have emerged since the end of World War II. It has entered the world of modern technology and science. It is the only successful transition from an agricultural to an industrialized-technological community.

Quote, 5-13:434.

3

[Criticizing Austria's capitulation to Arab terrorists by closing a transit camp for Israeli-bound Soviet Jews]: To abandon such an enterprise in deference to a pair of brutal gangsters has a terrifying meaning . . . While the civilized world stands with bowed head, along comes [Egyptian] President Sadat to celebrate the triumph of the young gunmen over a few aging, weary Jews [held hostage] and over the sovereignty and law of an enlightened European state . . . What is the future of a world in which two pirates and criminals can bring a proud nation to acceptance of their terms? What are the implications of transactions and engagements between civilized governments and violent extremists? Who is going to rule our world, governments or gunmen?

Before United Nations General Assembly,
New York, Oct. 3/
Los Angeles Times, 10-4:(1)17;
San Francisco Examiner & Chronicle,
10-7:(This World)13.

4

[On the recently-renewed Arab-Israeli warfare]: There is not a single man or woman in this hall who doesn't know deep inside his heart that Egypt and Syria have dealt a blow to the most cherished of causes—that of international cooperation. The premeditated, unprovoked attack [on Oct. 6] was one of the basest acts—coming on the Day of Atonement—of any government. We are determined that it will not succeed; because if it should, all hope for peace would die . . . One nightmare is always in the Israeli mind. Imagine that in a mood of suicidal stupidity we had gone back to the previous [pre-1967 war border] lines. If we had committed that folly, there would have been such destruction on October 6 that perhaps all of Israel's hope for the future might now have been lost, swept away. How right we were not to pull out [of captured Arab territory won in 1967].

At United Nations, New York, Oct. 8/
Los Angeles Herald-Examiner, 10-8:(A)2.

5

[On Arab claims that they want only evacuation of their lands by Israel and not the annihilation of Israel]: First, when the Arabs speak to their *own* people, their leaders say frankly that, if they got us back to the 1967 lines, this would be the first stage, to be followed by the decisive blow to the head and heart. Second, no man in his right senses believes that, if the massive thrust of Egyptian and Syrian tanks on October 6 [of this year] were to have succeeded in its objects, they would have come to a halt on the sand near the '67 boundaries, stepped on the brakes with a loud, victorious screech and said, "Here we stop." What nonsense! The very massiveness of the forces engaged proves that in October, 1973, they decided on a total assault on Israel.

Interview/Time, 10-29:45.

6

The Soviet objective is to dominate the Middle East. If the Soviets control the Middle East oil, Europe ultimately might fall into their palm like a ripe grape. And after Europe, the Soviets would want more . . . One of the key tests of whether the Russian desire for detente [with the West] is real or a strategem lies right here in the Middle East. While the Soviets were talking detente in the West, they were preparing, supplying and helping to plan a war in the Middle East. What we had in October was the rhetoric of detente but the reality of cold war.

Interview, Tel Aviv/
San Francisco Examiner, 11-1:16.

1

It is our greatest hope that the United States will respect the principle of free negotiations. America should let Israel play its own hand at the negotiating table [with the Arabs], to get the best deal Israel can, without being undercut by our friends. The Arabs will certainly not be undercut by their ally, the Soviet Union, which will give 100 per cent support to the Arab negotiation demands. The United States, therefore, should not press Israel to start negotiations with one hand bound behind its back.

Interview, Tel Aviv/
Los Angeles Herald-Examiner, 11-4:(A)12.

2

The acid test of the [Arab-Israeli] negotiations will be to see if the Arab offer of peace is real or is a glorified cease-fire. Peace means normal relations, trade, mutual accessibility, absence of the Arab support of Palestinian and other terrorists, a stop to hostile propaganda and the lifting of the Arab economic boycott against Israel that has lasted for the past quarter century. If there is to be a real peace in the Middle East, it should take the form of Israeli-Arab relations similar to the relations among partners of the European community. We reject a peace that simply is another truce maintaining until the next war.

Interview, Tel Aviv/
Los Angeles Herald-Examiner, 11-4:(A)13.

3

[On Arab threats to cut off oil shipments to countries supporting Israel]: Any country which changes its policy in respect to extortion becomes diminished in independence and sovereignty. The problem is not what Israel is doing about its independence but what those countries are going to do about theirs. Are they going to become dependencies of Kuwait and Libya?

News conference, Los Angeles, Nov. 18/
Los Angeles Times, 11-19:(1)3.

4

Israeli's aim at this [Middle East peace] conference is a peace treaty defining the terms of our coexistence [with the Arabs] in future years. Peace is not a mere cease-fire or armistice. Its meaning is not exhausted by the ab-

sence of war. Peace commits us not only to abstention from violence but also to positive obligations which neighboring states owe each other by virtue of their very proximity. The ultimate guarantee of a peace agreement lies in the creation of common regional interests in such degree of intensity, in such multiplicity of interaction, in such entanglement of reciprocal advantage, in such mutual accessibility of human contact, as to put the possibility of future war beyond rational contingency. Let us atone for 25 years of separation by working now toward a cooperative relationship similar to that which European states created after centuries of war.

At Middle East peace conference,
Geneva, Dec. 21/
The New York Times, 12-22:8.

Nzo Ekangaki
Secretary General,
Organization of African Unity

5

The cascade of countries severing relations [with Israel] has created a situation practically unprecedented in the annals of diplomacy and constitutes, at the African level, a significant defeat for Israeli diplomacy. After what occurred, the only true friend Israel has in Africa today is the Republic of South Africa.

Before Ministerial Council of Organization
of African Unity, Addis Ababa, Nov. 20/
The New York Times, 11-21:14.

David Elazar
Lieutenant General and Chief of Staff,
Israeli armed forces

6

[On Israel's just-completed raid on Arab guerrillas in Beirut]: We do not believe that the [Arab] terrorists will stop operating after this single blow to their headquarters. But their leaders have to realize our ability to fight them in every place. If they can attack us in Bangkok, Paris, Rome and other places, then there is no reason to believe that we cannot reach them anywhere in the world.

The Christian Science Monitor, 4-12:4.

Ismail Fahmy
Foreign Minister of Egypt

1

We hope that Israel now understands that Egypt—and for that matter all the Arab countries—cannot be conquered by force or allow its lands to remain occupied, nor would the Arab world accept that the Palestinians continue to be treated inhumanely and that Jerusalem, the city of peace, remain under the banner of the conqueror. Territories are the heritage most jealously guarded and defended by a people. They are handed from generation to generation. They are part of its history; they convey a profound sense of pride and, thus, of nationhood. Loss of territory deeply affects them and provokes a strong resolve to regain by all means what is by right theirs. Peoples do not bargain or barter over their territories, and the Arab nation is no exception. To expect the Arabs to give up part of their lands [to Israel] is to misread tragically their determination as to the contrary. To insist that this be done would wreck all hopes for this conference of peace to achieve what it has set out to do.

At Middle East peace conference, Geneva, Dec. 21/The New York Times, 12-22:8.

Faisal (Ibn Abdel Aziz)
King of Saudi Arabia

2

As friends of the U.S. and in the interest of maintaining and cementing this friendship, we counsel the U.S. to change its one-sided policy of favoritism to Zionism and support against the Arabs. We are deeply concerned that, if the U.S. does not change its policy, it will affect our relations with our American friends [and] place us in an untenable position in the Arab world. I want to draw the attention of my American friends to this serious situation so that we would not reach the point where we would be compelled to take other measures.

Interview/Time, 9-17:29.

Saud al-Faisal
Deputy Minister of Petroleum of Saudi Arabia

3

Arab diplomacy should strive to persuade

the U.S. . . . citizen that his interests are linked to the Arab cause, and that it is not our aim to inflict harm on him, but that it is the [pro-Israel] policy of his government which is creating a state of confrontation between us.

Interview/The New York Times, 9-4:3.

Suleiman Franjieh
President of Lebanon

4

[On the many Palestinian guerrillas based in Lebanon]: We have in Lebanon more than 300,000 Palestinians, and I do not think that any sister Arab country has given the Palestinians more than Lebanon. However, we wonder what our Palestinian brothers living among us want. Do they want residence and hospitality? If so, they are welcome, and I say this is our duty, not a favor. If they want coordination to serve a common cause, we also welcome this idea. But the existence of an occupation army in Lebanon is something no Lebanese can accept.

Los Angeles Times, 5-5:(1)5.

J. William Fulbright
United States Senator, D-Arkansas

5

The [U.S.] Senate is subservient [to Israel], in my opinion, much too much. We should be more concerned about the United States' interest, rather than doing the bidding of Israel. This is a most unusual development . . . The great majority of the Senate of the United States—somewhere around 80 per cent —are completely in support of Israel, anything Israel wants. This has been demonstrated time and again; and this has made it difficult for our government.

TV-radio interview/ "Face the Nation," Columbia Broadcasting System, 4-15.

6

One detects something less than advocacy, but more than simple apprehension, in warnings that the great wealth now accruing to the oil-producing states of the Persian Gulf may somehow pass into the hands of stronger powers . . . We [the U.S.] might now even have to do it ourselves with militarily potent surrogates in the region. The Shah of Iran is known to aspire to a "protecting" role for the Gulf region. A visiting Israeli scholar professes apprehensions that his government may move to "solve" the energy problems for the United States by taking over Kuwait, there being no force in the desert between Israel and the Persian Gulf capable of resisting the Israeli Army. There has also been ominous talk—one assumes unfounded—of a possible Israeli strike against Libya comparable to the recent reprehensible raid in Beirut. I am expressing apprehensions. I am most definitely not making predictions. I would like nothing better than to have them denied and repudiated by all concerned. In the meantime, I take the liberty of advising the Arab states not to underestimate the power and determination of the forces which may coalesce against them.

Before the Senate, Washington/
The Christian Science Monitor, 6-1:1.

1

There remains in the Arab world, despite everything, a remarkable reservoir of good will toward the United States. But as the mounting desperation of the Palestinians shows, that reservoir is fast being drained. To the Arabs, the United States seems not only hostile but gratuitously and irrationally so. In terms of our own national interests, I am bound to agree. In the service of a profound emotional commitment to Israel, we have all but kicked over the traces on our other interests in the Middle East: an economic interest in oil, a strategic interest in peace, and a perfectly ordinary human interest in the friendship of peoples who, whatever their quarrel with Israel, have never done anything to harm the United States.

May/The National Observer, 6-16:3.

2

. . . the general requirements [of an Arab-Israeli peace agreement] are clear: the recovery of lost lands by the Arabs and security for Israel. It is up to us [the U.S.] and up to the Russians, working through the United Nations, to apply whatever degree of persuasion we can, or whatever degree of pressure we must,

to bring about a compromise peace based upon the principles of the [UN] Security Council resolution of November, 1967. It would then be the responsibility of the Soviet Union and the United States, through the United Nations, to guarantee the settlement.

Before the Senate, Washington, Nov. 9/
San Francisco Examiner, 11-9:15.

3

[On the Arab cutback in oil shipments to pro-Israel Western countries]: To subject this big country [the U.S.], and our allies, to the possibility of a depression and economic chaos is an awfully high price to pay because Israel is not ready to go back to the 1967 cease-fire lines.

At Meeting with reporters, Washington,
Nov. 13/The Washington Post, 11-21:(A)14.

4

I think the Israelis have felt so confident of their source of power [the U.S.]—that is, their arms and their money—that they don't have to make a compromise. As long as we give them all-out support, they can hold their own and feel that they can expand. You see, they have been expanding their borders substantially. They have this program of immigration from the Soviet Union, which is estimated to come to between 30,000 and 35,000 this year. Now, we [the U.S.] pay the cost of that immigration. You look in yesterday's bill, and you will see we pay their transportation from Russia to Israel. There was $15 million to pay for apartments and mobile homes for the immigrants. There's money in there for a job-training program, university education, hospitals, for improvement of the [new] transit facilities in Austria. Politically, the present sentiment in the [U.S.] Congress is that we give them all that they request. The judgment here is on the psychology. If they can count on getting all that they want, in armaments and money, will this promote an attitude of we-stand-our-ground? My judgment is that the Israelis would be more likely to seek a settlement if they weren't too sure that we would support them if they continue to keep occupied Arab land.

Interview/The National Observer, 12-29:3.

Edouard Ghorra
Lebanese Ambassador/Permanent
Representative to the United Nations

1

[Appealing to Western countries not to support Israel]: The financial crisis, the energy crisis, the traditional bonds of friendship and cooperation and tourism are positive elements to further improve and develop relations between the Arab countries and the industrially and technologically developed countries. Mutually-beneficial relationships could be further developed on the basis of fairness, impartiality and justice. The disruptive forces of the Israeli policy of militarism, adventurism, intransigence and unbridled ambition should not be allowed to operate in such a way as to jeopardize these objectives.

Before United Nations Security Council,
New York, June 13/
The Dallas Times Herald, 6-14:(A)20.

Wayne E. Glenn
President, Western Hemisphere Petroleum
Division, Continental Oil Company

2

Two countries in particular, Saudi Arabia and Iran, will loom more important than ever because they have the reserves to increase [oil] production very substantially. Growing dependence on Middle East petroleum has ramifications for U.S. governmental policies that cannot be ignored. Our foreign policy will have to give increased attention to that area and to all the nations in it. And our economic policy will have to recognize that the balance-of-payments deficit from petroleum imports alone could reach $30 billion or more by 1985.

The Dallas Times Herald, 3-4:(N)2.

Andrei A. Gromyko
Foreign Minister of the Soviet Union

3

The Soviet Union harbors no hostility toward the state of Israel as such. The policy of annexation, the trampling of norms of international law and decisions of the UN—this is what has evoked the condemnation of Israel by all, including us . . . First of all, in the Soviet Union's firm conviction, it is necessary to implement the fundamental principle of international life—the principle that territory may not be acquired by means of war. Herein lies the key to the entire problem. Any document that may be adopted at the present [Middle East peace] conference must contain clear and precise pledges on the withdrawal of Israeli troops from all [Arab] territories occupied in 1967. Along with this, it is necessary to insure respect and recognition of the sovereignty, territorial integrity and political independence of all states of the Middle East, their rights to live in the world. This applies to Israel as well. Our position is clear and consistent from beginning to end—peace and security for all peoples of the region. This presupposes, naturally, that justice will be guaranteed with respect to the Arab people of Palestine.

At Middle East peace conference, Geneva,
Dec. 21/The New York Times, 12-22:8.

Lee H. Hamilton
United States Representative, D-Indiana

4

[On major countries' dependence on oil-rich Middle East and Persian Gulf nations]: One important challenge to the United States in the coming decade will be to come to grips with the fact that never before in the history of mankind have so many wealthy, industrialized, militarily-powerful and large states been at the potential mercy of small, independent and potentially unstable states which will provide, for the foreseeable future, the fuel of advanced societies. There are few traditional policies which can accommodate this difficult situation in an area of intense nationalism. The need for imaginative new types of policies involving the interdependence of the rich and poor, small and large, weak and powerful states has never been so great. There is a need, at the same time, to take all possible steps to minimize our future dependence on the energy resources of this [Middle East-Persian Gulf] region.

Before the House, Washington,
Jan. 11/Vital Speeches, 2-1:229.

Mohammed Hassanein Heikal
Editor, "Al Ahram," Cairo

1

We [Egyptians] do want peace. We want to open the [Suez] Canal, resurrect our ruined cities and build a new Egypt. We're ready to give the Israelis all the guarantees [of secure borders] they wish, but not on our territory. We might allow, here and there, for minor rectifications of our old frontiers. If the Israelis will be generous in their withdrawals, then we will be generous in our guarantees. If they relinquish their policy of arrogance, of imposing peace, then we can offer them the chance —at last—of being accepted in the Middle East. Israel can find its place amongst us, but not as the dominant power—not as a long arm, not as James Bond, not as Tarzan, not as Mighty Mouse.

Interview/
The New York Times Magazine, 11-18:120.

Haim Herzog
Major General and former chief
of intelligence, Israeli Army

2

The Arabs' general intention is to deal with Israel by phases. The first phase is to obtain an Israeli withdrawal to the pre-1967 borders, and then to attack again . . . A big issue is whether [Egyptian President Anwar] Sadat will be able to show he is independent of the other Arab states. This will emerge at the forthcoming Arab summit meeting set for this month. One thing is sure: Sadat will come to the summit with a great deal of prestige. He fought, and he is the only one [of the Arabs] who has gained anything [in the recent Arab-Israeli war]. His troops are still on the eastern side of the Suez Canal. So if he can maintain his independence from the others—he has shown an inclination of this by resuming diplomatic relations with the United States—then he stands a chance of making progress on his own policies. He wants the Sinai Desert back, as a prelude to another attack on Israel.

Interview,
Tel Aviv/
Los Angeles Herald-Examiner, 11-19:(A)8.

Amir Abbas Hoveyda
Prime Minister of Iran

3

The [Persian Gulf] is our economic lifeline. It must remain open to all countries for international navigation and commerce, and we have the determination and the capacity to see that it does. We also believe that the security of the Persian Gulf is the responsibility not of the American or the British taxpayer but of the states that border the waterway. There are two things that [we] do not want to see happen in the Persian Gulf. The first is that it become an area for big-power rivalries. The second is that it turn into a hotbed for subversion in the region. Any activity, directed from whatever source, that would aim to disrupt the free flow of oil will not be tolerated.

Interview/The New York Times, 7-4:3.

Hubert H. Humphrey
United States Senator, D-Minnesota

4

. . . the insistence by the Arabs on preconditions before negotiations [with Israel] stands as a serious obstacle to peace. If there are lessons to be learned from Vietnam, it is that achieving peace requires tireless hard bargaining and direct negotiations.

At Bnai Zion award dinner, New York,
Feb. 18/The New York Times, 2-19:7.

Hussein I
King of Jordan

5

Oil is a formidable weapon—if it is used properly. I believe it's a weapon that can be used for the development of this region, and for improving the lot of its people. It has not yet been used adequately for this purpose. But I can't believe it would be helpful to withhold the oil from anyone. It is an asset; it is needed by the world—including us. It could be used to narrow the economic gaps that exist in this area, the gaps between the "haves" and the "have-nots." This, after all, is part of the problem between the Arabs and the Israelis. The problem is not purely a mili-

427

(HUSSEIN I)

tary one, but is one of a genuine need for development, for giving our people the education they seek, for giving them the opportunities they seek—for narrowing the gaps. If these gaps were narrowed sufficiently enough, I believe many of the hatreds, many of the suspicions, many of the complexes would disappear. This is very vital. Let us not cut off our noses to spite our faces.

Interview, Amman/
U.S. News & World Report, 1-15:37.

1

I believe very firmly and honestly that Israel has not made any contribution whatsoever toward peace. I believe that the basis of a solution most obviously is the acceptance by Israel of [UN Security Council Resolution] 242 and the principles it contains. It offers the Israelis a great deal, and it offers the Arabs their rights. If this is unacceptable, if the Israelis continue to create changes and new facts in the occupied territories, I do not see how we are ever going to get out of this problem without a fresh disaster of great magnitude.

Interview, Amman/Time, 10-8:50.

2

We will defend the right of the Palestinian people to decide their fate without being submitted to any pressure, and to choose their path after they have liberated their territory [from Israel]. We remain at their side, forming a united family sharing the same hopes and pursuing the same objectives.

Before graduating Jordanian Army officers,
Nov. 22/The Washington Post, 11-23:(A)32.

Henry M. Jackson
United States Senator, D-Washington

3

The average American gets the idea that our trouble in the Middle East stems from our support for Israel. Nothing could be further from the truth. The facts are that, if Israel did not exist, Jordan would have disappeared. Saudi Arabia, which has over half the known oil reserves in the world outside the Soviet Union, would have disappeared from the map,

and maybe Lebanon, too. The problem in the Middle East is the have-not Arab countries against the haves. The two stabilizing factors in the Middle East are Israel and Iran. It's only Israel and Iran that could prevent an overrunning of the regime in Saudi Arabia. A key country that we're concerned about for oil for the U.S. is Iran. Iranians are Moslem, but they aren't Arab. They have a relatively close alliance with Israel. Iran is a crucial country. Then there is Kuwait. What's the threat to Kuwait? Israel? Not at all. It is Iraq, backed by the Soviet Union. What's the threat to Saudi Arabia? The have-not Arab countries: Egypt, operating through Yemen as they did several years ago; Syria; and Iraq, a country with a lot of oil but with an extremist government in power. These are the real threats to the security of oil supplies out of the [Persian] Gulf. It's not Israel that's the problem in the Middle East.

Interview/
U.S. News & World Report, 6-18:35.

4

Without Soviet support and material encouragement, without Soviet training and equipment, without Soviet diplomatic and political backing, this [current Arab-Israeli] war would not have been started. And yet, Dr. [Henry] Kissinger, the [U.S.] Secretary of State, comes before the American people . . . to say that Soviet behavior has been moderate and not irresponsible. I cannot agree.

Los Angeles/
Los Angeles Times, 10-19:(2)7.

5

I am astonished to hear it said that the best way to bring stability to the Middle East is to set up a peace-keeping force that would involve the sending of Russian and American troops into that volatile region. This seems to me a formula that carries with it the very great danger of dragging the superpowers into a military confrontation. There are few situations in the world that are more volatile than the Middle East, few places so endowed with an abundance of mischievous elements ·and unbridled passions. [It would be the height of

folly] for the United States to pour itself into that cauldron of instability.
> *Los Angeles Times, 12-31:(2)5.*

Abdul Salam Jalloud
Prime Minister of Libya

1

[On the Arab cutback of oil for Europe]: The oil embargo will not be lifted unless Europe begins to send modern weapons to the Arabs and to cooperate with us technologically. It would be totally unacceptable if Europe supplies Israel with arms and withholds such arms from us, the Arabs, who are struggling for the liberation of the usurped lands.
> *Interview/*
> *The Washington Post, 11-14:(A)13.*

Kenneth B. Keating
United States Ambassador to Israel

2

America's affinity for Israel touches both upon its oldness and its newness. On the one hand, the profound religious links we have with this country; on the other, our admiration for Israel as a pioneering and self-reliant nation which shares our ideals of free governments and free institutions.
> *Tel Aviv/*
> *San Francisco Examiner, 8-20:13.*

Edward M. Kennedy
United States Senator, D-Massachusetts

3

[The United States] has pledged to assure the people of Israel the arms they need to defend their nation. In the past, we have stood by that pledge. And I say that we will stand by the pledge today and tomorrow and for however long it takes for all nations to accept the existence and the independence of the state of Israel.
> *At conference of presidents of major*
> *Jewish-American organizations, Washington,*
> *Oct. 10/The New York Times, 10-11:18.*

4

There is now a concerted effort by the Arab [oil-] producer states to change our [U.S.] policy during the Middle East crisis by withholding oil from us and by restricting the supplies available to our allies. This challenge is more serious than it was in 1967, when we imported far less oil from the Arab states. And in the future, increasing imports of oil from the Arab world could make the challenge even more serious. Regardless of the strength of the oil weapon, however, our course as a nation is clear: We must never give in to this kind of pressure. This would be against our interests, against the faith placed in American commitments, against our principles as a nation and against our concern for action in the pursuit of peace.
> *Before the Senate, Washington,*
> *Dec. 6/Vital Speeches, 1-1('74):163.*

Malcolm Kerr
Professor of Political Science,
University of California, Los Angeles

5

The Egyptians are in a box. As they see it, the United States has let them down numerous times; it sold out to the Jews long ago. Russia let them down. They haven't had much support from any of the great powers. Yet they feel—and they are right—that they are supported by most countries of the world, as measured in the United Nations. So they don't feel they owe the world a damn thing. They have nothing to be ashamed of. They feel they're liberating Egypt [in their current war with Israel] the way the French liberated their country in 1944.
> *U.S. News & World Report, 10-22:50.*

Henry A. Kissinger
Secretary of State of the United States

6

We are now engaged in very serious, very open-minded consultations with many countries, trying to bring about an end to the hostilities in the [current Arab-Israeli war in the] Middle East. This crisis through which we are now living is a test of the possibilities of diplomacy and of the real meaning of detente. Because it must be clear that, while the United States is trying to make our nation safe from war, we will not do so at the price of making the rest of the world safe *for* war.
> *Oct. 17/The New York Times, 10-19:16.*

(HENRY A. KISSINGER)

1

The United States does not favor and will not approve the sending of a joint Soviet-U.S. force into the Middle East [to enforce the current cease-fire in the current Arab-Israeli war]. The United States believes that what is needed in the Middle East, above all, is a determination of the facts, a determination where the lines are and a determination of who is doing the shooting, so that then the [UN] Security Council can take appropriate action. It is inconceivable that the forces of the great powers should be introduced in the numbers that would be necessary to over-power both of the participants. It is inconceivable that we should transplant great-power rivalry into the Middle East, or alternatively that we should impose a military condominium by the United States and the Soviet Union. The United States is even more opposed to the unilateral introduction by any great power, especially by any nuclear power, of any military forces into the Middle East, in whatever guise those forces should be introduced.

News conference,
Washington, Oct. 25/
Los Angeles Times, 10-26:(1)23.

2

[On U.S. and Soviet involvement in Arab-Israeli negotiations]: The temptation is always there to exploit a situation to the advantage of one or the other of the superpowers. However, if the superpowers understand their own interests and the world interests, they ought to realize that the other side can always match them in terms of military equipment, and that the attempt to turn this into a super-power confrontation must lead to a constant-ly-increasing danger of war. The effort may be made. When it is made, we [the U.S.] will resist it as we have in the past. We hope—and that will certainly be our attitude—that the Soviet Union will approach these [Arab-Israeli peace] negotiations with the same spirit we shall—namely, that a settlement just to all parties is in the interest of everybody. If they

do not, then we will have to see what else can be done.

Interview, Peking, Nov. 12/
The New York Times, 11-13:16.

3

[On the cutback of Arab oil to countries which are pro-Israel]: The oil situation will continue for the indefinite future, and while we are highly respectful of the views of the Arab world, it is not possible for us to be swayed in the major orientation of our policy by the . . . temporary monopoly position enjoyed by a few nations.

Interview, Peking, Nov. 12/
The New York Times, 11-13:16.

4

In the land of Arabs and Jews, where the reality of mistrust and hate so tragically contradicts the spiritual message which originates there, it is essential for the voice of reconciliation to be heard. There is no acceptable alternative to a negotiated settlement of the issues so long in dispute, and to a determination on the part of all the parties who assemble here [at the about-to-begin Middle East peace conference in Geneva] to make these negotiations succeed. [In meetings with Arab and Israeli leaders in the Middle East,] I found none who wanted the war to continue; none who would not recognize that now is the time to break the cycle of uneasy truce and violent war. Upon us and what we do here depend the lives and hopes of people, and it is to the people we shall have to answer should we fail. The Middle East, whose dramatic, tragic and heroic peoples have produced three great faiths, is challenged today to another act of faith—that hatred can give way to reconciliation, that peace can become our purpose, compromise our method and hope our inspiration.

Geneva, Dec. 20/
Los Angeles Times, 12-21:(1)5.

5

We are concerned here, at a moment of historic opportunity, for the cause of peace in the Middle East and for the cause of peace in the world. For the first time in a generation, the peoples of the Middle East are sitting together to turn their talents to the challenge of a lasting peace . . . We are challenged by emotions so deeply felt—by causes so passionately believed and pursued—that the tragic march from cataclysm to cataclysm, each more costly and indecisive than the last, sometimes seems preordained. Yet, our presence here today—in itself a momentous accomplishment—is a symbol of rejection of this fatalistic view. Respect for the forces of history does not mean blind submission to those forces.

At Middle East peace conference, Geneva, Dec. 21/The New York Times, 12-22:8.

1

There are two schools of thought about Soviet objectives in the Middle East. One school of thought is that the Soviet Union has an interest in maintaining tension because that will guarantee permanent Arab hostility to the United States and enhances the possibilities of Soviet influence. The other school of thought is that, while this may have started out to be the Soviet policy in the 1950s, there have been since then three wars which have consumed a great deal of Soviet resources and whose outcome has been inconclusive. It has been demonstrated that the conflict in the Middle East can bring the superpowers into positions of potential confrontation. And it is, therefore, at least possible that the Soviet Union now has an interest in contributing to the stabilization of the situation in an area which neither superpower can really control by itself. As far as the United States is concerned, we will deal with the Soviet Union as long as its actions are consistent with the second interpretation. That is to say, if the Soviet Union makes a responsible contribution to peace in the Middle East, we will be prepared to cooperate—not at the expense of our traditional friends nor by imposing a settlement made together with the Soviet Union. We are in direct contact with all of the parties in the Middle East. But we are prepared to deal with the Soviet Union on an equitable basis as long as its motives—or as long as its actions—are consistent with a responsible course.

News conference, Washington, Dec. 27/ U.S. News & World Report, 1-7('74):66.

Teddy Kollek
Mayor of Jerusalem

2

Though my city has 70,000 Moslems in its population of 320,000, not a single hostile incident occurred during the recent [Arab-Israeli] war . . . Six years of treating each other with dignity and honesty, as equals, paid off well for the Arabs and Jews in Jerusalem. We have found the human solution that the Middle East must heed.

Los Angeles, Oct. 28/ Los Angeles Herald-Examiner, 10-29:(A)7.

Bruno Kreisky
Chancellor of Austria

3

[On criticism of his country's capitulation to Arab terrorists by closing a transit camp for Israeli-bound Soviet Jews]: The worst thing in this matter would be to put pressure on us. Nobody should forget that Austria has withstood other pressures. Rather, all other governments should consult with us [about] how the Jews emigrating from the Soviet Union can best be assisted . . . What we cannot accept is that Austria should become a secondary theatre of the Middle East conflict, with violence and confrontations of armed men from both sides.

Interview, Vienna, Sept. 30/ The New York Times, 10-1:3.

Robert J. McCloskey
Deputy Assistant Secretary for Press Relations, Department of State of the United States

4

[Criticizing some European countries for not cooperating with the U.S. in its attempts to supply Israel with arms during the current Arab-Israeli war]: We were and have been in a critical period which affects in many ways all of us . . . and we were struck by the number of allies going to some lengths to separate themselves publicly from us; and it raises the question for us as to how that action on their part can be squared with what the Europeans have often referred to as the indivisibility between us on matters of security.

The Christian Science Monitor, 10-27:1.

431

Muhammed Mehgi
Chairman, Arab-American Action Committee

1

If the U.S. supports Israel now [in the current Arab-Israeli war], as President Johnson did in 1967, American interests will pay the consequences. Arab oil might be cut off. This would paralyze Western industry . . . Millions of U.S. cars are thirsty for Arab oil. This is a natural link between the U.S. and the Arab world, and this is where American interests lie.

Interview, New York/
The Christian Science Monitor, 10-12:3.

Golda Meir
Prime Minister of Israel

2

It doesn't matter how you coat it: Arab sovereignty in Jerusalem just cannot be. This city will not be divided—not half and half, not 60-40, not 75-25, nothing. The only way we will lose Jerusalem is if we lose a war, and then we will lose all of it.

Interview/Time, 2-19:43.

3

Don't you think that . . . in a situation of this kind, where for 25 years there was no peace between Egypt and Israel—and certainly it was not because Israel did not want peace —and after a war like the war of '67, wouldn't it be proper, sensible and practical that the two sides should meet, and one side should tell the other, "These are the things that I want," and negotiations should be started? Is it possible to negotiate between two people through the press or through interviews or through public speeches? All that we have been asking for from the very beginning, immediately when the war was over, "Let us meet, as equals," we said; "Without any pre-conditions, let us negotiate."

TV-radio interview, Herzlia, Israel/
"Meet the Press,"
National Broadcasting Company, 5-6.

4

Let me tell you something that we Israelis have against Moses. He took us 40 years through the desert in order to bring us to the one spot in the Middle East that has no oil.

At dinner honoring West German Chancellor
Willy Brandt, Jerusalem, June 10/
The New York Times, 6-11:3.

5

[Criticizing Austria's capitulation to Arab terrorists by closing a transit camp for Israeli-bound Soviet Jews]: [The Austrian government's decision] will be regarded as a great victory throughout the terrorist organizations and the radio stations of the Arab world—and rightly so, because this is the first time a government has come to an agreement of this sort. Until now . . . terrorists often found themselves free to go through the same operation all over again; but now something much more has happened. The very principle of the freedom of movement of people has been put under a question mark. The four hostages taken in Vienna are alive and free; but I am convinced that—without this being the intention of the Austrian government and its Prime Minister—what has happened in Vienna is the greatest encouragement to terror throughout the world.

Before Council of Europe Parliamentary
Assembly, Strasbourg, France, Oct. 1/
San Francisco Examiner, 10-1:1.

6

I want you to know who we are fighting against [in the current Arab-Israeli war]. Since the [1967] Six-Day-War, a superpower, the Soviet Union, has decided to reinforce the enemy, sending him terrifying quantities of weapons of the most recent and sophisticated type, and that their limit was only the absorption capacity of Egypt and Syria.

Tel Aviv, Oct. 10/
The Washington Post, 10-11:(A)25.

7

For six years, like parrots, we have been repeating the same thing: We want to live in peace, in cooperation and in friendship [with the Arabs]. Therefore we say, "Let us sit down as equals. Let us negotiate without pre-conditions . . ." And you know exactly what the answer was for six years: no negotiations; pre-conditions. "Go back to the 1967 borders, and then maybe we will negotiate. Go back to the 1967 borders because it will be easier for us to attack you." That, of course, we could not agree to.

News conference, Oct. 13/
The Christian Science Monitor, 10-16:1.

1

Always, and especially this time, the friendship and assistance of the United States, its people and its government are dear to us. The United States is continuing to respond to our requests with the quantities and types of arms and the speed necessitated by the [current Arab-Israeli war] situation. We have no desire that anyone should fight in our place, but we are entitled to help in defending ourselves.

Before the Knesset (Parliament),
Jerusalem, Oct. 16/
The Christian Science Monitor, 10-18:1.

Richard M. Nixon
President of the United States

2

Israel simply can't wait for the dust to settle, and the Arabs can't wait for the dust to settle in the Mideast. Both sides are at fault. Both sides need to start negotiating. That is our position. We're not pro-Israel and we're not pro-Arab. And we're not any more pro-Arab because they have oil and Israel hasn't. We are pro-peace. And it's the interest of the whole area for us to get those negotiations off dead center. That is why we will use our influence with Israel; and we will use our influence—what influence we have—with the various Arab states . . . to get those negotiations on.

News conference, Washington, Sept. 5/
The New York Times, 9-6:26.

3

[On Arab countries' threats to use their oil supplies to retaliate against the U.S. and Europe's pro-Israel stands]: Oil without a market . . . doesn't do a country much good. We and Europe are the market. And I think that the responsible Arab leaders will see to it that, if they continue to up the price, if they continue to expropriate, if they do expropriate without fair compensation, the inevitable result is that they will lose their markets, and other sources will be developed.

News conference, Washington, Sept. 5/
The New York Times, 9-6:26.

4

[On Austria's capitulation to Arab terrorists by closing a transit camp for Israeli-bound Soviet Jews]: . . . I would hope that the [Austrian] Prime Minister [Bruno Kreisky] would reconsider his decision . . . for this fundamental reason that goes far beyond his country and even ours, and that is that we simply cannot have governments, small or large, give in to international blackmail by terrorist groups. That is what is involved. Not to mention, of course, the fact that we all have a concern for the emigres; they must have a place to come. So, on humanitarian grounds and on geopolitical grounds of the highest order, I believe that decision should be reconsidered; but naturally I am not going to put my friend, Mr. Kreisky, in the position of trying to dictate to him what it should be . . .

News conference, Washington, Oct. 3/
The Washington Post, 10-4:(A)6.

5

. . . I think, now, that all parties are going to approach this problem of trying to reach a settlement [in the Arab-Israeli conflict] with a more sober and more determined attitude than ever before; because the Mideast can't afford, Israel can't afford, Egypt can't afford, Syria can't afford, another war. The world cannot afford a war in that part of the world. And because the Soviet Union and the United States have potentially conflicting interests there, we both now realize that we cannot allow our differences in the Mideast to jeopardize even greater interests that we have—for example, in continuing a detente in Europe, in continuing the negotiations which can lead to a limitation of nuclear arms and eventually reducing the burden of nuclear arms and in continuing in other ways that can contribute to the peace of the world. As a matter of fact, I would suggest that, with all of the criticism of detente, that without that [U.S.-Soviet] detente, we might have had a major

(RICHARD M. NIXON)

conflict in the Middle East. With detente, we avoided it.

News conference, Washington, Oct. 26/
The New York Times, 10-27:14.

Mohammad Reza Pahlavi
Shah of Iran

1

We are not an atomic power; we do not intend to become an atomic power; but, nevertheless, I think that the deterrent there will be that a responsible country like mine—not only with our past history and this and that, but with our present and future—the best guarantee for peace will be this emerging power of Iran as an industrial, advanced country, a socially-advanced society, advanced agricultural country, a sophisticated country as such, at that, with enough, also, military power to make it understood that we mean what we say and that we have the means of meaning what we say. But I must reassure all that what we say will be always within the framework of the United Nations Charter, within decency, within reason and, I hope, wisdom.

TV-radio interview, Washington/
"Meet the Press,"
National Broadcasting Company, 7-29.

2

I've got this oil and I can't drink it. However, I know I can exploit it to the full without blackmailing the rest of the world and even attempting to prevent its being used to blackmail the rest of the world. I've therefore chosen the policy of ensuring its sale to everyone, indiscriminately. It wasn't a difficult choice. I've never thought of siding with the Arab countries who threaten to blackmail the West [by cutting back on oil shipments to pro-Israeli nations]. I've already said my country is independent, and everyone knows my country is Moslem but not Arab, and consequently, I don't act according to the convenience of the Arabs but according to the interests of Iran. Moreover, Iran needs money, and one can make a lot of money with oil. That's the whole difference between me and the Arabs. Because countries that say "we won't

sell the West any more oil" are countries that don't know what to do with their money. In many cases, they have a population of no more than 6- or 700,000 souls and so much money in the bank that they could subsist for three or four years without pumping a drop of oil, without selling a single barrel. I can't.

Interview/Los Angeles Times, 12-30:(6)4.

3

If you're asking me whom I consider our best friends, the answer is: the United States, amongst others. The United States understands us best for the simple reason they have many interests here: economic, therefore direct, interests; and political, therefore indirect, interests . . . Iran is the key, or one of the keys, of the world. I only have to add that the United States cannot withdraw within the frontiers of their country; they cannot revert to the Monroe Doctrine. They are compelled to respect their responsibilities to the world and, consequently, to attend to us. This detracts nothing from our independence, because everyone knows our friendship with the United States doesn't make us their slaves.

Interview/Los Angeles Times, 12-30:(6)4.

Robert Pierpoint
*News correspondent, Columbia
Broadcasting System (United States)*

4

For so long Americans have become used to thinking of the Israelis as the good guys and Arabs as the bad guys, that many react emotionally along the lines of previous prejudices. The fact is that both sides have committed unforgivable acts of terror; both sides have killed innocents; both sides have legitimate grievances and illegitimate methods of expressing them . . . The Israelis have and utilize a formidable political and propaganda force in this country [the U.S.] in the form of six million Jews. The Arabs, with only slightly less than a million descendants in America, are just beginning to organize a nation-wide counterforce. Perhaps this will help bring balance. In the meantime, the rest of us might apply more studied balance and fair play to the difficult problems of the Middle East.

News Commentary, March 7/
The Christian Science Monitor, 3-10:16.

Muammar el-Qaddafi
Chief of State of Libya

1

The Palestinian resistance movement does not exist any more. It has been destroyed by the Arabs in cooperation with Israel. This is not the fault of the Palestinians, because they have been over-powered by the Arab regimes. There is no front on Israel's border where the Palestinian resistance can operate from. What is being said on radios and in Arab conferences is all lies. The Arab nation needs someone to make it weep, not laugh, someone who can make it think rather than be emotionally carried away. In a matter of a few months, I shall escape from the trivial maneuvers of Arab politics. Once the Libya-Egypt merger is declared, my mission will end and I shall withdraw far from those crippled, barren and unsuccessful Arab politics.

Interview/Los Angeles Times, 4-26:(1)24.

2

[Saying Arab countries should nationalize U.S. interests, such as oil installations]: It is time for the Arab peoples to confront America. It is time to threaten American interests in the area, whatever the price . . . The United States, which thinks that she is controlling the world through the monopolistic oil companies and naval fleets, needs a severe slap in the face in the Arab region.

Tripoli, June 11/
Los Angeles Times, 6-12:(3)15.

3

[Saying the Arabs may use oil cutbacks as a weapon against a pro-Israel U.S.]: We must do something to change U.S. policy. We don't want to provoke you [Americans]. You have always acted in your national interest except in the Middle East. Perhaps the new oil situation will finally convince you that you should think of your national interest in the Arab world, as well as in the rest of the world. Oil in our hands may convince you that you can no longer afford to have the Israeli lobby dictate your foreign policy.

Interview/Newsweek, 9-24:53.

4

[On the current Arab-Israeli war]: A cease-fire imposed by the Americans and the Russians? Never! The Arabs must not accept the guardianship of the big powers or that of the [UN] Security Council. Israel has certainly violated all the resolutions of the United Nations; why should we be servile enough to buckle under to the will of others? I am in deep disagreement with [Egyptian] President Anwar Sadat and [Syrian] President Hafez Assad on even the objectives of their war. For me, the essential is not to take back from Israel the territories it won in 1967, but to liberate the Palestinians—all the Palestinians—from the Zionist yoke . . . . Even if Egypt and Syria should defeat Israel, I cannot give my backing to an operetta war.

Interview, Oct. 22/
Los Angeles Times, 10-23:(1)10.

5

[On the recent Arab-Israeli war, now at the cease-fire stage]: The war should have gone on, for years if need be, until the Arab or the Israeli side finished the other off completely . . . Only a long, devastating war could bring a final solution for the dispute. The Middle East has no room for both antagonists . . . I believe the war should go on until all Jews who immigrated to Israel after 1948 are forced to return to their original countries. They are foreigners and have no right to live with the Arabs. But Eastern and other Jews who coexisted peacefully with the Arabs before 1948 are to stay on and enjoy equal rights with the Palestinian Arabs.

Interview/Los Angeles Times, 11-13:(1)20.

Harry Reasoner
News commentator,
American Broadcasting Company

6

There are very grim projections on how much of our [the U.S.'s] oil we are going to have to get from abroad in the next dozen years if the U.S. is not going to grind to a halt. At the moment, there is simply not a real alternative to keeping on civil terms with the Arabs who have the oil. If this reality affects American policy, it is even more a factor in Western Europe, where several countries are not nearly as deeply tied to Israel by emotion and principle as is the U.S., and who have even fewer options in the energy field than the U.S. That is why there is new tension and no sign of an Arab willingness to compromise—and why Israel believes these are terribly critical years. It would be ironic and immoral but quite possible for the Arabs to win a victory with oil that they could not win with valor.

News commentary,
American Broadcasting Company, June 7/
The Christian Science Monitor, 6-16:14.

Zaid al-Rifai
Prime Minister of Jordan

1

Throughout the 25 years of its life, Israel failed to win the slightest degree of love or acceptance by its Arab neighbors. It has always been looked upon as an authority of terror and aggression, the conduct of which is always characterized with defiance and arrogance. The seeds of oppression which it planted in the Arab soil grew up with hatred. Israel's armed occupation of Arab territory constitutes an act of continued and escalating aggression which the world has watched in silence. It is from this position—the position of recourse, as a last resort, to rebellion against tyranny—that the Arabs had to take up arms. The fighting which broke out in our area at the Egyptian and Syrian fronts on last October 6 was a gallant effort by the Arab forces, dedicated to bring peace into reality. The economic measures taken by other Arab countries [cutbacks in oil exports to pro-Israeli nations] were another resolute expression demanding the compliance of Israel with the conditions of peace.

At Middle East peace conference, Geneva,
Dec. 21/The New York Times, 12-22:8.

Eugene V. Rostow
Professor of Law and
Public Affairs, Yale University

2

The United States does not support Israel out of sentiment, or out of sympathy, or because of the supposed influence of a Jewish lobby, or even to vindicate the promises of the international community under whose protection the Jewish National Home in Palestine was established and became the state of Israel. The United States is supporting Israel in order to protect vital national interests of the United States and of its allies and friends in Europe, the Middle East and Asia. All would be mortally threatened by Soviet control of the space and the resources of the great arc which extends from Morocco to Iran. There is no conflict between our feeling as Jews and our duty as American citizens. The national interests of Israel and of the United States in this prolonged conflict are parallel and compatible, and they are of nearly equal consequence.

Before National Executive Council,
American Jewish Committee, St. Louis,
Oct. 28/Vital Speeches, 12-1:104.

John Ruedy
Professor, Georgetown University,
Washington; Member, Middle East
Affairs Council

3

There can be no justice in the Middle East. This is no longer possible. If Jews are going to remain in Israel, some Palestinians lose their homes forever. On the other hand, I think none of us want to see Jews evicted on behalf of Palestine. So it is going to be a compromise. We [the U.S.] have to pressure our client [Israel], just as the Soviets have to be ready to pressure theirs [the Arabs].

Before Senate Appropriations Committee,
Washington, November/
The Washington Post, 12-16:(B)3.

Sabah al-Salim al-Sabah
Amir of Kuwait

4

[Saying he will cut off the flow of oil to the West if a new Arab-Israeli war breaks out]: We are committed to do so. When zero hour strikes, we shall use our oil as an effective weapon in the battle with Israel . . . This is our irrevocable position.

Quote, 4-22:362.

Anwar el-Sadat
President of Egypt

1

I have reached the limit of my patience [with U.S. pro-Israeli policy]. I find it strange that certain Arabs have not reached the same conclusion at the time Israel is still flooded with United States assistance . . . In certain Arab countries, United States interests today are more secure than ever before. Instead of forming a joint front to annoy Washington, we Arabs are eager to provide American interests with complete protection. Some Arabs have assured the United States of a smiling future in the area.

Interview/The New York Times, 1-9:3.

2

There are no doves or hawks on the other side—only Israelis. They have convinced themselves that they are quite happy where they are. It's hopeless to change it. Everything we have offered hasn't made the slightest difference in their outlook. And when the Libyan airliner was shot down [over Israel] with 108 civilians killed [earlier this year], every paper in Israel backed this barbarian act. So how can I change their thinking? The situation is hopeless and—make no mistake—highly explosive.

Interview/Newsweek, 4-9:45.

3

[Praising the recent nationalization in Libya of an American petroleum company]: [This is] the beginning of a battle against American interests in the whole Arab region. America must fully realize that it cannot protect its interests if it continues defying the Arab nation and supporting Israel without limitations. If America wants to entrust Israel with the task of protecting its interests, Israel will not be able to protect herself nor American interests in the area. [This expropriation of the oil company is] a fundamental part of

the formidable conflict . . . the first spark triggering the start of the battle.

Tripoli, Libya/
The Washington Post, 6-13:(A)1.

4

[Criticizing the U.S. for re-supplying Israel with arms during the current Arab-Israeli war]: [The U.S. was] not satisfied that her arms enabled Israel to block peaceful settlement [since the 1967 cease-fire]; but now she is involved in an action even greater and more grave than that. While we are fighting aggression, the United States is backing aggression. There are American naval and air lifts carrying new tanks, planes, artillery, rockets and electronic devices to Israel. We tell them [Americans] this will not terrify us. But we and you have to ask ourselves · a question before the matter reaches a point of no return. The question is, where to and until when?

Before Parliament, Cairo, Oct. 16/
The Washington Post, 10-17:(A)12.

5

We are fighting for the sake of peace, the only peace that is worth the name; that is, peace based on justice. The great mistake our enemy [Israel] has made is that he thought the force of terrorism could guarantee security. [The Israelis] are now faced with [a war of] attrition. That we can bear much better than they can. I would like to add, so they may hear me in Israel: We are not advocates of annihilation. Egyptian missiles are now on their pads ready to be launched to the deepest depths of Israel. We could have given the signal and issued the order. But we realize the responsibility of using certain kinds of weapons and we restrain ourselves. Yet they have to remember what I still say: an eye for an eye and a tooth for a tooth.

Before Egyptian People's Assembly/
Time, 10-29:29.

Pinchas Sapir
Minister of Finance of Israel

6

If you ask me about our [Israel's] achievements, I will tell you about the university in Beersheba. Do you know what Beersheba was

(PINCHAS SAPIR)

25 years ago? A couple of huts and some Arab Bedouins—the best place in the world to get murdered. There's a university there now, and that's achievement. All our life is a permanent revolution.

Time, 4-30:35.

Omar Saqqaf
Foreign Minister of Saudi Arabia

1

The puzzle is what is it that our American friends want. Why is the help always for Israel? There are more than 2.5 million Palestinian people either in refuge [abroad] or under occupation . . . If people think this question is going to be as it is now forever, they are wrong. We are friends with the United States. We want to be friends. But there is always a limit.

The Washington Post, 7-11:(A)25.

2

Our view is that no one can resolve the [Arab-Israeli] Middle East crisis except America. If America thinks that [Saudi Arabian] oil is guaranteed, we are not of the same opinion. There is a limit to our patience [with the U.S.'s pro-Israel stance]. We are not fighting the United States, but we want them to feel their responsibility.

San Francisco Examiner, 9-5:16.

John A. Scali
United States Ambassador/Permanent Representative to the United Nations

3

To the shame of all mankind, acts of violence and terror, often striking down innocent people, are on the verge of becoming a routine footnote to the tragic and unresolved Arab-Israeli conflict. The question now in the Middle East is not who started what but how this vicious cycle is to be broken. Assessing blame is secondary to the purpose of ending the misery and suffering on both sides. The overriding task of this Council is to seize the present opportunity and move to put an end to violence so that the political processes will have a chance to operate.

Before United Nations Security Council,
New York, April 17/
Los Angeles Times, 4-18:(1)18.

4

It seems clear to us that logically, politically, historically, realistically, the question of agreement of final boundaries [for Israel] must be viewed in the context of the total thrust and intent [of the 1967 UN resolution]. This question must, therefore, be resolved as part of the process of reaching agreement of all the complex factors governing new relationship[s] among the parties, to replace that defined in the 1949 armistice agreements . . . It could be begun as we have long favored, with an agreement on some Israeli withdrawal in Sinai and a reopening of the Suez Canal within the context of an extended cease-fire, as the first stage on the road to a final settlement. Such a first step would be firmly linked to a final settlement. But where a beginning is made in this or some other way is less important than [that] such a process be started without delay.

Before United Nations Security Council,
New York, June 14/
The New York Times, 6-15:7.

5

[On Israel's forcing down of an Arab commercial airliner in an attempt to capture an Arab guerrilla leader]: We deplore this violation of the United Nations Charter and of the rule of law in international civil aviation. It is high time to call a full stop to all such acts and related acts and threats of violence . . . National and international efforts to control terrorism must go forward. They must go forward, however, within and not outside the law. The commitment to the rule of law in international affairs, including the field of international civil aviation, imposes certain restraints on the methods governments can use to protect themselves against those who operate outside the law. My government believes actions such as Israel's diversion of a civil airliner on August 10 are unjustified and likely to bring about counteraction on an increasing scale.

Before United Nations Security Council,
New York, Aug. 14/The New York Times, 8-15:1.

Hussein Shafei
Vice President of Egypt

1

We ask God to give us strength to make the enemy [Israel] exhausted through guerrilla action and political and economic means. We are a nation of faith and know that Israel is not liked by anybody in this world . . . The Zionists are the enemies of humanity, and they cannot find anybody to love them.

At social-security conference,
Cairo, Feb. 23/
Los Angeles Herald-Examiner, 2-23:(A)1.

Joseph J. Sisco
Assistant Secretary for Near Eastern and
South Asian Affairs, Department of State
of the United States

2

While our [U.S.] interests in many respects are parallel to the interests of Israel, they are not synonymous with the state of Israel. The interests of the United States go beyond any one nation in the area. We have important political, economic and strategic interests in the entire area, whether you are talking about the Middle East as well as the area of the Persian Gulf and the Arabian peninsula. There is increasing concern in our country, for example, over the energy question; and I think it is foolhardy to believe that this is not a factor in the situation.

Israeli television interview/
The New York Times, 8-7:12.

Howard K. Smith
News commentator,
American Broadcasting Company

3

As homes [in the U.S.] grow colder and cars less mobile, it doesn't sound convincing to say the fuel crisis is going to turn out just fine. Still, that is what perspective indicates. The Arabs [by cutting back on oil shipments to pro-Israel countries] are applying what are in fact sanctions against the United States to change its policies. Well, history suggests sanctions don't work; indeed, they backfire. League of Nations sanctions against Mussolini only made him conquer Ethiopia faster. Roo-

sevelt's steel and oil sanctions against Japan didn't mend Japan's ways; it made war on the U.S. instead. United Nations sanctions against Rhodesia failed. America's against the Communists—called the ban on sale of strategic goods—has not made them less Communist. So with Arab oil sanctions. The victims may show a temporary deference. But in their hearts, the Europeans, the Japanese, the Americans are saying—never get so dependent on those "blanks" again. True, the U.S. may put more pressure on Israel to compromise; but it should have done that long ago anyhow. However, talk of abandoning Israel is ridiculous. Aside from the community the U.S. shares with the only democracy between Italy and India, it has a mighty geopolitical tie. With Russia all over the Mediterranean, America's hard national interest is to sustain the one strong, friendly bastion it can be sure of—Israel. And it will. The Arabs can hurt the U.S. for a while. But in the end, either they will come around—or the world will get around them.

News commentary,
American Broadcasting Company/
The Christian Science Monitor, 12-6:22.

Axel Springer
West German publisher

4

I can't say I didn't know what was happening [in Nazi Germany]. In 1933, I stood on the Kurfuerstendamm in Berlin and watched Nazi storm-troopers beating up old Jews. I was a young man, and I couldn't do anything about it. But I never forgot it. Now I think it is vitally important that my sons and all young Germans know what happened—that they are taught about it in school and read about it in the press and know why the survival of Israel is so important for Germany and the world.

Interview, West Berlin/
The Washington Post, 4-22:(B)1.

Zayed Ben Sultan
President, United Arab Emirates

5

It is important to understand that the Arab

(ZAYED BEN SULTAN)

world is collectively baffled and humiliated by its military defeats at the hands of tiny Israel. Rational leadership in the region is aware, moreover, that more defeat is in store in the event of further conflict. But suddenly, Arab leaders have realized they have this super-weapon of oil lying underground, and gradually they are getting together to decide how to use it.

Interview, Beirut/
Los Angeles Herald-Examiner, 8-28:(A)8.

Yosef Tekoah
Israeli Ambassador/Permanent
Representative to the United Nations

1

[Criticizing the UN Security Council for passing a resolution condemning Israeli retaliatory raids on Arab guerrillas in Lebanon]: [The resolution] demonstrates once more that the Security Council, like other United Nations organs, cannot, because of its structure and composition, its voting procedures and its pre-ordained results, deal equitably with questions pertaining to the Middle East situation. If it cannot examine and at least pronounce itself fairly and adequately on the murder of innocent men, women and children by Arab terrorist gangs, if it cannot recognize Israel's right to defend itself against sanguinary attacks, it is obviously not the body capable to act on any of the complex issues of the Arab-Israeli conflict.

At United Nations, N.Y., April 21/
The New York Times, 4-22:(1)6.

2

[Defending his country's forcing down of an Arab commercial airliner in an attempt to capture Arab guerrilla leader George Habash]: By making it possible for murderers such as . . . George Habash to operate from Beirut, to fly abroad without hindrance and then to return to Beirut, the Lebanese authorities show no regard for Israel's rights under the cease-fire and therefore cannot complain that Israel does not respect their rights . . . The real question is, why is Habash still free?

Before United Nations Security Council,
New York, Aug. 13/
San Francisco Examiner, 8-14:16.

3

[On the current Arab-Israeli war]: [The Soviet Union] must assume a great share of the responsibility for what has happened. The Soviet Union has identified itself with barbaric hatred and has supplied all kinds of weapons of war to the Arab states. If it were not for the policies and actions of the Soviet Union, the Middle East might today be in a state of peace instead of in a renewed state of suffering and bloodshed.

At United Nations Security Council
session, New York, Oct. 9/
The New York Times, 10-10:19.

4

What is Zionism? When the Jews, exiled from their land in the seventh century before the Christian era, sat by the rivers of Babylon and wept, but also prayed and sought ways to go home, that was already Zionism. When, in a mass revolt against their exile, they returned and rebuilt the Templar and re-established their state, that was Zionism. When they were the last people in the entire Mediterranean Basin to resist the forces of the Roman Empire and to struggle for independence, that was Zionism. When, for centuries after the Roman conquest, they refused to surrender and rebelled again and again against the invaders, that was Zionism. When, uprooted from their land by the conquerors and dispersed by them all over the world, they continued to dream and to strive to return to Israel, that was Zionism. When, during the long succession of foreign invaders, they tried repeatedly to regain sovereignty at least in part of their homeland, that was Zionism. When they volunteered from Palestine and from all over the world to establish Jewish armies that fought on the side of the Allies in the First World War and helped to end Ottoman subjugation, that was Zionism. When they formed the Jewish Brigade in the Second World War to fight Hitler, while Arab leaders supported him, that was Zionism. When, in the forests of Russia and the Ukraine and other parts of East Europe, Jewish partisans battled the Germans and sang of the land where palms are growing, that was Zionism. When Jews fought British colonialism while the Arabs of Palestine and the neighboring Arab states were being helped by it, that was Zionism.

At United Nations, N.Y./
Los Angeles Herald-Examiner, 11-11:(A)14.

Kurt Waldheim
Secretary General of the United Nations

1

[On the renewed Arab-Israeli war in the Middle East]: I have no illusions about how difficult it is for countries in conflict to turn from war to peace. I have no wish to deflect any government from what it believes to be its legitimate sovereign aims. I do, however, question whether the continuation of the war can possibly achieve these aims permanently for any of the parties. I am also deeply concerned at the wider threat to international peace and security which this situation may create.

Before United Nations Security Council,
New York, Oct. 11/
Los Angeles Times, 10-12:(1)10.

Harold Wilson
Member of British Parliament;
Former Prime Minister of the
United Kingdom

2

[On the recent military alert called by the U.S. in relation to possible Soviet intervention in the Arab-Israeli war]: The American decision not to consult [with Europe] was an outrage. On an issue potentially lethal for the world, it was a grave dereliction of duty owed by America to her allies.

U.S. News & World Report, 11-12:33.

Lester L. Wolff
United States Representative, D-New York

3

[Saying the U.S. should break diplomatic relations with Arab countries participating in the cutback of oil for the U.S.]: The United States can ill afford to conduct "business as usual" with nations whose illegal activities jeopardize our security and our ability to adequately meet the needs of our own people . . . [The diplomatic break] will serve to convince the Arab states that the U.S. is not weak and submissive, but rather a nation which deals firmly with those who resort to blackmail and threaten our security.

Before the House, Washington,
Dec. 5/Los Angeles Times, 12-6:(1)20.

Ahmed Zaki al-Yamani
Minister of Petroleum of Saudi Arabia

4

[On his country's policy of basing oil exports on the degree of support given the Arabs against Israel by the importing country]: If you are hostile to us, you get no oil. If you are neutral, you get oil, but not as much as before. If you are friendly, you get the same as before.

Interview/
Los Angeles Times, 11-19:(1)12.

5

Our [the Arabs'] natural inclinations are Western. Your interests and ours lie in working together for the betterment of all. We live together in the same world. But you will have to meet us, the Arabs, halfway. Perhaps if you do, we will all discover interesting things about one another and it will be a better world.

At luncheon, Taif, Saudi Arabia/
The Christian Science Monitor, 11-29:16.

6

[On his country's oil cutbacks to pro-Israel nations]: We are extremely disturbed by these cuts . . . We consider ourself part of the Free World, and any disturbance, any recession, in the European, Japanese or U.S. economy will hurt Saudi Arabia badly. [But the other side of the story is the] continuous occupation of our [Arabs'] territories by the Israelis and the very alarming policy of Israel to expand and take more territory.

Interview, New York, Dec. 4/
Los Angeles Times, 12-5:(1)15.

(AHMED ZAKI AL-YAMANI)

1

[On his country's cutbacks in oil shipments to the U.S. because of U.S. support for Israel]: I can tell you that, with regard to Saudi Arabia, if there is anything which we hate then it is to use this oil as a weapon. We were reluctant to use it. We came to this country begging you to change this [pro-Israel] policy, asking you to implement the [UN resolution] 242 and make peace with the area. All that we want is peace and nothing else. We hate to use oil as a weapon, and I don't think we will ever use it again, if that problem [Israeli occupation of Arab land], which is the only problem, is solved. There is nothing between the United States and Saudi Arabia as a bilateral dispute or difficulty. The only thing is this problem of, what you call it, the Arab cause: peace and removal of [Israeli] occupation.

TV-radio interview, Washington/
"Meet the Press,"
National Broadcasting Company, 12-9.

Mohammed Hassan el-Zayyat
Foreign Minister of Egypt

2

[On the recent Israeli raid on Arab guerrillas in Beirut]: The least the [UN] Security Council could do now is to call upon all member-states—including and, indeed, especially, the permanent members of the Council—to interrupt their economic assistance and their military supplies to Israel, which have and would facilitate their continuing of further aggression . . . Israeli authorities have served notice that such barbaric crimes will be repeated in Lebanon, Syria or any of the Arab countries. These statements suggest that Israel has assigned for itself an imperial role in our region.

Before United Nations Security Council,
New York, April 16/
Los Angeles Times, 4-17:(1)4.

3

Our intentions are not to occupy Israeli territory or to drive Israel into the sea. We say this not out of any tender love for Israel but because we understand the political reality. We have no policy for Israel's annihilation. What's our object? We really want peace—not as an ideological thing to please Washington or Moscow. We want it as a framework in which we can go on developing. But we cannot have peace *and* occupation. The cease-fire we want must be linked to complete evacuation by Israelis of all Egyptian, Syrian and Jordanian lands.

Interview/Time, 10-29:45.

AFRICA

Idi Amin
President of Uganda

1

You want to know why the British were so upset when I kicked out the Asians [from Uganda last year]? Because the British are the racists. They did not want the Asians in Britain. That's why.
San Francisco Examiner, 2-8:30.

2

There is plenty of food [in Uganda]. Sugar was short for a time, but now there is plenty of everything. This is a paradise country. The poorest man in Uganda is General Amin. It is better for me to be poor and the people richer.
Interview, Kampala/Time, 3-12:27.

3

[On his expulsion last year of Uganda's Asian population]: I am the hero of Africa. Even if I am killed, my operation is already a success. No single Ugandan will ever allow non-citizens to come back and control our economy.
News conference, Kampala/
Newsweek, 3-12:34.

4

We have outside the continent 80 million Africans [blacks]. During the Middle East war [of 1967], Jews are coming from the United States, from Russia, from Germany, from everywhere to help Israel. Why can't we [Africans] do the same? Why not African people from all over the world come to help us?
Before Organization of African Unity,
Addis Ababa, Ethiopia, May 25/
Los Angeles Times, 5-26:(1)5.

Habib Bourguiba
President of Tunisia

5

I am not a man who is angered easily; I do not believe that bad temper is a good example

of political behavior . . . I am not one of those who makes much noise boasting about the giant strides they have made. This kind of false boasting is not in my nature . . . I am a realistic man . . . A realistic person is he who prefers moderate reforms that pave the way for others to an impossible miracle . . . I only seek to accomplish what is possible.
Before International Labor Organization,
Geneva/Los Angeles Times, 7-8:(4)4.

Abba Eban
Foreign Minister of Israel

6

[On the breaking off of relations with Israel by several African countries]: We knew that the position of Israel in Africa was in fact not compatible with the geo-political situation in this continent where there are some eight Arab countries and where there are strong Moslem communities. When we developed our relations with Africa, we realized the risks and the possibility of the withdrawal of one country or another . . . But these setbacks are not tragic, and one cannot speak of our collapse in Africa.
Radio interview, Jan. 6/
The Washington Post, 1-7:(A)21.

Kenneth Kaunda
President of Zambia

7

I am leading a nation of drunkards . . . Zambians have hit the bottle so much that the situation is going from bad to worse. I don't want to be part and parcel of a nation of drunkards. I would rather die than accept the responsibility of running a drunken nation. If you [Zambians] fail to heed my warning, I am definitely going to quit.
At United National Independence
Party rally/Newsweek, 11-19:64.

Michael Manley
Prime Minister of Jamaica

1

We are willing to offer to the Organization of African Unity that, whenever it feels that volunteers from other countries can be trained to assist successfully in the overthrow of the racist regimes of South Africa and Rhodesia and the colonial regimes in Angola, Mozambique and Guinea-Bissau, we will undertake to recruit volunteers and send them across the ocean to Africa.

Before Organization of African Unity,
Algiers, Algeria, Sept. 8/
The Dallas Times Herald, 9-9:(A)16.

Mobutu Sese Seko
President of Zaire

2

We do not want to return blindly to all our traditional customs, but merely to choose those which can best be adapted to modern society. The recourse to authenticity has no other limit but to reach the goal of giving our country its own personality, its own culture.

Interview/Newsweek, 5-14:58.

Muammar el-Qaddafi
Chief of State of Libya

3

[On his country's "cultural revolution"]: We must purge all the sick people who talk of Communism, atheism, who make propaganda for the Western countries and advocate capitalism. We shall put them in prison . . . We live by the Koran, God's book; we will reject any idea that is not based on it. Therefore, we enter into a cultural revolution to refute and destroy all misleading books which have made youth insane and sick. These books must be burned.

April 15/The New York Times, 5-22:2.

4

If this world is a jungle, we [Libyans] are capable of becoming one of its beasts. We do not have atomic bombs or aircraft carriers, but we can die for our rights. [The] Libyan people are undergoing military training, and weapons will be distributed to the people if America or other powers decide tó embark on adventures . . . We will not die before we slap

those crazy people once at least or spit in their face. This should be enough for us.

News conference, Tripoli, May 13/
The Washington Post, 5-14:(A)5.

5

Socialism is my philosophy, and I'm interested in material progress for my people. Communism bans private property. That's against our principles. But capitalism is dead here.

Interview/Newsweek, 9-24:53.

Ian Smith
Prime Minister of Rhodesia

6

[On foreign economic sanctions imposed on his country because of Rhodesia's racial policy]: If we could break out of the sanctions straitjacket, I'm sure it would make a tremendous beneficial difference to Rhodesia. [But regardless of the sanction problem,] I think we can prove through statistics that the Rhodesian African is better off than any other African on the continent, that he enjoys a higher standard of living, that he has better educational and health and recreational amenities. We have done a lot, but we are far from complacent . . . The biggest priority in Rhodesia today is to raise the standard of living of the mass of the people. In order to do this, we want to ensure that we can get the economy moving, that we can break out of this straitjacket of sanctions which is harming, I believe, the African more than the European in Rhodesia.

Interview, Salisbury/
The Christian Science Monitor, 1-31:1,3.

7

[Criticizing Britain for insisting that Rhodesia's Constitution guarantee unimpeded progress toward majority rule by the majority black population]: Get off our backs and let us Rhodesians get on with the job. There is only one way to settle our Rhodesian problems. We Rhodesians have got to get together and do it among ourselves. Surely, anyone with a grain of common sense in his head can understand that simple, plain, stark fact . . . The main stumbling block [for improved British-Rhodesian relations] is the British government's participation in the issue. As long as Britain maintains the fiction that she can influence events here, so long will the Africans continue to look to Britain instead of coming to terms with reality in Rhodesia.

Before Parliament, Salisbury,
June 29/
The Washington Post, 6-30:(A)17.

1

[On sanctions placed against his country by various nations because of Rhodesia's racial policies]: History proves that sanctions gradually weaken. They get bigger and bigger holes blown through them until, in the end, those imposing them give up. I know of no case in history where the opposite trend applies, nor do I think we shall be any different.

Interview/
The Christian Science Monitor, 11-14:6.

William R. Tolbert, Jr.
President of Liberia

2

In Liberia we are determined today to take the first steps in a new direction, to help ourselves, to lift ourselves. And speed is truly the symbol of the new Liberia. For while in other developing countries men would speak of "the revolution," in the Republic of Liberia our people are seeking a speedy "evolution."

At White House dinner in his honor,
Washington, June 5/
The Washington Post, 6-7:(B)3.

3

For a century my country was the only free, democratic state on the African continent. She proved that black men could indeed determine their own destiny.

San Francisco Examiner & Chronicle,
6-10:(This World)2.

War and Peace

Zulfikar Ali Bhutto
Prime Minister of Pakistan

1

I have not been negatively critical of the United Nations. We have placed and we had placed great hopes in the United Nations. All small countries had placed great hopes in the United Nations. But we have seen that the United Nations has been bypassed, and it has been bypassed in very important crises, the most important of all being Vietnam. A cruel war was fought in Vietnam for a very long period of time, and the United Nations was bypassed in that war. There have been resolutions of the United Nations on the Middle East and on Kashmir, but these have not been implemented. The United Nations will undoubtedly gain in strength with the passage of time. This is a part of the evolution of contemporary political compulsions, provided that the detente does not decide to put the United Nations in a snuff box.

TV-radio interview, New York/
"Meet the Press,"
National Broadcasting Company, 9-23.

Willy Brandt
Chancellor of West Germany

2

There is nothing, as I see it, for years to come which can replace the U.S. deterrent as a force for world peace.

Interview/
U.S. News & World Report, 4-30:38.

3

We have finally begun to move toward world-wide peace. And now that we have, there can be no turning back. We must all go right on pursuing it actively, patiently and, above all, together. And while the final goal —an absolute peace—may not be something which I personally get to see in my lifetime,

I'll tell you this: I fully intend to see us get part of the way there.

Interview, Bonn/Parade, 9-23:7.

Leonid I. Brezhnev
General Secretary,
Communist Party of the Soviet Union

4

The Europe which repeatedly was transformed into a center for aggressive wars which resulted in wide-spread destruction and the death of millions of people must be relegated forever to the past . . . The war in Vietnam is ended. Soviet-American relations are developing satisfactorily. Broadly speaking, one can say that our planet today is closer than ever before to a condition of lasting peace.

Television address, Bonn, West Germany,
May 21/Los Angeles Times, 5-22:(1)6.

5

I have heard that the American political vocabulary includes the expression, "to win the peace." The present moment in history is, I believe, perhaps the most suitable occasion to use that expression. We [the U.S. and the Soviet Union] won the war [World War II]. Today, our joint efforts must help mankind win a durable peace. The possibility of a new war must be eliminated . . . The Soviet people are perhaps second to none when it comes to knowing what war means. In World War II we won a victory of world-historic significance. But in that war over 20 million Soviet citizens died, 70,000 of our towns and villages were devastated and one-third of our national wealth was destroyed. The war wounds have now been healed. Today the Soviet Union is a mightier and more prosperous country than ever before. But we remember the lessons of the war only too well; and that is why the peoples of the Soviet Union value peace so highly; that is why they strongly approve the peace policy of our Party and government. For us, peace is the highest achievement to which all men should strive if they want to make their life a worthy one.

Television address to the American people, San Clemente, Calif., June 24/ The New York Times, 6-25:18.

1

The cold war put the brake on the development of relations between nations and slowed down the progress and advance of economic and scientific ties. I ask myself, was that a good period? Did it serve the interests of the people? And my answer to that is no, no, no and again no. It was a war so cold that there came into being such means of warfare as atomic weapons, which must certainly cause us to start thinking, what are we preparing for—to destroy one another and to destroy our entire civilization, the product of thousands of years of man's efforts and labor, or should we endeavor to seek some other alternative? We have certainly been prisoners of those old [cold-war] trends; and to this day we have not been able fully to break those fetters and to come out into the open air, not only in the political field but in trade and economic ties.

Before U.S. business leaders, Washington/ Time, 7-2:10.

2

. . . are not the interests of universal pea᾿ served by the agreements between the Soviet Union and the United States on the mutual limitation of nuclear weapons and the prevention of nuclear war? The answer, I believe, is self-evident. At times, however, one hears contentions that the concluded treaties are allegedly unsatisfactory because they do not solve the existing problems once and for all. It is contended that, if agreements were reached at once on general and complete [disarmament], on the prohibition and destruction of nuclear weapons and on the dissolution of all military blocs, then, indeed, there would be a shift in world politics. All that is being done at present amounts, allegedly, to only half-measures. While it would be very good to achieve general and complete disarmament, including the

solution to the problem of nuclear weapons and military blocs, one can only wonder at the naivete of this approach. The Soviet Union has long and consistently struggled for the attainment of these aims; but our Western partners, alas, are still not yet prepared for such a solution. So should we sit on our hands and wait for God to rain manna? No, the principle "all or nothing" is absolutely worthless in international politics, an area where one should strive all the time to advance and to use any existing possibility for this.

Tashkent, U.S.S.R., Sept. 25/ Vital Speeches, 10-15:5.

3

The military preparations of the capitalist states are compelling the socialist countries as well to allocate the necessary funds for defense, diverting these from civilian construction, to which we should like to dedicate all our efforts and all our material resources. Dozens of newly-independent countries are also being drawn into the orbit of the arms race, as a result, of course, of the threat to their independence posed by imperialism—now in one part of the world, now in another. It goes without saying that the further extension of the arms race by the aggressive circles of imperialism, on the one hand, and the relaxation of international tension that has set in, on the other, are two opposite processes. The two cannot develop endlessly along what might be called parallel lines. If we want the detente and peace to thrive, the arms race must be stopped.

At World Peace Congress, Moscow, Oct. 26/ Vital Speeches, 11-15:72.

Chou En-lai
Premier of the People's Republic of (Communist) China

4

The great victories won by the people of Vietnam, Laos and Cambodia in their war against U.S. aggression and for national salvation have strongly encouraged the people of the world in their revolutionary struggles against imperialism and colonialism. A new sit-

(CHOU EN-LAI)

uation has emerged in the Korean people's struggle for the independent and peaceful re-unification of their fatherland. The struggles of the Palestinians and other Arab peoples against aggression by Israeli Zionism, the African peoples' struggles against colonialism and racial discrimination and the Latin American peoples' struggles for maintaining 200-nautical-mile territorial waters or economic zones all continue to forge ahead. The struggles of the Asian, African and Latin American peoples to win and defend national independence and safeguard state sovereignty and national resources have further deepened and broadened. The just struggles of the Third World as well as of the people of Europe, North America and Oceania support and encourage each other. Countries want independence, nations want liberation and the people want revolution—this has become an irresistible historical trend.

At Chinese Communist Party Congress,
Peking, Aug. 24/
The New York Times, 9-1:6.

1

There are a small number of people in the world who have a passion for encroaching on the independence of others. Living in the 1970s, they dream dreams of 18th-century feudal emperors. Their policy is one of holding nuclear weapons in one hand and declarations or treaties of what they call peace and security in the other, so as to deceive and impose their will on others . . . The danger of war still exists; relaxation is but a superficial phenomenon, and we must be well prepared against wars of aggression.

At dinner honoring French President
Georges Pompidou, Peking, Sept. 11/
The New York Times, 9-12:6.

Brian Crozier
Director, Institute for the
Study of Conflict, London

2

. . . I believe that a part of the Western intellectual establishment, through biased or negative criticism of our institutions and society, bears a heavy responsibility for fostering

an atmosphere that is favorable to . . . terrorists. Certain Western countries have a tendency to give hospitality in the media—particularly television—to extreme views and to grant terrorists a platform, while refusing time or space to moderates who want to offer rebuttals. This may make for exciting show business, but it breeds a taste for the real thing . . . I don't believe that most Western governments yet realize the special nature of the threat that terrorism poses for modern democratic societies. We're especially vulnerable to the daring and fanaticism of the man who is willing to die to get what he wants. We must learn to recognize and to combat this terrorist threat, or its specter will haunt us more and more in the years to come.

Interview/
The Reader's Digest, April:93.

Abba Eban
Foreign Minister of Israel

3

The United Nations has played no role in the settlement of any international conflict during the past few years. To cite a few examples: The Indo-Pakistan war, the Vietnam war, the conflict between the two Koreas, the Berlin problem, the European settlements, American-[Communist] Chinese tension and American-Soviet relations have all progressed toward a settlement without the UN. Even the present cease-fire between Egypt and Israel is not the result of a UN initiative. There is a general decline in the resonance and effectiveness of the UN, largely through its unbalanced resolutions and its failure to face such problems as international terrorism and piracy.

Interview, Jerusalem/
Los Angeles Herald-Examiner, 5-6:(A)15.

Andrei A. Gromyko
Foreign Minister of the
Soviet Union

4

The foreign policy of the Soviet Union is aimed at the continuation and consolidation of the current tendency for transforming international relations on peaceful lines. We proceed from the belief that this tendency will prevail in future. Behind it are the aspirations of all nations for peace. Behind it are the states for which peace is the chief goal of their foreign policy. And, last but not least, behind it is the understanding, spreading ever wider among the realistically-minded quarters in various countries, that there is no other alternative to nuclear war.

At Conference on Security and Cooperation in Europe, Helsinki, Finland, July 4/ Vital Speeches, 8-1:615.

Henry A. Kissinger
Assistant to the President of the United States for National Security Affairs

1

If we look at history, we see that there are certain periods and circumstances that have offered the opportunity for peace. Basic relationships are more important at such times than any conflict. We have [Communist] China entering the world, the Soviet Union acting like a great power and less like a revolutionary, and the United States understanding she is no longer on a crusade. The leaders of these nations have learned the limits of previous policy. They now relate to each other in a constructive way; the tensions we see now are a healthy sign of growing. We are developing a code of conduct with our former adversaries and a system of competition with our friends . . . These are all green shoots; they must be allowed to grow.

Interview, Washington/Time, 7-30:27.

2

The United States will never be satisfied with a world of uneasy truces, of offsetting blocs, of accommodations of convenience. We know that power can enforce a resigned passivity, but only a sense of justice can enlist consensus. We strive for a peace whose stability rests not merely on a balance of forces but on shared aspirations. We are convinced that a structure which ignores humane values will prove cold and empty and unfulfilling to most of mankind.

Before United Nations General Assembly, New York/ Los Angeles Herald-Examiner, 9-28:(A)10.

3

Under conditions of nuclear plenty, the decision to engage in general war involves consequences of such magnitude that no responsible statesman can base his policy on the constant threat of such a holocaust; and every leader with a responsibility for these weapons must set himself the task of bringing about conditions which reduce the possibility of such a war to a minimum and, indeed, over any extended period of time reduce this possibility to zero.

News conference, Washington, Dec. 27/ U.S. News & World Report, 1-7('74):64.

Charles A. Lindbergh
Aviator

4

It's still hard for me to realize that every city in this country could be destroyed, overnight. All it takes, quite literally, is the triggering. In the past, one of man's greatest protections was the time needed to move military forces: It took time to move an army; it took time to set up the weapons of destruction. All that has passed, in a single generation. The fundamental elements facing us today are unprecedented. We have destructive power greater than ever imagined; we have delivery systems making the whole world subject to destruction within minutes; and we have a population rise that throws man into competition for the fundamentals, like food, in a way unprecedented in history. These elements give man problems he has never faced before.

Interview, St. Paul, Minn./ The National Observer, 6-30:20.

Adam Malik
Foreign Minister of Indonesia

5

We must never allow the concept of "wars of liberation" to be used as a device to instigate or perpetuate civil war in an independent and sovereign country, or worse, to sanction with it the interference by foreign powers in the internal affairs of another country.

Before United Nations General Assembly, New York, Oct. 1/ Los Angeles Times, 10-2:(1)13.

Yakov A. Malik
*Soviet Ambassador/Permanent Representative
to the United Nations*

1

The Security Council can, and has a right
to, take the most severe measures against aggressors and to defend states which are victims
of aggression. This can be done only if none
of the permanent members, by an unjust veto,
paralyzes the Security Council and takes the
aggressor under its wing.

*Before UN Security Council,
New York, June 12/
Los Angeles Herald-Examiner, 6-13:(A)4.*

Richard M. Nixon
President of the United States

2

Let us build a structure of peace in the
world in which the weak are as safe as the
strong; in which each respects the right of the
other to live by a different system; in which
those who would influence others will do so
by the strength of their ideas and not by the
force of their arms. Let us accept that high
responsibility not as a burden, but gladly
—gladly because the chance to build such a
peace is the noblest endeavor in which a nation can engage . . .

*Inauguration address, Washington, Jan. 20/
U.S. News & World Report, 2-5:87.*

3

We often find . . . that after war . . . a
nation . . . tends to turn itself inward. And
rather than a period of peace being one that is
creative and positive, it is one that is negative,
one of withdrawal, one of isolation; and that
plants seeds for more conflict, not only at
home but abroad.

*At National Prayer Breakfast,
Washington/
The Christian Science Monitor, 2-5:10.*

4

The costs of peace are great, but the costs
of war are much greater.

*News conference, Washington, March 2/
The New York Times, 3-3:12.*

5

. . . the only thing more difficult than

getting the peace is keeping it . . .

*At swearing in of Henry Kissinger as
Secretary of State, Washington, Sept. 22/
The Dallas Times Herald, 9-23:(A)30.*

Paul VI
Pope

6

Just as it should be possible to defeat epi-
demics, illiteracy, misery and hunger, so it
should be possible to exclude the dangers,
menaces and ruptures which compromise the
peaceful existence of humanity on the earth.
[Such a dream is not easy,] above all when
part of the world's economy and the organization of peoples are founded on armaments,
and on the basis of prestige and the imposition of some over others. It is vital that peace
should become ever more a necessity in the
conscience of mankind. Then it will become
possible.

*On World Day of Peace, Vatican City, Jan. 1/
Los Angeles Herald-Examiner, 1-2:(A)4.*

7

Peace can never be a simple truce, an equilibrium of weapons between adversaries.

*Vatican City, Oct. 24/
Los Angeles Times, 10-25:(1)5.*

Philip Potter
*General secretary,
World Council of Churches*

8

We have seen many wars in which these
powers [the United States and the Soviet Un-
ion] have been involved—in Vietnam, India,
Pakistan, Nigeria, the Middle East, the Sudan
and elsewhere. No nation, however weak or
insignificant, has escaped or can escape the
bloody clutches of the great powers. ·

*Before World Council of Churches,
Bangkok, Jan. 2/
The Dallas Times Herald, 1-2:(A)4.*

Edwin O. Reischauer
*Professor, Harvard University; Former
United States Ambassador to Japan*

9

The greatest international problems are not

the balance of power and other military questions we have always focused on. Military might has gotten to the point where all you can do is destroy each other. War is a suicide pact. It is not a thinkable alternative to peace, as it once was.

Interview, Cambridge, Mass./
Los Angeles Times, 10-19:(2)7.

Charles S. Rhyne
President,
World Peace Through Law Center

1

The world's societies evolved law systems as a substitute for settlement of disputes by fighting. Likewise, in our nuclear age the international community must—if it is to exist and develop as a community—evolve a law system to replace the primitive solutions of balances of forces, war, haggling and plotting. Arms as a regulator of relations among nations has never worked. Every arms race has sooner or later, by accident or design, exploded into war. We must heed the message of history— that law is the only workable harness for power—and proceed to create that harness. Indeed, law is itself power, governing the behavior of men and nations more surely than coercive methods of force and threat of force.

At World Conference on World Peace
Through Law, Abidjan, Ivory Coast,
Aug. 27/Vital Speeches, 10-1:743.

Dean Rusk
Former Secretary of State
of the United States

2

. . . my generation came out of World War II with a rather simplistic answer—the notion of collective security. The next generation may have a much more complicated answer— no single theme as powerful as the notion of collective security. Maybe it will require action on many fronts. Maybe it's a whole bundle of sticks, no one of which will be decisive but which all together could in fact bring us nearer the durable peace which we must achieve. But we need more discussion about this, and I would like to see us address our-

selves to it in what might have been called, in an earlier stage, a great national debate, similar to the kind of national debate we had when we [the U.S.] went into NATO and went into the Marshall Plan and things of that sort . . . [The debate should be about] how the world is going to organize a peace in which these thousands of megatons will not be fired in anger, and what the component elements of that program for a durable peace ought to be. Unless we discuss that question in a realistic fashion, we're likely, through oversight or inertia or instinct, to drift back into a period of isolationism. I've said to some of my student friends that they will not improve their situation if they merely reject the mistakes of their fathers, merely to embrace the mistakes of their grandfathers. Their job is to find out what the answer of their generation is going to be to the question of organizing a durable peace.

Interview/The Washington Post, 8-5:(C)4.

Le Duc Tho
Member, North Vietnamese Politburo

3

I am a Communist and, according to Marxist-Leninist theories, so long as imperialism persists in the world, there will still be wars.

News conference, Paris, Jan. 24/
U.S. News & World Report, 2-5:18.

Kurt Waldheim
Secretary General of the
United Nations

4

In times of real danger—when confrontation seems to be leading inexorably into conflict—the great powers need the machinery of the United Nations for conciliation, for a settlement, even as a pretext for delay.

Before San Francisco United Nations
Association, San Francisco, Feb. 17/
Los Angeles Times, 2-21:(1)4.

5

The United Nations has increasingly become the last refuge of desperate governments, rather than the regular and orderly machinery for the settlement of disputes and

(KURT WALDHEIM)

the avoidance of conflict which its founding fathers intended it to be. This is an extremely dangerous trend.

San Francisco Examiner & Chronicle,
2-25:(This World)2.

1

Events at the United Nations reflect the realities of world politics. These realities are often difficult, unpleasant and uncomfortable. But any international policy which is not based upon global realities is doomed. To denigrate and ignore the United Nations because it reflects these realities is unwise and very dangerous.

The New York Times, 9-10:12.

2

We are a political organization in the first place. The United Nations was created in 1945 for political reasons, and it is evident that we have to stick to this purpose. Of course, economic, social and humanitarian aspects are very important, because if there is no economic stability in the world, we cannot expect that there will be political stability. But the main purpose was, is and always will be, political.

News conference, New York, Sept. 17/
The New York Times, 9-18:9.

Earl Warren
Former Chief Justice
of the United States

3

In his Inaugural Address, President Nixon declared that "the time has passed when America will make every other nation's con-

flict our own." A determination to refrain from unilateral assertions of our power should have the support of us all. But if the policy is to have any real meaning in a world where conflicts abound, there must be increased efforts to build better multilateral methods for building and keeping the peace. The multilateral half of any effective policy of unilateral restraint is not yet in evidence.

Before United Nations Association/
The New York Times, 2-12:27.

4

In these days when communications are so swift and pervasive, the people need no longer be led blindly into war. They can make up their own minds. It is fair to ask, I believe, if the people of the United States would have gone to war on the other side of the world in Indochina, which cost us over fifty thousands of lives and between $100- and $200-billion, if they had been given the right to assert their will.

At World Law Day dinner,
Oakland, Calif., Nov. 6/
San Francisco Examiner, 11-7:5.

Theodore H. White
Author, Historian

5

[U.S. President] Nixon believes peace is a deal: You don't fight me, I don't fight you; this is your turf, this is mine. It's a cold-blooded way to make peace, but he's done more than any other President since World War II . . .

Interview, New York/
The Christian Science Monitor, 8-1:11.

PART THREE

General

The Arts

Jacques Barzun
President, National Institute of
Arts and Letters (United States)

1

. . . the arts are kept alive by the concurrent energies of a great variety of talents, and not by geniuses alone. It is an illusion to suppose that the great genius, who by definition is unique, isolated and infrequent, could by himself insure the continuity of culture. It is therefore foolish to look askance at the coming together of the lesser geniuses and the higher talents in institutions and academies. These groups exist, not to create and revolutionize—no *group* can do that—but to connect and sustain.

At Ceremonial of American Academy of
Arts and Letters and National Institute
of Arts and Letters, May 16/
The New York Times, 5-27:(2)19.

Cecil Beaton
Author
Photographer, Designer

2

It [a return to tradition] has happened in the arts. Art students in London no longer drop a motor bicycle off the top of a building to make a sculpture. There was a time when they splashed paint on a canvas, rolled in it to make a picture. There is a realization that all that isn't valid any more. Young students are learning to draw, constructing careful, almost pre-Raphaelite drawings of a fern, say. They are thoughtful; they no longer look for a new gimmick. So-called sophistication is absolutely out. They are getting back to the simple rules of the craft.

Interview, Beverly Hills, Calif./
Los Angeles Times, 4-20:(4)12.

Harry Belafonte
Singer

3

Yes, President Nixon has more than doubled the [U.S.] Federal subsidy for the arts; but why is so much noise being raised for so little? It is indeed more than the nothing of only a few years ago; but it's not even enough to make a visible splash in the cultural capital of New York. Our country now spends 18 cents a person on the arts. Canada spends $1.40. West Germany leads the nations in this situation with $2.42. And the city of Vienna itself contributes $5.50 per person.

At National Press Club, Washington,
June 18/The Washington Post, 6-19:(B)8.

Michael Caine
British actor

4

[Criticizing the recent U.S. Supreme Court decision that individual states and localities must determine local standards for obscenity and pornography]: I believe people are entitled to make pornography, and those who want to are entitled to see it, providing young people—and by that I don't mean young adults—are protected. Setting up watch committees, local censors and the like is merely putting power back into the hands of local bigots and despots. We have them here in England. Anyone over 21 who wants to see a scene of explicit sex should be able to do so. To say it corrupts and depraves is nonsense.

San Francisco Chronicle, 8-7:40.

Emanuel Celler
Former United States Representative,
D-New York

5

To many Americans and to members of Congress, the idea of government support for

455

(EMANUEL CELLER)

the arts—and particularly the opera—may seem quite novel . . . We pledged $1 billion to protect investors against losses from Wall Street purchases. But we are niggardly when it comes to supporting art forms. It is startling to know that every time the curtain goes up at the Metropolitan [Opera], management loses $16,000.

Washington, March 15/
The Washington Post, 3-16:(B)8.

Marc Chagall
Painter

1

In every work of art there is both happiness and anguish; if you listen to Schubert, you find anguish. In love there's lots of anguish, but it's no good without the happiness. In painting, nowadays, you see a lot of anguish, but not much quality.

Interview,
Saint-Paul de Vence, France/
"W": a Fairchild publication, 9-7:14.

Schuyler Chapin
General manager,
Metropolitan Opera, New York

2

Unless the Federal government steps up with money, I don't see where support for institutions like this is going to come from. We are seeing the end of the era of private philanthropy. If somebody came here and said, "You may have what you want from the government," I would very simply ask for 20 per cent of my gross deficit—I'll take care of raising the other 80 per cent. This is not an unfair figure. Currently, we get from all public funds—Federal, state and city—$500,000 out of a $25-million-a-year budget. *Not* very much. Do you know what we pay for the upkeep of this building alone? Two million bucks a year. Nobody sees any of that on stage!

Interview, New York/
The New York Times Magazine, 9-23:53.

Salvador Dali
Painter

3

. . . right now I'm the greatest [painter]. I don't say this through vanity. It's just that the rest are so bad.

Madrid, May 29/
The Washington Post, 5-31:(C)5.

Naum Gabo
Sculptor

4

What I am trying to convey in my art is something of my consciousness that is neglected by science. The sciences are practical. Although there is an aesthetic sense in science —mathematics, for example, has its own kind of poetry, and many scientists even say that they are artists—basically, science is not connected with our feelings. Art has to do with our actual awareness of life, and it can affect our state of mind to such a degree that whatever we do in a practical way will be done better. Art and science are actions of our consciousness which come from the same roots, but they go in different paths. The scientist observes the world, thus separating himself from it and looking at it as an outsider. As an artist you do not observe the world, you live it, you experience it. Nothing is outside you. It is always coming from inside. If we could educate people to handle life in the same way as an artist handles his work, we would be enjoying life, you know, enormously more than we do now; because most of the time we are preoccupied only with our practical concerns. But we should actually have developed our sensitiveness to such a degree that, whatever we do, we do it as an art, as an artistic action.

Interview/
The Christian Science Monitor, 11-14:23.

Nancy Hanks
Chairman, National Endowment
for the Arts of the United States

5

[The] national awareness of the vital role of the arts has come not from some edict from Washington or any of the state capitals.

It has come, rather, from the interest of people in all of the arts, not just the traditional established forms. It has come from the involvement of people participating in cultural activities, and not merely being observers. It has come from a recognition that the description of "art" as a painting hanging, or dance on a stage, is inadequate, to say the least. It has come from an understanding that, as we move toward our third century, the pursuit of happiness, which was given equal billing in the Declaration [of Independence] as an inalienable right along with life and liberty, has been neglected.

Before Senate Appropriations Subcommittee,
Washington, April 12/
The Hollywood Reporter, 4-13:4.
1

It's exciting that so many people are getting involved in the arts. Every Congressman wants to get behind the arts bill because of what he hears from his own district. And after all, the bill is about joy and giving pleasure —not about baling out a folding aircraft company.

Newsweek, 12-24:86.

Thomas P. F. Hoving
Director,
Metropolitan Museum of Art, New York
2

I began as a collector, and my instincts are still there. When I see something I want, I do everything I can to get it. I've bought $300 million worth of stuff since I've been here [at the Museum], and I've never made a mistake . . . I'm a breed that won't happen again—not because of genius, but because of treaties and other complications. In the last waning hours of this thing, I will go through kafuffle to get the great objects.

Newsweek, 3-12:86.

Sol Hurok
Impresario
3

The Soviet Union is really popularizing the arts and music. Tickets to theatres and concerts are popularly priced. The best seat at the Bolshoi Opera House in Moscow costs three rubles [about $3.50]. The same thing applies to Germany; they spend a lot of money on the arts. In Austria [Vienna], every ticket costs the government more than half. Paris, too. We [the U.S.] are very much behind. We are beginning to appreciate the fact that we have to support the arts, but it is not fullheartedly.

Interview, New York/
The Christian Science Monitor, 5-17:(B)8.

Pauline Kael
Film critic, "The New Yorker" magazine
4

In the arts, the critic is the only independent source of information. The rest is advertising.

Newsweek, 12-24:96.

Yousuf Karsh
Portrait photographer
5

All I know is that within every man and woman a secret is hidden; and as a photographer it is my task to reveal it if I can. The revelation, if it comes at all, will come in a small fraction of a second with an unconscious gesture, gleam of the eye, a brief lifting of the mask that all humans wear to conceal their innermost selves from the world. In that fleeting interval of opportunity, the photographer must act or lose his prize.

Los Angeles Times, 3-9:(4)6.

Eric Larrabee
Executive director,
New York State Council on the Arts
6

The arts are the most precise and penetrating means of communication we have. Each artistic event is unique and self-contained: It cannot be explained by something else. Robert Frost was asked one time what one of his poems meant, and he answered: "If I could say it some other way, I wouldn't have had to write the poem." The Soviet government's fear of its poets and novelists is fully justified, for they cannot be countered; they can only be silenced. The artist informs us about the natural and man-made world. There is a sense

(ERIC LARRABEE)

in which we do not see or listen until the artist tells us to. How many ever noticed that the shadows cast by sunlight on snow were colored blue, until the impressionist painters showed us so? How many ever looked at decaying doorways and abandoned houses until photographers like Walker Evans taught us how? How many ever took seriously the environment of neon and billboards which is our natural habitat until the pop artist rubbed our noses in it?

At Memorial Art Gallery, Rochester, N.Y./
The New York Times, 9-2:(4)13.

1

The arts in this country [the U.S.] are, in fact, on a starvation diet. The institutions which nurture them are crushed between rising costs and rising demand for their services, and burdened as a result with income gaps which grow greater each year of continued inflation. Those that are lucky enough to have endowments are eating them away in the struggle to stay alive. Artists as professionals continue to be underpaid almost beyond belief, at levels which would horrify a self-respecting garbage collector.

Newsweek, 12-24:86.

Frank Lloyd
Owner, Marlborough Galleries, New York

2

I don't give a damn what anybody says. There's only one measure of success in running a [art] gallery: making money. Any dealer who says it's not is a hypocrite or will soon be closing his doors.

The New York Times, 5-21:40.

Zubin Mehta
Musical director,
Los Angeles Philharmonic Orchestra

3

No [U.S.] President has given as much as [President] Nixon to cultural affairs. He has even instituted what amounts to the first secretary for cultural affairs. Congress, on the other hand, seems unwilling to give as much

as the President to cultural affairs. Now, I don't know if Nixon is doing it because it is good politically for him—but it is certainly good for us.

Montreal/
Los Angeles Herald-Examiner, 9-16:(E)7.

Thomas Messer
Director, Guggenheim Museum, New York

4

[On the death of artist Pablo Picasso]: Not only is the art of the first half of this century unthinkable without Picasso, but I suspect the world itself would have been different and quite unimaginable without him.

April 8/The New York Times, 4-9:47.

Henry Miller
Author

5

[On the U.S. Supreme Court's ruling that local areas must determine obscenity and pornography standards]: The tenor of the times is totally against it. Never have we had such freedom of expression. I don't see how we can go backward. The Court is being very unrealistic.

Interview, California/
The Washington Post, 6-22:(B)9.

Robert Nathan
Author

6

. . . I have come to believe that art is a communication informing man of his own dignity and of the value of his life—whether in joy or grief, whether in laughter or indignation, duty or terror. Terror can be a catharsis. Indignation can dignify life . . . On the other hand, the communication which belittles man or dishonors him, though it may be thoughtful, is not thought—it is simply an exercise in malice; and in the great line between art and malice, there are only happenings. Man needs the comfort of his own dignity . . . and that's what the artist is for—to give him that comfort.

At Los Angeles Library Association's
Author's Luncheon/
Los Angeles Times, 4-8:(8)16.

Harry S. Parker III
Director-designate,
Dallas Museum of Fine Arts

1

A museum should try to involve all elements of the community, and that means anyone who has an interest in responding to art. It should be an open place, organized in a way so that everyone who wants to be part of it can . . . In order to get people to the museum you must generate a quality of excitement and a belief that a museum is not just a tourist point. As for specific ways to get people into a museum, you must first have an exciting permanent collection and then an equally exciting temporary exhibition program. Then, once you have those things, you can't hide the museum. People must be informed about what is going on, through the media and by word of mouth. You must let people know what you have and how it relates to them—that's an area that most museums are weakest in today. You must communicate why the art work you have is exciting; people must know about it and have exposure to it. There is a need to teach and a popular instruction job to be done.

Interview, New York/
The Dallas Times Herald, 10-14:(J)1.

Robert Scull
Art collector and patron

2

Art has all the aesthetics that we attribute to it, and all the culture, but it also has all the value. People are finally beginning to understand that maybe art is more powerful than gold. Art is a commodity that has to be treated with great respect, and there's nothing wrong with that. I think it's unique. You know, there are very few Jackson Pollocks around; there are very few Jasper Johns around; and if people want to own them, let them understand that great art is worth money. Why should art be on the low ring of international commodities? I think that art ought to be on top . . . Once you own art, you realize its tremendous value, its power, its ability to change your life, to make you think in terms of other things than crass commercial products. I think that art has the ability to ennoble a person, to involve a person with higher concerns than the usual commodities that are traded around the world. Art is like food. It's necessary to our spirits to be involved in art.

Interview, New York/
The Christian Science Monitor, 10-20:16.

William R. Tolbert, Jr.
President of Liberia

3

Art is an example of human skills and imagination. Through art lies communication. It makes us understand who we are and what it is to be human.

Washington, June 5/
The Washington Post, 6-6:(B)1.

Fashion

Hardy Amies
Fashion designer

1

To be radically new would be suicide in men's clothes. Men are more reluctant now than ever to accept a change of fashion.

Los Angeles Times, 5-10:(4)25.

Cecil Beaton
Author, Photographer, Designer

2

[On what he calls the ugly "clog" shoes of the 1940s which are appearing again today]: That is a terrible fashion. It reflects what is popular now—a sort of tackiness. You've got to be sleazy to have The Look. My opinion is that, if something is ugly, why bring it back? Luckily, this is on the way out. I see a reversion to tradition.

*Interview, Beverly Hills, Calif./
Los Angeles Times, 4-20:(4)12.*

Bill Blass
Fashion designer

3

The Current Look [in men's fashions in the U.S.] is more reminiscent of America than of England. We are looking back in fashion, but in an American way. Men are showing more interest in clothes, and I suppose it took the revolution of the 1960s to get the confidence that they have now. I think it interesting to note throughout the world the interest in America. Call it the Gatsby Look or the something of the 1920s, but it is an American look.

*Interview, New York/
The Dallas Times Herald, 2-5:(C)2.*

Joyce Brothers
Psychologist

4

I think that one of the things about any-

body's clothing is that he wears it to be noticed. In a field of daisies, one daisy is lost. That is one reason why a man might wear a bow tie—to stand out from the others who wear four-in-hands . . . In the past, a man dressed to impress a woman with the fact he could make a living for her. The more prosperous he looked, the more attractive he was. It showed he could go out and fight the world. Once, cavemen demonstrated this by wearing wild-animal skins. The caveman who wore them looked as if he could support a wife and propagate children. And this was part of the process of natural selection whereby the best survived. But now, women can support themselves. So men wear clothes that promise love and pleasure, rather than property and status. And I might say that women at all times dress with some man in mind—father, boyfriend, husband, even other men to stimulate her husband to notice her.

*Interview, New York/
San Francisco Examiner, 8-13:25.*

Oleg Cassini
Fashion designer

5

I'm a loner . . . an outdoor man. I'm the John Wayne of the dress business, and I'm still Number One whether they like it or not. I have star quality. All the things in my personal life have made me an image, while some designers remain faceless blobs.

*Interview, Detroit/
San Francisco Examiner, 9-3:15.*

Andre Courreges
Fashion designer

6

In the world of couture, evolution is slow; but this is a blessing. Anything good takes time to grow. The best vineyards, the best plants—new species do not grow overnight

. . . Someone capable of true creation is not born every day. Chanel is the Number One creative designer of our times. Most other designers are not that original. Many look for inspiration to the past. Any true creator in any field is a person who looks to the future.

Beverly Hills, Calif./
Los Angeles Times, 10-5:(4)2.

Oscar de la Renta
Fashion designer; President,
Council of Fashion Designers in America

1

For a long time, most European women have been interested in American fashion. It's been almost impossible for us [Americans] to bring our lines to Europe on a competitive basis. Now, with the dollar devaluation, it should be easier for us to compete. I see nothing now to stop the European buyer from coming to America to buy.

Los Angeles/
Los Angeles Times, 3-19:(4)11.

Erte
Fashion designer

2

Up until the 19th century, when women wore one fashion style—like lace or jewelry —the men wore them, too. This formed a beautiful image of men and women together, complementing each other in their dress styles. But from the 19th century the men began dressing in dark colors, even at night in black with tails; they all looked like a lot of waiters. At the same time, the ladies were brilliant with colors and diamonds and feathers and everything. It made me think that harmony should come back . . . I think that one of the achievements of unisex [fashions] is that it has brought about more harmony between the sexes. It makes things easier socially and sexually. Before, there was a terrible frontier and division between the two sexes.

Los Angeles/
The Washington Post, 12-16:(K)6.

Anne Fogarty
Fashion designer

3

The only thing that is out of fashion is spending a great deal of money on clothes. Ostentation is never fashionable. I know a great many women are spending $995 for a dress. But that's snobbery; or insecurity. That's not style. I've fought to keep my prices from $56 to $150. You can have great style for a very little amount of money. All you need is taste.

Los Angeles/
Los Angeles Times, 10-25:(4)8.

Rudi Gernreich
Fashion designer

4

[In the future,] people will want to look anonymous to distract attention. To attract attention invites violence and is an invasion of your privacy. People, therefore, will wear uniforms in public life . . . [But at home] in their own surroundings, where they are not challenged by hostility from strangers, people are expressing themselves freely in the way they dress.

New York/
The Christian Science Monitor, 5-25:10.

Halston
Fashion designer

5

Fashion is made by fashionable people. Designers only suggest. It is the way the client buys and edits clothing from a collection that makes it *a la mode.* The clientele tells you everything.

San Francisco, Sept. 15/
San Francisco Examiner, 9-17:26.

Edith Head
Fashion designer

6

No woman should leave a [clothes] store unless photographed from the rear. Then you'd see fewer women in pants. There should be a tag saying, "This is good for size 8, 10 and 12, but not for 14 or 16." The same dress can't be becoming to both sizes. This

461

(EDITH HEAD)

great fashion freedom is not a good thing. I think people are happier with rules.

Interview, Los Angeles/
Los Angeles Times, 4-1:(Calendar)17.

Mr. John
Fashion designer

1

Don't date your clothes by year or season. Forget Mardi Gras trends and gimmicks and seasonal extremes. Select things that can be in fashion any time, any month, for many years. A best-dressed woman can go into her closet blindfolded and be sure she will grab something appropriate, even if it's three years old.

San Francisco, Feb. 6/
San Francisco Examiner, 2-7:23.

Betsey Johnson
Fashion designer

2

I want people to talk to me with their clothes—to be fun to look at. I want to see people with their left sides different from their rights. I want people to look like a walking piece of sculpture. I want people to take chances, stop and feel, experiment, sparkle in the daytime, be red, shocking pink, magenta, chartreuse, yellow.

New York/
Los Angeles Times, 5-28:(4)1.

Charles Revson
Chairman, Revlon, Inc.

3

I have often said that in beauty, as in fashion, I believe in evolution—not revolution. I think the past has a lot to do with the present; and that's why we predict that my interpretation of the F. Scott Fitzgerald era will be significant. It should be one of the freshest looks in a long time, because it will launch the great comeback of femininity. Once again, a woman will be able to feel fashionable in the most feminine of all colors —pink . . .

"W": a Fairchild publication, 2-9:19.

Yves Saint Laurent
Fashion designer

4

In couture, one dress is a unique piece because of the price, the value, the workmanship. Yet, the most important mood of fashion today is the mix, the freedom to change, the melange. That is why it is so difficult to design for the couture. But I like difficulties.

Interview, Paris/
The Dallas Times Herald, 1-5:(D)1.

Vidal Sassoon
Hair stylist

5

[On long hair for men]: Fortunately, it doesn't mean anything any more. Hair is making a social statement, but from a point of fashion. We have come a long way from the youths who wore so much long hair it became a uniform—its own form of uniformity.

San Francisco Examiner & Chronicle,
7-15:(This World)2.

6

Hair is the only substance that grows in human form that you can mold, shape and cut to suit the individual body structure. It's a gutsy profession—and I love it.

Interview, Beverly Hills, Calif./
Los Angeles Times, 11-22:(4)25.

Elizabeth Taylor
Actress

7

I rarely buy couture clothes now because fashion changes so much. I don't think there is a set sort of style any more. That went out when Christian Dior died: the total look that encompassed everything—the hat, the gloves, the right handbag, the right shoes . . . Now you can almost get away with anything. I think it's rather nice and a lot of fun that you can create your own styles and that it doesn't have to cost you a lot of money.

Interview/
Ladies Home Journal, February:145.

John Weitz
Fashion designer

1

Clothes do not make the man. Achievement makes the man. But clothes can make a positive statement, express a man's personality in small, subtle ways.

Dallas/
The Dallas Times Herald,
10-28:(E)6.

Journalism

Spiro T. Agnew
Vice President of the United States

1

. . . some prestigious media spokesmen can be read and heard almost daily expressing fear for the future of the First Amendment. They assert that the American people are being kept in the dark by a deceptive government. A national network newsman has referred to an Administration "conspiracy" against the people's right to know. It is hard to find any factual basis for this hysteria. Almost nothing goes on in government that is not examined, re-examined, plumbed, analyzed, guessed about, criticized and caricatured by the media. All this affects the American people, as it should. But that doesn't mean that they necessarily accept it as revealed truth. They are not going to automatically embrace a [Harry] Reasoner dissertation, a [Carl] Rowan column or a Herblock cartoon any more than they automatically embrace a Nixon or a [Senator George] McGovern thesis . . . The fact is that the Nixon Administration is no more desirous of nor more capable of curtailing freedom of the press in America than any of its predecessors. On the contrary, despite the exaggerated and ill-founded charges of past decades regarding various Administrations' reigns of terror, news coverage of government today is more intensive than ever before in American history.

Before Minnesota Newspaper Association,
Minneapolis, Feb. 23/
Human Events, 3-17:12.

2

I haven't changed my basic opinions about the fact that bias still remains in segments of the most prestigious media . . . I don't think that one can say that *The New York Times* or *The Washington Post* are balanced publications. I don't think that the [broadcast] networks are balanced in their ideology. I don't

think there's a nickel's worth of difference between what Eric Sevareid thinks and what Walter Cronkite thinks. I think they see very much eye-to-eye. And I would like to see more balance in the commentary that comes out.

Interview, Washington/
The Christian Science Monitor, 3-30:7.

3

[Arguing against a blanket shield law to protect the confidentiality of newsmen's sources]: Now, I want a free press; I believe very much in a free press. But how can you say that reporters should have a shield law, a blanket shield law, that allows one of these reporters to refuse to give evidence before a grand jury? I don't see how you can get at the truth. How do you protect the 14th Amendment rights of the average citizen who is entitled to due process if he can't confront his accusers? . . . one must remember that we are talking very limitedly about grand-jury proceedings. Now, that's a private, a secret meeting. It is not the same as if it were spread all over the place. I think that, if a reporter's testimony is absolutely necessary to protect the rights of an individual against criminal accusations, then it is unconscionable to say that investigative reporting of that incident is more important than that man's right to keep from being convicted . . . Until the reporter has written his story, he's absolutely protected. But when he's ready to go public with an accusation of criminal conduct or very reprehensible conduct, at that point I think the person accused has the right to know what the source of the accusation is.

Interview, Washington/
The Christian Science Monitor, 3-30:7.

4

When government officials defend themselves from what they consider unfair slanting of news stories, the partisan newsman, outraged at unaccustomed criticism, too often hurls the counter-accusation of "repression" and "censorship." The news media really must learn to get over being so thin-skinned—particularly when they are so intolerant of thin-skinned officials.

At Freedom Forum, Harding College, Searcy, Ark., April 12/ The Washington Post, 4-13:(A)16.

George Anastapio
Professor of Law, University of Chicago

1

I do not know of a time in this century when the press [in the U.S.] has been so free as it has been the past five years. Despite the government threats, I still do not know of a professional journalist who would not publish secret documents or back down from a jail sentence if it means a good story.

At University of Dallas, April 27/ The Dallas Times Herald, 4-29:(A)23.

Harry S. Ashmore
Pulitzer Prize-winning journalist; President, Center for the Study of Democratic Institutions

2

There are going to be times when the media will be unpopular. It must go against the public pulse because the public is often wrong. The media have the role of arguing public policy. That is what editorial pages are for, and they are liable to be unpopular.

San Francisco Examiner & Chronicle, 4-29:(This World)2.

Benjamin C. Bradlee
Executive editor, "The Washington Post"

3

I think televised [Presidential] press conferences may be over the hill. Any President with any skill plays the press like a harp. Kennedy did it . . . so does Nixon.

Panel discussion sponsored by Columbia University Graduate School of Journalism, New York, Nov. 8/ San Francisco Examiner, 11-9:11.

Leonid I. Brezhnev
General Secretary, Communist Party of the Soviet Union

4

[On news conferences]: I don't like the question-and-answer system. A meeting with the press is not a school exam. A free discussion is better than just shooting questions. Journalists always ask too many questions.

News conference, Moscow/Time, 6-25:32.

David Brinkley
News commentator, National Broadcasting Company

5

There are numerous countries in the world where the politicians have seized absolute power and muzzled the press. There is no country in the world where the press has seized absolute power and muzzled the politicians.

Quote, 4-1:289.

Patrick J. Buchanan
Special Consultant to the President of the United States

6

. . . like the railroads at around the turn of the century, the [broadcast] networks in the United States have gained a position of power and dominance over the flow of ideas and information to the American people which I think is excessive. Now, the networks and the newspapers, the dominant newspapers—*The Washington Post* Company, *The New York Times*—have a tremendous power in this society to influence opinion. In our judgment, just as the First Amendment gives you [journalists] the right of a free press, the right of freedom of speech to criticize us, to say that the President of the United States is not doing a good job, so we [in government] can exercise the same freedom to say that the networks are not doing a good job, *The New York Times*, for example, might not be doing a good job, and *The Washington Post* might not be doing a good job. I think the First Amendment is a two-way street, as applies to

465

(PATRICK J. BUCHANAN)

us as well as to you.

Television interview/
"Morning News,"
Columbia Broadcasting System, 10-29.

Dean Burch
Chairman, Federal Communications
Commission of the United States

1

No matter how politicized a man is, he must leave politics behind in this job. I feel the government should stay the hell out of the news business, and I think this is a conservative position. What the hell is the cure for news objectivity? Is the cure for the FCC or some other government agency to authenticate the news? I really doubt it. We're aware of what both the President [Nixon] and the Congress think; but this is a regulatory agency which must have credibility. We don't make the law; we interpret it.

Interview/Variety, 2-21:28.

2

The Fairness Doctrine is the law of the land; has been practically since the inception of regulated communications in 1934. Admittedly, it's an imperfect instrument. Also, it's an intrusion on the broadcast journalist which the print journalist doesn't have to put up with. But the TV newsmen are public trustees and they are not to determine what the public is to see and hear, absolutely. They have to make sure the public has an opportunity to make up its own mind. I'm afraid that, under the rules of the game now, it's a burden the broadcasters will have to put up with.

Interview/TV Guide, 4-28:38.

John Chancellor
News commentator,
National Broadcasting Company

3

. . . we are living in a slightly different climate for journalism in America today than we did before the Vice President [Agnew] and this [Nixon] Administration made their attacks on us. One of the changes that I

perceive is that we may all be doing our jobs better because the Administration has accused us of being biased against them . . . there is more attention paid to the Administration because we are trying to answer to our own ethical standards—those standards having been brought into question by the Administration. It was, in fact, more relaxed in previous Administrations, and I think in some ways we may be doing a better job.

Panel discussion, New York/
The New York Times, 3-12:29.

4

. . . [U.S.] President Nixon virtually abandoned the press conference as a way of informing the people of his policies. I think the people have a right to see their President in action. And the press conference is a good direct way. Maybe not all of the conferences should be on the air—the President should be given room to choose his own options depending upon informational necessities. For instance, complicated material might best be presented in the East Room with no cameras, lots of experts. But if there are no complicated matters to explain, why not have the President submit himself to reporters, who are, after all, the surrogates of the people? . . . The institution of the press conference has begun to look bad under the Nixon Administration, and we are now in danger of losing something that is very important. When I was director of the Voice of America, I used to beg for press conferences because they were the best way of informing people abroad about the Presidency. I believe that the report function of the President is an essential one.

Interview, New York/
The Christian Science Monitor, 12-27:(B)6.

5

I don't think you can report the news on television without adding elements of your own personality, experience and judgment. I call it perspective, and it is sometimes confused by some people with commentary. I try not to comment on the news; but I do try to put things in perspective. I think a broadcaster ought to go beyond a mere recitation of that day's events.

Interview, New York/
The Christian Science Monitor, 12-27:(B)6.

Alistair Cooke
Chief United States correspondent,
"The Manchester (England) Guardian"

1

[Criticizing the Nixon Administration for its criticism of the press]: . . . this to me is a real threat to the First Amendment. It's the worst in my time. There do not seem to be enough people in power in the Administration—and I have my misgivings even about the courts—that realize you cannot tamper with the First Amendment. The moment you tamper with it, it falls apart. So you really have to lean over backwards and give people ludicrous expression. America's been getting a reputation as a bully, as a kind of military mammoth. But what would be much worse would be that America was afraid that its press was censored. The International Press Institute not long ago looked at the press of some 126-odd countries, decided that there were 20 that were free. But they actually had a warning note about the United States, of all the free ones.

Interview, New York/
The Christian Science Monitor, 4-26:9.

2

If [U.S. President] Nixon says the press is out to get him, he's absolutely right. We refer to a checks and balances system—a most unfortunate phrase. I prefer the term, "watchdog system." Under it, the Congress watches the President and the Supreme Court watches the Congress and the press is out to get all of them.

Before Women's National Democratic
Club, Washington, May 29/
The Washington Post, 5-30:(B)2.

Alan Cranston
United States Senator, D-California

3

[Advocating a bill to protect newsmen's confidential news sources]: A democracy can't operate unless the people have pretty good access to information about what's going on in the government . . . That's the basic issue here . . . Thomas Jefferson said that, if he had to choose between having a government and having a free press, he would choose the free press. I think the two are inseparable. You can't have a democracy, you can't have a republic like ours, without a free press that is operating freely.

Los Angeles Times, 1-30:(1)22.

Walter Cronkite
News commentator,
Columbia Broadcasting System

4

What I object to in the criticism [of the news media] from the White House is not the fact that there is criticism, not even the fact that they would try to raise their own credibility by attacking ours. But what has happened is that this [Nixon] Administration, through what I believe to be a considered and concerted campaign, has managed to politicize the issue of the press vs. the Administration to the point that now we come to the real crunch, which is the matter of our actual freedoms to operate, our freedom to criticize, our right to do that; our ability to function as journalists without harassment by an offended grand jury, whether it be county, state or Federal, or an investigative unit of the Federal government. We've come to that dangerous state now with the press in a position that to defend the right of the people to know—that is, to defend freedom of speech and press—is to somehow or other be anti-Administration. Thus politicizing the issue, they have again proved to be highly divisive in this society, and have created two Americas—one that believes in freedom of speech and press and one that doesn't. That's a vast over-simplification, of course; but still, when you get to the heart of it, we're down to that kind of a basic. And that is what concerns me today—the trend in this direction.

Panel discussion, New York/
The New York Times, 3-12:29.

5

I think that, in seeking truth, you have to get both sides of a story. In fact, I don't

(WALTER CRONKITE)

merely think, I *insist* that we present both sides of a story. It's perfectly all right to have first-person journalism; I'm all for muckraking journalism; I'm all for the sidebar, the eyewitness story, the impression piece. But the basic function of the press has to be the presentation of all the facts on which the story is based. There are no pros and cons as far as the press is concerned. There shouldn't be. There are only the facts. Advocacy is all right in special columns. But how the hell are you going to give people the basis on which to advocate something if you don't present the facts to them? If you go only for advocacy journalism, you're really assuming unto yourself a privilege that was never intended anywhere in the definition of a free press.

Interview,
New York/Playboy, June:76.

1

I think the [U.S.] Presidential press conference as now being conducted is not adequate in any way. It permits the President to use it as he pleases. He has complete control of whom he calls upon . . . What would really open it up would be if the President would conduct the 11 o'clock briefing himself. Let him invite the regular White House press corps—those correspondents who are there all day—into his Oval Office every morning and brief them personally. Why shouldn't he do it? Of course, the President is busy. Of course, he is probably the most over-worked man in the world. Of course, this would be a drain on him. But what is more important than the President of the United States having a constant liaison with the people of the United States? . . . if the President did a very brief session every morning and then met the entire press corps of the world, in the same way, every three months, nobody would have any complaints.

Interview,
New York/
The Christian Science Monitor,
10-26:(B)8.

Sam Cook Digges
President,
Columbia Broadcasting System Radio

2

[Criticizing "advocacy reporting"]: Those few [journalists] who would pervert their profession are like bacteria in a can of soup that causes botulism . . . [In the old days,] anyone who would have colored a story to fit his own ideology would have been considered in the same category as a common thief. As far as I am concerned, the comparison still holds. In addition to being corrupt, they are lazy. They are not interested in hard-hitting, factual investigative reporting—that takes work. They would rather cut corners, thinking they are twisting minds by twisting facts.

At University of Missouri School
of Journalism/Variety, 4-18:57.

Grant Dillman
Vice president and Washington bureau
manager, United Press International

3

Consider the news explosion . . . Datelines flood in today from Anloc, Amman, Da Nang, Damascus, Kano, Seoul, Taipei, Tel Aviv and Zambia, not to mention the traditional capitals of Rome, London, Paris and Moscow. And now Peking is joining the list . . . Thirty years ago, we were strangers to words like ecology, urban decay, deterrent capability, consumerism, participatory democracy and priestly celibacy . . . For better or worse, the problem promises to grow, and as our society becomes more and more complex, so will the problem of reporting it. Most Americans are weary of problems, and they resent the news media calling these problems to their attention.

Before Blue Pencil Club of Ohio,
Columbus, May 20/
The Dallas Times Herald, 5-21:(A)20.

Robert G. Dixon
Assistant Attorney General
of the United States

4

[Expressing the Nixon Administration's opposition to an absolute press shield law which would protect the confidentiality of a reporter's news sources]: Power without accountability is always dangerous, whether it be of the government, of big business, of big labor or of the press. We oppose an absolute privilege, because it would not even attempt to balance the competing and legitimate interest in open disclosure—so vital to the public, the government, the criminal defendant and others—against the blanket claim of total press secrecy.

Before Senate Judiciary Constitutional Rights Subcommittee, Washington, March 13/Los Angeles Times, 3-14:(1)6.

Thomas F. Eagleton
United States Senator, D-Missouri

1

[Saying newsmen should have the right to keep their sources confidential]: Some individuals may well have to pay the price of being the target of erroneous journalism . . . this is the price which simply must be paid in order not to jeopardize the free flow of news.

Before Senate Constitutional Rights Subcommittee, Washington, Feb. 21/The New York Times, 2-22:10.

Sam J. Ervin, Jr.
United States Senator, D-North Carolina

2

[Advocating legislation to protect reporters' news sources]: [In many cases,] if sources of information cannot be assured of anonymity, chances are they will not come forward. It is rather ironic, I think, that the reporters themselves are the ones who ultimately are jailed for refusal to reveal sources of stories which the public would never have been aware of had not the reporter himself decided to publish.

The Washington Post, 2-5:(A)4.

3

If we have a free press, then it follows that it will not always be "responsible." Any attempt by government to make it more "responsible" inevitably makes it less free. It is clear that the press does not always live up to the standards which editorial writers like to ascribe to it. I doubt if anyone in this room

feels that any of the nightly news programs or weekly news magazines is totally unbiased. But what might appear to some as a smirk on the face of [news commentator] Walter Cronkite might appear to others as an indication of sympathy. Bias, like beauty, is largely in the eyes of the beholder. If you don't think a television news show represents the truth, you can turn off your TV. If you don't think a magazine represents the truth, you can cancel your subscription. You have the right to expose yourself to whatever information you want. But to have the government prescribing what the truth is or limiting the information available for the citizen is contrary to the First Amendment.

At Texas Tech University/ The National Observer, 4-21:13.

William Farr
"Los Angeles Times" reporter who spent time in jail for refusing to divulge his news sources

4

[Advocating a shield law that would protect the confidentiality of a reporter's news sources]: . . . we do not want the legal right to protect sources as a favor to any newsman or all newsmen. We want such legislation to further the constructive processes of the press, so that the public will be fully and intelligently informed.

Before House Judiciary Subcommittee, Washington, March 7/ Los Angeles Times, 3-8:(1)12.

Fred W. Friendly
Professor of Journalism, Columbia University; Former president, Columbia Broadcasting System News

5

I think what has been proposed [by the White House for broadcast journalism] is chilling. The problem is that three different elements have been combined in a single package. Criticism from the White House—there is nothing wrong with that. Brandishing the "Fairness Doctrine"—that a station has to allow opposing views on important public questions—is all right, too. Threatening license rev-

(FRED W. FRIENDLY)

ocation is also all right. But when all three of these things are linked together in an attack from the Executive Branch of government —obviously with the President's [Nixon] knowledge and permission—then it does not bode well . . . I happen to take great pride in what broadcast journalism has accomplished in and after World War II, when Edward R. Murrow, Elmer Davis and Raymond Swing were all functioning in a different atmosphere. I don't want to see it all return to the Dark Ages that I remember in the early '30s, when there really was no such thing as broadcast journalism—just information conveyors. The [Nixon] Administration wants to make broadcasting a sterile form in which no aggressive investigative journalism and news analysis can take place.

Interview/
U.S. News & World Report, 2-19:51.

1

In the early days of radio, there used to be a few broadcasters who really used to sell their views, and who were in the business of being both reporters and editorialists. That doesn't go on now. I could count on my hand the number of times when Walter Cronkite has given personal opinion. I don't think that any broadcasters that I know of in network news abuse that right. They try not to. I remember once Dwight Eisenhower walked over to me when Cronkite and the former President were doing an interview, and President Eisenhower said to me: "What are Cronkite's politics?" I said, "I don't know, Mr. President. Why do you ask?" It was right in the middle of the Bay of Pigs incident and he said: "Well, I've just been letting off steam about the Kennedys, and Walter seems to be a little embarrassed. Is he a Kennedy man?" I said: "I don't know, Mr. President. My guess is that, like all good journalists, he's about 51 per cent against all politicians." That's a pretty healthy way to be. I don't think you should be 70 per cent, because that makes you not only a skeptic but a cynic, and I think cynicism is one of the deadly sins of

journalism. People such as Howard Smith, Walter Cronkite and John Chancellor take their duties very seriously. They know that, because they have a microphone and a camera and can speak around the curvature of the earth and to far corners of the country, they have a special responsibility. That responsibility is not to impose their views on the public, but to report and to try to make them understand all the salients of the story.

Interview/
U.S. News & World Report, 2-19:52.

J. William Fulbright
United States Senator, D-Arkansas

2

[Criticizing the Nixon Administration for attempting to stifle serious news and public-affairs programming on television]: As a number of commentators have noted, what the Administration wants is a situation similar to that which prevailed in France under [Charles] de Gaulle, where television served as a vehicle for government views which were never questioned or doubted.

Jan. 23/Daily Variety, 1-24:1.

Victor Gold
Former Press Secretary to
Vice President Spiro Agnew

3

An overwhelming number of Washington newsmen consider themselves to be elitists. That's because of training, inclination and intellectual cohabitation.

Interview, Washington/
Los Angeles Times, 2-8:(1)22.

Barry M. Goldwater
United States Senator, R-Arizona

4

The American people and the cause of freedom of information would be better served if small magazines—those with circulation of 250,000 or less—were provided with protection against the cost of mail rate increases. I believe that the smaller magazines, regardless of their political philosophy, have a great deal to contribute to American opinion. I believe that that contribution is sufficient to warrant its protection in law against rates that might put these smaller magazines out of business.

Quote, 1-21:64.

1

[Arguing against a proposed shield law that would protect the confidentiality of the news sources of anyone who called himself a newsman]: If the law attempts to define the term "newsmen," it would, in effect, be establishing a system for licensing members of the press [which would make press freedom meaningless] . . . [However,] if you do not define the term "newsmen," any irresponsible person in the country can get out a mimeographed scandal sheet and claim immunity under the law . . . I have encountered all kinds of newsmen, the majority of whom were responsible and honest. However, I have encountered some who were nothing more than liars and character assassins.

Washington, March 26/
Los Angeles Times, 3-27:(1)9.

2

[On press coverage of the Nixon Administration]: Some media representatives seem more interested in sinking the ship of state than in helping its crew save the passengers. Contrived attacks make it big on Page 1; actual rescues get minor coverage on Page 25.

News conference, Los Angeles, Nov. 13/
Los Angeles Times, 11-14:(1)18.

Julian Goodman
President,
National Broadcasting Company

3

I feel totally confident that a jury of fair men and women would judge that we, all three networks, are not "biased." But I do admit that we frequently report news that governments would prefer not be reported. So perhaps what the [Federal] Director of Telecommunications Policy [Clay Whitehead] hopes to achieve is not the prevention of bias, but the creation of it on behalf of the government he represents . . . There is only one Executive Branch of government, not 10. And to me, this places on it added responsibility to

be cautious and restrained in dealing with a news medium that is both licensed by the government and protected from the government by the First Amendment.

At Abe Lincoln Awards banquet of
Southern Baptist Radio & Television
Commission, Fort Worth, Tex.,
Feb. 8/Daily Variety, 2-9:14.

4

[Criticizing government interference in broadcasting]: If the government has a final say in how any program is done, broadcasters could be excused for taking a bland course rather than a brave one; we don't want that to happen. We don't want to see investigative reporting destroyed by narrow legal interpretations that do not take into account the damage done to public information . . . Each time a broadcaster weighs the criticism he has experienced after a controversial program, each time he allows innuendo and indirect pressure to affect his news judgment, broadcasting is inched further out from what ought to be a completely rainproof Constitutional umbrella.

Before American Women in Radio and
Television, Miami Beach/
Los Angeles Herald-Examiner, 5-19:(B)6.

5

Any news medium that exercises vigorously its right and responsibility to find the truth and to report and analyze the policies and actions of government will inevitably clash with the government. That is what the wise men who wrote the First Amendment intended and expected. But many of us find it difficult to believe that they intended government to defend itself with wiretaps, subpoenas, injunctions and other tools of harassment, containment and suppression. Yet it has.

At University of Florida commencement,
Aug. 25/Variety, 8-29:32.

6

[On public and government attacks on the news media]: I don't know that there will ever be any solution to this as long as problems abound and are honestly reported; or as long as mistakes in fact and judgment are made by individual newsmen, who are human,

(JULIAN GOODMAN)

too, and subject, as all humans are, to error. And I can understand the frustration of government leaders who would like to hear kind words and not unkind facts about the results of their efforts. I can understand them, but I cannot sympathize with their methods of correction.

At Central Presbyterian Church of Denver, Dec. 12/Daily Variety, 12-12:10.

Katharine Graham
Publisher, "The Washington Post"

1

In the long run I firmly believe that it all comes together: Good journalism is good public service, is good business.

At Gallaudet College colloquium, Washington, March 2/ The Washington Post, 3-3:(C)2.

2

. . . the news business imposes two sets of demands on its practitioners. The Post Company, like all of its competitors, is a business with an obligation to its stockholders to grow, prosper and return profits. But we also have a public obligation, a responsibility to serve the public by providing journalism of the highest quality. These two commitments are in no way contradictory . . . Financial independence is essential to support the talent and resources required for modern news-gathering, while . . . exciting, reliable news performance brings the public interest, audience and advertisers which produce profits.

At stockholders meeting, Washington, May 9/ The Washington Post, 5-10:(D)16.

Bruce Herschensohn
Deputy Special Assistant to the President of the United States

3

The national media is a kangaroo court, and the verdict is very clear from the outset. Some people only like dead Presidents. It's the live ones they try to discredit.

At "Support the President" rally, Albuquerque, N.M., Nov. 23/ The Washington Post, 11-25:(A)2.

Benjamin L. Hooks
Commissioner, Federal Communications Commission of the United States

4

I believe in a healthy tension between government and the press. Power corrupts in government. But power also corrupts the press. I believe in a free press; but a press that is too free can hurt people through irresponsibility.

Before National Association of Television Program Executives, New Orleans/Variety, 2-21:29.

Chet Huntley
Former news commentator, National Broadcasting Company

5

[On what changes he would make if he were head of a network news operation]: First, I would try to fill an hour of network news every evening. It may not succeed, but sooner or later it has to be tried. I became frustrated trying to work for any balance in what amounts to 23 minutes of airtime between the commercials. Second, I would take the young reporters and knock their heads together and tell them, "Forget about being Walter Lippmann for at least five years. Cover some agriculture stories and some economics. Don't get overly caught up in politics, particularly your own politics. There are some other things in the world."

Dallas/ The Dallas Times Herald, 12-14:(B)1.

Norman Isaacs
Professor and editor-in-residence, Columbia University Graduate School of Journalism

6

The tax laws are such that a man's a damn fool to hold onto a newspaper [he owns] rather than enter into a newspaper chain. The whole thing is constructed in such a way as to destroy independent newspaper[s]. The present system invites monopoly.

At Congressional conference on government and the media, Washington, April 12/ The Washington Post, 4-13:(B)12.

Nicholas Johnson
Commissioner, Federal Communications
Commission of the United States

1

[Since no national newspapers reach a significant percentage of the American people,] all you've got left is the TV network news. That's why the President [Nixon] is trying to get them out of the way. Once he intimidates them by getting you [the public] to turn them off, he has accomplished his goal. You are less well-informed today than you were three years ago. There are people who benefit from your not knowing what is going on, and there are people who benefit in your knowing only what they want you to know. [Power is no longer measured in terms of land, money] or even armies, but [by] control of ideas maintained through control of the little glass screen . . . The Washington game is to turn newsmen into repeaters, not reporters.

At Texas A&M University, Feb. 15/
Los Angeles Times, 2-16:(1)16.

2

If you can drive the networks and the networks news departments out of business, then the President's got the whole ballgame; be se there's nobody in the whole country tha an compete with him. As a practical matter, you've got an unchallengeable power in a nation that is built on a system of checks and balances.

Quote, 2-18:146.

Robert W. Kastenmeier
United States Representative, D-Wisconsin

3

[On why it would be difficult to draft a bill protecting the confidentiality of reporters' news sources]: I am convinced, by testimony before this Subcommittee and by events of recent months, that affirmative action is required to protect our free press from a growing subpoena threat . . . [Every member of Congress would] give a ringing endorsement to the concept of a free press when the idea is presented in the abstract. However, when the general principle is reduced to a specific instance of a reporter answering or not answering a court-issued subpoena under a given

set of circumstances, widely-divergent interpretations of the "free press" emerge. The dangers of doing harm to a "free press" through definition and delineation are real and cannot be overlooked.

At House Judiciary Subcommittee hearing,
Washington, March 20/
The New York Times, 3-21:18.

Henry A. Kissinger
Secretary of State of the United States

4

To those of you who are diplomats, be mindful of what you say, for you are surrounded by members of the press. And to those of you who are members of the press, be careful not to take too seriously everything you hear, for you are surrounded by diplomats.

At United Nations diplomatic corp dinner,
New York, Oct. 4/
San Francisco Examiner & Chronicle,
10-7:(A)1.

Irving Kristol
Professor of Urban Values, New York
University; Member of the Board-designate,
Corporation for Public Broadcasting
of the United States

5

The press has to get away from petty muckraking, petty scoops and the daily deadline. There is a certain juvenile quality about journalism which is sort of engaging but not appropriate. Everyone wants the little scoop, the piece of gossip, the exclusive stories no one else has. Instead, it should pay attention to information that's easily available but takes lots of work to understand.

The Washington Post, 4-15:(A)2.

Arthur Krock
Former Washington bureau chief,
"The New York Times"

6

[On the adversary relationship between government and the press]: They were born to fight each other, just like some warring tribes in Africa.

Newsweek, 1-15:42.

Jack Landau
News correspondent, Newhouse Newspapers;
Member, Reporters' Committee for
Freedom of the Press

1

[Supporting confidentiality for newsmen's sources]: If they [newsmen] violate their promises of confidentiality, they may never again be able to operate effectively, except to cover news which is offered by government handout or is a matter of public record. We ask you to consider what kind of nation we would be, for example, if the "Pentagon Papers," the Bobby Baker affair, the thalidomide horror, the My Lai massacre, among others, and hundreds of scandals involving state and local government, still lay locked in the mouths of citizens fearful that they would lose their livelihoods or perhaps even be prosecuted if their identities became known.

Before House Subcommittee/
Los Angeles Herald-Examiner, 2-19:(A)9.

Lee Kuan Yew
Prime Minister of Singapore

2

In the last few days in this country [the U.S.], I have discovered that any statement, any argument, however dispassionate . . . which can be faintly, directly or indirectly construed as in support of, or in sympathy with, any of the hopes, policies or aspirations of this [Nixon] Administration finds very scant space in the mass media.

At White House dinner in his honor,
Washington, April 10/
The New York Times, 4-12:55.

Bill Leonard
Senior vice president for public-affairs
broadcasts, Columbia Broadcasting System

3

It is perfectly clear what has aroused [U.S. President] Nixon's anger [toward the media]. It's perfectly simple: We've been reporting some of the things that have been happening in this country during the past year. We didn't create these things, only reported them. But they don't make the Nixon Administration look very good, and for that reason they be-

come [in the President's words] "outrageous, vicious and distorted."

San Francisco Examiner & Chronicle,
11-11:(This World)16.

Walter Lippmann
Author; Former political columnist

4

[On the proper relationship between newsmen and government officials]: I feel that newspapermen cannot be the personal or intimate friends of very powerful people. They just can't. It won't work. They'll either end in corruption of the press or a quarrel, and I've said that before. You cannot be in the confidence of a king.

Interview/The Washington Post, 3-25:(C)4.

5

I think raw news, raw fact, is not intelligible . . . to the public, and has to be explained. The explanation is as important as the fact itself. The duty of the press is to put forth not raw news but explained news.

Interview/The Washington Post, 3-25:(C)4.

Clare Boothe Luce
Former American diplomat and playwright

6

We used to have 12 newspapers in this city [New York]. Now there are three. Television has contributed to this, of course. But the real problem is the nature of the business. Editors inveigh against monopoly, but the news industry is the most monopolous of all. Syndicate eats syndicate; chain eats chain. They're making a frightful stew now about the issue of government and a free press. But the real question is: Is the press free at all? And the answer is no—and its least shackle is government.

Interview, New York/
The New York Times Magazine, 4-22:56.

Torbert H. Macdonald
United States Representative, D-Massachusetts

7

If I have a single message to send to the bosses of all the television and radio newsmen in the country, network and station alike, it's this: There's nothing that the Executive Branch [of the Federal government] can do to you or for you. Your job is to see to it that the news is reported accurately and fairly, by professional journalists, period. And, to the newsmen, I say keep on calling it as you see it. I'm not being so naive as to believe that the attacks from the White House will stop. I'm afraid that [President] Nixon's network neurosis is too far advanced for that.

At National Press Club, Washington, Nov. 15/San Francisco Examiner, 11-15:7.

Michael Manley
Prime Minister of Jamaica

1

A really free and democratic press has the obligation to create the vision of an ideal society for its readers—to spur the conscience of men toward the obliteration of human misery and injustice.

Before Inter-American Press Association, Jamaica/ San Francisco Examiner & Chronicle, 4-8:(B)2.

Mike Mansfield
United States Senator, D-Montana

2

[Criticizing the television networks for refusing to grant to Congressional opposition on-air time for rebuttal of Presidential TV addresses, etc.]: With the revolution of communications in this country, the whole notion of the separation of powers has been significantly diminished by the inordinate input the Executive Branch, through the President and the Cabinet officers, has on television. It is so much easier for the networks to cover the Executive Branch—it speaks with one voice. But ease of coverage is not effective coverage; and especially where Congress differs from the White House, it is difficult for the networks easily to present a balance. The designation by the joint leadership of the Congress of a spokesman to present a prevailing viewpoint was intended to meet the need of providing a viewpoint that accurately portrayed its input into national decisions.

Variety, 4-11:39.

Robert J. McCloskey
Former Deputy Assistant Secretary for Press Relations, Department of State of the United States

3

I have come to believe that there *can* be less of an adversary relationship between the press and the government than has commonly been assigned to them. If our respective and basic responsibilities sometimes conflict, they also complement one another, because each party must depend for understanding and acceptance on communication. Why, then, is there continuing difficulty? Because first, it is not sufficient merely for the government to state a conviction that a free and unintimidated media is essential to a democratic society. As the government performs, it must inform. Demands, assertions, pleas for credibility on faith might well in the end be vindicated and fulfilled; where they are not—because the government neither informed nor performed—the demands, assertions and pleas can end up mocking the government. The press and the public have a right to expect serious performance on the government's declarations of intent . . . Secondly, there is difficulty because it is not enough for the media to declare that, at all times and on all occasions, it is entirely objective. That our reach exceeds our grasp is less a poetic maxim than it is a reminder that total objectivity is unattainable. Therefore, to ask for an honest willingness to acknowledge error when it occurs—as the media's own critics recommend—is no more than to ask the government to be honest and continent in all its dealings with the press and the public. And third, we are in trouble because civility in an adversary relationship too frequently—and on both sides—falls victim to antagonism. There is no room for name-calling on either side in a relationship as subtle and sensitive as this, where both parties are, in effect, trustees of and accountable to the public interest. The point I make is that neither side has a corner on the market of infallibility or of being more sinned against than sinning; and, where differences arise, what is required is less religion and more Christianity toward one another. Too often, I fear, the approach

(ROBERT J. McCLOSKEY)

is more like that which created the search-and-destroy concept. What must be avoided at all costs is a slide toward alienating one another in dispute which runs the risk of putting the interests of the people last.

At National Press Club, Washington/
The New York Times, 5-21:31.

Carey McWilliams
Editor, "The Nation"

1

Without the small magazine, what would take its place? Where would the young writers go? Ideas don't get born on TV. They didn't get born at *Life* magazine. They get born here.

The Washington Post, 5-27:(L)17.

William G. Milliken
Governor of Michigan

2

[Advocating legislation to protect the identity of reporters' confidential news sources]: The press can best aid law enforcement by exposing activities that likely would not be exposed in any other way. To do this, it often must rely on sources who will not provide information unless confidentiality is respected. Legislative action should be taken primarily for the public, not for the press. It is the people themselves who can be cheated of their right to know when erosion of sources of information erodes freedom of information.

Lansing, Mich., March 15/
Los Angeles Herald-Examiner, 3-16:(A)18.

Clark R. Mollenhoff
Washington bureau chief,
"Des Moines Register"

3

[Arguing against a shield law that would protect the confidentiality of a reporter's news sources]: . . . it would create total chaos in these governmental bodies that must use the power of subpoena to obtain witnesses and documents in an effort to elicit the truth. It would be a greater boon to organized crime than the Fifth Amendment . . . it would be

disaster to organized government, business and labor. Eventually, an absolute shield law would hurt the press, because it would promote irresponsibility and lack of accountability.

Before House Judiciary Subcommittee,
Washington, March 7/
The Washington Post, 3-8:(A)2.

Walter F. Mondale
United States Senator, D-Minnesota

4

The longer I'm up here [in Washington], the more I'm convinced that the more important news is "leaked" [to the press]. Politicians and government just don't put out bad news about themselves. Most of the information I operate on is information that somebody leaked.

The Washington Post, 2-5:(A)4.

William Monroe
Washington editor, "Today" show,
National Broadcasting Company Television

5

The present uneasy condition of broadcasting—not quite free and not quite captive—will certainly change in one direction or another, toward greater freedom or toward a deeper captivity. If it slips down toward heavier obedience to government, I believe newspapers will find themselves slipping also . . . If government can make television news "fair and balanced," it can make newspapers "fair and balanced." If the assumption is valid, the logic is impeccable.

Before Minnesota Newspaper Association,
Minneapolis, Feb. 23/
Daily Variety, 2-26:12.

Reg Murphy
Editor, "Atlanta Constitution"

6

By describing himself as not being angry at people [news reporters] he couldn't respect, he [President Nixon] seems to think that we are not worthy of his personal feelings. That never has been our goal and ought never to be our goal. We ought to be involved in reporting news, and in fact that is what has created the problem for this Administration. Trying to blame a group of dedicated reporters for the outrages of his own Administration will make no sense to an American public which is already fed up with the activities of this Administration.

Oct. 26/San Francisco Examiner, 10-27:4.

Richard M. Nixon
President of the United States

1

Don't get the impression that you [the press] arouse my anger. You see, one can only be angry with those he respects . . . When a commentator takes a bit of news and then, with knowledge of what the facts are, distorts it viciously, I have no respect for that individual.

News conference, Washington, Oct. 26/
The New York Times, 10-27:14.

William S. Paley
Chairman, Columbia Broadcasting System

2

[On White House criticism of the news media]: It's been the same ever since I've been in the business: every government wants to be loved; and when the facts aren't lovable, they label it "opinion" . . . Some of the policies I set for CBS in the '30s are still in effect; that is, to fight hard and never surrender to government pressure, if that's the word you want to use, on any matter of news. The policies were to protect the public, but they've protected CBS as well.

At party honoring CBS president
Arthur Taylor, Washington,
March 14/The Washington Post, 3-16:(B)3.

John O. Pastore
United States Senator, D-Rhode Island

3

[Defending network TV newsmen]: By and large, with the exception of a little boo-boo here and there, these are usually independent people with a mind of their own and no axe to grind.

At Congressional conference on government
and the media, Washington, April 12/
The Washington Post, 4-13:(B)12.

Noel S. Paul
Secretary, British Press Council

4

. . . I think any moves by newspapers to accept a soundly-based machinery for the investigation and settlement of complaints [against the press] by the public would enhance the reputation of the press and not diminish it. I do believe that in Britain we have found an answer [through the Press Council] to the problem of promoting a responsible press without sacrificing freedom. And the danger which has always haunted me, and from which I feel much more protected now that we have a Press Council, is the danger that a government would feel obliged to legislate against the freedom of the press in order to insure responsibility in the public interest. I think the Press Council has lessened that danger considerably and, in the process, promoted a more responsible press.

The Washington Post, 4-29:(C)2.

Charles H. Percy
United States Senator, R-Illinois

5

The press, which has been accused of many indiscretions, has been fully and dramatically vindicated by [the] Watergate [political-espionage affair]. I doubt that the nation yet realizes how fortunate we are to have had an aggressive, unfettered press in this country in the past 12 months . . . But if we are going to have an unfettered press—and we must —then the press must accept the responsibility of disciplining itself in the public interest.

Before Inland Daily Press Association,
Chicago, Oct. 16/
The New York Times, 10-17:35.

Georges Pompidou
President of France

6

[Addressing newsmen who asked him why he has not been taking long countryside walks lately and who have speculated on his health]: If I haven't come out these last days, it's because of you. You give me a pain.

Carjac, France/
Los Angeles Times, 6-11:(1)2.

Dan Rather
News correspondent,
Columbia Broadcasting System

1

[On Nixon Administration criticism of the news media]: I'm certainly not saying that they all sit around a table and plan some grand strategy to hit the media on all fronts. But I am convinced that, in a broad, general way, the people around Nixon have come to know that it's okay to attack the media. I think people like [Presidential Assistants] Haldeman, Ehrlichman, Buchanan, et al, did set out to create this climate, knowing that just creating it would be enough to make the press pause.

Newsweek, 1-15:48.

2

When I go through the White House gates, insofar as is humanly possible I leave my own ideological opinions behind me. I'm not paid to tell people what I really think. I'm paid to tell them what I see, hear, feel and smell. Of course, I often fail to be totally objective. For instance, I feel very strongly about civil rights, and I think this [Nixon] Administration has been very insensitive in this area. In general, black people are treated shockingly in the United States. If that's [journalistic] bias, then so be it.

Interview, Washington/
San Francisco Examiner & Chronicle,
6-24:(Datebook)24.

Ronald Reagan
Governor of California

3

I believe in the First Amendment to the United States Constitution, which guarantees the freedom of speech and press. A free press is one of this country's major strengths, and the right to protect the source of information is fundamental to a newsman in meeting his full responsibilities to the public he serves.

After signing a bill protecting
newsmen's sources, Sacramento/
The Dallas Times Herald, 1-3:(E)7.

4

I believe in the tradition we've always observed for the right of a reporter to protect his sources and not reveal where he heard whatever it is that he writes. I believe in that . . . [But] I think there's a great deal of advocacy press today in contrast to objective reporting. Reporters today believe they have a right to even slant a news story to fit what philosophy they advocate. I disagree with that. I think they should leave that to the editorial page, and they should honestly and objectively report news.

Before high school students,
Sacramento, Jan. 29/
San Francisco Examiner, 1-30:11.

Elliot L. Richardson
Former Attorney General
of the United States

5

Because freedom of the press can be no broader than the freedom of reporters to investigate and report the news, the prosecutorial power of the government should not be used in such a way that it impairs a reporter's responsibility to cover as broadly as possible controversial issues.

Quote, 11-18:481.

Charles R. Richey
Judge, United States District Court
for the District of Columbia

6

[Barring a proposed subpoena of news-media material for use in the "Watergate" political-espionage trial]: This court cannot blind itself to the possible chilling effect the enforcement of these subpoenas would have on the flow of information to the press and, thus, to the public. This court stands convinced that, if it allows the discouragement of investigative reporting into the highest levels of government, that no amount of legal theorizing could allay the public's suspicions engendered by its actions . . .

Washington, March 21/
The Washington Post, 3-22:(A)1.

Nelson A. Rockefeller
Governor of New York

7

Government has an obligation not to in-

478

hibit the collection and dissemination of news. Freedom of the press is a fundamental principle on which this nation was founded. I'm convinced that, if reporters should ever lose the right to protect the confidentiality of their [news] sources, then serious investigative reporting will simply dry up. The kind of resourceful, probing journalism that first exposed most of the serious scandals, corruption and injustices in our nation's history would simply disappear.

Quote, 1-14:26.

A. M. Rosenthal
Managing editor, "The New York Times"

1

Most journalists believe that the right to maintain confidential [news] sources and information is an essential condition for the exercise of the First Amendment. We also believe that the very process of subpoenaing reporters, trying to get them to testify, attempting to use them as branches of government investigation by examining them even on published information, has created an atmosphere in which sources of news are losing confidence in reporters' pledges—not because of the reporters, but because the sources are aware of increasing court pressures on the press. I say flatly that, without the guarantee of confidentiality, investigative reporting will disappear. The erosion of confidentiality will mean the end of the exposure of corruption as far as the press is concerned.

Before House Judiciary Subcommittee,
Washington, March 5/
The New York Times, 3-6:25.

Stephen Rowan
Former news correspondent,
Columbia Broadcasting System

2

Whatever interest I have left in this business has diminished to maybe half a dozen major stations in this country that are doing a respectable job with their news. Let's not kid ourselves. I'm a 44-year-old veteran [newsman], and I do not fit into the kind of show-biz operation that most stations are

shooting for these days. I'm quite frankly distresse with the direction local TV news is going into—the flashy, show-biz atmosphere which I'm frankly not competent to compete in . . . Aside from the networks and a few big stations, they're all in the mad scramble to find another 27-year-old superstar. It's kind of sad. I think it spells the end of television news for a few years, at least till the pendulum swings back. I do think there is something more fulfilling for me to do with the rest of my life than to preside over a show-biz newscast that has no fewer than 13 film stories, each of which runs no longer than a minute-and-a-half, and provides a lot of excitement and frills to entertain the home viewer.

Buffalo, N.Y./Variety, 4-11:46.

Elton H. Rule
President,
American Broadcasting Companies

3

[Saying broadcasters should not be influenced by Nixon Administration attempts at bullying them and influencing news]: All those present fellows [in the Administration] will be gone some day, and another set will take their place, armed with new or disguised versions either of intimidation or of putting forward what they want the public to think is their best face . . . The pressures [on broadcasters] to back off, to forfeit responsibility, to forego courage, could be great if broadcasters were not true to their trust. What is important to remember is that broadcasting will always be with us. We are beholden to no man, no party, no corporation, no lobby. Our dedication is to report and investigate with impartiality and objectivity.

Before Comstock Club, Sacramento, Calif.,
April 18/The Hollywood Reporter, 4-19:6.

Robert W. Sarnoff
Chairman, RCA Corporation

4

Most visibly, we have had the unprecedented spectacle of high Federal officials attacking the national news media in general and TV network news in particular. It is plainly an

(ROBERT W. SARNOFF)

effort to impair the credibility of the news and to influence how it is reported. It seems aimed at a state of public information fed by government handout and starved by official secrecy on matters that are the public's business.

Before National Broadcasting Company
Television affiliates, Los Angeles,
May 7/Daily Variety, 5-8:1.

Thomas Sarnoff
Executive vice president,
National Broadcasting Company

1

[On criticism of broadcast news]: We welcome constructive criticism, but we do not welcome—nor must we allow ourselves to succumb to—destructive criticism. We must not only show the news when it is good [but also not] try to hide it when it is bad. It would indeed be an ironic waste if we were not to use the best means of communication to present to our people and to the world a true picture of our nation—warts and beauty marks alike.

Before Advertising & Sales Club of
San Diego and San Diego chapter, National
Academy of Television Arts and Sciences,
March 21/Daily Variety, 3-22:8.

Frank Sinatra
Singer, Actor

2

[On the press]: . . . I call them garbage collectors: the columnists without a conscience, the reporters who take longshots based on the idea that where there's smoke there's fire, all for the sake of a story. I'm blunt and honest. I could easily call them pimps and "hos." They'd sell their mother out. How dare they say what they do about me? . . . There's nobody to censure the press. Like [political columnist] Jack Anderson's attack on [Senator Thomas] Eagleton [during the 1972 Presidential election]—he didn't even apologize. I don't know Eagleton, but he's a human being. The poor bastard couldn't fight

back. I fight back. I would not think of not fighting back.

Interview, Culver City, Calif./
TV Guide, 11-17:34.

Chesterfield Smith
President-elect,
American Bar Association

3

The greatest of all Constitutional rights is freedom of the press, because that right is not just for the press but for the public.

Before Seattle-King County Bar Association/
The Dallas Times Herald, 2-16:(A)8.

Howard K. Smith
News commentator,
American Broadcasting Company

4

[On a proposed shield law to protect the confidentiality of reporters' news sources]: I'm against the shield law. Unless things get a lot worse than they are, I don't want a shield law for anybody. I think it involves too many complexities that haven't been thought out. For one thing, you've got to define who a reporter is . . . If you said that [it is] anybody who gives news out, what's to prevent a mobster from writing a newsletter and saying, "I'm a journalist; I can't testify"?

Panel discussion, New York/
The New York Times, 3-12:49.

Frank Stanton
Vice chairman,
Columbia Broadcasting System

5

We now believe it necessary to enact legislation to create an absolute newsman's privilege, which would apply not only to the Federal government but to the states, regardless of present shield laws or lack of them. [The legislation should provide that] no person shall be required in Federal or state proceedings to disclose either 1) the source of any published or unpublished information obtained for any medium of communication to the public, or 2) any unpublished information obtained or prepared in gathering or processing information for any public medium of communication. If anything less is accepted, we must accept, too, I think, the possibility of the ultimate irony—that reporters will never publish information which will tempt prosecutors to use their subpoena power, because they will possess absolutely no information worth having.

Before Georgia Radio-TV Institute,
University of Georgia, Atlanta,
Jan. 24/Daily Variety, 1-25:6.

Herbert Stein
Chairman, Council of Economic Advisers
to the President of the United States

1

In today's world, if you can look about you and see that things are pretty good, you're not fit to be an editorial writer for *The New York Times*, my son. Today, it is the bearer of *good* news who is in danger.

Before bankers, businessmen and educators,
Richmond, Va./Time, 2-26:12.

Carl B. Stokes
Former Mayor of Cleveland

2

News is whatever they [newspapers] print. If you don't print it, it ain't news.

Interview, Washington/
The Washington Post, 11-24:(D)3.

Arthur Ochs Sulzberger
Publisher, "The New York Times"

3

We do not think that the real threat to a free press arises from a failing of the press to be fair and accurate, [but from] people who are attempting to intimidate or to use the press for their own ends.

Newsweek, 1-29:62.

Arthur R. Taylor
President, Columbia Broadcasting System

4

Television has not created a new form of journalism; it has simply given the responsible reporter a new tool to employ. It is a tool with flaws, among them a lack of the perma-

nence any printed medium enjoys. But if properly employed, it is a tool with more than compensating virtues, chief among them immediacy and credibility. These characteristics derive from the lack of any necessary time delay in reporting an event to the public, and from its ability to show the event directly to the public, rather than being limited to description of the event. In addition, in the case of live broadcasts, the existence of national television networks permits an entire nation to participate in such an event simultaneously. It was not, however, until the launching of communications satellites that this role of television came into its own in the area of international affairs. Consider the impact of President Nixon's trips to the Soviet Union and, especially, the People's Republic of [Communist] China . . . millions of people, through the agency of television and satellites, could—and did—participate vicariously in the President's trips; and, as a result, our relations with the Russians and the Chinese became a subject of national discussion as they have not been for a decade.

Before Los Angeles World Affairs
Council, Oct. 24/
Vital Speeches, 12-1:111.

Lowell Thomas
News commentator,
Columbia Broadcasting System

5

You have to be a showman; that's been reflected in my [news] broadcasts; it's been part of my technique always. I don't use news over the wires; there are thousands who do that. When I started, there were no wires. I handle my material in my own funny way. Maybe that's one of the reasons I've survived. All the others that started with me have vanished. I work up to the minute I go on the air. I handle the news light. Even if the world is going to hell in a handbasket, we still might as well smile. Also, I'm on at the dinner hour—it's not my job to upset the digestive apparatus of the American public.

Interview, Los Angeles, Feb 14/
Daily Variety, 2-15:4.

Roger J. Traynor
Chairman, National News Council
(United States)

1

[Responding to press criticism of the Council, an organization that will deal with public complaints of unfair or inaccurate handling of the news by the news media]: An informed and intelligent public understanding of the vital role of the media in a free society—an understanding enlightened by an independent, responsible and objective evaluation of their preformance—would be a powerful defense to [government anti-media] attacks. I cannot believe that a council, completely detached from government and without any power to impose any sanctions whatever other than publicity, can be in any way a threat to press freedom or encourage an atmosphere of regulation . . . What have the media to fear from publicity, their very stock-in-trade? Are they so infallible as to be above criticism? Must the defense of freedom of the press be left solely to them?
Interview/The New York Times, 5-4:14.

Jerome R. Waldie
United States Representative,
D-California

2

[The press] is the only institution that is available to report to the people what their governors are doing to them—not *for* them but *to* them. We [in government] will tell the people what we are doing *for* them, but the press will tell the people what we are doing *to* them. And I think a balanced portrayal of what we are doing must include what we are doing *to* them as well as what we are doing *for* them.
Before Senate Judiciary Subcommittee on Constitutional Rights, Washington, Feb. 27/The Washington Post, 3-23:(A)30.

W. Allen Wallis
Chancellor,
University of Rochester (N.Y.)

3

Despite the self-congratulation of the newspapers that the exposure of [the] Watergate

[political-espionage affair] is a triumph of a free and unbiased press, it is at most a triumph of a free and biased press. *The Washington Post,* the prime mover in exposing Watergate, has been unsurpassed in its vitriolic hatred of [President] Richard Nixon ever since he attained prominence 25 years ago. Furthermore, quite apart from personal animus, *The Post* is one of the most ardent advocates of bigger, more pervasive and more centralized government—the views which sell best in its market; and no paper in the country is more opposed to the President's effort to reduce government. Had *The Post* made comparable efforts in the [U.S. Senator Edward Kennedy] Chappaquiddick affair, perhaps we would know as much about that as we know about Watergate. The Chappaquiddick affair, after all, was simpler and less-effectively hidden. I do not doubt that, if *The Post* had had the same animus toward Senator Kennedy that it has toward President Nixon, or even if it had been neutral instead of friendly toward the Senator, and that if it had had the same opposition to the Senator's policies that it has to the President's, or even if it had been neutral instead of friendly toward those policies, we would have known long ago more about Chappaquiddick than we now know about Watergate. The difference mocks the self-serving claims being made by and for the press. It has to be conceded for *The Post,* however, that exposing Chappaquiddick probably would not have been looked on by the Pulitzer Prize judges with the same admiration as exposing Watergate.
At Roberts Wesleyan College commencement, Rochester, N.Y./ The National Observer, 6-30:6.

Clay T. Whitehead
Director, Federal Office of
Telecommunications Policy (United States)

4

We are going to ask Congress to change the rules governing the process of renewing licenses for local television stations. Among other things, we believe [the stations] ought to be paying more attention to exercising their responsibility, on a voluntary basis, for what appears on TV in their communities. They're responsible for everything they transmit, from news to entertainment, whether it's locally produced or from the networks . . . [The controversy] was stirred principally by the initial reaction of the press that this responsibility of the broadcast-station owner was something new, something sinister that we were trying to impose. That was compounded by the fact that many people in the print media don't understand the current extent and the problems of broadcasting regulation that we have today. We think that, in this very important field of television, the responsibility for programming ought to come voluntarily from the people who head the stations.

The problem is that, over the years, a concept has evolved in network television that the news department should be insulated from its management. Well, organizations shouldn't be that insulated from checks and balances. If they are insulated from the government, their management, their advertisers and their viewers, to whom do they answer? I think that is an intolerable circumstance. News and public affairs ought to be presented as fairly and impartially as is humanly possible. That's what present regulations of the "Fairness Doctrine" —requiring broadcasters to present both sides of an issue—are all about.

Interview/
U.S. News & World Report,
2-19:48.

Literature

Richard Armour
Author; Professor Emeritus of English,
Scripps College, Claremont, Calif.

1

Wordsworth, in the *Prelude*, tells us of man's yearning for immortality . . . Wordsworth thinks that the closest man comes to immortality is his putting words together in the writing of books. In this way, man leaves something that outlasts his physical self—indeed, outlasts generation after generation of men. Perishable though the ink-and-paper or ink-and-parchment book is, its contents have a way of surviving. We possess nothing in the handwriting of Homer or Sophocles or Plato or Aristotle, and they lived many centuries before printing. Yet we have their words and are inspired by them today, more than 2,000 years after the deaths of their authors. They and many other great minds left us a verbal legacy far more valuable than any monetary legacy, and not subject to probate or inheritance tax.

At Claremont (Calif.) Men's
College commencement/
Los Angeles Times, 6-13:(2)7.

Brooks Atkinson
Former drama critic

2

Everything a man writes is autobiography, even when he's writing a novel; and criticism is pure autobiography. You can be more objective or less objective. I think it's psychologically impossible to be absolutely objective, except if you're running an adding machine.

Interview, Durham, N.Y./
The New York Times, 10-31:44.

Richard Bach
Author

3

[Thanking the American Booksellers Association for accepting his book, *Jonathan Livingston Seagull*]: It was like walking alone in a meadow and seeing, over by some reeds, a small phantom balloon and trying to touch it, and seeing your fingers pass through it! Then you rush home and try to duplicate the balloon in a model; but none of the balloon factories want to produce it. Your balloon is not "with it," they say. Finally, the best balloon factory of all, Macmillan, accepts it . . . And I want to thank all of your readers for flying my balloon!

"W": a Fairchild publication, 2-9:17.

Saul Bellow
Author

4

I think that people who write well are people who take a certain attitude toward themselves. Considerably more is involved than technique. One sees oneself as a certain kind of human being. I don't think that that peculiar act of initiation can be transmitted in a classroom. How am I going to describe to a young man or young woman the operation on one's soul which is necessary? You can't do that. So it's really misleading to say, "Well, I'll teach you to put together words on a page," or how to hook your reader or how to find a symbol or how to balance your narrative or anything of that sort.

Interview, New York/
Publishers Weekly, 10-22:76.

Heinrich Boll
Author

5

Novel-writing is like climbing a range of mountains. Five meters before each peak you feel like turning back. A big novel has at least 20 "climbing" crises. After each peak there's a downhill stretch, but then you have to climb again. Short stories are very different; the exercise is like jumping. Sometimes you make a great effort to jump a short distance; but in the last two or three years I stopped writing short stories because the jump was becoming too easy. An essay is a pentathlon, and sometimes I sit on essays for months.

Interview, New York/
The New York Times, 5-15:30.

Daniel J. Boorstin
Author; Director, National Museum of
History and Technology (United States)

1

Writing is like defecation: You do it to get rid of something.

The Washington Post, 8-12:(Potomac)29.

Jorge Luis Borges
Author

2

I think of writing as a pleasure. I don't think of it as an effort, and I never understood why people cared for praise or were bothered by criticism. The prizes and awards have their pleasure, but the lack of them would have given me no pain at all. Prizes and honors are like a lottery: If one wins, one is elated; if one loses, one doesn't give a hang about it.

Interview, Buenos Aires/
The Christian Science Monitor, 3-5:6.

Ray Bradbury
Author

3

You know what's wrong [with booksellers]? Most of those booksellers don't love books. They don't know about those books that help you make it past 3 a.m. They don't believe that what a man reads can give him the stuff to jump out of bed in the morning and live. Those people [the sellers] are looking at the profit sheets; they don't love the books; they don't love the words. There just aren't enough book-lovers in the booksellers.

Interview, Los Angeles, June 13/
Los Angeles Times, 6-15:(4)14.

Arthur C. Clarke
Science-fiction writer

4

Science fiction is often called escapism—always in a negative sense. Of course it's not true. Science fiction is virtually the only kind of writing that's dealing with real problems and possibilities; it's a concerned fiction. It's the mainstream that escapes from these things into small anxieties—away from fact, away from things that threaten or enrich our lives.

Interview, New York/
Publishers Weekly, 9-10:24.

Malcolm Cowley
Literary critic

5

[The writers of the 1920s] were much more ambitious to produce a masterpiece than writers today. They were ready to sacrifice their lives to producing it. Ambition like that is rare now. And the work of writing was more separate from the writer's personality. It was the work that succeeded, not the personality. But now the importance centers around creation of a *persona*. It was harder financially, too, in the '20s: There were none of the present opportunities for being supported by a foundation grant. There was only the rare publisher's advance, where an editor might take a gamble on you for $300. Well, on that you could live on potatoes for six months in Connecticut in those days.

Interview/Publishers Weekly, 9-17:20.

6

The public still reads novels to find out what life is like; but it is hard to find this out from a novel—that would be flatly impossible. People like to find a pattern in life, to see every evil punished and good rewarded. Thus every story becomes a fable with a moral. Even if a good man is ruined or sacrificed in a novel, there's a moral—that life is meaningless, perhaps. People will not like this moral, but it is there. Now, if you subtract the story from the writing and make it a phantasmagoria of events, there will be no satisfaction in it at all.

Interview/Publishers Weekly, 9-17:21.

Pete V. Domenici
United States Senator, R-New Mexico

1

A library is a keystone in every communi-ty. They are the fulfillment of Abe Lincoln's passion for books and learning which led him to walk miles to borrow them and study long hours before the dim fire. Libraries reflect freedom of opportunity to learn, to engage the best thinkers of the past. They are quiet places in a neighborhood where we can seek out higher ideas than the tawdry or mundane. Libraries are an important—even vital—aspect of our education[al], informational society, and we *must* preserve them in all communi-ties.

Quote, 12-2:538.

Jack Douglas
Writer

2

Once I lived in a big room over a garage and stared out at the ocean and never wrote a thing. I couldn't get in gear . . . I've found that, no matter where you are, you have to close the drapes and forget about where you are . . . There's no ideal place to write. You always think there is.

The Christian Science Monitor, 8-30:6.

Ralph Ellison
Writer

3

. . . the writer's morality is one which expresses a vision of human life. It contains a sense of what is right and wrong; what is life-preserving against that which is life-de-stroying. If he's a writer, his most serious way of expressing his sense of life and his identity is through his writing; and thus, if he is a moral man he will try to do that as well as he can . . . If you describe a more viable and ethical way of living and denounce the world or a great part of society for the way that it conducts its affairs, and then write in a sloppy way or present issues in a simplistic or banal way, then you're being immoral as an artist . . . Writers who are supposed to present vi-sions of the human condition which will lead to some sort of wisdom in confronting the

existence of experience and who do not do that in a disciplined and informed way are immoral.

Interview/The Washington Post, 8-21:(B)3.

James T. Flexner
*Author; Winner, 1973 (U.S.) National
Book Award in biography*

4

This negatively-labeled thing—non-fiction—is as much an art form as fiction; and it's within the realm of possibilities that it's more suited to our times. One of the advantages of being a biographer is that you can strain to under-stand someone bigger than you are, while a novelist can't spill out anyone bigger than himself.

*Interview, New York/
The New York Times, 4-15:(1)56.*

Paul Gallico
Author

5

We live in a rough, cold world today. But I make a different world when I write. I make it what I think it ought to be.

Publishers Weekly, 1-22:34.

Helen Gardner
*Author; Professor of English Literature,
Oxford University, England*

6

This is not a great creative era. In the 19th century the dominant art form was the novel, and the great form now is the memoir or autobiography. All the poetry one reads nowa-days is biographical or confessional: "My time in the loony bin" or "My attempts at suicide" or "My problems in getting straight with a dominating mama." What we're lacking now is the poetical imagination that transforms the raw material of experience into something more objective.

Interview/The New York Times, 6-7:56.

John J. Geoghegan
*President, Coward, McCann & Geoghegan,
publishers*

7

I firmly believe that everything publishable

is published in due course—plus a hell of a lot that would be no loss to civilization if it were not.

Los Angeles Herald-Examiner, 8-7:(A)12.

Eugene Ionesco
Author, Playwright

1

A good writer never has a vacation. For a good writer, life consists of either writing or thinking about writing.

Los Angeles Herald-Examiner, 1-6:(A)10.

John D. MacDonald
Author

2

[On why he uses the name of a color in the titles of all his "Travis McGee" stories]: It's a simple code. Nothing annoys a reader more than buying a book and then finding out that he's read it. The colors are a way of helping readers keep the titles straight . . . I looked at one of those leaflets of house-painter's samples and found out there are more than 30 colors still to go. I don't know what the titles will sound like when I get down to colors like fuchsia and puce, but we'll wait and see.

Interview, New York/
San Francisco Examiner & Chronicle,
8-26:(This World)36.

Norman Mailer
Author

3

There is a virtue in writing a book quickly; which is, sometimes if you write a book quickly, you start to take certain chances and a book takes on a sort of life . . . I've got 40 books I want to write yet. In other words, I like writing books quickly because I'd rather write 10 good but somewhat imperfect books than one or two perfect books.

News conference, New York, July 18/
The Washington Post, 7-19:(B)13.

Leland Miles
President, Alfred (N.Y.) University

4

A classic is a leech. It grabs you and won't let go. It refuses to die. It insists on sticking around. It's adhesive, durable and has staying power. It has to be a book at least 30 years old and should have survived at least a generation. A book is not a classic because it survived the first round or got out of the starting gate first. I've learned from experience that the first out of the gate is usually the last to finish the race. A classic, however, more often than not gets knocked down and almost out in the first round, but struggles and fights back to win in the 15th round. Classics upon publication are usually laughed at, ridiculed, spat upon, rejected, burned and condemned . . . Critics ridiculed *Leaves of Grass* as the work of a lunatic; and they tossed off *Moby Dick* as too philosophical, and even criticized it because there were no women in the book. The Irish burned [James] Joyce's book *[The Dubliners]* and [Edgar Allan] Poe couldn't get anyone to print his work and had to have it printed privately himself . . . What distinguishes men and women from machines are the four qualities lacking in computers: no imagination or compassion, no psychological insight, no capacity to make moral decisions and no ulcers or the capacity to care. These are qualities the classics can help develop within us; or as [Thomas] Wolfe put it, "What distinguishes us from animals [is] that we have loved great books."

At Dallas Women's Club, Jan. 17/
The Dallas Times Herald, 1-18:(C)3.

Henry Miller
Author

5

The taste for reading has diminished a great deal. There are more books being published, but less that mean anything. Today's books don't seem to carry the weight of those of 25 years ago. The cinema and television have taken over the public's attention. People won't read heavy books any more, unless they happen to be pornographic. I don't see any books existing in 100 years, maybe sooner. It seems to me that we are going to be able to acquire all the information we need through other media.

At National Booksellers Convention,
Los Angeles, June 14/Quote, 7-8:27.

Maurice B. Mitchell
Chancellor, University of Denver

1

You can watch television or go to the movies, but inside your head you have a television screen and a movie screen and an artist's canvas all ready to be put to work. When you read a book, you can paint pictures or invent television programs and do all kinds of things inside your head that you couldn't do outside. You can turn it on when you want it, and turn it off when you don't want it; and it's in color, too. That is something only books can give you. You can go to the library, take a book and read it, and bring it back; and unlike a snack or soft drink that is empty when you finish it, the book is as full as it was when you started; you can never take the insides out of it.

At elementary-school assembly marking end of Reading Week, Arvada, Colo./ The Wall Street Journal, 7-26:10.

Edna O'Brien
Author

2

When I'm writing well, that is akin to what saints call ecstasy. You know it's good, and no other kind of living can ever measure up to it . . . I always know when I'm not writing well. That's when I invent a flimsy excuse to leave my work—I have to go to Harrod's to get a lampshade.

Interview, London/Newsweek, 1-15:34.

Anthony Powell
Author

3

Autobiographies are very enjoyable to read, as long as you realize there is not a word of truth in them. Novels, on the other hand, are full of truth.

Interview, Frome, England/ The New York Times, 6-21:52.

Jeffrey St. John
Political commentator

4

Almost all the modern works of fiction fail to root the reader's mind in reality as [Jack]

London did. This is one reason why most of the modern works of fiction are fraudulent pieces of trash not worth the publisher's asking price. In comparison to London's works, much of modern fiction appears the product of minds who write about life-and-death situations without ever even a passing acquaintanceship with life or reality, which London learned and loved at an early age . . . London once wrote: "Let me glimpse the face of truth. Tell me what the face of truth looks like." What London was saying was that the search for truth was a search for reality, to grapple with life as one would grapple with an angry bear. This is what both the modern novelists and those who read such trash have lost—Jack London's lust for life. No wonder life today seems so dull.

Radio commentary/ The National Observer, 2-10:10.

Irwin Shaw
Author

5

People don't seem to be interested in short stories any more. And the magazines that printed them are closing down . . . And you don't make any money out of short stories, unless the movies pick one up. It's a more difficult form to express yourself than the novel, and it is satisfying to prove you can still do one. But short stories absorb a lot of energy, ideas and anecdotes you can put into novels.

Interview, Klosters, Switzerland/ Los Angeles Times, 2-25:(Calendar)14.

Jacqueline Susann
Author

6

[On why she doesn't give her readers a lot of trouble with words]: I learned that from Hemingway. He said, if you can take a four-syllable word and make it three, do it. He said cut every adjective there is, and then go through and cut again. I do it purposely, because I can write all the big words. If I'm writing a book and I'm telling a story, why should I use a word that maybe eight people [would] understand? It's so much easier to use big words, or use words that are more literary; even the flow goes well. But then you suddenly realize that people who are reading it may not quite get it, and I am most of all a story-teller. If you look up a definition of a novel, it's an extension of life. It should take people into a world or into a place where they haven't quite been, but when they're through, they should feel they've met people. I've always felt that I want to be a good story-teller. If I ever wanted to be literary, I could write a piece. But I think there are so many fine literary people around who are starving. And they hate me, because they think I purposely go out to write commercial books, and I don't. If I thought each book I wrote would be a commercial best-seller, it wouldn't take me three-and-a-half years and I wouldn't suffer . . . I think I'm a hell of a story-teller. And that's what I think a novelist should be.

Interview/
The Washington Post, 4-8:(Book World)2.

Literary critics have never liked any of the great story tellers. [Theodore] Dreiser wasn't supposed to be able to write; [Emile] Zola was called a yellow journalist; and Somerset Maugham never got a Nobel nomination because he was too popular. Popular writers never win prizes. It's like chocolate ice cream: You're not supposed to like it because it's too common . . . A good writer is one who produces books people enjoy, who communicates. So if I'm selling millions, then I'm good.

Interview, Los Angeles/
Los Angeles Times, 5-9:(4)9.

2

[On book clubs]: The Book-of-the-Month Club is still wearing corsets; they're still strait-laced in terms of their selections. But the Literary Guild is wearing pantyhose—they're modern.

The New York Times, 5-29:29.

Irving Wallace
Author

3

Even the most prestigious writers still sit by themselves, and, with their tortured psyches and numbed fingers, write and labor. That's the name of the game—work, patience and revision.

Los Angeles Herald-Examiner, 1-6:(A)10.

Robert Wedgeworth
Executive director,
American Library Association

4

[On proposed cutbacks in Federal funds for libraries]: It is imperative that Americans everywhere be made fully aware of the current plight of all types of libraries. Equal educational opportunities for all people without substantial support for information resources, in a variety of forms, is an unrealistic goal.

The New York Times, 4-25:47.

Thornton Wilder
Author

5

Lots of the works of our 19th-century authors—Melville, Emerson, Irving, Cooper—are unreadable now, although they were fine writers. There was too much Victorian plush and upholstery around them. The new tastes were partly influenced by Gertrude Stein—"A rose is a rose is a rose"—particularly toward prose that was as clean as a hound's tooth. She was a laughing, joyous, affectionate human being, full of insights. She had a gimlet eye for what the direction should be. "Is that adjective necessary?"—you know, that sort of thing. Her influence was toward writing that is clean of extravagance and subjective tumult. When the new frankness of language came in, I greatly approved of it, because the 19th century was a world of hush-hush for growing boys and girls. So now the new candor. All things go by pendulum. From the hush-hush and unspeakable we are now in the open sea of candor. It has gone too far; but it was a very valuable corrective, and we are coming back to equilibrium. You can already see the public is a little sick of revealing the animal impulses of man.

Interview, New York/
Los Angeles Times, 10-15:(2)7.

(THORNTON WILDER)

1

A writer should keep notebooks and write letters. Balzac and Flaubert were great letter-writers. It keeps your hand in. But you've got to learn to throw stuff away; the wastebasket is the writer's best friend.

Interview, New York/
The Washington Post, 11-18:(K)3.

Arthur M. Wilson
Author; Winner, 1973 (U.S.) National
Book Award in arts and letters

2

A biographer is like a contractor who builds roads: It's terribly messy, mud everywhere, and when you get done, people travel over the road at a fast clip.

Interview, New York/
The New York Times, 4-15:(1)56.

Tom Wolfe
Author, Journalist

3

There are really two reasons why the novel has faded. One is simply that people who wanted to write stories began to go into film, either in a theatre or on television . . . But the other thing, perhaps more important, is that young fiction writers, the serious writers, began to operate from a totally different point of view. Their idols were no longer the realistic writers of the past. Their heroes weren't Hemingway, Fitzgerald or Faulkner, much less writers of the 19th century like Dickens. But because they came out of a university atmosphere, the people they began to look at were Beckett, Pinter, Kafka and others, and these were all fable-tellers. And so this atmosphere meant the new fiction should have a mythic quality, which is very strong now; and you have all these young writers who all believe they should write myths because realism has been taken up by film and journalism. It's as if they are trying to write a perfect-enough myth, like the Greeks, which can be re-told and re-told.

Interview, New York/
Los Angeles Times, 7-18:(4)14.

Yevgeny Yevtushenko
Poet

4

I would like to write verses that would not seem banal to sophisticates and at the same time would be understood by unsophisticated readers. [Poetry] is a confession before everybody, and not before a narrow circle of spiritual esperantists.

Interview/
San Francisco Examiner & Chronicle,
4-8:(A)19.

Bella S. Abzug
United States Representative, D-New York

1

Which country in the world ranks 25th in life expectancy? Which country ranks 14th in infant mortality? Which country ranks 14th in literacy? Which country ranks 8th in doctor-patient ratio? The answer to each of these, I am sad to say, is the United States of America.

Quote, 3-25:270.

Lester Breslow
Dean, School of Public health,
University of California, Los Angeles

2

What we die of is influenced by what we eat, whether we smoke and so on. Doctors who treat diseases can do nothing about these things, but those who influence behavior can. Nothing that doctors can do can approach what can be accomplished by influencing behavior.

Interview, Los Angeles/
The Washington Post, 3-18:(G)11.

James L. Buckley
United States Senator, C-New York

3

The proposition is advanced, in support of some . . . health-insurance proposals, that the American system of health-care delivery is in some way fundamentally deficient and needs to be restructured from top to bottom. This criticism has been heard all too frequently in a variety of areas in recent years. The suggestion is made that everything in America is somehow corrupt and that existing forms must be torn out and replaced with new structures which, for the most part, must be under the control of the government. The American people happily now seem to have had their fill of this "what's-wrong-with-America" rhetoric.

Certainly, in the area of medical care, the facts suggest that no radical top-to-bottom changes are needed. I am unalterably opposed to any radical reorganization of our medical-care system by Federal legislation. I likewise oppose creation of a Federal bureaucratic administration to oversee all health-care delivery in this country. Needless to say, if the Federal government does become the source of payment for health-care services, it will have the controlling voice in how these services are rendered.

Nation's Business, April:31.

Morris E. Chafetz
Director, National Institute of Alcohol Abuse and Alcoholism of the United States

4

Parents who learn their children are not using the so-called other drugs, but the drug alcohol, are relieved. And while we are not getting into a competitive battle with other drugs, but a comparative one, parents are being relieved into a serious situation. Since no drug comes close in any measurement to the human and social destruction of alcohol problems, these parents are being relaxed into a situation that is like jumping from the frying pan into the fire.

Los Angeles Times, 6-28:(1)34.

Wilbur J. Cohen
Dean, School of Education, University of Michigan; Former Secretary of Health, Education and Welfare of the United States

5

One of the significant achievements of the now-much-criticized '60s was the general acceptance of the principle that health and medical care [in the U.S.] is a right and not a privilege. The Medicare program demonstrated that medical care can be extended to millions of persons by a governmental health-insurance system. The next step is to extend the principle of Medicare, which now applies to some 20 million senior citizens and the disabled—to all citizens irrespective of race, sex, religion, income or nationality. A national health-insurance program covering every individual from the day of birth to the moment of death is not only necessary and desirable, but, in my opinion, is inevitable. The only question is how and when.

Whitney M. Young, Jr., Memorial Lecture,
Wayne State University/
The National Observer, 4-7:13.

John A. D. Cooper
President,
Association of American Medical Colleges

1

[On the effect on medical schools of President Nixon's health budget cuts]: As grave as these proposed reductions are in their effect on programs for the coming year, implications for successive years are more serious. Dismantlement of faculty and loss of other resources affect not only the short-term prospect for progress in health; the prospect for achieving longer-term goals is also dimmed, since these resource losses are not easily reversible.

News conference, May 21/
Los Angeles Times, 5-22:(1)10.

Joseph D. Cooper
Professor of Political Science,
Howard University

2

I view the current review of over-the-counter medication, especially the speed with which it is to be executed, with concern. It should behoove us to proceed with deliberate slowness, for we might otherwise thrust new burdens on the medical-care system if we deny access by the general public to many remedies for symptomatic or even remedial relief. If anything, thought should be given to transferring some prescription medicines to self-prescriptive status.

Before American Academy of Allergy,
Washington, Feb. 12/
Los Angeles Times, 2-13:(1)17.

Charles C. Edwards
Assistant Secretary for Health,
Department of Health, Education and
Welfare of the United States

3

If the medical profession and the AMA were to take a hard line against reasonable attempts on the part of government to help solve the problems we face [in health care], such a defense position would be seriously counter-productive . . . The public is not going to accept a continuation of things as they are. The public will insist that some way be found to make sure that no one is priced out of the health marketplace, that no one gets care that is below a reasonable standard of quality, and that no one is forced to do without appropriate care simply because it is not available in his or her area of the country.

Before American Medical Association House
of Delegates, New York, June 27/
The New York Times, 6-28:19.

Thomas Elmendorf
President,
California Medical Association

4

[To stave off further government inroads in medicine, doctors must begin] rededicating ourselves to the really personal factors in medical care, [to] personal, compassionate, individual care. Nothing can replace this personal contact of the physician with his patient; and nothing can replace the art of the physician who "reads" his patient.

At his inauguration, Anaheim, Calif.,
March 13/San Francisco Examiner, 3-14:21.

Daniel X. Freedman
Chairman, Department of Psychiatry,
University of Chicago

5

[Saying the use of pills and other self-medication is not necessarily undesirable]: Societies have to self-medicate themselves. If we didn't, we'd have to go to a specially-trained person for everything, and our society is already falling apart when it comes to delivering knowledge.

Los Angeles Times, 2-16:(6)7.

Alan F. Guttmacher
President, Planned Parenthood Federation of America

1

[On the U.S. Supreme Court's ruling that abortions are legal during the first three months of pregnancy]: By this act, hundreds of thousands of American women every year will be spared the medical risks and emotional horrors of back-street and self-induced abortions. And as a nation, we shall be a step further toward assuring the birthright of every child to be welcomed by its parents at the time of its birth.

Jan. 22/The New York Times, 1-23:1.

Milton Helpern
Chief Medical Examiner,
City of New York

2

[On euthanasia]: I don't like this business. It leaves me cold. The arrogance of these doctors is so unnecessary. There are ways of making a patient comfortable. It usually turns out to be a case of impatience on the part of relatives and doctors—not the patient.

The New York Times, 7-1:(4)3.

Charles A. Hoffman
President,
American Medical Association

3

[On poor nutrition, excessive alcohol consumption, cigarette smoking, etc.]: Can anything be done to combat all this "personal pollution," this willful self-neglect and self-abuse? . . . Health must become the "thing to do." It must become a status symbol.

At Congress on Medical Education,
Chicago, Feb. 10/
San Francisco Examiner, 2-12:12.

John J. Horan
Senior vice president, Merck & Company

4

When the President of the United States tells the nation that "millions of citizens do not have adequate access to health care," he offers both an indictment and an opportunity for all of us concerned with health care. A reshaping process is now under way. And part of this process is to call into question the quality, the comprehensiveness and the methods of delivery of health-care services. Improvement of those services is a goal to which all of us—physicians, pharmacists and the pharmaceutical industry—can and do subscribe. We may wish, however, that those who make much of the flaws in the system were equally analytical in their consideration of alternatives; and we may wish that they insist on accurate information on which to base their judgments or indictments. We hear, for example, repeated accusations that physicians are misled or duped by prescription-drug promotion. Doctors are realists, with professional reputations to maintain. To say they are "manipulated" by promotional materials, which under the law must be truthful and balanced, is a fantasy. Yet, the misstatement continues to circulate, with the implication that only the crusader has eyes for the truth. The danger is that, if the man on the street is told continuously that doctors are incapable of making professional judgments, he may come to believe just that. What I do advocate is a strong defense for all that is good within our health system, coupled with a strong dedication to its improvement. We must lend our support and ideas to those who are working to correct abuses and inadequacies. At the same time, we must see things as they are.

Before National Association of
Retail Druggists, Portland, Ore.,
Oct. 16/Vital Speeches, 11-15:94.

Harold E. Hughes
United States Senator, D-Iowa

5

[On Nixon Administration opposition to his bill for additional Federal support for al-

(HAROLD E. HUGHES)

coholism programs]: To have this sort of rec- ommendation by the Administration is to be irresponsible, neglectful and not face up to the needs of the poor, defenseless alcoholic. It is a dark day as far as the future of alcohol- ism is concerned. It's a national tragedy. It's a day of shame for me [a reformed alcoholic] personally.

At hearings of Senate Subcommittee on
Alcoholism and Narcotics,
Washington/
The New York Times, 3-18:(1)44.

Peter B. Hutt
General Counsel, Food and Drug
Administration of the United States

1

Regulation of the safety of food and drugs should be an extremely simple and perfuncto- ry task. Unfortunately, this does not occur in the real world. In the 20 months that I have held my current position, I cannot recall one major safety decision by the FDA—regardless which way it was resolved—that has failed to provoke prolonged, and at times bitter, public dispute . . . Public policy design and execu- tion with respect to the safety of food and drugs is highly, and perhaps irretrievably, con- troversial.

San Francisco Examiner & Chronicle,
8-26:(This World)22.

Khir Johari
Malaysian Ambassador to the United States

2

It is difficult for a layman like me to understand why drug-abuse is rampant mostly in countries that have the highest standard of living. In these countries, religion is being free- ly practiced and the communication gap rarely exists. There must be something wrong some- where.

At International Police Academy meeting
on narcotics/
The Dallas Times Herald,
12-12:(A)3.

Edward M. Kennedy
United States Senator, D-Massachusetts

3

No one stands on a higher or more well- deserved pedestal in our national life today than the doctors of America. Think of the inspiration you give the young, the comfort you bring the old, the hope you give us all. The miracle of your healing power, your grace and skill, your learning and compassion are qualities that will never dim with time. They serve as beacons to the nation, continuing daily reminders of how much we could ac- complish in other areas of our nation's chal- lenge, if only we had your vision and commit- ment to meet the need.

Before American Academy of
Family Physicians, New York/
Quote, 3-18:245.

4

[Criticizing Nixon Administration medical- science budget cuts]: It is a crisis which devel- oped because a small group of men, isolated both from the scientific community and the people they are supposed to serve, decided that they alone knew best about what was important for the health of the country. They rejected the advice of outside consultants, leading scientists and their own great research agency [the National Institutes of Health]. If we have learned anything from the tragic events of the Watergate [political-espionage] scandal, it is that public policy must not be made in that arrogant fashion.

At National Institutes of Health, May 23/
The Washington Post, 5-24:(A)3.

John R. Kernodle
Chairman, American Medical Association

5

[Criticizing the Nixon Administration's Phase 3 price controls as they apply to the medical profession]: Controls are relaxed in other areas, yet the discrimination against physicians and some 3 million others who serve America's health needs is now even more sharply focused. A very real possibility exists that there will be a flight of allied, ancillary and support personnel from the health field, jeopardizing the quality of health care being delivered. How can the health-service industry, saddled with controls, compete for skilled personnel in an economy that is otherwise virtually free?

Chicago, Jan. 11/
Los Angeles Times, 1-12:(1)12.

Ancel Keys
Professor Emeritus of Physiology,
University of Minnesota

1

Much of the propaganda about over-weight goes far beyond scientific justification. There is no excuse to make people worry and feel guilty simply because they are a few pounds over "desirable" weight or even over the average for their height . . . In recent years, weight-reduction has become a considerable industry in the United States. Reducing clubs and "health spas" are spreading rapidly and obviously make money; books full of outrageous nonsense about dieting sell by the million. All this is not totally bad, perhaps. But in regard to preventive medicine and the maintenance of health, one could wish for other priorities.

At National Institutes of Health conference
on obesity, Washington, Oct. 2/
Los Angeles Times, 10-3:(1)7.

Sol Kittay
Industrialist, Philanthropist; President,
Kittay Scientific Foundation

2

[On why he decided to sponsor research in the mental-health field]: Some years ago, I read a story about a man who was a homosexual and didn't realize it. And when he did realize it and sought help, he was told that, if he had a heart attack, he would have a better chance of receiving a cure than he would with this condition. That stuck with me.

News conference, New York, April 11/
The New York Times, 4-12:53.

Arthur Kornberg
Nobel Prize-winning biochemist,
Stanford University

3

[Criticizing the Nixon Administration's pro-

posal to halt Federal support for training basic medical researchers]: [This constitutes] the most calamitous decision a government of the United States could make for the future of medicine and the welfare of our country. Were there an intentional effort to undermine the health and economic welfare of this country for the coming generations, I could imagine nothing more devastating than to stop training young people to do research in basic medical science . . . In the next 20 years, the chemistry of genes can become more precise, varied and extensive. The control of genetic functions and the replacement of defective genes will, if we don't sabotage on-going basic chemical and biologic research, transform the image of health and disease as dramatically as any advance in the history of medicine.

Before National Cystic Fibrosis
Research Foundation,
March 15/
The Washington Post,
3-16:(A)25.

Louis C. Lasagna
Professor, University of Rochester (N.Y.)
School of Medicine and Dentistry

4

My conclusion is that euthanasia is not something in the future, but that we are practicing the purposeful shortening of life right now and have been doing it for some time. Sometimes it's a merciful shortening of life, and other times it's a shortening of life that's achieved in a very cruel way . . . The choice is really not between euthanasia and no euthanasia; the choice is between secretive and uncontrolled shortening of life and more openly-discussed and handled controlled shortening of life. I prefer the latter, because I believe there is more chance of minimizing harm to patients, more who might benefit from treatment, or to relatives of the patient, and less chance, also, of damaging seriously the ethical fabric of our society if we do it in an open and controlled way rather than in the current way.

The National Observer,
4-28:13.

Henry L. Lennard
Professor of Medical Sociology,
University of California, San Francisco

1

Alcoholism treatment and rehabilitation programs must consider how difficult it is for persons already habituated to an alcoholic life to remain sober within an alcoholic society. Today's environment commands you to drink; you are considered a deviant if you don't. You go out to dinner or you go to a party —you turn down a drink and you are the odd one. There is an enormous advertising campaign which links alcohol with social success. Alcohol taxes are an important part of the national revenues. We have to change this—to construct a new landscape which commands you NOT to drink.

San Francisco Examiner, 9-19:28.

Harald Loe
Director, Dental Research Institute,
University of Michigan

2

The technical skill, time, effort and perseverance required to continually maintain a high standard of oral cleanliness exceed the ability of the average human being. The fact that the public has been purchasing power-driven brushes, water-irrigation devices and a multitude of other gadgets shows a general dissatisfaction with the handbrush-level of technology and a definite interest in improving the state of oral hygiene—provided this can occur without much personal effort. This is somewhat encouraging. What is not encouraging at all is the lack of constructive imagination on the part of the dental profession and industry in developing mechanical devices for the swift and effective cleansing of teeth.

At meeting commemorating the 25th
anniversary of the National Institute of
Dental research, Washington/
The New York Times, 7-1:(1)28.

Robert Q. Marston
Former Director, National Institutes
of Health of the United States

3

There is immorality in *not* carrying out

necessary research involving human subjects . . . There are several obvious reasons why such research must be carried on. First, in many instances there may not be a suitable animal model. Second, even if such an animal model exists, there always comes a time at which the test must be carried out in man. Even when the situation is as clear-cut as it was when it became possible to prevent the death of experimentally-infected mice by treatment with penicillin, it still was necessary to test the antibiotic in man. Medical history is full of examples in which the promise of animal experimentation failed to hold up in humans, or in which the results in man exceeded those that would have been predicted from animal experimentation. Finally, and most relevant to this discussion, is the need to test definitively in humans the procedures and therapies which are already part of the practice of medicine. The potency of modern procedures and therapies is such that the experimental method is often the only effective way to determine if their benefits are outweighed by undue hazard.

The National Observer, 2-24:17.

4

Nations have struggled for years with the problem of maintaining objectivity and the ultimate test of truth in the conduct and the management of biomedical research as that research has been supported increasingly with public funds. The solution in most countries except our own has been to separate medical research from the direct control of government because of the conviction that the political process is inherently incapable of resisting the temptation to misuse science for its own immediate political needs. Thus, throughout Western Europe the medical-research councils tend to be autonomous or semi-autonomous bodies supported by government but not controlled by government. Even in a country such as the U.S.S.R., the Academy of Medical Sciences, and not the Ministry of Health, has the major responsibility for the conduct and support of such research in the U.S.S.R. In this country [the U.S.], so far at least, enlightened leadership in both the Executive and Congressional Branches has resulted not only in a sound and healthy growth in biomedical research, but in [a] minimum of attempts to bend science to meet short-term political needs.

The National Observer, 6-2:11.

George S. McGovern
United States Senator, D-South Dakota

1

Currently-available diet plans run the gamut of the human imagination and vocabulary. Plans for the purchase at bookstores, health-food shops and through mail-order firms suggest: the water diet, the rice diet, the milk-and-bananas diet, the grapefruit diet, the drinking-man's diet, the lopsided-egg diet, the starvation diet, the crash diet, the loving-care diet, the macrobiotic diet, the eat-all-you-want diet, the raw-food diet, the organic-fruit diet, the baked potato-and-buttermilk diet, the bread, cheese and wine diet, and so on, ad infinitum. The benefits offered run from instant weight loss, lifetime thinness and sexual prowess, to psychic awareness, philosophical bliss and cures to cancer, paralysis, schizophrenia and syphilis. And while the prescription-drug and medical industries are under regulation by the Food and Drug Administration and other agencies, the diet industry, which produces potions and plans which often call for fundamental restructuring of an individual's dietary regimen, is virtually free from governmental restraints. The over-weight consumer is the most unprotected consumer of all.

The Wall Street Journal, 4-16:10.

John A. McMahon
President, American Hospital Association

2

Not long ago we regarded the idea of national health insurance as a socialistic plot that would rob America of its cherished heritage of free enterprise and individual initiative. But over the years we have come to realize that some form of universal health insurance —a more accurate term for what we believe will work best—is not only inevitable, but that the advantages—both to the consumer and the provider—could far outweigh the disadvan-

tages. And so, like regulation, the issue is not *whether* we will have it, but when and how.

At Town Hall, Los Angeles,
March 20/Vital Speeches, 5-1:435.

3

Americans are not concerned about getting well any more. They are concerned about what it's going to cost them—will an illness or injury bankrupt them.

At Town Hall, Los Angeles, March 20/
Los Angeles Herald-Examiner, 3-21:(A)6.

Margaret Mead
Anthropologist

4

I think that abortion is necessary as a back-up against our failure to protect and educate young women, our failure to provide contraception to anyone who needs or wants it, and our failure to provide people with enough to eat. I am in favor of a society where no woman has to turn to abortion as a result of these failures . . . The goal of this organization [Planned Parenthood] should be to prevent the births of unwanted children and to see that no more women need abortions. We should not be promoting abortion as a way of life. To argue for a woman's right to an abortion is absurd. Women have a right to institutions which will see to it that they never have an unwanted child.

Before Planned Parenthood Federation
of America, New York, Oct. 28/
Los Angeles Times, 10-29:(1)5.

Karl A. Menninger
Psychiatrist; Co-founder, Menninger Clinic

5

I used to believe that psychiatry was the great hope for America. But now I feel it's failed, and I don't really know why. People in analysis don't really seem to get better, as I once hoped and thought they would. Perhaps psychiatrists have become too arrogant, without enough love or compassion in their work. Did you see that study about a number of sane people who made up symptoms and had themselves admitted to mental institutions? As soon as they were there, they said they were all right; but the psychiatrists who examined them wouldn't believe them, and some of them were in there for months. The *patients* knew, though; they could tell who was sane better than the psychiatrists.

Interview, New York/
Publishers Weekly, 8-6:23.

1

I've spent most of my life treating people and teaching young doctors to do so. But more and more I see the still-greater importance of doing something preventive. Psychiatrists should eventually work themselves out of business by preventing illness or disorganization. But there's no money in prevention!

Interview/Time, 8-6:60.

Gaylord Nelson
United States Senator, D-Wisconsin

2

The drug industry is fleecing the people by trying to convince them through high-powered and expensive advertising that drugs sold under a brand name at exhorbitant prices are somehow or other more reliable than the same drugs sold under their official name, for one-half to almost one-thirtieth as much.

June 11/The New York Times, 6-12:15.

Richard M. Nixon
President of the United States

3

Law enforcement alone will not eliminate drug abuse. We must also have a strong program to treat and assist the addict. Two-thirds of my proposed anti-narcotics budget goes for treatment, rehabilitation, prevention and research. We are approaching the point where no addict will be able to say that he commits crimes because there is no treatment available for him. By providing drug offenders with every possible opportunity to get out of the drug culture, we need feel no compunction about applying the most stringent sanctions against those who commit crimes in order to feed their habits.

Radio address to the nation, March 10/
The Washington Post, 3-11:(A)4.

Abraham E. Nizel
Professor of Nutrition and
Preventive Dentistry, Tufts University

4

[Indicating the extent of tooth decay in the U.S.]: If all the 100,000 dentists in the United States restored decayed teeth day and night, 365 days a year, as many new cavities would have formed at the end of the year as were just restored during the previous year.

Before Senate Select Committee on
Nutrition, Washington/
The New York Times, 3-11:(4)10.

Albert S. Norris
Chief of Psychiatry,
Southern Illinois University Medical School

5

Most people do not realize the seriousness of the problems caused in trying to quit smoking. Cigarettes in their own way can be as addictive for many people as heroin. For heavy smokers, cigarettes have become the way to solve their problems. If you get tense, you take a cigarette. If you get bored, you take a cigarette. Under similar circumstances, a non-smoker would go for a walk, play badminton, plant flowers or bite his fingernails. Smokers have less of these outlets than any other people; they don't have to have them. They have learned *their* way of doing it. After 20 years, they've forgotten all the normal ways of dealing with tension.

Interview/Los Angeles Times, 6-7:(6)7.

Hans Popper
Dean, Mount Sinai Hospital School
of Medicine, New York

6

[On proposed Federal cutbacks in funds for general medical research]: A standard statement by the President [Nixon] is that you can't solve problems by throwing money at them. Research is a typical example where you only get results by throwing money at it. Even if somebody studied some colors of feathers of birds, next year the color of birds may solve the cancer problem. And I think we should not apologize for this.

Panel discussion, New York/
The New York Times, 4-15:70.

William Proxmire
United States Senator, D-Wisconsin

1

I think the American people are in a mess, physically. They're fat; they're lazy . . . When people are out of condition, they're less gentle, less friendly, less healthy, less kind. I think that being in shape is the way to have a better society and a better country.

Interview, New York/
The New York Times, 8-7:36.

2

It is no coincidence that in the decade of the '60s, when everything from golf carts to electric can-openers cut down on the effort we make to live in this affluent country, the rate at which young men between 25 and 44 died from heart attacks increased by an alarming 14 per cent. The heart is a muscle like any other; it needs exercise. The best, cheapest and most enjoyable way to exercise is to walk your way to health.

The Dallas Times Herald, 9-30:(A)37.

David L. Rosenhan
Professor of Psychology and Law,
Stanford University

3

How many people, one wonders, are sane but not recognized as such in our psychiatric institutions? How many have been needlessly stripped of their privileges of citizenship? How many have been stigmatized by well-intentioned but nevertheless erroneous diagnosis? Finally, how many patients might be "sane" outside the psychiatric hospital but seem insane in it? It is clear that we cannot distinguish the sane from the insane in psychiatric hospitals.

San Francisco Examiner & Chronicle,
3-18:(B)2.

Benno C. Schmidt
Chairman, (U.S.) President's Cancer Panel

4

The worst thing we can do is to indicate

that in a couple of more years, if we spend enough money, we will have a vaccine or a magic wand [to cure cancer]. Cancer is a terribly complicated subject. It is not a single disease and probably won't lend itself to a single cure. It is many diseases, and many approaches will be required. Progress will come on them one-by-one unless we have a miraculous cure, which none of us truly expects today.

News conference, Los Angeles, Oct. 11/
Los Angeles Times, 10-12:(2)1.

Raymond P. Shafer
Chairman, National Commission on Marijuana
and Drub Abuse of the United States

5

Drugs [are] an emotional thing. Our country has been running in great directions, but the first step in educating a community is to tell the truth. We want to put marijuana in its proper perspective, to show that it is relatively minor on the scale of social harm.

News conference, Rio de Janeiro, Jan. 14/
The Dallas Times Herald, 1-14:(A)15.

Jule M. Sugarman
Human Resources Administrator
of New York City

6

Medicaid [in New York] is already cut into too many pieces. Surveillance-utilization review is the responsibility of the state and city health agencies. Eligibility is supervised by the state Department of Social Services, but administered separately from income maintenance . . . All these functions rely on the same basic data. It is senseless to have separate systems running side by side. The amount of inter-system linkage required is extremely wasteful if not unmanageable. The opportunities for bureaucratic buck-passing are endless.

Before state commission studying social service
laws/ The New York Times, 2-4:(4)7.

Thomas Szasz
Professor of Psychiatry,
State University of New York, Syracuse

7

You have a right to have syphilis and go

untreated; you have a right to have tuberculosis and go untreated; but not mental illness. What right do psychiatrists have judging a person "mentally ill" and putting him into an institution, where the eventual effect of the institution leads to aberrent behavior that then becomes confused with the original "mental illness"? Why should people be locked up because psychiatrists cannot understand their language? If a man says, "I am Jesus Christ . . . eat my body, drink my blood," should we lock him up? At worst he is a liar. We do not demand that bees explain to us the meaning of insects or that Egyptian tablets explain to us the meaning of hieroglyphics, and we do not conclude that, if they fail to offer "explanations" which satisfy us, their languages are "incomprehensible" or "meaningless." Yet this is exactly what psychiatrists—and to a . . . large extent others—intellectuals, philosophers, laymen—have done with respect to so-called mental patients. They insist that the "patient" give them an account of himself satisfactory to them, and that if the person fails to do so, he is to be declared "dangerously ill" and treated as a menace to himself and others.

The Washington Post, 9-3:(A)25.

Lewis Thomas
President, Memorial Sloan-Kettering
Cancer Center, New York

1

As to mortality, I have a hunch that we will discover, some day, that disease and death are not as inextricably interrelated as we tend to view them today. All the rest of nature undergoes, in its variable cycles, the physiological process of death by the clock; all creatures, all plants age finally and, at the end, they all die. Diploid cells in tissue culture have finite life spans, which are different for different lines of cells, and characteristic of particular cell stocks. Some live for 40 generations and then die; others for 70. They do not develop fatal diseases; it is not a catastrophe; they simply reach the end of a life-span pro-

grammed for them in their own genomes, and, at the end of that span, they die. I believe that we [humans] are also like this. If we are not struck down, prematurely, by one or another of today's diseases, we live a certain length of time and then we die; and I doubt that medicine will ever gain a capacity to do anything much to modify this. I can see no reason for trying, and no hope of success anyway. At a certain age, it is in our nature to wear out, to come unhinged and to die, and that is that. My point here is that I very much doubt that the age at which this happens will be very drastically changed, for most of us, when we have learned more about how to control disease. The main difference will be that many of us will die in relatively good health, in a manner of speaking. Rather after the fashion of Bertrand Russell, we may simply dry up and blow away.

At Squibb Institute for Medical Research,
Princeton, N.J., Oct. 11/
Vital Speeches, 11-15:76.

Leslie T. Webster
Chairman, Department of Pharmacology,
Northwestern University

2

The average physician writes prescriptions for 75 per cent of his patients. Too many are for drugs that are unnecessary, ineffective as recommended and sometimes downright dangerous . . . Patients expect the doctor to prescribe something. They want a load of pills to show the doctor cares.

Los Angeles Times, 2-16:(6)7.

Paul Dudley White
Physician

3

Nature is on our side if we are reasonable. We can control our destiny by changing our way of life—by eliminating tobacco, getting real exercise, keeping our weight down and not eating too much fatty foods or foods with cholesterol. Keep moving and keep thinking. Don't let your brain atrophy. Too many people die from disuse of their bodies.

Interview, Belmont, Mass./
Los Angeles Times, 8-9:(1)8.

Ernest L. Wynder
President, American Health Foundation
1

It should be the function of medicine to have people die young as late as possible.
"W": a Fairchild publication, 5-18:16.

Richard E. YaDeau
Surgeon; Chairman,
Foundation for Health-Care Evaluation
2

Within the physician community, some still argue about whether the physician shall be accountable for his performance. As we physicians continue to debate this, the rest of the world has long since assumed that physicians *are* accountable—an assumption virtually unanimous throughout the non-physician community. Actually, the issue is no longer accountability, but: by what standards shall physicians be measured and who will be their architect.
The New York Times,
10-28:(1)52.

The Performing Arts

MOTION PICTURES

Muhammad Ali
*Former heavyweight boxing champion
of the world*

1

I turn down movie roles all the time. I ain't going to play in those movies made for black people. There's too much profanity, drinking, shooting up dope on the streets of Harlem, black women in bed with white men and black men in the shower with white women. You can't take your family to pictures like that. They're going to have to give me a superior role like they do to Charlton Heston or Peter O'Toole to get me in a movie.

*Interview, Las Vegas, Nev., Feb. 13/
Los Angeles Herald-Examiner, 2-14:(D)1.*

Lindsay Anderson
Director

2

I'm not a career [film] director, going from one movie to the next. I don't *enjoy* working in cinema the way I enjoy working in the theatre. It's difficult to relax when you're making a movie; the challenge is so great, like fighting a war. Some people *like* fighting wars, but I don't. I like to feel free, without pressures of money and time. Doing a play is more like a holiday.

*Interview, New York/
The New York Times, 7-1:(2)17.*

Fred Astaire
Actor

3

[On the cutback of film production by Metro-Goldwyn-Mayer]: The fact that the studio is no longer what it once was does not make me sad. I had a great time there and enjoyed it, as I've enjoyed almost every place I've ever worked. But I don't have nostalgia hangups like some people. I don't have sloppy feelings. It's been proved that there's no need

today for a big permanent establishment. Great movies can be made today without the great studio.

*Interview/
Los Angeles Times, 11-18:(Calendar)23.*

Lucille Ball
Actress

4

[On "permissive" motion pictures]: A lot of dirty old men have been on a ragged, jagged toot of making money and pandering to an audience's basest instincts. As soon as they are not making money—which is happening already—those pictures will sit in the vault. I know my audience is still out there, so I'm not worried. But it's a terrible thing as a mother—or father—to try to shape your children morally and in every other way and have it torn down in one short season of movie-going; because once they are 15 and a certain height, they are allowed into the theatres, and everything they were taught to believe in is ripped apart . . . Today's films leave the young people in a spiritual wasteland. No direction; everything is dirty, smelly, icky, lousy. They should have something to hope for, to dream about. We need a little fantasy; not just sexual fantasies. We give them no hope any place.

*Interview, Los Angeles/
San Francisco Examiner, 1-13:9.*

Richard Benjamin
Actor

5

I think everyone connected with movies is still partly childlike . . . I have my own theory that people see films absolutely as children, the way they always did from their school days. Movies are like dreams. You may not be able to understand or explain quite why some things work, but you can say that it had meaning or not. How can you criticize a dream? There's a level of fantasy in movies I'd like to sustain, the kind that keeps [Humphrey] Bogart alive today. Think of the enormous impressions you get of someone 15 feet high; a giant, unforgettable figure . . .

Interview, Cannes, France/
San Francisco Examiner & Chronicle,
2-11:(Datebook)14.

Ingmar Bergman
Director

1

Film-making is very hard work. It's a tough job. You must be on top of yourself every day. In the theatre you don't have to make your own stories; one can rely on Moliere, Strindberg, Ibsen. And if you feel that what you are doing is not good this day, there is always the hope that it will be better tomorrow or next week or in two weeks. Films offer no such consolation. Stage work is very un-neurotic; film work is, shall we say, a little bit stressy.

Interview, Copenhagen/
Los Angeles Times, 2-25:(Calendar)16.

2

I am sorry that we do not have more women directors. It is crazy that 99 per cent of all directors are men. If we had more women as directors, they could give us so many great and interesting [views] of them, just as women poets and writers can give us in literature. I would like to see at least 50 per cent or more women directors!

News conference, Cannes, France/
The Christian Science Monitor, 5-24:14.

3

There was someone who said that a film director is a person who never finds the time to think because of all the problems. That is the closest definition I can think of. Then, of course, one can think up a lot of things on the spur of the moment, all sorts of explanations. One can say that film direction is the transformation of visions, ideas, dreams and hopes in pictures which convey these feelings to the audience in the most efficient manner. One can also say that film direction can be given a strictly technical definition. Along

with an awful lot of people, performers and technicians, and a tremendous lot of machines, one produces a product. It's an everyday product or a work of art, whichever one prefers. What it is in reality–or if it is all of this or none of this–I'm unable to answer, although I have been directing films for 27 years.

The New York Times Magazine, 7-1:17.

Bernardo Bertolucci
Director

4

You can plot my career by listing the hotels I've stayed at in New York. First it was the Salisbury. Then the Warwick. Now the Sherry-Netherland. Where shall I stay for my next film?

Interview, New York/
"W": a Fairchild publication, 2-9:7.

5

There is no such thing as pornography. There are either good films or bad films. The term "pornography" was invented by the distributors of blue movies.

Interview, New York/
"W": a Fairchild publication, 2-9:7.

Robert Bolt
Playwright, Screenwriter, Director

6

In the theatre, a writer's work is paramount. He takes the lion's share of credit or blame. A skillful stage director can make a bad play seem better; but that's the limit of his power. Film is so much more flexible than theatre. The limits of what can be shown—from the twitch of an eyelid to the bursting of a dam—are so much wider that the director becomes the prime creative element. A filmwriter's work can be turned inside out and isn't much more than raw material for the director.

San Francisco Examiner, 2-16:29.

Ernest Borgnine
Actor

7

[On the villainous roles he plays]: What I do is so devilishly easy—no Stanislavsky. I

(ERNEST BORGNINE)

don't chart out the life history of the people I play. If I did, I'd be in trouble. I work with my heart and my head, and naturally my emotions follow. Like for *Emperor [of the North Pole]*, I said to myself, "You're an ugly sonofabitch," and really uglied myself up inside. Then, when we were ready to shoot, I prayed to the good Lord above and started to curse, because it took cursing to put me into the mood. If none of that works, I think to myself of the money I'm making.

Interview, New York/
The New York Times, 6-17:(2)13.

Charles Boyer
Actor

1

I hate acting in movies. It's not the same thing as acting on stage, because it's done forever and is sealed in celluloid.

Interview, Beverly Hills, Calif./
San Francisco Examiner & Chronicle,
3-25:(Datebook)24.

James Cagney
Actor

2

I was always, what do you call it, a journeyman actor. I never gave a damn about the rest of it. Do the job and run; I don't need the applause. My feeling always was that there was so much more living to do outside the [film] industry. By the time I'd finished each job, I'd have my reservations to get out of here [Hollywood]. There was all the nonsense going on here; and I figured the days aren't long enough for doing all the things that are fun and interesting.

Interview, Los Angeles/
Los Angeles Times, 5-6:(Calendar)1.

Michael Caine
Actor

3

[On working with Laurence Olivier]: He was totally cooperative, but not helpful. Let me explain the difference. The cooperation came from his complete professionalism. He was always early on the set, friendly and charming. But as far as any bits like, "Look, son, let's do it this way," forget it. For a man to be a truly great actor—and Larry is the greatest—he must be only aware of what he himself is doing. It was *my* worry to stand or fall on my own. If I needed help on the set, it was up to me to get a drama coach for the job, not Lord Olivier.

Interview, San Francisco, Jan. 15/
San Francisco Examiner, 1-16:19.

Frank Capra
Former director

4

Film has been liberated at such a rapid pace that some directors are drunk with freedom. These films [with sex and violence] can shock, yes; but they are not art. We must explore the human heart as well as our vices.

Before Seattle Film Society/
The Dallas Times Herald, 3-15:(C)8.

Leslie Caron
Actress

5

I always used to say that one should be very careful in selecting parts and just do the good things; but I think I was wrong. I think an actress should do everything that's offered to her, all the junk parts; because out of junk you will be good, and one day someone will notice you and give you that special part.

Interview, Los Angeles/
The Hollywood Reporter, 3-5:6.

6

I don't think Hollywood is an appropriate place for an actress of 40. In America you have to play freak parts—to swing a hatchet—if you're in that age category. In France you can still play love stories . . . Hollywood is all geared for men, because they are organized in a businesslike fashion and can find themselves parts. In France . . . I don't think women suffer from so much neglect.

The National Observer, 5-5:6.

Charles Champlin
Film critic, "Los Angeles Times"

7

It sounds pretentious to say it, but there is

no other reason for being in film criticism than to help raise tastes.

Newsweek, 12-24:96.

Sean Connery
Actor

1

The movie business isn't like other industries. You can't go in for market research. Who can say what the public really wants at any given moment? Look, if a certain size of boots is popular, and you can produce them at 75 per cent of the market price, and double your production . . . there's no doubt you're going to make a big gross profit, right? But with a film, you can't.

Interview, London/
San Francisco Examiner & Chronicle,
1-7:(Datebook)14.

Constantin Costa-Gavras
Director

2

All film-makers are political. They have a political purpose—in a certain way. The old Hollywood films are political. They rationalized the extermination of the American Indians. Always I remember, from the old Westerns, that if you saw Indians in the film, you knew that, at the end, they would die.

Interview, Washington/
The Washington Post, 4-6:(B)13.

Joan Crawford
Actress

3

I'm desolate at the thought I might be through [making films]. But today there just aren't jobs enough for women—they don't write for them any more. I wish I were Duke [John] Wayne, but I can't ride a horse well enough and I can't shoot straight.

At "Legendary Ladies of the Movies" series,
New York/Newsweek, 4-23:47.

4

[Criticizing the U.S. Supreme Court ruling giving local areas control over pornography standards]: Remember those days of the old Hays Office rulings, and I mean *rulings?* A

married couple could not be shown in bed at the same time . . . A screen kiss could last just a certain time, and that meant short . . . A seduction scene could only be suggested, like a man grabbing a woman by the shoulders and drawing her toward him before the fade-out began. Looking back, I wonder how the old films ever got past Cinderella! At least the Hays Office was one body to be pacified and appealed to. Now they are asking us to please an unlimited number of censors, perhaps hundreds of them, the local community censor. Can you imagine such an impossible situation? This would mean these local guardians would be looking over the shoulder of our directors, into the cameras of our cinematographers, impugning the integrity of our writers and inhibiting the work of our actors. How can the film industry submit to going backward after all the wonderful strides it has made forward over the years?

Interview, New York/
Los Angeles Herald-Examiner, 8-28:(B)4.

Judith Crist
Film critic, "New York" magazine

5

To be a critic, you have to have maybe 3 per cent education, 5 per cent intelligence, 2 per cent style and 90 per cent gall and egomania in equal parts.

Newsweek, 12-24:97.

Tony Curtis
Actor

6

. . . actors work very hard. We're not out on golf courses every day. I once sat down and figured it out that a guy like Henry Fonda or John Wayne—some big star who has made 130 movies or more—spends 18 years of his life in a dressing room waiting between shots. That's a lot of work.

Interview, Los Angeles/
The Hollywood Reporter, 3-19:6.

Hal David
Lyricist

7

In writing a love song for the stage, the

(HAL DAVID)

two lovers can sing to each other and still belt it out . . . things somehow become make-believe behind the proscenium. Film is just the opposite . . . things on the screen somehow tend to become more real. The effect all this has on music is that you have to understate things. A big love song that would be a knockout on the stage would look, in a film, too much like Jeanette MacDonald and Nelson Eddy.

Interview/
"W": a Fairchild publication, 3-9:16.

Bette Davis
Actress

1

I don't think the young [actors] are helped today by the freedom they have to choose or reject scripts. They have complete choice of what to do, and that means they do the thing they like and comes easiest to them. But is that the best way to learn? I learned from the pictures that were not ideal, that weren't easiest for me. The young shouldn't have absolute freedom of choice. That makes more sense later, when you really know more about what you are.

Interview, Los Angeles/
Los Angeles Herald-Examiner, 1-25:(B)6.

2

Think of where admission prices have gone. Tickets started out at 10 cents and now are up to $3.50 . . . For my son to take a date to dinner and a show today, it costs him about $25 for the one evening. So audiences now are much choosier. They used to just mark it off if the film was not good, because they didn't pay that much. But with today's prices, they really get mad if the picture is bad.

Interview, Los Angeles/
The Hollywood Reporter, 2-16:18.

Sammy Davis, Jr.
Entertainer

3

[On the cutback of film production by Metro-Goldwyn-Mayer]: When I am looking at

late-night TV wherever I happen to be appearing, I always wait for one of the old, great MGM musicals. It's very saddening to know that no more of these are going to be made under the great MGM banner. It's similar to the Titanic rolling over on its side.

Interview/
Los Angeles Times, 11-18:(Calendar)23.

Kirk Douglas
Actor

4

It's so easy for a director to become pretentious today and make what he thinks is a profound statement. They neglect to make a "movie," or what it was like when we were kids and we saw pirates and cowboys.

Interview, London/
The Hollywood Reporter, 1-11:6.

Clint Eastwood
Actor

5

[On violence in films]: . . . it's not the blood-letting or whatever that people come to see in the movies. It's vengeance. Getting even is a very important thing for the public. They go to work every day for some guy who's rude and they can't stand, and they just have to take it. Then they go see me on the screen and I kick the s— out of him . . . I feel that all this talk about violence in the movies is sort of over-done. Violence can be a catharsis for the audience. You might have, say, 90 people in a movie theatre and one nut; and the violence might inspire this one nut to do something, and everybody blames it on the movies. But we can't worry about that nut.

Interview, Washington/
The Washington Post, 4-24:(B)3.

Peter Falk
Actor

6

I like [making] movies best of all. There's not so much heat on you to get it done fast and cheap. I don't like the hurry of television. I feel very much the pressure and anxiety about schedules. I guess that's the way it has to be on TV. But if you care about something, you want it right—and movies have care and love in them.

Interview, Los Angeles/
The Christian Science Monitor, 4-9:9.

Bob Fosse
Director

1

[On his winning the "Oscar" and "Tony" awards this year]: I don't know what the awards mean, except maybe a few more zeroes on the end of my salary. You get all these awards and suddenly all these big actors want to work with you. People I haven't heard from in 20 years start calling me and saying, "I told you so," even though I don't remember them telling me anything. And you start thinking, "Gee, I must have the golden touch." And then you go back to work and come to grips with a new script and begin to realize all over again how inadequate you are and how tough it is to do something well.

Interview/Newsweek, 5-7:102.

James Franciscus
Actor

2

I'm certainly against censorship, and I feel the [U.S.] Supreme Court's ruling leaving moral judgment up to individual communities is frightful. But I must say that Hollywood has no one to blame but itself for the situation. It's the industry's own damn fault. Filmmakers had the latitude to control the quality of entertainment product, but they ignored their responsibility. Frankly, they deserve everything they get! . . . I just can't see where there is any excuse for nudity in any film made for public distribution.

San Francisco Examiner, 8-15:29.

Mike Frankovich
Producer

3

Cable TV, cassettes, discs that can play up to a two-hour film right in the home are coming, and you [theatre owners] should be making plans on ways to meet this new age of automation. I hope I don't sound downbeat, because I mean to sound upbeat. Entertain-

ment is the greatest business in the world, but we all have to be prepared for what is coming. Radio we ignored. TV we tried to ignore. We have to examine the way in which we can participate in the new developments taking place in our industry.

Before National Association of Theatre
Owners, Dallas, Feb. 1/
The Dallas Times Herald, 2-2:(E)10.

William Friedkin
Director

4

In the old days, we all used to see the same pictures. One week we'd see a Bette Davis picture, the next week a Bogart movie, then maybe a John Ford Western. Today, there's a black audience, a youth audience, what you might call a Middle American audience that sees Disney pictures. There are redneck films that do very well in the South, and New York-type hits, like *A New Leaf*, that die outside the cities. The movie audience has become as fragmented and polarized as the country itself.

Newsweek, 12-24:40.

Lillian Gish
Actress

5

We've got to get back to characters in movies. Building a character is the most difficult thing to do. Action or chases with cars don't take skill or work—they're just good exercise. But to build a character, make it true, not get caught at acting—that's difficult.

Interview, New York/
"W": A Fairchild publication, 11-16:2.

Ruth Gordon
Actress

6

A director is a nonentity. If he could create material, he'd be a writer. If he could interpret material, he'd be an actor. All he can do is sit in the background as the middleman, messing around with the work of artists and throwing up a lot when things go wrong. That's not to say that some directors aren't better than others. There are some who are

(RUTH GORDON)

great within the area which they serve. But I want to stay on the creative end—writing and performing.

At San Francisco Film Festival, Oct. 20/
San Francisco Examiner, 10-22:26.

Cary Grant
Actor

1

I don't wish to sound ungrateful, but the truth is I have very little to do with movies any more. I seldom go to the movies. I realize that they fill an enormous gap for many people, but not for me. I am more attracted to the world of reality. I won't say that I'll *never* make another picture, because I can't look into the future. I guess you can say that I'm retired from the movies until some writer comes up with a character who is deaf and dumb and sitting in a wheel-chair. At my age . . .

Interview, New York/
The New York Times, 7-22:(2)7.

Gene Hackman
Actor

2

It wouldn't be fair to say I haven't been affected by what has happened to me [his success in films]. The "Oscar," for example, is an affirmation of your worth by the standards of your peers; and unless you just don't care what people think of you, it's bound to have an effect. I do care; and winning it has definitely improved my opinion of myself as an actor.

Interview, San Francisco/
Los Angeles Times, 3-18:(Calendar)20.

Henry Hathaway
Director

3

People never remember what they hear in a movie. They only recall what they see. The big hits have unforgettable scenes in them, usually action. Pictures that are filled with dialogue do not do as well. So a conscientious director tries to make everything as visual as possible . . . One day I asked Alfred Hitchcock how he goes about shooting a script. He said sometimes he shoots 10 pages of dialogue in one day, and then spends 10 days shooting one page of something visual.

Interview, Los Angeles/
The Dallas Times Herald, 7-19:(C)12.

Goldie Hawn
Actress

4

In this business, you give and give, and they, your public, take and take and do not give anything back. They can be fickle, too. You get to feeling utterly drained, and you get selfish; you are terrified of giving any more because you're afraid you haven't got it to give. And your personal life sours. But if you know yourself, respect yourself, love yourself, you can keep giving freely, on and on; you replenish yourself.

Interview, Los Angeles/
The New York Times, 1-28:(2)14.

Katharine Hepburn
Actress

5

Everyone needs love at some time. God help us if we have never had any love in our lives. That's why I regret that we don't have any real love on the [film] screen any more. It's just sex, and that's old stuff.

Quote, 6-24:577.

6

A lot of hogwash is talked about acting. It's not all that fancy! When Nijinsky visited Chaplin on a set, Charlie was about to have a custard pie in his face, and Nijinsky said, "The nuances! The miraculous timing!" And it's a lot of bunk. You laugh, you cry, you pick up a little bit, and then you're a working actor. It's a *craft!* You're out there desperately doing something you hope people will come and see. Nowadays, directors, stars are constantly talking—pretentiously and a great deal more than they should—about their art. Talk, talk, talk, talk, *talk!* Spencer Tracy always said acting was "Learn your lines and get on with it"; so does Larry Olivier, so does John Gielgud, all the great ones.

Interview, Los Angeles/
The New York Times, 12-9:(2)21.

Charlton Heston
Actor

1

[On motion pictures]: More than any other [of the arts], it can leap national boundaries, break through language barriers. Indeed, it has done so. People, everywhere, see more film in a year than they read books or listen to music or look at paintings in a decade. I am not saying this is good or bad, simply that it is true. Film is the artform of the 20th century.

Before House Education Subcommittee,
Washington/
The Hollywood Reporter, 3-19:3.

2

When conglomerates started to acquire the [film] studios, the new managements were crazy about the idea of making movies, and they thought all that was needed was an infusion of new blood and new cash. One of the outcomes was that a studio like Paramount found itself with $100 million invested in five pictures—*On a Clear Day You Can See Forever, Catch-22, Paint Your Wagon, The Molly Maguires* and *Darling Lili*—none of which made its costs back at the box office. A little later, the managements decided that *Easy Rider* was the wave of the future, and a lot of money was squandered chasing the so-called youth market. During that period, I remember talking to one of the new heads of production. There was a film shooting on the lot [with] a first-time director, a first-time producer, but supposedly a story made to order for the youth market. This executive got a call informing him that this novice director had exposed 12,000 feet of film during the previous day's shooting. The executive wanted to know if that was good or bad. Well, that movie has still never been released.

Interview, Washington/
The Washington Post, 4-6:(B)1.

3

I wish we [in the film industry] could have more "moderate successes." But it seems to be a question of total failure or unheard-of success these days. It contributes to an all-or-nothing psychology that may not be good for the movie business in general. Perhaps it can't be helped. People seem to make a point of seeing certain pictures, maybe more than once, but avoid all the others.

Interview, Washington/
The Washington Post, 4-6:(B)1.

Alfred Hitchcock
Director

4

Some films are slices of life. Mine are slices of cake.

Interview, Los Angeles/
Los Angeles Herald-Examiner, 2-1:(C)1.

Dustin Hoffman
Actor

5

There's definitely a swing away from so-called "problem" pictures to more conventional entertainment. And that means larger budgets, big stars and established properties. And this works against serious or outspoken themes. When you spend six or seven million dollars, you tend to get very cautious.

Newsweek, 12-24:40.

Celeste Holm
Actress

6

Acting is controlled schizophrenia. That sounds neurotic, but isn't. You are playing someone else while being yourself.

Interview, New York/
The Dallas Times Herald, 8-18:(A)4.

Bob Hope
Actor, Comedian

7

No question about it, the movie audience has shrunk from 80,000,000 to about 14,000,000. Partly it was television, but also it's the dirty pictures. They're doing things on the screen today I wouldn't do on my honeymoon. I can't believe what they're showing on

(BOB HOPE)

the screen. I remember the days when Hollywood was looking for new *faces*.

Interview, North Hollywood, Calif./
Playboy, December:106.

Trevor Howard
Actor

1

"Faking" is a proper word for acting. I played Disraeli though I'm not a Jew, and Napoleon though I'm not French, and Wagner though I'm not a musician . . . Of course it's faking; we feel we're more real when we're not ourselves. I hope I'm not a dull, boring person, but I am afraid I am sometimes, and playing somebody important makes us feel better about ourselves.

Interview, New York/
San Francisco Examiner, 11-6:35.

Ross Hunter
Producer

2

Whatever they say, people go to the movies to be entertained. In life, we're surrounded by ugliness—wars and the cities . . . I believe [we in motion pictures are] dream-makers, and the public wants to dream. I want to keep all my movies beautiful and not glorify the anti-hero or anti-heroine. In an industry that does 300-400 movies a year, surely three or four should stress the good in life. I'm pro-man, not con-man.

Interview, Los Angeles/
Los Angeles Times, 3-11:(Calendar)11.

3

[On negative comments by New York film reviewers for his film, *Lost Horizon*]: Film critics! There aren't any New York film "critics." There are just people trying to make a name for themselves. They never hurt *Airport* or *Sound of Music* or *Love Story* or *Pillow Talk*. They tried to kill them, but the public doesn't believe what they say.

New York/
San Francisco Examiner, 3-20:35.

John Huston
Director

4

Unless an actor needs help, why, I try to interfere with him as little as possible, to get as much out of him and get him to develop his own personality, to reveal it to its fullest saturation, otherwise they'd be weaker shadows of myself . . . I direct actually as little as possible. I like to get my people to do it for me . . . Some of my best ideas have come from grips and electricians.

Interview, London/
The Christian Science Monitor, 8-11:11.

Jenkin Lloyd Jones
Editor and publisher,
"The Tulsa Tribune"

5

What generation . . . produced the Hollywood that's willing to do anything for a buck and comes out with movies that would better be described as peep-shows or as visual aids in an abnormal-psych class and that lards and meringues and whipped creams its hypocrisy by claiming that it is struggling toward new horizons in intellectual freedom? That's *our* generation. *We* sit behind the box office; *we* give the youngsters two bucks or two-and-a-half to go out and see GP rated up from R and R rated up from X. I remember in my generation we were lucky to get a dime to go out and see Tom Mix and Hoot Gibson kiss their horses.

Before Ohio Chamber of Commerce,
Columbus, March 14/
Vital Speeches, 5-15:473.

Pauline Kael
Film critic,
"The New Yorker" magazine

6

The young film-makers have already played a classic joke on the industry. After all those years of advertising about the expensive production values and the casts of thousands, Hollywood is now forced to imitate the rougher, faster techniques of the impoverished film-makers whose energy and originality have made it impossible for us to accept the glossy, luxuriantly wasteful movie-making of the old Hollywood.

Before House Education Subcommittee, Washington/The Hollywood Reporter, 3-19:3.

Sally Kellerman
Actress

1

Sex in movies is one thing. Let us have our jollies—no one's harmed by it. But violence is a crime. I saw *Straw Dogs* and came out hurt, angry, offended and scared. [Director Sam] Peckinpah should be hung by his kihonas. If there's any validity to religion, East and West, it's to combat violence like that.

Interview, Los Angeles/
"W": a Fairchild publication, 3-23:12.

Howard W. Koch
Producer

2

I've never won an "Oscar." I'd give my eyeteeth for an "Oscar." But there has to be more to the [Award] show than grabbing an "Oscar" and walking off. It has to be realized that this is a great public-relations opportunity for the movie business. Hollywood showmanship is supposed to be the best. We have to present glamor, well-dressed people. We have to remember that the world is looking at us. When that stage [at the Award presentations] first comes into sight, the audience should be amazed, and the hook is in.

Los Angeles Herald-Examiner,
3-25:(TV Weekly)5.

Stanley Kramer
Director

3

My critics are severe, but that only makes it more exciting. I read their stuff, all their pat, bourgeois intellectuality. I love approval as much as anyone, but I've also been around awhile. When I was younger, what I wanted to do was give a negative critic a cement overcoat. But I've sublimated that, so sometimes I just don't read them any more. Too much self-analysis is dangerous. I've survived failure.

I'm always pursuing the next dream, hunting for the truth.

Interview, Stockton, Calif./
Los Angeles Times, 1-7:(Calendar)38.

Jack Lemmon
Actor

4

In the old days, my generation thought of movies as escapist entertainment where stars would sell tickets even if the film was lousy. That's no longer true. I can't make *Avanti!* a success if it's no good. This is healthy. I no longer make a million dollars a picture. *The Great Race* made $25 million and still hasn't broken even after they got through paying Natalie Wood and Tony Curtis and me. It's asinine to assume actors are that important. *Save the Tiger* cost only $1,100,000 and it's all right there on the screen. Some stars still hold out for the big money; but they don't work much. I did *Save the Tiger* for nothing, and I'm prouder of it than all those movies I made millions on all rolled into one. That's how the business is changing, and I'm happy to change.

Interview, New York/
San Francisco Examiner & Chronicle,
2-18:(Datebook)10.

5

. . . some films supposed to be erotic aren't. Sex is supposed to be private. When it's done for an audience it isn't private any more. All the eroticism goes out of it for me when it's public. And for that reason I think it's difficult to do a truly erotic film.

Interview, New York/
Los Angeles Herald-Examiner, 10-6:(A)11.

Joseph E. Levine
President, Avco Embassy Pictures

6

My record for pictures has been one success in four. The ratio in the industry used to be one in seven. Now it's one in 15. The business has changed. Fifteen years ago, people went to the movies as a matter of course. Now they're more selective. In those days even a bad picture made a little money. Now it costs too much even to *open* a bad picture:

511

(JOSEPH E. LEVINE)

It costs you $1,000 to run the theatre, and you take in $50 . . . But the future of the motion picture business is not shaky. If I had seven sons, I would urge them to go into the motion picture business. When CATV is final, when there are enough sets out—say in five years—you'll be able to make a film and get all your money back in one night. It's not, by any means, a dying business. The only thing that's dying in our business is the people in it.

Interview, New York/
"W": a Fairchild publication, 12-14:10.

Joseph Losey
Director

1

Film is a dog: The head is commerce; the tail is art. And only rarely does the tail wag the dog.

Interview, Hanover, N.H., June/
The Christian Science Monitor, 7-18:9.

Daniel Melnick
Vice president in charge of production,
Metro-Goldwyn-Mayer, Inc.

2

[MGM's philosophy]: To make pictures that are "movie movies," not polemics or minority entertainment, not for special groups, not downbeat or about losers—and to make them in such a way that we are not so financially exposed that one unsuccessful picture can close down the studio. There isn't enough correlation between the cost of a film and its gross to justify the extravaganzas.

The New York Times, 4-29:(2)11.

Liza Minnelli
Actress

3

[On the Academy Awards]: I can understand male actors thinking the whole ceremony is a lot of baloney and that you shouldn't be working for awards—not that I think anyone is. But it is an honor given by the whole Academy. Anyway, a girl can get herself a new dress, take all day getting ready, and it is like going to a ball. The girl becomes a kind of princess, even if she doesn't win. The thing is, if you do win, the award only rubs off for a short while. After that, you're on your own.

Interview, London/
San Francisco Examiner & Chronicle, 6-3:
(Datebook)13.

Robert Mitchum
Actor

4

Acting is an avoidance of duty. Duty is to contribute. Acting contributes to the Bureau of Internal Revenue. It feeds a lot of hungry goldbrickers. Movies are a diversion to keep the populace distracted. It fills time, keeps them off the street, out of the rain.

Interview/The Dallas Times Herald, 7-6:(F)4.

Zero Mostel
Actor

5

In Hollywood, they're all camera-crazy. Directors fall in love with lenses. They're "close-up" crazy and they're "movement"-crazy. All the great things are really rather simple.

Interview, New York/
"W": a Fairchild publication, 1-12:13.

Paul Newman
Actor

6

[On his feelings about the "Oscar"]: You don't invest nine months of your life in a movie to see it open and die. The whole point is to make people see it, and Academy Award prestige will insure that. But on the other hand, I resent making acting and directing a competitive contest; it's wrong. It's funny, but medals and praise are important while you are trying to climb out of the barrel of molasses. After you've pulled yourself out, you don't need them.

Interview, Santa Monica, Calif./
San Francisco Examiner, 3-17:8.

Richard M. Nixon
President of the United States

7

I am a movie fan. Films are what entertainment should be. I would put it this way: sometimes we need to laugh, we need comedy; sometimes we need to be inspired; and always we need to be reminded of the greatness of our nation.

At tribute dinner for director John Ford,
Beverly Hills, Calif., March 31/
Los Angeles Times, 4-3:(4)11.

Jack Palance
Actor

1

Sometimes I hate being called an actor. What does an actor do? He just sits and waits. No one in the [film] industry is lower. Directors, producers, agents—they dominate. It's as though they spread out a bunch of cards, and the cards are the actors. From this bunch, they pick some cards and see if they can put together a picture. Grips, makeup people— when they look for jobs they maintain a certain prestige. They have a skill; they do a job. Actors aren't selected to do a job. Actors are selected so somebody can do a job with them. Of 35,000 actors here, how many are really actors? Actors are always in a state of limbo. They get a terrible shuffle. They wait for somebody to throw them crumbs.

Interview, Los Angeles/
Los Angeles Herald-Examiner, 10-7:
(TV Weekly)4.

David Picker
President, United Artists Corporation

2

The people in the [film] industry still underestimate the audience. The audience is very, very smart. They're 10 steps ahead of you all the time. And the audience is very specialized and very selective. They choose among family films the way they choose among sex films or Westerns: big hits, big flops, nothing in-between. They swarm to *Tom Sawyer* and stay away from *[Man of] La Mancha* . . . you can't generalize and go on what you *think* audiences want to see. What do you want to see a year-and-a-half or two years from now? You couldn't tell me. You can't make "now" pictures or "then" pictures

or some other kind of pictures. That's not the way you go about making movies. Films are totally individual today, personal and special. So you do your homework in terms of creators. You have to know who's around, here and also in Europe . . . You seek out the creators with lots of ideas and you listen to them. You follow your instinctive reactions and you hope you're latching on to the best of the ideas. You bet on your belief in ideas and your belief in talent.

Interview/Los Angeles Times, 7-11:(4)1.

Anthony Quayle
Actor

3

[On his being a character actor]: I'd hate to be a superstar. I don't know any of them who are really happy. I prefer to remain anonymous . . . When I was young, I had a sneaking feeling that it would have been fun to be really famous. Certainly, there have been times in my life when I've looked at some of the others and thought: Why not me? But now I wouldn't have the star image for anything. You're caught in it, trapped by it. I've seen it too often. You get dead bored, and you even lose the zest for living . . . If the world offers you superstardom, I don't know many people who would turn it down. But I would. I prefer to be a working actor, a character actor, and that's the truth.

Interview, Rome/
San Francisco Examiner & Chronicle,
9-9:(Datebook)10.

Robert Radnitz
Producer

4

We're never going to see the "panacea picture" again, the movie that everyone wants to see. *The Godfather* and *Airport* are exceptions. We can't stay in business with everybody trying to make such movies. It isn't only television that is diverting people; it's sports, camping, travel. You have to be more of a showman today, because movies are no longer the only show in town.

Interview, Los Angeles/
The Hollywood Reporter, 1-22:18.

Satyajit Ray
Director

1

I work under conditions of such extreme freedom. I write my films; I cut them; I do the designing; I operate the camera; I write the music, the advertising; I often dictate the theatre . . . I couldn't tolerate memos and front offices and temperamental stars. I often work with newcomers, people who just come up and knock on the door. In India we don't have that many professional actors, and I don't want to keep using the same people over and over. When I write a part, I get a definite image of my character, and I look for a person who fits that image. Sometimes I place ads in the papers, or I go into the streets and look for faces. When I find a particular face, I speak with the person, I listen to the voice, I watch them walk. If there's a willingness on the part of the person to act and face the camera, then the rest is easy. I like working with raw material.

Interview, Calcutta/
The New York Times, 8-3:16.

Martin Ritt
Producer, Director

2

I'm optimistic about the future of motion pictures. In the next 10 years America will make the best pictures in the world, because the restrictions are finally off. The sex kick is going to fade away fast . . . This country has the health and energy to do the best films, because, after years of difficulties, we can treat subjects realistically and with serious intent. It's been a long pull, but worth it.

Interview/
Los Angeles Herald-Examiner,
9-30:(California Living)29.

Ginger Rogers
Actress

3

I'd rather be involved in digging a very good-looking ditch from here to Albuquerque than to be involved in the filmed sexual fantasies of a sandwich-maker and a truck driver. Some of the [scripts] that have been offered

to me have just turned my stomach. If I had my druthers, I'd stay away from show business until it comes back to what I call entertainment.

Oklahoma City/
The National Observer, 10-6:7.

Paul Roth
President,
National Association of Theatre Owners

4

Selling [motion pictures] to television is quite often a disservice to movies. There is room for both, but neither does any good [when they are shown] too close together or confused together. There is a substantial difference between seeing a movie in a theatre and on television. A viewer cannot dominate a movie screen, [but] he can dominate a television set. They are two quite different experiences. *Patton* six inches high is a lot less effective than *Patton* 18 feet high.

Los Angeles Times, 12-3:(4)18.

George C. Scott
Actor

5

[Acting] is not the healthiest life in the world. It rewards you, but there is a price that has to be paid. Self-criticism can reach neurotic proportions. I've seen it in others, even in me. It's a strange way to make a living. You're very vulnerable, first, last and always. There is an inherent rejection factor —self-rejection, public rejection. If one is lucky, there comes a moment of acceptance, fame and glory; and then you may find you can't deal with that either, and you can spend a life on the shrink couch finding that out. Yet I've worked with very few actors who were aggrandizing or inconsiderate; I could count them on one hand with fingers left over. And the old saw that the bigger they are the nicer they are, that turns out to be true. That's my beef about awards . . . They set up an incredible false competition. They create cut-throatism where there isn't any—only admiration.

Interview, Los Angeles/
Los Angeles Times, 11-11:(Calendar)22.

Andrew Stone
Producer, Director

1

The emotions that made Mary Pickford a star are exactly the same today. I think there is a bigger audience for schmaltz than for pornography . . . There is a preponderance of pictures made today for avant-garde audiences. The market is glutted with violence and sex. But how many producers are making pictures for the long-lost audience that likes sentiment and straight entertainment? I'm going to stay with heart interest, schmaltz, sentiment—whatever you want to call it—and bring a lot of people back to the theatres.

Interview, Los Angeles/
The Hollywood Reporter, 1-2:11.

Gordon Stulberg
President, 20th Century-Fox Film Corporation

2

[On legal rulings designed to tone down allegedly obscene material in films]: The blander we make a scene, the safer we are. But if we adopt what is, in effect, television's standards . . . we are asking people to pay to see nothing more than television on a large screen. And that won't work.

Newsweek, 12-24:45.

Dimitri Tiomkin
Composer

3

[On producing his first film]: I call myself an observer and a son-of-a-bitch; if you combine the two, you come very close to the qualities of the ideal producer!

Interview, London/
San Francisco Examiner & Chronicle,
2-18:(Datebook)18.

Francois Truffaut
Director

4

Two generations of the world's youth were raised on Hollywood films. For us in France, cinema from Hollywood was a way of seeing the world, of learning about life. True, it was an idealized life we were witnessing; but what better form would you recommend for a nine-year-old boy? Films attracted the unhappy. The unhappier you were, the more you liked American films. It was popular art at its best.

Interview, Los Angeles/
Los Angeles Herald-Examiner, 9-2:(E)1.

5

It requires a sort of well-controlled madness to direct a film. Without the madness, there can be no film. One has a great feeling of power directing a film; but it is not like the power of a politician, since no one gets hurt. But the feeling that you have the power to create life is something fantastic.

Interview, New York/
"W": a Fairchild publication, 10-19:7.

Twiggy
British actress

6

There's nothing worse than a British actress attempting to play an American—unless it's an American girl trying an English accent.

Quote, 5-27:482.

Liv Ullmann
Actress

7

[Her impressions of Hollywood]: There you could forget what reality is. I like the glitter. It's seductive to get roses and cars and to have everything you say become suddenly important. You think what you say must be of world-wide interest since people are hanging on your every word. Then one day there aren't any roses in the dressing room, and you think they don't love you any more. You see how you can start to get unreal? Oh, Hollywood is fun, but I'm a little afraid of it, and a bit ashamed sometimes at the way a star is treated, and the way somebody who may be doing important work in the world is downgraded. I didn't say no to the money or the roses or the cars, but I do try to remember that the work is what's important, the roles you play. The work is what you went on the stage in the first place for. It meant so much you would go hungry for it. I don't forget that.

Interview, Washington/
The Washington Post, 6-23:(C)3.

Jack Valenti
President,
Motion Picture Association of America

1

[On the U.S. Supreme Court's ruling that local areas must determine obscenity and pornography standards, and that works need no longer be found utterly without redeeming social value to be banned]: [The Court is] talking about the obviously, patently and gratuitously pornographic material that comes out—the films that make a feeble attempt to redeem themselves by inserting "art," "entertainment" and "culture" into an obviously pornographic context . . . I think the saving thing in the Supreme Court decision is that "serious works of art" are not within its purview. I don't know yet whether the Court ruling will have an effect on creative freedom. It's under intense scrutiny in our legal department. Of course, the real problem is this: What happens if you send what you think is a serious work of art into the marketplace and the local law-enforcement officials harass it? You may win in court, but then you may have to spend so much money that you've doomed your picture to economic disaster. And a jury may say, "You think that's serious, but we think that's obscene." We're going to have to examine this very carefully.

June 21/
The Washington Post, 6-22:(B)1.

2

Movies have fascinated me since I was a small boy. They are the ultimate in drama and creativity. To tell a story in color, on the screen—no other form of drama has that. The stage is insular, confined. A book has no pictures. Paintings are static. Music is one dimensional. But a story on film has all these things. That's why it's so fascinating.

Interview, Washington/
Los Angeles Times, 12-27:(4)12.

E. Cardon Walker
President, Walt Disney Productions

3

If it says "Walt Disney Productions," a family can be assured that they're not going

to be shocked in any way—bored, maybe sometimes, but never shocked.

Time, 7-30:64.

Hal Wallis
Producer

4

Today, as soon as a man or woman has any degree of success in pictures, they form their own companies. They surround themselves with lawyers and tax people, they make fewer pictures and they're much more interested in what the deal is and what percentage of the gross they'll get than they are in what's in the script. Most of them just aren't equipped to combine business with artistry. And there's no way to build up a glamor stock company today. Today's stars want to make one picture a year, and even actors you never heard of won't sign a 40-week contract. Universal had Carrie Snodgress, who made one big hit, *Diary of a Mad Housewife.* Now they can't get her to answer the telephone. She apparently doesn't care if she never makes another picture. We've gone a long way from the likes of [Bette] Davis and [Barbara] Stanwyck, that's for sure.

Interview, Washington/
The Washington Post, 4-17:(B)8.

John Wayne
Actor

5

The men who control the big studios today are stock manipulators and bankers. Movies were once made for the whole family. Now, with the kind of junk the studios are cranking out—and the jacked-up prices they're charging —the average family is staying home and watching television. I'm quite sure that, within a few years, Americans will be completely fed up with a business that I feel is suffering from its own vulgarity.

Interview, Newport Beach, Calif./
Good Housekeeping, February:134.

6

I'm not preaching a sermon from the mount, you know; this is just my own opinion. But it does seem to me that, when our industry got vulgar and cheap, we began losing our regular customers. Sure, people are curious, and they'll go see any provocative thing once—maybe even four or five times—but eventually they'll just stay home and watch television. There used to be this little Frenchman in Hollywood who made all these risque movies . . . Ernst Lubitsch. He could make pictures just as risque as anything you'll see today, but he made them with taste and illusion. The only sadness in my heart for our business is that we're taking all the *illusion* out of it.

Interview, New York/
The New York Times, 12-30:(2)11.

William Wellman
Director

1

I'm not very fond of actors. They spend years looking in the mirror, studying their angles and so forth. You do that for any length of time and there are only two things that can happen: either you love what you see or you hate it. So far, I've never met anyone who hated it.

Interview/
"W": a Fairchild publication, 12-28:2.

Thornton Wilder
Author

2

[I] never stayed longer than six weeks in Hollywood. Corruption begins on the morning of the seventh week.

Interview, New York/
The Washington Post, 11-18:(K)3.

William Wyler
Director

3

There are some good new directors around who like to show off with the camera. These young men are tempted to draw attention to themselves because they are not up there on the screen with the actors. Many critics fall for this and think they are watching genius. When I began, the critics never paid any attention to the director. Today, they pay too

much attention to him and what he's thinking and doing. This only encourages the director to use more camera tricks. Directors have become a disturbing element in pictures, dreaming up ideas about what to do with the camera. But the camera isn't a toy. A disciplined director discards an idea if it doesn't help the scene. John Ford hardly ever moved the cameras in his movies, and look at his enormous success over the years.

Interview, Los Angeles/
The Dallas Times Herald, 12-1:(A)9.

Frank Yablans
President, Paramount Pictures Corporation

4

I'll admit it: I love the movies. As entertainment and as a communicative art, motion pictures have had a tremendous influence on our lives. Every childhood, including mine, was at least partially spent at the Saturday afternoon movies where larger-than-life figures involved us in incredible adventures, dazzling romances and chilling mysteries. The one thing that didn't change as we grew older was the impact of those movies and those stars on our lives. When I became president of Paramount, not only were doomsayers predicting the demise of the medium, they pointed their fingers at the fact that making pictures had become strictly a business stripped of its glamour and its fantasy. Nonsense! At last year's dinner honoring Paramount's founder, Adolph Zukor, on his 100th birthday, the crowds were lined up for blocks to get a look at their favorites. It's the same at every premiere, every important social event in Hollywood. The magic of movies will always be entwined with our lives.

Interview, New York/
The Dallas Times Herald, 7-27:(F)8.

5

The lost audience is lost only because we've been producing crap, by and large. If you eat lousy food at a restaurant, you might come back once more, figuring the chef had a bad night. But if the food's bad again, you're lost forever. Now, that's what has happened to a lot of the movie audience. But a really

(FRANK YABLANS)

good picture can still bring them back. The proof is that a *Godfather* or a *French Connection* will each make more money than a whole studio used to earn in a year of production.

Newsweek, 12-24:40.

Bud Yorkin
Producer, Director

1

That's where Hollywood fails us today —where do you find Cary Grants or James Stewarts? Or romantic couples like Myrna Loy and William Powell? . . . What does this do to motion pictures? It wipes out the glamor and paves the way for a cycle of *Last Tangos [in Paris]* that you won't believe.

Interview, San Francisco, March 13/
San Francisco Examiner, 3-14:23.

Darryl F. Zanuck
Producer

2

I'm a one-man institution. I don't even believe in dumb story conferences. What you get is scrambled eggs.

Los Angeles Herald-Examiner, 7-4:(A)8.

Franco Zeffirelli
Director

3

What I dislike most about films is the times of waiting for things to happen. All those filters an idea has to go through before you can really put your teeth into something. That is why I may decide to stop doing cinema entirely.

Interview, London/
San Francisco Examiner & Chronicle,
11-4:(Datebook)14.

Mai Zetterling
Director

4

For women directors, the problem is other women, most of whom are used to male direc-

tors; they are not used to taking orders from a woman. Directing an actor is a very complex and difficult thing, anyway. Most actors are extremely sensitive. You have to be fantastically delicate [with them] not to hurt anything, not to destroy their confidence as an actor . . . Being a director is harsh, difficult. Few people can do it. You're not trained to do that as a woman. We've learned, instead, to use our sensitivities, much more than men . . .

Interview/
Los Angeles Herald-Examiner, 12-28:(B)7.

Fred Zinnemann
Director

5

I'm from the very old Hollywood school, and we were there to entertain the public and not necessarily express ourselves as artists . . . How I feel personally is my own business in the sense that I would not want to be caught trying to preach to anybody. Subconsciously I probably have a preference for stories or characters of a kind, and if the audience reads something into them, that is up to them.

Interview, Pinewood, England/
The Christian Science Monitor, 6-22:11.

Adolph Zukor
Founder and chairman emeritus,
Paramount Pictures Corporation

6

If we knew in advance when we made any picture how it was going to be taken by the public, we'd have to hire a hall to hold the money. You make a picture you believe in. That doesn't mean the public will agree with us . . . I was fortunate. Failures were very few and far between, and successes were numerous. I always tried to make pictures that appealed to the young people. I always selected subjects the young people would be fascinated by. That's why we had more hits than the others.

Interview, Los Angeles/
The New York Times, 2-4:(2)13.

MUSIC

Vladimir Ashkenazy
Pianist

1

In the West [after fleeing the Soviet Union 10 years ago], I began to develop naturally as a man and then as a musician. For that you need independence. There's no limit to independence here in the West, and that is the greatest basis for finding yourself and the only basis for making music.

Newsweek, 3-26:99.

Pierre Boulez
Musical director,
New York Philharmonic Orchestra

2

[On noisy audiences]: At least I have the privilege of not looking at the audience, of only hearing them. But I must say that this makes me very angry. It is disturbing if you are telling something and somebody is not paying attention to it. It's exactly like in conversation. Sometimes you get the impression that you are just like a TV set—an expensive one. The sneezing and the coughing! The noise shows that you are going nowhere with this audience. It's discouraging.

Interview/
The New York Times Magazine, 3-25:32.

3

For me, the word "tradition" or "style" is quite different from what is usually understood. For me, the right tradition is to give a new face in each generation. A work, finally, is interesting because you change the approach . . . I don't think there is *one* style. Of course, you cannot play Mozart like you play Bruckner. But I am also sure that there is not only one way to play Mozart . . . Any approach is okay as long as it's musical and valid in accordance with the score. But I don't see a true style; I don't believe in it . . . I am

living in this year. I know more or less where music is going, and I cannot look back. To me, the most interesting point of view is to see why a score interests us *now*, what a score has to say to us *now*.

Interview/
The New York Times Magazine, 3-25:33.

Dave Brubeck
Musician

4

People speak of "pure" music, and I never know what they're talking about. People blindly believe in "musical tradition," even when it takes a wrong turn. Like classical music did when it abandoned improvisation; maybe that's why they're where they are today . . . Jazz came and said you could be more human and free. And this had a tremendous influence on art—painting, poetry, dance.

Interview/
The Christian Science Monitor, 5-1:11.

Maria Callas
Opera singer

5

There are too many people in opera telling each other how marvelous they are. But honesty takes courage. I remember my first class teaching at Juilliard. All the students applauded each other's efforts. I say, "What is this? Did they come to applaud or to learn?" They should start by holding their breath and not moving a muscle. When I came to opera, I came on my tiptoes. The stage is sacred. And opera is like going to church.

Turin, Italy/Newsweek, 4-23:100.

6

Some [opera singers] have brains and sensibilities. Others just sing and act like fools. I've never frequented them. They have nothing to talk about except their beautiful homes and

(MARIA CALLAS)

jewels and furs. Some of them have a talent with the press and with management, so they get reputations. They're good—anywhere but on the stage.

Turin, Italy/Newsweek, 4-23:100.

Pablo Casals
Cellist, Composer

1

The idea [in music] today is to do what no one has done before, at any cost. Instead of giving what they can give in a normal way, composers want to shock. They act like bad little boys. I have just read about a concert in which every member of a symphony orchestra was asked to play whatever pleased him at the moment. Then there was something about a piece for piano in which the pianist was not allowed to touch the keys . . . Experimentation is fine. But they should not call it music. They should call it something else.

Interview, Marlboro, Vt./
Los Angeles Times, 8-19:(Calendar)46.

Schuyler Chapin
General manager,
Metropolitan Opera, New York

2

In this age of over-image-saturation and over-communication, I don't think it's right that so little has been left to our imaginations. It's absolutely ridiculous that in an opera production everything has to be forced down one's throat. I think that the combination of music, drama, color, light and dance is a potent-enough basic series of ingredients so that you ought to be invited to find a visual complement to this. I have rejected—and I understand that it may have been for the first time in a long time—a design for a work that is coming up next season. I rejected it because one does not need to build D. W. Griffith's *Intolerance* for a piece that is essentially a display work for soprano, mezzo, tenor and bass. There is a practical reason for this. We are sinking under the weight of the productions that we have here—the amount of stage labor that it takes to mount an evening, strike it, score it, etc. We cannot operate on the basis of nothing but massive productions just because it's a big stage. We really do not need *Lawrence of Arabia* and Cecil B. DeMille.

Interview, New York/
The New York Times Magazine, 9-23:55.

Aaron Copland
Composer

3

[On conducting]: I get a real kick out of it. What could be nicer—it's a group effort for a wonderful end. Besides, it seems to be a very healthy occupation. Look at Toscanini, Stokowski. Conductors seem to live quite long—yes, the ones that live.

Interview, Croton, N.Y./
The Washington Post, 4-8:(L)2.

Arthur Fiedler
Conductor, Boston Pops Orchestra

4

What sustains me is a very simple thing: It is just trying to make music properly, as I believe the composer intended it to be. You have black notes on white paper, some of them like fly specks, and you bring them to life in your own way . . . A clown, a baseball player, an actress, and ice-cream vendor are all like me: We just happen to do things that people get enjoyment out of. But that isn't my main mission—giving joy. I like to make music, that's all.

Interview, Boston/
The Christian Science Monitor, 7-6:11.

Carlo Maria Giulini
Principal conductor-designate,
Vienna Symphony Orchestra

5

I don't like recording as much as concerts, because I love everything that is human—an audience is not just an audience but a part of the performance; also because fixing a given performance permanently [on a record] is a bit against the nature of performance, which can never be the same twice. That's why, when I do a recording, I always insist on playing the music all the way through, playing for the music, not the microphone. With recordings, it's always so tempting to try for perfection, to repeat, do over, listen, fix again. But you can end up with perfection, perfect sound, and still have the life of the music gone, dead.

Interview, Washington, June 15/
The Washington Post, 6-16:(B)7.

Benny Goodman
Jazz musician

1

The music of the last 10 or 15 years has been mainly influenced by rock, of course; but I consider rock a very immature musical form.

New York, Nov. 27/
The New York Times, 11-28:47.

Woody Herman
Band leader; Jazz musician

2

[On the life of a jazz musician]: Oh, I would recommend it for anybody. It's the happiest. A lot of pain, but you still have kicks that no one else does. And probably the greatest requisite of all—and you don't have to be a genius player, either—is when you're playing that ax, whatever the instrument is; no matter how great or how badly you play it, no one in the world can reach you. It's the greatest escape that God ever gave man, as far as I'm concerned. And that's why I believe that it's wonderful for anyone I like very much or love dearly—I want them to play something, to be involved in music. When you're playing, you're completely away . . . you're in your own world . . .

The Christian Science Monitor, 6-14:14.

3

It's the youth audience I want to cultivate. It's important for me to reach the young, fresh listeners. Frankly, I'm not interested in the older fans: I'm delighted many are still with me; but except for a handful of dyed-in-the-wool jazz buffs, most of them deserted me and the whole big-band scene for 25 years. Now they're coming around and they want to hear the same things they heard 25 and 30

years ago. We recently played a dance where the audience was split about 70/30—70 per cent pre-rock people, and the rest part of the Beatle generation. Since we had a preponderance of old fans, we gave them lots of the old book. And the youngsters listened to *The Woodchopper's Ball, Caledonia*, etc., with the patience of Job. Then we played *one* rock thing, and you should have seen the scowls on the oldsters' faces. *That's* why I'm interested in young people: Their tastes aren't frozen in 1945; they have the time, flexibility, interest and energy to really groove on all kinds of music. That's the audience I want to build on; and I'm not going to do it by confining myself to 30-year[-old] charts and 40-year-old songs.

Interview, New York/
The New York Times, 7-1:(2)21.

Lorin Hollander
Pianist

4

It is important for man to find out what is basically real: what is the phenomenon of the universe, what is really happening in our own bodies. And a musician speaks to all these questions in his music. The great musicians—Mozart, Bach—spoke about the most intimate emotional experiences of man. Whether they were themselves involved in a philosophical dialogue is unimportant. A performing musician has to research the man [composer] to understand what he was capable of speaking about in his music. A musician is not just out there moving his fingers and making sounds. He's saying something, otherwise he is not a musician, just a music player.

At Eastfield College/
The Dallas Times Herald, 3-2:(G)10.

Lena Horne
Singer

5

. . . I no longer sing the old songs—*Stormy Weather, Honeysuckle Rose, Two to Tango*—all that lot. I much prefer modern music and lyrics. I've had "Moon and June" and broken-hearted dames. When I came up in the '40s, those songs were right. Now things have

(LENA HORNE)

changed. The old ones bore me . . . Today's songs are more sensitive and realistic. They acknowledge that life is hard, that deep passion aroused by love or inhumanity is the stuff of which modern songs are made.

Interview, London/
San Francisco Examiner & Chronicle,
5-20:(Datebook)14.

Marilyn Horne
Opera singer

1

First of all, [to be an opera singer] you have the gift. I think the gift is a linking up of the vocal chords, the resonators, the ear and the mind. That comes first; you are born with that somehow. Then comes a lot of hard work and an awful lot of people helping you. And eventually you need terrific stamina—you really have to be as strong as a horse! And every singer needs somebody who is dead honest with him, somebody who tells him the absolute truth. Almost everyone I know who has had great success has had one person who has made the difference between a good career and a great career.

Interview,
Orange, N.J./
The Christian Science Monitor, 4-24:(B)9.

Sol Hurok
Impresario

2

The big change in the last 60 years has been the great increase in public appreciation of the better things. Today, we have 1,128 symphony orchestras in this country [the U.S.]. We can thank Hitler and Roosevelt for that: Hitler kicked the musicians out, and Roosevelt helped them find work with the WPA cultural activities in many cities. But in some ways we haven't advanced. Somehow we don't have as many great personalities among the performers as we did years ago: Marian Anderson, Josef Hofmann, John McCormack, Schumann-Heink, Harry Lauder, Fritz Kreisler

. . . People of that caliber, we don't have so many today.

Interview, New York/
The National Observer, 5-26:20.

Leon Kirchner
Composer

3

This has been a very discouraging period for a number of composers, a period in which the quality of music-making and inspired writing—the kind of thing we identify with music of the past—seemed less and less interesting. One had to be involved more with quantification than with quality of ideas . . . [People with this view] never consider excellence of sensual inspiration or sensitivities, but only statistical inspiration, something that can be counted by computers.

Interview, Cambridge, Mass./
The New York Times, 3-11:(2)15.

Andre Kostelanetz
Orchestra conductor

4

Criticism is upsetting. There is no person who is not susceptible to it. And there is always the curiosity to find out what people are saying. But you have to stand on your own two feet. There is no way of being accepted by everybody. It's like saying everybody must be Jewish or Protestant. After a while, you pay no attention to it and keep on doing what you think is right. Whatever concert life brings to me from now on—if it expands the meaning of music in terms of attendance, that's all that really matters.

Interview/ The New York Times, 5-6:(2)17.

Rolf Liebermann
Director, Paris Opera

5

[On the financing of opera]: One shouldn't talk about one's "artistic mission." If you have to produce an automobile, or whatever, you have to produce it for a price. It's exactly the same in opera. It's an organization that sells opera performances.

Interview, Paris/
The New York Times, 3-25:(2)17.

Lorin Maazel
Musical director, Cleveland Orchestra

1

I'd say there are more areas of dissimilarity of music-making between Boston and Chicago than between Vienna and Berlin. There is one characteristic, though, that one maybe could call American: a rhythmic tone. Faced with a new passage, an American musician would tend to play it absolutely evenly, without reference to its expressive context. The European player tends to have a built-in rubato. He sees a phrase and says to himself, "I know how that should go." Of course, if his ideas don't coincide with the conductor's, that may prove troublesome. There's another singular thing about Americans, and perhaps not only those in orchestras. There's a certain reticence about expressing oneself for fear of exhibiting bad taste; so that, unless a player is encouraged along these lines, he'll often end up with a kind of fine, respectable "no taste." I'm not talking about just turning a phrase tastefully and tipping one's hat to the stylistic niceties. I'm talking about that daring—at the risk of over-statement or under-statement—the Europeans seem to have; the impetus to say, "I'm going to infuse this phrase with my direct feeling about this music." But all of these considerations are peripheral. Pound for pound, American musicians, especially today, are more skilled and more educated, in non-musical matters too, than their European counterparts. And besides, none of this applies to the Cleveland Orchestra, which really is a special animal—like a chamber orchestra gone symphonic. That is to say, the Cleveland players have been trained in the basic axiom of chamber playing—listening to the other fellow—and they have applied it to all of their music-making.

Interview, Washington/
The Washington Post, 5-21:(B)7.

Charles Mackerras
Musical director,
Sadler's Wells Opera, London

2

Some people think symphony music is finished because young composers are not interested in writing for it. But as long as people are inspired and affected by Beethoven, Tchaikovsky and Mozart, the "conventional symphony" will continue.

Interview, London/
"W": a Fairchild publication, 5-18:19.

Mehli Mehta
Musical director,
American Youth Symphony Orchestra

3

I am a chamber musician . . . I treat all forms of music as chamber music, because to me chamber music is the highest form of the art. I regard an orchestra as a glorified chamber ensemble; and that's the greatest statement I can make about the orchestral medium.

Interview, Los Angeles/
Los Angeles Herald-Examiner, 4-22:(E)2.

Zubin Mehta
Musical director,
Los Angeles Philharmonic Orchestra

4

[Criticizing Europeans who look down on visiting American orchestras]: A central European who knows music belongs to him and is his own property can't stand the idea that the Cleveland [Orchestra] can play it like he's never heard it before. It would be silly to criticize a French orchestra that came to America because it can't play Gershwin. In any case, it could learn, just as Americans can learn the niceties of Mahler and Schubert.

Interview, Paris/
Los Angeles Times, 3-18:(Calendar)14.

Eugene Ormandy
Musical director, Philadelphia Orchestra

5

[Opera is] the most beautiful form of music-making, [but] it is too much aggravation. You rehearse with one cast, and one hour before the performance you are told that so-and-so is indisposed and someone else will be jumping in. Then they ask if you would like to use the remaining time to discuss tempi. Huh! Meanwhile, the singer has to get dressed,

(EUGENE ORMANDY)

put on makeup. Then you spend three or four hours in the orchestra, scared to death something will go wrong.

Interview, Philadelphia/
"W": a Fairchild publication, 5-18:19.

Dory Previn
Composer, Lyricist

1

There's something fascinating about how what we write with affects what we write. For years I wrote with a pen . . . and then, when it was stolen, I couldn't write for a long time. Finally, I transferred it all to an old Olympia typewriter. Still, I can't write lyrics on a typewriter. I have to use pen and paper and feel the words coming from the heart, through my body and into my arm. The typewriter is a machine, and anything you do in first draft on it has got to be much too rational.

Interview, Washington/
The Washington Post, 11-8:(B)1.

Julius Rudel
General director and conductor,
New York City Opera

2

As a conductor, I don't have to worry about keeping fit. My work is terrific exercise, and as somebody once said, conductors never develop psychosomatic disorders because they take out their hostilities on others. Most conductors live to be very old, probably for a combination of these reasons. If they worry about keeping in shape at all, it's only so that they present a reasonably svelte back to their audiences. Of course, they do get a fair amount of exercise just conducting, especially if they're the types that really throw themselves into the music. But it's the administrator in me that may yet do me in. Hours spent over schedules, reading librettos and scores, making momentous decisions often of a very unartistic nature, and arguing with boards and Congressmen are the things that make me physically unfit and keep me awake at night. My antidote is to conduct.

Interview/ Los Angeles Times, 12-14:(7)4.

Thomas Schippers
Conductor, Cincinnati Symphony Orchestra

3

Successful musicians are not insular in any way—and that's why it's important for Americans to have some exposure in Europe. You can't stay in Detroit or Toledo and expect to be a Toscanini. You've got to get around.

U.S. News & World Report, 9-24:64.

Dmitri Shostakovich
Composer

4

If I am composing, I do it around the clock. Unfortunately, I have not been able to develop a regimen for myself. Sometimes I am asked, "What do you need in order to compose? Perhaps you have to go to the seashore." Of course, I'd like to go to the seashore; but if some sort of idea has come to your mind, you could sit in a dog house and be quite comfortable, because everything is inside your head . . . I always dream. If any of my dreams cease, I'll cease being a composer. The reason I compose a current work is that I'm unhappy with a preceding one. If I would say, "Well, this I composed beautifully," then I'm finished as a composer.

Interview,
New York/
The New York Times, 6-24:(2)10.

Frank Sinatra
Singer, Actor

5

I don't think I've changed [musically]. What I'm singing is what I've always sung: a properly-integrated and well-rounded song with good contemporary rhythm sounds and a melody that suits me. Rock? It's influenced music but not me. Some of it I absolutely loathe. Now I see a shining light at the end of the tunnel. A lot of young composers like Neil Diamond, Joe Raposo, Jimmy Webb and Kris Kristofferson are writing a lot of wonderful things a la Larry Hart.

Interview,
Culver City, Calif./
TV Guide, 11-17:35.

Georg Solti
Musical director,
Chicago Symphony Orchestra

1

Why did Toscanini conduct from memory? Because he was nearsighted. Of course, he had that fabulous memory, but that wasn't really why he never used a score. Today, we have an entire generation of young conductors who think they must conduct from memory—all because Toscanini was nearsighted. It is total lunacy.

Time, 5-7:58.

2

The important thing [for a conductor] is that you must have an idea—good or bad, it doesn't matter, as long as you want something. A wild, tasteless conductor is better than one content to be merely exact, because he can at least interest the orchestra and the audience. They hate him if he just wants to go swimming with the orchestra. Bah! One must have ideas. It is a man's nature to follow ideas, not sticks. The baton matters hardly at all.

Interview,
San Francisco/
San Francisco Examiner & Chronicle,
5-20:(This World)31.

Stephen Sondheim
Composer, Lyricist

3

. . . [many years ago] I'd written a campus musical called *By George.* I thought it was terrific, so I asked him [his friend the late lyricist Oscar Hammerstein II] to read it as if he were a producer and didn't know me. The next day he called me over and said, "It's the worst thing I ever read in my life, and if you want to know why, I'll tell you." That afternoon, I learned what songwriting was all about—how to structure a song like a one-act play, how essential simplicity is, how much every word counts and, above all, the importance of content, of saying what *you*, not other songwriters, feel.

Newsweek, 4-23:61.

Janos Starker
Cellist; Professor of Music,
Indiana University

4

Recital life is dying. And the artists are killing it. They demand such huge fees that they need huge halls, which are usually no place to hear a solo instrument. It attracts audiences who respond to household names and to the theatrics of music-making instead of music itself.

Newsweek, 1-29:75.

Dimitri Tiomkin
Composer

5

Writing music for films is like making love to a woman: You have to see the face you are writing for, appreciate the subtleties of expression. I try to make each scene live in my music. And if I have any pleasure left at all, it's to think of all the unknown people listening to my music, people I'll never know . . . I'm an old ham at heart.

Interview, London/
San Francisco Examiner & Chronicle,
2-18:(Datebook)18.

Alec Wilder
Composer

6

. . . you cannot write a jazz phrase down on paper; it's absolutely impossible. It's an impulse; it's a way of phrasing; it's a way of attacking a note, a way of releasing a note, letting it go . . . Jazz players create instantaneously highly-imaginative music without any time to think about it. When I listen to these people, I am in literal awe of them. I have heard Charlie Parker create very rapid passages that were fantastically considered and responsible melodic lines, harmonically perfect—and doing it at the speed of light. You'd think he was just showing off a lot of digital dexterity, but it was not just a series of chromatic runs and pyrotechnics. Behind it all, the notes made sense; if you slowed them down, they all made sense. I once said to Marian McPartland, "What on earth did you do in the mid-

(ALEC WILDER)

dle of that piece where the harmony became so enormously complex and the rhythms became so complex?" And she just looked at me and said, "I don't know what you're talking about."

New York,
July 3/
The New York Times, 7-6:6.

THE STAGE

Alvin Ailey
Dancer, Choreographer

1

I'm interested in putting something on stage that will have a very wide appeal without being condescending; that will reach an audience and make it part of the dance; that will get everybody into the theatre . . . What do people mean when they say [depracatingly] we're "Broadway"? If it's art *and* entertainment—thank God; that's what I want to be.

Interview/
The New York Times Magazine, 4-29:21.

Edward Albee
Playwright

2

Commercial theatre needs [government] subsidy. The taste of the country is still formed by what happens in commercial theatre. Subsidizing the playwright while he creates has not been as frequent as it should. Somehow, the attitude has been if everything else is there, the playwright will just "arrive."

At House Committee hearing,
Washington, March 14/
The Washington Post, 3-15:(D)11.

3

A few years ago, a group of us approached a major New York newspaper and suggested [playwright] Arthur Miller for the drama critic's job, or even as an alternative critic. We were turned down. They seem to have a notion that the critic's basic function is not to serve the theatre, but the public. It's laughable, of course.

"W": a Fairchild publication, 10-19:7.

4

. . . I don't think a film ever has the same impact as a play. I think subconsciously everybody knows that film is an unreal experience —though not if you compare it with television, of course. But anyone who's ever been to the theatre, even street theatre, knows that's where the real thing is.

Interview, New York/
The Washington Post, 10-28:(L)2.

Judith Anderson
Actress

5

I can't stand the vulgarity that suffocates the theatre. Times have changed, and the theatre with them.

Newsweek, 12-17:54.

Robert Anderson
Playwright

6

Playwriting demands enormous energy— almost the energy of the 100-yard dash—because you have to protect your work against producers, directors and actors. Any one of them can ask for changes. It takes real dynamism to stand your ground and preserve what you've written until the play is a hit.

San Francisco Examiner & Chronicle,
9-9:(Sunday Scene)14.

Alan Bates
Actor

7

[On the "Tony" award]: Before you get it, you don't care. If you don't get it, you don't care. If you do get it, it gives you a bit of confidence; but one shouldn't let himself be pressured by it. I think it's a terrific sort of way to acknowledge a job well done, but I don't think winning an award should put one in the position of having to do better. It shouldn't change one's performance. After all, the performance one is doing is what was awarded, isn't it?

Los Angeles/Daily Variety, 3-30:16.

Ingmar Bergman
Director

1

In film-making, you make about three minutes of film every day, of the real film. In theatre, we just rehearse 8-10 weeks, and if it's not very good, we say perhaps it will be better tomorrow or the next day. But in film-making there is the enormous pressure that's so fascinating and terrifying. When I'm working on a film, there is often great stimulation; the demands of making it are just a part of the film every day. But I tell you, as a process of making, I prefer the theatre work.

News conference, Cannes, France/
The Christian Science Monitor, 5-24:14.

Abe Burrows
Director, Playwright

2

I never have been a critic-fighter, but there seems to be a desire these days to mold theatre in a certain way. Many critics are more concerned with their attitude than with the show. That is, they don't want to be caught "square." They'd rather be "with it."

New York/The New York Times, 12-9:(1)78.

Kitty Carlisle
Actress

3

I think people these days want plays about witty, well-dressed, attractive people who, when they fight with each other, use language and wit instead of four-letter words. I think they like to see pretty clothes. I think that's why *Light Up the Sky* was such a success. [In three of her recent summer tours] it played to more people than it did originally on Broadway.

Interview, Boston/
The Christian Science Monitor, 2-16:(B)9.

Gower Champion
Director, Choreographer

4

The present state of the Broadway theatre can be summed up in one word: tacky! And the musical theatre is shamefully threadbare.

Everybody knows that it costs too much money to mount a Broadway musical and that ticket prices are sky-high. What most people don't know is that the increase in ticket prices hasn't begun to keep pace with the increase in the cost of a musical production—making it take longer and longer for the production to get into the black. It's tough for the producers and backers, and few are willing to take a chance on anything but the most proven commercial talent available. Perhaps this nothing-ventured-no-new-talent-gained syndrome is one reason why the theatre is languishing and why there is a growing rumble in the arts about the possibilities of some sort of government support. All the money in the world, however, can't shore up a crumbling theatre when the key prop is missing. That prop is called writing invention. Writing invention is, in my opinion, the prime element missing in the theatre today. The writing on Broadway [has] become unimaginative, stale and repetitive, and the most inspired interpretive talents alive can't quite rescue a show with a mediocre book . . . The basic form of the Broadway musical has been pretty much the same for the last 40 years and, I think, desperately needs innovation, new directions conceptually. Unless somebody gets some fresh ideas and brings the musical into the '70s—at least—the American musical comedy is going to end up a relic like the melodrama or Gilbert and Sullivan instead of the vital, peculiarly American art form it once was.

Interview/
The Dallas Times Herald, 8-5:(F)15.

Carol Channing
Actress

5

I've heard so much about the theatre dying out, but I don't believe a word of it. The theatre can't die, because all the tribal feelings that mankind needs are unleashed only in the theatre and the sports arenas. We need those rites—laughing and crying together, warm and cozy together, that's the key word, under one roof. I feel about the theatre the way I do about a wild, passionate marriage—that I must

have that guy even if he does splatter tooth-paste all over the bathroom mirror.
News conference, San Francisco, Aug. 20/
San Francisco Examiner, 8-21:26.
1

I won't . . . make preference in media, because reaching people is what acting is all about. An actor is always a reflection of his audience; and I know there's a way through that lens, or through that microphone, just as there is across the footlights.
Los Angeles/
Los Angeles Times, 10-7:(Calendar)33.

Harold Clurman
Drama critic, "The Nation"
2

Critics should stop saying whether they like things; that's nobody's business. It's as if I were a chemist and the first thing I say about a piece of cheese is that I like it. What's important is: What's *in* that piece of cheese?
Newsweek, 12-24:96.

Alexander H. Cohen
Producer
3

[On shows that open and play from town to town away from New York City]: . . . those itinerant junk peddlers out there on the road. Those shows doing what appear to be fantastic grosses aren't doing all that well. You can only make money on the road by sitting still, because whopping costs are in-volved in traveling from one town to another, and those costs have to be added to a show's weekly operating "nut." It's impossible to pay off a pre-Broadway musical on the road. The reality is that they depend on Broadway, ulti-mately, for their success . . . Things that ori-ginate in out-of-town warehouses aren't Broad-way productions. I'm a hard-line Broadway producer, you see; and the road ain't where it's at, believe me . . . It *is* damned tough to succeed here [on Broadway]. We have tremen-dous problems. We are suffering from urban blight. But Broadway is still the fountainhead. A hit on Broadway is still worth a million bucks; and isn't that why shows come in, after all? How did *Fiddler on the Roof* make

it for seven years? And do *A Little Night Music, Pippin* and *Irene* look like six-week stands? You know what the road is? The road is what Broadway *was* last season. Broadway is still Mecca.
The New York Times, 11-4:(2)34.

Bette Davis
Actress
4

I hate the theatre and never intend to do it again. I hate the hours and the life. And half the New York audiences are not worth your time any more. If I did anything like that, it would be another tour of the country. The audience throughout the Midwest are great people. They love the theatre and act like they're glad you came to their town. But theatre parties have really wrecked the theatre in New York. By the time a guy has paid for dinner and $50-100 for tickets, which his wife made him do for her charity, he's not in any mood for a show, even if it is great.
Interview, Los Angeles/
The Hollywood Reporter, 2-16:18.

Simon Gray
British playwright
5

Our London theatre, which seems to be so flourishing, actually depends on American audiences. If it weren't for all the Yanks flocking to our shows, we'd have to shut up shop, at least in a lot of cases. And yet we're so contemptuous of Broadway.
Interview, New York/
The Washington Post, 10-28:(L)2.

Eileen Heckart
Actress
6

I don't know where the theatre is going. In New York they'll support Neil Simon and the high-gloss musicals and maybe Laurence Oli-vier for three months, but that's about it. The young people don't come to the theatre, be-cause if it's a hit musical, tickets are $12 each; then you have to pay for the baby sitter, transportation and dinner. It ends up

529

(EILEEN HECKART)

costing about $75 for one evening.

Interview, Los Angeles/
The Hollywood Reporter, 1-19:28.

1

After the first six months [of a play's run], the audience changes. Suddenly they don't react to subtleties. Then you realize all devoted theatre-goers have seen it and the "buyers" have taken over the seats. After a few more months, the people only laugh at the bloopers. Then you know it's gone to "twofers." At that point, I say, "Oh, Lord, when will my contract end?"

"W": a Fairchild publication, 10-19:7.

John Houseman
Producer, Director

2

We have allowed people to become purely speculative about going to the theatre. They decided that they would go to see "hits" or else nothing. They completely lost the habit of going to the theatre regularly. The trick of successful theatrical enterprise is to build continuity and habit.

Newsweek, 12-24:80.

Sol Hurok
Impresario

3

All the talk about live theatre dying because of television, muggings, fear of going out, bad location, weather—these are all alibis. If you have the attraction, the company, the artists that the public wants to see or hear, they will come.

Interview, New York/
The Christian Science Monitor, 5-17:(B)8.

Glynis Johns
Actress

4

Acting is a very difficult art. They were laughing backstage yesterday because I jumped the conductor in one of the musical numbers [in her current Broadway show, *A Little Night Music*], and I came off cursing myself. They said it was unusual to hear a star of a show cursing herself for doing something wrong; and I find it unusual that they should think it unusual. I don't see the point in being on the stage unless you are going to improve. It's up to you to be a damn sight better on the last night than you ever were on the first night. If someone is acting to pay the rent and to get money to have a good time away from the stage, he shouldn't be in this business. Any art is love, otherwise you cannot do it properly. It hurts too much; it's too much hard work for somebody who's playing at it.

Interview, New York/
The National Observer, 5-19:26.

Walter Kerr
Drama critic, "The New York Times"

5

The critic doesn't have any power except what's given to him voluntarily by the guy who reads him.

Newsweek, 12-24:96.

Angela Lansbury
Actress

6

The city of New York supports a hit [show] marvelously—the stores, the cabs, the restaurants. [But] I think one isn't really the toast of London—you settle down here; acting is a vocation here. I can't even get a table in a restaurant. "Lansbury?" they say. "How do you spell it?"

Interview, London/
Los Angeles Times, 10-27:(2)7.

Alan Jay Lerner
Playwright, Lyricist

7

I look with misgivings on efforts to attract the young to the theatre. Writers should write for themselves and for people who go to the theatre. Writing for a special group [like the young] is commercialism at its crassest. Write a good play, and people who go to the theatre will come.

News conference, San Francisco/
San Francisco Examiner & Chronicle,
5-20:(Datebook)9.

1

One of the unfortunate happenstances of the last 10 years [in the theatre] is not so much that young people with some musical talent have been over-praised as that the older and more experienced professionals have been so despised by the press that a lot of them are afraid to go back to work in their own medium—including a lot of fine playwrights like Paddy Chayefsky, who won't write for the theatre any more. Take the rock phase of the musical theatre, for example. I like good rock as much as anyone else, but I also know it has no dramatic value. I know as a craftsman you can't explore character with it, can't dramatize nuances of feeling, can't phrase . . . many gifted young composers are contemptuous of the musical-theatre form itself. The danger of revolt is always that a lot of good things are thrown out with the bad. The musical theatre has been around since Offenbach, and there are certain pillars that hold up the house—things that make the great musicals —and they are always going to be there. My sadness is when I see someone who doesn't deserve it being over-praised while he is alienating people who have loved and supported the musical theatre. The desire to attract the young has driven away a lot of people who have always cared about the theatre. The theatre has never been for one age group—and it never should be.

Interview, Beverly Hills, Calif./
The Christian Science Monitor, 8-30:7.

Natalia Makarova
Ballet dancer

2

We cannot build art only on technique. It helps, but it is not all. Not just technique for technique. If I have strong technique, I have to disguise this. I don't say to [the] public, "See how hard this is to do!" I work to make it look effortless, to make it look easy.

Interview, New York/
The Christian Science Monitor, 11-29:17.

Marcel Marceau
Mime

3

In the mime I do, I try to give invisible

objects heaviness, a light heaviness, so that you can see them. It is a matter of specific techniques, and it is a matter of belief, like Zen, you know, when the archer and the arrow are the same thing. In "Bip Tames the Lion," I am Bip and I am the lion. There is a relationship. In mime, you can do anything. You can defy gravity; you can walk on air. I do not need to go to the moon; I am already there.

Interview, New York/
Los Angeles Times, 5-20:(Calendar)42.

David Merrick
Producer

4

Plays are more difficult to put on as costs go up. I'm not having very much trouble at the moment because I haven't had a major flop recently; but give me a couple of musical flops and I'll have to scratch around, too. At the moment it's a little gloomy on Broadway, and I'm wondering if the number of plays produced each year will continue becoming fewer and fewer. I can't imagine why the situation should change, but even so I'm rather optimistic that it will stabilize at the present level.

Interview, New York/
The New York Times, 6-1:33.

5

I'm all for subsidies [for the theatre]. I know the argument that those who give subsidies finally choose the type of material that is produced, but I'll take my chances on it. Subsidized theatres work very well in England, and I'll take my chances on it here [in the U.S.].

Interview, New York/
The New York Times, 6-1:41.

Jason Miller
Playwright, Actor

6

Broadway right now is held together by mutual fear. People aren't going [to the theatre in New York], and Broadway lost $1 million last year. The theatre needs breaks —from producers, unions, landlords. And it

(JASON MILLER)

needs to encourage innovation, develop some good producers . . . I'm afraid Broadway is going to turn into a museum in 10 years or so unless something changes. But it still has magic, man, at least to me.

Interview, Los Angeles/
Los Angeles Times, 10-28:(Calendar)72.

Rudolf Nureyev
Ballet dancer

1

For me, dancing is the conquest of the body. There are so many things I must do before I can enjoy it. I wait in the wings sweating with fear. But it is exhilarating, too, and that is what saves me. You have to believe in your own power, your ability to do the impossible. Every small mistake I make, I live and relive a million times afterward. I cannot avoid that, but I have developed a number of devices to preserve myself. I know, for example, that I dance best when I am on my second wind; so, before the actual performance, I go through every move I will make on stage. I exercise every muscle so my body is near exhaustion. Then, when the body is under great stress, it will move, despite any mental block.

Interview, Milan, Italy/
The Christian Science Monitor, 11-2:13.

Joseph Papp
Producer

2

I can find faults in all our plays. The things that make money should support the others. And if a producer has staged one play by an author, he should agree, sight-unseen, to produce the second play. It's like a father to his son: You don't say I accept you only when you're good.

Interview, San Francisco/
San Francisco Examiner & Chronicle,
2-4:(Datebook)9.

3

Theatre is a social force. It must reflect the great issues of our times, which can only be reflected through writers now alive. Theatre is not just a place to put on plays. At its highest, it represents a commitment to art and society.

Interview/The New York Times, 3-7:46.

4

I believe theatre has to do with some human urge, basic to our condition, and therefore it will disappear only when we disappear . . . [There should be a push to] reach out into the country to get to those who have been "snobbed out" of the theatre. It is a disservice and distortion to perpetrate the notion that all Americans are cut from the same die—and that they are only interested in bread and circuses.

At House Committee hearing on funds for
the arts, Washington, March 14/
The Washington Post, 3-15:(D)11.

Christopher Plummer
Actor

5

Some actors tend, when playing a death scene, to feel sorry for themselves. I felt sorry for myself the first time I played Hamlet. I cried at my own death. It was very weepy. The audience, not the actor, is supposed to be moved. If you [the actor] are, you're doing their [the audience's] work. Some damn actor—I don't remember who—said you must be able to cry when you first experience the role in rehearsal. By the time you face the public, you must have the emotion licked.

Interview, New York/
The New York Times, 5-17:52.

Debbie Reynolds
Actress

6

[On her current show, *Irene*]: A lot of people are tired of shows with messages, and —like me—they enjoy seeing a warm show about a warm relationship. My approach to entertainment has always been to make people forget their troubles and enjoy the evening. Perhaps I'm a bit provincial in my thinking, but isn't that what entertainers are *supposed* to do?

Interview, Washington/
The New York Times, 2-25:(2)8.

Eva Marie Saint
Actress

1

. . . theatre in New York City is in disastrous shape. How encouraging for us then to discover an audience eager and waiting in Atlanta, Washington, D.C., Palm Beach, Detroit and Massachusetts. Theatre is alive and thriving everywhere but on Broadway.

Interview,
Los Angeles/
Los Angeles Herald-Examiner, 9-30:(E)1.

Donald Seawell
National chairman, American National
Theatre and Academy (ANTA)

2

I don't know if people don't go to Broadway because they are afraid for their lives or of what they see [at the theatre] there. But Broadway is not the mecca it once was. From what I've seen, some of the best theatre is coming from this [Western] part of the country.

At ANTA Southern California Chapter
meeting, Los Angeles, Jan. 29/
The Hollywood Reporter, 1-31:3.

Neil Simon
Playwright

3

Some critics never have liked what I've written, and there's absolutely nothing I can do about that. I do smile, of course, when they write that one work isn't as good as another, which, they forget, they didn't like in the first place. And when it comes to describing me . . . as the top money-making playwright of all time, that only makes me think of how wrong we are in our Western civilization to be labeling certain people by how much they're paid. The essential thing about all this money the plays have made is that it liberates me from worrying about money. It means I can work on my plays. After a certain point, money is just more money.

Interview/
The Dallas Times Herald, 1-12:(B)1.

Barbra Streisand
Actress, Singer

4

I don't want to return to the Broadway stage, because I don't like the feeling of being judged night after night. When people all over the world are watching me in a movie, I can be home taking a bath. But to have to stand out on stage every night and bear the brunt . . . it's exhausting.

Interview, New York/
The New York Times, 1-21:(2)3.

Walter Terry
Dance critic

5

There's been a tendency to keep modern dance something precious, as if popularity were not quite pure. But Shakespeare and Sophocles were the popular theatre of their day. The Rockettes are just as good as Martha Graham, only different.

The New York Times Magazine, 4-29:23.

Robert Whitehead
Producer

6

The theatre always has been special. It can't be anything else, because you shouldn't have more than 500, maybe 1,000 people, at a performance. What is important is that, if something is only seen by two or three per cent of the population, that is a lot of people. Plays that are part of our literature have probably been seen by only one per cent. What happens is that they are seen by the people who generate the taste, the influence of a civilization. Maybe only one per cent see a play, but a great many people are finally influenced by its existence. It has always been that way.

Interview, New York/
Los Angeles Herald-Examiner, 11-24:(B)8.

7

I hate to talk negatively about the theatre, because it's the last of the hand-made articles left—from the costumes to the emotions that find their own level each night. We're in an era of mass-produced arts. The theatre is still

(ROBERT WHITEHEAD)

carefully molded by hand. But unfortunately, in an era of rising costs and galloping inflation, it is no longer viable. I hope that will change. But it won't unless the economy of the country changes. That's why the last few seasons have been so skimpy—good business makes for good art. When lots of plays are being produced, the creative climate flourishes and we all benefit.

San Francisco, Dec. 11/
San Francisco Examiner, 12-12:71.

Tennessee Williams
Playwright

1

A writer cannot have any relationship with the critical establishment. I spent one evening with [*New York Times* drama critic] Clive Barnes, a gentleman and a good critic. It was a great ordeal. When a playwright meets the axman, it's terrifying. Later, Ruth Ford invited me to a party where Barnes would be. I said, "Honey, I can't meet Clive Barnes twice in a lifetime."

At University of Southern California,
March 18/Los Angeles Times, 3-22:(4)16.

2

. . . I only measure my work against my other work. I don't like the idea of rivalry among creative people. Rivalry is the root of all evil, not money. No one is the greatest living anything.

At University of Southern California,
March 18/The Hollywood Reporter, 3-21:15.

3

All my *great* characters are larger than life, not realistic. In order to capture the quality of life in two and a half hours, everything has

to be concentrated, intensified. You must catch life in moments of crisis, moments of electric confrontation. In reality, life is very *slow*. On-stage, you have only from 8:40 to 11:05 to get a lifetime of living across.

Interview/Playboy, April:80.

4

I'm strongest on characterization, dialogue, use of language. And I do have a sense of what is theatre, I believe. Oh, but weaknesses, I have so *many* . . . My greatest weaknesses are structural. And I over-do symbols; they're the natural language of drama, but I use them excessively. I'm also inclined to be overly introspective, but I don't know how to avoid it. I am an introspective person. I don't like writing that doesn't come deeply from the person, isn't deeply revealing *of* the person.

Interview/Playboy, April:84.

5

Regional theatre is the great hope of the theatre—regional theatre and subsidized theatre. I don't think much is going to happen of consequence until we [in the U.S.] have theatres like the National Theatre in England, where great plays are put in repertory, and subsidized to an extent—where you don't have to be smash hits in order to endure.

News conference, West Springfield, Mass./
The Christian Science Monitor, 11-29:21.

6

The price of tickets is the greatest hazard to the theatre. The tickets to Broadway shows are really getting out of people's sight. They just can't afford it, along with the rising cost of everything else. They'd rather stay home and see an old movie on TV. And you can't blame them.

News conference, West Springfield, Mass./
The Christian Science Monitor, 11-29:21.

TELEVISION AND RADIO

Howard H. Baker, Jr.
United States Senator, R-Tennessee

1

[On government concern about alleged obscene and pornographic programming on TV and radio]: It is obvious that a relationship exists between the level of governmental concern and the type and quality of programming. I deplore that linkage. It amounts to a commentary on the partial success of the industry to function as its own sensing system, and, as a result, the industry endures the dangerous practice of inviting governmental intervention in the monitoring of your [broadcasters'] activities.

Before National Association of Broadcasters,
Washington, March 27/
Daily Variety, 3-28:2.

Lucille Ball
Actress, Comedienne

2

I'm always aware of what people say to me, why they're watching [her TV show]. I have no intention of ever changing. I want some place on the dial you can turn to and know what you can expect. I haven't let changing times affect my writers. I'm trying to stay in the same old rut—the same old golden rut. My audiences are three generations in every home. I want it to stay that way.

Interview, Burbank, Calif./
Daily Variety, 2-9:19.

Patrick J. Buchanan
Special Consultant to the President
of the United States

3

[On political bias in public TV]: . . . if you look at public television, you find you've got [commentators] Sander Vanocur and Robin MacNeill, the first of whom, Sander

Vanocur, is a notorious Kennedy psychopath, in my judgment, and Robin MacNeill, who is anti-[Nixon] Administration. You have Elizabeth Drew—she personally is definitely not pro-Administration; I would say anti-Administration. *Washington Week in Review* is unbalanced against us. And you have Bill Moyers, which is unbalanced against the Administration. And then for a fig leaf, William Buckley's program. So they [Congress] sent down there a $165-million package [for public TV], voted 82-1 out of the Senate, thinking that Richard Nixon would therefore have to sign it; he couldn't possibly have the courage to veto something like that. And Mr. Nixon, I'm delighted to say, hit the ball about 450 feet down the right-field foul line, right into the stands; and now you've got a different situation in public television. You've got a new Board on the Corporation for Public Broadcasting; you've got a new awareness that people are concerned about balance. And all this Administration has ever asked on that, or on network [commercial] television frankly, is a fair shake.

On "Dick Cavett Show," New York,
March 22/The New York Times, 5-6:(1)55.

Dean Burch
Chairman, Federal Communications
Commission of the United States

4

[Criticizing pornography in broadcasting]: I simply do not believe that a "hell" here and "damn" there is going to destroy the nation's moral fiber. Nor am I talking about the greater and even refreshing candor with which such no-no's as homosexuality or VD or racial strife are now handled during prime-time, either on essentially entertainment shows or in a purely educational format. These *are* controversial public issues in most of the communi-

(DEAN BURCH)

ties I know anything about, and broadcasters ought to take them on in good taste . . . What I *am* talking about is the prurient trash that is the stock in trade of the sex-oriented radio talk show, complete with the suggestive, coaxing, pear-shaped tones of the smut-hustling host. I *am* talking about three, four, five solid hours of titillating chitchat—scheduled during daytime hours—in such elevating topics of urgent public concern as the number and frequency of orgasms . . . or the endless varieties of oral sex . . . or a baker's dozen of other turn-ons, turn-offs and turn-downs. This is garbage, pure and simple. And it's no less garbage because a sizable number of so-called adults seem to want to listen to it . . . In the last analysis, it is not dog-eared sex manuals we're talking about, or sexploitation comics, or peep shows, or "feelthy" postcards. We are talking about a medium whose transcendental quality is its pervasiveness; a medium that has no point of purchase, requires no admission ticket, no visit to a bookstore or a magazine counter; a medium available in the automobile, the living room, the bedroom—even in the nursery; a medium which, like the goddess of justice, is blind in that once unleashed it travels in every direction, uncontrolled and relentless. And for this reason it is a medium that is licensed to public trustees in order to serve the public convenience, interest and necessity. And if electronic voyeurism is what the authors of the Communications Act had in mind, I'll eat my copy.

Before National Association of Broadcasters,
Washington, March 28/
U.S. News & World Report, 5-7:40,41.

1

[On counter-commercials]: Does commercial advertising really fit very well with the Fairness Doctrine? Does an ad which says "Buy a Chevrolet" raise an issue of smog and pollution? I don't know. The courts have said so; we've not said so ourselves. But I think it's an overly simplistic view of the function of advertising; and after all, advertising is what pays the freight in the business. If you de-

stroy advertising, you've got to find another way of financing broadcasting.

Interview/TV Guide, 4-28:38.

Carol Burnett
Actress, Comedienne

2

Being a writer for a variety show is the hardest job in the world, because practically everything's written from scratch . . . And comedy is . . . well, dramatic actors think it's easy to jump in and be funny about anything. I think it's at least as difficult as doing drama. Most people cry at the same thing, but no two people laugh at the same thing.

Interview, New York/
The New York Times, 6-3:(2)17.

Michael Caine
British actor

3

. . . the British don't care about cinema. The British like television, because it shows them themselves . . . They're in the kitchen washing up and they hurry into the lounge and turn on the TV to watch people in the kitchen washing up. Britain's the only country with soap opera in prime-time. Soap opera —true life with only the boring bits left in.

Interview, Paris/
Los Angeles Times, 11-4:(Calendar)25.

William Castle
Producer

4

I have found [that] people who watch television are so literal . . . They want to know all the answers. When you do a movie, you can leave something to the imagination. If you do that on television, people don't like it . . . In a theatre, you're sitting there in the dark and you have to think. With television, there's always a distraction. That's why you have to hook them at once.

Interview, Los Angeles/
The Dallas Times Herald, 1-2:(A)11.

Dick Cavett
Television talk-show host

5

American TV is about 80 per cent junk; it

still is and probably always will be as long as it's in the hands of the junk-makers.

Television interview/
Los Angeles Times, 5-18:(4)23.

Alistair Cooke
Chief United States correspondent,
"The Manchester (England) Guardian"

1

[On educational television]: The people who go on the rampage to get into it are the worst people. They may be so-called educators, but you know Shaw's crack about he who does, does; and he who doesn't, teaches. Unfortunately, with of course great exceptions, it's frightfully true of educational TV. Some of the dullest people on earth are there. They have no fresh view of anything. They're enormously verbose. The discussion shows are intolerable.

Interview, New York/
The Christian Science Monitor, 4-26:9.

Alan Cranston
United States Senator, D-California

2

Those of us concerned with the lack of broadcast time for airing of public issues are disturbed also by the [Nixon] Administration's moves to gut public broadcasting by a combination of cutting off funds and attempting to control content by eliminating controversial programs. Commercial broadcast media have a direct interest in this issue; for if the regulators can push public broadcasting around and get away with it, they are going to push you around, too.

Before Hollywood Radio and Television
Society, Beverly Hills, Calif.,
June 22/Los Angeles Times, 6-25:(4)18.

Robert Culp
Actor

3

In a [TV] series, the one thing that matters is how much in love with the star the audience is; the rest is nonsense.

Time, 11-26:120.

Doris Day
Actress

4

There is really no reason why prime-time TV must devote so much of its time to pure entertainment. TV is the most powerful medium in the world; and Hollywood, its prime source of material, has used it almost entirely as an outlet for entertainment. Entertainment is a valuable and worthwhile commodity. It has provided me with a good living for many years. But it is not the alpha and omega of the world. Hollywood and the networks so often say, "We are giving the public what it wants." But the public never really knows what it wants until somebody gives it to them. It seems to me it is up to Hollywood and the networks to lead rather than follow.

Los Angeles, March 14/
Daily Variety, 3-15:6.

Marlene Dietrich
Actress, Singer

5

[On why she held out so long before agreeing to do a special on television]: Because I don't like people watching me for free. You don't get respect with people going out in the middle of my songs for a Coca-Cola . . . They [the audience] didn't laugh in any of the right places, so [the producers] told me they would edit-in a laugh-track later. "But you don't have my reaction to the applause," I told them. "We don't have time," they answered. They are robots, these people in TV.

Interview, New York/
The Washington Post, 1-7:(G)2.

Peter Falk
Actor

6

The general level of mediocrity on television is overwhelming.

Television interview, May 18/
Los Angeles Times, 5-18:(4)25.

Lewis Freedman
Producer

7

People have stopped writing seriously for

(LEWIS FREEDMAN)

television. There is more money in movies or books. There are 83 reasons why serious writers write for anything except for TV. Now we must find a new group. That's difficult. Young writers are writing forms we don't understand. They are writing in terms that middle-aged people like myself don't find nice. They write a language that we don't consider proper. They write about subjects we always were told we mustn't talk about. Young playwrights are treating casually what I treat importantly. *Jesus Christ Superstar* treats God and Christ and religion very casually. On PBS, the Easter Passion is performed with Christ in blue jeans. *Hair* is performed in ultra-conservative San Diego without one word of dissent. We in television are not really in tune with what the public is thinking today.

Interview, Los Angeles/
San Francisco Examiner,
4-1:(Sunday Scene)16.

Lillian Gish
Actress

1

[Television] is the greatest power on earth that exists to sway the minds of men.

Interview, San Francisco/
San Francisco Examiner, 10-29:23.

Hal Holbrook
Actor

2

I look for things [TV roles] that are good. Usually, when they're good they're different, and that's trouble. You see, the only thing left to do on television is to stir up trouble, to be controversial. But television is so meek that to be *real* is to be controversial.

Interview, New York/
The New York Times, 3-25:(2)19.

3

[On his former TV series *The Senator*]: I'm especially proud of that show; I was bitter and disappointed over its cancellation. We had the critical acclaim but not the rating. Too bad the democratic system gets turned over to

the so-called Madison Avenue psychology, wherein there is but one rule: Whatever sells and however you sell it is kosher . . . Here we were, proving you could deal with such controversial subjects as senility and the poverty program and the shooting of rioting students, and we were cancelled. TV cheated itself, robbed itself . . . All you can do in television is be a grain of sand. You can never be a mountain.

Interview, San Francisco/
San Francisco Examiner & Chronicle,
7-1:(Datebook)22.

Celeste Holm
Actress

4

The television camera is as revealing as a dermatological report.

Interview, New York/
The Dallas Times Herald, 8-18:(A)4.

Benjamin L. Hooks
Commissioner, Federal Communications
Commission of the United States

5

Unlike some FCC Commissioners, I *like* television, and for about 15 years was an ardent devotee of its programs. But I don't like it as much as I used to. You've made Marshall Dillon a psychological hero, and I used to like to see him shoot people once in a while.

Before National Association of Television
Program Executives, New Orleans/
Variety, 2-21:29.

Nicholas Johnson
Commissioner, Federal Communications
Commission of the United States

6

[Saying the FCC's power is too limited]: It is the Executive Branch that sets policy on cable television. It is the Executive Branch to which the Congress turns for recommendations on funding of public broadcasting. When there is no Executive recommendation, public broadcasting remains in limbo and subject to political control. It is the Executive Branch to which Congress turns for recommendations on the structure of the international common-carrier industry. It is the Executive Branch, not the FCC, that is proposing radical revisions in the Communications Act regarding [station] license renewal.

The New York Times, 5-6:(1)55.

1

. . . television [as it is constituted today] has nothing to do with serving anybody or with programs. Its business is to sell you, the viewer, to the advertiser. You, the viewer, are the product, not the consumer. The consumer is the advertiser. The purpose of programming is simply to capture your attention, in the same way a neon sign or a topless waitress would.

Interview/
San Francisco Examiner & Chronicle,
5-13:(Sunday Scene)14.

2

The greatest danger to broadcasters is broadcasters. It is the network executives who continue to dictate what the American people can see—not in terms of humanistic value, not in terms of what the best American writers and actors have to offer, but in terms of what will deliver audiences to advertisers, what will encourage values of materialism and conspicuous consumption in programs and commercials alike.

Quote, 12-23:602.

James Karayn
President, National Public Affairs
Center for Television

3

I have always felt that the function of public broadcasting is to be responsibly outrageous. Its great enemies are cowardice and caution, brought on in part by insecure financing . . . There must be an independent source of financing. Public television should be like, say, the Cancer Society or some other major national cause, wherein a giant kitty could be established into which corporations and foundations and government could funnel money without strings attached.

Interview/Los Angeles Times, 6-20:(4)16.

David Karp
Writer, Producer

4

Television used to be all live. It was marvelous. Everything was special then. The moment things were put on film, the whole business changed. It's depressing. Oh, sure, they might have made a lot of money through film. But the moment you put something on film, you want to run it forever. That's what they're doing.

Los Angeles Herald-Examiner,
3-11:
(TV Weekly)7.

Nira Kfir
Director,
Alfred Adler Institute, Tel Aviv

5

The invention that has had the greatest impact on mankind is television. Television should be a public servant. Instead, it is turning people into cop-outs who shrug and say, "What can we do about all that?" Or it turns them into spectators watching dramatic scenes in which they have no part. Or it turns them into consumers who think only of keeping up with the Joneses.

Before World Association of Women
Journalists and Writers, Jerusalem/
The Christian Science Monitor,
7-13:10.

Norman Lear
Writer, Producer

6

The so-called "adult" themes that television is currently dealing in are themes for which the American people have always been ready. We in television simply weren't trusting the people of this country to accept or reject as they saw fit. The TV think-tanks were telling us that the Bible Belt wouldn't accept this and the South wouldn't accept that and the [Federal] Administration wouldn't accept anything. I feel that we've reached a time in our national life where we must stop psyching each other out. We, especially in the media, must start to trust the American public more.

(NORMAN LEAR)

And to do that, we must begin to trust ourselves.

*Accepting International Radio and Television
Society's "Broadcaster of the Year"
award, New York, May 13/
The New York Times Magazine, 6-24:22.*

Robert Liebert
*Psychologist, State University of
New York, Stony Brook*

1

. . . the broadcasting industry tends to say that television is only "entertainment." It tends to see these two things—entertainment and socialization—as different. If it only entertains, they contend, then it doesn't socialize. That, of course, is preposterous. By interesting stories and parables, we've been socializing people—children and adults—from the beginning of our recorded history. It was very, very functional for tribes to sit around the fire and tell what great warriors did. That wasn't just entertainment; it was to get the kids who were sitting around the fire to be just like that. The industry tends to forget that entertainment is the greatest socializer there is.

*Interview/
The Christian Science Monitor, 11-9:13.*

Norman Lloyd
*Executive producer,
"Hollywood Television Theatre,"
Public Broadcasting Service*

2

As for [the] television medium, I'm convinced it positively improves upon plays written for the proscenium stage. When I go to the theatre to see a play nowadays, it never seems close enough. TV is a close medium; it lets you look into a person's eyes, a person's face, with an intimacy the theatre can never duplicate. [Playwright] Arthur Miller was astonished when he saw how *[Incident at] Vichy* came out. He swore it looked absolutely better on the television screen than it had ever looked on stage. And he said it without our asking.

Interview/ The Washington Post, 11-18:(K)5.

Torbert H. Macdonald
United States Representative, D-Massachusetts

3

I am against granting broadcast licenses in perpetuity . . . The door behind which licensees now operate is a big, thick, heavy door. It is our job in Congress to make sure that that door is not permanently bolted and barred . . . I cannot believe that every one of the more than 600 television stations currently on the air is doing as good a job as could possibly be done for its community; and I will not be a party to freezing out completely a prospective licensee who could do a better job just because he wasn't around at the right time to get the license in the first instance.

*Before National Association of Broadcasters,
New Orleans, Oct. 23/
Daily Variety, 10-24:10.*

Ward L. Quaal
*President,
WGN Continental Broadcasting Company*

4

[On criticism of American television]: . . . some of those of the newer generations, both within and outside our profession, either never learned or have forgotten the basic tenets of free enterprise in our free society. They have lost touch with the spirit, dedication, zeal and wisdom of the architects of what was then known as broadcasting by the American plan, and which since has been adapted in every free nation on earth in toto or in some modified fashion—adapted throughout the world because it is the most solid . . . [It is the broadcaster's] obligation to defend that which you and your predecessors fashioned by popular demand—the expressed wishes of a nation of 220 million Americans—including the 3 per cent of self-anointed intellectuals who preach what they seldom practice.

*Before National Association of Broadcasters,
Washington/Daily Variety, 3-27:1,2.*

Jean Renoir
Former motion picture director

5

TV cannot have the same artistic achievement as film because there's so little time to spend on technique. But today, some film-makers think of nothing but technique. Their films are sterile. With TV, the speed of production makes the medium exciting.

Interview,
Beverly Hills, Calif./
The New York Times, 2-5:24.

Debbie Reynolds
Actress

1

Making a TV series is like living in an old abandoned German tank in the desert. Television is just a big monopoly of money. You're wedged in between network power and advertising power. It's impossible to please both. A lot of people do succeed in TV, but I think they've had to downgrade their creative fibers and be big-business types.

Interview,
Washington/
The Washington Post, 2-6:(B)4.

Robert W. Sarnoff
Chairman, RCA Corporation

2

My projection for a bright future for television is rooted, I believe, in a realistic appraisal of the natural forces of economics, competition and technology. What it does not take into account, however, are the artificial forces that would be imposed by government restrictions. As a regulated industry, broadcasting has learned over the years how to live with government. The first three letters of our alphabet are FCC. We also deal with the FTC, the Department of Justice and other government agencies. And from the very beginning, the industry has maintained a dialogue, mostly a constructive one, with Committees in both houses of Congress. I think it is second-nature for us to be alert to the special nature of our public stewardship—and I don't think we're particularly thin-skinned about our regulated status. But the growing intensity of government assaults on broadcasting must give us new and genuine concern.

Before NBC-TV affiliates, Los Angeles,
May 7/Vital Speeches, 7-1:552.

Thomas Sarnoff
Executive vice president,
National Broadcasting Company

3

I stand before you today as a symbol of evil—a representative of the broadcasting industry. It has become fashionable to condemn broadcasting, particularly television, for most of the evils with which our country is currently beset. We are accused of influencing elections, fanning sparks of violence, of corrupting children and brainwashing people to buy advertised product[s]. To one charge we are definitely guilty, that of being accused of being the most potent of the mass media. If the pressures from Washington go unchallenged and unchecked, it is to consign our future to certain darkness. Not content to attack television on its programming side alone, our government has decided to launch a foray against the advertising as well. The Federal Trade Commission has recommended that ordinary product commercials be subject to offsetting counter-commercials. One finds it difficult to believe that its advocates are serious, but they are.

Before Advertising & Sales Club of
San Diego and San Diego chapter of National
Association of Television Arts and Sciences,
March 21/Daily Variety, 3-22:8.

Herbert S. Schlosser
President,
National Broadcasting Company Television

4

Television is truly the only national medium. It reaches every home in the country for more than 18 hours a day, and the average prime-time program during the regular season attracts about 22 million viewers. That makes television a communications force in which quantity is a singular quality.

Before Hollywood Radio and Television
Society, Sept. 11/
The Hollywood Reporter, 9-12:3.

5

[On "permissiveness" on TV]: This issue, in its basic terms, is how to balance a respect for creative freedom with an equal respect for

WHAT THEY SAID IN 1973

(HERBERT S. SCHLOSSER)

television as a home medium, a medium that
serves so wide a diversity of tastes and interests that it must observe certain limitations.
As a mass medium for home viewers, television will never lead any parade of permissiveness. But it should not lag so far behind the
march of an audience of millions that it can
be chained to the past by a few hundred
letters of complaint.

The New York Times, 10-25:83.

Walter A. Schwartz
President,
American Broadcasting Company Television
1

If in mass entertainment we [in TV] are
also evoking mass enlightenment, then we are
fulfilling a genuine moral obligation to our
viewers and ourselves.

Before ABC-TV affiliates, Los Angeles/
Variety, 5-30:31.

Arthur R. Taylor
President,
Columbia Broadcasting System
2

[Radio is] still the most ubiquitous and
most immediate of media . . . [No] medium
in the history of communications had ever
before achieved so much for so many people
. . . In a time of national emergency, it has
been and will be radio which will knit our
people together . . . [As a newcomer to the
communications industry,] there is one thing
that stands out to me . . . the enormous
flexibility of radio—its really irrepressible capacity to adjust to new circumstances, new
interests, new conditions. It has been the genius of radio to recognize quickly the need to
change and when to change. Radio . . . will
enlarge rather than diminish, regardless of
what the future holds in terms of communications.

At dinner honoring station KCBS'
Golden Mike Award, New York/
Variety, 3-7:36.

Clay T. Whitehead
Director, Federal Office of
Telecommunications Policy (United States)
3

There is no doubt that we're making two
overtures to the broadcasting industry. One is
the very straightforward statement that we
believe they should have more insulation from
government; they should have more stability
in their licenses; broadcasting should be run as
a business, not as an arm of the government.
On the other hand, we recognize the many
criticisms that have been brought to bear
against broadcasting. It's not only news—[it's]
the totality of broadcasting. And we are saying that the industry as a whole—networks
and local station managers—has to stand up
and say the responsibility that was enforced
from Washington will now be enforced voluntarily throughout the system.

Interview, New York/
The New York Times, 1-11:37.
4

[Saying the Nixon Administration does not
want to censor TV stations by threatening to
revoke their licenses]: The main value of the
sword of Damocles is that it hangs, not that it
drops. Once you take a guy's license away,
you no longer have any leverage against him.

News conference, Washington, March 8/
The Washington Post, 3-9:(A)17.
5

The core issue is, who should be responsible for assuring that the people's right to
know is served, and where should the initiative come from—the government or the broadcasters . . . Some, who now profess to fight
for broadcasters' freedom, would rely on regulatory remedies such as increased program category restrictions, burdening the broadcaster
and the audience with the clutter of counter-
advertising, banning ads in children's programs, ill-defined restrictions on violence, and
the like . . . clearly it is others, not this
[Nixon] Administration, that are calling for
more and more government controls over
broadcasting.

Before House Communications and
Power Subcommittee, Washington,
April 17/The Hollywood Reporter, 4-18:3.

542

Robert D. Wood
President,
Columbia Broadcasting System Television

1

[On audience complaints about controversial entertainment programming]: Part of being fully responsive to our public is to make sure that we do not allow a small, vocal and, at times, highly-organized minority to determine what can be seen on your television set. If we fell into this trap, we might be easily led to ban present-day equivalents of such literary classics as Nathaniel Hawthorne's *The Scarlet Letter*, Charlotte Bronte's *Jane Eyre*, George Bernard Shaw's *Mrs. Warren's Profession*, Theodore Dreiser's *An American Tragedy*, Emile Zola's *Nana*, even Walt Whitman's *Leaves of Grass.*

Before Better Business Bureau,
New York, Oct. 16/
The New York Times,
10-16:75.

Personal Profiles

Edward Albee
Playwright

1

It occurs to me, with some wonder occasionally, that I am as old as I am, because I think of myself as a good deal younger. Because I am younger. I am not settled into all the middle-aged things most people have settled into. I look around at all the people who are my age, and what do you see? I see a bunch of old people who I don't relate to at all.

Interview, Montauk Point, N.Y./
The Dallas Times Herald, 10-7:(K)5.

Michelangelo Antonioni
Motion picture director

2

If I had not become a director, I would have been an architect, I suspect, or perhaps a painter. I feel I am a person who has things he wants to show rather than things he wants to say. There are times when the two concepts coincide, and then we arrive at a work of art.

Interview, London/
Los Angeles Times, 12-30:(Calendar)16.

Fred Astaire
Actor, Dancer

3

. . . I never thought about bringing anything to dancing, or trying to say something with dancing, or trying to be something arty. I was just trying to make a buck. I never could take myself very seriously. I'm really a rat if you want to know the truth.

News conference, New York, April 30/
The Washington Post, 5-2:(B)13.

Howard H. Baker, Jr.
United States Senator, R-Tennessee

4

It's characteristic of some people to be public moralists, to express outrage, to be enthusiastic and aggressive. My personality tends to be more even—even more calculating—and I accept that. I make do with what I am.

Interview/
The New York Times Magazine, 9-30:93.

Brigitte Bardot
Actress

5

I find my equilibrium in nature, in the company of animals. I hate humanity—I am allergic to it. I see no one. I don't go out. I am disgusted with everything. Men are beasts—and even beasts don't behave as they do.

Interview/Newsweek, 3-5:45.

Abraham D. Beame
Controller, and Mayor-elect,
of New York City

6

I don't like to begin the day with work that has to be caught-up-on. I stay late in the office and finish up, or I take it home and finish it so that the morning is a new day. I take my problems to bed with me; I can never leave them behind. Sometimes I wake up in the night and make notes in the dark. Then I say to myself the next morning, "What the hell is this?"

The New York Times Magazine, 11-18:78.

Ernest Borgnine
Actor

7

I'm a simple guy. My friends are not in show business. I like to watch the boob tube [TV] and run down to my boat, and I like to play golf. My philosophy is that I deserve my comforts because I worked hard to achieve them. I have a 14-room house, but you can put your feet up on the coffee table and there's just enough carpet to keep you from getting a backache if you want to lie down on the floor. There's no keeping-up-with-the-Joneses for Borgnine . . . My idea of a good scene is a beautiful sunset, the ocean, a work of art, holding hands with a lovely girl, reading a good book, browsing in antique shops, looking at a piece of rock.

Interview, New York/
The New York Times, 6-17:(2)15.

Habib Bourguiba
President of Tunisia

1

[Addressing writers taking part in a poetry contest]: Not only is Bourguiba a man of political genius who has triumphed over French colonialism, but Bourguiba also is perhaps a great poet . . . When I have been called to God, these oratorical meetings will take on an elegiac tone to weep for the great man that I have been.

Tunis, August/
Los Angeles Times, 10-3:(1)2.

Jimmy Breslin
Author

2

My ambition is to become a hermit. I don't want to know anybody else; I'd like to buy back a million introductions. It started first as a fancy, developed as a yearning, now it's a driving, cold ambition. Where do I want to hermit? Where other people ain't.

Interview/
Los Angeles Times, 1-1('74):(4)1.

Leonid I. Brezhnev
General Secretary,
Communist Party of the Soviet Union

3

[On his gaining weight since cutting down on smoking]: One sits the whole day at the desk, and when I don't smoke, appetite is also standing next to me. "Away with you," I say. But comrade appetite does not budge from the spot.

Interview, Moscow, May 13/
Los Angeles Times, 5-17:(1)21.

Richard Burton
Actor

4

You must realize I met her [his wife, Elizabeth Taylor] 20 years ago and fell madly in love with her then. I'm afraid at first it was lust, but then I got to know her and it was love. I chased her for nine years; but she kept on marrying someone else all the time. Every time I found out she was divorced, she got married again and I arrived in time to congratulate the bridegroom. And when we did get together, it was a terrible thing. She didn't listen to my stories. She didn't laugh at the right time. She just looked at me through those strange eyes. I had to marry her to teach her.

Interview, Munich/TV Guide, 2-3:17.

Constantin Costa-Gavras
Motion picture director

5

When I was a small boy, I remember hanging on the back of the bus because I had no money to pay for a ride. Suddenly, the bus would stop and the conductor would come and hit me on the face and make me leave. I didn't have the money to take the bus to school, so I would either have to walk three kilometers or climb on the back of the bus and be humiliated. Today, I am violently opposed to almost any kind of humiliation. It is the thing that makes me angriest of all.

Interview, New York/
The New York Times, 4-22:(2)9.

Walter Cronkite
News commentator,
Columbia Broadcasting System

6

I really enjoy solitude and introspection. That's why I like sailing. I like sitting in the cockpit of my boat at dusk and on into the night, gazing at the stars, thinking of the enormity, the universality of it all. I can get lost in reveries in that regard, both in looking forward to a dreamworld and in looking back to the pleasant times of my own life.

Interview, New York/Playboy, June:84.

Sammy Davis, Jr.
Entertainer

1

Yeah, I got seven cars; yeah, I got 25 TV sets; I got 40 wristwatches, three Hasselblad cameras and God knows how many others . . . and I'm not ashamed of it. It's my life style. If it means first cabin, that's what I want . . . I love to live good. I could have bought Altovise [his wife] a Mercedes; but it makes me happy to have her drive a Rolls. I enjoy going to Cartier's. I say, "Gimme three of those and four of those." I bought that way when I couldn't afford it. So why not now? I didn't steal the money.

Interview, Beverly Hills, Calif./
TV Guide, 11-10:27.

Marlene Dietrich
Actress, Singer

2

It is such agony, being a legend in your own time . . .

Interview, New York/
The Washington Post, 1-7:(G)2.

Clint Eastwood
Actor

3

I'm not the guy you see on the screen. If I was, I'd go around drilling people with a .44. There are so many different elements that make up a man. I can be driven to great releases of temper just like any person, but I'm not a violent guy.

Interview, Washington/
The Washington Post, 4-24:(B)3.

Sam J. Ervin, Jr.
United States Senator, D-North Carolina

4

I am possessor of a great affliction, a Scotch-Irish conscience, which will not permit me to follow after a great multitude to do what I conceive to be evil.

Quote, 3-11:218.

Peter Falk
Actor

5

I don't bust into or out of anything. I get down on my hands and knees and crawl very slowly. It took me nine years to get married, ten to decide to become an actor.

Time, 11-26:122.

Eddie Fisher
Singer

6

Anyone who marries an actress is an idiot. Anyone who marries two actresses should be put up against a wall and shot at dawn. But three actresses? I don't know what that makes me.

Interview, Sparks, Nev./
San Francisco Examiner, 10-12:30.

Christina (Mrs. Henry) Ford
Wife of the chairman,
Ford Motor Company

7

People are full of fantasy. They think we are always sitting down formally to dinner and going to glamorous parties. They should see me in my dressing gown and Henry in his shirt, eating on a little tray and watching television.

Newsweek, 3-26:46.

Gerald R. Ford
Vice President of the United States

8

I may not have all the charisma in the world, but that's all right with me. I'd rather be sincere than have the kind of charisma you can turn on and off like a light switch. I'd rather be what I am than be a phony like a lot of people with charisma are.

Interview/
"W": a Fairchild publication, 12-14:16.

Paul Gallico
Author

9

I've got everything I want. And now I have a sense of impending extinction. How much longer can I wait? I've reached the life expectancy of this generation. I'm prepared for death, hoping I can go as my father did, who went to sleep and didn't wake up.

Interview, Antibes, France/
Publishers Weekly, 1-22:35.

Indira Gandhi
Prime Minister of India

1

I am one of those who always choose the most difficult paths. And between a straight road and a mountain road, I invariably go for the mountain road.

Interview/
McCall's, June:102.

Julian Goodman
President, National Broadcasting Company

2

I have been president of NBC for seven years by virtue of the fact that I never speak for more than one minute.

Beverly Hills, Calif./
San Francisco Examiner, 1-16:29.

Alfred Hitchcock
Motion picture director

3

A lot of people think I'm a monster . . . Well, I'm just the opposite. I'm more scared than they are of things in real life.

Television interview/
Los Angeles Herald-Examiner, 12-12:(C)15.

Sol Hurok
Impresario

4

I just can't be alone. I'm so attached to people; I love people. So if I'm not doing anything one night, I call up somebody and say, "Come over to the house, let's have dinner; let's sit around; let's have tea." If I go to a concert, I come home, get undressed, read the newspaper or a book, and suddenly I feel that I'd like to talk to somebody, to tell somebody the bad things and the good things.

Interview, New York/
The New York Times, 5-13:(2)1.

Michel Jobert
Foreign Minister of France

5

[On U.S. Secretary of State Henry Kissinger]: Some find him a bit overwhelming—I am sure he will not take offense at my choice of term—but this is normal because he revolves in so many spheres and tries to be present everywhere at once. He calculates like a politician. He also knows how to come to terms like a politician or lead the offensive like a man of this category, as well as how to abandon its pursuit when his position is in peril. Finally, Henry Kissinger is a man who lives each minute. This is my way of describing him: mobile, impassioned, calculating, very well organized, sometimes detached and most likely a dreamer, and unquestionably good-hearted.

The New York Times,
12-26:39.

Edward M. Kennedy
United States Senator,
D-Massachusetts

6

[On his brother, the late President John F. Kennedy, who was assassinated 10 years ago]: I miss him every time I see his children. I miss him every time I see the places, like Cape Cod, which had such meaning for him and still have for all of us. I miss him at the times our family used to get together, such as his birthday and Thanksgiving. I miss the chance to tell him about things I've done which I feel proud of, and I miss encouragement and advice at times of difficulty. I miss him as you'd miss your best friend.

Interview/
The Dallas Times Herald,
10-24:(E)11.

Henry A. Kissinger
Assistant to the President of the
United States for National Security Affairs

7

For me, women are only amusing, a hobby. Nobody spends too much time on a hobby.

Quote, 1-7:1.

Henry A. Kissinger
Secretary of State-designate
of the United States

1

[On whether he should be called "Dr. Kissinger" or "Mr. Secretary"]: I don't stand on protocol. If you just call me "Excellency," that will be sufficient.

News conference, San Clemente, Calif.,
Aug. 23/The Dallas Times Herald, 8-24:(A)2.

Andre Kostelanetz
Orchestra conductor

2

I'm extremely fortunate, and I don't mean with materialistic things. I survived revolutions, I heard Lenin speak, I crashed in a plane in Cambodia—all this in one lifetime. I was born totally unknown, and somehow or other it seems that now everybody knows me. I also think that most of the people like what I'm doing.

Interview/The New York Times, 5-6:(2)31.

Anita Loos
Author

3

Nothing that happens at night interests me. I hate parties, the theatre, television. So I go to bed early and I get up early, around 4 to 5 o'clock, and start writing.

Interview/The New York Times, 3-29:53.

Sophia Loren
Actress

4

I . . . think of myself in terms of food —like a pizza, which I happen to like very much. Being Neapolitan, I see myself as the classic pizza made with tomato and mozzarella. Why pizza? Because pizza is common; and I think I'm a very common housewife.

Quote, 12-2:530.

Joe Louis
Former heavyweight boxing champion
of the world

5

I just want one word on my tombstone:

"Even." I was born even, and I want to go out even.

Quote, 5-20:457.

Clare Boothe Luce
Former American diplomat and playwright

6

I remember standing there [on top of New York's Empire State Building in 1936 after her play *The Women* had just opened], staring out at a city of several million people, most of whom had never heard of me and didn't care, either. Then I thought of the people all over the country and the world, as far as China, for whom not a word I write, not anything I have done, will ever change their lives for the better. Fame seemed to be the most idiotic thing in the world. From then on, I have never had a very high opinion of myself.

Interview, New York/
The Washington Post, 4-29:(F)1.

John D. MacDonald
Author

7

No, I don't live like my [detective-story] heroes. I like to be home, feeding my duck and my goose, leaving the typewriter when Dorothy [his wife] rattles my dish.

Interview, New York/
San Francisco Examiner & Chronicle,
8-26:(This World)36.

Golda Meir
Prime Minister of Israel

8

I've known people who died too soon, and it was painful. I've known people who died too late, and it was equally painful. Listen: I feel insulted when I see the collapse of a fine brain. I don't want to undergo that insult. I want to die clear-headed. Yes, my only fear is living too long.

Interview/The New York Times, 3-15:49.

Robert Mitchum
Actor

9

I went into the movies thinking I'd be a

stuntman or extra, and I'd have been just as happy if I'd never got further than that. My life would have been a lot different—I wouldn't have met the people I've met, traveled the world and been recognized everywhere I go. But basically I'm a simple guy who likes simple things. The rest is frosting —cool and tasty but unnecessary. I don't need much to make me happy; good friends and a good bottle of whiskey are enough.

Interview, Los Angeles/
Los Angeles Herald-Examiner, 7-8:(D)1.

Richard M. Nixon
President of the United States

1

Great decisions, if they are to be good decisions, must be made coolly. Of course, I like to hear everyone, but then I go off alone.

Interview/
San Francisco Examiner & Chronicle,
6-17:(This World)7.

2

. . . I have a quality which is—I guess I must have inherited it from my Midwestern mother and father—which is that the tougher it gets, the cooler I get. Of course, it isn't pleasant to get criticism . . . But as far as I'm concerned, I have learned to expect it; it has been my lot throughout my political life. And I suppose, because I've been through so much, that maybe one of the reasons is, when I have to face an international crisis, I have what it takes.

News conference, Washington, Oct. 26/
The New York Times, 10-27:14.

Rudolf Nureyev
Ballet dancer

3

I am full of confusion, professional and private. If I don't allow my anger to burst out, then it stays in turmoil inside me and would explode. And when it comes, my anger is unlimited.

Interview, Milan, Italy/
The Christian Science Monitor, 11-2:13.

Jack Paar
Television entertainer

4

This is probably the last interview I'll ever give. I am tired of being analyzed. I've gone through the roughest kind of press, and I've said it all. Someone said that interviewing Paar is like dissecting a frog: both may die in the process.

Interview, Florida/
Los Angeles Herald-Examiner, 2-5:(B)6.

Prince Philip
Duke of Edinburgh

5

[Saying his reputation with the press is not very good]: That's the trouble with reputations: They cling much more tenaciously than the truth. If anyone can offer me any advice about how I can improve this reputation, or even offer any reason why I should have it, I shall be more than grateful. Perhaps I've made the mistake of saying what I think—but surely that's what every good journalist does every working day.

Before journalists, Glasgow, Scotland,
July 10/The Dallas Times Herald, 7-11:(A)5.

J. B. Priestley
Author, Playwright

6

[On what it was like to grow old]: It is as though, walking down [London's] Shaftesbury Avenue as a fairly young man, I was suddenly kidnaped, rushed into a theatre and made to don the gray hair, the wrinkles and the other attributes of age, then wheeled onstage. Behind the appearance of age I am the same person, with the same thoughts, as when I was younger.

Time, 9-24:58.

Robert Radnitz
Motion picture producer

7

God, how I love the ocean. I think the ocean cures anything. You have pneumonia? Go swimming every day. You have a broken leg? Float it in the ocean. I had a bad fall from a horse four years ago . . . The doctors

(ROBERT RADNITZ)

said, "You'll never be able to walk right again unless we operate." Instead, I had a friend carry me into the ocean—literally carry me —every day for six weeks. Two weeks after that, I was back playing tennis . . . My whole thing about the ocean borders on insanity. When you're a kid and you're very ill, you spend a lot of time dreaming of getting out. That was my life—reading and listening to music, and dreaming of islands and oceans.

Interview, Los Angeles/
Los Angeles Times, 3-18:(Calendar)18.

Sally Rand
Exotic dancer

1

I shall be here at the turn of the century. I will have a glass of pink champagne, dance the Vienna Waltz with a nice young man and sleep late the next morning. After that, I don't give a damn.

Interview, Washington/
The Washington Post, 6-10:(H)3.

Ralph Richardson
Actor

2

I don't feel 70. I always thought [that], when I was 70, I would be very wise, a very grand *seigneur*, full of grace but no doubt being pushed about in a little chair. But I find myself without any wisdom or graces, but at the same time I'm bounding about like mad.

San Francisco Examiner, 1-30:24.

Frank L. Rizzo
Mayor of Philadelphia

3

Basically, I'm a loner. I don't have a circle of friends, no hobbies, no sports. All I do is work.

Interview, Philadelphia/
Los Angeles Times, 1-21:(1)17.

Derek Sanderson
Hockey player

4

They say I'm a swinger and a playboy—and

I'm not. They say I'm thoughtless and I'm careless—and I'm not. I think about everything; I'm careless about nothing. I adapt to every situation, and they say I'm only one way. They say I'm an egomaniac, and I'm not.

Interview, Hollywood, Fla./
The National Observer, 2-10:16.

Norodom Sihanouk
Exiled former Chief of State of Cambodia

5

[On his life when he was leader of Cambodia]: I spent too much time on music and movie-making, and I had mistresses. Now I am like Buddha. I am faithful to my wife. I have no love adventures, no sports cars and no dancing parties . . . so I have more esteem for myself.

News conference, Peking/
The Christian Science Monitor, 8-27:6.

Stephen Sondheim
Composer, Lyricist

6

At least half my songs deal with ambivalence, feeling two things at once. I like neurotic people. I like troubled people. Not that I don't like squared-away people, but I *prefer* neurotic people. I like to hear rumblings beneath the surface.

Newsweek, 4-23:55.

Barbra Streisand
Actress, Singer

7

Fantasies can make a rich inner life. They can lead you places. If I never had a fantasy about being an actress, perhaps I wouldn't have become one. More than anything, I wanted to be recognized. That's why I started singing—so that somebody would *listen* to me.

Interview, New York/
The New York Times, 1-21:(2)3.

8

[Saying she will not do nude scenes in films]: Like the information about my love-life, my body is not for public display. Of course, it's a social thing. If society would say to hide your face and show your body, you'd see me hiding my face and showing my body. But that's me—one foot in the 19th century and one foot in the 20th.

Los Angeles Herald-Examiner,
6-29:(C)7.

Elizabeth Taylor
Actress

1

When I get old, either I'll be a fragile, sweet, grey-haired lady, or I'll be as fat as a piece of lard. But people will look at me anyway.

San Francisco Examiner, 3-5:26.

John Wayne
Actor

2

As an actor, I tried to bring a little bad and a lot of good to a character. The one thing I can't stand is pettiness; but I don't mind being cruel, or rough, or tough—in pictures or in life.

Interview/Newsweek, 3-19:85.

3

If it hadn't been for football and the fact I got my leg broke and had to go into the movies to eat, why, who knows? I might have turned out to be a liberal Democrat.

At National Football Foundation
Hall of Fame dinner, New York/
Newsweek, 12-17:55.

Tennessee Williams
Playwright

4

. . . the personal criticism of me is no better than the criticism of my plays. Some members of the press are still virulently against the outspokenly sensual person. I shall not name them, but they are significantly influential. One of them said I wasn't the sort of person one would take to dinner . . . Fortunately, there are also a great many people who don't think of me as a bum; a lot of them think of me as Tennessee Ernie Ford!

Interview/
Playboy, April:80.

Franco Zeffirelli
Motion picture director

5

I'm 51, not so young. I have not had time to either look nor act my age. I have not even found time in my hectic pursuit of two careers—music and films—to get married. I am sure that, if I had married, I would have produced a lot of children, hurriedly, and would always be dashing off somewhere, leaving them—which would give me a guilty conscience. My whole life has been jumping from here to there. Exhausting, but it keeps the physical and mental juices flowing, and that's youthful.

Interview,
Beverly Hills, Calif./
Los Angeles Herald-Examiner, 4-15:(F)3.

Philosophy

Spiro T. Agnew
Vice President of the United States

1

[Success is] not making $50,000 a year or a college degree or being fluent in three languages, [but] a state of mind satisfying the psyche.

Before his daughter's high-school graduating class, Washington, June 4/ The Washington Post, 6-5:(B)3.

2

I cannot stand here and tell you, in good conscience, that a world without war is visible on the horizon—or that a world without crime, without poverty, without oppression or discrimination is achievable in the foreseeable future . . . Such utopian preaching is fundamentally dishonest, hypocritical and insulting. Five thousand years of recorded human history attest to the imperfections of humankind. How can anyone really believe that every man and woman on earth, without divine intervention, can be ennobled to the extent that war, crime, discrimination and poverty are *eliminated* completely from the earth? Then why cannot we find sufficient inspiration in the articulation of reasonable and honest goals? . . . Is it not enough to promise that we will try to *reduce* crime by diligent policing, speedy justice, correction of known causes and rehabilitation of the offender? Is it not more believable to want to *diminish* poverty and oppression than to promise to *eliminate* them? In my opinion, a great deal of the discontent and frustration prevalent today can be traced to our failure to meet the impossible standards so casually set by many of us. It is the nature of man that, if he were promised eternal life, he would little appreciate learning that the best he can expect is to live 200 years. Because of such visionary pledges do gains appear as losses . . . I will point out that, when my generation messed things up, it was fre-

quently by failing to shun utopian promises and settle for pragmatic gains. It was by failing to look at the world realistically. It was by hoping for the best, but failing to prepare for the worst.

Before graduates, Drexel University/ The National Observer, 7-14:17.

William H. Armstrong
Author

3

There is violence in the world, but there is beauty. There is desolation, but there are dreams . . . there is sordidness and barbarities, but there is still reverence, loyalty and nobility . . . All are a part of the human condition . . . and always there remains the testimony of the night sky and the pages of history—testifying of both stars and men that they shine more brightly when it is darkest.

Before Phi Beta Kappa, Hampden-Sydney (Va.) College/ The Washington Post, 5-6:(B)7.

Charles Aznavour
Singer

4

You can age without growing old. An old man is a man who has given up questioning and accepts everything. To be young, one must remain inquisitive, dissatisfied, and never accept anything just because it's established, or law, or fashion, or because people love it the way it is.

Quote, 9-23:291.

George Balanchine
Director, New York City Ballet

5

I'm not interested in "later on." I don't have any "later on." We all live in the same time forever. There is no future and there is no past. So always I say when people talk to me about the future, "What's the matter with now? Now is when it is good; now is when it is beautiful . . ."

The Washington Post, 10-19:(B)19.

1

Our brains are a cemetery of words. There is no way except with inner vision to explain how you feel . . . As soon as I start speaking, I stop seeing.

Interview/Newsweek, 11-19:96.

William S. Banowsky
President, Pepperdine University

2

Remember, Columbus was looking for a direct route to India and stubbed his toe on what we call America . . . It may not be the thing that you are so cunningly pursuing that is the most important thing in life.

Before Junior League of Los Angeles,
Beverly Hills, Calif./
Los Angeles Times, 5-13:(4)3.

Brigitte Bardot
Actress

3

To be fulfilled, women must stay women. And there are no true women, nor true men. These days, you see a mutation of one sex into the other.

Interview/Newsweek, 3-5:45.

Cecil Beaton
Author, Photographer, Designer

4

. . . I am a bit starry-eyed. I like to watch people who have excelled and study them. Even if I don't know what they're about, it is fascinating to discover what quality of greatness has made them rise above others. Great people are very simple: They don't bother about pretense. There's no waffling about the perimeter. They slice through to the crux of the matter.

Interview, Beverly Hills, Calif./
Los Angeles Times, 4-20:(4)1.

Thomas Hart Benton
Artist

5

The real rewards that come to you in life are loyalties.

Joplin, Mo./
The New York Times, 4-8:(2)25.

Ingmar Bergman
Motion picture director

6

When I was younger, I was always afraid of death following me like a shadow. I was thinking of it every day; and there always existed the question of what would happen to me after death; would it seem an enormous feeling of loneliness after death? Then I had a small operation and was under anesthesia. I was sleeping five hours, but when I waked up, I thought it was a second. And I am feeling that death is exactly that sort of experience. So I have lost the whole terrifying feeling about death and what happens afterward . . .

News conference, Cannes, France/
The Christian Science Monitor, 5-24:14.

William Berkowitz
President, New York Board of Rabbis

7

The message of freedom linked with responsibility must be directed to vocal segments of our young people. The abandonment of all restraints, sexual and moral, and the tragic involvement with drugs has, in too many quarters, become synonymous with the quest for freedom.

Quote, 6-24:578.

Heinrich Boll
Author

8

The perfect scene of law and order is the cemetery. There we have the bankrupt and the bankers, Catholics and Protestants and atheists, homosexuals and heterosexuals, all together. Life is contradictory to law and order. Only the dead are in order and obey all the laws.

Interview, New York/
The New York Times, 5-15:30.

Gordon B. Carson
Executive vice president,
Albion (Mich.) College

1

People who know nothing about the courts feel free to criticize the courts; people who are ill-advised about the police feel free to criticize the police; and it is curious to me that the newspaper editors who denigrate the automobile industry and its executives for not producing a perfect vehicle every time—which vehicle involves some 15,000 parts—are at once the people who can't produce an edition of a newspaper without having errors in it. We suffer from a plethora of diagnosticians and only a modicum of persons who can suggest what the treatment should be, and carry it forward . . . all too frequently, the freedom to express oneself means the freedom to speak up with or without knowledge of the subject. It is now the time that the freedom to speak up should be accompanied by a knowledge of what one is speaking about. There is a well-known sign which one can see displayed in some of the research laboratories of our country; it is appropriate for all who think about the national problems confronting us today. The sign reads: "Caution: Be sure brain is engaged before putting mouth in gear."
At Rio Grande (Ohio) College commencement,
May 13/Vital Speeches, 8-15:663.

Pablo Casals
Cellist, Composer

2

The man who works and is never bored is never old.

Interview, Marlboro, Vt./
Los Angeles Times, 8-19:(Calendar)46.

Marc Chagall
Painter

3

To encounter a woman in your life is a strike of chance accorded by heaven . . . I don't think there was a creator who didn't depend on his wife's opinion; oh, there were some—Mozart was unhappy with his wife—but if the encounter is a success, what does she

give?—all of life!

Interview, Saint-Paul de Vence, France/
"W": a Fairchild publication, 9-7:14.

Charles W. Colson
Former Special Counsel to the
President of the United States

4

There are certain things about life that are basically unfair. I don't believe you can achieve Utopia. I don't believe you can reform human nature. A guaranteed equality probably assures the lowest common denominator for all of us. I would imagine in Upper Volta you probably have a hell of a lot more equality than you have in the United States: You probably have 10 per cent very wealthy and 90 per cent who are in abject poverty.

The Washington Post, 4-15:(C)5.

John B. Connally, Jr.
Former Secretary of the Treasury
of the United States;
Former Governor of Texas

5

Adversity breeds strength of character, and prosperity never will.

At Republican Party fund-raising dinner,
Dallas, Dec. 13/
The Dallas Times Herald, 12-14:(A)9.

Sean Connery
Actor

6

We all have our fantasies, don't we? We're all conditioned by the circumstances in which we were brought up. When I was young, there were no mini-skirts and see-through blouses. But nowadays the dolly-birds walk around in boots, fishnet stockings, short skirts, see-throughs and no bras. Okay, I admit it—they turn me on! But to the youngsters, it's all so commonplace . . . perhaps they're missing something. I tell you, *my* fantasies are pure and undiluted.

Interview, London/
San Francisco Examiner & Chronicle,
1-7:(Datebook)14.

Alistair Cooke
Chief United States correspondent,
"The Manchester (England) Guardian"

1

. . . as for our rage to believe we've found the secret of liberty in general permissiveness from the cradle on, I can only recall the saying of a wise Frenchman: "Liberty is the luxury of self-discipline." Historically, those people who did not discipline themselves had it thrust on them from outside.

On his "America" TV program, May 15/
Los Angeles Times, 5-17:(4)19.

Bill Cosby
Comedian

2

As far as my private life is concerned, show business is my job. My life at home doesn't differ from any other working man's, other than in dollars and cents. Every man becomes somebody else when he goes to work. You go to New York and get in one of those yellow cabs, and sitting up there on the driver's dashboard are color pictures of his kids smiling back at him. He's your cab driver, but he's their Daddy.

Los Angeles/TV Guide, 2-3:31.

Walter Cronkite
News commentator,
Columbia Broadcasting System

3

I get fearful about what the world is coming to. You know, most people are good; there aren't very many really evil people. But there are an awful lot of selfish ones. And this selfishness permeates society. It keeps us from the beauty of where we could go, the road we could travel. Instead of being always on these detours and bumbling along side roads that take us nowhere, we could be on a smooth highway to such a great world if we could just put these self-interests aside for the greatest good of the greatest number. It applies to the industrialist who puts out a product into which he builds obsolescence, and to the guy up in Harlem who throws his garbage out of the third-floor window. It's everybody's fault.

I just find it hard to understand how man could come so far, how he can be so damn smart and at the same time be so damn stupid.

Interview, New York/Playboy, June:86.

Dalai Lama
Exiled former Chief of
State of Tibet

4

No matter how hard you try, in 100 years or so you'll be dead. You must study about life, and in time you'll learn that death is unimportant.

Dharmasala, India/
The Washington Post, 7-15:(C)2.

Edward M. Davis
Chief of Police of Los Angeles

5

. . . there is nothing wrong with youth; most of us were youthful at some point. But we made some beautiful mistakes; and to surround ourselves with young men to create the illusion of youth in ourselves, or so that we can dominate others, is just bad business. Gray hair in itself has no intrinsic value; but what it represents, in terms of past mistakes in the learning experience, has great value. Throwing away the value of people who have been tempered in the fires of experience, to those who have yet to receive that kind of heat treatment, is shortsighted expediency.

Before Los Angeles County (Calif.)
Peace Officers Association/
Los Angeles Times, 6-6:(2)7.

William O. Douglas
Associate Justice,
Supreme Court of the United States

6

Free speech and free press—not spaceships or automobiles—are the important symbols of Western civilization. In material things, the Communist world will in time catch up. But no totalitarian regime can afford free speech and a free press. Ideas are dangerous—the most dangerous in the world because they are haunting and enduring. Those committed to

(WILLIAM O. DOUGLAS)

democracy live dangerously, for they stand committed never to still a voice in protest or a pen in rebellion.

Quote, 6-17:557.

Amitai Etzioni
Professor of Sociology,
Columbia University

1

If I had to predict—and I do so with great reluctance—I think that people [are] ripe for a great resurrection of the American family, and I think that people will start romanticizing marriage. They're getting tired of free-wheeling attitudes, and they're threatened by the removal of taboos. There is great insecurity caused by the fact that anybody can walk out [of a non-marriage relationship] at any moment, and people are searching for new, positive definitions. The forms that the return to the family and its revitalization will take are difficult to predict. They most likely will differ from those of the family of our parents, but they will be much more solid, stable and monogamous than the rotating partnerships of the hippie pads or the non-possessive "open" marriage.

The New York Times, 8-5:(1)54.

Oriana Fallaci
Journalist

2

I used to be intimidated when I was younger. I used to be scared of people . . . The point is that, since I have started to interview people in power, I have found how "everyday" they are. I don't know how to put it. Sometimes they are mediocre. Really, they are not better; they are not superior. I have met very few superior people. Now, if they are not superior, there is no reason to be intimidated. If they are superior, like the very few that I have found, they don't make you feel intimidated. They descend from their pedestal, and they come to you with their hand open and you feel at your ease. When they are more

intelligent, more clever, they are nicer.

Interview, New York/
The Christian Science Monitor, 2-9:12.

Charles O. Finley
Owner, Oakland "Athletics" baseball club

3

If anyone will pay the price for success, he can attain it. But the price is high. You have to do more work than your competitor, and sacrifice some of your competitor's enjoyments. You ask a thousand young people about success, and you'll find that 95 per cent of them have only desire. Desire is in the head. The other five per cent have determination. And determination is right here [in the heart].

Interview, La Porte, Ind./
Parade, 1-28:14.

Viktor Frankl
Professor of Neurology and Psychiatry,
University of Vienna

4

It's taboo today to talk about life as if it had any meaning. Man no longer is told by traditional values what he should do. He no longer knows basically what he wishes to do. As a result, he just wishes to do what others are doing, or he just does what others wish him to do.

Quote, 8-5:121.

Paul Gallico
Author

5

There's a lot of nonsense talked about people only being as old as they feel. It isn't true. The machinery breaks down. And when I'm fencing, I feel I can carry on, but my legs are saying "sit down, you clod, it's time for a rest."

San Francisco Examiner, 2-16:36.

Indira Gandhi
Prime Minister of India

6

Democracy is full of contradictions and confrontations; but these strengthen the people, who are the ultimate strength of our country . . . What other structure can have the flexibility to accommodate our contradictions, our diversity and our high aspirations? The prevailing mood amongst many intellectuals is one of cynicism and lack of faith in ordinary people, the inability to enjoy ordinary, every-day things and happenings. I have found that the way to replenish one's faith is to go to the people and to harness their enormous inner reserves of strength to meet the challenges which confront us.

Before One-Asia Assembly, New Delhi/
The Christian Science Monitor, 2-9:3.

1

My grandfather once told me there were two kinds of people: those who do the work and those who take the credit. He told me to try to be in the first group; there was much less competition there.

Quote, 3-25:266.

2

Happiness is such a matter of opinion, and continuous happiness doesn't exist. Only moments of happiness exist. And if by happiness you mean something like ecstasy . . . yes, I have known ecstasy, which is a great blessing; those who can say they have known it are very few. But ecstasy lasts a very little time and repeats itself very seldom.

Interview/McCall's, June:102.

Helen Gardner
Author; Professor of English Literature,
Oxford University (England)

3

When I was young, you were made to do things you really did not want to do. I hated going to dances; I just *loathed* dancing. I was bad at small-talk. I was hopeless at tennis . . . I thought, the time will come when I shan't mind that I can't play tennis; I shan't mind that I don't enjoy dancing. I shall just do what I want to and enjoy doing it. One loses an awful lot when one loses youth, but this is one of the rewards.

Interview/The New York Times, 6-7:56.

Paul H. Gebhard
Director, Institute for Sex Research,
Indiana University

4

I think we're [the U.S.] going to end up something like Scandinavia. This is a model which, by and large, strikes me as a reasonably healthy one. For a while we'll go through this chaos, this obsessive interest in sex, flooded with pornography. Then I think we'll get a little bit fed up with it and settle down, and things will probably be healthier in the long run. There hasn't been a [sexual] revolution in terms of behavior, because in my mind the term revolution means something rapid, rough. Really, what's happened is there's been a continuation of pre-existing trends, things that we can see beginning at the start of this century. However, in terms of the mass media, the changes have been abrupt enough to call it a revolution. When you stop to think that we still have things locked up in our cabinets that you can now buy at the local drugstore, that's a revolution.

Bloomington, Ind./
San Francisco Examiner, 1-5:27.

J. Paul Getty
Industrialist

5

Age doesn't matter, unless you're a cheese.
Quote, 2-4:97.

William W. Hagerty
President, Drexel University

6

Some nihilistic thinkers within and without the world of education are promulgating anti-intellectualism that could, if successful, presage a new Dark Age. Great numbers of our young are embracing new forms of old mysticisms that have for millennia impoverished entire continents on this globe; others are elevating old demons to altars of worship while at the same time casting down into a technological hell the engineer and scientist who have made possible the highest level of material well-being that the world has ever known. Somewhat allied to this—though certainly no-

(WILLIAM W. HAGERTY)

bler in intent even if unrealistic in practice—is a Rousseau-like "back to nature" movement, embraced as a panacea by young people who have never in their lifetimes seen a child die of diphtheria, or watch a grown man drag a body wasted by polio; youth who have never heard the word goiter, much less seen the disfigurement it embodies; youth who have never—until they returned to nature—feared to drink a glass of water or gone hungry because of a blighted or insufficient crop. They believe—strongly but wrongly—that billions of human beings can live in a simple world of simple comforts, worked with simple tools—but not, of course, without a stereo rig. The hard fact is that, uncontrolled, nature is the enemy. Nature is out to get us from the moment we are conceived. Without directing nature, without mastering and channeling those aspects of nature that are intrinsically inimical to our life form, some of us who survived would soon revert to a marginal existence, to a life of true savagery. There can be no doubt that an emotional malaise faces men in the Western world today—a spiritual crisis that stems in part, perhaps, from decades of fighting wars or trying to prevent wars; but this is a crisis that will not be cured by replacing old gods with new demons, or scrapping the tools of civilization in favor of a return by urban man to a rural ideal that never existed.

The National Observer, 5-5:13.

Walter J. Hickel
*Former Secretary of the Interior
of the United States*

1

[On youth's conviction that industry and government are the enemies of change]: If that attitude continues to be fostered in academic communities, we will write off the two greatest vehicles we have for change. The reality is that [they] are the most exciting arenas for those concerned about people and their needs . . . Wherever I go, I tell the young people if you don't like what's going on,

don't change the system, change the men.

*Before American Association of School
Administrators, San Francisco, March 19/
San Francisco Examiner, 3-20:5.*

2

The most important thing you can teach the young is to keep their conscience in their work. Unless they learn to keep learning, they have not been educated. Whether it is in the environment, social problems or world issues, we must not let the concern of the young become narrow. The only security in an everchanging world is constantly to search for that which is real.

*Before American Association of School
Administrators, San Francisco, March 19/
San Francisco Examiner, 3-20:5.*

Sidney Hook
*Professor of Philosophy,
New York University*

3

Equality in this country has meant a moral concern that all members of the society should be allowed to develop themselves to their full capacities as human beings. One can make a comparison with the family. Intelligent and benevolent parents don't treat all children in mechanically equal ways, but they have an equal concern for all. That is the moral ideal of equality, and it cannot be extended to mean mechanical "equality of result." It is true that Americans throughout history have broadened their moral concern. Just as one takes compensatory attitudes and actions toward a physically handicapped person, so can society look for ways in which to provide the person who is handicapped in other ways with an opportunity to display his or her talents. "Affirmative action" or "quotas," however, do not follow from equality of concern for the individual, because they deal with a whole class of persons. This means that emphasis on "equality of result" is a clear break with the American liberal tradition and with the Western ideal since ancient Greece— namely, individual merit and excellence. A downgrading of that emphasis is part of the glorification of the cult of mediocrity that seems to be growing in our society. When you set "equality of result" as the primary goal, then you must set standards in which the least-able becomes the denominator.

U.S. News & World Report, 4-9:41.

John A. Howard
President, Rockford (Ill.) College

1

There has been a generation collapse. The adults have not met their obligations. They have not transmitted to the young the standards of conduct which past generations had learned were necessary for a livable world. It is not the fault of the young if they are confused. It is the fault of those who should have transmitted understanding to them and didn't.

Before Rotary Club of Rockford/
Quote, 3-18:257.

Sol Hurok
Impresario

2

[Saying that, at 85, he has no thought of retirement]: You must love the things you do. Then you will eat well, digest your food well and sleep well. You don't age; you always remain young and the spirit is with you. Today is not so bad; tomorrow will be better. Don't think of the past; don't think of the future. Age is for the calendar. I hope the President [Nixon] pushes ahead with the space-shuttle program. I hope to live to see the day when we have music on the moon.

Interview,
New York/
The Christian Science Monitor,
5-17:(B)8.

Lee A. Iacocca
President, Ford Motor Company

3

My father always said, "Whatever you do—if you wait on tables—be the happiest, most efficient waiter that ever came down the pike. Whatever you do, do the damned thing well."

Interview,
Detroit/Parade, 5-20:9.

Masaru Ibuka
Chairman, Sony Corporation (Japan)

4

We Japanese enjoy the small pleasures, not extravagance. I believe a man should have a simple life-style—even if he can afford more.

Quote, 6-24:578.

Lady Bird (Mrs. Lyndon B.) Johnson
Widow of the late President
of the United States

5

. . . I put my thoughts into two categories: the "Aren't-you-glad-thats" and the "If-onlys." I try to keep the second column as short as possible. We should think about the first column ahead of time and savor things more when we have them. To be close to death gives you a new awareness of the preciousness of life, and the extreme tenuousness of it. You must live every day to the fullest, as though you had a short supply—because you do.

Interview, L.B.J. Ranch, Texas/
Time, 5-21:41.

Nicholas Johnson
Commissioner, Federal Communications
Commission of the United States

6

. . . the more you get into it, the more you discover that the whole process of communications is close to the core of what humanity is about. What distinguishes us [man] is our capacity to create and use symbols. With those symbols, we create alphabets, mathematics, architecture, civilization. Therefore, a proper functioning communications system is fundamental to everything that society is going to do.

Interview/
San Francisco Examiner & Chronicle,
5-13:(Sunday Scene)14.

Rafer Johnson
Former Olympic decathlon champion

7

I appreciate people who do things as well as they can—the guy who puts gas in my car,

(RAFER JOHNSON)

the plumber, the electrician. In a way, they're saying what I'm saying, that they owe themselves one thing—that they couldn't have done their job any better. If I can say that at the end of my life, I'll be happy.

Interview, Los Angeles/
Los Angeles Times, 3-20:(3)6.

Jenkin Lloyd Jones
Editor and publisher, "The Tulsa Tribune"

1

If someone could invent a narcotic guaranteed to make users deliriously happy with no bad side effects, humankind would probably last about three weeks, the time it takes to starve to death.

Quote, 7-22:74.

Eugene C. Kennedy
Professor of Psychology,
Loyola University, Chicago

2

The family is a rugged example of something that has reached its present state through evolution, which means it's tough in the sense of enduring. It is not a perfect vehicle, but there's nothing perfect about the human situation. It [the family] does fit man. It provides the context that can deal with our conflicts, with the fact that we hurt one another. It has survived because it can catch the winds and stand up under them.

The New York Times, 8-5:(1)54.

Henry A. Kissinger
Secretary of State of the United States

3

The great tragedies of history occur not when right confronts wrong, but when two rights confront each other.

San Francisco Examiner & Chronicle,
12-30:(This World)2.

Melvin Kranzberg
Professor of History,
Case Western Reserve University

4

The arts, science, social [concerns] and technology are not separate compartments of human knowledge and action. Instead, they all play a part in the great questions which have faced man in the past, face us in the present and will face our students tomorrow. To put it in another way, most of the urgent problems confronting man today and tomorrow involve technology, human values, social organization, environmental concerns, economic resources, political decisions and the like. These are "interface problems," that is, the interface between engineering and society; and they can only be solved—if they can be solved at all—by the application of scientific knowledge, technical expertise, social understanding and human compassion.

Quote, 2-4:112.

Irving Kristol
Professor of Urban Values,
New York University

5

[On the desire to achieve equality among people]: I think we lost our common sense in getting certain notions concerning to what degree equality could, in fact, be achieved—short of the use of terror; that is, to what extent human beings were naturally equal. That was because we had simply overlooked the idea of excellence; namely, to what degree human beings are not naturally equal. I must say I cannot think much [of] a democratic society which does not respect excellence . . . What's happened suddenly is a passionate confusion between democracy and equality. Now, democracy does involve equality; but it involves many other things besides equality. It involves liberty. It involves the rule of law. It involves excellence—namely, inequality of result.

The Washington Post, 4-8:(A)20.

Giovanni Leone
President of Italy

6

I adore women. To me, women are the most beautiful things around the world. I always say: The strongest evidence that God exists is a beautiful woman . . . Not only do I love women, I esteem them . . . And certainly I'd like to see a woman as President of the republic. I'm a feminist in my own way.

San Francisco Examiner & Chronicle,
4-29:(This World)2.

Wassily Leontief
Professor of Economics, Harvard University

1

A commodity or a resource is something that only one person, or a few people, can use. Then it's used up, gone. But ideas! Any number of people can use them, and they're never used up. That's the beautiful thing about them.

The National Observer, 12-15:7.

Clare Boothe Luce
Former American diplomat and playwright

2

Sex is a very private act. The minute it is made commonplace, it loses a great deal of its mystery and power. I saw in the paper this morning, which amused me no end, that Mae West walked out of [the film] *Last Tango in Paris.* What she walked out on was, of course, the destruction of the *mystique* of sex. I think the destruction of that mystique is a great, great loss.

Interview, New York/
The New York Times Magazine, 4-22:53.

Marcel Marceau
Mime

3

I do not get my ideas from people in the street. If you look at faces on the street, what do you see? Nothing. Just boredom. In the restaurants, the waiters look bored. In the courts, the judges look bored. It is the same in Europe as here. Life is so impersonal. It is the technology of life.

San Francisco Examiner & Chronicle,
5-13:(This World)2.

Lee Marvin
Actor

4

One of the good things about getting older is that you find out you're more interesting

than most of the people you meet. Sounds egotistical, but there it is.

Interview, Los Angeles/
San Francisco Examiner, 1-30:19.

Golda Meir
Prime Minister of Israel

5

. . . old age is like a plane flying through a storm: Once you're aboard, there's nothing you can do. You can't stop the plane; you can't stop the storm; you can't stop time. So one might as well accept it calmly, wisely.

Interview/Newsweek, 3-26:46.

Henry Miller
Author

6

I'm not very much interested in pornography as it is today. There's nothing without sex any more, which I think is phony. I prefer obscenity to pornography. Pornography is sly, but obscenity is forthright.

At American Booksellers' Association
convention, Los Angeles/
The New York Times, 6-13:37.

Walter F. Mondale
United States Senator, D-Minnesota

7

In the whole range of human problems I've dealt with in my nine years in the Senate—hunger, housing, labor, Indian education, migrant workers, children, aging—I kept getting back to one thing: the strength of the family. It's such a simple point, it should have been obvious.

Washington/
Los Angeles Times, 10-8:(4)10.

Akio Morita
President, Sony Corporation (Japan)

8

Men who insist only on their rights and forget their responsibilities must be reminded of their basic duties to society . . . it is clear that a nation whose people are disciplined will steadily grow, and a nation that lacks in discipline will decline.

The Washington Post, 11-19:(F)2.

Steven Muller
President, Johns Hopkins University

1

I believe in achievement, but I believe the crucial factor is the effort rather than the result. Who can do more than one's best? Who can ask more than to give the most one has? A successful person is one who is productive to the peak of his capacity and who is comfortable with his own self. This sounds so simple, but it is not commonly accepted. Success is equated with wealth, power, prestige and notoriety. These are dubious assets—some crave and possess them, but find no happiness or fulfillment in this application. Clearly, they are not equally available to all. But a successful life is possible for each of us. My argument is that as a people we try to shut out the realities of failure and of death—the ultimate failure—and that this is unhealthy. Each of us will die and each of us will fail at things. Can't we admit that and live with it?
Before graduating class, University of Maryland/
The Washington Post, 2-17:(A)14.

Rudolf Nureyev
Ballet dancer

2

I don't have definite opinions about everything. I never say, "This is good" or "This is bad"—tomorrow I may change my mind. Now you think this is black—10 days later it is rather gray, or white altogether. One doesn't set one's opinions. It's a matter of experiencing everything as much as possible.
Interview, Gary, Ind./
"W": a Fairchild publication, 5-4:7.

Bruce Ogilvie
Professor of Psychology,
California State University, San Jose

3

Success is a positive manipulation of failure. I know of no better definition of success.
. Interview/Los Angeles Times, 3-11:(3)9.

Paul VI
Pope

4

. . . modern man has been refined by all the progress of civilization, but he is still shortsighted in knowing how to use it wisely. Let us therefore say to ourselves: Enough of the outrages committed against the life and dignity of man. Enough of the impassive inhumanity which makes an attempt at the innocent and helpless life developing in the mother's womb [abortion]. Enough of crime, which today is becoming professional and organized. Enough of the strategy based on the race for the deadly power of scientific weapons. Enough of the degrading licentiousness of corrupt pleasure, which has been made into the ideal freedom, and of blind and selfish satisfaction. This denunciation could be extended as far as human degradations reach —which is a long way indeed.
Good Friday address, Vatican City,
April 20/Los Angeles Times, 4-21:(1)4.

5

Unfortunately, a broad and sad pornography market is spreading today with extreme ease and seems to find no embankment. It is a cause of modern immorality and growing permissiveness and a basis for cowardly earnings.
Castel Gandolfo, Italy, Aug. 26/
Los Angeles Herald-Examiner, 8-27:(A)9.

6

As he exists, man is not perfect. He is a being essentially in need of restoration, of rehabilitation, of fullness, of perfection and of happiness. His is a life which does not suffice to itself; he needs a complement of life, an infinite complement. Exalt man: You will make more evident his deficiency, his incompleteness, his inner need to be saved. We say it once and we say it in a word: his need for a savior.
Christmas message, Vatican City, Dec. 25/
Los Angeles Herald-Examiner, 12-26:(A)4.

Mary Quant
Fashion designer

7

A genius is someone who can come up with the obvious and it's revolutionary because no one else has thought of it. It's an ability to think simply. Then there is the perseverance to get the idea accepted—which is the hardest part of all.

San Francisco Examiner, 2-21:36.

William H. Rehnquist
Associate Justice,
Supreme Court of the United States

1

It is important to be friendly, or civil, to those with whom you disagree. Free discussion of ideas in a civil atmosphere is a necessary ingredient of free speech. Civility is important not just as a form of manner, but as an underlying attitude.

At Indiana University convocation,
Bloomington/
The Christian Science Monitor, 5-11:10.

Andrei D. Sakharov
Physicist

2

You always need to make ideals clear to yourself. You always have to be aware of them, even if there is no direct path to their realization. Were there no ideals, there would be no hope whatsoever. Then everything would be hopelessness, darkness—a blind alley.

The New York Times Magazine, 11-4:71.

Irving Shulman
Author

3

I believe man has the capacity to be as good as he wishes. Personal immortality means that someone will speak up after you die and remember you as a nice guy, someone who cared . . . These are the kind[s] of monuments people should build for themselves; but it's easier to build a cathedral than live that way.

Interview/
San Francisco Examiner & Chronicle,
4-22:(This World)35.

Boris T. Shumilin
Deputy Minister of the Interior
of the Soviet Union

4

Social inequality, the private-ownership psychology, individualism, the moral isolation of persons from society, lack of goals in life, the spirit of competition—all these things are inevitable concomitants of the capitalist system, which cultivate the lowest instincts in youth and motivate them to commit crimes; plus the cult of sex, brutality and violence on the movie and TV screens.

Interview/
The Christian Science Monitor, 4-10:4.

Simone Signoret
Actress

5

I am 52 and I look it . . . I am middle-aged and not ashamed of it. It is not something you catch, like a disease. It is not the flu. If a woman has been filled with life, with joy and love and tears, then waking up suddenly at middle-age can be a wonderful experience.

Los Angeles Herald-Examiner,
3-29:(B)6.

Athelstan Spilhaus
Former chairman, American
Association for the Advancement of Science

6

Everybody is doubting his fellow man these days. It's the adversary system, groups of people doubting other groups of people whom they always call "they." If you are an environmentalist, then the terrible "they" is big business. To the Republicans, the "they" is the Democrats, and vice versa. There is this fundamental disbelief in your fellow man or in society's ability to solve its problems. It's tantamount to doubting the original Creator.

The National Observer, 6-2:17.

Benjamin Spock
Physician

7

Obviously, the family is changing, and a lot of that change is to the good. More people who don't want a legal commitment are openly living together, and that's fine as long as there are no children. It doesn't hurt anyone. And some are marrying but don't want children, and that's fine, too. Only those people who can't resist children should have them;

(BENJAMIN SPOCK)

there's no practical reason ever to have children. But no matter how cynical we are about the family, there are a tremendous number of people who won't resist what Freud called "the repetition compulsion." Almost every child has been brought up in a family. The strongest impulse in a human being is to repeat the pattern set by parents.

The New York Times, 8-5:(1)54.

Rod Steiger
Actor

1

Now I know there is no such thing as success. If you find it young, you fight the rest of your life to sustain it. You have always the fear of age and being replaced by younger talent, which is inevitable. The important thing is, make an honest effort so they will say, "At least he tried."

Interview, New York/
San Francisco Examiner, 2-24:31.

Krister Stendahl
Dean, Harvard Divinity School

2

When he is afraid, man is a very vicious being. That is why increased knowledge is not only interesting, but is the road to learning what to fear and what not to fear.

At symposium on life beyond earth, Boston/
San Francisco Examiner, 1-27:11.

Maurice F. Strong
Executive Director,
United Nations Environment Program

3

In the final analysis, nations will be compelled to recognize that there can be no basic or enduring conflict between their national interests and the interests of the whole human community. The same compelling pressures of broader self-interest which induced man to form larger and larger social and political units in his rise from the family through the tribe, through the village, the town, the city, the city-state and the nation-state, must inevitably impel him toward taking his place within the structure of a planetary society.

Fairfield Osborn Memorial Lecture,
Rockefeller University, New York,
Oct. 18/The New York Times, 10-21:(1)19.

Jacqueline Susann
Author

4

Fame is just learning that the world is a first-class airplane and, as the [Richard] Burtons put it, getting used to the idea that you'll get the best table at Sardi's.

Interview, Los Angeles/
Los Angeles Times, 5-9:(4)9.

David Susskind
Motion picture-stage-television producer

5

In my view, the traditional disciplines have given way, not to a vacuum of morality, but to a new, highly-personalized morality. Young people today know what is right and wrong, they know viscerally the difference between truth and lies, and they recognize the ugly hypocrisy of preaching good and practicing evil.

At Roger Williams College commencement,
Bristol, R.I., June 11/Quote, 8-5:133.

Elizabeth Taylor
Actress

6

People who worry about their looks and their figures, and all that, lose what really makes a person. If you spend all your time worrying about how you look, then you are living totally within yourself. All I can see when I look in the mirror is a dirty face, an un-made-up face, or a made-up face! It's better to forget about keeping beautiful through diets and health farms. Enjoy life—it's much more important. No matter what people look like physically, some can have an inner glow and vitality much more beautiful than a 36-22-36 figure.

Interview/
Ladies Home Journal, February:143.

Gus Turbeville
President, Coker College, Hartsville, S.C.

1

Life is a series of paradoxes. Without evil, there would be no good; without darkness, there would be no light; without ugliness, there would be no beauty; without the valleys, there would be no mountains. Personalizing this, without others you would have no self-conception; you would not know if you were moral, or attractive, or intelligent, or superior unless there were others by whom you could measure your own attributes. Without a sense of self, you could not be evil, sinful, mean, selfish or attracted by all the temptations flesh is heir to. And without a self, you could not be good, generous, kind, considerate and godly. Although it is terrifying to think that Hitler formed a self identity through his reactions with others, it is encouraging to note that so did Schweitzer.

At Coker College, Sept. 12/
Vital Speeches, 10-1:763.

Barbara Ward
Economist

2

You commit yourself to where your attachments are, and if they are simply the consumption of material wants, you are terribly trapped psychologically, because you lack a certain freedom: You are caught by what the African calls "the wants" . . . And the more captured you are by "wants," the more captured you are by "what I must have, what I owe myself," and finally you are shredded, shredded, because you are never your own master. You are the prey of the shadows.

New York/
The Christian Science Monitor, 11-30:19.

John Wayne
Actor

3

Since communication is so much better, kids today are thrown in contact with temptations to new experiences that my generation wasn't. But what the hell, it hasn't seemed to affect the younger generation as much as the bluenoses would expect. The only generation gap I can see for some of these kids is soap and water. Goddamn, if they'd just wash a little more . . .

Interview,
Newport Beach, Calif./
Good Housekeeping, February:132.

Thornton Wilder
Author

4

Writing at this age [76] is not hard, not if you have the right idea—an idea deeply relative to yourself. Verdi wrote *Otello* at 78 and *Falstaff* at 79. Picasso was a beaver until his death in his 90s . . . Sophocles, at 90, was haled into court by his grandchildren, saying the old man was *non compos* and might will his estate to somebody else. When he went before the court, the judge said, "What do you have to say for yourself?" "I'll tell you something," Sophocles replied. "I wrote this morning the great chorus from *Oedipus at Colonus*." This work is a treasure. "Either I am crazy or you are," the judge said. "Case dismissed." This is an attractive story for us old men.

Interview,
New York/
Los Angeles Times,
10-15:(2)7.

Religion

Ernest T. Campbell
Pastor, Riverside Church, New York

1

The greatest failure of the church and synagogue may be that we are too "unexpectant." We have become so enamored with secular interpretations of things that we do not expect and anticipate the power that can come through God.

Quote, 5-27:482.

W. Sterling Cary
President, National Council of Churches (United States)

2

[On church involvement in politics]: I do not think you can be a Christian without being political. If you are Christian, you have got to be concerned about the real world: jobs, housing, justice. If you are concerned about that world, you have got to be involved in politics . . . If you want reconciliation and peace, you must enter the struggle to solve the issues which prevent them. We have a racist history as a society, for example. You have got to enter politics to resolve this.

News conference/
Los Angeles Times, 10-27:(1)29.

Harvey Cox
Professor of Divinity, Harvard University

3

Many of today's churches are not fulfilling their original purpose for existing. Religions, most of them, were traditionally formed as a means of allowing men to communicate, to tell their personal stories, to express their personal inferiority and to relate it to others. Christianity, Hinduism, Buddhism—all originated as clusters of stories passed on by men. And they traditionally celebrated them with songs, rituals, symbols, dances—all forms of

self-expression and personal experience . . . So many of our churches have become so mired in doctrine that there is little personal experience left . . . Kids I meet everywhere are looking for ways to feel themselves again, to enjoy the world around them. They want to meditate, to quiet their own minds, to tell their own stories. They don't want a barrage of directions and warnings and orders and behavior signals from their elders.

Los Angeles/
Los Angeles Times, 10-9:(4)8.

4

There's a real theological awakening. The undergraduates I teach can hardly be compared with the sophomore atheists I knew when I went to college in the early '50s. In those days, an interest in religion was considered intellectually reprehensible. Now when you announce a new course in religion, it's immediately over-subscribed.

"W": a Fairchild publication, 10-19:7.

Indira Gandhi
Prime Minister of India

5

. . . I don't go to temples and things like that. But I think religion is more than that. In my opinion, religion is believing in humanity and trying to make it better. So if we speak about that religion, the religion of man, then I am very religious.

Interview/McCall's, June:100.

Robert I. Gannon
Former president, Fordham University

6

The church is in crisis, but it has been there before. Happily, I believe it is returning to normalcy—that middle-ground between the "old mossback" extremists on the one hand and the "wild liberals" on the other. Right now, we are in a trough of moral decline, with the crest barely discernible. Society is in with us. The family is more pagan than it was 25 years ago, and sex and violence are everywhere.

Interview,
Manhasset, N.Y./
The New York Times, 4-8:(1)52.

Billy Graham
Evangelist

1

[Saying he knows of no town in America where the majority of people were real believing-Christians]: And I made a distinction between believing-Christians and church-goers who go to church for social, business or family-tradition reasons . . . The big issue [is] how far we can go on taking laws that were given to [biblical] Israel and apply them blanketly to a modern secular society. In the Bible, people were stoned to death for kidnaping, murder, fornication, adultery and a number of other crimes. I am sure no person today would say this is what we ought to do.

News conference, Atlanta/
Los Angeles Times, 4-26:(1)7.

Mark O. Hatfield
United States Senator,
R-Oregon

2

[On the National House-Senate Prayer Breakfast]: Events such as this prayer breakfast contain the real danger of misplaced allegiance, if not outright idolatry, to the extent that they fail to distinguish between the god of an American civil religion and the God who reveals himself in the Holy Scripture and in Jesus Christ. If we as leaders appeal to the god of an American civil religion, our faith is in a small and exclusive deity, a loyal spiritual adviser to American power and prestige, a defender of the American nation, the object of a national folk religion devoid of moral content.

At National Prayer Breakfast,
Washington, Feb. 1/
Los Angeles Herald-Examiner,
2-1:(A)2.

Will Herberg
Professor of Philosophy and Culture,
Drew University, Madison, N.J.

3

Who joins churches? People. So you have [at churches] men's clubs, women's clubs, youth clubs, basketball courts—a church, in America, necessarily has to be a kind of settlement house. Otherwise, you know what will happen? The young people will go to more-sinister places for their recreation. This sort of thing happens in every institution—churches, labor unions or whatever. Every institution goes through the process described by Charles Peguy, a Catholic publicist at the turn of this century, in these words: "It all begins with *mystique*; it ends with *politique*." That's the logic of institutions; but without institutions, you can't live.

Interview/
U.S. News & World Report, 6-4:55.

4

It's completely untrue that there is a widespread desire to get away from the institutional church. Certainly, the "Jesus people" say they don't like the institutional church. In its very nature, pietism or revivalism is anti-institutional—not in principle, however, but simply because so many of the established churches are felt to be in a rut. What do you suppose "revivalism" wants? Revival. Whom is it going to revive? The spiritually dead. Who are the spiritually dead? Members of churches that are in a rut. The pietists aren't out to destroy the institutional church, but to revive it. By their own logic, furthermore, they sometimes grow into established churches themselves.

Interview/
U.S. News & World Report, 6-4:56.

5

About 30 years ago, I was editor of a quarterly called *Judaism.* And in those days they worried a great deal about the survival of Judaism. They're worried about it now—everybody is always worrying. Anyway, I wrote then that the survival of Jewry was a matter of Divine Providence, not of a "strategy for survival." And that's true. If God has no purpose for Judaism and Christianity, why should

(WILL HERBERG)

they survive? If God has a purpose for them, all the forces of the world won't be able to destroy them.

Interview/
U.S. News & World Report, 6-4:60.

Theodore M. Hesburgh
President,
University of Notre Dame

1

I think the church is always going to have tension within it between those who would like to stay in the sacristy and those who would like to see it fighting all the battles in the slums and in the difficult areas of human endeaver. But I think it's got to be in both places. It's the old prayer and work and work and prayer, and faith and action and action and faith. We've got to somehow make it real by the total lives we live.

On "Washington Insight" TV program/
Quote, 9-16:277.

David Allan Hubbard
President, Fuller Theological Seminary,
Pasadena, Calif.

2

The growth of all kinds of prayer and meditation is a recognition of a need. They show a return to more spirituality at a time when our culture seems more secular. Americans growing up in the Depression thought greater affluence, raising the educational level and solving our social problems were good goals. Some of these goals have been achieved; but many Americans are without real happiness. Now we're seeing an expression of a human need that goes beyond what education, economics, technology and creature comforts can provide.

U.S. News & World Report, 8-27:36.

Franz Cardinal Koenig
Roman Catholic Archbishop of Vienna

3

Every action and activity in public in the world can be politics. In this sense, and only in this sense, does the church act politically.

An apolitical church would be as much of an absurdity as an apolitical labor union.

Before Federation of Austrian
Trade Unions/
The Washington Post, 3-16:(D)14.

James I. McCord
President, Princeton (N.J.)
Theological Seminary

4

This is an age in which man is exploring his inner self and the whole spiritual dimension of experience. As I see it, today is as much an age of faith as any we've ever known. Read history, and as every stage closes, the church is seen as ready to be swept away; but every time, in every new age, there she is again —fresher, leaner, purer, ready to go again.

Quote, 5-20:458.

John R. McGann
Roman Catholic Bishop of
Rockville Center, N.Y.

5

. . . many young people are bypassing the institutional church and giving allegiance to God in new movements which use the name of Jesus as their standard. While theologians are making progress in resolving historical and theological differences among Christian denominations, we are just beginning to realize and face up to the new gap that exists within Christian churches—that is, the distance between the church and its youth, those in the Jesus movements and those who have backed off from all religious affiliations.

At religious conference, Syracuse, N.Y./
The New York Times, 5-6:(1)62.

Golda Meir
Prime Minister of Israel

6

[On her recent meeting with Pope Paul VI, the first meeting between a Pope and an Israeli Prime Minister]: There were moments of tension. I felt that I was saying what I was saying to the man of the cross, who heads the church whose symbol is the cross, under which Jews were killed for generations. I could not escape this feeling. It stuck with me. And he felt it—that a Jewess was sitting opposite him—and he said: "This is an historic moment."

Interview/
Los Angeles Times, 1-20:(1)2.

James A. Michener
Author

1

I have always been very strongly in favor of the institutional church. I think the institutional church serves a marvelous role in helping people over the great transition periods of life. People ought to be married in a church, and they ought to be buried in a church. They ought to bring up their children at least with a knowledge of the church. I see great changes in the manifestations of religious faith, but none in the need.

Interview/
U.S. News & World Report, 12-10:54.

Robert V. Moss, Jr.
President, United Church of Christ

2

There is a great danger that, without a sound theological base, denominational social-action agencies . . . could become little more than baptized chapters of Americans for Democratic Action. For far too long, we have separated the theological resources of the church from the church as it lives from day to day. It is clear that future leadership is going to have to be theologically oriented and provide leadership that is reflective of the gospel and the tradition of the church. We simply cannot justify our involvement in the issues which the world is facing by quoting a few verses from the Bible. Leadership that puts aside the theological task is not leadership today.

Los Angeles, March 18/
Los Angeles Times, 3-25:(8)4.

Paul VI
Pope

3

[Saying there are places in the world where religion is controlled or banned by govern-

ment]: Remember in your prayers your brothers in the faith who cannot celebrate in the Easter festivities in the fullness of communion and joy. There still is a church obliged to live, rather survive, in the shadow of fear and in the asphyxiating and paralyzing darkness of an artificial and oppressing legality.

Vatican City, April 1/
Los Angeles Times, 4-2:(1)4.

John T. Pawlikowski
Professor, Catholic Theological Union,
Chicago

4

Mankind will not reach adulthood until we truly believe that the disappearance of any major religious tradition in the world would do irreparable harm to the understanding of mankind.

Quote, 6-24:577.

Michele Cardinal Pellegrino
Roman Catholic Archbishop of
Turin, Italy

5

[On the Roman Catholic Church by the year 2000]: Those who adhere to it formally probably will be less. Many who are Catholics by tradition or by birth and who are not sustained by a deep personal conviction of faith may easily break away from the Church. But those who remain will feel themselves part of a living Church, engaged in a more clear-cut mission, which will be more genuinely in keeping with the spirit of the gospels.

Turin/Los Angeles Times, 4-19:(7)8.

Joachim Prinz
Rabbi, Chairman of the governing
council, World Jewish Council

6

[Saying spiritual Judaism in the U.S. is headed for extinction]: If we continue an uncharted course toward the end of the 20th century, we might find ourselves not merely decimated in numbers, but utterly bereft of a spiritual existence which makes possible the unique contribution of Judaism to civilization. There are many discernible and definable phenomena which point to a possible disappear-

(JOACHIM PRINZ)

ance of American Jewry within the next two generations . . . Neither the horrors of the Hitler regime nor the creation of the State of Israel are relevant any longer to our young generation. The young people have American and human concerns. Thus, there is little to prevent them from intermarrying. The phenomenon of intermarriage alone, which according to some estimates amounts to almost 50 per cent of marriages contracted by Jewish partners, continues to be the main factor in any projection of the Jewish future. However important Israel is in our life, it cannot be said that a Jew, interested in Israel, traveling to Israel, is making a contribution to the continued existence of the Jew in his own country.

Before National Council of
Jewish Women, Miami Beach, March 29/
The New York Times, 3-31:33.

James S. Rausch
General secretary,
United States Catholic Conference

1

The function of informing, motivating and mobilizing a community of people, directing it toward a significant human problem and evoking from it a self-sacrificial response is preeminently the task of the church . . . in a very real sense, it is no less important for the church to be doing the work of social justice every day than it is for us to provide for the celebration of the Eucharist or to preach the Gospel.

Washington/
The Dallas Times Herald, 8-8:(E)4.

Edward C. Schillebeeckx
Belgian theologian

2

Pope Paul [VI] is very open to problems of peace and justice, and Rome is more progressive here than in church affairs. The Pope is confronted with the total collapse of inner church affairs. He cannot face this problem in

the way he faces the problem of the world. This is the tragedy of this Pope.

Los Angeles Times, 4-19:(7)8.

Alexander M. Schindler
Rabbi; President, Union of
American Hebrew Congregations

3

I think we're entering an age more amenable to the religious spirit. Increasingly, people are coming to the conviction that religion is essential, that the future of mankind cannot be entrusted to scientific rationalism.

Interview, New York/
San Francisco Examiner, 11-17:9.

Fulton J. Sheen
Former Roman Catholic Bishop
of Rochester, N.Y.

4

I do not mean that Christianity is over. I mean that society is not going to be influenced by it as it was before. We may be apt to despair at this, but history shows that Christianity undergoes a great crisis every 500 years or so, dying to be reborn.

Before Roman Catholic lawyers, Toronto/
Los Angeles Times, 5-17:(1)2.

George C. Wallace
Governor of Alabama

5

I believe in the separation of church and state; I do not believe in the separation of God and state.

Quote, 10-7:337.

Thornton Wilder
Author

6

The bottom dropped out of our religious convictions, and that was like an earthquake in modern society. Are there substitutes for traditional religion, you say? There are substitutes all over. Even the hippie movement, if that is the right word, is quasi-religious in character. Now Hindu and Eastern religion is pouring all through us. You are very isolated from what is happening if you do not know that. It's getting into jazz. Sexual liberation is part of what is going on. Eastern religious strains are now heavy in the American subculture. Yale has a meditation hall. Students can go for quasi-Buddhist reflection. You'll find similar things at Berkeley. What you are crazy about in your teens is going to affect you in life.

Interview, New York/
Los Angeles Times, 10-15:(2)7.

Tennessee Williams
Playwright

1

I've always been very religious. I was relig-
ious as an Episcopalian and I'm still religious as a Catholic, although I do not subscribe to a great many of the things you are supposed to subscribe to, like the belief in individual immortality. Nor in the infallibility of Popes. I think Popes are among the most fallible people on earth; so this is heresy, isn't it? And yet I *love* the poetry of the church. I love to go into either a high Anglican service or a Roman Catholic service. And I love to receive communion; but I'm usually working Sunday morning—so I take communion at funerals.

Interview/
Playboy,
April:84.

Space · Science · Technology

Robert Anderson
President, Rockwell International

1

. . . we know the universe will be filled, if not by our generation, then by the next. The earth already has been ringed by hundreds of satellites. Within a relatively short time, it may be ringed by thousands. The clamor of individual nations, and perhaps individual companies, for instant, economical world-wide communications, for day-to-day data on their natural resources, for hourly up-dates on weather predictions, will be enormous. There will be men and women scientists, engineers, industrialists, weather forecasters, forest rangers, not just circling above our earth, but living above it. We know that, within our lifetime, men will be speeding outside our solar system bringing the entire world into a new era of knowledge. We know all these things. We know because three-and-a-half years ago, when we landed men on the moon, the new knowledge gained showed old theories to be in error. Today, new parameters of understanding are unfolding concerning the relationship of the moon and the earth. And so I believe that during the next 15 years new knowledge, generated by the space program, will alter much of our present "earth bound" ideas. That's why an open-minded, unhampered imagination is a necessity as we look upward. And the one vehicle that can best spur our imagination is the space shuttle. The shuttle . . . is the Wright Brothers Kitty Hawk airplane of the space age. We know the Wright Brothers didn't have an easy time of convincing the nation of the usefulness of their airplane. And we face the same problem today with the shuttle. NASA is convinced. You're convinced. And I'm convinced. But in all honesty, not everyone is convinced that in the shuttle we have a forecast of man's future ability to use space to a degree far greater

than ever before thought possible. That lack of enthusiasm shouldn't discourage us.

At Goddard Memorial Symposium,
Washington, March 8/
Vital Speeches, 4-15:415.

Eugene A. Cernan
American astronaut

2

I'm one of those guys who has never seen a UFO. But I've been asked, and I've said publicly I thought they were somebody else, some other civilization . . . statistically, when you get out there and you look at the infinity of time and the infinity of space, which is something none of us can really understand, but exists—and I know it because I saw it—and you look how small our earth is . . . Statistically there has to be an infinite number of other earths and infinite numbers of other civilizations . . . I think it's exciting, scientifically and philosophically and any other way, for people young and old to think that in the future we may be able to go out there, or there may be other civilizations we can come in contact with.

News conference, Houston, Jan. 5/
Los Angeles Times, 1-6:(1)6.

Arthur C. Clarke
Scientist, Author

3

[Criticizing the critics of technology]: Our technology, in the widest sense of the word, is what has made us human. Those who attempt to deny this are denying their humanity. This currently-popular "treason of the intellectuals" is a disease of the affluent countries; the rest of the world cannot afford it.

Lecture at Smithsonian Institution,
Washington, March 14/
The Washington Post, 3-15:(B)8.

1

What we really seek in space is not knowledge, but wonder, beauty, romance, novelty —and above all, adventure. Let no one devalue these by fatuous charges of "escapism." They are essential to man because of his very nature.

Lecture at Smithsonian Institution, Washington, March 14/ The Washington Post, 3-15:(B)8.

Kurt Debus
Director, John F. Kennedy Space Center, National Aeronautics and Space Administration of the United States

2

The emphasis [in the space program] now will be more and more on the useful application of scientific findings. We are at the point of opening up space accessibility. We will use this accessibility to develop the tools that we will need to solve our future problems. I believe that mankind simply cannot otherwise solve its problems of the next 20 or 30 years connected with increasing population and the conservation of energy. We are identifying existing sources of energy from space now. Soon, other sources of energy will have to be developed. And here again, space tools will help solve that problem.

Interview, Kennedy Space Center, Fla./Nation's Business, April:46.

Otto J. Glasser
Lieutenant General and Deputy Chief of Staff for Research and Development, United States Air Force

3

We [the U.S.] are pricing ourselves out of the aerospace business, not only in the foreign-trade field, but domestically as well . . . We are running the risk of becoming a second-rate technological power. The only way to solve the gold-flow problem is to get some U.S. products flowing overseas. But if there isn't a thriving high-technology world here, we won't be selling abroad . . . We are somewhat complacent. When foreign aircraft began to compete with us, we used to be able to say: "Oh, well, we are selling them all those parts —gyros, pumps, radar." But if you had been at the recent Paris air show, you would see we are no longer even in the parts business. So unless we get moving, we are in trouble. And I'm talking as much about commercial business as I am about military.

Interview, Washington/ The New York Times, 7-1:(5)13.

William R. Gould
Senior vice president, Southern California Edison Company; Chairman, Atomic Industrial Forum

4

. . . the technological revolution promised to give every American a life of comfort and luxury. Now, however, our children have been told that the affluent society has been achieved at the cost of frightful pollution and irreversible damage to the environment. Science has been blamed for designing the flood of consumer products, and industry for producing them. We have heard shrill calls for a no-growth economy, for a return to a more primitive life. Fortunately, most young people—and most Americans—realize intuitively that there is no turning back the clock of history. And they would not wish to do so if they could . . . the problems created by advancing technology can only be solved, or alleviated, by more and better technology.

Before National Science Teachers Association, Detroit, April 2/ Vital Speeches, 7-15:605.

William W. Hagerty
President, Drexel University

5

At the very time that a new and more highly-sophisticated level of technology is needed, at the very time when world-wide population pressures cry for immeasurably greater levels of production in all areas, a great wave of disillusionment about the applications of scientific knowledge has begun to sweep no small sector of this country [the U.S.]—and this, amazingly enough, in the generation that has profited by the greatest technical advances in the entire history of the human race.

The National Observer, 5-5:13.

Charles A. Lindbergh
Aviator
1

. . . the space program doesn't destroy the environment. In fact, it has given us information that we wouldn't have had, to use in preserving the environment. If the money hadn't been spent on the space program, the question is, how would it have been spent? I think we can be sure that it wouldn't have been spent on conservation in the way we would have liked. Life just isn't like that. The space program has another benefit, a defense benefit. It's a way to keep men in training and factories in being.

Interview, St. Paul, Minn.|
The National Observer, 6-30:20.

George M. Low
Deputy Administrator, National
Aeronautics and Space Administration
of the United States
2

[When man first saw earth from the moon,] he suddenly realized how fragile and how precious it appeared to be in the vast universe around it. He quickly came to realize that he had better learn how to manage his planet earth; and to manage it, he must first understand it. But understanding the earth is not enough. Since so much of what happens here on earth depends on our sun, a detailed understanding of the sun becomes of first importance.

Los Angeles Times, 5-14:(1)8.

Ernest R. May
Director, Institute of Politics,
Kennedy School of Government,
Harvard University
3

We [the U.S.] have been and have perceived ourselves as the leader of the world in technological innovation and industrial production. That—and quite apart from the apparently temporary energy crisis—is probably over. I think you can see the evidence of this. A Brazilian economist put it to me once: "What kind of country do you have? You put a man on the moon, but you have to watch

him on a Japanese television set." The capacity of the Japanese in particular, and of other nations, to outdo us in technological innovation and production seems to me quite clear. So it is possible that we will revert by the next century to the kind of role that we were playing in the mid-19th century, with our great strength being agriculture rather than industry. That is certainly a place where we retain our comparative advantage.

Interview, Cambridge, Mass.|
Los Angeles Times, 11-22:(2)7.

Gerald M. Monroe
Executive vice president,
LTV Aerospace Corporation
4

Space exploration means far more than spending a lot of money to launch rockets and walk on the moon. It means using satellites for educational television in remote parts of the world, improving our weather forecasting, protecting our food supplies and developing our ocean resources.

At American Astronautical Society's
International Congress of Space
Scientists, Dallas|
The Dallas Times Herald, 6-22:(B)2.

John R. Quarles
Deputy Administrator,
Environmental Protection Agency
of the United States
5

Like it or not, we will still be dependent upon our technology, and it has brought us great blessings. But we must now begin to differentiate between the blessings and the curses of technology.

San Francisco Examiner, 11-1:36.

John J. Riccardo
President, Chrysler Corporation
6

Technology and the various industries which apply it have become first the heroes and then the villians in what we have come to know as the revolution of rising expectations . . . Our resources, both intellectual and financial, however huge, are finite. There simply is not enough money or knowledge to do everything we want to do, even if we knew how to do it.

U.S. News & World Report, 1-22:38.

Robert W. Sarnoff
Chairman, RCA Corporation

1

The Industrial Revolution was a powerful centralizing force; it transformed peasant societies and local markets into a complex structure of industrial and business enterprises with world-wide connections. The Electronic Revolution will encourage flexibility and decentralization of organized activities; it will free those who make and execute decisions to base themselves almost wherever they choose. The Industrial Revolution tended to subordinate the individual to the organization even as it multiplied human physical capabilities, productivity and material wealth. The Electronic Revolution will shape electronics into a personal tool of universal application. It will compress a multitude of systems and devices —with the energy to run them—into packages small enough to carry in the hand. It promises to enhance the status of the individual by amplifying the power of the human mind and the precision of human control just as the Industrial Revolution amplified the power of human muscle. The result through the rest of this century will be a fundamental and growing shift in patterns of working and living, based on improved ways of using the brain. A growing variety of inexpensive, compact and versatile devices will perform the menial tasks of the mind—calculating, remembering, searching for references, measuring risks and opportunities—the whole variety of non-creative mental activities that precede decision or creation.

At Commemoration Day ceremony of Imperial College of Science and Technology, London, Oct. 25/Vital Speeches, 12-15:131.

Harrison Schmitt
American Astronaut

2

[On the reduced U.S. space budget]: There's a leadership failure in all levels of administration in leading the country in recognizing the inherent worth of the exploration of frontiers.

Before New Mexico Legislature, Jan. 31/ The Dallas Times Herald, 2-1:(A)2.

Edward Teller
Physicist

3

This country [the U.S.] has become great and strong because technology was placed on the highest pedestal in the late 19th century and early part of this century. But the situation has been changing among young people ever since World War II ended. Today, technology has a bad name. Young people believe it is irrelevant. If they continue to believe this, we, and particularly they, will soon be irrelevant.

At Republican Governors Conference, New York/ The New York Times, 5-13:(1)46.

James A. Van Allen
Professor of Physics, University of Iowa

4

It is sometimes remarked that the entire astronomical universe, except for the earth, the sun and the moon, could disappear and that the man-in-the-street would never know the difference. This statement has a certain grubby truth to it. But I wish to remark that man's image of himself and of his role in the universe is dependent in large measure on astronomy.

The New York Times, 12-2:(4)6.

Wernher Von Braun
Former Deputy Associate Administrator, National Aeronautics and Space Administration of the United States

5

At the time [Lyndon] Johnson served as Vice President under [John] Kennedy, it was he who virtually designed the objectives of NASA, culminating in the objective to land a man on the moon in the '60s. It is very certain to all of us in NASA that, without his

(WERNHER VON BRAUN)

support, we could never have landed a man on the moon. There was more and more questioning why such expense was necessary. People were concerned particularly after the fire in which three astronauts died. They thought it was reckless to send people to the moon. Johnson steadfastly stuck with the agency, stuck to his guns.

Kansas City/
Los Angeles Times, 2-11:(1)10.

Jesse Werner
Chairman and president,
GAF Corporation

1

In times past, the only nations which accumulated a disproportionate share of worldly goods were those fortunate enough to be blessed with a wealth of natural resources, good harbors and military strength. Science has made radical changes in this equation. It has become the great leveler among nations. I know of no clearer proof of this than the rise of Japan from a handcraft civilization to the third major industrial power of the world in well under 100 years. In spite of a dearth of raw materials, the Japanese have achieved this unparalleled transformation.

Quote, 7-22:80.

Jerome B. Wiesner
President,
Massachusetts Institute of Technology

2

For several years I have been concerned that improperly-exploited computer and communication technology could so markedly restrict the range of individual rights as to eliminate meaningful life as we appreciate it. In other words, 1984 could come to pass unnoticed while we applaud our technical achievements. The great danger which must be recognized and counteracted is that such a depersonalizing state of affairs could occur without specific overt decisions, without high-level encouragement or support, and totally independent of malicious intent. The great danger is that we could become "information-bound," because each step in the development of an "information tyranny" appeared to be constructive and useful. I used to suspect that it would be much easier to guard against a malicious oppressor than to avoid being slowly but most surely dominated by an information Frankenstein of our own creation. [The] Watergate [political-espionage affair] has demonstrated I was clearly not worried enough about improper uses of technology.

At International Communications
Association Conference/
The National Observer, 8-4:11.

Henry Aaron
Baseball player, Atlanta "Braves"

1

[Saying he doesn't like the attention being paid to him because of his nearing Babe Ruth's home-run record]: I used to love to come to the ball park. But now I hate it. Every day becomes a little tougher because of all this—writers, tape recorders, microphones, cameras, questions and more questions. Roger Maris lost his hair the season he hit 61 [home runs]. I still have my hair; but when it's all over, I'm going home to Mobile and fish for a long, long time.

Interview, Atlanta, June 28/
The Washington Post, 7-1:(D)4.

2

[On the possibility of his passing Babe Ruth's home-run record of 714]: All I'm trying to do is hit 715, and people can debate the merits of the two of us as much as they want. They can argue about comparative times at bat, about stadiums and about the lively ball, and they can reach any conclusions they wish. I don't want anyone to forget Ruth. But I hope they remember Henry Aaron, too.

Los Angeles Herald-Examiner, 9-23:(C)3.

Red Adams
Pitching coach,
Los Angeles "Dodgers" baseball club

3

My job is to help a pitcher, not discipline him. If I embarrass you one day, I can't expect you to accept my help the next day. Three words are important: flexibility, communications and common sense. I also feel it's very important to acquaint myself with each player as a person as well as [a] pitcher . . . I try not to get carried away with my importance. I think the role of a coach is often overplayed; but I realize that, as baseball moves more toward specialization, I can help.

If I have a philosophy it's that I want my pitchers to pitch to their own strength rather than the hitter's weakness.

Interview, Vero Beach, Fla./
Los Angeles Times, 3-28:(3)4.

Muhammad Ali
Former heavyweight boxing champion
of the world

4

I still believe in the Golden Gloves idea: you fight and eliminate. The heavyweight title has been ruined by people who don't fight. If a man is ranked seventh, he may not get a shot for seven years. [Floyd] Patterson and [Ingemar] Johansson tied up the title for three years. [Joe] Frazier wouldn't fight. The only champions who were willing to put it on the line were Sonny Liston and me.

Interview, Las Vegas, Nev./
Los Angeles Herald-Examiner, 2-14:(D)1.

5

I've put a couple of pages in the boxing book. I'm greater than boxing. I *am* boxing. Muhammad Ali is the biggest thing in the history of all sports—Rose Bowl, Super Bowl, Kentucky Derby, all of them.

Quote, 2-18:165.

Sparky Anderson
Baseball manager, Cincinnati "Reds"

6

[On his rule against long hair for his players]: I talk to the players and try to explain that a guy without all that hair is more businesslike and gives a better impression. If they answer I have no right to tell them how to look, I agree. I say, "If you want to take me to the Supreme Court, you're going to win, sure as hell. But one thing the Supreme Court can't do is make up my line-up card."

Interview, Tampa, Fla./
Los Angeles Herald-Examiner, 3-8:(C)1.

(SPARKY ANDERSON)

1

[On the wildness of New York *Mets* fans when their team won the pennant last week against the *Reds*]: It isn't New York that's to blame, or the people of New York. It's us. I'm talking about me, the players and everyone else who are supposed to set an example for the fans. After a pennant-clinching, the players are supposed to salute each other's performance, enjoy their victory and maybe take a couple of sips of champagne. But do they? Of course not. They throw it all around the clubhouse, douse everybody with it and what not. You see how they carry on, the wild way they act. If the players do this, why not the fans? I did the same things. I'm no better than them. Here I am calling them animals and lunatics, and I'm doing the same thing. How can I sit here and criticize the behavior of the fans when mine isn't any better?

The New York Times, 10-13:40.

Arnold "Red" Auerbach
General manager,
Boston "Celtics" basketball team

2

To legalize betting on all sports has an insidious potential to corrupt. I want to emphasize the effect that such legislation could have on the athletes themselves. They will be suspect, suspect and suspect. Every time a shot is missed, there will be shouts from the stands of "dump, dump, dump." Athletes will be accused of playing the point spread.

Boston, May 31/
The Dallas Times Herald, 6-1:(F)7.

Bob Bailey
Baseball player, Montreal "Expos"

3

. . . there are cases when a crowd should boo a player; like when it's obvious he isn't trying. But the kind of booing that gets me is when you're going bad and the fans get on you. It doesn't help. It never helps to be booed when you're trying.

The New York Times, 6-7:63.

Vida Blue
Baseball pitcher, Oakland "Athletics"

4

[On his team's just winning the American League Western Division championship]: Sure it's nice to win; but there is only one thing that's important to me and that's the money that we're going to get, win or lose. It's a business with me, and I refuse to lie to all the Little Leaguers and try to con them. I don't love baseball. I like it. And to me baseball means money, and that's all I care about.

Chicago, Sept. 23/
Los Angeles Herald-Examiner, 9-24:(C)1.

Teddy Brenner
President,
Madison Square Garden Boxing, New York

5

World-championship boxing in the U.S. has about disappeared, and we must do something to correct the situation. The WBA and WBC have made it a point to avoid U.S. fighters in most categories; and we've reached a point where heavyweight George Foreman and lightweight Bob Foster are our only world champions. At one time, we dominated almost all the divisions of boxing.

New York, June 20/
The Washington Post, 6-21:(G)6.

Paul Brown
Football coach, Cincinnati "Bengals"

6

If you live sloppy, you will play sloppy. I can't stand it when a player whines to me or his teammates or his wife or the writers or anyone else. A whiner is almost always wrong. A winner never whines.

Quote, 8-5:141.

Clay Carroll
Baseball pitcher, Cincinnati "Reds"

7

[Baseball is] a hitter's game. They have pitchers because somebody has to go out there and throw the ball up to the plate.

The Christian Science Monitor, 5-1:15.

Jim Colbert
Golfer

1

My reaction to anything that happens on the golf course is no reaction. There are no birdies or bogeys, no eagles or double bogeys; they are only numbers. If you can get that way, you can play this game. It's my way.

Jacksonville, Fla./
The Dallas Times Herald, 3-19:(C)1.

Alistair Cooke
Chief United States correspondent,
"The Manchester (England) Guardian"

2

Except for boxing, all sports have changed. They have changed quite drastically and always in the same direction. The evolvement is from sport and fun to entertainment and big business; from competitors to performers. It's a sad thing, really. The athletes have turned into entertainers.

Interview, Los Angeles/
Los Angeles Times, 6-12:(3)1.

3

I share the English prejudice in favor of the amateur, the all-round athlete who is well-behaved and well-read, who can perhaps write or do other things and who plays golf and billiards well, along with tennis and other games. Such an individual is more attractive than the man who capitalizes professionally on one talent, who specializes intensively just to make a lot of money. Amateur means lover—it's the French word for lover. And it is love of sport that has vanished. Money has killed off the amateur.

Interview, Los Angeles/
Los Angeles Times, 6-12:(3)7.

4

I have no regrets but one: I wish I had taken up golf at the age of 15 instead of at 55. I have a passion for landscapes, and the golf courses of the world are microcosms of landscapes obliterated elsewhere by billboards. And it is a game you play against yourself; you have to earn every reward. Intellectually, the greatest delicacy; a sobering game.

Interview, San Francisco/
San Francisco Examiner, 11-5:23.

Jack Kent Cooke
President,
Los Angeles "Lakers" basketball team

5

I like the highly-refined competition in professional sports. I like competition, period. Do the pleasures outweigh the problems? It's like comparing night with day. The pleasures are so transcendent, there is no problem.

Interview, Los Angeles Times, 5-13:(3)8.

Margaret Court
Tennis player

6

[On her losing to Bobby Riggs]: One minute in this sport you're on top of the world; then the next minute brings disappointment. It's either up or down in tennis.

May 14/Los Angeles Times, 5-22:(1)1.

Bruce Crampton
Golfer

7

A player like [Lee] Trevino, joking and chattering, is great for the tour. I'm the first to recognize it. But I don't think the tour could handle 150 Trevinos. I'm out there trying to do a job. I'm not an actor. If I were, I should be in Hollywood. I'm an entertainer only to the extent that people get entertainment from watching me hit the golf ball. The only thing I'm trying to do on the course is hit good golf shots. If that's not enough for the fans, they're watching the wrong player.

Interview, San Diego/
Los Angeles Times, 2-18:(3)6.

Joe Cronin
President, American (Baseball) League

8

[On the American League's new designated-hitter rule]: We think this rule will be a great boon to young talent. There may be a lot of gawky, strong kids who ordinarily may not feel they have the all-around skills to come into baseball who will be lured into the game by the knowledge they could make a career in hitting alone. After all, Babe Ruth was a big, awkward boy who started out as a pitcher and

579

(JOE CRONIN)

who became the greatest home-run hitter of them all.

News conference, New York, Jan. 30/
The Washington Post, 1-31:(D)1.

Augie Donatelli
Former baseball umpire, National League

1

[On being an umpire]: It's not an easy profession. The way some players and managers beef about the close calls—well, it knocks the morale right out of you. But mine always stayed up because, as a young man, I loaded coal onto railroad cars. Things like that you don't forget.

The Christian Science Monitor, 12-31:(B)5.

Don Drysdale
Former baseball player,
Los Angeles "Dodgers"

2

[On baseball rule changes]: I don't think they should monkey around with the rules. The game has been the same all these years, and I think if you fool around with it you're just asking for trouble. Where do you stop?

Los Angeles Times, 3-30:(3)7.

Charles (Chub) Feeney
President, National (Baseball) League

3

[Criticizing the American League's new designated-hitter rule]: . . . the National League is scoring runs at a slightly higher pace than the American. But the main reason I was against the rule when it was adopted, and still am, is that I like the strategy in the game. The fans do, too. And I think the DH rule takes some of that away. It deprives them of thinking along with the managers. As for the attendance figures, I'm happy the American League's are up. But we're running about 1.8 million ahead of them. I think the closeness of their pennant races has helped bring people into the parks more than the designated hitter.

Interview/
San Francisco Examiner, 9-5:61.

Bob Feller
Former baseball pitcher

4

Everywhere I go today, kids are asking me how to throw a spitter or some other kind of trick ball. They're asking me everything but how to get the fastball over the plate, and that's the most important thing in pitching.

The Christian Science Monitor, 9-7:13.

Charles O. Finley
Owner, Oakland "Athletics" baseball club

5

I can turn a profit because I don't have many unessential employees to pay big money to. I put my money into player development, and I don't worry about paying $20,000 to a public-relations man who can't put any extra people in the seats anyway . . . Baseball owners tell me they can't make any money. But there's a feeling that every ex-player has to be put on the payroll as a $25,000-a-year scout. I don't see that I'm a charitable organization. A player ought to plan for his future while he's playing and while he has a big name. I've made $100,000 business loans to some of my players; I've given them tips on the market, and I've tried to give them sound business advice. I don't need some ex-player hanging around turning in scribbled, useless scouting reports. I pay the money and the profit should go to me, not him.

The New York Times Magazine, 7-15:32.

Curt Flood
Former baseball player

6

[On baseball's reserve clause]: The problem with the reserve clause is that it ties a man to one owner for the rest of his life. There is no other profession in the history of mankind, except slavery, in which one man was tied to another for life.

Interview, Majorca/
The National Observer, 4-14:6.

Gerald R. Ford
Vice President of the United States

7

People who play to win don't bother me if

they're playing within the rules. Although some folks have these soft ideas about wanting to downgrade competition, you're destroying a lot of the benefits of sports if you don't play to win—as hard as you can—always within the rules . . . Two of the most important things in sports—or in politics, business or anything else—are teamwork and leadership. If you don't play competitively to win, there's no way to develop effective teamwork, and it's hard to develop leaders.

Interview,
Washington/
Los Angeles Times, 12-12:(3)1.

George Foreman
Heavyweight boxing champion
of the world

1

[On his just-won victory over Joe Frazier]: I did it! . . . I did it! . . . I did it! I'm the heavyweight champion of the world!

Kingston, Jamaica, Jan. 22/
Los Angeles Herald-Examiner, 1-23:(C)2.

2

The [championship] title is borrowed from the people and must be given back. I plan to take advantage of it while I can, treat everybody good, and when it's time to give it up, I'll do so, smiling.

Time, 2-5:45.

A. J. Foyt
Auto racing driver

3

The Indy 500 is the World Series, the Masters and the Kentucky Derby all wrapped up in one event. In the other races, you're running for $75,000 or $100,000; but at Indianapolis, you're running for a million dollars. That's what the exposure is worth in publicity and endorsements. If you win that race, or even come in second, the rest of the season is so lovely. But if you don't, it's a long, hard year.

Los Angeles/
The New York Times, 5-6:(5)4.

Joe Frazier
Former heavyweight boxing champion
of the world

4

When you're champ, you have to live like a champ. You've got to have big cars, fancy clothes, rings and mink coats for the missus. [Current heavyweight champion] George [Foreman] doesn't have all those things yet. So he's got to come looking for me again. I represent the big payday. After all, he can't take that title and hide with it.

Los Angeles Times, 5-28:(3)2.

Roman Gabriel
Football player, Los Angeles "Rams"

5

You don't win when you have too many bitchers. Things don't go the way certain people thought they should go, and you have one guy complaining and then another, and after a while everyone starts falling into that complaining mood . . . The biggest problem [with the *Rams*] right now is that we have too many selfish players—by that I mean players not motivated to play as a team but rather as individuals. In any business, you should be involved first in making that the best there is. But we've got guys on our club who are thinking about recognition for themselves first and . . . the team second.

Interview, Los Angeles, Jan. 24/
The Dallas Times Herald, 1-25:(D)6.

Ed Garvey
Executive director, National
Football League Players' Association

6

[Saying the NFL commissioner is partial to management in player-management relations]: . . . we took a survey of the membership last year and again this year. We put in a couple of questions on the commissioner: "Whom does he represent? Does he represent you or is he neutral or does he represent owners only?" Eighty-five per cent of the players said he represents owners only . . . One of the first things you learn in life, certainly in law school, is conflict of interest. How in the

WHAT THEY SAID IN 1973

(ED GARVEY)

world can you be paid by one side [as the commissioner is by the owners], have them approve your contract, chair their meetings, be their chief executive, and then turn around and be neutral? It's crazy. You can't do it.

Interview, New York/
Los Angeles Times, 2-13:(3)7.

Abe Gibron
Football coach, Chicago "Bears"
1

[His standards for NFL team competence]: . . . forty guys who want to play football that punishes the opposition on offense and defense. Anybody that doesn't want to, let him go some place else, squeeze grapes and throw the juice at other people. I want none of that stuff here.

Los Angeles Times, 7-27:(3)2.

Althea Gibson
Tennis player; Golfer
2

Tennis is tougher mentally and physically [than golf]. Anybody can play golf, but not everybody can play tennis. In tennis, you've always got somebody across the net from you who won't let you do what you want to do. But in golf the course doesn't move and par doesn't change. Now, wait a minute. I'm sorry but I've got to take some of that back. Tennis does require a lot more stamina than golf, but actually golf is tougher mentally. Once you've learned to play tennis, things come pretty automatically. You don't have to think too much because it's all been instilled in you on the practice court. But there are so many things which can go wrong with your golf game that you are forced to think constantly.

Interview, Boston/
The Christian Science Monitor, 7-23:10.

Dan Goich
Football player, New York "Giants"
3

[In football,] you have to prove your manhood more times in one season than most men do in a lifetime. When you don't make

it, when you can't perform or you get beat or you get cut, you're cut as a man. Not everyone can take that. Having the intelligence to think about those things can actually hinder you in football. There are a lot of irrational things football demands—the insular existence, the pain, the emotionalism. I'm no intellectual, but I do think about these things. Some guys just accept them. Even on the field, sometimes when you should just react physically, you want to think too much. It inhibits you.

Interview/
Los Angeles Times, 11-23:(1)36.

Tom Gorman
Tennis player
4

. . . consistency is directly connected with your mental approach to the game. You know, the difference in talent on the pro tour isn't that great. We all have days sometimes when we beat guys we're not supposed to beat and lose to people we usually handle without too much trouble. But generally, when you're the wrong half of an upset, it's because you left your concentration back in the clubhouse.

Interview/
The Christian Science Monitor, 7-30:4.

Billy Graham
Evangelist
5

I think sports is a great thing for our nation [the U.S.], as long as it doesn't become an idol. It is a positive force in American life. I believe you'll find more dedicated Christians in athletics than in any other facet of American life . . . but I don't think the team with the most Christians is necessarily going to win. The Lord may be helping their characters and souls, but I don't think He's any more for the *Dodgers* than He is for the *Braves*. More than being concerned with who's going to win the Super Bowl, I feel the Lord is probably more concerned that they might find a day other than Sunday to play on.

Los Angeles Times, 6-30:(3)2.

Andy Granatelli
President, STP Corporation;
Racing-car owner

1

. . . I have repeatedly tried to interest auto-club and track officials in a planned program for reducing speeds [in auto races] by restricting fuel consumption and fuel loads. My pleas have largely gone unheeded. All of us in racing must face the fact that we are simply going faster than our tracks and drivers can safely handle these flying missiles. This is not only a demand for reform, but a sincere and sad plea to all of my fellows in racing to assist me in obtaining this kind of reform.

Indianapolis, May 31/
Los Angeles Herald-Examiner, 6-1:(C)6.

Whitey Herzog
Baseball manager, Texas "Rangers"

2

[Saying today's professional players don't have the minor-league experience he had]: These kids today have missed out on a lot. Expansion has had something to do with it, but they come up so fast now. When I started, it was a very common thing for each player to spend an average of five years in the minors. A player would have 700 games under his belt before he reached the majors; a pitcher would have worked 800 innings . . . When I played, we didn't worry about money. We were a bunch of kids the same age having a good time. We were professional baseball players. That was what counted, not the money. Kids today worry too much about money. They want to make it and make it fast.

Interview/
The Dallas Times Herald, 7-11:(E)1.

Jesse Hill
Commissioner,
Pacific Coast Athletic Association

3

[The U.S. Olympic Committee is] an unfortunate example of those with the minimum of sports expertise trying to control, organize and direct America's most prestigious athletic competition. The groups which control our Olympic affairs realize their authority is not based on merit. To secure their position, they manipulate the USOC constitution as necessary to maintain their voting control. Thus, the USOC, year by year, becomes further removed from those who are really responsible for the success of our nation's sports programs. The USOC is not aware of the changing times. The USOC is out of date.

The Washington Post, 3-31:(C)1.

Bob Howsam
General manager,
Cincinnati "Reds" baseball club

4

Baseball is as much a part of America as the freedoms we cherish and the liberties we defend. If one understands baseball, he understands America.

Before Rotary Club,
Cincinnati/
Los Angeles Herald-Examiner,
2-18:(B)4.

Lamar Hunt
President, Kansas City "Chiefs"
football team

5

[On the World Championship of Tennis series which he founded]: Probably tennis is a sport that was held down because of its own image. It was a gentleman's game played at clubs and not looked on as a public game. We tried to get away from that concept. We play in public arenas, and we have a meaningful schedule from January 15 to May 15, where before there were just isolated tournaments along with a few traditional dates such as Wimbledon and Forest Hills. I think our scheduling format, where we make the competition into a kind of horse race, has helped win public interest. And television coverage has helped a good deal. All of this has had the impact of putting tennis on the same plane with basketball, hockey or football, where you have a schedule and you can see who is winning or losing during the season.

Dallas/
The New York Times, 5-6:(5)8.

Jim (Catfish) Hunter
Baseball pitcher, Oakland "Athletics"

1

Know what I hate to do? I hate to walk a man. It bugs me something fierce. Because every time you put a man on base for free, it seems like he scores. I'd rather give up a hit than a walk—that's how strongly I feel about it.

Interview, Oakland/
The Christian Science Monitor, 10-20:12.

Robert Trent Jones
Golf-course designer

2

[On professional-golfer criticism of his course designs]: Pros want fairway traps from which they can reach the green. They want dead-flat greens with no rolls or contours. They don't want any hole too long or the rough too deep. They usually get their way, and a lot of tournaments turn into boring putting contests . . . I don't build courses just for the pros. That's like designing an office building just for executives. I worry more about the effect of a course on a duffer. Besides, I've never built a course that a pro can't score 65 on if he's playing well. They want me to build a course they can shoot in the 60s on when they're playing lousy.

Interview/Los Angeles Times, 2-9:(3)9.

Kip Keino
Kenyan track star

3

I am really terribly disappointed with the attitude of amateur track officials in the United States. They never seem to want to serve the athletes, only themselves, and that is a terrible pity. In Kenya, it is just the reverse: the athlete comes first.

San Francisco Examiner, 2-7:53.

Jack Kelly
Vice president,
United States Olympic Committee

4

Some say the Olympic Games are too big. That's possibly so if you hold them all at one site. They could be diversified; split them up around the world. They could be held within a month or so and allocated where the best facilities and organization exist for a particular sport. As an athlete, I enjoyed world championships in my own sport more than the Olympics. We were bigger fish in a smaller pond.

At General Assembly of International
Sports Federations, Oklahoma City, May 25/
Los Angeles Herald-Examiner, 5-26:(B)3.

Billie Jean King
Tennis player

5

. . . I'm definitely in the minority with my fellow players on the subject of yelling at tennis matches. I say let the crowd roar if a good shot turns them on. After all, without paying customers you've got no pro sports. Yelling wouldn't bother my concentration, but some of the others think it would bother theirs. But as I've told them, they'd adjust to it.

Interview/
Los Angeles Herald-Examiner, 2-21:(B)2.

6

[Advocating less audience noise during play]: The quality of play is better when there aren't any distractions. You depend so much on hearing the ball come off your opponent's racket. It helps in judging the speed of the shot and getting a feel for the tempo of play. In baseball, it doesn't matter how many people are cheering at Yankee Stadium: You can still hear the crack of the bat.

Los Angeles Herald-Examiner, 4-17:(C)2.

7

Women can be great athletes. And I think you'll find in the next decade that women athletes will finally get the attention they've deserved through the years, that people will respect us as athletes and not just whether we're good-looking and whether she's cute. We're changing, you know; and I think people, and in particular businessmen, are realizing that we're marketable, that we can help them make money for their companies, and that we're professional athletes.

The New York Times, 9-22:24.

Bowie Kuhn
Commissioner of Baseball (United States)

1

Both sides [players and owners] are trying to avoid a [player] strike. The owners would like to make it a three-year contract this time. They need three years of peace. The players need three years of peace. And I need three years of peace.

At baseball dinner, Cincinnati/
San Francisco Examiner, 2-10:27.

2

. . . baseball always has been a contentious sport—and that's good. In that way, it mirrors our contentious democracy.

News conference/
The Christian Science Monitor, 5-21:13.

3

[Advocating a "designated runner" similar to the American League's current designated hitter]: I think it would do a lot for the game. My favorite play is the stolen base; it's the most beautiful play in the game. We even have drawn up a model rule on it, stipulating that a team could use a designated runner up to three times in a game. Then you'd see teams drafting track stars, and we'd restore some of the strategy that the designated hitter has removed. I can hear the fans screaming now, screaming for Jones, the mythical designated runner, when the manager doesn't want to use him until later.

Dec. 13/
Los Angeles Times, 12-14:(3)2.

Abe Lemons
Former basketball coach,
Oklahoma City University

4

I think I'd rather be a football coach. That way, you can never lose more than 11 games in a season. As a basketball coach, I once lost 11 games in December alone!

The Christian Science Monitor, 12-31:(B)5.

Joe Louis
Former heavyweight boxing champion
of the world

5

A heavyweight champion shouldn't think so much about money. A champion should help the boxing game by fighting often. When he doesn't fight often, it hurts boxing, because he's the man at the top, the one everyone looks up to. When he's idle, boxing's idle.

Interview, New York/
Los Angeles Herald-Examiner, 6-24:(B)2.

Billy Martin
Baseball manager, Detroit "Tigers"

6

[On the American League's new designated-hitter rule]: I don't like the rule because it isn't baseball. Maybe it will bring more hitting into the game, and I guess that's what the fans want. But at the same time, it also takes some of the strategy out of baseball, particularly in the areas of pinch-hitters and relief pitchers. I'll admit I've thought a lot about how the designated hitter can be used. For example, if I batted Frank Howard in the lead-off position in Boston, he'd have five shots at hitting that short left-field wall in Fenway Park. That's a situation which is intriguing even to me. But over-all, I don't like the rule.

Interview,
Lakeland, Fla./
The Christian Science Monitor, 3-30:13.

Willie Mays
Baseball player, New York "Mets"

7

[Announcing his retirement from baseball]: It's been a wonderful 22 years, and I'm not just getting out of baseball because I'm hurt. I just feel that the people of America shouldn't have to see a guy play who can't produce. I have three cracked ribs; and at 42 you can't play the way you could at 20, anyway. If the *Mets* get in the World Series, I'm playing in it—I don't know how, but I'm playing. But I've got to face facts. I've been in a lot of slumps and come out of them; but now I'm running out of time.

News conference,
New York,
Sept. 20/
The New York Times, 9-21:27.

John McKay
Football coach,
University of Southern California

1

[On criticism that college football is a farm system for professional sports, and thus does not merit college support]: More college players go into teaching, business and the professions than into pro ball. And in the end, the pros leave pro ball and go into something else they were trained for in college. We're a farm system for dentists.

Los Angeles Times, 2-18:(3)11.

Fred McLeod
Golfer; 1908 U.S. Open champion

2

If we [in 1908] had played as slowly as young players on the tour today, we would have been arrested for vagrancy.

Los Angeles Times, 7-3:(3)2.

George Meany
President,
American Federation of Labor-
Congress of Industrial Organizations

3

The Olympic Games are an old tradition and are supposed to be the essence of pure sport. But the Russians use the Games for their own political purposes . . . Our disadvantage in this country [the U.S.] is that we practice pure amateurism—but not the Russians. The Russians can't drop prejudice. They can't run a race for the simple pleasure of competition and sport. They have to build up a national ego. Take Olga Korbut, that little girl gymnast. She is absolutely wonderful. But I keep thinking that, compared to our kids, she has it made. No economic problems or feeding problems for her and her family. She gets a good education and leads a good life —and she is supposed to be an amateur. Over here, we hold our Olympic athletes to a rigid and impractical amateur code.

Interview,
Washington/
The Washington Post, 11-7:(D)1.

Art Modell
Owner,
Cleveland "Browns" football team

4

[On the pleasures of owning a football team]: It was much more interesting and fun a decade ago. The single biggest change is the relationship with players. We used to have a mutual trust. Ten years ago, I felt a strong obligation to help the players in their private lives. In the last few years, they have turned to lawyers, agents and a union. Call it paternalism, call it big-daddyism, call it anything you wish: We had a fine relationship that we both enjoyed and that is now gone. I am dismayed and disappointed by the way things are now. Another thing wrong is the stress on winning, by comparison with what it was 10 years ago. I like to win as much as anybody, but I don't believe in winning-at-any-price. This is no part of my philosophy, this tampering with other people's assistant coaches, luring players to play out their options, the winning-at-all-costs-and-the-hell-with-everything-else. There's an honorable way to win, and I'm on that side.

Interview/
Los Angeles Times, 5-13:(3)1.

Jack Nicklaus
Golfer

5

Power is over-emphasized in modern golf to a point where it's become totally out of proportion to the basic nature and enjoyment of the game. Golf is a game of *precision*, not strength. I grew up on a course that demanded precision; and the courses I've always enjoyed the most are those that demand precision over power. This has become so important to me that it's a major factor in my tour schedule. I just don't want to play those long, wide-open, dull, repetitive, unimaginative tracks any more. Where's the fun, where's the challenge in just beating at the ball? Any idiot can do that; and if he's strong enough, he'll score well. That's not what golf's about. It's a thinking man's game. Beyond that, for a golf course to be enjoyable it has to be within everyone's capabilities, and it has to have variety. Sure, you're going to put in some holes where power would be an advantage. It's a factor in the game. But it shouldn't be *the* factor.

Esquire, April:152.

1

[On his victory by one stroke over Lee Trevino in the just-concluded Tournament of Champions]: Oh, that's fun. That's the whole thing. That's what this game is about. Here was Lee in a spurt, and then I made birdies on three of the last seven holes. That's the whole thing—responding to a challenge, playing the way you want to play, doing the things you want to do, and winning. On the other hand, if you lose, it kills you.

Rancho La Costa, Calif./
The Dallas Times Herald, 4-23:(C)2.

Bruce Ogilvie
Professor of Psychology,
California State University, San Jose

2

In sports, it takes a man who can live with the reality of fan rejection. You can't win them all. So you have to learn to tolerate unfair and unreasonable fan reaction. If you let it interfere with your talent, you're in trouble. Talent doesn't necessarily mean ability. The great athlete has talent plus attitude —the right attitude toward failure, for instance . . . He realizes he can't win them all, and he makes it a point to learn from his defeats.

Interview/Los Angeles Times, 3-11:(3)9.

Bob Oliver
Baseball player, California "Angels"

3

[On the Oakland *Athletics'* use of orange-colored baseballs]: You can take your orange baseballs, wrap them in a blue blanket and dump them in the Red Sea.

Palm Springs, Calif./
Los Angeles Times, 4-3:(3)1.

Merlin Olsen
Football player, Los Angeles "Rams"

4

. . . I love this game; I really do. Oh, sure,

I make good money; but I couldn't justify it for the money alone. You have to make too many sacrifices, physically and emotionally. You play 10 years and you're lucky if you still have a head full of teeth and one good knee and just one or two joints without traumatic arthritis. The emotional drain is tremendous. You only have so much to give emotionally, and if you use up so much for football, you don't have enough left for your family. Inevitably, they suffer, and your relationship with them suffers.

Interview,
Los Angeles/
Los Angeles Times, 11-23:(1)34.

Jesse Owens
Former Olympic track champion

5

The United States, and every country of power in the world, should do everything possible to keep—indeed, to improve—the Olympic program. Only an Olympian can fully realize and appreciate the grip the games have on the youth of the world, and this is especially true throughout the U.S. The Olympic image has far more influence than a great majority realize, and I still have the mail to prove it. Problems can be solved—must be solved. If we lose the Olympics and all they represent, our civilization will have taken a sad step backward.

Scottsdale, Ariz./
The Christian Science Monitor, 3-7:14.

Milt Pappas
Baseball pitcher, Chicago "Cubs"

6

I'm walking fewer batters. There's nothing more demoralizing than the base on balls. It can destroy you. You walk a guy; they bunt him around to second or he steals; he moves to third on a ground ball and scores on a wild pitch or passed ball—one run without a base hit. You're just making life a whole lot easier for the opposition.

Interview,
San Diego/
The Christian Science Monitor, 4-19:9.

Wes Parker
Former baseball player,
Los Angeles "Dodgers"

1

[Criticizing player "greed" in asking too much from management]: Basically, I'm against anything that will harm baseball. In my opinion, what's happening this year between owners and players is harming baseball, as it did last year . . . There are definitely two sides in a situation like this; but if I had to pick a side at this point, I would lean more toward the owners. My reason is I feel the players are pushing a good thing too far. If the players are not careful, greed will be the death of professional baseball . . . I think it's an over-all thing. I think the pension plan was good enough as it was. I think the players are paid good enough salaries now so they don't have to worry about freedom to negotiate [with more than one club]. I think players in general are treated extremely well by the teams and that to threaten the future of baseball over the issues they're concerned with is putting the entire thing out of proportion. What I wonder is, where are the guys who just love to play baseball?
Interview/Los Angeles Times, 2-23:(3)1.

George Parnassus
Boxing promoter

2

There is no time like the present [in sports]. It is a lot of bunk when oldtimers tell you today's fighters aren't as good as they were 30 or 40 years ago. All athletes—football, baseball, runners, basketball—are better today than they were yesterday. The same is true for boxing. Boxers are better-conditioned, faster, more intelligent and better-prepared than ever before. And they all will be better tomorrow than they are today. This is life, the way the spinning-wheel spins.
Los Angeles, April 19/
Los Angeles Times, 4-20:(3)3.

Joe Paterno
Football coach, Pennsylvania State University

3

Winning is the most important thing, but it isn't everything. In football or anything else, there's often a difference between aspiration and achievement. If you're licked, you're licked. The idea then is to learn something from losing . . . If you're licked by a better man, you're still a winner. Our definition of a loser is a guy who doesn't do the best he can.
Interview/Los Angeles Times, 8-31:(3)8.

Maurice Phillippe
Racing-car designer

4

[Disputing the opinion that racing cars go too fast for safety]: That's a purely relative argument. What speed is too quick? These cars are more controllable today than they ever have been because of the wings and the tires and all the developments. When you have a series of accidents as we had at Indianapolis [in the 500-mile race] this year, you'll always have people who say the speeds are too high. I'm sure they said the same thing when the speeds were 100 miles per hour.
Los Angeles/
The Washington Post, 6-24:(D)7.

John Ralston
Football coach, Denver "Broncos"

5

Football's first commandment is know thyself. And that takes time. It isn't easy [for a coach] to become intimately acquainted with 47 ballplayers, and seven or eight assistant coaches. But that's only a start. You should know the 1,200 other players in the league almost as well as you know your own.
Interview/Los Angeles Times, 11-30:(3)1.

Willis Reed
Basketball player,
New York "Knickerbockers"

6

I don't care how much natural ability you have, you don't get anywhere in this world without working for it. I have no idea where I got my drive; it was just there, I guess. But I know this: I put in the practice hours; I just didn't walk in and take it. I think most kids who make it big in life, or in the pros, are winners by the time they leave high school. I don't say a man can't change and become a winner later; but it's tougher then. I've found the really good ones win early and never lose the habit. I can't explain it, but if kids like that go into the pros, they eventually wind up . . . a winner.

Interview/
The Christian Science Monitor, 2-7:16.

Bobby Riggs
Tennis player

1

[On his defeat the day before by Billie Jean King in their "battle of the sexes" tennis match]: She beat me so easily that I almost cried . . . I don't think I'll ever see anybody do as well as she did. I mean, she played tennis. I love this game, and she did so well that I wanted to hide.

San Francisco Examiner & Chronicle,
9-23:(C)2.

Clifford Roberts
Chairman,
Masters (Golf) Tournament Committee

2

[On complaints that the Masters is segregated because of the ruling of ineligibility of black golfer Lee Elder]: There is not now and never has been player discrimination, subtle or otherwise. We have much respect for Mr. Elder as an American representative in the game of golf. He tied last year with Lee Trevino for first place in the Greater Hartford Open and would have won an invitation [to the Masters] had he not lost in the playoff. Moreover, to invite Mr. Elder without his having qualified by personal achievement would be practicing discrimination in reverse. [The late Bob Jones, father of the Masters,] made it clear, in writing, that any black golfer who qualified to play in the Masters would automatically receive the invitation which had been earned . . . If we were to make an exception in favor of Mr. Elder or any other golfer who had failed to qualify, we might properly be condemned by all other golfers, including the growing number of black players who are

making a career of tournament golf.

Augusta, Ga., April 4/
The Washington Post, 4-5:(D)1.

Brooks Robinson
Baseball player, Baltimore "Orioles"

3

[Advocating revision of the reserve clause]: We [players] are conscious of owners' problems. They must maintain expensive farm systems, a burden that football and basketball don't have. But we still think a man, somewhere in his lifetime, should have a chance to decide his destiny.

Interview, San Juan, P.R., Feb. 5/
Los Angeles Herald-Examiner, 2-5:(B)2.

4

[On why the general public looks down on player salary demands]: Sports are big business. But to the average fans, we aren't like people who work for airlines or in a bank. We all get big salaries for having fun.

Interview, San Juan, P.R., Feb. 5/
Los Angeles Herald-Examiner, 2-5:(B)2.

Pete Rose
Baseball player, Cincinnati "Reds"

5

Hitting a baseball is the hardest thing to do in all of sport. Think about it: You've got a round ball, a round bat, and the object is to hit it square. No one can help you. There's nobody blocking for you or setting a puck.

Los Angeles Times, 6-22:(3)3.

Carroll Rosenbloom
Owner,
Los Angeles "Rams" football team

6

When interviewing coaches, I always try to get them mad by asking them: "What makes you think you can be a head coach?" The good ones react the same way. Before answering, [Don] Shula stuck his jaw out a mile, and I thought [Chuck] Knox was going to spit in my eye.

Los Angeles, Jan. 24/
Los Angeles Times, 1-25:(3)6.

589

(CARROLL ROSENBLOOM)

1

A successful coach is a man who loves football, who loves winning and who loves his family. This is a great sport. It's worth a man's love—if you win. If you lose, it's the saddest sport in the world.

Interview, Los Angeles/
Los Angeles Times, 1-28:(3)10.

Derek Sanderson
Hockey player

2

I've always maintained there are three things you need to make money in professional sports. One is talent. The second is points. The third is color [showmanship].

Interview, Hollywood, Fla./
The National Observer, 2-10:16.

Tex Schramm
President,
Dallas "Cowboys" football team

3

You hear a lot of talk about over-emphasis, but people don't really think college football is over-emphasized. They don't think their money is wasted on football by the universities. By comparison with some other public expenditures, they know it isn't a lot of money. And they accept college football as standing on its own, not as somebody's farm system. I think the thing underlying this acceptance is that football is such a vital force in so many American communities. It's a unifying agent, a rally point. This goes for baseball and other sports, too, but it's more universal in football. The team is the one thing that can bring together all or most of the elements of the campus, city, region, state and even country in a common interst.

Los Angeles Times, 2-18:(3)11.

4

From a standpoint of competitiveness and attractiveness, the thing that's made the Super Bowl the Number One single sports event in the country is that it's one spectacular game that decides the world championship. This has been a concept of football throughout the years. Football never has been a series sport. The popularity of college bowl games has been this way. Further, by going to a series you depreciate regular-season games that lead up to the end. It takes away the sudden-death aspect of no-tomorrows. You put your best on the line in one gigantic shot. You know when the day's over, one team will be world champion.

The Dallas Times Herald, 3-25:(C)3.

Tom Seaver
Baseball pitcher, New York "Mets"

5

[Arguing against the American League's new designated-hitter rule]: I think fans appreciate the total athlete more than the owners give them credit for. Part of the game is being a total athlete, doing more than one thing.

Interview, Greenwich, Conn.,
Jan. 12/The New York Times, 1-13:21.

6

[On the playing of the national anthem before each game]: I think it should be played. It's become a tradition. At times, especially in bad weather, it bothers me to stand on the mound after warming up while it's been played, but that's purely a relationship to my job. Everybody I know accepts it [the anthem] as a part of baseball. It's been a part of baseball as long as we can remember.

Interview/
The New York Times, 1-21:(5)1.

Robert E. Short
Owner, Texas "Rangers" baseball club

7

The problem [in baseball ownership] is not to make money—though I'm not averse to that—but not to lose a lot. The problem is how to put enough people into the ballpark to keep the books balanced and stay in business.

Los Angeles Times, 4-23:(3)8.

O. J. Simpson
Football player, Buffalo "Bills"

8

Pick the best player on the other team—

and stay away from him. Pick on weakness instead. It's WHO you play against that counts—not what. Don't worry about what defense they're in. Worry about WHO is playing what in that defense. Watch where they put their best man in every defense—and run away from him. Most coaches worry themselves sick about zone defenses and odd-man lines, things like that. Forget it. WHO is the odd-man and can our center handle HIM? Football is a match-up of players, not playbooks.

Interview/
Los Angeles Times, 10-12:(3)6.

Terry Slater
Hockey coach, Los Angeles "Sharks"

1

[On team motivation]: Pride is the basic factor; it all begins with pride. Good athletes have tremendous pride, but each is different. You've got to find the different ways to bring out the pride . . . Sometimes I rip up tables, throw things, scream. I'm crazy . . . You never know. Not long ago, I put up a sign in the dressing room pointing out that winning the playoffs will be worth $15,000 extra per man. We lost two straight. Nobody seemed impressed. I took the sign down and put it up in my own room. I'm impressed with $15,000.

Interview, Los Angeles/
Los Angeles Times, 2-8:(3)3.

Steve Smith
Pole vaulter

2

[One reason he is turning professional]: I was tired of competing with East Europeans and walking around after meets in ripped jeans and faded sweatshirts. They wear $250 suits and get into their Mercedes and drive to the best restaurants.

The New York Times, 11-4:(5)11.

Warren Spahn
Pitching coach, Cleveland "Indians"
baseball club; Former pitcher

3

[On the American League's new designated-hitter rule]: As a baseball man, I think the

rule is good. It should produce more runs and put more people in our ballparks. Now, as a pitcher, I think it stinks.

San Francisco Examiner, 1-26:58.

4

I wouldn't trade my years [in baseball] for anything. We really enjoyed playing [when he was an active player]. Today, it seems to be all money. The kids are always looking at their bankbooks and talking about pension plans. I wonder if they can really enjoy it as much as we did.

The Christian Science Monitor, 1-30:6.

John Thompson
Executive director, National Football League Management Council

5

[On NFL Players' Association charges that the NFL commissioner is partial to management in player-management relations]: We're in a unique business. The winning of games is foremost on the minds of owners and players. It's not like industry. Nobody cares if Ford beats General Motors or vice versa. But cutting across this whole thing you have the players and owners in a lateral confrontation on some issues. And you have another element: the fans. We have to be careful on both sides. If you destroy public confidence in the owners or the players, you've destroyed the game . . . Our view is that the commissioner has the expertise and overall view needed to serve as arbitrator of disputes. The union's argument is that he is selected by the owners, paid by the owners and therefore can't be impartial. We just don't accept that. We *pay* him to be impartial. This commissioner [Pete Rozelle] has grown in stature to where he doesn't have to be beholden—and isn't—to either party.

Interview, New York/
Los Angeles Times, 2-13:(3)6.

Lee Trevino
Golfer

6

There's no need for the national anthem at sports events. The public doesn't come to hear it. Eighty per cent don't know the words; I

(LEE TREVINO)

don't. A short prayer might be better. Everyone respects the flag; you don't have to play the national anthem to prove it.

Interview/The New York Times, 1-21:(5)3.

Thomas Tutko
Professor of Psychology,
California State University, San Jose

1

. . . in a nation with millions of amateur athletes, the thing that's missing today is an awareness that professional athletes are different from the rest of us. Professional sports is a business, and the pro athlete is essentially a businessman. His product, he thinks, is winning games. The more games he wins, the more money he makes . . . The trouble starts when he is thought of as a model for the rest of us, and particularly our children. Unfortunately, kids don't differentiate between the Super Bowl and a Little League game unless it's carefully and repeatedly explained. That's what's missing: an understanding of the difference . . . [The professionals] project a win-or-else attitude that kids copy. I have no doubt that their language reflects their attitude: "Kill 'em! Zap 'em!" The coach who loses the Super Bowl says: "Losing is like dying." The winner says: "Winning isn't everything—it's the only thing." All this may be true on the pro level. But it's destructive to children and other young athletes . . . it's a fact that almost everybody fails in some things sooner or later. The question is how to adjust to losing—and there's no better place to learn this than in sports.

Interview/
Los Angeles Times, 2-25:(3)1,8.

Vernon O. Underwood
Chairman, Hollywood (Calif.) Turf Club

2

I think [horse] racing is a much more exciting sport than baseball or football. There is something different every day. If you go to a game, it may turn out to be a bad one. At the racetrack, there are nine "games" every

afternoon. If there is a bad one, there are always eight more.

Interview, Los Angeles/
Los Angeles Times, 6-5:(3)6.

Al Unser
Auto racing driver

3

[On the fear of crashing]: I think all of us have fear at times. I don't want to get hurt —no way. But they wouldn't pay me the money they do if racing was 100 per cent safe.

Los Angeles Times, 11-9:(3)2.

Bill Veeck
Former baseball-club owner

4

Baseball is the only competitive game left for humans. You have to be 7 feet tall for basketball. You have to be 7 feet wide for football. You have to be made of ice to play hockey.

Los Angeles Times, 7-25:(3)2.

Hubert Vogelsinger
Soccer coach, Yale University

5

I am convinced that, if soccer gets hold of the American athlete, then the rest of the world better watch out. I've never seen a more talented athlete in terms of speed, power, agility, strength, courage, or anyone more coachable than the American player. If he gets proper techniques and tactical tools and sufficient challenge in play, there will be no way of stopping him.

The New York Times, 8-19:(5)6.

Tom Weiskopf
Golfer

6

[His theory of golf]: It's all a combination of confidence and maturity and control of yourself. It's not letting yourself get flustered, or in a panic. It's playing your own game, playing within yourself, playing at your tempo. It's not letting yourself get too fast. It's like those old pro quarterbacks: They've got two minutes to play, but you don't see them getting flustered; they take their time and let things happen—they don't force them to happen—and they make those two minutes stretch out forever. That's the thing. You've got to let things happen—not try to force them to happen.

Interview, Harrison, N.Y./
Los Angeles Times, 8-6:(3)3.

1

[Criticizing hero-worship by fans of professional golfers]: I would rather go down to the old bar and drink beer and eat peanuts like the rest of the guys and have a good time about it, rather than have somebody tell you how great you are . . . I think if people would realize that Jack Nicklaus and Arnold Palmer are just like the guy that's probably their next-door neighbor—they enjoy the same things that they like to do—I think they wouldn't hero-worship. It's kind of silly in a way that people look at us that way. Sure, we have a talent, we play our talents with much greater efficiency than other people do and we're respected for that; but that's the way it should be left. The excitement and the hero-worship should be left at the golf course.

New York/
Los Angeles Times, 9-23:(3)1.

Bobby Winkles
Baseball manager, California "Angels"

2

[On the slowness of baseball games]: Ballplayers are in the habit of walking. When there's an out at first and the ball is thrown around the infield, everybody *walks* back to his position; nobody gives it a little bounce. When there's a pick-off play at first base, the first-baseman lobs it back to the pitcher. Why can't he *throw* it right back, show a little zip? A guy hits a fly ball and doesn't even get to first base. Or he hits a ground ball and doesn't run through the base. On a routine grounder, he's thrown out by 20 feet; and that's just not possible if he's running. He stands in the batter's circle till his name is announced; then he swings the lead bat, walks up to the plate in 30 seconds, is in and out of the batter's box on every pitch. He runs out a foul ball,

and it takes him a minute to get back in the box. An outfielder makes a catch and lobs it back into the infield 55 feet high. I realize that people are going to say these are petty things. They're all small; but when you eliminate all of them, you'll have some excitement you wouldn't see otherwise.

Los Angeles Times, 3-30:(3)7.

3

[On the American League's new designated-hitter rule]: It was a great help when the pitcher used to bat, because even if you weren't sure if he was tired, if he was up and you had a man on and were down by a run, you'd take him out. Now [with the DH rule] you try to make sure he's tired, and you might go just one man too long.

Los Angeles Times, 4-27:(3)9.

Wilbur Wood
Baseball pitcher, Chicago "White Sox"

4

This is just a job to me. I get paid to get somebody out.

Newsweek, 5-28:78.

John Wooden
Basketball coach,
University of California, Los Angeles

5

I like the custom of playing the national anthem at public gatherings, including major sports events. However, perhaps it is not necessary at every game. Frequently, I take my team to the dressing room for last-minute instruction rather than having them stand around cooling off during the anthem. I have received letters from super-patriots taking me to task for that. I wonder if those super-patriots are always standing. Times are changing. I tell my players, "If you are on the floor when the anthem is played, I don't expect you to stand at attention—but don't do anything disrespectful."

Interview/The New York Times, 1-21:(5)3.

6

In basketball, we meet adversity head on. It's so much like life itself: the ups and downs, the obstacles—they make you strong.

(JOHN WOODEN)

A coach is a teacher, and like any good teacher, I'm trying to build men.

Time, 2-12:67.

Philip K. Wrigley
President, Chicago "Cubs" baseball club

1

When a club draws 1.3 million [attendance] as the *Cubs* did, and still loses money, baseball is in trouble. If this continues, you know where we'll be?—in the same boat with an opera company, which means the only way baseball will survive will be through public subscriptions, outright donations. Baseball cannot live on gate receipts now. If it were not for radio and TV, we would have no chance at all.

Interview/Los Angeles Times, 5-13:(3)8.

The Indexes

A

Aaron, Henry, 577
Abdallah, Saad al-, 417
Abdesselam, Belaid, 417
Abernathy, Ralph D., 55, 309
Abourezk, James, 148
Abrams, Creighton W., 148, 230
Abzug, Bella S., 242, 491
Adams, Red, 577
Adams, Russell, 112
Addabbo, Joseph P., 363
Agnew, Spiro T., 67, 98, 124, 165, 242-243, 268-269, 309, 320, 363, 464, 552
Agustsson, Einar, 392
Aiken, George D., 269
Ailey, Alvin, 527
Akins, James E., 417
Alarcon (Quesada), Raul, 339
Albee, Edward, 527, 544
Albert, Carl, 44, 124, 165, 309, 364
Alexander, Herbert E., 244
Ali, Muhammad, 502, 577
Alioto, Joseph L., 326
Allende (Gossens), Salvador, 339
Amies, Hardy, 460
Amin, Idi, 443
An Chi-yuan, 348
Anastaplo, George, 465
Anderson, John B., 165, 270, 364
Anderson, Judith, 527
Anderson, Lindsay, 502
Anderson, Robert (playwright), 527
Anderson, Robert (Rockwell Int.), 572
Anderson, Robert O., 67
Anderson, Sparky, 577-578
Androutsopoulos, Adamantios, 392
Antonioni, Michelangelo, 544
Arafat, Yasir, 417
Arbatov, Georgi A., 392
Armour, Richard, 484
Armstrong, Anne, 331
Armstrong, William H., 552
Ash, Roy L., 67, 124, 166, 198, 230
Ashkenazy, Vladimir, 392, 519
Ashley, Thomas L., 166
Ashmore, Harry S., 465
Askew, Reubin, 112
Aspin, Les, 124, 231
Assad, Hafez al-, 417
Astaire, Fred, 502, 544
Atkinson, Brooks, 484

Auerbach, Arnold "Red," 578
Aznavour, Charles, 552

B

Bach, Richard, 484
Bagley, Worth, 392
Bailey, Bob, 578
Bailey, Mildred C., 44
Baker, Howard H., Jr., 222, 244, 270, 535, 544
Balanchine, George, 552-553
Ball, George W., 166, 393
Ball, Lucille, 502, 535
Ball, Robert M., 309-310
Balles, John, 198
Bamberger, E. Clinton, 310
Banowsky, William S., 112, 553
Bao Dai, 364
Barber, James D., 167, 270
Barber, Stephen, 271
Bardot, Brigitte, 331, 544, 553
Barker, James R., 67
Barnhart, Don, 112
Barre, Raymond, 67
Barrett, David, 339
Barzel, Rainer, 393
Barzun, Jacques, 455
Bates, Alan, 527
Bayh, Birch, 68, 167
Bazelon, David L., 222
Beam, Jacob D., 68, 393
Beame, Abraham D., 544
Beard, Robin, 271
Beaton, Cecil, 455, 460, 553
Beer, Lawrence W., 348
Beer, Samuel, 271
Belafonte, Harry, 455
Bellow, Saul, 484
Ben-Gurion, David, 418
Benjamin, Richard, 502
Bennett, Lerone, Jr., 112
Benson, Lucy Wilson, 271
Benton, Thomas Hart, 553
Bentsen, Lloyd M., 44, 68, 98, 167, 222, 340, 364, 394
Bergman, Ingmar, 503, 528, 553
Berkowitz, William, 553
Berrigan, Philip, 364
Berti, Gianluigi, 394
Bertolucci, Bernardo, 503
Bhutto, Zulfikar Ali, 348, 446

Biaggini, Benjamin F., 198
Bible, Alan, 98
Bickel, Alexander M., 112, 167
Biddle, James, 124
Biden, Joseph R., Jr., 244
Billecoq, Pierre, 394
Binh, Mrs. Nguyen Thi, 365
Bjelke-Petersen, Johannes, 349
Blackburn, Ben B., 231
Blackburn, Clark W., 310
Blackmun, Harry A., 168, 222, 271
Blass, Bill, 460
Bloede, Victor G., 68
Blue, Vida, 578
Blum, Richard, 98
Bok, Derek C., 272
Boll, Heinrich, 44, 484, 553
Bolt, Robert, 503
Bombard, Alain, 124
Bond, Julian, 245
Boo, Ben, 326
Boorstin, Daniel J., 168, 485
Booth, Arch N., 199
Borges, Jorge Luis, 485
Borgnine, Ernest, 503, 544
Borlaug, Norman E., 125
Botha, John S. F., 68
Boucher, H. A., 125
Boulez, Pierre, 519
Boumedienne, Houari, 418
Bourassa, Robert, 340
Bourguiba, Habib, 418, 443, 545
Bowen, William G., 113
Boyd, Alan S., 320
Boyer, Charles, 504
Bradbury, Ray, 485
Bradlee, Benjamin C., 465
Bradley, Tom, 55, 126, 169
Bradshaw, Thornton F., 68
Brandt, Willy, 365, 394-395, 446
Brennan, Peter J., 199, 245
Brenner, Teddy, 578
Breslin, Jimmy, 545
Breslow, Lester, 491
Brewster, Kingman, Jr., 45, 245, 272
Brezhnev, Leonid I., 69, 148, 231, 272, 349, 365, 395-397, 418-419, 446-447, 465, 545
Brinegar, Claude S., 320
Brinkley, David, 465
Briscoe, Dolph, 98, 200, 245
Brock, William E., III, 55, 169
Brooke, Edward W., 272-273, 365
Brothers, Joyce, 460
Brown, B. Frank, 113
Brown, George S., 231
Brown, Paul, 578
Browne, Secor D., 321
Brownstein, Irwin, 222
Broyhill, Joel T., 365
Brozen, Yale, 69
Brubeck, Dave, 519

Brunthaver, Carroll G., 70
Brzezinski, Zbigniew, 148
Buchan, Alistair, 45, 149
Buchanan, Patrick J., 246, 465, 535
Bucher, Jeffrey M., 70
Buckley, James L., 126, 169, 200, 246, 273, 491
Bundy, McGeorge, 169, 246, 365
Bunker, Ellsworth, 366
Burch, Dean, 466, 535-536
Burger, Warren E., 45, 99, 222-223
Burgert, Frank J., 70
Burke, Yvonne B., 55
Burnett, Carol, 536
Burns, Arthur F., 70, 126, 169, 200
Burns, James MacGregor, 169-170, 273
Burrows, Abe, 528
Burton, Richard, 545
Busch, Joseph P. 223
Bush, George, 246-247, 273
Butz, Earl L., 70-71, 113, 126, 149, 170, 201-202, 247
Byrd, Don, 99
Byrd, Harry F., Jr., 170, 340
Byrd, Robert C., 99, 126, 170, 247, 273, 340, 366
Byrne, William M., Jr., 366

C

Caetano, Marcelo, 397
Cagney, James, 504
Caine, Michael, 455, 504, 536
Calder, Alexander, Jr., 71
Callas, Maria, 519
Callaway, Howard H., 232
Camara, Helder, 341
Campbell, Charles F., 99
Campbell, Ernest T., 566
Caplin, Mortimer, 202
Capra, Frank, 504
Carleson, Robert B., 310
Carlisle, Kitty, 528
Carlson, Norman A., 99
Carmichael, Stokely, 55
Caron, Leslie, 504
Carpenter, Liz, 331
Carr, Robert, 397
Carroll, Clay, 578
Carson, Gordon B., 554
Carter, Jimmy, 247
Cary, W. Sterling, 566
Casals, Pablo, 520, 554
Cassini, Oleg, 460
Castle, William, 536
Castro, Fidel, 341, 397
Cavett, Dick, 536
Cawley, Donald F., 99
Ceausescu, Nicolae, 397
Celler, Emanuel, 248, 455

Cernan, Eugene A., 572
Chafetz, Morris E., 491
Chagall, Marc, 456, 554
Chamberlain, John, 71, 127
Champion, Gower, 528
Champlin, Charles, 504
Chancellor, John, 45, 466
Channing, Carol, 528-529
Chapin, Schuyler, 456, 520
Chiang Ching-kuo, 350, 366
Chiao Kuan-hua, 397
Childers, Erskine, 170, 398
Chiles, Lawton M., Jr., 171
Chisholm, Shirley, 171
Chou En-lai, 351, 367, 398, 419, 447-448
Chukovskaya, Lydia, 398
Church, Frank, 149
Clague, Ewan, 203
Clark, Kenneth B., 45, 56, 113
Clark, Mark W., 233, 367
Clark, Ramsey, 100, 149, 274, 367
Clarke, Arthur C., 485, 572-573
Clausen, A. W., 149, 203
Clements, William P., Jr., 71, 233, 398
Clifford, Clark M., 233
Clurman, Harold, 529
Coffin, William Sloane, 46
Cohen, Alexander H., 529
Cohen, Wilbur J., 491
Colbert, Jim, 579
Colby, William E., 171
Cole, Edward N., 127
Coleman, James, 113
Collins, James M., 203
Colson, Charles W., 56, 274, 554
Commager, Henry Steele, 274
Conese, Eugene P., 72
Connally, John B., Jr., 46, 72, 100, 127, 149-150, 171, 203-204, 224, 248, 274-275, 367, 398, 419, 554
Connery, Sean, 505, 554
Connor, John T., 275
Connor, Reginald, 72
Constantine II, 399
Conte, Silvio O., 46
Cook, G. Bradford, 72
Cook, Leon F., 56
Cooke, Alistair, 46, 127, 171, 275, 467, 537, 555, 579
Cooke, Jack Kent, 579
Cooney, Patrick, 399
Cooper, John A. D., 492
Cooper, John Sherman, 172
Cooper, Joseph D., 492
Cooper, Owen, 276
Copland, Aaron, 520
Cort, Stewart S., 419
Cosby, Bill, 555
Costa-Gavras, Constantin, 505, 545
Cotton, Norris, 172, 276, 367
Courreges, Andre, 460

Court, Margaret, 579
Cowley, Malcolm, 485
Cox, Archibald, 276
Cox, Harvey, 566
Coyne, Thomas J., 46
Crampton, Bruce, 579
Cranston, Alan, 172, 233, 248, 419, 467, 537
Crawford, Joan, 505
Crist, Judith, 505
Cronin, Joe, 579
Cronkite, Walter, 56, 172, 277, 467-468, 545, 555
Crozier, Brian, 448
Culp, Robert, 537
Culver, John C., 172
Curtis, Carl T., 277
Curtis, Tony, 505

D

Dalai Lama, 351, 555
Daley, Richard J., 310
Dali, Salvador, 456
Dash, Samuel, 277
Daud, Sardar Mohammed, 351
David, Hal, 505
Davis, Bette, 506, 529
Davis, Edward M., 100, 555
Davis, Sammy, Jr., 506, 546
Day, Doris, 537
Dayan, Moshe, 420
Dean, John W., III, 277-278
Debus, Kurt, 73, 573
de Butts, John D., 73
Decter, Midge, 331
Degler, Carl N., 331
de Guiringaud, Louis, 420
de la Flor, Miguel Angel, 341
de la Renta, Oscar, 461
DeLorean, John Z., 128, 321
Denenberg, Herbert S., 73
Dent, Frederick B., 204, 311
Dent, John H., 73
de Olloqui, Jose Juan, 341
DiBona, Charles J., 128
Dickinson, William L., 150, 204
Diebold, John, 74, 204
Diederichs, Nicholaas, 74
Dietrich, Marlene, 46, 537, 546
Digges, Sam Cook, 468
Dillman, Grant, 468
Dinitz, Simcha, 420
DiSalle, Michael, 205
Dixon, Robert G., 468
Dobriansky, Lev E., 150
Dole, Robert J., 248, 278
Domenici, Pete V., 486
Dominick, Peter H., 278
Donatelli, Augie, 580
Dong, Pham Van, 368
Doolittle, James, 368

Doub, William O., 128
Douglas, Jack, 486
Douglas, Kirk, 506
Douglas, William O., 47, 150, 173, 224-225, 555
Douglas-Home, Alec, 150, 399-400, 421
Drapeau, Jean, 321
Drysdale, Don, 580
Dubos, Rene, 128
Duc, Nguyen Phu, 368
Dunn, Winfield, 278
du Pont, Pierre S., IV, 279

E

Eagleton, Thomas F., 469
East, Catherine S., 332
Eastwood, Clint, 506, 546
Eban, Abba, 421-423, 443, 448
Echeverria (Alvarez), Luis, 351
Eckhardt, Bob, 128
Eckstein, Otto, 205
Eddy, Edward D., 332
Edwards, Charles C., 113, 492
Egan, William A., 129
Ehrlich, Paul R., 129
Ehrlichman, John D., 129, 173, 249, 279
Eisenhower, Julie Nixon, 173
Ekangaki, Nzo, 423
Eklund, Coy G., 74
Elazar, David, 423
Elizabeth II, 400
Ellison, Ralph, 486
Ellsberg, Daniel, 368
Elmendorf, Thomas, 492
Engman, Lewis A., 74-75
Erte, 461
Ervin, Sam J., Jr., 47, 100, 151, 174-175, 225, 250, 279-281, 368, 469, 546
Etzioni, Amitai, 556
Evans, Daniel J., 175
Ewing, Maurice, 129

F

Fahmy, Ismail, 424
Faisal (Ibn Abdel Aziz), 424
Faisal, Saud al-, 424
Falk, Peter, 506, 537, 546
Fallaci, Oriana, 556
Farr, William, 469
Fasi, Frank, 326
Feeney, Charles (Chub), 580
Feller, Bob, 580
Fiedler, Arthur, 520
Fiedler, Edgar R., 205
Finklea, John F., 130
Finley, Charles O., 556, 580
Fischer, John H., 47, 57, 114

Fisher, Eddie, 546
Flanigan, Peter M., 75
Flemming, Harry S., 250
Flexner, James T., 486
Flood, Curt, 580
Flood, Daniel J., 342, 369
Flournoy, Houston I., 175
Fogarty, Anne, 461
Folsom, Richard G., 130
Fonda, Jane, 369
Fong, Hiram L., 250, 369
Fooner, Michael, 100
Ford, Christina (Mrs. Henry), 546
Ford, Gerald R., 57, 151, 175-176, 250-251, 281, 311, 546, 580
Ford, Henry, II, 47, 75, 130
Ford, Wendell H., 281
Foreman, George, 581
Fosse, Bob, 507
Foy, Lewis W., 130
Foyt, A. J., 581
Franciscus, James, 507
Franjieh, Suleiman, 424
Frankl, Victor, 556
Frankovich, Mike, 507
Frazier, Joe, 581
Freedman, Daniel X., 492
Freedman, Lewis, 537
Freeman, S. David, 131
Frenzel, Bill, 251
Fri, Robert W., 131
Friedan, Betty, 332
Friedkin, William, 507
Friedman, Milton, 57, 131, 205
Friendly, Fred W., 469-470
Frizzell, Kent, 57
Fromm, Eric, 48
Fruchart, Armond, 131
Fukuda, Takeo, 351
Fulbright, J. William, 151-152, 176, 369, 400-401, 424-425, 470

G

Gabo, Naum, 456
Gabriel, Roman, 581
Galbraith, John Kenneth, 76, 205-206
Gallico, Paul, 486, 546, 556
Gandhi, Indira, 352, 369, 547, 556-557, 566
Gannon, Robert I., 566
Gardner, Helen, 486, 557
Gardner, John W., 281, 311
Garment, Leonard, 58
Garvey, Ed, 581
Gebhard, Paul H., 557
Geoghegan, John J., 486
Gernreich, Rudi, 461
Gerstacker, Carl A., 76, 131
Gerstenberg, Richard C., 76, 132, 206, 321
Getty, J. Paul, 76, 557

Ghorra, Edouard, 426
Gibron, Abe, 582
Gibson, Althea, 582
Gibson, Weldon B., 76
Gillespie, Alastair, 342
Giscard d'Estaing, Valery, 73, 401
Gish, Lillian, 48, 507, 538
Giulini, Carlo Maria, 520
Gizikis, Phaidon, 401
Glasser, Otto J., 573
Gleazer, Edmund J., Jr., 114
Glenn, Wayne E., 426
Goich, Dan, 582
Gold, Victor, 470
Goldberg, Arthur J., 225
Goldman, Eric F., 48, 251, 282
Goldmark, Peter C., 326
Goldwater, Barry M., 49, 77, 152, 176, 233-234, 251-253, 282-283, 369-370, 470-471
Goodman, Benny, 521
Goodman, Julian, 471, 547
Goodpaster, Andrew J., 234, 401
Gordon, Kermit, 311
Gordon, Ruth, 507
Gorman, Tom, 582
Gott, Edwin H., 77
Gould, William R., 573
Graham, Billy, 49, 58, 370, 567, 582
Graham, Katharine, 283, 472
Granatelli, Andy, 583
Grant, Cary, 508
Gray, L. Patrick, III, 101, 225, 284
Gray, Mary W., 332
Gray, Simon, 529
Grayson, C. Jackson, Jr., 206-207
Grechko, Andrei A., 402
Green, Marshall, 370
Greenstein, Fred I., 177
Greer, Germaine, 333
Griffin, Robert P., 284
Griffith, William E., 352, 402
Griffiths, Martha W., 333
Gromyko, Andrei A., 353, 370, 402, 426, 448
Gross, H. R., 371
Grunert, Horst, 402
Guinan, Matthew, 207
Gurash, John T., 152
Gurney, Edward J., 284
Guttmacher, Alan F., 493
Gwinn, William P., 321

H

Hackman, Gene, 508
Haggerty, William W., 557, 573
Haig, Alexander M., Jr., 284-285
Haldeman, H. R., 101, 253, 285
Hall, Paul, 207
Halston, 461

Hamilton, Lee H., 426
Hammer, Armand, 77, 403
Hanks, Nancy, 456-457
Harper, John D., 49, 77
Harriman, W. Averell, 153
Harrington, Michael J., 207
Harris, Leslie, 77
Harrison, John S., 207
Hart, Philip A., 77, 285
Hartley, Fred T., 132
Hatcher, Richard G., 58, 311, 326
Hatfield, Mark O., 49, 77, 153, 177, 234, 371, 567
Hathaway, Henry, 508
Hathaway, William D., 253
Hawn, Goldie, 508
Hayakawa, S. I., 114-115
Hays, Wayne L., 285, 371
Head, Edith, 461
Heath, Edward, 78, 403
Hebert, F. Edward, 234, 371
Hechler, Ken, 132
Heckart, Eileen, 529-530
Heckler, Margaret M., 78
Heide, Wilma Scott, 333
Heikal, Mohammed Hassanein, 427
Heller, Walter W., 78
Helms, Jesse A., 78, 153, 208, 285
Helpern, Milton, 493
Hepburn, Katharine, 508
Herberg, Will, 153, 567
Herman, Woody, 521
Herschensohn, Bruce, 472
Herzog, Haim, 427
Herzog, Whitey, 583
Hesburgh, Theodore M., 334, 568
Hester, James M., 115
Heston, Charlton, 509
Hewitt, William A., 78-79
Heyns, Roger W., 115
Hickel, Walter J., 115, 558
Hill, Jesse, 583
Hitchcock, Alfred, 509, 547
Hoadley, Walter E., 208
Hodgson, James D., 208
Hoffer, Eric, 101
Hoffman, Charles A., 493
Hoffman, Dustin, 509
Hogan, Lawrence J., 177
Holbrook, Hal, 538
Hollander, Lorin, 521
Hollings, Ernest F., 285
Holm, Celeste, 509, 538
Holman, Carl, 58
Holt, Marjorie S., 115
Holton, Linwood, 59, 254
Homer, Sidney, 208
Hood, Edwin M., 79
Hook, Sidney, 116, 558
Hooks, Benjamin L., 59, 472, 538
Hope, Bob, 50, 509
Horan, John J., 493

Horn, Stephen, 59
Horne, Lena, 521
Horne, Marilyn, 522
Houseman, John, 530
Hoveyda, Amir Abbas, 427
Hoving, Thomas P. F., 457
Howard, John A., 559
Howard, Trevor, 510
Howsam, Bob, 583
Hruska, Roman L., 79
Huang Hua, 342, 353, 371
Hubbard, David Allen, 568
Hudnut, William H., III, 177
Hughes, Harold E., 101-102, 178, 254, 311, 371-372, 493
Hughes, Thomas L., 154
Humphrey, Hubert H., 79, 132, 154, 178, 208, 234, 254, 286, 312, 372, 404, 427
Hunt, E. Howard, 286
Hunt, Lamar, 583
Hunt, Sherman, 132
Hunt, William H., 178
Hunter, Jim (Catfish), 584
Hunter, Ross, 510
Huntley, Chet, 116, 472
Hurok, Sol, 457, 522, 530, 547, 559
Hurwitch, Robert A., 342
Hussein I, 427-428
Huston, John, 510
Hutchins, Robert M., 116, 254
Hutchinson, Edward, 287
Hutt, Peter B., 494

I

Iacocca, Lee A., 80, 178, 321, 559
Ibuka, Masaru, 559
Ichord, Richard H., 404
Ikard, Frank N., 80, 133
Inayama, Yoshihiro, 353
Inbau, Fred E., 225
Inouye, Daniel K., 255, 287
Ionesco, Eugene, 487
Isaacs, Norman, 472

J

Jackson, Henry M., 81, 133, 154, 209, 287, 404, 428
Jackson, Jesse L., 59
Jackson, Joseph H., 102
Jackson, Maynard H., Jr., 59
Jacoby, Neil H., 81
Jalloud, Abdul Salam, 405, 429
James, C. L. R., 343
James, Daniel, Jr., 372
Jenner, Albert E., Jr., 225
Jobert, Michel, 405, 547
Johanneson, Olafur, 405

Johari, Khir, 494
John, Mr., 462
Johns, Glynis, 530
Johnson, Betsey, 462
Johnson, Ladybird (Mrs. Lyndon B.), 559
Johnson, Nicholas, 81, 473, 538-539, 559
Johnson, Rafer, 559
Jones, James H., 82
Jones, Jenkin Lloyd, 178, 510, 560
Jones, Mary Gardiner, 82
Jones, Reginald H., 133
Jones, Robert Trent, 584
Jordan, Barbara, 59, 178
Jordan, Vernon E., Jr., 60, 179, 312

K

Kael, Pauline, 457, 510
Kahn, Herman, 60, 116, 154, 255, 353
Kaiser, Edgar F., 82
Kalmbach, Herbert W., 287
Kanowitz, Leo, 334
Kaplan, John, 102
Karayn, James, 539
Karp, David, 539
Karsh, Yousuf, 457
Kastenmeier, Robert W., 133, 473
Katzenbach, Nicholas deB., 102
Kaunda, Kenneth, 443
Kauper, Thomas E., 82, 209
Keating, Kenneth B., 429
Keino, Kip, 584
Kellerman, Sally, 511
Kelley, Clarence M., 102-103
Kelly, Arthur F., 322
Kelly, Jack, 584
Kemp, Jack, 179, 372
Kendall, Donald M., 82, 353, 405
Kenna, E. Douglas, 209
Kennedy, Edward M., 50, 60, 155, 179-180, 209, 255-256, 288, 312, 372-373, 405-406, 429, 494, 547
Kennedy, Eugene C., 560
Kernodle, John R., 494
Kerr, Malcolm, 429
Kerr, Walter, 530
Keys, Ancel, 495
Kfir, Nira, 539
Kheel, Theodore W., 210
Kiernan, Edward J., 104
Kim Jong Pil, 354
King, Billie Jean, 584
King, Kerryn, 133
Kinnear, George, 180
Kirchner, Leon, 522
Kirk, Dudley, 134
Kirk, Norman, 354
Kirk, Russell, 116
Kissinger, Henry A., 134, 155-157, 180, 235, 288,

343, 354, 373-374, 406-408, 429-431, 449, 473, 547-548, 560
Kittay, Sol, 495
Kleindienst, Richard G., 61, 83, 104, 226
Klutznick, Philip M., 104
Knauer, Virginia H., 210
Koch, Howard H., 511
Koenig, Franz Cardinal, 568
Kollek, Teddy, 431
Kornberg, Arthur, 495
Kosciusko-Morizet, Jacques, 83
Kostelanetz, Andre, 522, 548
Kosygin, Alexei N., 355, 408
Kramer, Stanley, 511
Kranzberg, Melvin, 560
Kreisky, Bruno, 431
Kreps, Juanita M., 334
Kristol, Irving, 83, 473, 560
Krock, Arthur, 473
Krogh, Egil, Jr., 288
Kuchel, Thomas H., 61
Kuhfuss, William J., 83, 210
Kuhn, Bowie, 585
Kurland, Philip B., 226
Ky, Nguyen Cao, 374

Lindsay, John V., 104, 181, 256, 326
Link, Arthur S., 181, 289
Linowitz, Sol M., 327
Liotard-Vogt, Pierre, 84
Lippmann, Walter, 50, 182, 474
List, Robert, 104
Lloyd, Frank, 458
Lloyd, Norman, 540
Loe, Harald, 496
Loevinger, Lee, 84
Lon Nol, 375
Long, Robert W., 84
Long, Russell B., 256
Loos, Anita, 334, 548
Loren, Sophia, 548
Losey, Joseph, 512
Louis, Joe, 548, 585
Love, John A., 134-135
Low, George M., 574
Luce, Charles F., 135
Luce, Clare Boothe, 158, 256, 289, 334, 355, 474, 548, 561
Luns, Joseph, 235, 409
Lyman, Richard W., 50, 117
Lynn, James T., 327

L

LaFontaine, Hernan, 117
Laird, Melvin R., 157-158, 180, 235, 288, 313, 375
Lam, Pham Dang, 375
Lamborn, Robert L., 117
Landau, Jack, 474
Landon, Alfred M., 181, 289
Lansbury, Angela, 530
Larrabee, Eric, 457-458
Larry, R. Heath, 84, 210
Lasagna, Louis C., 495
Lasch, Christopher, 181
Lastiri, Raul, 343
Lawrence, Mary Wells, 84
Lear, Norman, 539
LeBailly, Eugene B., 343
Leber, Georg, 408
Lee, Harold B., 50
Lee Kuan Yew, 355, 474
Leggett, Robert L., 181
Leigh (Guzman), Gustavo, 343
Lemmon, Jack, 511
Lemons, Abe, 585
Lennard, Henry L., 496
Leonard, Bill, 474
Leone, Giovanni, 560
Leontief, Wassily, 561
Lerner, Alan J., 530-531
Levine, Joseph E., 511
Liebermann, Rolf, 522
Liebert, Robert, 540
Lindbergh, Charles A., 134, 449, 574

M

Maazel, Lorin, 523
MacDonald, John D., 487, 548
MacDonald, Peter, 61
Macdonald, Torbert H., 474, 540
MacInnes, William C., 117
Mackerras, Charles, 523
Madden, Carl H., 85
Magruder, Jeb Stuart, 290
Mahon, George H., 182
Maier, Henry W., 327-328
Mailer, Norman, 50, 487
Makarova, Natalia, 531
Malek, Frederic V., 182
Malik, Adam, 449
Malik, Yakov A., 450
Mandel, Marvin, 182, 290
Manglapus, Raul, 355
Mankiewicz, Frank, 256
Manley, Michael, 444, 475
Mann, Forbes, 235
Mannes, Marya, 118
Mansfield, Mike, 158, 182, 235, 257, 290, 375-376, 475
Mao Tse-tung, 376
Marceau, Marcel, 531, 561
Marcos, Ferdinand E., 355
Marland, Sidney P., Jr., 118
Marston, Robert Q., 496
Martin, Billy, 585
Martin, George C., 313
Martin, William McChesney, Jr., 85
Marvin, Lee, 561

Mast, Hans, 210
Mathias, Charles McC., Jr., 183, 290
Mavros, George, 409
May, Ernest R., 574
May, William F., 51
Mayhew, David R., 183
Mays, Benjamin E., 61
Mays, Willie, 585
McCall, Tom, 135
McCarthy, Eugene J., 183, 291
McClellan, John L., 105
McCloskey, Michael, 135
McCloskey, Paul N., Jr., 183
McCloskey, Robert J., 431, 475
McCollister, John Y., 376
McCord, James I., 568
McCord, James W., 291
McCracken, Paul W., 85, 183, 210
McDonagh, Edward C., 136
McDonnell, George F., 136
McGann, John R., 568
McGee, Frank, 183
McGill, William J., 118
McGovern, George S., 62, 183-184, 236, 257-258, 291-292, 313, 376-377, 497
McKay, John, 586
McKay, K. Gunn, 377
McKay, Robert B., 105
McKetta, John J., Jr., 136
McKinney, George W., Jr., 211
McLaughlin, Joseph, 226
McLeod, Fred, 586
McMahon, John A., 497
McNamara, Francis J., 158
McWilliams, Carey, 476
Mead, Margaret, 136, 313, 497
Means, Russell, 62
Meany, George, 85-86, 158, 184, 211-213, 258-259, 292, 328, 377, 586
Meeds, Lloyd, 62
Mehgi, Muhammed, 432
Mehta, Mehli, 523
Mehta, Zubin, 458, 523
Meir, Golda, 335, 432-433, 548, 561, 568
Melinkoff, David, 226
Melnick, Daniel, 512
Menninger, Karl A., 497-498
Merrick, David, 531
Meserve, Robert W., 227
Messer, Thomas, 458
Michener, James A., 569
Miles, Leland, 487
Milford, Dale, 378
Miller, Arnold R., 136, 213
Miller, E. Spencer, 322
Miller, Henry, 458, 487, 561
Miller, Jason, 531
Millett, John D., 118
Milliken, William G., 476
Mills, Wilbur D., 51, 137, 184, 213, 378, 409
Millstein, Ira M., 335

Minh, Duong Van, 378
Minnelli, Liza, 512
Minow, Newton N., 185
Mintoff, Dom, 409
Mitchell, John N., 292-293
Mitchell, Martha (Mrs. John N.), 293
Mitchell, Maurice B., 488
Mitchell, Parren J., 62
Mitchum, Robert, 512, 548
Mitterrand, Francois, 410
Mobutu Sese Seko, 410, 444
Modell, Art, 586
Mollenhoff, Clark R., 476
Mondale, Walter F., 62, 185, 214, 236, 293, 314, 476, 561
Monroe, Gerald M., 574
Monroe, William, 476
Moorer, Thomas H., 159, 236, 378, 410
Moos, Malcolm C., 119, 185, 293
Morita, Akio, 86, 561
Morris, Richard B., 259
Morton, Rogers C. B., 63, 137
Moss, John E., 185
Moss, Larry, 137
Moss, Robert V., Jr., 379, 569
Mostel, Zero, 512
Moynihan, Daniel P., 356
Mujibur Rahman, 356
Muller, Steven, 562
Murphy, Patrick V., 105-106
Murphy, Reg, 476
Muskie, Edmund S., 138, 186-187, 214, 294, 322, 379, 410

N

Nader, Ralph, 138, 187
Nakasone, Yasuhiro, 214
Nathan, Robert, 458
Neal, Fred Warner, 159
Neaman, Samuel, 86
Nedzi, Lucien N., 63
Needham, James J., 86
Nelson, Gaylord, 314, 498
Neustadt, Richard E., 187
Newcomer, Leland B., 119
Newell, Barbara, 119
Newman, Paul, 512
Nicholson, E. L., 87
Nicklaus, Jack, 586-587
Nixon, Richard M., 25-27, 28-43, 51, 63, 87, 106, 138-139, 159-160, 188-189, 214-215, 237, 259-260, 294-297, 314-315, 328, 356, 379-382, 433, 450, 477, 498, 512, 549
Nizel, Abraham E., 498
Nizer, Louis, 227
Norris, Albert S., 498
Nunn, Sam, 189
Nureyev, Rudolf, 532, 549, 562
Nyquist, Ewald B., 119-120

O

O'Brien, Edna, 488
O'Connell, David, 410
Ogilvie, Bruce, 562, 587
Ohira, Masayoshi, 357
Olds, Glenn A., 106
Oliver, Bob, 587
Olsen, Merlin, 587
O'Neill, Thomas P., Jr., 160, 190
Ormandy, Eugene, 523
Owens, Jesse, 587
Owens, Wayne, 190

P

Paar, Jack, 549
Packwood, Robert, 190, 260
Pahlavi, Mohammad Reza, 87, 139, 335, 357, 434
Palance, Jack, 513
Paley, William S., 477
Palme, Olof, 383, 411
Papadopoulos, George, 411
Papp, Joseph, 532
Pappas, Milt, 587
Parker, Harry S., III, 459
Parker, Wes, 588
Parnassus, George, 588
Pastore, John O., 160, 477
Paterno, Joe, 588
Paterson, Basil A., 298
Patman, Wright, 87, 190, 215
Patolichev, Nikolai S., 88
Paul VI, 450, 562, 569
Paul, Noel S., 477
Pawlikowski, John T., 569
Pechman, Joseph A., 215
Pell, Claiborne, 411
Pelligrino, Michele Cardinal, 569
Pepper, Claude, 107
Percy, Charles H., 107, 139, 215, 298-299, 315, 477
Perez, Carlos Andres, 344
Peron, Juan D., 344
Perot, H. Ross, 88
Petersen, Henry E., 260
Peterson, Peter G., 140, 190
Pettis, Jerry L., 357
Philip, Prince, 549
Phillippe, Maurice, 588
Phillips, Howard, 190, 299, 316
Picker, David, 513
Pickle, J. J., 190
Pierpoint, Robert, 434
Pike, Otis G., 238
Pinochet (Ugarte), Augusto, 344-345
Pitts, James, 140
Plaza, Galo, 345
Plummer, Christopher, 532

Poage, W. R., 216, 316
Podell, Bertram L., 216
Pomerance, Rocky, 107
Pompidou, Georges, 477
Popper, Hans, 498
Porter, George, 140
Portman, John, 322
Potter, Philip, 450
Powell, Anthony, 488
Powell, Lewis F., Jr., 227
Previn, Dory, 524
Price, Raymond K., Jr., 260
Priestley, J. B., 549
Prinz, Joachim, 569
Proxmire, William, 140, 160, 191, 216, 238, 260, 299, 383, 499

Q

Qaddafi, Muammar el-, 412, 435, 444
Quaal, Ward L., 540
Quant, Mary, 562
Quarles, John R., 574
Quayle, Anthony, 513

R

Rabin, Itzhak, 160
Radnitz, Robert, 513, 549
Ragle, Thomas B., 120
Railsback, Thomas F., 191
Ralston, John, 588
Rand, Sally, 550
Randolph, Jennings, 322
Rangel, Charles, 63
Rarick, John R., 160
Rather, Dan, 478
Rausch, James S., 120, 570
Ray, Dixy Lee, 140, 335
Ray Satyajit, 514
Raynes, Burt F., 52, 120
Reagan, Ronald, 107, 140, 191, 216-217, 299-300, 383, 478
Reasoner, Harry, 261, 300, 345, 435
Reed, Willis, 588
Reedy, George E., 261
Regan, Donald T., 52, 88-89, 120
Rehnquist, William H., 227, 563
Reinecke, Ed, 261
Reinert, Paul C., 121
Reischauer, Edwin O., 121, 140, 161, 358, 450
Reiss, Paul, 121
Renoir, Jean, 540
Reston, James, 261
Rettaliata, John T., 121
Reuss, Henry S., 300
Revson, Charles, 462
Reynolds, Debbie, 532, 541
Rhodes, John J., 300

Rhyne, Charles S., 227, 451
Ribicoff, Abraham A., 108, 217, 328, 412
Riccardo, John J., 574
Richardson, Elliot L., 64, 108, 191-192, 238, 262, 301, 316, 383, 478
Richardson, Ralph, 550
Richey, Charles R., 478
Rickover, Hyman G., 52, 239
Riegle, Donald W., Jr., 262
Rifai, Zaid al-, 436
Riggs, Bobby, 589
Riles, Wilson, 52, 122
Ripa, Louis C., 323
Ritt, Martin, 514
Rizzo, Frank L., 108, 262, 550
Roa, Raul, 345
Roberts, Clifford, 589
Robinson, Brooks, 589
Robison, Howard W., 383
Roche, James M., 89
Roche, John P., 141
Rockefeller, David, 89, 141, 358
Rockefeller, John D., III, 52
Rockefeller, Nelson A., 53, 108, 141, 228, 262, 317, 478
Rockwell, W. F., Jr., 323
Rogers, Ginger, 514
Rogers, William P., 161, 192, 262, 345-346, 358, 384
Romney, George W., 53
Romulo, Carlos P., 358
Ronan, William J., 323
Roosa, Robert V., 89
Rose, Daniel, 328
Rose, Pete, 589
Rosenbloom, Carroll, 589-590
Rosenhan, David L., 499
Rosenman, Samuel I., 301
Rosenthal, A. M., 479
Rosenthal, Benjamin S., 161, 412
Rostow, Eugene V., 436
Roth, Paul, 514
Rowan, Stephen, 479
Ruckelshaus, Jill, 335
Ruckelshaus, William D., 108-109, 142, 262, 301
Rudel, Julius, 524
Ruedy, John, 436
Rule, Elton H., 479
Rush, Kenneth, 359, 384, 412
Rusk, Dean, 161-162, 239, 263, 302, 451
Rust, Edward B., 90, 217
Rustin, Bayard, 64
Ryan, Leo J., 142

S

Sabah, Sebah al-Salim al-, 436
Sadat, Anwar el-, 437
Saint, Eva Marie, 533
St. John, Jeffrey, 488
Saint Laurent, Yves, 462

Sakharov, Andrei D., 412-413, 563
Salinger, Pierre, 263, 302
Samuelson, Paul A., 90
Sanders, Beulah, 317
Sanderson, Derek, 550, 590
Santarelli, Donald E., 109
Sapir, Pinchas, 437
Saqqaf, Omar, 438
Sarasin, Ronald A., 217, 302
Sarnoff, Robert W., 479, 541, 575
Sarnoff, Thomas, 480, 541
Sassoon, Vidal, 462
Saunders, Charles B., Jr., 122
Saxbe, William B., 192, 228, 263, 302, 385
Scali, John A., 162, 346, 438
Scammon, Richard M., 263
Schaber, Gordon, 228
Schaefer, A., 217
Scheel, Walter, 413
Scherle, William J., 303
Schillebeecky, Edward C., 570
Schiller, Bradley R., 317
Schindler, Alexander M., 570
Schippers, Thomas, 524
Schlafly, Phyllis, 239
Schlesinger, Arthur M., Jr., 162
Schlesinger, James R., 162-163, 239
Schlosser, Herbert S., 541
Schmidt, Benno C., 499
Schmidt, Helmut, 385, 413
Schmitt, Harrison, 575
Schramm, Tex, 590
Schroeder, Patricia, 335
Schwartz, Bernard, 228
Schwartz, Walter A., 542
Scott, George C., 514
Scott, Hugh, 53, 109, 163, 192-193, 303, 317, 359, 385
Scott, Stanley S., 64
Scott, William L., 385
Scull, Robert, 459
Seaborg, Glenn T., 142
Seaver, Tom, 590
Seawell, Donald, 533
Servan-Schreiber, Jean-Jacques, 414
Sevareid, Eric, 264, 303
Seymour, Whitney N., Jr., 110
Shafei, Hussein, 439
Shafer, Raymond P., 499
Shapiro, Irving S., 90
Shaw, Irwin, 488
Sheen, Fulton J., 570
Short, Robert E., 590
Shostakovich, Dmitri, 524
Shriver, R. Sargent, 304, 317
Shulman, Irving, 563
Shultz, George P., 91, 142, 218
Shumilin, Boris T., 563
Shumway, Forrest N., 143
Signoret, Simone, 563
Sihanouk, Norodom, 163, 359, 385-386, 550

Sikes, Robert L. F., 359
Simkin, William E., 218
Simmons, Richard P., 219
Simon, Neil, 533
Simon, Norton, 323
Simon, William E., 143
Simpson, O. J., 590
Sinatra, Frank, 480, 524
Singh, Swaran, 359
Sirica, John J., 228, 304
Sisco, Joseph J., 439
Sisouk Na Champassak, 386
Sizemore, Barbara, 122
Slater, Terry, 591
Smith, Arnold, 414
Smith, Austin, 193
Smith, Chesterfield, 304, 480
Smith, Howard K., 91, 193, 219, 239-240, 304, 439, 480
Smith, Ian, 444-445
Smith, Rufus Z., 346
Smith, Steve, 591
Soames, Christopher, 92, 414
Solti, Georg, 525
Solzhenitsyn, Alexander I., 414
Sondheim, Stephen, 525, 550
Sosthene Fernandez, 387
Souvanna Phouma, 387
Spahn, Warren, 591
Speer, Edgar B., 219
Spencer, William I., 92
Spiegel, John P., 53
Spilhaus, Athelstan, 563
Spock, Benjamin, 563
Springer, Axel, 415, 439
Staats, Elmer B., 194
Stair, Clark E., 323
Stanmeyer, William A., 110
Stans, Maurice H., 264, 305
Stanton, Frank, 480
Stark, Fortney H., 305
Starker, Janos, 525
Steele, Robert H., 387
Steiger, Rod, 564
Stein, Herbert, 220, 481
Steinem, Gloria, 335-336
Steiner, George, 415
Stendahl, Krister, 564
Stennis, John C., 240
Stern, Herbert Jay, 229
Stevenson, Adlai E., III, 194, 240, 305
Stewart-Smith, Geoffery, 415
Stokes, Carl B., 481
Stokes, Louis, 64, 318
Stone, Andrew, 515
Strauss, Robert S., 264-265, 305
Streisand, Barbra, 533, 550
Strong, Maurice F., 144, 564
Stulberg, Gordon, 515
Sugarman, Jule M., 499
Sullivan, James R., 324

Sullivan, William H., 387
Sultan, Zayed Ben, 439
Sulzberger, Arthur Ochs, 481
Sunkel, Osvaldo, 346
Surrey, Stanley S., 220
Susann, Jacqueline, 488-489, 564
Susskind, David, 564
Symington, Stuart, 92, 163
Szasz, Thomas, 499

T

Talese, Gay, 329
Talmadge, Herman E., 92
Tanaka, Kakuei, 53, 93, 359-360
Tannenbaum, Stanley, 93
Tanner, N. Eldon, 336
Taylor, Arthur R., 93, 481, 542
Taylor, Elizabeth, 462, 551, 564
Taylor, Maxwell D., 240
Taylor, Rod, 54
Tekoah, Yosef, 440
Teller, Edward, 144, 575
Terry, Walter, 533
Thach, Nguyen Co, 388
Thanom Kittikachorn, 388
Thieu, Nguyen Van, 388-389
Tho, Le Duc, 389, 451
Thomas, Lewis, 500
Thomas, Lowell, 481
Thompson, James R., 265
Thompson, John, 591
Thompson, Robert, 390
Thomson, Meldrim, Jr., 194
Thone, Charles, 194
Thurmond, Strom, 240-241
Tiomkin, Dimitri, 515, 525
Tito, Josip Broz, 415
Tolbert, William R., Jr., 445, 459
Tondel, Lyman M., Jr., 229
Torrijos (Herrera), Omar, 347, 415
Tower, John G., 195, 318
Train, Russell E., 144
Traynor, Roger J., 482
Trent, Darrell M., 145
Trevino, Lee, 591
Trudeau, Pierre Elliott, 347
Truffaut, Francois, 515
Tuchman, Barbara, 163, 265, 306
Tung, Hoang, 390
Tunney, John V., 110, 145, 265, 306
Turbeville, Gus, 565
Turk, Edmund J., 145
Tutko, Thomas, 592
Twiggy, 515

U

Udall, Morris K., 145

Udall, Stewart L., 324
Uhlman, Wesley C., 324, 329
Ullman, Al, 195
Ullman, Liv, 515
Underwood, Vernon O., 592
Unser, Al, 592
Ushiba, Nobuhiko, 93, 361

V

Valenti, Jack, 516
Van Allen, James A., 575
Van Andel, Jay, 94
Veeck, Bill, 592
Verity, C. William, 94, 145
Vilar, Esther, 336
Vinson, Carl, 54
Vogelsinger, Hubert, 592
Volcker, Paul A., 94
Volpe, John A., 324
Von Braun, Wernher, 575

W

Wagner, Robert F., 265
Wakefield, Stephen A., 146
Waldheim, Kurt, 164, 441, 451-452
Waldie, Jerome R., 306, 482
Walker, E. Cardon, 516
Walker, Walter, 241
Wallace, George C., 265-266, 570
Wallace, Irving, 489
Wallis, Hal, 516
Wallis, W. Allen, 195, 482
Walske, Carl, 146
Walum, Laurel, 336
Ward, Barbara, 146, 565
Warner, Rawleigh, Jr., 94-95, 146
Warren, Earl, 195, 266, 452
Watson, Thomas J., Jr., 220
Wattenberg, Ben J., 306
Wayne, John, 122, 516, 551, 565
Wearly, W. L., 95
Webster, Leslie T., 500
Wedgeworth, Robert, 489
Weeden, Donald E., 95
Weicker, Lowell P., Jr., 54, 195, 266, 306-307, 324
Weinberger, Caspar W., 65, 146, 195-196, 318
Weiskopf, Tom, 592-593
Weisner, M. F., 241
Weitz, John, 463
Welch, Louie, 329
Wellman, William, 517
Werner, Jesse, 576
West, Frederic W., Jr., 95, 325
Weyand, Frederick C., 390
Whitaker, John C., 65
White, Paul Dudley, 500

White, Theodore H., 452
Whitehead, Clay T., 482, 542
Whitehead, Robert, 533
Whitelaw, William, 416
Whitlam, Gough, 307, 361-362, 390
Whitman, Marina v. N., 96
Wickman, Krister, 390-391, 416
Wiesner, Jerome B., 576
Wildavsky, Aaron, 196, 266, 307
Wilder, Alec, 525
Wilder, Thornton, 489-490, 517, 565, 570
Wilkins, Caroline, 266
Wilkins, Roy, 65-66, 110
Williams, Hosea, 66
Williams, John J., 196, 307
Williams, Tennessee, 534, 551, 571
Wilson, Arthur M., 490
Wilson, Charles, 267
Wilson, Harold, 416, 441
Wilson, James Q., 110
Wilson, Malcolm, 196
Wilson, William R., 325
Winkles, Bobby, 593
Winpisinger, William W., 221
Wirin, A. L., 229
Wolfe, Tom, 490
Wolff, Lester L., 441
Wolfgang, Marvin E., 111
Wood, Robert D., 543
Wood, Wilbur, 593
Woodcock, Leonard, 96-97, 221
Wooden, John, 593
Wrigley, Philip K., 594
Wriston, Walter B., 97, 329
Wyler, William, 517
Wynder, Ernest L., 501

Y

Yablans, Frank, 517
YaDeau, Richard E., 501
Yamani, Ahmed Zaki al-, 441-442
Yarborough, Ralph W., 196
Yarrington, Blaine J., 147
Yasukawa, Takeshi, 362
Yeo, Edwin H., 221
Yevtushenko, Yevgeny, 490
Yorkin, Bud, 518
Yorty, Samuel W., 147
Young, Andrew, 66
Young, Stephen M., 111
Younger, Evelle J., 111, 147, 267

Z

Zahedi, Ardeshir, 164
Zamyatin, Leonid M., 416
Zanuck, Darryl F., 518

Zayyat, Mohammed Hassan el-, 442
Zeffirelli, Franco, 518, 551
Zetterling, Mai, 518
Ziegler, Henri, 325

Ziegler, Ronald L., 197
Zinnemann, Fred, 518
Zukor, Adolph, 518
Zumwalt, Elmo R., Jr., 241, 391

Index to Subjects

A

A Little Night Music (play), 529:3, 530:4
A New Leaf (film), 507:4
Abortion—*see* Medicine
Achievement, 562:1
Acting/actors, 503:7, 504:1, 504:2, 504:3,
    504:5, 505:6, 506:1, 507:6, 508:4, 508:6,
    509:6, 510:1, 510:4, 512:4, 512:6, 513:1,
    514:1, 514:5, 515:6, 517:1, 518:4, 527:6,
    529:1, 530:4, 532:5, 546:6, 551:2
    character actors, 513:3
    character, building a, 507:5
    salaries, 511:4
ADA—*see* Americans for Democratic Action
Adams, John, 250:2
Aden, 410:5
Adversity, 554:5
Advertising, 81:5, 84:2, 277:1, 286:2, 290:2
    belief in, 77:5
    dishonesty of, 93:2
    disloyalty, creation of, 69:2
    fraud in, 74:4
    harassment of, 68:4
    television, 539:1, 539:2, 541:1
        counter-commercials, 536:1, 541:3,
        542:5
        Fairness Doctrine, 536:1
        Madison Avenue psychology, 538:3
Aerospace—*see* Space
Affluence—*see* Wealth
Afghanistan, 351:4
AFL-CIO—*see* American Federation of Labor-
    Congress of Industrial Organizations
Africa, pp. 443-445
    colonialism in, 447:4
    Israeli relations, 423:5
    Soviet subversion in, 398:2
    U.S. bases in, 158:3
    See also specific countries
Age/youth, 544:1, 549:6, 551:5, 552:4, 554:2,
    556:5, 557:3, 557:5, 559:2, 561:4, 561:5, 563:5,
    565:4
Aged—*see* elderly
Agency for International Development (AID), 149:3
Agnew, Spiro T., 266:1
    bribery and kickback scandal, 243:1, 243:2, 243:3,
    243:4, 252:5, 261:4, 264:1, 265:1, 265:3, 299:2
    election victory (1972), 253:4
    Nixon, relationship with, 242:2
    political weaknesses, 242:3
    poverty-program attorneys, 310:2

press/news media, 261:4, 466:3
Republican presidential nomination (1976), 242:4
resignation as Vice President, 243:3, 243:4,
    252:5, 255:1, 264:1, 265:1, 265:3, 300:3
tax evasion, 243:3
Agriculture/farming, 52:2, 68:1, 70:1, 70:5, 71:1,
    78:1, 83:4, 96:1, 125:1, 126:4, 201:1, 201:2,
    201:3, 201:4, 211:3, 216:1, 217:2, 288:6,
    312:2, 317:6, 574:3
    agri-business, 217:3
    Green Revolution, 125:1
    price supports, 92:4
    prices/costs, food/farm, 46:2, 67:3, 78:4, 96:1,
    126:4, 199:3, 201:1, 201:2, 201:3, 201:4,
    201:5, 202:3, 205:1, 206:4, 210:3, 210:4,
    211:3, 216:1, 216:5, 218:2, 219:2
    See also Food
Agriculture, U.S. Dept. of, 317:6
AID—*see* Agency for International Development
AIM (American Indian Movement)—*see* Indian, Ameri-
    can
Air—*see* Environment—pollution
Air Force, U.S.—*see* Defense
Air transportation—*see* Transportation
Airport (film), 510:3, 513:4
Alabama, 266:1
Alaska oil pipeline—*see* Environment
Albert, Carl, 264:3
Alcatraz, 63:1
Alcoholism—*see* Medicine
Algeria, 410:5
Alien and Sedition Act, 250:2
Allende (Gossens) Salvador, 339:1, 343:5, 344:4,
    344:6, 345:1, 345:2, 345:4, 346:4
Alliance for Progress, 47:4
AMA (American Medical Association)—*see* Medicine
Amendments, Constitutional—*see* Constitution, U.S.;
    specific amendments
American (Baseball) League—*see* Baseball
American Booksellers Association, 484:3
American Dream, 49:3, 64:1
American Federation of Labor-Congress of Industrial
    Organizations (AFL-CIO), 70:3, 317:6
American Indian Movement (AIM)—*see* Indian, Ameri-
    can
American Legion, 232:3
American Medical Association (AMA)—*see* Medicine
American Petroleum Institute, 133:5
American scene, the, pp. 44-54
Americans for Democratic Action (ADA), 569:2
Americas/Latin America, pp. 339-347
    arms supplies/purchases for, 343:3, 345:3

Americas (*continued*)
    foreign investment, 346:1
    Organization of American States (OAS), 340:4, 347:3
    territorial waters, 447:4
    U.S. relations, 340:4, 343:3, 345:6
    See also specific countries; Caribbean
Amtrak—*see* Transportation—railroads
An American Tragedy (book), 543:1
Anderson, Jack, 480:2
Anderson, Marian, 522:2
Angola, 444:1
Antitrust—*see* Commerce
ANZUS—*see* Australia-New Zealand-U.S. Treaty Council
Appalachia, 64:3, 132:4
Appeasement—*see* Foreign affairs
Arabs, pp. 417-442, 447:4
    British relations, 412:1
    Communism, 417:3
    dinar vs. dollar, 405:1
    European arms for, 429:1
    guerrillas/terrorists, 158:6, 421:4, 423:2, 424:4, 438:5, 439:1, 440:2
        Austrian transit camps, 422:3, 431:3, 432:5, 433:4
        Black September, 158:6
        Israeli Beirut raid, 420:2, 423:6, 424:6, 440:1, 442:2
        Munich Olympics, 158:6
        U.S. diplomats in Sudan, 158:6, 159:4
    Israeli relations, 420:3, 423:2, 432:7, 436:1
    Japanese relations, 353:4
    oil embargo—*see* Middle East
    Soviet relations, 158:6
    U.S. relations, 425:1, 431:1, 441:3
        control of U.S. business, 75:3
        nationalization of U.S. interests, 435:2, 437:3
    See also Middle East
Argentina, 344:2
Aristotle, 484:1
Armco Steel Corp., 145:5
Arms control—*see* Defense
Armstrong, Neil A., 234:5
Army, U.S.—*see* Defense
Arts, pp. 455-459, 560:4
    as communication, 457:6, 458:6, 459:3
    critics, 457:4
    freakishness in, 46:4
    galleries, 458:2
    geniuses, 455:1
    mass-produced, 533:7
    museums, 457:2, 459:1
    painting, 456:1, 456:3, 457:6, 509:1, 516:2, 519:4
    photography, 457:5, 457:6
    pornography/obscenity, 487:5, 557:4, 561:6, 562:5
        Supreme Court decision, 455:4, 458:5, 505:4, 507:2, 516:1
    private philanthropy, 456:2
    public interest in, 456:5, 457:1
    rivalry in, 534:2

    science compared with, 456:4
    sex in, 455:4
    sophistication in, 455:2
    in Soviet Union, 457:3
    support/subsidy for:
        in Austria, 455:3, 457:3
        in Canada, 455:3
        in France, 457:3
        in Soviet Union, 457:3
        in U.S., 455:3, 455:5, 456:2, 457:1, 457:3, 458:1, 458:3, 459:2, 527:2, 528:4, 531:5, 534:5
        in West Germany, 455:3, 457:3
    tradition, return to, 455:2
    value of, 459:2
    See also Censorship; Literature; Performing arts
Aruba, 343:1
Ash, Roy L., 371:1
Asia/Pacific, 161:5, 181:1, 314:2, pp. 348-391, 436:2, 447:4
    Chinese (Communist) aspect, 357:1
    collective security, 348:1, 353:1
    Communist aspect, 366:5, 367:5
    European aspect, 357:1
    It'l. Conference of Asian Nations, 359:6
    Japanese aspect, 357:1, 360:4, 360:7
    Soviet aspect, 348:1, 353:1, 357:1, 398:2
    U.S. aspect, 348:2, 354:1, 357:1, 359:5, 374:1
Assad, Hafez al-, 435:4
Astronomy—*see* Space
Atheism—*see* Religion
Athletics, Oakland (baseball), 587:3
Atlantic Alliance—*see* North Atlantic Treaty Organization
Atlantic Charter, 408:1
Atlantic Richfield Corp., 68:6
Attica (N.Y.) Prison, 107:1
Australia, 307:3
    accommodation with Communist countries, 349:1
    automobile seat-belt law, 320:4
    British relations, 349:1
    China (Communist) aspect, 361:3
    Indochina aspect, 361:2, 390:4
    isolationism, 362:1
    Labor Party (ALP), 349:1
    North Vietnamese relations, 349:1, 362:1
    Soviet relations, 349:1
    U.S. relations, 349:1, 361:2, 361:4
    Vatican relations, 362:1
Australia-New Zealand-United States Treaty Council (ANZUS), 362:1
Austria, 422:3, 425:4, 431:3, 432:5, 433:4
Auto racing—*see* Sports
Automobiles—*see* Transportation
Avanti! (film), 511:4

B

Bach, Johann Sebastian, 521:4
Baker, Bobby, 474:1

Baker, Howard H., Jr., 244:2, 297:2
Balance of Payments—*see* Trade, foreign
Balance of power—*see* Defense
Ball, George, 73:4
Ballet—*see* Dance
Balzac, Honore de, 490:1
Bangladesh, 348:4, 352:4, 356:2
Banking—*see* Commerce
Barnes, Clive, 534:1
Baseball, 584:6, 585:7, 588:2, 590:3, 592:2
    Aaron/Ruth home-run records, 577:1, 577:2
    American League, 579:8, 580:3, 585:3, 585:6, 590:5, 591:3, 593:3
    blacks in, 58:3
    as a business, 580:5, 589:4, 594:1
    coaching/coaches, 577:3
    colored baseballs, 587:3
    competition, 592:4
    contentious sport, 585:2
    designated-hitter rule, 579:8, 580:3, 585:3, 585:6, 590:5, 591:3, 593:3
    designated runner, 585:3
    fans booing a player, 578:3
    fans, wildness of, 578:1
    hitter's game, 578:7
    hitting, 589:5
    long hair for players, 577:6
    minor leagues, 583:2
    national anthem, 590:6
    ownership, 590:7
    part of America, 583:4
    pitching/pitchers, 577:3, 578:7, 591:3, 593:3, 593:4
        fastball, 580:4
        spitter, 580:4
        walking, 584:1, 587:6
    player-management relations, 588:1
    reserve clause, 580:6, 589:3
    rule changes, 580:2
    salaries/money, 583:2, 589:4, 591:4
    strike by players, 585:1
    slowness of game, 593:2
    stolen bases, 585:3
    TV/radio aspect, 594:1
    umpire, 580:1
    winning, 578:4
Basketball, 583:5, 588:2, 588:6, 589:3, 592:4
    coaching/coaches, 585:4, 593:6
    national anthem, 593:5
Beauty, 462:3
Beckett, Samuel, 490:3
Beethoven, Ludwig van, 523:2
Berlin—*see* Germany
Berrigan brothers, 252:2
BIA (Bureau of Indian Affairs)—*see* Indian, American
Bible, the—*see* Religion
Bicentennial Era, U.S., 52:5
Bill of Rights, U.S.—*see* Constitution, U.S.
Birth control—*see* Medicine
Blacks—*see* Civil rights
Block, Herbert (Herblock), 464:1

Boer War, 415:2
Bogart, Humphrey, 502:5, 507:4
Bolshoi Opera House (Moscow), 457:3
Book-of-the-Month Club, 489:2
Books—*see* Literature
Boredom, 554:2, 561:3
Bork, Robert H., 297:3
Boxing—*see* Sports
Bradley, Tom, 58:3
Brandeis, Louis D., 223:2, 271:4
Brazil, 341:1
Brennan, Peter J., 211:5
Brezhnev, Leonid I., 151:5, 371:2, 398:2, 404:2, 407:3
Brice, Lord, 195:5
Britain—*see* United Kingdom
British Columbia (Canada), 339:5
British Press Council, 477:4
British Steel Corp., 95:5
Broadcasting—*see* Radio; Television
Broadway—*see* Stage
Bronte, Charlotte, 543:1
Bruckner, Anton, 519:3
Buchanan, Patrick J., 478:1
Buckley, William F., Jr., 535:3
Buddhism—*see* Religion
Budget, Federal—*see* Government
Bulgaria, 404:4
Bureau of Indian Affairs (BIA)—*see* Indian, American
Burger, Warren G., 225:6, 228:4
Burke-Hartke bill, 91:3
Burton, Richard, 564:4
Buses—*see* Transportation
Business—*see* Commerce
Busing for racial balance—*see* Civil rights
Butz, Earl L., 216:2
By George (play), 525:3
Byrne, W. Matthew, Jr., 176:3

C

Caledonia (song), 521:3
California, 329:1
Cambodia, 265:4, 375:1, 375:4, 380:3, 386:4, 388:2, 389:4, 447:4, 550:5
    becoming Communist, 366:5, 386:1
    Communist bases in, 381:4
    Fascism in, 386:1
    French occupation of, 386:2
    Khmer Rouge, 386:1, 386:2, 386:3
    Lon Nol, deposing of, 371:5
    North Vietnam aspect, 381:3, 382:1, 384:4, 387:1, 387:3
    Soviet relations, 398:2
    U.S. bombing in, 272:5, 306:5, 363:1, 363:6, 369:3, 370:3, 371:2, 371:6, 372:1, 372:4, 372:5, 376:2, 377:1, 377:3, 379:2, 382:2, 383:4, 384:4, 385:4, 387:2, 387:3, 388:1, 391:1, 391:2
Camp David (Md.) 173:4

Canada:
　tax system, 202:5
　U.S. relations, 346:3
　　oil for U.S., 342:2, 347:4
　　if Watergate happened in Canada, 301:3
　See also British Columbia; Quebec
Cancer—*see* Medicine
Capital gains—*see* Commerce
Capital punishment—*see* Crime
Capitalism, 339:3, 346:4, 359:4, 412:6, 418:6, 444:3,
　444:5, 447:3, 563:4
　black, 64:3
　in Soviet Union, 398:2, 403:1
Cardozo, Benjamin N., 223:2
Caribbean, 342:1, 343:1
　See also specific countries
Cars—*see* Transportation—automobiles
Castro, Fidel, 340:4
Catch-22 (film), 509:2
Catholic Conference, U.S., 120:3
Catholicism—*see* Religion
CBS—*see* Columbia Broadcasting System
Censorship, 455:4, 505:4, 507:2
Census Bureau, U.S., 306:5
Central Intelligence Agency (CIA), U.S., 171:3, 286:3,
　290:2, 293:4, 307:4, 339:1
Chancellor, John, 470:1
Chanel, Coco, 460:6
Chaplin, Charles, 508:6
Character, strength of, 554:5
Charisma, 546:8
Chayefsky, Paddy, 531:1
Chiang Kai-shek, 350:4
Chicanos—*see* Civil rights
Chile:
　capitalism in, 339:3
　civil war in, 339:4, 345:2
　Constitution, 345:4
　coup overthrowing Allende, 339:1, 343:5, 344:4,
　　344:6, 345:1, 345:2, 345:4, 346:4
　democracy in, 339:3
　dictatorship in, 339:4
　Fascism in, 339:1, 339:4, 349:2
　freedom in, 339:3
　ITT affair, 84:3
　junta, 344:5, 344:6, 345:1, 349:2
　Marxism in, 339:3, 344:6
　socialism in, 339:2, 339:3
　standard of living in, 344:6
China (Communist), 152:3, 160:5, 213:2, 357:5,
　449:1
　aggressiveness, 361:3
　Asian aspect, 357:1, 360:7
　Australian attitude toward, 361:3
　coveted by all, 351:2
　economic aspect, 360:7
　foreign policy, 349:2
　gross national product, 360:3
　Indian relations, 348:5, 360:3
　Indochina attitude, 360:3, 390:1
　Japanese relations, 348:2, 353:4, 360:5, 360:7

　Mexican relations, 351:5
　Nationalist China life compared with, 350:4
　Nationalist China, liberation of, 351:1
　Nationalist China recovery of mainland, 350:2
　Nationalist Chinese relations, 350:1, 359:4
　"ping pong diplomacy," 350:5
　population, 360:3
　Soviet aspect, 152:5, 163:6, 352:5, 354:1, 355:1,
　　355:3, 358:3, 360:3, 386:1, 398:2, 404:4
　as superpower, 360:3
　Tibetan relations, 351:3
　totalitarian society, 350:5
　U.S. relations, 156:4, 157:3, 158:2, 158:6, 161:1,
　　253:3, 275:3, 306:5, 340:1, 340:4, 342:5,
　　348:2, 351:3, 354:3, 354:5, 355:3, 358:2,
　　358:3, 359:3, 373:4, 374:1, 381:2, 385:5,
　　448:3
　　feeding of China, 52:2
　　negotiations with China, 189:2
　　Nixon China trip (1972), 149:2, 152:5, 352:5,
　　　356:4, 481:4
　　recognition of China, 350:5
　　secondary enemy of China, 386:1
　　trade with China, 342:5
　Vietnam aspect, 376:4
　See also China (Nationalist)
China (Nationalist)/Taiwan, 348:2
　anti-Communist policy, 350:3
　Communist China liberation of, 351:1
　Communist China life compared with, 350:4
　Communist Chinese relations, 350:1, 359:4
　fall to Communists, 366:5
　countries breaking relations with, 359:4
　free and open society, 350:5
　recovery of mainland, 350:2
　U.S. relations with, 354:4, 359:4
　　U.S. troops, 354:4
　See also China (Communist)
Chou En-lai, 348:2, 350:5
Christ, Jesus—*see* Religion—Christianity
Christianity—*see* Religion
Church—*see* Religion
Churchill, Winston S., 193:5
CIA—*see* Central Intelligence Agency
Cinema—*see* Motion Pictures
Cities—*see* Urban affairs
Citizens Committee (Conference) on State Legisla-
　tures, 171:1
Civil rights/racism, pp. 55-66, 161:5, 232:1, 247:4,
　247:5, 314:4, 334:1, 334:2, 369:6, 443:1, 444:1,
　444:6, 445:1, 447:4, 478:2, 552:2, 566:2, 589:2
　backlash, 56:2
　"benign neglect," 60:3
　Black Caucus, Congressional, 63:4
　Black Muslims, 66:3
　Black Panthers, 66:3
　blacks/Negroes, 55:1, 55:2, 55:5, 56:1, 56:2,
　　56:5, 57:1, 58:4, 58:5, 59:1, 60:1, 60:4, 61:1,
　　61:2, 61:4, 62:4, 62:5, 63:4, 64:3, 64:4, 64:5,
　　64:6, 65:3, 65:4, 66:1, 66:2, 66:3, 149:4,
　　232:1, 312:2, 312:3, 312:4, 326:5, 478:2

Civil rights—
   blacks (*continued*)
      in baseball, 58:3
      capitalism, 64:3
      crime, 110:4
      education/schools/faculties, 55:2, 112:5, 119:3
      employment/unemployment, 55:4, 60:2, 65:3
      golfers, 589:2
      in government, 58:3, 59:2, 61:2
      intellectuals, 112:5
      movies, 502:1, 507:4
      NAACP, 56:2
      in Rhodesia, 447:1
      self-respect, 66:2
      studies, black, 112:1, 113:4
      in U.S. compared with other countries, 57:3
      in Vietnam, 65:3, 66:3
      women's movement compared with, 334:1
   business aspect, 58:3, 59:1
   busing for racial balance, 55:3, 56:3, 56:5, 57:2,
      61:4, 62:7, 63:2, 64:2, 65:1, 247:5
   Chicanos, 334:1
   marches, 64:4
   in 1960s, 60:2, 64:6
   Philadelphia Plan, 58:5
   Plessy vs. Ferguson, 60:1
   political aspect, 59:5
   segregation/integration, 55:3, 56:1. 56:2, 56:5,
      57:1, 58:4, 58:5, 59:4, 61:4, 62:4, 64:2, 65:1,
      66:2, 113:4, 149:4
   See also Indian, American
Civil War, U.S., 280:5, 378:1
Civilisation (TV Show), 415:2
Civility, 563:1
Clark, Kenneth, 415:2
Clark, Ramsey, 109:4, 376:5
Classification, gov't.—*see* Government—secrecy
Clements, William P., Jr., 239:3
Cleveland Orchestra, 523:1, 523:4
Coexistence—*see* Foreign affairs
Cold war—*see* Foreign affairs
College—*see* Education
Colonialism—*see* Foreign affairs
Colson, Charles W., 290:2
Columbia Broadcasting System (CBS), 477:2
Columbus, Christopher, 553:2
Commerce/industry/finance/business, 52:1, pp. 67-97,
   198:4, 204:3, 206:6, 264:4, 339:5, 580:7
   ability and achievement in, 76:5
   antitrust/mergers/monopoly, 77:6, 79:3, 82:4
   Arab control of U.S., 75:3
   banking, 209:5
   big business, 181:1, 242:1, 244:4, 309:4, 563:6
   capital gains, 67:5, 88:2, 89:1, 92:3, 213:5, 213:6,
      214:1
   capital spending/investment, 203:4, 210:5, 213:6,
      217:6
   change, enemy of, 558:1
   civil rights aspect, 58:3, 59:1
   competition, 73:3, 76:4, 79:4, 81:4, 82:4, 86:3
   confidence/credibility/faith in, 49:3, 51:1, 90:1,
      262:4

   consumerism, 44:1, 71:3, 75:1, 80:3, 81:4, 82:2,
      90:1, 90:2, 497:1
   corporate conscience, 86:1
   dominating society, 81:4
   education aspect, 112:3
   environment aspect, 88:3
   government relations, 74:1, 75:5, 75:6, 76:4,
      80:1, 83:1, 84:1, 93:3, 242:5
   heartless corporations, 49:3
   interest rates, 70:4, 87:6, 198:1, 201:5, 205:4,
      208:5, 208:6, 209:5, 211:1, 212:4, 215:2
   integrity in, 94:4, 95:1
   leaders in, 87:1
   lost its voice, 77:4
   monetary system, 67:1, 73:5, 76:1, 87:3, 87:5,
      89:4, 93:4, 210:5
      dollar, U.S., 67:3, 68:5, 80:2, 85:1, 85:2, 93:1,
         96:1, 97:2, 211:1, 214:4
         devaluation of, 70:2, 72:3, 77:1, 78:3,
            83:2, 85:3, 87:3, 87:5, 94:3, 152:5,
            204:2, 216:3, 284:5, 461:1
      exchange rates, 85:3, 89:4, 94:3
      gold, 67:5, 68:5, 74:2, 77:7, 85:2, 208:5,
         284:5, 573:3
   multinational/world corporations, 76:2, 76:6,
      84:3, 85:1, 90:4, 92:3, 95:2, 346:4
   nationalization, 75:2, 95:5
      of railroads—*see* Transportation—railroads
   one-man head of company, 71:2
   political aspect, 82:1, 93:3
   help for poor, 88:3
   Presidency, relations with, 209:1
   profits, 68:6, 70:3, 74:1, 82:2, 82:3, 88:3, 89:2,
      90:4, 94:2, 199:5, 209:5, 210:3, 210:5, 211:3,
      212:4, 217:6, 219:2, 219:3, 221:3, 329:4,
      343:3
      excess-profits tax—*see* Taxes
   running of a business, 67:4
   small business, 209:5
   social responsibility of, 74:1, 74:3, 84:4, 88:3,
      90:1
   stocks/securities industry, 72:4, 77:1, 86:5, 86:6,
      89:2, 95:3, 95:4, 208:5, 284:5
      brokerage rates, 89:2
      New York Stock Exchange (NYSE), 86:5,
         86:6, 95:4
      Securities and Exchange Commission (SEC),
         72:4, 290:2
      Wall Street, 52:2, 95:3, 95:4, 290:2, 455:5
   taxes, corporate—*see* Taxes
   wage-price responsibility, 206:6
   youth "turned off" on, 120:4
   See also specific industries; Advertising; Economy;
      Trade, foreign
Committee for the Re-election of the President,
   259:1, 283:2, 290:1, 291:3, 291:4
Common Market—*see* Europe—European Economic
   Community
Communication Act, 535:4, 538:6
Communications—*see* Science
Communications (philosophical), 559:6
Communism, 150:3, 154:4, 156:4, 160:6, 163:6,

Communism (*continued*)
    350:3, 355:3, 357:5, 359:4, 371:2, 388:4, 393:4,
      400:1, 408:3, 451:3, 555:6
    trade with Communists, 86:2, 153:3
    See also specific countries; Marxism; Socialism
Competition, 47:3, 73:3, 76:4, 79:4, 81:4, 82:4,
    86:3, 202:2, 207:5, 209:3, 216:3, 217:4, 563:4,
    574:3, 579:5, 580:7, 586:3, 590:4, 592:4
Compromise, 119:1
Concorde (SST)–*see* Transportation–air
Congress, U.S., 166:3, 171:2, 171:4, 172:1, 172:3,
    191:5, 192:5, 194:1, 272:3, 318:4, 363:1
    committees, 172:6
    constituency/representation, 166:2, 288:6
    drinking habits of members, 249:2
    FBI, overseeing of, 109:2
    foreign affairs aspect, 162:1
      Kissinger disregard for Congress, 148:1
    House of Representatives, 181:4, 196:2
      age requirement, 167:2
      term of office, 189:1
    impoundment, Presidential–*see* Government
    military aspect, 152:4
    Nixon Administration relations, 180:4
    pluralism and factionalism of, 172:3
    Presidency, loss of power to/relations with, 165:4,
      167:4, 169:2, 169:3, 169:6, 172:2, 175:5,
      176:1, 178:7, 181:1, 181:3, 182:2, 182:5,
      183:7, 184:1, 186:2, 187:1, 189:3, 190:2,
      190:3, 193:1, 193:2, 194:2, 196:2, 271:4.
      272:5, 312:5, 467:2
    respect for, 171:1
    salaries of members, 177:5
    Senate, 167:3, 196:2, 266:3
      age requirement, 167:2
      hearings open to public, 171:1
    spending/power of purse/budget aspect, 165:4,
      167:4, 170:3, 174:2, 190:1, 195:2, 198:1,
      198:2, 200:2, 201:5, 211:4
    Supreme Court aspect, 222:7, 467:2
    TV coverage of sessions, 185:1
    war-making authority, 152:4
    young people in, 167:2
    See also specific committees; Government
Connally, John B., Jr., 248:3
Conservatism (political), 76:1, 108:4, 148:4, 242:3,
    247:4, 252:2, 252:3, 259:4, 261:3, 267:1, 283:2,
    291:4, 318:4, 466:1
Constitution, U.S., 46:3, 47:1, 182:1, 269:3
    Amendments:
      First, 174:6, 176:3, 179:3, 249:1, 464:1,
        465:6, 467:1, 469:3, 471:3, 478:3, 479:1
      Fifth, 476:3
      Fourteenth, 464:3
      Twenty-second, 168:4
    Bill of Rights, 44:1, 265:4
    checks and balances aspect, 114:2
    "color blind," 65:4
    foreign affairs aspect, 151:2
    judiciary aspect, 222:7
    Presidential powers aspect, 174:7
      impoundment, 174:5

    regional government aspect, 194:3
    See also constitutions of specific countries
Consumer Price Index, 220:1
Consumerism–*see* Commerce
Coolidge, Calvin, 242:1
Cooper, James Fenimore, 489:5
Corporation for Public Broadcasting–*see* Television
Courts–*see* Judiciary
Cox, Archibald, 290:4, 305:3
Crime/law enforcement, 49:3, pp. 98-111, 134;1,
    141:2, 247:5, 312:5, 328:2, 328:4, 552:2
    capital punishment/death penalty, 101:4, 102:3,
      104:1, 104:2, 105:3, 106:5, 107:4, 110:3,
      312:5
    citizen involvement in, 101:3
    courts aspect, 99:6, 110:2
    criminal responsibility for, 106:3
    drug-related, 498:3
    education related to, 115:1
    fear of, 111:1
    gun control, 104:6, 105:1, 106:2, 107:5, 111:4
    journalism aspect, 102:6, 476:2, 476:3
    juvenile delinquency, 334:2
    law and order, 110:4, 264:4, 553:8
    Negro/black, 110:4
    no-knock laws, 100:4
    organized crime, 53:1, 104:3, 476:3, 562:4
    police, 99:2, 100:3, 102:6, 102:7, 103:3, 105:5,
      106:1, 107:3, 554:1
    poverty as cause of, 100:6
    preventive detention, 100:4
    prisons/correctional system, 99:1, 99:4, 99:5,
      101:1, 105:4, 107:1, 108:3, 109:3, 110:5,
      111:5
      training of prisoners, 107:2
      work release, 107:3
    punishment, 102:2
    search and seizure, unreasonable, 222:3
    sex roles related to, 334:2
    subversion, 103:4
    victims of crime, 111:3
    white-collar crime, 98:3, 102:1
    See also Federal Bureau of Investigation
Crimean War, 415:2
Cronkite, Walter, 464:2, 469:3, 470:1
Crosby, Bing, 50:1
Cuba, 257:5, 343:1, 347:3
    aggression against, 341:2
    Soviet aspect, 340:4, 397:4
    subversion of other governments by, 342:4
    U.S. relations, 340:1, 340:4, 342:5
      hijacking agreement, 340:4
Cubs, Chicago (baseball), 594:1
Curtis, Tony, 511:4
Custer, George Armstrong, 63:1
Cynicism, 51:1, 556:6
Cyprus, 409:4, 410:5
Czechoslovakia, 411:1
    Soviet relations, 395:5, 404:4
      Soviet invasion (1968), 370:2, 398:2, 413:3,
        416:3

D

Dance, 519:4, 520:2, 527:1, 544:3
  ballet, 531:2, 532:1
  modern, 533:5
Darling Lili (film), 509:2
Data banks, 184:3
Davis, Angela, 252:2, 271:2
Davis, Bette, 507:4, 516:4
Davis, Elmer, 469:5
Day-care—*see* Social Welfare
Dean, John W., III, 168:2, 249:1, 265:5, 270:5, 274:2, 284:1, 287:2, 290:2, 291:2, 294:3, 295:4, 299:3, 303:3
Death (medical aspect)—*see* Medicine
Death (philosophical), 546:9, 548:8, 553:6, 555:4, 559:5, 562:1
Death penalty—*see* Crime
Decisions, great, 549:1
Declaration of Independence, U.S., 167:5, 456:5
Deere, John, 127:4
Defense/military, 46:4, 53:5, 186:3, pp. 230-241, 242:1, 447:3, 574:1
  Air force, U.S., 233:5, 234:1
    women in, 240:3
  aircraft carriers, 241:4
  arms control/race/disarmament, 101:2, 152:1, 152:3, 159:3, 161:5, 189:2, 231:3, 234:4, 235:1, 235:2, 235:6, 237:1, 237:2, 241:3, 349:2, 365:3, 433:5, 447:2, 447:3, 562:4
    strategic arms limitation talks (SALT), 152:5, 155:3, 156:4, 234:5, 235:6, 306:5
  Army, U.S., 230:2, 232:2, 232:3, 234:1
    racial quotas, 232:1
    representative, 230:3
    reduction of size, 230:1, 231:3, 239:3
    volunteer Army, 230:3, 232:1, 232:2, 232:3, 233:2, 240:1
    women in, 240:3
  Backfire bomber (Soviet), 233:5
  B-1 bomber, 233:5
  B-52 bomber, 233:5
  balance of power/forces, 158:2, 403:2, 406:3, 408:3, 409:1, 417:4, 450:9, 451:1
  bases, closing of U.S., 233:4
  confidence in, 51:1
  Congress meddling in, 152:4
  conventional forces, 406:3, 412:5
  critical attitude toward, 236:6, 240:5, 241:1
  deterrence, 253:3, 360:6, 408:3, 412:5, 446:2
  democracy, military not, 236:3
  draft, 117:4, 230:3, 232:3, 234:3, 238:2
    draft-dodgers, 239:2
  elite, military, 305:2
  flight pay for desk-bound officers, 238:1
  fuel shortage effect on, 236:7
  Marine Corps, U.S., 234:1
  military-industrial complex, 231:5, 236:4, 240:5, 241:1

  missiles:
    intercontinental ballistic, 239:3
    MIRV, 231:2, 239:5
    SAM-6, 240:1
    SS-18, 231:2
    Trident, 234:5
  Navy, U.S., 234:1
    fleet reduction, 241:3
    Mediterranean fleet, 240:1
  officers:
    number of, 236:2, 238:3, 239:1
    servants of, 231:1
  Pentagon, 186:3, 236:1, 238:3, 239:1, 240:1, 240:5, 302:3, 339:1, 363:1
  Polaris submarine, 239:3
  President's responsibility for, 235:3
  sea/maritime power, 392:5
  size of forces, 233:3
  spending/costs/budget, 208:6, 230:4, 231:5, 234:5, 235:5, 235:6, 237:1, 239:4, 240:1, 240:2, 240:4, 240:5, 240:6, 313:2, 410:3
  strength, reduction of, 148:2, 234:4, 235:6
  weapons development, 231:3
  See also specific countries and areas
Defense, U.S., Dept. of, 186:3, 189:2, 231:4
de Gaulle, Charles, 470:2
DeMille, Cecil B., 520:2
Democracy, 44:3, 46:5, 114:2, 168:1, 168:3, 172:3, 177:2, 184:2, 185:2, 194:1, 195:5, 227:5, 282:1, 350:3, 352:2, 355:5, 358:4, 358:5, 383:1, 392:2, 399:1, 411:4, 421:3, 467:3, 555:6, 556:6, 585:2
  See also specific countries
Democratic Party, 245:4, 248:2, 265:2, 328:1, 551:3, 563:6
  bugging by, 251:5
  campaign costs (1972), 255:1
  campaign tactics, 245:5
  compromise, necessity for, 254:4
  Democratic Convention (1972), 258:1
  Democratic National Committee, 280:1
  economy aspect, 200:1
  fragments and factions, 257:6
  image of, 247:3, 247:5, 258:1
  principles of, 254:1
  product of big labor, 244:4
  wins/losses in 1972 election, 257:2
Demonstrations, political, 249:1, 277:5
Dentistry—*see* Medicine
Depression, the, 282:3, 568:2
Detente—*see* Foreign affairs
Devaluation of U.S. dollar—*see* Commerce—monetary system
Diamond, Neil, 524:5
Diary of a Mad Housewife (film), 516:4
Dickens, Charles, 490:3
Dictatorship, 184:2
Dior, Christian, 462:7
Diplomacy—*see* Foreign affairs
Disarmament—*see* Defense—arms control
Discipline, 555:1, 561:8
Disney, Walt, 127:1, 507:4

Disraeli, Benjamin, 259:4
Doctors—*see* Medicine
Dollar, U.S.—*see* Commerce—monetary system
Dominican Republic, 343:1
Douglas-Home, Alec, 405:4
Douglass, Frederick, 55:1
Draft, military—*see* Defense
Dreiser, Theodore, 489:1, 543:1
Drew, Elizabeth, 535:3
Drugs—*see* Medicine
Dubliners, The (book), 487:4
Dulles, John Foster, 386:2
Dutch Guiana, 343:1

E

Eagleton, Thomas F., 480:2
East Europe—*see* Europe
East Germany—*see* Germany
Easy Rider (film), 509:2
Ecology—*see* Environment
Economic Stabilization Act, 211:3
Economy, the, pp. 198-221, 245:4, 284:5, 285:6, 288:6, 318:3
    black markets, 200:4, 202:1, 204:3, 215:1
    boycotts, food, 201:5, 210:5, 216:5
    controls/freeze, wage/price/economic, 78:4, 198:3,
        199:1, 200:2, 200:4, 201:4, 202:1, 203:4,
        204:2, 205:2, 205:3, 205:5, 206:5, 208:2,
        209:1, 209:4, 209:4, 210:3, 211:1, 211:3,
        211:4, 212:4, 213:3, 215:1, 216:2, 217:3,
        217:5, 219:2, 219:3, 220:1, 220:2, 221:2,
        494:5
    diplomacy, economic, 204:1
    free/private enterprise/market system, 70:3, 77:6,
        90:1, 120:4, 202:1, 204:3, 206:6, 207:5,
        208:1, 209:3, 215:1, 218:4, 219:3, 231:5,
        322:2, 497:2, 540:4
    gross national product (GNP), 141:2, 141:3,
        195:6, 198:2, 237:1, 240:1, 253:4, 358:1,
        360:3
    growth of, 124:6, 573:4
    inflation, 46:2, 48:3, 52:2, 70:4, 167:4, 175:5,
        187:1, 198:1, 200:2, 200:4, 201:5, 202:2,
        203:2, 203:3, 203:4, 204:2, 205:2, 205:3,
        206:4, 208:4, 208:6, 209:5, 210:4, 210:5,
        210:6, 211:1, 213:3, 214:2, 214:4, 214:6,
        215:1, 215:4, 216:4, 217:1, 217:2, 217:6,
        218:2, 219:2, 219:3, 220:1, 264:4, 278:3,
        285:6, 297:4, 298:1, 311:6, 351:6, 401:2,
        458:1, 533:7
    one-world economics, 90:4
    Phases of Nixon program:
        Phase 1, 205:2, 211:4
        Phase 2, 204:2, 209:1, 218:1
        Phase 3, 218:1, 494:5
        Phase 4, 96:1, 198:4, 199:1, 202:4, 209:4,
            215:1, 216:2, 221:4
        Phase 5, 202:4
    productivity, 72:1, 76:4, 77:1, 84:4, 113:3,

202:2, 214:4
    rationing, 202:1, 204:3, 215:1
    recession/depression, 203:6, 210:5, 213:6, 215:1,
        215:2
    regulated economy, 218:4
    ripple effect, 207:1
    supply and demand, 205:3
    teaching of economics, 206:1
    See also specific countries and areas; Commerce;
        Labor; Prices; Wages
Eddy, Nelson, 505:7
Edison, Thomas A., 127:4
Education/schools, pp. 112-123, 215:3, 288:6,
    312:4, 489:4, 557:6, 558:2, 568:2
    academic life, 115:2
    academic mystique, 115:2
    aid to, 112:4, 113:6, 120:3, 122:2, 311:4,
        314:1, 315:2
    bankrupt schools, 328:4
    black faculties, 119:3
    black schools, 112:5
    black studies, 112:1, 113:4
    bridging of past and present, 118:1
    British, 116:5
    business, relations with, 112:3
    character and education, 114:2
    class of '73, 119:1
    coeducation, 119:3
    college/university, 114:3, 114:5, 115:2, 120:5,
        121:2, 121:5, 315:3
        admissions, 120:1
        cost of, 120:5
        critics of, 115:2
        degree, the, 119:5, 552:1
        draft, protection from the, 117:4
        enrollments, 117:4, 119:2
        finances of, 113:1
        football, 586:1, 590:3
        politically active, 118:4
        private, 121:2
        women's, 119:3
    compensatory, 57:2
    costs of, 120:5, 314:4
    credit, academic, 116:2
    crime related to, 115:1
    degrees and diplomas, 119:5, 120:1, 122:1,
        552:1
    diversity in, 117:2
    equal opportunity in, 55:2, 113:5, 489:4
    faculty labor unions, 121:4
    foreign languages, 121:3
    freedom, academic, 112:6
    government relations, 115:3
    high schools, 113:2, 122:1
    law school, 227:1, 229:2
    liberal academicians, 335:7
    liberal education, 117:3
    limitations of, 116:3
    male domination of, 119:3
    master planning for, 118:5, 121:2
    medical school/students, 113:6, 492:1

Education (*continued*)
mediocrity in, 116:5
myths, educational, 120:1
private/parochial, 117:2, 118:5, 120:3, 120:5, 121:1, 121:2
protest, era of, 115:2
psychological education, 115:5
public attitude toward, 49:3, 115:2, 118:3, 118:4
purpose of, 118:3
reality, process of, 115:4
relevance in, 115:5
role of, 121:5
"schooling" vs. "education," 116:5
social experimentation, 115:5
standards, academic, 112:6
students:
  disruptive tactics, 112:6
  dress, 114:4
  faculty decision-making, control of, 112:6
Swiss, 116:5
teaching/teachers/professors, 118:2, 119:4, 121:4, 122:4, 188:4
technically oriented, 113:3
technology in, 119:4
tests, 117:1
time, too much, 115:1
"training" vs. "education," 117:3
women on faculty, 119:3
Education, U.S. Office of, 122:2
Egypt, 418:1, 418:5, 422:5, 424:1, 427:1, 428:3, 429:5, 432:6, 433:5, 435:4, 437:5, 442:3, 448:3
Israeli relations, 432:3
Libya, merger with, 435:1
Soviet relations, 398:2, 429:5
U.S. relations, 427:2
See also Middle East
Ehrlichman, John D., 193:3, 270:2, 284:1, 290:2, 302:2, 306:5, 478:1
Eisenhower, Dwight D., 157:3, 470:1
Air Force, 233:5
civil rights, 61:2
wiretaps, 109:4
Elder, Lee, 589:2
Elderly/aged/old, the, 309:4, 313:5, 314:1, 314:3, 315:2, 315:3, 326:5
Elections/campaigns:
British system, 245:3
costs/expenses, 244:1, 245:3, 255:1, 254:3, 254:6, 257:1
fair and foul in, 277:3
fund-raising/contributions/financing of, 243:3, 243:4, 244:4, 246:6, 248:4, 254:3, 255:4, 256:3, 260:3, 261:1, 262:5, 264:2, 272:1, 281:5
government/public financing of, 242:5, 244:4, 246:6, 255:4, 257:1, 261:1
1960: 302:2, 304:4
1968: 259:6
1972: 246:2, 247:5, 248:2, 250:3, 252:3, 253:4, 255:1, 255:2, 257:1, 257:2, 257:3, 257:4,
258:1, 258:2, 258:3, 258:4, 259:1, 259:6, 261:2, 280:1, 291:3, 293:1, 304:4, 480:2
1973: 265:2
1974: 271:4, 282:2, 328:1
1976: 252:1, 263:6, 282:3, 282:4, 299:2, 304:4
stealing elections, 250:5
tactics/dirty tricks, 245:5, 246:2, 246:3, 251:5, 255:1, 255:5, 258:3, 259:1, 264:3, 264:4, 275:2, 291:4
TV aspect, 245:3, 251:3
vote, 18-year-old, 178:6
voter apathy, 262:6
voter registration methods, 255:3
  by mail, 250:4, 250:8
young people's attitude toward, 245:1
See also specific countries; Government; Politics
Electronic Revolution, 575:1
Eliot, T.S., 115:5
Ellsberg, Daniel, 176:3, 252:2, 271:2, 279:3, 288:5, 365:6, 366:4
Emerson, Ralph Waldo, 489:5
Emperor of the North Pole (film), 503:7
Employment—*see* Labor
Energy, 92:2, 128:3, 128:4, 134:4, 135:1, 138:2, 139:2, 140:1, 142:3, 142:4, 143:1, 144:2, 144:4, 145:1, 145:4, 156:5, 176:1, 210:4, 288:6, 426:4, 435:6, 439:2, 573:2
coal, 137:3
crisis/shortage, energy/fuel, 124:3, 124:4, 125:2, 126:1, 127:2, 128:1, 130:2, 130:3, 131:1, 132:1, 132:3, 132:5, 132:6, 133:1, 133:3, 133:4, 133:5, 133:6, 134:2, 135:1, 135:2, 136:1, 136:2, 136:3, 136:5, 137:1, 137:2, 137:3, 138:4, 139:1, 139:4, 140:2, 140:4, 142:2, 143:4, 143:5, 144:5, 145:3, 146:1, 146:2, 146:3, 146:5, 147:1, 285:6, 439:3, 574:3
  air transportation, effect on, 322:1
  Arab oil embargo—*see* Middle East
  automobile aspect, 320:6, 322:4, 324:2
  blackouts, 125:2, 144:3
  Canada oil supply for U.S., 342:2, 347:4
  military, effect on, 236:7
  rationing of gasoline, 126:1, 127:2, 138:4, 146:5
nuclear/atomic power, 128:3, 133:4, 138:2, 139:3, 144:3, 146:2
self-sufficiency, U.S., 136:3, 139:1, 143:3
solar energy, 139:3, 140:3
Energy Action Group, 408:1
England—*see* United Kingdom
Environment/ecology, 74:3, 81:4, pp. 124-147, 156:5, 277:1, 327:3, 328:5, 558:2, 560:4, 563:6, 574:1
animals and plants, decimation of, 129:2
business, help from, 88:3
growth, 132:2, 135:3, 141:3, 146:3, 147:3
international cooperation, 124:6
land, preservation of, 124:5
oceans, 129:4, 138:1, 549:7, 574:4

Environment (*continued*)
oil pipeline, Alaska, 125:2, 129:1, 133:2
oil spills, 129:4
parks, 134:3
pesticides, 125:1, 126:4
pollution, 44:1, 48:1, 49:3, 124:1, 127:4, 131:3,
  131:5, 134:1, 141:2, 145:4, 145:5, 573:4
  air, 128:3, 130:1, 130:4, 131:2, 131:4,
   134:4, 135:2, 136:4, 140:7, 141:1, 142:1,
   144:4, 144:5, 145:2, 146:4
  Clean Air Act, 128:5, 130:1, 143:2, 144:5
  water, 44:1, 124:6, 129:3, 129:4, 130:4,
   131:4, 134:4, 136:4, 140:7, 141:1, 144:4,
   146:4
  Water Pollution Control Act, 128:5
population, 70:5, 127:4, 129:2, 129:3, 134:1,
  140:7, 143:2, 161:5, 573:2, 573:5
recycling, 124:6, 136:4, 145:5
strip mining, 132:4
technology aspect, 124:1, 131:3, 138:3
wilderness, 127:1
zero economic growth, 124:6
See also Energy
Environmental Protection Agency (EPA), U.S.,
  128:5, 131:2, 143:2, 321:6
Equal Rights Amendment, 332:1, 333:4, 335:7
Equality, 47:3, 554:4, 558:3, 560:5, 563:4
Erie, Lake, 130:4
Ervin, Sam J., Jr., 268:3, 269:1, 297:2
Ethiopia, 341:5, 439:3
Europe, 380:4, pp. 392-416, 433:5, 436:2, 446:4,
  447:4, 448:3
aircraft-manufacturing industry, 325:2
Asian aspect, 357:1
cohesion in, 414:3
Common Agricultural Policy, 78:1
defense, 394:6, 403:2, 410:4, 412:3
  force levels, 237:1, 239:5, 406:3
Eastern Europe, 400:1
  freedom in, 399:5, 404:3
  sports in, 591:2
economic aspect, 152:5, 205:2, 210:5, 400:3,
  408:3, 441:6
European Economic Community (Common Market), 73:1, 78:1, 91:3, 92:1, 395:4, 397:5
  British entry, 152:5, 398:5, 403:4, 403:6
  French entry, 401:2
European Security Conference, 155:3, 396:6,
  397:1, 408:2
foreign-policy aspect, 414:3
Indochinese aspect, 385:2
Latin America, arms supplies for, 343:4
Middle Eastern aspect, 405:6
  Israel, arms for, 429:1, 431:4
music aspect, 523:1, 523:4, 524:3
oil aspect, 133:3, 419:4, 429:1, 435:6
productivity, 202:2
quality of life in, 141:2
regionalized political power, 414:1
relations among states, 423:2, 423:4

Soviet aspect, 393:1, 395:6, 396:6, 403:2, 408:3,
  410:3, 422:6
standard of living, 141:2
tension, reduction of, 396:6, 410:3
U.S. relations, 155:3, ·156:4, 161:4, 385:2,
  399:4, 405:6, 406:2, 407:4, 408:1, 408:3,
  441:2
  aid to Europe, 313:2
  defense/troops aspect, 237:1, 393:2, 394:1,
   394:4, 394:6, 395:3, 400:3, 401:5, 401:6,
   404:1, 405:3, 405:6, 406:3, 407:1, 410:3,
   410:4, 412:3, 412:4, 412:5, 413:3
  trade, 78:1, 92:1, 399:4
unity, European, 398:5, 407:4, 408:1
Year of Europe, 406:2
See also specific countries
European Economic Community—*see* Europe
Euthanasia—*see* Medicine
Evans, Walter, 457:6
Excellence, 558:3, 560:5
Executive—*see* Presidency, U.S.
Experience, 555:5
Exports—*see* Trade, foreign

F

Fairness Doctrine—*see* Advertising—television; Jour-
  nalism—broadcast
Faisal, King, 417:3
Fall, Albert, 300:2
Falstaff (opera), 565:4
Fame, 548:6, 564:4
Family, the, 310:3, 556:1, 558:3, 560:2, 561:7,
  563:7
Fantasies, 550:7, 554:6
Farming—*see* Agriculture
Fascism, 154:4
  See also specific countries
Fashion, pp. 460-463
American, 460:3, 461:1
anonymity, 461:4
"clog" shoes, 460:2
couture, 460:6, 462:4, 462:7
dating clothes, 462:1
designing, 461:5
European interest in American, 461:1
F. Scott Fitzgerald era, 462:3
Gatsby look, 460:3
hair styling, 462:5, 462:6
men's, 460:1, 460:3, 463:1
ostentation in, 461:3
pants, 461:6
psychological aspect, 460:4
spending on clothes, 461:3
unisex, 461:2
Faulkner, William, 490:3
FBI—*see* Federal Bureau of Investigation
FCC—*see* Federal Communications Commission
FDA—*see* Food and Drug Administration
Fear, 564:2

Federal Bureau of Investigation (FBI), U.S., 99:3,
101:2, 108:6, 284:1, 290:2, 293:4, 307:4
   Congressional aspect, 109:2
   Constitutional rights infringed by, 103:2
   Director of, 109:1, 110:1
   intelligence aspect, 99:3, 100:1
   limits of investigative techniques, 109:1
   monolithic institution, 110:1
   political independence of, 98:2, 102:5
   public informed about, 103:6
   as secret police, 109:2
Federal Communications Commission (FCC), U.S.,
466:1, 538:5, 538:6, 541:2
Federal Trade Commission (FTC), U.S., 74:4, 541:2,
541:3
Fiddler on the Roof (play), 529:3
Films—*see* Motion pictures
Finance—*see* Commerce
Fitzgerald, F. Scott, 462:3, 490:3
Flaubert, Gustave, 490:1
Florida, 171:1
Fonda, Henry, 505:6
Fonda, Jane, 213:2, 376:5, 378:5, 387:6
Food, 156:5, 574:4
   foreign affairs aspect, 149:2
   moral right, 125:1
   rationing, 202:1
   See also Agriculture
Food and Drug Administration (FDA), U.S., 494:1,
497:1
Food stamps—*see* Social welfare
Football, 583:5, 588:2, 589:3, 592:2, 592:4
   coaching/coaches, 585:4, 588:5, 589:6, 590:1,
590:8
   college, 586:1, 590:3
   the commissioner, 581:6, 591:5
   competence, team, 582:1
   competition, 590:4
   manhood, proof of, 582:3
   National Football League (NFL), 581:6, 582:1
   National Football League Players' Assoc., 591:5
   ownership, 586:4
   player/management relations, 581:6, 586:4,
591:5
   players:
      complaining and selfish, 581:5
      family life, 587:4
      money, 587:4
      whiners, 578:6
   Super Bowl, 590:4
   vital force in community, 590:3
   winning, 586:4, 588:3, 590:1, 591:5
Ford, Gerald R., 159:2, 248:5, 264:3, 275:2
Ford, Henry, 52:4
Ford, John, 507:4, 517:3
Ford, Ruth, 534:1
Foreign affairs, pp. 148-164, 180:5, 186:3, 196:2,
259:4, 272:1, 274:4, 288:1, 291:1, 297:1,
299:2, 302:1, 304:3, 342:5, 354:5, 406:2,
414:3, 419:5, 420:1, 426:2, 435:3, 452:3
   appeasement, 163:6, 350:3

coexistence, 148:3, 157:3, 349:2, 350:3, 373:4,
387:4, 419:1, 423:4
cold war, 79:1, 148:3, 151:4, 152:5, 153:3,
159:2, 253:3, 392:3, 395:6, 400:4, 407:2,
422:6, 447:1
collective security, 348:1, 353:1, 451:2
colonialism, 347:2, 386:2, 415:5, 444:1, 447:4,
545:1
confrontation, 157:2, 159:3, 161:2, 232:2,
233:3, 236:4, 366:1, 407:3
Congressional aspect, 162:1
credibility in, 380:4
detente, 148:2, 148:3, 149:5, 150:5, 153:1,
154:3, 155:1, 156:4, 157:2, 157:3, 158:1,
159:2, 163:1, 164:1, 230:2, 232:2, 234:2,
234:4, 235:2, 235:4, 351:3, 352:1, 352:5,
387:4, 394:4, 394:5, 400:3, 404:4, 407:2,
407:3, 410:3, 411:1, 413:1, 413:2, 422:6,
429:6, 433:5, 447:3
diplomacy/diplomats, 164:2, 473:4
   "grandmotherly" diplomacy, 161:4
   superpower diplomacy, 155:3
domestic affairs relations to, 156:6, 161:3
food aspect, 149:2
foreign aid, 151:1, 151:4, 158:3, 160:3, 161:5,
162:2, 314:1, 384:5
imperialism, 50:4, 156:5, 341:2, 341:3, 376:4,
386:1, 397:4, 397:6, 398:2, 402:1, 447:3,
447:4, 451:3
intelligence, foreign, 160:4, 162:4, 171:3
isolationism, 152:3, 154:1, 155:2, 159:1, 161:5,
362:1, 383:1, 406:2, 412:5, 450:3, 451:2
leaks, foreign-policy, 101:2
"linkage theory," 154:2
military orientation of, 185:6
Monroe Doctrine, 434:3
Nixon Doctrine, 154:4, 157:4, 180:5, 345:6,
354:4
policeman of world/cop on beat, 149:6, 154:4,
157:4, 163:5
Presidential/Executive aspect, 151:2, 162:1
public demonstrations, effect of, 249:1
secrecy in, 148:1
self-help, 154:4
superpower relationships, 390:1
terrorism, 159:4, 448:2, 448:3
   See also Arabs
treaties/commitments, 150:1, 159:3, 235:3,
363:4, 383:4, 429:4
unpopular governments, identification with,
160:3
Watergate aspect, 154:1
See also specific countries
Foreign Service, U.S., 163:6
Foreman, George, 578:5, 581:4
Foster, Bob, 578:5
France, 410:5, 414:1, 515:4
   British relations, 399:5
      tunnel link, 394:3
   Cambodia occupation, 386:2
   colonialism, 545:1

France *(continued)*
  Common Market entry, 401:2
  defense, 405:2
  economy, 401:2
  elections in, 410:1
  foreign investment in, 401:2
  French National Railways, 325:1
  motion pictures, 504:6
  nuclear tests, 405:2
  productivity, 72:1
  television, 470:2
Franco, Francisco, 355:5
Frankfurter, Felix, 268:3
Franklin, Benjamin, 127:4, 179:3
Frazier, Joe, 577:4, 581:1
Freedom/liberty, 47:2, 47:3, 76:4, 84:4, 150:3,
  159:3, 172:4, 180:1, 184:3, 191:4, 191:5,
  195:6, 206:6, 223:1, 236:3, 261:3, 268:3,
  291:4, 302:1, 350:3, 404:4, 553:7, 562:4
  of assembly, 184:3, 404:2
  of choice, 332:1, 332:2, 333:1
  of expression, 153:3, 174:6, 185:6
  of information, 476:2
  of the press—*see* Journalism
  of religion, 404:2
  of speech, 68:4, 296:1, 339:3, 374:6, 467:4,
  478:3, 555:6, 563:1
Free enterprise—*see* Economy
French Connection, The (film), 517:5
French Guiana, 343:1
Freud, Sigmund, 563:7
Frost, Robert, 457:6
FTC—*see* Federal Trade Commission
Fuel shortage—*see* Energy
Fulbright, J. William, 159:2
Future, the, 552:5, 559:2

G

Gabor, Zsa Zsa, 305:3
Galbraith, John Kenneth, 216:2
Gambling/lotteries/betting, 95:3, 190:4
Gandhi, Indira, 125:1
Gasoline shortage—*see* Energy
GATT—*see* General Agreement on Tariffs and Trade
Gaza Strip, 420:4
General Agreement on Tariffs and Trade (GATT),
  79:4
General Federation of Women's Clubs, 332:1
General Motors Corp., 321:4
Geneva accords—*see* Indochina
Genius, 562:7
Germany, 375:2, 439:4, 440:4
  Berlin, 155:3, 257:5, 359:4, 448:3
    Berlin Wall, 153:3, 404:3, 411:1
  division of, 353:2, 375:2, 387:7, 415:1
  Japanese relations, 353:4
  Middle East aspect, 420:3
  Nazism, 395:2, 439:4
  unity between East and West, 395:1

East Germany:
  lack of freedom, 415:1
  shooting escapees, 402:5
  admission to UN, 353:2
West Germany, 359:4
  anti-Americanism in, 393:3
  British relations, 399:5
  anti-Communism in, 393:3
  defense budget, 394:4
  freedom in, 415:1
  German Federal Railway, 325:1
  Indochina aspect, 365:2
  Israeli relations, 439:4
  neutralism, 393:3
  the past, 395:2
  productivity, 72:1
  Soviet relations, 155:3, 396:3
  admission to UN, 353:2
  U.S. post-war aid for, 384:5
  anchored in West, 394:5
Gershwin, George, 523:4
Gettysburg Address, 167:5
Gibbon, Edward, 46:4
Gibraltar, 409:4, 415:5
Gibson, Hoot, 510:5
Gibson, Kenneth, 58:3
Gielgud, John, 508:6
Gilbert and Sullivan, 528:4
Gladstone, William, 193:5
GNP (gross national product)—*see* Economy
Godfather, The (film), 513:4, 517:5
Golan Heights, 418:1
Gold—*see* Commerce—monetary system
Goldwater, Barry M., 287:4
Golf, 579:1, 579:4, 587:1, 592:6
  black golfers, 589:2
  courses, 584:2, 586:5
  golfers as entertainers, 579:7
  Greater Hartford Open, 589:2
  hero-worship by fans, 593:1
  Masters Tournament, 589:2
  power over-emphasized, 586:5
  slow play, 586:2
  tennis compared with, 582:2
  Tournament of Champions, 587:1
Government, pp. 165-197, 318:3
  ability to solve nation's ills, 178:4
  agreement binding a ruler, 265:4
  big government, 181:1, 202:4
  blacks in, 58:3, 59:2, 61:2
  blame placed on, 169:1
  budget/spending, 77:1, 166:1, 167:4, 169:5,
  170:3, 174:2, 175:5, 177:3, 178:3, 178:7,
  179:2, 183:5, 184:1, 186:1, 187:1, 190:1,
  190:6, 191:1, 195:1, 195:2, 196:1, 198:1,
  198:2, 200:4, 201:5, 208:6, 214:5, 216:4,
  217:2, 230:4, 267:1, 272:5, 309:3, 309:4,
  311:6, 312:3, 314:1, 315:1, 315:2, 316:5,
  317:4, 371:1
  business-government relations—*see* Commerce
  Cabinet, reconfirmation of, 170:4

Government (*continued*)
centralized/concentrated, 170:2, 172:4, 181:1, 191:5, 482:3
change, enemy of, 558:1
chauffeuring of officials, 191:1
checks and balances, 114:2, 194:2, 227:5, 257:2, 272:3, 467:2, 473:2
city government—*see* Urban affairs
coalition, 275:3
compromise in, 175:7
confidence/credibility/belief in, 49:3, 50:6, 51:1, 181:2, 185:5, 192:2, 192:3, 262:4, 271:2, 285:7, 290:2, 292:4, 302:1
corruption in, 196:3, 259:2, 286:2, 289:2, 300:3, 307:5, 312:5
debate in, 184:2
deceptive, 464:1
dissent in, 186:3
economic aspect, 199:1, 200:5, 204:3, 206:6, 216:4
education aspect, 115:3
Federalism, 166:3, 170:2, 180:2, 191:5, 194:3, 329:2
glorification of officials, 175:1
helping people, 343:3
honesty of officials, 49:3, 271:2, 274:3
impeachment, 186:2, 191:3
See also Watergate
impoundment, Presidential, 165:4, 172:2, 173:2, 174:2, 174:5, 175:5, 182:2, 190:2, 191:2, 195:1, 272:5, 288:1, 312:5, 317:4, 371:1
law, government respect for, 192:4, 195:4, 225:4
law, government without, 228:2
leaks, 101:2, 172:5, 176:2, 192:4, 277:5, 476:4
local/state, 177:2, 179:1, 180:1, 180:2, 192:3, 186:1, 191:5, 198:2, 327:3, 474:1
loyalty in, 195:4, 307:4
medicine/health aspect—*see* Medicine
mediocrity in, 114:2
morality in, 272:5, 289:3
in nautical terms, 168:1
neighborhood, 177:2
one-man rule, 187:1, 262:2
paperwork in, 167:5
press aspect—*see* Journalism
regional, 194:3
regulatory agencies, 193:4, 242:5
reliance on/expectations from, 170:5, 192:3, 202:1
too much responsibility, 188:2
revenue-sharing, 166:3, 175:2, 175:4, 177:2, 179:1, 180:5, 182:3, 186:1, 253:3, 326:2, 327:2, 329:2
secrecy/classification, 148:1, 166:4, 169:4, 172:5, 176:2, 176:3, 178:3, 185:5, 186:3, 189:2, 479:4
separation of powers, 151:2, 165:4, 188:5, 280:2, 280:4, 283:1, 472:2
size/growth/power of, 56:3, 174:3, 177:3, 195:3, 195:6, 202:4, 259:6
return of power to people, 253:3, 259:6

states vs. Federal, 194:3
Supreme Court restraint of, 226:2
surveillance/wiretapping/intelligence, 98:1, 99:3, 100:1, 100:2, 100:5, 101:2, 109:4, 184:3, 263:1, 265:4, 276:5, 293:4, 471:5
See also Federal Bureau of Investigation—intelligence; Politics—intelligence
television regulation—*see* Television
transportation aspect—*see* Transportation
virtue, 303:4
White House, living in the, 173:4
"yes men," 197:1
young people's attitude toward, 194:1, 196:3
young people in, 173:3
See also specific departments, bureaus, etc.; Elections; Politics; Presidency
Graham, Billy, 206:2, 242:1
Graham, Martha, 533:5
Grant, Cary, 518:1
Grant, Ulysses S., 282:1, 289:2, 303:4
Gray, L. Patrick, III, 284:1
Great Race, The (film), 511:4
Great Society, the, 50:4, 257:5
Greatness, 553:4
Greece, 409:4, 411:3
ancient, 558:3
Constitution, 401:4
coup overthrowing Papadopoulos, 392:2, 399:2, 401:3, 409:2
democracy in, 392:2, 399:1, 411:4
elections in, 392:2
monarchy, abolition of, 399:1
totalitarianism in, 399:2
U.S. relations, 411:5
Greer, Germaine, 331:3
Griffith, D. W., 520:2
Gross national product (GNP)—*see* Economy
Guadalupe, 343:1
Guinea-Bissau, 444:1
Gulf of Tonkin Resolution, 181:1
Gun control—*see* Crime
Guyana, 343:1

H

Habash, George, 440:2
Haig, Alexander M., Jr., 185:6, 253:2
Hair (play), 537:7
Haiti, 343:1
Haldeman, H. R., 193:3, 270:2, 270:5, 278:1, 290:2, 302:2, 306:5, 478:1
Hamilton, Alexander, 213:2
Hamlet, 532:5
Hammerstein, Oscar, II, 525:3
Handicapped, the, 312:1
Happiness, 557:2, 568:2
Harding, Warren G., 209:2, 282:1, 289:2, 300:2, 303:4, 306:5
Hardin, John, 65:4
Harlan, John, 65:4
Harlow, Bryce N., 253:2

Hart, Lorenz, 524:5
Hart, Philip A., 105:3
Hawthorne, Nathaniel, 543:1
Health—*see* Medicine
Health, Education and Welfare (HEW), U.S. Dept. of, 316:5
Hemingway, Ernest, 488:6, 490:3
Herblock—*see* Block, Herbert
Heroin—*see* Medicine—drug abuse
Heston, Charlton, 502:1
HEW—*see* Health, Education and Welfare, U.S. Dept. of
Highways—*see* Transportation
Hinduism—*see* Religion
Hiss, Alger, 302:2
History, 52:5
Hitchcock, Alfred, 508:3
Hitler, Adolf, 154:4, 163:6, 341:1, 355:5, 395:2, 396:3, 415:1, 419:5, 440:4, 522:2, 565:1, 569:6
Ho Chi Minh, 386:2
Hockey—*see* Sports
Hofmann, Josef, 522:2
Hollywood—*see* Motion pictures
Holmes, Oliver Wendell, 223:2
Homer, 484:1
Honeysuckle Rose (song), 521:5
Hoover, Herbert, 200:1, 209:2, 242:1, 282:3
Hoover, J. Edgar, 98:2, 102:5
Horse racing—*see* Sports
House Committee on Roads, 322:5
House Interior Committee, 58:1
House of Lords, British—*see* United Kingdom—government
House of Representatives, U.S.—*see* Congress
House Ways and Means Committee, 72:1
Housing—*see* Social welfare
Housing and Urban Development (HUD), U.S. Dept. of, 191:1
Howard, Frank, 585:6
Hudson Institute, 255:2
Hughes, Charles Evans, 342:1
Human condition, the, 552:3
Human nature, 554:4
Humanity, 45:1, 45:5, 544:5, 559:6, 566:5
Humankind, 552:2
Humiliation, 545:5
Humor, 183:6
Humphrey, Hubert H., 266:1
Hungary, 411:1
Hunt, E. Howard, 300:2, 306:6
Hypocrisy, 564:5

I

Ibsen, Henrik, 503:1
Iceland:
  British fishing dispute, 405:4
  U.S. forces in, 392:1
IDA—*see* International Development Association
Ideals, 563:2
Ideas, 555:6, 561:1

Immortality, 484:1, 563:3, 571:1
Impeachment—*see* Government; Watergate
Imperialism—*see* Foreign affairs
Imports—*see* Trade, foreign
Impoundment, Presidential—*see* Government
Incident at Vichy (TV show), 540:2
India, 125:1, 352:3, 450:8
  arming herself, 348:5
  Communist Chinese relations, 348:5, 360:3
  democracy in, 352:2
  Japanese relations, 353:4
  motion pictures, 514:1
  Pakistani relations, 348:5, 356:3, 357:4
    war with (1971), 348:3, 348:4, 356:3, 448:3
  population, 352:2
  Soviet relations, 349:3, 352:4, 353:1, 356:3, 359:2
    arms aid, 356:3
  U.S. relations, 356:1, 356:3, 359:1, 359:2
    arms aid, 356:3
    feeding of India, 52:2
Indian, American, 56:4, 57:4, 58:1, 59:3, 61:3, 62:1, 62:2, 63:1, 65:2, 312:2, 505:2
  Alcatraz occupation, 63:1
  American Indian Movement (AIM), 62:1, 62:2
  Bureau of Indian Affairs (BIA), U.S., 61:3, 65:2
  Navajos, 59:3, 61:3, 62:3
  Oglala Sioux, 62:3
  paternalism, 59:3
  unemployment, 62:3
  Wounded Knee protest, 57:4, 58:1, 63:1, 65:2, 151:5
Indian Ocean, 349:1
Indianapolis 500 race—*see* Sports—auto racing
Individuality, 114:1, 563:4
Indochina, 257:5, pp. 363:391, 452:4
  amnesty for U.S. draft-dodgers/deserters, 239:2, 363:3, 367:3, 377:4, 379:1, 380:2, 383:5, 384:3
  Australian attitude toward, 361:2, 390:4
  blacks in, 65:3, 66:3
  bombs dropped in, 376:3
  Communist Chinese attitude toward, 360:3, 390:1
  Communist takeover of, 385:5
  European attitude toward, 385:2
  Four-Party Joint Military Commission, 384:1
  Geneva accords, 378:4, 390:4
  gradualism in, 378:6
  half-hearted/no-win policy of U.S., 367:2, 370:2, 383:3
  International Control and Supervisory Commission, 384:1
  peace agreement, 363:6, 364:1, 364:4, 365:1, 365:3, 366:2, 367:1, 368:1, 369:7, 370:3, 370:5, 372:4, 373:2, 373:3, 378:1, 379:2, 380:1, 384:1, 386:5, 387:4, 388:2, 388:3, 388:4, 389:4, 390:5
    violations by North Vietnam/Viet Cong, 382:1, 383:4, 385:4, 387:1
  peace with honor, 367:5, 373:1, 377:5, 379:3,

Indochina (*continued*)
379:4, 380:4, 381:4, 390:3
prisoners of war (POWs), U.S., 237:3, 249:1, 275:3, 364:5, 369:2, 369:3, 372:3, 377:1, 377:2, 379:3, 380:2, 381:4, 383:2, 383:4, 384:3, 385:4, 388:4
racist policies in, 369:6
reconstruction aid, post-war, 365:4, 365:5, 366:3, 368:3, 370:1, 371:1, 371:3, 372:2, 374:3, 375:5, 376:5, 376:8, 378:2, 381:3, 383:2, 384:2, 384:5, 385:3
Soviet attitude toward, 365:3, 390:1
Swedish attitude toward, 383:1, 411:1, 411:2, 416:2
U.S. withdrawal from, 352:5, 390:3
West German attitude toward, 365:2
See also specific countries
Indonesia, 380:3
Industrial Revolution, 575:1
Industry—*see* Commerce
Inflation—*see* Economy
Installment purchasing, 83:3
Insurance industry, 73:3, 136:2
no-fault insurance, 131:3
Integration—*see* Civil rights—segregation
Intellectualism/intellectuals, 228:5, 242:3, 255:2, 262:4, 380:2, 448:2, 540:4, 556:6, 557:6, 572:3
black, 112:5
Intelligence, foreign—*see* Foreign affairs
Intelligence/surveillance—*see* Federal Bureau of Investigation; Government; Politics
Interest rates—*see* Commerce
Internal Revenue Service (IRS)—*see* Taxes
International Development Association (IDA), 360:4
International Press Institute, 467:1
International Telephone & Telegraph Corp. (ITT), 84:3, 282:2, 309:1
Intolerance (film), 520:2
IRA (Irish Republican Army)—*see* Northern Ireland
Iran, 426:2, 434:1, 436:2
Israeli relations, 428:3
Pakistani relations, 357:4
Shah of Iran, 424:6
U.S. relations, 434:3
Iraq, 420:4, 428:3
Ireland, 398:1
See also Northern Ireland
Irene (play), 529:3, 532:6
IRS (Internal Revenue Service)—*see* Taxes
Irving, Washington, 489:5
Isolationism—*see* Foreign affairs
Israel, 149:4, 160:5, 396:4, pp. 417-442, 443:4, 447:4, 448:3, 569:6
achievements, 437:6
African relations, 423:5
Arab relations, 420:3, 423:2, 432:7, 436:1
negotiations—*see* Middle East
borders, 427:1, 438:4
countries breaking relations with, 423:5, 443:6
democracy in, 421:3, 422:2
Egyptian relations, 432:3

European arms for, 429:1, 431:4
Iranian relations, 428:3
Japanese relations, 353:4
Kuwait, Israeli takeover of, 424:6
Libya, Israeli strike against, 424:6
occupation of Arab territory—*see* Middle East
oil, lack of, 432:4
South African relations, 423:5
Soviet relations, 426:3
Soviet emigration, 404:3, 425:4, 431:3
U.S. support/relations, 417:3, 417:4, 419:3, 420:5, 421:1, 424:2, 424:3, 424:5, 425:1, 425:4, 428:3, 429:2, 429:3, 431:4, 432:1, 433:1, 437:1, 437:3, 437:4, 438:1, 438:2, 439:2, 439:3, 442:1
West German relations, 439:4
See also Middle East
Italy, 399:5, 560:6
ITT—*see* International Telephone & Telegraph Corp.

J

Jackson, Andre, 303:4
Jackson, Henry M., 151:5, 159:2
Jamaica, 343:1, 441:1
Jane Eyre (book), 543:1
Japan, 380:4, 408:1, 439:3, 559:4
Arab relations, 353:4
Asian aspect, 357:1, 360:4, 360:7
Communist Chinese relations, 348:2, 353:4, 360:5, 360:7
currency realignment, 353:5
defense aspect, 358:1
militarism, 355:6, 360:2
nuclear aspect, 360:1, 360:6
economic aspect, 152:5, 205:2, 351:6, 355:6, 359:6, 360:4, 360:7, 441:6
gross national product (GNP), 353:4, 358:1
productivity, 72:1, 202:2
energy aspect, 135:1
German relations, 353:4
government, 196:5
Japanese National Railways, 325:1
Indian relations, 353:4
Israeli relations 353:4
Korean relations, 353:4
Middle East oil, dependence on, 419:4
Pakistani relations, 353:4
peace aspect, 351:6, 359:6
Soviet relations, 353:4, 360:5
technology, 574:6, 576:1
territorial aggrandizement, 360:7
tourist manners, Japanese, 353:3
trade, 93:1, 93:4, 353:4
with U.S., 353:5, 361:1
U.S. relations, 53:5, 156:4, 348:2, 353:4, 357:2, 357:3, 360:5, 361:1, 362:2
U.S. bases, 158:3, 358:1, 360:1
U.S. post-war aid, 384:5
security treaty, 358:3, 360:6
trade, 353:5, 361:1

Japan (*continued*)
Vietnamese relations, 353:4
Jaworski, Leon, 305:3
Jazz—*see* Music
Jefferson, Thomas, 127:4, 258:2, 467:3
Jersey City (N.J.), 229:1
Jerusalem—*see* Middle East
Jesus Christ Superstar (play), 537:7
Jobs—*see* Labor—employment
Johansson, Ingemar, 577:4
Johns, Jasper, 459:2
Johnson, Lyndon B., 181:1, 187:3, 190:7, 193:5
Indochina, 367:4, 367:6, 377:5, 378:6, 381:1
Middle East, 432:1
monarchist, 265:4
space, 575:5
White House staff, 251:4
Jonathan Livingston Seagull (book), 484:3
Jones, Bob, 589:2
Jordan, 420:4, 428:3, 442:3
Journalism/the press/news media, 52:3, 68:4, 184:3,
186:3, 187:3, 189:2, 247:1, 272:3, 286:3,
294:5, 336:2, 358:4, 448:2, pp. 464-483, 490:3,
549:5
advocacy type, 467:5, 468:2, 478:4
analysis, news, 469:5
bias/objectivity in, 277:2, 464:2, 464:4, 466:1,
466:3, 467:5, 469:3, 471:3, 478:2, 478:4,
479:3, 482:1, 482:3, 482:4
in Britain, 477:4
broadcast/TV/radio, 464:2, 465:6, 466:2, 466:5,
469:3, 469:5, 470:1, 470:2, 471:3, 472:5,
473:1, 473:2, 474:6, 474:7, 476:5, 477:3,
479:3, 479:4, 480:1, 481:1, 481:5, 482:4,
542:3
Fairness Doctrine, 466:2, 469:5, 482:4
show-biz atmosphere, 479:2
as a business, 472:1, 472:2
crime/law enforcement aspect, 476:2, 476:3
definition of news, 481:2
editorializing, 470:1, 478:2
elitist newsmen, 470:3
explained news, 474:5
freedom of the press, 44:4, 179:3, 339:3, 404:2,
413:2, 464:1, 464:3, 465:1, 465:6, 467:3,
467:4, 467:5, 469:3, 471:1, 472:4, 473:3,
474:6, 475:1, 475:3, 476:5, 477:4, 478:3,
478:5, 478:7, 480:3, 481:3, 482:1, 482:3,
555:6
glamorizing the White House, 170:1
good news, 481:1
government aspect, 472:4, 473:6, 474:4, 474:6,
475:3
regulation/criticism of press, 288:1, 465:6,
466:1, 466:3, 467:1, 464:4, 467:4, 469:3,
469:5, 470:2, 471:3, 471:4, 471:5, 471:6,
473:1, 473:2, 474:7, 476:5, 477:2, 477:4,
478:1, 478:5, 479:3, 479:4, 482:1
"leaks" to press, 476:4
secret documents, publication of, 465:1
subpoenaing of newsmen, 174:6

watchdog over government, 467:2
government, news coverage of, 186:3, 464:1,
464:4, 465:6, 466:3, 467:2, 471:2, 471:3,
471:5, 472:3, 474:1, 474:2, 474:3, 474:7,
475:2, 476:4, 476:6, 479:3, 482:2, 482:3
a human press, 336:2
investigative type, 469:5, 471:4, 478:6
juvenile quality of, 473:5
magazines, 469:3, 470:4, 476:1, 488:5
monopoly in, 472:6, 474:6
muckraking, 467:5, 473:5
muzzling of, 465:5
National News Council, 482:1
news explosion, 468:3
newspapers, 68:4, 473:1, 476:5, 481:2, 554:1
chains vs. independents, 472:6
influencing public opinion, 465:6
of New York City, 474:4
Nixon aspect, 259:6, 466:3, 467:1, 467:2, 467:4,
469:5, 470:2, 473:1, 474:2, 474:3, 474:7,
476:6, 478:1, 482:3
phobic elements of, 363:5
Presidential addresses, rebuttal to, 475:2
Presidential press conferences, 307:3, 465:3,
465:4, 466:4, 468:1
responsibility, 472:4, 477:4, 477:5
shield law/confidentiality of sources, 186:3,
288:1, 464:3, 467:3, 468:4, 469:1, 469:2,
469:4, 471:1, 473:3, 474:1, 476:2, 476:3,
478:4, 478:7, 479:1, 480:4, 480:5
Supreme Court, news coverage of, 225:1
Vietnam aspect, 368:4, 390:3
Joyce, James, 487:4
Judaism—*see* Religion
Judaism (magazine), 567:5
Judges—*see* Judiciary
Judiciary/courts, 182:4, pp. 222-229, 247:1, 272:3,
554:1
accusatory vs. inquisitional system, 229:3
adequacy of, 228:1
British system, 110:2
caseload/workload, 223:2, 227:3
confidence in, 49:3, 51:1, 77:5
Constitutional aspect, 222:7
crime/law enforcement aspect, 99:6, 110:2
demands on system, 222:6
ethics, 229:2
independence of, 222:5
judges, 223:5, 225:2
impeachment of, 191:3
intellectual, 228:5
lawyers/attorneys, 222:1, 227:5
dedication of, 226:4
education of, 227:1, 229:2
intellectual, 228:5
manners, 223:3
office vs. trial types, 227:2
omni-competence of, 227:1
over-worked, 226:1
qualifying of, 223:4
legal assistance/poverty aspect—*see* Social welfare

Judiciary (*continued*)
  Presidential/Executive aspect, 222:5, 222:7, 224:1
  respect for, 227:5
  Supreme Court, U.S., 99:6, 194:1, 222:4, 225:6
    abortion, 493:1
    arbiter, ultimate, 224:1
    Burger Court, 225:6, 228:4
    changes on, 224:4, 227:4
    confidence in, 51:1, 77:5
    Congressional aspect, 222:7, 467:2
    dissent on, 224:3
    government, restraining of, 226:2
    integration decision, 62:4
    Justices, 222:7, 224:2
    moral leadership, 225:1
    news coverage of, 225:1
    opinion-writing, 224:3
    over-burdened, 226:2
    parochial-school aid, 120:3
    pornography decision, 455:4, 458:5, 505:4, 507:2, 516:1
    Presidential/Executive aspect, 222:7, 224:1
    public-opinion aspect, 222:7, 228:4
    Warren Court, 224:4
    wars, enjoining of, 150:4
    women on, 333:3
    workload, 223:2
  trials:
    challenging witnesses, 222:2
    delays, 226:1
    evidentiary rules, 222:3, 225:7
    juries, 223:5
      grand jury, 464:3
    manners, courtroom, 223:2
    truth, seeking of, 223:5
  See also Law
Juilliard School, 519:5
Justice, U.S. Dept. of, 98:2, 174:6, 228:2, 260:3, 285:3, 290:2, 291:2, 301:1, 307:4, 541:2
Juvenile delinquency—*see* Crime

K

Kafka, Franz, 490:3
Kahn, Herman, 242:3
Kashmir, 446:1
Kennedy, Edward M., 266:1, 304:4
  Chappaquiddick affair, 252:1, 263:2, 282:4, 482:3
  running for President in 1976, 252:1, 263:6, 282:4
  Watergate, criticism of, 252:1, 282:4
Kennedy, John F., 50:2, 76:4, 98:2, 169:6, 261:1, 273:3, 304:4, 575:5
  assassination, 254:2
  impoundment, Presidential, 191:2
  Indochina, 381:1
  monarchist, 265:4
  press conferences, 465:3
  reminiscences about, 547:6

Kennedy, Robert F., 50:2
  assassination, 254:2
  wiretaps, 109:4
Kettering, Charles F., 127:4
Khrushchev, Nikita S., 398:2
King, Billie Jean, 589:1
King, Martin Luther, 55:1, 64:4, 254:2
Kinmen (Nationalist China), 350:3
Kissinger, Henry A., 78:4, 148:4, 149:1, 161:1
  Congressional aspect, 148:1
  detente, 159:2
  Indochina, 364:2, 388:4
  Middle East, 428:4
  personal characteristics, 547:5
  Secretary of State nomination, 148:1
Kleindienst, Richard G., 165:5, 290:2
Knowledge, 564:2
Knox, Chuck, 589:6
Knox, Frank, 275:3
Koran, the—*see* Religion
Korbut, Olga, 586:3
Korea, 340:4, 348:2, 350:5, 390:4, 417:4, 448:3
  division of, 353:2, 375:2
  Japanese relations, 353:4
  Korean war, 187:3
  reunification of, 447:4
  North Korea:
    admission to UN, 353:2
  South Korea:
    admission to UN, 353:2
    Communist takeover of, 366:5
    U.S. troops in, 354:1
Kreisky, Bruno, 433:4
Kreisler, Fritz, 522:2
Kristofferson, Kris, 524:5
Kristol, Irving, 242:3
Kroc, Ray, 264:2
Kuwait, 423:3, 424:6, 428:3

L

Labor, 52:1, 207:2, 217:6, 311:4
  arbitration, compulsory, 199:2
  bargaining, 92:4, 207:4, 208:1, 210:1, 212:1, 218:1, 218:4
  big labor, 181:1, 244:4
  ecology aspect, 135:5
  employment/unemployment/jobs, 73:4, 205:4, 208:6, 209:2, 210:5, 214:6, 215:1, 217:6, 281:3, 312:2, 312:3, 312:4, 314:4, 318:3, 318:5, 327:3, 403:4
    black, 55:5, 60:2, 65:3
    Indian, American, 62:3
  layoffs, 220:4
  management, relations with, 199:4, 199:5, 206:3, 207:3, 212:2, 217:4
  Presidential relations, 209:1
  retirement, 203:1, 310:3
  safety, 213:4
  shrinkage of work force, 203:1

Labor (*continued*)
strikes, 199:4, 207:2, 207:3, 207:4, 208:1, 208:3, 210:1, 212:1, 212:2, 218:5, 221:1
food stamps/welfare for strikers, 203:5, 204:4, 207:4, 208:1
public-employee strikes, 329:4
unions, 77:1, 81:4, 85:1, 204:4, 206:4, 211:2, 212:3, 218:1, 221:1, 221:3, 312:2, 317:6, 329:4
civil-rights aspect, 58:3
confidence in, 49:3
maritime, 207:3
school-faculty type, 121:4
wage/price responsibility, 206:6
work, 554:2, 557:1, 559:3, 559:7
work ethic, 83:3, 202:2
working conditions, 204:5, 219:1
workmen's compensation, 212:3
See also Economy
Labor, U.S. Dept. of, 317:6, 333:4
Laird, Melvin R., 253:2
Laos, 375:1, 375:4, 378:4, 380:3, 386:5, 387:5, 388:2, 389:4, 447:4
Communist takeover, 366:5
North Vietnam threat to, 381:3, 382:1
Pathet Lao, 387:5
U.S. bombing in, 376:1, 377:1
Last Tango in Paris (film), 518:1, 561:2
Latin America—*see* Americas
Lauder, Harry, 522:2
Law, 223:1, 223:5, 225:4, 228:4, 274:1, 281:6, 296:1, 302:3, 384:3, 451:1, 552:4, 560:5
applied to all, 229:1
government without, 228:2
law school, 227:1, 229:2
respect for, 98:5, 100:3, 226:1, 226:3, 229:1
governmental/Presidential, 185:3, 192:4, 195:4, 225:4, 281:1
See also Judiciary
Law and order—*see* Crime
Lawrence of Arabia (film), 520:2
Lawyers—*see* Judiciary
League of Communists, 415:4
League of Nations, 341:5, 439:3
League of Women Voters, 332:1
Lincoln, Abraham, 167:5, 177:6, 355:5, 486:1
Lindbergh, Anne Morrow, 331:3
Lippmann, Walter, 472:5
Liston, Sonny, 577:4
Literacy, 120:2, 491:1
Literary Guild, 489:2
Literature/books, pp. 484-490, 509:1, 516:2, 537:7
biography/autobiography, 484:2, 486:4, 486:6, 488:3, 490:2
book clubs, 489:2
booksellers, 485:3
candor in, 489:5
classics, 487:4
criticism/critics, 485:2, 489:1
the future of, 487:5
immortality through, 484:1

libraries, 486:1, 489:4
morality in, 486:3
mythic quality in, 490:3
of the 1920s, 485:5
of the 19th century, 486:6, 489:5
non-fiction, 486:4
novels/novelists, 484:2, 484:5, 485:6, 486:4, 486:6, 488:3, 488:5, 488:6, 490:3
of the past, 118:1
poetry/poets, 457:6, 486:6, 490:4, 519:4, 545:1
women poets, 503:2
pornographic, 487:5
prizes and awards, 485:2
publishing, 486:7
reading, 487:5
science fiction, 485:4
short stories, 484:5, 488:5
writing/writers, 484:4, 484:5, 485:1, 485:2, 485:5, 486:2, 486:3, 486:5, 487:1, 487:3, 488:2, 488:6, 489:1, 489:3, 490:1, 548:3, 548:6, 565:4
women writers, 503:2
Little Big Inch line, 133:2
Lockheed Aircraft Corp., 309:1, 318:1
London, Jack, 488:4
Lon Nol, 371:5, 386:1, 391:1, 398:2
Los Angeles Council on Foreign Affairs, 355:3
Lost Horizon (film), 510:3
Lotteries—*see* Gambling
Love, 508:5
Love Story (film), 510:3
Loy, Myrna, 518:1
Loyalty, 195:4, 307:4, 553:5
Lubitsch, Ernst, 516:6

M

MacDonald, Jeanette, 505:7
Macmillan Co., 484:3
MacNeill, Robin, 535:3
Magazines—*see* Journalism
Magruder, Jeb Stuart, 286:4, 290:2
Mahan, Alfred T., 342:1
Mahler, Gustav, 523:4
Malaysia, 366:5, 380:3
Malraux, Andre, 332:2
Malthus, Robert, 70:5
Man of La Mancha (film), 513:2
Mansfield, Mike, 264:3
Mao Tse-tung, 348:2
Marcos, Ferdinand E., 355:4
Mardian, Robert, 290:2
Marijuana—*see* Medicine—drug abuse
Marine Corps, U.S.,—*see* Defense
Marriage, 556:1, 563:7
Marshall Plan, 82:5, 97:2, 451:2
Martinique, 343:1
Marxism, 318:2, 331:5, 339:3, 344:6, 451:3
See also Communism; Socialism

Mary Queen of Scots (book), 415:2
Maryland, 243:3, 243:4
Materialism, 48:1, 565:2
Matsu (Nationalist China), 350:3
Maugham, W. Somerset, 489:1
Mayors—*see* Urban affairs—government
McCarthy, Joseph R., 100:4, 271:3, 299:3
McCord, James W., 306:6
McCormack, Cyrus, 127:4
McCormack, John, 522:2
McGovern, George S., 248:2, 250:3, 258:4, 261:2,
    304:4, 464:1
McPartland, Marian, 525:6
Meany, George, 317:6
Medicaid—*see* Medicine—insurance
Medicare—*see* Medicine—insurance
Medicine/health, 313:1, 314:1, 315:2, pp. 491-501
    abortion, 336:4, 493:1, 497:4, 562:4
    alcoholism, 311:6, 491:4, 493:3, 493:5, 496:1
    American Medical Association (AMA), 492:3
    birth control, 336:4
    cancer, 499:4
    cholesterol, 500:3
    death/mortality, 500:1, 501:1
    dentistry, 496:2, 498:4
    diets/over-weight, 495:1, 497:1, 500:3
    doctors/physicians, 491:2, 492:4, 493:2, 493:4,
      494:3, 500:2, 501:2
      doctor-patient ratio, 491:1
    drug abuse/addiction/narcotics, 55:2, 103:5,
      108:5, 247:5, 311:6, 318:1, 328:2, 491:4,
      494:2, 498:3, 553:7
      crime related to, 98:4, 498:3
      heroin, 98:4, 108:1
      marijuana, 103:5, 106:4, 499:5
      trafficking, 106:6, 108:1
    drugs, 500:2
      drug industry, 498:2
      promotion of, 493:4
      safety, 494:1
    euthanasia, 493:2, 495:4
    exercise, 499:2, 500:3
    genetics, 495:6
    government aspect, 491:3, 491:5, 492:3, 492:4,
      496:4
      budget/fund cuts, 492:1, 494:4, 495:3, 498:6
    health care/services, 44:1, 310:3, 311:6, 312:4,
      314:4, 317:2, 317:4
      cost/price of, 201:5, 497:3
    heart attacks, 499:2
    hospitals, 188:4
    infant mortality, 491:1
    insurance, 491:3, 497:2
      Medicaid, 499:6
      Medicare, 212:3, 314:1, 491:5
    life expectancy, 491:1
    mental health/psychiatry, 495:2, 497:5, 498:1,
      499:3, 499:7
    nutrition, 493:3
    research, 495:3, 496:3, 496:4, 498:6
    a right, not privilege, 491:5

schools/students, medical, 113:6, 492:1
self/over-the-counter medication, 492:2, 492:5
smoking, 493:3, 498:5, 500:3
in Soviet Union, 496:4
as status symbol, 493:3
tension, 498:5
Mediocrity, 114:2, 558:3
Mediterranean, 352:5, 392:5, 409:4, 439:3, 440:4
Melville, Herman, 489:5
Men, 544:5, 553:3
Mental health—*see* Medicine
Metro-Goldwyn-Mayer, Inc., 502:3, 506:3, 512:2
Metropolitan Opera (N.Y.C.), 455:5
Mets, New York (baseball), 578:1, 585:7
Mexico, 341:5
    Communist Chinese relations, 351:5
    U.S. relations, 343:2
Middle East, the, 101:2, 134:2, 138:4, 149:4, 281:3,
    349:2, 407:3, pp. 417-442, 446:1, 450:8
    Arab/Israeli negotiations/peace conference, 420:7,
      421:4, 421:5, 423:1, 423:2, 423:4, 426:3,
      427:4, 430:2, 430:4, 432:3, 432:7, 433:2
    Arab/Israeli war (1967, Six Day), 417:2, 418:1,
      432:3, 432:6, 443:4
    Arab/Israeli war (1973), 134:2, 144:5, 155:1,
      417:5, 418:5, 418:6, 419:2, 420:5, 422:4,
      422:5, 427:2, 428:4, 429:5, 429:6, 430:1,
      431:2, 431:4, 432:1, 432:6, 433:1, 435:4,
      435:5, 436:1, 437:4, 440:3, 441:1, 441:2
    Austria and Arab terrorism, 422:3, 431:3, 432:5,
      433:4
    German aspect, 420:3
    Israeli occupation of Arab land, 349:2, 418:1,
      418:6, 419:1, 421:2, 422:4, 424:1, 425:2,
      425:4, 426:3, 427:2, 428:1, 428:2, 435:4,
      436:1, 436:2, 441:6, 442:1
    Israeli downing of Arab airliner, 437:2, 438:5,
      440:2
    Jerusalem, 418:1, 421:5, 424:1, 431:2, 432:2
    oil, 419:5, 420:1, 422:6, 424:6, 425:1, 426:2,
      426:4, 427:3, 428:3, 433:2, 435:2, 435:6,
      438:2, 439:5
      Arab embargo/cutback/weapon, 126:3, 128:1,
        134:2, 135:2, 139:4, 143:5, 342:2, 347:4,
        395:4, 417:1, 417:2, 418:3, 419:4, 423:3,
        425:3, 427:5, 429:1, 429:4, 430:3, 432:1,
        433:3, 434:2, 435:3, 436:1, 436:4, 439:3,
        441:3, 441:4, 441:6, 442:1
    Palestine/palestinians, 158:6, 410:5, 418:2,
      419:1, 419:2, 420:4, 423:2, 424:1, 424:4,
      425:1, 426:3, 428:2, 435:1, 435:4, 435:5,
      436:2, 436:3, 438:1, 440:4, 447:4
    Soviet aspect, 155:1, 352:5, 418:1, 418:5, 422:6,
      423:1, 426:3, 428:3, 428:4, 429:5, 430:2,
      431:1, 432:6, 433:5, 436:2, 436:3, 440:3,
      441:2
      peace keeping—*see* U.S., *below*
    Suez Canal, 420:7, 427:1, 427:2, 438:4
    superpower aspect, 419:2, 428:5, 430:2, 432:6
    United Nations Resolution 242, 442:1, 428:1
    U.S. aspect:
      policy, 405:6, 433:2, 434:4, 435:3

Middle East—
  U.S. aspect (*continued*)
    Soviet/U.S. peace-keeping guarantee, 425:2, 428:5, 430:1
    Zionism, 435:4, 439:1, 440:4, 447:4
    See also specific countries; Arabs
Military—*see* Defense
Miller, Arthur, 527:3, 540:2
Miller, Glenn, 138:4
Missiles—*see* Defense
Mitchell, John N., 286:4, 290:2, 291:2, 293:2, 293:3
Mix, Tom, 510:5
Moby Dick (book), 487:4
Moliere, Jean Baptiste, 503:1
Molly Maguires, The (film), 509:2
Monarchy, 195:5, 265:4
Monetary system—*see* Commerce
Mongolia, 398:2
Monopoly—*see* Commerce—antitrust
Monroe Doctrine—*see* Foreign affairs
Moon—*see* Space
Morality, 45:1, 553:7, 562:5, 564:5, 566:6
Morocco, 420:4, 436:2
Moslemism—*see* Religion
Motion pictures/cinema/films, 487:5, 488:1, 490:3, pp. 502-518, 537:7
  Academy Awards/"Oscar," 507:1, 508:2, 511:2, 512:3, 512:6
  admission prices, 506:2, 516:5
  all-or-nothing psychology, 509:3
  audiences/public, 506:2, 506:5, 507:4, 509:7, 513:2, 515:1, 517:5, 518:6
  automation, 507:3
  black-oriented, 502:1, 507:4
  business aspect, 505:1, 512:1, 516:4, 516:5
  cassettes, 507:3
  censorship, 505:4, 507:2
  conglomerate acquisition of studios, 509:2
  costs of production, 509:2, 509:5, 511:4, 511:6, 512:2
  criticism/critics, 504:7, 505:5, 510:3, 511:3, 517:3
  directing/directors, 503:3, 503:6, 506:4, 507:6, 508:3, 508:6, 510:4, 512:5, 512:6, 513:1, 515:5, 517:3
    women directors, 503:2, 518:4
  as diversion, 512:4
  as entertainment, 510:2, 511:4, 512:7, 514:3, 515:1, 517:4, 518:5
  family-type, 513:2, 516:3, 516:5
  French, 504:6
  future of, 511:6, 514:2
  glamor, 518:1
  Hays Office, 505:4
  Hollywood, 504:2, 504:6, 505:2, 507:2, 509:7, 510:5, 510:6, 511:2, 512:5, 515:4, 515:7, 516:6, 517:2, 517:4, 518:1, 518:5, 537:4
  illusion, 516:6
  in India, 514:1
  love in, 508:5

magic of, 517:4
MGM production cutback, 502:3, 506:3
music for, 505:7, 525:5
"panacea picture," 513:4
political-type, 505:2
pornographic/obscene/permissive, 503:5, 509:7, 510:5, 515:2, 516:6
  sex/nudity, 502:4, 504:4, 507:2, 508:5, 511:1, 511:5, 513:2, 514:2, 514:3, 515:1, 550:8, 561:2, 563:4
  Supreme Court ruling, 505:4, 507:2, 516:1
preaching-type, 518:5
"problem" pictures, 509:5
producers, 513:1, 515:3
ratings, 510:5
schmaltz in, 515:1
stage/theatre compared with, 502:2, 503:1, 503:6, 504:1, 505:7, 516:2, 527:4, 528:1, 533:4
stars, 511:4, 513:3, 515:7, 516:4
the great studios, 502:3
success ratio, 511:6, 518:6
television compared with, 506:6, 514:4, 515:2, 540:4
television, selling films to, 514:4
violence in, 48:1, 504:4, 506:5, 511:1, 515:1, 563:4
visual aspect, 508:3
Westerns, 505:2, 507:4, 513:2
women, parts for, 504:6, 505:3
writing/writers, 503:6, 507:6
young film-makers, 510:6
youth-oriented, 507:4, 509:2
See also Acting
Moyers, Bill, 535:3
Moynihan, Daniel P., 60:3
Mozambique, 444:1
Mozart, Wolfgang Amadeus, 519:3, 521:4, 523:2, 554:3
Mrs. Warren's Profession (play), 543:1
Ms. (magazine), 336:2
Murrow, Edward R., 469:5
Museums—*see* Arts
Music, 509:1, 516:2, pp. 519-526
  American musicians compared with Europeans, 523:1
  American musicians, European exposure for, 524:3
  audiences, noisy, 519:2
  chamber music, 523:1, 523:3
  classical, 519:4
  composing/songwriting, 520:1, 520:4, 521:4, 522:3, 523:2, 524:1, 524:4, 524:5, 525:3, 531:1
  conducting/conductors, 520:3, 524:2, 525:1, 525:2
  criticism, 522.4
  experimentation, 520:1
  imagination of audience, 520:2
  improvisation, 519:4
  independence required, 519:1

Music (*continued*)
    jazz, 519:4, 521:2, 521:3, 525:6, 570:6
    for motion pictures, 505:7, 525:5
    opera, 519:5, 523:5
        financing of, 522:5
        massive productions, 520:2
        singers, 519:6, 522:1
        support/subsidy for, 455:3, 455:5, 456:2
    orchestras, 522:2
        U.S. orchestras, European attitude toward, 523:4
    pure music, 519:4
    purpose of, 521:4
    quality of, 522:3
    the recital, 525:4
    recording, 520:5
    rock music, 521:1, 521:3, 524:5, 531:1
    singing/singers, 521:5, 524:5
        opera, 519:6, 522:1
    in Soviet Union, 457:3
    for the stage, 505:7
    style, 519:3
    symphony music, 523:2
    tradition in, 519:3, 519:4
    youth audience, 521:3
Muskie, Edmund S., 263:6, 266:1
Mussolini, Benito, 355:5, 419:5, 439:3

N

NAACP (National Association for the Advancement of Colored People)—*see* Civil rights
Nader, Ralph, 71:3, 80:3, 90:1
Nana (book), 543:1
Narcotics—*see* Medicine—drug abuse
NASA (National Aeronautics and Space Administration)—*see* Space
National Advisory Commission on Crime, 104:6
National Aeronautics and Space Administration (NASA)—*see* Space
National Association of Women Lawyers, 332:1
National Broadcasting Co (NBC), 547:2
National Federation of Business and Professional Women's Clubs, 332:1
National Football League (NFL)—*see* Football
National Institutes of Health, 494:4
National News Council—*see* Journalism
National Organization for Women (NOW)—*see* Women
National Rifle Association, 106:2
National Security Council, 109:4, 185:6, 189:2
National Theatre of England—*see* Stage—England
Nationalism, 355:3
Nationalization—*see* Commerce; Transportation—railroads
NATO—*see* North Atlantic Treaty Organization
Nature, back to, 557:6
Navajos—*see* Indian, American
Navy, U.S.—*see* Defense
NBC—*see* National Broadcasting Co.

Nazism—*see* Germany
Negroes—*see* Civil rights—blacks
Neurotic people, 550:6
New Deal, the, 177:1, 257:5
New Frontier, the, 257:5
New York City, 329:1
    newspapers, 474:6
    politics, 245:2
    Social Services Dept., 499:6
    theatre—*see* Stage—Broadway
New York Stock Exchange (NYSE)—*see* Commerce—stocks
New York Times, The (newspaper), 333:4, 464:2, 465:6, 481:1, 534:1
New Zealand, 354:2
News—*see* Journalism
News/press conferences, Presidential—*see* Journalism—Presidential
Newspapers—*see* Journalism
Newsweek (magazine), 275:4
NFL (National Football League)—*see* Football
Nicklaus, Jack, 593:1
Nigeria, 450:8
Nijinsky, Vaslav, 508:6
Nile River, 418:4
Nixon, Richard M./Nixon Administration, 63:4, 213:1, 242:1, 246:4, 250:1, 250:2, 255:6, 256:1, 263:3, 283:2
    accomplishments, 247:2, 253:3, 274:4, 275:3, 281:3, 285:3, 306:5, 452:5
    Agnew, relationship with, 242:2
    aides/staff, 185:6, 193:3, 246:1, 248:6, 251:4, 259:1, 260:4, 260:5, 262:1, 273:3, 276:2, 279:2, 290:1, 303:5
    controversy, dealing with, 261:4
    Constitution, disregard for, 265:4
    credibility/believability/trust—*see* Presidency—credibility
    crises, appetite for, 270:5
    deviousness, 248:1
    emotional instability, 292:4
    impeachment—*see* Watergate
    a loner, 182:5, 253:1, 253:2
    mentality, 302:2
    Nixon Doctrine—*see* Foreign affairs
    as peacemaker, 377:3
    political power, 261:2
    master politician, 258:4
    relaxation of, 173:4
    resignation—*see* Watergate
    role in history, 50:4
    successes, blowing up of, 153:1
Nobel Prize (literature), 489:1
Nobel Prize (peace), 377:3
North Atlantic Treaty Organization (NATO)/Atlantic Alliance, 161:5, 231:3, 385:2, 392:5, 394:1, 394:4, 394:6, 400:1, 400:3, 401:5, 405:6, 406:3, 408:1, 408:3, 409:1, 410:2, 410:4, 411:5, 451:2
North Korea—*see* Korea
North Vietnam—*see* Vietnam

Northern Ireland:
British authority in, 403:3, 403:5, 410:5
Catholics in, 403:3, 416:1
Irish Republican Army (IRA), 399:3
Libyan aspect, 412:1
sharing power in, 416:1
Protestants in, 403:3
Unionist Party, 398:1
unity with Ireland, 399:3, 403:3
Novels—*see* Literature
NOW (National Organization for Women)—*see* Women

O

OAS (Organization of American States)—*see* Americas
Obsolescence, 555:3
Oceans—*see* Environment
Oedipus at Colonus, 565:4
OEO—*see* Office of Economic Opportunity
Offenbach, Jacques, 531:1
Office of Economic Opportunity (OEO), 316:3, 317:5, 317:6
Office of Federal Contract Employees, 333:4
Office of Management and Budget, 174:1
Oglala Sioux—*see* Indian, American
Oil/petroleum, 80:4, 344:1, 405:1
Alaska pipeline, 125:2, 129:1, 133:2
companies, 68:6
depletion allowance—*see* Taxes
government corporation, 80:4
public-utility regulation, 81:3
European aspect, 133:3, 419:4, 429:1, 435:6
imports, 75:3, 92:2, 426:2, 429:4, 435:6
Israeli lack of, 432:4
prices, 87:4, 139:3
spills, 129:4
See also Middle East
Oil Policy Committee, 143:5
Old people—*see* Elderly
Olivier, Laurence, 504:3, 508:6, 529:6
Olympics—*see* Sports
On a Clear Day You Can See Forever (film), 509:2
Onassis, Jacqueline, 336:2
Opera—*see* Music
Opinions, 562:2
Oppenheimer, J. Robert, 127:4
Oppression, 153:3
Ordinary/superior people, 556:2, 556:6
Organization of African Unity, 444:1
Organization of American States (OAS)—*see* Americas
Organized Crime Control Act, 105:3
Orwell, George, 195:3
Otello (opera), 565:4
O'Toole, Peter, 502:1
Ottoman Empire, 440:4

P

Paint Your Wagon (film), 509:2
Painting—*see* Arts
Pakistan, 450:8
Bangladesh, recognition of, 356:2
Indian relations, 348:5, 356:3, 357:4
war with India (1971), 348:3, 348:4, 356:3, 448:3
Iranian relations, 357:4
Japanese relations, 353:4
Soviet aspect, 348:1, 398:2
U.S. relations, 348:3, 356:3
U.S. arms aid, 348:3, 356:3
Palestine/Palestinians—*see* Middle East
Palmer, Arnold, 593:1
Panama:
Canal, 340:3, 342:1, 342:3, 345:5, 346:2, 347:1, 347:2, 415:5
Communism in, 340:3
Soviet aspect, 342:1
Panov, Valery, 412:2
Papadopoulos, George, 392:2, 399:2, 401:3, 409:2
Paramount Pictures Corp., 509:2, 517:4
Parker, Charlie, 525:6
Parks—*see* Environment
Past, the, 552:5, 559:2
Patriotism, 44:3, 49:3, 54:1, 103:4, 213:2, 304:1
Patterson, Floyd, 577:4
Patterson, Robert P., 275:3
Patton (film), 514:4
Paul VI, Pope, 568:6, 570:2
PBS (Public Broadcasting Service)—*see* Television—public
Peace, 82:6, 125:1, 148:3, 149:5, 150:3, 151:5, 152:1, 156:3, 157:3, 159:1, 159:3, 160:1, 232:2, 234:2, 236:6, 237:1, 237:2, 237:3, 238:4, 253:3, 354:3, 369:5, 381:2, 381:3, 392:3, 394:2, 394:4, 395:6, 396:5, 401:5, 401:6, 402:4, 410:3, 412:2, 415:3, 423:4, 427:4, 437:5, 441:1, 446:2, 446:3, 446:4, 446:5, 447:2, 447:3, 448:1, 448:4, 449:1, 449:2, 450:2, 450:4, 450:5, 450:6, 450:7, 450:9, 451:2, 452:3, 452:5, 566:2
See also War; War and Peace
Peace Corps, U.S., 94:2, 377:4, 380:2
Peckinpah, Sam, 511:1
Peguy, Charles, 567:3
Penghu (Nationalist China), 350:3
Penn Central Railroad—*see* Transportation—railroads
Pennsylvania Fish Commission, 130:4
Pentagon—*see* Defense
"Pentagon Papers," 174:6, 176:2, 176:3, 252:2, 279:3, 363:5, 365:6, 366:4, 368:5, 474:1
Performing arts, pp. 502-543
See also Dance; Motion pictures; Music; Radio; Stage; Television
Permissiveness, 106:3, 225:6, 286:2, 502:4, 541:5, 555:1
Persian Gulf, 424:6, 426:4, 427:3, 428:3, 439:2
Personal profiles, pp. 544-551

Peru, 341:4
Pesticides—*see* Environment
Petroleum—*see* Oil
Philadelphia Plan—*see* Civil rights
Philippines:
    Constitution, 355:5
    democracy in, 358:4, 358:5
    dictatorship in, 355:5
    martial law in, 355:4, 355:5, 358:4, 358:5
    North Vietnamese threat to, 381:3
Phillips, Howard, 317:5
Philosophy, pp. 552-565
Photography—*see* Arts
Picasso, Pablo, 458:4, 565:4
Pickford, Mary, 515:1
Pillow Talk (film), 510:3
Pinter, Harold, 490:3
Pippin (play), 529:3
Planned Parenthood, 497:4
Playwriting—*see* Stage
Poe, Edgar Allan, 487:4
Poetry—*see* Literature
Poland, 398:2
Police—*see* Crime
Politics, pp. 242-308, 580:7
    business/industry aspect, 82:1, 93:3
    campaigns—*see* Elections
    confidence in, 284:5
    corruption, 247:1, 282:1, 301:3
    "enemies list," White House, 265:5
    ethical standards, 291:3
    giving up politics, 250:7
    intelligence/espionage, political, 249:2, 251:5,
        255:1, 263:1, 277:3, 277:5, 286:1, 289:2,
        291:4, 303:4
        See also Watergate
    ITT favoritism affair, 282:2
    political parties, 196:3, 266:4
        two-party system, 244:4, 251:6, 289:2
    politicians, 262:3, 265:6, 284:3, 547:5
        character ingredients, 255:1
        decency among, 285:4
        honesty of, 259:3, 277:1
        laughable figures, 266:3
        violence against, 254:2
    scandals, 262:6, 289:3, 303:4
        Teapot Dome, 282:1, 300:2
        See also Watergate
    television aspect, 245:3, 251:3, 259:3
    as warfare, 171:5, 266:2
    women in, 266:5
    young, disenchantment of, 247:1
    See also specific parties; Conservatism; Govern-
        ment; Liberalism; Watergate
Pollock, Jackson, 459:2
Pollution—*see* Environment
Poor, the—*see* Social welfare
Population—*see* Environment
Pornography—*see* Arts
Portugal:
    democracy in, 410:2

    liberalization in, 397:2
    military forces, 410:2
Postal Service, U.S., 80:4, 178:5, 179:3, 189:4,
    194:4
    mail rate increases, 470:4
    Postmaster General, 179:3
Poverty—*see* Social welfare
POWs (prisoners of war)—*see* Indochina
Powell, William, 518:1
Pravda (newspaper), 400:1
Prayer Breakfast, National House-Senate, 567:2
Prejudice—*see* Civil rights
Prelude (poem), 484:1
Presidency/Executive, U.S., 167:1, 177:4, 182:4,
    184:4, 188:5, 268:4, 273:3
    abolition of, 163:6
    aides/advisors, 171:5
    blamed for what goes wrong, 171:4
    British-type vote of confidence, 193:5
    broadcasting authority, 538:6
    budget/spending aspect, 167:4, 170:3, 178:7,
        184:1, 187:1
    business, relations with, 209:1
    Congressional/legislative relations—*see* Congress
    credibility/confidence/integrity/trust in, 260:2,
        273:1, 278:5, 282:1, 287:4, 290:2, 290:4,
        292:2, 297:4, 300:3, 304:1, 304:3, 305:4,
        306:3, 306:4
    defense/military aspect, 235:3
    as demanding position, 188:1
    economy aspect, 211:4
    foreign-affairs aspect, 151:2, 162:1
        war-making powers/authority, 150:2, 150:4,
            152:4, 153:2, 160:2, 161:2
    Gaullist view of, 196:2
    glamorization of, 170:1
    governing as thinks best, 165:3
    growth of Executive office, 168:2
    humility of, 183:4
    impeachment, 186:2, 191:3
        See also Watergate
    impoundment—*see* Government
    institutionalized, 177:1
    invisible, 177:1
    Judiciary aspect, 222:5
        Supreme Court aspect, 222:7, 224:1
    labor relations, 209:1
    and the law, 185:3, 281:1
    living in luxury, 185:4
    power/authority, 166:4, 169:6, 174:7, 181:5,
        183:7, 185:2, 185:3, 186:2, 187:1, 187:3,
        193:2, 222:5, 272:1, 289:4
    press/news conferences, 307:3, 465:3, 465:4,
        466:4, 468:1
    prisoner of Pennsylvania Avenue, 175:3
    privacy/confidentiality of, 165:5, 167:6, 296:2,
        297:2, 301:1
    privilege, Executive, 165:5, 174:4, 175:6, 182:1,
        187:2, 273:2, 276:4, 279:4, 288:1, 312:5
    responsibilities of, 249:1
    satisfaction of, 196:2

Presidency (*continued*)
taping White House conversations, 292:3
tariffs, control over, 96:2
term of office, 168:4
Vice President, relationship with, 165:2, 242:2
vigilance, target of, 172:3
See also specific Presidents; Congress; Government
Press—*see* Journalism
Press conferences, Presidential—*see* Journalism—Presidential
Price Commission, U.S., 207:1, 264:2
Prices, 198:4, 204:3, 205:2, 206:6, 210:6, 212:4, 215:1, 216:3, 217:2, 217:5, 217:6, 219:3, 315:2
food—*see* Agriculture
price fixing, 82:4
See also Economy
Public Broadcasting Service (PBS)—*see* Television—public

Q

Quality of life, 128:4, 134:3, 141:2, 141:3, 149:5, 335:6
Quebec (Canada), 340:2

R

Racism—*see* Civil rights
Radek, Karl, 81:1
Radio, 507:3, 535:1, 535:4, 542:2, 594:1
See also Television
Railroads—*see* Transportation
Rams, Los Angeles (football), 581:5
Raphael (Santi), 455:2
Raposo, Joe, 524:5
Reasoner, Harry, 464:1
Recycling—*see* Environment
Reds, Cincinnati (baseball), 578:1
Redskins, Washington (football), 61:2, 188:3
Religion/church, 48:1, 404:2, 424:2, 511:1, 537:7, pp.566-571
atheism, 444:3, 566:4
Bible, the, 567:1, 569:2
Buddhism, 566:3, 570:6
Catholicism, 403:3, 416:1, 569:5
Christianity/Christian, 566:2, 566:3, 567:1, 567:5, 568:5, 570:4
in athletics, 582:5
Christ, Jesus, 567:2, 567:4, 568:5
civil religion, 567:2
credibility/confidence in, 49:3, 51:1, 262:4
crisis in, 566:6, 570:4
definition, 566:5
disappearance of, 569:4
doctrine, mired in, 566:3
failure of, 566:1
government control or banning of, 569:3
heresy, 571:1
Hinduism, 566:3, 570:6
institutional, 567:4, 568:5, 569:1

intermarriage, 569:6
"Jesus people," 567:4
Judaism/Jews, 406:1, 409:3, 418:4, 420:4, 421:3, 422:3, 429:5, 430:4, 431:3, 432:5, 433:4, 434:4, 435:5, 436:2, 436:3, 439:4, 440:4, 443:4, 567:5, 568:6, 569:6
Zionism, 435:4, 439:1, 440:4, 447:4
Koran, the, 444:3
Moslemism, 428:3, 431:2, 434:2, 443:6
political/activist, 566:2, 568:3, 570:1
Pope, the, 570:2, 571:1
popularity of, 566:4, 570:3
Protestantism, 398:1, 403:3
public return to, 568:2
purpose of, 566:3
revivalism, 567:4
secularism, 566:1, 567:1, 568:2
separation of church and state, 570:5
as social club, 567:3
substitutes for, 570:6
tension within, 568:1
theological base for, 569:2
Republican Party, 213:2, 245:4, 248:3, 251:6, 252:3, 253:4, 254:1, 255:1, 265:2, 269:1, 272:5, 563:6
businessmen's party, 244:4, 264:4
campaign tactics, 245:5, 246:2
dissenters purged from, 262:2
economy aspect, 200:1, 264:4
law-and-order party, 264:4
principles of, 248:3, 254:1
Republican National Committee, 282:2
Watergate responsibility—*see* Watergate
Reputation, 549:5
Responsibility, 561:8
Retirement—*see* Labor
Revenue-sharing—*see* Government
Revolution, 367:1, 557:4
American Revolution/Revolutionary War, 152:4, 195:5, 255:6, 279:4
Rhodesia, 149:4
black majority rule, 444:7
British relations, 444:7
Constitution, 444:7
economy, 444:6
racism in, 444:1, 444:6, 445:1
sanctions against, 439:3, 444:6, 445:1
standard of living, 444:6
Richardson, Elliot L., 295:1, 297:2, 298:2
Riggs, Bobby, 579:6
Right vs. wrong, 560:3, 564:5
Robinson, Jackie, 58:3
Rockettes, the, 533:5
Rogers, Will, 183:6
Roman Empire, 156:5, 440:4
Romania, 404:4
Roosevelt, Franklin D., 169:6, 246:2, 254:4, 258:2, 273:3, 275:3, 439:3, 522:2
Roosevelt, Theodore, 342:1
Rousseau, Jean Jacques, 557:6
Rowan, Carl, 464:1

Rozelle, Pete, 591:5
Rural affairs—*see* Urban affairs
Russell, Bertrand, 500:1
Russia—*see* Soviet Union
Russo, Anthony, Jr., 176:3, 366:4
Ruth, Babe, 577:1, 577:2, 579:8

S

Sadat, Anwar el-, 422:3, 427:2, 435:4
Sailing, 545:6
Sakharov, Andrei D., 409:3
SALT (strategic arms limitation talks)—*see* Defense—
    arms control
San Marino, 394:2
Sanders, Colonel, 52:4
Satellites—*see* Space
Saudi Arabia, 419:5, 426:2, 428:3, 438:2, 441:6,
    442:1
    U.S. relations, 417:3, 424:2
Scandinavia, 557:4
    See also Sweden
Scarlet Letter, The (book), 543:1
Schools—*see* Education
Schubert, Franz, 456:1, 523:4
Schumann-Heink, Ernestine, 522:2
Schweitzer, Albert, 565:1
Science/technology, 52:2, 52:4, 78:5, 125:1, 134:3,
    136:4, 204:5, 235:1, 282:1, 557:6, 560:4,
    568:2, pp. 572-576
    aerospace industry, 325:2, 573:3
    arts compared with, 456:4
    blessings and curses of, 574:5
    communications, 481:4, 572:1, 576:2
    computers, 576:2
    criticism of/disillusion with, 572:3, 573:4, 573:5,
        574:6, 575:3
    in education, 119:4
    environment aspect, 124:1, 131:3, 138:3
    "information tyranny," 576:2
    Japanese, 574:3, 576:1
    U.S. decrease as technological power, 573:3,
        574:3
    women scientists, 572:1
    See also Space
Scotland, 403:6
Scott, Hugh, 264:3
Seas, freedom of the, 71:4
Seat belts, 320:4
SEC (Securities and Exchange Commission)—*see*
    Commerce—stocks
Secrecy in government—*see* Government
Securities and Exchange Commission (SEC)—*see*
    Commerce—stocks
Securities industry—*see* Commerce—stocks
Segregation—*see* Civil rights
Selective Service System, U.S., 234:3, 238:2
    See also Defense—draft
Selfishness, 555:3, 562:4
Senate, U.S.—*see* Congress
Senate Foreign Relations Committee, 368:5

Senate Interior Committee, 58:1
Senator, The (TV show), 538:3
Sevareid, Eric, 464:2
Sex, 46:4, 336:4, 557:4, 561:6, 566:6, 570:6
    in the arts, 455:4
    in motion pictures, 502:4, 504:4, 507:2, 508:5,
        511:1, 511:5, 513:2, 514:2, 514:3, 515:1,
        550:8, 561:2, 563:4
    in television, 563:4
Shakespeare, William, 533:5
Shaw, George Bernard, 537:1, 543:1
Shield law—*see* Journalism
Shula, Don, 589:6
Siberia—*see* Soviet Union
Sierra Club, 127:1
Sihanouk, Norodom, 382:2
Simon, Neil, 529:6
Sinai Desert, 427:2
Sinatra, Frank, 50:1, 317:5
Singapore, 355:2, 380:3
    fall to Communists, 366:5
Sirica, John J., 294:5, 297:2
Six Crises (book), 270:5
Six Wives of Henry VIII, The (TV show), 415:2
Skepticism, 51:1
Skyjacking—*see* Transportation—air
Smith, Howard K., 470:1
Smithsonian Agreements, 78:3, 87:3
Smoking—*see* Medicine
Snodgrass, Carrie, 516:4
Soccer—*see* Sports
Social Security System—*see* Social welfare
Social welfare, pp. 309-319
    day/child care, 310:5
    food stamps, 313:1
        for labor strikers, 203:5, 204:4, 207:4, 208:1
    guaranteed income, 318:5
    housing, 188:4, 215:2, 310:3, 312:3, 312:4,
        313:1, 314:1, 315:1, 315:2, 318:1
    migrant workers, 312:2
    poverty/the poor, 55:4, 57:3, 125:1, 188:4,
        209:2, 215:3, 229:1, 242:3, 309:1, 309:4,
        311:4, 311:6, 312:3, 313:4, 313:5, 314:1,
        314:2, 314:3, 314:4, 315:2, 316:1, 317:3,
        317:4, 317:5, 317:6, 318:1, 318:3, 326:5,
        327:1, 552:2, 554:4
        business help for, 88:3
        cause of crime, 100:6
        education aspect, 122:3
        legal assistance, 309:2, 310:2, 316:2
        as profession, 314:5
        "trickle down" theory of poverty program,
            311:1, 316:3
        war on poverty, 47:4, 310:5, 318:2
    rent controls, 211:3
    Social Security System, 309:5, 310:1, 310:3,
        311:4, 314:1
    welfare, 46:4, 53:1, 77:1, 188:2, 204:4, 208:1,
        309:1, 310:4, 311:2, 312:2, 316:1, 317:1,
        318:5
    See also Elderly

Socialism, 52:1, 148:3, 339:2, 339:3, 339:5, 349:2, 396:2, 396:6, 397:2, 397:6, 398:2, 402:3, 403:1, 415:4, 447:3, 497:2
  See also specific countries;
    Communism; Marxism
Solar energy—*see* Energy
Solzhenitsyn, Alexander I., 409:3
Sophocles, 484:1, 533:5, 565:4
Sound of Music, The (film), 510:3
South, the U.S., 507:4, 539:6
South Africa, 149:4, 441:1
  Israeli relations, 423:5
South Korea—*see* Korea
South Vietnam—*see* Vietnam
Soviet Academy of Medical Sciences, 496:4
Soviet Ministry of Health, 496:4
Soviet Union/Russia/U.S.S.R., 57:3, 149:4, 152:3, 392:4, 393:2, 407:1, 409:1, 412:4, 412:5, 440:4, 447:2, 449:1, 450:8
  Africa, subversion in, 398:2
  Arab relations, 158:6
  arts in, 457:3
  Asian aspect, 348:1, 353:1, 357:1, 398:2
  Australian relations, 349:1
  Bulgarian relations, 404:4
  capitalism in, 398:2, 403:1
  Caribbean aspect, 342:1
  citizenship in, 414:5
  Communist Chinese aspect, 152:5, 163:6, 352:5, 354:1, 355:1, 355:3, 358:3, 360:3, 386:1, 398:2, 404:4
  Communist Party, 365:3, 446:5
  Cuban aspect, 340:4, 397:4
  Czechoslovakian relations, 395:5, 404:4
    Soviet invasion (1968), 370:2, 398:2, 413:3, 416:3
  defense/military aspect, 158:2, 189:2, 234:5, 235:2, 239:3, 239:5, 240:1, 241:2, 241:3, 393:4, 397:4, 398:3, 404:5
    missile strength, 352:5
    Navy/sea power, 79:2, 241:3, 392:5
    submarine fleet, 398:4
  economic aspect, 397:4, 402:2, 404:5, 412:6
  Egyptian relations, 398:2, 429:5
  emigration, 151:5, 396:4, 404:2, 404:3, 406:1, 409:3, 425:4, 431:3
  European aspect, 393:1, 395:6, 396:6, 403:2, 408:3, 410:3, 422:6
  Fascism in, 398:2
  foreign affairs aspect, 158:5, 365:3, 393:4, 402:1, 402:3, 407:2, 408:2, 448:4
  freedom in, 399:5, 404:2, 408:2
  imperialism of, 397:4, 397:6, 398:2
  Indian relations, 349:3, 352:4, 353:1, 356:3, 359:2
  Indochina/Vietnam aspect, 365:3, 370:5, 390:1
  Israeli relations, 426:3
  Japanese relations, 353:4, 360:5
  KGB, 414:4
  medical research in, 496:4
  Mediterranean aspect, 352:5, 439:3

Middle East aspect—*see* Middle East
  Mongolian aspect, 398:2
  music in, 457:3
  Olympics aspect, 586:3
  Pakistani aspect, 348:1, 398:2
  Panamanian aspect, 342:1
  poets and novelists, fear of, 457:6
  Polish rebellion, suppression of, 398:2
  repression in, 153:3, 406:1, 412:2, 414:4
  Romanian relations, 404:4
  Russian Revolution, 400:4
  Siberia, 396:2
  standard of living, 393:4, 396:2
  trade, 213:2, 413:1
    See also U.S., *below*
  U.S. relations, 69:1, 152:1, 155:3, 156:4, 157:2, 157:3, 158:1, 158:6, 161:1, 234:4, 253:3, 275:3, 306:5, 340:1, 340:4, 373:4, 381:2, 385:5, 392:3, 395:6, 401:1, 402:4, 405:6, 407:2, 407:3, 410:4, 431:1, 433:5, 446:4, 446:5, 448:3
    feeding of Soviets, 52:2
    Nixon Soviet trip (1972), 152:5, 239:5, 481:4
    trade, 68:2, 81:2, 82:6, 88:1, 89:3, 151:5, 153:3, 155:1, 342:5, 404:3, 404:5, 405:5, 416:4
      grain/wheat sale to Soviets, 68:3, 78:4, 81:1, 91:2, 201:2, 216:2, 264:4
  West German relations, 155:3, 396:3
  Western technology, importation of, 231:2, 402:2
  Yugoslavian relations, 404:4
Space, 321:5, 573:1, 573:2, 574:1, 574:4
  astronomy, 575:4
  energy aspect, 573:2
  extra-terrestrial life, 572:2
  moon landing/walks, 234:5, 572:1, 574:4, 575:5
  National Aeronautics and Space Administration (NASA), 572:1, 575:5
  satellites, 572:1, 574:4
    commercial, 73:1
    communications, 481:4
  shuttle, 572:1
  spending/budget, 313:2, 575:2
  the sun, 574:2
  unidentified flying objects (UFO), 572:2
Spain, 341:5, 355:5, 415:5
Speech, freedom of—*see* Freedom
Sports, 513:4, pp. 577-594
  amateur, 579:3
  auto racing, 583:1, 592:3
    Indianapolis 500 race, 581:3, 588:4
  betting, legalized, 190:4, 578:2
  boxing, 577:5, 578:5, 579:2, 581:1, 588:2
    championships/champions, 581:2, 581:4, 585:5
    Golden Gloves, 577:4
  as business, 579:2, 589:4, 592:1, 594:1
  competition, 579:5, 580:7, 586:3
  East European, 591:2
  entertainers, athletes as, 579:2, 579:7
  fan rejection, 587:2

Sports (*continued*)
  hockey, 583:5, 591:1, 592:4
  horse racing, 592:2
    off-track betting, 190:4
  money in, 590:2
  national anthem, 590:6, 591:6, 593:5
  old vs. new, 588:2
  Olympics, 583:3, 584:4, 586:3, 587:5
    Soviet aspect, 586:3
    U.S. Olympic Committee (USOC), 583:3
  pole vaulting, 591:2
  soccer, 592:5
  track and field/running, 584:3, 588:2
  winning/losing, 578:4, 580:7, 586:4, 587:2,
    588:3, 590:1, 591:5, 592:2
  women athletes, 584:7
  See also Baseball; Basketball; Football; Golf;
    Tennis
SST (supersonic transport)—*see* Transportation—air
Stage/theatre, 490:3, pp. 527-534
  audiences, 529:4, 530:1, 532:5, 533:6
    regularity of theatre-going, 530:2
    young audiences, 529:6, 530:7, 531:1
  Broadway/New York City, 527:1, 528:3, 528:4,
    529:3, 529:4, 529:5, 529:6, 530:6, 531:4,
    531:6, 533:1, 533:2, 533:4, 534:6
  costs of production, 528:4, 529:3, 531:4, 533:7
  criticism/critics, 527:3, 528:2, 529:2, 530:5,
    534:1, 551:4
  death of, 528:5, 530:3
  directing/directors, 503:6, 527:6
  in England, 529:5, 530:6, 531:5, 534:5
  as entertainment, 532:6
  message-type, 532:6
  mime, 531:3
  motion pictures compared with, 502:2, 503:1,
    503:6, 504:1, 505:7, 516:2, 527:4, 528:1,
    533:4
  music for, 505:7
  musicals, 528:4, 529:3, 529:6, 531:4
    rock musicals, 531:1
  parties, theatre, 529:4
  playwriting/playwrights, 503:6, 527:2, 527:6,
    528:4, 530:7, 531:1, 532:3, 533:3, 534:1,
    534:2, 534:3, 534:4, 537:7
  regional, 534:5
  repertory, 534:5
  road, shows on the, 529:3
  as social force, 532:3
  support/subsidy for, 527:2, 528:4, 531:5, 534:5
  television compared with, 536:4, 540:2
  ticket prices, 528:4, 529:4, 529:6, 534:6
  "Tony" award, 507:1, 527:7
  vulgarity in, 527:5
Stalin, Josef, 341:1, 400:3, 406:1
Standard of living, 88:2, 88:3, 125:1, 125:2, 147:2,
  212:1, 214:6, 221:1, 494:2
  See also specific countries
Stanislavsky, Konstantin, 503:7
Stans, Maurice H., 290:2
Stanwyck, Barbara, 516:4

State, U.S. Dept. of, 186:3, 189:2, 346:3
Steel industry, 94:2, 141:1, 145:5
Stein, Gertrude, 489:5
Steinem, Gloria, 332:2
Stennis, John C., 297:2, 301:1
Stewart, James, 518:1
Stimson, Harry L., 275:3, 303:4
Stocks—*see* Commerce
Stokes, Carl, 58:3
Stokowski, Leopold, 520:3
Stone, Clement, 264:2
Stormy Weather (song), 521:5
Strategic arms limitation talks (SALT)—*see* Defense
  —arms control
Straw Dogs (film), 511:1
Strikes, labor—*see* Labor
Strindberg, August, 503:1
Strip mining—*see* Environment
Students—*see* Education
Suburbs—*see* Urban affairs
Subversion, 103:4, 304:4
Subversive Activities Control Board (SACB), 158:5
Success, 552:1, 556:3, 562:1, 562:3, 564:1
Sudan, 450:8
Suez Canal—*see* Middle East
Sun, the—*see* Space
Superpowers, 155:3, 390:1, 409:4, 411:1, 419:2,
  428:5, 430:2, 432:6, 450:8
Supersonic transport (SST)—*see* Transportation—air
Supreme Court, U.S.—*see* Judiciary
Surveillance—*see* Government
Sweden, 133:3, 416:2
  Indochina/Vietnam attitude, 383:1, 411:1, 411:2,
    416:2
  neutrality, 411:1
  Social Democratic Party, 411:2
  U.S. relations, 411:1, 411:2, 416:2
Swing, Raymond, 469:5
Switzerland:
  economy, 217:6
  education aspect, 116:5
Syria, 418:5, 420:4, 422:5, 428:3, 432:6, 433:5,
  435:4, 442:2, 442:3

T

Taft, William Howard, 223:2, 342:1
Taiwan—*see* China (Nationalist)
Tariffs—*see* Trade, foreign
Taxes, 88:3, 89:1, 167:4, 177:2, 180:2, 190:6,
  191:4, 196:1, 198:2, 201:5, 209:5, 213:6,
  214:3, 214:5, 216:4, 217:1, 217:2, 218:3,
  220:3, 309:4, 309:5, 310:3, 315:2, 472:6
  British system, 202:5
  capital gains—*see* Commerce
  compliance, 202:5
  corporate, 70:3, 72:1, 203:2
    excess-profits tax, 211:3
  depletion allowance, 67:2, 92:3, 137:1, 200:3,
    214:1

Taxes (*continued*)
  foreign tax credit, 92:3
  import tax/surcharge, 85:4, 86:3
  Internal Revenue Service (IRS), U.S., 265:5, 293:4, 512:4
    Code, 213:6
  investment tax/credit, 72:1, 213:5
  loopholes, 72:1, 137:1, 200:3, 214:1, 215:3, 314:1
  minimum tax, 214:1
  property tax, 327:4
  surcharge, 203:2
Taylor, Elizabeth, 545:4
Tchaikovsky, Piotr Ilich, 523:2
Teachers College (Columbia Univ.), 114:2
Teaching—*see* Education
Teapot Dome—*see* Politics—scandals
Technology—*see* Science
Television, 448:2, 476:1, 487:5, 488:1, 490:3, 507:3, 509:7, 513:4, 516:6, 530:3, 534:6, pp. 535-543
  adult themes, 539:6
  advertising—*see* Advertising
  the audience, 535:2, 536:4, 537:3, 537:5, 539:6, 541:4, 541:5, 543:1
  baseball coverage, 594:1
  British, 536:3
  cable (CATV), 507:3, 511:6
  children's programming, 542:5
  controversial programming, 538:2, 538:3, 543:1
  criticism/condemnation of, 540:4, 541:3, 542:3
  educational TV, 537:1, 574:4
  as entertainment, 537:4, 540:1, 542:1, 543:1
  French, 470:2
  future of, 541:2
  government aspect, 174:6, 535:1, 541:2, 541:3, 542:3, 542:5
    Presidency, broadcasting authority of, 538:6
  journalism—*see* Journalism—broadcast
  junk on, 536:5
  licenses, broadcast, 482:4, 538:6, 540:3, 542:3, 542:4
  live TV, 539:4
  mediocrity on, 537:6
  motion pictures compared with, 506:6, 514:4, 515:2, 540:4
  motion pictures sold to, 514:4
  political aspect, 245:3, 251:3, 259:3
  pornography/permissiveness/sex on, 535:1, 535:4, 541:5, 563:4
  public TV/broadcasting, 535:3, 537:2, 538:6, 539:3
    Corporation for Public Broadcasting, 535:3
    political bias of, 535:3
    Public Broadcasting Service (PBS), 537:7
  public issues, airing of, 537:2
  soap operas, 536:3
  as socializer, 540:1
  stage/plays compared with, 536:4, 540:2
  tennis coverage, 583:5
  violence on, 542:5, 563:4

  Watergate hearings, televising of—*see* Watergate
  writing for, 536:2, 537:7
  See also Federal Communications Commission; Radio
Tennis, 579:6
  audience noise, 584:5, 584:6
  consistency in, 582:4
  golf compared with, 582:2
  King/Riggs match, 589:1
  television coverage of, 583:5
Terrorism—*see* Foreign affairs
Thailand, 380:3, 380:4, 388:2
  fall to Communists, 366:5
  North Vietnamese aggression against, 375:3
Theatre—*see* Stage
Thieu, Nguyen Van, 363:2, 374:6, 390:5
Third World, 359:3, 447:4
Tho, Le Duc, 374:5
Tibet, 351:3
Time (magazine), 152:5, 275:4
Tito, Josip Broz, 404:4
Tom Sawyer (film), 513:2
Toscanini, Arturo, 520:3, 524:3, 525:1
Totalitarianism, 255:2, 350:3, 350:5, 415:1, 421:3, 555:6
Trade, foreign, 67:1, 76:3, 78:5, 79:1, 79:2, 79:4, 82:5, 83:4, 85:4, 86:3, 87:2, 91:1, 91:3, 93:1, 93:4, 96:1, 152:1, 202:2, 203:4, 342:5, 344:1, 353:4, 397:5, 447:1, 573:3
  balance of payments, 71:1, 73:5, 79:2, 82:6, 83:4, 92:3, 96:1, 128:3, 133:2, 137:1, 208:5, 410:3, 426:2
  Communists, trade with, 86:2, 153:3
  deficits, 75:4, 353:5
  East-West Trade Relations Act, 81:1
  imports/exports, 67:3, 70:1, 71:1, 72:1, 73:4, 76:3, 78:5, 83:4, 92:2, 96:1, 161:5
    oil/petroleum, 75:3, 92:2, 426:2, 429:4, 435:6
    surcharge/taxes, 85:4, 86:3
  protectionism, 76:3, 78:1, 78:5, 90:3, 91:3, 92:2, 200:2
  quotas, 72:2, 76:3, 78:5, 91:3
  shipping, 79:2
  tariffs, 72:2, 76:3, 78:1, 78:5, 92:1, 93:1, 96:2
  See also specific countries
Trains—*see* Transportation—railroads
Transportation, pp. 320-325
  air transportation, 321:1, 321:3, 321:6, 323:1, 324:5
    gasoline shortage effect on, 322:1,
    skyjacking, 324:4
    subsidies for airlines, 324:1
    supersonic transport (SST), 321:5
      Concorde, 325:3
    vertical take-off transports, 321:5
  automobiles/cars, 321:1, 323:1, 328:5
    complements mass transit, 321:6
    dependence on, 320:1
    energy/gasoline shortage effect on, 320:6, 322:4, 324:2

Transportation—
  automobiles (*continued*)
    gives freedom, 321:4, 322:4
    the industry, 321:2, 322:3, 554:1
    love affair with, 324:3
    misused, 322:4
    pollution aspect, 131:2
      catalytic converter, 142:1, 145:2
    seat belts, 320:4
    sex symbols, 324:3
  buses, 321:4, 323:1, 324:2, 324:3
  highways, 320:5, 322:5, 324:2, 324:5
  mass transit, 320:6, 321:3, 321:6, 323:1, 323:3
  modes, cooperation between, 323:1
  railroads/trains, 320:2, 320:3, 320:6, 321:4,
    321:6, 323:1, 324:2, 324:5
    Amtrak, 324:6
    British Railways, 325:1
    French National Railways, 325:1
    German Federal Railway, 325:1
    government nationalization/regulation/running
      of, 178:5, 198:4, 322:2, 323:4, 324:6,
      325:1
    Japanese National Railways, 325:1
    monorail, 321:6
    Penn Central Railroad, 318:1, 323:4
  space travel, 321:5
  subsidies, 323:3, 324:1
  tires, 323:5
  trucks, 324:1
Transportation, U.S. Dept. of, 290:2, 320:6
Treasury, U.S. Dept. of the, 290:2
Treaties—*see* Foreign affairs
Trevino, Lee, 579:7, 587:1, 589:2
Trials—*see* Judiciary
Truman, Harry S., 169:6, 187:3, 266:2, 307:5,
  315:2
Tunisia, 443:5
Tweed, William M. (Boss), 289:3
Two to Tango (song), 521:5
Tyranny, 174:3, 184:3, 228:2, 294:1, 404:4

U

UFO (unidentified flying object)—*see* Space—extra-
  terrestrial life
Uganda, 443:2
  Asians, expulsion of, 443:1, 443:3
  British relations, 443:1
  economy, 443:3
UN—*see* United Nations
Under-developed countries, 344:1, 346:4, 360:5
Unemployment—*see* Labor—employment
Unidentified flying object (UFO)—*see* Space—extra-
  terrestrial life
Unions—*see* Labor
United Kingdom/Britain/England, 440:4
  Arab relations, 412:1
  arts censorship, 455:4
  Australian relations, 349:1
  British Railways, 325:1

  Common Market entry, 152:5, 398:5, 403:4,
    403:6
  the Commonwealth, 400:2, 414:2
  criminal jurisprudence in, 110:2
  economy, 403:4
  education aspect, 116:5
  French relations, 399:5
    tunnel link, 394:3
  government:
    cabinet system, 181:5
    civil servants, 397:3
    House of Lords, 183:7
    political campaign system, 245:3
    vote of confidence, 193:5
  history, pre-occupation with, 415:2
  Iceland, fishing dispute with, 405:4
  Italian relations, 399:5
  journalism/the press in, 477:4
    British Press Council, 477:4
  malaise, English, 403:4
  oil reserves, 133:3
  population, 134:1
  racism in, 443:1
  Rhodesian relations, 444:7
  as "service" country, 75:4
  stage/theatre, 529:5, 530:6, 531:5, 534:5
  tax system, 202:5
  television, 536:3
  Ugandan relations, 443:1
  unemployment in, 403:4
  Watergate:
    attitude toward, 271:1
    if happened in England, 301:3
  West German relations, 399:5
  See also Northern Ireland; Scotland
United Mine Workers of America, 136:5, 213:4
United Nations (UN), 47:4, 158:6, 230:1, 371:5,
  420:3, 426:3, 429:5, 438:4, 439:3, 446:1,
  448:3, 451:4, 451:5, 452:1, 452:2
  Charter, 341:5, 434:1, 438:5
  Conference on the Environment, 125:1
  German admission, 353:2
  Korean admission, 353:2
  Security Council, 417:2, 425:2, 428:1, 430:1,
    435:4, 440:1, 442:2, 450:1
Universal Pictures Corp., 516:4
University—*see* Education—college
Updike, John, 48:3
Upper Volta, 554:4
Urban affairs/cities, 215:3, 312:4, 314:2, pp.326-330
  crisis in, 48:3, 326:1, 327:1, 327:4, 328:1, 328:4
  development, urban, 315:1
  fun to be in cities, 328:5
  government, city, 329:4
    Mayors, 326:3, 326:6
      black, 58:3, 61:2
  impractical/inefficient aspect, 328:5
  respositories for poor, black, etc., 326:5
  rural affairs, 314:1, 314:2, 316:4, 328:3
  suburbs, 326:4, 327:1, 328:5
  "Vietnamization" of, 327:4

Urban League, 56:2
USOC (U.S. Olympic Committee)—*see* Sports—Olympics
U.S.S.R.—*see* Soviet Union
Utopia, 552:2, 554:4

V

Vanocur, Sander, 535:3
Vatican, the, 362:1
VC (Viet Cong)—*see* Vietnam
Verdi, Giuseppe, 565:4
Veterans of Foreign Wars, 232:3
Vice Presidency, U.S., 165:1, 183:2, 250:9
  elimination of, 183:3
  President, relationship with, 165:2, 242:2
Viet Cong (VC)—*see* Vietnam
Vietnam, 48:1, 48:3, 101:2, 153:2, 153:4, 155:2,
  161:5, 163:2, 163:4, 187:3, 193:5, 236:4,
  239:5, 240:2, 240:5, 252:2, 253:3, 277:2,
  306:5, 347:1, 348:2, 350:5, 354:1, pp. 363-391,
  410:5, 417:4, 427:4, 446:1, 446:4, 450:8,
  447:4, 448:3
  Japanese relations, 353:4
  My Lai massacre, 474:1
  reunification/division of, 375:2, 387:7, 389:4,
    390:2
  Soviet aspect, 370:5
  Viet Cong (VC), 387:1, 387:3
  Vietnamization, 180:5
  North Vietnam, 249:1, 368:2
    Australian relations, 349:1, 362:1
    Cambodian aspect, 381:3, 382:1, 384:4,
      387:1, 387:3
    Communist Chinese aid for, 376:4
    Laos aspect, 381:3, 382:1
    negotiating with, 388:1
    Philippine aspect, 381:3
    Thailand aspect, 375:3
    U.S. aspect:
      bombing, 364:2, 371:4, 375:4, 376:6,
        377:3, 381:4, 385:1
      invasion, 378:4
      mining, 381:4
      negotiations, 189:2, 370:3, 373:5
      relations, 342:5, 368:3, 373:2, 373:4,
        374:1
  South Vietnam:
    Army, 389:1
    Communist takeover of, 368:2, 374:2
    Constitution, 388:3
    corruption in, 368:4, 374:6
    democracy in, 389:5
    elections in, 389:2, 389:5
    freedom in, 368:4, 374:6
    political prisoners in, 368:4
    press attitude toward, 368:4
    press, controlled, 374:6
    U.S. withdrawal of forces from, 390:3
    See also Indochina

Vietnam Reconstruction Conference, 360:4
Violence, 48:1, 566:6
  in motion pictures, 48:1, 504:4, 506:5, 511:1,
    515:1, 563:4
  in the 1960s, 45:3, 48:3, 296:1
  on television, 542:5, 563:4
Voice of America, the, 466:4

W

Wages, 77:1, 206:6, 212:3, 217:2, 217:6
  minimum wage, 92:4, 214:2
  See also Economy
Wallace, George C., 60:4, 63:4, 252:1
  attempted assassination of, 254:2, 265:7
  campaign methods, 255:5
War, 157:2, 158:2, 161:2, 230:1, 230:2, 231:5,
  233:1, 237:1, 369:5, 381:3, 383:4, 394:2,
  396:5, 423:4, 426:3, 429:6, 441:1, 446:4,
  447:2, 448:1, 448:4, 449:3, 449:4, 450:3,
  450:4, 450:9, 451:1, 451:3, 452:4, 552:2, 557:6
  liberation wars of, 449:5
  undeclared, 150:4
  See also specific wars; Peace; War and Peace
War and peace, 334:2, 407:2, pp. 446-452
Warren, Earl, 224:4, 225:6
Warsaw Pact, 231:2, 232:2, 400:1, 408:3, 409:1
Washington, George, 367:3
Washington Post, The (newspaper), 283:4, 464:2,
  465:6, 482:3
Washington Week in Review (TV show), 535:5
Water—*see* Environment
Watergate, 44:4, 48:3, 51:2, 52:2, 53:1, 77:1, 94:4,
  102:1, 114:2, 151:5, 168:2, 168:3, 182:4,
  187:1, 193:5, 194:1, 239:5, 243:4, 245:4, 245:5,
  246:2, 247:1, 252:1, 253:4, 255:4, 255:5, 258:3,
  259:6, 260:5, 261:2, 262:6, 263:2, 265:2, pp.
  268-308, 336:3, 477:5, 478:6, 482:3, 494:4,
  576:2
  Canada, if happened in, 301:3
  as coup d'etat, 293:5
  British attitude toward, 271:1
    if happened in England, 301:3
  Civil War compared with, 280:5
  effect on elections:
    1974: 271:4
    1976: 282:3
  foreign affairs aspect, 154:1
  how/why it happened, 268:4, 269:2, 270:2,
    273:3, 276:2, 278:2, 283:2, 285:7, 286:3,
    287:5, 288:5, 291:2, 296:1, 304:4
  impeachment of Nixon, 269:3, 273:1, 275:2,
    275:3, 275:4, 277:1, 278:4, 287:1, 290:4,
    291:1, 292:1, 292:2, 292:4, 304:3
  overblown, 284:4
  as partisan political issue, 269:1, 271:3, 275:3,
    277:2, 285:6, 287:1, 299:2, 299:4, 306:2
  pay-offs to conspirators, 278:1, 287:5
  the people as final judge, 270:3

Watergate (continued)
  prosecutor, independent special, 298:2, 301:1, 305:3
  Republican Party responsibility for, 268:2, 273:4, 274:4, 275:1, 278:2, 282:3, 299:1, 306:2, 307:2
  resignation of Nixon, 269:3, 273:1, 277:1, 278:5, 290:3, 291:1, 292:4, 295:2, 297:1, 297:4, 299:2, 300:3, 304:1, 304:3, 306:3
  Senate Watergate Committee/hearings, 279:3, 280:1, 284:4, 284:5, 287:2, 287:4, 294:2
    absence of legal concepts, 270:4
    televising of, 268:1, 268:3, 276:3, 278:3
  tapes/papers, 273:2, 276:4, 276:5, 278:4, 280:2, 280:4, 281:1, 283:1, 287:3, 290:4, 292:1, 296:2, 297:2, 301:1, 304:2
  Teapot Dome compared with, 282:1, 300:2
  not typical of politics/only few people involved, 269:2, 271:2, 272:1, 284:3, 285:4, 290:1, 291:3, 302:1, 307:1
  Washington Post coverage of, 283:4
  young, impact on, 272:2
Wayne, John, 54:1, 242:1, 460:5, 505:3, 505:6
WBA—see World Boxing Association
WBC—see World Boxing Council
Wealth/affluence. 546:7, 568:2
Welfare—see Social welfare
Wellesley College, 119:3
Wellington (book), 415:2
West Germany—see Germany
West, Mae, 561:2
Whitehead, Clay T., 471:3
Whitlam, Gough, 349:1
Whitman, Walt, 543:1
Whitney, Eli, 127:4
Winning—see Baseball; Football; Sports
Wiretapping—see Government—surveillance
Wolfe, Thomas, 487:4
Women/women's rights, 64:1, pp. 331-336, 547:7, 553:3, 554:3, 560:6
  athletes, 584:7
  credit access, 78:2, 335:2
  education aspect, 119:3
  equal pay for equal work, 332:4, 334:3, 335:7
  Equal Rights Amendment, 332:1, 333:4, 335:7
  film directors, 503:2, 518:4
  freedom of choice, 332:1, 332:2, 333:1
  men, equality with, 44:1
  men, women trying to be like, 331:2
  militancy necessary, 333:4
  militant/lunatic fringe, 331:1, 331:4
  military, women in, 240:3
  National Organization for Women (NOW), 332:3, 333:4
    news coverage of, 336:2
    poets, 503:2
    in politics, 266:5
    as President of Italy, 560:6
    scientists, 572:1
    sex roles, 334:2
    on Supreme Court, 333:3
    writers, 503:2
Women, The (play), 548:6
Women's Equity Action League, 332:1
Wood, Natalie, 511:4
Woodchopper's Ball, The (song), 521:3
Wordsworth, William, 484:1
Work—see Labor
Works Progress Administration (WPA), 522:2
World Bank, 360:4
World Boxing Association (WBA), 578:5
World Boxing Council (WBC), 578:5
World War I, 48:3, 440:4
World War II, 47:4, 91:3, 97:2, 176:1, 202:1, 257:5, 376:3, 384:5, 395:2, 440:4, 446:5, 451:2
World War III, 401:6
Wounded Knee, S.D.—see Indian, American
WPA—see Works Progress Administration
Wright Brothers, 572:1
Writing—see Literature; Motion pictures; Stage

Y

Yale University, 570:6
Yemen, 420:4, 428:3
Young people, 564:5, 565:3
Young Women's Christian Association (YWCA), 332:1
Youth—see Age
Yugoslavia:
  Communist Party of, 415:4
  Soviet relations, 404:4
YWCA—see Young Women's Christian Association

Z

Zahir Shah, Mohammed, 351:4
Zaire, 444:2
Zambia, 443:7
Ziegler, Ronald L., 253:2
Zionism—see Middle East
Zola, Emile, 489:1, 543:1
Zukor, Adolph, 517:4